FIELDS OF
APPLIED PSYCHOLOGY

FIELDS OF
APPLIED
PSYCHOLOGY
SECOND EDITION

ANNE ANASTASI

Professor of Psychology
Fordham University

McGRAW-HILL BOOK COMPANY

New York/St. Louis/San Francisco/Auckland/Bogotá/Düsseldorf/Johannesburg
London/Madrid/Mexico/Montreal/New Delhi/Panama/Paris/São Paulo
Singapore/Sydney/Tokyo/Toronto

Library of Congress Cataloging in Publication Data

Anastasi, Anne, date
   Fields of applied psychology.

   Bibliography: p.
   Includes index.
   1.   Psychology, Applied.   I.   Title.
   BF636.A53   1979   158   78-21267
   ISBN 0-07-001602-X

FIELDS OF APPLIED PSYCHOLOGY

1 2 3 4 5 6 7 8 9 0 D O D O 7 8 3 2 1 0 9

This book was set in Helvetica by Black Dot, Inc. (ECU).
The editors were Richard R. Wright and David Dunham;
the designer was Anne Canevari Green;
the production supervisor was Charles Hess.
The drawings were done by Tek/Nek Inc.
R. R. Donnelley & Sons Company was printer and binder.

CONTENTS

PART IV
CONSUMER PSYCHOLOGY

PART V
CLINICAL, COUNSELING, AND COMMUNITY
PSYCHOLOGY

PART VI
PSYCHOLOGY AND OTHER PROFESSIONS

APPENDIXES

PREFACE

THIS REVISION has retained the objectives and basic approach of the first edition. Yet within that framework, it is largely a new book. In practically all fields of applied psychology, the mid-sixties marked the beginning of an era of unprecedented activity. This growth is reflected in the present edition insofar as about 70% of the references now cited postdate the 1964 edition. In fact, slightly over half of the references are from the 1970s. This chronological distribution takes on added significance in the light of my continued efforts to provide historical perspective for each topic. The earliest reference cited is dated 1873; many topics are traced to their origins in the late nineteenth and early twentieth centuries. Thus within a span of approximately 100 years, more than half of the publications cited cover less than a decade.

With regard to similarities between the two editions, the primary aim of the book is still to provide an overview of what psychology has to offer in practical contexts. I have again tried to show what psychologists do when they are not engaged in teaching or basic research in an academic setting. It is noteworthy that an increasing proportion of psychologists are devoting part or all of their time to the various fields of applied psychology surveyed in this text.

Throughout the book, attention is again centered on the specialized research methodologies that represent the psychologist's most distinctive contribution to each field. By focusing on method, the book provides the reader with the needed skills for critical evaluation of psychological findings, conclusions, and practices encountered in daily life. A special effort has been made to alert the reader to common types of methodological pitfalls and misinterpretations in each field.

Another major aim of the book is to present an integrated and comprehensive picture of applied psychology. Combining such disparate fields as clinical, engineering, and consumer psychology within a single book makes it possible to perceive relations among their findings that may have previously gone unnoticed. Fresh insights often emerge from the juxtaposition of similar problems that have been studied in different contexts by investigators with diverse orientations. For this reason, cross-references have been used liberally throughout the text, and every effort has been made to note connections and unify the various areas.

The differences between the two editions reflect both quantitative and qualitative changes that have occurred in the 15-year interval. A conspicuous development has been the emergence of new fields that had been dimly foreshadowed in the earlier edition. Among the most vigorous are organizational (Ch. 6), environmental (Ch. 9), and community (Ch. 13) psychology. Consumer psychology has been reoriented toward a greater concern with the consumer as such rather than merely as purchaser of goods and services (Chs. 10 and 11). There has also been increasing activity in the evolving psychoeducational (Ch. 17), psychomedical (Ch. 18), and psycholegal (Ch. 19) specialties. All these recent developments are characteristically interdisciplinary. Applied psychologists are working more and more with members of many other professions.

Another noteworthy trend in all fields of applied psychology is a sharp rise in theoretical and methodological sophistication. Among the many examples may be mentioned the development of such assessment techniques as behaviorally anchored rating scales, the refinement of job analysis procedures, new systems of job classification geared to worker traits, varied applications of decision theory, and the measurement of interaction effects within comprehensive person-environment systems. Increasing attention is being given to the utilization of appropriate experimental designs and statistical procedures for applied research, especially in consumer and clinical psychology. The growth of program evaluation, particularly in community psychology, has stimulated further methodological explorations. Another significant development has been the increasing application of the concepts and methods of operant conditioning and contingent reinforcement, often as part of broadly formulated behavior modification programs. This trend can be seen most clearly in connection with occupational training (Ch. 4), worker motivation (Chs. 5 and 6), consumer behavior in relation to environmental protection (Ch. 11), clinical and community interventions (Chs. 13 and 14), education (Ch. 17), and medical practice (Ch. 18). Finally, several fields show evidence of the growing awareness of cultural differences, especially with reference to developing nations and to ethnic minorities within a pluralistic society. Although examples can be found throughout the text, this topic has received special attention in connection with personnel assessment (Ch. 2), industrial training (Ch. 4), worker motivation and managerial styles (Chs. 5 and 6), equipment and environmental design (Chs. 8 and 9), clinical and community psychology (Chs. 13 and 14), and education (Ch. 17).

While directed principally to the college student, this book is also appropriate for beginning graduate students; for students in various professional schools, including education, business, medicine, and law; and for practitioners who may wish an overview of what contemporary psychology has to offer to business and the professions. In the interest of flexibility of use at different levels, selected references have been included throughout the test as a source of further information on the topic under discussion.

A book spanning so wide a range of topics draws upon the contributions of thousands of specialists. The list of references acknowledges my debt to those authors whose work has been directly cited. I am grateful to the many on this list who sent me reprints. Several provided unpublished materials, answered numerous queries by mail, telephone, or personal conferences, and generally contributed well beyond the normal exchange of information expected among professional colleagues. In this connection, I owe special thanks to: Barbara J. Andrew, National Board of Medical Examiners; Cynthia and Martin Deutsch, Institute for Developmental Studies, New York University: Jerome E. Doppelt, Psychological Corporation; Robert C. Droege, U.S. Department of Labor; Marvin D. Dunnette, University of Minnesota; John C. Flanagan, American Institutes for Research; Edwin A. Fleishman, Advanced Research Resources Organization; Harry F. Harlow, University of Arizona; Jacob Jacoby, Purdue University; Helen L. Leroy, University of Wisconsin Primate Laboratory; Howard Leventhal, University of Wisconsin; Peter M. Lewinsohn, University of Oregon; Kenneth E. Lloyd, Drake University; Lloyd F. Lofquist, University of Minnesota; Howard H. McFann, Human Relations Research Organization; John W. Menne, Iowa State University; Blythe Mitchell, Psychological Corporation; D. Morgan Neu, Starch INRA Hooper, Inc.; Frank L. Schmidt, U. S. Civil Service Commission; Julius Segal, National Institute of Mental Health; Benjamin Shimberg, Educational Testing Service; and Jane D. Hildreth, Willo P. White, and Thomas J. Willette, American Psychological Association.

To my colleagues in the Fordham University Psychology Department, I am grateful for their continued interest in the progress of the book and their readiness to discuss questions and provide pertinent materials. I acknowledge particularly the contributions of Mary-Carol Cahill, David R. Chabot, David T. Landrigan, Henryk Misiak, and Warren W. Tryon, and the special assistance of Marvin Reznikoff, who not only read the five chapters on clinical, counseling, and community psychology but also served as a continuing resource in these areas throughout the preparation of the book. For unusually helpful bibliographic services, I am grateful to several members of the Fordham University library, particularly Mary F. Riley, Chief Reference Librarian; Lucy Valentino, of the Circulation Staff; and Victoria Overton, of the Periodicals Staff. I want to express my appreciation to Stanley Friedland for skillful assistance in indexing, preparation of examination questions in the Instructor's Manual, and other essential production tasks. Special thanks are due my husband, John Porter Foley, Jr., for his participation in the solution of innumerable problems of both content and form at all stages in the preparation of the book.

Anne Anastasi

INTRODUCTION

PART ONE

WHAT IS APPLIED PSYCHOLOGY?

ONE

PPLIED PSYCHOLOGY is coming to play a significant role in more and more facets of modern society. During the first half of the twentieth century, the majority of psychologists were engaged in university teaching and basic research. Today at least half of the members of the American Psychological Association are working in business, industry, clinics, hospitals, schools, community agencies, correctional institutions, rehabilitation centers, or government. It is the object of this book to provide an overall view of the types of functions performed by such applied psychologists. Within each field, attention will be focused upon what psychologists as such can contribute to the solution of problems that are the joint concern of many different specialists.

FIELDS OF APPLIED PSYCHOLOGY

The varied and growing activities of psychologists cannot be readily classified into neat and mutually exclusive categories. The multiplicity of ways in which psychologists perceive themselves is well illustrated by the nearly 40 divisions of the American Psychological Association (see Appendix A). Some of these, such as the Divisions of General Psychology, Experimental Psychology, and Physiological and Comparative Psychology and the Division on the Teaching of Psychology, clearly draw most of their members from university faculties. Others, such as the Divisions of Industrial and Organizational, Consumer, Clinical, Counseling, Consulting, Rehabilitation, and Community Psychology, and the Divisions of Psychotherapy, School Psychologists, Engineering Psychologists, and Psychologists in Public Service, are composed largely of applied psychologists. Still other divisions represent interest areas that cut across teaching or basic research and professional applications. It should be added that many APA members belong to more than one division. This multiplicity of divisional membership is itself a reflection of the overlapping and changing roles of contemporary psychologists.

Traditionally, the term "applied psychology" has been most closely identified with the applications of psychology in business and industry. The *Journal of Applied Psychology,* established in 1917, is still concerned largely with industrial psychology. Early textbooks, as well as college courses entitled "Applied Psychology," which began to appear in the 1920s, usually covered problems of personnel selection, efficiency of work, and advertising. The first two of these areas were included in 1913 in a book entitled *Psychology and Industrial Efficiency* by Hugo Münsterberg, a Harvard professor who has been called the first all-around applied psychologist in America. Münsterberg did much to define the field of applied psychology and to outline the possible uses of psychology in business and industry, as well as in other areas.

Another pioneer in applied psychology was Walter Dill Scott, whose book, *Psychology of Advertising,* appeared in 1908. With his appointment as professor of applied psychology at Carnegie Institute of Technology in 1915, he became the first psychologist to hold such a title in an American university. Scott initiated research in several areas of personnel selection and in 1919 founded The Scott Company, the first consulting firm in this country devoted to industrial psychology. The reader interested in historical perspectives can find a comprehensive list of landmarks of professional psychology, from 1860 to 1939, in a handbook edited by Fryer and Henry (1950, pp. vii–x). These landmarks include antecedent developments in general psychology that contributed to the rise of applied psychology, as well as noteworthy events within the entire area of applied psychology itself.

Within industrial psychology, later developments led to the differentiation of three major areas. These areas grew out of three corresponding traditions in general psychology. The area of personnel selection and classification evolved from psychological testing and differential psychology; that of human-factors engineering, from experimental psychology; and that of employee relations, from research on personality and social psychology.

Further development and re-sorting of areas is reflected in the current field of *industrial and organizational psychology,* covered in the first major division of this book (Part II). Those psychologists who identify with this field are generally concerned with personnel selection and classification procedures, the closely related area of training, and employee relations and management problems. Although some specialize in one or another of these areas, most psychologists qualified to work in one of them can and frequently do work in the others. There is considerable similarity in the interests, training, and experience of industrial psychologists concerned with any of these areas.

A distinctly different group, however, is engaged in *engineering psychology,* treated in Part III. Such psychologists deal with problems of work and fatigue, the improvement of work methods, conditions in the working and living environment—such as lighting, air pollution, and noise—and the design of equipment and working space for more efficient use by the human operator. In the 1970s, engineering psychologists began to apply their techniques increasingly to the design and use of living space. They joined forces with urban planners, architects, social psychologists, and other specialists in the emerging field of *environmental psychology.*

Consumer psychology, discussed in Part IV, started as a part of business and industrial psychology but now represents a distinct field. Beginning at the turn of the century in laboratory studies of individual features of advertisements, this field has expanded to include extensive research on consumer characteristics, wants, and preferences. Such research merges into studies of economic behavior on the one hand and product design on the other. With regard to methodology, consumer surveys have much in common with public opinion polling. Psychological work in these areas has many points of contact with economics and sociology. Research on mass media of communication has also been broadened to include many aspects of consumer behavior besides the purchase of advertised products. Similarly, the "consumerism movement" has shifted the focus toward the interests and rights of consumers, as illustrated by the demand for "truth in advertising" and for products better designed for safety and convenience of use.

In Part V, the reader is introduced to *clinical psychology.* One chapter considers techniques for the assessment of emotional and intellectual disorders; another, intervention procedures; and a third, research in clinical psychology. Although the first psychological clinic in America was established by Lightner Witmer at the University of Pennsylvania as early as 1896, the practice of clinical psychology dates largely from World War II. Prior to that time, clinical psychologists were chiefly mental testers, and most of their clients were children. The years since World War II witnessed a phenomenal rise in the number of psychologists working in the clinical area, as well as an expansion of their activities to include more work with adults and more psychotherapy at all age levels. Research on clinical problems has also increased sharply both in quantity and in methodological sophistication. The rise of *community psychology* in the late 1960s influenced both the orientation and practice of clinical psychologists and further broadened their sphere of operation.

That the work of psychologists often defies classification is well illustrated by the distinction between clinical psychology and *counseling psychology* (also covered in Part V). In general, counseling psychologists are concerned with milder forms of emotional disturbance than are clinical psychologists. They deal, too, with a variety of problems encountered by essentially normal persons. Nevertheless, the functions of many individual clinical and counseling psychologists undoubtedly overlap.

Since career counseling constitutes a major part of the functions of many counseling psychologists, special attention will be given to the nature of occupational choices, the factors affecting them, and their significance in the life of the individual. It is noteworthy, too, that the field of counseling psychology, although now much broader, originated in the vocational-guidance movement (Brewer et al., 1942). The first vocational-guidance bureau was opened in Boston in 1908 by Frank Parsons, whose book, *Choosing a Vocation* (F. Parsons, 1909), was published the following year. The National Vocational Guidance Association was organized in 1913. And in 1914 the first vocational-guidance unit in a public school system was established in Cincinnati. In its subsequent growth, the vocational-guidance movement itself was greatly influenced by the development of psychological testing. Still later, the emerging and broader field of counseling psychology incorporated many concepts and procedures originating within clinical psychology.

Part VI, covering *psychology and other professions,* is concerned with areas in which psychologists function chiefly as consultants to other professional personnel. Major examples can be found in education, medicine, and law (including government and public affairs). Psychologists also contribute indirectly to these fields through the training of professional personnel, particularly in education. It is characteristic of these fields that, although potentially they provide many opportunities for the application of psychology, their contacts with psychology have been slow to develop. Today there are many indications of a growing participation by psychologists in all these fields.

THE SCIENCE AND PROFESSION OF PSYCHOLOGY

Applied psychology does not differ in any fundamental way from the rest of psychology. In terms of training and orientation, every applied psychologist is a psychologist first and an applied specialist secondarily. This point of view has been repeatedly reaffirmed in national conferences on graduate education in psychology, convened under the auspices of the American Psychological Association (Hoch, Ross, & Winder, 1966; Raimy, 1950; Roe, Gustad, Moore, Ross, & Skodak, 1959). Psychology is probably unique in its status of "professional science" or "scientific profession," and *that,* the conferences concluded, is the way psychology should remain if it is to be maximally effective. Psychologists are not sharply separated into basic scientists and professional practitioners. All have had essentially the same type of academic preparation; specialization occurs chiefly at the level of practicum training and on-the-job experience. The clinical, counseling, or personnel psychologist, for example, has received training in experimental psychology, and the experimental psychologist in his research utilizes concepts or hypotheses that may have originated in the clinic or factory.

Scientific Method. The unique contribution that applied psychologists can make in industry, government, hospitals, clinics, schools, and other practical settings stems principally from their research approach to problems of human behavior. When psychologists go to work in an applied context, they bring with them, not a set of rules or specific facts, but a *method* for attacking problems. This is essentially the scientific method, common to all sciences. Applied psychologists have been trained in the many techniques for utilizing this basic method in the study of human behavior. It is for this reason that the major emphasis in this book will be placed on the particular methodologies appropriate to each field of applied psychology.

What, specifically, is meant by the statement that applied psychologists use the scientific method? First, like their colleagues in all fields of psychology, they rely on *empirical observation* rather than on subjective opinion. Their choice of a personnel selection test, training method, or type of therapy is *not* based on their "superior wisdom" as psychologists, nor on the recommendation of leading authorities, standard texts, or "hundreds of satisfied clients." Instead, psychologists gather data to evaluate empirically the effectiveness of different tests, training methods, or forms of therapy. They will, of course, draw upon previous knowledge and whatever wisdom they possess to choose promising procedures and to formulate testable hypotheses. Their familiarity with psychological facts and principles and their prior experience in similar practical situations will greatly facilitate the selection or development of effective procedures. But their effectiveness cannot be assumed—it always needs to be demonstrated.

It is also characteristic of the scientific method that full *records* of observations are made without delay, with the aid of instruments when feasible. Even when relying on unaided observation, however, psychologists do not trust to memory for their facts. As psychologists, they are particularly aware of the selectivity of attention and memory. We tend to notice and to recall just those observations that support our preconceived expectations or biases and to forget contradictory facts. Or we may recall the most dramatic instances, which are likely to be atypical and less representative than the more readily forgotten ordinary cases.

Another prerequisite of scientific observation is *replication.* Observations must be repeated. Generalizing from a single observation or from a few cases is especially hazardous in psychology because of the extensive individual differences in behavior, as well as the variability in the responses of the same person on different occasions. Many repetitions are needed to establish a conclusion with adequate certainty.

But numbers are not enough. Statistics *may* lie when improperly employed. The cases observed must be *representative* of the groups about which conclusions are to be drawn. The samples utilized must be carefully scrutinized for possible selective bias. Perhaps the most vivid demonstration of the effect of such selective bias is provided by public opinion polls that "went wrong" in their predictions because certain income levels or other categories of persons happened to be either overrepresented or underrepresented in the samples interviewed.

One of the chief distinguishing features of the scientifically trained applied psychologist is that he never fails to specify the *margin of error* of his procedures. No technique is perfect; and the extent of error inherent in each must be taken into account in any administrative decisions based upon its application. Such error itself must be empirically determined before the technique is ready for operational use. An example of the type of chance errors that affect psychological measurement is provided by temporal fluctuation. Thus a job applicant might score lower on a test on one day because he is sleepy and depressed, and higher on another day when he feels alert and confident. Or he might perform better on one form of the test and poorer on another because of the particular sample of items in the two forms, thereby illustrating another type of measurement error.

Still another example is to be found in the use of personnel selection tests to predict an applicant's job performance. Since so many factors influence an employee's achievement on the job, it is obvious that no test could make such a prediction with perfect accuracy. Some variation between the predicted and actual outcome is inevitable. Through follow-up studies, it is possible to determine the magnitude of such prediction errors for any given test and any given job.

A different kind of chance error can be seen in an attitude survey, when one sample of 50 employees reports more dissatisfaction with management policies than another sample of 50. Even though both samples were chosen with equal care to represent a cross section of the company's employees in all important characteristics, the first sample happened to include more disgruntled individuals than the second. Any statistical measure, such as an average, percentage, or correlation, should be accompanied by some indication of the fluctuation in its value to be expected from sample to sample. With such a sampling error, we are able to estimate the limits within which results in other samples are likely to fall. Thus, we might be able to predict that the percentage of dissatisfied employees in the company falls between 24 and 32, even though we cannot say definitely whether it is 27, 31, or some other specific figure.

Although all of the above procedures are characteristic of the scientific method, the very heart of the method is to be found in the design of experiments that permit observations under *controlled conditions.* Only under such circumstances can we identify cause-and-effect relations. To establish the effectiveness of a particular form of therapy, it is not enough to report that 63% of the patients recovered. We must also know what percentage recovered in an untreated control group equated in all relevant respects with the treated group. As long as the two groups differed in only one respect, namely, the presence or absence of a given treatment, then differences in outcome can be attributed to the treatment.

It should not be inferred, however, that the scientific method is limited to the study of a single variable at a time. With more complex experimental designs, it is possible to investigate simultaneously the effects of two or more variables, as well as the interaction between them. Table 1-1 gives a hypothetical example of an

TABLE 1-1
Schematic Illustration of Interaction between
Instructional Method and Aptitude Level

Group	Range of Academic Aptitude Scores	Mean Arithmetic Scores after Instruction		
		Method A	Method B	Total
I	120-140	41	60	50
II	90-110	38	25	31
III	60-80	21	8	14
Total		33	31	

experimental design in which two methods of teaching arithmetic are employed systematically with three groups of children differing in academic aptitude. Of the 40 subjects in Group I, with aptitude scores between 120 and 140, 20 are taught by Method A and 20 by Method B. The 40 subjects in Group II are similarly assigned to the two teaching methods, and the same procedure is followed with Group III. The mean scores obtained by the six subgroups, showing amount of improvement following the course, indicate that Method B is more effective than Method A with the higher aptitude subjects (Group I), while the reverse is true of the less able groups. If the appropriate statistical analyses reveal that these differences exceed those expected by chance, we can conclude that there is a significant *interaction* between teaching method and ability level.[1] The joint analysis of both variables thus permits the discovery of relationships that would have gone undetected if either variable had been investigated separately. Under the latter conditions, we would know only that children with higher academic aptitude scores learn more arithmetic than do those with lower scores, as shown by the row means in Table 1-1, and we would conclude that instructional Methods A and B do not differ significantly in their effectiveness, as indicated by the two column means.

Interaction of variables, in the sense in which this concept was used in the preceding example, is receiving increasing attention in all fields of applied psychology; many examples of it will be encountered throughout this book. In clinical psychology, for instance, the relative success of different types of therapy

[1]The statistical procedure required for this purpose is *analysis of variance.* Descriptions of it can be found in any recent text on psychological statistics, such as Guilford and Fruchter (1978).

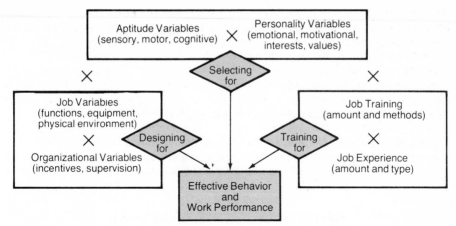

Figure 1-1. Conceptualization of interactions among human-factors system variables as related to human performance effectiveness. *(Adapted from Uhlaner, 1970, Schema I.)*

may vary with such client characteristics as educational level or cultural background.

In a still different context, job performance is being viewed increasingly as the result of complex interactions between many variables of both the worker and the work situation. This comprehensive orientation is illustrated by human-factors *systems research.* Cutting across all areas traditionally included under industrial and engineering psychology, this approach permits an analysis of the combined effects of personnel selection, training, and job variables upon work performance. The interrelationships of these factors are shown schematically in Figure 1-1. Proposed by Uhlaner (1970, 1972) with special reference to military occupational specialties, this schema provides a "measurement bed" for assessing work effectiveness in any context. It includes aptitude and personality variables of the worker, job training and experience, nature of the job activities, physical characteristics of the working environment, and such organizational variables as incentives and supervisory techniques.

Basic and Applied Research. Since applied psychologists follow the same fundamental procedures as their laboratory colleagues in solving problems, how can they be differentiated? When the applied psychologist is engaged in research—as is true much of the time for many applied psychologists—the distinction hinges on the difference between basic and applied research. This difference is one of degree. Although examples can be found that fall clearly into the basic or applied categories, some research could be classified in either. One determining factor is how the problem is chosen: to help in theory construction or in making administrative decisions. For instance, is the investigation concerned primarily with the nature of learning or with the most effective method for training airplane pilots?

A closely related difference pertains to the specificity or generality of the results. The findings of basic research can usually be generalized more widely than those of applied research. The latter characteristically yields results pertaining only to narrowly limited situations. Similarly, applied research permits less analysis of causal relationships, since situations are likely to be compared in their totality, rather than being broken down into more elementary components. For instance, applied research may demonstrate that one of two training procedures, in all their operational complexities, yields better results than the other within a particular context. But it may not be possible, under these circumstances, to specify *why* the one method was superior.

In terms of the example given in Table 1-1, basic research might compare two instructional methods differing in a single, clearly defined variable, such as size of instructional unit, i.e., how much new material is introduced at one time. In fact, the experimental design might include the systematic sampling of different unit sizes, so that speed of learning could be expressed as a function of unit size within each aptitude level. Applied research, on the other hand, would be illustrated by the comparison of two composite instructional methods differing from each other in many variables. These variables would have been chosen and optimized in the light of available knowledge regarding the conditions that facilitate learning by children with high and low academic aptitude.

The Applied Psychologist's Service Functions. The continuum along which are found examples of basic and applied research can be further extended to include development, evaluation, system installation, and practice or service functions. Not only are we still dealing with a continuum, rather than with sharply separated functions, but any single psychological project or professional activity may also cover a wide range along this continuum. Moreover, the basic features of the scientific method characterize the work of the applied psychologist throughout this continuum.

Some applied psychologists spend all or most of their time in service rather than research functions. How do such psychologists use the scientific method when engaged, for example, in psychotherapy with an emotionally disturbed client, in testing a child with a learning disability, in interviewing an applicant for an executive position, or in planning a consumer survey for a toothpaste manufacturer? They do so in at least two ways. First, they evaluate and choose their procedures, not on the basis of subjective opinion, but in the light of available published research conducted in comparable situations. Being unable under the circumstances to carry out their own empirical evaluations, they nevertheless are guided by whatever empirical data are available regarding tests, questionnaire techniques, types of psychotherapy, or any other procedure they plan to use.

In a still more general way, the scientific training of psychologists influences their approach to every problem they encounter in their service functions. Through such training, they have formed habits of accurate and objective observation and recording of facts and have learned to guard against preconceived notions and premature acceptance of conclusions. They have learned to reserve judgment and to modify or discard conclusions as fresh facts become available. In their service functions as in their research, applied psychologists often need to formulate hypotheses and verify them against subsequent data. In trying to discover the sources of a person's neurotic fear, the causes of a child's reading difficulty, or the leadership potential of a job applicant, psychologists form a succession of tentative hypotheses. Each hypothesis suggests what further facts must be elicited and is in turn either confirmed or disconfirmed by such facts.

To be sure, not all applied psychologists have profited so fully from their scientific training. But it is the goal of such training to foster this type of problem-solving attitude. Such an attitude represents an important difference between the professional psychologist and either the well-meaning but untrained psychologizer or the deliberate impostor.

THE PROBLEM OF CHARLATANISM

Nature and Extent. Some of the areas in which applied psychologists work have traditionally proved attractive to charlatans, pseudoscientists, and self-styled experts. In this flourishing psychological underworld are found phrenologists, physiognomists, astrologers, and others who try to diagnose your aptitude and personality traits or prescribe a specific career by examining the shape of your skull, the angle of your jaw, or the date of your birth. Here, too, are the many systems for improving your personality, developing your memory or your selling ability, overcoming your fears and other emotional problems, and generally attaining health-wealth-and-happiness for the payment of a small fee. On the borderland are the practitioners who assume a semblance of scientific respectability by administering tests. They may, however, rely on a single test of unknown validity for which extravagant claims are made. Or they may send a batch of tests by mail, which are taken under uncontrolled conditions and interpreted without any other knowledge about the individual. All these practices represent flagrant misuses of tests and yield meaningless results.

Charlatanism is against the public interest under whatever guise it is practiced. But charlatans have often called themselves psychologists, thus further confounding the public and undermining its confidence in psychology. When the glowing promises go unfulfilled and the anticipated benefits fail to materialize, psychology gets the blame. Some charlatans hold "degrees" from diploma mills and dubious correspondence schools offering bizarre or token curricula (see Brophy & Durfee, 1960; Lebo, 1953).

The prevalence of charlatanism in the behavioral domain arises partly from the widespread misconceptions and lack of knowledge about the nature of psychology itself (see, e.g. Sherman, 1960). Psychology is one of the youngest of the sciences. Modern experimental psychology dates from about 1875; and until the 1940s, few psychologists worked outside of universities. Consequently, the general public is still vague about the functions of psychologists and is thus more receptive to the claims of the charlatans.

Even more important in accounting for the spread of charlatanism is the public's strong desire for the sort of help the charlatans offer. People believe the claims—however fantastic—because they want to believe them. And the charlatan, unhampered by facts, promises easier and more satisfying solutions to life's problems than does the reputable psychologist. The charlatan offers shortcuts to self-evaluation, quick cures for your neuroses, a new personality in ten easy lessons, and decisive vocational advice in a neat package—all with the bland assurance of 99$\frac{1}{2}$% accuracy. The hard realities of science look unattractive against such prospects.

Still another reason for the spread of pseudopsychology is that laws controlling the use of the title "psychologist" have only recently been enacted. Prior to World War II, there were no such laws in the United States. By the 1970s, most of the 50 states had either certification laws, which limit the use of the title to qualified practitioners, or licensing laws, which define and control the practice of psychology.

Among their clients, charlatans include not only individuals seeking personal help but business organizations as well. In fact, certain consulting firms using highly questionable procedures specialize in personnel selection for business and industry. Even the more obvious forms of quackery, such as phrenology and physiognomy, have not been without adherents among business executives (Blackford & Newcomb, 1919). Such gullibility is not so prevalent today as it was early in the century, when psychology was largely unknown to the layperson. But it is still encountered. As late as 1953, for instance, *Fortune,* a magazine read widely by business leaders, published a serious and sympathetic account of a personnel selection system based on facial characteristics (Stryker, 1953). The article refers to the use of this system by a number of high-level business executives as an aid in personnel decisions. The personnel and industrial-relations director of one large manufacturing company, for instance, was quoted as saying that this system "is one of the greatest contributions ever made to the field of executive selection and development" (Stryker, 1953, p. 146).

Efforts to judge personality and aptitudes from physical appearance date back to antiquity. Today this accumulated folklore survives, not only in the organized systems of charlatanry but also in common social stereotypes. Literature and art have done much to perpetuate these stereotypes. And our very language makes it difficult to escape them. Thus, we associate "highbrow" with the intellectual, red hair with a fiery temper, and a square jaw with firmness of character. These familiar examples illustrate one source of popular stereotypes, namely, analogy and superficial resemblance. Red is the color of fire, and a square jaw looks more solid and firm than a receding chin. Similarly, the association between head size or shape and intelligence is bolstered by the vague knowledge that the brain plays an important part in behavior.

A little knowledge about the brain was also the basis for the doctrine of phrenology, formulated by the eighteenth- and early nineteenth-century anatomist Franz Gall. Going far beyond the meager data then available on the localization of cortical functions, Gall proposed that different areas of the brain control specific and complex traits, such as mechanical ingenuity, conscientiousness, and combativeness. He maintained further that overdevelopment or underdevelopment of these traits could be diagnosed by examining the protuberances on the skull. The identification of a particular "bump" was taken to mean that the function allegedly controlled by the corresponding cortical area was highly developed in the individual. In the hands of its later exponents, Gall's theoretical formulation degenerated into a popular system for quick personality assessment and vocational guidance (Fowler, 1873).

Common Fallacies. An examination of the rationale underlying phrenology will serve to illustrate the sort of fallacious reasoning prevalent in such pseudoscientific systems. First, the assumed correspondence between skull shape and brain shape ignores the cerebrospinal fluid and the several layers of membrane that intervene between brain and skull. Second, size is not a dependable index of the degree of development of different parts of the brain. Efficiency of function is more likely to be related to complexity of interrelations among neurones and other microscopic and biochemical characteristics of nerve matter. Third, the type of trait that phrenologists ascribe to different brain areas is quite unlike the functions identified through research on cortical localization. Connections have been demonstrated between certain muscle groups or sense organs and specific brain areas, the very areas where phrenologists localize such traits as veneration and parental love.

Fourth, and probably most important, is the nature of the evidence cited by phrenologists in support of their doctrine (Fowler, 1873). Such evidence vividly illustrates the popular fallacy of citing selected cases. In their published writings, phrenologists amassed examples of eminent men whose cranial protuberances corresponded to the alleged cerebral location of their special talents. Similarly, they cited cases of intellectual leaders who had unusually large skulls. A favorite example is Daniel Webster, whose massive skull measured over 24½ inches in circumference and who had a cranial protuberance in the exact spot where phrenologists locate literary talent. But of course the phrenologists ignore all the other eminent men with average or small skulls and with bumps in the wrong places. Phrenologists also refer to microcephalics, who have abnormally small skulls and very low intelligence. But they overlook the other clinical varieties of mental retardates with normal skulls or with characteristically large skulls, such as hydrocephalics. Investigations conducted by psychologists on large, unselected samples of children and adults have revealed very low correlations between cranial capacity and intelligence (Anastasi, 1958, Ch. 5; Paterson, 1930, Ch. 3). Similarly, precise measurements of head shape have shown no consistent relationships with either general intellectual level or special aptitudes.

Closely related to phrenology is the doctrine of physiognomy, under which are loosely grouped a number of characteristics pertaining to facial structure, hand shape, skin texture, and hair and eye color. Drawing partly from ancient lore and partly from selected examples of the physiognomies of famous persons, Johann Lavater wrote extensively on this system in the eighteenth century. Early in the present century, Katherine Blackford elaborated certain aspects of it with special reference to its use in personnel selection (Blackford & Newcomb, 1919). In this form, the system enjoyed considerable vogue for a number of years.

In this area, too, psychologists have conducted several investigations designed to check on various alleged associations between physical and psychological traits (Hull, 1928, Ch. 4; Paterson, 1930, Ch. 7). Carefully measured facial dimensions and indices were correlated with aptitudes and personality characteristics as determined by tests or associates' ratings. Among the physical traits investigated were convexity of profile, height of forehead, blondness, and a variety of other facial measures chosen to test traditional claims of physiognomists. All the relationships investigated yielded insignificant correlations. It might be added that when psychologists invited practicing physiognomists or phrenologists to participate in controlled investigations, they repeatedly met with refusal (see, Hull, 1928, p. 121).

The Barnum Effect. A favorite sales appeal of charlatans and borderline "consultants" is to invite business executives to undergo their particular brand of personality analysis so that they may "judge it for themselves." The sort of personality description that they provide consists of vague generalities applicable to most people. When confronted with such a description, the recipients are impressed with its apparent accuracy and insight and conclude that the method will work equally well with their employees. This pseudovalidation has been called the "Barnum effect" (see Dunnette, 1957, p. 223; Meehl, 1956, p. 266) after Phineas T. Barnum, the famous showman and acknowledged expert in the art of humbug.

The readiness with which these general personality descriptions are accepted as true was demonstrated at a conference of personnel managers (Stagner, 1958). A standard personality inventory was administered to the group, and the papers were then collected for scoring. Before getting the actual scores, each participant received an identical copy of an alleged "personality analysis." The analysis consisted of a list of descriptive statements, in which the same 13 had been marked for each person. These 13 statements had been chosen because they were assertions applicable to the large majority of people; most were flattering, thus increasing their acceptability. Examples include:

You have a great need for other people to like and admire you.

You have a tendency to be critical of yourself.

You have a great deal of unused capacity which you have not turned to your advantage.

You pride yourself as an independent thinker and do not accept others' statements without satisfactory proof.

The unmarked statements, interspersed among the others, were generally unfavorable comments about the personality traits tested.

After examining his own report, each man was asked to rate the accuracy of the description on the following 5-point scale: amazingly accurate, rather good, about half and half, more wrong than right, almost entirely wrong. Of the 68 personnel managers in the group, 50% marked the description "amazingly accurate," 40% "rather good," and 10% "about half and half." When given the genuine test scores and told about the hoax, the personnel managers were quite vocal in their surprise. Apparently none had doubted the authenticity of the original reports.

Similar results have been obtained with other groups, including industrial managers and college students.[2] Not only were the personality descriptions as a whole accepted as accurate by the large majority of all these groups but most of the individual statements marked for each person were also classified as predominantly correct. It will be recognized that this Barnum effect also accounts for much of the success of fortune tellers, astrologers, and similar charlatans. All these systems provide only random assortments of universally applicable generalities and fail to indicate how one person actually differs from another. And it is this differentiation of individuals that is the primary function of testing and other assessment procedures in industrial, clinical, counseling, and any other contexts.

WHO IS AN APPLIED PSYCHOLOGIST?

Qualifications. The prevalence of charlatanism provides one reason for inquiring into ways of identifying genuine psychologists. In addition, the phenomenal growth of applied psychology since midcentury means that more and more

---

[2]See Forer (1949), Merrens and Richards (1970), Snyder and Larson (1972), Stagner (1958), Sundberg (1955), Ulrich, Stachnik, and Stainton (1963). There is also evidence that such reactions occur in other cultures (Diamond & Bond, 1974). Professional status of examiner is unrelated to acceptance of a favorable personality description, but unfavorable descriptions are more readily accepted from higher-status examiners (Halperin, Snyder, Shenkel, & Houston, 1976).

psychologists are working with laypersons or with members of other professions who may lack the technical knowledge to evaluate the psychologist's qualifications. Hence it has become increasingly important to set up standard procedures for identifying psychologists and judging their special competencies.

Typically, psychologists hold the PhD degree in psychology from the graduate school of an accredited university. They should not be confused with psychiatrists or psychoanalysts. Psychiatrists are trained in medicine. After receiving the MD degree, they undergo several years of supervised experience in the diagnosis and treatment of mental disorders. Their preparation thus parallels that of other medical specialists, such as surgeons or pediatricians. The *psychoanalyst* may be either a psychiatrist or a psychologist who utilizes a particular approach to the treatment of emotional disorders, an approach originating in the psychoanalytic theories of Sigmund Freud. The *clinical psychologist,* like psychologists in other fields, has earned a PhD degree in psychology, with additional experience in working with emotionally disturbed persons. More will be said in Part V of this book regarding the functions of clinical psychologists and their relations with psychiatry.

Some psychologists in all fields have only the MA degree. Such persons are often qualified to function as psychological technicians, in a limited area or under supervision, rather than as professional psychologists. With the growing need for psychological services, a succession of task forces, committees, and boards has endeavored to formulate effective ways of training and utilizing psychologists at different levels of professional qualifications. For the independent practice of psychology, however, the completion of doctoral-level training is considered essential (see, e.g., American Psychological Association, 1975b).

A significant step, both in raising professional standards and in helping the public to determine who is a psychologist, has been the enactment of state certification and licensing laws for psychologists. Nearly all states now have such laws and publish directories of licensed or certified psychologists.[3] Although varying in details, the basic requirements are similar in most states. These include a doctoral degree in psychology plus supervised experience (usually one or two years) and a qualifying examination. Most states employ a uniform multiple-choice examination assessing knowledge of the major fields of psychology at a level that the psychologist should have attained regardless of his or her own specialty. Additional requirements, such as essay examinations, oral examinations, or interviews, may be set up by the individual states.

Generally, the applicant is licensed or certified for the practice of psychology as a whole, rather than in a specialty. Moreover, these procedures are concerned with the attainment of minimal competence for acceptable practice. A higher level of accreditation is provided by the American Board of Professional Psychology (ABPP), an independently incorporated board within the profession itself, originally established by the American Psychological Association. ABPP grants diplomas in four specialties: Clinical, Counseling, Industrial and Organizational, and School

---

[3]In those few states still without licensing or certification laws, the state psychological associations administer nonstatutory certification and publish lists of qualified psychologists. For clinical psychologists qualified to function at the level of independent practice, a comprehensive national source is the *National Register of Health Service Providers in Psychology* (1975; see also Zimet & Wellner, 1977).

Psychology. Requirements include a PhD in the psychological specialty in which the diploma is sought plus five years of experience in the specialty. In addition, ABPP requires an oral examination in the individual's own specialty, which may include field observations of the candidate's professional work or standardized skill assessments in simulated professional situations. The function of ABPP is essentially to provide information on qualified psychologists; and it does so by publishing a directory of diplomates in each specialty. As a privately constituted board within the profession, it has no legal authority for enforcement. Only the state laws pertaining to psychology have such authority.

The American Psychological Association (APA) is the national association to which most psychologists belong (see Appendix A). Membership in this association does not imply that the psychologist is certified for the performance of any service functions. Nevertheless, the Biographical Directory of the APA is a source of considerable information about the location, training, and professional functions of its members. The APA also performs numerous other functions designed to improve and systematize training standards, raise the level of professional practice, and clarify the public image of psychology. Descriptions of the activities of psychologists in various specialties have been published from time to time as a means of informing the public and assisting students in their career choices. The most comprehensive of these surveys, prepared under APA auspices, are *Careers in Psychology* (1975) and *Career Opportunities for Psychologists: Expanding and Emerging Areas* (Woods, 1976).

Of particular importance was the formulation of a professional code of ethics, *Ethical Standards of Psychologists*. First published by the American Psychological Association in 1953 and subsequently revised and amended, this code is especially relevant to the problems encountered by applied psychologists in their relations with the public. A copy is reproduced in Appendix B. Specialized sets of standards and guidelines for psychologists working in particular areas have also been developed as the need arose. Examples include Standards for Providers of Psychological Services (APA, 1975b) and Guidelines for Psychologists Conducting Growth Groups (APA, 1973).

Professional Settings. A final question that may be asked about applied psychologists is where they work. We may begin by examining the primary work settings of psychologists in general. Pertinent data, obtained in a 1974 questionnaire survey conducted by the American Psychological Association, are summarized in Figure 1-2. It will be noted that slightly under half ($46\frac{1}{2}\%$) of the respondents were employed by colleges, universities, and professional schools. A substantial number of these, however, were working primarily in student counseling, administration, or research, with little or no involvement in classroom teaching. At least some would undoubtedly be classified as applied psychologists. The remaining categories in Figure 1-2 fall clearly within the fields of applied psychology surveyed in this book.

Against the background provided by Figure 1-2, we may consider more specifically the various channels through which applied psychologists provide their specialized services to the public. Many industrial psychologists operate through consulting firms and applied research institutes staffed largely by psychologists. Several of these organizations were established after World War II, often by groups of psychologists who had been engaged in psychological work in the military services. Some consulting firms are broader in scope, having been formed

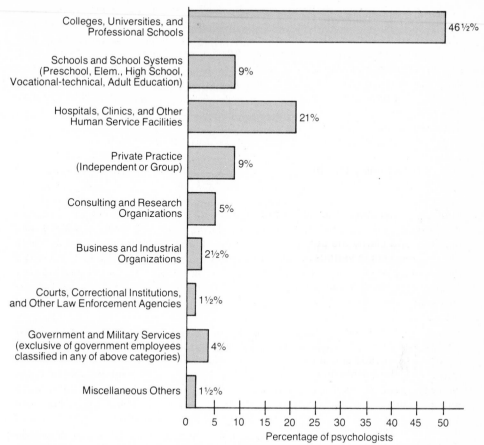

Figure 1-2. Primary work settings of psychologists: Distribution of responses in a survey conducted in 1974 by the Human Resources Department, American Psychological Association. *(Data by courtesy of American Psychological Association.)*

by business consultants or engineers, but employing a number of full-time psychologists. All perform services for industry or government on a contract basis as needed.

Other psychologists are employed directly by business and industry. They can now be found in practically every type of business, including manufacturing, retailing, transportation, advertising, insurance, and many others. An example of an industrywide cooperative organization that has been using the services of psychologists for many years is the Life Insurance Marketing and Research Association (LIMRA). With a psychologist as its research director, this association develops and evaluates personnel selection techniques for life insurance agents and performs other personnel research functions.

Many clinical or counseling psychologists are employed by hospitals, clinics, and counseling agencies. Institutions for mental retardates or for emotionally disturbed patients, Veterans Administration hospitals, outpatient clinics, and community mental health centers are examples of such organizations. A much smaller number of psychologists work in courts, prisons, schools for juvenile delinquents, and other correctional and law enforcement settings. A growing specialty area is that of the school psychologist, employed by public school systems and by some private schools. In addition, a considerable number of counseling, clinical, and educational psychologists work in school systems.

Full-time private practice claims a small proportion of psychologists. In the 1974 APA survey cited in Figure 1-2, fewer than 10% of all respondents listed independent or group practice of clinical psychology as their primary work activity. Private practice in other fields, such as business and industrial psychology, totaled less than 1%.

A highly productive area of applied psychology is represented by military psychology. The functions of psychologists working for the armed services cut across all major fields of applied psychology. They cover most aspects of engineering psychology and systems research, test construction, personnel selection and classification, training and educational technology (especially in the development of vocational skills and literacy training), and leadership and other organizational problems. Clinical psychology is also represented in a variety of research and service functions. In all these areas, the research conducted by military psychologists has produced results relevant to many civilian endeavors (M. P. Crawford, 1970). Such research offers a number of advantages over research conducted in other settings, including access to large samples for relatively long periods of time, better facilities for control and systematic manipulation of experimental variables, and organizational continuity permitting large-scale programmatic research.

A large number of psychologists are employed by civilian government agencies, such as the United States Civil Service Commission, the United States Employment Service, and the many divisions of the Department of Health, Education, and Welfare. Beginning in 1922, when the first government psychologist, L. J. O'Rourke, was appointed director of research in the United States Civil Service Commission (Kavruck, 1956), the employment of psychologists in public service has undergone prodigious growth. Psychologists are also employed in many capacities by state and local governments. Test construction and the development and evaluation of other personnel selection and classification procedures represent one example of the functions commonly performed by such psychologists. It might be added that the total number of psychologists employed by government includes many persons classified elsewhere in Figure 1-2, such as state hospitals, school systems, state universities, and municipal colleges.

From another angle, mention should be made of the special channels for the application of psychology available in university settings. Most universities have counseling centers where counseling and clinical psychologists provide service for the university's own students. Where an active clinical training program is under way, the university may also have hospital facilities, clinics, and counseling centers that serve the public. Some universities have research centers in industrial and organizational psychology which operate much like a consulting firm, carrying out contract research and development programs for industry or government. To this should be added the contract research conducted by individual faculty members, usually under government sponsorship. Although many of these individual research grants are for basic research, some clearly belong in applied psychology.

SUMMARY

Prior to World War II, psychology was primarily an academic discipline. Today, about half of America's psychologists work outside of universities. Employed largely by government agencies, industry, school systems, hospitals, clinics, and community centers, these applied psychologists are contributing in such areas as personnel assessment and training, management and organizational practices, the improvement of work methods and of working and living environments, consumer research and mass communication, the diagnosis and treatment of behavioral disabilities and disturbances, and career and other types of personal counseling. Some psychologists work with members of other professions, as consultants or in the training of other professional personnel. This relationship is currently illustrated in the fields of education, law, and medicine.

Like all psychologists, applied psychologists are trained in the basic science of psychology. Their unique contribution stems from their application of the scientific method to problems of human behavior. The experimental method common to all the sciences consists essentially in the empirical observation and recording of facts under systematically controlled conditions. It requires replication, the use of representative samples, and a determination of the margin of error inherent in its procedures. The distinction between basic and applied research is one of degree. In their service functions, applied psychologists are influenced in many ways by their training in scientific method. In this regard, they differ from the charlatan, who has traditionally invaded several areas of applied psychology. Such professional developments as state certification and licensing of psychologists, the establishment of the American Board of Professional Psychology, and the formulation of *Ethical Standards of Psychologists* and other specialized professional standards and guidelines represent significant steps in combating charlatanism and in clarifying the public image of psychology.

INDUSTRIAL AND ORGANIZATIONAL PSYCHOLOGY

PART TWO

PERSONNEL SELECTION AND CLASSIFICATION

TWO

ONCERNED WITH THE FIELD of industrial and organizational psychology, Part II of this book deals with the application of psychology to personnel selection and classification; personnel development and training; employee attitudes, motivation, and morale; and the many facets of organizational psychology.[1] In accordance with the systems approach introduced in Chapter 1, all these areas of industrial psychology need to be considered in relation to each other as well as to the areas of engineering psychology covered in Part III. We should remain constantly aware of possible interactions among variables of the worker, the job, and the work context, as illustrated in Figure 1-1 and the systems measurement bed. For example, in the effective utilization of human resources, the matching of persons with jobs through personnel selection and classification should be coordinated with development and training. Thus, if selection standards are lowered because of a shortage of qualified applicants, training programs must be strengthened in order to achieve the desired level of job performance. Similarly, changes in the physical and interpersonal work context and the redesign of jobs and equipment may reduce the demands on the worker and thus result in a performance level that could not have been reached by either selection or training, or both. The familiar observation that an individual's job performance is a resultant of his abilities and his motivation provides still another example of interaction. In this and the following section, different aspects of human-factors systems must necessarily be considered sepa-

---

[1]A major publication in this field is the *Handbook of Industrial and Organizational Psychology*, edited by Dunnette (1976), where extensive treatments of all these topics can be found.

rately for practical reasons of presentation. But their interrelations will be frequently noted and should always be borne in mind.

The first two chapters in Part II deal with basic problems and procedures in personnel selection and classification and with available techniques for the assessment of personnel. In industry, such procedures and techniques are used not only in hiring new employees but also in connection with promotions, discharges, transfers, and other personnel decisions. Nor are they limited to industrial psychology. Essentially the same procedures are applicable to the selection and classification of military personnel, the admission of students to college and professional schools, or the identification of clients most likely to benefit from a particular form of therapy. Although first discussed in this section within the context of industrial psychology, these techniques provide an introduction to methodology that is of basic importance in most fields of applied psychology, since they concern the fundamental goal of the utilization and conservation of human resources. For this reason, they will be examined more fully than more specialized procedures of limited application. A timely survey of major problems and procedures in this broad area can be found in Dunnette and Borman (1979).

JOB ANALYSIS

Nature and Objectives. The purpose of a job analysis is to provide a description of what workers do on the job for which selection procedures are being developed. The description should cover operations performed, equipment used, conditions of work, hazards and other special characteristics of the job, nature and amount of training provided, opportunities for promotion or transfer, relation to other jobs, and any other pertinent information. Such a *job description* provides the basis for the *job specification,* or list of worker qualifications for which tests or other selection devices must be prepared. To be effective, a job analysis must be specific to the job being studied. A description in terms of vague generalities that would be equally applicable to many jobs is of little use for purposes of personnel selection and classification. The job analysis must focus on those requirements that differentiate the particular job from other jobs.

An even more important characteristic of an effective job analysis is that it indicate those aspects of performance that differentiate most sharply between the better and the poorer workers. In many jobs, workers of different levels of proficiency may differ little in the way they carry out most parts of their jobs—only certain features of the job may bring out the important differences between successes and failures. In his classic book, *Aptitude Testing,* Hull (1928) stressed the importance of these differentiating aspects of job performance, which he called "critical part-activities." Later, this concept was reemphasized by Flanagan (1949, 1954) under the name of "critical requirements." It also underlies the job-element method of job analysis developed by the U. S. Civil Service Commission (Primoff, 1975).

Although for the present purpose we are considering job analysis as the first step in developing a personnel selection program, it should be noted that it has other important uses in industry. It can serve as a basis for setting up or modifying training programs, improving operating procedures, reducing accident hazards, and redesigning equipment. Job analyses also help in arriving at job evaluations for adjusting pay rates. For this purpose, different jobs are rated with regard to certain major factors, such as training and experience required, physical and psychological demands, degree of responsibility, and working conditions. By assigning weights to these factors, one can obtain an overall evaluation for each job, which is then used in setting up the wage scale. Still another application of job analysis is to be found in the preparation of job descriptions and classifications used in vocational counseling. More will be said about such sources of occupational information in Chapter 16.

Procedures. For whatever purpose it is conducted, job analysis requires systematic data-gathering techniques if it is to yield usable information.[2] Job analysts should preferably combine several sources of information to obtain a well-rounded picture of job activities. They may consult *published sources,* including descriptions of similar jobs as well as training and operating manuals prepared for the particular job. *Performance records* may be examined, especially those that contain qualitative descriptions of common errors, learning difficulties, and reasons for failure on the job. Records of customer complaints may provide clues useful in the analysis of sales jobs.

Direct observation of a representative sample of workers is always desirable. This technique may involve no more than unaided personal observation, as when the job analyst accompanies a house-to-house salesperson or a delivery truck driver on regular rounds. When applicable, tapes, films, and other objective performance records may be utilized. In the analysis of manual operations, the job analyst may use the techniques of time and motion study, to be discussed in Part III. To be sure, the mere presence of an observer may affect performance somewhat in many types of jobs. Nevertheless, this type of observation provides the job analyst with a fuller and more vivid picture of job activities than could be obtained through more indirect sources.

An important source of information for any kind of job is provided by *interviews*—with supervisors, job instructors, and workers of varying degrees of experience and job success. Such interviews have a number of advantages as job-analysis techniques. It is obvious that persons who have been carrying on the job are in a good position to report what occurs on such a job. Moreover, the participation of workers and supervisors in the job analysis gives them a better understanding of what the psychologist is trying to do and increases their ultimate acceptance of the results of the project. On the other hand, workers, however experienced in job activities, may have little insight into the reasons for their own or other workers' success or failure. Nor can they readily translate job activities into worker qualifications. Semantic problems may also interfere with communication. Such terms as "good judgment," "sense of humor," or "dependability" may have very different connotations for different persons. For all these reasons, such interviews should cover objective facts as much as possible, focusing on what workers do and what happens.

An attempt to introduce more objectivity into workers' reports is illustrated by another technique, which may be described as a *diary* or *activity log.* Rather than relying on memory during an interview, the worker is required to keep a running

---

[2]For a survey and critical evaluation of some major techniques, see McCormick (1976b), Prien and Ronan (1971).

record of all the tasks performed during a specified period of time. Such a procedure reveals many activities that may be overlooked when one relies on the recollections of a small sample of workers. An example of this method is provided by R. Stewart's (1967) study of 160 British managers, who kept diaries of daily job activities on specially prepared forms for a period of four weeks.

A procedure that utilizes some of the features of the diary method is the *critical-incident technique* described by Flanagan (1954). Essentially, this technique calls for factual descriptions of specific instances of job behavior that are especially characteristic of either satisfactory or unsatisfactory workers. It thus centers attention on the previously discussed critical job requirements, leaving out of consideration job behavior that does not differentiate successful from unsuccessful workers. Depending on the nature of the job and other circumstances, the incidents may be reported by supervisors, co-workers, subordinates, or other associates. To ensure frankness in reporting, anonymity of the data should be preserved. The incidents may be recorded as they occur over a designated period, such as two weeks. Growing out of Air Force research during World War II, the critical-incident technique has been employed with such varied groups as commercial airline pilots, research personnel in physical science laboratories, factory workers, dentists, and department store salesclerks.

In the effort to make job analysis more systematic and quantitative, increasing use is being made of *structured job analysis inventories.* These instruments provide lists of job tasks, as well as working conditions and other appropriate job characteristics. Workers may be asked to check items that are applicable to their jobs, or they may rate each item in terms of relevant scales, such as time spent on the task or importance for the job. This method of job analysis has been applied to Air Force personnel (Morsh, 1962), clerical workers (Prien, 1965), and industrial executives (Hemphill, 1959), among others.

Another methodological development is the growing focus on worker-oriented job analysis, in terms of psychological characteristics required for the performance of job tasks. An example is the Position Analysis Questionnaire, or PAQ (McCormick, Jeanneret, & Mecham, 1972). Developed through several years of research, this instrument provides quantitative measures of the degree of involvement of different sensory, motor, and cognitive attributes in each job that is analyzed. For instance, how much arithmetic reasoning, spatial visualization, or manual dexterity does a particular job demand? Also included are situational characteristics of the job context (physical and psychological) that require the individual to adapt to given working conditions (e.g., dealing with people, working against time pressure).

A similar approach is represented by the work of Fleishman and his associates (Fleishman, 1972, 1975; Theologus & Fleishman, 1971) on task taxonomy. Drawing upon their own long-term research on psychomotor and physical abilities (subsequently extended to include sensory functions) and on the accumulated published findings on cognitive traits,[3] these investigators have proposed a behavioral taxonomy as a basis for describing job functions.

An example of a job analysis prepared by the United States Employment Service (USES) is given in Appendix C. The job chosen for this illustration is that of dough

---

[3]For those familiar with factor-analytic research, it should be added that these traits include the most widely verified factors in Guilford's Structure-of-Intellect model.

mixer in the bakery products industry—a job covering relatively few different tasks. It is noteworthy that, even for such a simple job, a proper job description is considerably fuller and more detailed than an untrained observer would assume. The USES job analysts utilize a combination of direct observation of the worker performing the job and interviews with workers, supervisors, and others who may have information about the job.

In translating the job description into worker qualifications, the USES employs a variety of ratings, as illustrated in Appendix C. First, there is an evaluation of the level of work performance in relation to data, people, and things. Jobs are also grouped into broad Occupational Interest Areas of Work, such as artistic, scientific, industrial, humanitarian. In this classification, the job of dough mixer is placed in the "industrial" category. Worker requirements are specified in reference to general educational development, kind and amount of specific vocational preparation, and aptitude test scores (when available for the particular occupation). The job analyst also records under "temperaments" the characteristic types of job situations to which the worker must adapt (e.g., a variety of duties requiring frequent change) and indicates the physical demands and environmental conditions associated with the job.

DEVELOPMENT AND EVALUATION OF PREDICTORS

Job analysis enables the personnel psychologist to define the problem by specifying the critical worker requirements for success in the given job. Such an analysis may suggest, for example, that the job demands finger dexterity, perceptual speed, computational accuracy, and the ability to work effectively under confusing and distracting conditions. The next step is to prepare tests, questions, rating scales, or other selection devices designed to assess the applicant's standing in these traits. All such selection instruments are known as *predictors,* since they are used to predict each individual's subsequent job performance.

The predictors assembled at this stage may include previously available published tests, instruments developed specially for this project, or a combination of the two. In choosing a predictor or in preparing a new one, the psychologist is, in effect, formulating a series of hypotheses, namely, that the score on each test or the answer to each question on an application or recommendation form is significantly related to eventual success on the given job. The correctness of these hypotheses depends upon several factors, such as the effectiveness of the job analysis in bringing out important job requirements, the proper utilization of previous research data obtained with available instruments in similar job situations, the psychologist's ingenuity in devising new instruments, and his general familiarity with psychological facts and principles. Much can be done in advance to increase the chances that correct hypotheses will be formulated. Nevertheless, some empirical confirmation within the particular job context is always desirable.

The technical procedures for constructing and evaluating tests and other assessment instruments are beyond the scope of this book. For surveys of such procedures, the reader is referred to texts on psychological testing and personnel assessment (e.g., Anastasi, 1976, Chs. 4–8, 15; Guion, 1965a; Lawshe & Balma, 1966; McCormick & Tiffin, 1974, Chs. 5–7). General guidelines for test evaluation are provided by the *Standards for Educational and Psychological Tests* (1974), published by the American Psychological Association. A more specialized set of guidelines for the validation of personnel selection instruments was prepared by the APA Division of Industrial and Organizational Psychology (1975a). Critical reviews of published tests can be found in the series of *Mental Measurements Yearbooks* (Buros, 1978). For the present purpose, we shall focus on the major concepts needed to understand the use of tests with industrial personnel, particularly with reference to the reliability and validity of tests and the use of test results in reaching personnel decisions.

Reliability. The reliability of a test refers to its consistency. Will individuals retain the same relative positions in the group if they are examined on two occasions with the same finger dexterity test? Obviously, if there were broad shifts in position, so that the person who was best in the group on one day scored near the bottom when retested on another day, the test could have no value as a predictor of subsequent job performance. As suggested by this example, the temporal stability of a test can be determined by comparing the scores obtained by the same persons on two administrations of the test.

Another aspect of test reliability pertains to consistency of scores on parallel forms of the test. Although designed to measure the same ability, such parallel forms are composed of different items. For example, two forms of a vocabulary test might yield slightly different scores because some individuals happen to know more words on one list, while others know more words on the other list. This type of reliability can be measured by comparing the scores obtained by the same persons on two forms of a test. When two forms are not available, the reliability is often estimated by comparing scores on two halves of a single form, such as the scores on odd and even items.

In the event that the test cannot be objectively scored but requires evaluation or interpretation of responses by the examiner, a further type of reliability that should be checked is scorer reliability. This can be done by having a sample of papers independently scored by two examiners and computing the degree of scorer agreement between the two sets of scores. Scorer reliability is more likely to represent a problem in certain types of personality tests than in aptitude tests, although it needs to be considered in some of the latter too.

Whatever the type of reliability under consideration, it can be expressed in terms of a *correlation coefficient.*[4] This statistical technique, which is used for many purposes in psychological research, shows the degree of relationship or correspondence between two sets of scores. The correlation coefficient, conventionally designated by the symbol r, provides a single index of the closeness and direction of relationship within the whole group. It can vary from +1.00 (a perfect positive correlation), through 0, to −1.00 (a perfect negative, or inverse, correlation). A +1.00 correlation means that the individual receiving the highest score in one variable also receives the highest score in the other, the one who is second best in the first is second best in the second, etc., each person falling just as far above or below the mean in one variable as he does in the other. A −1.00 correlation, on the other hand, indicates that the highest score in one variable is paired off with the lowest in the other, a corresponding perfect reversal occurring throughout the

---

[4]Procedures for computing correlation coefficients can be found in any elementary statistics book, such as Guilford and Fruchter (1978). For further discussion of test reliability, see any recent text on psychological testing, such as Anastasi (1976) and Ebel (1972).

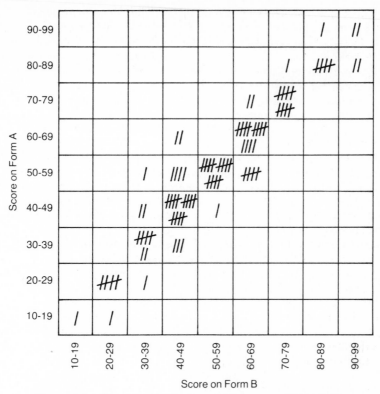

Figure 2-1. Bivariate distribution yielding a correlation of .94.

group. A zero correlation signifies no relationship at all between the two sets of scores, or the sort of arrangement that would result if the scores were shuffled and paired off at random.

The correlations found in actual practice are almost never equal to +1.00 or −1.00 but fall on some intermediate value. The numerical size of the coefficient represents the closeness of relationship, in either a positive or negative direction. An example of high positive correlation is given in Figure 2-1. This figure shows a bivariate distribution, indicating the scores obtained by each of 100 examinees on Forms A and B of a test. Each tally mark shows the score of one person on both forms. It can be seen, for example, that seven persons obtained scores between 30 and 39 on both forms, while three scored between 30 and 39 on Form A but between 40 and 49 on Form B. When computed, the correlation between the two forms proves to be .94. Such a correlation indicates a strong tendency for individuals to maintain the same relative standing on the two forms, although it can be seen that the correspondence is not perfect.

Validity. The most important practical question about any psychological test concerns its validity, i.e., the extent to which the test actually measures what it purports to measure. Do the applicants who score high on this test perform well on the job, while those who score low perform poorly? High reliability is a necessary but not a sufficient condition for high validity. If a test has low reliability, it cannot have high validity, because scores on this test depend to a large extent on erratic, chance factors. A high reliability, on the other hand, does not ensure high validity. The test could be measuring with a high degree of consistency abilities that are not related to performance on the particular job. In this context, job performance is the *criterion* against which the validity of the test is measured. In technical usage, the criterion is defined as an independent measure of the behavior that the test is designed to assess or predict.

The validity of a test may be investigated in many ways. In the APA test *Standards* (1974), these procedures are classified under three major types of validity: content, criterion-related, and construct. *Content validity* involves essentially the systematic examination of the test content to determine whether it covers a representative sample of the behavior domain to be measured. Educational achievement tests, such as tests of arithmetic or spelling, are commonly evaluated in terms of their content validity. In industry, content validity is generally employed for job-sample tests, in which the task set for the examinee is a representative part of the work to be performed on the job. Familiar examples include driving tests and tests for such office skills as typing, stenography, bookkeeping, and the operation of various business machines. Many job-sample tests are custom-made to fit specific jobs. The representativeness of the job sample is an important consideration in all forms of content validation.

Job samples merge imperceptibly with simulators, which call for the same behavior functions required on the job but, for practical reasons, may employ specially designed equipment, compressed time schedules, and artificially contrived situations. Examples of these tests will be examined in Chapter 3. Certain other refinements and elaborations of content validation, which are widely applicable in the design of personnel selection procedures, will be described in a later section of this chapter.

Criterion-related validity is based essentially on the comparison of test scores with some index of criterion behavior, such as job performance. Ideally, it would seem to be the most appropriate procedure for validating tests for personnel selection and classification. Its application in industrial settings, however, is limited by several practical difficulties. Both its uses and limitations will be examined further in the next two sections. Criterion-related validity may be subdivided into *predictive* and *concurrent* validity, which differ essentially in the time relations between test administration and the gathering of criterion data. In an industrial context, predictive validity involves the testing of applicants or newly hired employees on whom criterion data are obtained after a sufficient period of employment, such as six months, a year, or longer. In concurrent validation, the test is administered to present employees on whom criterion data are already available.

The *construct validity* of a test is the extent to which the test may be said to measure a theoretical construct or trait. Examples of such constructs are verbal aptitude, mechanical comprehension, manual dexterity, emotional stability, and dominance. Such traits are frequently identified by intercorrelating scores from a large number of tests and applying a further statistical technique known as factor analysis.[5] Essentially, the factors, traits, or constructs thus identified represent

---

[5]For brief introductions to factor analysis, see Adcock (1954), Anastasi (1976, Ch. 13), and Nunnally (1978, Chs. 9–10). A comprehensive treatment of the statistical methodology of factor analysis, at a more advanced level, can be found in Harman (1976).

behavioral characteristics that are common to many specific activities. Utilizing a broader kind of behavioral description than do other types of validity, construct validation requires the gradual accumulation of information from a variety of sources. Its relevance to the industrial use of tests is receiving increasing recognition and will be illustrated in a later section on component and synthetic validity. Construct validation is also implied by some tests designed by job simulation.

CRITERION-RELATED VALIDITY IN PERSONNEL ASSESSMENT

Criterion-related validation has three essential requirements: (1) an adequate sample of persons to be tested, (2) a suitable criterion measure of job performance, and (3) appropriate statistical techniques for analyzing the relation between test scores and criterion measures.

Validation Sample. The ideal procedure would be to test an unselected sample of applicants, all of whom are then hired and retained on the job long enough to accumulate adequate and stable criterion data. For practical reasons, it is rarely, if ever, feasible to study such an unselected sample. At the very least, however, applicants in the validation sample should be hired without reference to their scores on the test under investigation. The problem here is that of *preselection,* which reduces the variability or range of individual differences in job-relevant variables within the sample, thereby lowering any correlation computed between test and criterion. The validity of the test will thus be underestimated under these conditions. Such reduction in the validity coefficient normally occurs unless a completely unselected applicant sample is followed up. If the sample were to be selected on the basis of scores on the test itself, the artificial reduction in measured validity would be so great as to render the results almost meaningless.

If time restrictions or other conditions necessitate the use of present employees rather than applicants, yielding concurrent rather than predictive validation, several additional features of the experimental design are sacrificed. Attrition over time will not only shrink sample size but will also further reduce variability, with a corresponding lowering of validity coefficients. Present employees will also have had varying amounts of job experience, which may be reflected in their test performance, thereby confounding the relation between test score and criterion. Furthermore, when employees are given tests "for research purposes only," their motivation and test-taking attitudes may be quite unlike those of genuine job applicants; and these conditions are likely to be reflected in their test performance.

Criterion Measures. The measures employed to represent the employees' criterion status obviously constitute a key element in this type of validation. Industrial psychologists have given much attention to what has come to be known as "the criterion problem" (Ronan & Prien, 1966). It is widely recognized that the criterion measures employed in most personnel research leave much to be desired with regard to their reliability as well as to their coverage of job performance. Job success is a complex concept, and it can be assessed in many ways. Production records provide a criterion measure available for many kinds of jobs. Quantity and quality of output, waste through spoilage of materials, amount of sales, and merchandise returned are among the records that can be used for this purpose. Length of time the individual remains on the job represents a more comprehensive criterion measure, especially important in jobs having rapid turnover. Whether employees are discharged for incompetence or whether they leave spontaneously, they contribute to turnover costs. In certain jobs, performance in training provides useful criterion data. Other sources include records of accidents, absenteeism, tardiness, and disciplinary actions. In concurrent validation with present employees, industrial psychologists sometimes compare the mean test performance of persons in different jobs or different levels of the same job. This job-status criterion is based on the expectation that, in general, individuals tend to move into and remain in jobs that are in line with their aptitudes.

Regardless of how much objective information may be available, it is usually desirable to include ratings among criterion measures. Depending upon the nature of the job, such ratings may be obtained from supervisors, co-workers, subordinates, instructors, or other personnel. If secured under satisfactory conditions, ratings represent a particularly good source of criterion data. Specific rating techniques, as well as ways of reducing common judgment errors, will be discussed in Chapter 3. A special advantage of rating procedures is that the rater can make allowances for unusual conditions affecting an individual's production record or other facets of job performance. For example, one factory worker may turn out fewer articles than another because he has poorer equipment, or one salesperson may sell more life insurance than another because she operates in a higher income territory. Either the criterion measures should be obtained solely from persons working under closely similar conditions or they should be adjusted in some way for existing inequalities.

An essential precaution in criterion-related validation is to guard against *criterion contamination,* whereby the test scores themselves influence an individual's criterion status. For example, if a supervisor knows that one employee scored low and another high on an aptitude test, this knowledge may affect the ratings they receive for job performance. Such influences will artificially inflate the correlation between test scores and criterion. It is therefore imperative that anyone who participates in the assignment of criterion ratings have no access to test scores or other predictor data. While the predictors are being validated, they must not be used for operational purposes in either selecting or evaluating personnel.

Statistical Indices of Validity. The validity of each predictor may be determined by analyzing the relationship between predictor scores and criterion scores. Suppose the validation sample includes two contrasted groups of life insurance agents, one composed of highly successful salespersons, the other of near failures. With such a dichotomous, or twofold, criterion, we may compare the mean predictor scores obtained by the two groups. If the successful agents achieve higher predictor scores than the unsuccessful, then the predictor has some validity for this criterion.

To answer the question conclusively, we need to determine the *significance of the difference* between the means of the two groups. Measures of statistical significance are widely used in psychological research, being required in nearly all types of investigations. The computational details can be found in any elementary textbook of statistics (e.g., Guilford & Fruchter, 1978). For interpretive purposes, we shall be concerned only with the basic rationale. From a practical standpoint, statistical significance refers essentially to the chances that similar results will be obtained if the investigation is repeated. How likely is it that the successful salespersons would again score higher than the unsuccessful if another sample were tested and followed up? A certain amount of variation in results will always occur through *sampling error,* as well as through the unreliability of measuring instruments discussed in an earlier section. Every investigation utilizes only a sample of the total relevant population. In personnel selection research, for instance, the sample on which validity is determined is never the same as the groups on whom the predictors will be used operationally. How far, then, can we generalize from the validation sample to other samples?

The sampling fluctuation (or standard error) of a mean depends upon the number of cases *(N)* and the variability, or extent of individual differences in the group. Variability is normally measured by the standard deviation *(SD),* based on the difference between each person's score and the group mean.[6] The standard error of the difference between two means can itself be computed from the standard errors of the two means. The end-product of such computations is always a *p* value, giving the probability that the difference between the two means is small enough to have resulted from chance errors of sampling. If this probability is less than 1 out of 100 ($p <$ .01), we generally conclude that the difference is large enough to be significant. In other words, we conclude that, in the total population from which this sample was drawn, the difference would still favor the same group (e.g., the successful salespersons). The chances of such a conclusion being wrong are less than 1 out of 100. It might be added that a lower level of significance, such as .05, is sometimes accepted. In every investigation, however, the level used is specified.

A finer breakdown of the relation between predictor and criterion may be presented in the form of an *expectancy chart,* illustrated in Figure 2-2. This chart

[6] $SD = \sqrt{\dfrac{\Sigma(X - M)^2}{N}}$ *SD* is also symbolized by the Greek letter sigma (σ).

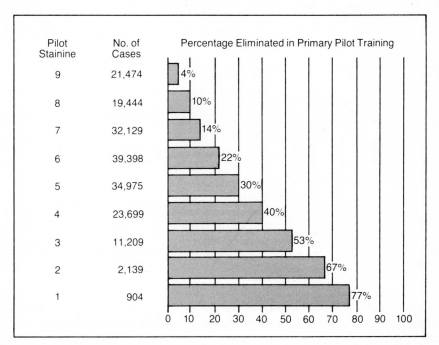

Figure 2-2. Expectancy chart showing relation between pilot stanine and elimination from primary flight training. *(From Flanagan, 1947, p. 58.)*

shows the percentages of student pilots who failed primary flight training within each stanine score[7] on the pilot selection battery developed by the Air Force. Figure 2-2 shows that 77% of the trainees with the lowest stanine score (1) were eliminated, while only 4% of those receiving the highest stanine score (9) failed to complete the course satisfactorily. The percentage of failures decreases consistently over the intervening stanines. These percentages, given in Figure 2-2, provide an estimate of the probability that student pilots tested subsequently would pass or fail. For example, it can be predicted that approximately 40% of candidates scoring 4 will fail and 60% will pass. Similar statements can be made about the expectancy of success or failure on the part of individuals. Thus, an individual with a pilot stanine score of 4 has a 60:40, or 3:2, chance of completing primary flight training.

Another example of an expectancy chart is given in Figure 2-3. This chart shows the performance of 83 participants in a training program for technicians in a utility company. The training program consisted of six progressively more complex steps or modules. The chart shows the percentage of trainees who successfully completed five or six modules, in relation to their scores on the Numerical Test of the Personnel Tests for Industry (to be discussed in Chapter 3). These percentages range from 0, among those scoring below 10 on the test, to 80, among those scoring 20 and above.

[7]The stanine (contraction of *"standard nine"*) is a widely used type of standard score, expressed on a 9-point scale, with a mean of 5 and an *SD* of approximately 2 points. All standard scores give the individual's distance above or below the mean in terms of *SD* units. To avoid negative numbers and decimals, the scores are usually translated into a new scale with conveniently chosen values for mean and *SD*.

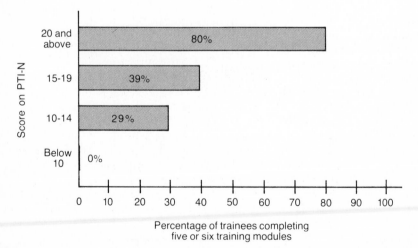

Figure 2-3. Relation between scores on Personnel Tests for Industry—Numerical (PTI-N) and performance of 83 technician trainees in a utility company. *(Data by courtesy of The Psychological Corporation.)*

The most precise expression of the relation between predictor and criterion is provided by a *validity coefficient*. Such a coefficient is customarily computed when both predictor and criterion scores are in the form of continuous variables. In that case, the relation can be represented in a bivariate distribution such as that illustrated in Figure 2-1 and the correlation computed by the same method. Other types of correlations, however, can be employed when predictor or criterion or both are in the form of dichotomies or of multiple categories. These techniques are described in standard statistics texts. Like all statistical measures, validity coefficients must be evaluated for significance. If we find that a validity coefficient is significant at the .01 level, we conclude that it is too high to have resulted from chance errors, and we accept it as evidence of genuine validity.

Whether a validity coefficient is high enough for practical significance, as contrasted with statistical significance, depends on the way the test is to be used. For example, will the test be used singly or in combination with other predictors? What sort of personnel decisions will be made from the test scores? We shall return to these questions in later sections on the combination of predictors and their use in decision strategies.

ALTERNATIVE APPROACHES TO TEST VALIDATION

Limitations of Criterion-Related Validation Studies. When the same or similar tests were correlated with performance on presumably similar jobs in industrial validation studies, the validity coefficients were found to vary widely. In one extensive survey of published studies, for example, spatial relations tests correlated from −.55 to +.65 with job performance of machine tenders (Ghiselli, 1959, 1966). Such findings led to widespread pessimism regarding the generalizability of test validity to different job situations. The variability among validity coefficients may stem from several sources. When results are reported for different tests designed to measure the same aptitude (e.g., spatial relations), some variation may arise from differences in reliability and other properties of the specific test. Substantial differences in validity have been reported, however, even when the identical test is used with different samples.

In a sophisticated statistical analysis of the problem, Schmidt and his co-workers (Schmidt & Hunter, 1977a, 1977b; Schmidt, Hunter, & Urry, 1976) demonstrated that much of the variance among obtained validity coefficients may be a statistical artifact resulting from small sample size, criterion unreliability, and preselection. The industrial samples available for test validation are generally too small to yield a stable estimate of the correlation between predictor and criterion. For the same reason, the obtained coefficients may be too low to reach statistical significance in the sample employed and may thus fail to provide evidence of the test's validity. It has been estimated that about half of the validation samples used in industrial studies may include no more than 40 or 50 cases (Schmidt et al., 1976, p. 474). With such small samples, the application of criterion-related validation is not technically feasible. The unavailability of adequately large samples should therefore be added to the other obstacles that lie in the way of applying criterion-related validation mentioned in the preceding section.

Still another condition that may contribute to the variability of criterion-related validity coefficients is to be found in the criterion measures employed in industrial studies. For example, the correlation of a clerical aptitude test with the job performance of office clerks may be high in one department or company and low in another because the duties of office clerks may differ substantially from one department or company to another. Test validities may also vary when checked against different criteria of success in a single job. For example, a test may fail to correlate significantly with supervisors' ratings and yet show appreciable validity in predicting who will resign and who will be promoted at a later date (Albright, Smith, & Glennon, 1959). When different types of criteria are compared for the same individuals, moreover, their intercorrelations are often quite low. For instance, accident records or absenteeism may show virtually no relation to productivity or error data (Seashore, Indik, & Georgopoulos, 1960).

There is also evidence that job criteria may change over time, for various reasons, such as amount of practice or experience, advancement in rank, changing nature of the same job, and shifts in organizational goals (Fleishman, 1972; Ghiselli & Haire, 1960; MacKinney, 1967; Prien, 1966). Similarly, tests that predict performance in training may fail to predict subsequent job proficiency (Ghiselli, 1966). In summary, extensive research on "the criterion problem" has clearly demonstrated that job criteria are complex and dynamic rather than static; that various types of criterion data, or subcriteria, for any one job may have little relation to each other; and that different jobs bearing the same name often represent a different combination of subcriteria.

Because of criterion complexity, validating a test against a global criterion of job proficiency may be of questionable value and is certainly of limited generality. If different subcriteria, or job elements, are relatively independent, a more effective procedure is to validate each test against the particular job element that it is designed to measure. An analysis of these more specific relationships lends meaning to the test scores in terms of the multiple dimensions of criterion behavior (Dunnette, 1963b; Ebel, 1961; Wallace, 1965). For example, one test might prove to be a valid predictor of a clerk's perceptual speed and accuracy in handling detail work, another of his ability to spell correctly, and still another of his ability to resist distraction.

If, now, we turn to the practical question of evaluating a test or a combination of tests for effectiveness in predicting a complex criterion such as success on a given job, we are faced with the necessity of conducting a separate validation study in each local situation and repeating it at frequent intervals. This is admittedly a desirable procedure and one that is often recommended in test manuals.[8] In many situations, however, it is not feasible to follow this procedure because of almost insurmountable practical obstacles. Even if adequately trained personnel are available to carry out the necessary research, most criterion-related validity studies conducted in industry are likely to prove unsatisfactory for at least three reasons. First, it is difficult to obtain dependable and sufficiently comprehensive criterion data. Second, the number of employees engaged in the same or closely similar jobs within a company is often too small for significant statistical results. Third, correlations will very probably be lowered by restriction of range through preselection.

For all these reasons, personnel psychologists have been exploring several alternative validation procedures. These procedures usually represent refine-

[8]Some test publishers (e.g., Psychological Corporation, Science Research Associates) provide consulting services at a nominal cost in the validation of their own tests within specific companies.

ments, elaborations, or combinations of one or more of the traditional validation methods. To suggest the directions in which this research is proceeding, three approaches will be cited. These vary from procedures that are already operational on a large scale to those that are at the stage of theoretical exploration and pilot studies. It is beyond the scope of this text to describe the statistical techniques or the operational details for these approaches; such information can be found in the sources cited.

Identification and Assessment of Job Elements. One approach utilizes detailed, standardized rating procedures in a combination of job analysis and content validation. This is illustrated by a test development program designed for personnel selection in a state civil service system and adopted by several states and municipalities (Menne, McCarthy, & Menne, 1976). Essentially, the program follows systematic and objective procedures for collecting and analyzing ratings from job incumbents and supervisors. Ratings are obtained for three types of material. The first is a list of task statements covering the major tasks that a worker on the particular job is expected to perform. These statements are rated with reference to such characteristics as time spent on each task, frequency, criticality and consequence of error, and relation to successful job performance. The second set consists of worker requirements, including knowledge, abilities, skills, and personal characteristics. These worker qualifications are rated in various ways in relation to the previously described task statements. The third set consists of test items to be rated for degree of relatedness to one or more of the worker qualifications needed for the job.

Computers are utilized to process the data from all ratings and to maintain a large item bank from which appropriate tests can be assembled for each job. When items are used in a test, data on examinee job performance are likewise analyzed and stored to provide material for supplementary criterion-related validations. The same approach can be used in assessing the job-relatedness of requirements with regard to education, training, experience, and other background data.

Synthetic Validity. First introduced by Lawshe (1952), the concept of synthetic validity was later defined by Balma (1959, p. 395) as "the inferring of validity in a specific situation from a systematic analysis of job elements, a determination of test validity from these elements, and a combination of elemental validities into a whole." Several procedures have been developed for gathering the needed empirical data and for combining these data to obtain an estimate of synthetic validity for a particular complex criterion (see, e.g., Guion, 1965b; Lawshe & Balma, 1966, Ch. 14; McCormick, 1959; Primoff, 1959, 1975). Essentially, the process involves three steps: (1) detailed job analysis to identify the job elements and their relative weights; (2) analysis and empirical study of each test to determine the extent to which it measures proficiency in performing each of these job elements; and (3) finding the validity of each test for the given job synthetically from the weights of these elements in the job and in the test.

In a long-term research program conducted with United States Civil Service job applicants, Primoff (1959, 1975) developed the J coefficient (for "job coefficient") as an index of synthetic validity. Among the special features of this procedure are the listing of job elements in terms of worker behavior and the rating of the relative importance of these elements in each job by supervisors and job incumbents. Correlations between test scores and self-ratings on job elements are found in total applicant samples (not subject to preselection of employed workers). Various checking procedures are followed to ensure stability of correlations and of weights derived from self-ratings, as well as adequacy of criterion coverage. For these purposes, data are obtained from several different samples of applicant populations. The final estimate of correlation between test and job performance is found from the correlation of each job element with the particular job and the weight of the same element in the given test.[9] There is evidence that the *J* coefficient has proved helpful in improving the employment opportunities of minority applicants and persons with little formal education, because of its concentration on job-relevant skills (Primoff, 1975).

Bayesian Statistics. Schmitt and Hunter (1977a, 1977b) describe still another approach, based on an application of Bayesian statistics (Novick & Jackson, 1974). Following a job analysis of the job under consideration, the investigator chooses a test (or a set of tests) found to predict the relevant job behaviors in prior research. Statistical procedures are given for estimating the extent of variability in prior validity coefficients attributable to chance errors associated with sample size, criterion unreliability, and range restriction. From such an analysis, it is possible to assess the degree of generalizability of prior validity findings to the present job situation. If the validity coefficient anticipated from such an analysis of prior data is high enough, no further research is needed. If not, local, criterion-related validation is conducted on the limited available sample. However, with a Bayesian approach, the data obtained on the present sample are interpreted in *combination* with the data accumulated in prior studies, thereby strengthening the confidence that can be placed in the findings.

COMBINING PREDICTORS

Having determined the validity of various predictors for a given job criterion and having on that basis chosen the predictors to be retained for operational purposes, the personnel psychologist must now formulate an appropriate strategy for using these predictors in making personnel decisions. In the terminology of decision theory, a strategy is a technique for utilizing information in order to reach a decision about the individual. The simplest kind of strategy involves the use of a single predictor. If circumstances of supply and demand determine the proportion of applicants to be hired, then all that is required is to start selecting individuals from the top of the predictor distribution and continue downward until the required number of persons has been hired. If only persons likely to fall above a minimum criterion level are acceptable, then a cutoff point in predictor scores can be established by examining the bivariate distribution of criterion and predictor scores. How high a test score should applicants have, for example, to ensure that 90% of those hired will reach or exceed a specified standard of job performance?

Most selection programs, however, are not so simple as this. Since criteria are complex, several predictors are usually required for adequate criterion coverage. With multiple predictors, the question arises as to how they are to be combined in

---

[9]The statistical procedures are essentially an adaptation of multiple regression equations, discussed in the next section. For each job element, its correlation with the job is multiplied by its weight in the test, and these products are added across all appropriate job elements.

reaching a decision about the individual. Given five scores earned by an individual on tests or other selection devices, how are they to be used in deciding whether to accept or reject the applicant?

Clinical Judgment. When tests or other predictors are employed in the intensive study of individual cases, as in selection of high-level personnel, executive evaluation, clinical diagnosis, or counseling, it is a common practice for scores to be interpreted by the examiner in arriving at a decision without further statistical manipulation. To be sure, the individual's scores are evaluated with reference to any available general or local norms. But no statistical formula or other automatic procedure is applied in combining scores from different predictors or in interpreting the individual's score pattern. Through a relatively subjective process, the examiner interprets the individual's scores in terms of his own past experience with similar cases, his familiarity with particular job requirements, or his knowledge of psychological theory and relevant published research. The results are usually presented in the form of a detailed description of aptitudes, interests, motivation, and other job-relevant variables, supplemented by specific predictions regarding performance on the job under consideration. The use of clinical judgment to synthesize test results and data from other sources is prevalent in assessment centers. These centers represent a growing approach to the evaluation of high-level personnel, to be described in Chapter 3.

There is a substantial body of research on what the clinician or interviewer does when evaluating and combining data to reach a decision. Some investigators have tried to compare the relative effectiveness of clinical and statistical methods of combining data in situations where both are applicable. But, in practice, both are rarely applicable to the same situation. We may lack either the extensive quantitative data needed to develop statistical prediction formulas or the time and personnel needed for clinical prediction. Further discussion of clinical judgment will be found in Chapter 12.

Multiple Cutoff Scores. A simple statistical strategy for combining scores utilizes multiple cutoff points. This procedure requires the establishment of a minimum score on *each* predictor. Every applicant who falls below the minimum score on any one of the predictors is rejected; only those reaching or exceeding the cutoff scores on all predictors are accepted. This is the technique followed, for example, in the General Aptitude Test Battery (GATB) developed by the United States Employment Service for use in the occupational counseling program of its State Employment Service offices (U.S. Department of Labor, 1970a). This battery yields nine aptitude scores, only some of which are considered for any one occupation. For example, accounting was found to require a minimum score of 105 in General Learning Ability and 115 in Numerical Aptitude; plumbing called for a minimum of 85 in General Learning Ability, 80 in Spatial Aptitude and in Manual Dexterity, and 75 in Clerical Perception. These are standard scores on a scale having a mean of 100 and an *SD* of 20.

The multiple cutoff strategy is readily applicable to predictors that are not linearly related to the criterion. Up to a certain point, for example, speed of hand movement may be closely related to output in an assembly-line job. But, beyond that point, greater speed may be of no avail because of the mechanical limitations of the operation. The relevance of speed to performance in such a job would be reflected in the failure of persons below a certain speed. Yet the correlation between speed and performance level among employed workers may be low and negligible. The multiple cutoff technique is also especially suitable for jobs in which superior ability along one line cannot compensate for a deficiency in an essential skill. Operators of sound-detection devices, for example, need good auditory discrimination. Anyone incapable of making the necessary discriminations will fail in such a job, regardless of how well qualified he or she may be in other respects.

Multiple Regression Equation. The most precise strategy for combining predictor scores is that using the multiple regression equation. This equation yields a predicted criterion score for each individual. Specific techniques for computing regression equations can be found in many texts on psychological statistics. In such an equation, each predictor is weighted in direct proportion to its criterion correlation and in inverse proportion to its correlation with other predictors in the battery. Thus a test that overlaps other tests in the battery receives less weight than one that measures a unique aspect of the criterion, even if their validity coefficients are equally high. The weights employed are also such as to translate all predictor scores into the same units, so that they may be added. Finally, a constant is added to the total so as to express the predicted criterion score in terms of some convenient scale, usually the same scale employed in reporting the original criterion scores.

The use of a multiple regression equation in predicting an applicant's job performance can be illustrated with the following equation:

$$X'_c = .23X_1 + .32X_2 + .18X_3 + .39X_4 + 46.$$

Let us suppose that an applicant, Audrey Barclay, earns the following scores on four predictors, in the order listed in the above equation: 15, 8, 11, and 13. Her predicted criterion score (X'_c) is then computed by substituting these values in the equation, as follows:

$$X'_c = (.23)(15) + (.32)(8) + (.18)(11) + (.39)(13) + 46 = 59.06.$$

Rounding the total to two significant figures, we would report applicant Barclay's estimated criterion score, or index of expected job performance, as 59. This score can then be evaluated either in reference to the scores of other applicants or in reference to an empirically established cutoff score.

It can be seen that, unlike the multiple cutoff strategy, the multiple regression equation makes it possible for high scores in some predictors to compensate for low scores in others. For this reason, this technique should not be used when deficiencies in key skills ought to disqualify an applicant. With such jobs, a combination of multiple cutoff and regression equation may be employed, whereby applicants are first screened on key skills and then the regression equation is applied to the remaining cases. An advantage of the regression equation is that it provides an index of each individual's predicted job performance, permitting a comparison of the relative qualifications of applicants. With multiple cutoff procedures, individuals are simply identified as falling above or below each cutoff point.

Cross-Validation. When a set of predictors has been selected on the basis of their individual validities, the validity of the set as a whole should be checked in a new sample. Such an independent determination of validity in a second comparable sample is known as "cross-validation." This step is especially important when we start with a large number of predictors, such as individual items for an application form, and retain a small proportion for final use. Cross-validation is advisable in making up a battery of tests, especially if a relatively large number of the original tests are discarded because of low validities. The validity of the composite—be it test battery, application form, or total test whose items were individually validated—should not be computed on the same sample used for choosing the individual predictors. If it were so computed, the validity coefficient would capitalize on chance errors within the original sample and would consequently be spuriously high. In fact, a high validity coefficient will result under these circumstances, even when the set of predictors has no validity at all for the particular criterion.

Let us suppose that, out of a sample of 100 salesclerks, the 30 with the highest and the 30 with the lowest sales records are chosen to represent contrasted criterion groups. If, now, these two groups are compared in a number of traits actually irrelevant to success in selling, certain chance differences will undoubtedly be found. Thus, there might be an excess of urban-born and of red-haired salesclerks within the upper criterion group. If we were to assign each individual a "score" by crediting him with one point for urban residence and one point for red hair, the mean of such scores would undoubtedly be higher in the upper than in the lower criterion group. This is not evidence for the validity of the predictors, however, since such a validation process is based upon a circular argument. The two predictors were chosen in the first place on the basis of the chance variation that occurred in this particular sample. And the same chance differences operate to produce the mean differences in total score. When tested in another sample, the chance differences in frequency of urban residence and red hair are likely to disappear or be reversed. Consequently, the validity of the scores will collapse.

A specific illustration of the need for cross-validation is provided by an early study with the Rorschach inkblot test (Kurtz, 1948). In an attempt to determine whether the Rorschach could be of any help in selecting sales managers for life insurance agencies, this test was administered to 80 managers, including an upper criterion group of 42 considered very satisfactory by their companies and a lower criterion group of 38 considered unsatisfactory. The 80 test records were studied by a Rorschach expert, who selected 32 signs, or response characteristics, occurring more frequently in one criterion group than in the other. A scoring key was developed in which signs occurring more often in the upper group were scored +1 and those more frequent in the lower group, −1. When this scoring key was reapplied to the original 80 managers, 79 of the 80 were correctly classified in the upper or lower group. The correlation between test score and criterion would thus have been close to 1.00. However, when the test was cross-validated on a second comparable sample of 41 managers, 21 in the upper and 20 in the lower group, the validity coefficient dropped to a negligible .02.

That such results can be obtained under pure-chance conditions was demonstrated by Cureton (1950), who determined the "scores" of 29 students on each of 85 nonexistent test items by shaking 85 numbered tags and letting them fall, once for each student. If a tag fell numbered side up, the item was scored right; if blank side up, it was scored wrong. An item analysis conducted with these chance scores against the students' grade-point averages yielded a 24-item "test." Total scores on this test correlated .82 with the criterion of college grades in the original group of 29 students. This correlation, of course, does not demonstrate validity, but the operation of pure chance—or, to use Cureton's more vivid term, "baloney."

Cross-validation concerns not only the selection of test items and of tests within a battery, but also the weights with which the separate test scores are combined in a regression equation. When the predictor battery is applied to a new sample, the multiple correlation (R) between battery and criterion will tend to drop, inasmuch as the weights are not optimal for the new sample. Because of chance errors in the original correlation coefficients, the weights will vary somewhat from sample to sample. The amount of shrinkage in R can be estimated by applying a shrinkage formula; or it can be determined empirically by cross-validating the battery. The anticipated shrinkage in cross-validation will be greater the smaller the initial sample. Since the inflated validity in the initial sample results from an accumulation of sampling errors, the smaller groups (which yield larger sampling errors) will undergo more validity shrinkage.

Classification Decisions. So far we have considered only selection decisions, in which each individual is either accepted or rejected. Deciding whether or not to hire a job applicant, admit a student to medical school, or accept a candidate for officer training are examples of selection. In classification decisions, on the other hand, every individual must be utilized. The question is where to assign each person so as to maximize the effectiveness of the total organization. Classification always involves more than one criterion—be it jobs, military occupational specialties, courses of study, or clinical treatments.

In the military services, classification is of major importance. After preliminary screening, everyone in the remaining personnel pool must be assigned to the military specialty where he or she can serve most effectively. An example of a classification battery is that developed by the Air Force during World War II for assigning men to training programs for pilot, navigator, and other aircrew specialties. Similar batteries are now used by all branches of the armed services. Another example of classification decisions is provided by the choice of a field of concentration by a college student. Career counseling, too, is based essentially on classification, since clients are told their chances of succeeding in different kinds of work. Clinical diagnosis is likewise a classification problem, the major purpose of each diagnosis being a decision regarding the appropriate type of therapy. In industry, classification decisions are required when new employees are assigned to different training programs or different jobs within the company.

For classification purposes, predictors must have *differential validity.* Such validity is higher the larger the difference between the correlations of the predictor with the separate criteria to be predicted. In a two-criterion classification problem, for example, the ideal test would have a high correlation with one criterion and a zero correlation (or preferably a negative correlation) with the other criterion. General intelligence tests are of little use for classification decisions, since they predict success about equally well in many kinds of work. Hence, their correlations with the criteria to be differentiated tend to be too similar. Individuals scoring high on such a test would often be classified as successful for either assignment, and it would be impossible to predict in which they would do better. In a classification battery, we need some tests that are good predictors of criterion A and poor predictors of criterion B, and other tests that are poor predictors of A and good predictors of B.

In classification batteries, each criterion requires a different regression equation. Depending on the correlations of the tests with each criterion, some tests may

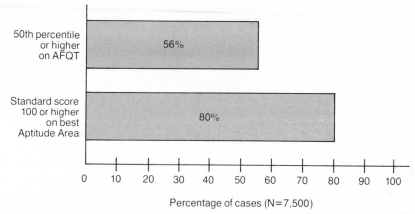

Figure 2-4. Percentages scoring above average on AFQT and on best Aptitude Area of Army Classification Battery in a sample of 7,500 applicants for enlistment. *(Data from U.S. Army Research Institute for the Behavioral and Social Sciences. Courtesy J. E. Uhlaner, 1974.)*

be included in all the equations, albeit with different weights in each; other tests may appear in only one or two equations, having zero or negligible weights for some of the criteria. Thus the combination of tests employed, as well as the specific weights, differs with the particular criterion.

With the gradual shift from the limited goal of filling a particular job to the broader goal of placing every individual in the work he or she is best qualified to perform, classification is assuming increasing importance in modern society. Differential prediction of criteria with a battery of tests permits a fuller utilization of resources than is possible with a single general test or with a composite score from a single regression equation.

A practical illustration of the advantages of classification strategies is provided by the use of Aptitude Area scores in the assignment of personnel to military occupational specialties in the U.S. Army (Maier & Fuchs, 1972). Each Aptitude Area corresponds to a group of jobs requiring a similar pattern of abilities, knowledge, and interests. From a 13-test classification battery, combinations of three to five tests are used to find the individual's score in each Aptitude Area. Figure 2-4 shows the results of a study of 7,500 applicants for enlistment, in which the use of Aptitude Area scores was compared with the use of a global screening test, the Armed Forces Qualification Test (AFQT). It will be noted that only 56% of this group reached or exceeded the 50th percentile on the AFQT, while 80% reached or exceeded the average standard score of 100 on their best Aptitude Area. Thus, when persons are allocated to specific jobs on the basis of the aptitudes required for each job, a very large majority are able to perform as well as the average of the entire sample or better. This apparent impossibility, in which nearly everyone could be above average, can be attained by capitalizing on the fact that nearly everyone excels in *some* aptitude.

DECISION MODELS

Statistical decision theory was developed by Wald (1950) with special reference to the decisions required in the inspection and quality control of industrial products.

Many of its implications for the construction and use of psychological tests and other predictors were systematically worked out by Cronbach and Gleser (1965). Essentially, decision theory is an attempt to put the decision-making process into mathematical form, so that available information may be used to arrive at an optimal decision under the specified circumstances. Although the detailed mathematical procedures required in specific practical situations are in an early stage of development, some of the basic concepts of decision theory are proving helpful in the reformulation and clarification of personnel procedures.

Basic Concepts of Decision Theory. Suppose that 100 applicants have been given an aptitude test and followed up until their job performance could be evaluated. Figure 2-5 shows the bivariate distribution of test scores and criterion measures for the 100 persons. The correlation between the two variables is slightly below .70. The minimum acceptable job performance, or criterion cutoff, is indicated on the graph by a heavy horizontal line. The 40 cases falling below this line represent job failures; the 60 above the line, job successes. If all 100 applicants are hired, therefore, 60% will succeed on the job (base rate = .60). Similarly, if a smaller number were hired without reference to test scores, the percentage who succeeded would probably be close to 60. Suppose, however, that the test scores are used to select the 45 most promising applicants out of the 100 (selection ratio = .45). In that case, the 45 employees falling to the right of the heavy vertical line would be selected. It can be seen that within this group of 45, there are 7 job failures, or *false acceptances,* falling below the heavy horizontal line, and 38 job

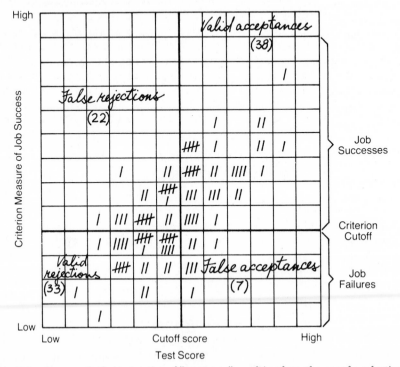

Figure 2-5.   Increase in the proportion of "successes" resulting from the use of a selection test.

successes. Hence the percentage of job successes has risen from 60 to 84 (38/45 = .84).

For a complete evaluation of the effectiveness of the selection strategy illustrated in Figure 2-5, another category of cases must also be examined. This is the category of *false rejections,* comprising the 22 applicants who scored below the cutoff on the test but fell above the criterion cutoff. From these data, we infer that 22% of the total applicant sample are potential job successes who would be lost if the test is used with the given cutoff point. In setting a cutoff score, attention should be given to the percentage of false rejects as well as to the percentages of successes and failures within the accepted group. In some situations, this cutoff should be set sufficiently high to exclude all but a few possible failures. This would be true when the job is of such a nature that a poorly qualified worker could cause serious loss or damage, as in the case of a commercial airline pilot. Under other circumstances, it may be more important to admit as many qualified persons as possible, at the risk of including more failures.

It is characteristic of decision theory that the total effectiveness of personnel strategies is assessed on the basis of several parameters. We have seen that such evaluation takes into account not only the validity of tests in predicting a particular criterion but also such parameters as base rate and selection ratio. Another important parameter is "cost" or *utility* of expected outcomes. Both concepts refer essentially to the assignment of values to outcomes, in terms of some judgmental scale of favorableness or unfavorableness. In industrial situations, a dollar value can often be assigned to different outcomes, so that what is estimated is cost in the usual sense. For the assessment of less tangible factors, such as employee morale, public image, and societal goals, any numerical scale can be used to express the relative judged value of alternative outcomes. It should be noted that decision theory did not introduce the problem of values into the decision process but merely made it explicit. Value systems always enter into decisions; but they are not always recognized or systematically handled.

In choosing a decision strategy, the goal is to maximize expected utilities (or minimize costs) across all outcomes. Reference to the schematic representation of a simple decision strategy in Figure 2-6 will help to clarify the procedure. This diagram shows the decision strategy illustrated in Figure 2-5, in which a single test

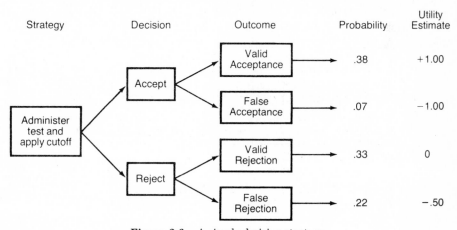

Figure 2-6. A simple decision strategy.

is administered to a group of applicants and the decision to accept or reject an applicant is based on the chosen cutoff score on the test. There are four possible outcomes: valid and false acceptances and valid and false rejections. The probability of each outcome can be found from the number of persons in each of the four sections of Figure 2-5. Since there are 100 applicants in the sample, these numbers divided by 100 give the probabilities of the four outcomes listed in Figure 2-6. In the last column of Figure 2-6, typical utility estimates have been entered for each outcome.

The expected overall utility of the strategy can be found by multiplying the probability of each outcome by the utility of the outcome, adding these products for the four outcomes, and subtracting a value corresponding to the cost of testing (here estimated as .10 on the utility scale). The total expected utility (EU) for the above strategy is

$$\text{EU} = (.38)(1.00) + (.07)(-1.00) + (.33)(0) + (.22)(-.50) - .10 = +.10.$$

This EU can then be compared with other EUs found with different cutoff points, different tests (differing in validity and cost), or with a battery of tests. Comparisons can likewise be made with different decision strategies, such as: accept cases above high cutoff, reject cases below low cutoff, and administer a second test to those in the intermediate or uncertain range.[10]

Optimizing Personnel Procedures. An early precursor of decision theory in psychological testing is to be found in the Taylor-Russell tables (1939), which provide estimates of the net gain in selection accuracy attributable to the use of a test. The information required includes validity coefficient of the test, base rate, and selection ratio. A change in any of these three factors will alter the predictive efficiency of the test.

For purposes of illustration, one of the Taylor-Russell tables is reproduced in Table 2-1. This table is designed for use when the base rate, or proportion of successful employees selected prior to the use of the test, is .60; additional tables are available for other base rates.[11] The entries in the body of Table 2-1 indicate the proportion of successful employees expected after the use of the test for selection purposes. Thus the difference between .60 and any table entry shows the increase in proportion of successful selections attributable to a test of given validity, with the given selection ratio. Obviously, if the selection ratio were 100%, that is, if all applicants had to be accepted, no test, however valid, could improve the selection process. Reference to Table 2-1 shows that, when as many as 95% of applicants must be hired, even a test with perfect validity ($r = 1.00$) would raise the proportion of successful employees by only 3% (60 to 63). On the other hand, when only 5% of applicants are hired, a test with a validity of only .30 can raise the percentage of successful workers from 60 to 82.

It is apparent that, with a test of given validity, the proportion of successful employees can be increased by lowering the selection ratio, i.e., by hiring a smaller proportion of applicants. In order to fill the available job openings, however, this

---

[10]Examples showing all computational steps can be found in Wiggins (1973), Ch. 6.

[11]The complete set of tables can be found in the original source (Taylor & Russell, 1939). They have also been reproduced in McCormick & Tiffin (1974, Appendix B).

TABLE 2-1
Proportion of Successful Employees as a Function of Selection Ratio
and Test Validity: Base Rate = .60

(From Taylor & Russell, 1939, p. 576. Copyright 1939 by American Psychological Association. Reproduced by permission.)

Validity	Selection Ratio										
	.05	.10	.20	.30	.40	.50	.60	.70	.80	.90	.95
.00	.60	.60	.60	.60	.60	.60	.60	.60	.60	.60	.60
.05	.64	.63	.63	.62	.62	.62	.61	.61	.61	.60	.60
.10	.68	.67	.65	.64	.64	.63	.63	.62	.61	.61	.60
.15	.71	.70	.68	.67	.66	.65	.64	.63	.62	.61	.61
.20	.75	.73	.71	.69	.67	.66	.65	.64	.63	.62	.61
.25	.78	.76	.73	.71	.69	.68	.66	.65	.63	.62	.61
.30	.82	.79	.76	.73	.71	.69	.68	.66	.64	.62	.61
.35	.85	.82	.78	.75	.73	.71	.69	.67	.65	.63	.62
.40	.88	.85	.81	.78	.75	.73	.70	.68	.66	.63	.62
.45	.90	.87	.83	.80	.77	.74	.72	.69	.66	.64	.62
.50	.93	.90	.86	.82	.79	.76	.73	.70	.67	.64	.62
.55	.95	.92	.88	.84	.81	.78	.75	.71	.68	.64	.62
.60	.96	.94	.90	.87	.83	.80	.76	.73	.69	.65	.63
.65	.98	.96	.92	.89	.85	.82	.78	.74	.70	.65	.63
.70	.99	.97	.94	.91	.87	.84	.80	.75	.71	.66	.63
.75	.99	.99	.96	.93	.90	.86	.81	.77	.71	.66	.63
.80	1.00	.99	.98	.95	.92	.88	.83	.78	.72	.66	.63
.85	1.00	1.00	.99	.97	.95	.91	.86	.80	.73	.66	.63
.90	1.00	1.00	1.00	.99	.97	.94	.88	.82	.74	.67	.63
.95	1.00	1.00	1.00	1.00	.99	.97	.92	.84	.75	.67	.63
1.00	1.00	1.00	1.00	1.00	1.00	1.00	1.00	.86	.75	.67	.63

can only be achieved by recruiting more applicants. Thus, recruiting costs would increase, as would selection costs, inasmuch as more persons must be screened and evaluated. Mathematical procedures for taking these factors into account were developed by Sands (1973) in a comprehensive decision model designated as Cost of Attaining Personnel Requirements (CAPER). This model utilizes cost estimates per person for recruiting, selection, induction, and training of new employees. Estimates are also entered for the relative cost of false acceptances and false rejections. With these data inputs, it is possible to identify the selection ratio—and hence the cutoff score on the test—that will minimize total cost (or maximize expected utility) for the entire personnel process. A computer program has been developed for the CAPER model. It might be added that the increasing availability of computer facilities makes the use of such complex decision models quite feasible. With a computer, different combinations of parameters can be readily simulated and the resulting changes in total cost ascertained.

Moderator Variables. The validity of a test for a given criterion may vary among subgroups of persons. The classic psychometric model assumed that prediction errors were characteristic of the test rather than of the person and that these errors were randomly distributed among persons. With the flexibility of approach ushered in by decision theory, there has been increasing exploration of prediction models involving interaction between persons and tests. Such interaction implies that the same test may be a better predictor for certain classes of persons than it is for others. For example, a given test may be a better predictor of criterion performance for men than for women, or a better predictor for applicants from a lower socioeconomic level than for applicants from a higher socioeconomic level. In these examples, sex and socioeconomic level are known as *moderator variables,* since they moderate the validity of the test (Saunders, 1956).

When computed in a total group, the validity coefficient of a test may be too low to be of much practical value in prediction. But when recomputed in subsets of persons differing in some identifiable characteristic, validity may be high in one subset and negligible in another. The test could thus be used effectively in making decisions in the first group but not in the second. Perhaps another test or some other assessment technique can be found that is an effective predictor in the second group.

Interests and motivation often function as moderator variables in individual cases. Thus, if an applicant has little interest in a job, he will probably do poorly regardless of his scores on relevant aptitude tests. Among such persons, the correlation between aptitude test scores and job performance would be low. For individuals who are interested and highly motivated, on the other hand, the correlation between aptitude test score and job success may be quite high.

Empirical evidence for the operation of moderator variables comes from a variety of sources (Zedeck, 1971). Ghiselli (1956, 1960, 1963, 1968) has investigated the role of moderator variables in several industrial situations. In a study of taxi drivers (Ghiselli, 1956), for example, the correlation between an aptitude test and a job-performance criterion in the total applicant sample was only .220. The group was then sorted into thirds on the basis of scores on an occupational interest test. When the validity of the aptitude test was recomputed within the third whose occupational interest level was most appropriate for the job, it rose to .664.

At this time, the identification and use of moderator variables are still in an exploratory phase. Considerable caution is required to avoid methodological pitfalls (see, e.g., "Moderator Variables," 1972; Zedeck, 1971). The results are usually quite specific to the situations in which they were obtained; and cross-validation is especially important. It is also desirable to check the extent to which the use of moderators actually improves the prediction that could be achieved through more direct means (Pinder, 1973; Zedeck, 1971).

Situational and Organizational Variables. The concept of moderator variables is gradually being absorbed into more comprehensive models that incorporate interactions of personal variables not only with predictors but also with variables of training, job processes, and work environment (Campbell, Dunnette, Lawler, & Weick, 1970; Dunnette, 1963a; Schoenfeldt, 1974). An example is a model described by Dunnette (1963a) and illustrated in Figure 2-7. While representing the same general orientation underlying the systems measurement bed sketched in Chapter 1 (Fig. 1-1), this model concentrates on features especially pertinent to selection and classification problems. A noteworthy element is the differentiation between process and product (or outcome) in job performance. An implication of this distinction is that the same job behavior (process) may lead to different organizational consequences or criterion outcomes in different job situations. Thus, behavior that could prove effective in one organizational environment might prove ineffective in another. The model also calls attention to the feedback

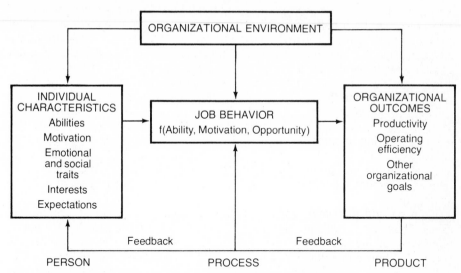

Figure 2-7. A comprehensive model of job performance. *(Adapted from Campbell, Dunnette, Lawler, & Weick, 1970, p. 11. Copyright © 1970 by McGraw-Hill, Inc. Reproduced by permission.)*

individuals receive from the organizational outcomes of their behavior. This feedback in turn affects their subsequent job behavior, as well as the further development of such personal characteristics as expectations, motivation, and job-related abilities.

THE QUESTION OF TEST FAIRNESS

Social and Legal Implications. The decades of the 1960s and 1970s witnessed increasing public concern with the rights of minorities, a concern reflected in the enactment of civil rights legislation at both federal and state levels. In connection with mechanisms for improving educational and vocational opportunities of minorities, psychological tests received widespread attention, both favorable and unfavorable. Much of the concern centers on the possible lowering of test scores by cultural conditions that may have influenced the development of aptitudes, interests, motivation, attitudes, and other traits of minority group members. At the same time, it is recognized that, when social stereotypes and prejudice may distort personal evaluations, properly used objective tests provide a safeguard against favoritism and arbitrary or capricious decisions (see APA, 1969; Anastasi, 1976, Ch. 3; EEOC, 1970).

Since 1960 there have been rapid legal developments pertaining to personnel testing, including legislative actions, executive orders, and court decisions (Fincher, 1973; Albright et al., 1976). The most pertinent federal legislation is provided by the Equal Employment Opportunity Act (Title VII of the Civil Rights Act of 1964 and its subsequent amendments). Responsibility for implementation and enforcement is vested in the Equal Employment Opportunity Commission (EEOC), which developed a set of guidelines for this purpose (EEOC, 1970). In 1978, in the interests of simplified procedure and improved coordination, the *Uniform Guidelines on Employee Selection Procedure* were jointly adopted by the EEOC, the Civil Service Commission, and the Departments of Justice, Labor, and Treasury.

Some major provisions of the *Guidelines,* which are reproduced in Appendix D, should be noted. The Equal Employment Opportunity Act prohibits discrimination on the grounds of race, color, religion, sex, or national origin in selection procedures leading to employment decisions. In the *Guidelines,* the same equity regulations specified for tests are also applied to all other formal or informal selection procedures, such as educational or work-history requirements, interviews, and application forms (Sec. 2B, 16Q). When the use of a test or other selection procedure results in a substantially higher rejection rate for minority than for nonminority applicants ("adverse impact"), its utility must be justified by evidence of validity for the job under consideration (Sec. 3, 4). In defining acceptable procedures for establishing validity, the *Guidelines* make explicit reference to the APA test *Standards* (1974). A major portion of the *Guidelines* covers minimum requirements for acceptable validation (Sec. 14). The reader may find it useful to examine these requirements in the light of the treatment of test validation in earlier sections of this chapter.

Levels of Cultural Differentials in Test Scores. Cultural differences affect behavior at many levels, ranging from superficial, narrowly limited, and temporary effects to those that are basic, far-reaching, and lasting (Anastasi, 1976, Ch. 12). When testing persons from diverse cultural backgrounds, it is important to differentiate between cultural factors that affect *both* test and criterion performance and those whose influence is restricted to the test. It is the latter, test-restricted differences that reduce test validity for minority groups. Examples of such factors include previous test-taking experience, motivation to do well on tests, rapport with the examiner, and test anxiety. A desirable procedure is to provide adequate test-taking orientation and preliminary practice, as illustrated by the pretesting orientation techniques developed by the United States Employment Service (U. S. Department of Labor, 1968, 1970b, 1971a, 1971b) and by some test publishers (e.g., Bennett & Doppelt, 1967).

Specific test content may also influence test scores in ways that are unrelated to criterion performance. In a test of arithmetic reasoning, for example, the use of names or pictures of objects unfamiliar in a particular cultural milieu would represent a test-restricted handicap. Ability to carry out quantitative thinking does not depend upon familiarity with such objects. On the other hand, if the development of arithmetic ability itself is more strongly fostered in one culture than in another, scores on an arithmetic test should not eliminate or conceal this difference.

By far the most important consideration in the testing of culturally diverse groups—as in all testing—pertains to the interpretation of test scores. The most common misgivings about the use of tests with minority groups arise from popular misinterpretations of test scores. It is important to bear in mind that tests measure current behavior and hence reflect the cumulative influences of experiential background. Test scores cannot in themselves explain why the individual behaves as he or she does. Tests do *not* reveal innate, fixed, or unchangeable characteristics of the organism—they only assess current status. With suitably designed training programs, and with situational and organizational settings that may alter attitudes and motivation, both the test scores and the behavior they assess may be expected to change. Again we see the implications of the systems approach and the concept of interaction. Test scores need to be interpreted in the light of the interactions between aptitudes (or other traits) and situational variables, both past and future.

Statistical Analyses of Test Bias. To predict outcome in some future situation, such as job performance, we need tests with high predictive validity against the specific criterion. This requirement was often overlooked in the development of so-called culture-fair tests. In the effort to include in such tests only those functions common to different cultures or subcultures, we may choose content that has little relevance to any criterion we wish to predict. A better solution is to choose criterion-relevant content and then investigate possible differences in test validity as a function of the examinees' experiential backgrounds. It should also be noted that the predictive validity of a test is less likely to vary among cultural groups when the test is intrinsically relevant to criterion performance. If a verbal test were employed to predict nonverbal job performance, a fortuitous validity might be found in one group and not in another. But a test that directly samples criterion behavior, or one that measures essential component job skills, is likely to retain its validity in different groups. Since the mid-1960s, there has been a rapid accumulation of research on possible ethnic differences in the predictive meaning of test scores.

The concept of test bias can be visualized if we refer again to the bivariate distribution in Figure 2-1. For the present purpose, the horizontal axis *(X)* represents test scores and the vertical axis *(Y)* represents a criterion measure of job performance. The tally marks, showing the position of each individual on both test and criterion, indicate the direction and general magnitude of the correlation between the two variables. The line of best fit drawn through these tallies is known as the regression line, and its equation is the regression equation. In this example, the regression equation would have only one predictor. The multiple regression equations discussed earlier in this chapter have several predictors, but the principle is the same.

When both test and criterion scores are expressed as standard scores $(SD = 1.00)$, the slope of the regression line equals the correlation coefficient. For this reason, if a test yields a significantly different validity coefficient in two groups, this difference is described as *slope bias*. Figure 2-8 provides schematic illustrations of regression lines for several bivariate distributions. The ellipses represent the region within which the tallies for each sample would fall. Case 1 shows the bivariate distribution of two groups with different means in the predictor, but with identical regression lines between predictor and criterion. In this case, there is no test bias, since any given test score *(X)* corresponds to the identical criterion score *(Y)* in both groups. Case 2 illustrates slope bias, with a lower validity coefficient in the minority group.

Even when a test yields the same validity coefficients in two groups, it may show *intercept bias*. The intercept of a regression line refers to the point at which the line intersects the axis. A test exhibits intercept bias if it systematically underpredicts or overpredicts criterion performance for a particular group. Let us look again at Case 1 in Figure 2-8, in which majority and minority samples show identical regressions. Under these conditions, there is neither slope nor intercept bias. Although the groups differ significantly in mean test score, they show a corresponding difference in criterion performance. In Case 3, on the other hand, the two groups have

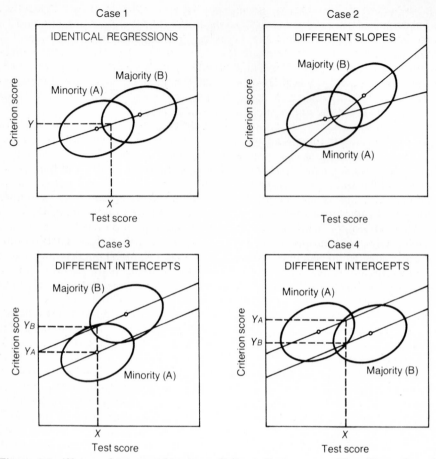

Figure 2-8. Slope and intercept bias in predicting criterion scores. The ellipses show the regions within which members of each group fall when their test scores are plotted against their criterion performance. *(Cases 1, 2, and 3 adapted from Gordon, 1953, p. 3.)*

regression lines with the same slope but with different intercepts. In this case, the majority group (B) has a higher intercept than the minority group (A); that is, the majority regression line intersects the Y axis at a higher point than does the minority regression line. Although the validity coefficients are equal in the two groups, any test score (X) will correspond to a different criterion score in the two groups, as shown by points Y_A and Y_B. Because of the intercept difference, the use of the majority regression line for both groups would *overpredict* the criterion performance of minority group members. If a single cutoff score were applied to both groups, it would discriminate in favor of the minority group. Intercept bias discriminates against the group with the higher intercept.

Psychologists who are concerned about the possible unfairness of tests for minority group members visualize a situation illustrated in Case 4. Note that, in this case, the majority excels on the test, but majority and minority perform equally well on the criterion. The minority group now has the higher intercept. Selecting all applicants in terms of a test cutoff established for the majority group would thus discriminate unfairly against the minority. Under these conditions, use of the majority regression line for both groups *underpredicts* the criterion performance of minority group members. This situation is likely to occur when a large proportion of test variance is irrelevant to criterion performance and measures functions in which the majority excels. A thorough job analysis and component validation provide safeguards against the choice of such a test.

It has been demonstrated mathematically that Case 3 will occur if the two groups differ in a third variable (e.g., sociocultural background) which correlates positively with both test and criterion (Reilly, 1973). Under these conditions, the test overpredicts the performance of minority group members, and the use of a single cutoff score for both groups favors the minority. It has also been shown that intercept bias can be eliminated if group membership is included as an additional, binary or dichotomous variable in the regression equation (McNemar, 1975).

What do empirical investigations show regarding slope and intercept bias? Careful statistical analyses of the results of over 30 published studies of test validity in black and white samples demonstrated that the obtained discrepancies in validity coefficients did not differ from chance expectancy (Boehm, 1977; Katzell & Dyer, 1977; O'Connor, Wexley, & Alexander, 1975; Schmidt, Berner, & Hunter, 1973). Because of methodological limitations, the results of several of these studies are merely inconclusive. However, the lack of significant validity differences has been corroborated by some well-designed studies on industrial samples (Campbell, Crooks, Mahoney, & Rock, 1973; Gael, Grant, & Ritchie, 1975a, 1975b) and army personnel (Maier & Fuchs, 1973).[12]

With regard to intercept bias, well-controlled studies have found either no significant difference or, more often, a tendency for the tests to overpredict the criterion performance of minority groups. Such results have been obtained for a wide variety of industrial jobs (Campbell et al., 1973; Gael et al., 1975a, 1975b; Grant & Bray, 1970; Ruch, 1972) and in military training programs (Gordon, 1953; Maier & Fuchs, 1973; Shore & Marion, 1972). It is interesting to note that the same results have been obtained in comparisons between groups classified according to educational or socioeconomic level. For example, the Army Classification Battery tended to overpredict the performance of high school dropouts and underpredict the performance of college graduates in training programs for military occupational specialties (Maier, 1972).

The problem of selection bias is still being actively investigated at both empirical and theoretical levels (Hunter & Schmidt, 1976; Novick & Ellis, 1977; "On Bias," 1976; Schmidt & Hunter, 1974). Some have proposed comprehensive decision models, which provide for the explicit inclusion of value judgments in assessing the relative utility of different outcomes (Gross & Su, 1975; Hunter, Schmidt, & Rauschenberger, 1977; Petersen, 1974; Petersen & Novick, 1976). In our present state of knowledge, there is insufficient basis to justify different cutoff scores for minority groups. It is likely that ethnic and socioeconomic categories are too crude and heterogeneous to serve as effective moderator variables in sorting

[12]Further discussion of methodological questions on the problem of differential validity can be found in Hunter and Schmidt (1978), in the replies to this article in the same issue of the journal, and in Linn (1978).

individuals into subgroups and exploring interactions between personal characteristics and predictors. These categories cover a vast number of experiential
differences whose combination varies from person to person. More specific and
clearly defined experiential variables would probably prove more productive.

Statistical adjustments in test scores, cutoffs, and prediction formulas hold little
promise as a means of correcting social inequities. More constructive solutions are
suggested by other approaches discussed earlier in this chapter. One approach is
illustrated by multiple aptitude testing and classification strategies, which permit
the fullest utilization of the diverse trait patterns fostered by different cultural
backgrounds. Another approach is through adaptive treatments, such as individualized training programs. In order to maximize the fit of such programs to
individual characteristics, it is essential that tests reveal as fully and as accurately
as possible the person's present level of development in the requisite abilities.

SUMMARY

In developing a personnel selection and classification program, the first major step
is a job analysis, including a detailed study of job tasks with special reference to
the worker traits required for performing these tasks. Predictors are chosen or
developed to assess the traits identified in the job analysis. All predictors should be
evaluated for reliability and validity. Although criterion-related predictive validity is
logically the most appropriate procedure for personnel selection instruments, it is
not technically feasible in most industrial contexts. Various forms of content,
construct, and synthetic validity are more suitable, especially with complex and
multidimensional job criteria.

Predictors may be combined by clinical judgment, multiple cutoff procedures,
or multiple regression equations. Cross-validation in a new sample is advisable,
especially when only a small proportion of the original predictors survive initial
validation. For classification decisions, predictors should have differential validity
for the separate criteria. Classification strategies result in maximum utilization of
human resources.

The concepts of decision theory permit an optimization of many parameters in
personnel programs. Test characteristics can be combined with base rate, selection ratio, the relative cost of false acceptances and false rejections, and other
pertinent factors in estimating the overall effectiveness of alternative selection
programs. More complex decision models that include moderator variables and
situational-organizational variables represent the application of comprehensive
systems approaches to personnel procedures. The use of objective and valid
predictors can help to ensure equal employment opportunities for minorities.
Research on test bias, including both slope and intercept biases, indicates that
statistical adjustments in cutoff scores and prediction formulas hold less promise
than do classification strategies and complex decision models that combine
selection, training, job design, and other system variables.

PERSONNEL ASSESSMENT TECHNIQUES

THREE

HAPTER 2 was concerned with basic procedures for the development and evaluation of predictors. In the present chapter, we shall look at the specific kinds of predictors most often used in personnel selection and classification. These include tests for the measurement of abilities and personality traits, ratings, application forms, reference reports, interviews, and the multiple techniques employed in assessment centers.

ABILITY TESTS

In this section, we shall consider types of cognitive tests most appropriate for the assessment of industrial personnel, illustrating them with a few specific tests. For a more comprehensive survey of available instruments, the reader is referred to textbooks on psychological tests, such as those cited in Chapter 2 (Anastasi, 1976; Guion, 1965a; Lawshe & Balma, 1966), as well as to the *Mental Measurements Yearbooks* (MMY). A convenient source is *Vocational Tests and Reviews* (Buros, 1975), which covers instruments of special relevance to occupational testing, taken from all the MMYs from 1938 to 1972 and including approximately 650 items. Information on currently available tests can be found in the catalogues of test publishers. A comprehensive directory of test publishers is included in each MMY. The names and addresses of major American test publishers from whom catalogues can be obtained are given in Appendix E.

Short Screening Tests. Several tests of general mental ability have been specially developed for the rapid, preliminary screening of industrial personnel. These tests are short, usually requiring between 10 and 30 minutes. They are easy to administer and can be objectively scored by a clerk or by computer. Early tests of this type that have enjoyed wide popularity are the Otis Self-Administering Test of Mental Ability and the Wonderlic Personnel Test.[1] Such tests are sometimes loosely described as "intelligence tests"; but this term is misleading because it implies more stability of developmental level and greater breadth of coverage than can properly be inferred from the scores. Since most of these tests measure largely verbal and numerical abilities and correlate highly with school achievement, a more appropriate label for them is "scholastic aptitude."

A still better practice, however, is to characterize each test more precisely in terms of the functions measured and its empirically established behavioral correlates. This practice is illustrated in the Wesman Personnel Classification Test, which provides separate Verbal, Numerical, and Total scores. From the nature of the items, as well as from the distribution of scores reported for various educational and occupational groups, this test appears to be better suited for higher level than for lower level jobs.

A short battery of screening tests, more appropriate for lower level jobs, is the Personnel Tests for Industry, which includes a 5-minute Verbal Test, a 20-minute Numerical Test, and a 15-minute Oral Directions Test. In the last-named test, both instructions and test items are presented on either phonograph records or tape, thus ensuring more uniform procedure than would be possible through oral administration by different examiners. A Spanish edition is also available. This test is rather heavily weighted with perceptual and spatial items and also depends to a considerable extent on immediate memory for auditory instructions. Available data suggest that it may be especially useful in screening applicants for such jobs as laborer, maintenance and service worker, and messenger. Reference may also be made to several basic literacy tests for adults, specifically designed to assess the attainment of minimum educational skills required for particular jobs. An example is the Basic Occupational Literacy Test (BOLT) developed by the U.S. Employment Service. A number of similar tests are available from commercial test publishers.

The usual paper-and-pencil screening tests predict performance in training somewhat better than they predict subsequent job performance (Ghiselli, 1966). When such tests are correlated with criteria of job proficiency, moreover, the correlations vary widely with the nature of the job. In general, clerical and supervisory jobs tend to yield the highest validity coefficients with this type of test. Validity is also likely to be high for any other type of job requiring substantial use of the verbal and numerical abilities measured by these tests. In other jobs, the validity coefficient may be low or negligible, once the required minimum is exceeded. This might be the case, for instance, when job success depends largely upon traits not measured by these tests, such as mechanical aptitude, artistic sensitivity, manual skills, or personality factors. Even in such jobs, however, persons falling below a certain minimum in general scholastic aptitude are likely to fail.

Special Aptitude Tests. In the assessment of personnel for most jobs, tests of special aptitudes are particularly appropriate. Such aptitude tests are sometimes

---

[1]Complete references for each test cited in this book, including publisher and other pertinent information, can be found in the MMYs. *Tests in Print II* (Buros, 1974) provides an index for all tests listed in the MMYs prior to 1974. A classified list of commonly used tests, with publishers, is given in Anastasi (1976), Appendix E.

custom-made to fit the demands of the job. For certain aptitudes common to many jobs, however, published tests are available. Most of these standardized tests for general use are in the areas of vision, hearing, psychomotor abilities, mechanical aptitude, and clerical aptitude.

Many industrial jobs call for minimum standards in vision or hearing (McCormick & Tiffin, 1974, Ch. 6). Considerable research is available showing the effects of sensory capacities upon quantity and quality of output, spoilage and waste of materials, job turnover, and accidents. Many types of military occupational specialties likewise make heavy demands upon visual or auditory capacities.

Both visual and auditory sensitivity include not one but many functions. Among the *visual* characteristics found to be of greatest practical importance may be mentioned: near acuity at "reading distance" (13 to 16 inches), far acuity (usually measured at 20 feet), perception of distance or depth, muscular balance of the eyes (phoria), and color discrimination. Composite instruments have been developed for measuring all these aspects of vision. An example is the Ortho-Rater, illustrated in Figure 3-1. Providing measures of each of the above characteristics, the Ortho-Rater is widely used in industry. In *hearing,* the aspect of most general concern is auditory acuity, measured by finding the faintest sound that the individual can just barely hear. Both individual and group audiometers are available for measuring such acuity (Hirsh, 1961). Other hearing characteristics

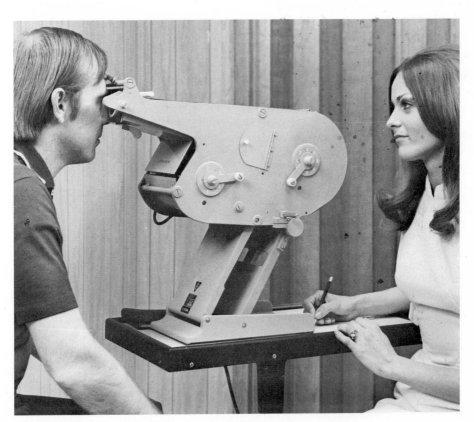

Figure 3-1. Ortho-Rater for testing visual functions. *(Courtesy of Bausch & Lomb.)*

important for certain industrial and military functions include discrimination of pitch and of loudness.

Tests of *psychomotor abilities* are used widely in the selection of industrial and military personnel. Usually such tests are tailored to meet specific job requirements. Of considerable help in this connection is the previously cited research of Fleishman (1972) and his associates on the identification of distinct motor abilities. Most commercially available tests of psychomotor abilities call for very simple types of movement. Often they require manipulation of small objects, as in the Purdue Pegboard, illustrated in Figure 3-2. In one part of this test, the examinee inserts a pin in each hole, using the right hand, the left hand, and both hands simultaneously, in successive trials. In another part of the test, pins, collars, and washers are assembled and fitted into each hole, both hands being employed in a prescribed procedure. Tests such as these are utilized in selecting workers for assembling, packing, routine machine operations, and similar jobs.

Tests commonly classified under the heading of *mechanical aptitude* cover a variety of functions. Psychomotor abilities enter into some of these tests, either because the test may call for rapid manipulation of materials or because special subtests designed to measure motor dexterity are included. Perceptual speed and accuracy also play a part in certain tests. The major factors measured by mechanical aptitude tests, however, are spatial visualization and mechanical comprehension.

A test designed to measure the first of these abilities is the Minnesota Paper Form Board, illustrated in Figure 3-3. Each item consists of a geometric figure cut into two or more pieces. The examinee must visualize how the pieces fit together and choose the drawing that shows the correct arrangement. A large number of studies conducted with this test indicate that it is one of the most valid available instruments for measuring the ability to visualize and manipulate spatial relations. Among the criteria employed in this research were performance in shop courses, grades in engineering and other technical and mechanical courses, supervisors' ratings, and objective production records. The test has also shown some validity in predicting the achievement of dentistry and art students. Another test that has been widely employed for industrial purposes is the Bennett Mechanical Compre-

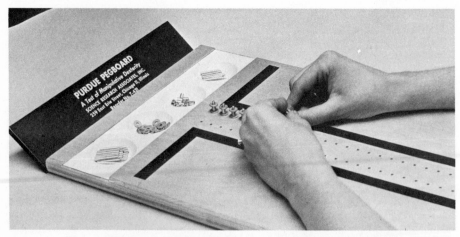

Figure 3-2. Purdue Pegboard. *(Courtesy of Science Research Associates.)*

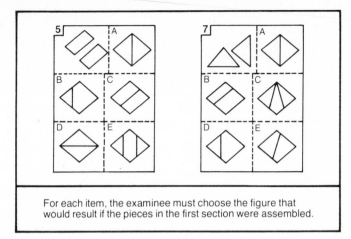

For each item, the examinee must choose the figure that would result if the pieces in the first section were assembled.

Figure 3-3. Sample items from the Revised Minnesota Paper Form Board. *(Reproduced by permission. Copyright © 1941, renewed 1969 by The Psychological Corporation, New York, N.Y. All rights reserved.)*

hension Test, illustrated in Figure 3-4. Several studies of this test provide evidence of both concurrent and predictive validity for mechanical trades and engineering. Correlations ranging from the .30s to the .60s have been found with either training or job-proficiency criteria in many kinds of mechanical jobs (Ghiselli, 1966; Patterson, 1956).

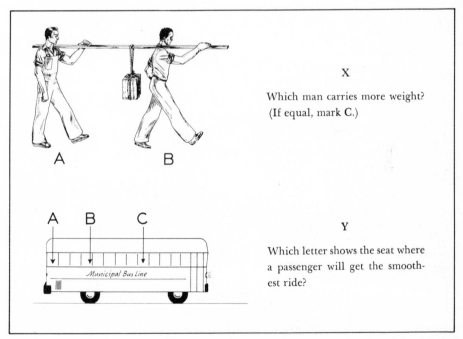

X

Which man carries more weight?
(If equal, mark C.)

Y

Which letter shows the seat where a passenger will get the smoothest ride?

Figure 3-4. Sample items from the Bennett Mechanical Comprehension Test. *(Reproduced by permission. Copyright © 1969 by The Psychological Corporation, New York, N.Y. All rights reserved.)*

When the two numbers or names in a pair are <u>exactly the same,</u>
make a check mark on the line between them.

66273894 _____ 66273984

527384578 _____ 527384578

New York World _____ New York World

Cargill Grain Co. _____ Cargil Grain Co.

Figure 3-5. Sample items from the Minnesota Clerical Test. *(Reproduced by permission. Copyright © 1933, renewed 1961 by The Psychological Corporation, New York, N.Y. All rights reserved.)*

Tests designed to measure *clerical aptitude* are primarily concerned with perceptual speed and accuracy. A well-known example is the Minnesota Clerical Test, illustrated in Figure 3-5. In the two parts of this test, the examinee compares pairs of numbers and names, respectively, to determine whether the two paired items are the same or different. Although a deduction is made for errors, the scores depend predominantly on speed. Moderately high correlations have been reported between scores on this test and ratings by office supervisors or by commercial teachers, as well as performance records in courses and in various kinds of clerical jobs. Several studies compared the scores obtained by different levels of clerks, by clerks and by persons in other occupations, and by employed and unemployed clerks. All these comparisons yielded significant mean differences in the expected directions.

It is apparent that such a relatively homogeneous instrument as the Minnesota Clerical Test measures only one aspect of clerical work. Clerical jobs cover a multiplicity of functions. Moreover, the number and particular combination of duties vary tremendously with the type and level of job. Even specific jobs designated by the same name, such as typist, filing clerk, or shipping clerk, may differ considerably from one company to another. Despite this diversity of activities, however, job analyses of general clerical work indicate that a relatively large proportion of time is spent in such tasks as classifying, sorting, checking, collating and stapling, stuffing and sealing envelopes, and the like. Speed and accuracy in perceiving details are thus of primary importance for the clerical worker, especially in the lower level, routine clerical jobs. For higher level clerical jobs, the verbal and numerical abilities measured by scholastic aptitude tests are undoubtedly more relevant. Several clerical aptitude tests combine verbal and numerical tests with tests of perceptual speed and accuracy in a single battery. Such composite tests are useful provided they yield separate scores for each part, since the relative weights of these abilities may vary widely from one clerical job to another.

Multiple Aptitude Batteries. In the history of psychological testing, so-called intelligence tests, such as the individually administered Stanford-Binet and group tests designed to measure the same general composite, preceded the special aptitude tests. Particularly in vocational testing, it soon became apparent that the available intelligence tests did not cover all requisite abilities. Mechanical, clerical, and other special aptitude tests were originally developed to supplement intelligence tests. Concurrently, analyses of intelligence test performance revealed conspicuous intraindividual differences from one intelligence test to another or among different parts of the same test. A person might do well on a written test but poorly on a performance test requiring spatial orientation; or, in the traditional written test, he might be consistently better on the numerical than on the verbal items. It thus appeared that the intelligence tests themselves might be measuring a small number of relatively independent aptitudes in which the same individual could vary appreciably.

A parallel development in basic research was the study of the nature and organization of intelligence by the techniques of factor analysis. Essentially such techniques involve the administration of a large number of tests to the same persons. The scores on all the tests are then intercorrelated and the correlations subjected to further statistical analyses in order to determine which tests tend to cluster together and which are relatively independent. Examples of the separate abilities, or "factors," thus identified include verbal comprehension, numerical computation, quantitative reasoning, perceptual speed, spatial visualization, and mechanical comprehension. Through factor analysis, what had formerly been called intelligence could now be subdivided into relatively independent abilities, and these abilities could be combined with those underlying the special aptitude tests to provide a more comprehensive picture of intelligence.

The construction of multiple aptitude batteries was the direct outcome of factor-analytic research. Rather than yielding a single global score, such as an IQ, these batteries provide a profile of scores on separate tests, most of which correspond more or less closely to traits identified through factor analysis. Several batteries of this sort are now commercially available (see Anastasi, 1976, Ch. 13). An example is the Differential Aptitude Tests (DAT), for which the largest amount of validity information is available. The DAT yields scores in eight abilities: Verbal Reasoning, Numerical Ability, Abstract Reasoning, Clerical Speed and Accuracy, Mechanical Reasoning, Space Relations, Spelling, and Language Usage. Because this type of test is especially useful in counseling, the DAT will be illustrated more fully in Chapter 15.

Other major examples of multiple aptitude batteries, previously cited in Chapter 2, include the classification batteries developed for use in the military services and the General Aptitude Test Battery (GATB) prepared by the USES. The latter consists of 12 tests yielding the following nine scores: General Learning Ability, Verbal Aptitude, Numerical Aptitude, Spatial Aptitude, Form Perception, Clerical Perception, Motor Coordination, Finger Dexterity, and Manual Dexterity. The General Learning Ability score is a factorially complex but practically useful measure based on performance in vocabulary, arithmetic reasoning, and spatial visualization tests. The other scores correspond more nearly to independent abilities identified through factor analysis. In order to adapt testing procedures to the needs of educationally disadvantaged adults, a parallel Nonreading Aptitude Test Battery (NATB) was constructed. Requiring no reading or writing, the NATB was designed to yield the same nine aptitude scores as the GATB. Research on the NATB is still needed, however, particularly with reference to the comparability of its occupational cutoff scores with those established for GATB and its applicability to persons unaccustomed to testing.

Thus far, multiple aptitude batteries have been used more widely for vocational counseling of individuals than for industrial selection or placement. With the growing emphasis on classification programs, however, such batteries may come to play a more prominent part in industrial personnel programs. When selecting applicants for a single job, most personnel psychologists rely on a combination of specific aptitude tests chosen to fit the particular job. But when the problem is that of maximum utilization of an available personnel pool, a multiple aptitude battery measuring a few broad abilities that cut across many different jobs is more effective.

Occupational Proficiency Tests. A distinction proposed by Fleishman (1972) between ability and skill is relevant to the type of test under consideration. "Abilities" refer to relatively broad traits the individual brings with him when he begins to learn a new task. These traits reflect the cumulative effects of prior learning. They are also related to a variety of tasks. For example, spatial visualization has been found to correlate with performance on such varied tasks as aerial navigation, blueprint reading, and dentistry. "Skills," on the other hand, refer to proficiency in a particular task, such as piloting a plane or operating a machine. Abilities influence skill learning through transfer of training from earlier learning. Occupational proficiency tests measure skills in the performance of particular occupational tasks. All presuppose some specialized training or experience for the job in question.

Specialized *information tests,* written or oral, represent one type of occupational proficiency test. Examples of commercially available tests for general use are provided by the Purdue Vocational Tests, which cover such trade areas as welding, engine lathe operation, and carpentry. In the large majority of jobs, information is a necessary but not a sufficient condition for satisfactory performance. Information tests therefore need to be supplemented by standardized *work-sample tests,* which closely reproduce actual job processes. Among the best known examples are tests for certain clerical skills, such as typewriting. Other examples include tests for a driver's license and a pilot's license.

Of particular interest is a work-sample test for executives, the in-basket test. Simulating the familiar "in-basket" found on the administrator's desk, this test provides a carefully prepared set of incoming letters, memoranda, reports, papers to be signed, and similar items. Before taking the test, the examinee has an opportunity to study background materials for orientation and information regarding the hypothetical job. During the test proper, his task is to handle all the matters in his in-basket as he would on the job. All actions must be recorded in writing but may include letters, memos, decisions, plans, directives, information to be obtained or transmitted by telephone, agenda for meetings, or any other notes. Performance may be rated in terms of many indexes of managerial style, such as "involves subordinates," "postpones decision," "explains to peers," and "takes final action."

The in-basket technique has yielded promising results with such groups as business executives, school principals, government administrators, and military officers (Frederiksen, 1962, 1966; Frederiksen, Saunders, & Wand, 1957; Hemphill, Griffiths, & Frederiksen, 1962; Lopez, 1966; Meyer, 1970). Although clearly representing a job sample and calling for specialized administrative skills, in-basket tests also belong with situational tests, discussed in the next section as methods of assessing personality characteristics. All situational tests involve both cognitive and noncognitive variables, although the relative proportion varies from test to test.

PERSONALITY TESTS

It is widely recognized that many job failures result from personality deficiencies. Having the required intellectual level, knowledge, and skills does not ensure that the individual will be an effective producer, a satisfied employee, or a well-liked co-worker. Personality characteristics may determine success or failure on *any* kind of job. Nevertheless, it is obvious that they play a particularly important part in jobs requiring extensive interpersonal contacts, such as selling and supervisory work.[2] Understandably, the possible contributions of available personality tests to personnel selection have been somewhat more fully explored in these fields than elsewhere.

Other types of jobs, however, make special demands upon the worker, for which particular personality variables may be critical. Examples include working at routine and repetitive tasks, working under distracting conditions, and working against time pressure. A job requiring close attention to minute details and one calling for rapid shifts of attention amid constant confusion present an obvious contrast in the emotional qualifications for successful performance. The importance of such personality requirements is recognized in some of the techniques of job analysis described in Chapter 2, such as the Position Analysis Questionnaire and the system of job analysis followed by the USES. Approaching the problem through job analysis represents a beneficial influence in personality assessment, insofar as it focuses attention on specific, job-relevant personality variables.

At this stage in their development, personality tests in general are not as effective in assessing most job-related personality variables as are the various judgmental techniques to be considered in later sections of this chapter. A few standardized personality tests are promising but still require more validation research in specific job situations. Some are useful in the hands of a trained psychologist; but even in such cases, they should be used in combination with other supporting data about the individual.

The validity of personality tests against industrial criteria has generally run lower than that of ability tests (Ghiselli, 1966). Similarly, an extensive survey of industrial validation studies of both personality inventories and projective techniques yielded generally disappointing results (Guion & Gottier, 1965). To be sure, the validity of most of the instruments surveyed can be most aptly described as unproven rather than disproved, because of methodological weaknesses in the validation research. Nevertheless, their validity cannot be assumed. It is also noteworthy that the empirical results on the relative merits of ability and personality tests for job applicants are correctly reflected in public opinion. In a carefully designed interview survey of a national adult sample (Fiske, 1967), over 75% of the respondents evaluated tests as good for assessing abilities and likes and dislikes (interests), but only about 50% considered tests good for investigating a job

---

[2]Special features of supervisory jobs will be considered in Chapter 6.

applicant's social relations and personal problems. Bearing in mind the limitations of current personality tests, we may briefly examine the types of instruments that have been used in personnel psychology.

Measurement of Interests. An early instrument that has stood the test of time unusually well is the Strong-Campbell Interest Inventory (SCII). First developed by E. K. Strong, Jr. in 1928, this test has undergone continuing revision, extension, and research—including long-term longitudinal validation (Campbell, 1971, 1974; Strong, 1943, 1955). In this test, examinees record their liking or dislike for a wide variety of activities, objects, or types of people commonly encountered in daily living. Preliminary research demonstrated that persons engaged in a given occupation tend to have common interests, not only in job activities by also in school subjects, hobbies, sports, types of plays or books, social relations, and the like. It thus proved feasible to question individuals about their interests in familiar things and thereby determine how closely their interests resemble those of persons successfully engaged in each occupation.

The SCII is scored with a different key for each occupation. The items to be included in each key, as well as the weights assigned to each response, were found empirically by comparing the percentage of persons in the particular occupation choosing each response with the percentage of men or women in the general reference sample who chose it. Responses occurring significantly more often among lawyers, for instance, than in the general reference group receive positive weights in the lawyer's key; those occurring significantly less often among lawyers receive negative weights. By such empirical criterion keying, about 125 occupational keys have been developed. New occupational keys are added as adequate samples become available.

Besides the occupational scores, the SCII also provides scores on six general occupational themes, including Realistic, Investigative, Artistic, Social, Enterprising, and Conventional. These themes were derived from the classification of interests developed by Holland (1973) and supported by extensive research both by Holland and by other independent investigators. Each theme characterizes not only a type of person but also the type of working environment that such a person would find most congenial. Finally, scores are reported on 23 basic interest scales, which consist of clusters of substantially intercorrelated items. In general, these 23 scales correspond to broad occupational categories, such as science, art, agriculture, and business management.

Another widely used set of interest inventories is that developed by Kuder (1963, 1966, 1970). The best known of these inventories is the Kuder Vocational Preference Record, which assesses relative interest in a few broad areas, including Outdoor, Mechanical, Computational, Scientific, Persuasive, Artistic, Literary, Musical, Social Service, and Clerical. Another version, the Kuder Occupational Interest Survey, reports degree of similarity between the individual's interest pattern and the interest patterns of each of a number of specific occupations. Both this form of the Kuder inventories and the SCII can be scored only by computer, at several designated scoring agencies.

Mention may also be made of the Allport-Vernon-Lindzey (1970) Study of Values, which assesses the relative strength of six basic motives or evaluative attitudes, designated as Theoretical, Economic, Aesthetic, Social, Political, and Religious. In use for many years, this test revealed characteristic value patterns for a number of occupational groups. Despite superficial differences in terminology, there is substantial similarity between this set of six values and both Holland's occupational themes (incorporated in the SCII) and the interest areas of the Kuder Vocational Preference Record.

Interest inventories were originally developed for vocational counseling rather than for employee selection; they will be discussed from the standpoint of counseling psychology in Chapter 15. The importance of assessing interests for occupational selection and classification, however, is being increasingly recognized.

Personality Inventories. This type of personality test originated in the attempt to identify emotional maladjustment and neurotic behavior. A number of current personality inventories—especially those designed for use in clinical contexts— still focus primarily on emotional abnormality. Most of the newer inventories, however, are concerned with individual differences in emotional, motivational, and social traits among essentially normal persons. Moreover, such inventories typically provide a profile of scores in a number of traits, rather than a single score. The norms on such tests generally fall near the center of the score range. Deviations in either direction from such a norm need to be interpreted in terms of particular job requirements. Desirable score patterns for each type of job may be empirically established by the usual follow-up procedures described in the preceding chapter.

An example of a personality inventory is the Guilford-Zimmerman Temperament Survey, which yields separate scores on the following 10 traits: General Activity, Restraint, Ascendance, Sociability, Emotional Stability, Objectivity, Friendliness, Thoughtfulness, Personal Relations, and Masculinity. The items measuring these traits are presented in random order and not identified as such to the examinee. Three typical items are:

You start work on a new project with a great deal of enthusiasm	YES	?	NO
You are often low in spirits	YES	?	NO
Most people use politeness to cover up what is really "cutthroat" competition	YES	?	NO

This inventory has been used extensively in personnel testing, and some suggestive validation research against industrial criteria has been reported.

Two more recently developed examples of multivariate personality inventories are the California Psychological Inventory (CPI) and the Comrey Personality Scales. Both are characterized by a high level of technical quality, and both have been employed in a continuing research program. Among the many different populations studied with the CPI are several occupational groups. From these data, regression equations have been developed for predicting performance in many fields of work. Because the Comrey scales are much newer, the amount of data gathered thus far with the finished instrument is less extensive. A special feature of this inventory is its use of a 7-point scale for recording item responses, in place of the usual two or three response options. It might also be noted that its trait categories have held up well in cross-cultural studies.

A common difficulty limiting the usefulness of personality inventories in personnel selection is their susceptibility to *faking*. Many investigations have demonstrated that, on self-report inventories, respondents can frequently identify the socially desirable answers and will mark such answers instead of those corresponding to their own habitual behavior (Anastasi, 1976, Ch. 17). The motivation to create a favorable impression is of course stronger in a selection than in a counseling situation, although not totally absent even in the latter. Several techniques have been devised for reducing or at least detecting such faking. The Guilford-Zimmerman, for example, provides three verification keys, based on the responses to certain items, to detect falsification and carelessness in responses. Similar check scores are included in the CPI and the Comrey scales.

A procedure designed to reduce the tendency to fake is the forced-choice technique. In a forced-choice item, the respondent must choose between answers that appear equally acceptable (or unacceptable) but that differ in validity for a specific criterion. It should be noted, however, that this technique reduces but does not eliminate faking, especially by the applicant for a specific job (Dunnette, McCartney, Carlson, & Kirchner, 1962). Even when items are equated for general social desirability, the individual may recognize that certain responses are more relevant to the particular job. Still another procedure, which is gaining recognition, is to orient the examinee more fully to the purposes of testing in order to elicit frank responses. It is certainly not in the individual's best interests to be placed on a job that is incompatible with his or her personality characteristics.

Projective Techniques. It is principally in clinical psychology that projective techniques have enjoyed their greatest popularity. Hence they will be discussed more fully in Chapter 12. These techniques, however, are also used to a limited extent in industry, especially for intensive individual evaluation of executives and other high-level personnel. Typically in a projective test the examinee is assigned an *unstructured* task, which permits an almost unlimited variety of possible responses. The test stimuli are usually vague and equivocal and the instructions brief and general. Such tests are based on the hypothesis that the way the individual perceives and interprets the test material, or "structures" the situation, reflects basic personality characteristics. The test stimuli thus serve as a sort of screen on which respondents "project" their own ideas. Since the examinees are generally unaware of the way their responses will be scored or evaluated, projective techniques are less susceptible to faking than are self-report inventories; but they are not entirely immune to it.

A widely used projective technique, which has also served as a model for the development of many later instruments, is the Thematic Apperception Test (TAT). First developed by H. A. Murray and his associates (1938, 1943), this test consists of a set of pictures, for each of which the respondent makes up a story. As in most projective tests, there is no objective scoring procedure, the stories being interpreted by the examiner in terms of Murray's theory of needs and of environmental forces that either facilitate or interfere with the satisfaction of these needs. Several adaptations of the TAT have been developed for special purposes. Extensive research has focused on the needs for achievement, affiliation, and power (Atkinson, Raynor, et al., 1974; McClelland, 1971).

Pictures are employed in a somewhat different way in the Tomkins-Horn Picture Arrangement Test (PAT), a projective technique originally designed for the selection and guidance of industrial personnel. Each item of the PAT consists of three sketches presented in a round-robin arrangement so as to minimize positional set (see Fig. 3-6). The respondent's task is to indicate the order of the three pictures "which makes the best sense" and to write a sentence for each of the three pictures to tell the story. Most items deal with interpersonal relations, more than

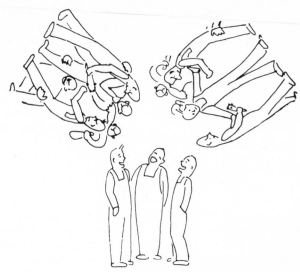

Figure 3-6. Sample items from the Tomkins-Horn Picture Arrangement Test. The respondent indicates the sequence that makes the best sense for the three pictures and writes three sentences explaining them. (*Copyright © 1944, 1957, 1959 by Silvan S. Tomkins & Daniel Horn. Reproduced by permission of authors and Springer Publishing Company, Inc.*)

half of them portraying work situations in an industrial setting. Advantages of this test are that it can be group-administered and machine-scored. The norms are also unusually good for a projective test, having been obtained on a large, representative sample of the United States population. Subjective interpretation has not been entirely eliminated, however. After the objective score pattern is found for each person, it must still be interpreted by a clinical psychologist. In exploratory research on such varied groups as high level executives, salespersons, and workers engaged in routine, repetitive tasks, the PAT yielded promising results in assessing several job-relevant personality characteristics (Miner, 1960, 1961, 1962; Miner & Culver, 1955).

In the light of available knowledge regarding their reliability, validity, and other technical characteristics, projective techniques in general must still be regarded as research instruments. None is ready for regular operational use in personnel selection (Kinslinger, 1966). A few of these techniques, however, have been yielding some useful information when interpreted by experienced clinical psychologists in the assessment centers to be discussed later in the chapter (Grant, Katkovsky, & Bray, 1967).

Situational Tests. Although the term "situational test" first came into prominence during World War II, tests of this type had been developed before that time. Essentially a situational test is one that closely resembles or simulates a "real-life" criterion situation. In this respect such tests are similar to the work-sample tests discussed earlier in this chapter. In situational tests, however, the criterion behavior that is sampled is more varied and complex. Moreover, interest is centered, not on aptitude or achievement, but on emotional, social, attitudinal, and other personality traits. Several kinds of situational tests have been developed for evaluating the leadership behavior and human relations skills of management personnel. In fact, such techniques constitute a characteristic feature of assessment centers.

A promising type of situational test is the Leaderless Group Discussion (LGD). Requiring a minimum of equipment and time, this technique has been widely used in the selection of such personnel as military officers, civil service administrators, industrial executives, management trainees, sales trainees, teachers, and social workers (see Anastasi, 1976, Ch. 20; Bass, 1954; Guilford, 1959, pp. 260–263). In this test, a group of examinees is assigned a topic for discussion during a specified period. Examiners observe and rate each person's performance but do not participate in the discussion. Although often used under informal and unstandardized conditions, the LGD has been subjected to considerable research, and some objective scoring procedures have been worked out for it.

Validity studies suggest that LGD techniques are among the most effective applications of situational tests. Many significant and sizable correlations have been reported between ratings from LGD performance and follow-up or concurrent ratings obtained in military, industrial, and social settings. Some of these correlations are as high as .60. Neither LGD nor other, more elaborate situational tests, however, have proved valid as devices for assessing broad personality traits. All such tests appear to be most effective when they approximate actual work samples of the criterion behavior they are designed to predict. The LGD tests in particular have some validity in predicting performance in jobs requiring a certain amount of verbal communication, verbal problem solving, and acceptance by peers. Another factor that seems to increase the predictive validity of situational tests is job familiarity on the part of the raters. Such a finding again suggests that situational tests work best when the participants' performance is interpreted as a work sample rather than in terms of underlying personality variables.

RATING PROCEDURES

Long before the appearance of the first psychological test, job applicants were being selected through letters of application, references from past employers, and personal interviews. Tests have by no means replaced these traditional procedures of personnel selection. In fact, no reputable industrial psychologist would evaluate an applicant on the basis of tests alone. Test scores must be interpreted in the light of other information about the individual's background. Moreover, good tests are not available for all traits, especially in the area of personality. A rating obtained from a well-conducted interview, or from persons who have observed the applicant adequately in previous relevant situations, is preferable to a poor test or a test of unknown validity. It is also likely that for certain interpersonal traits, involving as they do the reactions of the individual to other persons, ratings will always provide the most valid predictors.

Application forms, references, and interviews may all be used to obtain *biographical data* pertaining to education, special training, job history, and other relevant facts of past experience. When properly interpreted, an accurate record of what an individual has done in the past is an effective predictor of what he or she will do in the future. Interviews and references also provide *interpersonal data* based on the interaction of the applicant with the interviewer and with previous acquaintances, respectively. The following sections are concerned with ways of improving application forms, reference reports, and interviews and with an evaluation of the effectivenss of these techniques. But first we shall consider rating procedures in general, since they underlie both reference reports and interviewing, besides having other important uses in personnel psychology.

In Chapter 2 we have already seen that ratings constitute an important source of criterion data for most jobs. The evaluation of each person's job performance against which predictors can be validated represents one application of rating procedures in personnel psychology. An important operational use of rating is to be found in the merit rating systems regularly employed by many companies. Such periodic performance ratings serve as an aid in administrative decisions regarding promotions, salary increments, transfers, or discharges. They also provide information needed for the improvement of worker performance through conferences or additional training. In personnel selection, rating procedures can be effectively incorporated into reference forms and interview reports. Although many rating procedures have been developed in the effort to make judgments more objective and precise, they can be conveniently classified under six major types: order-of-merit comparisons, rating scales, scaled checklists, forced-choice technique, nominating technique, and field review method.

Order-of-merit Comparisons. In order-of-merit procedures, the rating is done by ranking, comparing, or classifying people. Thus a supervisor may be asked to *rank* the 27 employees in a department in order of merit for overall job performance or for any specified trait. A more precise but time-consuming procedure is that of *paired comparisons,* in which each individual is paired in turn with every other and the judge merely indicates which is the better in each pair.

Even order-of-merit ranking becomes laborious when the group is large. As a result, it may be done carelessly and inaccurately by the busy rater. A less demanding variant, which nevertheless yields results of sufficient accuracy for most purposes, is the *forced distribution.* In this procedure, the rater may be given a rating scale similar to those to be discussed shortly, but the number of persons to be placed in each category is specified—either rigidly, or, more often, approximately.

An example of a forced distribution with 40 cases is given in Table 3-1. The

TABLE 3-1
A Forced Distribution with 40 Cases

Rating	A	B	C	D	E
Number of persons to be assigned each rating	3	10	14	10	3

numbers in each category are derived from normal curve frequencies, on the assumption that the trait under consideration is normally distributed in the group. If this assumption is correct, the trait categories in the scale can be treated as equal units of amount. In fact, they have the mathematical properties of the previously described standard scores (Ch. 2). Such equality of units is a further advantage of the forced distribution as compared with ordinary ranking. Ranks cannot be treated as equal units. The difference in job proficiency between two employees ranked first and second in a group of 27 is likely to be much greater than the differences between those ranked 13th and 14th in the same group. This follows from the fact that in a normal distribution individuals cluster more closely in the center and are more widely scattered as the extremes are approached.

All order-of-merit techniques presuppose that the same judge evaluates all members of the group on a single occasion. Such a procedure is feasible in certain situations, as when a supervisor rates the employees in his or her department. But there are obviously other situations to which this procedure is inapplicable, notably reference forms submitted on individual applicants and interview reports prepared as each applicant is interviewed. Another limitation of order-of-merit techniques is that they provide information only on the relative position of each individual within a group; they do not permit evaluation in terms of absolute standards. Thus from order-of-merit data alone it would be impossible to determine which individuals if any fall below minimum proficiency standards required for a job or to compare different groups that have been independently rated.

Rating Scales. To obtain a record of absolute judgments in terms of an external standard, various types of rating scales have been developed. With such scales, each individual is independently evaluated. In the preparation of all rating scales, the basic problem pertains to the choice of units for expressing degrees of the trait to be rated. These units must be easily understood and uniformly interpreted by all raters.

A common type of rating scale utilizes *descriptive adjectives* as its units. For example, an individual's punctuality, accuracy, or sense of humor might be rated as very inferior, inferior, average, superior, or very superior. In the effort to make the units more meaningful, different sets of adjectives may be substituted to fit each trait. Thus in the rating of general ability level, the adjectives might be: retarded, dull, mediocre, clever, brilliant. Although still frequently encountered, the descriptive-adjective rating scale is one of the least satisfactory. Whether general or specific adjectives are employed, different raters are likely to interpret them with considerable variation. Not only are the terms themselves vague but each rater may also apply a somewhat different standard in making a judgment. Because of differences in their previous experiences with employee groups, one rater may describe as mediocre the same job behavior that another rater considers clever.

Nor should we be misled by the false impression of objectivity and quantification created by *numerical rating scales.* Substituting the numbers 1 to 5 for the previously cited descriptive terms in no way clarifies the meaning of the units. To rate a person "4" in sense of humor is just as vague and subjective as to say he is "superior" in this regard. Both types of ratings are subject to the same misunderstandings and judgment errors. The use of finer units in a numerical scale, moreover, does not necessarily increase the precision of the ratings. To rate sense of humor on a 100-point scale is probably no more accurate than to rate it on a 10-point scale. Raters cannot reliably discriminate between, let us say, ratings of 73 and 74 in such a trait. Hence, either they will not use the intervening values or they will use them in a haphazard and nondiscriminating manner.

A more effective way to make the scale units meaningful is to utilize critical incidents, or *scaled behavior samples,* for the scale units. Smith and Kendall (1963) developed a refinement of such behaviorally anchored rating scales whereby both the qualities or dimensions to be rated and the behavior samples are empirically formulated and scaled by groups of judges drawn from the same populations as the raters who will eventually use the scales. To ensure that the behavior samples or incidents are consistently perceived by raters as instances of the dimensions they represent, a process of "retranslation" is followed. For this purpose, a new group of judges sorts each incident into what appears to be the most appropriate dimension. Only those incidents ascribed to the original dimensions by the large majority of respondents are retained. The same group (or a similar group) rates the incidents for effectiveness of the behavior illustrated. The mean of these ratings provides the scale value for each item retained in the scale. This procedure has proved effective in the development of rating scales for such diverse groups as hospital nurses, department managers in retail stores, naval officers, and college professors (Borman & Dunnette, 1975; Campbell, Dunnette, Arvey, & Hellervik, 1973; Harari & Zedeck, 1973; Smith & Kendall, 1963; Zedeck, Imparato, Krausz, & Oleno, 1974). There is also some evidence that behaviorally based rating scales

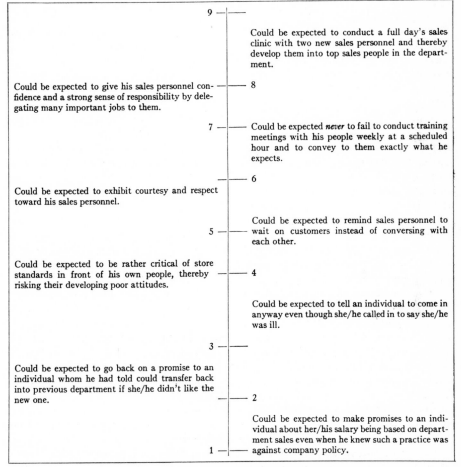

Figure 3-7. A behaviorally anchored graphic rating scale for the effectiveness with which department managers supervise their sales personnel. *(From Campbell, Dunnette, Arvey, & Hellervik, 1973, p. 17. Copyright © 1973 by American Psychological Association. Reproduced by permission.)*

need not be job specific. Such a scale was successfully developed for use with a wide variety of nonnursing hospital jobs, ranging from floor sweepers and dishwashers to laboratory technicians and social workers (Goodale & Burke, 1975).

An example of a behaviorally anchored rating scale is given in Figure 3-7. This is one of nine scales developed for use in the rating of retail-store department managers by their immediate supervisors (J. P. Campbell et al., 1973). The scale illustrated pertains to the manager's supervision of sales personnel. Other scales in the set cover such dimensions as handling customer complaints, merchandise ordering, and communicating relevant information to associates and to higher management.

Since human traits are continuous variables, any assignment of individuals to discrete categories is artificial. Raters often report difficulty in placing an individual into any one of the given categories, objecting that the ratee seems to fall between two categories. This difficulty is obviated in *graphic rating scales,* in which the individual's trait rating may be indicated by checking any position along a continuous line. To ensure uniformity of interpretation by different raters, it is desirable to anchor the graphic scale at several points by giving behavioral descriptions, as illustrated in Figure 3-7. Raters are usually told, however, that these behavioral descriptions do not represent separate categories but indicate only the direction of the line. This type of rating scale thus combines the continuity of graphic ratings with the interpretive clarity of scaled behavioral descriptions. For most purposes, it is the most satisfactory type of rating scale. In recording or combining ratings from such a scale, it is customary to divide the line into segments, the number usually varying from 5 to 9. While leaving the rater free to check anywhere he or she chooses, such a procedure recognizes the fact that very small differences in the position of the checkmarks are of no significance because of limitations in the discriminative ability of raters, as well as the negligible increase in rating reliability with increase in number of scale units (Lissitz & Green, 1975; G. A. Miller, 1956).

Scaled Checklists. In another type of rating procedure, the rater checks all statements in a given list that characterize the individual. Although presented in random order, these statements range from very favorable to very unfavorable and cover a variety of traits. To find the individual's overall rating, the scale values of all statements checked for him are averaged. These scale values, which do not appear on the rating form, are derived during the construction of the checklist by a procedure first employed by Thurstone and his co-workers (1929) in developing attitude scales. First, a large number of descriptive statements about workers are assembled. These statements are then presented one at a time to individual judges, who sort them into piles (usually 11), from least to most favorable. The scale value given to each statement is the mean position assigned to that statement by all the judges.

It has been found that different groups of judges, such as supervisors, personnel workers, college professors, and students, agree closely in the mean position assigned to such statements (Uhrbrock, 1961b). Within each group, any statement showing too wide a variability in the positions assigned to it by individual judges is discarded as ambiguous. The final list of statements is selected so as to cover a wide range of favorableness and to comprise statements spaced by approximately

TABLE 3-2
Illustrative Statements from a Scaled Checklist for Rating Workers
(Data from Uhrbrock, 1961b.)

Statement	Scale Value[a]	SD[b]
Is seriously lacking in judgment	13	8.45
Is poor at following instructions	25	6.12
Is a steady worker	69	8.57
Occasionally develops new ideas	74	12.23
Effectively coordinates departmental activities	89	12.18
Is dynamic leader who stimulates enthusiasm	109	2.42

[a]Statements were sorted into 11 piles by 16 judges. Scale values are mean positions multiplied by 10 to eliminate decimals.
[b]Standard deviation of positions assigned by 16 judges, also multiplied by 10.

equal distances in scale values. In Table 3-2 will be found some typical checklist statements, together with their scale values and variability measures.

Forced-choice Technique. Earlier in this chapter the forced-choice technique was described as a procedure for reducing faking on personality inventories. The same technique has been employed for rating purposes in the effort to minimize certain rater biases, such as the tendency to rate an individual too high or too low. Table 3-3 shows a typical forced-choice item designed for the rating of Air Force instructors by their supervisors (Berkshire & Highland, 1953). This was one of many items employed in a study of the relative effectiveness of different forms of forced-choice items, varying in the following features: number of statements per item; inclusion of favorable or unfavorable statements, or both; and raters' instructions to choose the one or two most descriptive or least descriptive statements, or both. Items of the type illustrated in Table 3-3, in which all statements are equally "favorable" and only the *most* descriptive are to be marked for each person, proved more effective and more acceptable to raters than other combinations. It will be seen in Table 3-3 that the alternative statements are approximately equated in favorableness index (FI) but differ sharply in dis-

TABLE 3-3
Typical Item from a Forced-choice Rating Report
(From Berkshire & Highland, 1953, p. 363.)

Item	FI	DI
a. Patient with slow learners	2.82	1.15
b. Lectures with confidence	2.75	.54
c. Keeps interest and attention of class	2.89	1.39
d. Acquaints classes with objective for each class in advance	2.85	.79

Note. Raters mark the two statements that are *most descriptive* of each individual. FI and DI do not appear on rating form.

crimination index (DI), or ability to differentiate between high and low criterion groups.

The statements marked for each individual are scored in terms of their empirically established weights, which are based on their criterion correlations or discrimination indexes. Of course, such weights never appear on the rating forms. But insofar as a rater can detect the difference in job relevance between two equally desirable statements, the rater's evaluation of a given individual can still be deliberately slanted in either a favorable or an unfavorable direction. For this reason, the forced-choice technique cannot entirely eliminate rater bias, although it can probably reduce it in most situations.

Nominating Technique. A promising approach to rating is based on the nominating technique. Originally developed in sociometry for investigating group structure, this technique is generally used in obtaining peer ratings, as when a group of co-workers, trainees, or officer candidates rate each other. It is also being employed increasingly in industry. The nominating technique can be applied in any group whose members have been together long enough to ensure a necessary minimum of acquaintance, as in a factory, office, class, or military unit. Each person is asked to choose or nominate the group member with whom he or she would most like to work, eat lunch, spend free time, or carry out any other specified activity. Or the person may be asked who would make the best department supervisor, district manager, officer, or group leader. The technique may also be applied to more specifically labeled behavioral variables, such as maturity, originality, or dependability. The total number of nominations received by each person represents that person's rating.

Peer ratings apparently reflect much more than mere popularity. There is considerable evidence from military studies indicating that these ratings may be more reliable and valid than supervisors' ratings of the same individuals (Campbell, Dunnette, Lawler, & Weick, 1970, pp. 113–114; Downey, 1974; Downey, Medland, & Yates, 1976). Their superiority is particularly evident in ratings of interpersonal traits, such as leadership. Validity studies of peer nominations in industry have also yielded promising results. Life insurance agents in one company, for example, submitted peer nominations on a 14-item questionnaire, from which an overall rating was computed for each individual (Weitz, 1958). Without any knowledge of these ratings, the company subsequently promoted 100 of the agents to supervisory jobs. Performance ratings of these men after six months on their supervisory jobs were significantly and substantially related to their initial peer ratings, as shown in Table 3-4. The performance ratings were assigned by supervisors who had no access to the original peer nominations. Other studies of the validity of the nominating technique have shown it to be a good predictor of several practical criteria dependent upon interpersonal relations.

Although it is only applicable to certain types of situations, the nominating technique has proved to be one of the most dependable of rating techniques. These findings are not surprising when we consider some of the features of peer nominations. First, the number of raters is large, including all group members. Second, an individual's peers are often in a particularly favorable position to observe his or her typical behavior. They may be better judges of certain interpersonal traits than shop supervisors, superior officers, instructors, or other outside observers. Third, and probably most important, is the fact that the opinions of group members—right or wrong—influence their actions and hence partly

TABLE 3-4
Relation between Peer Nomination Ratings
and Subsequent Supervisory Performance
(Data from Weitz, 1958.)

Peer Nomination Score	Number of Men	Percentage Rated Good or Excellent in Supervisory Performance[a]
10-14	33	76
4-9	28	54
0-3	39	39

[a]The significance of the relationship is indicated by a x^2 of 10.08, $p < .01$.

determine the nature of the individual's subsequent interactions with the group. Other comparable groups may be expected to react in a similar way toward the individual. Peer ratings thus have the same kind of validity as work samples.

Field Review Method. Another procedure designed chiefly to improve qualitative evaluations of employee performance is the field review method. In this method, a consulting psychologist or a member of the personnel department interviews each supervisor regarding the performance of employees in his or her department. Although the discussion is kept informal, the interviewer sees to it that certain points are covered and adequately followed up in the course of the interview. Special efforts are made to elicit supporting facts for each statement, such as the specific ways in which one employee's performance is outstanding, the particular weaknesses another has exhibited in relations with co-workers, and the like.

On the basis of such an interview, the personnel worker may rate the overall job effectiveness of the employee into rough categories, such as definitely outstanding, satisfactory, or definitely a problem. These ratings, for example, could serve as a criterion measure if more precise quantitative ratings are unobtainable. Frequently, however, the object of the field review method is merely to stimulate the supervisor to evaluate the employee more objectively and to plan appropriate action.

Factors Influencing the Accuracy of Ratings. Like other predictors, ratings can be evaluated in terms of reliability and validity. Reliability of ratings covers temporal stability as well as interrater agreement. The former may be found by comparing the ratings assigned by a single judge to the same individuals on different occasions, the latter by comparing the ratings assigned by different judges to the same individuals.

The validity of ratings has been investigated much less frequently than their reliability, probably because of the difficulty of finding adequate criterion measures. It cannot be assumed, however, that high rating reliability implies high validity. Raters may be highly consistent over time and may agree closely with each other while subject to common errors and biases which reduce validity. For the same reason, the use of a consensus or average rating by a group of judges as a criterion does not provide conclusive evidence of validity, except for such traits as popularity or leadership, which are defined largely in terms of social interaction. For most traits, follow-up data on the ratee's behavior in relevant situations represent the most satisfactory criteria against which to validate ratings. This is particularly true when ratings are used as predictors of future proficiency, in connection with selection or classification decisions.

Ratings are subject to a number of common errors and distortions. A well-known example is the *halo effect.* This is a tendency on the part of raters to be unduly influenced by a single favorable or unfavorable trait, which colors their judgment of the individual's other traits. One way to reduce halo effect is to define traits in terms of concrete behavior. In some graphic rating scales, the favorable and unfavorable ends of the line are reversed in random order for different traits. This device serves to emphasize the distinctness of each trait and forces the rater to read the anchoring statements rather than marking a similar position indiscriminately for all traits. When several persons are to be rated by the same rater, a recommended procedure is to rate all persons in a single trait before rating anyone in the next trait. Thus, all ratees are first rated in cooperativeness, then all are rated in productivity, and so on. This procedure tends to focus the rater's attention on each trait separately rather than on a general impression of each person.

Another common error, known as the *error of central tendency,* refers to judges' avoidance of extreme scale positions and their tendency to place an excessive number of persons in the center of the scale. This error is eliminated in forced-distribution and other order-of-merit procedures. Explaining the purpose of the rating so that judges are motivated to identify rather than to conceal individual differences helps to reduce the error. It should be noted, however, that, if judges do not have an adequate basis for making the required discriminations, encouraging them to use the ends of the scale leads to overdifferentiation and increases the overall amount of judgment error. In such a situation, reduction in range is desirable and corresponds to the regression toward the mean that occurs in statistical prediction.

The *leniency error* denotes the reluctance of many raters to assign unfavorable ratings, especially when ratings are used for administrative purposes. The ratings actually given may thus range from average to excellent, or they may even cluster entirely near the upper end of the scale. Like the error of central tendency, the leniency error reduces the effective size of the scale and makes ratings less discriminative. It, too, can be eliminated through the use of a forced distribution. Providing more favorable than unfavorable terms in the scale is another way to reduce this error. Judges may be less reluctant to characterize an individual as "only slightly cooperative" than to call him "uncooperative." The forced-choice technique and some of the other special rating procedures described in the preceding section were designed partly to avoid the leniency error. There is evidence that the forced-choice technique reduces but does not entirely eliminate this error (Taylor & Wherry, 1951). Under certain conditions, moreover, graphic rating scales may be just as satisfactory as forced-choice procedures in this regard (Berkshire & Highland, 1953).

Judgment errors may also arise from *social stereotypes.* Controlled experiments have demonstrated, for instance, that ratings for such traits as intelligence, dependability, industriousness, talkativeness, and conscientiousness may be influenced by the wearing of eyeglasses (Thornton, 1944). Other stereotypes stemming from folklore or from the pseudoscientific systems of phrenology and physiognomy may also affect ratings in many psychological traits (Secord & Muthard, 1955). The association of a high forehead with intelligence, a square jaw with determination, or a steady look with honesty are familiar examples. Such stereotypes may influence ratings even when the rater is unaware of their operation. What the rater accepts as a hunch or general impression may in fact stem from an unrecognized response to some irrelevant physical cue. Judgment errors resulting from social stereotypes tend to be most prevalent in ratings based on a brief interview or other initial contact. The less behavioral information raters have about the individual, the more likely are they to rely upon stereotypes and snap judgments.

One of the conditions that affects the validity of ratings is the extent of the rater's *relevant acquaintance* with the person to be rated (Freeberg, 1969). It is not enough to have known the person for a long time. The rater should have had an opportunity to observe him in situations in which the behavior in question could be manifested. For example, if an employee has never had an opportunity to make decisions on the job, his ability to do so cannot be evaluated by his supervisor. Increase in duration of personal acquaintance, without a corresponding increase in opportunities to observe the trait rated, may actually reduce the accuracy of ratings. Both halo effect and leniency error, for instance, tend to increase with very long acquaintance (Freeberg, 1969). In many rating situations, it is desirable to include a space to be checked in lieu of a rating if the rater has had no opportunity to observe the particular trait in a given individual. A request for supporting evidence or specific examples of behavior is a further way of encouraging respondents to rate only those traits they have actually observed.

Ratings may vary in a number of ways as a function of *rater characteristics.* Some raters are typically "hard," while others are "easy." Thus the same group of persons may cluster at different parts of the scale when evaluated by different judges. Raters may also differ in the spread, or variability, of their ratings, some utilizing only a narrow portion of the scale, others spreading their ratings over a much wider range. Finally, ratings may vary in the relative positions they assign to particular individuals. Rater A may regard Alice Brown as much more dominant than Janet Green, while Rater B holds the opposite view with equal conviction. To some extent these differences may reflect idiosyncrasies of the raters, arising from their past experience, their differing concepts of the traits, and similar factors. Some of the variation, however, may result from the fact that the ratees have been observed in different situations by the two raters. Even in similar situations, the raters' own manner, appearance, reputation, and other characteristics may evoke different behavior from the same individual. Thus, some of the variation among the ratings assigned by different judges may reflect genuine differences in the behavior of the ratee under different circumstances.

While much more research is needed to spell out all the qualifications of a good rater and the reasons for such qualifications, it is clear that differences among raters are large and significant. A number of experiments using a variety of rating procedures agree in one conclusion: Who does the rating makes more difference in the ratings received than do the characteristics of the rating scale, the rating technique employed, or the conditions under which ratings are made (Campbell et al., 1970; pp. 114–116; Fiske & Cox, 1960; Schneider & Bayroff, 1953).

There is some evidence that the rater's own job effectiveness influences his ratings (Campbell et al., 1970, pp. 114–115; Kirchner & Reisberg, 1962). For example, more effective and less effective supervisors tend to have different concepts and expectations about what constitutes effective job behavior in the persons they evaluate. The same individual may thus receive high ratings from one rater and low ratings from another because the two raters are judging different traits. Still another factor is the rater's job level and his relation to the ratee.

Supervisors, co-workers (or peers), and subordinates are likely to have different views of the same individual. Such considerations suggest the desirability of obtaining evaluations from more than one rater. Especially in the case of managerial performance, ratings from observers at different levels or in different organizational roles are helpful.

Much of what has been said regarding factors that influence the accuracy of ratings suggests the desirability of *rater training.* Research in both industrial and military settings has demonstrated the effectiveness of training in increasing the validity of ratings and in reducing such judgment errors as halo effect and leniency error (Bernardin & Walter, 1977; Borman, 1975; Latham, Wexley, & Pursell, 1975). Training programs are especially appropriate for supervisors who must assign periodic merit ratings as part of their regular duties. They are also helpful for selection interviewers who must rate applicants and for anyone who is asked to provide criterion ratings.

Rater training programs vary in duration and thoroughness depending upon their purposes and the available facilities. Even a relatively simple orientation session lasting only an hour or two will produce noticeable results. In general, such a training program should explain the aims and purposes of the ratings, provide information on common judgment errors such as halo effect and stereotypes, stress the importance of obtaining maximal differentiation and avoiding both leniency and central tendency errors, clarify and illustrate the meaning of the traits to be rated and of the scale units, and give supervised practice in the assignment of ratings.

APPLICATION FORMS AND REFERENCE REPORTS

Application Forms. One of the best known procedures of personnel selection is the evaluation of candidates through letters of application or application forms. The traditional *letter of application* stating the applicant's availability and qualifications for the job is subject to many errors. Owing to inadequate knowledge of job requirements, the applicant may be unable to determine what personal characteristics or background facts are most relevant to the job. Moreover, adverse factors are not likely to be included and qualifications may be deliberately falsified. Characteristics of the letter itself, such as neatness, handwriting, grammatical or spelling errors, organization of content, and effectiveness of expression may influence the reader in many ways. Of course, when the job duties include extensive letter writing, the letter of application may be regarded as a job sample. But in many jobs, such skills are quite irrelevant. If a photograph is included for jobs in which appearance is of little relevance, physical stereotypes may further distort judgment.

Application forms, or biographical inventories, ensure more uniformity in the facts ascertained, since the employer determines what items are to be included. Like the personality inventories described in an earlier section, the biographical inventory is a self-report instrument, but most of its questions pertain to relatively objective and readily verifiable facts. Typical items deal with amount and nature of education, previous job history, special skills, hobbies, and recreational activities. Some of these items, which may seem far-removed from job functions, have proved useful as indicators of job-relevant personality dimensions, especially in the areas of motivation, interests, and interpersonal relations. Extracurricular and community activities, for example, may furnish information about the individual's leadership qualifications and interpersonal skills. Frequently, the applicant's reaction to prior experiences is also sought, as when respondents are asked to list the courses they liked best and least in school or what they liked and disliked in their prior jobs. Some biographical inventories also include items quite similar to those found in interest inventories.

By providing information about relevant biographical data, application forms can serve as effective aids in personnel selection. But the relevance of items and the significance of specific responses must be empirically determined. Otherwise, the application form may prove wasteful and misleading. In developing an application form, personnel psychologists are guided in their original choice of items by available research on the relationships between biographical data and job criteria. A further, more specific guide is provided by a job analysis of the job under consideration. The final selection of items, however, requires an empirical validation of specific responses against a criterion of job success. This process is similar to test validation. It includes the selection and weighting of items in one group of employees and a cross-validation of the complete application form in another group (see Ch. 2). However relevant a biographical item may seem for a particular job, its validity cannot be assumed without such empirical verification.

The procedure followed in developing a *weighted application blank* is described in detail in several sources (see especially England, 1971; Guion, 1965a, pp. 381–396; McCormick & Tiffin, 1974, pp. 69–78). Essentially, it involves a comparison of the relative frequency of each response in high and low criterion groups. For example, if job turnover is the criterion, the employees might be divided into those that remained on the job one year or longer (High Group) and those that left within the first year (Low Group). An item response chosen by 60% of the High Group and 29% of the Low Group would probably receive a weight of +2; one marked by 9% of the High Group and 30% of the Low Group would receive a weight of −3; one marked about equally often in the High and Low groups would receive a weight of zero or be eliminated from the form. The individual's total score is the algebraic sum of all his item weights. When the form thus developed is administered to a new sample for cross-validation, the total scores obtained by this group are correlated with the job tenure criterion. This correlation represents the validity of the application form.

Beginning in the early 1920s with a form for the selection of salesmen (Goldsmith, 1922), weighted application blanks have been developed for many types of jobs. One of the most extensive users of this technique is the Life Insurance Marketing and Research Association (1973, 1975), which developed a system of scoring weights for evaluating biographical data of life insurance agents. When appropriate procedures have been followed, biographical inventories have proved to be consistently good predictors of performance in a wide diversity of contexts. They have been successfully developed against such varied criteria as job turnover of bank clerks (D. D. Robinson, 1972), productivity of research scientists (Taylor & Ellison, 1967), artistic creativity of high school students (Anastasi & Schaefer, 1969; James, Ellison, Fox, & Taylor, 1974), and performance of divers and aquanauts in naval training programs (Helmreich, Bakeman, & Radloff, 1973). Weighted application blanks have proved valid as predictors of job performance in groups ranging from unskilled seasonal workers, office clerks, and service station dealers to chemists, engineers, and high-level executives.[3]

In the development and use of weighted application blanks, certain cautions should be observed. It is important to check for possible *nonlinear relationships* between items and criterion. In some jobs, for instance, maximal proficiency may be associated with the intermediate ages or educational levels. In such cases, lower or negative weights would be assigned to both extremes, while the intermediate values would receive the highest positive weights. Another point to check is *preselection.* If applicants have already been screened on the basis of any of the characteristics included in the blank, a comparison of successful and unsuccessful workers among those hired may fail to reveal any validity for this characteristic. For example, when only high school graduates are hired, amount of education may show no relation to later job success of employees. But if education is in fact related to success on this job, dropping this item will worsen rather than improve the selection process. There are several ways of handling preselection, depending upon specific circumstances. But in no case can we *assume* either the absence of preselection or the irrelevance of preselection items.

Still another problem is the possible *situational specificity* of biographical inventory items. The predictive validity of individual items may be quite specific to the job for which they were empirically selected and validated. A personal or background characteristic that is favorable for one job may be irrelevant or unfavorable for another. Such specificity may extend to very similar jobs, such as selling different products. It may also hold for different criteria within the same job. For example, different scoring weights may be required to predict earnings, turnover, accident rate, or promotion potential for the same job. On the other hand, there is a growing body of research indicating that clusters of interrelated items may reflect more stable and widely applicable behavior dimensions. Through factor analysis of individual item responses, several investigators have identified certain dimensions characterizing the life-styles and experiential patterns of different persons. These dimensions, revealed in responses to item clusters, are meaningfully related to subsequent job attitudes and performance (Baehr & Williams, 1967; Cassens, 1966; Morrison, Owens, Glennon, & Albright, 1962; Schmuckler, 1966).

Subsequent progress in the construction and application of weighted application blanks is characterized by other methodological innovations. In the development of a biographical inventory for navy divers, for example, longitudinal data were elicited through the use of a question-by-year response matrix. Thus for most of the items, questions were answered with reference to each appropriate age up to 18 years (Helmreich et al., 1973). In a different context, Lee and Booth (1974) applied utility analysis in estimating the potential saving in personnel costs resulting from the use of a weighted application blank to predict turnover of clerical employees.

[3]Surveys of biographical inventory studies, with references, can be found in such sources as McCormick and Tiffin (1974, Ch. 4), Owens (1976), and Owens and Henry (1966). Many examples of more recent investigations, not covered in these surveys, are reported in the late 1960 and 1970 issues of the *Journal of Applied Psychology.* A catalogue of life history items was prepared on behalf of the APA Division of Industrial and Organizational Psychology by Glennon, Albright, and Owens (1966).

Reference Reports. Another common selection procedure is to investigate the applicant's "references." This involves essentially the obtaining of information about the applicant from persons acquainted with him. Such persons are usually former employers, although teachers, co-workers, and personal acquaintances may also be included. A major use of references is to verify the job experience claimed by the applicant. It is also expected that the applicant's performance in previous jobs or other situations will be predictive of his performance in the prospective job. Since this second objective requires the identification and appraisal of relevant behavior, it presents a much more difficult task.

The reference may be in the form of a *letter of recommendation,* in which the writer is left free to choose the content. It has been aptly said of such letters that "they are often sealed with a shrug and opened with a smile. The letter may be only one way of speeding the parting guest. The enthusiasm of the writer may indicate only his joy over a separation long overdue."[4] This criticism is particularly applicable to the open letter given to the applicant upon termination. Not being confidential, it is likely to contain only favorable statements. It will also tend to be vague and general, since the writer has no knowledge of the specific jobs for which it will eventually be used.

A letter mailed directly to the prospective employer can be made more relevant to the prospective job, since at least the job title and the company are known to the writer. Even under these conditions, however, the writer may have little familiarity with actual job requirements. A still better type of letter is one written in response to an inquiry from the prospective employer. In such an inquiry, the nature of the job can be further specified and relevant items of information can be requested.

From the third type of letter it is a short step to an *employment recommendation form.* Such forms are coming to be used more and more in place of the open-ended testimonial letter and narrative recommendation. Recommendation forms can be developed by the same procedures as weighted application blanks. Items can be chosen on the basis of their empirical validities in predicting any desired criterion. The responses can be scored in terms of empirically established weights, and a total score on the entire form can be computed. Insofar as certain items may call for the rating of the applicant's previous job performance, abilities, or personality traits, rating procedures can be incorporated into the form. The previously discussed graphic rating scales and the forced-choice technique are especially suitable for this purpose.

Unlike application blanks, however, recommendation forms have so far been subjected to little research. Although widely used, they usually consist of subjectively chosen items of unverified validity. Either the responses are examined qualitatively, or crude scoring weights are assigned to them in terms of their "face value." Under these conditions, it is not surprising that follow-up studies have revealed little or no validity for the personel evaluations based on such forms.

Among the few research publications dealing with recommendation forms is a series of studies conducted for the U.S. Civil Service Commission with the Employment Recommendation Questionnaire, or ERQ (Goheen & Mosel, 1959; Mosel & Goheen, 1958a, 1958b, 1959). In one of these studies (Mosel & Goheen,

---

[4]Quoted in an early text on applied psychology (Poffenberger, 1942, p. 238), but unfortunately still true.

1958b), the ERQs of 1,193 employees in 12 skilled trades were analyzed. The standard recommendation forms had been mailed prior to employment to the references listed on each man's application blank. An average of about four ERQs were sent out for each applicant. Of these, 56% returned completed, 23% returned incomplete, 18% failed to return, and 3% returned unopened. These figures are described as typical of the return rate of federal ERQs. Total scores for each applicant, found by applying "rational" rather than empirical weights to the ERQ items, yielded low and generally insignificant correlations with a criterion of subsequent job performance based on supervisory ratings. An analysis of separate items on the ERQ showed poor discriminative power, with heavy concentration of responses on the favorable answers.

Another technique for investigating references is the *telephone checkup*. This procedure has several practical advantages over mailed questionnaires. It is likely to yield a much larger proportion of completed inquiries. Respondents are generally less reluctant to give a frank and full evaluation of the applicant orally than in writing. Through skillfully worded questions, proper sequence of items, and other devices, trained telephone interviewers can do much to reduce suggestion, halo effect, and other judgment errors. Frequently they can also pick up clues in the respondent's remarks, tone of voice, inflection, hesitation, or other expressive behavior that suggest the need for further probing. As a result, they may elicit important facts that would not have been provided spontaneously or in answer to routine questions.

A more time-consuming but effective procedure is the full-scale *field investigation*. Relying on face-to-face interviews with several persons who know the applicant, these investigations can provide the most comprehensive and unbiased record of past performance. They generally cover not only job proficiency but also other information bearing on abilities, personality, and character. In one of the previously cited civil service studies (Goheen & Mosel, 1959; Mosel & Goheen, 1959), field investigation findings on 109 applicants for three professional positions (economist, budget examiner, and training officer) were compared with the ERQ scores for the same persons. Although significant correlations were obtained for two of the three positions, none of the correlations was high. In several cases, moreover, the ERQ failed to detect extremely disqualifying features revealed by the field investigation. This failure may have resulted in part from a selective bias in ERQ returns. Persons who have adverse information about an applicant and cannot recommend him favorably often fail to respond at all to a written inquiry. To determine how much confidence can be placed in field investigation data, however, the investigator should also evaluate the respondent in the course of the interviews, checking on his accuracy and dependability as well as on any possible biases toward the applicant.

INTERVIEWING

Interviewing techniques are used for many purposes in journalism, law, medicine, social work, clinical psychology, counseling, public opinion polling, and consumer research. Within personnel psychology, interviews are commonly employed not only as selection procedures but also in conducting employee attitude surveys, as a means of communication between management and workers, in handling grievances, and in other supervisory functions. A special application is provided by the exit interview, held with employees who are leaving the company. Apart from dealing with the routine details of termination, such an interview can serve a public relations function by ensuring that workers leave with a more favorable attitude toward the company. It can also yield valuable data on the causes of turnover as found both in worker characteristics and in conditions within the company. Still another type of personnel interview is that used for employee development. Related both to merit rating and to training programs, this type of interview is designed to let employees know how well they are doing on the job and to help them improve. It is used especially with supervisory and executive personnel in management development programs.

Psychological discussions of the interview can be found in a number of books. Some cover all types of interviews (Bingham, Moore, & Gustad, 1959; Kahn & Cannell, 1957); others concentrate on personnel selection interviews (Bellows & Estep, 1954; Fear, 1973); and one focuses entirely on the employee development interview (N. R. F. Maier, 1958). Some include a survey of published research on the interview (Bellows & Estep, 1954; Bingham et al., 1959; Kahn & Cannell, 1957); others are essentially how-to-do-it books on interviewing procedures (Fear, 1973; N. R. F. Maier, 1958). Within the present chapter, we shall be concerned only with the interview as a personnel selection tool. Much of what is said about interviewing in this context, however, will also apply to other uses of the interview.

Nature of the Selection Interview. Through face-to-face conversation with the applicant, the selection interview provides two major sources of information, namely, a behavior sample and a reactional biography. As a behavior sample, the interview permits the direct observation of certain traits such as voice, speech, use of language, nervous mannerisms, and general appearance. Since the interview is a dynamic interaction between two persons, it may also yield clues to certain complex social traits, such as poise, dominance, emotional control, and social sensitivity.

The second source of interview information is the biographical data reported by the applicant in response to questioning. Such data should not be limited to job experiences but should be drawn from the complete life history. Moreover, they should cover not only what has happened to the individual but also how he reacted to it and how he now perceives it. To have been fired because of a fight with the supervisor may have a different significance if the individual perceives it as an instance of his own inexperience in interpersonal relations, as plain tough luck, or as systematic persecution. Similarly, we want to find out not only what grades he received in school but also what subjects he liked and disliked, and why.

On the interviewer's part, the interview requires skill in data gathering and in data interpreting. An interview may lead to wrong decisions because important data were not elicited or because given data were inadequately or incorrectly interpreted. An important qualification of the successful interviewer is sensitivity in picking up clues in the respondent's behavior or in facts he reports. Such clues then lead to further probing for other facts that may either verify or contradict the original hypothesis. Thus the interviewer engages in the cycle of hypothesis formation and hypothesis testing discussed in Chapter 1.

The chief potential contributions of the interview to the selection process include, first, the assessment of traits for which no satisfactory tests are available.

It would be foolish to try to gauge numerical or mechanical aptitude, for instance, through an interview, since tests can do the job quicker and better. For many social, emotional, and motivational traits, however, an intensive interview may provide the best source of information. A second advantage of the interview is that it permits fuller coverage of biographical data then is possible through application blanks. Through selective probing, the interview makes it possible to explore a particular area more intensively as the individual's own responses point the way. This individual adaptability of procedure, of course, is impossible with such mass techniques as the application blank. In fact, interviewers often use application blank responses as a starting point in identifying areas for further questioning.

A third contribution of the interview concerns the combining of data to arrive at final evaluations or decisions. Characteristically, the interviewer utilizes a clinical approach in combining both interview data and information obtained from tests and other sources (see Ch. 2). Such a procedure permits the qualitative interpretation of trait patterns, of the interaction of different factors, and of rare circumstances that may be important in individual cases but unsuitable for statistical treatment. A fourth function of the interview is to provide the applicant with accurate information about the job under consideration. Once respondents understand clearly what a job entails, they are themselves better able to decide whether a particular job fits their own interests, goals, and qualifications.

Form of the Interview. The *traditional* personnel selection interview is haphazard, unsystematic, and impressionistic. It is generally brief and unplanned. As such, it is likely to vary at random from one applicant to another and to elicit as much irrelevant as relevant information. At the other extreme is the completely *standardized* interview, which may be little more than an orally administered questionnaire. Because of its rigid and artificial nature, such a procedure sacrifices the opportunity for personal interaction and flexibility that an interview can provide, while requiring more staff time than the administration of a written questionnaire.

Between these two extremes is the *patterned* interview. Also known as "guided," "structured," and "systematic," this type of interview covers certain specified areas, such as work history, education, early home background, present domestic and financial condition, and social and recreational activities (Fear, 1973; McMurry, 1947). The sequence of areas is usually uniform, and each is introduced with a comprehensive standardized question. Within these limits, however, the interviewer has considerable latitude. His role is to steer the conversation into relevant channels and make sure that all areas are adequately explored. Through follow-up questions, he checks on any points that may have been omitted by the applicant or that seem unclear or suspect.

Sources of Error in Interviewing. Interpretation of interview data is subject to the various *judgment errors* discussed in connection with rating. Since evaluations must be made on the basis of a brief contact, halo effect and social stereotypes are especially likely to operate. The interviewer's "hunches" and "intuitions" often arise from just such judgment errors. Some hunches may result from a chance resemblance to a former acquaintance. If a previous employee who embezzled company funds happened to have widely spaced eyes which gave him a distinctive appearance, the interviewer may respond with a vague feeling of distrust when he encounters an applicant with the same facial peculiarity. This feeling may be aroused without the interviewer's awareness of the basis of his response—hence the mysterious and awesome nature of many hunches.

Hunches as such should not be summarily dismissed in the course of the interview. Rather, they should be examined. First, we should try to identify the basis of the hunch. Recognizing the underlying cue will in itself go far toward showing whether the hunch was based on a stereotype or chance resemblance, or whether it occurred in response to a relevant fact in the applicant's behavior or past record. Second, the hunch should be regarded, not as conclusive in itself, but as a hypothesis to be tested by further probing.

Another type of error that may affect interview findings has been called *contagious bias*. This error refers to the effect that the interviewer's own beliefs, expectations, or preconceived notions may have upon the interviewee's responses. The term "contagious bias" was first used by S. A. Rice (1929) in an early analysis of sociological survey data. More recent studies, some using tape recordings, have repeatedly corroborated the effect of interviewer bias and have thrown some light on its operation (Kahn & Cannell, 1957, Ch. 7). Significant differences in the findings of different interviewers may occur through incorrect recording of data, misunderstanding of ambiguous answers, or actual differences in the responses elicited. Interviewers may inadvertently inject their ideas into the conversation by their wording of questions, by reacting to the respondent's answers in ways that differentially reinforce certain types of answers, or by suggesting appropriate answers when the respondent hesitates. They may also slant the results by accepting some ambiguous answers while following up others by further probing.

The *total time* covered by the interview is also an important consideration. In actual practice, the duration of selection interviews may range from 1 or 2 minutes to several hours per applicant; a total time of 15–20 minutes is not unusual for rank-and-file jobs. When lasting only a few minutes, the interview can provide little more than a general impression of appearance and a few superficial behavioral characteristics. Stereotypes and other judgment errors are also likely to play a major part in such brief interviews. For intensive evaluation of high-level personnel, more than an hour is generally required.

Interviewer Training. Since the interviewer himself is an important element in the interviewing process, the most effective way to improve the interview is by better selection and training of interviewers. In all too many companies, however, personnel interviewers are still chosen because of their "interest in people" and clean-cut appearance. In some cases, they are persons lacking special qualifications, who cannot be fitted into any other job. Actually, interviewers should be selected like any other technical personnel, in terms of relevant abilities, personality traits, educational level, and specialized training.

Intensive training courses in interviewing itself, often conducted by an outside consulting psychologist, have proved successful in many companies. Such courses should include an introductory orientation in interviewing principles, followed by skill training. The latter may utilize any convenient combination of direct observation of interviews, tape recordings, transcripts, role playing in which trainees assume in turn the roles of interviewer and applicant, and supervised practice in interviewing genuine applicants.

In the course of such training, the interviewer is alerted to the operation of various judgment errors and biasing effects. He is also introduced to other practices designed to improve the effectiveness of interviewing, such as recording of facts promptly rather than trusting to memory, citing supporting evidence for judgments, and preparing for each interview by studying both the job specifications and any available information about the applicant from tests, application blank, telephone checkups, and other sources. Such preparation ensures that the interviewer focus on relevant qualifications and provides hypotheses to be checked in the course of the interview.

The importance of establishing good rapport and putting the applicant at ease at the opening of the interview should also be recognized. Most applicants are inclined to be tense on first contact with the interviewer, especially if they are eager to get the job. In fact, unusual freedom from tension in such a situation may indicate either lack of interest in the job or extensive interview experience because of frequent job changes. In both instances, the attitude would be an unfavorable sign, although it may, of course, have other explanations that would emerge in individual cases.

Training programs often employ interviewing manuals and forms specially developed for the particular company. Much of the orientation material, as well as areas to be covered, opening questions, and other interviewing aids, can be succinctly presented in such fashion.

Interview Research. Despite its long history of use as a selection device, the interview has, until recently, generated little research. Although scattered studies on isolated features have appeared from time to time, systematic, coordinated research programs on the interview date largely from the 1960s (e.g., Carlson, Thayer, Mayfield, & Peterson, 1971; Hakel, Dobmeyer, & Dunnette, 1970; Matarazzo & Wiens, 1972; Webster, 1964).

As in the case of tests, a basic question about interview results concerns their *reliability and validity.* Reliability of interviews includes both intrarater and interrater consistency. Intrarater reliability may be studied by having the same interviewer either reinterview the same persons at different times or independently reappraise the applicants from tape recordings or transcripts of the identical interviews after a time interval. When an overall interview rating is computed from the ratings on individual items, odd–even correlations can also be found for each interview. Interrater consistency can be measured either by comparing the results of interviews of the same persons by different interviewers or by having different interviewers evaluate the applicants from tape recordings of single interviews. All of these procedures provide somewhat different information. Differences in the applicant's own behavior at different times or with different interviewers, for example, are eliminated as a source of variation when recordings of single interviews are used.

Validity is sometimes determined globally, by checking final interview prediction against a composite criterion of job success. Other investigators analyze the validity of individual trait evaluations in terms of subsequent manifestations of the same traits. It must be recognized that any general statements about reliability or validity of *the* interview are bound to be misleading. Interviews vary widely in both reliability and validity, depending upon many factors, such as the form of the interview (traditional, standardized, or patterned), its duration and thoroughness, and the qualifications of the interviewer. Since the interviewer, like the clinician, is an integral part of the process, research designs on the reliability and validity of interviewing should take into account individual differences among interviewers.

In the light of the above considerations, it is not surprising to find marked variations in the reliabilities and validities of interviews reported in published surveys (Ulrich & Trumbo, 1965; O. R. Wright, 1969). In general, early studies of "experienced" but untrained interviewers (usually sales managers) using the traditional, unplanned type of interview reveal very poor interrater agreement. Later studies of patterned interviews conducted by trained interviewers yield much more promising evidence of reliability and validity. In one such study, for example, significant correlations ranging from .43 to .68 were found between interview ratings of predicted job success and subsequent criterion measures (McMurry, 1947). These validity coefficients were obtained on groups comprising from 84 to 587 employees in three companies; the criteria included foremen's ratings and turnover data. There is also evidence that reliability may be improved by using behaviorally anchored, scaled expectation rating scales (as in Fig. 3-7) to record interview results (Maas, 1965).

Much of the later research has focused on a study of the *interviewing process* itself. A better understanding of what actually occurs during the interview should provide a basis for devising ways of improving the accuracy of interview results. An example of such research is the series of investigations by Matarazzo and his co-workers (see Matarazzo & Wiens, 1972) on the factors associated with the duration of the interviewee's responses (utterances) and of the silent pauses following interviewer questions. A major condition affecting response delay and duration was the respondent's current interest and involvement in the content area under discussion. Another was the interviewer's behavior, including the length of the interviewer's own utterances, nodding and other expressions of attention, and the use of neutral versus interpretive comments. All these variables were positively related with duration and speed of interviewee responses.

From another angle, C. W. Anderson (1960) found that interviewers themselves tend to talk proportionately longer with applicants they accept than with those they reject; with the rejected cases, more time is spent in silent pauses. Unlike the Matarazzo procedure, in which duration of interviewer utterances was experimentally controlled, this study analyzed recordings of actual selection interviews, in which speaking time was unrestricted.

Some investigators have been systematically exploring the factors influencing interviewers' final decisions about a candidate (see Carlson et al., 1971; Hakel et al., 1970; Webster, 1964). An example is a well-designed investigation of interviewers' reactions to favorable and unfavorable information (Bolster & Springbett, 1961). For this purpose, synthetic protocols of interview information were assembled so that favorable and unfavorable items could be matched in number and strength and could be presented in predetermined orders. An initial set to accept or reject the applicant was established by providing the interviewer with a preliminary test score. Figure 3-8 shows the effect of successively presented favorable items (in protocol A) and unfavorable items (in protocol C) in shifting the interviewers' ratings away from the initial position. Each graph is based on mean ratings of 16 interviewers. It can be seen that an average of 8.8 favorable items was required in protocol A to shift the ratings from "reject" to "accept." In contrast, an

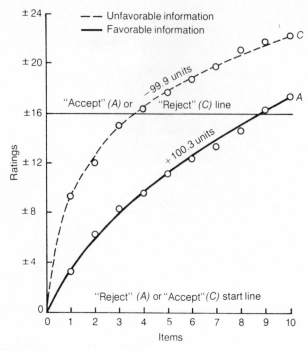

Figure 3-8. Shift in interviewer judgment in response to favorable and unfavorable items. Units noted on each curve represent total item weight of the 10 items in each protocol. *(From Bolster & Springbett, 1961, p. 99. Copyright © 1961 by American Psychological Association. Reproduced by permission.)*

average of only 3.8 unfavorable items was sufficient to shift ratings from "accept" to "reject" in protocol C. The greater influence of unfavorable items on final decisions has been corroborated in other studies conducted in different settings (Carlson, 1971; Miller & Rowe, 1967).

ASSESSMENT CENTERS

Since midcentury, increasing use has been made of assessment centers, especially in the evaluation of managerial or administrative personnel. This procedure has been adopted by several large industrial organizations, such as AT&T, IBM, and Standard Oil, as well as by certain government agencies and by the armed services (Bray, Campbell, & Grant, 1974; Dunnette, 1971; Finkle, 1976; Finkle & Jones, 1970; Olmstead, Cleary, Lackey, & Salter, 1974). This approach was first developed for the selection of specialized military personnel during World War II. During the intervening years, it has been used in personality research, principally at the Institute of Personality Assessment and Research (IPAR) of the University of California (Taft, 1959).

In the typical assessment center, a small group of persons to be evaluated for the same type of job are brought together, usually for two to three days. During this period, multiple assessment techniques are utilized, including interviewing and a variety of ability and personality tests. A distinctive feature of this approach is the inclusion of situational tests, such as the previously cited in-basket tests and the Leaderless Group Discussion. The program usually employs specially designed job simulations, role playing, group problem solving, and business games. Another common feature is the use of multiple assessors, often including one or more trained in clinical psychology. Frequent use is also made of peer ratings, usually through a nominating technique. Many of the traits evaluated pertain to motivation, interpersonal skills, and other personality variables.

Studies of the predictive validity of assessment center evaluations have yielded promising results. In a well-controlled, longitudinal investigation of the AT&T program, substantial correlations were found between assessment-staff predictions regarding recent appointees to first-level management positions and such criteria as subsequent advancement to higher management levels and salary growth (Bray et al., 1974; Bray & Grant, 1966). In such predictions, the staff judgments proved superior to paper-and-pencil tests. Both the situational tests and the interview made important contributions to the overall evaluation. Among the major conditions that affect the predictive validity of assessment center evaluations are the qualifications of the assessors; the rating of behaviorally oriented and job-specific variables rather than broad, general traits; and the relevance of the behavior sampled in the assessment center to the job under consideration. A thorough job analysis helps to ensure such relevance.

Although the original AT&T study included only men, the same assessment center procedures were later found to be equally effective in predicting the managerial performance of women (Moses & Boehm, 1975). An abridged version of the AT&T assessment center program has also been developed (Moses, 1973). Requiring only one day, this shortened approach yielded overall ratings that correlated in the .70s with those obtained in the full assessment procedure.

There is evidence that assessment center evaluations are more predictive of advancement than of first-level management performance. Suggested by the findings of several studies, this hypothesis was directly tested in a well-designed longitudinal investigation of 254 Standard Oil Company managers attending a company assessment center (Mitchel, 1975). Correlations of both peer and assessor ratings were computed against a criterion of salary growth after intervals of 1, 3, and 5 years. These correlations rose consistently over time, being highest for the 5-year interval. A methodological implication of such findings is that validation of assessment center techniques should not rely on concurrent or short-term predictive validity.

A note of caution is sounded by Hinrichs (1969). In a study of 47 senior IBM employees, ratings of their management potential based on information already available in the personnel records correlated .46 with ratings of management potential from a two-day assessment center. From this and similar findings, Hinrichs suggests that a careful analysis of personnel records, possibly supplemented with an interview, may provide much of the information obtained in the more lengthy and expensive assessment center program. At the same time, the investigator noted certain limitations to this conclusion. First, the use of personnel records is not suitable for the early identification of management potential among new employees with little job history; the participants in this study had been with the company for an average of 7 years. Second, no information is available on the predictive validity of the two sets of ratings. It should also be noted that the actual overlap between the two sets of ratings appears quite small when we consider the possible substitution of one set for the other; a correlation of .46 indicates only about 20% common variance.[5] This study nevertheless highlights the need for comprehensive utility analyses of assessment centers, in which long-term validity and personnel costs are combined in a comparative evaluation of alternative procedures. This is the type of analysis cited earlier in the chapter in connection with the use of weighted application blanks (Lee & Booth, 1974).

SUMMARY

Industrial psychologists utilize a variety of ability and personality tests. Short screening tests of mental ability have been developed for different job levels. Special aptitude tests, such as those for measuring psychomotor, mechanical, and clerical aptitudes, are particularly appropriate for personnel selection. Multiple aptitude batteries, covering a small number of relatively broad and widely applicable abilities, are especially suitable for personnel classification programs. Occupational proficiency tests measure skill in the performance of particular occupational tasks. Including both information tests and work samples, many such tests are custom-made for specific jobs.

Personality tests may be used with any type of worker but have found their greatest application in jobs requiring extensive interpersonal contacts, such as selling and managerial work. It is especially important in this area to guard against common misuses of tests, such as undue reliance on test scores in the absence of other information or the use of inadequately validated instruments. The major types of personality tests used in personnel selection include interest tests, personality inventories, projective techniques, and situational tests. Being among the most successful of all personality tests, interest tests rely chiefly on the empirical criterion keying of reported interests in a variety of familiar experiences.

For most personnel selection and classification purposes, tests need to be supplemented by other procedures. Application blanks, references, and personal interviews utilize combinations of biographical and interpersonal data. What the individual has done in the past is an effective predictor of future performance. Interpersonal evaluations provide appropriate indices for many social traits. Rating procedures, utilized for many personnel purposes, include order-of-merit comparisons, rating scales, scaled checklists, forced-choice technique, nominating technique, and field review method. Ratings are susceptible to halo effect, leniency and central tendency errors, and social stereotypes. They are influenced by amount and kind of acquaintance and by many rater characteristics.

Letters of application and traditional application blanks are being replaced by weighted application blanks, found to be valid for a wide variety of jobs. Letters of

---

[5]Percentage of common variance, or coefficient of determination, equals r^2 (see any recent statistics text, such as Guilford & Fruchter, 1978, pp. 358–359).

recommendation are often too general and insufficiently discriminative. Standard-ized recommendation questionnaires are a potentially useful selection device but have been inadequately developed. Telephone checkups and field investigations yield fuller and more dependable information. The selection interview provides a behavior sample as well as a reactional biography. Common interviewing errors, besides those shared with other rating procedures, include hunches based on irrelevant cues and contagious bias. Patterned interviews conducted by trained interviewers have yielded promising evidence of reliability and validity. Assessment centers, employing multiple assessment procedures and multiple assessors, are being used increasingly, especially in the prediction of management potential.

DEVELOPMENT AND TRAINING

FOUR

THAT PSYCHOLOGY has much to contribute to training programs is apparent when we realize that the psychology of training is the applied psychology of learning. Learning theory is at the very core of the science of psychology and has been especially productive of well-designed research. Yet psychologists have not been so widely involved in industrial training as they have in personnel selection. The missing link was a dearth of applied research in this area. Such applied research was needed to bridge the gap between the wealth of available basic research on learning and the vast number of practical situations where training was going on. It is only since World War II that psychologists have come to play a major part in training programs. The significant contributions of psychologists to military training during the war undoubtedly did much to demonstrate their potential contribution to training problems in general. Although the necessary applied research is now being conducted in industrial contexts as well, much of it is still done under military sponsorship.

NATURE AND SCOPE OF INDUSTRIAL TRAINING

Traditionally, training is differentiated from education in terms of breadth of goals. The primary objective of training is the acquisition of specific skills and information, as in learning to drive a truck, operate a lathe, or fill out a sales slip. Education is concerned with the development of more widely applicable skills, knowledge, and attitudes, as in reading, solving arithmetic problems, understanding modern society, or enjoying music. Industrial training, however, is being increasingly directed toward broader, long-range goals and is thus taking on more and more of the earmarks of education. This trend is exemplified by the increasing use of the term "development" in connection with industrial training programs. The term "training" itself is coming to be used in a more comprehensive sense, to include development. Particular emphasis is now placed on the role of training programs in the development of attitudes, especially with regard to interpersonal relations. However broadened in scope, though, industrial training is necessarily job-oriented. While recognizing that the development of the "whole person" may in the long run be the best way to train more effective workers, industry is still primarily concerned with improving job performance.

The Place of Training in Personnel Systems. Selection and classification do not provide industry with all the skills it requires. Many of these skills must be learned by employees after they are hired. The relative weight placed on selection and training varies with the nature of the job. Typists, for instance, have generally learned to type before they are employed, while salesclerks are usually trained on the job. The emergence of new industries and the rapid changes in industrial operations characteristic of modern society create especially heavy demands for training. When there is a personnel shortage in any field, moreover, improved and augmented training programs must make up for the necessary lowering of selection standards. An example is provided by the training innovations introduced during the U.S. Army's conversion to an all-volunteer status (Lee & Parker, 1977, Ch. 9; Taylor & staff, 1975; Taylor, Michaels, & Brennan, 1972). This action led to an upsurge of training research and the development of special training programs. As a result, persons with marginal entry skills and limited learning aptitudes were trained to perform effectively in several military occupational specialties. Such training also prepared them for similar civilian occupations, for which they could subsequently qualify. Another illustration is to be found in the efforts of industrial organizations to hire more members of ethnic minorities, many of whom had serious limitations in formal education and in relevant job experience.

In this connection, reference should be made to the systems measurement bed portrayed in Figure 1-1 and discussed in Chapter 1. Within the total human factors system, selection and classification sort out persons in terms of job-relevant skills. Training undertakes to bridge the gap between the initially available skill pool and the skills actually needed for job performance. From another angle, equipment and jobs may be redesigned to simplify worker skill requirements. This approach represents still another means of coordinating jobs and persons within the total system.

Who Is to Be Trained? Training is not limited to the new employee. It is a continuing process from which old as well as new workers can benefit. In addition to the orientation and skill training provided for the incoming worker, training is a means of preparing promising workers for promotion to a higher job level. Such training is particularly important for promotion to a supervisory post, in which employees must assume functions not covered by their present jobs. Training may also take the form of refresher courses for experienced workers, to ensure the continuance of effective work methods or to update information and procedures.

A comprehensive and continuing training program is one way to maintain and improve operating procedures throughout the company. An important function of the training department is to make periodic surveys of training needs through analyses of production, accident, turnover, and other records; interviews and conferences with supervisors; questionnaire surveys of employees; and other appropriate techniques (see McCormick & Tiffin, 1974, Ch. 10; McGehee & Thayer, 1961, Chs. 2–4). These procedures serve to locate departments or areas of operation in which training is particularly desirable. Similarly, the examination of merit ratings and other individual evaluation techniques help to identify workers most in need of training. With regard to job level, the area of training is coextensive with the full range of jobs, from unskilled labor to top management. Widespread adoption of management development programs is, in fact, one of the chief characteristics of modern industrial training.

Kinds of Training. The number and variety of training programs that may be found within a single company are very great. Such programs may cover the learning of verbal or cognitive content, psychomotor skills, or human relations skills. Some may pertain to the modification of attitudes, feelings, and motivation. In duration, the training may range from a one-hour orientation lecture to a four-year course in a company school. In large companies, each of the major functions (i.e., marketing, finance, manufacturing, engineering, and employee relations) often has its own training program. And, within each function, separate programs are available for many different activities. In employee relations, for example, there might be training programs on merit rating, interviewing, safety, wage and salary administration, and labor relations.

Most training programs for manual and clerical jobs are concerned chiefly with *job skills.* Training programs in *technical and professional* areas deal with many specialized techniques, from drafting to job evaluation. Cutting across training in the different company functions are *management development* programs for supervisory and executive personnel. Human relations training plays a particularly important part in such management development programs, although it also enters into more specialized programs, as in the training of sales and employee-relations personnel. Because of the growing interest in management development, this type of training will be discussed more fully in a separate section of the chapter.

Another companywide type of training is *orientation.* Also known as "induction" or "indoctrination," orientation training is designed to acquaint new employees with company practices, policies, and regulations. It should also provide information about the company and its products or services in such a way as to increase the employee's identification with the company and to foster desirable attitudes toward the job. Although traditionally associated with incoming employees, orientation training is now regarded as a continuing process. Keeping *all* employees informed about the company through lectures, conferences, handbooks, employee newsletters, and more informal personal contacts is the comprehensive aim of modern orientation programs. There is also an increasing emphasis on the development of attitudes, as contrasted with the imparting of routine facts.

Some companies also provide *general education* in practically any field in which there is enough employee interest. As a service to employees, courses of a purely cultural or recreational nature—from sociology or American literature to folk dancing or contract bridge—may be offered in company schools. Certain employees may also be sent under company auspices to colleges or universities to complete educational requirements for promotion to higher level jobs or possibly just to obtain the broad perspectives of a liberal education.

TRAINING MEDIA AND PROCEDURES

In view of the wide diversity of trainees, objectives, and content, it is to be expected that industrial training programs utilize many different media and training methods. Although two or more media are frequently combined and the distinctions among procedures are not at all sharply drawn, a few major types can be identified.

Lectures. Consisting essentially of a single oral presentation, a lecture may be given in person as well as through recordings, sound films, or closed-circuit television. In itself, the lecture does not provide for active participation by the learner, nor for repeated practice. Frequently it is used for preliminary explanation of procedure, which is then followed by demonstration, practice, discussion, or other techniques. The lecture itself can also be supplemented with such training aids as charts, slides, or models. Lectures are often employed in orientation training to provide simple factual information such as plant organization or safety rules.

Printed Materials. Training manuals, handbooks, and similar instructional materials also present information in verbal terms and—like the lecture—may include pictures and diagrams. Such printed materials are likewise suitable for orientation purposes. Unlike the lecture, however, they permit repeated exposure, since the trainee may consult the printed instructions as often as necessary. For this reason, this instructional medium is appropriate for the learning of long sequences or complicated procedures which could not be acquired in a single oral presentation. Training manuals are often combined with lectures and with practice in actual job performance. A training manual should be much more than a list of steps to be followed. Much can be done to make such a manual interesting to read and easy to understand. Learning principles can be utilized in its preparation, as in the development of any training procedure.

Films and Television. Both films and closed-circuit television may be used as a substitute for the formal lecture and demonstration. When so employed, they share the advantages and limitations of the personally delivered lecture. They do, nevertheless, provide uniformity of presentation in a large-scale program. And they permit maximal utilization of the best qualified instructors. Short films are frequently combined with ordinary lectures as a training aid.

Certain intrinsic features of the motion picture medium, as well as television, make it particularly suitable for training purposes. Since they permit the controlled presentation of visual stimuli in motion, films can be used in discrimination training, as in learning to recognize aircraft or read a radar scope. They are well adapted to learning a sequence of movements. The fact that the operation can be slowed down without altering its nature gives the film an added advantage over a live demonstration, where this is often impossible. The editing of a film by cutting and splicing may also increase its training effectiveness through focusing attention on important details, eliminating irrelevant material, altering sequences for increased comprehension, and similar modifications.

Films can present a situation realistically, while avoiding the hazards of direct experience. For instance, a film can show the consequences of incorrect procedures, as in an automobile or airplane crash. Still another intrinsic advantage of films arises from the use of the camera in the "subjective" point of view, that is, showing objects and movements as seen by the person performing the task rather than by an observer facing him.

Training Devices and Simulators. In contrast to the previously discussed, "passive" training procedures, training devices provide learner participation, with repeated practice in actual job skills and immediate feedback. They may be employed as a substitute for real equipment when use of the latter by an inexperienced operator might entail risk to materials or personnel or when the equipment is too costly to use in the early stages of instruction. Training devices may also isolate or recombine different job functions so that the learner may spend more time on the more difficult or critical part activities.

Although training devices call for the manipulation of equipment, they are by no means limited to the teaching of motor skills. They may provide training in sensory discrimination, tracking skills (as in steering a vehicle or keeping a pointer on target), and the performance of complex sequences of manipulative responses. Some require the understanding of operating principles and their application to problem solving, as in training technicians in troubleshooting and maintenance of complex electronic equipment. In such a device, typical malfunctions are set into

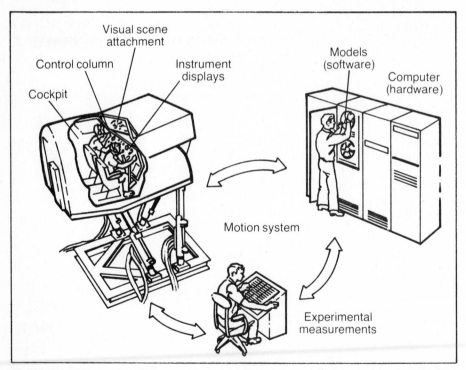

Figure 4-1. The basic components of a dynamic aeronautical flight simulator, including cockpit, visual scene attachment, motion system, computer control system, and measurement equipment. *(From Huff & Nagel, 1975, p. 427. Copyright © 1975 by American Psychological Association. Reproduced by permission.)*

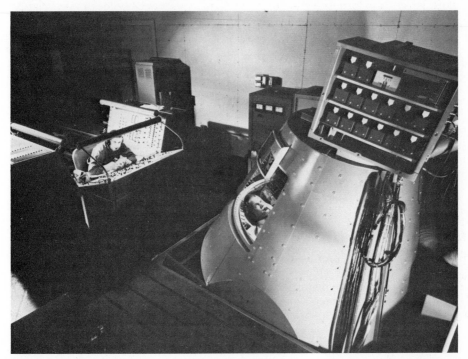

Figure 4-2. Astronaut training in spacecraft simulator. *(Courtesy of National Aeronautics and Space Administration.)*

the system, and the trainee traces the source of the malfunction by carrying out the appropriate checking operations.

The terms "training device" and "simulator" are often used interchangeably. Insofar as the terms are differentiated, "training device" covers a relatively broad category, ranging from simple devices for the acquisition of isolated skills to complex, ground-based devices for basic flight training. Simulators, on the other hand, are generally complex and reproduce job characteristics more closely than do training devices. Their design emphasizes realism in equipment and operations. For example, flight simulators are usually built for each new major aircraft. These simulators reproduce with a high degree of fidelity the instrument panels in the cockpit, the "feel" of the controls, the sound of the engines, cockpit motion, and other characteristics perceptible to the operator. To provide realistic practice in contact flying, a view of the runway and other ground features can be shown through the cockpit window by film, closed-circuit television, or computer-generated graphics. Without leaving the ground, the trainee can thus perform all necessary operations for specified flight maneuvers, including both contact and instrument flying, while receiving feedback on the effects of each action as though he or she were in actual flight. Figure 4-1 shows a schematic diagram of the basic components of a flight simulator. Several investigations have shown that such ground training transfers well to aircraft flying and can effect considerable saving in costly aircraft training (see, e.g., Caro, 1973; Caro, Isley, & Jolley, 1973; Valverde, 1973).

Although simulators have been developed for several types of jobs, their major application is in aviation (J. A. Adams, 1973; Caro, 1973; Huff & Nagel, 1975; "Learning to Fly," 1977; Valverde, 1973). Flight simulators are regularly employed by commercial airlines as well as by the military services, often in advanced stages of training. They can also provide experienced pilots with periodic practice in handling emergencies that would rarely be encountered during ordinary operations. Another function is to introduce the pilot to a new type of aircraft. Before practicing in the air, the experienced pilot may spend several hours operating the simulator for the new model.

Both simulators and training devices proved especially useful in the preparation of astronauts for space travel. Fixed-base simulators of the type shown in Figure 4-2 were used regularly in the manned space program. They provide actual spacecraft controls and displays in normal and emergency operating procedures. The instructor's console permits the insertion of different problems, as well as the simulation of ground facilities such as the launch control center and remote sites.

Programmed and Computer-administered Instruction. Programmed training involves essentially the preparation of a series of instructional steps through which the learner is guided in a systematically established sequence. The sequence may be uniform for all learners, or it may follow different routes determined by the learner's own responses. Once the program, or instructional content, has been prepared, it can be presented to the learner through various media, ranging from programmed textbooks, through specially developed mechanical gadgets or "teaching machines," to digital computers.

From the standpoint of the psychology of learning, programmed instruction has much in common with the previously discussed training devices. Both require active learner participation and provide immediate feedback after each response. Both allow for individual differences insofar as the individual may progress at his or her own pace. Because they deal with verbal learning, however, the techniques generally classified under programmed instruction usually present far greater complexities of programming than do training devices. In general, programmed instruction has proved most effective as a supplement to other instructional techniques. As such, it can provide intensive training on specific units having clearly defined objectives, such as the use of logarithms needed in performing an otherwise nonmathematical job. It is especially appropriate when there are wide individual differences in prior knowledge of a topic among the trainees.

The possibilities of automated teaching have received widespread attention in education, where programs have already been developed in many areas of instruction from the preschool to the college level. Such automated teaching programs will be discussed more fully and illustrated in Chapter 17, dealing with the contributions of psychology to education. That industry is interested in the potentialities of automated training is suggested by the many conferences, seminars, institutes, and workshops on the subject conducted by various organizations, including the American Management Association. Discussions from the standpoint of industrial training directors can be found in Levine and Silvern (1960–1961), Margulies and Eigen (1962), and Shoemaker and Holt (1965). Programmed learning has been incorporated into the ongoing training activities of several large companies in such varied fields as manufacturing, life insurance, public utilities, and retail selling. The armed services have also made extensive use of programmed instruction, along with other types of automated instructional devices (Bryan & Nagay, 1965; Lumsdaine & Glaser, 1960).

Increasingly, programmed instruction has been linked with the use of computers, which are especially suited to the automated administration of learning programs.[1] A particularly important feature is the flexibility provided by computers, whereby the choice of material presented to the learner may be continuously adjusted to the learner's own previous responses. On the other hand, the effectiveness of a learning program depends much more on the content of the program ("software") than on the computers or other mechanical gadgets ("hardware") used to administer the program. In fact, the principal contribution of the wave of interest in programmed instruction probably stems from the attention it has focused on the application of sound learning principles to the development of training procedures in general. This important by-product of programmed instruction will become apparent in a later section of this chapter, dealing with the development of training programs.

Job Performance. Undoubtedly, the most direct way to learn a job is by actually working under the guidance of an experienced worker, a supervisor, or an instructor. *On-the-job training* is an age-old method for transmitting job skills. All too often, however, it provides little more than unguided experience, including the learner's own trial and error, his undirected observation of experienced workers, and some casual, unsystematic instruction. Supervisors and experienced workers often lack the time, motivation, and teaching skills to provide the necessary instruction. It is well known that a successful performer is often a poor teacher. On-the-job training can be improved by training supervisors or other selected employees in effective instructional methods and by ensuring that they have enough time for training new workers. The substitution of systematic on-the-job training for traditional haphazard procedures has regularly led to marked improvements in speed of learning and quality of performance. There is considerable research demonstrating that "experience" is *not* the best teacher, when it is in the form of unguided exposure to the task. Individuals do not work out the most effective procedures when left to their own devices. The conspicuous rises in production often found when experienced workers are put through a systematic training program demonstrate the same point.

The *vestibule school* represents one way of increasing the effectiveness of job-performance training. Such a school may use regular job equipment, as well as training devices and other instructional procedures. It provides training in a separate area or training center, free from the distractions and pressures of the working environment. Instruction is conducted by a training-oriented instructor rather than by a production-oriented supervisor. Depending upon the skills to be taught, vestibule training may last from a few days to several months.

[1] It should be noted that computers are also frequently employed with the training devices and simulators discussed in the preceding section. In fact, the trend in the development of sophisticated flight simulators is toward completely automated, computer-based instructional systems that include automated performance assessment during learning and the adjustment of task difficulty and instructional sequences to the learner's skill level (see, e.g., Knoop, 1973).

Systematic job-performance training is also provided in *apprenticeship programs*. Developed for the preparation of skilled artisans, such programs combine classroom instruction with directed shop practice. Detailed specifications have been worked out for apprentice programs in different crafts, such as machinist or toolmaker, which may require as much as four years. Unlike the vestibule school, whose goal is the rapid teaching of one or more semiskilled operations, the apprenticeship provides training for a total skilled job covering many different activities.

Small-group Interactive Techniques. Several related training procedures involving group discussion and social interaction have come into prominence with increasing interest in the development of human relations skills (Olmstead, 1974). Like training devices and job-performance methods, they are characterized by active learner participation. The training activities involve many of the interpersonal skills required in supervisory and executive jobs, such as solving problems by group discussion, effective conference leadership, and face-to-face contacts with individuals in handling realistic supervisory problems. Because they are used chiefly in management development, these training methods will be discussed in the later section on that topic.

Problem-solving Interview. Still another training medium is the problem-solving interview. Closely related to both merit rating and employee counseling, such interviews are held periodically by supervisors or training officers as a means of improving the job effectiveness of individual workers. Although applicable to all types of employees, this technique is most widely employed in management development and will be discussed further in that connection.

GUIDELINES FROM LEARNING RESEARCH

As in many other personnel functions, the principal role of psychologists in industrial training is that of consultant. Their major contribution is in the development, installation, and evaluation of training programs. They may also carry out applied research on training problems. And they may conduct specialized training courses in such functions as interviewing, merit rating, or the human relations aspects of supervision. Frequently, too, they "train the trainers," who then carry out the bulk of the company's training in all areas.

In their development of training procedures, psychologists may be guided by certain commonly accepted generalizations about learning. Derived largely from basic research on learning, these generalizations are supported by applied research conducted in industry and the armed services (see, e.g., Bass & Vaughan, 1966; I. L. Goldstein, 1974; R. E. Silverman, 1970).

Motivation. It is well established that motivation helps learning. Such motivation may be in the form of higher pay, security, promotion, other forms of recognition or status, or even the satisfaction of succeeding on the job. To be effective, the anticipated reward must be one that is significant for the particular learner. In addition, the training itself may provide intrinsic motivation through definite and realistic goals. If the learning is broken down into units and if performance standards are set neither too high nor too low, the individual's feeling of accomplishment as he achieves each goal motivates him to continue learning. Under these conditions, performance level is higher than when merely "trying one's best" (Locke, 1967; Locke, Bryan, & Kendall, 1968). Unrealistic goals, on the other hand, may produce frustration and resentment and retard learning.

Stress. Learning is also hindered by stress, which may result from anxiety, embarrassment, distraction, or confusion. Stress is especially detrimental in the learning of complex functions requiring discrimination, problem solving, and flexibility of approach (Klier & Linskey, 1960). Freedom from stress is one of the advantages of the vestibule school as compared with training on the job. After essential skills have been mastered, the worker is better able to cope with the more stressful working environment.

Learner Participation. The familiar adage, "Practice makes perfect," is well grounded in learning theory and has several implications for the management of training. Active participation by the learner is a prerequisite for effective learning. Elaborate visual aids and impressive demonstrations may be of little use unless they lead to some action on the part of the learner. Moreover, the task should be practiced as it will eventually be performed. Verbal description of a sequence of movements, for instance, is no substitute for carrying them out ("hands-on" training). At the same time, the learner should have sufficient guidance, especially in the early stages of training, to prevent the practicing of errors. Practicing the wrong response makes it necessary to unlearn it later on. It is for this reason that correctness and accuracy are generally emphasized in the early stages of training, speed in the later stages. This approach is effective except when reduction of speed alters the nature of the responses. In that case, the learner would not be practicing the responses he or she ultimately needs to make.

Feedback. One of the best established learning principles pertains to feedback, or knowledge of results (Bilodeau, 1969, Chs. 8 & 9; Locke, 1967). Letting learners know how well they are doing serves to identify and thus differentially reinforce the correct responses. Such reinforcement is more effective if it is immediate and specific. With increasing delay, the effect of the reinforcement drops off rapidly. Precise information about nature and extent of errors produces faster improvement than simply being told whether a response is right or wrong.

Part versus Whole Learning. The relative merits of part versus whole learning have been repeatedly investigated (Briggs & Naylor, 1962; Naylor, 1962; Naylor & Briggs, 1963). Performing the whole task during each trial has the advantage of affording practice in the activity that is ultimately required. In many situations, whole learning also makes the task more meaningful and permits the proper establishment of relations among parts. In many industrial tasks, however, some operations or units are more difficult to learn than others. Hence, uniform practice by the whole method would lead to overlearning of some parts and underlearning of others. The degree of organization or interrelatedness of units within the total task is also relevant, as are individual differences in prerequisite aptitudes and in prior learning. Under most circumstances, some combination of part and whole methods usually proves best.

Distribution of Learning Time. Another common distinction in studies on learning effectiveness is that between "massed" and "distributed" practice. This is a question of the optimum distribution of training periods over time. Obviously, excessive massing of effort, as in "cramming" the night before an examination, produces fatigue and reduces alertness and attention. Working under these conditions interferes with performance of any sort. It also makes for shorter retention of newly learned material. Beyond this extreme, however, the optimum duration and spacing of learning sessions depends on many factors related to the nature of the learning task and the characteristics of the learner. The length, difficulty level, and complexity of the task are clearly relevant, as is the type of learning required. For example, the acquisition of psychomotor skills and rote memorization gain more from distributed practice than does the learning of meaningful verbal content. Even in learning a single task, a different distribution of effort may be best at different stages of learning. The optimum distribution of learning time may also vary with the learner's ability level, prior learning experience, interest, and motivation.

Behavior Modification. A direct utilization of major learning principles in the practical management of training is illustrated by the techniques subsumed under "behavior modification" (Bandura, 1969). Basically, these techniques represent the application of operant conditioning principles to the acquisition and strengthening of wanted behavior, such as safe operating procedures or effective interpersonal relations, and the elimination of unwanted behavior, such as stage fright, uncontrollable temper, or excessive drinking. Thus far, behavior modification has been most widely employed in clinical psychology and, to a lesser extent, in childhood education. Its use in industrial training is being explored in many contexts, and its potential contributions have aroused widespread interest (Brown & Presbie, 1976; Luthans & Kreitner, 1975; Nord, 1969; Porter, 1973).

A major procedure of behavior modification is the *contingent reinforcement* of the desired behavior by immediately following such behavior with a reward. The variety of possible rewards, or reinforcers, is almost limitless; to be effective, each reinforcer should be chosen to fit the individual's interests, preferences, and wants. Reinforcers may range from candy, money, or free time to public recognition or the satisfaction experienced from successful solution of a difficult problem. A second important procedure pertains to the retention of the desired behavior through the use of appropriate *schedules of reinforcement.* For instance, if a response is reinforced continuously during training, but only at rare intervals (or never) on the job, the response will soon disappear through the process known as "extinction." Such extinction may be prevented by following an intermittent schedule of reinforcement during training, possibly increasing the interval between reinforced responses as the training proceeds.

An application of behavior modification to the reduction of absenteeism among industrial workers is described by Pedalino and Gamboa (1974). A sample of 215 hourly employees in one plant of a manufacturing and distributing center constituted the experimental group, while the employees in four adjoining plants served as the comparison groups. The reinforcement consisted of financial rewards in the form of a lottery, administered as follows (Pedalino & Gamboa, 1974, p. 696):

> Each day an employee *comes* to work and is *on time,* he is allowed to choose a card from a deck of playing cards. At the end of the five-day week, he will have five cards or a normal

poker hand. The highest hand wins $20. There will be eight winners, one for approximately each department.

This lottery was in operation *each week* for 6 weeks (phase 1). For the following 10 weeks, the reinforcement schedule was stretched, the lottery being operated *every other week* (phase 2). Results showed that absenteeism decreased significantly in the experimental group but did not decrease in any of the comparison groups during the same period. The lower rate of absenteeism was maintained during phase 2.

The successful application of a similar lottery system to reduce absenteeism and tardiness among industrial workers has been reported by other investigators (Johnson & Wallin, 1976; Nord, 1969, 1970; Wallin & Johnson, 1976). Other operant conditioning techniques have been used to improve performance on a variety of jobs, including mechanical, clerical, sales, and supervisory functions. Still other operant conditioning studies have obtained promising results in training "hard-core unemployed" in the skills needed for finding and applying for jobs, as well as in job performance (Azrin, Flores, & Kaplan, 1975; Brown & Presbie, 1976).

Interaction. In the discussion of scientific method in Chapter 1, interaction was illustrated with a hypothetical example in which two methods of teaching arithmetic were compared in each of three groups of children differing in academic aptitude. The decades of the 1960s and 1970s have witnessed an upsurge of research on interactions between learner characteristics and instructional methods or other aspects of the learning situation[2] (Berliner & Cahen, 1973; Cronbach & Snow, 1977). For example, whether a person learns better in a structured or an unstructured situation and whether he learns rules better by inductive or deductive methods may depend on his anxiety level and on his verbal ability (Berliner & Cahen, 1973).

As more and more interaction studies were conducted, however, there was a discouraging accumulation of conflicting and negative results. In a searching analysis of the problem, Cronbach (1975) observed that the reason for this disappointing state of affairs could probably be found in higher order interactions. In other words, most learning situations are complex and involve more variables than had been investigated in the usual interaction studies. Suppose that there is a significant Method × Sex × Grade interaction in learning arithmetic. This could mean that Method A is better for girls and Method B for boys in Grade 3, while the relative merits of the two methods are reversed for boys and girls in Grade 6. A single investigation combining children from Grades 3 to 6 would probably reveal no interaction, and different investigations studying single grades would report conflicting results. A further difficulty is that, in order to identify statistically significant higher order interactions, the investigator needs very large samples. Yet the variables that actually interact in most learning situations are probably quite numerous, and their effects can only be detected through higher order interactions.

A solution proposed by Cronbach (1975) is to conduct descriptive, local studies, whose findings are interpreted within the total context, rather than designing studies from which broad generalizations can be drawn directly. As results from

---

[2]This research has been variously designated as ATI (Aptitude- or Attribute-Treatment Interaction) or TTI (Trait-Treatment Interaction).

such local studies accumulate, they may lead to insights regarding the effects of relevant variables, which will eventually be generalizable. It should be noted that the findings of the local studies also provide applied research data of immediate use within the particular context. An example of the practical application of this approach is provided by an investigation of training procedures with army enlistees selected from the upper and lower extremes of aptitude, as measured by the Armed Forces Qualification Test (Bialek, Taylor, & Hauke, 1973; Cooper, 1974).

In the first part of this study, a systematic experimental manipulation of variables was attempted, including learner aptitude, task complexity and difficulty, and a large number of instructional method variables. It soon became apparent, however, that this experimental design was methodologically unfeasible—for both theoretical and practical reasons. As a result, the first approach was replaced by an optimizing strategy whereby preliminary instructional programs were prepared for high- and low-aptitude learners on the basis of prior knowledge about each variable. The programs were then tried out on groups of trainees, modified, applied to new groups, and eventually accepted or rejected.

Certain practical guidelines for effective instructional programs emerged from this research. For instance, low-aptitude trainees learned best by methods that maximized contacts with a live instructor, as in small groups. These trainees did most poorly with programmed texts or videotape. High-aptitude trainees, on the other hand, performed well with self-instructional materials, providing much of their own feedback and requiring a minimum of explanation and demonstration by the instructor. This study is an example of well-planned applied research on a problem on which the more systematic basic-research approach would probably have yielded inconclusive and uninterpretable results.

Transfer of Training. A final and most important consideration in any training program is transfer of training. To be of practical use, industrial training must transfer to job performance. A trainee may become highly proficient in the use of a training device; a supervisor may exhibit sophisticated human relations attitudes and skills in the course of group-discussion training; but if these newly learned responses are not manifested in improved job performance, the training has failed. Learning research suggests that transfer of training is more likely to occur between situations that have many common elements. This again highlights the desirability of making the training tasks as similar as possible to the job task. However, it is not the physical but the psychological similarity that counts. The essential point is that the trainee learn the operations required on the job in the appropriate working context. Elaborate efforts to achieve a high degree of physical realism in a simulator, for example, may prove to be a needless expense in many training situations (Blaiwes, Puig, & Regan, 1973; Caro, 1973).

Another way of increasing transfer is to provide a variety of tasks in the learning situation. Such variation helps the individual to generalize his learning to new situations. Variation in the irrelevant parts of the stimulus situation forces the learner to respond to its critical aspects. Finally, giving the learner an understanding of principles facilitates transfer. But merely stating a principle verbally is not enough. A more effective way is to have the learner observe its application in a number of different situations. The relative merits of these different techniques for achieving transfer depend to some extent on the nature of the task and the type of learning required (Gagné, 1970, pp. 333–339).

DEVELOPING A TRAINING PROGRAM

In the design of training programs, the psychology of learning can provide general guidelines. Training programs, however, are highly specific and require information gathered within the particular context in which they are to be used. The psychologist approaches the problem armed with the appropriate methodology for collecting and utilizing such information. The basic procedures can be summarized in three steps: (1) perform a task analysis to discover what must be learned; (2) construct the training program, with special attention to the choice of appropriate instructional media and techniques and the optimum sequencing of learning units; (3) evaluate the effectiveness of the training program.

It might be noted that the interest in programmed learning and automated instructional devices has done much to focus attention on the need for task analysis and proper sequencing of learning units. Moreover, the above steps are usually embodied in the approach designated by such terms as "performance-oriented instruction," "competency-based education," and the like (see, e.g., Burke, Hansen, Houston, & Johnson, 1975; J. E. Taylor et al., 1972). These terms, however, have been used with such a variety of different meanings and with such confusing definitions as to render them of doubtful value for purposes of communication.

Task Analysis. The purpose of task analysis is to determine the content of the training program. Such a task analysis is similar to the job analysis conducted for selection programs, in that both emphasize the skills needed to perform the job. Both begin with a full listing of operations to be performed and indicate which are the critical part activities (see Ch. 2). In task analysis, however, the operations to be performed are generally broken down into finer units. To be most effective, moreover, the task analysis should yield specific training objectives expressed in the form of observable actions to be performed, such as "compute percentages" or "set dials to required pressure and temperature." Through task analysis, it should be possible to identify any activities requiring little training because they are already in the learner's behavior repertory. Similarly, task analysis should indicate which activities require the most intensive training because of intrinsic difficulty, importance for the job, or both.

Many of the procedures followed in task analysis are similar to those described in Chapter 2 for use in job analysis (McCormick, 1976b; McGehee & Thayer, 1961, Ch. 3). Observation of the job by the analyst and consultation with workers and supervisors are common procedures. Previously prepared checklists and questionnaires are often used to facilitate task description. These techniques may be supplemented by examination of operating manuals and of available records and reports that might indicate causes of job failure and special sources of difficulty. The critical-incident technique has also been used in this connection (see, e.g., Folley, 1969; Glickman & Vallance, 1958).

Factor analysis can help in identifying the skills that are of primary importance in different stages of learning a task. The value of this approach was demonstrated in an investigation of a complex sensorimotor task similar to that required in flying an interceptor aircraft (Parker & Fleishman, 1961). Factorial analyses of this training task had shown that performance in early practice sessions depended largely on spatial orientation, while performance in later sessions depended increasingly on multilimb coordination. On this basis, an experimental training program was devised in which the instructions to trainees focused on different aspects of the operation at different learning stages. Performance records showed that the group taught by this method learned significantly better than a group taught by conventional methods.

Program Construction. A major decision in constructing a training program pertains to the choice of suitable *instructional media and techniques.* The principal available types were described earlier in this chapter. The choice should be made in the light of known interactions of instructional method with content to be learned and relevant learner characteristics. Another consideration is the relative cost-effectiveness of the different media. The anticipated transfer of training to job performance is a major element in assessing the overall cost effectiveness of different types of programs.

In the actual preparation of a specific training program, the principal process is *sequencing.* Once the component units to be learned have been identified through task analysis, they should be arranged in optimal sequence for maximum transfer to the performance of the total task. One naturally thinks that a training program should advance from the easy to the difficult units, but this rule is too vague and general to be readily applicable. A useful guide is to begin with what the learner already knows and introduce unfamiliar content by a gradual progression. Among other advantages, this procedure tends to reduce errors and to maximize positive reinforcement, thus enhancing the learner's motivation and favorable attitude toward the task.

The most fundamental sequencing principle is based on the simple notion of prerequisite skills and knowledge. Beginning with the learning objectives derived from the task analysis, we can examine each unit performance and ask what the learner must be able to do and what he or she needs to know in order to learn this performance. We thereby identify the prerequisite learning unit on the next lower level of the hierarchy. By asking this question about each unit in turn, we can work back until we reach skills and knowledge already available to the learner. This is essentially what is meant by constructing learning hierarchies (Gagné, 1970, Ch. 9). For example, trainees must be able to identify the controls on a piece of equipment and know the function of each before they can learn to use these controls in a coordinated pattern to operate the equipment. Similarly, a learner needs to progress from defining concepts, to formulating rules utilizing these concepts, to solving problems involving these rules.

Evaluation of Training. Like selection programs, training programs should be objectively and systematically evaluated. We cannot *assume* that training improves job performance. Nor can we rely on expressions of opinion, as is done in many companies. Workers and supervisors may believe they have benefited from training without manifesting any genuine improvement. To evaluate a training program, we need to compare the job performance of the same group before and after training, or the performance of a trained group with that of a control group, or the performance of two or more groups trained by different methods.[3] Like the content

---

[3]Detailed analyses of the appropriate experimental designs, with relative merits and limitations of each, can be found in J. P. Campbell et al. (1970, Ch. 12).

of training, the criteria for evaluating its effectiveness must be derived from a task analysis. Whether or not training was successful can be determined only in the light of the specific objectives of the training program.

The criteria for evaluating the effectiveness of industrial training may be conveniently classified into four levels: (1) participant reaction to program, (2) learning of program content, (3) changes in job performance, and (4) impact on organizational outcomes (Catalanello & Kirkpatrick, 1968). The first two levels provide internal evaluations of the training program itself; the last two represent external evaluations, including transfer of training to the trainee's job performance, as well as more indirect effects on such variables as production costs, productivity, and job performance of subordinates (in the case of management training). Although the ultimate value of a training program depends on its external effects, assessment on all four levels is desirable, provided that objective and reasonably well-controlled procedures are employed. Carefully constructed questionnaires to gauge trainee satisfaction or dissatisfaction with different features of the training program can yield useful data. Performance tests for essential job skills are an integral component of well-designed training programs. Objective written tests of needed factual information are appropriate for some jobs. When all participants are trained to a preestablished performance standard, the time required to reach this standard is an important criterion for evaluating alternative training programs.

Internal performance criteria, especially if based on a thorough task analysis of the job, are particularly useful in *formative evaluations* of the program. This type of evaluation refers to the tryout and revision that go on while a training program is being developed. Its use is illustrated in the previously cited research on training programs for high-aptitude and low-aptitude army enlistees (Bialek et al., 1973). The successful development of training programs suited to a particular job context or type of learner owes much to good formative evaluation.

External criteria of training effectiveness, while more difficult to apply than internal program criteria, are essential to justify the continued use of any training program. The appropriate criterion measures obviously depend upon the nature of the job. Any aspect of job performance that was included in the training program can be measured, observed, or rated in the effort to assess the extent to which the training transferred to the job. Other external criterion data are illustrated by output records, breakage and use of supplies, amount of sales, customer complaints, accidents, absenteeism, and job turnover.

The evaluation of a training program should also include an analysis of its *cost effectiveness*. In the design of simulators, for example, cost effectiveness depends in part on the relative cost per hour of training in the simulator and in the regular job equipment (such as an aircraft). The total number of hours of simulator and of aircraft training required to reach a given performance standard should be included in such evaluation. The question of fidelity of simulation is also relevant. For example, increasing fidelity through visual displays and cockpit motion may or may not appreciably increase transfer of training. Moreover, even if greater fidelity of simulation does improve transfer, so that the needed hours of actual aircraft training are thereby reduced, this improvement must be balanced against the increased development and operating costs of the more realistic simulator. There is considerable evidence, in fact, that training effectiveness depends more on the organization and content of the training program than on the physical characteristics of the simulator. For many training purposes, maximum effectiveness can be achieved with relatively simple and inexpensive training devices (Blaiwes et al., 1973; Caro, 1973).

Finally, the effectiveness of a training program should also be considered within the broader framework of the total human factor system. How does the contribution of a particular training program interact with other facets of the system, such as recruiting, selection, classification, job and equipment redesign, and organizational structure? This question places the evaluation of training within the systems measurement bed introduced in Chapter 1 and cited at the beginning of this chapter.

MANAGEMENT DEVELOPMENT

Management development takes many forms, from personal counseling to subsidized university courses (J. P. Campbell et al., 1970, pp. 40–50 & Ch. 10). In content it may range from reading skills to interpersonal attitudes. Managers need thorough and continuing orientation regarding company policies; they need supervisory skills in handling the many face-to-face situations encountered in their daily work; they need knowledge of management principles for effective planning and organizing; in some departments, such as engineering, they obviously need to keep up with the latest technical and scientific developments in their field; and they need the imagination and breadth to take a comprehensive and long-range view of company functions. Not all these needs are equally strong at all levels. In general, supervisory functions assume more importance at the lower management levels. They play a particularly important part in the job of foreman, or first-line supervisor. At the higher or executive levels, planning, organizing, and creativity become increasingly more important.

In view of its many objectives, it is understandable that management training utilizes a variety of procedures. An important component of management development is on-the-job training. This training may include job rotation in order to acquaint the prospective executive with different jobs and departments in the company. It may involve service as assistant to a manager, who delegates specific assignments to the trainee. In all cases, the amount and quality of coaching provided by an experienced company manager are of basic importance in the success of such training. In the progression to higher levels of management, actual job performance at lower managerial levels serves both a selection and a training function. Longitudinal as well as retrospective studies of managers in large corporations are providing data on the nature of managerial functions and on the conditions determining managerial succession (Bray et al., 1974; Glickman, Hahn, Fleishman, & Baxter, 1968; MacKinney, 1967).

Among the many specialized types of management development programs, three are of special interest. These are concerned with human relations training, management games, and creativity training. The first has been chosen for discussion because it covers a major portion of current management training programs. More has undoubtedly been written about human relations training than about any other phase of management development. The other two, on the other hand, represent little more than promising ventures into relatively unexplored territory.

Human Relations Training. The broad category of human relations training includes not only the development of effective interpersonal skills but also an increase in self-knowledge and the improvement of attitudes toward one's job and one's associates. The principal techniques employed for such training utilize either individual interviews or various small-group interactive methods.

The use of the *problem-solving interview* as an instrument of human relations training has been fully described by N. R. F. Maier (1958). If the individual seeks help because of a personal problem or job difficulty, the interview or series of interviews conducted to solve the problem would usually be considered counseling. The appraisal interview, on the other hand, is either initiated by the individual's supervisor because of a perceived job difficulty or is held periodically as a regular supervisory procedure. Essentially, the object of all such interviews is to give the individual an opportunity to bring up, talk about, and work out solutions for his or her own problems. The interviewer serves chiefly as an active listener. His function is to create a permissive climate conducive to free discussion and constructive problem solving, and to help clarify the individual's own feelings. Since this type of interview is patterned closely after the nondirective interview developed in clinical psychology, it will be discussed more fully in Chapter 13. Illustrations of its use in industrial contexts can be found in Maier's books (1958; 1973, Ch. 20). Problem-solving interviews with top executives represent one of the growing functions of the consulting psychologist in industry.

In the course of solving his problems in the interview, the supervisor also learns how to use the interview as a supervisory tool with his own subordinates. This dual function runs through much of human relations training. Such training is designed to give the individual, not a set of ready-made solutions or rules, but a *method* for solving interpersonal problems. It is also designed to induce the individual to become active in his or her own self-training. Another important objective is the development of sensitivity to the feelings and attitudes of others. Thus the supervisor must learn to respond to slight cues in the behavior of others which may suggest underlying reasons for what they say and do.

All of these objectives are illustrated in the various supervisory training techniques that utilize *group discussion and social interaction* (Maier, Solem, & Maier, 1957; Olmstead, 1974). As used in this context, "discussion" means active individual participation and group interaction in reaching decisions. It does *not* refer to the question-and-answer type of discussion that often follows a formal lecture. The discussion methods used in human relations training provide direct practice in interpersonal relations, group problem solving, conference leadership, and other skills needed in a supervisory job. Participants have a chance to observe feelings and attitudes as manifested in their own and their associates' behavior. They may discover that the same objective events are differently perceived by different persons. And they should learn to recognize and avoid snap judgments, pat solutions, and stereotypes in solving human relations problems.

Several special techniques and training aids have been developed to increase the effectiveness of discussion methods for these purposes. One is the *case method,* whereby the group is given specific cases to discuss. Each case provides a description of a realistic human relations problem for which the group undertakes to work out a solution. The many collections of cases that have been published for this purpose bear witness to the popularity of the method (e.g., Glover, Hower, & Tagiuri, 1973; Kindall, 1969; McLarney & Berliner, 1970). A variant of the case method, designed to increase active participation by discussants, has been described as the "incident process" (Pigors & Pigors, 1961). In this method, the case is introduced by reporting a specific incident, about which the discussants then ask questions to elicit background facts. When sufficient information has been accumulated, the discussants proceed to summarize the case, identify the problem, propose courses of action, and evaluate the relative merits of the proposals.

A much less structured approach is illustrated by a technique commonly designated as *sensitivity training*[4] (Back, 1972; Bradford, Gibb, & Benne, 1964). Typically, a group of about a dozen trainees meet for a short period (usually a week) in a relatively isolated place, with a minimum of outside contacts and distractions. The group leader undertakes in a variety of ways to induce an atmosphere of frank and uninhibited airing of problems and feelings in group sessions. In this context, the participants are encouraged to study their own reactions and those of other group members as they occur. Having much in common with group psychotherapy (to be considered in Chapter 13), sensitivity training is designed to increase insight into oneself and others, promote acceptance of self and associates, and improve interpersonal behavior.

Some sensitivity training groups include only a single person from each organization, on the assumption that greater freedom of expression is likely to be achieved among strangers. Under these conditions, however, single participants may find it difficult to apply their newly learned approaches upon returning to their companies. Moreover, important interpersonal issues may not emerge in a group of strangers, and there is little opportunity for coming to grips with existing conflicts and interpersonal problems within each organization. For these reasons, an increasing number of practitioners of sensitivity training prefer to work with a "family group," that is, a group of persons who actually work together in a particular company.

Another technique, which can be combined with either the case method or sensitivity training, is *role playing* (N. R. F. Maier et al., 1957). In its basic form, role playing requires individuals to assume designated roles and enact a human relations incident. A typical case may be presented orally, in written instructions, on a film, or through a dramatized version with prepared script and dialogue. The prepared material stops at the point where the problem has fully developed. Beyond that point, the trainees must carry on in their own way, assuming the roles of workers, supervisor, or whatever the case requires. Each individual, however, is instructed always to play himself, that is, to act as *he* would if placed in that situation. Other group members serve as observers. Following the role playing, the entire group discusses what was done. The number of role players in different cases may vary from two to a dozen or more. Trainees take turns in assuming the roles of employees, supervisors, and observers.

Empirical evaluations of human relations training procedures generally report significant improvement in attitudes, sensitivity, and problem-solving behavior when trainees are tested in the training situation itself (J. P. Campbell et al., 1970, Ch. 13). Few studies, however, have obtained evidence of transfer of training to the job situation.

In a well-designed longitudinal study conducted at the International Harvester Company, Harris and Fleishman (1955) assessed on-the-job supervisory behavior through questionnaires filled out by the workers in each foreman's work unit. A random sample of workers in each group completed a Supervisory Behavior

---

[4]Also known by several other names, such as "T-group training" and "laboratory training."

Description on two occasions, 11 months apart. During this period, 39 of the foremen had attended a two-week course in leadership training conducted at a central company school; the remaining 59, who had received no such training, constituted the control group. On the Supervisory Behavior Description, each worker indicated how often his foremen did what the item described, such as planning each day's activities in detail, insisting that everything be done his way, or helping his men with their personal problems. These questionnaires were scored for two independent leadership dimensions, which had been identified through factor analyses in earlier research. One of these dimensions was described as "Consideration," representing a friendly, warm, and considerate supervisory relation, as contrasted with an impersonal and authoritarian relation. The other dimension, designated as "Initiating Structure," concerned the extent to which the supervisor actively plans and directs group activities oriented toward goal attainment. A comparison of the mean scores obtained by the foremen in both leadership dimensions on the two occasions revealed no significant change in observed supervisory behavior in either the trained or the control group.

In an earlier study conducted in the same company (Fleishman, 1953b), significant differences had been found in the foremen's supervisory attitudes as reported in a questionnaire filled out by foremen themselves at the beginning and end of training. However, a comparison of matched groups of foremen who had been back on the job for varying periods showed no significant mean differences between trained and untrained groups in either attitudes or behavior. These findings suggest that what was learned in training did not transfer to the job context. To explore the situation further, Fleishman administered additional questionnaires designed to elicit the attitudes and expectations of the foreman's own supervisor, as well as the foreman's description of his supervisor's behavior and his perception of what the supervisor expects. An analysis of the responses indicated that the "leadership climate" in which the foreman operates is a major determinant of his own attitudes and behavior. In other words, the supervisor's behavior toward his subordinates is itself affected by the behavior of his own supervisor toward him. Similar results have been obtained in other industrial research in which leadership climate was investigated. One practical implication of these findings is the importance of conducting supervisory training from the top down. To train supervisors who will then resume their duties in a leadership climate that is inconsistent with their training may be worse than useless.

The ultimate test of the effectiveness of any supervisory training program is its impact on the job performance of subordinates. Even if training produces lasting changes in the job behavior of a supervisor, the effect of these changes on such criteria as productivity, absenteeism, and turnover needs to be ascertained. For example, the relation between productivity and supervisory style (i.e., relative emphasis on Consideration and Initiating Structure) is quite complex and involves interactions with both employee characteristics and type of job. This topic will be considered further in the next two chapters.

Special mention should be made of the research on the effects of sensitivity training (Back, 1974; Campbell & Dunnette, 1968; P. B. Smith, 1975). Although more extensive than that on any other form of human relations training, much of this research is inconclusive because of inadequate experimental controls. The results show that attitudes and self-concepts generally do change in the course of sensitivity training. The specific behavioral effects, however, vary not only with the job context but also with the prior personality characteristics of the trainees. Those behavioral changes that transfer to the job situation, moreover, do not necessarily lead to greater job effectiveness. There is also need for more data on possible detrimental side effects on the individual and on his or her job performance.

Management Games. Not all management decisions deal with interpersonal relations. It is in handling personnel problems that the previously described group problem-solving methods are likely to prove most effective. Decisions reached jointly by all persons concerned are more likely to fit all the idiosyncracies of those particular individuals than would decisions reached by a single person. Such a joint decision will also tend to be more acceptable to the group than would a decision imposed from without, however reasonable the latter decision may be when evaluated objectively. Executives, however, are called upon to make many other kinds of decisions, concerning other matters besides personnel relations. Often these decisions require specialized knowledge and skills that only a few members of the organization may possess. Reaching a correct decision in such areas is not merely a matter of choosing a course of action that satisfies all group members. Other procedures are required to enable the executive to balance different company objectives, to secure and evaluate relevant information, and to predict the probability of different outcomes. Special mathematical techniques, designated as "operations research," have been developed to systematize many aspects of this decision-making process.

In training executives to make this type of decision, the previously mentioned *case method* has again proved useful. Several published collections of "cases" deal not only with personnel problems but also with many other types of management decisions in such areas as production, research, distribution, advertising, and financing. A more specialized technique that has aroused considerable interest utilizes *management games,* or *simulation* (Dill, 1974; Kibbee, Craft, & Nanus, 1961). Gaming as a training procedure is not new, having been used for a long time by the armed services in their "war games." The application of this concept to business, however, is more recent, dating from the late 1950s. The first management game was developed by the American Management Association for use in its executive training seminars (Appley, 1957). Since then, several hundred games have been constructed for use in schools of business and company training programs. One of the most elaborate was developed in 1960 at the Carnegie Institute of Technology (Cohen, Dill, Kuehn, & Winters, 1964).

In a management decision game, one or more teams, each representing a business firm, make a series of decisions controlling the operations of their firm during a specified period. The simulated time period may be as short as a week or as long as a year or more. Decisions may range from the pricing of a single product to opening a new plant, obtaining funds by issuing debentures or common stock, or conducting research to develop new products. A mathematical model of how the industry operates is used to calculate the outcomes of each team's decisions. With simple models, such calculations can be performed manually; with more complex models, a computer is required. In either case, the trainees receive immediate feedback. It is the object of management games not only to give the players an awareness of the complexity of the economic environment in which they must operate but also to train them to cope with such complexity through systematic analysis and effective problem-solving procedures. It should be added, however, that available research evidence of the effectiveness of such training procedures in executive problem solving and decision making is meager.

Creativity Training. Industry is constantly clamoring for new ideas—from a catchy trade name to the complex creations of modern engineering. In today's rapidly changing world, industry needs creative and imaginative management more than ever before. It is therefore not surprising to find that the development and facilitation of creative thinking have received considerable attention in management development programs, as well as in the training of scientists and engineers (Stein, 1975, Ch. 17).

Psychological research on creativity has concentrated chiefly on ways of identifying creative persons. It is being increasingly recognized, however, that creative talent should be not only identified but also developed. There is growing interest in the organizational conditions conducive to creative achievement, in the work methods followed by creative producers, and in procedures for developing creative productivity (C. W. Taylor, 1972).

A widely publicized technique designed to favor original and creative thinking is known as "brainstorming" (Osborn, 1963; Stein, 1975, Ch. 13). By this method, the individual segregates in time the production of ideas from their evaluation. It is argued that an evaluative set makes the individual too critical and inhibits the development of new ideas. Hence the instructions emphasize quantity rather than quality of ideas. Participants are told to express any idea that occurs to them, however foolish or unsatisfactory it may seem. Any form of criticism is strictly taboo. Selection and evaluation of ideas occur in a completely separate, later stage. The hypothesis is that brainstorming will produce not only more ideas in general but also more ideas of high quality than will the more critical traditional procedure.

Research on the effectiveness of brainstorming generally supports the hypothesis that deferment of judgment increases the quantity of ideas produced (Stein, 1975, Ch. 13). The results pertaining to quality, however, are less certain. There is a substantial positive correlation between the quantity and quality of ideas produced by different individuals, regardless of whether or not brainstorming procedures are used. Moreover, any advantage of brainstorming with regard to quality may disappear when the quality criterion gives little weight to sheer originality (Weisskopf-Joelson & Eliseo, 1961). It is also likely that the response set established by brainstorming may simply alter standards of what is an acceptable response rather than increasing ability to produce ideas. This possibility is suggested by an experiment on the formulation of hypotheses from given data (Frederiksen & Evans, 1974). After recording their responses to each problem, participants in this study were given model lists of acceptable responses. One group received long lists (quantity model); the other group received short lists of the best ideas, carefully worded (quality model). Both the quantity and quality models proved effective in significantly modifying responses in the expected direction. Contrary to one of the common assumptions of brainstorming, the instructions that emphasized quality produced higher quality of responses than did the instructions that emphasized quantity.

Another question that has generated considerable research is whether brainstorming is more productive when participants work individually[5] or when they work together in real interacting groups. On the basis of rather casual evidence, it

[5]Such participants are often described as a "nominal group," because the total number of ideas thus produced still represents the contribution of all persons in the group.

had been commonly accepted that brainstorming is more effective when carried out in groups than individually. In a well-designed experiment, on the other hand, individual performance was found to excel group performance significantly in mean number of ideas produced, mean number of unique ideas, and quality of solutions (Taylor, Berry, & Block, 1958). These findings have been corroborated in later studies (Bouchard, Barsaloux, & Drauden, 1974; Dunnette, Campbell, & Jaastad, 1963; Madsen & Finger, 1978). It is possible that group interaction may contribute more to the subsequent evaluation of ideas than to their initial production. The relative effectiveness of individual and group procedures may also vary with the nature of the problem and with the specific ways in which brainstorming techniques are applied (Madsen & Finger, 1978; Stein, 1975, Ch. 13).

TRAINING AND CULTURAL DIVERSITY

The years since midcentury have been characterized by greatly increased contacts among persons from different cultures or subcultures. Interactions across cultural boundaries present many kinds of difficulties. Among the varied approaches proposed to overcome these difficulties, we find a number of specialized training programs. Considerable research and development effort, for example, has been devoted to job training of culturally disadvantaged minorities in the United States (Doeringer, 1969; I. L. Goldstein, 1974; Salipante & Goodman, 1976). These include such groups as ethnic minorities, persons with foreign-language backgrounds and inadequate mastery of English, marginal workers, "hard-core unemployed," school dropouts, and residents of inner-city and other poverty areas.

From a different angle, training programs concerned with cross-cultural contacts are needed for overseas work assignments. Such programs are directed principally to American personnel working in foreign countries. Examples include managerial and technical personnel in overseas branches of transnational corporations, government personnel (both civilians and military), and participants in various volunteer programs in developing countries. Technical and professional personnel who conduct basic educational programs or job-skills training for local groups in the host country encounter still other combinations of cross-cultural problems. For a survey of cross-cultural training research, the reader is referred to Barrett and Bass (1976).

By way of illustration, we shall examine three types of programs based on well-designed research and development procedures. Although the principal research in this training area has been conducted under military sponsorship, it has wide applicability in civilian contexts. It has been observed, for example, that only about 13% of army jobs are strictly military; the remaining 87% are represented in counterpart civilian occupations (Wool & Flyer, 1969).

Training in Job Skills. A job-training program adapted to educationally and culturally disadvantaged trainees was cited earlier in this chapter as an example of interaction between training procedure and learner aptitude (Bialek et al., 1973; Cooper, 1974). The study was specifically concerned with the development of effective training procedures for military personnel accepted under "Project 100,000" (Wool & Flyer, 1969). The goal of this project was to admit, each year, 100,000 men who would previously have been rejected because of low aptitude test score. In this respect, the military services were joining federal agencies in the "war against poverty" by reconsidering job entrance requirements and offering useful job training to persons generally regarded as unemployable. This approach assumed even greater importance with the subsequent establishment of the all-volunteer army. Despite the lowered admission standards, however, performance requirements in military jobs were to be maintained. This was the problem that training had to help solve within the total personnel system.

In developing the specialized training program for low-aptitude trainees, the investigators considered both cognitive and motivational handicaps arising from the trainees' experiential backgrounds. They were mindful of the fact that poor performance on the aptitude test probably reflected "a history of nonreinforcement in a learning situation" which would elicit unfavorable attitudes toward subsequent learning in a school-like context (Bialek et al., 1973, p. 34). Among the principal features of the training program found to be most effective with these trainees was the use of manipulative ("hands-on") rather than verbal or conceptual instructional modes. Demonstration and practice with real equipment predominated. Complex tasks were broken into small subunits which could be more readily mastered. Feedback was provided as soon after each response as possible and preferably was made an inherent property of the response (e.g., if two wires are spliced correctly, the phone rings).

In teaching job skills that did not themselves require reading, the use of reading as a training procedure was kept to a minimum. Verbal communication was provided by a live instructor interacting with a small group of trainees. A particularly effective technique in this connection was the utilization of peer instruction, whereby trainees who have already mastered a skill teach it to fellow trainees, usually in a one-to-one ratio. Not only does this benefit the learners by increasing personal contact and providing a model closely similar to themselves, but it also gives the peer instructors further opportunity to apply and consolidate their own knowledge.[6] All the procedures incorporated in this prototype program provide useful guidelines in the development of other training programs for similar trainee populations.

Functional Literacy and Basic Skills. Another series of investigations stimulated by Project 100,000 was the eight-year research program conducted by the Human Resources Research Organization (HumRRO) on literacy training (Sticht, 1975).[7] For purposes of this program, "functional literacy" (FLIT) refers to the attainment of minimal reading (and listening) skills required for effective performance of a specified job. The first step in the FLIT research was to establish realistic reading requirements for specific military occupational specialties, such as cook, repairman, and supply clerk. Job analyses included an investigation of the relation between reading aptitude and tests of both job knowledge and job performance on

---

[6]Peer instruction has proved promising as a training procedure at all aptitude levels and in various civilian as well as military contexts (see, e.g., Weingarten, Hungerland, & Brennan, 1972).

[7]This summary volume, entitled *Reading for Working,* is a useful source for anyone wishing to pursue this topic further. An adaptation of this program, directed specifically to functional literacy in daily living, was subsequently developed for use in schools and other civilian training programs (HumRRO, 1978).

the part of present incumbents. It also included the development of a Job Reading Task Test for each type of job, based on a sample of actual, commonly used, job reading materials. For each job, the goal of reading instruction was defined in terms of performance on this test.

The overriding purpose of the entire project was to reduce the gap between the literacy demands of the jobs and the literacy skills of the workers. To achieve this purpose, a dual approach was followed. On the one hand, both job performance and job training were redesigned to reduce literacy requirements that were not intrinsic to the job. This redesign is illustrated by the following procedures: extensive simplification and clarification of training and operating manuals; the preparation of job performance aids, such as manuals, checklists, or diagrams, for storage and retrieval of job information that would otherwise have to be "stored" in the worker; and the substitution of listening for reading whenever feasible as a mode of training and of communication on the job.

The other side of the dual approach consisted in the design of a prototype literacy training program, whose goal was the attainment of a seventh-grade reading competence with job-related materials within the available six-week training period. This training program utilizes reading tasks that will actually be

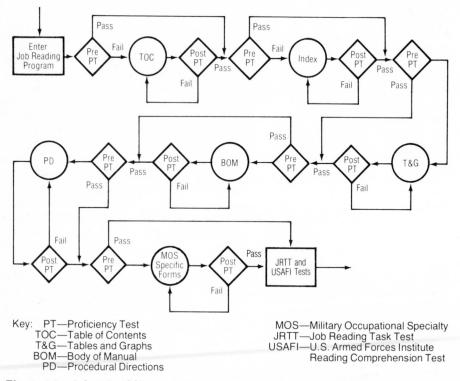

Key: PT—Proficiency Test
       TOC—Table of Contents
       T&G—Tables and Graphs
       BOM—Body of Manual
       PD—Procedural Directions

MOS—Military Occupational Specialty
JRTT—Job Reading Task Test
USAFI—U.S. Armed Forces Institute
             Reading Comprehension Test

Figure 4-3. A functional literacy training program. *(Adapted from Sticht, 1975, p. 124. Copyright © 1975 by Human Resources Research Organization. Reproduced by permission.)*

encountered both in job training and in later job performance, thereby ensuring greater transfer of training as well as better motivation for the learner. The training is individualized in that reading materials are selected from the type of job for which the individual has already been selected. Self-pacing permits each learner to proceed at the rate determined by his or her own performance.

Learning is programmed into a series of modules, each with its own pretest and posttest,[8] as illustrated in Figure 4-3. The skills sampled by the modules include locating information in the table of contents and index of job manuals, reading tables and graphs, extracting information from the body of the manual, following procedural directions, and reading specific printed forms used in the individual's military occupational specialty. Immediate feedback is provided after completion of each module, with provision for additional training in the particular skill until the content of that module is mastered. Peer instructors from the same program are utilized as assistants and instructional aides.

Another HumRRO project had the broader goal of enhancing the basic learning capacity of army personnel with initially low aptitude scores (Jealous, Bialek, Pitpit, & Gordon, 1975). Through a highly individualized instructional program, trainees developed basic language and arithmetic skills and improved in both cognitive performance and self-direction. Although these findings were based on a small sample, they suggest a promising line of investigation with far-reaching educational and industrial implications.

Cultural Awareness Programs. Communication and collaboration across cultures and subcultures are often hampered by failure to understand the causes of each other's behavior. The same behavior may have quite different explanations when encountered in persons with diverse cultural backgrounds. Several investigators have addressed themselves to ways of increasing one's awareness of cultural differences in the significance of verbal and other overt behavior. The *culture assimilator* is a printed instructional program concerned with explaining the actions of persons in a culture other than one's own (Fiedler, Mitchell, & Triandis, 1971; O'Brien & Plooij, 1977). Based on a detailed study of the characteristic customs, values, and interpersonal attitudes of the cultures involved, this instrument requires a different version for each pair of interacting cultures.

Essentially, the culture assimilator provides short descriptions of incidents of cross-cultural conflict or misperception. Each incident is followed by four plausible attributions of the behavior of the person in the other culture; one attribution is that typically made by members of the other culture; the other three are attributions commonly made by members of one's own culture. As soon as a trainee selects a response option, the program provides an explanation of why the choice was correct or incorrect and (if incorrect) directs the trainee to reread the material and choose another option.

Although the culture assimilator requires extensive research and development effort, its use by trainees is quite simple; and the total training period generally

---

[8]These are examples of criterion-referenced tests, a type of test that has come into prominence in individualized training programs. It is designed to test for mastery of skills and knowledge required for a specified purpose (Anastasi, 1976, pp. 96–100).

covers two to five hours. The training is admittedly at the cognitive level. However, it appears to provide an effective substitute for merely reading or hearing lectures about another culture, since it involves active participation by the learner in the understanding of typical concrete behavior. This program may also be used as an introduction to more extensive training with such techniques as role playing and behavior modification. Cultural assimilators have been developed with reference to Arab countries, Iran, Thailand, Central America, and Greece (Fiedler et al., 1971), as well as to an aboriginal culture of South Australia (O'Brien & Plooij, 1977). Adaptations have also been proposed for use within the United States with reference to workers from ethnic and socioeconomic minorities (Triandis, Feldman, Weldon, & Harvey, 1974).

Approaching the problem from a different angle, the *HumRRO workshop in intercultural communication* (Kraemer, 1973, 1974, 1975) seeks to improve one's own cultural self-awareness. The participants are taught to recognize the restrictive cultural influences in their own thinking and behavior. These restrictive influences stem from the unwarranted assumption that thought patterns characteristic of one's own culture are shared by all cultures. Organized into a two-day workshop, the program utilizes video recordings of excerpts of conversations between an American and a host national in an imaginary "non-Western culture." The conversations occur in work situations involving Foreign Service, Peace Corps, business, or military personnel. Each excerpt illustrates a manifestation of at least one cultural influence in the background of the American speaker, either in what he is saying or in the way he says it. For each excerpt, the participants try to identify the restrictive cultural element. Excerpts involving different manifestations of a single cultural element are grouped into sequences to facilitate identification of the common element. Examples of such cultural elements include individualism, action orientation, competition as a way of motivating people, reasoning in terms of probability, and the tendency to quantify aspects of experience even when no quantification is required.

SUMMARY

In the effective utilization of human resources, training is closely interlocked with selection and classification. Industrial training is a continuing process that can benefit all employees, from beginner to experienced worker and from unskilled labor to top management. Training programs in industry serve a variety of functions, including orientation, acquisition of job skills, technical and professional training, management development, and general education. Among the principal training media employed for these purposes are lectures, training manuals and other printed materials, films and television, training devices and simulators, programmed and computer-assisted instruction, job performance, small-group interactive techniques, and problem-solving interviews.

Basic research on learning provides general guidelines for the development of training procedures, as illustrated by the accumulated findings on the role of motivation, the effects of stress, active learner participation, feedback, part versus whole learning, the distribution of learning time, conditioning principles as applied to behavior modification, trait-treatment interactions, and transfer of training. In developing a particular training program, the major steps are task analysis, program construction (with special attention to sequencing of units in a learning hierarchy), and evaluation of training (both formative and terminal, with both internal and external criteria).

The broad area of management development covers many types of training and utilizes a diversity of training techniques. Much of it is concerned with the development of human relations skills and attitudes through such techniques as problem-solving interviews, the case method, sensitivity training, and role playing. In other aspects of management development, two techniques of special interest are management games (or simulation) and creativity training.

Special training needs arise from cultural pluralism and the problems associated with movement and communication across cultural boundaries. Programs to meet these needs are illustrated by adaptations of job-skills training procedures for educationally and culturally disadvantaged workers, functional literacy training, and cultural awareness programs.

ATTITUDES AND MOTIVATION

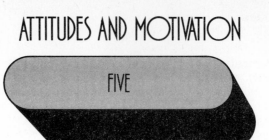

FIVE

SELECTION AND TRAINING provide qualified personnel to do each job. But to get the job done, the individual must also *want* to work. The motives that impel people to work are complex, and the incentives for which they strive include more than the paycheck. Within the limits set by their qualifications, what individuals actually accomplish may vary widely as a function of their attitudes toward the company, toward their immediate superior, toward their fellow workers, and toward other aspects of the job. Low morale can make a brilliant worker totally unproductive; high morale can lead ordinary persons to well-nigh incredible feats.

To be sure, employee selection and classification are concerned not only with abilities but also with attitudinal and motivational factors. Similarly, training programs contribute to the development of attitudes. Nevertheless, the nature of the work and the conditions under which it is performed may substantially affect employee motivation. It is chiefly in terms of these job and organizational variables that worker motivation will be considered in the present chapter.

Today's widespread concern with problems of industrial motivation and morale dates from the classic Hawthorne studies, which first focused attention on the part played by employee attitudes in productivity. Following an examination of these studies, we shall consider procedures for assessing employee attitudes, typical findings about the relation between job satisfaction and job performance, and major theories of work motivation. In terms of the total human factors system diagrammed in Chapter 1 (Fig. 1-1), we are now ready to focus on the third major subsystem, covering job and organizational variables. The present chapter is concerned with the assessment and understanding of worker attitudes and motivation and with their relation to job behavior. In the next chapter, we shall look at typical organizational procedures for the effective management of this facet of the human factors system. With regard to the contribution of psychology, it is apparent that selection and classification represent chiefly the application of psychometrics (testing and the assessment of individual differences); and training is most closely linked to the psychology of learning. Within this framework, the present topic draws most heavily from personality theory and social psychology. In fact, it is sometimes designated as "industrial social psychology."

THE HAWTHORNE STUDIES

The series of investigations that came to be known as the "Hawthorne studies" began in 1924 at the Hawthorne Works of the Western Electric Company, in the outskirts of Chicago, and extended over 15 years (Mayo, 1933; Roethlisberger & Dickson, 1939). The focus of these studies shifted toward human relations in 1927, when the research came under the general direction of Elton Mayo of the Harvard Business School. This change in viewpoint, however, was gradual and was not fully effected until several years later. The first studies were designed to investigate the effects of such variables as illumination, rest pauses, and length of working days on productivity. It soon became apparent, however, that output did not bear a simple relation to these factors. Some of the studies yielded apparently haphazard results that defied interpretation. In others, productivity rose steadily, regardless of what experimental changes were introduced. Even when poorer conditions were reinstated in the course of some experiments, worker performance continued to improve instead of dropping back to the earlier level.

An examination of the actual procedures followed in the course of these experiments reveals what would now be recognized as an astounding number of uncontrolled factors. In their efforts to secure cooperation, the investigators had made conditions as pleasant as possible for their subjects. Thus, in addition to their exposure to the systematically controlled experimental variables, the subjects were released from their customary close supervision, worked in a small group of congenial co-workers of their own choice, were assigned to a more cheerful and comfortable workroom, were allowed to converse more freely during work, received considerable attention from the experimenter and other company personnel, and were consulted about the changes that were introduced.

Following their recognition of the role of supervisory practices and other factors influencing employee attitudes, the Hawthorne investigators embarked upon an intensive attitude survey through interviews of over 21,000 workers. These interviews began as highly structured inquiries into what each employee liked and disliked about working conditions, supervision, and the job itself. It was soon discovered, however, that employees often talked about "irrelevant" topics which were usually of interest in their own right. As a result, the structured interviews were replaced by longer, unguided interviews in which employees were allowed to bring up any problem they considered important. This survey served several purposes. It was noted that most employees welcomed the opportunity to express their views and exhibited more favorable attitudes as a result of it. Specific complaints registered during the interviews were studied by management with a view to correcting the conditions that evoked them. Principally, however, the results of the interviews were used as a basis for the discussion of human relations problems in the company's supervisory training program.

The interview survey also suggested other problems for investigation. It was found that the expressed satisfaction or dissatisfaction often bore little relation to the actual condition cited. One employee might be satisfied and another dissatisfied with the same condition, such as wages, hours of work, or specific features of the working environment. The meaning of these items for the individual seemed to depend in part upon their value as status symbols, and this in turn often depended upon the attitudes of the group in which he or she worked. There was also evidence of voluntary restriction of output as a result of pressures from the work group. The formation of informal social groups within the organization and the influence they exert upon individuals' attitudes and job performance thus became the subject of the next phase of the Hawthorne studies.

Accordingly, an intensive observational study was initiated with a small group of workers assigned to a special room. Data were gathered over a six-month period by two investigators: an observer stationed in the room who recorded verbal and overt behavior; and an interviewer who explored individual attitudes, meanings, and values and sought information on the individual's personal history and life outside the plant. Special attention was given to the existence of informal groupings among the workers, the relation of these groupings to the formal supervisory organization of the department, and the types of social pressures whereby the group controlled individual work performance.

The last stage of the Hawthorne studies is represented by the installation of a plantwide program of employee counseling. This program provided professional counselors for problem-solving interviews with any worker having a problem to discuss. Its objectives were to help employees in the solution of their personal problems and to provide management with general guides for improving personnel and supervisory procedures.

All this research activity did much to launch the "human relations" movement in industrial management. A vast literature on employee attitudes and work motivation has subsequently accumulated. Management theory and practice have put heavy emphasis on interpersonal relations, as illustrated by the management development programs discussed in the preceding chapter. Insofar as the Hawthorne studies have stimulated research in these areas, they undoubtedly served a good purpose. Nevertheless, later analyses of the actual findings indicate that the final interpretation offered by the Hawthorne investigators may be just as faulty as the original experimental design.

In 1974, 50 years after the initiation of the first "Hawthorne experiment," a conference of behavioral scientists and industrial managers was held at the original site in Hawthorne (Christiansen, 1975). The predominant impression at this conference was that the so-called Hawthorne effect, its causes, and its implications for management were differently perceived and interpreted depending upon the participant's theoretical orientation. The many different models of worker motivation that have since been proposed could each claim support from the Hawthorne data.

From another angle, there have been several reexaminations of the original data which have cast considerable doubt on the predominantly interpersonal interpretation (Carey, 1967; H. M. Parsons, 1974). The evidence showed that a change in the *pay rate system* was a major influence on productivity. In one of the principal experiments, the additional incentive pay was based on the output of the five workers in the experimental group rather than the 100 workers in the entire department, as heretofore. As a result, each worker's pay more closely reflected her individual performance. The importance of this financial variable was corroborated in other experiments of the series. In an unusually thorough reanalysis of the data, Parsons (1974) identified *information feedback* as another major variable. Detailed performance records were available to each participant and were frequently consulted by them. Applying the principles of operant conditioning, Parsons demonstrated that the contingent reinforcement provided by such feedback in combination with the more highly individualized financial reward could best explain the observed output changes.

In addition to their historical role in management research and practice, the Hawthorne studies also served to highlight the need for controlling attitudinal variables in the design of psychological experiments. The term "Hawthorne effect" is now commonly used to refer to the influence that participation in an experiment may have upon the subject's behavior. Insofar as being a subject in a particular experiment may in itself involve certain interpersonal relations with the research personnel, as well as associated changes in status, self-concept, or environmental milieu, a control group should be exposed to the same conditions in order to separate their effects from those of the experimental variable. Similarly, participants should not have access to their records during the experiment, nor should they be rewarded in accordance with their performance, unless these contingent reinforcements are themselves variables under investigation (H. M. Parsons, 1974). Under certain circumstances, the Hawthorne effect may refer not so much to experimental design as to oversimplified interpretation of results (Sommer, 1968). For example, a single experimental variable, such as illumination or noise in a working environment, is likely to influence performance both directly and indirectly. It may also interact with individual characteristics in its effects on performance. Thus, a favorable change in such an environmental variable may not only make a task easier to perform but may also enhance positive attitudes toward the task; and an unfavorable change may cause a highly motivated person to work harder to overcome the environmental handicap.

ASSESSING WORKER OPINIONS AND ATTITUDES

Systematic surveys of employee attitudes are now an accepted management practice. Some of the uses of these surveys were already suggested by the Hawthorne studies: to identify needed changes in policies, procedures, or facilities; to provide a realistic basis for supervisory training programs; and to help in evaluating the effect of different conditions upon job performance. Attitude surveys have also been utilized in more general research on work motivation to find out what people want in a job and how these wants vary in relation to age, sex, education, occupational level, or other personal characteristics. In such research, data are often gathered on a communitywide or nationwide basis, rather than being limited to a single company or plant.

The major procedures for gathering data on employee motivation and attitudes include interviewing, projective and other indirect techniques, opinion surveys, and attitude scales for measuring degree of job satisfaction. Two or more of these techniques may be combined in a single investigation. To ensure frankness, the respondent's anonymity and the confidentiality of the data should be preserved, whatever technique is employed.

Interviewing. Because well-conducted interviews are quite time-consuming, they rarely constitute the sole data-gathering technique. Interviews may be used in the early stages of research to identify topics and items for inclusion in a questionnaire.

They are sometimes employed as a more intensive supplement to other survey techniques. For this purpose, interviews may be conducted with every member of a small organizational unit or with a representative sample of a larger unit, such as a plant or company. A rich source of employee attitude data is often available in interviews conducted for other purposes, such as appraisal and problem-solving interviews held periodically by supervisors and exit interviews held with employees who are about to leave the organization. Exit interviews, however, are likely to yield more information, especially with regard to sources of job dissatisfaction, if conducted by an outside consultant (Hinrichs, 1975).

Projective and Other Indirect Techniques. Projective techniques provide a relatively unstructured stimulus situation, allowing the respondent considerable freedom of expression. Insofar as they are indirect, these techniques are believed to be less subject to rationalization and other face-saving devices and hence more likely to reveal genuine attitudes. Several familiar projective techniques, such as word association, sentence completion, or picture interpretation, have been adapted for attitude measurement. Another example is provided by an early survey conducted at General Motors and known as "My Job Contest" (Evans & Laseau, 1949). Employees were invited to participate in a letter-writing contest on the topic, "My Job and Why I Like It," for which 5,000 prizes were awarded. The letters, which totaled nearly 150,000, were content-analyzed with reference to 58 "themes," or factors associated with favorable job attitudes. A number of other indirect testing techniques have been applied to the assessment of attitudes (D. T. Campbell, 1950; Shaw & Wright, 1967; Summers, 1970), but they are rarely used in industrial settings except for research purposes.

Opinion Surveys. Utilizing written self-report questionnaires, opinion surveys make it possible to reach a large number of employees in a short time. Anonymity can be easily provided by having employees drop the questionnaires in a ballot box or mail them directly to an outside survey agency. Typically, opinion question-naires include questions on specific items within such areas as working conditions, relation to fellow workers, supervisory relations, company policies, pay, employee benefits, and opportunity for advancement. Responses may be analyzed so as to identify major areas of dissatisfaction; to single out specific items, such as employee cafeteria or vacation policy, about which opinions may be outstandingly favorable or unfavorable; to compare the frequency of dissatisfaction in different departments or different kinds of jobs within the company; or to answer other questions pertinent to the local circumstances.

In contrast to other attitude questionnaires, opinion surveys are primarily concerned with the percentage of persons who report satisfaction or dissatisfaction with *specific items* of company policy, procedures, or facilities. Opinion questionnaires may also provide an opportunity for write-in comments, which can be studied by content analysis. Through a preliminary review of the comments, a list of content categories is prepared. These categories, or types of statements, are then used to code each comment, and the percentage of respondents making each type of statement is recorded. Examples of such content categories might be "working equipment should be updated" or "poor selection of food in cafeteria."

Measures of Job Satisfaction. The most common procedure involves the use of attitude scales. Like opinion surveys, attitude scales are suitable for mass administration in written form. Rather than indicating frequency of satisfaction or dissatisfaction with a wide variety of specific items, however, attitude scales yield an index of intensity of favorable or unfavorable attitude toward a broad area; several provide a single, overall index of job satisfaction, covering all aspects of the job situation.[1]

The measurement of attitudes and the development of psychometrically sophisticated attitude scales has for many years been an active area of research in social psychology. Surveys of available procedures and scales designed for a variety of purposes can be found in Shaw and Wright (1967) and Summers (1970); descriptions and evaluations of instruments constructed specifically to assess job attitudes are provided by Robinson, Athanasiou, and Head (1969). With regard to item form, a common distinction is that between Thurstone-type and Likert-type attitude scales (see Anastasi, 1976, Ch. 18; Summers, 1970, Ch. 8).

The typical Thurstone scale provides a series of statements ranging from very favorable, through neutral, to very unfavorable. The statements are selected and their scale values determined through procedures similar to those described in Chapter 3 for the construction of scaled checklists. A few items of the sort used in employee attitude scales are reproduced in Table 5-1, together with their empiri-

TABLE 5-1
Illustrative Statements for Use in an Employee Attitude Scale
(Selected from Uhrbrock, 1934.)

Scale Value	Statement
10.4	I think this company treats its employees better than any other company does.
8.9	A man can get ahead in this company if he tries.
7.4	On the whole, the company treats us about as well as we deserve.
5.1	The workers put as much over on the company as the company puts over on them.
2.1	You've got to have "pull" with certain people around here to get ahead.
0.8	An honest man fails in this company.

cally derived scale values. In the actual scales, all the statements are printed in random order, without their scale values. The respondent's attitude score is found by taking the mean scale value of the statements he endorses.

In the Likert-type scale, the respondent is required to mark *each* statement by choosing one of five alternatives: Strongly Agree (**SA**), Agree (**A**), Undecided (**U**), Disagree (**D**), Strongly Disagree (**SD**). The individual statements are either clearly favorable or clearly unfavorable. Responses are scored by crediting 5, 4, 3, 2, or 1, respectively, to each alternative from the favorable to the unfavorable end. For example, **SA** for a favorable statement receives a score of 5, as does **SD** for an unfavorable statement. The sum of the item credits is the individual's total score on

---

[1] A few instruments serve a dual function and may be scored to yield both attitude measures for individuals and frequency of specific responses in the group.

the scale. Likert scales may also be constructed entirely from favorable statements, since unfavorable attitudes can be expressed simply by disagreeing with such statements. This feature is sometimes considered an advantage of Likert scales over Thurstone scales, because some respondents may be reluctant to endorse clearly unfavorable statements. Other practical advantages of the Likert-type scale are that its development is less laborious and that satisfactory reliability can be achieved with fewer items than are required in a Thurstone-type scale (Summers, 1970, Ch. 8). For these reasons, the Likert item format is more common in attitude scales administered in industrial settings.

Several other item types have been used in attitude scales, some of which represent variants or adaptations of Thurstone or Likert types or a combination of the two. Recent methodological developments include a number of psychometric refinements, as well as such practical improvements as shortening the time required and simplifying the respondent's task. A conspicuous trend is the measurement of satisfaction with different facets of the job, often identified through prior factor-analytic research.

An example of a well-constructed and practicable attitude questionnaire is the Job Descriptive Index (P. C. Smith, 1974; Smith, Kendall, & Hulin, 1969). This instrument yields measures of job satisfaction for five aspects of the work situation: work itself, supervision, co-workers, pay, and opportunities for promotion. The first three categories contain 18 items each; the last two contain 9 each. Items consist of an adjective or short descriptive phrase, as illustrated in Table 5-2.

TABLE 5-2
Typical Items from Job Descriptive Index (JDI)

(Copyright 1975 by Bowling Green State University. Reproduced by permission. Information may be obtained from Patricia Cain Smith, Department of Psychology, Bowling Green State University, Bowling Green, Ohio 43403.)

Work	Supervision	Co-workers
Y Satisfying	Y Asks my advice	N Slow
N Boring	N Hard to please	Y Smart
Y Useful	N Quick-tempered	N Hard to meet

Pay	Promotions
Y Satisfactory profit sharing	N Dead-end job
N Underpaid	Y Good chance for promotion

Respondents are instructed to write **Y** (yes) next to each item if it correctly describes the particular aspect of their job, **N** (no) if it does not, and **?** if they cannot decide. Although the items obviously pertain to the respondents' evaluations and attitudes, they are presented as job descriptions, in order to facilitate the understanding of the task, especially by respondents with limited education and reading comprehension. The terms were chosen so as to be applicable to a wide variety of jobs and easily understood by respondents regardless of educational background.

As part of the extensive research that preceded the development of the final form of the JDI, the original item pool was administered to the same persons three times with instructions to respond in terms of their present job, the "best" job they could think of, and the "worst" job they could think of. On the basis of these responses, the most discriminating items were retained. For example, an item checked just as often to describe "best" and "worst" jobs would be discarded as probably irrelevant to job satisfaction. The score on each of the five job facets is a weighted sum of the responses to each item in the category. About half of the items in each category are favorable (requiring a **Y** answer to be counted) and half are unfavorable (requiring **N** as an answer). Available research data indicate good reliability and validity for the scores.

Another instrument illustrating features of special interest is the Minnesota Satisfaction Questionnaire (Weiss, Dawis, England, & Lofquist, 1967). Also developed through many years of research, this scale utilizes an adaptation of Likert-type items. In the terminology of operant conditioning, each item describes a reinforcer in the work environment. There are five items for each of 20 scales representing such reinforcers as ability utilization, advancement, financial compensation, relations with co-workers and with supervisors, creativity, variety of work, and working conditions. Items from each scale are distributed throughout the form with no scale identification. For each item, respondents mark one of five alternatives, indicating their degree of satisfaction with the specified element on their present job. Typical items are reproduced in Table 5-3. Item responses are scored 1 to 5, and the score on each scale is the sum of the item scores in that

TABLE 5-3
Minnesota Satisfaction Questionnaire (MSQ): Instructions and Sample Items

(Copyright 1967 by Work Adjustment Project, Department of Psychology, University of Minnesota. Reproduced by permission.)

Ask yourself: How *satisfied* am I with this aspect of my job?

"1" means I am *not satisfied* (this aspect of my job is much poorer than I would like it to be)

"2" means I am *only slightly satisfied* (this aspect of my job is not quite what I would like it to be)

"3" means I am *satisfied* (this aspect of my job is what I would like it to be)

"4" means I am *very satisfied* (this aspect of my job is even better than I expected it to be)

"5" means I am *extremely satisfied* (this aspect of my job is much better than I hoped it could be)

On my present job, this is how I feel about . . .	1	2	3	4	5
The variety in my work	☐	☐	☐	☐	☐
My job security	☐	☐	☐	☐	☐
The chance to try out some of my own ideas	☐	☐	☐	☐	☐
The amount of pay for the work I do	☐	☐	☐	☐	☐
The chance to do the kind of work that I do best	☐	☐	☐	☐	☐
The way I get full credit for the work I do	☐	☐	☐	☐	☐
The chance to be responsible for planning my work	☐	☐	☐	☐	☐
The way my boss provides help on hard problems	☐	☐	☐	☐	☐
The physical working conditions of the job	☐	☐	☐	☐	☐
The friendliness of my co-workers	☐	☐	☐	☐	☐

scale. A General Satisfaction score can also be found by summing the scores on 20 designated items, one from each scale.

The MSQ is self-administering and requires no more than a fifth-grade reading level. While research is still in progress to improve this instrument, available data on reliability and validity are generally satisfactory. Although the MSQ and the previously described JDI were developed from different orientations, it is noteworthy that a joint investigation of the two instruments revealed important correspondences and yielded data that contributed to the validation of both (Gillet & Schwab, 1975).

Of particular interest is the inclusion of the MSQ in a set of four instruments designed for a coordinated approach to the investigation of *work adjustment*, defined as "the continuous and dynamic process by which the individual seeks to achieve and maintain correspondence with his work environment" (Lofquist & Dawis, 1969, p. 46). This correspondence implies that the individual fulfills the requirements of his or her work environment (through appropriate aptitudes, skills, motivation, etc.) and that the work environment fulfills the requirements of the individual (by satisfying needs that have a high value for the worker). In addition to the MSQ, the following instruments have been developed:

Minnesota Satisfaction Scales (MSS), to measure how satisfactorily individuals perform on their jobs (Gibson, Weiss, Dawis, & Lofquist, 1970);

Minnesota Importance Questionnaire (MIQ), to assess the relative value of different vocational needs for the individual (Gay, Weiss, Hendel, Dawis, & Lofquist, 1971); and

Minnesota Job Description Questionnaire (MJDQ), to measure the kinds and amount of reinforcers provided by each job (Borgen, Weiss, Tinsley, Dawis, & Lofquist, 1968b).

To illustrate the joint application of these instruments, consider the hypothesis that the degree of correspondence between the individual's vocational needs (as measured by the MIQ) and the reinforcers available on his job (as measured by the MJDQ) should predict the amount of job satisfaction he experiences (as measured by the MSQ), provided that his abilities correspond to the ability requirements of the job. Several other similar hypotheses have been formulated and can be tested through the combined use of the four parallel questionnaires (Lofquist & Dawis, 1969). Considerable research has been stimulated by this model. It should be added that the assessment of jobs with regard to their reinforcer or need-fulfilling potentialities is being explored by several investigators (Jenkins, Nadler, Lawler, & Camman, 1975). The techniques employed for this purpose include not only questionnaires completed by supervisors or job holders, as in the MJDQ, but also interviews with supervisors or job holders and direct, on-site observations by a trained job analyst.

JOB SATISFACTION AND JOB PERFORMANCE

The improvement of job satisfaction is a desirable goal in its own right. Workers spend a large proportion of their waking hours on the job—and this part of their life should be made as pleasant and satisfying as possible. Furthermore, individuals' on-the-job experiences are likely to color their off-the-job attitudes and general feeling of well-being (Kornhauser, 1965). A satisfied work force also has many values from the standpoint of organizational effectiveness. Favorable employee attitudes tend to be associated with fewer grievances and complaints; more harmonious labor-management relations; lower rates of accidents, tardiness, absenteeism, and job turnover; more successful personnel recruitment; and better community relations. Through their influence on such behavioral outcomes, employee attitudes may have a substantial financial impact on the operation of an organization (Mirvis & Lawler, 1977).

Following misinterpretations of the Hawthorne studies, however, early management theories tried to justify a concern with job satisfaction in terms of its effect on productivity. This approach rested on a shaky foundation and was not supported by subsequent research. The relation between worker attitudes and job behavior is complex. Both the sources and the effects of job satisfaction are being extensively reexamined within a systems framework, with due attention to reciprocal causal relations and interaction of variables.

Nature and Sources of Job Satisfaction. It should be noted that attitudes often "spread" beyond their source. Employees in one department, for example, may criticize the food in the cafeteria or the vacation schedule because of a generalized dissatisfaction arising from an unreasonable supervisor. The individual may be only vaguely aware of the true source of his discontent; or he may be aware of it but still feel dissatisfied with other features of his job which he would otherwise find acceptable. In still other cases, the worker may himself correctly localize the source of dissatisfaction; but in a questionnaire or interview he may focus on other, more overtly acceptable dislikes because of a reluctance to report the real cause. In interpreting the results of attitude surveys, the investigator should be alert to these possibilities and should probe further, through intensive interviews or other procedures, in order to identify the actual source of dissatisfaction.

Job variables may interact with worker characteristics in their relation to job satisfaction. In other words, the same job variable may have a different effect on workers' job satisfaction depending upon their own interests, needs, expectations, or other personal characteristics. An example of such interaction is provided by a study of the effects of role ambiguity and role conflict on job satisfaction (Johnson & Stinson, 1975). Role ambiguity is illustrated by workers' uncertainty about their job duties, responsibilities, and authority and by lack of clarity about their supervisors' evaluation of their work. Role conflict is illustrated by receiving incompatible requests concerning the work and by being assigned tasks which one feels should not be part of the job. Both of these job variables have generally been found to be negatively correlated with job satisfaction. In this study, however, the relation was moderated by the strength of the workers' needs for achievement and for independence. Thus the effect of these role variables was not uniformly aversive; a condition that led to considerable job dissatisfaction in workers with strong achievement and independence needs might have little or no effect on workers in whom these needs were weak.

Essentially, job satisfaction depends upon the degree of correspondence between each worker's needs and the reinforcing or need-fulfilling characteristics of the job. This formulation was cited in the preceding section as a basic element in the concept of work adjustment. Since the relative value individuals place on different needs varies widely, the same objective job situation may provide a high degree of job satisfaction for some workers and dissatisfaction for others. From a somewhat different angle, job satisfaction can be considered in terms of "met expectations" (Porter & Steers, 1973). Job dissatisfaction is associated with marked discrepancies between what individuals expect to find on a job and what they actually find.

In a well-designed study of the reasons why college graduates leave jobs, the effect of such discrepancies was clearly demonstrated (Dunnette, Arvey, & Banas, 1973). When measured across 15 major job characteristics (working conditions, salary, nature of work, etc.), the discrepancies between job expectations and job experiences were considerably greater in the terminated group than in a closely comparable group of employees who remained on their jobs. A practical implication of such findings is the desirability of giving applicants accurate and realistic information about the prospective job, rather than focusing only on the more generally attractive features as in the traditional recruiting film (Wanaus, 1973).

The role of financial compensation in job satisfaction is of particular interest because money may have different meanings for different workers (Opsahl & Dunnette, 1966). For some, pay is a means of obtaining food and other necessities for oneself and one's family; for others, it signifies security; for still others, it permits the enjoyment of specific luxuries, fulfilling a variety of individual needs (e.g., for pursuing a favorite hobby or sport). The symbolic function of money also contributes to its motivational value. The amount of one's financial compensation may be perceived as recognition or concrete feedback for one's job performance, as a mark of successful achievement, as a tangible sign of social status and prestige, or simply as equitable and just compensation for one's services relative to what others receive for similar work (Finn & Lee, 1972; Pritchard, Dunnette, & Jorgenson, 1972).

A considerable body of data has also accumulated on cultural differences in the relative importance of different needs (Barrett & Bass, 1976). Such differences reflect in part deep-rooted national differences in traditional value systems. They are also affected by current social and economic conditions, as illustrated by studies in developing nations. As living conditions change over time, the relative strength of different worker needs shows corresponding changes.

Relation of Job Satisfaction to Job Behavior. One aspect of job behavior found to be clearly and consistently related to job satisfaction is *job turnover* (Brayfield & Crockett, 1955; Locke, 1976; Porter & Steers, 1973; Vroom, 1964). When surveyed as much as a year in advance, workers who left their jobs reported significantly less favorable attitudes toward various aspects of their jobs than did those who remained. Insofar as unfavorable job attitudes also tend to be correlated with absenteeism and tardiness, some investigators conceptualize a continuum of withdrawal from an aversive job situation, ranging from tardiness through absenteeism to turnover (Locke, 1975; Porter & Steers, 1973). Such withdrawal behavior is most commonly associated with discrepancies between what the worker expects and what the job provides with respect to pay, opportunities for promotion, treatment by supervisor, and such features of the work itself as responsibility, autonomy, and task variety (Porter & Steers, 1973).

In contrast to the results on withdrawal behavior, research has failed to support the hypothesized effect of job satisfaction on *productivity* (Brayfield & Crockett, 1955; Locke, 1976; Schwab & Cummings, 1975). The relationship between worker attitudes and productivity depends in part on how productivity is related to the individual's own work values and goals. For example, workers who are strongly motivated to advance to a higher level in the company may produce more for this reason and at the same time be dissatisfied with their present jobs. Or acceptance by co-workers may be of prime importance to an employee, and such acceptance may be contingent upon restriction of output to conform to a norm set by the group. This would be especially true in a cohesive group with high morale and strong feelings of loyalty. Under some circumstances, quantity and quality of output may bear a different relation to the individual's goals, as when a skilled artisan resists efforts to increase speed if he believes the quality of his work will suffer. For some persons, a high degree of expressed job satisfaction may mean no more than complacency, a condition not especially conducive to the exertion of great effort.

When a correlation is in fact found between job satisfaction and productivity, the causal relation is quite likely to be in the reverse direction from that traditionally expected (Greene, 1975; Porter & Lawler, 1968). Thus, in certain persons, successful performance produces satisfaction with their work, rather than vice versa. This type of relation has been demonstrated by means of longitudinal studies in which both variables were measured at two points in time (Greene, 1973; Wanaus, 1974). Such findings suggest that the objectives of job selection and classification, whereby applicants are placed in jobs that maximize their chances of successful performance, are fully as important for the worker as for the organization.

The relation between performance and satisfaction may also vary as a function of worker characteristics. For example, there is evidence suggesting that successful achievement is a source of task liking or satisfaction for persons with high self-esteem but not for persons with low self-esteem (Jacobs & Solomon, 1977; Korman, 1968). Similarly, the closeness of fit between the worker's abilities and the ability requirements of the job has been found to influence the relation between job satisfaction and performance (Carlson, 1969). Job satisfaction was more highly correlated with performance among those persons whose abilities closely matched job requirements than among those with poorer job fit. This finding supports the theory of work adjustment cited in the preceding section (Dawis, Lofquist, & Weiss, 1968). The investigation of such interactions among person variables, job satisfaction, and job performance is a promising area of research within the systems approach to worker attitudes.

THEORIES OF WORK MOTIVATION

The Hawthorne studies shifted the emphasis in managerial theories of worker motivation from pay and other material benefits to human relations. From the present viewpoint, both approaches appear equally limited and simplistic. The decades of the 1960s and 1970s witnessed a proliferation of theories of work motivation, with a corresponding increase in systematic, theory-oriented research. It is clearly beyond the scope of this book to survey all major theories or even to describe any one of them fully. Instead, only the highlights of representative theories will be presented. A comprehensive and well-balanced discussion of theories of work motivation is provided by Steers and Porter (1975). Shorter surveys can be found in J. P. Campbell et al., (1970, Ch. 15) and Miner and Dachler (1973).

Several current theories of work motivation represent variants, modifications, or combinations of a few focal theories. Because of such overlap, any classification of available theories is somewhat arbitrary. A convenient subdivision, which will be followed in the present discussion, is that between content and process theories (J.P. Campbell et al., 1970; Miner & Dachler, 1973). Content theories are concerned principally with those conditions or factors in the individual or his environment that energize and direct his behavior. They ask *what* motivates worker performance. Process theories, on the other hand, endeavor to explain *how* behavior is motivated. They focus on the mechanisms whereby variables of the individual and of his environment combine and interact in producing job behavior.

Content Theories. Originating in clinical psychology, the *need hierarchy* theory of Maslow (1943, 1970) was subsequently applied to an understanding of worker motivation (Maslow, 1965; McGregor, 1960). According to this theory, needs are uniformly organized into a hierarchy of prepotency, beginning with (1) basic physiological needs (e.g., air, food, water) and proceeding through needs for (2) safety and security, (3) belongingness or social acceptance, (4) esteem (achievement and recognition), and (5) self-actualization (using one's capacities to the fullest extent). When a need is satisfied, it no longer serves to motivate behavior, and the next higher need in the hierarchy emerges.

The need hierarchy theory is consistent with the common finding that workers in lower level jobs tend to stress such work values as security and pleasant relations with co-workers and supervisors, while those in higher level jobs put more emphasis on opportunities for achievement, self-expression, and challenging work (Friedlander, 1965). The nature of the jobs themselves, however, may account for some of these differences. If a job is so organized as to allow workers little or no self-expression, they must seek satisfaction in factors extrinsic to the work. This situation can be seen in semiskilled factory jobs as well as in the more routine types of clerical work. A direct test of Maslow's theory requires a fairly prolonged longitudinal study. Few investigators have undertaken such a test, and the available empirical data offer little or no support for the theory (Lawler & Suttle, 1972). It has been suggested that a simple hierarchy, possibly with only two levels, may fit the facts more closely, but this possibility remains speculative at present.

While the need hierarchy theory approaches motivation in terms of the individual's wants, the Herzberg two-factor, or *motivation-hygiene*, theory concentrates on the conditions in the work situation that can satisfy these wants (Herzberg, 1966). In the initial investigation that led to the formulation of this theory, data were gathered through intensive interviews of about 200 engineers and accountants in nine industrial plants (Herzberg, Mausner, & Snyderman 1959). In each interview, the employee was asked to think of a time when he felt exceptionally good or exceptionally bad about his job and to describe what happened. An account of both a "good" and a "bad" situation was obtained from each person. The interviewer also inquired into the duration of the situation itself and of the attitudes it engendered, the factors leading to the satisfaction or dissatisfaction (including both objective events and the individual's perception of them), and the effects of the situation on the individual's feelings, health, job performance, interpersonal relations, and other behavior.

In interpreting their findings, the authors differentiated between "satisfiers" and "dissatisfiers." Their results showed that the satisfiers (motivators), producing favorable job attitudes, usually pertain to the *job itself.* Predominant among such factors, in order of their frequency, were achievement, recognition, characteristics of the work, responsibility, and advancement. These factors center around opportunities for self-actualization and growth. Recognition was most effective when related to genuine achievement and progress. Otherwise, its effects tended to be trivial and short-lived. The dissatisfiers (hygiene factors), on the other hand, more often referred to *job context*, as illustrated by ineffective or unfair company policies, incompetence of supervisor, poor interpersonal relations with supervisor, and unsatisfactory working conditions.

It might be noted, too, that salary appeared with intermediate frequency among both satisfiers and dissatisfiers. However, mention of salary nearly always pertained to obtaining raises or failure to receive an expected raise. Thus, salary was perceived either as an instance of unfairness in supervision and company policy or as tangible recognition for achievement and as a sign of progress. With regard to the effects of attitudes, the authors concluded that dissatisfiers (contextual factors) influence principally emotional adjustment, job turnover, absenteeism, and the like. But only the satisfiers (intrinsic job factors) can provide the positive motivation to greater productivity. Thus, human relations programs and fringe benefits can at best eliminate dissatisfaction, but they cannot provide motivation for better job performance, especially of a creative nature.

An important effect of the Herzberg theory has been to point up the limitations of the human relations approach to work motivation. The theory has also stimulated extensive research, much of it by its critics. Nevertheless, this research did provide a mass of data that added to our understanding of worker attitudes and motivation. With regard to its specific propositions, however, the motivation-hygiene theory has not been supported by the findings of well-designed studies (Dunnette, Campbell, & Hakel, 1967; House & Wigdor, 1967).

The procedures followed by Herzberg and his co-workers have been widely criticized. A major weakness of their methodology is that, in the recall of satisfying and dissatisfying job incidents, respondents are likely to attribute the cause of satisfaction to their own achievement (intrinsic work factors) and to attribute dissatisfaction to external conditions (job context). This methodological artifact was further compounded by the coding process, whereby the experimenters interpreted and classified each reported incident as a satisfier or dissatisfier. When different procedures were employed to control for these methodological deficiencies, both intrinsic work factors and context factors were identified as sources of satisfaction and dissatisfaction. Whether a particular factor leads to satisfaction or dissatisfaction depends on other variables, including the nature of the job, the occupational level, and the age, education, and other characteristics of the respondent. As for the claim that satisfiers lead to greater productivity, the findings regarding job satisfaction and productivity cited in the preceding section fail to support such a causal relation. It is only when the so-called satisfiers (e.g., achievement, recognition, advancement) are made contingent upon performance that they lead to improved productivity. Under these conditions, any factor that is valued by the individual will serve as a reinforcer.

Process Theories. Two major theories address themselves principally to the motivational process rather than to specific individual needs or environmental reinforcers. *Equity* theory has its roots in several independently formulated theories of human motivation. In its application to industrial settings, it is most closely associated with the writings of J. S. Adams (1965). According to this theory, a major determinant of both job satisfaction and performance is the worker's perception of equity or inequity in the job situation.

The definition of equity is outlined in Figure 5-1. It involves essentially a

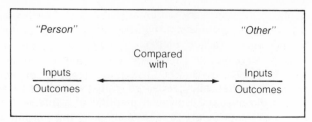

Figure 5-1. Basic elements in the concept of equity. *(As defined by J. S. Adams, 1965.)*

comparison of the person's perceived ratio of his inputs to outcomes with his perceived ratio of inputs to outcomes of a reference "other." The "other" chosen for this purpose could be a particular fellow worker, a class of workers (such as bank clerks), or even the individual himself in a prior job. Inputs refer to the individual's contributions to the job, including not only his present job performance (time, effort) but also any other attributes he perceives as relevant to the work situation, such as education and length of time on the job. Outcomes cover such rewards as pay, promotions, fringe benefits, status and privileges, and intrinsic satisfaction from the work itself. They may also include negative factors, such as poor working conditions, monotonous work, and unpleasant personal relations. It should be emphasized that the ratios refer to the individual's *perceptions* of the situation, which may or may not correspond to the objective facts or to the perceptions of another observer.

Equity theory proposes that perceived inequity between the ratios for "person" and "other" leads to dissatisfaction and to attempts to reduce the inequity by any available means.[2] An obvious way to decrease the inequity is by lowering one's productivity in response to perceived underreward (or raising it in the case of overreward). But there are a number of other possible procedures, such as trying to increase one's outcomes, as in asking for a raise, or altering one's perceptions, as in devaluing a promotion.

Although equity theory is applicable to any type of outcome, most of the relevant research has dealt with pay (Goodman & Friedman, 1971; Lawler, 1968; Pritchard, 1969; Pritchard et al., 1972). While the major hypotheses of equity theory have generally been supported, others have either been inadequately tested or have produced mixed results. It has also been suggested that the theory is limited in scope and that parts of it could most effectively be incorporated into a more comprehensive theory.

A theory of work motivation that is widely accepted by industrial psychologists and is stimulating an increasing amount of research is commonly known as *expectancy* theory.[3] Like equity theory, expectancy theory is expressed in cognitive terms, taking as its starting point the worker's perceptions of the job situation. As applied to work settings, the theory was first formulated by Vroom (1964) and has been elaborated by Porter and Lawler (1968) among others. Its basic proposition is

---

[2]The reader familiar with the theory of cognitive dissonance (Festinger, 1957) will recognize its similarity to equity theory in this regard.

[3]Also designated by such names as instrumentality theory, expectancy/valence theory, and valence-instrumentality-expectancy theory (V-I-E), although these names are sometimes used to identify variants of the theory.

that an individual's behavior is motivated by his expectation that the behavior will lead to certain outcomes, together with his evaluation of these outcomes. A major concept of the theory is "valence," or an individual's affective preference for particular outcomes. Valences may be positive or negative, insofar as outcomes may be desirable or undesirable. Another major concept is "expectancy," or an individual's estimate of the probability that a certain act will be followed by a particular outcome. Expectancies depend upon such factors as self-confidence, prior experiences in similar situations, observation of the present situation, and communications from others (Lawler, 1973).

Essentially, expectancy theory proposes that the motivational force to perform an act is the product of the expectancy of an outcome by its valence. The overall expectancy can itself be divided into two types (Steers & Porter, 1975, p. 182):

1. $(E \rightarrow P)$: Expectancy that a certain action or effort (E) will lead to a desired performance (P). For example, if a salesperson increases the number of calls per day (E), what is the likelihood that his or her sales will increase (P)?
2. $(P \rightarrow O)$: Expectancy that the performance (P) will lead to a particular outcome (O), such as a pay raise or bonus.

The more detailed formula for motivational force (F) would thus read:

$$F = (E \rightarrow P) \times (P \rightarrow O) \times V$$

Further elaborations are illustrated in Figure 5-2. For example, the individual's effort could lead to success (Performance A) or failure (Performance B) in achieving the desired result, such as increased sales. Moreover, some outcomes (X) provide intrinsic satisfaction, while others (Y) are instrumental in achieving more remote outcomes (Z). Still other outcomes (N) will occur regardless of the success or failure of the individual's action. In such an expanded model, motivational force is conceptualized as a function of the net combined effect of all relevant expectancies and valences.

Among the criticisms of expectancy theories are their increasing complexity and the lack of clarity of some of their implications. Both conditions make hypothesis testing difficult and the interpretation of negative results ambiguous (Locke, 1975; T. R. Mitchell, 1974). Some of the difficulties stem from the use of unobservable, cognitive processes as causal constructs. The substitution of operant conditioning models would probably avoid such difficulties.

Overview. It should now be apparent that none of these theories of work motivation is complete in itself. Each has limitations, and its usefulness may vary with the type of situation to which it is applied. Some investigators utilize composite theories which incorporate features of two or more theories. Elements of all four can be recognized in some formulations. Each theory has expanded our understanding of work motivation by focusing attention on an important set of variables or relationships within the total job-performance system, and each has stimulated systematic, theory-oriented research.

The general picture that emerges shows work motivation to be complex in its interrelationships and multivariate in its coverage. It encompasses many worker needs (whose relative strength varies among individuals) and many features of both the work itself and the job context. The determinants and effects of worker motivation can be best conceptualized through a systems approach, with due

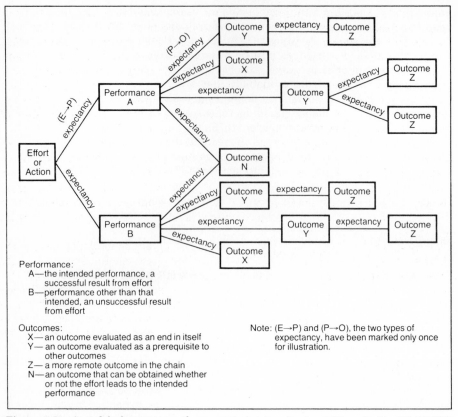

Figure 5-2. A model of expectancy theory. *(Adapted from Lawler, 1973, p. 50. Copyright © 1973 by Wadsworth Publishing Company, Inc. Reprinted by permission of the publisher, Brooks/Cole Publishing Company, Monterey, California.)*

attention to interactions among variables of both the person and the job.

The concepts and methods of *operant conditioning* are gradually being introduced into the study of work motivation (Hamner, 1974; Jablonsky & DeVries, 1972; Nord, 1969).[4] This approach can provide hypotheses that are at once simpler, more widely applicable, and more amenable to experimental verification than are the hypotheses proposed by other theories. It also holds promise of unifying and coordinating the contributions of different theories. A fundamental principle of operant conditioning is that of *contingency*. To be effective, a "reward" or reinforcement should be immediately contingent on the desired performance and proportional to the performance level. Nord (1969) suggests, for example, that the chief difference between Herzberg's motivators and hygiene factors is that the former are usually contingent on the individual's own responses and the latter are not. Hence the motivators are more likely to reinforce good performance.

---

[4]For an account of a successful practical application in an industrial setting, see Tosi and Hamner (1974), pp. 113–122.

An effective *schedule of reinforcement* is a further way of assuring the establishment and maintenance of the desired behavior (Hamner, 1974). One of the most successful is the variable ratio schedule, whereby reinforcement is received after a certain number of desired responses, this number varying around an average. Lotteries, slot machines, and other forms of gambling provide rewards on a variable ratio schedule—a fact which may help to explain the strong motivation and sustained interest of the players. Again referring to Herzberg's motivators, Nord (1969) observes that these rewards, which derive from the intrinsic nature of the work, are most likely to follow a variable ratio schedule.

Jablonsky and DeVries (1972) describe an extended operant-conditioning model that incorporates some of the concepts of expectancy theory. This model attempts to meet many of the objections that have been raised against the application of an oversimplified operant-conditioning model to worker behavior. The authors also include in their model the multiple sources of reinforcement that are likely to operate in an industrial situation, as when supervisors and co-workers reinforce incompatible behavior in the worker.

It should be noted that expectancy theory and operant conditioning have much in common. Both emphasize the need for contingent reinforcement. A major difference between them, however, pertains to schedules of reinforcement. According to expectancy theory, continuous reinforcement should be more effective than a variable ratio schedule, while the opposite is predicted by the operant-conditioning model. Although research to test these alternative predictions in a job situation is meager, available data from at least one suggestive study support the operant conditioning hypothesis (Yukl, Wexley, & Seymore, 1972).

SUMMARY

Worker attitudes and motivation combine with the effects of selection and training in determining both job satisfaction and job performance. The Hawthorne studies focused attention on human relations in management, but later research demonstrated the limitations of this approach. From a methodological standpoint, the Hawthorne effect highlighted the need to control for the influence of attitudinal variables and feedback in the design of psychological experiments.

The principal procedures for assessing worker attitudes include interviewing, projective and other indirect techniques, opinion surveys regarding specific features of the job, and attitude scales for measuring job satisfaction. Attitudes may spread beyond their source. They often reflect an interaction between job variables and worker characteristics. Job satisfaction depends on the degree of correspondence between the individual's needs and the reinforcing or need-fulfilling characteristics of the particular job. Job satisfaction is inversely related to tardiness, absenteeism, and turnover. Its relation to productivity is more complex, depending upon individual and situational variables. When a relation is found, it is more likely that high productivity causes job satisfaction, rather than the reverse. To improve productivity, rewards must be contingent upon performance.

Theories of work motivation may be classified into those concerned chiefly with content (needs, incentives) and those concerned with process (how motivating variables operate and interact). Content theories are illustrated by the need

hierarchy and the motivator-hygiene theories. Process theories are best represented by equity theory and expectancy theory. Each of these theories has advanced
the understanding of work motivation by calling attention to an important set of
motivational variables or relationships. Elements of these theories may be effectively combined in a more comprehensive systems approach to motivation. The
principles of operant conditioning may help in integrating the contributions of
different theories and in providing more clearly formulated and more readily
testable hypotheses.

ORGANIZATIONAL PSYCHOLOGY

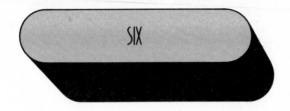

SIX

RGANIZATION THEORY is an interdisciplinary field concerned with the structure and functioning of organizations and the activities of the people within them. Its contributors have been drawn from such disciplines as economics, engineering, sociology, and psychology (Dunnette, 1976, Sect. V; Hackman, Lawler, & Porter, 1977; Lichtman & Hunt, 1971; Pugh, 1966). Traditionally, organization theorists have applied various generalized models of human behavior, with little attention to individual differences or interaction effects.

The more recently emerging field of organizational psychology represents the application of psychological methodology to the behavior of individuals in organizational settings. In its broadest sense, it covers the whole of industrial psychology, approaching all problems of effective performance from a systems orientation. In this sense, organizational psychology includes the previously considered areas of recruiting, selection, classification, training, and motivation, as well as engineering psychology (discussed in later chapters). Organizational goals and objectives clearly underlie and affect all personnel policies and procedures (Bass, 1968). In evaluating the job performance of a salesperson, for example, one needs to balance such organizational goals as number of nonrepeat sales versus long-term customer satisfaction.

More commonly, the term "organizational psychology" is used to designate those areas of industrial psychology derived chiefly from personality theory and social psychology. It is in this sense that the term is used in this book. Within this narrower definition of organizational psychology, Chapter 5 was concerned with research and theories about worker attitudes and motivation. The present chapter focuses on the managerial policies and procedures formulated on the basis of such available knowledge. Although most research and writings on organizational psychology refer to industrial settings, the field covers all types of organizations, such as school systems, hospitals, government agencies, and military units. Increasingly, organizational psychology is being applied in these other contexts. A number of psychologists are engaged in the growing professional specialty of organization development (OD), which is concerned with the dual goal of increasing organizational effectiveness and enhancing worker satisfaction (Alderfer, 1977; Friedlander & Brown, 1974).

Modern organizational psychology is essentially systems-oriented in its approach to personnel problems. By its very nature, it should bring together many variables that were traditionally considered independently, such as worker traits, characteristics of job tasks, and features of the working environment. Not surprisingly, research in organizational psychology is identifying significant interactions among such variables. Apparently inconsistent results of earlier fragmentary studies are gradually being fitted into more comprehensive—and comprehensible—patterns. These promising developments do not gainsay the fact that the vast accumulation of writings about organizational and managerial psychology reveals much confusion, an abundance of empty verbiage, and a plethora of new catchwords for weak theories. It is against this dismal background that signs of genuine progress are becoming discernible.

LEADERSHIP AND SUPERVISION

The type of leadership provided by one's immediate supervisor is undoubtedly a significant determiner of both job satisfaction and job performance. The Hawthorne studies ushered in a long period of overemphasis on the human relations role of the supervisor, which is still reflected in simplistic views of supervisory functions. A brief look at a sample of research on supervisory behavior will provide some notion of the actual complexities involved.

The Michigan Studies. A series of investigations conducted at the Institute for Social Research of the University of Michigan has been concerned with the characteristics of successful supervisors (Likert, 1961). Over 70 studies were carried out in many different industries, as well as in hospitals, government agencies, and voluntary organizations. Data were gathered at all management levels and on workers in a wide variety of jobs, from unskilled labor and clerical work to scientific research. The general design of these studies involved essentially a comparison of the supervisory practices followed in the "best" and "poorest" units of an organization. These units were identified on the basis of such criteria as productivity, job satisfaction, turnover, and absenteeism. A major finding of the Michigan studies was that supervisors of the high-producing units were more often "employee-centered," while supervisors of low-producing units were more often "job-centered." By "employee-centered" the investigators mean specifically that the supervisors place the primary emphasis on the human problems of the workers; they are friendly and supportive toward the worker, trying to build and maintain the individual's sense of personal worth; and they provide only general supervision, allowing considerable individual freedom in carrying out the job. In contrast, the job-centered supervisors place primary emphasis on production itself, seeing that the workers use the prescribed methods and overseeing their work closely.

The investigators recognized, of course, that such comparative studies do not in themselves permit an analysis of cause-and-effect relations. It is conceivable, for example, that low group productivity leads to closer supervision and more pressure on the part of the supervisor, rather than vice versa. There is some suggestive experimental data indicating that worker output can in fact produce changes in supervisory behavior (Farris & Lim, 1969; Lowin & Craig, 1968). In subsequent publications, Likert and his associates (Likert, 1967; Likert & Bowers, 1969) call attention to the need for longitudinal studies in order to identify causal relations, and they report that such studies are in progress at Michigan. Moreover, in commenting on the inconsistent results of different investigators regarding the effects of supervisory style on worker attitudes and productivity, they observe that such effects may require several years to become fully manifested and hence would not be detected in short-term studies.

The Ohio State Studies. Another approach to supervision is illustrated by the Ohio State Leadership Studies, one of which was cited in Chapter 4 in connection with the evaluation of human relations training. That study identified two major dimensions of supervisory behavior: "Consideration," characterized by a friendly, warm, considerate supervisory relationship, as contrasted with an impersonal and authoritarian relationship; and "Initiating Structure," pertaining to the extent to which the supervisor actively plans and directs group activities oriented toward goal attainment (Fleishman, 1953a; Stodgill & Coons, 1957).

These two dimensions will be recognized as bearing a general resemblance to the employee-centered and job-centered orientations identified by the Michigan group. In the Ohio State research, however, the two characteristics were found to be independent dimensions. In other words, an individual's rating on one is unrelated to his rating on the other. It was found further that supervisors rating low on both traits proved to be weak and ineffective leaders who were often bypassed by their own subordinates (Fleishman, Harris, & Burtt, 1955). Although the results varied somewhat with the situation, in general the most effective leaders were above average in both Consideration and Initiating Structure. Supervisors emphasizing either dimension at the expense of the other tended to be less effective. It might be added that the Michigan investigators, too, observed that the foremen in charge of high-producing units tended to be *both* employee-centered and oriented toward high production goals (Likert, 1961, p. 8). But this relationship is not clearly demonstrated or emphasized in the published accounts of the Michigan research.

Further research on the dimensions of Consideration and Initiating Structure indicated that the relation between these supervisory characteristics and certain indices of employee morale may be curvilinear (Fleishman & Harris, 1962). Thus, both employee grievances and turnover within different units of a manufacturing plant were related to supervisors' ratings in these dimensions only at the extremes of low Consideration and high Structure. Beyond certain critical levels, increasing Consideration or decreasing Structure had no effect on grievance and turnover rates. The same investigation revealed some interaction effects between the two supervisory dimensions. Grievance rates were uniformly high among workers whose foremen were low in Consideration, regardless of the degree of Structure the foremen exhibited. Similarly, for foremen high in Consideration, grievance rates were low regardless of degree of Structure. For foremen at intermediate levels of Consideration, however, grievance rate rose steeply from low to high levels of Structure. A similar interaction of Structure and Consideration was found against a criterion of quality of performance (Cummins, 1971).

Interactions of Supervisory Style with Worker and Job Variables. There is considerable evidence that the relative effectiveness of different supervisory styles depends on the cultural background and personality characteristics of the workers, as well as on the nature of the work. Neither Consideration nor Structure shows a consistent relation to worker satisfaction or performance criteria (Korman, 1966). Research in different countries has revealed national differences in preferred supervisory styles on the part of both workers and supervisors (e.g., Barrett & Bass, 1976; Gough, Misiti, & Parisi, 1971; Haire, Ghiselli, & Porter, 1966; Ryterbrand & Barrett, 1970). Other studies have found significant interactions between supervisory style and personality characteristics of workers and supervisors (Herold, 1974; Runyon, 1973; Vroom, 1964; Weed, Mitchell, & Moffitt, 1976).

On the basis of research with a wide variety of work groups, Fiedler (1967; Fiedler & Chemers, 1974) developed a model of leadership effectiveness involving the interaction of leadership style with variables of the task and the work context. Other things being equal, nondirective, human-relations-oriented leadership tends to be more effective with unstructured tasks in which performance is relatively undefined. Directive, task-oriented leadership, on the other hand, tends to be more effective with highly structured tasks, performed according to standard operating procedures. Other moderating variables include the quality of leader–member relations (trust, acceptance of leader) and the degree of official power of the leader (e.g., power to hire and promote, permanence of one's own position).

Fiedler combines the three moderator variables into a scale of favorableness of the leadership situation. Within this framework, he analyzes group performance effectiveness under different leadership styles. His results indicate that the human-relations-oriented style (Consideration) is most effective in situations of intermediate favorableness, while the task-oriented style (Initiating Structure) is most effective at the extremes of either very favorable or very unfavorable leadership. These two extremes could be illustrated by a well-liked supervisor of a construction crew working from a blueprint (favorable or easy extreme) and an unpopular chairman of a volunteer committee preparing a policy statement (unfavorable or difficult situation). A leadership situation at an intermediate degree of favorableness could be illustrated by a department chairman in a large university. Pertinent features of this situation include: (1) the work task of specialized teaching and research is highly unstructured; (2) the chairman would not occupy his position unless he enjoyed the trust and esteem of at least a sizable majority of his department; and (3) his own position is not permanent and carries limited administrative power.

Although most research has concentrated on the effects of leadership style on worker performance, some investigators have been concerned with the variables that influence leader behavior (Barrow, 1976). There is evidence from several sources indicating that leaders do adapt their behavior to situational contingencies. It appears, moreover, that Initiating Structure is more responsive to task complexity, while Consideration is more responsive to level of worker performance.

Overview. It is evident that there is no one simple formula for improving supervision. Here, as in all situations involving interpersonal relations, there is no set of rules for "getting along with people." As Likert (1961) pointed out, effective supervision must be adaptive and relative. Procedures that work for one person or in one situation may be useless or harmful with another person or in a different situation. Because of differences in past experiences, workers vary in the way they perceive the same behavior on the part of a supervisor. Employees also vary in their values, goals, and expectations. Personality differences, too, may make one worker welcome additional responsibility and freedom from supervision, whereas another feels lost and insecure in the same situation.

A second important factor is the personality and habitual behavior of the supervisor himself. Any sudden change in the supervisor's manner or procedures, such as might occur after a supervisory training program, may be viewed with suspicion and distrust by his subordinates. Moreover, supervisory practices that are inconsistent with the supervisor's personality and run counter to his deep-rooted behavior patterns are likely to be superficial and insincere. In this lies one of the chief fallacies of the popular books and high-pressure courses on how to get along with people. Such an approach to interpersonal relations leads to behavior that is contrived and deliberate, rather than spontaneous and forthright.

Another significant factor is the leadership climate or managerial context within which supervisors must function. Important as their jobs are, first-line supervisors cannot operate in a vacuum. Their overall success as supervisors, as well as the relative effectiveness of specific supervisory practices, depends upon the company's organizational structure, the attitudes of higher management, and other situational conditions. It will be recalled from Chapter 4 that a follow-up study of the effects of supervisory training, conducted at the International Harvester Company, revealed the importance of "leadership climate" as represented by the behavior, attitudes, and expectations of the foreman's own supervisor. In a still later follow-up, it was found that the supervisors rated as most proficient those foremen whose scores (unknown to the raters), were high in Initiating Structure and low in Consideration (Fleishman & Bass, 1974, p. 292). This occurred despite the fact that foremen with this trait pattern had work groups with higher rates of accidents, absenteeism, and turnover than did those with other patterns. Apparently these foremen received high ratings because they fitted the stereotype of effective leadership. The merit ratings were thus reinforcing supervisory practices that were inconsistent with those taught in the supervisory training course.

Finally, it must be recognized that, for effective supervision, an employee-centered, human relations point of view is not enough. Some traditional, directive organizational programs function effectively, while some human relations programs are rejected by workers (Katzell, 1962). Argyris (1974), a leading exponent of the human relations approach, has published a candid report of an attempt at organizational development focused on the improvement of interpersonal relations in a newspaper office, which proved an utter failure (see also Dubin, 1975). The limitations of the human relations approach were noted by some of the Michigan investigators, were more clearly demonstrated in some of the Ohio State studies, and were vigorously expounded by Herzberg and his associates (1959) in the report of their previously cited investigation of employee atttiudes. Herzberg emphasized the importance of the sense of achievement that can be provided by the work itself. Part of the supervisor's role in this connection is to recognize good work and to reward it selectively—rather than praising indiscriminately just because to do so is "good human relations"! It might be noted that such selective rewarding, or contingent reinforcement, is also indicated by the principles of operant conditioning.

PARTICIPATIVE MANAGEMENT

One of the chief results of the human relations movement in management has been a growing emphasis on employee participation in decision making (Frost, Wakeley, & Ruh, 1974; Likert, 1961, 1967; McGregor, 1960). There is some variation, however, in the nature and extent of participation that is advocated, the mechanics for implementing it, and the extent to which it involves group or individual responsibility.

The Group-Dynamics Approach. Likert (1961, 1967) typifies the group-dynamics approach in his advocacy of group-decision processes at all levels. To this end, he proposes a "linking-pin" type of organizational structure consisting of many overlapping groups that extend across adjacent management levels. Each foreman, for example, would participate in decision-making conferences with the employees in his work unit and would also participate with other foremen and their supervisor in similar conferences at the next level. Thus the supervisor in one group is a subordinate in the next, and so on at successive levels. Horizontal as well as vertical linkages are built into this system. The emphasis on groups rather than on individuals is quite evident in this approach, as illustrated by Likert's statement that "an organization will function best when its personnel function not as individuals but as members of highly effective work groups with high performance goals" (1961, p. 105).

Group participation in decision making has been incorporated by Likert and his associates into an elaborated version of the employee-centered management style, designated as "System 4." Likert (1967) classifies management systems into four types, which he labels: (1) exploitative authoritative, (2) benevolent authoritative, (3) consultative, and (4) participative group.[1] Each system is described in terms of detailed items of managerial behavior, classified under such headings as motivations, communications, interactions, decision making, goal setting, and control. In a questionnaire used by the Michigan researchers in studying management beliefs and practices, these items are rated on graphic rating scales ranging from typical System 1 behavior to typical System 4 behavior. Figure 6-1 illustrates three of the items from the decision-making category.

The Harwood-Weldon Studies. One of the most widely quoted early studies of employee participation was conducted at the Harwood Manufacturing Company, a pajama factory (Coch & French, 1948). Certain necessary changes in the design of the garments required new work assignments for the operators. As is usually the case, the workers had reacted with considerable resistance to previous changes. Even when their earnings are protected, workers resent having to learn new work methods. As a result, production drops, and grievances, absenteeism, and turnover increase. At the time of the investigation, four equated work groups were formed. One group of 13 served as a control, being merely informed of the change in the usual way. Two groups of 7 and 8 workers actively participated with management in planning the changes. A fourth group of 18 was represented by two members,

---

[1]Systems 1 and 2 correspond roughly to McGregor's (1960) Theory X, Systems 3 and 4 to his Theory Y.

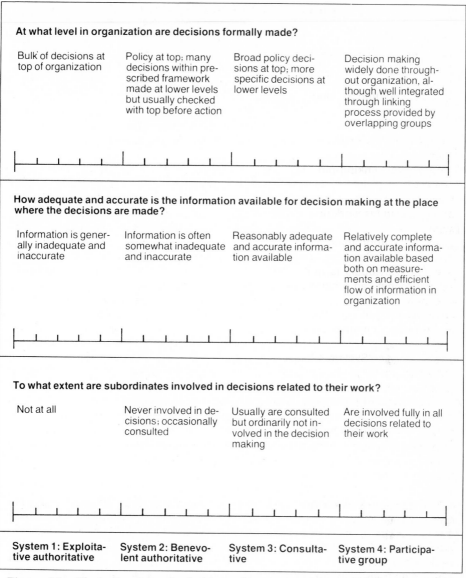

Figure 6-1. Illustrative items in decision-making category from Likert rating scale of managerial style. *(Adapted from Likert, 1967, pp. 205, 207. Copyright © by McGraw-Hill, Inc. Reproduced by permission.)*

who participated with management in making the changes and discussed developments with the rest of the group.

With regard to productivity, the two groups with full participation showed less drop after the changeover, faster recovery, and higher ultimate level of output than did the control group. The group with limited participation yielded intermediate

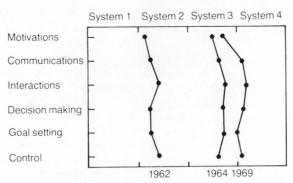

Figure 6-2. Change in managerial style at Weldon Plant as reported by supervisors and managers. *(Adapted from Seashore & Bowers, 1970, Fig. 3, p. 231. Copyright © 1960 by American Psychological Association. Reproduced by permission.)*

results.[2] The experimental groups also had fewer grievances and turnover after the change than did the control group. Several months after the original experiment, the control group was given full participation before undergoing another change of procedure. On this occasion, its productivity record equaled that of the experimental groups. A later report from the same company records the successful introduction of extensive changes in production methods with the help of a companywide program of employee participation (French, Ross, Kirby, Nelson, & Smyth, 1958).

In 1962, the Harwood Manufacturing Company purchased the Weldon Company, another pajama manufacturer which had been unprofitable for several years. At the time of acquisition, a number of changes in management procedures were introduced. The effects of these changes were analyzed in a longitudinal study conducted by Michigan researchers in collaboration with Harwood's board chairman, himself an industrial social psychologist (Marrow, Bowers, & Seashore, 1967; Seashore & Bowers, 1970). Figure 6-2 shows the managerial style followed at the Weldon plant as perceived by its managerial personnel and recorded on the Likert questionnaire at the time of acquisition, as well as two and seven years later. The shift from the authoritative toward the participative end of the scale is clearly apparent. Similar changes in reported worker satisfaction with various aspects of their jobs were found over the same period. Concurrently, productivity increased, as shown in the two-year comparison given in Figure 6-3. Although comparable productivity data are not available for later years, the investigators report that productivity remained approximately stable (Seashore & Bowers, 1970).

Although the findings of the Harwood-Weldon studies have been widely cited as evidence of the effects of increased worker participation in decision making, it should be noted that many organizational changes were introduced within a short time. Like much applied research, these field studies were designed to evaluate the impact of a composite program of organizational development which comprised a

[2]But note that Fleishman (1965), in a similar study in the garment industry, found evidence that the critical factor in productivity was not individual participation but rather the awareness that the group was *represented* in decision making.

multiplicity of variables. Not only were there other interrelated changes in managerial practices, as reflected in the perceived shift toward Likert's System 4, but there
were also various other kinds of innovations in personnel procedures. Among the
latter were several training programs, including especially the retraining and
coaching of poor performers; new production methods with a pay rate increase;
the introduction of tests for employee selection; and the discharge of chronic low
performers and chronic absentees. Some attempts were made to identify the
contribution of different factors to productivity by analyzing productivity data
immediately following the introduction of each change. But the results of such an
analysis are highly tentative (Marrow, Bowers, & Seashore, 1967, Ch. 12).

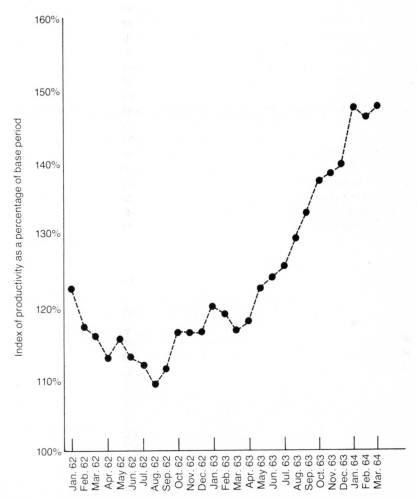

Figure 6-3. Index of productivity based on average hourly earnings per month of employees
on piece rate in the Weldon plant, expressed as percentage of base period. *(From Likert, 1967,
Fig. 3-9, p. 37. Copyright © 1967 by McGraw-Hill, Inc. Reproduced by permission.)*

Limitations in the Effectiveness of Participation. While participation in decision making is undoubtedly a fruitful managerial procedure to explore in specific
situations, its effects on both job satisfaction and job performance are not
uniformly favorable (Heller & Clark, 1976; Lowin, 1968). More research is needed
on the interaction of participation with variables of the workers and the work
situation. There is evidence that worker traits moderate the effects of participation
(Vroom, 1959). For example, degree of perceived participation was found to
correlate significantly with both job attitudes and job performance ratings among
persons with a high need for independence. But it showed no significant relation
with these criteria among those with a low need for independence.

That the nature of the work may moderate the effects of participative management was demonstrated in a study of four organizational units by Morse and
Lorsch (1970). Two of the units had been selected as a highly effective and a
relatively ineffective unit in a company manufacturing containers on high-speed,
automated production lines; the other two units were similarly chosen in a
research and development company in the field of communications technology. In
the manufacturing company, the high-performing unit was characterized by more
tightly prescribed procedures, many more rules and regulations, and much less
worker influence on decision making than was the low-performing unit. In the
research and development company, the differences in worker influence and
organizational climate between high-performing and low-performing units were in
the opposite direction. These results were confirmed in later studies in other,
similar organizations (Lorsch & Morse, 1974). The investigators explained their
results in terms of the fit between task and organizational variables. The effectively
performing units are those in which management practices are appropriate to the
nature of the job tasks and to the predominant characteristics of the workers.

From another angle, whether individual or group decisions are superior depends on the nature of the problem to be solved. Such questions as degree of
technical knowledge or expertise required would certainly affect the optimal extent
of effective participation in decision making. There has been considerable research, too, on the so-called risky shift, or the tendency for group decisions to
involve more risk taking than do decisions reached by individuals (R. D. Clark,
1971; Wallach, Kogan, & Bem, 1964). Still another pertinent consideration is the
effect of group decision making on the worker's perception of his or her own
individuality. Although there are many conditions in the work situation that
contribute to the individuation or deindividuation of the person (J. P. Campbell et
al., 1970, pp, 428–440; Ziller, 1964), the implications of group participation need to
be examined from this viewpoint.

Management by Objectives. A special application of participative management is
to be found in management by objectives (MBO). First popularized in the 1950s
(Drucker, 1954; McGregor, 1957), MBO received increasing attention in the next
two decades. It was introduced principally as a means of making performance
appraisal more systematic and realistic. In applying MBO, different levels of
management jointly define the goals or objectives of an organization. These
objectives are communicated to workers and used as a guide for evaluating each
worker's performance. Such a procedure should reduce role ambiguity and clarify
job expectations besides providing an objective and job-related basis for assessing
performance.

Obviously, MBO involves wide participation in goal setting at all management levels, from top executives to first-line supervisors of small work units. The extent to which nonsupervisory workers participate in influencing decisions, however, may vary from the total participation implied in Likert's System 4 to simply having each supervisor communicate specific objectives to the workers in his or her unit. The optimum level and nature of such participation depends upon the previously cited variables of the job and the worker.

To be effective, MBO requires the systematic and explicit formulation of genuine, realistic goals. Much attention has been given to procedures for identifying goals (Carroll & Tosi, 1973; Gross, 1965; Steers & Porter, 1974). Broad-based organizational objectives must be translated into specific task goals for successively smaller organizational units, extending ultimately to the individual worker. Action plans for implementing the objectives must be specified and performance standards established to gauge the attainment of goals. The total system of objectives should be comprehensive and should take into account the relative importance of different goals. Possible conflicts between objectives need to be resolved. While clarity of goal formulation should be sought, there should still be sufficient flexibility to permit the exercise of initiative when appropriate and to provide for adaptation to changing conditions.

Management by objectives provides several advantages, apart from the benefits of broad participation in decision making. At higher management levels, the clear formulation of goals permits better planning and more efficient utilization of resources. It facilitates coordination of the activities of different units and helps to reduce overlap, duplication, and conflict of functions. At all levels, working toward clearly defined goals leads to better performance and higher productivity than can be attained by merely trying to "do one's best." Goals are especially effective if their difficulty is adjusted to the skill and other characteristics of the individual. There is evidence from both laboratory and industrial studies that, regardless of who sets the goals, performance is favorably affected by the presence of goals (Kim & Hamner, 1976; Latham & Kinne, 1974; Locke, 1968, 1975; Ronan, Latham, & Kinne, 1973; Steers & Porter, 1974). From another angle, when task goals are communicated to workers and the relation of these goals to broader organizational objectives is clarified, the workers' jobs may become more meaningful to them, thereby enhancing job satisfaction. Still another advantage of MBO stems from its feedback procedures, which facilitate learning and performance improvement.

In terms of operant conditioning, MBO can be regarded as one more application of contingent reinforcement. Insofar as performance appraisal focuses on specific elements of performance that are consistent with the attainment of clearly defined objectives, the required performance is reinforced by the feedback given the worker. Such contingent reinforcement will be especially effective if performance appraisal is linked with the reward system, as illustrated by pay increases, bonuses, promotions, fringe benefits, and the like.

JOB DESIGN

The process of job design includes three phases: identification of individual tasks to be performed; specification of the method for performing each task; and combination of tasks into jobs to be assigned to individual workers. In the effort to reduce operating costs, industrial engineers relied chiefly on the principle of *specialization* in job design. The objectives of specialization are to minimize skill requirements and learning time for each job and to limit the number and variety of tasks to be performed by each worker. At the same time, there has been growing recognition of the adverse effects of extreme specialization on the worker, notably through the increase in monotony and the loss of a sense of personal achievement. Traditionally, however, industrial psychologists have accepted the content of each job as fixed by the production process and have tried to improve worker satisfaction through interpersonal relations and other factors extrinsic to the work.

Since the mid-1960s there has been an upsurge of interest in modifying job content itself in the effort to improve both job satisfaction and performance. One of the first and most vigorous exponents of this approach was Herzberg (1968), whose motivation-hygiene theory had focused attention on the work itself as a source of motivators or satisfiers (Ch. 5). It should be added that, with the increasing automation of industrial processes, there is less need for human operators to perform routine tasks and more and more need for skilled personnel to carry on the varied and demanding jobs of maintenance, troubleshooting, and equipment development.

Several ways of reversing the trend toward job specialization have been explored (Friedlander & Brown, 1974; Maher, 1971). At a very simple level, *job rotation* may reduce monotony by having each worker perform different operations in a rotated order rather than performing a single operation all the time. A procedure developed chiefly in England and the Scandinavian countries replaces the assembly-line type of operation with small, cohesive *work groups* operating as semiautonomous teams (Emery & Thorsrud, 1969; Emery & Trist, 1965; R. B. Goldman, 1976; Hill, 1971; Trist & Bamforth, 1951). *Job enlargement* tackles the problem by increasing the number and variety of operations performed by each individual. This approach involves the horizontal extension of job functions, since all operations are at the same level of skill and responsibility.

In contrast, *job enrichment*[3] includes both vertical and horizontal extension. It comprises not only more varied work content but also more autonomy and responsibility in planning and carrying out the work. The operations are self-paced, rather than being automatically paced as in an assembly line. Workers are responsible for quality control, inspecting their own work and correcting errors. The job also becomes more meaningful insofar as it usually entails the completion of a whole, identifiable unit task or product. Performance feedback is often an integral part of the process. Participation in job redesign may or may not be included. Herzberg (1968), for instance, argues against worker participation in this situation, whereas the Michigan group advocates it strongly.

Several field studies have demonstrated beneficial effects of job enrichment (Ford, 1969; Herzberg, 1968; Lawler, 1969). Although most studies have used control groups, the experimental designs still make the identification of causal relations difficult. Especially is this true because of the large number of changes in work content and procedures introduced simultaneously by job enrichment programs. In general, the observed effects of job enrichment include a rise in job satisfaction and a drop in turnover and absenteeism. Job performance shows improvements in quality more often than in quantity of output. It is possible that the rise in quality results partly from the fact that workers inspect and correct their own

---

[3]The terms "job enlargement" and "job enrichment" have been used with inconsistent meanings by some writers (see, e.g., Herzberg, 1968; Hulin & Blood, 1968).

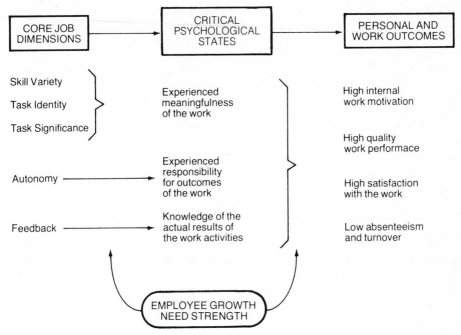

Figure 6-4. A theoretical model of job enrichment. (*From Hackman & Oldham, 1975, Fig. 1, p. 161. Copyright © 1975 by American Psychological Association. Reproduced by permission.*)

work rather than from their making fewer errors in the first place (Hulin & Blood, 1968). Moreover, the type of worker satisfactions enhanced by job enrichment are more likely to reinforce job behavior associated with quality than with quantity of production.

The analysis of job enrichment has been substantially clarified and systematized by Hackman and Oldham (1975), who offer a conceptual model and a measuring instrument. The model, reproduced in Figure 6-4, brings together the principal features (core job dimensions) and the effects of job enlargement.[4] Each of the core job dimensions is measured in the Job Diagnostic Survey (JDS), a questionnaire completed by workers in the job under investigation. The score on each core job dimension is combined through the following formula to find a Motivating Potential Score (MPS) for the job:

$$\text{MPS} = \left[\frac{\text{Skill Variety} + \text{Task Identity} + \text{Task Significance}}{3} \right] \times \text{Autonomy} \times \text{Feedback}$$

The MPS may be used to assess jobs both before and after enrichment. The JDS also provides measures of three "critical psychological states" that serve as

[4]It is likely that, with further research, this model may be simplified or otherwise modified (Dunham, 1976). In its present form, it should be regarded chiefly as a means of advancing constructive thinking about job enrichment.

intervening variables in the model, as well as measures of several indices of job satisfaction and work motivation. Finally, it includes a measure of "employee growth need strength," chosen as the most relevant worker variable which interacts with job characteristics in moderating the effects of the job enrichment program. This variable refers to the value the individual places on deriving feelings of accomplishment and personal growth from his or her work.

At this point, we again encounter the familiar refrain about interaction. There is a growing body of data indicating that the effects of job enrichment on job satisfaction and work motivation vary with worker characteristics and contextual variables (Hackman & Oldham, 1975; Hulin & Blood, 1968; Locke, Sirota, & Wolfson, 1976; Oldham, Hackman, & Pearce, 1976; Porter, Lawler, & Hackman, 1975, Ch. 10). Cultural background has been found to affect workers' reactions to job enrichment. For example, white-collar workers, as well as blue-collar workers from small-town or rural backgrounds, tend to respond favorably to increased job complexity and responsibility, while blue-collar workers from large urban centers tend to respond unfavorably. Hulin and Blood (1968) explain these differences in terms of the extent to which the workers have internalized middle-class work values, which stress achievement, responsibility, and advancement. In a provocative theoretical analysis, Nord (1977) raises serious questions about the feasibility and desirability of job enrichment for the majority of modern industrial workers.

Reactions to job enrichment have also been found to differ as a function of such individual variables as skill level, cognitive style, and needs for achievement, growth, and social contacts. Simple, repetitive jobs do not necessarily produce boredom in all workers; increasing job complexity and responsibility may arouse anxiety and insecurity in some persons. In this connection, reference should also be made to the programs of job simplification developed as a means of adapting job requirements to the skills of marginally qualified workers in industrial and military settings. Essentially, the goal should be to locate the optimum point on the simplification-enrichment continuum for each worker. This point not only varies with the individual's cultural and personal characteristics but may also vary over time as the person acquires new experiences.

At a more basic theoretical level, Nord (1969) suggests a possible interpretation of the effects of job enrichment in terms of operant conditioning. To be effective, reinforcers must represent valued rewards for the individual. Thus, for those workers who value recognition and the feeling of achievement associated with successful task completion, job enrichment provides effective reinforcers. Usually, it also provides such reinforcement on a variable ratio schedule, similar to the reinforcement schedule associated with solving crossword puzzles and playing games of chance. This schedule, it will be recalled, is highly effective in eliciting the reinforced responses. The task variety characteristic of enriched jobs will itself serve as another reinforcer, especially when initial level of stimulation was very low, as in a highly repetitive job.

ORGANIZATIONAL STRUCTURE

Concepts. Essentially, the structure of an organization refers to the nature and interrelations of its units, that is, of the individuals and groups who carry out its various functions. The links in an organization chart show who reports to whom and who supervises whom. They represent lines of authority with regard to decision making and control. Generally, organization charts also indicate such relationships as relative status, promotion ladders, work flow, functional dependencies among units, and formal channels of communication. Role definitions are usually incorporated in organization charts, as in such designations as Vice-President for Research and Development, Sales Manager, Personnel Director, or Superintendent of the Red Sands Plant. The literature on organizational structure is voluminous, both within the broad field of organization theory and in the more recently developing area of organizational psychology. For a well-balanced introduction to this topic, the reader is referred especially to Porter et al. (1975, Chs. 8 & 9).

A closely related concept encountered frequently in modern organizational psychology is that of *organizational climate* (Forehand & Gilmer, 1964; James & Jones, 1974; Payne & Pugh, 1976). This term has been loosely used and variously defined by different writers. Some use it to refer to those objectively observable characteristics of an organization that are especially effective in influencing the attitudes and performance of its members. While covering major structural variables of the organization, these characteristics may also include such features as leadership style, extent of participation, and nature of communication. Other theorists define organizational climate in terms of members' perceptions of organizational characteristics, which serve as intervening variables in mediating the effects of organizational variables on behavior.

Structural Variables. Organizational structures can be described in terms of a number of variables. Size of units or subunits is an important feature. It has been repeatedly shown that, at least among blue-collar workers, small work units are associated with higher job satisfaction and lower rates of absenteeism and turnover than are large units (Porter & Lawler, 1965). Another major feature is shape. Is the organization chart tall, with many levels, or flat, with few levels? A closely related characteristic is span of control, or number of subordinates supervised. Organizations can also be characterized in terms of degree of centralization or decentralization, concentration or dispersion of authority and control, and amount of autonomy of individual units. Specialization of function is another major characteristic of organizational structure. Organizations also differ in the degree of standardization of procedures and the prevalence of formal rules and regulations.

Organizational Contexts and Contingencies. No single type of organizational structure is most effective for all organizational contexts and all types of workers. In fact, in most organizations, the optimal type of structure may vary from one major unit to another (e.g., manufacturing, sales, research and development). Among the context factors that in part determine the appropriate organizational structure are type of organization (e.g., manufacturing plant, retail store, government agency), size of whole organization, and nature of the work. Another important contingency factor is represented by the human resources of the organization. This includes the nature, level, and distribution of skills, abilities, education, job experience, needs, and personality characteristics of the organization's members.

In summarizing the research on the effects of different organizational structures on worker attitudes and behavior, Lorsch and Morse (1974) speak of a "contingency approach" and Porter et al. (1975) refer to certain more beneficial "combinations" of context and structure. Expressed in these terms, the principal conclusions from available studies reduce to the following contingent relationships: (1) closely controlled, high-structured organizations, with formally defined and standardized procedures, tend to be most effective for relatively unskilled and inexperienced workers who have strong needs for security and stability and are engaged in work that is simple, clearly specified, and unchanging; (2) low-structured organizations, with few rules and regulations and considerable automony and dispersion of control, are most effective for workers who have relatively high skills, extensive job-related training and experience, high self-esteem, and strong needs for achievement and self-actualization, and who are engaged in work that is nonroutine, complex, and rapidly changing. These contingent relations will be recognized as another example of interaction between organizational variables and variables of the job tasks and the individuals.

COMMUNICATION

Systematic research on communication as an aspect of organizational functioning is relatively meager. The development of appropriate theory and models of organizational communication has lagged behind other facets of organizational theory. Considerable communication research has been conducted by social psychologists, often in laboratory settings, but its applicability to industrial contexts needs to be directly investigated. A comprehensive examination of theories, models, and needed research on organizational communication can be found in Porter and Roberts (1976). Despite the paucity of broad, theory-based research projects in this area, industrial psychologists have been approaching communication problems from a variety of angles and gathering data on specific questions for several decades. A sample of these approaches is illustrated in this section. It should also be noted that discussions of other aspects of organizations, such as type of structure and leadership styles, often have important implications regarding the nature and extent of communication.

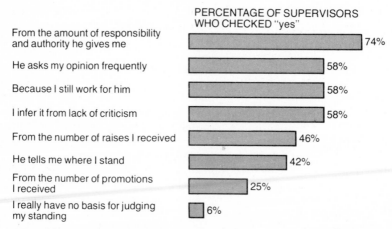

Figure 6-5. Replies of supervisors to the question: "On what basis do you judge your standing with your immediate superior?" *(From Likert, 1961, p. 54. Copyright © by McGraw-Hill, Inc. Reproduced by permission.)*

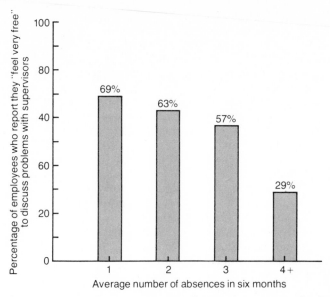

Figure 6-6. Relationship between absenteeism and supervisory communication in different departments. *(From Likert, 1961, p. 18. Copyright © 1961 by McGraw-Hill, Inc. Reproduced by permission.)*

Nature and Scope of Industrial Communication. With the increasing size of industrial organizations, communication assumes more and more importance as a means of linking the various parts together, channeling incoming information to the appropriate outlets, and ensuring coordinated action. Industrial communication may take many forms. It can be as personal as a luncheon conversation between two vice-presidents or as impersonal as an announcement over the plant's public address system. It can be as succinct as a one-sentence bulletin board notice or as detailed as a 100-page report, as formal as a stockholders' meeting or as informal as the transmission of a rumor over the grapevine. A common and effective medium of communication is the face-to-face interview in all its forms, such as performance-appraisal, problem-solving, and counseling interviews. Group meetings are among the most widely used communication techniques in all types of organizations. Company training programs serve a communication function, as do employee attitude surveys. Suggestion systems are a traditional means of routing employee ideas to management.

Within an organization, communication may flow downward, as when policy statements, operating procedures, and the like are transmitted from management to employees; upward, as illustrated by employee suggestions and grievances; horizontally, or across units at the same level; and diagonally, or across units at different levels. The mere presentation of material in oral or written form does not assure communication. The complete communication process comprises transmission, reception, comprehension, and acceptance or rejection. What is communicated includes not only cognitive material, such as facts, procedures, policies, and ideas, but also emotional climate, feelings, and attitudes. Such information is often transmitted through nonverbal channels, as illustrated by the tone of voice, facial expression, gestures, and stance that accompany speech.

We must bear in mind, too, that actions speak louder than words and are thus a part of the communication system. A raise, a promotion, or a reduction in job responsibility are likely to be perceived by the employee as evaluations of his or her job performance—and as such they will carry more weight than a verbal communication. When supervisors in a large public utility were asked, "On what basis do you judge your standing with your immediate superior?" many more of their replies referred to actions than to verbal appraisals (Likert, 1961, p. 54). Figure 6-5 shows the percentage who checked each answer.

That communication has an important influence on employee attitudes and morale is quite generally recognized. Some suggestive data are reproduced in Figure 6-6. Based on a survey of white-collar workers in a large public utility, this graph shows a consistent relation between freedom of communication and absenteeism in different departments. Apparently those departments in which employees felt free to discuss their problems with the supervisor had fewer absences than those in which the atmosphere was less conducive to free communication. Similar results were obtained with blue-collar workers in the same company. In another investigation (Burke & Wilcox, 1972), degree of job satisfaction reported by each of 323 telephone operators was found to be positively related to their perceived openness of communication with their supervisors.

The Communication Process. Industrial psychologists have investigated the communication process from many angles. Some have been concerned with the relative effectiveness of different media. In one such study (Dahle, 1954), information was transmitted by five different methods in various departments of an industrial plant. Later, tests were administered to determine how much the individual employees had actually received and retained. The results are shown in Table 6-1. It will be noted that the combination of oral and written communication gave the best results but that oral only was more effective than written only. Bulletin board and grapevine yielded the poorest results.

TABLE 6-1
Mean Information Test Scores of Employees
Receiving Communication through Different Media
(From Dahle, 1954, p. 245. Copyright 1954 by
American Management Association. Reproduced by permission.)

Medium	Number of Employees	Mean Test Score[a]
Combined oral and written	102	7.70
Oral only	94	6.17
Written only	109	4.91
Bulletin board	115	3.72
Grapevine only (control group)	108	3.56

[a]All differences are significant at the .05 level or better except that between the last two means in the column.

Written and oral communications each have certain intrinsic advantages that make them suitable for different purposes. Written communications are more accurate and provide a permanent record. They permit fuller coverage of detail and can be cited as an official, authoritative reference. Oral communications, on the other hand, are more personal, permit the give-and-take of two-way communication, and can be adapted to the individual listener.

In a series of studies (Leavitt, 1972; Leavitt & Mueller, 1951), one-way communication was compared with two-way communication in which varying kinds and amounts of feedback from the recipients were permitted. Accuracy was considerably improved by free feedback in which the listeners could ask questions to clarify points at any time during the communication. Such two-way communication, however, required more time than did one-way communication. In general, feedback is most helpful when presenting complex and relatively novel content. With repeated contacts between speaker and audience, moreover, the need for feedback tends to decrease. As the participants learn to communicate in terms of a "common code," the words used will acquire the same meanings for speaker and listeners. This is also true of persons who have had similar backgrounds of training and experience.

With regard to written communication, a number of studies have been concerned with the content and readability of such publications as instructional manuals, handbooks, plant magazines, and company bulletins (Carlucci & Crissy, 1951; Sexton and Staudt, 1959a; Sticht, 1975). Using a measure known as the Flesch Index (to be discussed in Ch. 11) or some adaptation of it, these studies demonstrated that the large majority of job publications are too difficult for workers to read. Rewriting them in a style better suited to the educational level of their readers would increase their effectiveness as communication media. The same techniques have been applied to checking the readability of union-management agreements, with similar results (Lauer & Paterson, 1951; Tiffin & Walsh, 1951).

Another approach has focused on the improvement of communication skills, including both the transmitting and the receiving of information. There has been considerable interest, for example, in the development of reading improvement programs for executives. A more comprehensive and individualized type of training is represented by the "communication clinic," which has been successfully employed in a number of organizations (Sexton & Staudt, 1959b). Concerned with both psychological and linguistic aspects of communication, this approach provides whatever remedial procedures are needed to increase the individual's effectiveness in reading, writing, and speech.

Communication Networks. The typical organization chart, showing who reports to whom, may be regarded as a map of the organization's formal communication channels. That information often flows through other, informal channels, even in a highly structured organization, is well known. The routing of information through an organization has important implications for decision making. The decisions made by top executives depend upon the information they receive. The larger the organization, the more likely it is that information is highly screened, condensed, and interpreted before it reaches the top management levels. Persons at lower organizational levels may thus influence decisions by their selective filtering of information. Of particular interest is the type of communication network illustrated in Figure 6-7, in which all information going to a top executive must filter through

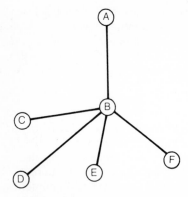

Figure 6-7. A communication network in which B plays an important filtering role. *(Adapted from Leavitt, 1972, p. 196.)*

an assistant. As a result, the assistant may become the one who really makes the decisions and runs the organization. Such a situation may not only limit organizational effectiveness but also disrupt morale.

A number of techniques have been employed to analyze the flow of communication in both large organizations and small groups (see Porter & Roberts, 1976, pp. 1579–1584). Asking individuals with whom they spend their time during working hours is one approach. Having a trained observer stationed in a workroom, as in the Hawthorne studies, is another. Other techniques study the communications more directly. For instance, a record is made of all communications passing a particular spot, such as a given executive's desk, throughout the day. In a "cross-sectional analysis" each person is asked what communication (if any) was in progress at a specified point in time.

Another technique, known as "ecco analysis" (episodic communication channels in organization), follows a specific unit of information throughout the communication network (K. Davis, 1953, 1972). In applying this method, for example, the investigator might ask each individual whether he knows some particular item of information. If so, the respondent is further asked from whom and through what medium he learned of it and in what respects, if any, the information he received differed from that presented by the investigator. This method has been used to study grapevine and other informal types of communication, as well as communications transmitted through official channels. Data can be analyzed in various ways to show, for instance, extent and direction of information flow, distortion of facts in the process of transmission, and relative use of different media.

Still another approach is represented by laboratory studies of communication nets in small task-oriented groups (Bavelas & Barrett, 1951; Burgess, 1968; Leavitt, 1951; 1972, Ch. 18). Figure 6-8 shows some of the communication nets investigated in these studies. Participants are seated around a table but are separated by radial partitions so that they cannot see each other and must communicate by passing notes through slots in the partitions. Each group is assigned problems whose solution requires the pooling of information by all group members. The experimenter sets up different communication nets by opening some slots and closing others.

In the star pattern (Fig. 6-8), all information must be sent to a central person C,

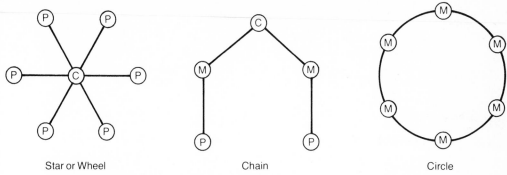

Star or Wheel   Chain   Circle

Figure 6-8. Three types of communication nets. *(Adapted from Leavitt, 1951.)*

who transmits the answers back to each individual member. In the chain, information is sent by the two peripheral members P, through the middle members M, to C. In the circle, there is no centralized organization, information traveling back and forth among all members. With regard to speed and accuracy of problem solving, the star yielded the best results and the circle the poorest. However, circle nets had better morale and were better able to adapt to sudden and confusing changes of task. A leader and a stable form of organization emerged most readily with the star pattern, more slowly with the chain, and failed to emerge with the circle.

It is quite likely that different kinds of communication nets may be most effective for different purposes. Moreover, group size limits the applicability of certain patterns. The circle, for example, is practicable only with very small groups. As group size increases beyond a certain point, some preliminary sifting and screening of information is essential, before it is transmitted to a central recipient. There is also evidence that the differences in speed of problem solving with different types of nets tend to disappear with increasing practice and with stronger motivation (Burgess, 1968).

Communication Barriers and Breakdowns. Special attention has been given to factors associated with communication failures (Haney, 1960; Leavitt, 1972, Chs. 11, 19). Supervisory practices that weaken morale may reduce the effectiveness of upward communication. Attitudes of hostility and distrust not only may reduce the flow and acceptance of information but also may lead to deliberate distortion of communication at all organizational levels. Status relationships and organizational climate may likewise hamper the upward flow of communication. In some organizations, superiors are told only what subordinates think they want to hear.

A common cause of communication failures is to be found in the different frames of reference against which individuals may perceive a situation. It is well known that perception is selective and that each person tends to perceive what fits in with his or her own experiences, interests, and needs. This fact was demonstrated when 23 middle-management executives participating in a company training program were requested to identify the major problem facing a company about which they had read (Dearborn & Simon, 1958). Although the instructions asked for the problem that should be dealt with first by a newly appointed company president—and thus emphasized a broad, companywide perspective—the executives tended to perceive chiefly problems in their own areas, such as sales, organizational structure and policy, or human relations.

Communication breakdowns often result from preconceived notions, prejudices, stereotypes, and strong emotional associations with certain words (see Haney, 1960). A tendency to overgeneralize or to jump to conclusions may also seriously retard communication. The "evaluative tendency" has been described as another barrier to effective communication (Rogers & Roethlisberger, 1952). When we hear or read a statement made by another person, often our first reaction is to express agreement or disagreement with it, i.e., to evaluate it within our own frame of reference, rather than trying to understand it from the other person's point of view. The attempt to remove this communication barrier underlies the nondirective or client-centered techniques developed by Carl R. Rogers and his associates for use in counseling and psychotherapy (see Ch. 13). These techniques have also been applied to other areas of interpersonal relations.

Gibb (1964) argues that communication barriers and breakdowns can be most effectively handled, not by superficial attempts to improve the mechanics of communication itself, but by identifying and correcting more basic organizational problems. Ineffective communication is regarded as a symptom of underlying managerial defects. Effective communication should occur as a natural constituent of job performance and problem solving, not as a separate program conducted for purposes of persuasion or morale building. Undue emphasis on the communication process itself may lead to a contrived and artificial approach that is likely to be self-defeating.

CONFLICT RESOLUTION

Nature and Scope. Although union-management conflicts have undoubtedly received the widest publicity, conflicts are likely to occur between any interacting and interdependent groups. Within industrial settings, such conflicts may arise, for example, between middle and top management, between production and sales divisions, or between manufacturers and dealers (see, e.g., Assael, 1973). When two mutually dependent groups seek incompatible goals, conflict ensues. The major psychological sources of such conflicts can be found in group differences in motivation (or needs) and in perception (Stagner & Rosen, 1965).

Groups may differ in the needs they seek to satisfy in a given situation and in the ways they consider most effective for satisfying those needs. Frustration in achieving such satisfactions often leads to hostility and aggression, which may be expressed in angry disputes, disruptive actions, or physical violence. Group conflicts may also arise or be intensified by the different ways in which the groups perceive a situation. Differences in the experiential backgrounds of the two parties to a dispute often result in very different perceptions of the same objective facts. The groups may have dissimilar frames of reference, not only because of their diverse job roles and functions but also because of educational, socioeconomic, and other broad cultural differences that determine relatively durable attitudes. The resulting perceptual differences extend to individuals' perceptions of themselves and of the members of the other side, as well as to their perceptions of issues and proposed actions. Working through these perceptual differences and thereby promoting mutual understanding is one of the techniques for resolving conflicts.

Research Approaches. The causes and management of intergroup conflicts have been extensively discussed by specialists in many fields, including economics, sociology, political science, engineering, and organization theory. Psychologists have focused largely on understanding the behavior of participants in conflict situations, drawing upon knowledge from personality theory, clinical psychology, and social psychology. Research on conflict resolution has followed a variety of procedures. Some investigators have conducted questionnaire surveys to assess the perceptual and attitudinal differences among such groups as union members, union officials, management personnel, and different levels of workers (McCormick & Tiffin, 1974, pp. 387–389; Stagner & Rosen, 1965, Ch. 2).

A most prolific area of research, yielding more than 1,000 references over some 15 years, has utilized controlled laboratory experiments with bargaining games (Rubin & Brown, 1975). These games represent highly simplified and artificial situations, in which two or more participants choose courses of action designed to maximize their gains and minimize their losses. The action strategies may be cooperative, individualistic, or competitive. Various criteria of bargaining effectiveness were applied to assess the influence of a large number of variables, ranging from the physical arrangement of the setting, the presence of an audience, and the role of third parties to the amount of communication, the bargaining strategy followed, and the personality characteristics of the participants. Although a mass of valuable data has been accumulated by this method, a large gap still remains between the results of these laboratory studies and the complex bargaining situations encountered in industry.

Some investigators have used more realistic simulations of industrial conflict situations (Shapira & Bass, 1975; Shepard, 1961). In these studies, the participants are management personnel enrolled in executive training workshops. They are divided into teams and assigned typical industrial problems to solve by negotiation or other types of group discussions. This approach merges imperceptibly with organization development and other action programs conducted in companies by outside consultants. Some of these programs have concentrated on improving the interpersonal relations between the representatives of the two parties to the negotiations (Blake, Mouton, & Sloma, 1965; Blake, Shepard, & Mouton, 1964; French & Bell, 1973). While the participants in such workshops do show improvement in mutual understanding and attitudes, little or no information is available regarding subsequent individual behavior or organizational performance. Still another approach utilizes field studies of real-life conflicts (Assael, 1973; for other examples, see Rubin & Brown, 1975). Data may be gathered from objective records, observer reports of public events, and interviews with key persons. Analysis of a particular situation over a period of several years may provide clues regarding causal relations among variables.

Constructive Solutions. From the wide diversity of approaches to the study of conflict resolution, one recommendation emerges with considerable consistency, namely, that problem-solving strategies are more effective than bargaining strategies in providing lasting and mutually satisfactory solutions (Thomas, 1976). It has been repeatedly observed that conflicts as such need not be disruptive or destructive in their effects. On the contrary, they may provide a stimulus for reexamining procedures and developing new and better ways of attaining organizational objectives. In the typical bargaining situation, each party to a dispute sacrifices some part of its demands in order to reach a mutually acceptable compromise. Thus, neither side is completely satisfied. In a predominantly problem-solving approach, on the other hand, a creative and integrative alternative is sought, which differs from the solutions initially proposed by each side but meets the needs of both. Admittedly, this is not an easy task. In many conflict situations, moreover, a combination of some bargaining and some joint problem solving may be required.

Several guidelines have been proposed to facilitate a problem-solving approach to conflict resolution (Blake et al., 1964; N. R. F. Maier, 1973, Ch. 22; Shepard, 1961; Simkin, 1964; Stagner & Rosen, 1965, Ch. 6). An important step is to clarify issues and improve each party's understanding of the other's position. Closely related to such understanding is a rapprochement in the diverse perceptions of the two sides and a reduction in hostile attitudes. These objectives can be aided by the services of a third party, functioning as a mediator or consultant. One technique proposed for this purpose is to prepare two columns on a chalkboard, one listing the merits of Group A's position, the other, those of Group B's. Participants are asked to provide specific, concrete arguments for either position; the leader ensures that each argument is fully understood before proceeding (N. R. F. Maier, 1973). Several other suggestions of this type have been offered in the effort to focus attention on understanding as a necessary antecedent to rebuttal or persuasion. Separating broad issues into more manageable and clearly defined units also facilitates constructive discussion of solutions.

Another procedure conducive to integrative solutions is to identify a common or superordinate goal that is important to both sides. A familiar example would be the desire of both company and workers to avoid the heavy costs of a long strike; another is the joint concern about loss in sales resulting from a steep rise in the sales price of the company's products. Still other recommended procedures include the establishment of continuing mechanisms for resolving conflicts as they arise, in order to minimize crisis bargaining and eleventh-hour negotiations (Simkin, 1964). Finally, conflict resolution should be viewed against the framework of the entire organization. The frequency, intensity, and potential destructiveness of conflicts can be reduced by improving other organizational features, ranging from selection, classification, and training to job design, communication, and grievance procedures.

CORPORATE SOCIAL RESPONSIBILITY

Since the early 1970s, corporations have become increasingly aware of the broad societal implications of their actions. To be sure, large corporations have for many decades manifested their sense of social responsibility by such actions as the support of higher education through grants and scholarships and by sponsoring "institutional advertisements" which publicize social causes unrelated to the marketing of the company's own products or services. It is also evident that, in order to survive, any business must reflect, at least in part, the values of the community in which it operates. More recently, however, corporate social responsibility has taken on new meanings and has reached a new order of magnitude. A clear and thoughtful introduction to the topic can be found in Bauer and Fenn (1972).

Many social developments of the late 1960s and 1970s have contributed to the heightened social awareness of business organizations. Among the most familiar examples is consumerism, with its concerns about such matters as product safety, "truth in advertising," and full and accurate product labeling. The ecology movement has focused attention on environmental protection, the reduction of air and water pollution, and the conservation of natural resources. Civil rights, minority problems, and the women's liberation movement have highlighted another cluster of problems and pressures. Political and international concerns have generated demands that companies scrutinize the buyers and consumers of their products and services and evaluate the purposes for which their commodities are used.

The pressures for corporate actions on behalf of social objectives come from several sources. Investors, customers, employees, students, and special activist groups have all been raising questions about the direct and indirect societal consequences of the ordinary pursuit of each corporation's business. Each group, through both its verbal protests and its actions, has been defining in part what constitutes responsible corporate behavior. The confusing multiplicity of issues, as well as the conflicting pressures to move in incompatible directions, makes it particularly difficult to reach effective and wise organizational decisions.

In an effort to introduce some clarity, coordination, and objectivity into the situation, Bauer and Fenn (1972) examine the development and application of the *corporate social audit*. Such audits have been undertaken in rudimentary and exploratory form by business organizations as self-audits, by investment groups (e.g., mutual funds created to offer investors a "socially responsible" portfolio), and by public interest groups (e.g., church organizations, citizens' councils). The purpose of such audits is to provide a systematic assessment of the activities of corporations in relation to a range of social issues. In practice, audits have varied widely in their coverage, with such areas as employee satisfaction, safety, and pollution control predominating. Data may be gathered from several sources, including printed reports, company records, questionnaire surveys, and interviews with corporate officers and other key persons.

From the corporation's viewpoint, a comprehensive and accurate self-audit serves two major purposes: (1) to aid in its own decision making and (2) to inform its various publics about the implementation of its social responsibility policies. The coverage should include both internal matters (e.g., employee benefits, health, and safety) and external issues (e.g., product safety, nature of advertising, environmental protection). As Bauer and Fenn (1972, pp. 73–74) observe, however, the list must remain flexible and responsive to society's evolving value system and emerging problems. Moreover, the relative importance of specific issues will differ with the industry, geographical region, and other contextual variables. Nor does it seem desirable to obtain a composite index for any given company, since the relative weight of different factors depends so largely on the individual user's value system. The audit will thus be more generally useful if numerical ratings (or other summary evaluations) are kept separate for each factor or issue covered. Finally, a company's activities with regard to social issues, like all its other functions, need to be evaluated in terms of the most effective allocation of its available resources within the total organizational system. Decisions should be based on a comprehensive analysis of the net, long-term societal consequences of corporate actions, taking into account the many interacting and sometimes conflicting objectives.

SUMMARY

Organizational psychology represents a comprehensive systems approach to the problems of human performance in work settings. Although focusing chiefly on managerial policies and procedures, it is concerned with the combined effects and the interactions of many variables of the workers, the job tasks, and the organizational context. It is now well established that there is no single organizational formula, management system, or supervisory style that fits all jobs and all individuals.

A major area within organizational psychology deals with such leadership or supervisory dimensions as Consideration and Initiating Structure, as illustrated by the Michigan group-dynamics approach, the Ohio State Leadership Studies, and Fiedler's interaction model. Closely related to leadership styles is the research on participative management, as exemplified by the Harwood-Weldon studies. Management by objectives (MBO) combines major aspects of participative decision making with the explicit formulation of realistic performance goals and objective appraisal procedures. Job-enrichment programs are multifaceted, involving more varied and meaningful job tasks as well as increased autonomy and responsibility in carrying out the work. Their benefits, along with those of MBO, are understandable in terms of contingent reinforcement and other operant conditioning principles.

Organizational structure pertains to the nature and interrelationships of organizational units. Organization charts typically show lines of authority and control, relative status, promotion ladders, work flow, functional dependence, and formal channels of communication. The optimal organizational structure varies with the nature of the work and the characteristics of the workers. Effective communication in all directions is a key concept in organizational performance, but it cannot be developed apart from the total organizational context. Conflict resolution is a major problem in both internal and external organizational relations. In general, problem-solving strategies yield more generally satisfying and durable solutions than do bargaining strategies. The social responsibility of corporations has received increasing attention during the 1960s and 1970s. The corporate social audit represents an attempt to provide a clear, balanced, and objective evaluation of the societal consequences of organizational activities.

ENGINEERING AND ENVIRONMENTAL PSYCHOLOGY

PART THREE

HUMAN PERFORMANCE

SEVEN

N EARLIER CHAPTERS, reference was made to the areas of basic psychological research that contributed most to particular fields of application. We saw that personnel selection and classification draw most heavily from psychometrics and differential psychology, training from the psychology of learning, and organizational psychology (including theories of work motivation) from social psychology and personality theory. Although such attributions of influence obviously represent an oversimplification, they help to identify the characteristic orientation of the different fields of applied psychology. Within this framework, engineering psychology comes closest to being "applied experimental psychology"—a title by which it has sometimes been designated (Chapanis, Garner, & Morgan, 1949). It was chiefly the experimental research on human sensation, perception, and motor behavior that provided the groundwork for the development of engineering psychology.

SCOPE AND ORIGINS OF ENGINEERING PSYCHOLOGY

In current usage, "engineering psychology" is a rather flexible term (see Alluisi & Morgan, 1976; Chapanis, 1976; McCormick, 1976a). This flexibility also characterizes other terms commonly employed to refer to the more comprehensive area to which engineering psychology contributes, such as "human factors," "human factors engineering," or (in most European countries) "ergonomics." The "human factors" problems to which engineering psychologists address themselves typically draw upon many other sciences and professions, including anatomy, physiology, anthropology, sociology, several varieties of engineering, industrial design, and architecture, among others. The term "engineering psychology" is sometimes used in a broad sense to cover practically every topic in industrial psychology, including selection and classification, training, motivation, work methods, equipment design, and work environment. A more common usage restricts its coverage to the last three topics, as is done in this book. In simple terms, the three chapters in this section will consider in turn *how* work is performed, with *what*, and under what *conditions.*

The present chapter, concerned with human performance, begins with an examination of the nature of work and fatigue and the problem of monotony in relation to fatigue. We shall then inquire into work schedules, or the distribution of work over time. This will be followed by a discussion of methods design, concerned with the effectiveness of worker procedures in carrying out a task. Finally, we shall consider accident prevention and industrial safety as one aspect of methods design, as well as in their broader research implications. The second chapter in this section deals with the design and arrangement of equipment and with the more inclusive problem of developing efficient man-machine systems. The third chapter is concerned with working and living environments. In it will be considered the effects of such factors as illumination, ventilation, air pollution, noise, and crowding, as well as other emerging concerns of environmental psychology.

Although engineering and industrial psychology have many points of contact and are drawing closer together, they can probably be best differentiated in terms of their approach to the worker and his or her job (Chapanis, 1976). While the industrial psychologist is oriented toward fitting the worker to the job (through selection, classification, training, and incentives), the engineering psychologist is oriented chiefly toward fitting the job to the worker (by designing appropriate operating procedures, equipment, and work environments). Another distinctive feature of engineering psychology is its emphasis on a systems approach to problems of human performance. Engineering psychologists pioneered in such a systems orientation—an orientation that has since found its way into all fields of applied psychology. The concept of human performance systems, with their interacting variables, was presented in Chapter 1. Reference to it occurred repeatedly in the chapters on industrial and organizational psychology; we shall return to it time and again in the later sections of the book.

From another angle, modern engineering psychology extends beyond occupational settings to all spheres of daily living. Increasing the effectiveness of human performance and minimizing fatigue are certainly relevant to all human activities—in the home, in sports, and in other avocational pursuits, as well as on the job. Psychologists have been contributing not only to the designing of industrial machinery, military equipment, and aerospace vehicles but also to the designing of such consumer products as kitchen stoves, telephones, and automobile seats. Still another example is provided by the improvement of highway design, road signs, traffic lights, and other features of concern to the general driver.

Although engineering psychology has only recently attained the status of a fully developed field of applied psychology, its antecedents can be traced to the earliest beginnings of industrial psychology. As early as 1898, Frederick W. Taylor, best known for his time study of manual operations, applied systematic observation of worker performance to the designing of shovels (Copley, 1923, Vol. 2, Ch. 5). Taylor found that, owing to the haphazard selection of shovel shapes and sizes, shovelers in a steel plant were lifting loads varying from $3\frac{1}{2}$ to 38 lbs. Through empirical tryout of different loads, he concluded that $21\frac{1}{2}$ lbs. constituted an optimal load for men working regularly as shovelers. When either heavier or lighter loads were tried, total daily output declined. Accordingly, he designed different sizes of shovels for different materials, so as to yield approximately this load. Thus a small spade-shovel was provided for handling heavy iron ore and a large scoop for shoveling ashes.

Frank B. Gilbreth, of motion-study fame, also devoted considerable effort to designing special chairs for different types of work, in order to minimize strain and fatigue (Gilbreth & Gilbreth, 1916). One of these was a high chair with a footrest, to be used with a tall desk or worktable. With such an arrangement, the operator could work equally well while either sitting or standing and could thus shift body posture to relieve muscular strain. Among his classic "rules" for motion economy, Gilbreth included several dealing with the arrangement of the workplace, the position of tools, and the design of equipment. His writings include many observations and recommendations on all these ways of improving worker efficiency (e.g., Gilbreth, 1911, Ch. 3).

During the following two or three decades, there were isolated studies in several countries pertaining to the improvement of work processes, equipment, or the work environment. A more systematic, continuing research program was initiated in the 1920s by the Industrial Fatigue Research Board of Great Britain, later renamed the Industrial Health Research Board. In one survey sponsored by this board, the focus of interest was described as "a large class of machines requiring frequent manipulation of a release or control or some other manual operation in which . . . the worker and the machine form a single system (Legros & Weston, 1926, p. iii), a statement that has a remarkably modern ring to it. The survey led to recommended improvements in several types of laundry and leather-working machines; in certain machines used in the manufacture of textiles, shoes, and brushes; in sheet-metal work; and in tobacco processing.

It was during World War II, however, that engineering psychology rose into prominence as a separate discipline. The immediate impetus for its emergence came from the increasing complexity of the machines that men were called upon to operate. High-speed aircraft, rockets, and radar were among the many new instruments whose operation taxed human capacities to unprecedented degrees. It soon became apparent that selection and training were inadequate to provide a sufficient number of operators who could function at the required level of proficiency. The solution was to redesign the equipment so as to make the operator's job simpler, less confusing, less demanding, or in other ways more manageable. This might be accomplished by improving the displays (such as dials) through which information is received, by making the controls easier to operate, or by having the machine take over some of the complicated intervening processes formerly carried out by the human operator.

Present-day engineering psychology differs in a number of ways from earlier work. The most conspicuous difference is in its magnitude. Since its formal beginnings in World War II, engineering psychology has been expanding at a prodigious rate. Its bibliographies run into many thousands of titles (Alluisi & Morgan, 1976). Much of the work in the United States has been done for the military services and the aerospace industry. Applications to a wider range of industries have been more common in several European countries and are now increasingly evident in this country (H. L. Davis, 1973). In contrast to early, scattered efforts, modern engineering psychology characteristically approaches problems more systematically, through comprehensive, long-term research and development projects. Another noteworthy contribution is the publication of handbooks summarizing normative data on sensory, motor, and other relevant human capacities for use by engineers in the design of equipment (e.g., Van Cott & Kinkade, 1972).

WORK AND FATIGUE

The Concept of Efficient Human Performance. The principles of efficient work apply to any situation involving human performance, whether in a factory, in an office, in a classroom, at home, or on a tennis court. Basically, the concept of efficiency refers to the ratio of output to input. A machine that requires 50 units of power to produce 10 units of work is more efficient than one requiring 70 units of power to produce the same 10 units of work. When the concept is extended to human work, many more factors need to be considered, both on the input and on the output side. Thus, in addition to the time required to perform a task, one must take into account the worker's energy expenditure, the feelings of strain and effort, and the emotional costs of persistent worries, disagreeable obligations, or unpleasant interpersonal contacts. Similarly, a long-range comprehensive measure of output would include not only quantity of production but also quality of original contributions and other creative achievements, errors and wastage, accidents, absenteeism, turnover, grievances, labor unrest and strife, physical and mental health of workers, and many other indirect or remote consequences of the work.

Changes over time in any output variable may be visualized by means of a work curve. This curve usually shows quantity of production, but it may also be plotted in terms of errors or other measures of performance. Figure 7-1 illustrates some of the concepts commonly used in describing the course of output over time. These include the initial "warming up" before peak productivity is reached, the eventual work decrement presumably indicating the onset of fatigue, and a possible "end spurt" as the end of the work period is anticipated. Random, momentary fluctuations are also characteristic of work curves. Not all the features shown in Figure 7-1, of course, need be found in any individual work curve.

Fatigue: Nature and Assessment. A major goal of effective human performance is the reduction of fatigue. Everyone "knows" what fatigue is, but definitions and

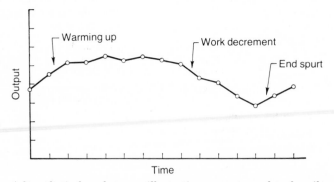

Figure 7-1. A hypothetical work curve, illustrating concepts used to describe performance changes.

indicators of it reveal an overwhelming diversity (McCormick, 1976a, Ch. 7; Geacintov & Peavler, 1974; Grandjean, 1968; Hashimoto, Kogi, & Grandjean, 1971). Sometimes the term is used to refer to feelings of tiredness, sometimes to a reduction in output, and sometimes to the physiological conditions resulting from continued activity. It might be argued that these three classes of phenomena are just different manifestations of the same general state of the organism. But the difficulty is that they often disagree. Pronounced feelings of tiredness may be accompanied by no drop in output; output may decline in the absence of corresponding physiological changes; and output and feelings may remain unchanged for some time after the physiological onset of fatigue.

Feelings of fatigue, moreover, may take many forms, depending upon the type of activity that evoked them. They may range from muscular soreness, localized stiffness, and aches to sleepiness, mental confusion, muscular tensions, and general weariness. Sometimes such feelings are difficult to distinguish from sheer boredom and loss of interest. The decline in output, too, may take different forms, such as decrease in speed of performance, deterioration of quality, loss in originality, increase in errors and spoilage, rise in accident frequency, attention lapses, and greater variability of performance. Several of these output changes may occur together, of course. But, under certain circumstances, output may continue unchanged in some respects while showing marked deterioration in others.

It should likewise be noted that feelings of tiredness as well as output indices of fatigue are highly specific to the task. Transfer of fatigue to other tasks declines rapidly as task similarity decreases. Even with very similar tasks, a sharp drop in output from continued performance of the one task is unlikely to produce an equally pronounced drop in the other. Change of activity, even though slight, will usually decrease the effects of fatigue.

Both feelings of fatigue and output decrement depend in part upon motivation and attitude. Everyone has undoubtedly had the experience of tiring quickly when performing a job he disliked but working for long stretches with no noticeable change in output or feelings at something that fired his enthusiasm. It is partly for this reason that many investigators have turned to physiological indicators of fatigue. The many bodily indicators investigated for this purpose (McCormick, 1976a, Ch. 7) can be classified as chemical (e.g., blood or urine content, oxygen consumption), electrical (e.g., electroencephalogram, electromyograph for specific muscle groups, galvanic skin response), and physical (e.g., blood pressure, heart rate, body temperature). It should be noted that these measures refer to different effects of work on the organism and will not necessarily yield consistent results when applied to different tasks or to different persons.

Rate of oxygen consumption during work has often been used to assess the comparative energy cost of different kinds of work. One technique (respirometer) requires the subject to breathe through a mask connected with a container in which the expired air is collected (see Fig. 7-2). Chemical analyses of air samples taken at different points in the work period show the amount of oxygen consumed per unit of time, which can be translated into Calories.[1] For example, approximate estimates of the Calories per minute required to perform common tasks include:

[1] A Calorie (or kilocalorie) is the amount of heat required to raise the temperature of 1 kilogram of water 1° Celsius. It is a unit commonly used in reporting both the energy expended in bodily activities and the energy-producing value of foods—as anyone on a weight-reducing diet soon learns!

Figure 7-2. Oxygen consumption and heart rate measured on an industrial job. *(From Davis, Faulkner, & Miller, 1969, Fig. 1. Copyright © 1969 by The Human Factors Society, Inc. Reproduced by permission. Photograph by courtesy of Human Factors Section, Health, Safety, and Human Factors Laboratory, Eastman Kodak Company.)*

2.2 Calories for light manual work while seated at a table, 6.8 for sawing wood, 7.7 for mowing the lawn with a hand mower, 8.0 for chopping a tree, and 9.0 for carrying a 17-lb suitcase upstairs (McCormick, 1976a, p. 173). Although indicating the broad range of energy expenditure for different types of work, these figures would vary considerably with rate of work (such as speed of walking), work methods, and working conditions (e.g., temperature), as well as with age and other characteristics of individual workers.

Although some occupations still require substantial physical effort (especially in industrially underdeveloped countries), human energy is being replaced more and more by other sources of energy in industrial work. With the increasing use of laborsaving devices—from baggage pushcarts to automated production plants—heavy muscular work has been steadily declining as a major cause of occupational fatigue. In fact, concern for the effective and safe use of one's body in task performance may gradually shift from job functions to avocational and "leisure-time" activities. Many persons today perform their most demanding physical work, not on the job, but in caring for their own homes (shoveling snow, gardening, painting); in vigorous sports; and in hiking, camping, and other strenuous recreational pursuits. Perhaps "weekend workers" and inexperienced, part-time athletes will become as much of a menace as the proverbial Sunday driver—although they will rarely injure anyone but themselves.

The Question of Mental Fatigue. Since occupational work has been shifting from the predominantly physical toward the psychomotor and strictly "mental," there is an increasing interest in the nature of so-called mental fatigue and in the psychologically stressful work conditions that produce it. What, for instance, constitutes the fatigue that a student may feel after long periods of solving mathematical problems or reading a difficult textbook? First it should be noted that the physiological effects of intellectual activity are slight but of the same kind as those following physical work. It is likely that these slight changes are the result of the muscular responses that always accompany even the most "purely intellectual" work. For example, there are contractions of the eye muscles in reading; subvocal contractions of speech muscles during silent thought; postural reactions in the head and neck, as well as in the rest of the body; hand and arm movements in writing; and various muscular tensions from such tangential acts as gripping the pencil hard, setting the jaw, and frowning while trying to concentrate. Measures of muscle-action potentials taken while children or adults solve arithmetic problems without the use of paper and pencil show evidence of muscle activity which increases as the difficulty of the problems increases (e.g., Shaw & Kline, 1947). In general, increased muscular tension is associated with sustained attention.

Among the other components of what is commonly called mental fatigue are general feelings of strain and effort. Boredom, drowsiness, and sleepiness are often included. Emotional reactions to frustration and conflict may also be an integral part of the experience. Frustration may arise from failure to solve a problem, indecision, inability to comprehend a difficult idea, and other stressful experiences accompanying mental work.

A growing number of industrial operations call for continued alertness, or *vigilance* (Buckner & McGrath, 1963; Davies & Tune, 1969; McCormick & Tiffin, 1974, Ch. 18). The clearest example is provided by monitoring tasks, which are needed more and more as industrial processes become mechanized and automated. Essentially, monitoring involves constant attention to an operation in order to detect any malfunction or other condition demanding action. The "signal" that something is wrong may be provided by dials, gauges, or other instruments; or it may be perceived through direct observation of the operation, as in listening to the sound of a machine. Typically, the monitor is required to react to irregularly appearing and infrequent signals, although he or she must watch for them and be ready to respond at all times. Understandably, there is a sharp decline in the monitor's signal detection over time. The introduction of rest periods, with short watches of 30 minutes or less, can usually maintain performance at a satisfactory level. There is also some evidence that a higher signal rate may improve both signal detection and speed of responding to signals. In practical situations, signal rate can be increased by introducing noncritical, artificial signals to which the monitor must make some designated response (McCormick & Tiffin, 1974, pp. 495–499).

Another common operation calling for vigilance is the inspection of products for quality control (Harris & Chaney, 1969). Inspection errors include both failure to detect defects and incorrect rejection of acceptable items. The task has several psychological features in common with monitoring. Although most inspection processes are visual, some involve hearing, touch, and even taste (as in tea tasting). Research has shown that the accuracy of inspection varies with the nature of the defects to be identified, their frequency of occurrence, and the inspection methods employed. Considerable improvement can be effected by providing various aids for observing and evaluating item characteristics.

In still another type of situation, the effect of fatigue on attention control has been demonstrated with airplane pilots. Research with flight simulators indicated that, as the pilots became fatigued following several continuous hours in the simulator, their standards of performance accuracy declined, their range of attention shrank, and they tended to respond to instrument readings in isolation without reference to other concomitant readings (McFarland, 1971). Such behavioral signs of fatigue may be too slight to be manifested in gross output measures. They may show up only in an occasional slip, a brief confusion of signals, or a slight interruption of the smooth rhythm of a skilled performance. But such minor lapses may have serious consequences in certain kinds of occupations.

From all the research that has been conducted on fatigue, one point emerges clearly: fatigue is not one but many things, and each should be investigated in its own right. Different indices, whether they be introspective reports, physiological changes, output measures, or special behavioral tests, all have their place and should be chosen with reference to the specific problem under investigation.

Monotony and Boredom. Any comprehensive psychological discussion of fatigue includes frequent references to monotony and boredom. These feelings are difficult to differentiate from fatigue, although they can be distinguished under certain circumstances. Thus an individual may become appreciably tired from a long spell of interesting and absorbing work which he at no time found boring. Or he may find a light, repetitive task highly boring but not feel tired from it. Nevertheless, boredom and fatigue are frequently associated. In a monotonous task we generally find greater output decrement and more energy expenditure than in a varied and absorbing task. Like feelings of fatigue, boredom is an unpleasant experience, often characterized by difficulty in keeping attention fixed on the task at hand. Part of the unpleasant emotional tone comes from a conflict between wanting to turn away to more attractive activities and realizing that one must continue with the dull task.

There is some evidence to suggest that the effects of monotony are most severe for tasks requiring an intermediate degree of attention (Schachter, Willerman, Festinger, & Hyman, 1961; Wyatt, Frost, & Stock, 1934). With completely routine tasks demanding a minimum of attention, individuals are free to think of other matters, talk to their co-workers, or attend to other stimuli in their surroundings. At the other extreme, a complex and varied task tends to hold the attention because of its intrinsic features. It is the semiautomatic task, requiring constant attention but providing little intrinsic interest, that is likely to produce the greatest strain. When performing such a task, the worker must repeatedly resist the tendency to attend to other stimuli or to pursue other thoughts that have greater pulling power than the work at hand. The previously cited vigilance tasks are, of course, a prime example of this type of strain.

It is apparent, too, that monotony cannot be understood solely in terms of task characteristics. The identical task may be boring in one set of circumstances and not boring in another. Monotony depends upon the relation of task, surroundings, and individual. Work may become more boring when performed under distracting conditions, because of the strain of fighting off the pull of competing stimuli. The distracting stimuli may be of many sorts, from other people talking or moving about to thoughts about last night's date or tomorrow's holiday. On the other hand, with highly routine types of work, giving the individual an opportunity to converse with neighbors may reduce monotony. Under certain circumstances, the introduction of music, or even noise, may help to alleviate monotony. Incentives also affect the degree of boredom experienced on a job, higher motivation tending to lessen monotony. In one series of experiments, setting a specific performance goal, as compared to instructing subjects to do their best, enhanced interest and reduced boredom for routine, repetitive, and attention-demanding tasks (Locke & Bryan, 1967).

Individuals differ widely in their susceptibility to monotony when performing the same job. To some, even a highly repetitive job, such as packing light bulbs, is challenging and satisfying. To others, a complex and varied job, such as teaching, may be boring. Among workers engaged in any one type of work, a certain amount of self-selection has undoubtedly occurred. Persons likely to find a particular type of work highly boring and distasteful would tend to leave or avoid such work in the first place. Investigations of individual differences within a single job are thus limited by a certain amount of preselection. Nevertheless, any significant relations that do emerge in such studies between personal characteristics and susceptibility to monotony are of interest. In an investigation of 72 sewing-machine operators, for instance, susceptibility to monotony was significantly related to certain other indications of discontent and restlessness (P. C. Smith, 1955). In comparison with the workers reporting less boredom, those reporting stronger feelings of boredom more often preferred active leisure activities, disliked regular daily routine, and indicated dissatisfaction with their personal and home life as well as with their job situation. Feelings of boredom were also reported by significantly more workers under 20 years of age and by significantly fewer over 35; there was no relation between boredom and age in the intervening group. The investigator describes those less susceptible to boredom as being relatively placid, contented with the existing state of affairs, and possibly rigid in their behavior.

Many remedies have been proposed for monotony in industry. Each undoubtedly has something to contribute in specific situations. The findings on individual differences in susceptibility to monotony suggest the importance of personnel selection and placement, with reference to relevant personality characteristics as well as job aptitudes. The study of sewing-machine operators suggests the possibility of utilizing biographical and interview data to identify individuals more likely to find repetitive work satisfying.

Changes in working conditions and working environment may also serve to reduce monotony. The introduction of rest breaks often relieves monotony as well as fatigue. Eliminating distractions in the case of work requiring constant attention reduces conflict and strain. With more automatic jobs demanding little attention, on the other hand, such activities as conversation with co-workers or listening to music often help.

A third approach concentrates on making the work itself more varied or interesting. Setting specific goals or grouping repetitive work into broad units tends to give the worker a sense of accomplishment. Work done in batches is usually less monotonous than work done with a continuous—and endless— succession of items. Films or plant tours showing where the individual's work fits into the total production picture or giving information about uses and characteristics of the product are also sometimes employed to increase interest. Finally, the various procedures for job enrichment discussed in Chapter 6 represent more basic attacks on the problem of industrial monotony.

WORK SCHEDULES

Among the many conditions affecting human performance is the distribution of work over time. Several questions can be asked in this connection. What is the effect of introducing rest periods during work and what is the best way to distribute and utilize these breaks? How is productivity related to total length of workday and workweek? How does night work or work on other special shifts affect the worker's job performance and general well-being?

Rest Periods. It is undoubtedly true that a judicious distribution of work and rest will improve working efficiency for anyone, be he schoolchild, college student, office worker, farmer, or assembly-line operator. The practice of having rest breaks is now well established in business and industrial settings. Such breaks usually provide an opportunity to obtain refreshments (as in the well-known coffee break), move about, relax in an employee lounge, chat with co-workers, and generally experience a change of activity and surroundings. The optimum duration and distribution of rest periods varies with the nature of the work and with the skill, experience, and other personal variables of the worker. Heavy work or tasks demanding close concentration generally require more rest than does lighter or more routine work. The novice may tire more quickly than the skilled performer, hence requiring more rest. Ordinarily, rest periods will yield the maximum benefit if introduced just as performance (or interest) begins to lag. If the rest break comes too soon, it may simply disrupt peak performance, requiring a new warming-up period when work is resumed. If the rest break is delayed too long, on the other hand, workers will continue to perform at a needlessly low level and will not be making the best use of their time and effort.

These common generalizations about work and rest are manifestly reasonable and can serve as useful guidelines for anyone wanting to use his or her time effectively. The industrial research on the effect of rest breaks on most work functions, however, provides meager data. There are scattered studies spanning some 50 years that quite consistently show favorable changes following the introduction of rest periods. In the early research of the Industrial Fatigue Research Board, relevant data were gathered on various industrial operations ranging from light to heavy work. The results usually showed a rise in daily output, even though the employees spent less time working after the introduction of scheduled rest periods. For example, in a group of women assembling bicycle chains, the introduction of a 5-minute rest at the end of each hour reduced total working time by 7% while increasing average daily output by 13% (Vernon & Bedford, 1924).

In a more recent study (Bhatia & Murrell, 1969), mean weekly productivity level improved, although the rest schedules reduced total working time from 8 to 7 hours a day. Equally favorable results have been obtained with office workers. In an American study of comptometer operators, a significant rise in output rate followed the introduction of short mid-morning and mid-afternoon rest breaks (McGehee & Owen, 1940). Most of these investigations used small samples and experimental designs that do not permit a clear identification of the factors accounting for improved productivity. Among the changes reported are increased rate of work, reduction of errors, decrease in unscheduled rest breaks, and improvement in attitudes and job satisfaction. With light manual operations and with office work, rest breaks undoubtedly serve to reduce boredom and drowsiness.

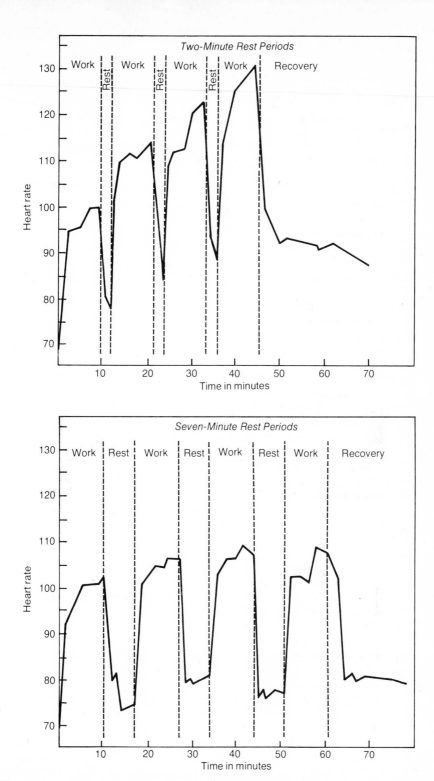

Figure 7-3. Heart-rate patterns during a lifting task performed with a 2-minute and a 7-minute rest break after every 10-minute work period. *(From Davis, Faulkner, & Miller, 1969, Figs. 2 and 3. Copyright © 1969 by The Human Factors Society, Inc. Reproduced by permission.)*

Two types of work in which the effects of rest periods can be clearly demonstrated with empirical data are heavy physical work and vigilance tasks. Figure 7-3
shows the physiological stress, as indicated by heart rate, resulting from a lifting
task carried out under two conditions: (1) with a 2-minute rest and (2) with a
7-minute rest after every 10-minute work period (Davis, Faulkner, & Miller, 1969). It
is apparent that the 2-minute break is inadequate, since the heart rate continues to
increase in successive 10-minute work periods. The 7-minute break, on the other
hand, permits the heart rate to remain at approximately the same level and below
110 in each work period.

Using a different indicator of the physiological cost of work, Murrell (1965)
proposed a formula for estimating the amount of rest required for different levels of
physical work. The formula utilizes the average Calories per minute expended
when working at the given task, as well as the number of Calories per minute
chosen as an acceptable standard over the entire working day. This standard takes
into account the maximum energy output per day a normal man can comfortably
maintain over a long period, including the amount of energy ordinarily expended
during sleep and other nonworking hours. Figure 7-4 illustrates the application of
this formula, with standards ranging from 3 Cal/min to 6 Cal/min. For instance, if
the energy cost of a given task is 8 Cal/min, as in chopping a tree, we can achieve a
standard of 4 Cal/min over the working day when the worker rests an average of 37
minutes per hour, or slightly under 5 hours during the 8-hour working day. The 4
Cal/min standard is consistent with estimates of desirable limits for men engaged
in physical work. This standard will vary, of course, with age, sex, physical
condition, and other worker variables.

At the other end of the energy-expenditure scale, vigilance tasks require
frequent breaks in order to ensure continued concentration during long periods of
relative inactivity. The effect of rest breaks in a typical monitoring task is illustrated
in a laboratory study (Bergum & Lehr, 1962) in which subjects watched a rotating

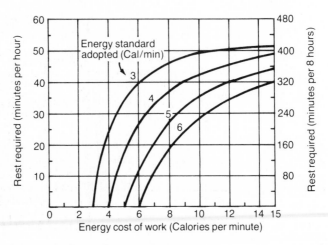

Figure 7-4. Rest requirements for work activities of varying energy costs for maximum
expenditure standards of 3, 4, 5, and 6 Calories per minute. *(From McCormick, 1976a, Fig. 7-12,
p. 177, based on formulation by Murrell, 1965, p. 376. Copyright © 1976 by McGraw-Hill, Inc. Reproduced by
permission.)*

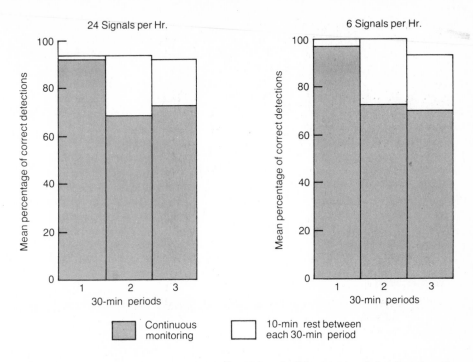

Figure 7-5. Performance in monitoring tasks with and without rest periods. *(Data from Bergum & Lehr, 1962, p. 426.)*

circular panel containing 20 half-inch red lamps, which illuminated in sequence. The signal to be detected consisted of the failure of a lamp to illuminate in its normal sequence. Control subjects worked continuously for a 90-minute period. Experimental subjects had a 10-minute rest period after each 30 minutes of work. In one experiment with 40 subjects, the signal rate was 24 per hour; in another, with 20 subjects, it was 6 per hour. Subjects responded to each signal by depressing a hand-held pushbutton. Figure 7-5 shows performance with and without rest pauses. Under the conditions of this experiment, signal rate (6 vs. 24 per hour) did not significantly affect percentage of correct signal detection. It appears that signal rates must vary more widely in order to make an appreciable difference in monitoring performance. The major finding of the study, of course, is that rest periods significantly improved signal detection for both higher and lower signal rates and were able to maintain detection at an acceptable level throughout the monitoring period.

Workweek. Among the conditions that affect human performance are *length* of workweek and workday. A workweek totaling from 35 to 40 hours has been standard for many decades. Concern about the effect of longer workweeks focuses principally on overtime work, especially during periods of national emergency. During World Wars I and II, unusually long workweeks were instituted in some plants to meet critical shortages. It thus became possible to study changes in productivity following increases and subsequent decreases in hours of work. A survey of about 3,500 men and women workers in 34 industrial plants in the United

States showed maximal efficiency with an 8-hour day and a 40-hour week (Kossoris & Kohler, 1947). Although longer hours usually increased total weekly output, the hourly output rate decreased sharply; the resulting increases in output thus lagged far behind the increase in working time. Beyond certain limits, moreover, total output may actually decline with a longer workweek, as illustrated in several early studies by the British Industrial Fatigue Research Board. In one large munitions plant, for example, shortening the workweek from 66 to $47\frac{1}{2}$ hours increased total weekly output by 13% (Vernon, 1920).

Several additional findings from studies on the workweek help to explain the decline in productivity associated with longer hours. A major reason is that the rate of work is likely to drop when the number of working hours rises. It may also take longer to reach peak productivity at the beginning of the day. The tendency for persons to slow down automatically as length of work period increases has been observed in laboratory experiments as well as in industrial investigations. It is a natural tendency to conserve one's energy in various ways as one faces the prospect of a long period of activity and to increase one's energy expenditure when a short period of activity is anticipated. The industrial studies also found that, with longer hours, much more time was lost through absenteeism, tardiness, and unscheduled rest breaks. Errors and accident rate also tended to increase.

Another question pertains, not to the total number of hours in the workweek, but to the *distribution* of working hours during the week. The early 1970s witnessed a vigorous movement toward work-schedule innovations in American industrial and governmental organizations, following an earlier similar movement in Europe (Glickman & Brown, 1973). Although some of the changes include a decrease in the total number of working hours per week, interest centered largely on alternative work patterns with the same number of hours. The most popular arrangement, adopted by hundreds of companies in the United States, was the 4-40 pattern, consisting of four 10-hour working days.[2] Research on the effects of the 4-day week has yielded mixed results with regard to advantages and disadvantages.

In a relatively well-designed study (Ivancevich, 1974), workers in two closely comparable but geographically distant divisions of a manufacturing company were compared on several measures of job satisfaction, anxiety-stress, and job performance over a 13-month period. The first month provided preconversion data. During the next 12 months, one division worked on a 4-40 schedule while the other remained on the 5-40 schedule. The findings of this study were generally favorable to the 4-40 group, which showed significantly greater improvement than did the 5-40 group in nearly all measures within the three areas investigated. A later investigation (Ivancevich & Lyon, 1977) included both a replication of the original 13-month study in another division of the same company and a later follow-up of the original experimental group after a total 25-month period. The results of the replication corroborated the generally positive findings of the original study. But the initial advantage of the first experimental group over the control group had virtually disappeared after 25 months. These findings suggest that the favorable impact of a 4-40 workweek may be limited to short-term effects.

Other studies, using principally self-report questionnaires, explored the effects of the 4-day week on workers' personal life, as well as on their job attitudes and

---

[2]Since the length of the working week varied somewhat in different organizations, the number of working hours per day varied accordingly but rarely fell below 9.

performance (Goodale & Aagaard, 1975; Nord & Costigan, 1973). The results suggest that, while workers' general attitude toward the 4-day week is favorable, more specific questions elicit a variety of complaints. Although several benefits were reported regarding personal, domestic, and leisure activities, disadvantages were also cited. Moreover, such negative reactions tended to increase over time. Workers often reported loss of sleep: even after one year of the altered working schedule, the earlier rising time had not been compensated by earlier bedtime. While absenteeism usually declines, end-of-day fatigue and slowing down are often mentioned. In several types of jobs, the unavailability of individual workers on different days creates problems with regard to communication, the scheduling of meetings, and customer contacts and service. One conclusion that clearly emerges from this research is that the benefits and deficits of the 4-40 schedule differ widely with the nature of the job and with the age, sex, and probably other characteristics of the workers.

Another scheduling innovation that is arousing considerable interest is "flexitime," whereby the 5-day week is retained but arrival and departure time may vary over a limited range (Schein, Maurer, & Novak, 1977). Such arrangements are especially attractive to workers with responsibilities for child care or other personal commitments. They also provide a means of recognizing individual differences in preference for different diurnal work patterns.

Shift Work. A much older type of variation in work schedules is illustrated by shift work. Several types of functions, as in emergency services and continuous industrial operations, must be performed on a 24-hour basis. Other types of work may be continued through all or part of the night for consumer convenience (e.g., transportation, restaurants). In still other work settings, extended operating schedules are often followed for fuller utilization of costly equipment and facilities. The need for shift workers spans a broad range of work skills and occupational levels, from residents in neurology to security guards.

Shift work must be evaluated not only in terms of productivity but also in terms of its long-range effects upon the worker's health and well-being. The problem is twofold, involving, first, the relative effectiveness of day and night work and, second, the effect of adapting to periodic changes in work cycle. By following socially established schedules of work, recreation, meals, and sleep, the human organism has developed a daily rhythm in physiological activities as well as in efficiency of work (see Colquhoun, 1971, 1972; Kleitman, 1963). Body temperature, for example, reaches a low point between 2 and 5 A.M. and a high point in midafternoon. Similar cycles have been observed in blood pressure, pulse rate, chemical composition of the blood, activity of endocrine glands, and other physiological functions. With regard to behavioral indices, corresponding cycles have been found in laboratory studies using tests of sensory, motor, and intellectual functions, as well as in investigations of the output of industrial workers. It should be noted that by altering living schedules all these cycles can be shifted forward or backward by several hours or completely reversed with regard to day and night. It is more difficult, however, to lengthen or shorten the basic 24-hour cycle, at least in some physiological processes, even when subjects live under experimentally controlled conditions.

Research on the effects of industrial shift work has been conducted in a number of countries over a period of several decades (Colquhoun, 1971, 1972; de la Mare & Walker, 1968; Malaviya & Ganesh, 1977; Mott, Mann, McLaughlin, & Warwick,

1965). In general, night workers report disturbances in sleeping, eating, and digestion. The most common problem is inability to get enough sleep in the daytime because of light, noise, and conflicts with the living habits of family and friends. Also mentioned are interference with family relations, social activities, and recreation. Although such objections are common, they are by no means universal. Some workers prefer night work for a variety of personal reasons, ranging from less traffic congestion in commuting to work to a friendlier and pleasanter atmosphere on the night shift; and for some, productivity may be higher in the night than in the day shift (Malaviya & Ganesh, 1977).

Rotating shifts call for periodic readjustment of physiological rhythms and would thus seem to be more deleterious than fixed shifts. This expectation is borne out by performance records, including errors and accident rate, as well as by adverse effects on health. A comparable situation is provided by flight across time zones. For example, a flight over the Atlantic, which involves a 5-hour change in daily schedule, requires a week for complete readjustment of physiological rhythms. The change from day to night shift may require an even longer period for such physiological adaptation. Typically, workers are given a break of 24 hours or more between shift changes to provide an opportunity for some readjustment.

Even with regard to rotating shifts, however, wide individual differences have been found. Some workers express preference for the variety afforded by a rotating shift and can apparently function effectively under such conditions. Perhaps traditional shift work should be regarded as a more extreme form of flexitime. When practicable, individual preferences for both particular shifts and rotation pattern should be taken into account. Individual decisions, however, must be based on careful consideration of possible adverse effects of both night work and frequent shift rotation. The optimal arrangement probably varies with the nature of the job functions, the work setting, the physical and psychological characteristics of the worker, and the worker's value system and life-style.

METHODS DESIGN

Time and Motion Study. In 1881, Frederick W. Taylor, a mechanical engineer, began his observations of steelworkers which led to the development of *time study* (Copley, 1923; Merrill, 1960, pp. 67–113; F. W. Taylor, 1911). His aim was to increase productivity by improving the performance of the workers. This approach represented a radical departure from engineering practices prevailing at the time, since it shifted attention from the machines to the worker. Even in the simplest unskilled operation, Taylor argued, the way in which the worker carries out the job can make a substantial difference in productivity. Time study was essentially a process of analyzing an operation into its component parts and noting the time required by the best workers to perform each part. Although Taylor defined time study to include the elimination of useless movements and the selection of the best way to perform each of the remaining movements (Copley, 1923, Vol. 1, p. 227), little was done along these lines prior to the work of Gilbreth, to be discussed below. Taylor himself concentrated on establishing optimal times for different operations and setting pay rates in accordance with such times. He was also a strong advocate of the selection and training of workers and the introduction of rest periods.

Taylor's time-study procedures were incorporated into the more elaborate techniques of *motion study* developed by Frank B. Gilbreth (1909, 1911; Gilbreth &

Gilbreth, 1917; Merrill, 1960, pp. 245–291). Like Taylor, Gilbreth was an engineer; his wife, psychologist Lillian M. Gilbreth, collaborated in much of his work and continued it after his death. Gilbreth's observations of many kinds of workers convinced him of the prevalence of wasted effort. When left to their own resources, he noted, most workers use many unnecessary and inefficient movements. It was chiefly through the elimination of unnecessary movements that Gilbreth believed output could be increased and fatigue decreased at the same time. In one of his most famous investigations, he was able to reduce the number of separate movements required in bricklaying from 18 to 5. He thereby increased the average number of bricks that could be laid in an hour from 120 to 350.

In motion study, movements are broken down into much smaller elements than was done in the earlier time study of Taylor. In mapping out the path of motion followed by the hand of the operator, Gilbreth utilized many special observational aids, such as photographs, motion pictures, stereoscopic slides, and three-dimensional wire models. The motion-picture camera is now standard equipment in time and motion analysis. Through an examination of films showing what is done by each hand of the operator and the time spent in each activity, the time and motion analyst eliminates unnecessary movements and rearranges the remaining movements in what appears to be the quickest and easiest pattern.

In working out an improved method for performing an industrial operation, the time and motion analyst is guided by certain commonly accepted rules. Lists of such guidelines can be found in standard contemporary works on time and motion analysis (e.g., Barnes, 1968; Karger & Bayha, 1965). One of the most important rules is to minimize the number of motions by eliminating unnecessary movements. Another is to minimize the length of motions, as illustrated by reducing the distance that the worker must reach in obtaining tools or materials or in operating machinery. Other common objectives are to utilize rhythmic motions whenever feasible and to employ continuous, curved movements in preference to straight-line movements involving sudden and sharp changes of direction. Still another example is the principle of bimanual symmetry, providing for the use of both hands simultaneously in opposite and symmetrical movements.

When first introduced, time and motion study did not prove to be the boon that its enthusiastic exponents had anticipated. A major obstacle was that it became linked with managerial practices evoking widespread worker hostility and lack of cooperation. Apart from such organizational problems, we can now recognize several weaknesses in the original approach—weaknesses that have been substantially corrected in current applications.

The additive treatment of movements characteristic of early time and motion studies overlooked the fact that the speed of a given movement may be influenced by other movements that precede or follow it. The identical element of motion may require appreciably more time when performed in one context than when performed in another. These interaction effects were demonstrated by means of specially designed apparatus, which permits separate timing of the elements of a movement sequence (Hecker, Green, & Smith, 1956; Schappe, 1965; Wehrkamp & Smith, 1952). In one experiment, the time required to turn on switches was longer, the longer the distance the hand had to travel between switches. In another, travel time was found to vary as a function of the time required to manipulate different types of switches, as by pulling, pushing, turning, and dial setting. When the subject had to perform a more time-consuming manipulation, as in setting dials, his hand also moved more slowly from one position to the next than it did when he performed quicker manipulations. It thus appears that, when a person is set for more precise and slower movement, this set carries over to all components of the movement sequence. For this reason, it is necessary for the time and motion analyst to check the times of the total movement sequence in its final form, rather than relying on estimates obtained for separate components or for these components observed in a different sequence.

Another difficulty is that a movement pattern that looks simple on a chart may be awkward and fatiguing to the human operator. Today, more emphasis is put on the anatomic and behavioral characteristics of the human operator and less on the geometry of the path of motion. For example, although bimanual symmetry is generally a useful guideline, it does not always yield the most efficient pattern of movement (e.g., Barnes, Mundel, & MacKenzie, 1940; Lauru, 1954). In certain tasks, a single-handed operation or the use of one hand at a time may be faster or may require less energy expenditure.

From the psychologist's viewpoint, a fundamental weakness in the approach of the early time and motion analysts was their failure to recognize individual differences in work methods. They were firmly convinced that there is "one best way" for performing each job. We now know that there may be an interaction between work methods and individual variables. As a result of differences in physical or psychological characteristics among workers, one method may be best for individual A and another method for individual B. An interesting illustration is provided by research on the performance of older workers (Welford et al., 1951), showing that older persons tend to modify their method of performing a task so as to compensate for any decline in perceptual skills and other minor disabilities. When a task permitted a variety of approaches and the method was largely under the performer's control, compensatory changes occurred and performance showed no age decrement. In tasks whose performance was rigidly set by the conditions of the experiment, on the other hand, performance declined with age.

A related point pertains to the desirability of worker participation in any methods-improvement program. With good two-way communication, many suggestions for improving work methods will originate with the workers themselves. If workers become "motion-minded," moreover, they can readily discover ways of eliminating waste motion and increasing operating efficiency. It has been proposed (Likert, 1961) that workers and supervisors should be trained in the basic techniques of work simplification, so that they may themselves apply these procedures, with technical assistance and advice from experts when needed. Under these conditions, work methods can remain sufficiently flexible to allow for individual differences. No longer need the "one best way" be prescribed for all individuals by an outside expert.

Broad Scope of Modern Methods Design. Today, time and motion analysis is carried on largely by industrial engineers, although psychologists may employ its techniques among other procedures for improving human performance. Work methods include more than movements. Attention must also be given to the improvement of perceptual, cognitive, and decision-making processes. Any activity could probably be performed more efficiently if persons habitually engaged in it were to examine it systematically from this point of view. The broader scope of the current approach is also evidenced in the utilization of more comprehensive criteria for evaluating efficiency of work methods. More use is now made of qualitative indices of output, such as errors, rejects, and spoilage, in addition to measures of sheer quantity. Safety has also become a major goal in the improvement of work methods.

Methods-design programs merge imperceptibly with several other programs for improving human performance. Some are concerned with a group of persons working on a task as an integrated team. In this respect they border on some of the organizational problems considered in Chapter 6. Certain features of the working environment, to be discussed in Chapter 9, have a direct bearing on performance effectiveness. Equipment design and layout, treated in Chapter 8, are probably most closely linked to methods design. For example, research on inspection jobs has identified many ways for improving the required discrimination and thus reducing error rate (see McCormick & Tiffin, 1974, pp. 503–509). Some pertain to better inspection procedures, such as scanning for only one type of defect at a time or examining the article while it is lying flat rather than in motion. Several, however, involve specially devised inspection aids, such as magnification of the features to be observed or the use of an overlay for quick spotting of defects. In many kinds of jobs, the availability of performance aids, such as charts, tables, and diagrams for ready reference, can greatly facilitate the worker's task. The preparation of operating manuals that are clear, easy to follow, and suited to the reading level of their users is a significant aspect of job simplification (see, e.g., Sticht, 1975).

Research on work methods is concerned with a wide range of human activities, from the least tiring posture for picking strawberries and the optimal speed for climbing stairs to the safest way to operate the controls in the cockpit of a jet. Many examples of such applications can be found in texts on engineering psychology (e.g., McCormick, 1976a, Ch. 7).

As one illustration, we may consider research on methods of *carrying loads.* Despite the development of mechanical devices, loads are still being carried by persons in many contexts—from farm laborers to restaurant waitresses and from travelers with luggage to students with piles of books. In industrially underdeveloped countries, moreover, transporting loads by human carriers is still prevalent for a variety of purposes. Experimental studies in this area have used several measures of energy cost to the organism, such as pulse rate and oxygen consumption. In general, the best position in carrying loads is one that interferes least with the carrier's normal postural balance and center of gravity. The optimal method varies somewhat with the weight of the load. High positions, as on a tray, are better for lighter loads, while low positions are better for heavier loads. Similarly, the shape of the load may affect the carrier's posture and hence the efficiency of operation.

A specific experiment, illustrated in Figure 7-6, compared the oxygen consumption of seven methods of carrying loads which are used in various cultures (Datta & Ramanathan, 1971). The participants were seven normal, healthy volunteers. Each carried a 30-kilogram load of granite chips at a prescribed walking rate over a level 1-kilometer route. The methods were rotated in random order among the participants, one method per day. In Figure 7-6, the methods are arranged in increasing order of oxygen consumption, with the most efficient method used as a base (100). The methods are described briefly as follows:

1. *Double pack*—load equally divided between front and back packs, which are strapped across shoulder and tied loosely together at bottom;
2. *Head*—load balanced on head, with straw ring as padding, and kept in position by one or both hands;

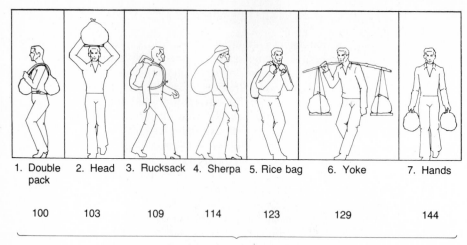

1. Double pack	2. Head	3. Rucksack	4. Sherpa	5. Rice bag	6. Yoke	7. Hands
100	103	109	114	123	129	144

Relative oxygen consumption

Figure 7-6. Relative oxygen consumption of different methods of carrying loads. *(Data from Datta & Ramanathan, 1971.)*

3. *Rucksack*—strapped across shoulders as a high backpack;
4. *Sherpa*—carried in a sack supported by strap around forehead (used by hill-climbing sherpas, since it frees both hands);
5. *Rice bag*—carried in a sack on back, upper two corners held by hands or hooks;
6. *Yoke*—divided equally and suspended by three ropes at each end of a resilient bamboo strip placed across shoulder;
7. *Hands*—divided equally and carried by two hands, as in water pails.

A second and quite different illustration concerns the accuracy of *blind positioning movements*. This is the type of movement required when one operates some control device without looking at it, usually because one must look at something else at the time. Examples can be found in driving a car and in landing a plane. In an experiment on this problem (Fitts, 1947), the subjects wore blindfolds and had to touch various targets with a sharp-pointed marker, as shown in Figure 7-7. There were three tiers of targets, the middle one being at approximately shoulder level and the others at about 45° above and below. Horizontally, the targets extended from front to 135° to the subject's right and left. Mean error scores for each target position showed greatest accuracy for the front positions and least for the extreme lateral positions. With regard to level, accuracy tended to be highest for the bottom tier and lowest for the top tier. Right-hand targets could be reached with slightly more accuracy than left-hand ones.

INDUSTRIAL SAFETY AND ACCIDENT PREVENTION

Extensive effort is now devoted to the problems of industrial safety and accident prevention. Besides a sharp rise in both basic and applied research pertaining to accidents, the years since 1965 have witnessed a flood of handbooks, new

Figure 7-7. View of left side of target stand used in study of blind positioning movements. *(Data from Fitts, 1947. Photograph by courtesy of United States Air Force.)*

journals, symposia, and national and international conferences devoted to safety (see, e.g., *Encyclopedia*, 1971). A large proportion of this activity has centered around highway safety (Forbes, 1972). Psychologists have investigated not only the behavior of drivers but also that of passengers, bicycle riders, and pedestrians of different sorts, including children. Research has been concerned with the general driver as well as with taxi, bus, and truck drivers, outside repairmen, and other commercial drivers. Increasing attention is also being given to safety in the home, where a substantial proportion of accidents occur.

The procedures employed in industrial safety programs vary widely, from the development of safety devices and protective clothing to safety campaigns and competitions. One of the recognized objectives of methods improvement is to increase operational safety. Studies of fatigue, rest periods, length of workweek, and shift work have frequently employed accident rate as a criterion. In fact, accident prevention is related to nearly every topic in industrial psychology, including selection, training, and employee attitudes. For several types of jobs, screening out individuals likely to have many accidents is an important aspect of personnel selection. Training employees to follow safe operating procedures is a significant part of many training programs. And the role of employee attitudes in the observance of safety rules and in other behavior related to accidents is widely recognized. Characteristics of the working environment and equipment design have also been investigated with reference to safety.

Psychology's contribution to industrial safety consists chiefly in research on the causes of accidents. Some typical approaches will be examined below. They have been chosen because they either illustrate important methodological problems or concern some explanatory concept that has been used widely in accident research.

Accidents and Human Factors. It has been estimated that the vast majority of industrial accidents are caused by human factors, that is, by something that a person does or fails to do. Such causes include not only unsafe operating procedures but also faulty or inadequate inspection of equipment or materials. Thus even accidents attributed to equipment failure may in many cases be traceable to human errors. It is therefore understandable that many investigators have looked for a relationship between accident rate and personal characteristics. A large number of variables have been studied in this connection, including job-related aptitudes, psychomotor skills, emotional and interpersonal traits, attitudes, sensory deficiencies, health and physical characteristics, job experience, age, sex, educational level, and socioeconomic background factors. Although a few clear-cut relationships have been established, results are often difficult to interpret because so many of these variables are interrelated and there are probably some significant interactions.

Some of the methodological problems involved in isolating the contribution of different factors are illustrated in a well-designed study of the relation of age and experience to accident rate (Van Zelst, 1954). A frequent difficulty in evaluating the relation of job experience to accident rate stems from selective turnover. Since workers with the worst accident records tend to be separated from the company, the longer an employee remains on a job the more highly selected is he or she likely to be with regard to safety. This progressive selection could bring about a spurious negative relation between length of job experience and accident rate. In the above study, monthly accident records were plotted separately for 1,237 male employees who remained with the company during a five-year period and for 1,317 male employees who were hired at the same time but who had left or been discharged during that period. Figure 7-8 shows the results. It can be seen that accident rate drops sharply for both groups during the first five months on the job. Beyond that point, however, there is a general leveling off in both groups. Of particular interest is the finding that, after the initial adjustment period, accident rate is consistently higher for the turnover than for the nonturnover group.

In the same study, accident records were similarly plotted for 387 male workers hired after a systematic training program had been installed in the company. These men thus had the benefit of formal training in correct job procedures and safety methods. The result was a lower initial accident rate and a more rapid drop than in the untrained group. The trained group required only three months of job experience to reach the safety level achieved by the untrained group after five months.

In still another part of the same study, age was found to be significantly associated with accident rate, when the effect of job experience was ruled out. Figure 7-9 gives the average monthly accident rates for three groups of workers. Groups A and B were equated in job experience, each having spent an average of three years on their present job. Group A, however, was younger than Group B, their mean ages being 29 and 41 years. It can be seen that the younger group had a consistently higher accident rate throughout the experimental period. Group C was in the same general age bracket as Group B (mean age 39 years) but unlike the first two groups had no job experience. It is interesting to note that, after the usual

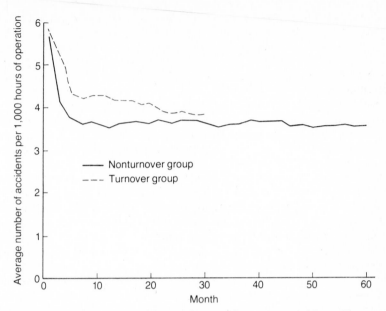

Figure 7-8. Relationship between job experience and average monthly accident rate for a nonturnover and a turnover group. *(From Van Zelst, 1954, p. 315. Copyright © 1954 by American Psychological Association. Reproduced by permission.)*

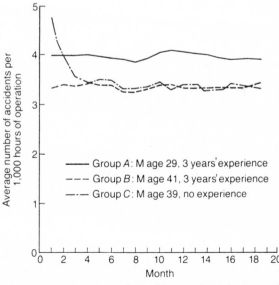

Figure 7-9. Relationship between age of employee and average monthly accident rate. *(From Van Zelst, 1954, p. 316. Copyright © 1954 by American Psychological Association. Reproduced by permission.)*

adjustment period, this group's accident rate dropped to a level that practically coincided with that of Group B.

The interpretation of statistics regarding motor vehicle accidents is especially beset with pitfalls. In studies of the relation between frequency of traffic accidents and personal characteristics of drivers, for example, it is necessary to control mileage and exposure hazard. Thus, if drivers in certain age ranges drive more miles per year than those in other age brackets, or if they drive under more dangerous conditions with regard to weather, illumination, or traffic volume, they are more likely to have accidents. Another problem arises from the incomplete reporting of accidents in official records (F. L. McGuire, 1973). A substantial proportion of legally reportable accidents are not recorded, although the proportion of underreporting decreases with the seriousness of the accidents. The underreporting, moreover, varies with geographic location and with such driver variables as age, sex, and occupation. It is difficult to generalize about such apparent reporting biases, however, because of interrelations among some of these driver variables as well as their possible relation to seriousness of accidents.

Surveys of automobile drivers have generally failed to reveal any close association between personal characteristics and accident frequency, although measures of attitudes and personality factors appear somewhat more promising than do other variables investigated (e.g., Brown & Berdie, 1960). Even in the case of personality characteristics, however, it seems likely that different response patterns account for accidents on the part of different individuals. For example, some may have accidents because of habitual unconcern with the rights of others, some because of a compulsion to hurry at all times, some because of strong feelings of hostility and competitiveness toward other drivers, and so on. It is also interesting to note that two studies of young automobile drivers found no significant relation between accident frequency and either habitual driving speed or number of traffic violations (Comrey, 1958; R. G. Stewart, 1957). All these results suggest that the type of behavior that produces accidents may be quite specific and cannot be identified in terms of broad personality traits or general driving habits.

The need to relate *specific* type of accident to *specific* personal characteristics is illustrated by an exploratory study of 104 taxi drivers (Babarik, 1968). Laboratory tests of different types of reaction time indicated that those drivers who were relatively slow in initiating a motor response but fast in carrying out the movement had significantly more rear-end collisions and fewer front-end collisions than did the drivers with more nearly typical ratios of initiation (or perceptual) and movement speeds. The results fit the hypothesis that drivers with relatively slow perceptual and relatively rapid movement responses tend to stop their vehicles abruptly, thereby increasing the chances that a following driver runs into them. These findings are also consistent with the results of an early study indicating that workers with faster reactions on motor than on perceptual tests had more industrial accidents than did those exhibiting the reverse reaction pattern (Drake, 1940).

A promising approach to accident research is provided by a series of studies based on a perceptual-information-processing model of driver behavior (Barrett & Thornton, 1968; Barrett, Thornton, & Cabe, 1969; Kahneman, Ben-Ishai, & Lotan, 1973; Mihal & Barrett, 1976). Criterion data on accident-related behavior were obtained both from detailed company records of commercial drivers and from reactions to emergency situations in a realistic simulator using a televised road scene. The driver's perceptual and information-processing behavior was assessed through three types of measures: (1) tests of perceptual style; (2) tests of reaction time; and (3) a selective attention test for different series of auditory stimuli presented to each ear. The tests of perceptual style, derived from the research of Witkin and his associates (Witkin, Dyk, Faterson, Goodenough, & Karp, 1962), deal essentially with the observer's ability to extract salient information from a complex background. Persons exhibiting a high degree of this ability are described as field-independent; those whose responses are more strongly influenced by the perceptual field in which a particular stimulus is embedded are designated as more field-dependent. The research findings supported the hypothesis that the "safer" drivers tend to be more field-independent and to excel significantly in selective attention and in complex reaction time. Field independence as a factor in auto safety has itself been the focus of considerable research (Goodenough, 1976). Several hypotheses have been proposed and are being tested in the effort to understand how field-dependent drivers differ from field-independent drivers in their response to emergencies and in their other driving behavior.

Accident Proneness. The possibility of going astray in the interpretation of accident statistics is well illustrated by the concept of accident proneness, which refers essentially to the tendency of an individual to retain his or her relative accident liability over a long period of time. Often this concept has been used with the further implications of generality and causality. Thus it is assumed that a highly accident-prone person will tend to incur many accidents in all situations, from opening a can to driving a car, and that his or her accident liability is a reflection of personal characteristics leading to unsafe behavior. In the early research, the distribution of accidents within a group was often cited as evidence of accident proneness. For example, if 10% of the group have 50% of the accidents, these individuals are identified as accident prone. It would then seem that, if we could either remove these persons from hazardous jobs or possibly retrain them, we should be able to cut the accident rate in half.

The fallacy in this reasoning stems from the assumption that by chance everyone should have the same number of accidents. Hence, any marked deviation from the average accident rate is regarded as accident proneness. Actually the distribution of accidents obtained in most groups closely approximates the distribution expected by chance (Mintz & Blum, 1949). With rare events, such as serious accidents, this distribution is highly skewed, since most persons will have no accidents during the period covered.[3] Suppose a total of 10 accidents occur in a group of 100 persons. Obviously at least 90 persons will have had no accident. In fact, since some will have two or even more accidents by chance, more than 90 will have had no accident. As the total number of accidents in the group increases, the distribution becomes less skewed and approaches a symmetrical curve. This was illustrated empirically by comparing the distributions of accidents among 59 streetcar motormen over increasingly longer periods, ranging from 1 to 13 months (Ghiselli & Brown, 1955, pp. 343–344). The longer the observation period, the larger the total number of accidents and hence the more nearly symmetrical the curve.

The only sure test of accident proneness is to compare the accident records of the same individuals for two periods of time (Maritz, 1950). In this way we can

---

[3]When the number of events (e.g., accidents) is small compared with the number of persons to whom such events can happen, the appropriate chance distribution is the Poisson distribution, a highly skewed curve with the peak at the low frequencies.

ascertain whether the *same* individuals have high accident records during both observation periods. This procedure was applied in a classical study of about 29,500 automobile drivers over a six-year period. During the total period, slightly over 4% of the drivers accounted for over one-third of the accidents. Reanalysis of the same data with regard to the first and second three-year intervals, however, revealed that the high-accident records during the two periods were obtained largely by *different individuals*. As a result, if those drivers having two or more accidents during the first three-year period had been prevented from driving during the second period, the total number of accidents during the second period would have been reduced by only 3.7%. To put it differently, those identified as "safe drivers" during the first three years (because they had either one accident or none) accounted for 96.3% or all the accidents during the next three years.

In the case of industrial accidents, the correlations between accident records of the same persons during two time periods vary widely with the nature of the job, the sample, the working conditions, and other variables. There is little or no evidence that persons maintain their level of accident-prone behavior across *different situations*. Within some occupations, however, there seem to be consistent individual differences in unsafe or accident-inducing behavior. McCormick and Tiffin (1974, p. 520), for example, report correlations of .74, .86, and .88 between accident rates during two six-month periods in three groups of production workers. In this study, all persons within each group were engaged in the same kind of work. When large groups of workers performing varied functions were investigated, the resulting correlations may be inflated by consistent individual differences in exposure to hazard. Under these conditions, persons performing relatively hazardous work will probably be doing so during both observation periods and will thus tend to have higher accident rates in both periods than will workers in safer jobs. In a study of 9,000 steelworkers, however, close agreement was found in the number of accidents during two successive years, even when the data were corrected for job hazard (McCormick & Tiffin, 1974, p. 521).

In conclusion, accident proneness may serve as a useful descriptive concept in investigating industrial accidents within specific jobs. In the far more complex and varied situation presented by traffic accidents, however, it is likely that the identification of accident-prone drivers as a group is far too simplistic an approach to yield fruitful results. It is more productive to investigate the influence of specific conditions that impair the driver's ability to operate a car safely. Extensive research has been conducted on the effects of fatigue, loss of sleep, alcohol, and drugs on driving behavior (Forbes, 1972). These conditions create serious hazards by reducing alertness, vigilance, psychomotor coordination, and speed of response. Other adverse changes are likely to occur in judgment, attitudes, and emotional responses.

Task Variables. With the growing realization that accidents can be best understood in terms of specific behavior, attention has turned more and more to the contribution of task variables. Any conditions that increase the complexity or difficulty of the operator's task will lengthen response time and raise the likelihood of error. When a driver becomes confused because of inadequate road marking, for example, he or she is likely to slow down or stop abruptly, make an improper turn, get on a one-way lane in the wrong direction, or engage in other unsafe and hazardous behavior.

Psychologists first approached the problem of traffic accidents by developing tests for the selection of drivers (DeSilva, 1942; Lauer, 1960). A later development was the establishment of "drivers' clinics" for rehabilitating accident-prone drivers by making them aware of deficiencies and of faulty operating habits. More recently, interest has shifted to the application of human engineering to the design of highways and equipment (Forbes, 1972; R. J. Kaplan, 1976). For example, research has been conducted on the dimensions and placement of controls, displays, seats, and windows in buses and trucks. A number of studies have been concerned with characteristics of highway signs, such as position, size, color, and lettering. Others have dealt with the perceptibility of stop signs and blinker lights; the clarity and comprehensibility of traffic symbols; and the relative effectiveness of different types of vehicle markings, signaling devices, and headlights. Drivers' responses to the yellow phase of traffic signals (Konečni, Ebbesen, & Konečni, 1976) and drivers' judgments of the speeds of their own and of other cars on the highway (Olson, Wachsler, & Bauer, 1961; Schmidt & Tiffin, 1969) have also been investigated.

Situational Variables. Among the variables investigated in relation to accident rate are various working conditions subsumed under the concept of psychological climate (Keenan, Kerr, & Sherman, 1951; Kerr, 1957; Slivnick, Kerr, & Kosinar, 1957). One study (Keenan et al., 1951) analyzed all lost-time accidents of 7,103 employees of a tractor factory over a five-year period. Mean accident rate per person was computed for each of 44 shop departments. The same departments were also rated on a number of situational variables by a panel of eight raters from the company's managerial personnel. The mean accident rate for departments was then correlated with each of these rated situational variables. Partial correlation technique was employed in the effort to tease out the effects of variables that were themselves intercorrelated. One of the closest relationships found in this study was that between accident rate and physical discomfort of the shop environment, as from excessive heat, noise, vibration, or dust. The investigators concluded that the annoyance and distraction occasioned by these conditions increase accident liability. It was also interesting to note that the presence of an obvious danger, such as glowing molten metal, increased the likelihood of unrelated accidents that did not involve the particular hazard. It may be that the presence of an obvious danger reduces the attention given to other, less conspicuous accident hazards.

In a survey of published findings pertaining to psychological climate and accident rate, Kerr (1957) proposed two major explanatory mechanisms, based upon alertness and stress. First he argued that accidents are simply one kind of low-quality work behavior, similar to errors or spoilage. Conditions that improve the quality of work tend also to reduce accident rate. One of these is alertness; another is freedom from distracting negative stresses. With regard to alertness, Kerr maintained that a psychological climate that encourages passive compliance and discourages individual initiative is likely to reduce alertness and thereby increase accident frequency. One survey of different factory departments, for instance, found a correlation of −.40 between promotion possibilities and accident rate. In the same survey, departments with the best suggestion records tended to have the fewest accidents. It is apparent that psychological-climate theories of accidents link the problem of industrial safety with questions of organizational structure and supervisory practices discussed in Chapter 6.

Overview of Emerging Trends. A conspicuous feature of current research on industrial and vehicular safety is its increasing breadth of coverage. Reference has already been made to operational safety as a recognized objective of selection, training, and organizational-development programs. Some of the research cited in this section, particularly in reference to traffic accidents, deals with the design of equipment and environments, to be discussed in Chapters 8 and 9. Clinical, counseling, and community psychology can all contribute from their specialized vantage points. And a number of safety problems fall within the areas of medical and legal psychology (Chs. 18 and 19).

A second prominent feature of the present approach is its systems orientation. Although certainly apparent in research on industrial safety, this orientation is most clearly illustrated in the investigation of traffic safety. In this area, we can see applications of systems concepts on at least three levels. First, the driver, vehicle, and road can be regarded as a feedback-controlled continuous tracking system of the sort to be considered in Chapter 8. The driver's behavior is constantly responsive both to stimuli from the road and to the feedback from his or her own prior reactions in controlling vehicle movement. Second, the variables of the driver (human abilities and limitations) interact with variables of the vehicle (equipment) and variables of highway design and traffic control (environment). The safety and effectiveness of system performance can be altered by changes in any of these interacting variables. Third, there is increasing attention to cost-benefit analysis and trade-offs within the broader societal system in which vehicular safety is embedded. For example, in the design of cars and the legal control of their operation, several significant objectives need to be examined and balanced, such as those pertaining to safety, air pollution, noise, fuel conservation, and consumer wants with regard to costs (initial, operating, maintenance), operating convenience, and the like.

A third major trend is the increasing recognition of the behavioral specificity of safe and unsafe operating procedures. The most productive research has dealt with the relation between specific task demands and specific behavioral characteristics. This approach is aided by the development of theoretical models regarding the operator's behavior. It contrasts with the blind empiricism of earlier studies, in which the frequency of miscellaneous accidents was correlated with any available variables.

Finally, there is an increasing amount of research on near-accidents and unsafe behavior as such. This type of study provides more data under better controlled conditions than does the slow accumulation of accident statistics. Related to this approach is the study of safe behavior in the activity under investigation. These more direct and positive approaches to safety research require the same sorts of job analyses and task analyses that underlie the development of sound selection and training programs (Chs. 2 and 4).

SUMMARY

The principal goal of engineering psychology is the design of operating procedures, equipment, and environments to fit human capabilities, limitations, needs, and preferences. Some engineering psychologists contribute to this goal through research on human performance. Others work closely with specialists from other fields, within the broad area of human factors engineering, in developing appropriate procedures, products, and operating systems.

Minimizing fatigue is an important objective in the improvement of human performance. Fatigue has been variously defined in terms of feelings of tiredness, decline in output, and physiological changes. Measures of oxygen consumption and heart rate illustrate physiological indices of fatigue. So-called mental fatigue may include, in varying combinations, feelings of boredom, drowsiness, lapses of attention and difficulty in concentrating, muscular tension, and other vague discomforts. Reactions to repetitive, monotonous jobs depend upon the interaction of worker, task, and situational variables.

In most types of work, the introduction of scheduled rest periods is generally accompanied by improvement in job satisfaction and slight increases in productivity. In heavy physical work, properly spaced rest breaks of adequate duration are essential to prevent serious fatigue effects. Tasks calling for continuous vigilance also require frequent rest periods to maintain a dependable performance level. Length of workday and workweek affect productivity, output rate tending to decline beyond an 8-hour day and a 40-hour week. Shift work involves disruption of diurnal physiological rhythms, especially with rapid rotation between different shifts. However, individuals differ in both preferences and ability to adjust to different work schedules. Extensive empirical tryouts of scheduling innovations, including the 4-day week and flexitime, have yielded mixed results; they are probably effective ways of meeting the needs and preferences of some workers in certain types of jobs.

Beginning with the early contributions of Taylor and Gilbreth, time and motion study has now become part of more comprehensive methods-design programs. These programs are characterized by a broadened scope of problems and procedures, a recognition of individual differences, and a firmer grounding on basic research in the physiology and psychology of human performance.

Accident prevention is a recognized objective of modern methods-improvement programs, besides being related to nearly every other aspect of industrial and engineering psychology. Studies on the relation of accident rate to personal characteristics must take into account the interrelation of many personal variables. Accident proneness can be conclusively demonstrated only through the correlation of individual accident records over different time periods. Increasing attention is being given to the role of task and situational variables in eliciting safe or unsafe behavior both in industry and on the highway. Research on accident prevention has been advanced by the application of theoretical models relating specific behavior to specific types of accidents and by the study of near-accidents and unsafe behavior in direct comparison to safe behavior in particular situations. The analysis of safety problems provides especially clear illustrations of the systems approach characteristic of all engineering psychology.

HUMAN FACTORS IN EQUIPMENT DESIGN

EIGHT

CHAPTER 7 WAS CONCERNED with the improvement of human performance through the design of work methods and work schedules. Among the major criteria of effective human performance are reduction in accident and health hazards, lessening of fatigue, increase in worker satisfaction, and improvement in quantity and quality of output. In the present chapter, we shall see how performance can be enhanced through the design and arrangement of equipment to fit human capabilities. The improvement that can be effected by such procedures is usually far greater than that ordinarily obtained through the selection or training of operators or the introduction of more efficient work methods. Moreover, equipment redesign permits a fuller utilization of available human resources by reducing the ability requirements of the job or by making provision for special disabilities. For instance, research has been done to identify ways in which equipment can be modified for more effective use by older workers or by physically handicapped persons. It should also be borne in mind that equipment design finds many applications in the manufacture of consumer products, such as household appliances, cooking utensils, office furniture, automobiles, toys, and sports equipment. In some of these areas, engineering psychology overlaps consumer psychology in both objectives and procedures.

A major feature of current engineering psychology is its comprehensive approach. Beginning as "knob-and-dial" research, which dealt with rather specific equipment problems, engineering psychology has become increasingly concerned with man-machine systems. The latter involve a composite analysis of all that is done by the machines and by the operator or team of operators required to carry out a complex task. It is in such systems research that the most spectacular progress can be made. Moreover, it is chiefly through this orientation that engineering psychology has begun to make contributions to basic psychological knowledge, as well as to other fields of applied psychology.

MAN-MACHINE SYSTEMS

Basic Concepts. If we were to name the one most distinctive contribution of modern engineering psychology, it would probably be the concept of man-machine systems. A schematic diagram of such a system is given in Figure 8-1. Essentially, this approach requires that we consider the human operator and the machine as interacting components of a single system. Psychologists began to use such an approach in their efforts to communicate with engineers. It is characteristic of man-machine systems that the functions of the human operator are described in engineering terminology. These functions include sensing or information receiving, data processing, and operation of controls. Inputs, such as temperature, amount of gasoline, direction and speed of motion, and the like, are translated by the mechanisms into signals, which are transmitted to the human operator by the displays. In many situations, of course, the operator receives at least some information directly, as from looking at the road when driving a car. The operator combines the new information with his or her stored knowledge and thereby decides upon a course of action, such as the operation of a particular control. The mechanism activated by the control in turn leads to a corresponding output, such as turning the car to the right or increasing the altitude of the plane.

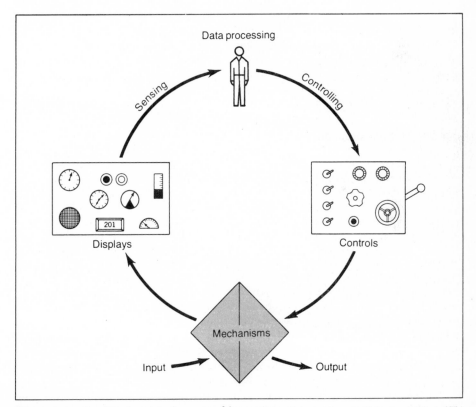

Figure 8-1. Simplified model of man-machine system. *(Adapted from F. V. Taylor, 1957, p. 250.)*

Apart from facilitating interdisciplinary communication, the concept of man-machine systems has served to advance our understanding of human performance. This approach makes it evident that what has often been regarded as the performance of the human operator is actually total system performance. Altering some feature of the equipment, for example, may greatly improve the output of the man-machine system. But it cannot be assumed that the performance of the human operator has improved under these circumstances. Improvement in system output resulting from changes in task variables should be distinguished from improvement in operator performance, such as that resulting from selection or training.

By investigating the performance of the whole man-machine system, it is possible to specify the proportion of total system error attributable to each of its components. As a result, effort can be focused on improving those components of the total operation that account for a major proportion of performance errors. Such an analysis may indicate that changes could most profitably be introduced in display characteristics, in control characteristics, or in the intervening data processing that the operator must perform. By altering the system dynamics, some of the data-processing load may be removed from the operator and built into the machine. The operator's task is thereby simplified, and the speed and accuracy of overall system performance may be increased to unprecedented levels.

Engineering psychologists were in large part responsible for introducing the systems approach in the study of human performance, an approach that is now followed increasingly in all fields of applied psychology. In our overview of industrial and organizational psychology, we have already encountered certain major features of this approach, including interaction and trade-offs. Interaction refers to situations wherein the effect of any one variable on system performance depends upon the nature and/or amount of another variable. Within the personnel subsystem, this relationship was illustrated by interaction of worker aptitude level with training method. In a man-machine system, it can be illustrated by interactions between operator skills and response demands of the equipment. For example, if a piece of equipment is designed for on-the-spot repairs, the operator may need sophisticated electronic skills; if it is designed with replaceable modules, the operator may need no such skills.

Systems design usually involves trade-offs in the allocation of functions to different system components, including human and mechanical components (see Chapanis, 1976). The advantages of using a particular kind of component must be balanced against the costs (or disadvantages) associated with its use. Alternative arrangements and allocations of functions may have to be investigated (through laboratory simulations, computer simulations, or other procedures) to evaluate the resulting cost-effectiveness of the total system. It should be kept in mind that the use of the term "cost" in this context includes not only economic considerations but also other applicable social, organizational, and personal values.

The interchange of functions between man and machine is facilitated by the use of engineering models to describe human behavior. If the machine is to take over some of the functions of the human, these functions must first be specified in the terminology of physics and mathematics. Analyzing human behavior in terms of a new set of constructs and models will in turn provide psychologists with fresh insights, sharpen their concepts, and open up new fields of research. The rapidly growing body of psychological research on information theory and on decision making illustrates some of the effects of engineering psychology upon basic psychological research.

Tracking Experiments in Closed-Loop Systems. The simple system diagrammed in Figure 8-1 represents a *closed-loop system,* in which the results of the
operator's actions are fed back into the displays, and such feedback produces
constant readjustments in the operator's responses. A familiar closed-loop system
not involving a human operator is a heating system controlled by a thermostat.
When the room temperature drops below the setting, the thermostat turns on the
burner. When this action causes the room temperature to rise to the designated
level, the thermostat turns off the burner. Examples of man-machine closed-loop
systems include driving a car, steering a ship, and operating a power shovel.

An *open-loop system,* on the other hand, is one which, once activated, cannot be
further controlled. Illustrations are provided by driving a golf ball and by target
shooting. To be sure, by observing performance in one trial, the individual can
improve his or her golf drive or come closer to the bull's eye in the next trial. But
such feedback does not permit the continuing control process characteristic of
closed-loop systems.

In their investigation of the variables influencing the performance of closed-
loop systems, engineering psychologists have conducted several hundred experiments involving the tracking of a moving target (J. A. Adams, 1961; McCormick,
1976a, pp. 213–235; Poulton, 1974). In such experiments, the operator must make
continuous adjustments with a crank, wheel, or other control device in order to
maintain alignment between a "target" and a "cursor," or indicator (Fig. 8-2).
Tracking may be of the pursuit or the compensatory variety. In *pursuit tracking,* the
target moves, and the operator must follow this movement with the cursor, which
he controls. In *compensatory tracking,* there is a fixed center reference mark, and
the operation of the control counteracts the target movement so as to keep the
target aligned with this fixed mark. In compensatory tracking, the operator does
not directly observe either the experimentally controlled stimulus movement or the
response movement, which he himself controls. What he does observe is the error,
or difference, between the two movements. Under most conditions, compensatory
tracking is more difficult than pursuit tracking.

Among the many task variables whose effects on tracking performance have
been studied are characteristics of the target, such as its rate of movement and
size; characteristics of the control, such as its position, size, plane of rotation, rate

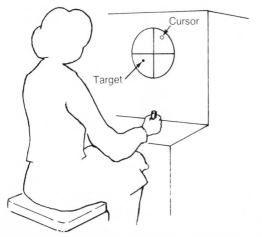

Figure 8-2. A typical tracking task.

of motion, friction, and inertia; ratio between rate of motion of control and of cursor; and type of control exerted, that is, position, velocity, or acceleration. Some studies have employed two-handed tracking, in which one hand controls right-left movement of the cursor and the other hand controls front-back or up-down movement. Other research has investigated the interaction of task variables with operator variables. Still other studies have been concerned with an analysis of the person's behavior in carrying out a tracking operation.

In some complex tracking systems, the operator's task may overtax human capability, especially within the available response time; some may require mathematical operations beyond the ability of most persons, even if sufficient time were available. For such situations, several procedures have been developed to facilitate the operator's task (McCormick, 1976a, pp. 219–223). In each case, part of the operator's data processing is shifted to the machine, and either the resulting display or the control action is appropriately adjusted. An example is *quickening,* whereby the derivative information provided in the display can be translated directly into action without further processing by the operator. Quickening is especially helpful where the observable response of the system to the operator's control actions is delayed. Another procedure is the use of *predictor displays,* which may show, for example, the future position of a vehicle that is being guided in a particular direction at a particular rate. Approaching the problem from the opposite angle, other experimenters have demonstrated that delayed feedback about one's own motor behavior in such activities as writing or drawing, as well as in steering action, can substantially degrade performance (Coleman, Ruff, & Smith, 1970; K. U. Smith, 1962).

System Simulation. Among the procedures utilized by engineering psychologists is system simulation, which permits the investigation of man-machine systems under controlled laboratory conditions (H. M. Parsons, 1972b). We already encountered the use of simulators for training purposes in Chapter 4. Such simulators are frequently used by a single trainee at a time. System simulation, on the other hand, typically involves a group of persons working together on several equipment components. This type of simulation may be employed in system design, system evaluation, and experimental investigations of system variables. Investigators can simulate the environment, the equipment, and even the behavior of the human operators, as in a complete computer simulation. Simulations of the physical components of the system may range from miniatures, photographs, maps, and diagrams to replicas or adaptations of real objects or parts of objects (e.g., cockpit of an airplane). Most major projects have used realistic simulations of equipment and environment with human operators. Frequently the inputs that are simulated are signals or messages (e.g., blips on a radarscope, radio messages) instead of the original objects from which they would normally emanate.

A major application of system simulation is found in long-term projects on air traffic control systems. In the mid-1950s a pioneer project in this field was launched by Paul M. Fitts and his associates at the Laboratory of Aviation Psychology of Ohio State University (H. M. Parsons, 1972b, Ch. 10). By means of a specially designed electronic analog simulator, it was possible to present 30 independently controlled "aircraft," or target blips, on simulated radarscopes. A "pilot room" and a "radar control room" were set up in the laboratory, each providing multiple response stations for groups of subjects functioning simultaneously, as in a real airport. The subjects were trained air traffic controllers and pilots. Several criteria of system performance were employed to study the effects of different task and procedural variables. Among these criteria were average fuel consumption, average amount of time required to bring an aircraft in or to take it out to a point 50 miles from takeoff, amount of deviation of incoming aircraft from the heading of the runway, and number of conflicts (defined as failure to maintain minimum separation between aircraft). Among the many conditions investigated were various display characteristics; load variables, as illustrated by the rate at which aircraft enter the terminal area; and procedural variables, including communication procedures, types of instructions that controllers may issue to pilots, and ways of allocating responsibility to individual controllers working in pairs.

Since the early studies at Ohio State University, air traffic control problems have been widely investigated, both in this country and abroad (H. M. Parsons, 1972b; Rohmert, 1971). An outstanding example is the sophisticated, large-scale research that has been under way for many years at the National Aviation Facilities Experimental Center of the Federal Aviation Administration, in Atlantic City, New Jersey (H. M. Parsons, 1972b, Ch. 15). The facilities available at this center can be adapted for many kinds of studies, such as the comparison of different control procedures, problems of coordination within and between centers in en route control, and other general operating problems. At such a research center, it is also possible to design studies for different geographic locations, simulating local airport characteristics, traffic load, available communication facilities, and operating procedures. This type of study has been conducted for a number of locations, such as New York City, Washington, D.C., and Honolulu.

Simulators have also been used widely in the development of man-machine systems for space flight (H. M. Parsons, 1972b, pp. 422–429). Psychological research has been conducted with subjects confined for extended periods in sealed cabins that reproduce most of the living conditions of space cabins. In these studies, the subjects perform realistic control and maintenance tasks, as well as observational and research functions pertaining to space exploration. The effects of different system variables on the performance of all these activities can thus be investigated. A related application of system simulation is to be found in the development of remote-control systems for unmanned earth-orbital satellites and lunar or planetary vehicles.

DISPLAY PROBLEMS

In the terminology of engineering psychology, a display is a device used to present information indirectly by symbolic or pictorial means. Examples of common displays include speedometers, thermometers, pressure gauges, gas meters, altimeters, doorbells, and fire gongs. With advancing automation, there is an increase in the number and complexity of displays to which the human operator must successfully respond. Research has shown that improvements in the design of displays can lead to substantial savings in time and energy and a marked reduction in accident risk.

Visual Displays. By far the most common types of displays are visual. Such displays may become very complex, as illustrated by the instrument panels of modern aircraft. Engineering psychologists have studied many aspects of visual displays, such as dial size and shape, length of scale units, number and spacing of scale markers, direction of pointer movements, size and style of letters and numerals, and ease of identifying and interpreting different graphic symbols (McCormick, 1976a, Ch. 4).

Many experiments have been concerned with dial design. One experiment with 60 male college students compared the five types of dials reproduced in Figure 8-3, including vertical, horizontal, semicircular, round, and open-window (Sleight, 1948). In the first four dial types, the pointer moves along the dial scale; in the open-window type, the pointer remains fixed and the dial scale moves, only a small segment appearing behind the window. Seventeen settings were presented with each dial, each setting falling on one of the scale markers (i.e., either a whole number or a half number). Exposure time for each setting was 0.12 second. An error was scored when the observer either gave an incorrect reading or was unable

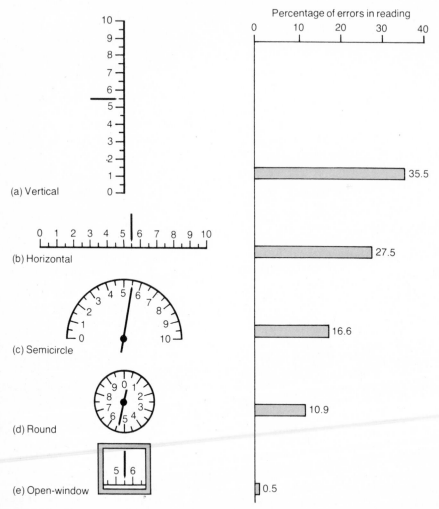

Figure 8-3. Percentage of errors in rapid reading of five types of dials. *(Adapted from Sleight, 1948, pp. 177, 181.)*

to give a reading during the brief exposure. As can be seen in Figure 8-3, the smallest percentage of errors (0.5) was obtained with the open-window design, the largest with the vertical dial (35.5).

One factor determining the accuracy of rapid reading of different types of dials seems to be the area that the observer must scan in order to make a reading. In the above experiment, the greater the area, the higher was the error frequency. The open-window type provides the most compact design, the circular the next most compact. The semicircular and horizontal scales require the eye to cover increasingly more ground. It is also relevant to note in this connection that with semicircular and horizontal scales errors were more common at the extreme positions. The difference between horizontal and vertical scales, on the other hand, is undoubtedly related to the fact that horizontal eye movements are easier and faster than vertical eye movements. Customary reading habits, involving the horizontal scanning of the page, would also tend to favor the horizontal type of scale. It is noteworthy that the advantage of horizontal as compared with vertical scales persists when longer exposure times are used (Graham, 1956).

In practical situations, many other variables determine the relative effectiveness of different types of dials. The results depend upon the nature of the information presented and the purpose for which it is used. For example, a vertical scale proved best for airplane altimeters (Roscoe, 1968). In this case, an important feature was the *compatibility* between the meaning of "up" on the scale and the meaning of "up" in altitude of the plane. The greater the pictorial realism of a scale, the easier it is to read.

When *precise readings* are required (e.g., to two or three digits), both speed and accuracy can be greatly improved by the use of a digital display, in which the complete reading appears in a window (McCormick, 1976a, p. 69; Weldon & Peterson, 1957). In Figure 8-4, this type of display is illustrated with a common

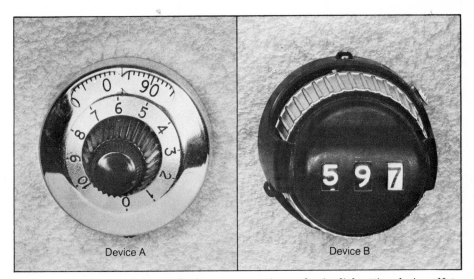

Device A   Device B

Figure 8-4. The use of digital display versus moving scales in dial-setting devices. Note relative difficulty of reading the two dials. Both settings read 597. *(From Chapanis, 1976, p. 705. Copyright © 1976 by Rand McNally College Publishing Company, Chicago. Reproduced by permission. Photographs by courtesy of A. Chapanis.)*

device used in setting a dial at a desired value. In device A, the correct adjustment of the knob requires observation of two moving scales that are difficult to read; in device B, the control is simply rotated until the correct three-place number appears in the centrally located digital display. Another disadvantage of device A is that the knob moves the scale until the desired setting coincides with the fixed pointer at the top; a fixed scale with a moving pointer would be easier to handle.

Another variable that affects the results of dial-reading experiments is the type of reading required. The examples cited thus far called for *quantitative reading,* in which the actual numerical value must be determined. In *qualitative,* or *check reading,* on the other hand, the purpose may be simply to determine whether the indicator is within a normal or safe range or whether the equipment is or is not functioning properly. Moreover, qualitative reading may be concerned with the direction and rate of movement of an indicator, as well as with its position. For this type of reading, the dial and moving-pointer display is superior to the open-window and digital displays. In such cases, the "critical" segment of the dial should be clearly marked with a dark band, color, or some other easily perceptible symbol. When a whole panel of dials is to be monitored for any deviation from normal conditions, the normal position of all dials should be aligned so that any deviation immediately stands out as a break in a continuous line. Such an arrangement greatly increases the speed and accuracy of monitoring a large number of dials (McCormick, 1976a, pp. 77–79). It should be added that dials with moving pointers can serve a dual function, providing both quantitative readings and check reading. If all that is wanted is an indication of malfunctioning or emergency conditions, a simpler display, such as a red light, would be adequate.

Visual displays may also be used to convey short, simple, but important messages in a variety of settings. Familiar examples are road signs for the guidance of the motorist and signs in waiting rooms, airports, and other public places for the information of users. In industry, such displays are employed both in the working environment and on equipment. They may serve to identify parts of machinery, indicate the function of given parts, and provide information about actions to be taken. Many thousands of *graphic symbols* have been devised and investigated for use in these various situations (Dreyfus, 1972; McCormick, 1976a, pp. 97–106). The growth of international travel and the increasing demand for machinery to be used in diverse cultures have further stimulated the search for symbols that are readily and widely understood.

Considerable research has been done on such questions as the ease of identifying and differentiating pictorial symbols and the frequency of correct interpretation of particular symbols. Certain general guidelines are suggested by such research (Cahill, 1975; 1976; McCormick, 1976a, pp. 105–106). Prior experience influences the interpretation of all symbols, a fact that assumes special importance when such symbols are to be used across cultures. The effectiveness of different types of symbols also varies with the context in which they appear and with the nature of the information to be communicated. Nevertheless, certain characteristics, such as simplicity and unity of design, tend to make some symbols generally easier to identify and interpret than others. In most situations, symbols that are recognizable representations of common, everyday objects are also more effective than are abstract or arbitrary forms.

Auditory Displays. Although not so widely applicable as visual displays, auditory signals are familiar in many contexts. Common examples are provided by alarm clocks, doorbells, telephones, fire sirens, and foghorns (McCormick, 1976a, Ch. 5). Because of their attention-compelling nature, auditory signals are especially suitable for reporting emergencies. While the observer might be looking elsewhere or might close his eyes, his ears are always "open" to stimuli. Auditory communication is suitable under conditions of low illumination and when the operator must move about and cannot continuously observe a visual display. Auditory displays are also useful in situations where heavy demands are made upon visual attention. The substitution of auditory displays for one or more visual displays in these situations would remove some of the overload from the visual modality. There is also some evidence that, in a monitoring task, auditory signals are detected more frequently than visual signals; and combined visual and auditory signals give a still higher detection rate (McCormick, 1976a, pp. 53–54). In general, redundancy of input through more than one sensory channel increases the probability that the information is received.

An example of auditory displays is provided by the radio range signals employed in aircraft navigation. These signals are produced by using two directional radio beams at right angles to each other. One beam transmits the letter A by Morse code (dot-dash); the other beam transmits the letter N (dash-dot). The signals are so generated that if the aircraft is "on the beam," or flying just between the two crossed beams, a steady tone results. If the airplane veers too far to the left or right, the A or N will be heard instead. Still another illustration of auditory displays is to be found in sonar, a technique for identifying underwater objects and for determining the direction of their movement. Pitch discrimination is crucial in this operation.

To all these examples of auditory displays we must of course add the very important medium of speech communication (Chapanis, 1976, pp. 707–710; McCormick, 1976a, Ch. 6). Some reference to research on speech intelligibility will be found in Chapter 9. In that chapter, we shall also consider investigations on the effects of noise on all forms of auditory communication, an area of research that constitutes a major part of the present topic.

Other Sense Modalities. In recent years, some exploratory research has been conducted on the communication possibilities offered by still other sense modalities, notably the kinesthetic and the tactual. Thus the "feel," or amount of resistance encountered in operating a stick, lever, or other control, may convey relevant information to the operator. The distance over which a control is moved may also be perceived through kinesthetic cues. And different controls may be identified tactually by the shape of their knobs. Some illustrative research on the shape coding of knobs will be cited in the following section, dealing with control problems. The skin senses have also been investigated as a more general medium of communication, through the use of either electrical or mechanical (vibratory) stimulation (Kirman, 1973; McCormick, 1976a, pp. 136–140).

Of particular interest are recent advances in tactile display equipment for use by the blind (McCormick, 1976a, pp. 137–140; Sherrick, 1975). One example is the Optacon (optical-to-tactile converter) developed at Stanford University (Bliss, Katcher, Rogers, & Shepard, 1970; Bliss & Moore, 1974, 1975). This instrument permits a blind person to read directly from a printed page by means of an optical "camera," which picks up the visual images, and a tactile stimulator, which translates these images into vibrations conveyed to the fingertip. Figure 8-5 shows the Optacon in use by a blind child who is learning to read. With one hand, the user

Figure 8-5. Blind child learning to read with the Optacon, a device for converting visual images into tactile vibrations. *(Photograph by courtesy of James C. Bliss, Telesensory Systems, Inc.)*

scans the print with a small camera; with the forefinger of the other hand, he receives a vibratory image of what the camera sees. Available results suggest that learning to read with the Optacon takes longer than learning to read Braille, and the rate of reading is slower. However, this device can be applied directly to any printed matter, without the restrictions, bulkiness, and production time and costs associated with Braille materials.

Another major research program has addressed the broader objective of developing man-machine communication and control systems for the handicapped (Kafafian, 1973).[1] Concerned with both sensory input and motor output, this research program has developed a wide assortment of devices for use by the blind, the deaf, and the deaf-blind, as well as for the orthopedically and neurologically handicapped. A particular goal of the program is to enable severely handicapped children to communicate and thereby enhance their capability for education and intellectual development. Of special interest are a group of related cybernetic aids that permit persons with motor handicaps to operate a remote control electric typewriter by any one of several specially developed keyboards.

[1]Although the devices developed in this program cut across several sections of the chapter, they are cited together at this point for simplicity.

Depending on the nature and extent of the individual's handicap, the keyboard may have 14, 7, 2, or even a single control key. Appropriately constructed keyboards may be operated with almost any part of the body over which the individual has muscular control, including finger, fist, elbow, toe, foot, tongue, or stylus attached to the head. The same types of keyboards can be adapted to operate telephones, computers, and other home, office, or factory equipment. Instructional programs developed for use with these devices have yielded promising results regarding practical feasibility.

CONTROL PROBLEMS

In man-machine systems, a control is a device for utilizing human effort in activating or directing a machine. Controls include a wide variety of handles, levers, handwheels, cranks, foot pedals, and the like. The steering wheel of an automobile is a familiar example. In designing controls, engineering psychologists draw upon much of the basic research on human motor activities, such as the studies cited in Chapter 7. They might, for example, take into account the relative accuracy, speed, or strength of hand movements in different directions, the accuracy of blind positioning movements at various points, or the conditions that affect the speed of serial movements. In addition, a considerable body of applied research has dealt more specifically with the operation of controls (McCormick, 1976a, Chs. 8 & 9; Van Cott & Kinkade, 1972, Ch. 8). As examples, three problems that have been widely investigated will be examined.

Display-Control Compatibility. The spatial relationships between display and control affect the speed and accuracy with which the control is operated. Isomorphism, or similarity in pattern of displays and controls, facilitates response (Chapanis & Mankin, 1967; Fitts & Deininger, 1954; Fitts & Seeger, 1953). For

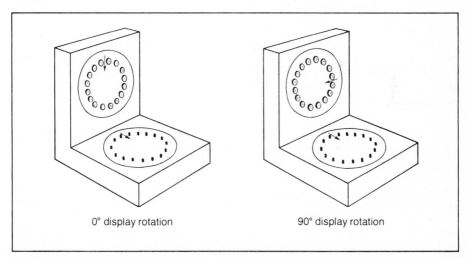

0° display rotation   90° display rotation

Figure 8-6. Two combinations used in studying effects of display-control relations on task difficulty and on abilities required. *(From Fleishman, 1957, p. 523. Copyright © 1957 Educational and Psychological Measurement. Reproduced by permission.)*

example, if the operator must push a button corresponding to the particular light that flashes on a panel, he can do so faster and with fewer errors if lights and buttons follow the same pattern. If the lights are arranged in a square, the buttons should also form a square; if the lights are in a column, the buttons should also be in a column, and so on. And of course, within such a pattern, the light and button that belong together should occupy corresponding positions. The greater the display-control compatibility, the less "translating," or data processing, will be required of the operator.

As the correspondence between display and control patterns decreases, not only does the difficulty of the task increase, but there may also be changes in the number and nature of the abilities required by the task. These effects were demonstrated in an experiment with the task illustrated in Figure 8-6 (Fleishman, 1957). When a stimulus light flashed on the vertical display panel, the subject was to push the corresponding button on the response panel as quickly as possible. The position of the arrow on display and control panels served as a reference point. Thus, if the light that flashed on was the third to the left of the arrow, the subject was to push the third button to the left of the arrow. The first illustration in Figure 8-6 shows the two arrows in identical positions on both panels. Seven other positions were investigated, in which the display panel was rotated by different amounts. The 90° position is shown in the right-hand half of Figure 8-6.

The effect of such rotations on accuracy of performance can be seen in Figure 8-7. It is evident that a 0° display rotation, representing complete isomorphism of display and control panels, yields a far greater number of correct responses than do any of the other arrangements. The participants in this study had also taken several tests chosen so as to measure a number of abilities previously identified through factor analysis. Performance on the easiest task, with 0° rotation, correlated .47 with perceptual speed and had negligible correlations with all the other abilities tested. With a 90° display rotation, performance correlated only .25 with perceptual speed, but it correlated .69 with spatial orientation. With 180° rotation, the correlation with perceptual speed dropped to a negligible .04, but performance now correlated .40 with spatial orientation and .40 with response orientation.

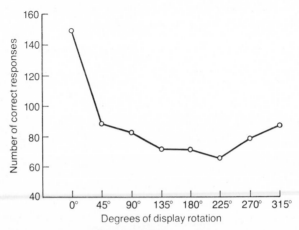

Figure 8-7. Number of correct responses in relation to display-control compatibility. Display rotation of 0° represents complete compatibility. *(From Fleishman, 1957, p. 527. Copyright © 1957 by* Educational and Psychological Measurement. *Reproduced by permission.)*

Changing the relationship between display and control thus altered the nature of the task performed by the subject.

A practical application of display-control compatibility to a familiar domestic object, the kitchen stove, is illustrated in a study of the relation between positions of burners and controls (Chapanis & Lindenbaum, 1959). Figure 8-8 shows the four arrangements of burners and controls employed in the study, together with the total number of errors in 1200 trials (80 trials by 15 different participants tested with each design). It will be seen that design I, in which the burners are directly aligned with the controls, produced no errors. The other three designs yielded increasingly more errors in the order shown. Mean response times showed similar differences, I requiring significantly less time than II throughout, and II requiring significantly less time than III and IV after practice (during the last 40 trials). The designs investigated were representative of those used on stoves manufactured at the time, although design I, the most effective, was the least common. It should also be noted that lack of uniformity in the spatial relations between burners and controls

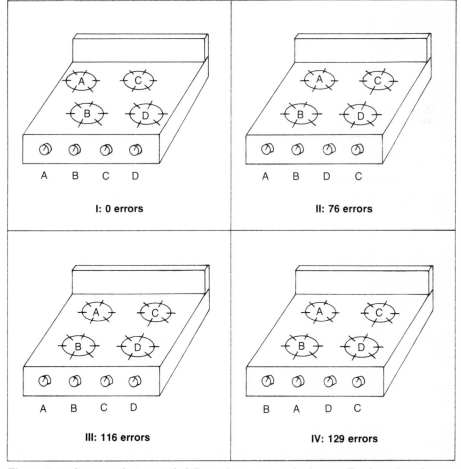

Figure 8-8. Stove-top designs with different burner-control relations. Total number of errors is given for each design. *(Data from Chapanis & Lindenbaum, 1959.)*

on different makes or models of stoves leads to confusion, annoyance, and difficulties in shifting from one stove to another. Uniform arrangement is highly desirable in the position of any widely used controls, such as hot and cold water faucets or the accelerator and brake pedals on a car.

Population Stereotypes. A related problem concerns situations in which movement of a control determines the direction of change in system output. Such system output may be observed directly, as in steering a car or turning on a radio, or it may be observed through a change recorded by a display, as in the movement of the speedometer needle when the foot presses down on the accelerator. In either case, there are certain expected relations between control movement and resulting effect on system performance. Known as population stereotypes, these expectancies are undoubtedly affected by prior experience and may therefore vary in different cultures (Chapanis, 1975, pp. 72–74 & Ch. 8).

Some of these population stereotypes are well known. For example, the large majority of persons brought up in industrialized Western cultures find it "natural" to turn the steering wheel in a clockwise direction in order to turn the car to the right. In other contexts, we expect a clockwise movement of a radio dial to increase the volume of sound, but we expect a clockwise movement of a faucet to reduce the flow of water. The latter stereotype also applies to steam valves. In the United States, pushing a toggle switch *up* is typically associated with starting or turning *on* (e.g., lights), but the reverse association was found in Great Britain (Chapanis, 1975, p. 73). It should also be noted that items of standard equipment that violate the expected relation can readily be found. Chapanis (1965, p. 108) illustrates four toggle switches observed on equipment in a single psychology laboratory in an American university in which the "on" position was up, down, right, and left, respectively. Controls that violate well-established population stereotypes are likely to cause annoyance, delay, and errors.

A typical investigation designed to explore some of these population stereotypes was conducted by Warrick (1947). Using panels such as those illustrated in Figure 8-9, the subject was to "move" a light to the center position by rotating the knob. Actually rotation of the knob caused the lights in the row to turn on and off in sequence. Unknown to the subject, the equipment was so adjusted that the light moved toward the center regardless of the direction in which the knob was turned at the start of any one trial. Thus no direction was differentially reinforced during the experiment itself. Any preferred directional association revealed by the data would therefore indicate the subject's own predisposition.

The three panels yielding the most clear-cut results are reproduced in Figure 8-9. Examination of panels A and B would suggest that clockwise movements are associated with "right" and "up," while counterclockwise movements are associated with "left" and "down." That the relation is not so simple as this, however, is indicated by the results obtained with panel C. Here most subjects chose counterclockwise for upward and clockwise for downward movements. The answer seems to be that the preferred relation is one in which the display moves in the same direction as the side of the control *nearer to it*. When the position of the control is reversed, as in panels B and C, the "meaning" of clockwise and counterclockwise rotation is correspondingly reversed.

Several other types of expected effects of control movements have been investigated in other research (Chapanis, 1965, Ch. 5; Loveless, 1962; McCormick, 1976a, Ch. 8). Among them are relationships involving displays and controls

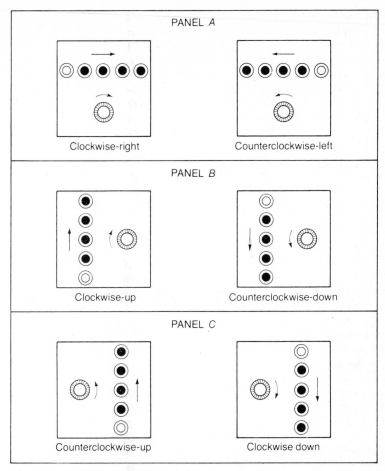

Figure 8-9. Some examples of population stereotypes in display-control relationships. The light (white circle) must be moved to the center position by turning the control knob. *(Adapted from Warrick, 1947.)*

mounted on different planes, concentric knobs which control different displays, and both wheel- and stick-type vehicular controls set in different planes. Controls have also been studied in relation to auditory displays (e.g., Simon, Mewaldt, Acosta, & Hu, 1976). For instance, subjects responded more quickly when directed to move a toggle switch up in response to a high-pitch signal and down in response to a low-pitch signal than when this relation was reversed. Moving the switch toward the source of sound (up, down, right, or left) elicited faster responses than did moving it away from the source of sound. There is also some evidence that these two stereotypes interact in their effect on speed of response.

Coding of Controls. The rapid and correct identification of controls is important in many situations. Turning on the hot-water faucet when we want cold water may be annoying or momentarily painful. Stepping on the accelerator instead of the brake pedal in a car or reaching for the wrong control in an airplane can prove fatal. In an Air Force survey conducted during World War II, for example, confusion between landing-gear and flap controls was reported to have caused 457 aircraft accidents within a 22-month period (McFarland, 1946, p. 607).

The identification of controls can be facilitated by coding each control in terms of some readily observable characteristic, such as its location, size, shape, texture, or color. Thus if the cold-water faucet is always on the right and the hot-water faucet on the left, or if the cold-water faucet has a blue knob and the hot-water faucet a red knob, confusion will be greatly reduced. *Standardization* of such features is thus one way to facilitate the use of controls. The fact that controls are often in different positions in different models of cars, airplanes, or other equipment interferes with their effective operation. Under these conditions, uniform coding of controls with regard to shape, color, or some other characteristic will reduce the interference effects when the operator changes from one model to another.

Another factor determining the ease of identifying controls is their *discriminability*. Many experiments have been conducted to determine how far apart two controls must be, how much they must differ in size, or what shape they must have to be differentiated with a minimum of error (McCormick, 1976a, pp. 132–136). Shape of control handles is of particular interest because of its many usable variations, as contrasted, for instance, with the limited number of practicable sizes. Unlike colors, moreover, shapes can be identified tactually, when the operator's vision is otherwise occupied or when the control must be operated in dim light.

In one Air Force experiment on the tactual identification of control knobs (Jenkins, 1947), 25 plastic shapes were mounted on rods that were bolted into a turntable. Each subject, wearing blindfold goggles, was given a test knob to explore for one second. The turntable was then rotated to a predesignated point, and the subject felt each knob in turn until he found one that he thought was the test knob. The same procedure was repeated with each shape as a test knob. The order of test and comparison knobs was varied systematically to balance out intraserial effects.

An analysis of the frequency with which each shape was confused with every other shape revealed certain sets of shapes that were most clearly distinguishable. Comparison of results obtained with gloves and with bare hands showed no essential differences in the relative discriminability of shapes, although more errors were made in general when gloves were worn. Similarly, the investigation of horizontally mounted controls yielded about the same results as those obtained with vertically mounted controls, suggesting that mode of mounting or position in which the knob is grasped is not a critical factor in its identification.

A third way to facilitate identification of controls is to utilize *meaningful associations*. This technique is somewhat similar to the use of population stereotypes in establishing display-control directional relations. Certain well-known color symbols can be relied upon in coding controls. The association of red and green lights with "stop" and "go" and the identification of red with fire or danger of any sort are familiar examples. Meaningful symbols can also be incorporated in shape coding of controls. The Air Force now uses several control knobs whose shapes suggest their functions, as illustrated in Figure 8-10. The landing-gear knob, for example, is shaped like a landing wheel and the flap-control knob is shaped like a wing.

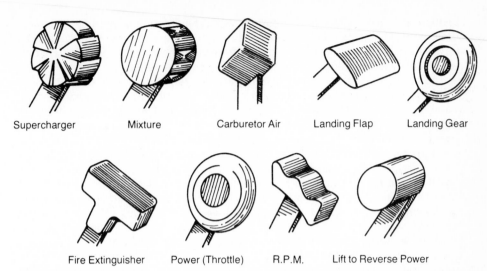

| Supercharger | Mixture | Carburetor Air | Landing Flap | Landing Gear |

| Fire Extinguisher | Power (Throttle) | R.P.M. | Lift to Reverse Power |

Figure 8-10. Shape-coded aircraft control knobs for use in United States Air Force. *(From Human Factors Engineering, 1977, Ch. 2, Sect. 2D18, p. 3.)*

PROBLEMS OF SPATIAL CONFIGURATION AND ARRANGEMENT

Substantial improvements in human performance can often be achieved by spatial rearrangements of equipment. These rearrangements may pertain to such varied problems as the relative position of different machines to be operated by a team of workers; the location of different controls to be manipulated by a single operator; the layout of parts to be assembled by a single person; the dimensions and forms of chairs, which affect sitting posture; and the shape of tool handles, which determine hand position in grasping and using the tool.

Among the earliest recommendations of time and motion analysts were those pertaining to the spatial arrangement of the workplace, tools, and supplies. Materials should be arranged in the order in which they are to be used, so that the worker need not cross and recross his path of motion. Moreover, having a regular place for each article eliminates search. Further savings are effected by prepositioning tools in holders in such a way that they are grasped in the position in which they will be used. Holders for pens represent a simple and familiar example of this principle. Additional examples are provided by holders for prepositioning screwdrivers and other small tools.

Many types of data and several specialized methodologies have been employed in working out optimal spatial arrangements in different situations. Much can be accomplished by such simple procedures as observing persons while they use existing equipment and soliciting user criticisms, comments, and suggestions. An example is provided by a survey of homemakers regarding equipment and layout characteristics that increase or decrease the difficulty of a wide variety of household tasks (Steidl, 1972). To illustrate more specialized procedures, we shall consider some of the techniques of (1) applied anthropometry and biomechanics and (2) link analysis.

Applied Anthropometry and Biomechanics. The procedures of applied anthro-pometry and biomechanics[2] consist essentially in measuring the human body at rest and in motion and designing equipment to fit these measurements. Height, weight, arm and leg length, hand and finger dimensions, length of reach, and force exerted and energy expended in carrying out different movements are among the many measurements taken. Extensive compilations of such measures are now available, and procedures for collecting and applying anthropometric data have been described (Hertzberg, 1972; McCormick, 1976a, Ch. 10; Roebuck, Kroemer, & Thomson, 1975). Although for certain purposes "average" dimensions are appro-priate, in other situations extremes must be considered. For instance, steps should be low enough to accommodate the shortest users and entrances high enough to accommodate the tallest. In certain types of equipment, such as work chairs and automobile seats, individual differences can be accommodated by providing an adjustable range.

In the design of both consumer products and industrial equipment, anthropo-metric differences between the sexes and among ethnic groups must also be taken into account. As more products are designed for international markets, ethnic and cultural differences are receiving increasing attention (Chapanis, 1975). Relevant population differences have been recorded in such characteristics as height and weight, separate bodily dimensions, muscular strength, and traditional working and sitting postures. In certain cultures, for example, squatting rather than sitting or standing postures are customary among artisans as well as in the preparation of food in the home (Daftuar, 1975). All these differences have obvious implications for the design of agricultural and industrial equipment as well as household appliances.

A few examples will serve to suggest the variety of situations to which biomechanics can contribute. An application to work layout is provided by the *semicircular work space.* In an assembly job, for example, the bins containing the parts to be assembled should be arranged, not in a straight line, but in a semicircle in front of the worker. Such an arrangement eliminates the excessive reaching required for the end bins in a linear arrangement. Figure 8-11 shows the outer dimensions of the so-called normal and maximum working areas. The former is determined by sweeping the forearm across the table, with the upper arm hanging against the body and with the elbow as a pivot. The latter is found in the same fashion, except that the whole arm is now rotated, with the shoulder as a pivot. The area where the semicircles defined by the right and left hands overlap represents a zone where two-handed work can be performed most conveniently.

The semicircular work space is appropriate for any situation where the operator must reach for a number of items in a repetitive sequence. The collating of papers and the stuffing of envelopes by a clerk represent familiar examples. It might appear that the saving in time and energy effected by the semicircular work space is trivial. This is true if we consider the collating of a single set of papers or the assembly of a single article. But in a repetitive job the savings mount up to impressive figures. In one large radio manufacturing company, for instance, it was estimated that, by shortening the reach to each supply bin by 6 inches, the total

---

[2]Although anthropometry focuses on anatomical dimensions and biomechanics on muscular activity, the two approaches overlap in their applications to equipment design and will therefore be discussed together.

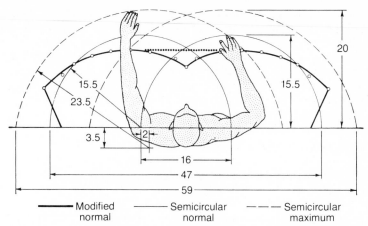

▬▬▬ Modified	▬▬▬ Semicircular	─ ─ ─ Semicircular
normal	normal	maximum

Figure 8-11. Modified normal working area, with traditional normal and maximal semicircular areas superimposed. Dimensions shown are in inches. *(Adapted from Squires, 1956, p. 2.)*

saving in time was 34,000 hours a year and the saving in distance traveled by the operators' hands was 98,500 miles a year! (Barnes, 1968, pp. 263–264).

For most purposes, the semicircular pattern provides a sufficiently accurate guide for defining the most effective work space. Human movements, however, rarely fit into such simple geometric forms. A detailed empirical study conducted under Navy auspices demonstrated that the normal working area is more limited in extent and is defined by a more complex figure, known in mathematics as a "prolate epicycloid" (Squires, 1956). This figure—which does not look quite so complicated as it sounds—is shown in heavy solid line in Figure 8-11. The traditional semicircular areas corresponding to normal and maximum working space are included for comparative purposes. The deviation from a semicircle results chiefly from the fact that, when the forearm moves outward, the elbow does not remain in a fixed position but moves out and away from the body. Consequently, the figure is somewhat flattened, and the right and left corners are chopped off. This type of curve is useful not only in designing a flat working surface but also as a guide for the construction of control panels and other vertical working areas. For the latter purpose, the vertical surface is erected perpendicularly along the outer contour of the figure, which is first flattened out at the center as shown by the dotted line in Figure 8-11.

Considerable attention has been given to the design of *chairs and seats* for different purposes. The importance of seat design in maintaining good posture and providing adequate support has long been recognized. Discomfort over long periods of time, as in driving a car or piloting a plane, can lead to serious operating deficiencies. The amount of force an individual can exert in operating a control also depends on his bodily position relative to the control, as well as on the type of bodily support available. In industrial and office work, improper height, position, or shape of seats can produce excessive muscular strain and fatigue in the course of the work period.

Research on seat design utilizes both anthropometric techniqes and subjective ratings of comfort (Grandjean et al., 1969; Grandjean, Hunting, Wotzka, & Shärer, 1973; McCormick, 1976a, pp. 282–288). The results have led to the formulation of guidelines for evaluating seating facilities in terms of general human requirements. Specific design details, however, vary with the purpose of seats (e.g., typing, driving, assembly operations, resting) and with individual differences in bodily dimensions. Insofar as practicable, adjustable seats, work surfaces, or both provide an effective way of allowing for individual differences. For some types of work, it is desirable to utilize arrangements of work surface and seat heights that permit the worker to alternate between standing and sitting, in order to provide for change of posture. It is interesting to note that the advantages of such flexibility were recognized in the pioneer work of Gilbreth, as illustrated by his elevated chair with its own footrest cited in Chapter 7. The same objective can of course be achieved by adjustable height of either chair or work table.

Another application of biomechanics dating from the early 1900s, which is now showing an upsurge of activity, is in the design of *tools and instruments.* Improperly designed hand tools can produce muscular strain and cumulative fatigue, especially when the tool is used for long periods during the work day. The redesign of such simple tools as pliers can markedly reduce hand and wrist strain (Tichauer, 1966). As an aid in choosing optimum tool design to minimize muscular effort, the investigator may take electromygraphic recordings of the person's hand muscles while using the tool (Khalil, 1973). This technique was employed in the redesign of a type of forceps used by neurosurgeons. The improved design provided a firmer grasp and reduced finger fatigue (Miller, Ransohoff, & Tichauer, 1971). When examined from the viewpoint of biomechanics, many familiar and widely used consumer products, from snow shovels and stepladders to frying pans and telephone dials, can be redesigned for easier and safer use (see, e.g., "Building a Better Mousetrap," 1969).

A noteworthy development in biomechanics is the increasing attention devoted to the design of space and equipment adapted to the needs of the *physically handicapped.* Major examples are provided by the previously cited research on devices that permit blind persons to read regular print and those that permit persons with multiple sensory and motor handicaps to communicate and to operate equipment. Another approach is illustrated by a study of energy expenditure in the use of crutches by unilateral leg amputees (Ganguli, Bose, Datta, Chatterjee, & Roy, 1974). Reach and space requirements for the handicapped and for persons in wheelchairs, as well as adaptations of bathroom and kitchen fixtures for use by the orthopedically handicapped, represent further examples. The growing movement to enable physically handicapped persons to lead productive, independent, and personally satisfying lives is clearly reflected in this phase of contemporary engineering psychology. Recent enactment of federal legislation requiring public buildings to accommodate the needs of the handicapped will undoubtedly accelerate the development of appropriate adaptations of equipment and facilities.

Link Analysis. In the design of optimal spatial arrangements of system components, whether operated by a single person or a team, link analysis can provide valuable information. By this method, data are gathered regarding operational connections between different components within a system. The components thus investigated may be individual dials or other signals on a display panel, individual controls on a control panel, different machines operated in succession by the same worker or by different workers, and individual operators working together within a system. A strong link between two controls, for example, would mean that they are often used in sequence and should therefore be placed close together. A strong link between two operators would mean that they must frequently communicate, hand each other materials, or interact in other ways.

The purpose of link analysis is to utilize the empirically observed connections among components in order to improve the arrangement of displays, controls, machines, and persons. Although essentially a problem of the spatial layout of work, link analysis also bears some relation to display and control arrangements discussed earlier in this chapter, to architectural psychology to be considered in Chapter 9, and to communication nets and organization theory discussed in Chapter 6. There are basically two methods for obtaining link data: through observation of the system in operation and through the judgments of operators. Observational techniques are more suitable for determining frequency of link usage, while judgment techniques must usually be employed to estimate the relative importance of links. When the use of observational methods is not practicable, judgments must be relied upon for frequency data as well.

Direct or unaided observation may be adequate for a simple system consisting of few components. Motion pictures help in recording the manipulation of controls or the movement of persons from one work station to another. For link analysis of visual displays, an eye camera may be employed. The eye camera photographs reflections of light from the eye. These reflections show the sequence of fixation points and the duration of each fixation. This method was used in an intensive link analysis of aircraft display instruments (Jones, Milton, & Fitts, 1949; Milton, Jones, & Fitts, 1950). The percentage of times eye movements occurred from each display to every other was determined during different flight maneuvers, such as climbing, banking, and landing. In the same way, information was obtained regarding length of fixation, number of fixations per minute, and proportion of time spent fixating on each instrument. On the basis of all this information, the best arrangement of the instruments was identified, and this arrangement was adopted in all military and commercial planes in the United States (see McCormick, 1976a, p. 297).

An application of link analysis to a very different context can be found in an exploratory study concerned with the spatial layout of a general hospital (Souder, Clark, Elkind, & Brown, 1964, pp. 115–118). Focusing on the importance of facilitating and expediting essential interdepartmental contacts, the investigators collected data on traffic between different departments in each of two hospitals. For each kind of trip, the record showed origin and destination, duration, time distribution, and categories of persons involved. The last item permits an estimate of "skill-weighted" time consumed by the trip. For example, did the trip involve a clerk, a highly skilled technician, or a surgeon? Computers can be effectively utilized in at least two ways in this procedure: (1) to process the large quantities of empirical data, and (2) to simulate planned hospitals on the basis of estimated patient load, hospital facilities, and other anticipated institutional characteristics. The traffic data generated in the computer simulation can then be used to evaluate alternative spatial arrangements and arrive at an optimal choice. A similar application of link analysis and computer simulation to the redesign of a surgical unit is described by Whitehead and Eldars (1964).

Approaching hospital design from a different angle, Lindheim (1966) calls attention to the increased flexibility of spatial planning made possible by technological advances. She speaks of the "uncoupling" of traditional spatial linkages between functionally related units as a result of improved methods of communicating information and transporting materials. Oral messages can be transmitted by telephone or intercom, and written messages by teletype or pneumatic tube; objects of varying sizes can be transported by dumbwaiters, conveyors, or other devices. Citing a study of the radiology departments of three different types of hospitals, Lindheim illustrates the lessening of spatial constraints resulting from such technological advances as the possible transmission of x-ray and fluoro-scope images through closed-circuit television. The implication seems clear: in the design of new facilities, link analysis of existing facilities must be combined with a consideration of relevant technological developments and other changing condi-tions.

SUMMARY

A major goal of engineering psychology is to enhance human performance through the design and arrangement of equipment to fit human needs and capabilities. The comprehensive approach of modern engineering psychology is exemplified by its focus on man-machine systems. Such an approach permits an assessment of interactions among system variables, as well as trade-offs among system objectives and an evaluation of cost-effectiveness of the total system. By describing the functions of the human operator in engineering terminology, the systems approach makes it possible to transfer some of these functions to the machine. Research on simple, closed-loop systems is illustrated by experiments on tracking, most of which deal with the effects of task variables on tracking performance. System simulation is an important procedure in the development and evaluation of complex systems involving many components.

One of the problems of equipment design pertains to the design of displays through which information is transmitted to the operator. Although visual displays are the most common, auditory displays are particularly useful in certain situa-tions. Some research has also been done on the potentialities of tactual displays. With regard to visual displays, extensive research has been conducted on the factors influencing speed and accuracy of dial reading, such as dial size and shape, length of scale units, number and spacing of scale markers, and direction of pointer movements. Research has also been conducted on the identification, discrimination, and interpretation of graphic symbols.

Among the problems investigated with regard to controls are display-control compatibility and population stereotypes in the expected effects of control move-ments. Another example is provided by research on the coding of controls in terms of position, size, shape, or color. Confusion among controls can be reduced by standardizing similar controls, increasing the discriminability of different controls, and utilizing meaningful associations for the identification of controls.

Spatial arrangement and configuration of equipment may substantially improve performance and reduce muscular strain and fatigue. Applied anthropometry and biomechanics are concerned with the design of products, equipment, and work space to fit empirically assessed anatomical and motor characteristics of the human body. Design decisions must take into account not only average population requirements but also individual differences, differences associated with sex and with ethnic and cultural groups, and the special needs of physically handicapped persons. Examples of the contributions of biomechanics can be found in the semicircular work space, the design of seats, and the improvement of tools and household articles. Link analysis utilizes data on frequency and importance of operational connections between system components to design an optimal spatial layout. This technique is applicable to a wide variety of problems, ranging from the arrangement of aircraft display instruments to the design of hospital buildings.

HUMAN FACTORS IN ENVIRONMENTAL DESIGN

NINE

I HAS LONG BEEN RECOGNIZED that human performance and well-being depend in part upon the characteristics of the physical environment. For many years, engineers have been active in the establishment of illumination standards for different types of work, the maintenance of suitable temperature and other atmospheric conditions, the reduction of noise, and similar problems. It is apparent that such problems pertain not only to factories and offices but also to schools, libraries, homes, waiting rooms, and other environments designed for prolonged human use. Social and clinical psychologists have become increasingly concerned about the influence of all aspects of the environment on interpersonal behavior, emotional and cognitive development, and mental health. From a different angle, the development of the space program, as well as arctic and undersea exploration, has stimulated intensive research on the effects of certain extreme environmental conditions on human performance.

An important contribution of psychologists to all these problems is methodological. Research in this field has been advanced by the introduction of experimental designs that control for such factors as suggestion and attitude changes. The Hawthorne studies, one of which was originally concerned with the effects of illumination, focused attention on the need to control these more subtle variables. Psychology has also stimulated the investigation of individual differences in the effects of environmental variables. It is now recognized that in the working environment, as in work methods, certain individual characteristics must be considered in setting optimum standards.

ENVIRONMENTAL PSYCHOLOGY

The 1970s have witnessed the emergence and rapid growth of a broad and rather amorphous specialty designated as environmental psychology (Craik, 1973;

Heimstra & McFarling, 1974; Ittelson, Proshansky, Rivlin, & Winkel, 1974; Moos, 1976; Proshansky, 1976; Wohlwill & Carson, 1972). The concept of environment has certainly played a significant part in psychological theory and research from the earliest beginnings of the field. As traditionally used in psychology, however, "environment" has been contrasted to "heredity" as a source of behavior development and individual differences. In this sense, environment is closely related to learning. It refers to the cumulative effects of the individual's responses to the environmental stimuli he or she encounters throughout life. Thus child-rearing practices, formal schooling, and interpersonal contacts represent major components of environment in this sense. In contrast, the emerging field of environmental psychology, as well as the broader interdisciplinary area of behavior-environment relations, focuses on human interaction with specific aspects of the "physical environment" (Wohlwill, 1970), including both the built and the natural environment.

Reflecting in part the mounting public concern about the deteriorating environment on planet Earth, environmental psychology spans a wide and heterogeneous array of problems. It covers not only the planned effects of human actions on the environment but also the unplanned and unanticipated side effects. The problems investigated range from air and water pollution and the depletion of natural resources to the design of offices, psychiatric wards, and playgrounds. When broadly defined, environmental psychology overlaps major areas of traditional engineering psychology, as well as portions of consumer, community, and clinical psychology. In fact, insofar as the mutual influence or dynamic interchange between man and his environment pervades all human behavior, the definition of environmental psychology presented by many of its exponents could cover virtually all of psychology.

The problems actually investigated by environmental psychologists, although certainly diverse, can be identified somewhat more clearly. For the purposes of this book, we can differentiate between research on the effects of environmental variables on human behavior and research on the effects of human behavior on the environment. The latter type of research deals with what people do, such as littering, causing forest fires, or wasting fuel. Its practical objective is to devise ways of altering such behavior in large masses of people. Insofar as the goals and methodology of this research have much in common with those of consumer psychology, it will be considered in that connection (Chs. 10 and 11). Research on the effects of the physical environment on human behavior fits more naturally into the area of engineering psychology and has been incorporated in this chapter. The next four sections provide a brief look at the sort of problems investigated, with reference to illumination, atmospheric conditions, weightlessness and related gravitational phenomena, and sensory stimulation (e.g., noise). Most of the research in these areas has been conducted by engineering psychologists with a background in experimental psychology. However, illustrative studies typical of the contributions of the environmental psychologists will be cited in the appropriate sections.

The last section, dealing principally with the built environment, is more closely identified with the characteristic approach of contemporary environmental psychologists. This area is concerned with the design and arrangement of space for optimal human use. Many environmental psychologists are primarily social psychologists by training, and this orientation is reflected in their approach to such design problems. Much of their research deals with the effects of various design features on the attitudinal, emotional, and interpersonal behavior of persons within the particular settings.

Like other newly emerging specialties in psychology, environmental psychology has close linkages with other fields, such as architecture, urban planning, engineering, sociology, anthropology, and biology. Environmental psychologists often function as consultants or on interdisciplinary teams. The strongly interdisciplinary nature of this specialty is clearly reflected in the available publications, which typically include or cite contributions by specialists from a variety of fields (e.g., Proshansky, Ittelson, & Rivlin, 1976; Wohlwill & Carson, 1972). The broad field of man-environment relations provides opportunities for novel psychological careers in both research and practice (Bass & Bass, 1976; Woods, 1976). From another angle, the environmentalist orientation is having an impact on traditional fields of applied psychology. For example, Bass and Bass (1976) cite suggestive evidence that regional migration and choice of work site, as well as job satisfaction, are related to various environmental characteristics ranging from weather conditions to population density and recreational facilities. More and more, employees at all levels are considering the attractiveness of the working and living environments in making job decisions, along with pay, fringe benefits, nature of work, and the other factors long familiar to the industrial-organizational psychologist. In clinical psychology, to cite another example, increasing attention is being given to the spatial layout as well as to the interpersonal aspects of therapeutic environments (Proshansky et al., 1976, pp. 340–351, 459–479).

ILLUMINATION

Amount of Light. The establishment of optimal illumination levels for different types of work is a complex undertaking which must take many factors into account. The use of different approaches to the problem accounts in part for a controversy that began in the 1930s and is not yet completely resolved. Traditionally it has been assumed, especially by illuminating engineers, that task visibility can generally be improved by increasing the level of illumination. Faulkner and Murphy (1973) point out that, as developments in lighting technology made higher levels of illumination available, these higher levels were quickly adopted and recommended as optimal. For instance, a steady rise in the recommended illumination levels for office work can be observed from 1910 to 1960. On the other hand, several investigators, including some psychologists, have questioned the conclusion that increasing amount of light always improves task visibility (Faulkner & Murphy, 1973; Hopkinson & Collins, 1970; Tinker, 1948, 1959, 1963). With the growing concern about fuel conservation and reduction in the use of electricity, the avoidance of unnecessarily high illumination levels takes on added importance. Moreover, under certain conditions, high levels of illumination may actually reduce visibility and increase eye strain and fatigue.

The study of the effects of different lighting conditions on human performance presents many methodological problems. The simple, obvious procedures do not yield readily interpretable results. Several early industrial studies, for example, showed the effects of increasing illumination on worker output (for a summary, see McCormick, 1970, p. 460). Most of these merely compared performance records before and after the introduction of some improvement in illumination, usually an increase in the amount of available light. Many kinds of work were covered by these studies, including card punching, mail handling, weaving, machine-shop work, inspection, assembly, and various other skilled or semiskilled manufacturing operations. Initial illumination was generally quite low, varying from less than 1 fc[1] to slightly over 28 fc for different types of work. When illumination was raised to levels ranging from 5 to 50 fc (still considerably below current standards), output improved by amounts varying from 4% to 35%. Other, similar studies have shown a decrease in errors and spoilage or a sharp drop in accident rate following improvements in lighting conditions.

This general type of experimental design, of course, is subject to the Hawthorne effect. Rises in output may have resulted partly or wholly from better employee attitudes. On the other hand, if employee attitudes *can* be improved by slight increases in illumination, such changes may be fully justified on those grounds alone. Because the initial illumination levels were so low in the studies cited, some of the output increases very probably did result from improved task visibility. At least part of the performance improvement, however, may be attributable to the more attractive and cheerful work environment brought about either by the brighter lighting itself or by other associated changes, such as cleaning or painting the working area and equipment. From a practical standpoint, anything that increases job satisfaction or productivity is desirable. From a scientific standpoint, however, we would like to identify just what factors led to improved job perform- ance and to learn how they operated. This information is needed if we want to be able to generalize beyond the immediate situation in which data were gathered. Another methodological consideration pertains to the durability of the higher output level. The improvement occurring when a change is introduced may be followed by a gradual decline to the original level. This effect will not be detected unless records are kept over a sufficiently long period.

With regard to feelings of comfort, strain, fatigue, and other subjective effects, it would seem that judgments of preference for different levels of illumination should provide a useful guide. Unfortunately, the solution is not that simple. In a well-designed series of early experiments, Tinker (1954) demonstrated that sub- jects' choices of preferred illumination levels depend upon visual adaptation. Groups of students reading individually under either diffuse indirect illumination or a local reading light chose markedly different illumination levels, depending upon the initial level to which they had been exposed. Table 9-1 summarizes the results of one of these experiments. It will be seen that in both series the largest percentage of readers chose the light to which they had been adapted, the frequency of choice declining gradually for both higher and lower intensity levels. When subjects were adapted to 8 fc, their median preference fell roughly at 12 fc; when they were adapted to 52 fc, it fell approximately at 52 fc. The principal implication of these experiments is that expressed preferences based on short observation periods are highly susceptible to prior visual adaptation.

It is also noteworthy that in the above experiment individual differences in preferred illumination level were very large. With the exception of 1 fc, every given level of illumination was chosen by some subjects. In the setting of illumination standards, allowance must be made for individual differences in visual acuity and

[1]A footcandle (fc) is the amount of light from a 1-candlepower source falling on a surface 1 foot away; 1 footcandle equals approximately 1.076 decalux units in the International System of Units (SI). For fuller explanation of the units employed in the measurement of illumination, see McCormick (1976a), Ch. 12.

TABLE 9-1
Effect of Visual Adaptation upon Intensity of Light Preferred
for Reading under Diffuse General Illumination
(From Tinker, 1954, p. 63. Copyright 1954 by American Academy of Optometry.
Reproduced by permission.)

Adapted to 8 fc (Standard)								
Footcandles	1	2	3	5	8	12	18	26	41
Percentage of times preferred	0.0	1.2	1.5	4.4	26.2	24.0	17.1	13.9	11.7

Adapted to 52 fc (Standard)								
Footcandles	18	30	41	46	52	59	62	71	100
Percentage of times preferred	5.4	8.0	11.4	14.0	21.0	11.6	11.9	9.1	7.6

Note. N = 144.

in other variables that may substantially affect both performance and feelings of comfort. Persons with subnormal visual acuity or other visual deficiencies can improve their performance through the use of brighter illumination. Customarily, individual differences are taken into account by setting the recommended illumination high enough to meet varied personal requirements. Provision for individual adjustment of illumination level, if feasible, is a better solution. Aging also affects illumination requirements. Beginning approximately in the forties, acuity decreases progressively with age. Older persons thus need a higher level of illumination in order to perform a given task as well as is done by younger persons. Approximate ratios for this purpose have been worked out for different age levels (Blackwell & Blackwell, 1971; Fortuin, 1963).

An extensive collection of recommended illumination levels for a wide variety of situations is given in the *IES Lighting Handbook* (1972). The Illuminating Engineering Society (IES) based these standards primarily on the laboratory research conducted over many years by Blackwell (1959, 1961; *IES,* 1972, pp. 3–14 to 3–33). Although the procedure is quite complex, its essential features can be briefly summarized. In the basic experimental procedure, the subject is seated in a cubicle facing a translucent screen whose level of illumination can be varied by the experimenter. The visual task is to watch for a small disk that appears on the screen during an interval signaled by a buzzer. The disk is actually projected during one out of every four intervals delineated by the buzzer. The subject is instructed to press a button during the interval that the disk is seen.

In setting illumination levels for any visual task, three task characteristics are taken into account: (1) time available for visual response, (2) size of detail to be discriminated, and (3) brightness contrast of the detail to be discriminated against the background. The effects of the first two characteristics are undoubtedly familiar. With more time to examine the material and with larger details (e.g., reading larger vs. smaller print) lower levels of illumination suffice. The third characteristic can be illustrated by the greater visibility of black print on white paper in comparison with grey print on the same paper.

In his research, Blackwell systematically varied exposure time, size of disk, and contrast between disk and background. His results are in the form of curves showing the interaction among these variables and between these variables and illumination level. From such data it was possible to specify the illumination level required to attain threshold performance (i.e., correct responses 50% of the time) under different time, size, and contrast conditions. These illumination levels were then adjusted upwards to take account of realistic visual demands, including moving objects, unknown location of objects within field, and requirement of 99% rather than 50% correct responses.

The application of these basic data to the known characteristics of many visual tasks in factories, offices, homes, hospitals, and other settings led to the recommended illumination levels of the IES handbook. A few examples, chosen to illustrate the wide range of illumination requirements, are shown in Table 9-2. It

TABLE 9-2
Examples of Illumination Levels Recommended by the
Illuminating Engineering Society (IES) for Different Types of Visual Tasks
(Items selected from IES Lighting Handbook, 1972, pp. 9–81 to 9–90.)

Task or Situation	Recommended Illumination (fc)[a]
Surgical operating table	2500
Very difficult inspection (industrial)	500
Drafting, cartography	200
Proofreading	150
Food preparation in home kitchen	150
Reading handwritten material	70
Wrapping, packing, and labeling	50
Reading books, magazines, newspapers	30
Loading trucks or freight cars	20
Hotel lobby (except for reading and working areas)	10

[a]These values can be converted to decalux units by multiplying by 1.076.

should be noted that Faulkner and Murphy (1973), among others, have pointed out that many of these levels may be higher than necessary—or even higher than desirable in certain situations. It is also noteworthy that these levels are higher than those recommended by comparable organizations in other countries. Faulkner and Murphy (1973) observe that, according to Blackwell's own data, increasing illumination beyond certain points has a negligible effect on minimum detectable size and contrast. The curves showing this effect flatten out as the higher illumination levels are reached.

It is also unlikely that a single illumination level can be recommended as optimal for the broad types of tasks listed in the IES handbook. For example, reading ordinary black print on a typical book or journal page, which provides high contrast, rarely shows performance improvement when illumination is increased beyond 10 to 20 fc. Reading from a poor, dim copy of the printed page, on the other hand, may show performance improvement when illumination is increased up to 50 or 100 fc (Faulkner & Murphy, 1973). More recently developed procedures provide a general method for relating quality of illumination to task performance, without recommending a specific level for each type of task (A. M. Marsden, 1972).

Distribution and Type of Light. Other characteristics of light besides its intensity affect visual efficiency. Of particular importance is the degree of uniformity of illumination. Poor distribution of light is likely to produce glare, which may cause discomfort, visual fatigue, poor performance, and accidents. Glare may result from the presence of direct light sources in the visual field or from highly reflecting surfaces, such as polished metal or glossy paper. The closer the glare source is to the observer's line of vision, the more serious is the loss in performance. In one experiment, the loss in visual effectiveness ranged from 42% when the glare source was at an angle of 40° from the line of vision to 84% when it was at an angle of 5° (McCormick, 1976a, p. 325).

The effects of glare result in part from *phototropism,* the natural tendency of the eye to turn toward a source of light or other bright spot in the visual field. Muscular effort is expended in turning the eyes back and forth between fixation points, as well as in the accompanying convergence and accommodation changes. The presence of brights spots in the visual field thus heightens visual fatigue, which is largely fatigue of the eye muscles. To maintain fixation on the work surface with a minimum of strain, the surroundings should be somewhat darker than the work area. At the same time, the contrast should not be so great as to require shifts from light to dark adaptation. It has been generally recommended (although without much empirical verification) that the brightness ratio should be no greater than 3:1 between work area and immediate surroundings and no greater than 10:1 between work area and more remote parts of the room (McCormick, 1976a, p. 328). Excessive uniformity of light may also be undesirable, because of its emotional effect on the worker. Such lighting may produce boredom and sleepiness. In most practical situations, satisfactory results can be obtained through a combination of diffuse general illumination of fairly low intensity and local light units near the work surface.

Many types of special-purpose lighting have been developed to facilitate the performance of highly demanding visual tasks. Examples are provided by the many

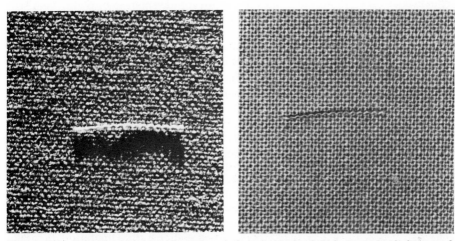

Figure 9-1. Visibility of a loose thread on cloth under 75 fc of surface-grazing lighting and under 650 fc of general diffuse illumination. *(From Faulkner & Murphy, 1973, pp. 154, 155. Copyright © 1973 by The Human Factors Society, Inc. Reproduced by permission. Photograph by courtesy of Human Factors Section, Health, Safety, and Human Factors Laboratory, Eastman Kodak Company.)*

inspection tasks performed to maintain quality control of manufactured products, in which minute defects or deviations may produce serious malfunctions. For the detection of such imperfections, intensity of illumination is usually less important than the position and direction of the light and other special characteristics of the light source. Faulkner and Murphy (1973) describe 17 different types of special-purpose lighting suitable for particular inspection tasks, such as spotlighting, edge lighting, polarized light, stroboscopic lighting, and surface-grazing or shadowing. An example is provided in Figure 9-1. The left-hand picture shows the effectiveness of surface-grazing illumination in utilizing shadows to facilitate detection of a loose thread on cloth. In the right-hand picture, the texture and other surface cues have been virtually washed out by the very high level of general illumination. Thus, 75 fc of appropriate lighting provided far better visibility than did 650 fc of general diffuse lighting.

ATMOSPHERIC CONDITIONS

Regulation of Body Heat. In the process of metabolism, the body generates heat. When the organism is at rest, metabolic rate is slower and less heat is generated than when the organism in engaged in physical activity. The more strenuous the activity, the greater the amount of heat generated. To maintain its normal temperature, the body must give off excess heat. If body heat is dissipated too slowly, one feels uncomfortably warm; if it is dissipated too fast, one feels chilled. Body heat is dissipated chiefly through *evaporation* of perspiration, *radiation* of heat from the body to cooler surfaces in its environment (such as walls), and *convection* of heat by the air around the body.

The cooling power of a particular environment depends upon other characteristics besides its temperature. There is a sound factual basis for the popular cliché that "It's not the heat, it's the humidity" that often causes discomfort. High humidity reduces the rate of evaporation of perspiration and thus decreases the effectiveness of an important mechanism for the dissipation of bodily heat. The role of humidity can be illustrated by the reactions of a group of men exposed for one hour to different combinations of temperature and humidity (C. L. Taylor, 1946). When the humidity was only 10%, temperatures as high as 140° Fahrenheit were judged to be tolerable. On the other hand, when the humidity reached 80%, a temperature of 110°F proved intolerable. Similar interactions of temperature and humidity have been found when the ability to carry on physical work was the criterion.

Circulation of the air also affects its cooling power. The effectiveness of fans derives from this principle. Dissipation of bodily heat is accelerated if the blanket of warm air that surrounds the body is carried away and cooler air replaces it. However, if air temperature is near or above body temperature and humidity is high, fans will be of no avail.

In the effort to provide a measure of the joint effect of interacting atmospheric variables on human comfort and performance, several composite indexes have been developed (McCormick, 1976a, pp. 339–343). One of the best known is *effective temperature* (ET), which combines the effects of temperature, humidity, and air movement (*ASHRAE,* 1972). This index was developed in a series of studies in which feelings of thermal comfort and discomfort were the principal criterion. Any given ET corresponds to the temperature of still, saturated air (100% humidity) that would give the same perceived warmth. Thus an ET of 80° is equivalent to a temperature of 80°F with 100% humidity and completely stagnant air. It follows that ET 80° would be considerably more uncomfortable than a temperature of 80° experienced under ordinary conditions of humidity and air movement encountered in everyday life.

It should be added that kind and amount of clothing worn, as well as activity level, also interact with atmospheric variables in their effects on feelings of comfort, physiological changes, and task performance. The tolerance limit for both heat and cold can be considerably extended by appropriate clothing (McCormick, 1976a, pp. 353–354). The use of loose-fitting, white apparel in hot climates, for example, facilitates heat loss through evaporation and convection and minimizes absorption of heat from the sun. Another relevant condition is duration of exposure to extreme thermal conditions. Tolerance can be increased by following an appropriate schedule of work and rest.

Effect of Temperature on Task Performance. A number of early British studies focused attention on the effects of atmospheric conditions in factories and mines (Bedford, 1953). Temperature, humidity, and air motion were found to be related to such performance indices as productivity, spoilage and waste, number and severity of accidents, and absenteeism. With the increasing use of air conditioning and improvements in heating and insulation of interior working environments, such studies in job contexts have become less frequent. It is mostly when the nature of the task or the location of the work requires performance under atypical conditions that the problem persists. Outdoor work in certain climates is an obvious example.

Most laboratory studies on the influence of temperature on task performance have investigated interactions between effective temperature (or a similar composite index), the energy expenditure required by the task, and duration of the work period. Some of these relationships are illustrated in the research of Mackworth (1946, 1961). One study was concerned with the performance of telegraph operators under extreme climatic conditions. The average number of errors made by 11 operators in receiving Morse code was compared under different combinations of temperature and humidity. The operators had been acclimatized to the atmospheric conditions under investigation for periods of 7 to 11 weeks prior to the experiment. Results were reported in terms of ET. Figure 9-2 shows average number of errors per hour with effective temperatures of 79°F and above. It can be seen that when ET exceeds 95°F there is a sharp rise in errors. Of particular interest is the finding that the increase in errors is greater during the third hour than during the first hour of work, indicating the cumulative effects of working for long periods of time under such uncomfortable conditions. Analysis of individual records showed that deterioration under adverse atmospheric conditions was greater for operators who were initially less skilled than for the more highly skilled.

Other studies were conducted with heavy physical work, as in raising and lowering a 15-lb. weight, or with a combination of intermittent heavy physical work and work requiring accurate muscular control, as in a pursuit type of tracking task. In contrast to the results of the telegraphy study, these tasks showed larger performance decrements, which began at ETs considerably below 95°F.

With regard to the effect of cold temperatures on human performance, a critical factor is the lowering of hand-skin temperature (Fox, 1967). Finger dexterity is especially susceptible to low temperatures (Lockhart, 1968). Some research has

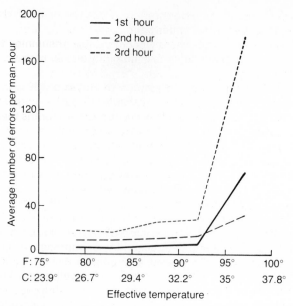

Figure 9-2. Relation between effective temperature and average number of errors in Morse code receiving. *(Data from Mackworth, 1946, p. 148.)*

been done on the effects of warming the hands with radiant heat from infrared heaters (Lockhart & Keiss, 1971). Such auxiliary heat produced significant improvement in task performance in a variety of dexterity tasks, such as inserting pegs in holes, block stringing, knot tying, and screw tightening.

The effects of both heat and cold on mental work are considerably less than their effects on physical work, especially during short exposure periods. What little research has been done with cold temperatures has failed to demonstrate any significant effects. With regard to heat, a review of available research (Wing, 1965) led to the preparation of curves showing the relation between effective temperature and exposure time below which unimpaired mental performance could be expected. As might be anticipated, at uncomfortably high temperatures there is evidence of deterioration of mental performance. Despite the fact that relatively little heat is generated during mental work, feelings of discomfort occurring during very warm (or very cold) temperatures are likely to distract the individual from the task at hand and to reduce motivation. Hence over long work periods, productivity is likely to drop in mental tasks also.

Weather and Related Conditions. The various atmospheric variables considered in the preceding sections are obviously related to the broader and more pervasive conditions subsumed under weather, seasons, and climate. Theories regarding the effects of climate upon human behavior and upon the development of civilizations date back to Aristotle and probably earlier. During the first quarter of the present century, Huntington (1924) wrote extensively on this subject and conducted several field surveys to test his hypotheses. Of particular interest were his analyses of seasonal variations in the output of piece-rate workers in different latitudes. For example, 410 operatives in three Connecticut hardware factories, surveyed over a period of four years, showed production peaks in the spring and fall, with a steep production drop in midwinter and a smaller drop in midsummer. One year when the summer was exceptionally cool, the midsummer drop in output failed to appear. These factories were chosen because working conditions were unusually uniform throughout the year and there seemed to be no major external constraints affecting production. When the output curves of 120 workers in South Carolina cotton factories were similarly analyzed, the spring and fall peaks were found to be farther apart, both falling closer to the winter months than was true in the Connecticut survey. Moreover, the midsummer production drop was now steeper than the midwinter drop. These trends became more pronounced in the output curve of 2,300 cigar makers in Tampa, Florida. In this group, there was a single output peak in midwinter, as well as a steep midsummer drop.

In a more recent, comprehensive investigation of English secondary school students, Aulciems (1972) found significant effects of both outdoor and indoor climatic conditions on performance in arithmetic and on general intelligence tests. The effects were more pronounced on the more difficult tasks. Both this study and the pioneer research of Huntington illustrate one approach to the behavioral effects of weather. These investigators concentrated on identifying optimal climatic conditions for human performance, comfort, and well-being. The behavioral indices employed are typically performance records and reports of thermal comfort, mood, and other subjective feelings. In drawing conclusions from such studies, acclimatization and adaptation must be taken into account. Within broad limits, both task performance and feelings depend upon the temperature, humidity, and other climatic conditions to which persons have become accustomed.

Another approach focuses on the effects of climatic stress on such behavioral indices as performance deterioration, accidents, crimes of violence, riots, suicide, and admissions to psychiatric hospitals. The procedure usually involves the compilation of masses of data on daily weather conditions, on the one hand, and available institutional or governmental records about human activities, on the other. An example can be found in the *Report of the National Advisory Commission on Civil Disorders* (1968), which provides temperature data for 18 major street disorders occurring in 1967 in the United States. In all these cases, the temperature was 79°F or higher; in half of the cases it was above 90°F. Although such survey data suggest useful hypotheses, it is difficult to interpret the results because of the large number of uncontrolled and often unknown factors involved.

A particularly well-documented finding pertains to seasonal variations in the number of admissions to psychiatric hospitals (Moos, 1976, Ch. 3). Surveys in several countries located on all five continents reveal a consistent pattern of increasing admissions in the spring, with an annual peak in late spring or summer. The peak months differ in the expected directions in northern and southern hemispheres. Moreover, some investigations demonstrated a relationship between number of admissions and actual temperature records for specific periods. It has been suggested that rising temperature and increasing hours of daylight may augment the stress of persons already under emotional tension. Some of this effect may be a direct result of the climatic conditions. However, the effect may be mediated, at least in part, by the increase in interpersonal contacts associated with warm weather and longer daylight periods. The fact that children are not in school and some adults are on vacation from jobs further increases the crowding in already overcrowded homes and neighborhoods.

Other climatic conditions for which a variety of adverse effects have been reported include low barometric pressure, sudden atmospheric changes occurring before and during storms, and certain winds (Moos, 1976; Muecher & Ungeheuer, 1961). Of special interest is the foehn, a warm, dry wind characteristic of Alpine regions. A study of the automobile accident rate in Zurich, for example, showed a significant rise during a four-hour period preceding the onset of this wind and a still higher increase during the actual foehn.

In view of the many interacting variables involved in even the more carefully planned field studies, there is an obvious need for systematically controlled studies in bioclimatology. To be sure, many of the traditional studies on the effect of temperature and other clearly defined atmospheric variables on task performance, cited in the preceding section, contribute to our understanding of the role of weather in human behavior. Other investigators are beginning to address themselves to different kinds of questions through appropriate experimental designs. This approach is illustrated by research with a controlled-climate chamber, in which persons can live comfortably in a hotel-like setting for long periods while temperature, humidity, rate of air flow, and other atmospheric conditions are systematically varied (Hollander & Erdman, 1964; Hollander & Yeostros, 1963). By this means, it was possible to verify, for example, that arthritic patients experience an increase in pain and motor difficulties with rising humidity and falling barometric pressure.

Other investigators have been exploring the association of hot weather with hostile and aggressive behavior, so frequently reported in the survey literature. In one study (Griffitt, 1970), college students rated the attractiveness of a "stranger" on the basis of his alleged responses to an attitude questionnaire. In some cases 25% and in other cases 75% of the stranger's responses agreed with those of the subject. As anticipated, attractiveness ratings were higher when responses indicated closer attitude similarity. Both sets of ratings were obtained under hot (ET 90.6°F) and under comfortable (ET 67.5°F) room temperatures. Attractiveness ratings were consistently higher under comfortable temperatures. Ratings of subjective mood were also more favorable under the cooler temperature and were positively correlated with attractiveness ratings. Another investigation (Baron & Lawton, 1972) provided evidence that persons exposed to an aggressive model are more likely to manifest anger and aggressive behavior in hot than in comfortable temperatures. Such a finding suggests interesting implications regarding the development of riots. As more research accumulates from well-designed studies of clearly defined hypotheses, it should become possible to sift myths from facts in the lore about weather and human behavior.

Air Pollution. The 1970s witnessed mounting concern regarding the pollution of air and water. In this context, pollution refers principally to man-made environmental hazards, most of which are by-products of advanced technology. Chief among such pollutants are toxic gases released in industrial smoke and automobile exhaust fumes, insecticides, herbicides, and ionizing radiation.

Among the first air pollutants investigated were those endangering the health of certain types of *industrial workers.* Protective clothing, face masks, and other safety measures were introduced over the years to guard against such hazards. The current approach to the problem is distinguished principally by its comprehensiveness, in terms of (1) the contexts and types of hazards covered, (2) the variety of groups that participate in developing solutions, and (3) the evaluation of the many interacting variables and trade-offs to be taken into account (Ashford, 1976). A major step in raising occupational health standards was the enactment in 1970 of the federal Occupational Safety and Health Act, commonly known as OSHA. Against this background, behavioral toxicology is emerging as a growing field. A major aspect of this field is the assessment of the long-term effects of noxious substances on human performance and mental health. From another angle, psychologists are exploring the applicability of behavioral monitoring as a sensitive indicator in the detection of noxious stimuli in the environment.

Active concern with the effects of air pollution on the *general public* is of relatively recent origin. Research on the effects of pollutants on mental health is still meager and limited to a few toxic agents (Moos, 1976, Ch. 6; Williams, Karp, & Wilson, 1972). Moreover, inadequate controls in survey and epidemiological studies limit the causal interpretation of results. Nevertheless, some effects are well established. It has long been known, for example, that high concentrations of carbon monoxide (as from automobile exhaust and heating systems) cause severe physiological symptoms and, within short periods, can lead to collapse and even death. Less is known about the cumulative effects of long-term exposure to low levels of carbon monoxide. There is some research evidence that exposure to everyday levels (50 to 250 parts per million), as in peak rush-hour traffic, may impair vigilance and psychomotor performance and lengthen reflex reaction time. The results also indicate wide individual differences in both physiological and behavioral response to any given concentration.

In the effort to demonstrate that precise measurement of psychological effects of air pollutants is feasible, M. H. Jones (1972) reports a well-controlled experiment on eye irritation resulting from smog. The psychophysical method of limits was employed to establish pain thresholds in the eye in response to an "experimental" smog produced by combining the exhaust from two automobile engines and submitting it to a variety of treatments. Odor cues were controlled by introducing the smog through an eye mask while the subject was breathing fresh air.

Of particular interest are the findings of chronic lead poisoning among children living in deteriorating slum housing (Lin-Fu, 1967; Williams et al., 1972). Although the use of lead-based interior paints was discontinued by 1950, this paint is still found in old houses. Young children, mostly between the ages of 1 and 3, ingest the poison when they peel off and swallow bits of flaking wall paint. The effects of the resulting lead poisoning include mental retardation, behavioral problems, perceptual disabilities, distractibility, and emotional instability. Follow-up studies indicate persisting damage several years after the poisoning. Relatively little is known about the possible behavioral effects of the more widespread, continued exposure to low levels of lead poisoning from auto exhausts, food, and other common sources.

Air Pressure and Oxygen Deficit. Although relatively restricted in its applications, considerable research has been done on more extreme atmospheric conditions than those discussed in the preceding sections. Among the factors investigated are extreme cold, as found in arctic regions; rapid changes in barometric pressure, such as might be encountered during escape from a submarine or in a sudden emergency loss of pressure in high-altitude pressurized aircraft; and oxygen deficiency, or hypoxia,[2] as found at high altitudes.

---

[2]Often loosely called "anoxia," which actually means oxygen lack rather than oxygen deficit.

Of all these conditions, the one whose psychological effects have been most thoroughly investigated is hypoxia (McCormick, 1976a, Ch. 13; McFarland, 1937, 1946, Ch. 3). By placing subjects in experimental chambers, it is possible to expose them to atmospheric conditions corresponding to different altitudes, to present these conditions in random sequence, and to intersperse them with control sea-level sessions in order to rule out the effects of suggestion. Although individuals differ widely in their responses to oxygen deficit, behavioral effects of hypoxia usually begin at an altitude of approximately 10,000 feet and increase in extent and severity with increasing altitude. Loss of consciousness and collapse generally occur at about 20,000 feet. It should be noted, of course, that modern high-altitude aircraft are regularly equipped with pressurized cabins that reproduce the atmospheric conditions prevailing at low altitudes. Under such conditions, the symptoms of hypoxia do not occur.

The individual is usually unaware of the onset of hypoxia, a fact that makes it all the more important that persons who may be exposed to oxygen deficit take proper precautions in advance. The first symptoms are often emotional: the individual may become irritable and belligerent or—more often—euphoric and jolly. These initial changes are not unlike the effects of mild doses of alcohol. With increasing altitude, there is progressive loss of sensory and motor functions. Night vision may be impaired even below 10,000 feet in some persons. Visual acuity, color discrimination, and other visual functions are among the first to decline. Hearing is affected later. Complex motor processes are disrupted earlier than simpler activities. Attention is weakened, as indicated by poorer detection of both visual and auditory signals in vigilance tasks (Cahoon, 1973). Handwriting deteriorates, and speech becomes slurred and unintelligible. At higher altitudes, reaction time is lengthened. Intellectual functions are likewise affected in the order of their complexity. The more complex functions requiring memory, reasoning, and judgment are lost first; at higher altitudes, even such simple functions as canceling letters deteriorate.

Rapid ascent to very high mountains, as in a railroad or airplane, produces hypoxic effects similar to those described above. Slower ascent, as in ordinary mountain climbing, produces a rather different set of symptoms, which may include illness and depression (McFarland, 1937). Persons reared at high altitudes show considerable physiological adaptation to such altitudes. This is true of the residents of certain villages in the Andes, who normally live at altitudes close to 15,000 feet. Such persons also exhibit much greater tolerance to acute and severe hypoxia when experimentally exposed to simulated altitudes beyond 30,000 feet (McFarland, 1937; Velasquez, 1959).

WEIGHTLESSNESS AND OTHER GRAVITATIONAL PHENOMENA

As human exploration pushed toward more remote frontiers—in the deep sea, in high-speed air travel, and into outer space—research on the biological and psychological effects of unusual environments proceeded apace (Berry, 1973; McCormick, 1976a, Ch. 15; Poulton, 1970, Chs. 16 & 17; Sells & Berry, 1961). Various phenomena have been investigated with special reference to space travel, ranging from the emotional and interpersonal effects of isolation and confinement to the physiological and motor effects of drastic alterations in gravitational force.

Weightlessness. The experience of weightlessness resulting from zero gravity represents one of the most spectacular problems with which the space traveler must cope. Human posture and locomotion are adapted to the Earth's normal gravitational pull. Under highly reduced or zero gravity, locomotion is difficult, movements are erratic and uncoordinated, and perception becomes disoriented. Cardiovascular changes and other physiological disturbances may also occur. Prolonged exposure may lead to muscular weakening from disuse. Return to normal Earth gravity conditions is accompanied by temporary disruption of psychomotor performance and some physiological reactions. No permanent disabilities have been noted, however, following space flights of one month or less thus far investigated. It is difficult to predict the effects of longer space missions, lasting a year or more. Much would probably depend on living conditions and activity programs within the spaceship.

Zero gravity and highly reduced gravity, as on the moon's surface, also affect human performance by eliminating traction. The tractionless environment calls for drastic alterations not only in locomotion but also in carrying out simple maintenance tasks, as in using a screwdriver or a wrench. Data on the physiological and behavioral effects of gravitational changes have been collected both by simulation and by observations during actual space flight. With regard to zero gravity, some effects can be simulated through special procedures. For instance, subjects can be floated in water-filled tanks for several hours at a time while the effects on both physiological condition and task performance are measured. True zero gravity can be simulated for periods of only about one minute by flying an aircraft in a parabolic trajectory so that centrifugal force exactly balances the pull of gravity (Moran, 1969). Data on the effects of prolonged exposure to zero gravity come from observations by the astronauts themselves during space flights and from analyses of records and films obtained during such flights (e.g., Kubis & McLaughlin, 1975).

With regard to task performance, extent of disruption and loss in speed depend upon whether the person is strapped down with a harness, free-floating in the spacecraft, or operating outside the spacecraft, as in making external repairs. Disruption of performance is least when strapped down. Extravehicular activities performed outside the spacecraft are slower and more fatiguing. The nature of the task also affects results. Not only do some tasks show much less disturbance than others, but certain tasks can also be performed more easily and quickly in reduced or zero gravity (e.g., moving or guiding large objects). All tasks, however, show an initial performance decrement and increase in time due in part to the need to master simple zero-gravity skills, such as body restraint and guidance systems. Adaptation and learning occur fairly rapidly, and most tasks can subsequently be performed as well as they were under normal gravity or even better.

Acceleration. A related problem pertains to the high accelerative forces experienced during launch and reentry. In a sense, this condition is the opposite of weightlessness, since the gravitational force acting upon the body is increased many times (T. M. Fraser, 1973; McCormick, 1976a, Ch. 15; Poulton, 1970, Ch. 16). High acceleration can be simulated in a human centrifuge. This device has been used experimentally to determine the amount of accelerative force that can be safely tolerated for different periods of time, the optimal body position and other conditions that affect such tolerance, and the effect of different amounts of force upon the subject's ability to operate controls and perform other tasks. The centrifuge capsule has been used not only to assess the physiological and behavioral effects of accelerative stress but also for adaptation and training in preparation for space flight.

Illusions. Many psychological problems investigated with reference to ordinary aircraft are also relevant to space travel. This is true of the research on various illusions resulting from the interaction of information received through different sense modalities when one is in motion (Clark & Graybiel, 1955, 1957). In the flight situation, for example, familiar sensory cues are often encountered in unfamiliar contexts and hence misperceived. As a result, the position and motion of the aircraft may be misjudged. The gravity receptor (otolith organs) located in the inner ear play an important part in our spatial orientation. In the absence of suitable visual cues, these gravity receptors may lead to disorientation because of the unusual conditions of gravity and acceleration encountered in flight. Some accidents attributed to "pilot error" have probably resulted from such spatial disorientation. Major protection against perceptual errors is provided by prior knowledge about the nature and sources of these common illusions and by training in correct procedures that avoid reliance on misleading sensory cues.

SENSORY STIMULATION

Sensory stimulation represents an environmental hazard when the organism is exposed to overstimulation or understimulation in one or more sense modalities. At one extreme, we find the effects of prolonged sensory deprivation, as experienced by individuals lost at sea, living through the arctic night, or working in solitary outposts. A closely related area of research pertains to the effects of isolation and confinement on both single individuals and groups. The other extreme is illustrated by the "noise pollution" characteristic of so many industrialized or urban environments.

In discussions of the effects of noise on human behavior, the term "noise" is often used to mean unwanted sound. With specific reference to task performance, noise has been identified with auditory stimuli that bear "no informational relationship to the presence or completion of the immediate task" (Burrows, 1960). Regardless of its physical properties, noise in this context customarily refers to sounds that are injurious, disruptive, distracting, or annoying.

Noise and Hearing Loss. It is well established that continued exposure to very loud sounds is likely to cause hearing loss (Kryter, 1970, Ch. 5; McCormick, 1976a, Ch. 14). The effects depend not only on loudness (intensity) but also on pitch (frequency) and duration of exposure. Figure 9-3 shows the intensity in decibels (dB) of some familiar sounds. For continuous exposure during an eight-hour working day, upper limits between 85 dB and 100 dB have been proposed, depending upon the frequency range of the sound. Somewhat higher intensities are tolerable with intermittent exposures of shorter duration. With exposures of $1/4$ hour or less, intensities of 115 dB are considered acceptable (*OSHA*, 1971).

Some of the hearing loss resulting from noise is temporary. Partial or total recovery may occur within periods ranging from a few hours to several months. Rate of recovery depends on nature and duration of the sound, as well as on

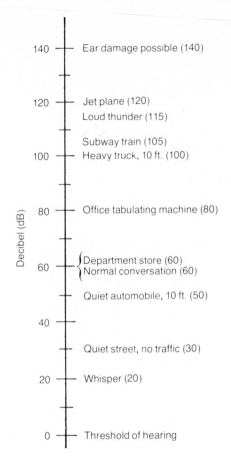

Figure 9-3. The decibel scale of sound intensity illustrated with some common sounds. (Adapted in part from McCormick & Tiffin, 1974, p. 471, and Morgan & King, 1975, p. 317.)

individual differences. With repeated exposure, however, recovery becomes gradually less and less, with some permanent residual loss. Such permanent hearing loss has been shown to increase with years of exposure, when the effects of age are controlled. When sound intensity exceeds the established upper limits for the conservation of hearing, the risk of hearing loss can be reduced by such procedures as redesign of equipment, improved layout, installation of baffles and soundproofing materials, and the wearing of earplugs and muffs.

It might be added that damage risk is not limited to industrial and transportation noises. Discotheques and rock-and-roll band concerts often involve several hours' exposure to sound of 110 dB or even higher intensities (Heimstra & McFarling, 1974, p. 181; Kryter, 1970, pp. 199–205). At these levels, according to the standards established by the Occupational Health and Safety Administration, exposure should be limited to periods of $\frac{1}{2}$ hour or less (*OSHA,* 1971). There is also some research showing temporary hearing loss in rock music performers immediately following an 85-minute performance, as well as less severe residual hearing loss when their hearing was tested at other times (Kryter, 1970, pp. 199–205). The hearing loss extended over a wide range of frequencies.

Noise and Auditory Communication. In work requiring the proper response to auditory cues, noise may interfere directly with task performance. Considerable research has been done on the *masking* of sounds by different kinds of noise (Kryter, 1970, Ch. 2). The effect of such masking is to raise the auditory threshold for various sounds. We can thus determine how much the loudness of a sound signal or other auditory stimulus must be increased for the stimulus to be just barely audible against the given noise.

A problem of widespread practical importance concerns the *intelligibility of speech* under different noise conditions (Kryter, 1970, Ch. 2; McCormick, 1976a, Ch. 6). Whether in face-to-face contacts, over the telephone, in an intercom system, or in radio transmission, many situations demand accurate voice communication. Accordingly, extensive research has been devoted to testing the effects of noise on the understanding of speech under different circumstances. The intelligibility of speech under given noise conditions can be assessed by various indexes based essentially on the speech-to-noise intensity ratio at the appropriate frequency levels. Attention has also been given to ways of improving communication that must be carried out under adverse noise conditions (McCormick, 1976a, Ch. 6). For example, the substitution of a set of easily identifiable words (like "Roger") for letters improves the intelligibility of the message itself. When standard information is to be transmitted, intelligibility is greatly enhanced by limiting the messages to a small number of previously chosen and clearly distinguishable key words. Training personnel in communication techniques that have proved effective also helps. It has been found, for instance, that under noisy conditions, intelligibility improves if the pauses between syllables and words are shortened and the speech sounds themselves are prolonged.

Noise as Distraction and Annoyance. Consider the following statements:

"I can study much better with the radio going full blast—commercials and all."
"I never turn the radio on myself when I want to work, but it doesn't bother me if my roommate turns it on. I just ignore it."
"I simply can't work in the library. With people walking around or whispering, it's impossible to concentrate."
"How can New Yorkers ever get any work done? Trucks rumbling past, sirens screaming, buildings going up or coming down, streets periodically torn up—you can't hear yourself think!"

These represent a few of the many opinions people express about the effect of distraction on work. What do the facts show?

Any attention-arousing stimulus that is irrelevant to the task at hand may serve as a distractor. Besides noise, common sources of distraction include the presence of other persons, anything in motion, bright lights or vivid colors, internal sensations of pain or discomfort, excesses of temperature, pleasant thoughts, and worries. In industrial settings, offices, and other work situations, however, noise is probably the most common distractor. Hence investigations of distraction have usually been concerned with noise. The results would probably be quite similar if other distractors were used.

Research on the effects of noise on performance has yielded many apparently inconsistent results (Kryter, 1970, Ch. 13; McCormick, 1976a, Ch. 14). This does not mean that the question is unanswerable, but rather that the answer is complex. Let us begin by noting the fact that laboratory experiments often show no decline in gross output measures, even when fairly drastic noise distractions are introduced. The results do, however, show some relation to the nature of the task. Thus vigilance or monitoring tasks, requiring constant attention, tend to be adversely affected. In general, complex mental or psychomotor tasks and those calling for a high level of perceptual capacity exhibit more decrement under noisy conditions than do simple, automatic, and thoroughly learned tasks. The effect of noise may even vary within a single task as a function of the performance measure employed, insofar as different aspects of performance are assessed by different measures (Theologus, Wheaton, & Fleishman, 1974).

Performance on monotonous tasks may actually improve when noise is introduced, a finding that has been explained in terms of an arousal hypothesis (McBain, 1961). An optimum level of arousal, it is argued, is conducive to alertness and effective performance.

The nature of the noise is another significant variable. Continuous noise is less disturbing than intermittent noise. Unexpected and unpredictable noise is most likely to disrupt performance (Finkelman & Glass, 1970; Glass & Singer, 1972; Theologus et al., 1974). It has been suggested, too, that the "intelligibility" of noise for the individual affects its distracting power (McBain, 1961). Noise that has little meaning for the individual is less likely to attract attention away from the task at hand. This hypothesis would help to explain why students whispering across a library table may prove more distracting than the drilling, pounding, and crashing noises from the construction job across the street, or why a political speech on the radio is more distracting than music. A related factor is that, in many situations, the disruptive effects of a distraction result not so much from the intrinsic properties of the stimulus as from the individual's emotional response to it. This is particularly true when the distraction is caused by some inconsiderate action on the part of another person, such as co-worker, fellow student, or neighbor. In this connection, too, some investigators have presented experimental evidence that the effects of noise are less disruptive when the individual has some control over the noise (Glass & Singer, 1972). The experimental procedure followed in these control studies, however, precludes a clear interpretation of results (Wohlwill, 1975).

Numerous experiments, spanning several decades and utilizing a variety of approaches, suggest that under noise stress subjects tend to maintain their normal performance level by putting more effort into the task. Although individual investigators reflect different theoretical slants, their descriptions of performance under noisy conditions contain statements indicating that subjects take more care, attend more closely, work harder, utilize their total information-handling capacity, or draw upon reserve energy. Some experimenters have approached the problem through the use of a primary task and a subsidiary task, in which the primary task is clearly perceived by the subject as having first priority (Boggs & Simon, 1968; Finkelman & Glass, 1970). When noise was introduced, performance on the secondary task was disrupted, while performance on the primary task remained unchanged.

Studies utilizing direct measures of energy expenditure do in fact support the hypothesis that work is more costly to the organism when performed under noisy conditions than when performed under quiet conditions. In trying to overcome the effects of noise (or other distractions or stresses), the individual puts forth more energy, with the result that performance level is maintained or even raised. Examples of this reaction may readily be found in everyday life. When a distraction is introduced, we may grip the pen more tightly, press harder on the typewriter keys, and move our lips or even vocalize while reading. These reactions tend to focus attention more strongly on the task at hand and thereby help us to resist the pull of the distracting stimulus.

An experimental example is provided by a study in which the task was to add columns of figures under quiet and under noisy conditions (Freeman, 1939). A system of rotation was used to balance out practice and other cumulative effects. Although the introduction of noise caused a temporary drop in number of correct additions per work period, output gradually reached the same level observed during quiet periods. During noisy periods, however, the subjects used more energy, as indicated by measures of both oxygen consumption and muscle-action potentials. Figure 9-4 gives the average results for action potentials from the four limbs. The graph shows that muscular tension was greater under noisy than under quiet conditions. Over the 12-day period, however, muscle-action potentials decreased until they reached approximately the level of the quiet periods. Essentially the same results were obtained with regard to oxygen consumption.

The above experiment thus demonstrates a further point, namely, physiological adaptation to noise with continued exposure. It seems that, when unfamiliar noises are first introduced, they produce a startle reaction that may interfere with work. When well motivated, subjects quickly bring output up to their normal level by exerting more effort. With time, however, the noise is no longer distracting, and energy expenditure itself drops back toward a normal rate. Whether such adaptation is partial or complete cannot be ascertained without more evidence. It may be that work under noisy conditions will always remain at least a little more costly than work under quiet conditions. Moreover, the amount and rate of adaptation

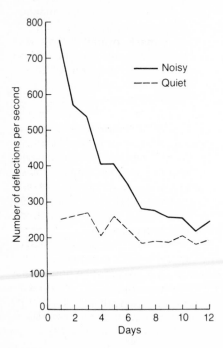

Figure 9-4. Average magnitude of muscle-action potentials on successive days of work under quiet and noisy conditions. *(Adapted from Freeman, 1939, p. 358.)*

undoubtedly vary with the intensity of the distraction, the nature of the task, and the intellectual and emotional characteristics of the individual.

It should also be noted that, even when persons are not working on any specific task, mere exposure to noise produces an increase in muscle tension and other physiological changes similar to those occurring during emotional excitement (Kryter, 1970, Ch. 12). Under these conditions, too, adaptation effects have been observed. Nevertheless, there is some evidence suggesting that exposure to high noise levels over a period of years—besides representing an annoyance in the home, in school, or at work—may constitute a health hazard (Glass & Singer, 1972; Jones & Cohen, 1968; Kryter, 1970, Ch. 12; McCormick, 1976a, pp. 368–370). Hard data to test this hypothesis are meager, and the interpretations of research findings are controversial in view of the possible influence of uncontrolled variables in the samples studied.

Music in Industry. Industrial music had its origins in early work songs, which served chiefly to pace the rhythm of motor activities but undoubtedly helped also to relieve monotony and improve morale. Although music is now used widely in American industry, there are few controlled studies of its effects and results are inconclusive (Uhrbrock, 1961a). Several investigations of simple assembly operations and other repetitive jobs reported slight increases in output, reduction in scrappage rate, and no change in accident frequency following the introduction of music during work (Kerr, 1945; H. C. Smith, 1947). Other well-controlled studies of both simple and more complex industrial jobs, however, failed to find any significant improvement in performance attributable to music, although they also found no detrimental effects (McGehee & Gardner, 1949; Newman, Hunt, & Rhodes, 1966).

It is reasonable to expect that music would be more beneficial in simple, monotonous tasks than in more demanding, varied, and complex tasks. Even in simple tasks, however, individual differences in response to music in general and in preferences for particular types of music could mask overall effects on performance, especially in small samples of workers (Newman et al., 1966). With certain types of tasks, moreover, the introduction of music may prove to be distracting and may adversely affect quality of work (Uhrbrock, 1961a).

In contrast to the results on productivity, surveys of employee attitudes have consistently revealed predominantly favorable reactions to the introduction of music during work. When workers were asked whether they wanted the music continued, the large majority replied that they did. In the same studies that demonstrated no effect of music on objective output records, most workers reported that they got more work done when music was played. Among the most frequently cited effects of music on work were that it reduces monotony, makes time pass more quickly, makes work easier, and gives you a lift.

It is entirely possible that, at least in some jobs, music serves to improve attitudes and job satisfaction without appreciably affecting output. Such a finding would be quite consistent with the results of research on employee attitudes discussed in Chapter 5. If music is introduced to enhance employee satisfaction, however, it is well to ascertain in advance preferences and aversions for particular types of music within the group. Not only have wide individual differences been found in this regard, but also some of the commonly accepted stereotypes about appropriate music have not been supported by survey results (Newman et al., 1966).

Sensory Deprivation. The term "sensory deprivation" is used to designate a reduction in the absolute level, variability, or patterning of sensory stimulation. In milder forms it produces boredom and restlessness; in more severe forms it may lead to hallucinations and other serious aberrations. Although research on the effects of sensory deprivation is of recent origin, its implications have aroused interest in many connections, from child development to psychotherapy, and from ideological indoctrination ("brainwashing") to space travel (Poulton, 1970, Ch. 6; Radloff & Helmrich, 1968; Rasmussen, 1973; Schultz, 1965; Weinstein, Fisher, Richlin & Weisinger, 1968; Zubek, 1968). From a theoretical standpoint, it has been suggested that variety of stimulation contributes to the activation level, or "alertness," of the organism and that activation level is in turn related to the effectiveness of behavior. Underlying neurological mechanisms have been proposed to explain this phenomenon.

Under certain circumstances, highly repetitive visual tasks may induce sleep or mild hypnosis. Similarly, when driving on a superhighway with little to do and few objects to see along the roadside, some drivers become drowsy and sleepy. In long-distance truck driving, hallucinations are a possible accident hazard (McFarland & Moseley, 1954, pp. 124–125). In experimental studies of sensory deprivation, adult volunteers have usually been confined individually in a small enclosure providing a minimum of visual, auditory, and touch stimuli for periods ranging from a few hours to several days. Among the observed effects are perceptual distortions and cognitive disorientations, major disturbances of time estimation, hallucinations, inability to concentrate, decline in test performance, and unpleasant emotional states. Some subjects voluntarily terminate the experiment ahead of schedule because they find it intolerable. It is noteworthy, too, that subjects in such isolation experiments characteristically show an abnormal concern with time (M. B. Mitchell, 1962).

Individuals vary widely in their reactions to all aspects of sensory deprivation and isolation. Such individual differences are especially marked with regard to emotional responses. In general, persons who adjust well to the psychological stresses of isolation are those who adjust well in other everyday-life situations. Motivation is an important factor in counteracting the adverse effects. Personnel selection is thus a major way to prevent such effects. Habituation and training, including a knowledge of expected phenomena and specific ways of circumventing them, are also effective. Isolation stress may be further reduced by maintaining communication and by providing activity and stimulation for the operator, as is typically done with astronauts during space missions. When a crew must work together in prolonged confinement, careful consideration should be given not only to individual personality characteristics but also to interpersonal compatibility.

THE BUILT ENVIRONMENT AND RELATED PROBLEMS

Much of what is currently included within the emerging area of environmental psychology could be more accurately described as architectural psychology. Environmental psychologists have been largely concerned with the spatial layouts of cities, buildings, rooms, and furnishings as they affect human behavior, with special emphasis on interpersonal behavior, feelings, and attitudes. They are also interested in human reactions to natural environments, such as campsites, parks, landscapes, and wilderness trails. With rare exceptions, however, such "natural" environments have been modified and in part designed by human intervention, if only to provide safe access and perhaps to select an optimum lookout for scenic enjoyment.

Concepts from Social Psychology. Environmental psychologists who surveyed the state of their burgeoning discipline in the 1970s often deplored the lack of a coherent theoretical framework and expressed a need for unifying constructs (Craik, 1973; Ittelson et al., 1974; Proshansky et al., 1976). Nevertheless, contemporary treatises incorporate several social-psychological constructs, derived largely from field observations and case studies of both animal and human behavior.

Among the antecedent developments that helped to shape their field, environmental psychologists recognize especially the contributions of Kurt Lewin (1951) and Roger Barker (1968). According to Lewin's field theory, behavior is a function of the interaction between the individual's personality (needs, values, feelings, etc.) and his perceived environment, or life space. Although the concept of life space was defined largely in terms of social and cultural features of the environment, its physical attributes were often included by implication.

Barker's ecological psychology focused more directly on the objective, enduring context of behavior, as contrasted with the individually perceived life space. He was concerned especially with the regularized forms of behavior elicited by such institutional settings as church, schoolroom, hotel lobby, or football stadium. In each setting, behavior is affected by the physical arrangement and properties of seats, tables, and other furniture, as well as by the intended purpose of the setting, its social traditions, and the types of persons who use it. Following several years of detailed field observations in real-life settings—mostly in a Midwestern American community—Barker commented:

> We found . . . that we could predict some aspects of children's behavior more adequately from knowledge of the behavior characteristics of the drugstores, arithmetic classes, and basketball games they inhabited than from knowledge of the behavior tendencies of particular children (Barker, 1968, p. 4).

It should be noted that this orientation is quite consistent with the emphasis on situational specificity characteristic of social learning theory and behavior modification, discussed in several other parts of this book.

Still another source of influence can be traced to Henry Murray's (1938) theoretical model of individual needs and environmental press. The assessment of such individual needs as achievement, order, autonomy, and affiliation underlies several widely used personality tests. The term "press" refers to environmental forces that either facilitate or thwart the satisfaction of needs. Being criticized, receiving affection, and facing competition are examples of environmental press. Following Murray's theoretical model, G. C. Stern (1970) developed two parallel self-report inventories for use by college students: the Activities Index (AI) to measure 30 needs and the College Characteristics Index (CCI) to measure 30 corresponding press descriptive of college environments. Data on each institution are obtained by having the CCI filled out by a student sample. Mean scores for each environmental press are then used to plot the institutional profile. The index thus describes the *perceived environment* of each institution.

Perceived environment is also the basis of a series of Social Climate Scales developed by Moos (1974, 1975a, 1975b, 1976). These scales were constructed for use in a variety of contexts, including hospital-based and community-based psychiatric treatment programs, correctional facilities, military companies, university student residences, high school classrooms, community groups, work milieus, and families. Each scale consists of 80 to 100 true-false items with which respondents describe their perception of the given environment. Items were originally written to tap theoretically chosen environmental dimensions, such as press toward involvement, autonomy, or order; final items were empirically selected on the basis of their ability to discriminate among contexts, as well as their internal consistency within subscales. Each environmental context is described in terms of 7 to 10 subscale scores. It is noteworthy that the Social Climate Scales were designed for relatively small units within complex and heterogeneous institutions—for example, a classroom rather than a whole school, a treatment program rather than a whole hospital, a university student residence rather than a whole university. In this respect, these scales yield more readily interpretable and less ambiguous data than would be obtained from a composite assessment of an entire organizational setting.

Currently there is a growing recognition of the need for *perceived environmental quality indices* as a major component of the comprehensive assessment of environmental quality for policy formation and decision making (Craik & Zube, 1976). Such indices can contribute data on both favorable and unfavorable human reactions to characteristics of air, water, and sound, as well as to more complex features of the environment. While grappling with numerous methodological problems, researchers from several disciplines have begun to develop perceived environmental indices for a variety of domains, such as scenic and recreational sites, residential environments, and institutional contexts.

A group of interrelated concepts frequently encountered in treatises on environmental psychology includes personal space, privacy, territoriality, and crowding (Altman, 1975; Freedman, 1975; Hayduk, 1978; Ittelson et al., 1974). All these constructs have been studied extensively in animal research, both by field observations of wild animals and by controlled laboratory experimentation. More recently, they have been extended to human behavior and investigated by both survey and experimental methods. *Personal space* refers quite literally to the physical space surrounding the person, i.e., the distance each prefers to maintain between himself or herself and others. *Privacy* has been variously defined. It may refer to (1) the need for occasional isolation and solitude, (2) freedom from observation by other persons, and (3) protection of one's anonymity and reserve against unwanted intrusion. The common objections to "invasion of privacy" through computer data banks, covert observation, and questions about personal matters provide examples of the last-named category.

The concept of *territoriality* has played a prominent part in the writings of ethologists and has been profusely illustrated from field observations of many species of wild animals. Staking out one's own piece of ground and defending it against intruders may serve several useful functions, such as safeguarding one's food supply and protecting one's young. Extrapolations of this concept to human behavior, however, have sometimes been carried to fanciful extremes. Freedman (1975, Ch. 3) provides a sobering critique of some of these attempts. To be sure, persons often identify an area that they can control and from which they may exclude intruders. The area may be one's home, one's room or office, a workbench, desk, or file drawer. But there are many practical reasons for such behavior, and we need not look for a biological basis in animal behavior to explain it.

Crowding has received particular attention by environmental psychologists because of its relation to such societal concerns as the hazards of overpopulation, the stresses of life in urban centers, and the overcrowded housing conditions of the poor. The research in this area has yielded conflicting results and led to controversial interpretations (Freedman, 1975; Ittelson et al., 1974; Moos, 1976, Ch. 5; Proshansky et al., 1976, pt. 3; Wohlwill & Carson, 1972, pp. 3–58). Controlled experiments on population density as such (i.e., amount of space per person) suggest that task performance is unaffected (Freedman, 1975). In such experiments, the same number of persons were compared when working in a large and a small room. Under the same conditions, high density tended to *augment* whatever feelings the individual had toward the situation or the persons in it. Thus intrinsically pleasant situations became pleasanter and intrinsically unpleasant situations became more unpleasant. The same dual effect was observed on interpersonal feelings and behavior, such as friendliness, hostility, or aggression.

It should be noted that many of the unpleasant effects ordinarily attributed to crowding may result from associated sources of discomfort and frustration rather than from the number of persons present or the amount of space available per person. Exposure to heat and odors, having to stand for long periods in a subway car or on a waiting line, and being pushed and jostled by fellow shoppers are intrinsically unpleasant experiences, quite apart from the presence of a crowd. Similarly, overcrowded living conditions often occur in association with deteriorated housing, poverty, unemployment, low educational level, broken homes, and other deleterious circumstances. It has also been suggested that the number of persons with whom one must interact may be more important than sheer physical density (number of persons per unit space).

One general finding that emerges from research on the related areas of crowding, personal space, privacy, and territoriality is that reactions in all these areas exhibit wide individual, cultural, and situational differences. Optimal requirements for personal space (interpersonal distance), as well as concepts of privacy, vary markedly among cultures and subcultures (e.g., Lomranz, 1976). In the design of housing, it is particularly important to take traditional behavior patterns and life-styles into account (Chapanis, 1975, Ch. 16; Zeisel, 1975). Individual differences in personality characteristics also affect preferences and behavior in these regards. Territoriality likewise varies as a function of individual and cultural variables. Perceptions of crowding are especially subject to cultural and subcultural differences (Ittelson et al., 1974, Ch. 6; Schmidt, Goldman, & Feimer, 1976). With regard to situational variables, it is evident that both the perception of crowding and its behavioral effects are quite different in a football stadium, theater, library, or shopping center. Whether exposure is temporary or continued and of short or long duration is also relevant. The reaction to living or working in crowded conditions is quite unlike the reaction to riding in a crowded train or shopping in a crowded supermarket.

Freedom of choice has been proposed as a unifying concept to account for the many diverse findings regarding personal space, privacy, territoriality, and crowding (Proshansky et al., 1976, pp. 170–181). Crowding is experienced adversely if it frustrates the achievement of an individual's goal or purpose. It is unpleasant if it blocks the individual's behavior and restricts freedom of choice. If at any given time and in any particular situation individuals are not free to control their personal space, privacy, and use of space (as in territoriality), an oppressive experience of crowding is likely to ensue. In a similar vein, Altman (1975) uses privacy as a unifying concept, defining privacy as an active process whereby one achieves selective control over access to oneself and regulates interaction with other persons.

Methodology. Environmental psychologists utilize a large and varied repertoire of methods (Craik, 1973; Ittelson et al., 1974, Ch. 8; Michelson, 1975; H. M. Parsons, 1972a; Proshansky, 1976; Proshansky et al., 1976, pt. 5; Wohlwill, 1970). Data are typically gathered in naturalistic, intact, real-life settings, with no artificial isolation or manipulation of variables. Considerable emphasis is placed on attitudes and affective reactions to features of both natural and built environments. At the same time, environmental psychologists recognize the need for direct observation of behavior, since persons are often unaware of the influence of the physical setting, while their actions reveal its effects. Significant relations have been found, for example, between the design features of residential buildings and the extent of communication and socializing among neighbors. Other studies have investigated use of playgrounds, parks, and gardens in relation to their location, layout, and equipment. Longitudinal studies are also desirable to detect long-term effects. When people move into or away from a community or region, can such actions be related to identifiable physical features of these particular settings? Because of the complexity of the situations investigated and the multiplicity of variables, it is recognized that many studies provide at best descriptive results and do not permit the clear identification of causal relations. The findings of such field studies, however, may suggest hypotheses that can be tested under controlled experimental conditions.

The subjects employed in research on environmental design may consist of random samples of the public, user groups (e.g., residents of a housing unit, office workers, schoolchildren), special client groups (e.g., elderly, handicapped), or special competence groups (e.g., architecture students, city planners, institutional managers). The types of settings that have been studied range widely, as illustrated by campsites, parks, playgrounds, museums, offices, schools, hospital wards, prisons, university dormitories, transportation systems, neighborhoods, homes, and individual rooms (bathroom, bedroom, kitchen, living room).[3] The environments to be assessed may be presented in many different ways, ranging from real-life contexts to simulations of varying degrees of realism (Proshansky et al., 1976, pp. 326–340). The participants may be persons who inhabit the real-life setting under investigation, or they may be invited to walk or drive over a specified route as part of the research. Simulations may employ such devices as scale models, films, photographs, drawings, or computer-generated models. For some purposes, only the name or brief verbal identification of an environmental entity may be presented, in order to evoke the respondent's memories or image of it.

The specific procedures employed in gathering data from respondents range widely but can be grouped into two broad categories, namely, self-report techniques and observation of overt behavior. *Self-report techniques* may investigate how space is used, the time distribution of activities in specific contexts, the problems and difficulties encountered, and self-estimates of performance effectiveness within different spatial settings. Even more often, respondents are asked

---

[3]Examples of studies in many of these contexts can be found in H. M. Parsons (1972a) and Proshansky et al. (1976).

about their preferences, feelings of enjoyment or annoyance, and esthetic and ethical values. The specific methods range from intensive interviews of small samples to large-scale public opinion polls. Several adaptations of familiar testing procedures have also been developed, such as projective techniques, adjective checklists, statements to be marked true or false, and multiple-choice items. Examples of published instruments include the Landscape Adjective Check List for describing natural scenery (Craik, 1971) and an Environmental Response Inventory for assessing attitudes toward such environmental concepts as pastoralism, urbanism, the need for privacy, and mechanical orientation (McKechnie, 1974). Several studies have employed the Semantic Differential, whereby ratings are recorded on a set of 7-point scales, each defined by a pair of contrasting adjectives, such as roomy-cramped, welcoming-unwelcoming, and comfortable-uncomfortable.

In a well-designed study employing self-report procedures, college freshmen living in high-rise, "megadorm" housing were compared with those living in low-rise dormitories on the same campus (Wilcox & Holahan, 1976). The social climate of the two residential environments was assessed with the University Residence Environment Scale, or URES (Moos & Gerst, 1974), which yields scores on 10 variables. Significant differences were found on several variables, residents in high-rise buildings rating their environments lower on Involvement, Support, Order and Organization, and Student Influence and higher on Independence than did residents of low-rise dormitories. Within the high-rise dormitories, residents of the upper floors (7 to 10) rated their environments lower on Involvement, Support, Student Influence, and Innovation than did residents of lower floors (1 to 5). Such results are helpful in planning design features of future buildings, as well as in suggesting operating procedures for minimizing the unwelcome feelings of isolation associated with high-rise buildings.

In another study of college dormitories (Mandel & Baron, 1976), the characteristics and uses of rooms were investigated. When rooms had clearly identified territory for each occupant, the students were more likely to study in their rooms and also got along better with their roommates. At the same time, students who studied in their rooms obtained higher grade-point averages than did those who studied elsewhere.

A very different approach is illustrated by the use of trade-off games (Michelson, 1975, Ch. 3). This simulation technique is similar to that employed in the management games described in Chapter 4. Its object, however, is to assess the relative values that individuals place on different environmental features. Participants make decisions under conditions of constrained choice, i.e., with limited resources to be allocated to competing wants.

An example is the University of Southern California Trade-off Game (Robinson, Baer, Banerjee, & Flaschbart, 1975), which was one of the procedures employed in a comprehensive research project on the design of residential environments. The sample was drawn from the Los Angeles area and was stratified with respect to ethnicity, income level, and stage in life cycle (e.g., families with young children, elderly persons). In the USC game, the respondent is given 11 cards, each describing an environmental attribute and listing different amounts or conditions of the attribute. Six cards cover accessibility (e.g., to schools, work, shopping, recreational facilities) and five cover character of residential area (e.g., adequacy of dwelling space, air quality). The game itself involves several steps, but the major step requires the allocation of 25 poker chips to the 11 attributes. The underlying principle in this allocation is that a higher level of one environmental attribute can be attained only by accepting a lower level of another attribute. Some individuals, of course, can eliminate certain attributes at the outset, such as accessibility to schools or work for an elderly retired person.

Methodologically, an important advantage of the game approach is that it avoids certain intrinsic weaknesses of traditional methods of assessing trade-offs (I. M. Robinson et al., 1975). On the one hand, most questionnaires and other self-report techniques explore unconstrained choices or wants, which may yield unrealistic rankings of goals. On the other hand, analyses of the choices people actually make under existing conditions (e.g., moving into or out of particular neighborhoods or types of homes) gives little information about what they would do if other settings became available.

The second major procedure for studying the effects of the built environment, *direct observation of overt behavior,* has been applied less often than have the self-report techniques. In scope, this approach spans a diversity of techniques, ranging from highly subjective, global impressions to objective observation and recording of minute behavioral details. At one extreme, we find community studies by participant observers, illustrated by Gans' (1962) description of a low-income Boston neighborhood. The author and his wife lived in the area for an extended period, participated in the life of the community, and made close personal contacts with the residents. The information thus obtained was supplemented by interviews with various community leaders who were familiar with neighborhood problems and customs. Gans concluded that, contrary to expectations, such conditions as crowding and decrepit physical environment were not in themselves a significant cause of mental illness. In fact, the uprooting of inhabitants that resulted from an urban renewal project appeared to be a more likely contributor to pathology, because it disrupted the inhabitants' strong family and ethnic ties and threatened their sense of security.

The previously cited ecological approach of Barker (1968) involves systematic observation and recording of behavior in representative settings within a community. Observations are detailed and precisely recorded. Time sampling is followed, with 30-minute continuous observation periods. Behavior is described as it occurs in the intact real-life settings, with no attempt by the observer to control or manipulate variables. The principal object is to identify the enduring behavioral attributes of diverse settings.

Another procedure is behavioral mapping, illustrated by the extensive research of Proshansky and his associates in the psychiatric wards of three large metropolitan hospitals (Proshansky et al., 1976, pp. 340–351). This method traces the movements of inhabitants through existing physical settings and provides information on how they use space. By means of time sampling and specially prepared forms, observers record where individuals go and what they do in different locations. In the study of psychiatric wards, behavior was classified into such categories as "isolated passive," "isolated active," and "social." The relation between characteristics of the physical setting and the frequency of different types of behavior provides clues for the improvement of existing facilities and the design of future facilities.

Various forms of behavioral mapping have also been employed in research on museum visitors (Bechtel, 1970; Melton, 1972; Winkel & Sasanoff, 1976). One procedure is to have observers stationed at key positions to map the movements of visitors and to record time spent in viewing each exhibit and in such other activities as resting or conversing. A composite map of the movements of a sample of visitors can also be obtained with the *hodometer,* which records the total number and location of footsteps across a floor (Bechtel, 1970). This device utilizes a cluster of electric switch mats covering an entire floor space, each mat being connected to an electric counter. Use of the hodometer to study the movements of museum visitors yielded promising results. For instance, there was close correspondence between hodometer records of relative number of persons who had stood in front of each exhibit in one sample of visitors and the rank order of preferences for the same exhibits reported by another sample.

In still another museum study (Winkel & Sasanoff, 1976), a simulation procedure was developed and compared with on-site observations of visitor behavior. A simulation booth was constructed in which large colored photographic slides of three views of the museum interior were projected simultaneously on adjacent screens. The first sets of photographs showed the visitors' view of the museum as they walked into the main entrance and on into the main gallery. From that point on, the photographs were chosen to take the participants wherever they said they wanted to go and to show them what they wanted to see. Initial exploratory research revealed promising similarities between the results of the simulation and the on-site observations.

SUMMARY

The emerging field of environmental psychology has its roots in both traditional engineering psychology and social psychology. The effects of illumination, atmospheric conditions, noise, and other environmental variables on human performance have been investigated by engineering and experimental psychologists for many decades. Recent developments have extended this area of research to include a wide variety of both living and working environments. Increasing attention has also been given to the behavioral and attitudinal effects of spatial features of the built environment.

Illumination research has provided minimum standards of light intensity for different activities. Such standards must take into account the interaction of several variables of task, person, and illumination. Distribution and type of lighting are often more important than intensity of light. With regard to human reactions to atmospheric conditions, an important mechanism is the regulation of body heat by evaporation, radiation, and convection. Studies of task performance under extremes of temperature show more deterioration in physical than in mental work. A variety of available data suggests behavioral effects of weather, seasons, and climate, which are gradually being tested under controlled conditions. Psychological research on air pollution is slowly accumulating. The psychological consequences of oxygen deficit (hypoxia) are well established. There is also a growing body of data on the behavioral effects of weightlessness (zero gravity), reduced gravity, and high accelerative forces. Space travel and undersea exploration have both stimulated such research and provided rich sources of data.

Environmental hazards associated with sensory stimulation may be illustrated by excessive noise at one extreme and by prolonged sensory deprivation at the other. Noise has been investigated as a cause of temporary or permanent hearing impairment, as a source of interference with auditory communication, and as a major form of distraction. The effects of noise distraction on performance are complex and depend upon the interaction of several variables of the noise, the task, and the individual. While music in work settings is generally favored in employee opinion surveys, output records reveal slight improvement in routine tasks but a negligible or adverse effect on more complex or attention-demanding functions. Research on extreme sensory deprivation has identified several adverse psychological effects. These effects, however, vary widely among individuals and can also be substantially reduced by appropriate procedures.

A growing area within environmental psychology can best be characterized as the social psychology of architecture. In their approach to the built environment, the psychologists who identify with this area have made extensive use of such concepts as personal space, privacy, territoriality, and crowding. Research in this area utilizes a large and heterogeneous repertoire of methods, including both self-report techniques and direct observation of overt behavior.

CONSUMER PSYCHOLOGY

PART FOUR

SCOPE AND METHODS OF CONSUMER PSYCHOLOGY

TEN

HILE INDUSTRIAL and engineering psychology are concerned primarily with the behavior of the individual as a producer, consumer psychology deals with his behavior as a consumer. This field of psychology began with the psychology of advertising and selling, whose object was effective communication from the manufacturer or distributor to the consumer. Through advertising, the consumer is informed about available products or services and about the particular ways in which they may meet his needs. Advertising itself dates from the earliest recorded periods of human history (Presbrey, 1929; Sampson, 1875). The excavations of Pompeii, for example, disclosed advertisements for a variety of products or services, painted on the walls of public buildings. Newspaper advertising appeared shortly after the establishment of the first newspapers in the seventeenth century. Advertising psychology was launched during the first two decades of the present century with scattered laboratory studies and with the publication of books by such pioneers as Walter Dill Scott (1908) and H. L. Hollingworth (1913).

Consumer research was later broadened to cover two-way communication, from consumer to producer as well as from producer to consumer. Communications from the consumer were first sought in the 1920s as a means of preparing more effective advertisements (Link, 1932). Systematic inquiry into consumer needs and wants enabled the advertisers to identify those features of their products that would be of greatest interest to the consumer. Such consumer surveys led directly to the next step, which involved the consideration of consumer wants and preferences in the actual designing of products. At this stage, the psychology of advertising was already being absorbed into the broader, emerging field of consumer psychology.

THE FIELD OF CONSUMER PSYCHOLOGY

Since the 1960s, consumer psychology has undergone phenomenal growth. In the second edition of a major text on consumer behavior, the authors wrote, "Between 1968 and 1972 there has been more published research than during all years prior to 1968" (Engel, Kollat, & Blackwell, 1973, p. 622). In the chapter on consumer psychology in the *Annual Review of Psychology,* Jacoby (1976b, p. 331) estimated that 7,000 to 10,000 directly relevant papers had been published since the end of 1967. One indication of the increasing vigor of this field of research was the formation in 1960 of a division of consumer psychology in the American Psychological Association and the establishment, that same year, of the *Journal of Advertising Research.* Dissemination of research results was further facilitated by the advent of the *Journal of Marketing Research* in 1964. The interdisciplinary nature of current approaches to consumer behavior is highlighted by the formation of the Association for Consumer Research in 1969. The members of this association are drawn from many fields, including psychology, marketing, economics, architecture, law, and medicine, among others. Another demonstration of such interdisciplinary orientation is to be found in the *Journal of Consumer Research,* first published in 1974 under the joint sponsorship of ten organizations representing a variety of professional specialties.

In the development of consumer psychology, the most conspicuous trend has been the shift of focus from consumer qua purchaser to consumer qua consumer (Jacoby, 1976b; Perloff, 1968). This shift has been manifested in at least four distinct ways.[1] First, the locus of interest has been extended *beyond the act of purchase.* Consumer behavior is being more broadly defined to include "the acquisition, use, and disposition of products, services, time, and ideas" (Jacoby, 1976b, p. 332). Consumer research covers not only the activities leading to acquisition but also the ways in which individuals use what they have acquired and dispose of products that have outlived their original function (e.g., discard, resell, repair, adapt for a different function). From another angle, consumer psychology concerns the relation of consumers with organizations, including not only private industry but also government agencies, educational institutions, hospitals, religious organizations, and any other institutions that provide goods or services.

A second major development in consumer psychology is the increasing tendency to approach problems from the *consumer's viewpoint.* This orientation can be recognized in the earliest surveys of consumer wants and preferences, as well as in the use of consumer data in product testing and product design. The development of products to fit consumer characteristics, capabilities, and use patterns links consumer psychology with certain aspects of engineering psychology (Ch. 8).

A more recent manifestation of this consumer orientation is the emphasis on ways to safeguard consumer interests and well-being. Some consumer psychologists have played an active part in the consumerism movement of the late 1960s and 1970s (Asker & Day, 1974; Engel et al., 1973, Ch. 25; Jacoby, 1975; Perloff, 1968). For example, they have provided research and technical services to

---

[1]The term "consumer qua consumer" has been widely used by consumer psychologists to designate all four manifestations. Because it seems to correspond more clearly to the first two, however, more descriptive terms have been substituted for the last two in the present discussion.

consumer organizations and to government agencies in connection with the formulation and implementation of such legislature as the Fair Packaging and Labeling Act of 1967, popularly known as the "Truth-in-Packaging" law. Psychologists have contributed to such areas as product safety; adequacy of consumer information regarding products and services; and consumer education programs, covering not only the transmission of specific knowledge related to consumer affairs but also instruction in effective decision making and in resistance to undue persuasive pressure.

A third trend in consumer psychology is the emerging recognition of the consumer as a living organism whose behavior is of *scientific interest* in its own right (Jacoby, 1975; Katona, 1967; Perloff, 1968). Because humans spend a large share of their waking life in consumer behavior (broadly defined), the study of such behavior in real-life contexts has much to contribute to basic psychological knowledge. Jacoby (1975) presents a particularly convincing analysis of the many ways in which social psychology can be enriched by research on consumer behavior, particularly in such areas as communication and persuasion, information processing, decision making, motivation, attitude formation, social norms and conformity, and interpersonal reactions. He cites several social psychological hypotheses and constructs which could be effectively tested through consumer research, and he calls attention to the increasing use of sophisticated data analysis techniques in such research. Elsewhere, Jacoby (1976a) examines opportunities for mutual contributions between consumer and industrial psychology. It might be added that, with increasing specialization among psychologists, any efforts to establish linkages between initially disparate fields are of particular importance for mutual corroboration and strengthening of explanatory concepts.

A fourth trend characterizing the work of consumer psychologists is a growing concern with *social issues.* This orientation may be described as one that regards the consumer as citizen (Jacoby, 1975, 1976b; Perloff, 1968; Sheth & Wright, 1974). In this connection, psychologists are asking: How can the knowledge generated about the acceptance of commercial products be utilized to stimulate the acceptance of practices that benefit the individual and society? This approach to consumer behavior is two-faceted. On the one hand, it refers to the responsibilities of society toward the individual consumer. Examples include the provision of effective health care facilities and programs, the dissemination of health care information in comprehensible and persuasive ways to ensure its acceptance; the design of transportation systems to suit consumer needs and wants; and the planning of leisure-time and recreational facilities, such as cultural centers and national parks, on the basis of consumer behavior and preferences.

On the other hand, the conception of consumer as citizen refers to the responsibilities of the consumers themselves as members of society. This facet of consumer psychology overlaps a large segment of the environmental protection movement. Its object is to modify the behavior of large masses of consumers with regard to such problems as littering, forest fires, air pollution, noise, conservation of energy and other natural resources, preservation of endangered animal species, and population control.

Examples of research illustrating these four major trends in consumer psychology will be given in Chapter 11. It is apparent that modern consumer psychology spans a wide variety of topics; its methods are correspondingly diverse. In the present chapter, we shall examine some of the typical research procedures followed in six major areas: testing advertising effectiveness, consumer opinion surveys, assessment of consumer attitudes through rating scales and projective techniques, psychological market segmentation, product testing, and studies of consumer behavior in natural settings.

TESTING ADVERTISING EFFECTIVENESS

The present section provides an overview of typical procedures followed to evaluate the effectiveness of ads of all sorts, including magazine, newspaper, direct-mail, car-card, billboard, radio, and television advertising. The diversity of these procedures well-nigh defies classification. There are almost as many variants, adaptations, and combinations of techniques as there are investigators. Moreover, each technique could be classified along several dimensions, such as type of experimental design, type of subjects, data-gathering procedures, and nature of instruments employed. Nevertheless, we can recognize certain clusters of techniques that have major features in common and can serve as convenient categories for discussion.

Experimental Simulation. One of the earliest procedures employed in psychological research on advertisements was based on different types and degrees of simulation; this remains the method of choice to investigate the effect of individual ad variables on observer reactions. Whether data are gathered in laboratory or field situations, this approach involves some control by the investigator over ad content, method of presentation, or mode of observer response. Hundreds of studies by this method, spanning several decades, have provided data on the influence of specific ad features, such as size, position, color, printing type, wording, or illustration. Although much of this research has been conducted with college students, other consumer populations have also been sampled.

One type of simulation utilizes a specially prepared *dummy magazine,* so constructed as to hold constant all variables except those under investigation. Thus, if we wanted to test the effect of size of ads upon their attention and memory value, we would insert ads of different sizes in which such other characteristics as color, illustration, and position were equated. Such a dummy magazine can be used in a laboratory situation, in which the subjects are instructed to look through it at their own pace, turning each page in order. The subjects' behavior may be investigated in various ways, as by observing how long they look at each page or part of a page or by testing their recall of the content of different ads. Similar dummy magazines, with controlled ad variables, may be distributed to consumer samples at their homes and followed up with recall or recognition tests in a subsequent interview (e.g., Blackwell, Engel, & Kollat, 1969, pp. 88–94). In still another variant of this approach, ads may be exposed in a store window in accordance with a predetermined plan while an operator records the proportion of persons passing by who stop to look at each ad.

A different type of simulation is illustrated in a well-designed study by Szybillo and Jacoby (1974b). A total of 90 black and 90 white male college students were asked to evaluate six proposed ads for attractiveness of ad and for likelihood that they would purchase the product advertised. The six products were Irish whisky, dress shirt, umbrella, attaché case, deodorant, and underwear. The proposed ads were presented entirely through verbal descriptions, which included fictitious brand names, three to four sentences of product-descriptive copy taken from actual ads, and the number, sex, and race of the models in the ad. For each product, the ratio of black-to-white models in different ads was 4:0, 3:1, 2:2, 1:3, or 0:4. The experimental design thus permitted a three-way analysis of variance, including race of respondent, racial ratio of ad, and product (2×5×6 factorial design). A control group of 15 black and 15 white students received the identical ad descriptions without the information about race of models. Each individual in both experimental and control groups was given only one ad for each product. Although this study is cited principally for its methodological features, it is of interest to note that blacks responded most favorably to ads with a 2:2 ethnic ratio; the two least favored ratios were no blacks and a single black. The responses of the whites yielded no significant differences with regard to ethnic ratio of ads.

Mechanical Devices. In certain situations, consumer reactions to ads can be assessed more objectively and precisely by the use of well-known laboratory instruments to control ad exposure, record subject responses, or both (Blackwell, Hensel, Phillips, & Sternthal, 1970; Caffyn, 1964). Several devices have been developed for the *visual presentation* of ads under controlled conditions. Some are adaptations of the tachistoscope, which permits the rapid exposure of visual stimuli. Such instruments have been employed to determine what the subjects see on the page during their first quick glance. Immediately after each exposure, subjects are asked what they saw. Since the exposure is usually too brief to permit eye movements, the subjects will see only that which first catches the eye. Small portable models have been developed for use in supermarkets and other real-life settings. An example is the Port-T-Scope designed by the Starch organization and employed in testing not only ads but also other visual materials, such as package designs and point-of-purchase displays.[2]

Another type of exposure device, developed for use in an extensive research project, provides measures of the distance, illumination level, and duration of exposure at which each ad can first be correctly recognized (Advertising Research Foundation, 1962; Caffyn, 1964). It also utilizes binocular rivalry to determine which ad dominates when a pair is presented simultaneously. These indices were employed in assessing the visual effectiveness of ads and in identifying desirable ad features, such as unity of organization, white space, color, and informative headline.

Eye cameras have been employed to photograph the observers' eye movements while they are looking at ads. This method provides a continuous record of all eye fixations. With it, one can determine the order in which different ads are examined, the amount of time spent looking at each, and the path followed by the eye as it explores the different parts of a single ad. Portable models of the eye camera have been developed for use in advertising field studies. Certain physiological changes have also been explored as possible indicators of interest, attention, and emotional responses aroused by different ads. One is the *galvanic skin reaction* (GSR), manifested by a rise in the electrical conductivity of the skin resulting from the increased secretion of the sweat glands during arousal and emotional excitement. Another is the *pupil dilation response* (PDR) found to accompany the presentation of interest-arousing stimuli (Blackwell, Hensel, & Sternthal, 1970; Krugman, 1964, 1965, 1968). Changes in pupil size are measured from continuous photographs of the eye. Through the use of control slides matched with the ad slides, the effect of

---

[2]Unpublished brochures provided by Dr. D. Morgan Neu, Starch INRA Hooper, Inc., Mamaroneck, N. Y., January 1977. Also described in "On-the-spot Size-up of Package Design" (1973).

light intensity on pupil size can be ruled out. This technique has been applied to printed ads, television commercials, packages, and product designs. There is some research evidence suggesting that, when used in this context, both GSR and PDR may indicate chiefly the degree of attention aroused and hence the amount of information processed from the incoming stimuli.

Several types of *"push-button" response devices* have also been developed to facilitate the subject's recording of his own reactions. For instance, push-button voting machines may be temporarily installed in supermarkets to enable shoppers to register their preferences for alternative package designs of a particular product (see, e.g., "A Robot Redesigns Vicks," 1961). A more elaborate response device has been used in research on audience reaction to radio and television programs. Members of small consumer samples meet in a studio to view or listen to a program. Each participant is given a red and a green push button and is instructed to push the green button during the parts of the program he or she likes and to press the red button during the parts he or she dislikes. Since time is simultaneously recorded on the same tape as the responses, the parts of the program that each participant liked or disliked can be identified.

Mention should also be made of the various *electronic recorders* for radio and television usage, which can be installed in the homes of cooperating families. Such instruments keep a record of the times when the sets are in use each day, as well as the stations or channels to which they are tuned. Other devices, placed in the same room as the television set, can provide a *photographic record* of the audience at any given time, from which it is also possible to observe each person's activity and facial expression (C. L. Allen, 1965). The use of these devices has revealed, for example, that there may be no one in the room during a substantial proportion of the time that a set is on.

Consumer Panels. A widely applicable technique utilizes consumer panels. Essentially, a consumer panel is a representative sample of consumers (or households) selected in terms of geographical distribution, age, sex, ethnic identity, socioeconomic level, education, or other relevant variables. For certain purposes, the panel is chosen to represent the general population; for others, it may be specially selected to sample prospective users of particular commodities, such as baby foods or Cadillacs. The same panel may be employed over a period of time. If the same persons are used too often, however, their behavior may be affected by their panel participation, so that they will no longer react like typical consumers.

The consumer panel may be utilized in various ways. In the pretesting of ads, for example, alternative ads may be submitted to panel members by mail or personal interview in order to solicit their reactions to the ad as a whole, the illustration, the written copy, the headline, or any other feature of interest. A common form of consumer panel technique requires the keeping of a diary of brand purchases, television viewing, magazine or newspaper reading, or other relevant consumer behavior during a designated period (Sudman, 1964). Such information may be analyzed within an experimental design that permits the identification of causal relations between advertising exposure and product or brand use. Consumer panels are also employed in product testing, to be discussed in a later section. Moreover, it has been suggested that, in the introduction of new products, panel members may serve the function of innovators and change agents in their community (Jacoby, 1976a, pp. 1041–1043; Mancuso, 1969).

Readership and Audience Surveys. Several specialized commercial organizations conduct regular sample surveys of the audience reached by different media, such as newspapers, magazines, radio, and television. The information collected in these surveys may cover audience size and composition; recall or recognition of specific ads; and attitudes toward particular ads, products, or brands. In radio and television research, many techniques have been devised for finding out how many people listen to each program and who they are in terms of sex, age, education, socioeconomic level, geographical distribution, and other relevant characteristics. The results of such surveys form the basis of the widely publicized "ratings" of programs. No one survey method is completely satisfactory. Each has its own advantages and weaknesses, and each provides a somewhat different kind of audience information.

One simple technique utilizes a *hidden offer.* At some inconspicuous point in the program, a free article is offered. The article chosen is one that is generally desirable and need not be related to the products advertised on the program. It is assumed that, owing to the "hidden" position of the offer, those who write in for the article have actually listened to all or most of the program, rather than having heard only the offer. This assumption is probably correct in general, although some respondents may have heard about the offer from a friend or neighbor. At best, the hidden-offer technique can provide only a rough comparison of the relative audience coverage of two or more programs in which similar offers are made.

Telephone inquiries are now a well-established method for evaluating the audience coverage of different programs. The survey may cover a designated period, such as the preceding day. In that case, the respondent is asked during what hours the radio or television was on and what programs were heard. The respondent might also be asked who was listening to the program—how many men, women, and children. The replies to such a survey are obviously subject to errors of memory and other inaccuracies of report, despite the recency and brevity of the period covered. The same limitations apply to the use of both mailed questionnaires and personal interviews that rely on the respondent's memory.

To avoid these difficulties, the *coincidental technique* was evolved. In a telephone inquiry, the respondents are asked whether the radio or television is on at the time and if so what program is tuned in and what is the name of the sponsor or product advertised. The calls are made to a random sample of telephone owners, drawn from the telephone directory of each city. A limitation of all telephone surveys, however, arises from the fact that a sizable proportion of households that own radios and television sets may have either no telephone or an unlisted number. Moreover, the loss in coverage is likely to be selective in terms of income level. Households without a phone are most often at lower income levels. Unlisted phones tend to be more common at both the lowest and highest income levels, albeit for different reasons (Perloff, 1968, p. 448). Since the relative popularity of different programs, as well as the total amount of radio listening or television viewing, varies with socioeconomic level, the results of telephone surveys may be somewhat distorted.

Readership surveys are regularly conducted for a number of magazines and newspapers. In addition to estimates of the size and composition of the total audience reached by each of these media, the surveys provide comparative data on the percentage of persons who remember each of the ads appearing in them. Both recall and recognition methods may be used in such surveys. In the *aided recall* method, respondents who have read a given issue of the magazine or newspaper are given a set of brand or company names and are asked whether they remember seeing an ad for any of them in that issue. For each ad they claim to have seen, the respondents are asked to report, in their own words, all they can remember about the ad. To elicit the full report, the interviewer may also ask a series of probing questions pertaining to what the ad looked like, what it said, and so forth. The relatively subjective and unstandardized nature of this procedure tends to lower its reliability (Lucas, 1960). The results are also more dependent on the skill and competence of the interviewers than is true of more objective procedures.

The surveys conducted by the Starch organization typically rely on the *recognition* of ads. All respondents who have seen the issue under investigation are shown each ad in turn and are asked three questions about it: whether they remember seeing the ad, whether they noticed the name of the product or advertiser, and whether they read 50% or more of the written matter in the ad. From the replies to these questions, three corresponding Starch scores are computed, known as the "noted," "seen-associated," and "read most" scores, respectively. Because readership scores tend to be higher for ads presented earlier in the interview, each interview begins on a randomly selected page (Lucas, 1960; Starch, 1966).

In recognition tests, some persons will usually report that they saw an ad even if it has not yet appeared in any medium. These false recognitions may result in part from confusion with other similar ads, especially in the case of a widely advertised commodity. Some respondents, too, may deliberately falsify their responses so as to impress the interviewer with their powers of observation or for the many other reasons that prevent frankness in a face-to-face interview. In order to allow for false recognitions, some ads that have not yet appeared may be interspersed with the regular ads. The percentage of persons who falsely recognize the control ads could then be used as a correction term in adjusting the percentages obtained with the published ads. Since ads vary widely in the frequency of false recognition, however, the ideal procedure would be to determine this frequency for each ad prior to its publication and to use these figures to correct the postpublication results for each ad separately (Lucas, 1940). There is some evidence that the inflation of readership scores is higher for ads of well-known brands than for ads of less familiar brands (Koponen, 1956). It has also been shown that the proportion of false recognitions is much lower if respondents are told in advance that the magazine may contain ads not appearing in the issue they had read (Neu, 1961). It is apparent that survey results may reflect subtle influences which should be taken into account in comparing the findings of different investigators.

Large-scale recognition surveys can achieve some degree of control over ad variables by selecting ads for comparative analysis. In this way, they can approximate the previously mentioned experimental simulation studies. This application of readership data is illustrated in an early investigation by Rudolph (1947). Using Starch readership figures for 2,500 half-page and full-page ads from a single magazine, Rudolph analyzed the effect of each ad characteristic while holding other features constant. Ads were regularly matched for product, company, size, and use of color, unless one of the latter variables was itself under investigation. For example, when studying the readership of right- and left-hand pages, Rudolph compared black-and-white full-page ads for a single brand of a product appearing on right and left pages. Readership ratios found in such subgroup comparisons were then averaged across all ads, brands, and products. Rudolph's findings were corroborated in readership studies of more limited scope by Starch and other investigators.

A more direct control of certain conditions can be attained through the *split-run technique,* whereby the ads to be compared appear on the same page of the same issue of the same magazine or newspaper. This is accomplished by placing one ad in half the copies and the other ad in the other half. Comparable distribution to all outlets can be assured by alternate stacking of the two forms.

An adaptation of the split-run technique was employed in a survey of 150 magazine subscribers in Rochester, New York (Politz, 1960). By means of specially prepared copies of one issue, some readers were exposed to certain ads twice, some once, and some not at all. Each reader underwent all three conditions, but with different ads. As a check on actual exposure to the ad, a tiny glue seal held the test pages together in each copy. Only when this seal was broken was the exposure counted for that reader. In interviews conducted a few days after the last exposure, all participants were asked to name the first brand that came to mind for various products. It was thus possible to determine how far exposure to an ad had raised the percentage of respondents who named a given brand above the percentage who named it in the unexposed control group. Reference to Figure 10-1 shows that, in terms of this index of brand familiarity, two exposures were about twice as effective as a single exposure. The advantage of two exposures proved to be equally large when interviewees were questioned about their knowledge of and belief in the claims made by the different brands and when they were asked what brand they thought they would buy if they were to purchase the product on that day. Results pertaining to the respondent's willingness to buy the advertised product are also illustrated in Figure 10-1.

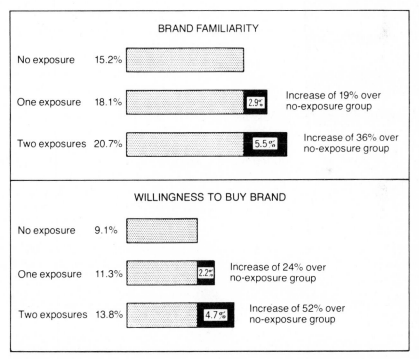

Figure 10-1. Effect of repetition of magazine advertisements upon readers' reactions to advertised brands. *(From Politz, 1960, pp. 14, 20. Copyright © 1960 by Curtis Publishing Company. Reproduced by permission.)*

Mail-Order Purchases and Inquiries. In the case of direct-mail advertising, mail-order sales can be keyed to specific ads. Analysis of sales records thus permits a comparison of the sales effectiveness of different ads. Under ordinary circumstances, the mailed ads differ in many variables, including the product and brand offered for sale, the time of year when mailed, and the many features of the ads themselves. For research purposes, however, it is possible to hold all variables constant except the one under investigation. For example, two ads for the same article could be mailed simultaneously to random halves of the recipient population; the ads themselves could be identical in all features except one, such as the illustration.

With newspaper and magazine advertising, the analysis of coupon returns provides a similar opportunity to assess the effectiveness of particular ads. By keying the coupons in some convenient way, those belonging to each ad can be identified. Actual buying behavior can be studied if the coupon is used for mail-order purchases. When the coupon is inserted merely to test the attention value of different ads, it may offer a free sample, a recipe booklet, an informative brochure about the product, or some other inducement. Under these circumstances, however, we cannot assume that coupon returns indicate potential sales. Coupons are often filled out by children or by habitual clippers, who may clip the coupon just because they like to receive mail or because they cannot resist a free offer of any article. Thus, unless actual mail-order sales are involved, coupon returns indicate only the relative attention value of the ads themselves.

In any event, it is essential that both the nature of the offer and the physical characteristics of the coupon be held constant if the difference in returns is to reflect the relative effectiveness of the ads. The position of the coupon, for example, will greatly affect frequency of returns. Coupons in the outside bottom corner of the page are more conspicuous and easier to clip than coupons in the lower center of the page. And returns are nearly twice as frequent for the former than for the latter position (Starch, 1930). The ads themselves should also be comparable in all characteristics except those under investigation. Ideally the ads should appear on the same page of the same issue of the same magazine. If less than full page in size, the ads should occupy the same position on the page. This apparently impossible feat can be accomplished through the previously mentioned split-run technique.

Some investigators have analyzed written inquiries in response to large numbers of ads, either with or without coupons. In one of the most extensive of these studies, Starch (1959, 1966) obtained from 75 companies confidential records covering 8,200 advertisements. The total number of inquiries analyzed was approximately 12 million, distributed over a 10-year period. As in the previously described analyses of readership records, the ads compared in studying any one variable, such as color, were matched as closely as possible in other variables, such as size, kind of product, company, kind of offer, and presence or absence of coupon. Differences in size of circulation among magazines were controlled by expressing number of inquiries in terms of per million circulation.

The results with regard to size of ad, color, and position are essentially the same as those obtained in readership studies. The only significant differences between the two types of criteria were found in the case of repetition. Although readership scores remain virtually the same when an ad is reinserted in different issues, inquiries do decline. The drop for the second insertion is about 25%. There are smaller declines for successive insertions, the returns leveling off at about 60% of the original number. Such a decline is understandable, since readers who send a written request in response to an ad are unlikely to write again when they see the ad a second time. Thus the later returns come largely from new readers.

Brand Use and Sales Records. Except for the analysis of mail-order sales, which has limited applicability, the methods discussed thus far have been concerned with reactions to the ads as such. Does the ad attract and hold attention? Does it make a lasting impression, so that it can be recalled or recognized later on? It is obvious that these are necessary but not sufficient conditions for effective advertising. The ultimate question is whether the ad succeeds in leading to appropriate action. Although more difficult to measure under controlled conditions than the attention or memory value of ads, buying behavior provides the most comprehensive index of advertising effectiveness.

Brand use surveys represent one technique for the investigation of buying responses. The survey may be conducted by mail, telephone, or house-to-house interviews. The respondent is merely asked what brand of a certain commodity, such as coffee or soap, is currently being used in the household. A single survey can conveniently cover a number of common household commodities. The frequency of brand use can be tied in with advertising by including questions about the magazines and newspapers that are read regularly in the home. Thus if brand A is advertised in magazine X, we can compare the frequency of use of brand A among readers and nonreaders of magazine X.

Several procedures may be followed to check on the accuracy of replies in brand use surveys. For example, the interviewer may arrange to return and collect empty containers, for which the respondent receives some premium. Or the interviewer may offer to buy old magazines for a nominal sum. A "pantry check" of the brands actually on the shelves at the time of the interview is sometimes feasible.

Starch (1961b) reported a 16-year study in which some 400,000 interviews were conducted to determine the relation between ad readership and reported product purchases. The study covered a total of about 45,000 ads appearing in two widely read magazines. Ad readership was measured by the seen-associated score obtained by the usual Starch procedure. In addition, respondents were questioned about purchases they had made during the first week after the publication of each ad. Results were analyzed so as to yield an index of net-ad-produced purchases. This index was derived from the proportion of ad readers who bought the product and the proportion of nonreaders of the ad who bought it. On this basis, Starch concluded that, on the average, the net effect of these magazine ads in increasing the number of buyers was 13.04%. A limitation of this type of survey stems from the difficulty of analyzing cause-effect sequences. Did respondents begin using the product because they saw the ad, or did they notice the ad because they were already using that brand?

Some attempt to disentangle these relations was made in special parts of the Starch study. For instance, 898 ad readers were paired with nonreaders of the same ads who had the same buying rate for the product before the ad appeared. Following the publication of the ads, those who had read the ads made 14.5% more purchases than the nonreaders of the ads.

It would seem that the most direct way to find out how well an ad works is to see what happens to sales after the ad is run. Although apparently simple, such sales tests are expensive and difficult to conduct. A major difficulty is that of ruling out the effect of other variables on sales. If there is a sudden spell of bad weather with a resulting increase in colds, the sale of cold remedies will rise regardless of advertising. In order to rule out these extraneous influences, control data of some sort are needed. In testing the sales impact of a radio or television commercial, for example, control data may be obtained from an area in which the brand is not advertised in these media. The control area should, of course, be as nearly comparable to the test area as possible in population characteristics and in other forms of advertising of the product and brand. In such studies, sales records are analyzed for an extended period prior to and after the introduction of the test ads. Changes in sales in the test area can then be evaluated in terms of concurrent changes in the control area.

Analyses of sales records were combined with telephone interviews in an extensive and well-designed investigation of advertising effectiveness for instant coffee (Aaker & Day, 1974). The experimental design permitted a sequential analysis of causal relations by including measurements at more than one point in time (see Campbell & Stanley, 1966; Rozelle & Campbell, 1969). Data were gathered in 19 telephone surveys, each covering a national probability sample of 1,200 households that had used instant coffee within the preceding 60 days.[3] The surveys were spaced at two-month intervals over three years and were timed to coincide with bimonthly sales audit periods. In the telephone interviews, data were collected on three major questions: (1) brand awareness, (2) attitude toward brands, and (3) advertising exposure. For brand awareness, respondents were asked to name all instant coffee brands "that can be bought around here." The results were expressed as the proportion of respondents who named any one brand of the five being studied. The brand attitude index was based on a weighted average of the proportion of the sample naming any one brand as "the best" and the proportion saying it was "one of several better brands." Advertising exposure was assessed by asking respondents to name all brands of instant coffee seen or heard advertised during the past 30 days on radio or television, or in magazines or newspapers. As a check, the respondents were asked for any specific facts they recalled from ads of the named brands, and these facts were checked against actual ad copy for the brand at the time of the survey. The measure of advertising exposure was based on the proportion of respondents who correctly recalled one or more specific copy claims being made by the named brand.

During the same time periods, sales data were obtained from bimonthly audits of a national sample of retail stores. It was thus possible to analyze the relationships among the four variables measured at any two successive time periods. As illustrated in Figure 10-2, such an analysis yields three types of correlations: (1) same variable on two occasions (e.g., brand awareness at time period 1 and time period 2), (2) different variables on same occasion (e.g., brand awareness and advertising exposure at time period 2), and (3) *cross-lagged* correlations (e.g., brand awareness at time period 1 and market share of sales at time period 2). In the Aaker and Day study, such correlations were used in finding regression equations to predict brand awareness, brand attitude, and market share of sales at one period from the same three variables at the preceding period, along with advertising exposure. Contrary to the traditional model of the causal flow of advertising effects, the results showed that the influence of advertising may go directly from

---

[3]In order to locate the required number of user households, 3,000 households had to be contacted in each survey. A total of 57,000 telephone contacts were thus required.

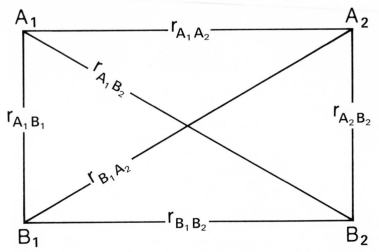

Figure 10-2. Cross-lagged correlations, correlations between variables, and correlations between occasions. A and B refer to variables, 1 and 2 to occasions.

awareness to behavior, not necessarily through attitude. It was further found that, although attitude change generally preceded behavior change, some effect also occurred in the reverse direction.

CONSUMER OPINION SURVEYS

Purposes of Opinion Surveys. It is now generally recognized that the development and marketing of consumer goods and services requires two-way communication. It is wasteful for the manufacturer to devise a product that *he* thinks consumers want and then use advertising and selling techniques to try to convince consumers that they do want it. A more effective procedure is to investigate consumer wants first and then develop products and services to meet those wants. It is better to avoid sales resistance than to overcome it.

Consumer surveys may be used as a guide in designing new products, in modifying existing products, or in preparing advertisements for products already on the market. The utilization of consumer research in product design may be regarded as an extension of engineering psychology (see Ch. 8). Consumer survey data may help not only in developing the product itself but also in designing the package or in choosing a trade name. For the advertiser, consumer research provides information on those features of the product that are most important to the consumer. Do people who own electric clocks like them chiefly because of their high level of accuracy, because of their dependability, or because they do not require daily winding and setting? Consumer surveys may also reveal new uses for a product. When Kleenex was first developed, it was marketed as a facial tissue to remove cleansing cream. Its makers later learned, however, that many purchasers used it as a handkerchief. Accordingly, subsequent advertising focused on the merits of Kleenex for this purpose, stressing the fact that as a handkerchief it is cheap and sanitary and requires no laundering.

The procedures followed in conducting consumer surveys are essentially the same as those employed in *public opinion polls.* Although the preelection polls are undoubtedly the best known examples, public opinion polls are regularly conducted to ascertain prevailing opinions on many political, economic, and social questions. The information gathered in such surveys over the years provides a valuable pool of raw data for social science research. Public opinion polls and consumer surveys are often handled by the same organizations. Many are conducted by commercial survey organizations. Certain universities have research bureaus that specialize in this type of survey, such as the Survey Research Center at the University of Michigan. Public opinion polls are also regularly conducted by several government agencies. The consumer opinion survey is a particularly useful tool in the rapidly expanding area of research pertaining to consumer safety and well-being and to the consumer's role as citizen (see, e.g., Andrews & Withey, 1976; Campbell, Converse, & Rodgers, 1976).

Sampling Problems. Even when based on impressively large samples, opinion surveys may yield totally misleading results because of either poor methodology or a deliberate attempt to support a foregone conclusion. It is not difficult to find examples of surveys rendered worthless by inadequately trained or unscrupulous investigators. The best protection against such misrepresentations is a knowledge of how to evaluate an opinion survey. The basic problems, pitfalls, and procedures of opinion surveys have been fully discussed in numerous publications that may be consulted for further details (e.g., Dunnette, 1976, Ch. 9; Dunnette & Kirchner, 1965, Ch. 9; Sudman & Bradburn, 1974; Survey Research Center, 1976; Warwick & Lininger, 1975).

Once we have decided what we want to ask in a survey, we need to determine *whom* to ask and *how* to ask it. The first question concerns sampling. Although there are several kinds of sampling procedure, a basic distinction is that between random and stratified sampling. A *random sample* is one in which each individual in the given population has an equal chance of being chosen and each choice is independent of every other choice. It could be illustrated by taking every tenth name in an alphabetical list of all names in the population. The familiar practice of "pulling a name out of a hat" accomplishes the same purpose.

A *stratified sample* is a miniature replica of the total population with respect to chosen variables. For example, if a sample is to be stratified with regard to education, the proportion of persons in each educational level, or "stratum," must be the same as that in the total population. If 21% of the given population are college graduates, then 21% of the persons included in the sample must be college graduates, and so on. The sample may be stratified separately with regard to several variables, such as age, sex, education, income level, and geographical location. In this case, the distribution of each of these variables in the sample should match its distribution in the population. A more precise procedure is to stratify the sample for all chosen variables simultaneously so that each cell in the cross-classification contains the correct proportion of persons. One cell of such a sample, for instance, might call for five female high school graduates between the ages of 30 and 35.

A number of surveys employ *area sampling,* in which small geographic units are sampled, rather than persons. In national surveys, this procedure may involve the sampling of counties. When applied within a city, it requires the sampling of blocks and even smaller units, such as dwellings. Each interviewer is then given specific addresses at which to call. Area sampling may itself be random, stratified, or a combination of both types.

Sample size is not as important as representativeness. Through the use of stratified samples it is possible to obtain precise estimates of population data with fewer cases than are needed with random sampling. Many national surveys use between 3,000 and 5,000 cases. The percentages of each response obtained in such samples have sufficiently small sampling errors for most purposes.

By computing sampling errors, the investigator can determine the range within which the corresponding population percentages are likely to fall, as well as the significance of the differences between obtained percentages. For instance, he might find that 35% of the respondents in the sample are dissatisfied with the refrigerator service provided by Company A. By computing the standard error of this percentage, he finds that the percentage of such dissatisfied customers in the population from which the sample was drawn may range from 33 to 37. By the same statistical procedures, he may establish that the percentage of complaints is significantly smaller for the refrigerator manufactured and serviced by Company B than it is for Company A's refrigerator.

Although a certain minimum sample size is required for reliable results, further increases in number of cases are generally wasteful. Moreover, large samples provide no guarantee that the results are accurate. A classic example of this point is the *Literary Digest* poll, based on the replies of $2^1/_2$ million cases (Albig, 1956). This poll, which in 1936 predicted the election of a presidential candidate who was actually defeated by an overwhelming majority, highlights two faulty sampling procedures. First, the sampling was biased, since the mailing lists were obtained from telephone directories and automobile registrations. These sources yielded a sample that overrepresented higher income groups and underrepresented lower income groups. Second, the proportion of nonrespondents was high. Although there were approximately $2^1/_2$ million respondents, the number of ballots sent out was 10 million.

Considerable research is now available on the effects of *nonresponse bias* and *volunteer error* upon the representativeness of samples (e.g., Bell, 1961; Burchinal, 1960; Howe, 1960; Macek & Miles, 1975; Weaver, Holmes & Glenn, 1975). This research demonstrates that survey respondents differ from nonrespondents in a number of characteristics that may be correlated with the answers they give. Similarly, persons who volunteer for any sort of investigation, whether in the laboratory or in the field, differ from those who do no volunteer. Differences have been found not only in such demographic variables as age, sex, education, occupation, and income level but also in general aptitude level and in such personality characteristics as self-esteem, conventionality, and emotional adjustment (Bell, 1961). The specific differences undoubtedly vary with situational factors, such as the nature of the survey, the topics covered, the sponsoring organization, and the data-gathering procedures.

In house-to-house interviews, some of the nonrespondents are persons who were not at home when the interviewer called. Unless proper precautions are taken, a daytime survey will underrepresent employed persons and will overrepresent elderly retired persons and mothers of young children. Other nonrespondents are those who refuse to cooperate when contacted. Still a different situation is involved when a general call is issued for volunteers to participate in a laboratory study. With regard to mailed questionnaires, it has been found that those who respond are more likely to be favorably disposed toward the company or product than those who fail to respond.

Various procedures have been proposed for minimizing the effect of nonresponse bias in survey results. The most direct way, of course, is to increase the proportion of respondents. Much research has been conducted over the decades to identify the conditions that affect the return rate of surveys—and the problem is still being actively investigated (see, e.g., Anderson & Berdie, 1975; Dillman & Frey, 1974; Doob, Freedman, & Carlsmith, 1973; Etzel & Walker, 1974; Huck & Gleason, 1974; Matteson, 1974; Sheth & Roscoe, 1975). Much of this research has dealt with mail questionnaires, which typically yield the lowest return rate. Among the variables studied are preliminary contacts (by phone or letter), different kinds of follow-up techniques, survey sponsorship (university or commercial organization), small monetary rewards, personalized letter form, hand-addressed envelope versus typed address labels, type of postage, inclusion of return envelope, and use of colored paper. Additional factors that obviously affect response rate include length of questionnaire, ease of filling it out, and the interest it evokes in the particular respondent sample. The style and general tone of the follow-up letters may also make a significant difference, as was demonstrated in a well-designed study which compared a whimsical, a humorous, and a formal style (Anderson & Berdie, 1975). Not surprisingly, the relative effectiveness of these three styles varied among different recipient populations.

In order to assess the extent of nonresponse bias in the returns of a particular survey, the demographic characteristics of the respondents may be compared with those of the total population or with the specifications originally laid down for the stratified sample. The nature and extent of bias in the results may also be estimated by comparing the replies obtained from early and late respondents or from those who responded to the initial request and those who responded to the follow-up. These findings may then be extrapolated to those who failed to respond at all.

Questionnaire Construction. A second major aspect of opinion-survey methodology is questionnaire construction. Poorly formulated questions can play as much havoc with survey results as can improper sampling procedures. The wording of questions and the general appearance and layout of the questionnaire are of primary importance in surveys conducted by mail. Questions used in telephone or house-to-house surveys, however, also need to be carefully formulated in advance.

The question writer can profitably examine the extensive research literature on the effects of different question forms upon replies (e.g., Bingham et al., 1959, Ch. 7; Cantril, 1944; Sudman & Bradburn, 1974). Acquaintance with the findings of this research will alert the investigator to certain common pitfalls that should be avoided. The trend of opinion revealed in survey replies can be significantly altered and even reversed by changing the grammatical form of the question, the number of response options provided, the order in which questions are presented, or the format for recording responses (Cantril, 1944, Ch. 2; Jacoby, 1978). In a questionnaire on cooking ranges, significantly different percentages of preferences were obtained when alternatives were presented verbally or pictorially (Weitz, 1950). The inclusion of emotionally toned terms such as "liberal" or "democratic" or the insertion of the name of a prominent person in an opinion questionnaire can substantially affect results.

Leading questions should of course be avoided. But some leading questions may appear innocuous to the investigator. Ambiguities are also difficult to detect, however well informed and experienced the writer may be. Since the writer knows what he wanted to say, he can rarely perceive other possible meanings in his question. Although much can be done in advance to improve the formulation of questions, *pretesting* provides the only sure way to iron out all difficulties. The questions should be pretested on persons typical of the respondent populations for which the survey is designed. Several revisions may be required to develop a satisfactory questionnaire.

The social desirability variable discovered in personality test responses also affects the answers given in consumer surveys. The tendency to give what the respondent perceives as the socially more desirable answer is particularly strong in face-to-face interviews. If people are asked directly what magazines they read, for example, the replies will grossly overestimate the readership of prestige magazines and will show negligible readership for the pulp magazines, which actually sell by the millions (Lucas & Britt, 1963, pp. 223–229). For this reason, magazine and newspaper readership surveys employ indirect and check questions to ascertain whether or not the respondent has read the latest issue of a particular medium.

The growing body of research on individual response styles in questionnaire replies is highly relevant to consumer surveys. Such studies have revealed consistent individual differences in response styles, which may be correlated with other behavioral characteristics of the respondents. For instance, individuals differ in their tendency to answer "Yes" or "No" when asked whether they use a certain product, read a particular magazine, or look at a TV program (Wells, 1961). The "yea-sayers" are also more likely to express a clear-cut preference between two articles than are the "nay-sayers" and to give more favorable ratings to products, programs, and other items on which opinions are solicited. Insofar as these response styles reflect broad personality differences, they may serve as useful predictors of other behavior, such as impulse buying, susceptibility to persuasion, or preference for certain media (Becker & Myers, 1970; Couch & Keniston, 1960). From another angle, however, a disproportionate number of yea-sayers or nay-sayers in a sample could distort results in a variety of ways. Either an independent measure of this response tendency should be obtained for each participant, or questionnaires should be formulated so as to minimize its operation (Jacoby, 1978).

Interviewer Variables. In telephone and face-to-face surveys, the selection, training, and supervision of field interviewers represent an important phase of the project (Hauck & Steinkamp, 1964; Steinkamp, 1966; Survey Research Center, 1976). Survey results may be influenced in many ways by the interviewer's appearance and behavior. The interviewer's race, sex, and socioeconomic level have been found to affect responses to questions pertaining to race relations, sexual behavior, and labor or economic issues, respectively (Athey, Coleman, Reitman, & Tang, 1960; Cantril, 1944, Ch. 8; Kahn & Cannell, 1957, Ch. 7).

The interviewer's own opinion on the question under investigation likewise affects results (Cantril, 1944, pp. 107–112). It is interesting to note that when results have been analyzed with regard to community size, interviewers' opinions have been found to affect the distribution of responses in small towns and rural areas, but not in large cities. Among the possible reasons for this difference, the investigators pointed out that in smaller communities interviewers are more likely to be acquainted with their respondents. This fact may operate in two ways. First, interviewers consciously or unconsciously tend to choose respondents who share their views. Second, the respondents are more likely to know the interviewer's views and hence express an opinion that agrees with those views.

Anything in the interviewer's appearance, dress, manner, or comments that tends to associate her or him with a certain point of view may bias interview results.

This is true even when the cue may be false, as in the case of popular stereotypes. In a survey on the use of hard liquor, two interviewers happened to look like the popular stereotype of a "prohibitionist." The samples interviewed by these two investigators reported much less use of liquor than did those questioned by the other interviewers (Skelly, 1954).

Respondents are also influenced by the interviewer's behavior during the interview. Any indication of agreement or disagreement by gesture, facial expression, or comment may affect subsequent responses. An experiment on verbal reinforcement was conducted in the form of a telephone survey of public opinion (Hildum & Brown, 1956). Interviewers in one group were instructed to say "Good" when the respondent expressed agreement with the question, those in another group to say "Good" when the respondent expressed disagreement. In two other groups, "Mm-hmm" was used as a reinforcement in the same ways. The response "Good" proved to bias the results significantly, while "Mm-hmm" did not.

When interviewer bias affects the respondent's answer—through appearance, behavior, or known opinion of the interviewer—the effect may be regarded as a special instance of the social desirability variable that operates in self-report techniques generally. Social desirability may be defined in terms of different groups with which the respondent identifies. There are very broad norms with regard to the moral and lawful behavior of civilized society; there are narrower national, regional, or class norms with reference to many questions of group relations, economic policy, patriotism, and the like; and there are still narrower norms established by the characteristics and behavior of the individual interviewer. "Interviewer bias" in the replies of respondents may thus be regarded in part as the respondent's effort to give the "right answer" as defined by the immediate situation. Even with an interviewer who is a total stranger and whom they never expect to see again, most people are reluctant to "make a bad impression."

ASSESSMENT OF CONSUMER ATTITUDES
THROUGH RATING SCALES AND PROJECTIVE TECHNIQUES

Research on consumer attitudes toward products and services has borrowed a number of techniques from psychological testing and clinical psychology. Rating scales represent one way of obtaining readily quantifiable responses from large groups of persons. Projective techniques, on the other hand, have been explored as a possible means of detecting emotional responses that might not emerge through direct questioning.

Semantic Differential. Among rating techniques, the Semantic Differential, originally developed by Osgood and his associates (Osgood, Suci, & Tannenbaum, 1957), has proved especially popular in consumer studies. This technique involves essentially the presentation of appropriately selected pairs of adjectives or descriptive phrases which define the ends of a set of rating scales. Each scale usually contains seven units, although fewer units are sometimes used. The respondent marks the scale unit that best represents his or her own attitude toward the object. The Semantic Differential has often been employed to investigate the consumer's image of a product, brand, store, or organization. For example, in a comparison of consumer attitudes toward two competing brands of a common food product, Barclay (1964) administered 12 Semantic Differential scales defined by such contrasting terms as fair tasting vs. excellent tasting, very healthful vs. not very healthful, and average value for money vs. excellent value. Analysis of reported brand purchases during the preceding month revealed small but significant differences in attitudes in favor of the purchased brand.

In another study (Bearden & Woodside, 1976), Semantic Differential scales were employed in assessing attitudes toward five brands of bottled soft drinks. Following a complex and sophisticated model for data gathering and analysis, the investigators obtained ratings on the following sets of 7-point scales: (1) beliefs about each brand (e.g., for young people vs. not for young people); (2) how strongly individual feels about each product attribute, such as taste, degree of carbonation, or value for price; (3) likelihood of drinking soft drinks in different situations (e.g., entertaining at home, participating in sports, or with "fun" foods during a work break); (4) likelihood of having each brand in each situation; (5) likelihood of each situation arising in the next four weeks; and (6) likelihood of buying each brand in the next four weeks. The results revealed significant interactions between brand attitudes and situational variables. The prediction of brand-purchase likelihood could be improved by taking the situational data into account.

Projective Techniques and Related Procedures. Finding out *why* people buy a certain product—or why they do anything, for that matter—is difficult. In answer to a direct question about the reasons for their choices or actions, people are likely to give rationalizations or socially desirable answers which may differ from their real motives. It was to meet these difficulties that certain clinical techniques were introduced into consumer psychology. The proponents of this approach to consumer behavior labeled their work "motivation research"—a term that rose to prominence in the 1950s and 1960s and then fell into disuse as the rather extreme claims initially made for these techniques failed to materialize (Dichter, 1964; Henry, 1958; Hill, 1968; G. H. Smith 1954). Nevertheless, if examined from a less grandiose viewpoint, these procedures may have something to contribute. In general, this approach refers to the use of intensive, individual, qualitative methods in the study of consumer attitudes and buying decisions. One of these techniques is *depth interviewing,* which may itself vary widely in the hands of different investigators (G. H. Smith, 1954, Chs. 3–5). At one extreme we find a fairly structured approach, with predetermined opening questions followed by nondirective probes. At the other extreme is psychoanalytic interviewing designed to explore emotional contexts, symbolic meanings, and fantasies that may be associated with a product. Another variant is the *group interview,* which may be conducted either with a natural group such as a family or club or with a specially assembled consumer panel (G. H. Smith, 1954, Ch. 6). This situation gives the respondents an opportunity to interact with each other, as well as to react directly to questions, sample products, demonstrations, films, or other stimuli presented by the interviewer.

The Impression Studies conducted by the Starch organization employ semi-structured interviews to investigate the attitudes aroused by the ad as a whole, the product, the illustration, and the written matter. Through a series of probing questions, the interviewer explores what the ad means to the respondent, whether any part of it arouses resistance, the extent to which claims are accepted, and the like.

Extensive use has also been made of almost every available kind of *projective technique* (G. H. Smith, 1954, Chs. 7–14). Among those most commonly employed may be mentioned both free and controlled word-association tests, sentence completion, and picture interpretation tests patterned after the Thematic Apperception Test. A number of studies have used cartoons in which the respondent must supply the speech of one of the characters. One such cartoon, used in a survey of factors influencing brand choice of aspirin (Engel & Wales, 1962), shows a druggist saying to a customer:

> This widely known brand of aspirin gives you 100 tablets for 67 cents, and that brand gives you 100 tablets for 27 cents. Which would you like?

The respondent fills in the customer's reply. In the group shown the cartoons, 30% of the replies indicated a choice of the 27-cent aspirin, while only 18% of a similar group who were asked direct questions chose the less expensive brand. The authors suggest that the projective cartoon procedure minimizes the pressure of prestige and social desirability to respond in terms of "quality" rather than price. Such tests try to capitalize on the fact that respondents are often willing to put in the mouth of a third person an opinion that they themselves hold but are unwilling to express. The same idea can be utilized by merely wording an ordinary question in the third person. Instead of asking, "What do you think are the objectionable features of this cleanser?" we can say, "Some women who use this cleanser find a lot of faults with it. I wonder if you can guess what they are objecting to."

Another common technique is role playing, or visualization (Henry, 1958, pp. 74–79; G. H. Smith, 1954, Ch. 10). This technique was employed in a widely quoted early study of consumer attitudes toward instant coffee (Haire, 1950). Although some form of powdered instant coffee had been on the market for many years, it had not been widely adopted at the time of this study. When directly questioned about their reasons for not using instant coffee, most respondents said that they did not like the flavor. Suspecting that this might be a rationalization, the investigator showed other samples of consumers a shopping list, with the request that they try to project themselves into the situation and describe the personality of the woman who bought the groceries. One group of 50 women was given list A; another group of 50 was given list B. As shown below, the two lists were identical except for the fifth item:

List A	*List B*
1½ lb hamburger	1½ lb hamburger
2 loaves Wonder bread	2 loaves Wonder bread
bunch of carrots	bunch of carrots
1 can Rumford's Baking Powder	1 can Rumford's Baking Powder
Nescafé instant coffee	Maxwell House coffee, drip grind
2 cans Del Monte peaches	2 cans Del Monte peaches
5 lb potatoes	5 lb potatoes

The descriptions obtained with the two lists were distinctly different. Among the women shown list A, which contained instant coffee, 48% characterized the shopper as lazy, and an equal percentage said she did not plan her purchases well; 12% called her a spendthrift; and 16% said she was not a good homemaker. In the group shown list B, which contained a well-known brand of ground coffee, laziness was mentioned by only 4% and bad planning by 12%; no one in this group described the shopper as a spendthrift or said she was not a good homemaker.

Adding a pie mix to *both* shopping lists, which were used with two new samples of women, brought the personality descriptions of the regular-coffee buyer closer to those of the instant-coffee buyer. Evidently it was the inclusion of a prepared food item that evoked the stereotype. This part of the study also suggests, however, that the responses were influenced by the *other* items in the list, even though the lists differed only in the coffee item. The generalizability of the numerical results regarding the one item under investigation is severely limited by such contextual influences. This methodological limitation is emphasized by Hill (1968). In a modified version of the Haire study, Hill obtained further evidence that the responses are influenced by the affective connotations of the other items in the two lists.

In still another part of the Haire study, responses to the original instant-coffee list were obtained from users and nonusers of instant coffee, as determined by a pantry check. The personality descriptions revealed several significant differences between the two groups of respondents. Unfavorable descriptions of the instant-coffee shopper were much more common among the nonusers than among the users.

In consumer research, the principal contribution of projective techniques (and depth interviews) is probably as a source of hypotheses which can subsequently be tested by more objective, quantitative, large-scale procedures. They are thus most useful in the preliminary, exploratory stages of a consumer study. Usually, this clinically oriented research is conducted with small, unrepresentative consumer samples. Because many of these techniques require considerable expenditure of time on the part of trained investigators, they are too costly for large-scale surveys. At the same time, the type of data they yield is subject to wide individual differences. The emotional associations and motives investigated in this research are often of a highly personal nature and cannot be readily generalized. Once certain behavior patterns or feelings have been identified, it is necessary to determine what proportion of consumers in large, representative samples react in a similar way toward a given product.

In visualization, or role-playing, studies, such as those dealing with instant coffee, we cannot be sure that the associations between product use and personality stereotypes are as strong or prevalent as the results suggest, nor that they actually affect buying behavior (Hill, 1968). When the interviewer asks respondents to give a personality description from a shopping list, for instance, he is forcing them to hunt around for any stereotype they can think of in the effort to comply with his request. Sad as it may be, few respondents have the self-confidence and courage to tell the interviewer that it can't be done. It is thus possible that many of the women who described the instant-coffee buyer as lazy did so only because they thought that was what the interviewer wanted them to say. The results merely show an awareness of the stereotype. They do not indicate its prevalence or strength. The fact that the undesirable stereotype was mentioned by more nonusers than users could mean simply that respondents are less likely to express disapproval of something that they themselves do. But this does not tell us what is cause and what is effect.

Projective techniques have generally yielded little or no evidence of validity in personality studies. We certainly cannot assume that they provide valid indices of buying motives. In this area, as in personality testing, their validity remains to be demonstrated. The fact that in projective testing and depth interviewing respondents may talk at great length does not necessarily mean that what they say is deep, nor that it is relevant to the behavior we are trying to predict. Moreover, the results may reflect the investigator's preconceived notions. Because of the relatively uncontrolled and subjective nature of many of these techniques, it is virtually impossible to rule out the investigator's biases and expectations.

PSYCHOLOGICAL MARKET SEGMENTATION

Knowledge about the characteristics of various consumer publics has been one of the objectives of consumer research from its earliest beginnings. Media research provides information on demographic characteristics of the audience reached by specific newspapers, magazines, and radio or television programs. Armed with this information, advertisers can choose the medium most suitable for their products and can adapt the appeal, wording, and other features of their ads to the particular audience. Thus food ads will be more successful if placed in a magazine read by homemakers. Ads for any given product, such as a camera, may be very differently formulated for a college paper, a trade journal, or a general family magazine. Within one medium, placing book ads on the book review page not only selects the persons interested in books but reaches them at a time when they are specifically oriented toward books.

To choose their medium effectively, as well as to prepare effective ads, advertisers need to know as much as possible about the consumers who use their products. Beginning with such simple demographic variables as sex, age, and socioeconomic level, studies of market segmentation have been extended to include psychological dimensions. Some researchers have used depth interviewing and projective tests to find out how users of a product or brand differ from nonusers. Other investigators have employed personality inventories for the same purpose.

An unusually extensive and well-designed study, illustrating the early exploratory approach to psychological market segmentation, was conducted by Koponen (1958, 1960) with a national consumer sample. The Edwards Personal Preference Schedule (EPPS) was administered to 8,963 adult men and women who were classified as heads of households. The EPPS is designed to measure the relative strength of 15 needs, such as achievement, affiliation, dominance, or change. In this study, significant mean differences in several needs were found among subgroups classified according to such demographic variables as age, sex, annual income, city size, and United States region. Such findings provide the advertiser with useful information about consumers in different markets.

A major part of the analysis consisted in the comparison of EPPS scores of consumer subgroups classified according to reported purchase of various commodities, such as cars, cigarettes, cosmetics, and paper towels. Subscribers to different magazines were similarly compared. In still another part of the study, mail order purchases made in response to different appeals were checked against EPPS scores. In each case, two groups were chosen from persons who scored at opposite ends of the distribution in the need under investigation but who were matched in such variables as age, income, and city size. A sales promotion piece was deliberately written to appeal to individuals high in that particular need. These advertisements were mailed to the members of both groups, and the resulting sales in the two groups were compared. A mail-order ad written around the appeal for change, for example, brought in over twice as many returns from the group scoring high on the need for change as from the group scoring low in this need. In general, these validation studies revealed significant but low relationships between EPPS scores and buying behavior. Other factors, such as price, product characteristics, and nature of the offer proved to be more imporant in determining frequency of returns.

Many studies of more limited scope followed the same approach, with rather meager results. Few significant relations were established, and personality variables usually accounted for only a small proportion of the variance of consumer behavior. These disappointing outcomes led to some searching critical evaluations of methodology, as well as suggestions for more promising approaches (Engel et al., 1973, pp. 290–306, 651–655; Jacoby, 1971, 1976b; Kassarjian, 1971). A major weakness of the early exploratory studies stems from their lack of clearly formulated hypotheses regarding expected relations between specific personality variables and specific aspects of consumer behavior. The traits investigated were usually those covered by available personality inventories, without explicit consideration of how these personality variables operate within a comprehensive theoretical model of consumer behavior. Such a purely empirical approach, utilizing large numbers of variables, is also likely to yield some chance associations which will disappear when the study is replicated on a new sample.

Another common criticism pertains to the use of inadequate or inappropriate personality measures. The self-report inventories employed had often been developed for different purposes, such as the diagnosis of personality problems. Moreover, the reliability and validity of their scores may have been low, especially when the instruments were used with populations unlike the standardization samples. The assumption of generalized personality traits has also been criticized, in view of the growing evidence for situational specificity of personality traits. For instance, an individual's dominance or sociability may vary in different contexts, such as office, home, or sports and recreational settings. The situations sampled in the chosen personality inventories may not have corresponded closely to those most relevant to consumer behavior. Finally, it has been argued that the study of personality influences in consumer behavior requires multivariate statistical procedures (e.g., cluster analysis, factor analysis, canonical correlation). These methods are needed to deal with the interaction of variables and to reveal the combined effects of trait patterns. Traditional analyses of isolated personality variables by means of correlations or subgroup mean comparisons may fail to detect genuine relations or may yield inconsistent results in different studies.

More recent investigations have been designed to meet one or more of these criticisms. A few examples will serve to suggest the scope of this research. Sparks and Tucker (1971) administered the Gordon Personal Profile and the Gordon Personal Inventory to 190 male college students. The eight trait scores obtained with these personality inventories were analyzed against responses to a product-use questionnaire covering frequency of use of 14 common products and including a question about the adoption of new clothing fashions. Single correlations between personality variables and product usage yielded the usual weak and spotty results. For example, cautiousness accounted for about 2% of the variance in the use of mouthwash; sociability accounted for about 6% of the variance in the use of men's cologne. More promising results were obtained with canonical correlation,[4] through which clusters or types of consumers could be characterized in terms of both high (or low) usages of certain products and high (or low) scores on certain personality variables. Evidence of personality trait interactions can be illustrated by the results on early and late adopters of new fashions. Both groups scored high in sociability. But the early adopters combined high sociability with high emotional stability and low responsibility, while the late adopters combined high sociability with low emotional stability and high cautiousness.

Some investigators have been trying to develop composite portraits of designated consumer groups. This approach has been variously described as "psychographic," "life-style," or "activity-interest-opinion" (AIO) research. The last-named term refers to the use of tailor-made questionnaires covering activities, interests, and opinions. Rather than administering standardized inventories designed to assess broad personality traits, these investigators construct and choose items in terms of their relevance to the products and the types of consumer behavior under study.

This psychographic approach is illustrated in a study of 1,000 female homemakers who were members of a consumer mail panel (Wells & Tigert, 1971). Besides demographic and product-use items, the questionnaire contained 300 AIO statements to be rated on a 6-point scale ranging from "definitely agree" to "definitely disagree." Cross-tabulation of the three types of items yielded psychographs of the heavy users of each product with regard to both demographic and personality variables. For example, frequent users of eye makeup were clearly differentiated from frequent users of shortening in their usage of other products (e.g., other cosmetics in the former and other cooking and household products in the latter), as well as in their media usage (e.g., types of magazines and television programs). The two groups were likewise sharply contrasted in demographic variables (e.g., age, size of family, type of community, geographical region) and in expressed interests, attitudes, values, and life-style. The authors point out that such psychographs could be developed for other target populations, such as nonusers, light users, or other market segments for any given product or service. They also cite examples of major changes made in the type of advertising or the packaging of particular products as a result of AIO studies of consumers.

In still another type of study (Jacoby, 1971), personality research was applied, not to types of products, but to a facet of consumer behavior, namely innovation proneness. The purpose of the study was to test the hypothesis that innovators, or early adopters of new products, tend to be less dogmatic than late adopters. The rationale was carefully worked out on the basis of both personality theory and prior research findings regarding the association of high dogmatism with resistance to change in many contexts. The subjects were 60 unmarried female college students. They were shown 15 sets of photographs, each set depicting five varieties of a given product (cosmetics, women's clothing, and a few miscellaneous products). Within each set of five, there were four traditional varieties and one innovation. Subjects were instructed to select one item in each set that they would buy if given the choice. The "innovation score" (0 to 15) for each subject was correlated with her score on the Rokeach Dogmatism Scale, a standardized self-report inventory.

---

[4]In canonical correlation, the variables in each of the two sets to be correlated are weighted so as to yield the maximum correlation between the two sets. For details, see R. J. Harris (1975, Ch. 5).

The significant negative correlation between the two variables ($-.316$) confirmed the hypothesis. The less dogmatic the person, the more likely she was to select innovative products. Another study of innovation proneness, using male college students, found that low tolerance for ambiguity was associated with unwillingness to buy products perceived as new by the respondent (Blake, Zenhausern, Perloff, & Heslin, 1973).

PRODUCT TESTING

Product testing is concerned with actual products as used by typical consumers. It covers a variety of problems, ranging from consumer's ability to differentiate among brands and consumer preference for particular brands, through more basically oriented research on taste preferences in food and water, to the design of products to fit consumer needs and wants.

Brand Identification and Brand Preference Studies. It has often been asserted that different brands of many consumer goods are indistinguishable once the brand labels and other artificial cues are removed. So-called blindfold tests require careful methodological controls. Otherwise, either positive or negative results may be spurious. It is essential, of course, that all extraneous cues be effectively ruled out. For instance, touch cues might facilitate the identification of some brands of cigarettes. On the other hand, negative results need not indicate lack of discrimination. Subjects may be unable to name brands correctly—especially in the case of obscure brands whose names are unfamiliar—even though they can discriminate the taste in a paired comparison test and may consistently prefer one of the brands. Another methodological problem arises from the presentation of several brands during the same experimental session. The procedures followed to eliminate sensory adaptation, prevent mixture of sensations, and otherwise ensure independence of observations may be inadequate or may themselves introduce cumulative effects. Product testing provides an opportunity to apply the psychophysical methods of the psychology laboratory to consumer research. Both laboratory and field studies have been conducted on brand identification and brand preference with such commodities as cigarettes, cola beverages, shaving creams, bread, and beer (e.g., Allison & Uhl, 1964; Fleishman, 1951; Littman & Manning, 1954; Thumin, 1962).

For purposes of illustration, we may consider a well-designed field investigation of beer consumption in a representative sample of families in one city (Fleishman, 1951). The consumer panel consisted of 20 families that were regular beer purchasers, were willing to cooperate in the study, and constituted a stratified sample of the general beer-drinking population of that city with regard to social level. In contrast to most laboratory and field studies, which call for momentary expressions of preference, this study allowed a seven-day period for the development of preferences. Each day, 48 identical-looking bottles of free beer were delivered to each family. Included were 8 bottles of each of six brands, identified by the colors of the bottle caps. On any one day, subjects could thus continue to use the first brand tried or could keep trying new brands until they found one they liked. From one day to another, however, the color code was changed. Thus the subjects had to make a new set of choices each day. The subjects recorded the brands they drank each day (by color of caps), as well as their preferences. Empty bottles, bottle caps, and unused bottles were collected daily. Significant brand differences were found both in number of bottles consumed and in recorded preferences. Expressed brand preferences agreed with data on consumption. Apparently beer drinkers *can* differentiate among certain brands even in the absence of brand names.

On the other hand, no significant differences in brand preference were found in another study, in which beer was presented in unlabeled bottles for less extensive taste tests and subjects were asked to rate the contents of each bottle (Allison & Uhl, 1964). Moreover, adding correct labels in a second test under similar conditions did yield significantly higher ratings for the participant's regular brand. These taste preferences probably reflected both the cumulative effect of advertising and the individual's prior experience with particular brands. It should also be noted that conditions were not identical in the two parts of the study. In the blind test, for example, subjects received two bottles of each of three brands but were unaware of this fact. In the labeled test, they received one bottle of each of six brands. This condition could affect subjects' ability to perceive differences within each set.

The discrepant results of these two studies of beer brands point up the need to specify exact methodology when drawing conclusions from any single study. Although always desirable, this precaution is especially relevant to brand identification and preference studies. When procedures differ in several respects, as they did in the two studies cited, the investigators are actually asking different questions—and they may well get a different answer.

Food and Water Acceptability Studies. The United States Army conducts extensive laboratory and field studies on food preferences. Although the immediate object of this research is to improve meal planning in the armed services, it has made significant methodological contributions to consumer psychology as a whole. Some of the techniques developed in this work have been widely adopted in the food industry.

Much attention has been given to the development and evaluation of methodology. For instance, recorded food preferences have been compared with actual food consumption of different foods under natural conditions, including regular mess-hall feeding and the use of rations in field maneuvers (Peryam, Polemis, Kamen, Eindhoven, & Pilgrim, 1960). Several different kinds of rating procedures have been employed to investigate both overall acceptance (Schutz, 1965) and specific perceptual attributes of foods, such as sweetness of a beverage, texture of ground meat, or amount of mayonnaise in a tuna-fish spread (Moscowitz, 1972). Laboratory techniques in which individual attributes were systematically varied under highly controlled conditions have shown that respondents are able to state the direction and amount of change needed to increase overall acceptability of a given food sample.

Another investigation was concerned with an analysis of preferences for lists of named foods (Schutz & Kamenetsky, 1958). This technique, which is a type of consumer opinion survey, had generally yielded higher mean preference ratings for each food than those obtained with laboratory taste tests. One reason for this discrepancy may be found in the frame of reference used by respondents in rating named foods. The individual's actual liking for any given food, such as beef stew, will vary from one occasion to another partly as a function of variability in ingredients, manner of preparation, and other characteristics of the particular serving. In a laboratory taste test, the individual responds to the food as presented. In a purely verbal opinion survey, however, he is asked to judge the generalized food rather than a particular version of it. Are these generalized judgments based upon the respondent's average experiences with this food, upon the best examples he has encountered, or upon the poorest?

To answer this question, three groups of subjects were asked to rate 54 foods and beverages. The first group was given the standard instructions, which simply call for a rating of how much the respondent likes or dislikes the item. Subjects in the second group were asked to rate the "Best Serving" of each food they had ever eaten, and those in the third group were asked to rate the "Poorest Serving." The mean ratings obtained in the three groups clearly demonstrated that, under standard survey conditions, subjects tend to rate the best example of each food they have encountered. For each class of foods, as well as for all classes combined, mean ratings with standard instructions were practically identical with those obtained for "Best Servings." The ratings for "Poorest Servings," on the other hand, were appreciably lower.

Many of the procedures employed in food research have been adapted for studying potability, or consumer acceptability, of water for drinking purposes (Bruvold, 1968, 1970; Bruvold & Gaffey, 1969; Dillehay, Bruvold, & Siegel, 1967). Much of this research has been supported by the United States Public Health Service and other public agencies. The methods vary from consumer surveys of attitudes toward community water supply to highly controlled laboratory studies of small consumer panels tested with synthetic water samples. It has been repeatedly found that potability is inversely related to total mineral content of water but that the type of chemical compound containing any given mineral is also an important determiner of taste acceptability (Bruvold, 1968; Bruvold & Gaffey, 1969). There is also evidence that consumer ratings of community water can be predicted quite closely from laboratory ratings (Bruvold, 1970).

Product Development Studies. A major use of product testing is to aid in the development of new products or the improvement of existing products. The experimental techniques employed for this purpose are quite varied, as are the problems investigated. Any feature of any product or service may be the object of inquiry. All the techniques employed in food and water acceptability studies are of course applicable to the development of specific products. Procedures may range from verbal evaluations and ratings to actual use of products or services in natural settings. There is suggestive evidence from various sources that fairly simple tests may yield reasonably accurate predictions of the results of more elaborate, full-scale studies. This has been demonstrated in some of the previously cited food and water research. An illustration from a very different area is provided by a study of dinnerware patterns (D. H. Harris, 1964). The preference ratings assigned to ten fine china patterns by a sample of 140 women shoppers correlated .91 with the actual sales of the patterns during the preceding six months. As a result, the company was able to use a similar rating procedure to pretest 70 proposed new patterns and to select 14 of them as the most promising for actual marketing.

Although opinion surveys, ratings, and other verbal techniques are used extensively in product testing, they are by no means essential. Direct behavioral observations and records of product usage permit product testing with a wide variety of subjects. Food testing with a rather special kind of consumer population is illustrated in Figure 10-3.

Mention should also be made of the use of anthropometric data in designing such consumer products as clothing; seats for railway cars, airplanes, automobiles, and auditoriums; household furniture; and telephone booths, to name only a few examples (see Ch. 8). Although the collection and analysis of anthropometric measures are not, strictly speaking, product testing, they are consumer research in a broad sense. In the design of certain products, anthropometric measures are utilized together with behavioral data and consumer preferences.

OBSERVING CONSUMER BEHAVIOR IN NATURAL SETTINGS

Certain aspects of consumer behavior can be directly observed either through motion picture films or by means of trained on-the-spot observers (Wells & LoSciuto, 1966). This technique derives from the work of Roger Barker in ecological psychology, discussed in Chapter 9. It will be recalled that Barker and

Figure 10-3. Some consumers are not human. A subject participates in a cat-food taste test. The different varieties of the product presented in the three pans are weighed before they are offered to the animal and again after removal. *(Courtesy of The Quaker Oats Company.)*

his associates made highly detailed records of the behavior of children and young people in particular settings, such as classroom, ball park, and drugstore.

A closely similar procedure was followed by Wells and LoSciuto (1966) in recording the behavior of shoppers in supermarkets. Among the advantages of this method, they mention that it concentrates on what people do, not what they say they do; it does not depend on memory; and it is not subject to misinterpretation of questions nor to the tendency to rationalize behavior. They also observe, however, that to avoid sampling bias it is important to consider when and where observations are made. Day of week and hour of day, for example, influence the proportion of men and women, employed workers, and schoolchildren in the sample. Type and location of store may affect the socioeconomic and ethnic composition of the sample. This method also yields predominantly qualitative data that may be difficult to summarize, Moreover, in some cases, the reasons why a consumer behaves as he or she does may not be apparent, although some clarification may be obtained through brief questioning.

In their own study, Wells and LoSciuto (1966) stationed trained observers at cereal, candy, and detergent counters of supermarkets. A total of 1,500 distinct "episodes" of consumer behavior were recorded during 600 hours of observation. Each episode began when the shopper entered the aisle with apparent intention of making a purchase and ended when he or she left the aisle. In their analysis of the data, the investigators sought answers to such questions as the following: Who buys the product (proportion of women, men, children)? Who influences the purchase when more than one person is present? Do shoppers look for a particular brand? Do they examine and compare prices? Do they inspect packages and read labels before buying?

The same approach is illustrated by research on the behavior of museum visitors, cited in Chapter 9. Behavioral mapping can be applied in many settings. The behavior of large groups of persons over a period of time may sometimes be explored through available records or even physical traces (Webb, Campbell, Schwartz, & Sechrest, 1966). For example, physical signs of uneven floor wear may suggest the relative popularity of different paths in public rooms. The magazines or empty bottles discarded in a neighborhood may provide some indication of the use of different printed media, products, or brands. Relative popularity of radio stations among automobile drivers can be estimated by having mechanics record the position of radio dials in all cars brought in for service. The amount of litter that accumulates in public places can serve as a direct indicator of the effectiveness of different antilitter posters. All these types of data have been used in particular situations to suggest hypotheses or to supplement information gathered by other methods. Many sources of data about real-life behavior are available; their effective utilization in specific settings depends on the alertness and sophistication of the investigator in detecting meaningful relations and in sorting out irrelevant and confounding influences.

SUMMARY

Beginning with the psychology of advertising and selling, consumer psychology has broadened its scope to include research on the consumer as purchaser, as consumer, as citizen, and as a source of data in basic behavioral sciences. The methods of consumer psychology span a wide diversity of experimental designs, subjects, data-gathering procedures, and instruments. Six major categories of research include: testing advertising effectiveness, consumer opinion surveys, the assessment of consumer attitudes through rating scales and projective techniques, psychological market segmentation, product testing, and studies of consumer behavior in natural settings.

Among the techniques employed in testing advertising effectiveness are experimental simulation of ads, mechanical devices, consumer opinion panels, readership and audience surveys, analysis of mail-order purchases and inquiries, and collection of brand-usage data and sales records. In consumer opinion surveys, the basic methodological problems concern sampling procedures and questionnaire construction. Sampling may be random or stratified, the latter requiring fewer cases. In area sampling, households in small geographical units are sampled, rather than persons. Sample size should be evaluated in terms of the resulting standard errors of percentages. Survey results must be checked for nonresponse bias and volunteer error. The questions employed in a consumer survey need to be formulated with care and pretested on a representative sample. In telephone and face-to-face surveys, interviewer variables must be taken into account. Consumer attitudes toward products or services may also be assessed through rating scales (e.g., Semantic Differential) and through projective techniques (e.g., picture interpretation, role playing, visualization) and depth interviews of small samples.

Psychological market segmentation provides composite descriptions of the personalities and life-styles of typical users of particular products, media, or services. Product testing may take many forms, as illustrated by the investigation of brand identification and brand preferences, food acceptance and water potability research, and product development studies. The study of consumer behavior in natural settings, such as supermarkets or museums, is a growing area of research traceable to the work of Roger Barker and his associates in ecological psychology.

THE STUDY OF CONSUMER BEHAVIOR

ELEVEN

HEREAS CHAPTER 10 FOCUSED on the methodology of consumer psychology, this chapter will describe typical applications and illustrative findings. As noted in Chapter 10, modern consumer psychology has its roots in the psychology of advertising, which was essentially an application of the psychology of communication and persuasion to marketing problems. Its basic objectives included the transmission of information about a product or service in such a way that the message is noticed, understood, accepted, and retained; that the brand name and trademark are correctly identified and recognized; and that the probability of a particular action (e.g., buying the product) is increased by appealing to consumer wants and arousing appropriate associations and attitudes. With the broadening scope of consumer psychology, the findings regarding effective procedures of communication and persuasion have been applied increasingly to a wide spectrum of problems of societal concern. Some major applications will be examined in the last two sections of this chapter, dealing with the safeguarding of consumer rights and well-being and with social and environmental problems. Consumer psychology has also been expanding with regard to the aspects of consumer behavior covered by its research. This expansion is exemplified by studies of consumer decision-making behavior and by the interdisciplinary area described as economic psychology or behavioral economics.

PERCEPTUAL AND COGNITIVE FACTORS

Physical Features of Printed Ads. Some of the earliest studies in the psychology of advertising were concerned with the effect of such ad characteristics as size, repetition, position, color, and illustration upon attention and retention. Continued research on these factors by a variety of methods has led to the accumulation of a considerable body of data that can serve as a general guide in the preparation of ads and other forms of mass communication. Results have been derived largely from readership surveys of magazines or newspapers and from analyses of written inquiries, although eye cameras, tachistoscopes, stereoscopes, and other laboratory techniques have also been utilized.

Increasing the *size* of an ad will generally increase its readership but not in direct proportion to size. An obvious advantage of a large ad, of course, is that it encounters less competition for attention from other ads on the page. In a Starch (1957) survey covering a four-year period, the percentage of magazine readers who recognized each ad was compared for half-page and full-page black-and-white ads in the same product category and appearing in the same magazine. The same analysis was repeated with two-color and with four-color ads. The average Starch "noted" score[1] was 13.3 for the half-page and 25.2 for the full-page ads. Other investigators have found that ads covering a two-page spread are noticed more often than are one-page ads, although the differences are not large (Assael, Kofron, & Burgi, 1967). In a survey of newspaper ads, Troldahl and Jones (1965) reported that size was the feature accounting for most of the variance in readership scores.

Apart from the diminishing returns of continued size increases, the rate of increase in readership will itself depend upon the attention value of the original ad. A small ad that is noticed by a large proportion of readers has less to gain from an increase in size than one noted by few readers. It should also be noted that the additional space available in a large ad may be used in various ways. It is possible, of course, merely to magnify a small ad so as to fill up the space, but this is rarely done. In a larger ad, there is an opportunity to include more illustration and more text. Sometimes, the additional space is utilized simply as "white space," or unfilled background. Ads with a large proportion of white space tend to attract attention because of their novelty, stark simplicity, and startling appearance. White space may also be used to create a desired atmosphere.

A second major factor that increases the number of readers reached by an ad is *repetition* (Batten, Barton, Durstine, & Osborn, 1967). Each time an ad is repeated in a different issue of a magazine, it will be seen by a certain number of new readers, as well as by some who had seen it in the earlier issue. As a result, the total number of readers who notice the ad, as well as the number who read it, tends to remain approximately the same on successive repetitions. Starch (1960a; 1966, pp. 93–97) analyzed the readership data for 80 ads that had been inserted from two to eight times unchanged in different issues of the same magazine. The intervals between insertions ranged from two weeks to several months, the most common interval being one month. The results showed that each ad tended to retain the same readership level through all repetitions. Those ads with low initial readership were noted by a small proportion of readers on successive repetitions; those with high initial readership were noted by a large proportion of readers on each repetition. Such findings suggest the desirability of using successful ads repeatedly. Similar results have been obtained in other studies with business magazines (McGraw-Hill, 1962) and with outdoor poster advertising (Starch, 1960b).

For those readers who notice the ad on more than one occasion, the repeated

[1]See Ch. 10 for explanation of these Starch recognition scores.

exposure serves to strengthen whatever impact the ad makes on them. A laboratory study in which pairs of ads were exposed in a stereoscope for a brief interval provided some evidence that repeated observation of certain ads may lower the perceptual threshold for those ads (Berg, 1967). During a five-week interval between pretest and posttest, the young women in the experimental group had much more contact than did those in the control group with ads for brassieres and girdles that included a picture of a model. On the posttest, the experimental group perceived this type of ad significantly more often than did the control group.

Considerable attention has been given to the *position* of an ad within magazines or newspapers. This question actually covers several independent questions. One has to do with choice of page within the medium. Extensive data have been gathered on the proportion of readers who look at each page in a newspaper or magazine. The results indicate that the content of different pages has more effect on reader traffic than does the physical position of the page. Placing an ad near a popular editorial feature gives it an advantage.

In magazines, ads on the cover pages (inside front cover, page 1, inside and outside back cover) do have a significant readership advantage of 30% to 64% over inside pages (Starch & staff, 1961). Among the inside pages, however, physical location seems to make little difference (Starch, 1961a). This uniformity of attention value probably results from the efforts of magazine publishers to distribute the editorial content evenly throughout the medium. Whenever possible, of course, ads should be placed near relevant editorial features. For example, book ads should be on or near the book review pages. Such placement helps to select an interested audience and also reaches the reader when he or she is particularly receptive to the product. Advertisers have also been concerned about right- and left-hand pages, as well as right and left halves of single pages. Readership data, however, have shown negligible differences between these positions when comparisons are made under adequately controlled conditons (Rudolph, 1947). What differences are found probably result from a variety of factors, including reading habits (from left to right in our culture), habits of holding and turning pages, and customary placement of ads and features.

Color is now employed in the majority of magazine ads, and it is often introduced in newspaper ads as well. How effective is such a use of color in attracting reader attention? In Rudolph's analysis of ad readership data for one magazine, two-color ads, which use only one color besides black, had only about 1% higher readership than comparable black-and-white ads (Rudolph, 1947, pp. 35–37). However, four-color ads, in which all colors can be realistically reproduced, averaged 54% higher than black-and-white ads in readership figures. These findings have generally been corroborated by later investigators (Assael et al., 1967; Starch, 1956). There is also evidence in these studies, however, that color interacts with size in its effect on ad readership. The advantage of colored ads over black-and-white ads is much greater for half-page than for full-page ads, and it is greater for one-page than for two-page spreads. It is understandable that a large ad, which is already attracting a large proportion of readers, is not likely to show marked gains in readership as further improvements are introduced.

It might be noted that in two-color ads color is generally used not for realistic portrayal but as an attention-getting device. When the printed matter in a medium is largely black and white, the introduction of even a modicum of color will catch the eye. This advantage is lost, however, in a medium which uses color as lavishly as is done in most present-day American magazines. Where color is still a novelty, as in newspapers, the addition of even a single color to an ad will enhance its attention value. Much depends, too, upon the way color is used in an ad. Some ads can be effectively presented without color and might gain little from the arbitrary addition of one or more colors. Others depend upon color to achieve realism, to display the attractive features of the product, or to create a suitable atmosphere. Average readership figures may be misleading when applied indiscriminately to individual ads. The introduction of color may produce spectacular gains in the effectiveness of some ads and negligible gains in others.

Like color, *illustrations* serve many functions. They may be used to facilitate comprehension of ideas, to aid in the later identification of the product at the point of sale, or to arouse appropriate affective associations. For certain classes of products, the illustration lets the product "speak for itself," as in the photograph of an attractive dessert, a warm coat, or a decorative floor covering.

With regard to attention value, pictures of people generally rate high. An analysis conducted by Starch (1946) indicated that ads portraying people were more often read than those showing only the product. Using the read-most index, which is based on the proportion of respondents who have read half or more of the text of an ad, Starch selected the 50 most widely read and the 50 least widely read ads from his records. The illustrations centered about people in 29 of the former and only 10 of the latter. Pictures of the product alone were found in none of the former and in 32 of the latter. On the other hand, it should be noted that some of the most successful ads portray appetizing foods that can be prepared with the given product. This type of ad would feature, for example, not a package of flour, but a cake baked with that flour, along with a recipe for the cake.

An important consideration in the choice of illustration is its congruity with the product and the verbal appeal. There is evidence suggesting that, when human models are used in a printed ad, the "fittingness" or appropriateness of the model for the product may influence judgments of product quality (Kanungo & Pang, 1973). In the use of illustrations to attract attention, there is the danger that the ad comes to be regarded as an end in itself. Advertisers should always remember that they are trying to sell the product, not the ad. Irrelevant, bizarre, or "arty" illustrations may attract attention to themselves but usually fail to associate the ad with the product or brand name. A related question pertains to the specific audience that the advertiser wants to reach. The content and form of the illustration tend to preselect those who will read the ad.

Trademarks and Other Reduced Cues. From a psychological standpoint, every trademark is a reduced cue. Its function is to serve as a conditioned stimulus for the recall of the product and company name. The trademark also tends to evoke the feelings and ideas that have become associated with the product through previous advertising and through the consumer's own contacts with the product. When the trademark is a direct representation of the brand name, as with Camel cigarettes or Quaker Oats cereals, the association is particularly easy to establish and the chances of confusion with other products or brands are minimized. Frequently, the trademark is chosen so as to symbolize a characteristic advantage of the product or service, which the advertiser wants to highlight. An example is the Prudential Life Insurance Company's Rock of Gibraltar (the enduring strength of Gibraltar).

It is not only the registered trademark that serves as a reduced cue. Any distinctive recurring feature of a company's advertising comes to stand for the product. Examples include slogans, printing type, layout, writing style, decorative design, nature of illustration, and characteristic color combinations. When a certain style of advertising has become strongly identified with one company, any attempt by a competitor to imitate it generally benefits the original company more than it benefits the imitator. Most observers attribute the ad to the original company, not even noticing the competitor's name. The effect is likely to be a greater rise in sales for the original company than for the competitor (Engel et al., 1973, p. 218).

To achieve continuity while avoiding monotony, advertisers often combine repetition of a major feature with variation of details. This type of advertising frequently takes the form of variations on a basic theme. Thus individual ads in a series may appeal to the same consumer need by means of different incidents. Each ad would thus present the same message but express it differently. Or the same character may be portrayed in different settings. The use of familiar "trade characters" who recur in a company's advertisements not only facilitates product recognition but also helps to provide human interest and encourages the consumer to identify with the product.

Psychological research on the selection of trademarks, logos, and brand names has been concerned with such questions as distinctness and ease of identification, cognitive and affective connotations, and recognition and recall—especially the association of brand name or other symbol with the appropriate product. Common research techniques include association tests, Semantic Differential and other types of rating scales, and various recall and recognition tests. Tachistoscopic exposure has been used to investigate the speed with which different trademarks could be perceived and recognized (Burdick, Green, & Lovelace, 1959). It is noteworthy that perceptual speed, rated favorableness, and frequency of recall were highly intercorrelated among the trademarks investigated (r's from .75 to .82). Using a paired-associate technique, another study (Lutz & Lutz, 1977) showed that a pictorial logo or trademark incorporating both product and brand name is a better memory aid than one based on either product or brand name alone.

In a well-designed series of studies of brand awareness, Kanungo (1968, 1969) found that both meaningfulness and appropriateness of brand names significantly influenced recall. Meaningfulness refers principally to familiarity and frequency of usage of words. In the case of newly coined names, it depends on the closeness of resemblance to familiar words. Appropriateness, or "fittingness," of a brand name was defined in terms of its resemblance (in form, sound, or meaning) to a word associated with the product. A brand name with high fittingness for the product resembles a commonly associated word; one with low fittingness resembles a rarely associated word. Both meaningfulness and fittingness were verified by ratings for these qualities obtained from participants in the experiment. The results showed that recall of the brand name corresponding to each product was significantly related to both variables, although there was also a significant interaction between them. With high-fitting brand names, recall of brand-product associations was uninfluenced by meaningfulness; with low-fitting names, the more meaningful names were better recalled. For instance, there would be little or no recall difference between two high-fitting brand names for folders, such as Paper-Safe (high-meaning words) and Filex (low-meaning, newly coined name). On the other hand, with such low-fitting names for adhesive tape as Sporty (high meaning) and Landes (low meaning), the high-meaning name was recalled significantly more often.

Sometimes a brand name becomes so strongly identified with a product that it comes to be used as a product name. Thus people may say Kleenex to mean any cleansing tissue or Jell-o to mean any gelatin dessert. Such a generic use of brand names has both legal and psychological implications. Legally, a company may lose its exclusive right to the name if it can be demonstrated that the name is commonly employed to designate a product category. This was the fate of such brand names as aspirin, cellophane, nylon, and linoleum. Psychologically, the generic use of brand names may lead to the indiscriminate purchasing of competing brands. It may also cause increasing dissatisfaction with the original brand as a result of the unrecognized use of inferior brands by the consumer.

Another legal problem, that of brand-name infringement, arises from the psychological facts of verbal perception and discrimination. When reading a word, we do not normally perceive every letter in it. A few letters provide enough cues for the recognition of the whole word. Consequently, if certain letters are omitted, added, or substituted, the word may still be perceived in its original form.

The frequency with which brand names are actually confused can be assessed through recognition tests administered to consumer samples. Such procedures can be used both in testing the distinctness of proposed names for a new brand and in providing data to help evaluate legal claims regarding infringements. The percentage of respondents who incorrectly "recognize" a new name as a preexisting brand name provides an empirical index of degree of confusion. A special adaptation of the recognition method for measuring brand-name confusion is described by Weitz (1960). In this method, four groups of respondents are examined by means of four different experimental procedures. In the first group, the original names appear on the initial list, while the imitations appear on the test list; in the second, the procedure is reversed. In the third, the originals appear on both lists; and in the fourth, the imitations appear on both. Several control measures can thus be obtained.

Readability. The term "readability" is most commonly used to mean the *difficulty level* of reading matter. In this sense, the easier a passage, the more readable it is. Reading ease is also affected by legibility of type, layout, and other mechanical features of the printed page. Similarly, one's interest in the topic influences the ease of reading. The measurement of readability, however, has centered on reading ease as determined by linguistic form. The principal question has been, "How can the writer express what he or she is trying to say so as to simplify the reader's task?"

One factor that affects reading ease is the difficulty level of individual words. Frequency of use can serve as an index of word comprehension. Common words are more likely to be understood than are rare words. Standard compilations of frequency of word usage can be consulted to assess the appropriateness of vocabulary for specific purposes.[2] Besides vocabulary level, several other linguistic factors have been investigated in relation to reading ease. Those characteristics of reading matter found to correlate most highly with criteria of reading ease (such as comprehension, reading speed, or grade level of content) have been combined into readability formulas (see Chall, 1958; Klare, 1963). These formulas are designed to estimate the difficulty level of a passage on the basis of such factors as

---

[2]E.g., Thorndike and Lorge (1944), Carroll, Davies, and Richman (1971).

word frequency, word length, number of abstract words, sentence length, sentence structure, and number of personal references. Since most of these factors are highly intercorrelated, the various formulas derived from them yield similar results. Computer programs have also been developed for many of these formulas (Coleman & Liau, 1975).

One investigator who did much to publicize readability research is Rudolf Flesch. After completing a doctoral dissertation on readability, Flesch (1946) published a popular book entitled *The Art of Plain Talk.* This book was followed by a series of other writing guides which also provided revisions and simplifications of the Flesch readability formula (Flesch, 1949, 1958). In developing his original formula, Flesch used as his criterion a series of graded passages from the McCall-Crabbs *Standard Test Lessons in Reading.* These passages had been standardized on the basis of number of questions correctly answered by children of known reading ability. The criterion of reading ease was thus based on empirically determined comprehension.

The most widely used form of the Flesch formula (1949, pp. 213–216) yields two measures, a "reading ease" score *(RE)* and a "human interest" score *(HI).* Reading ease is based on average word length in syllables *(WL)* and average sentence length in words *(SL).* These figures are inserted in the following formula:

$$RE = 206.835 - .846WL - 1.015SL$$

The human interest score is derived from the percentage of "personal words," such as proper names and personal pronouns, and the percentage of "personal sentences," such as spoken sentences, questions and other remarks directed to the reader, and exclamations. The unit to which all these measures are applied is a continuous 100-word passage. For reliable results, several random 100-word samples from the given selection are analyzed, and the counts are averaged. Table 11-1 provides an interpretive frame of reference for reading ease scores in terms of academic levels and types of magazines. Levels of human interest scores are also referred to typical magazines, ranging from fiction, through digests and trade publications, to scientific journals.

TABLE 11-1
Interpretation of Flesch Reading Ease Score
(Data from Flesch, 1949, pp. 149–150)

Description of Style	RE Score	Estimated Reading Grade	Typical Magazine
Very Easy	90–100	5th	Comics
Easy	80– 90	6th	Pulp fiction
Fairly easy	70– 80	7th	Slick fiction
Standard	60– 70	8th–9th	Digests
Fairly difficult	50– 60	High school (10th–12th)	Quality
Difficult	30– 50	College (13th–16th)	Academic
Very difficult	0– 30	College graduate	Scientific

Of all the readability formulas, those developed and popularized by Flesch have had the greatest impact upon journalists, advertising copywriters, and others interested in reaching mass audiences. Concern with the "Flesch index" of one's writing soon spread through these fields, with a resulting simplification of style. Scattered attempts have been made to test the effects of such simplifications on readership.

Split-run readership tests with easy and hard versions of the same articles have been conducted in such varied media as a Midwestern farm paper (Lyman, 1949), a campus newspaper (Swanson, 1948), and a company paper sent to employees (Swanson & Fox, 1953). The readership gains reported for the simpler version range from zero (or a slight loss) to as high as 66%. Among the factors determining these results are the absolute difficulty level of the versions as well as the amount of difference between them. Intrinsic interest of the content for the readers may also partly erase differences in reading ease. Another difficulty in interpreting results is that some of the versions differ in ways not measured by the Flesch scores. For example, the pair of articles yielding the largest readership difference (66%) also differed in organization, the easier version being more systematically and clearly organized. In another case, the more difficult version sounded stilted and unnatural. It contained inappropriate words and circumlocutions that seemed to have been deliberately inserted to increase reading difficulty.

Another type of study compared reading ease with readership data for published material, rather than employing specially prepared versions. In an analysis of all major articles appearing in one issue of a single popular magazine, readership and degree of satisfaction were surveyed in a national sample of 340 readers (Haskins, 1960). An abstraction index computed for each article correlated $-.79$ with "finishing index," or proportion of readers starting the article who finished it. On the other hand, among those who finished an article, the proportion who rated it "excellent" correlated $+.80$ with the abstraction index.

Readability formulas have met with a varied reception. They have been hailed enthusiastically as guides to good writing and attacked vigorously as mechanistic devices to stifle creativity and debase literature. After looking with horror at figures such as those reported in Table 11-1, the critics have asked, "Should writers of science and literature try to raise their 'Flesch index' by imitating the style of pulp magazines and comic strips?"

The truth lies somewhere between these extreme views. Readability research *can* improve writing, but its findings must be used with discretion. Good writing depends on other factors besides those included in readability formulas. Then, too, there is undoubtedly an optimum difficulty level for different kinds of materials, as there is for different audiences. Intrinsically simple material becomes stilted, pretentious, and obscure when expressed in long words and intricate sentences. On the other hand, literary or scientific writings may lose in aesthetic value or in intellectual precision when oversimplified. Unusual words and subtle figures of speech may be a source of artistic delight in poetry. And the technical terms of science, mathematics, and logic represent a way of simplifying and clarifying complex masses of information that might otherwise prove unmanageable.

Simplicity and clarity of expression cannot be achieved by routine procedures. They are general goals of good writing that need to be pursued by whatever means are appropriate to the subject matter. Readership formulas *are* appropriate when the object is to maximize the communication of simple messages. This is the purpose of advertising copy, cookbooks, instruction sheets, training manuals, government bulletins, and similar forms of writing designed for mass audiences. It is to these forms of writing that readability formulas are most directly applicable.

EMOTIONAL AND MOTIVATIONAL FACTORS

Why do consumers use certain commodities or services? What do they like or dislike about a product? Why do they buy one brand rather than another? How can advertising arouse a desire for a product and lead to actual purchase? Although modern techniques of consumer research have focused attention upon questions such as these, the importance of emotional and motivational factors was recognized in the earliest writing on advertising psychology.

Motivation. The message of an advertisement links the product or services advertised with consumer wants and needs. Whether presented through printed copy, illustration, spoken word, or television commercial, its object is to show how the commodity may satisfy consumer wants. In Chapter 5, human needs or wants were examined from the standpoint of worker motivation. The individual's behavior as a consumer is a function of the same needs, ranging from basic physiological drives, such as hunger, thirst, and the avoidance of pain and discomfort, to higher order, socially acquired drives, such as the need for status, social approval, and achievement.

By looking through any current magazine or newspaper, one can easily find examples of ads appealing to each of these drives. One can also find evidence of the operation of one or more of these drives in most human activities. But merely labeling an activity as a manifestation of the hunger drive or the achievement drive tells us little about it. Nor are traditional lists of drives of much help to the ad writer, being too general to serve in the choice of advertising appeals. The hunger drive could be employed to advertise any food, from soup to candy. Yet there are vast differences between the appeal of a steaming bowl of soup on a cold day and that of a gift box of candy on one's birthday. Safety or the avoidance of danger is undoubtedly an important consideration in buying a car, but the actual choice between specific cars may be based on the automobile's role as a status symbol. Furthermore, buying decisions often reflect multiple interlocking motives. In choosing a particular cake mix, for example, a purchaser may be influenced by a personal craving for sweets, by pride in achievement as a gourmet cook, and by the need for social approval from family and guests.

The strength of any drive is not a fixed quantity. Strength of basic organic needs depends upon degree of deprivation. When thwarted, such drives may become overpowering. If breathing is hampered, the individual will fight violently for air. To a starving man, food becomes extremely important. But advertisers are not addressing their messages to starving consumers. When these basic drives are satisfied, higher order drives become prepotent. The relative strength of these higher order drives is also influenced by learning. Hence their strength will vary from one culture or subculture to another. New drives develop as the individual's experiences change. For every drive, moreover, learning determines in large part what the individual does to satisfy it and what incentives are sought. Cultural differences in eating customs and in food preferences provide a dramatic illustration of this fact.

Finally, the advertiser must take into account the specificity of buying motives. It is not so much a question of whether economy or prestige represents the stronger drive for a consumer. Rather it is a question of which is uppermost in the consumer's choice of a specific commodity. For the same consumer, economy may be foremost in the purchase of a washing machine, while prestige predominates in the choice of a car. The absurdity of trying to use the same "tried and true" appeal for very dissimilar products inspired the cartoon reproduced in Figure 11-1. The distinguished-looking man with the eye patch, featured repeatedly in Hathaway shirt ads, may sell shirts; but an eye patch on a dog would probably have little appeal for purchasers of dog food.

In selecting an effective appeal for a specific commodity, the advertiser can turn to the findings of opinion surveys and other types of consumer research. These techniques provide information on what typical consumers like or dislike about a product; what specific features led them to change brands; under what circumstances they made their most recent purchase of some durable commodity; how

"I know it's worked before, but will it sell <u>dog food</u>?"

Figure 11-1. Appeals are specific to the commodity.(*From* The New Yorker, *Dec. 30, 1961, p. 32. Drawing by O'Brian;* © 1961 The New Yorker Magazine, Inc. Reproduced by permission.)

they use a particular product; and many other concrete questions about the role a particular product plays in the consumer's daily life. An example is provided by an early consumer study conducted for M & M candy. For many persons, candy eating was found to be "associated with accomplishment of a job that the person who ate the candy considered disagreeable. The candy was a sort of reward or compensation for doing a tough job." Accordingly, M & M switched its advertising theme in two test markets from "Smooth, rich, creamy coated chocolate—everybody likes 'em" to "Make that tough job easier—you deserve M & M candy" (Yoell, 1952). Following this change in advertising appeals, sales in the two test areas rose from 17% to 35% of the national M & M total.

Considerable attention has been given to the relative merits of *positive* and *negative appeals* in advertising (Higbee, 1969; Ray & Wilkie, 1970; Spence & Moinpour, 1972). Essentially, a positive appeal portrays a pleasant situation that will follow the use of the product, while a negative or fear appeal portrays an unpleasant situation that can be avoided by using the product or following the recommended course of action. For certain products, negative appeals can be made more dramatic and arresting than the corresponding positive appeals. Examples of negative appeals can be found in the ads for products designed to protect against bad breath, body odor, "coffee nerves," "tired blood," and many other familiar advertiser diseases.

That negative appeals can be quite successful has been repeatedly demonstrated by survey data. In one extensive analysis of readership data, ads showing the unfavorable results of not using the product received much more attention than did ads showing the favorable results of using the product (Rudolph, 1947, p. 69). The former were also read by a larger proportion of persons than were the latter. On the other hand, there are many types of products for which negative appeals are inappropriate. The age and other characteristics of the consumers may also influence the relative effectiveness of positive and negative appeals. The results may likewise be affected by the specific way in which the negative appeal is presented. Thus, if the situation portrayed is too unpleasant, as in a detailed picture of a serious accident, people may simply turn away from the ad. Moreover, the emphasis should be placed on the action the individual may take to avoid the unpleasant situation. It is escape from fear, rather than fear itself, that reinforces the desired learning. An investigation of the use of fear appeals to promote better dental hygiene found that fear appeals were more effective than positive appeals in arousing anxiety, but they were not more successful in modifying attitudes or behavior (Evans, Rozelle, Lasater, Dembroski, & Allen, 1970). The behavioral effects undoubtedly depend upon several interacting variables. No simple generalization emerges from all the findings about negative appeals.

With the growing concern about consumer protection, the use of fear appeals to advertise commercial products is being increasingly questioned (Spence & Moinpour, 1972). If fear appeals actually arouse anxiety, it has been argued, the cumulative effects of continued exposure to many such appeals may produce in some persons a heightened state of chronic anxiety, lowered self-esteem, or other undesirable effects. Moreover, the relation between the product advertised and the unpleasant situation it allegedly prevents is often tenuous. Popularity and social acceptance will *not* necessarily follow the use of a particular toothpaste, mouthwash, or bath soap, although the ad message may clearly imply that they will. Yet purchasers have no recourse against such indirect claims. They cannot request a refund, as they could if an electric clock failed to run.

Although the large majority of ads appeal to specific consumer wants, there are two well-known exceptions. One is the *reminder ad,* whose object is simply to keep the brand name before the public. Such ads serve to reinforce the associations with brand names that were established by other, conventional ads. They are effective with brands that are already familiar and widely advertised. Unless supported by other ads that do contain appeals, reminder ads would probably have little effect on sales.

Another type of ad that contains no appeal is the *institutional ad.* Although showing the name of the company, such ads make no mention of the merits of any products. Their object is to advertise the company as a whole, rather than any specific product. The ad may publicize some worthy cause, or it may feature the company's own beneficent activities. Insofar as the name of the company is included, such ads serve a reminder function. Their principal effects on product sales, however, presumably stem from the association of desirable ideas and feelings with the company and its products. The implications of this type of advertising will be seen more clearly in the light of the discussion of feelings and attitudes and of corporate image in the next two sections.

Attitudes and Feelings. While the message in a printed ad or sales talk tells consumers explicitly why they should purchase a commodity, other aspects of advertising may influence their reactions to the product in more subtle ways. Such effects have been variously described as "feeling tone," "atmosphere," "mood," and "attitudes." A pleasant or unpleasant feeling aroused by any element of an advertisement may influence the consumer's reaction to the product. For this reason, the advertiser must inquire into the feelings associated with all aspects of the ad. It is relatively easy to recognize the role of illustrations in associating appropriate feelings with the product. In advertising soup, for instance, pictures can vividly suggest the glowing health of happy children, or the warmth and comfort of piping-hot soup on a blustery day, or the graciousness of an elegant dinner party. Other less obvious features of the ad may also arouse strong feelings that will spread to the product. An effective appeal in the ad's primary message may be worthless if an undesirable or inappropriate association is evoked by the colors, the printing type, or even a border design surrounding the ad. If the appeal is directed to elegance and daintiness while the printing type suggests cheapness and strength, the effects will clash and tend to cancel out rather than reinforcing each other.

The association of *colors* with different feeling tones is widely recognized. Studies on the suitability of different colors for advertising various commodities were among the earliest conducted in the psychology of advertising. Apart from its possible attention value and its realism in portraying the commodity, color may arouse strong affective associations. Through common experiences, most people have learned to associate red with fire, blood, and danger; blue with cool rivers and lakes; orange and yellow with sunlight and comfortable warmth, and so on.

In one investigation (Wexner, 1954), 94 college students were shown eight colors and were given a list of 11 "moods" described in such terms as: exciting, stimulating; distressed, disturbed, upset; calm, peaceful, serene; powerful, strong, masterful. The instructions were to name the one color that best represented the feelings described by each group of words. For each of the 11 moods, the choices showed a significant predominance of certain colors. For instance, for exciting and stimulating, 61 subjects chose red. Repetition of this experiment with different groups indicated that certain color associations, including those cited above, are quite consistent (Murray & Deabler, 1957). Others vary with the demographic characteristics of the population, particularly its socioeconomic level. It should be added that changing the saturation or brightness of colors will considerably modify their affective associations. Deep red and pink would hardly be expected to arouse the same feelings, nor would navy and sky blue.

The *printing type* used in brand name, headline, or advertising copy should be legible, attractive, and appropriate. In a book, poor legibility of type may decrease speed and accuracy of reading and increase visual fatigue. But in an ad poor legibility reduces the motivation to read further. Even more important is the fact that the frustration experienced in trying to read such material will cause annoyance that may spread to the product.

Psychologists have done considerable research on the legibility of type (McCormick, 1976a, pp. 88–97; Poulton, 1967, 1969a, 1969b; Tinker, 1963). Among the criteria employed to measure legibility are accuracy of perceiving letters or words in brief tachistoscopic exposures; reading speed and comprehension for long passages; distance at which letters, words, or sentences can be correctly read; indices of eye fatigue after continuous reading; and number and nature of eye movements made during reading. With more difficult reading, there is an increase in the number and duration of eye fixations and in the number of retracing movements.

Through all these techniques, it has been demonstrated that printing types vary significantly in legibility. Simple types are generally read faster than Old English or other types with elaborations and curlicues. The relative legibility of different types also varies with other factors, such as size, width of margins, interlinear spacing, and brightness contrast between letters and background.

Another factor that influences legibility is familiarity of both type and arrangement. Any unfamiliar feature tends to slow down reading. It is partly for this reason that a passage or headline printed in lowercase is read at a faster rate than one set entirely in capitals. The chief advantage of a headline set in capitals is that it can be read at a greater distance than one set in lowercase. This advantage is pertinent to the designing of billboards and road signs. Familiarity of layout also facilitates reading. Bizarre arrangements of printed matter, sometimes used by advertisers as a means of gaining attention, may be self-defeating because of the frustration and annoyance they engender. With adult readers who have established certain reading habits, any change in layout of printed matter will increase reading difficulty, even when the new layout is better adapted than the old to the characteristics of human vision (Coleman & Kim, 1961).

Besides legibility, one needs to consider the ideas and moods associated with different printing types. That printing types arouse distinctive feelings has been repeatedly demonstrated (Burt, Cooper, & Martin, 1955; Kastl & Child, 1968; Tannenbaum, Jacobson, & Norris, 1964). For example, such moods as sprightly, sparkling, dreamy, and soaring tend to be associated more often with curved, light, and ornate types, while such moods as sad, dignified, and dramatic are more often associated with angular and heavy (boldface) types. Advertisers have long tried to utilize these reactions by choosing types that express feelings appropriate to their products and to the appeals they wish to convey. Figure 11-2 illustrates a variety of types used in brand names to express such diverse qualities as elegance, dependability, dignity, informality, sturdiness, and so on.

That distinct moods can be suggested by *sounds* as well as by shapes is

Figure 11-2. Printing types that arouse widely different affective associations.

illustrated in Figure 11-3. Given the two meaningless forms and the two meaningless "words" shown in this figure, the vast majority of persons will associate the word containing the l and m sounds with the gently curving shape, and the word containing the t, r, and k sounds with the sharply angular shape. The feelings aroused by different sounds should be considered in devising brand names, as well as in selecting appropriate words for advertising copy. In the choice of a brand name, meaningful associations should also be investigated, preferably in a consumer survey.

Another important factor in the success of a brand name is *ease of pronuncia-*

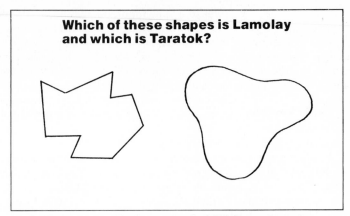

Figure 11-3. Moods associated with forms and sounds.

tion. Just like type that is difficult to read, a brand name that is difficult to pronounce tends to arouse annoyance and hostility. Because of the possible embarrassment resulting from mispronouncing the name, moreover, many customers will hesitate to ask for the product and will buy a more pronounceable competing brand instead. There are a number of instances in which a manufacturer became aware of the sales handicap resulting from a hard-to-pronounce brand name and did something about it. The makers of Baume Bengué, for example, began to insert "pronounced Ben Gay" under the name. Later, the name was changed to Ben Gay altogether. Another classic example is that of Suchard chocolate (Grube, 1947). Recognizing the difficulties that American consumers were having in pronouncing this name, the company began to print the slogan "Say Soo Shard" on the wrapper of each chocolate bar. This in turn led to the decision to adopt a live trademark in the form of an attractive little girl who was to be known as "Sue Shard." Eventually this little girl was featured in all advertisements for the company, through photographs, comic strips, radio commercials, and personal appearances.

Apart from word choice, many *other aspects of language* serve to arouse feelings that may be pleasant or unpleasant, appropriate or inappropriate. A passage consisting of short sentences, with a choppy, jerky rhythm, for example, is likely to suggest pep, sparkle, and liveliness; one written in longer sentences, with strings of modifiers and a slow, languorous rhythm, is more likely to suggest relaxation and reverie. The imagery evoked by language also needs to be considered. To say that "evaporated milk makes a fine curd in the stomach and is therefore more digestible than regular milk" could be factually correct, but it arouses imagery that is unappetizing.

Product Image. The term "product image" refers to the composite of attitudes and ideas associated with a product. Tea, for instance, was at one time associated with old ladies, invalids, delicate china, and the affectations of the "tea shoppe." In the effort to change this image and to appeal to a wider public, advertisers began to feature pictures of young people and of rugged-looking men drinking tea for relaxation after work or sports. For the same reason, such terms as "brisk," "robust," and "hearty" were used more and more to describe tea in adversiting copy. Product image may also refer to a specific brand. Marlboro cigarettes were originally considered elegant and somewhat feminine. In the effort to alter this brand image, the company undertook an advertising campaign in which ranchers, hunters, and other sturdy outdoor types were shown smoking Marlboros.

Brand names and trademarks are often chosen so as to strengthen the desired brand image. Of particular interest is the story of Green Giant peas (J. W. Crawford, 1960, pp. 86–89). A small company in Minnesota—The Minnesota Valley Canning Company—began to market canned peas grown from a seed that produced extra large peas. The company chose the brand name Green Giant and displayed a picture of a smiling green giant on the cans and in all advertisements of this product. Soon the green giant began to appear also on other canned goods prepared by this company, such as corn, and some of the other brand names were changed accordingly. Recognizing the popularity and effectiveness of this symbol, the company itself eventually changed its name to the Green Giant Company.

The Green Giant story illustrates a deliberate effort to transform a successful brand image into a corporate image. The reverse process is more common. In a well-established company, the strength of the corporate image increases public acceptance of each of its products. In some situations, however, it is better not to identify all products with a single corporate image. If a company makes both breakfast food and fertilizer, it would undoubtedly be desirable to have different brand names for the two lines and to keep the brand images distinct.

Even when two very similar products are involved, the use of a single brand name may be undesirable when the products are designed for different consumer markets or when some of their characteristics might conflict. This is illustrated by what may be regarded as a postscript to the Green Giant story recounted above. The same company subsequently began marketing a type of canned peas whose principal feature is that they are *small.* Typical advertising copy for these peas asserted that "Their small size tells you, the minute you open the can, that these are not ordinary peas. . . . They have a subtle sweetness . . . that rivals the famed petits pois of France" (Le Sueur advertisement, 1962). Under these conditions, it is understandable that the Green Giant company chose a *different* trade name for these peas.

Institutional advertising, mentioned in an earlier section, is one of the recognized methods of developing a favorable *corporate image.* But to be effective, a corporate image needs to be much more than merely favorable—it must be specifically related to company objectives. A corporate image might, for example, suggest scientific advancement, old-fashioned goodness and dependability, elegance and distinction, or sturdiness and vigor. To combine or exchange these images might prove disastrous. A corporation cannot be all things to all people. It needs to formulate its objectives clearly and then set about developing a corporate image that fits these objectives. Conflicting and contradictory impressions tend only to confuse and weaken the corporate image. For conglomerates providing a heterogeneous assortment of products or services, different corporate names are often retained for this reason.

To be sure, any organization may be somewhat differently perceived by its different publics, including stockholders, employees, suppliers, distributors, customers, government officials, the press, and the communities in which it operates. Although recognizably different, these various corporate images will have a common core and will tend to influence each other. If a company's plants spread soot over the townspeople's homes or pollute their streams, these actions become a part of its corporate image. Advertising cannot do the whole job. The corporate image is affected by every aspect of a company's operation, from the quality of its products and the nature of its employee relations to the appearance of its buildings and grounds and the printing type used on its letterheads.

Nearly all techniques of consumer research have been used to investigate the public images of products, brands, or corporations. The motivation researchers of the 1960s, who did much to popularize the concepts of product image and corporate image, relied heavily on depth interviews and projective techniques. Among the more objective procedures employed for image research are adjective checklists and the Semantic Differential, described in Chapter 10. For instance, one study comparing three brands of beer used four forms of Semantic Differential scales to obtain separate ratings of the beer itself, the company, the advertising, and the type of consumers who use it (Mindak, 1961).

It has frequently been argued that consumers tend to select products and brands whose images fit their own self-concept. In fact, there is evidence that individuals can readily describe themselves and their associates by using a list of product and brand names instead of adjectives (Kassarjian, 1971). Descriptions of the "typical user" of a particular product or brand have also been obtained through the "shopping list" technique described in Chapter 10. This procedure was employed by Woodside (1972) in comparing the consumer image associated with two brands of beer.

Taste tests have also been adapted for investigating the brand images of such products as turkey meat (Makens, 1965) and beer (Jacoby, Olson, & Haddock, 1971). It has generally been found that judgments of quality can be significantly influenced by attaching familiar brand names to the product samples. With suitable experimental designs, however, it is possible to assess the relative magnitude of this influence and to measure the interactions of brand name with other variables, such as price and actual product composition as detected through taste cues (Jacoby et al., 1971).

A substantial amount of research has been done on *store image* (Jacoby, 1976b, p. 335). An example is the study of supermarket chains by Stanley and Sewall (1976). In a well-designed investigation using multidimensional scaling, actual store patronage by a group of 93 female homemakers from a single neighborhood was analyzed against three variables: size of store (as an index of assortment of merchandise available), driving time from neighborhood to store, and rated image of the supermarket chain. During a home interview, each respondent rated the 7 supermarket chains to which the 12 supermarkets in the area belonged. She was also asked where she shopped for most of her groceries. The results showed that, although driving time was the most important single variable in predicting store patronage, addition of the chain image measure explained about 40% of the variance remaining after driving time was accounted for.

DECISION PROCESSES

Model of Consumer Behavior. There is a growing body of research on how the consumer makes decisions. The focus is on the process of decision making and the conditions that influence it, rather than just on the final act of purchase. Some investigators have designed comprehensive models of purchasing behavior, like the one illustrated in Figure 11-4. Such models incorporate all aspects of

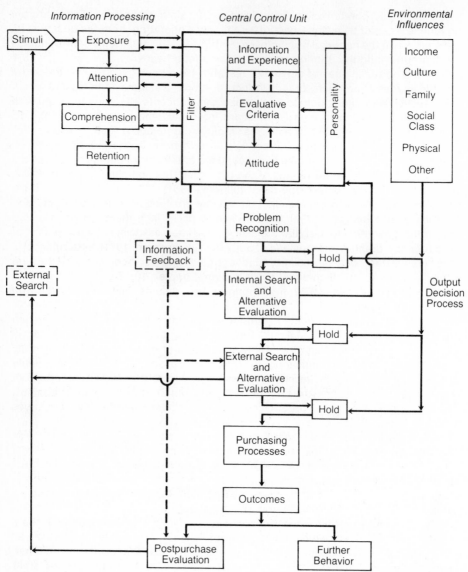

Figure 11-4. A comprehensive model of consumer decision making. *(From Engel, Kollat, & Blackwell, 1973, p. 58. Copyright © 1973 by Holt, Rinehart and Winston, Inc. Reproduced by permission.)*

consumer behavior, ranging from the perception, comprehension, and recall of ads and other product-related information to the purchasing act and the subsequent evaluation of the product in use. They are thus designed to span nearly all of consumer psychology and to provide a general framework for investigating specific variables. Although the model shown in Figure 11-4 may look quite complex, a few principal features can readily be noted. The Central Control Unit represents the individual consumer with his or her stored experiences, personal traits, attitudes, and criteria for evaluating particular products. All these individual variables influence the filtering and processing of incoming product information. The rest of the model pertains to the consumer's problem-solving behavior, whereby the consumer fulfills his or her needs by choosing and purchasing a particular product or service.

For many purchases, the decision process is considerably abbreviated. This would be true for minor and habitual purchases, such as cereal or toothpaste. The full-scale process is more likely to be followed when deciding on major and less frequent purchases, such as television set or car. Essentially, the full decision process includes: (1) the recognition of a need or problem; (2) an internal search and evaluation of alternatives, based on stored information; (3) an external search and evaluation of alternatives, ranging from increased attention to relevant ads to seeking information from associates and shopping for the product; (4) purchase of a chosen brand; and (5) outcomes, including degree of satisfaction with purchase. At any stage in the decision process, new (or newly perceived) influences may intervene to halt or postpone action ("Hold" in Fig. 11-4).

Sources of Information. Some of the research on consumer decision making deals with the sources of information employed by the consumer and their relative effectiveness in influencing the final purchasing decision. For instance, 5,000 householders who had recently bought carpeting were interviewed to find out how they had heard about the specific brand purchased and which information source had been most influential in their decision to buy (Blackwell et al., 1969, pp. 196–204). Although the results varied somewhat across brands, salesclerks and personal acquaintances were found to be more frequent and more effective sources for this product than were radio, television, magazine, or newspaper advertising.

Of particular interest is the research on informal, word-of-mouth communication (Arndt, 1967; Engel et al., 1973, Ch. 17; Jacoby, 1976a, 1976b). Information transmitted in face-to-face conversation or over the telephone has been repeatedly shown to have more impact on consumer behavior than do more formal information sources. In general, mass media appear to be better equipped to create product and brand awareness, while word-of-mouth communication is more effective at the later, evaluative stages of the decision process. Consumers tend to have more confidence in information they spontaneously seek, which is often the case with word-of-mouth communications about products. Moreover, they perceive their personal contacts as unbiased, in contrast to salespersons and marketer-dominated sources. A personal acquaintance is just as likely to transmit negative as positive information about a product, thereby strengthening credibility. Still another advantage stems from the fact that two-way communication is involved, thus increasing the likelihood that the information provided fits the needs and interests of the individual recipient. Much research has been done on the roles and characteristics of opinion leaders, persons who are likely to be sought by their associates as sources of product information.

Family Participation in Purchasing Decisions. Another area of investigation is the role of different family members in purchasing decisions. Most research has dealt with the influence of husbands and wives on family purchases, although some attention has also been given to the role of children. One type of study analyzed husband-wife discussions on what to purchase with a hypothetical monetary gift (Kenkel, 1961).

Another approach uses interviews or questionnaires to assess the relative contribution of husband and wife to purchasing decisions. In one such study (Blackwell et al., 1969, pp. 156–163), husbands and wives from 301 households were questioned regarding the role they played in the purchase of nine product categories, ranging from automobiles and refrigerators to toothpaste and coffee. The questions covered different stages in the decision process, from initiation and planning, through information seeking, to the buying and postpurchase evaluation stage. The relative contribution of the spouses was found to vary with both product category and decision-making stage.

From a different angle, H. L. Davis (1970) explored the dimensions of husband and wife roles in buying decisions. Focusing on two types of durable goods—automobiles and living room furniture—Davis questioned the spouses about specific facets of the decision, including when and where to buy, how much to spend, and such product characteristics as model, make, style, and color. The results suggested that the degree to which decisions are dominated by one or the other spouse, or are made jointly, depends not only on the product but also on the dimension or facet. Within each product category, one influence cluster was associated with product-related decisions (e.g., model, style, color) and another with allocation and scheduling decisions (e.g., how much to spend, when to buy). Other data pertained to differences in the reports of husbands and wives regarding their own and their spouse's influence on buying decisions. In general, these differences seemed to be largely of the sort expected from the unreliability of single reports, although some genuine differences in role perceptions may also have operated.

There is also research indicating that children may exert some influence on the family's purchasing decisions for certain types of products. Ward and Wackman (1972) administered a questionnaire to 132 mothers of 5- to 12-year-old children in an East Coast metropolitan area. The questions covered frequency of child's request for product purchase and frequency of mother's yielding to the request, for each of 22 products. Both showed significant relations to age of child and to type of product. There was substantial evidence of child influence in the purchase of such products as breakfast foods, snack foods, candy, games, and toys.

Perceived Risk. One of the concepts that has stimulated considerable research on consumer behavior is that of perceived risk (Cox, 1967). The decision to purchase a product or service involves the risk of unsatisfactory performance, as well as possible financial, social, psychological, or physical risks. The higher the purchase price and the longer the expected use of the product, the greater is the perceived risk. A wrong decision in choice of car or washing machine involves more financial risk than does a wrong decision in buying a detergent. Social risks incurred with an incorrect purchasing decision are illustrated by disapproval on the part of associates and loss of status. Highly visible items, such as wearing apparel, rate relatively high on social risk. Psychological risk covers a multiplicity of personal dissatisfactions and disappointments with the product or service in use. Physical risks refer to possible health or safety hazards that may be associated with a wide variety of products, from cars to toys and patent medicines.

Research on these components of perceived risk indicates that ratings of performance risk are the best predictors of overall perceived risk for most products (Kaplan, Szybillo, & Jacoby, 1974). Product categories differ widely in the level of overall perceived risk. The rank order of perceived risk components also differs for certain classes of products. For example, social and psychological risks rank at the top of the list for wearing apparel but at the bottom for toothpaste and aspirin. Risk perception is a function not only of the product but also of the buying environment (e.g., store selection, buying from a catalogue) and of the individual consumer (Jacoby, 1976b). Some research has been done on the personality characteristics of high and low risk-perceivers. A more promising approach, according to some investigators, is to study the information-processing models followed by consumers in utilizing data to assess overall risk and to reach a buying decision (Bettman, 1974, 1975). One of the questions investigated, for example, pertains to the way in which consumers combine ratings of the certainty of making a satisfactory brand choice with ratings of the importance of so doing, within any given product category.

Consumers employ a variety of risk-reduction strategies, depending upon their own psychological characteristics, the product category, the purchasing context, and other features of the particular situation (Engel et al., 1973, pp. 378–383; Jacoby, 1976b). A widely applicable and effective strategy is to seek more information through further external search of various sources. Another strategy is to continue to use familiar brands as opposed to shifting to new or untried brands. Other things being equal, brand novelty is associated with high perceived risk. A related strategy is to buy standard, nationally advertised brands rather than private brands, i.e., those owned by retailers (Bettman, 1974). Still another strategy is to buy only the more expensive brands. The opposite strategy, that of buying only the least expensive brands, may be followed when financial risk ranks high for the particular product and consumer, while other risk components rank relatively low.

The role of price in consumer decision making has itself been the subject of extensive research (Jacoby, 1976b; Jacoby et al., 1971; Peterson & Jolibert, 1976; Szybillo & Jacoby, 1974a; Woodside, 1974). Much of this research concerns the role of price as an indicant of perceived product quality. The studies have used such varied products as beer, soft drinks, nylon hosiery, and an electric lunch box. In general, the findings suggest that, when price is one of several available cues, it has no significant effect on perceived product quality. In the absence of other cues, however, price will influence perceptions of product quality. Other things being equal, consumers tend to judge the higher priced product to be of superior quality.

That extrinsic cues are relied upon when intrinsic differences in product characteristics are imperceptible was already noted in other connections.[3] Under these conditions, judgments of taste and of other product features reflect brand name familiarity, brand image, store image, and other characteristics of the buying environment. Absence of intrinsic cues regarding product quality may result not only from actual product similarity (as in several experimental studies) but also from lack of expertise and information on the consumer's part. The continuing efforts of government agencies and consumer organizations to increase consumer information and awareness of relevant product characteristics should eventually reduce reliance on extraneous cues.

Behavioral Economics. A special application of the study of consumer decision making is illustrated by the area of research variously designated as economic psychology, psychological economics, or behavioral economics. Much of this research has been conducted by Katona and his associates at the Survey Research

---

[3]See, e.g., discussion of product testing in Ch. 10 and of brand image in this chapter.

Center of the University of Michigan (Katona, 1967, 1975). This approach utilizes interviews with representative samples of consumers to investigate motives, attitudes, and expectations regarding broad economic questions. For instance, consumers may be asked "Do you think that a year from now you people will be better off financially, or worse off, or just about the same?" and "Do you think that in the country as a whole during the next twelve months we will have good times financially, or bad times, or what?" From the replies to a series of such questions, the investigators compute an Index of Consumer Sentiment, which represents the overall degree of optimism or pessimism expressed by the respondent.

When combined with the usual economic indices of disposable personal income, the Index of Consumer Sentiment substantially improves the prediction of buying behavior, especially the purchase of such durable goods as automobiles and household applicances. Changes in buying behavior over the years are more closely related to consumer attitude changes than they are to income changes. In a society in which the majority of families have discretionary purchasing power, beyond that needed for necessities, fluctuations in available money are not sufficient to predict economic behavior. Under these conditions, consumer buying behavior is a function of both ability to buy and willingness to buy—the latter stemming from feelings of security or insecurity, confidence or uncertainty, and other measurable attitudes. These findings were supported not only by comparisons of attitude changes with sales of durable goods in cross-sectional surveys but also by longitudinal studies of the same families. Repeated interviews of the same individuals permit an analysis of changes in attitudes, the factors leading to such changes, and the effect of the changes on individual buying behavior.

Among the questions investigated in behavioral economics is that of "saturation." What happens to purchases after consumer needs have been satisfied through the extensive availability of consumer goods? The results support the view that, when existing needs are gratified, other needs take their place. When a family buys their longed-for home, they need new appliances and furnishings. When they have acquired all the appliances they can use, they want new models with improvements, and so on. Consumer attitudes have also been studied in relation to other types of economic behavior, such as saving, borrowing, purchase of life insurance, investing in stocks and bonds, use of credit cards, and installment buying. In general, the results indicate that consumers respond differently to changes in such economic indicators as income, prices, interest rates, and taxes, depending upon their perceptions of the current economic situation and their expectations for the future.

Some of the consumer research conducted at the Survey Research Center has a very broad orientation and reflects the growing concern with the consumer as citizen. This is illustrated by a longitudinal study of a representative sample of 5,000 American families over nearly a decade (Duncan & Morgan, 1977). Through repeated interviews, the changing status of these families was documented with regard not only to income and expenditures but also to housing, jobs, marriage, children and child care, shifting family composition, and many other facets of daily living.

A still broader orientation is evidenced in a series of studies which explored consumer attitudes of satisfaction and dissatisfaction with their economic condition as well as their overall quality of life (Katona, 1975, Chs. 24, 25; Strumpel, 1976). The complex interactions of objective and subjective components in consumer's perceptions of well-being were analyzed from several viewpoints.

Special attention was given to the societal implications of the findings, in relation to dwindling natural resources and the widespread questioning of materialistic expansion. In commenting on the results, Katona calls for a redefinition of progress "so that people identify an improvement in their situation less with an increase in the quantity of material goods and more with other aspects of the quality of life" (Katona, 1975, p. 397). He observes further that "consumer expenditures on services and for knowledge or cultural purposes contribute much less to the exhaustion of natural resources than expenditures requiring the production of an increased quantity of consumer goods" (p. 393). He also reports some movement in this direction, insofar as the proportion of income spent on services and the acquisition of knowledge has been increasing.

This type of research reflects the growing demand for social indicators, concerned with general well-being and the quality of life, to supplement the traditional economic indicators, such as changes in gross national product (GNP). It should be noted that, like economic indicators, social indicators include both objective and subjective components (i.e., attitudes, satisfactions, expectations). Psychologists such as Katona and his associates have focused attention on the need to include subjective components in *both* types of indicators.

SAFEGUARDING CONSUMER RIGHTS AND WELL-BEING

Consumer as Purchaser. The broadened scope of consumer psychology characteristic of the 1960s and 1970s was manifested in several distinct trends. One major development, stimulated by the consumerism movement, can be described as research in the service of the consumer as purchaser of products and services. Its focus is on safeguarding the interests of consumers in their relations with commercial organizations. An example is provided by the growing concern with *product safety,* including both the reduction of health and accident hazard in the product itself and the provision of safeguards against dangerous misuses by inadequately informed consumers (Engel et al., 1973, Ch. 25; Stark, 1976).

A second major trend relates to the accuracy and adequacy of consumer *information* about products and services. This concern obviously underlies the enactment of such legislature as the Fair Packaging and Labeling Act of 1967. Psychologists have made substantial research contributions toward this goal (Jacoby, 1975; Perloff, 1968). At a purely perceptual level, shoppers' ability to identify ingredients printed on food packages has been investigated in relation to size of print and to brightness contrast between print and background (Poulton, 1969a, 1969b). Several studies have dealt with the purchaser's assessment of relative cost of differently sized packages (M. P. Friedman, 1966, 1972; Gatewood & Perloff, 1973). Widespread consumer confusion was found when information on quantity (number, size, weight) and price was presented for the entire package in the traditional way. The difficulty increased when the quantities in different packages were not exact multiples (e.g., 2 lbs. vs. 5 lbs.) and when they included fractions (e.g., $2^{1}/_{4}$ lbs.). Price comparisons were greatly facilitated by dual-price labeling, whereby unit price (e.g., per pound) is provided in addition to price for the package.

Consumer as Citizen. Another burgeoning area of research is the evaluation, from the consumer's viewpoint, of the services provided by government and other public or semipublic agencies. Logically, this area represents an extension of product (and service) design to fit consumer needs and preferences. It thus overlaps both engineering psychology and commercially sponsored consumer surveys and product testing. Typically, however, the research now under consideration involves long-term planning and large-scale projects. It is illustrated by the use of consumer attitude and behavior data in the placement and design of parks, beaches, artistic and cultural centers, transportation systems, highways, airports, and other public facilities.

A broad field of application, rich in opportunities for consumer research, is provided by the planning of *transportation systems* (McCormick, 1976a, pp. 431–441). Consumers' reactions to a transportation system depend upon its intrinsic transportation features, such as convenience, speed, flexibility of routing, and frequency and location of available stops, as well as upon associated usage features, such as comfort and attractiveness of vehicle interior, characteristics of stations and waiting areas, and methods of fare collection (e.g., passes, tickets, tokens, exact fare, cash with change). A series of questionnaire and interview surveys sponsored by the Research Laboratories of the General Motors Corporation provide data on consumer preferences regarding many of these features (see Alluisi & Morgan, 1976; McCormick, 1976a, pp. 436–441). One of these surveys assessed the relative values that consumers assigned to a set of 32 system characteristics, ranging from stylish vehicle exterior and the sale of coffee and newspapers on board, at the low end of the scale, through a variety of features affecting comfort and convenience of trip, to being able to complete a trip without changing vehicles, having a seat, and arriving when planned.

Other consumer studies have dealt with such questions as passenger preferences for different types of British railway carriages (West, Ramagge, West, & Jones, 1973), drivers' attitudes toward the use of automobile seat belts (Fhanér & Hane, 1975), and consumer reactions to private cars versus public transportation with regard to a wide variety of attributes (Paine, Nash, Hille, & Brunner, 1969). It is also noteworthy that human factors considerations were especially influential in the design of the San Francisco Bay Area Rapid Transit (BART) system, with its many innovative features (Sundberg & Ferar, 1966).

A more narrowly limited area of application is illustrated by surveys of *consumer complaints about noise* (McCormick, 1976a, pp. 369–371; Moos, 1976, pp. 180–184). Most of these studies have dealt with aircraft noise as it affects residents of metropolitan areas in the vicinity of airports (Fiedler & Fiedler, 1975; Kryter, 1968). Some research has also been done with highway traffic noise, using experimental noise simulation over extended time periods in naturalistic situations (Ward & Suedfeld, 1973).

The results of such studies of noise complaints present certain apparent inconsistencies, particularly between verbally reported attitudes and behavioral indices. Unless the noise level is very high, considerable habituation is likely to occur. Selective factors may also operate, the persons who move into and remain in noisy areas tending to be those less disturbed by noise. Other desirable features of a neighborhood, moreover, frequently counterbalance the noise disturbance in the general satisfaction reported by residents. Apart from specific noise problems, some methodological research has been conducted on techniques for assessing the significance of consumer complaints in general and identifying the causes of complaints (Kurth, 1965; Namias, 1964).

Still another type of investigation is concerned with consumer evaluations of *personal contacts with governmental agencies.* This research is illustrated by a pilot study of "bureaucratic encounters," reporting the results of a national survey of consumer experiences with various government services (Katz, Gutek, Kahn, & Barton, 1975; see also Conner, 1976). The study covered seven "service areas," including employment, job training, workmen's compensation, unemployment compensation, welfare assistance, hospital and medical care, and retirement benefits. Also included were four types of "regulatory areas," dealing with drivers' licenses, traffic violations, income tax, and police activities. The study focused on three major questions: (1) the extent to which government services were actually utilized, (2) what recipients thought of the services, and (3) the relation between respondents' evaluation of government services and their more general attitudes toward government. Among other findings, the survey revealed some underutilization of available services, usually resulting from lack of knowledge.

Promoting Self-care. A vigorous area of research in consumer psychology pertains to the consumer's own role in the delivery of health services. The goal of this research is to develop effective ways of promoting such sound health practices as proper dental hygiene, regular medical examinations (e.g., chest x-rays), immunization, early treatment (e.g., breast cancer), and adherence to prescribed medical regimens. Considerable research is being conducted on mass communication of health information, in the effort to increase both its clarity and persuasiveness. Such research thus represents the application, in the interest of public health, of the familiar procedures of advertising psychology: attracting and holding attention, presenting understandable messages, appealing to relevant motives, arousing appropriate attitudes, and evoking the desired behavior.

Some psychologists have utilized survey techniques to explore the variables associated with effective and ineffective health-related behavior. This approach is illustrated by a study of the reasons why patients with high blood pressure do or do not follow the prescribed medical regimens (Caplan, Robinson, French, Caldwell, & Shinn, 1976). Patient education and social support techniques were also investigated as means of improving adherence to prescribed procedures. Another study analyzed the questionnaire responses of smokers, ex-smokers, and nonsmokers in a sample of 200 male administrators, engineers, and scientists employed by a single government agency (Caplan, Cobb, & French, 1975). Results showed that persons who had been unable to quit smoking, compared with those who had succeeded, tended to perceive and report more job stress, as indicated by quantitative work load, deadlines, and responsibility. In terms of personality, the nonquitters were more competitive, hard-driving, and involved in their work. Social factors, such as group pressure for smoking, also influence the outcome.

Other psychologists have concentrated on improving the effectiveness of health care communication. Considerable research has been concerned with the use of mass media (films, television, booklets) to educate the public in various disease-preventive behaviors pertaining to diet, inoculations, smoking, and other common problems (e.g., Evans, 1976). Of particular interest is a series of experiments by Leventhal (1971) and his associates on the communication of health information both in mass media and in face-to-face contacts. Much of this research was concerned with the role of fear appeals in persuasive communications regarding preventive health behavior. On the basis of both his own research and his analysis of other published studies, Leventhal proposed an information-processing model in which emotional responses (such as fear) and adaptive responses (such as changes in belief and protective health acts) represent parallel rather than serial responses to the awareness of danger. Depending upon concomitant circumstances and his or her own personality characteristics, the individual may respond to the danger message predominantly by danger control (through problem-solving activity) or by fear control. The latter is a response to internal emotional cues which may actually lead to avoidance of the desired behavior, such as not obtaining a chest x-ray for fear of what it may reveal.

In his own research, Leventhal found that the recommended action was most likely to follow when clear and objective information regarding danger was combined with specific action instructions (Leventhal, Jones, & Trembly, 1966; Leventhal, Watts, & Pagano, 1967). In connection with smoking, for example, the action instructions were designed to help participants to identify specific cues in their everyday environments that elicited the purchase and smoking of cigarettes and to substitute new responses to each of these cues. It should be noted that the preparation of such specific action plans, tailored to the individual's own life situations, represents a major technique in self-administered behavior therapy programs, to be discussed in Chapter 13.

CONSUMER BEHAVIOR IN RELATION TO SOCIAL AND ENVIRONMENTAL PROBLEMS

It was noted in Chapter 10 that psychological research focusing on the consumer as citizen addresses two kinds of questions. The first concerns the responsibilities of society toward the consumer. Psychologists' contributions to this area were considered in the preceding section. The second type of question, to which we now turn, concerns the consumer's responsibilities toward society. Consumer behavior in this category is illustrated by an individual's contributions of services, products, or money to various enterprises in the public interest. The myriad volunteer services, fund-raising drives, and periodic appeals provide familiar examples. Recent psychological research in this general area is illustrated by studies of volunteer blood donors in comparison with nondonors (Cialdini & Ascani, 1976; Condie, Warner, & Gillman, 1976). This research sheds light on the reasons why some persons do and others do not donate blood, as well as the relative effectiveness of techniques to promote participation. Similarly, contributions to charity have been studied in relation to verbal modeling, i.e., telling subjects the percentage of neighbors who had contributed and the average amount of contribution (Catt & Benson, 1977). The findings of such studies have suggestive implications for other types of volunteer programs.

Although psychologists have been concerned with many kinds of behavior that contribute to the public good, they have been especially active in research on problems of environmental protection. Stimulated by the environmental orientation of the 1960s and 1970s, this research should be considered in relation to the environmental psychology discussed in Chapter 9 as a subdivision of engineering psychology. Those studies dealt essentially with the effects of environmental conditions on human behavior; the present group of studies deals with the effects of human behavior on the environment. The problems investigated range widely, including the prevention of forest fires, the reduction of air and water pollution, the use of reclaimed water, the fostering of antilittering behavior, the conservation of energy and other natural resources, the preservation of endangered species, and the promotion of population control. Some investigations concentrate on consumer attitudes toward various environmental questions; others deal with overt behavior.

Attitude Studies. It is now widely recognized that technological solutions to ecological problems, such as environmental pollution and depletion of natural resources, are not enough. The solution depends also upon the modification of maladaptive human behavior, the development of public awareness of the long-term cumulative consequences of certain human actions, and an informed evaluation of trade-offs and priorities. It follows that an important step in moving toward a solution is to assess current attitudes toward ecological problems. Data about what people know and how they feel about environmental problems are needed in order to design effective procedures for altering relevant behaviors.

A scale for assessing general ecological attitudes and information was designed by Maloney and Ward (1973; Maloney, Ward, & Braucht, 1975). It consists of an objectively scored, self-report inventory yielding subscale scores in (1) verbal commitment—what respondents state they are willing to do in reference to specific environmental issues, (2) actual commitment—what they actually do, (3) affect, or degree of emotionality related to each issue, and (4) knowledge about specific factual matters related to ecological issues. Preliminary findings suggested a high degree of verbal commitment and affect about ecological problems but a lower degree of actual commitment and a particularly low degree of pertinent knowledge. The latter deficit indicates a strong need for public educational programs in this area.

Focusing on a more specific question, Bruvold (1971) constructed Thurstone-type attitude scales to assess affective reactions to the use of reclaimed water for drinking, swimming, and laundry. Public reactions to air pollution have been widely investigated by opinion polling techniques (Swan, 1972). The results indicate widespread adaptation and passive acceptance, with little awareness of the effects of air pollution on health. Several procedures have been proposed for increasing public awareness of pollution problems and stimulating citizen participation in environmental planning and policy making (Buckhout, 1972; Swan, 1972).

Still another type of study involves the experimental evaluation of different techniques for modifying ecological attitudes. This approach is illustrated by a well-controlled analysis of the relative effectiveness of (1) an informative message, (2) modeling through face-to-face presentation of "expert" judgment, and (3) social norms in the form of average judgments of a trained group (Simpson, Rosenthal, Daniel, & White, 1976). Different combinations of these techniques were used in the effort to influence subjects' esthetic judgments of forest areas that had been treated by ecologically sound procedures, such as thinning or clear-cut patches with no trees, which are employed for fire and disease control. The results clearly indicated that esthetic judgment could be altered by information regarding the ecological benefits of the visually unpleasing forest treatments. The social anchors also influenced judgment but were less effective than the didactic message.

Another example is provided by a well-designed investigation of the effect of fear appeals upon attitudes toward energy conservation (Hass, Bagley, & Rogers, 1975). Fear appeals representing two levels of severity of consequences of an energy shortage and two levels of probability of occurrence of such a shortage were presented in essays read by the subjects. The results indicated a significant relation between experimental treatments and conservation attitudes, although the effect depended only on severity and not on probability of occurrence.

Behavioral Research. A rapidly proliferating body of research comprises experimental studies of treatment strategies designed to influence overt behavior. Many of these studies employ techniques of behavior modification, such as modeling, prompting, and contingent reinforcement with financial incentives. Various forms of feedback, didactic information, formulating and facilitating specific action plans, and social influences (through group or "leader" opinion, commendation, etc.) are also among the techniques investigated. This type of research will be illustrated with studies of two types of consumer behavior, namely, littering and energy consumption.

Research on *littering* has been conducted on adults and children in both laboratory settings and such naturalistic settings as an urban high-density area (Chapman & Risley, 1974), a forest campground (Clark, Burgess, & Hendee, 1972), a grocery store (Geller, Witmer, & Tuso, 1977), and a football stadium (Baltes & Hayward, 1976). A closely related area of investigation pertains to the consumer's role in the recycling of materials, such as returning used bottles, depositing papers in special receptacles, and the like (Geller, Chaffee, & Ingram, 1975; Geller, et al., 1977; Reid, Luyben, Rawers, & Baily, 1976; Witmer & Geller, 1976).

To illustrate the methodology followed in this research, we may consider the study by Baltes and Hayward (1976), which compared four treatment strategies employed to modify adult littering behavior in a football stadium. Data were gathered at two football games on five random samples of spectators selected from comparable seating sections. One sample served as the control group, receiving no experimental treatment. Each person in the four experimental samples received an individual litterbag before being seated. The four experimental treatments were (1) operant conditioning with positive reinforcement in the form of a $1 prize for each of 20 winning litterbag numbers, to be collected at exit when turning in filled litterbag; (2) positive prompting message ("You will be a model for other people . . ." etc.) on printed instruction card attached to litterbag; (3) negative prompting message ("Don't be a litterbug . . ." etc.) similarly presented; and (4) litterbag only, with no message. The dependent variable was the amount of improperly disposed ground litter, which was collected from each section in labeled bags and weighed immediately after the game. The principal finding was that the experimental conditions, in comparison with the control condition, accounted for a 45% reduction in ground litter. The four treatment strategies, however, did not differ significantly among themselves under the conditions followed in this experiment.

Psychological research on *energy conservation* manifested an impressive upsurge in the late 1970s. Most of this research deals with residential consumption of either electricity or fuel oil (e.g., Hayes & Cone, 1977; Kohlenberg, Phillips, & Proctor, 1976; Palmer, Lloyd, & Lloyd, 1977; Seaver & Patterson, 1976; Seligman & Darley, 1977; Winett, Kagel, Battalio, & Winkler, 1978). Typical procedures are illustrated by a study of the effects of daily feedback regarding the consumption of electricity (Seligman & Darley, 1977). Data were obtained in 29 physically identical townhouses in which air conditioning was the largest single source of electricity usage during the summer. For a three-week period, daily meter readings were taken for each home in both feedback and control groups. For the feedback homes, daily consumption was expressed as a percentage of predicted consumption and was displayed to the home owner on a Lucite device attached to the kitchen window. Prediction of daily consumption for each home was based on daily temperature records and consumption data obtained in the same home during a three-week preexperimental period. Thus, if in terms of their own past performance home owners were using either more or less energy on any one day, they would immediately be aware of it. Both control and feedback groups received a letter explaining the daily meter readings and urging them to save electricity by reducing their air conditioning usage. The only difference between the two groups was in the presence or absence of daily feedback. The results demonstrated the effectiveness of such feedback. Although the pretreatment period showed no significant difference between the two groups in electricity consumption, during the treatment period the feedback group used 10.5% less electricity than did the control group. This difference was both statistically significant and large enough to have practical meaning.

SUMMARY

For effective communication, the advertising message (or any other public information message) should be so presented as to be noticed, understood, accepted, and retained. The success of an ad in attracting and holding attention depends in part upon such physical factors as size, repetition, position, color, and illustration. Any feature that is repeated in a series of advertisements comes to serve as a reduced cue for the product and the company. Such reduced cues include not only registered trademark, logo, and brand name but also slogan, color combination, printing type, layout, writing style, nature of illustration, and any other recurring aspect of the ads. Psychological research on trademarks and brand names has dealt chiefly with such questions as ease of identification, cognitive and affective connotations, recognition and recall, and brand name confusion. Readability research pertains to the difficulty level of reading matter, which can be assessed by the Flesch indexes and similar formulas.

The message of an ad links the particular product or service with consumer needs and wants. By providing data on how consumers use products and what they like or dislike about different products, consumer surveys help in the choice of effective appeals. For some products, negative or fear appeals may be more effective than positive appeals. Attitudes and feelings aroused by any element of an ad, such as colors or printing type, may generalize to the consumer's reaction to the product. The concepts of product image, brand image, store image, and corporate image refer to the composite of attitudes and ideas associated with the particular object.

Comprehensive models of purchasing behavior incorporate all stages of product-related activities, from the perception, comprehension, and recall of ads and other sources of relevant information to the purchasing act and subsequent evaluation of the product in use. Particular attention has centered on consumer decision-making processes, as illustrated by research on the utilization and relative impact of different sources of information, the role of different family members in the various stages of purchasing decision, and the influence of perceived risk on product selection and buying decisions. Behavioral economics represents a special application of the study of consumer decision making, which focuses particularly on the long-range effects of consumer attitudes and expectations on discretionary buying of durable goods and other economic behavior. The accuracy of economic forecasts can be substantially improved by adding consumer attitude survey data to the usual economic indices.

The broadening scope of consumer psychology is evidenced by research pertaining to product safety, perceptibility and comprehensibility of product information, and the use of consumer survey data in planning and evaluating public facilities and services, such as recreational areas, transportation systems, and airports. Systematic analyses of consumer complaints and consumer evaluations of contacts with governmental agencies are further examples of this phase of consumer psychology. Programs to promote public health goals are making increasing use of psychological research on techniques of effective communication and behavior modification. From another angle, a growing body of psychological research is concerned with altering both consumer attitudes and overt behavior with regard to littering, recycling, energy consumption, and many other broad societal and ecological problems.

CLINICAL, COUNSELING, AND COMMUNITY PSYCHOLOGY

PART FIVE

CLINICAL PRACTICE: APPRAISAL PROCEDURES

TWELVE

LINICAL PSYCHOLOGISTS work with persons who have problems in coping with the demands of daily life. Today, clinical psychologists are functioning in a variety of settings, including not only clinics, hospitals, and community centers but also industry, schools, prisons, courts, government agencies, and the military services. In industry, for example, the number of employees with emotional problems is large enough to merit serious concern. Such emotional difficulties occur at all levels, from unskilled labor to top management, and range from the mild problems of essentially normal persons to full-blown psychoses. The effects of these conditions upon job performance may take many forms, including excessive absenteeism, increased accident rate, deterioration of output, and disruption of co-worker morale.

The practice of clinical psychology utilizes findings and techniques from many branches of psychology, such as abnormal psychology, personality theory, learning theory, and psychological testing. The specific activities of clinical psychologists include a variety of service functions, as well as research, training, and supervision (Garfield & Kurtz, 1976). The particular combination of activities varies widely with the work setting and the interests and background of the individual psychologist. To describe their service functions, clinical psychologists originally adopted such medical terms as "diagnosis" and "therapy." Although clinical psychologists vary widely in their orientations, a growing number have been rejecting this medical model since the 1960s. The altered terminology reflects fundamental changes in theory and practice. The disease model is being replaced more and more by a behavioral model that focuses on problem solving in daily life. Even when the terms "diagnosis" and "therapy" are used for brevity and convenience—as they are at times in this book—they do not imply the disease model. Their specific connotations will emerge as the work of the clinical psychologist is examined in these three chapters.

Both clinical psychology (Chs. 12–14) and the closely related field of counseling psychology (Chs. 15–16) are marked by an abundance of unresolved issues and active controversies. In part, this situation stems from complexity of subject matter and from the comparative youth of these fields. Another factor making for diversity of opinion, however, is that both theory and practice in these fields tend to be highly colored by human values. Discussions of the objectives of counseling and psychotherapy, or definitions of "mental health," for example, often touch closely upon one's concept of a "good life." Thoughtful clinical and counseling psychologists have faced these issues, as will be noted in several connections in these chapters. But unanimity has by no means been attained. While complacency certainly does not characterize any field of applied psychology, turbulence and struggle are especially typical of the clinical and counseling areas. Although this introductory book focuses primarily upon what is presently known, many problems remain to be solved. The fact that much can be found in the common ground, about which considerable agreement exists, should not lull the reader into assuming an absence of controversy.

OBJECTIVES OF CLINICAL APPRAISAL

To avoid the unwanted connotations of the term "diagnosis," many clinicians today prefer such terms as appraisal, assessment, and evaluation. In the present context, all these terms will be used interchangeably to designate the clinician's fact-finding process. Covering a wide variety of procedures, this is the process whereby the clinical psychologist attempts to define the problem requiring attention in each individual case. Among the various objectives of appraisal in clinical psychology, the following can be clearly identified: (1) screening and classification, (2) personality description, (3) self-understanding, (4) treatment decisions, and (5) prediction of outcome.

Screening and Classification. To the layman, diagnosis generally means attaching labels to people. This is the traditional approach to diagnosis, which clinical psychology inherited from nineteenth-century psychiatry. In psychiatric hospitals, a good deal of attention is still given to the categorizing of patients by various diagnostic labels. It is generally recognized, however, that such labels can serve only for purposes of preliminary screening and rough classification.

A major distinction is that between mental retardation and psychopathology. In terms of intelligence test performance, *mental retardation* usually corresponds to an IQ below 70, found in about 2% of the population. Within this category, further subdivisions are made into four levels of retardation:[1] mild (IQ 52–68), moderate (IQ 36–51), severe (IQ 20–35), and profound (IQ below 20). A more functional classification recognizes those cases requiring custodial or nursing care, those that are trainable by specialized individual procedures, and those that are educable in school classes. Decisions regarding the disposition of individual cases, moreover, must be based on a comprehensive study of the individual's present functioning level, developmental history, experiential background, and physical condition. For

---

[1]These levels are defined to correspond to cutoff points at 2, 3, 4, and 5 *SD*s below the mean of the general population (Grossman, 1973). The IQs specified above are those for the Stanford-Binet (*SD* = 16).

these purposes, the IQ on a standardized intelligence test needs to be supplemented by an equally systematic assessment of the individual's adaptive behavior in his or her own life environment (for available instruments, see Anastasi, 1976, pp. 238–239, 269–271; Grossman, 1973).

Although psychological research on mental retardation has lagged behind the investigation of other mental disorders, it now constitutes an active area of research (Baroff, 1974; Robinson & Robinson, 1976). Some progress has already been made toward an understanding of the nature and causes of mental retardation. Organic defects underlying certain forms of mental retardation, such as phenylketonuria (PKU) and Down's syndrome (formerly called "mongolism"), have been identified. Some suggestive research has been done on the role of cultural deprivation in the development of other forms of intellectual retardation. There has also been an upsurge of activity in the training and rehabilitation of mental retardates.

Within the domain of psychopathology, psychoses are commonly distinguished from neuroses. *Psychoses* represent the more severe disorders, usually disrupting the individual's ability to conduct normal activities of daily life. The largest single group of psychotics, accounting for over half of all hospitalized cases, are diagnosed as schizophrenic. Although including several forms with identifiable behavior patterns, schizophrenia as a whole is characterized by disturbances of thought processes, loss of contact with reality, and extreme withdrawal from social contacts. Also common in schizophrenia are hallucinations and bizarre mannerisms of speech and gesture. In the paranoid type, the schizophrenic experiences delusions, in which he may believe, for example, that he is being persecuted by enemies who are plotting against him.

Although less common than schizophrenia, manic-depressive psychoses constitute another widely recognized category. These conditions are characterized, on the one hand, by periods of extreme depression, hopelessness, and slowing down of thought and action and, on the other, by periods of elation, overactivity, and flight of ideas in which one thought leads to the next through superficial association. The same person may exhibit both phases at different times (circular type), or either phase alone may alternate with periods of normality (manic or depressive types). Hallucinations and delusions may occur during both depressed and manic phases. The term "depressive disorders" is often used to designate a broad category including manic-depressive psychoses and other affective disturbances (Secunda et al., 1973).

Mention should also be made of organic psychoses, which have identifiable physical pathology resulting from such factors as drugs, alcohol, senile deterioration, or other sources of brain damage. By contrast, such disorders as schizophrenia and manic-depressive psychoses are sometimes described as functional or psychogenic, since no physiological basis has been conclusively demonstrated for them. Many psychologists object to these terms, however, because they imply more knowledge of etiology than is currently available. Although extensive research on the causes of these disorders is in progress, their etiology still remains largely unknown.

Neuroses represent relatively mild personality disturbances in which the individual remains in touch with reality and shows no gross disorders of thought or action. These conditions are generally considered to be psychogenic and amenable to treatment by psychological techniques. Neurotics typically feel miserable.

Often their emotional problems interfere with interpersonal relations and lower their productive capacity in school or on the job. Because they are aware that something is wrong and are unhappy about their condition, neurotics are more likely to seek and continue treatment than are psychotics, and they are more likely to cooperate actively in the treatment.

One of the most characteristic neurotic reactions is anxiety. The individual experiences feelings of dread and apprehension out of all proportion to the situations that arouse them. The anxiety may also be diffuse, or free-floating, rather than being associated with any particular stimulus. In some cases, specifically classified as anxiety neurosis, minor environmental stresses produce attacks of acute anxiety accompanied by palpitation of the heart, profuse sweating, difficulty in breathing, and tremors.

Some neurotics exhibit phobias, or irrational fears of particular objects or situations, such as claustrophobia (fear of closed spaces) or acrophobia (fear of high places). Still another example is the obsessive-compulsive type, characterized by persistent thoughts of a useless or nonsensical nature or by a strong urge to perform certain meaningless acts, like repeated hand washing. Another major category is that of hysterical neurosis, including a conversion type and a dissociative type. In the conversion type, the individual develops an apparent physical ailment, such as paralysis of the right arm, which enables him to escape from an unbearable emotional situation. A particularly dramatic form of neurotic behavior is illustrated by the dissociative type, in which the individual removes himself from unpleasant life situations by forgetting who he is and other details of his life. In rare cases, such amnesia may last for several years, the individual assuming a new name, working at a different occupation, and living his life apart from his earlier contacts. Also rare is the condition of multiple personality, in which the individual alternates between two or more distinct personalities (see, e.g., Schreiber, 1973; Thigpen & Cleckley, 1957)

These and other types of neurotic reactions have been traditionally classified as specific syndromes, or associated groups of symptoms. Surveys of such diagnostic categories, as well as fuller descriptions of both psychotic and neurotic behavior, can be found in textbooks of abnormal psychology (e.g., Page, 1975; Ullmann & Krasner, 1975) and especially in psychiatric texts and manuals (American Psychiatric Association, 1968; Freedman, Kaplan, & Sadock, 1975; Schacht & Nathan, 1977). Most clinical psychologists, however, avoid the use of specific diagnostic labels in evaluating individual cases. More and more it is being recognized that the syndromes of the classical diagnostic systems do not fit the cases encountered in practice. In fact, "textbook cases" that do fit the descriptions are hard to find.

Some attempts have been made to develop new systems of classification, especially for psychotic behavior, by investigating the empirical concomitance of "symptoms," or specific behavioral manifestations, within individual cases. Several studies have employed the techniques of correlation and factor analysis for this purpose and have proposed sets of categories corresponding to the factors thus identified (Lorr, 1966; Lorr, Klett, & McNair, 1963). Other investigators have proposed systems of classification based on course, intensity, and etiology of the disorder (see Phillips & Draguns, 1971).

From a different angle, many clinical psychologists reject all attempts to place individuals into diagnostic categories. They point out that, even when derived from empirically established correlation of symptoms, these categories still represent only group trends. The combination of specific manifestations of disturbance is unique to each individual. Then, too, behavior traits vary in degree from person to person. Any classification in terms of presence or absence of a given symptom is therefore unrealistic. Several quantitative scales have been proposed as a substitute for symptom classification (Phillips & Draguns, 1971).

Still another argument against the use of diagnostic categories is that psychological disorders are not "disease entities," like pneumonia or scarlet fever. To classify an individual as a paranoid schizophrenic tends to create the misleading impression that he is suffering from a specific psychological "disease." In reality, however, he manifests a collection of loosely related disorders of behavior that may have complex causes and probably require different treatment in individual cases. Rather than being identified as symptoms of "mental illness," such behavior disorders are coming to be recognized more and more as direct manifestations of the conflicts and problems of daily living. This point of view was first publicized by Szasz (1961) in a book entitled *The Myth of Mental Illness*. Similar views have been repeatedly expressed by several clinical psychologists and personality theorists (e.g., Albee, 1969).

A frequent objection to diagnostic classification arises from the potential misuse and misinterpretation of such diagnostic labels as mentally retarded or schizophrenic (Bogden & Taylor, 1976; Hobbs, 1975; Phillips & Draguns, 1971). Labeling persons in terms of deviant behavior is likely to have a detrimental effect on their subsequent development. Such labels may influence the individual's own self-concept, as well as the expectations and reactions of his or her associates. Thus they establish a self-fulfilling prophecy. Diagnostic labels may also carry unwarranted and simplistic assumptions about etiology and modifiability. Labels all too often suggest that the source of the difficulties is to be found in some "internal" and permanent deficiency of the organism itself.

When stripped of its misuses and unwarranted implications, however, a well-designed system of classification can serve important functions (Kendell, 1975; Tryon, 1976). In clinical practice, it helps to identify and define the individual's problem and to plan the direction of further inquiry. It should enable the clinician to select and apply available knowledge regarding similar problems. Although each individual is unique, there are enough uniformities in behavioral disturbances to provide the clinician with useful guidelines in the study of any one person. In clinical research, it is particularly important to try to identify behaviorally homogeneous populations in order to obtain meaningful results. In fact, the lack of adequate classification systems accounts for many of the inconclusive or ambiguous results obtained in clinical research on etiology and treatment (see, e.g., Bergin & Strupp, 1972; Secunda et al., 1973).

Personality Description. A major objective of the clinical psychologist's assessment function is to provide a personality description of the individual case (F. McKinney, 1960, 1965; McKinney, Lorion, & Zax, 1976). Such a description is unique for each person, covering the specific behavioral difficulties the individual manifests as well as the antecedent circumstances that led to their development. In contrast to traditional diagnostic labels, such a personality description is a full and detailed report. Its object is to facilitate the understanding of what makes the individual behave as he or she does and to serve as a guide for planning specific therapeutic procedures. It also differs from the traditional diagnostic approach in its utilization of a normal rather than a pathological frame of reference. The individual's behavior is seen as an exaggeration or distortion of behavior mechanisms commonly used by normal persons in meeting the conflicts and frustrations of daily living. Through such an approach, moreover, the clinician focuses more on the person's assets than on his or her liabilities, looking for residues of strength on which to build.

The terms, concepts, or constructs employed in such personality descriptions vary somewhat with the personality theory favored by the particular clinician. The psychologist's theoretical orientation also influences the relative emphasis placed on the client's own behavior and on the environment in which the client functions, particularly within familial and other interpersonal contexts. Similarly, some clinical psychologists concentrate on the individual's present behavior; others explore behavioral and environmental history; still others consider early childhood experiences as of primary etiological significance.

Whatever their theoretical orientation, most clinical psychologists include personality descriptions of some sort in the case reports they prepare as part of their regular clinical functions (Garfield, 1974, pp. 93–100; Sundberg, Tyler, & Taplin, 1973, Appendix F). A major purpose of such reports is to communicate the clinician's findings and recommendations to persons who need such information. Depending on the situation, the report recipients could include the client himself, family members, teachers, psychiatrists, social workers, or other professionals. Even when a written report is not required for transmittal, clinicians generally prepare the report as a record for future reference and as an aid in clarifying and organizing their own thinking about the case.

Because of the recognized importance of report writing in clinical practice, several books provide guidelines and suggestions for preparing case reports (Hammond & Allen, 1953; Huber, 1961; Klopfer, 1960). The form, length, and content of such a report should be adapted to the needs and characteristics of the intended recipients. In its selection and organization of content, the report should be oriented toward possible solutions of the individual's immediate problems. In style, it should be simple and direct; technical terms should be included only when they truly facilitate communication in reports directed to knowledgeable professionals.

Self-understanding. An important goal of the fact-finding, or exploratory, aspect of the clinical process is the attainment of insight, or self-understanding, by the client. Although any discussion or sharing of diagnostic findings with the client may contribute to such insight, certain clinical approaches are primarily oriented toward this objective. In nondirective, or client-centered, therapy, the principal goal is to encourage clients to verbalize their anxieties and examine their problems. Through such self-exploration, the clients come gradually to understand their motives and actions. The insight thus gained, it is believed, will enable them to resolve their own conflicts and to manage their behavior more effectively.

Similarly, psychoanalysis is specifically designed to make clients aware of the origins of their emotional difficulties, which are often traced back to early childhood experiences. Free association and dream analysis are among the psychoanalytic techniques used for this purpose. Other common clinical procedures, such as play techniques and psychodrama, are also employed, with the dual objective of furthering the clinician's understanding of the clients and the clients' understanding of themselves.

The utilization of diagnostic techniques for the promotion of client insight illustrates the interrelation of diagnosis and therapy in clinical psychology. Insight plays an important part in several forms of psychotherapy. The methods cited above for the attainment of insight represent well-known therapeutic procedures. As such, they will be considered more fully in Chapter 13. They are mentioned here simply to highlight the fact that, in much current clinical practice, diagnosis and therapy cannot be differentiated with regard to temporal sequence, methods, or objectives. Even a brief contact during which the client has an opportunity to describe the problem to a clinician may have therapeutic value. For that matter, when the client decides to consult a clinician and puts that decision into practice by keeping the first appointment, that action itself may contribute to the rehabilitation process.

Treatment Decisions. A growing number of psychologists reject not only diagnostic classification but also traditional personality descriptions in the practice of clinical psychology. They maintain that the primary objective of clinical appraisal should be the formulation of a plan of action to treat the client's problem (A. Z. Arthur, 1969; Linder, 1965). The focus is not so much on describing or understanding as on problem solving and decision making. Some psychologists argue specifically against the concept of personality traits as fixed, unchanging, underlying causal entities (Mischel, 1968; D. R. Peterson, 1968). They also question the value of tracing present behavioral difficulties to early origins in the individual's childhood experiences.

It is certainly true that psychological traits, as empirically identified through correlational and factor-analytic techniques, reflect only certain regularities in the individual's behavior and do not themselves represent causal or unchanging entities. Research results on both cognitive and noncognitive traits support this view (Anastasi, 1970; 1976, pp. 376–378, 521–524). Furthermore, noncognitive or personality traits are likely to exhibit less generality across situations than do abilities. The individual's numerical aptitude or mechanical comprehension, for example, will not vary much from one situation to another; but a person may be quite sociable and outgoing at the office, while shy and reserved at a dinner party. There is an extensive body of empirical evidence indicating that persons do exhibit considerable situational specificity in such behavior as aggression, social conformity, dependency, and rigidity (Mischel, 1968; D. R. Peterson, 1968). Personality development occurs under less uniform and standardized conditions than does intellectual development, with its heavy dependence on formal school instruction. In the personality domain, moreover, the same response may lead to social consequences that are positively reinforcing in one situation and negatively reinforcing in another. Thus the individual may learn to respond in quite different ways in different contexts.

The rejection of personality descriptions in terms of broad traits is especially clear among psychologists who practice behavior modification as a treatment procedure. More will be said about this approach elsewhere in this chapter and in the following chapter. For the present, it will suffice to note that these psychologists seek to identify the particular "behavior of interest" that is to be altered, such as anxiety in public speaking or insufficient self-assertiveness. The highly specific behavior thus defined is then used as a basis for mapping out the treatment program.

Prediction of Outcome. Closely related to the selection and formulation of appropriate treatment programs is the prediction of outcome. Since outcome may be defined in many ways, the prediction problem covers several more or less related questions. One question pertains to the probability of improvement, recovery, or deterioration in the absence of therapy. Such information is useful, for example, in matching control and experimental samples in research on the effects of therapy. It also contributes to practical decisions regarding the disposition of individual cases.

Another question concerns the individual's response to particular methods of therapy (Bordin, 1974, Ch. 8). Thus, if an outpatient clinic has a long waiting list, cases can be selected on the basis of their estimated chances of improving with the available therapy. If those who fail to return after one or two visits and those who continue in therapy but derive no benefit from it can be weeded out in advance, available therapeutic resources can be more effectively utilized. In accepting clients for psychotherapy, moreover, most clinical psychologists make an effort to screen out the type of cases that do not respond well to this form of therapy.

With institutionalized cases, a further question is that of posthospital adjustment. Decisions regarding discharge depend upon this type of prediction. The criteria against which such predictions can be tested include rehospitalization within specified periods of time, as well as various indices of the individual's level of functioning in the community. Among these indices may be mentioned objective records of educational or vocational achievement, ratings by family members and other associates, and the individual's own report of his or her feelings.

Considerable research has been done on the prognostic use of both tests and case history data in the effort to provide a systematic basis for clinical prediction (Clum, 1975). Analysis of case history material on schizophrenics has suggested a useful distinction between process and reactive schizophrenics (Higgins & Peterson, 1966; Kantor & Herron, 1966). One of the chief differentiating features of these two groups is found in the onset of the disorder, which is slow and gradual in the process group and sudden in the reactive group. In the latter cases, too, the psychotic condition is often precipitated by a highly stressful experience. There is fairly extensive evidence to show that prognosis is more favorable for the reactive than for the process group.

Another approach to the prediction of outcome is illustrated by a survey of posthospital adjustment of discharged patients (Dinitz, Lefton, Angrist, & Pasamanick, 1962). In terms of both rehospitalization and community-adjustment criteria, this study showed that the environmental milieu to which patients return is a major factor in the success of their posthospital adjustment. For instance, married women with young children were more likely to make a good adjustment than were single women living with their parents or other relatives. Data regarding the condition of these cases at the time of admission and discharge indicated that this difference in adjustment could not be attributed to selective factors. The investigators suggest that a family milieu in which the patient is required to take responsibility, as in managing a home and caring for young children, is more conducive to recovery than one in which the "sick" role is accepted and even encouraged by solicitous relatives.

The same study found that educational and socioeconomic variables are significantly related to outcome. Women who were college graduates, for instance, made a much more successful posthospital adjustment and were less often rehospitalized than women with only an elementary school education. A similar relation was found between outcome and socioeconomic status. It should be noted that educational and socioeconomic factors may enter the picture in at least two ways. They not only determine certain features of the posthospital milieu to which individuals return but also reflect characteristics of the patients themselves—such as intellectual level, persistence, and self-confidence—that may be directly related to outcome.

SOURCES OF INFORMATION IN CLINICAL APPRAISAL

In the effort to understand the client's problems, clinical psychologists may turn to three major sources of data, namely, case history, psychological tests, and diagnostic interview. Depending upon their theoretical orientation, the setting in which they function, and the type of client with whom they are dealing, clinicians will vary in the extent to which they employ each of these sources. To facilitate all aspects of clinical appraisal, the utilization of computers is steadily increasing.

Case History. Utilizing a reverse longitudinal approach, the case history, or anamnesis, provides data about the client's reactional biography. It covers family background and current familial situation, educational and vocational history, and other important facts regarding the individual's physical and psychological development from the prenatal stage to the present. Information may be gathered through interviews with the client, family members, teachers, employers, co-workers, friends, or anyone else who has had contact with the client. School and employment files, agency reports, court records, and other official sources may be consulted. Unless an adequate medical report is already available, a medical examination is usually requested to round out the picture and to identify any conditions that may require treatment by a physician. In certain settings, the services of a social worker are utilized in obtaining at least part of the case history material.

Psychological Tests. In clinical practice, psychological tests are commonly employed to determine general level of intellectual functioning and to check for evidence of intellectual impairment or deterioration. A wide variety of personality tests is also available for investigating emotional disorders, strength of various needs, interests, attitudes, adjustment mechanisms, self-concepts, interpersonal relations, and many other facets of behavior. Major types of tests used in clinical practice will be examined in later sections of this chapter.

Interviewing Techniques. The diagnostic interview represents a particularly important part of the process of clinical assessment (Bingham et al., 1959, Ch. 13; Burdock & Hardesty, 1969; Matarazzo, 1965). Although a single intensive interview may serve for this purpose, frequently a series of interviews is required. In a diagnostic interview, the client has the opportunity to describe his problem as he sees it and to talk freely and fully about himself. Interest generally centers on how the client perceives events in his life and how he reacts to them, rather than on the objective events as such. Clinicans differ, however, in the extent to which they ask questions designed to elicit information about specific behavior difficulties, sources of conflict, or symptoms. In the nondirective approach, for example, the client is simply encouraged to talk about anything he considers important.

Although the interview is largely a medium for verbal communication, it also provides many opportunities for direct behavioral observations. Facial expressions, laughter, crying, blushing, muscular tics and grimaces, gestures, posture, and other expressive reactions serve as additional cues to the client's feelings. In the more severely disturbed cases, such symptoms as hallucinations, delusions, and flight of ideas may become apparent in the course of the interview.

For maximal effectiveness, the interview requires good rapport between clinician and client. Essentially this means that clients must have confidence in the clinician, so that they feel free to communicate. Ordinarily an individual shows some resistance to discussing or even thinking about certain highly emotional matters. There are several ways in which the clinician may help to overcome such resistance. Privacy and confidentiality of communication are, of course, essential. Through his own comments and behavior, moreover, the clinician can indicate that he is interested, attentive, and seriously concerned about the client's problems. The clinician's manner should be warm, friendly, and relaxed, while at the same time remaining impersonal and professional.

Most clinical psychologists today put the greatest emphasis on the establishment of a permissive atmosphere. By this is meant that the clinician refrains from judging or evaluating anything the client communicates—the clinician expresses neither approval nor disapproval but concentrates on understanding and clarifying the client's own feelings. Although "permissiveness" is most closely associated with the client-centered school of clinical practice, its advantages—at least at certain stages—are quite generally recognized. In actual practice, however, it is difficult for any clinician to withhold entirely all expressions of approval or disapproval. Differential reinforcement of topics for discussion or of different types of patient responses is likely to be provided even by the most nondirective of clinicians. Some research findings on the effects of subtle cues in the clinician's behavior upon the course of client responses will be considered in Chapter 14.

It should also be noted that in much current clinical practice the diagnostic interview merges imperceptibly with the therapeutic interview. This is particularly true of those approaches that stress the therapeutic value of client-therapist relationship.

Computer Utilization. Computers are used for a variety of purposes in clinical psychology. Several tests employed in clinical assessment can now be scored by computers. Such automated scoring is most helpful for tests yielding multiple scores, especially when the pattern or interrelationship of these scores has diagnostic relevance. A traditional use of computers, particularly in clinical research, is in the statistical analysis of test scores and other assessment data. A growing application is in the systematic and uniform maintenance of case records (Spitzer & Endicott, 1971).

More innovative applications of computers are illustrated by what Kleinmuntz (1975) has termed "noncomputational" uses. These uses take advantage of the computer's flexibility in applying decision rules and its capacity for storing and utilizing vast quantities of relevant data. One such application, already available for certain tests,[2] is the computer formulation of detailed clinical interpretations of individual score profiles. In this situation, the computer simulates the synthesizing and interpretive function of the clinician. Another potential application, whose

---

[2]Among them are Minnesota Multiphasic Personality Inventory, California Psychological Inventory, Rorschach, Holtzman Inkblot Technique, Differential Aptitude Tests.

practical implementation is still in the future, is computer interviewing. For this purpose, the computer presents a series of questions covering a wide range of diagnostic signs. The questions are answered by the client or some other person familiar with the client's behavior, such as family member, nurse, or ward attendant. The computer output from the processing of these responses indicates the relative likelihood of different diagnoses.

NATURE OF CLINICAL JUDGMENT

Two more or less related questions can be asked about the clinician's diagnostic function: "*What* does he do?" and "*How well* does he do it?" A substantial amount of research and considerable discussion have been devoted to both questions. Nevertheless, psychologists are still a long way from reaching definite answers.

Person Cognition. What the clinician does in assessing a client may be regarded as a special case of person cognition, or interpersonal perception (Bakan, 1956; Bieri et al., 1966; Sarbin, Taft, & Bailey, 1960; Wiggins, 1973, Ch. 4). Through what process does *anyone* come to know and understand another person? This is a broad question that has been approached from the standpoints of epistemology, the psychology of perception, and information theory, among others. Investigations of the accuracy of interpersonal perception and of the factors that affect it are beset with methodological pitfalls. Generalizations about one's ability to judge others are misleading unless they specify the type of judgment and the circumstances under which it is made. Moreover, spurious impressions of accuracy can arise from failure to control certain variables, such as degree of resemblance between judge and subject or degree of resemblance between subject and a group stereotype in terms of which the judge may be responding (Cronbach, 1958).

In understanding another person, individuals often rely upon *assumed similarity* to themselves. They can thus use their own experiences in interpreting the behavior of another. Although they cannot directly observe another's aches and pains or feelings of joy and sadness, they can identify them through facial expressions, gestures, verbal reports, and other overt cues that they have learned to associate wth their own feelings. Assumed similarity between a newcomer and familiar others, such as one's relatives, friends, or former clients, is an extension of this mechanism. When this approach is followed in trying to understand someone quite unlike oneself—or unlike one's earlier acquaintances—it is likely to prove misleading. Errors may thus arise when clinicians make diagnostic or prognostic inferences about a client whose cultural background, education, or socioeconomic level differs markedly from their own (see, e.g., Wainwright, 1958).

The Clinician's Data-gathering Function. The diagnostic role of the clinician can be described in terms of data gathering and data interpreting. We shall begin by considering what the clinician can contribute to the process of data gathering. First, by establishing and maintaining rapport, he may elicit from the client facts about his life history not readily accessible in other ways. Such life-history data provide a particularly sound basis for understanding an individual and predicting his future behavior (Dailey, 1960). The life history has been aptly described as "an unbiased population of events which is as convincing an operational definition of a person as one can hope for" (Dailey, 1960, p. 21). It might be added that the more factual data one has from the life history, the less filling-in needs to be done in the interpretive process.

In his search for facts, the clinician is also guided by the client's own responses. He may thus form tentative hypotheses that suggest the direction of further probing. Such interlocking of data gathering and interpretation represents both an advantage and a potential danger of clinical interviewing. On the one hand, it permits more flexibility of search and more effective utilization of cues than would be possible with a test, questionnaire, or other standardized procedure. On the other hand, if the clinician puts undue confidence in his early hypotheses, he may look only for data that support them. By the type of questions he asks and the way he formulates them or by subtle expressions of agreement or disagreement, he may influence what the client reports. Sarbin and his associates (1960) call this process "soliciting" as contrasted to "probing." Such biased data-gathering techniques undoubtedly account for the remarkably uniform etiologies found among the clients of some psychoanalysts.

Another way in which the clinician contributes to the fact-finding process is by serving as a stimulus in an interpersonal situation. In this respect, the clinical interview may be regarded as a situational test (see Ch. 3). It provides a sample of the client's interpersonal behavior, observed under more or less controlled conditions.

The Clinician's Interpretive Function. There has been much discussion of the interpretive, or data-processing, function of the clinician. Some have argued for a special process of "clinical intuition" that is qualitatively different from other forms of inference. Belief in such a process arises partly from the fact that clinicians are often unable to report the cues they employ in reaching a conclusion (Sarbin et al., 1960, Ch. 8). The mystery disappears, however, when we realize that many of our perceptions utilize cues that are inaccessible to self-examination. A classical example is visual depth perception. We regularly perceive the world in three dimensions, without being able to specify the cues we employ in this process. Similarly, after exposure to a test protocol, a set of test scores, a case history, or a face-to-face interaction with a client, the clinician may assert that the patient is creative, or a likely suicide, or a poor psychotherapy risk, even though the clinician cannot verbalize the facts used in reaching such a conclusion. Being unaware of the cues that mediated his inference, the clinician is also unaware of the probabilistic nature of the inference. As a result, he may attribute a higher degree of certainty to his inference than is justified.

A number of investigations have been concerned with the comparative validity of clinical versus statistical predictions (see Meehl, 1954; Sarbin et al., 1960, Ch. 10; Sawyer, 1966; Wiggins, 1973, Ch. 5). Given the same set of facts, such as test scores or life-history data, will clinical judgment provide more accurate predictions of subsequent behavior than would be obtained by the routine application of a regression equation or other empirically derived prediction formula? The large majority of studies have found statistical prediction to be at least as good as clinical prediction, and sometimes better.

It is difficult to generalize from such studies, however, because the results are undoubtedly affected by the nature of the data to be interpreted, the type of criterion behavior to be predicted, and the characteristics of the clinician. Not only the amount of training and experience of the clinician, but also the soundness of the theoretical framework within which he operates, will influence the validity of his judgments. If a clinician is guided by a weak and unverified personality theory, his prediction success may be poorer than that of the crudest statistical procedures. The process of clinical judgment probably varies widely from one clinician to another. Insofar as the clinican functions as an instrument, he needs to be individually validated, just like a test. Moreover, since clinical judgment is probably not a single trait, the clinician's validity must be separately investigated for different types of prediction, which have been classified according to type of client, type of outcome, and other relevant variables.

Several attempts have been made to analyze what clinicians do to arrive at their inferences (see Wiggins, 1973, Ch. 4). It is frequently claimed that clinical judgment, as contrasted to statistical data-processing techniques, is peculiarly suited to understanding the uniqueness of individuals. In the course of their interactions with clients, clinicians are able to develop constructs, categories, or trait concepts that are specifically fitted to each individual case. They can also take into account patterns of traits or events. Their interpretations of any single fact, such as a test score, can be made contingent upon other variables, such as another test score or some biographical facts.

Furthermore, in their interpretations, clinicians are able to incorporate rare events, whose frequency is too low to permit their use in statistical prediction. Although any one such event occurs very infrequently, it may significantly affect outcome in an individual case. Moreover, *different* "rare events" will be encountered often enough to have a substantial effect upon the decisions reached in large numbers of cases. In this connection, Meehl (1954, p. 25) quotes the old paradox that "an improbable event is one that hardly ever happens, but nevertheless something improbable happens almost every day."

In focusing upon the uniqueness of the individual case, we must not lose sight of the fact that people also exhibit a great deal of similarity. Without such similarity, the science of psychology could never have developed. In fact, society and civilization would be impossible, and human relations would be chaotic. In the clinical context, it is the pronounced similarity among individuals that enables the clinician to utilize the technique of assumed similarity, to refer to test norms, or to draw upon personality theories developed through research on other persons. With regard to the clinician's consideration of patterns and interrelations of facts, it should be noted that such analyses can also be incorporated in statistical prediction formulas (Wiggins, 1973, Ch. 4). Although for most purposes linear regression equations based on simple additive combination of terms have proved sufficiently accurate, more complex combinations of variables can be handled by appropriate mathematical techniques. Such mathematical models have in fact been used in an effort to discover the type of model actually followed by different clinicians. An interesting finding from such studies, known as "bootstrapping," is that a statistical model of a clinician's own behavior will usually yield more valid predictions than does the clinician himself (Dawes & Corrigan, 1974). Because such a model reflects only the regularities in the clinician's behavior, it reduces the influence of random procedural errors.

With diagnostic procedures in their present stage of development, there is much that the clinician must do, because neither tests nor statistical prediction formulas are available to do the whole job. For many years to come, clinicians will probably continue to use a combination of clinical judgment and such statistical aids as norms, expectancy tables, and regression equations. Clinicians need to be constantly aware of the probabilistic nature of all their inferences, whether derived from clinical judgment or statistical procedures. And they should make continuing efforts to check the validity of their predictions in terms of empirical follow-ups.

ASSESSING COGNITIVE FUNCTIONS

Almost every type of test may be used by a clinician in individual cases. Tests of academic achievement, for example, are often useful in clinical work with children. Vocational aptitude and interest tests may be required to help solve a special problem with an adolescent or adult client. Certain types of tests, however, were designed chiefly as clinical instruments. It is with these tests that we shall be concerned in the remaining sections of this chapter. Only a few examples of tests in each category will be cited. For a fuller discussion the reader is referred to textbooks on psychological testing (e.g., Anastasi, 1976; Cronbach, 1970) and to books on the practice of clinical psychology (e.g., Garfield, 1974; Sundberg et al., 1973). Apart from providing an overview of the sort of tests used by clinicians, the present survey will familiarize the reader with certain concepts relevant to the discussion of therapy and of clinical research to be given in the next two chapters.

Stanford-Binet Intelligence Scale. Among the best established clinical instruments are tests of general intellectual level. Traditionally designated as "intelligence tests," such instruments typically yield a composite index of the individual's performance in several cognitive functions. The test that has been used for this purpose longest is the Stanford-Binet. Originally developed by Terman at Stanford University from an earlier test introduced by Binet in 1905, the Stanford-Binet has been periodically revised and updated (Terman & Merrill, 1973). The current form of the test extends from the age of two years to the superior adult level, but it is used most commonly with children. Most of the items are oral, although some require the examinee to read, write, draw, or carry out simple manipulative tasks.

Like most tests designed for clinical use, the Stanford-Binet is an individual test. It can be administered to only one person at a time and requires a trained examiner. Although more time-consuming and much harder to give and score than group tests, individual tests provide additional information for the clinician. Thus in such a situation it is possible to observe the individual's work methods, attitudes, and problem-solving techniques, as well as the finished product. Interpersonal reactions, emotional responses, and other incidental behavior can likewise be noted. Individual tests also provide a better opportunity for establishing rapport with each examinee than do group tests.

The Stanford-Binet yields a single standard score,[3] expressed as a deviation IQ (intelligence quotient) with a mean of 100 and an *SD* of 16. A particular advantage of this test stems from the wealth of interpretive data that has accumulated through many years of clinical use. Clinicians have thus had a chance to learn inductively what to expect from individuals at different Stanford-Binet IQ levels.

The Wechsler Scales. The Wechsler Adult Intelligence Scale (WAIS) was specially developed as a clinical instrument for adult testing (Matarazzo, 1972; Wechsler, 1978). Standardized on a representative nationwide sample, this test provides separate norms for successive age levels between 16 and 75 years. The WAIS yields a total deviation IQ ($M = 100$, $SD = 15$), as well as separate Verbal and Performance

---

[3]For an explanation of standard score and standard deviation (*SD*), see Chapter 2.

Figure 12-1. Easy item from WAIS-R Picture Arrangement Test. *(Reproduced by permission. Copyright © 1976 by The Psychological Corporation, New York, N. Y. All rights reserved.)*

IQs. The Verbal IQ is based on six orally administered tests utilizing verbal and numerical content; the Performance IQ is derived from five subtests using nonverbal symbols, pictures, geometric forms, and cutout parts of objects to be assembled by the examinee. A simple item from one of the picture tests is reproduced in Figure 12-1. The task in this test is to rearrange a set of cards in proper order so as to tell a story. Figure 12-2 illustrates another of the performance tests, in which the pieces of familiar objects are to be assembled by the examinee.

The Wechsler Intelligence Scale for Children (WISC) was prepared as a downward extension of Wechsler's adult scales (Wechsler, 1974). It, too, provides

Figure 12-2. Administration of WAIS-R Object Assembly Test. *(Courtesy of The Psychological Corporation.)*

Verbal, Performance, and Full Scale IQs and is quite similar to the WAIS in form and content. Norms are available for every four-month interval between the ages of 6 and 17 years. The third member of the series is the Wechsler Preschool and Primary Scale of Intelligence (WPPSI), designed for ages 4 to 6½ years (Wechsler, 1967). The WPPSI follows closely the model of the other two scales, with norms for every three-month interval. Most of its subtests are adaptations or simpler versions of WISC subtests.

Performance and Nonlanguage Scales. A number of less well-known tests have been developed for use with special groups, such as infants and preschool children (see Anastasi, 1976, Ch. 10). Others have been designed for testing persons unable to take the usual type of test, such as the deaf, the orthopedically handicapped, children with reading disabilities, illiterates, and foreigners with a language handicap. There are several nonlanguage group tests that require no reading; some can be administered without the use of language altogether, the instructions being presented by means of gestures, pantomime, and demonstrations. For individual testing, performance tests are generally employed for several of the special handicaps mentioned above. Since most nonlanguage and performance tests tap chiefly perceptual and spatial rather than verbal and numerical functions, they are also used in clinical practice to provide a better rounded picture of the individual's cognitive development. The Performance Scale of the previously mentioned Wechsler scales was included chiefly for this purpose.

A nonlanguage test that has been widely used in both clinical practice and research is the Progressive Matrices (Raven, 1956). Each of the 60 items in this test consists of a matrix, or arrangement of elements, from which a piece has been removed. The examinee must choose the correct insert from the given options, as illustrated in Figure 12-3. The early items in the series require primarily accuracy of discrimination, as in the first item in Figure 12-3. Later, more difficult items involve analogies, permutation and alternation of pattern, and other logical relations, as illustrated in the second item of Figure 12-3. Because it is a nonverbal test requiring the eduction of relations among abstract elements, this test is particular-

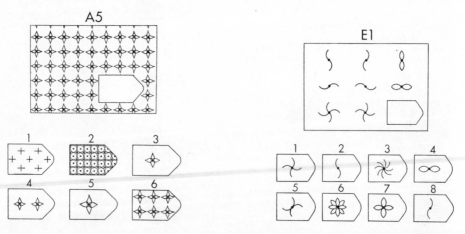

Figure 12-3. Typical items from Progressive Matrices. *(Copyright © 1956 by J. C. Raven. Reproduced by permission.)*

ly useful in clinical practice as a supplement to the usual verbal type of intelligence test. Still another application is in the testing of persons with severe motor handicaps, as in cerebral palsy, with whom the Progressive Matrices test has proved quite successful. When administering the test to such cases, the examiner points to each response option in turn, while the respondent signifies assent or dissent through some convenient signal.

Detecting Cognitive Dysfunction. Several types of tests have been designed as clinical instruments for assessing cognitive dysfunction (see Anastasi, 1976, Ch. 16). Such tests are used to detect intellectual deterioration resulting from brain damage (or "organicity"), psychotic disorders, senility, or other pathological conditions. They are sometimes employed to help differentiate between mental retardation and psychosis, as well as between mental retardates with or without brain damage. Many of these tests are only loosely standardized, being designed chiefly to give the clinician an opportunity to make qualitative observations. Others have relatively standardized procedure and empirical norms.

Available tests of cognitive dysfunction are based on the premise of a differential deficit in different functions. Among the functions found to be most sensitive to pathological processes are memory for newly learned material, perception of spatial relations, and abstraction, or concept formation. The individual's performance on these tests is usually compared with his performance in a function that is relatively resistant to deterioration. Vocabulary test scores or scores on predominantly verbal intelligence tests are often used for the latter purpose. An index of the individual's prior intellectual level, from which he subsequently deteriorated, can also be obtained from his educational or occupational status or from intelligence tests he may have taken in the past.

The Wechsler scales are often used to identify diagnostic signs of particular clinical syndromes, such as brain damage, schizophrenia, or anxiety states (Matarazzo, 1972). All these applications are based on *score patterns*, that is, on an analysis of inequalities of performance from one subtest to another. Qualitative observations regarding atypical performance on subtests, or even items, may provide useful cues for the experienced clinician. Many of the proposed quantitative indices for score pattern analysis, however, are subject to technical weaknesses that render them of doubtful value. For most of these diagnostic signs, more research is needed to establish their possible validity (Anastasi, 1976, pp. 465–471).

Among the special tests used widely by clinical psychologists for assessing intellectual impairment is the Bender-Gestalt Test. In this test, the examinee copies nine simple designs, presented one at a time. Other tests require the drawing of designs from memory, after a brief exposure. Another well-known type of test utilizes the sorting of objects or forms to assess concept formation (e.g., Goldstein-Scheerer Tests of Abstract and Concrete Thinking). In such tests, interest is focused on the methods employed by the respondent in grouping objects, as well as on his ability to shift from one basis of classification to another. For example, the examinee is given a set of circles, squares, and triangles in different colors, with the instructions to place together those that belong together. Whether he groups the pieces according to form or color, he is then asked to sort them in another way. In another series of tasks, common objects are employed in a variety of sorting situations. For example, the examiner selects an article and asks the respondent to pick out the others that belong with it. The examiner also places objects in groups on some basis, such as color, shape, material, or use, and asks why they belong together. The same object may be included in several different groupings, such as eating utensils, toys, and metal objects. Hence the individual is again required to shift from one attribute of an object to another in the reclassifications.

Identifying Learning Disabilities. The late 1960s witnessed an increasing recognition of the widespread incidence of learning disabilities among schoolchildren (Johnson & Myklebust, 1967; Lerner, 1971; McCarthy & McCarthy, 1969). As a result, extensive efforts were launched to identify and remedy these handicaps. Typically, children with learning disabilities show normal or above-normal intelligence, in combination with pronounced difficulties in learning one or more basic educational skills (most often, reading). In addition, they manifest various combinations of related behavioral difficulties, such as perceptual disorders, motor incoordination, deficiencies in memory and attention control, impairment in conceptual skills, undirected and impulsive hyperactivity, and emotional and interpersonal problems. Whether or not brain dysfunction is involved in learning disabilities is still an unresolved issue, although there is evidence suggesting such involvement (Rourke, 1975).

Because of the uncertain etiology of learning disabilities, the complexity of their behavioral manifestations, and the diverse combinations of handicaps in individual cases, it is understandable that the test batteries administered to such cases include a wide assortment of measures (Anastasi, 1976, pp. 478–482, 717–718). Besides the previously mentioned tests of cognitive dysfunction, the selection often includes general intelligence tests, such as the Stanford-Binet or WISC, and tests of educational achievement—particularly those permitting an analysis of specific strengths and weaknesses. Several test series have been specially developed for both screening and intensive evaluation of children with learning disabilities. Some of these concentrate on sensorimotor or perceptual functions. Others provide detailed analyses of communication skills, as illustrated by the Illinois Test of Psycholinguistic Abilities and the Porch Index of Communicative Ability in Children. Programs for children with learning disabilities illustrate the close intertwining of diagnosis and remediation so characteristic of contemporary clinical psychology.

ASSESSING NONCOGNITIVE FUNCTIONS

In traditional psychometric terminology, "personality tests" are instruments for assessing such noncognitive functions as emotional, motivational, and attitudinal behavior. Although the investigation of behavior can be facilitated by differentiating between cognitive and noncognitive functions—and between aptitude and personality tests—it should be noted that essentially we are describing different *aspects* of the individual's behavior. Everything individuals do reflects both cognitive and noncognitive characteristics. How well individuals perform a task depends not only on their relevant aptitudes but also upon their motivation, interests, and emotional state. Similarly, the way in which they resolve an emotional conflict and their reaction to different remedial procedures are influenced by their intellectual level and problem-solving style.

Although personality tests vary widely with respect to reliability, validity, and adequacy of norms, such tests as a whole are not so well constructed nor so successful as ability tests. For this reason, personality tests are employed chiefly as exploratory tools in clinical practice. In assessing personality traits, most clinicians rely heavily upon life-history and interview data. Of the many noncognitive assessment techniques available to the clinician, we shall consider four major types: (1) self-report inventories, (2) projective techniques, (3) measures of self-concepts and personal constructs, and (4) assessment techniques used in behavior modification programs.

Self-report Inventories. In a self-report inventory, the respondents answer a series of written questions about their typical feelings, attitudes, and actions. This technique has been used in measuring such varied characteristics as vocational interests, attitudes, interpersonal relations, and neuroticism. Standardized inventories have been prepared for use with different age groups, from the elementary school to the adult level. Some were developed within clinical settings to detect manifestations of psychopathology; others were designed for essentially normal persons. Examples of the latter were cited in Chapter 3 in connection with the appraisal of industrial personnel. The use of self-report inventories in the measurement of interests is discussed in Chapters 3 and 15.

Among clinically oriented inventories, the most widely used is the Minnesota Multiphasic Personality Inventory (MMPI). Originally developed "to assay those traits that are commonly characteristic of disabling psychological abnormality," the MMPI consists of 550 statements to be marked "True," "False," or "Cannot say." The items range widely in content, covering such areas as: health, psychosomatic symptoms, neurological disorders, and motor disturbances; sexual, religious, political and social attitudes; educational, occupational, family, and marital questions; and common neurotic or psychotic behavior disturbances, such as obsessive and compulsive states, delusions, hallucinations, ideas of reference, phobias, and the like. A few illustrative items are reproduced below:[4]

> I do not tire quickly.
> I am worried about sex matters.
> When I get bored I like to stir up some excitement.
> I believe I am being plotted against.

In its regular administration, the MMPI provides scores on the following 10 scales:

1.	Hs:	Hypochondriasis		6.	Pa:	Paranoia
2.	D:	Depression		7.	Pt:	Psychasthenia
3.	Hy:	Hysteria		8.	Sc:	Schizophrenia
4.	Pd:	Psychopathic deviate		9.	Ma:	Hypomania
5.	Mf:	Masculinity-femininity		0.	Si:	Social introversion

Eight of these scales consist of items that differentiated between patients with specified clinical syndromes and a normal control group of approximately 700 persons. These scales were developed empirically by criterion keying of items, the criterion being traditional psychiatric diagnosis. Items for the Masculinity-femininity (Mf) scale were selected in terms of frequency of responses by men and women. High scores on this scale indicate a predominance of interests typical of the opposite sex. The Social Introversion (Si) scale was added later, on the basis of research on normal persons. A special feature of the MMPI is its utilization of so-called validity scales (L, F, K). These scales are not concerned with validity in the technical sense but provide checks on carelessness, misunderstanding, faking, and the operation of special response sets and test-taking attitudes.

Scores on the MMPI scales are expressed as standard scores with a mean of 50 and an *SD* of 10. These standard scores are used in plotting profiles, as illustrated in Figure 12-4. A score of 70 or higher—falling 2 *SD*s or move above the mean—is

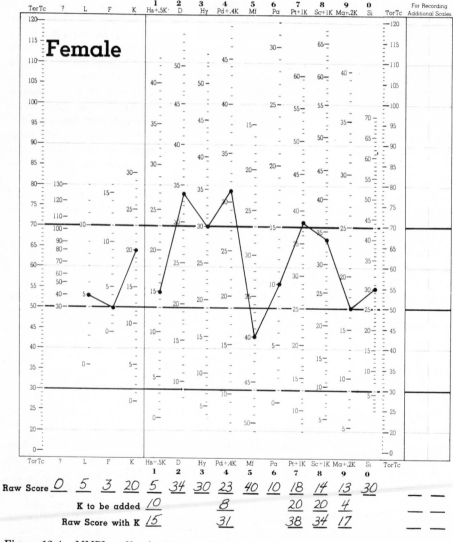

Figure 12-4. MMPI profile of a 28-year-old woman. *(Data by courtesy of David R. Chabot. Profile chart reproduced by permission. Copyright © 1948 by The Psychological Corporation, New York, N. Y. All rights reserved.)*

generally taken as the cutoff point for identifying possible pathological deviations. The interpretation of MMPI profiles is much more complex than the labels originally assigned to the scales might suggest. The test manual and related publications now caution against literal interpretation of the clinical scales. For example, we cannot assume that a high score on the Schizophrenia scale indicates the presence of schizophrenia. Other psychotic groups show high elevation on this scale, and schizophrenics often score high on other scales. Moreover, such a score may occur in the record of a normal person. It is partly to prevent possible misinterpretations of scores on single scales that the code numbers 0 to 9 have been substituted for the scale names in later publications on the MMPI.

The original clinical scales of the MMPI were based on a traditional psychiatric classification which rests upon a questionable theoretical foundation. As we saw in the first section of this chapter, the artificiality of these categories has been a matter of concern in clinical psychology for a long time. The fact that such categories prove unsatisfactory in actual practice is now generally conceded. Current interpretations of the MMPI treat the scales primarily as linear measures of personality traits identified in terms of the salient characteristics of the groups used in developing the scales. For example an elevated score on Scale 6 (originally labeled "Paranoia") suggests a high degree of suspiciousness and resentfulness. Another consideration is that a high score on any one MMPI scale may have different implications depending upon the individual's scores on other scales. It is the score pattern, or profile, rather than the scores on individual scales, that must be considered. To facilitate the interpretation of score patterns, a system of numerical profile coding has been developed. In such codes, the sequence and arrangement of scale numbers show at a glance which are the high and which the low points in the individual's profile.

A mass of research data has been collected on the characteristics of persons yielding each of a large number of coded profiles, and various handbooks, codebooks, and atlases have been prepared to aid in the interpretation of these profiles (Dahlstrom, Welsh, & Dahlstrom, 1972). A further step in the evolution of MMPI interpretation is the development of several computerized systems for automated profile interpretations. These automated systems are usually derived from profile interpretations by skilled clinicians, which are coded and programmed for computer retrieval. For proper utilization, such computer outputs still need to be evaluated by a trained clinician in the light of (1) fuller knowledge about the individual client from other sources, and (2) the research literature on such questions as the effect of cultural differences on MMPI responses (Dahlstrom, Welsh, & Dahlstorm, 1975).

The MMPI has also served as an item pool for the construction of about 300 special scales, most of them developed by independent investigators to meet specific needs (Dahlstrom et al., 1975). Both normal and clinic populations have been employed in selecting items for these scales against a wide variety of criteria. Examples include scales assessing Ego Strength, Dependency, Prejudice, and Social Status. Several of these scales have been used widely in clinical research.

Projective Techniques. Although projective techniques have been employed for a variety of purposes—including personnel selection, executive evaluation, and consumer surveys—their principal application is in clinical psychology (Klopfer & Taulbee, 1976). Most of them require individual administration by a specially trained examiner. And they yield a mass of qualitative data along with (or in place of) quantitative scores. It will be recalled from Chapter 3 that projective techniques as a group are characterized by the use of a relatively *unstructured* task, which allows considerable freedom in the examinee's response. The underlying hypothesis is that, when test stimuli and instructions are vague and equivocal, the individual's responses will reveal his or her own basic personality characteristics.

There is almost no limit to the kinds of tasks or situations that can serve as a basis for projective testing. Available techniques are many and varied. One of the earliest was the "free association test," in which examinees are given a list of disconnected words, to each of which they must respond with the first word that comes to mind. Another test employing verbal stimuli is the sentence completion test. Examinees are given the opening words of a series of sentences and are required to write suitable endings. Frequently the instructions stress the fact that the sentences should express the individual's own feelings. The sentence stems are chosen so as to permit wide latitude in the responses. Typical examples are: "I feel . . ."; "What annoys me . . ."; "My father. . . ." The responses are evaluated or coded in various ways. Thus they might be rated for degree of disturbance indicated, or they might be checked for the number of references to a particular theme, such as insecurity, hostility, or parental conflict.

One of the best known projective instruments, the Rorschach, utilizes inkblots as stimuli. Developed in 1921 by the Swiss psychiatrist Herman Rorschach, this test utilizes 10 cards, each containing a bilaterally symmetrical but otherwise irregular blot, similar to that illustrated in Figure 12-5. Some of the cards are in black, white, and gray; others are in color. As the respondent is shown each blot, he is asked to tell what he sees—what the blot could represent. Different systems of administration vary in the details of procedure and scoring, but all require a good deal of qualitative interpretation in translating the responses into broad personality characteristics. Although content is considered to some extent, the traditional scoring systems are based predominantly on formal characteristics of the responses. For example, scores are derived from such data as: number of associations elicited by the whole blot and number elicited by details of the blot; number of times the person responds to form and to color; frequency with which he

Figure 12-5. An inkblot of the type employed in the Rorschach technique.

perceives movement, as well as kind of movement perceived (human, animal, etc.); and the ways in which he perceives shading.

Because the extensive research literature on the Rorschach and other projective techniques has generally failed to validate many of the proposed interpretations, there has been some decline in the use of these techniques (Thelen, Varble, & Johnson, 1968). Later developments have proceeded in two principal directions. On the one hand, an attempt has been made to construct projective techniques that meet the technical requirements of psychometric instruments with regard to standardization of administration and scoring, norms, reliability, and validity. This approach is illustrated by the Holtzman Inkblot Technique, which was modeled after the Rorschach but sought to eliminate the major technical deficiencies of that instrument (Holtzman, 1968, 1975). On the other hand, many clinicians utilize the Rorschach chiefly as an aid in the clinical interview, rather than as an objectively and quantitatively scored psychometric instrument (Klopfer & Taulbee, 1976; Aronow & Reznikoff, 1976). In such an approach, responses are interpreted by the clinician within the context of other knowledge about the individual case; and the major emphasis is on content rather than on formal response characteristics. A promising application is illustrated by the consensus administration of the Rorschach, in which the inkblots are presented for joint interpretation by family members, co-workers, or other natural groups. In these situations, the technique is used as a basis for observing interpersonal behavior.

Several projective techniques employ pictures as stimuli. In the Thematic Apperception Test (TAT), which was cited in Chapter 3, black and white pictures are presented individually with the instructions to make up a story to fit each picture. The respondent is told to describe what is happening in the picture, to indicate what the characters are feeling and thinking, and to give the outcome. The content of the pictures is sufficiently unstructured to permit wide freedom of interpretation. Evaluation of responses is largely qualitative, drawing heavily upon Murray's personality theory. Among the many adaptations of the TAT may be mentioned special forms for children (Bellak, 1975) and for the aged (Bellak, 1975; Wolk & Wolk, 1971).

With regard to the contributions they can make to clinical assessment, projective techniques differ widely among themselves. Some appear more promising than others because of sounder theoretical orientation, more favorable empirical findings, or both. About some there is a voluminous research literature; about others little is known. Although each instrument obviously must be evaluated on its own merits, certain general statements can be made about the projective approach to personality assessment.

On the positive side, projective techniques are effective in "breaking the ice" and establishing rapport during initial contacts with a client. They are also applicable to a wide variety of examinees. Several available techniques involving nonverbal media can be used successfully with young children, illiterates, or persons with language handicaps. Projective tests, moreover, are less susceptible to faking than are self-report inventories, since their purpose is generally disguised. In addition, the respondent soon becomes engrossed in the task and is hence less likely to resort to the habitual restraints and defenses of interpersonal communication. At the same time, because of its unstructured nature, the task is usually less threatening than those encountered in aptitude tests.

When evaluated in terms of their technical qualities as tests, however, projective instruments generally fare rather poorly. Most are inadequately standardized with regard to both administration and scoring procedures. Consequently, results are likely to vary as a function of the examiner. With a few notable exceptions, norms are inadequate. Normative data either are lacking or are based on small unrepresentative samples. Frequently, not enough information is given about normative samples to permit an evaluation of the norms. For many projective tests, reliability is difficult to determine because of the nature of the test and the absence of parallel forms. When obtained, reliability coefficients are often low. Empirical studies of validity have also yielded disappointing results for most projective tests. Positive findings have sometimes been obtained because of inadequate controls and other methodological deficiencies.

Some of the special problems encountered in the evaluation of projective techniques will be considered in Chapter 14, in connection with clinical research (see also, Anastasi, 1976, Ch. 19). In their present state of development, most projective techniques should be regarded as interviewing aids rather than as psychometric tools. Their chief usefulness lies in providing leads to be followed up by the clinician.

Self-concepts and Personal Constructs. Although self-report inventories and projective techniques represent the most numerous and best known devices for personality assessment, many other approaches are being actively pursued (Anastasi, 1976, Ch. 20). Investigators have experimented with tests of perception, aesthetic preference, and humor responses, among others. Of particular interest for clinical psychology are techniques for exploring self-concepts and personal constructs. These techniques are closely allied with some of the personality theories and systems of psychotherapy to be discussed in the next chapter. A common feature of such techniques is their concern with the way in which the person views himself and others. In this respect, they reflect the influence of phenomenological psychology, which focuses on how events are perceived by the individual. The individual's self-description thus acquires primary importance in its own right, rather than being regarded as a substitute for other types of behavioral observations. Interest also centers on the extent of self-acceptance shown by the individual.

One of the special procedures for investigating self-concepts is the Q sort, developed by Stephenson (1953). In this technique, the examinee is given a set of cards containing statements or trait names and is asked to sort them into piles according to their applicability to himself, from "most characteristic" to "least characteristic." The items may come from a standard list but more often are designed to fit the individual case. To ensure a uniform distribution of ratings, a forced-normal distribution may be used, the respondent being instructed to place a specified number of cards in each pile (see Chapter 3).

Q sorts have been employed to study a variety of psychological problems. In the clinical investigation of individual personality, the person is often asked to re-sort the same set of items according to different frames of reference. For example, he may sort the items as they apply to himself and to other persons, such as his father, mother, wife, or therapist. Q sorts can also be obtained for the individual as he actually thinks he is (real self) and as he would like to be (ideal self). A cumulative measure of the differences between real- and ideal-self sorts provides an index of self-acceptance. To observe change, Q sorts may be obtained repeatedly at different stages in the course of psychotherapy.

Q technique represents an attempt to systematize self-rating procedures. It can also be employed as a basis for rating others. For example, clinicians may use the *Q* sort to record their evaluations of individuals. The *Q* sort provides a widely applicable rating technique for both clinical practice and research (Block, 1961; S. R. Brown, 1968; Rogers & Dymond, 1954).

Another relevant technique is the *Semantic Differential*, originally developed by Osgood and his associates (1957) as a tool for research on the psychology of meaning. This technique has subsequently proved useful in a variety of fields, including that of personality assessment. The Semantic Differential represents a standardized and quantified procedure for measuring the connotations of any given concept for the individual. Each concept is rated on a 7-point bipolar graphic scale defined by a pair of opposites such as good-bad, strong-weak, or fast-slow. Every concept to be investigated is rated in turn on each scale, as illustrated in Figure 12-6. Some of the scales can be applied literally to a particular concept, as in the rating of CHILD on the large-small scale. Many of the scales are obviously interpreted figuratively, as when a person is described as "cold." When a scale appears totally inapplicable to a concept, the respondent would presumably check the middle position.

Intercorrelations and factorial analyses of the original set of 50 scales revealed three major factors: *Evaluative*, with high loadings in such scales as good-bad, valuable-worthless, and clean-dirty; *Potency*, found in such scales as strong-weak, large-small, and heavy-light; and *Activity*, identified in such scales as active-passive, fast-slow, and sharp-dull. The evaluative factor is the most conspicuous, accounting for the largest percentage of total variance. Responses on the Semantic Differential can be analyzed in several ways. For quantitative treatment, the ratings on each scale can be assigned numerical values (e.g., from -3 to $+3$). The overall similarity of two concepts for an individual can be assessed in terms of their positions on all scales. The connotations of any one concept can be analyzed by finding its "score" on the three principal factors cited above. For example a

CHILD

Large _____:_____:_____:_____:_____:_____:_____ Small

Tense _____:_____:_____:_____:_____:_____:_____ Relaxed

Strong _____:_____:_____:_____:_____:_____:_____ Weak

Valuable _____:_____:_____:_____:_____:_____:_____ Worthless

Cruel _____:_____:_____:_____:_____:_____:_____ Kind

Warm _____:_____:_____:_____:_____:_____:_____ Cold

Figure 12-6. The Semantic Differential technique. In rating the concept CHILD, respondent checks the appropriate segment on each scale. Usually 15 or more scales are provided for each concept.

person's concept of "My father" may rate −2 in the evaluative factor, +2.7 in potency, and +0.5 in activity.

The concepts to be rated may be selected to fit whatever problem is being investigated. Respondents may, for instance, be instructed to rate: themselves, family members, friends, employers, teachers, or public figures; members of different ethnic or cultural groups; persons engaged in different occupations; activities, such as studying or outdoor sports; abstract ideas, such as confusion, hatred, sickness, peace, or love; product names or brand names; and radio or television programs. The Semantic Differential has been applied not only in clinical practice but also in research on such diverse problems as clinical diagnosis and therapy, vocational choices, cultural differences, and consumers' reactions to products and brand names (Snider & Osgood, 1969).

Assessment Techniques in Behavior Therapy Programs. Earlier in this chapter, reference was made to those clinical psychologists who practice behavior modification, which in the clinical context is generally referred to as behavior therapy.[5] In general, such psychologists reject personality description in terms of broad, stable, and causal traits. Instead, they emphasize the situational specificity of all behavior. In their assessment functions, they concentrate on the immediate "behavior of interest" that the individual seeks to modify (Bijou & Peterson, 1971; Dickson, 1975; Kanfer & Saslow, 1969; D. R. Peterson, 1968).

The principal objectives of assessment in behavior therapy programs can be grouped under three headings. First, assessment techniques help in defining the individual's problem through a functional analysis of relevant behavior. Such an analysis involves a detailed specification of the treatment target, such as the reduction of anxiety when taking examinations, overcoming a fear of air travel, improving self-assertiveness, or acquiring specific social competencies. This process includes a description of the stimuli that elicit the behavior of interest; the situations in which such behavior occurs; and the nature, magnitude, and frequencies of particular responses. It is also important to investigate the conditions that tend to maintain unwanted behavior, i.e., to ascertain what are the usual consequences of the target behavior in the individual's present environment. It should be noted that the targets for behavior therapy may include not only overt behavior but also cognitions and feelings.

A second requirement in behavior therapy programs is the identification of effective reinforcing stimuli for use in the reconditioning process. Although such common reinforcers as food (e.g., candy), social approval, and attention from associates may often prove efficacious, a systematic survey of the relative value of available reinforcers in individual cases will enhance the probability of successful retraining.

Third, there is need for assessing the behavior change resulting from treatment. Such assessment should include techniques for monitoring change in the course of the program, so as to permit evaluation of treatment effectiveness and the introduction of procedural alterations at any treatment stage. It should also include terminal measures to establish the individual's attainment of satisfactory status and follow-up observations to ensure maintenance of satisfactory status.

---

[5]These terms are used rather loosely and are sometimes given specialized meanings by different writers.

Because of the rapid growth of behavior therapy programs, the development of specialized assessment techniques has lagged far behind. A survey of leading clinical psychologists engaged in behavior therapy revealed the use of a variety of makeshift local devices and widespread dissatisfaction with available techniques (Kanfer, 1972). Among the procedures commonly employed are: direct observations of behavior, in both naturalistic settings and specially designed standardized situations; role playing; checklists and rating scales filled out by the individuals themselves or by such observers as parents, teachers, classmates, and nurses or other hospital personnel; diaries of the daily occurrence of target behaviors; physiological measures, as in the assessment of anxiety or sexual arousal; and interviewing techniques specially directed to the behavior of interest (D. R. Peterson, 1968, pp. 121–122).

A number of instruments have been prepared for use in specific research projects or treatment programs. Several are fear-behavior surveys, which list items frequently found to evoke anxiety and ask the respondent to indicate degree of disturbance aroused by each. An example is the Fear Survey Schedule (Wolpe, 1973; Wolpe & Lang, 1964), one of the few that have been published. It comprises over 100 items, ranging from "flying insects" and "the noise of vacuum cleaners" to "open wounds" and "taking written tests." For each item, respondents indicate how much they are disturbed by it, by marking one of five options from "not at all" to "very much." Another area of interest in surveys of target behaviors is that of self-assertiveness. For example, the Conflict Resolution Inventory (McFall & Lillesand, 1971) contains 35 items describing situations in which the person is asked to do something unreasonable or inconvenient. For each situation, respondents indicate whether or not they would be likely to refuse the request and how comfortable they would feel about refusing or acquiescing. This technique can be used not only in the initial assessment but also in monitoring the course of assertive training.

Some instruments have been designed to aid in choosing appropriate reinforcers for use in behavior modification programs. Examples include the Reinforcement Survey Schedule (Cautela & Kastenbaum, 1967), the Pleasant Events Schedule (MacPhillamy & Lewinsohn, 1974, 1976), and the Mediator-Reinforcer Incomplete Blank (Tharp & Wetzel, 1969). Constructed for use with children, the Mediator-Reinforcer form provides a set of incomplete sentences, such as "The thing I like most to do is _____ " and "I will do almost anything to get _____ ."

SUMMARY

In its broadest sense, clinical appraisal, or "diagnosis," corresponds to the fact-finding aspect of clinical practice. Its chief objectives include screening and classification, personality description, self-understanding by the client, the formulation of treatment decisions, and the prediction of outcome. In the classification of psychological disorders, a basic distinction is that between mental retardation and psychopathology, the latter being further subdivided into psychoses and neuroses. More specific syndromes have been identified, but the application of these traditional psychiatric categories has many drawbacks. Characteristically, the clinical psychologist is interested in a detailed personality description of the individual case, with its unique combination of problems, adaptive mechanisms, and antecedent circumstances. The interrelation of diagnosis and therapy is illustrated by those forms of psychotherapy that emphasize the therapeutic value of the client's insight into the nature and origin of his or her problems. From another angle, the close linkage of assessment and treatment functions is clearly apparent in behavior therapy, as well as in programs for children with learning disabilities.

Considerable research and discussion have been concerned with the nature and effectiveness of clinical judgment. The clinician's diagnostic task has been described as a special case of the process of person cognition. With regard to both data gathering and interpretation, there are a number of ways in which the services of a skilled clinician are needed. Whether objective assessment techniques and statistical prediction formulas can eventually assume the entire appraisal function remains a debatable question.

The major sources of data available to the clinician include case history, diagnostic interview, and psychological tests. Computers are being utilized increasingly to serve a variety of functions in clinical practice and research. Among the types of tests most frequently employed in clinical practice are individual intelligence tests, instruments for detecting cognitive dysfunction and for identifying learning disabilities, self-report personality inventories, projective techniques, and measures of self-concepts and personal constructs. Special assessment procedures are being developed for use in behavior therapy programs.

CLINICAL PRACTICE: INTERVENTION PROCEDURES

THIRTEEN

THE CHANGES THAT HAVE occurred in clinical practice since the 1960s are reflected in the increasing use of the broad term "intervention" in place of the more medically oriented terms "treatment" and "therapy." In certain contexts, the two latter terms are still appropriate in designating the services rendered; but the wide variety of functions now performed by clinical psychologists call for a more inclusive name. The activities of clinical psychologists have undergone expansion and diversification in several directions. Although a substantial proportion of clinical psychologists still rely chiefly on individual psychotherapy involving continued verbal communication between clinician and client, several new types of intervention and goals are evident. Examples include individually designed relearning programs (as in behavior modification), planned manipulations of the client's environment, a growing concern with prevention as contrasted with remediation, and a positive orientation toward the enhancement of well-being and effectiveness.

Both the types of clients served and the kinds of problems treated by clinical psychologists have become greatly diversified. With the recognition of the widespread need for psychological services and the limited number of available clinical psychologists, efforts are being made to utilize psychologists in innovative ways so as to extend the reach of their services. Among the diverse ways of meeting this problem may be mentioned: short-term psychotherapies; various forms of group therapy; the psychologist's role as a consultant to persons who are in key positions to implement intervention programs; and the utilization of a wide variety of nonprofessionals to perform many direct client services. These developments suggest that at least some clinical psychologists will be spending less of their time in client contacts and more in training, supervision, and consulting functions.

The variety of intervention procedures currently available in clinical psychology is large and growing. The choice of procedure depends partly on the nature and severity of the problem and partly on such client characteristics as age, education, socioeconomic level, and cultural background. To a considerable extent, the type of procedure employed also reflects the training and theoretical persuasion of the clinician, the available facilities, and other extraneous factors. The same behavioral symptoms may be treated quite differently by different therapists, and several types of therapy may be combined in treating a single individual. There are very few forms of treatment that are wholly specific to a given condition. Nevertheless, there is a growing number of clinical psychologists who follow an eclectic approach, choosing the particular form of therapy or combination of therapies to fit the needs of the individual client (see, e.g., Dimond, Havens, & Jones, 1978).

In the present chapter, the different types of intervention will be considered under five major headings: somatic therapies, individual psychotherapy, group therapies, behavior therapy, and community psychology.

SOMATIC THERAPIES

All somatic therapies are administered by a medical practitioner or under his or her immediate supervision. In the use of these therapies, psychologists may collaborate with physicians in several ways. The clinical psychologist may help in determining which patients are most likely to benefit from a particular therapy and in evaluating progress in the course of therapy. Often, psychotherapy, conducted by a psychologist, is combined with somatic therapy. In some cases, in fact, somatic therapy may be administered chiefly to make the patient more amenable to psychotherapy. Perhaps the most important contribution psychologists can make to the development of somatic therapies is in the area of research. The special methodological controls and experimental designs required in this type of research provide a fruitful field for the psychologically trained investigator. It is chiefly as background for some of the research problems to be considered in Chapter 14 that somatic therapies are introduced in this section.

Somatic therapies are themselves quite varied, being grouped together only because of their common medical nature (Suinn & Weigel, 1976). The introduction of a new somatic therapy usually arouses widespread optimism and exaggerated expectations, only to be followed by skepticism and a more sober evaluation. Some therapies that were popular in the 1950s have been largely replaced by newer techniques. In the practical application of any somatic therapy, one must consider the likelihood of undesirable side effects, of either a physiological or psychological nature. Some side effects have been demonstrated with all the commonly used somatic therapies, although the incidence and severity of such effects vary with the individual patient, the dosage level, and other circumstances. Little is known, however, about the specific patient variables that determine the rather pronounced individual differences found both in side effects and in responsiveness to the various somatic therapies. Among the major somatic therapies are psychosurgery, shock therapy, and the many therapies covered by the broad area of psychopharmacology.

Psychosurgery. The results of animal experiments on the extirpation of brain tissue, as well as the observation that human personality changes sometimes followed brain injuries or the removal of frontal lobe tumors, led some neuropsychiatrists to try brain surgery in the treatment of severe psychopathology (Brown, Wienckowski, & Bivens, 1973; Freeman & Watts, 1950; Hitchcock, Laitinen, & Vaernet, 1972). Psychosurgery is a general name for the application of surgical techniques to the brain in the absence of organic pathology. Several specific procedures have been developed for this purpose. The original technique, commonly known as "lobotomy," involved the severing of the corticothalamic tracts that connect the thalamus with the frontal lobes of the cerebral cortex. Later variations limited the operation to more narrowly circumscribed areas and employed simpler surgical procedures.

Various combinations of neurological and psychological mechanisms were proposed to account for the therapeutic effects of psychosurgery, but the evidence in support of any of these explanations is meager. Later, more precise research with animals suggested that this form of therapy may be most useful in controlling violent emotional outbursts and aggressive behavior (M. Goldstein, 1974). Through improved clinical techniques for investigating responses to cortical stimulation, it has proved possible to pinpoint the exact locus in the brain that controls the unwanted behavior in individual cases. Hence the lesion can be limited to a minute area.

There is still insufficient knowledge, however, about the variables associated with the relative effectiveness of psychosurgery with different persons. More information is also needed regarding the conditions determining the occurrence of adverse side effects, which may include memory defects and other cognitive or emotional disturbances. Today, psychosurgical techniques are considered only when other, less drastic forms of therapy have failed. It should also be noted that several professional associations and government agencies have been very active in developing ethical standards, guidelines, and review procedures to safeguard the rights and well-being of patients treated by psychosurgery (B. S. Brown et al., 1973).

Shock Therapy. Several forms of shock therapy for artificially inducing comatose or convulsive states have been tried from time to time. The specific techniques were usually suggested by accidental observations made either in the treatment of other disorders in human patients or in the course of animal experimentation. Although several hypotheses have been formulated to explain the rationale of such therapies, in either physiological or psychological terms, none has been conclusively established.

In *electroconvulsive therapy* (ECT), convulsive seizures are induced by passing an electric current through the cerebral cortex. The patient feels no pain, since the electric shock produces unconsciousness immediately. The seizure lasts about a minute, but the patient usually remains stuporous for about an hour. Treatments are generally administered several times a week, the total duration of the series depending upon the patient's response to treatment and the rate of improvement. ECT is used chiefly with cases in which depression is either the principal feature or a major symptom (Secunda et al., 1973). Confusion and memory loss are immediate effects of the treatments but lessen gradually. Whether there is any permanent cognitive loss as a result of ECT is difficult to ascertain because of inadequate controls in most investigations with human patients. Animal experiments, however, suggest that some permanent cognitive changes may occur. In the decision to utilize any somatic therapy, the therapist must weigh the possibility of permanent deleterious side effects against the chances that the patient will remain in a seriously disturbed condition or even deteriorate if untreated.

Psychopharmacology.[1] Drugs have been used in the treatment of psychological disorders in many ways and for a long time (Efron, 1968; Greenblatt, 1975; Iverson, Iverson, & Snyder, 1978; Uhr & Miller, 1960). Prior to the introduction of electroshock, several drugs were employed to induce convulsions. A different application of drugs is to be found in research on the nature of mental disorders. Data have been obtained both in animal experiments and in clinical observations of human patients. Certain drugs, when taken by normal individuals, produce temporary symptoms similar to those found in psychotic patients. Because they "mimic" psychotic symptoms, these drugs are sometimes described as *psychotomimetic.* Some of this research used lysergic acid diethylamide (LSD), which induces schizophrenic-like symptoms, including disturbances of perception and thought, hallucinations, and mood changes.

Among the *psychotherapeutic drugs*, those that have aroused the widest interest are undoubtedly the tranquilizers. The major tranquilizers (or antipsychotic drugs) are used in mental hospitals to calm hyperactive and aggressive patients. Generally they are also effective in reducing other typical psychotic behavior, such as delusions, hallucinations, disorders of thinking, and bizarre mannerisms.

The introduction of tranquilizers in the 1950s led to a sharp decline in the need for physical restraint, isolation, locked wards, and other traditional methods for controlling highly disturbed patients. Figure 13-1 shows the results of a five-year survey conducted in the state mental hospitals of New York. The findings are typical of those obtained in other American state hospitals following the introduction of tranquilizers. It will be seen that, as the number of patients put on tranquilizing drugs rises, the number requiring restraint drops sharply. Beginning in the second year of drug therapy, the total state hospital population also declined. This decline resulted from an increase in the number of patients discharged as improved, rather than from changes in number of admissions. Representing the first reversal in the rising trend of American state mental hospital populations, this finding was particularly dramatic.

While indicating that the introduction of tranquilizers into overcrowded and understaffed mental hospitals was undoubtedly a wise move, this type of survey fails to identify the specific factors that brought about the improvement. The investigators themselves pointed out that during the last three years of the survey conspicuous administrative changes were made in the state hospitals. That these changes were themselves of major therapeutic value is now generally recognized. Even prior to the official innovations in hospital organization and procedures, the use of tranquilizers probably affected the attitudes of the hospital staff toward the patients. As patients become easier to manage, the behavior of the hospital personnel toward them takes on more constructive and therapeutic qualities. It has been observed, in fact, that the administration of tranquilizers to mental hospital patients may improve the behavior of the staff as much as that of the patients (Ewalt, 1961, p. 39).

Surveys such as the one cited illustrate forcefully the distinction between

---

[1]Also known as "behavioral pharmacology," a term that is increasing in popularity.

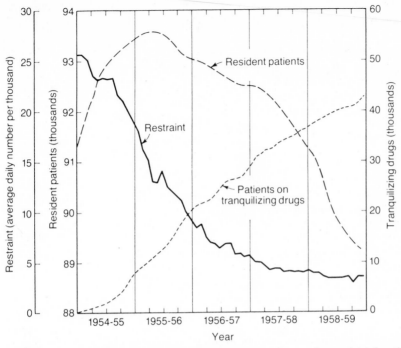

Figure 13-1. Trend in adoption of tranquilizers, use of restraint, and total patient population in New York State mental hospitals, 1954–1959. *(From Brill & Patton, 1959, p. 498. Copyright © 1959 by* American Journal of Psychiatry. *Reproduced by permission.)*

applied and basic research. Although the results are clear with regard to the introduction of tranquilizers within a specific context, with its peculiar complex of circumstances, they tell us little that can be generalized to other situations and other sets of circumstances. For the latter purpose, we need the more highly controlled experimental designs to be considered in Chapter 14. In this connection it is relevant to note that tranquilizers have failed to produce such dramatic effects in other countries where the shift to therapeutic environments in mental hospitals had antedated the advent of tranquilizers (Ewalt, 1961, p. 47; Trouton & Eysenck, 1961, pp. 681–682).

Even the most enthusiastic exponents of tranquilizers recognize that not all types of cases are helped by these drugs. Moreover, it is quite generally acknowledged that for maximum effectiveness tranquilizers need to be combined with some form of psychological intervention. Drug administration and dosage also need to be carefully adjusted to each individual case in order to minimize adverse side effects of both a medical and a behavioral nature.

Another group of psychotherapeutic drugs, sometimes called minor tranquilizers, are the antianxiety drugs. These are used chiefly with neurotic disorders. Still another category, the antidepressant drugs, have proved effective in the treatment of psychotic depressions (Secunda et al., 1973). Promising results have also been obtained with an antimanic drug, lithium carbonate (commonly called lithium). This drug not only helps in controlling the hyperactivity, flight of ideas, and other typical behavior of acute manic attacks but has also proved effective in preventing recurrence of manic episodes after discharge from the hospital (Prien, Caffey, & Klett, 1973).

Despite the waves of enthusiasm that have greeted each new somatotherapy, there is no one "miracle cure" for mental disorders. The various somatic therapies described above continue to be used with different cases, the choice of specific therapy depending upon the nature of the disorder, individual patient characteristics, and other circumstances. Several therapies may be tried in turn with the same individual. Since so many mental disorders originate in the individual's inability to cope with problems of daily life, somatic therapies are coming to be regarded more and more as adjuncts to psychotherapy. The psychoactive drugs, even more than earlier forms of somatic therapy, are used increasingly to render the withdrawn, uncommunicative, unresponsive, agitated, or aggressive patient accessible to psychotherapy. It should be borne in mind that to reduce the anxiety arising from unsolved problems is not in itself a solution.

INDIVIDUAL PSYCHOTHERAPY

General Characteristics. In the New York State certification law for psychologists, psychotherapy is defined as "the use of verbal methods in interpersonal relationships with the intent of assisting a person or persons to modify attitudes and behavior which are intellectually, socially, or emotionally maladaptive" (*Psychology*, 1967, p. 47). Elsewhere psychotherapy has been described as "a series of very specialized conversations with a skilled clinician" (Shaffer & Shoben, 1956, p. 514). To be sure, psychotherapy is not always strictly verbal, especially when applied to young children, but it always involves some means of communication between therapist and client.

Regardless of their theoretical persuasion, practically all clinical psychologists agree that the *interpersonal relationship* between therapist and client is an important element in psychotherapy—if not the most important. The personality of the clinician and his or her behavior toward the client during the session are thus an integral part of the therapeutic process. Typically, the client-therapist relationship can be characterized as concerned, nonthreatening, and accepting. In his interactions with the therapist, the individual gradually discovers that, no matter what he says, he will not be criticized, blamed, or rejected. The strict confidentiality observed also reassures him that his behavior during the therapy hour will lead to no aversive consequences in his daily life. The therapeutic relationship thus provides a "safe" situation in which the individual can try out new interpersonal behavior. In this respect, the clinician serves the same function as the training devices and simulators used in flight training. The learner can make mistakes without danger to himself. The client's interaction with the therapist helps him to understand his reactions to people in general and enables him to develop new ways of feeling and thinking about himself and others.

Psychotherapy can also be regarded as a *learning process*. Maladaptive responses are acquired through learning. Psychotherapy offers the individual a method for unlearning these responses and replacing them with new responses of a more adaptive nature. Several psychologists have tried to explain the process of psychotherapy in terms of learning principles (Bandura, 1961; Dollard & Miller,

1950; Mowrer, 1950; Shoben, 1949). Since psychologists differ in their theoretical orientation with regard to both learning and psychotherapy, no one explanation would find general acceptance. It should also be borne in mind that therapeutic procedures developed largely on an empirical basis; it was only later that theoretical rationales were formulated to support them. A few examples will suffice to illustrate how learning theory has been applied to psychotherapy.

A major goal of all psychotherapy is the overcoming of anxieties and the elimination of defenses built up against these anxieties in the form of behavioral symptoms. Within the context of a secure and emotionally satisfying therapeutic relationship, the client is encouraged to verbalize his anxieties and the situations that led to them. Talking about an anxiety-provoking situation approximates the experience of reliving it. The symbolic, verbal reinstatement of the situation arouses much of the anxiety associated with the situation itself. Through the processes of extinction and counterconditioning, the original responses to these situations tend to disappear and are replaced by the more positive affective responses of security and confidence aroused by the therapeutic situation. Through stimulus generalization, these newly acquired responses tend to be evoked by similar situations subsequently encountered outside of therapy. The individual may also develop a generalized learning set that will make him better able to solve emotional and interpersonal problems in the future.

In psychotherapy, timing is important. If too much anxiety is aroused early in therapy, conditioning may occur in the wrong direction. The therapeutic situation itself might thus become anxiety provoking and intolerable for the client. Anxiety must be aroused very gradually and only after a sufficiently secure therapeutic relationship has been established. As the client overcomes his initial anxiety and learns to cope with it, he can safely progress to a consideration of situations evoking more severe anxiety. As anxiety is reduced, the individual is able to examine his problems rationally and work out more effective ways of handling them.

In the course of therapy, the client's self-concept also tends to change in a favorable direction. Under the influence of the therapist's accepting attitude, the client experiences a growing sense of his own personal worth. Insofar as this response generalizes to other persons he encounters outside of the therapeutic situation, the client will exhibit more confidence and security in interpersonal relations. There is evidence to suggest that feelings of personal worth tend to be accompanied by a more favorable evaluation of others. These newly aroused attitudes on the client's part will in turn elicit more favorable responses from his associates. Hence a cycle of positive behavior and reinforcement is started in the individual's real-life experiences whereby the effects of therapy are further generalized.

Scope of Psychotherapy. Many clinical psychologists set a number of limitations upon the type of client they will accept for psychotherapy. The requirements vary considerably with the theoretical orientation of the therapist and the form of psychotherapy he or she practices. Because of the heavy reliance upon verbal communication in most types of psychotherapy, minimum educational and intellectual levels are often specified. Background factors that would affect the client's motivation for therapy are sometimes considered. The various indices for predicting response to therapy that were cited in Chapter 12 are also relevant in this connection. Psychotherapy has been traditionally employed with neurotics and with essentially normal persons who want help with some of their emotional problems. More recently, however, there has been a growing interest in the application of psychotherapy to schizophrenics and other severely disturbed cases. It will be recalled that somatic therapies have been used increasingly for the purpose of making psychotics accessible to psychotherapy.

Surveys of the relationship between type of therapy employed and client variables have consistently shown that *socioeconomic level* is an important factor. The higher the individual's socioeconomic level, the greater are his or her chances of being accepted for psychotherapy in outpatient clinics and of continuing in therapy (Baekeland & Lundwall, 1975; Lorion, 1973, 1974). These differences remain even when cost, availability of therapists, and similar extraneous factors are ruled out. Since socioeconomic level is itself related to educational level, the latter undoubtedly accounts in part for the more limited use of psychotherapy by persons at lower socioeconomic levels. Another contributing factor is the discrepancy between the socioeconomic levels of therapist and client. The more similar the client's and therapist's cultural background are, the easier it will be for the therapist to understand and communicate with the client. The concept of assumed similarity discussed in Chapter 12 may be recalled in this connection. Still another reason is to be found in the motivations, attitudes, and expectations of persons with different experiential backgrounds. Motivation for therapy will tend to be higher when the client has more to look forward to in terms of vocational achievement, social status, and other tangible rewards of improved personal effectiveness.

Upper-middle-class clients are also more likely to respond favorably to the predominantly verbal and introspective nature of most psychotherapeutic techniques and to accept such goals as self-understanding and tracing the origins of their difficulties. Persons from other cultural backgrounds are often puzzled and disappointed by traditional psychotherapy. They are more likely to expect either a physical remedy for their difficulties or an immediate practical solution for a specific problem of daily life. They may also expect the therapist to assume a more active role in giving advice than is characteristic of most psychotherapists (Baekeland & Lundwall, 1975; Hollingshead & Redlich, 1958, Ch. 11; Padilla, Ruiz, & Alvarez, 1975). For cultural minorities and other clients with diverse educational and cultural backgrounds, other forms of therapy, to be discussed later in this chapter, are frequently more successful.

Two further points should be noted, however. First, lower-class clients are by no means homogeneous; they exhibit wide individual differences in response to therapy. Those who overcome sociocultural pressures to drop out do show good success rate from therapy (Lorion, 1974). Second, there is evidence that preparatory orientation techniques regarding client and therapist role expectations reduce dropout rate and lead to greater improvement from therapy (Heitler, 1976).

Because children have difficulty in verbalizing their emotional problems, *play therapy* is often employed in either individual or group forms (Ginnott, 1961). In the play session, the child has an opportunity to act out his anxieties, hostilities, aggressions, and other disturbing feelings. Among the media utilized for this purpose are puppets, dolls, toy furniture, clay, sand, and finger paints. Therapy sessions are usually conducted in a room that is as indestructibly furnished as possible, and the child is allowed to do what he wishes, within broad limits. Through an accepting and nonthreatening manner, the therapist establishes a warm, secure interpersonal relationship with the child, just as is done in the verbal interaction with adult clients. In this safe context, the child obtains emotional release from his manipulations of the play materials. With the aid of interpretations or clarification by the therapist, the child may also gain insight into his own motives and feelings.

A conspicuous recent trend is the growing utilization of *brief psychotherapy*. Introduced in response to the expanding demands for psychotherapy and the pressure of long waiting lists, short-term intervention techniques have proved effective in treating a wide range of emotional disturbances (Barten, 1971; Bellak & Small, 1965; Small, 1971). The actual time covered by short-term psychotherapy varies with the type of therapy, the nature of the problem, and other circumstances. The intervention could involve a single contact; more likely, 10 to 15 sessions may be required, and the upper limit is well over 100 sessions. Many different procedures have been adapted for this purpose, representing a variety of theoretical orientations. In general, however, brief psychotherapy concentrates on treating immediate psychological problems, rather than trying to restructure the individual's personality.

Among the goals of short-term psychotherapy is early intervention to prevent the development of more serious disturbances. Its procedures are particularly appropriate for emergency and crisis intervention. Although also employed in private practice, brief psychotherapy is especially characteristic of the services provided in community mental health centers. It is being used increasingly to meet the needs of cultural minorities and economically underprivileged clients.

Thus far, we have concentrated on common features of psychotherapy. Even these features, however, are more characteristic of some forms of psychotherapy than of other forms. In the field of psychotherapy, "schools" still thrive. There are currently many varieties of psychotherapy, each with its loyal adherents (Bergin & Strupp, 1972; Corsini, 1973). It is heartening to note, however, that the trend is toward eclecticism. Well-trained clinical psychologists recognize that different forms of psychotherapy may be required for different clients and that no one form is universally to be preferred. In a survey of the members of the APA Division of Clinical Psychology, 55% of those engaged in psychotherapy described their orientation as "eclectic" (Garfield & Kurtz, 1976). Like its clients, psychotherapy itself becomes better integrated as it grows toward maturity.

To illustrate more fully what psychotherapists do, we shall briefly examine in the next sections two of the best known theoretical orientations of clinical psychology, namely psychoanalysis and client-centered therapy. The influence of these two approaches has permeated most current forms of psychotherapy.

Psychoanalysis. The theory and techniques of psychoanalysis originated during the last quarter of the nineteenth century in the work of Sigmund Freud, a Viennese physician who became interested in the treatment of emotional problems. Freud's approach to these problems still provides the general framework for psychoanalysis, although many changes in specific therapeutic procedures and in theoretical rationale have been introduced. The principal object of psychoanalysis is to uncover repressed impulses and forgotten experiences that are believed to underlie present behavioral symptoms. The client is thereby given an insight into possible causes of his maladaptive behavior. He is also enabled to relive emotionally the incidents in which the repression occurred. As he becomes aware of his repressed impulses in a context of reduced anxiety, he is able to bring them under rational control. In the classical psychoanalysis of Freud, the origins of emotional difficulties were traced to early childhood experiences. Among neoanalysts, the causes of symptoms are more often sought in the individual's present interpersonal relations. Partly for this reason, the newer psychoanalytic therapies generally require less time than classic psychoanalysis, a condition which makes them applicable to a wider range of clients.

Among the special techniques employed by psychoanalysts are free association and dream analysis. In the former, the client is asked to report everything that comes to mind; nothing is to be held back, however irrelevant, absurd, or embarrassing it may seem. To facilitate such free association, the client traditionally reclined on a couch, with the analyst seated outside his field of vision. Today the procedure is often more flexible: the client may sit, lie down, or walk around as he wishes. Although the couch has remained the symbol of psychoanalysis in popular thinking, some contemporary analysts have discarded it altogether. Dream analysis is utilized by psychoanalysts as another source of cues to unconscious or repressed impulses, which, they maintain, appear in dreams in disguised and symbolic form. The dreams reported by the client may be interpreted directly by the analyst in terms of common psychoanalytic symbols, or they may serve as the starting point for further free association by the client.

With regard to the client-therapist relationship, psychoanalysts emphasize the process of transference. By "transference" is meant that in the course of therapy the client identifies the therapist with a parent or some other important person in his life and projects upon the therapist the emotions he feels toward that person. These feelings may be positive, such as dependence and love, or negative, such as hostility and antagonism. The therapist uses the transference relationship as a device to help the client relive his earlier emotional experiences. As the treatment progresses, the transference itself is gradually terminated by explaining its source to the client.

It is apparent that active interpretation by the therapist is a major feature of psychoanalysis. The analyst interprets the client's dreams, his casual remarks and slips of the tongue, the apparently irrelevant content of his free associations, and the feelings the client expresses toward the analyst. When resistance is encountered in free association, the analyst interprets it as evidence of repression and calls the client's attention to the defenses he is using against anxiety-provoking content. By bringing together disparate bits of information that the client provides, the analyst offers him an explanation of the source of his symptoms. In building up such an explanation, the psychoanalyst asks probing questions to elicit additional facts. All too often the inquiry may take the form of what Sarbin and his associates describe as "soliciting" rather than "probing" (see Ch. 12). There is thus a strong likelihood that the resulting explanation will reflect the psychoanalyst's theoretical views more closely than it does the personality dynamics of the particular client.

Different schools of psychoanalysis quickly emerged, each with its theoretical and procedural variations, its recognized leader, and its highly partisan protagonists. The entire psychoanalytic movement flourished during the first half of the twentieth century, to the extent that the term "psychoanalysis" was often used as a synonym for "psychotherapy." Today, the popularity of psychoanalysis has waned conspicuously (see, e.g., Davids, 1975). In a survey of the APA Division of Clinical Psychology (Garfield & Kurtz, 1976), only about 11% of the respondents described their theoretical orientation as psychoanalytic; this percentage rose to 19 if certain later adaptations were included.

Among the reasons for the decline of psychoanalysis are the duration and resulting expense of the treatment, which exceed those of any other form of psychotherapy. In addition, the cultural milieu in which psychoanalysis originated was quite dissimilar from that in which most clinical psychologists operate today. Consequently, its approach is less appropriate for the types of clients and problems now encountered. Currently the influence of psychoanalysis is surviving largely in the insights and concepts incorporated in other forms of psychotherapy.

Client-centered Therapy. Also known as "nondirective counseling," client-centered therapy was first described in 1942 by Carl R. Rogers, an American psychologist (Rogers, 1942, 1951, 1961). In contrast to psychoanalysis, client-centered therapy reduces interpretation by the therapist to a minimum. The basic postulate of client-centered therapy is that individuals have the capacity to identify the sources of their emotional problems and to work out effective solutions, once they are freed from disabling anxieties and feelings of insecurity. To accomplish this goal, client-centered therapists establish a permissive, accepting, nonthreatening therapeutic relationship. They refrain from probing, interpreting, advising, persuading, or suggesting. They serve the function of active listeners, trying to understand fully what the client says and feels, and making every effort to perceive situations from the client's point of view.

An important part of the therapist's task is to reflect and clarify the client's feelings by restating the client's remarks. This clarification of feeling is illustrated in the following excerpt from a recorded interview with a 20-year-old woman. The excerpt begins near the end of the first interview (Snyder, 1947, pp. 140–141).[2]

> **Cl.** I don't know whether that's exactly right or not. I can't put my finger on it. Sometimes I feel lonely and sometimes I feel another way. Do you have cases this bad?
> **Th.** You really wonder whether anybody else could be—
> **Cl.** I think I'm worse than anybody that I know. That's just it. I feel as though I am terribly, terribly low. It just does not seem worth—bothering with it, it doesn't seem worthwhile, that I can't get up there to first base.
> **Th.** You think about making the struggle, but it doesn't seem possible.
> **Cl.** That's right. I just wonder what other people do when they find problems and stuff. I just wonder whether they see it through or try to find out something else.
> **Th.** You feel that you'd like to know how somebody else would handle it.

Through systematic analyses of recorded interviews, client-centered therapists have conducted extensive research on the therapeutic process itself. These studies indicate that in the course of client-centered therapy there is an increase in the number of statements showing insight and self-understanding, as well as in statements regarding client plans and decisions. Similarly, a comparison of early and late therapeutic sessions shows an increase in number of statements expressing positive attitudes toward self and a decrease in statements expressing negative attitudes toward self. The individual's self-concept comes to resemble his or her

[2]Cl. stands for "client," Th. for "therapist." Copyright 1947 by Houghton Mifflin Company. Reproduced by permission.

ideal concept more closely in the course of therapy. Acceptance of others and respect for others also increase with the growing acceptance of oneself. The methodology of these studies and their broader implications regarding the effectiveness of therapy will be considered in Chapter 14.

In the previously cited survey of clinical psychologists (Garfield & Kurtz, 1976), less than 2% of the respondents characterized their theoretical orientation as Rogerian. In our contemporary culture, this approach shares some of the drawbacks of psychoanalysis. It appeals to highly verbal clients interested in exploring their own thoughts and feelings and willing to accept a nondirective therapist. Like psychoanalysis, however, this form of therapy has left its mark on the broad category of eclectic psychotherapists. From another angle, the Rogerian approach is identified with so-called *humanistic psychology*, which permeates several of the more recently developed therapies (Burton, 1967; Page, 1975, pp. 128–134). This rather vaguely identified orientation emphasizes the importance of subjective experience, self-actualization, and the individual's responsibility for directing his or her own life. Among the emotional disorders of particular interest to humanistic psychotherapists is existential neurosis, considered to be especially prevalent in contemporary society. This condition is characterized by alienation and a sense of the futility and meaninglessness of one's life. The humanistic orientation is prominent in some forms of group therapy, to be discussed in the next section.

GROUP THERAPY AND OTHER GROUP-RELATED PROCEDURES

Traditional Group Psychotherapy. Although group activities and group discussions were utilized therapeutically in different settings since the beginning of the century, the widespread adoption of current methods of group psychotherapy dates from the 1950s (Kaplan & Sadock, 1971). First introduced as a means of coping with a shortage of therapists, group therapy was soon seen to have a number of intrinsic advantages. In its most usual form, it has much in common with individual psychotherapy. A group of 5 to 10 persons meet once or twice a week for several months to discuss their emotional problems. The therapist, who serves as discussion leader, tries to create a permissive atmosphere that reduces resistance and defensiveness. Each participant describes his own experiences and difficulties as he feels inclined and comments upon the experiences of other group members. An informal atmosphere is maintained, with group members sitting around a table or in some other casual grouping.

Most persons are eventually able to relive emotionally charged experiences as well in group therapy as they can in individual therapy—and sometimes better. Recognizing that others have similar problems enables them to consider their own problems more objectively. Participation in group therapy helps to break down feelings of isolation so common among emotionally disturbed persons. It provides opportunities to try out interpersonal behavior. And it enables each person to test his or her perceptions against those of others and to correct distortions and maladaptive behavior through feedback from other members of the group.

To ensure maximal effectiveness, participants in group therapy are usually screened for various characteristics, and groups are assembled with special reference to age and sex distribution, type of problems, and other relevant variables. Group therapy may be employed exclusively or in combination with individual psychotherapy. When the two approaches are combined, they may run parallel, or individual psychotherapy may be used in advance to prepare the client for group therapy.

There are fully as many varieties of group as of individual psychotherapy. The therapist may play a very active role in steering discussion and interpreting member reactions; or he may be nondirective, limiting his remarks to acceptance, restatement of content, and clarification of feelings. Psychoanalytically oriented group therapists utilize transference reactions, which develop not only toward the therapist but also toward other group members.

Psychodrama. A long-established variety of group therapy is psychodrama (Moreno, 1971, 1975). In this technique, the client acts out unrehearsed parts on a stage, with other clients in the audience. The therapist usually assigns roles, directs the performance, and interprets the individual's behavior. Supporting parts are played by therapeutic assistants or by other clients. The individual may play himself in realistic situations from his daily life; he may play the roles of other persons in his life, such as his father; or he may improvise imagined roles. Psychodrama is designed to provide emotional release as well as self-insight. Role playing is a simplified version of psychodrama which does not require a theatrical setting or special props. It is used with clinical groups, as well as in certain types of training, some of which were illustrated in Chapter 4.

Personal Development Groups. A conspicuous popular movement of the 1960s and 1970s was the emergence of a diversity of personal development groups known by such names as encounter, growth, sensitivity, training (T), and marathon groups (Burton, 1970; Gottschalk & Davidson, 1971; Suinn & Weigel, 1975). Although they frequently include some emotionally disturbed persons, most of these groups are directed to essentially normal persons seeking to develop their "human potential" and live fuller lives. Persons who feel alienated, lonely, or bored are among those attracted to such programs, along with those having more specific emotional difficulties they wish to overcome. The use of sensitivity groups to improve interpersonal skills was cited in Chapter 4 in connection with management training.

Although varying widely in procedures, most of the personal development groups identify with a humanistic-existential orientation. Within this rather amorphous and vaguely defined framework, the various groups set up such objectives as self-fulfillment, self-acceptance, uninhibited emotional expression, heightened awareness of sensory experience, and openness and trust in interpersonal relations. The actual programs fall short of these goals, and many of the techniques are of questionable value. Although personal development groups may make a significant contribution to human well-being in our contemporary culture, most of them arouse rather unrealistic expectations. Evidence of their effectiveness is meager and was generally obtained under inadequately controlled conditions that preclude clear interpretation of results (Kilmann & Sotile, 1976). Moreover, adverse effects, ranging from weakened self-confidence to psychotic episodes, have been reported in an appreciable proportion of cases (Hartley, Roback, & Abramowitz, 1976; Lieberman, Yalono, & Miles, 1973).

The need for informing and protecting participants in personal development groups is widely recognized. Within this context, the American Psychological Association (1973) prepared a set of guidelines for psychologists conducting growth groups. These guidelines address themselves to three major requirements:

(1) the sort of advance information that group leaders should give prospective participants; (2) the need to screen participants to ensure that the particular group experience offered is appropriate for the individual and not likely to harm her or him; and (3) the qualifications of group leaders relative to the type of groups they conduct (e.g., psychotherapeutic, educational, social-recreational). It should be noted that a number of growth groups are conducted by laymen who would not be reached or influenced by such professional guidelines. In most groups, the leaders are called trainers or facilitators, rather than therapists or psychologists. Hence their activities are not subject to regulation by available state licensing or certification laws.

Self-help Groups for Special Problems. Another type of group is organized around a specific goal, shared by all its members. A long-standing and well-known example is Alcoholics Anonymous, together with the parallel groups organized for spouses and for teenage children of alcoholics. Similar groups have been established for the control of drug addiction, gambling, smoking, and obesity. Still other groups have been formed by former mental hospital patients and by ex-prisoners. Such groups are typically peer-organized and peer-managed. Persons with a common problem meet periodically for mutual support and sharing of experiences; often there are also provisions for member contacts on a crisis or emergency basis. Other specific activities included in the programs vary widely with the nature of the problem—and even among different organizations devoted to the same problem, as illustrated by the diverse groups available for drug addicts. Professionally trained leaders may or may not be involved in these programs, some of which employ various psychotherapeutic techniques (see, e.g., Bassin, 1975).

Family Therapy. In contrast to group therapy, which utilizes group techniques to alter the individual's feelings and behavior, family therapy is directed toward improving the functioning of the family group (Bowen, 1971; Erickson & Hogan, 1972; Guerin, 1976; Minuchin, 1974). Applying a systems approach, the family therapist recognizes that altering the behavior of any family member will affect the behavior of other members, as well as the operating effectiveness of the whole family unit, or system. A program of family therapy may include various combinations of individual psychotherapy with different family members; conjoint therapy, in which spouses (or parents and children) meet together with one or two therapists; and group family therapy in which, for example, several couples may meet together to talk about their problems and learn from the feedback they receive from other couples, as in the typical group therapy situation. Several families with children may likewise meet in group sessions.

The practice of family therapy, a rapidly growing specialty in clinical psychology, serves several functions. It is obviously appropriate in the solution of marital problems; it is an essential component of child therapy; and it is a valuable adjunct to the treatment of any individual, insofar as the family constitutes a major part of the real-life environment in which that individual must function. Family therapy can play a significant part in the return of a hospitalized patient to community living. The chances of successful rehabilitation are increased by a favorable family environment, which provides understanding and support while discouraging dependence and a continuation of the sick role.

The techniques employed by family therapists reflect the usual diversity of theoretical approaches. Among the most common are programs to clarify and improve interpersonal communication and programs designed to alter specific family roles and behaviors. Family therapy is making increasing use of the various techniques of behavior modification, to be considered in the next section (Jacobson & Martin, 1976). Crisis intervention is another growing facet of family therapy, especially when conducted through community-based centers.

BEHAVIOR THERAPY

General Characteristics. Although employing a wide diversity of techniques, behavior therapy is essentially the systematic application of learning principles to therapeutic intervention. Its roots can be identified in early experiments on the acquisition and elimination of children's fears conducted by John B. Watson and his co-workers (M. C. Jones, 1974; Watson & Watson, 1921). Its subsequent development can be traced through several decades of basic research on learning and personality theory. Since the 1960s, there has been a sharp upsurge of interest in behavior therapy, and its procedures have been incorporated in the practice of clinical psychology in a wide variety of settings. At the same time, behavior therapy has gradually broadened to include an ever-widening repertory of intervention techniques. Various types of cognitive therapies have been included in behavior therapy programs, and there is increasing evidence of a merging of cognitive and behavioral approaches (Goldfried & Davison, 1976; Lazarus, 1971, 1976, 1977; Mahoney, 1974, 1977; Rimm & Masters, 1974, Ch. 10).

A distinctive feature of behavior therapy programs is their detailed specification of objectives. Such specifications should include a precise description of the desired target behavior. For example, a target behavior for a withdrawn schizophrenic might be that he converse with his associates and respond to them in other appropriate ways. In addition, more immediate subgoals are set up as a sequence of graded steps, beginning with the most readily attainable behavior, such as "glances at person speaking to him," "nods," or "utters one word." It will be recalled that the specification of performance objectives and the appropriate sequencing of learning steps are important guidelines to follow in all programs of training and performance improvement (Chs. 4 & 6).

The specific techniques of behavior therapy utilize many types of learning, including both classical and operant conditioning, observational and imitative learning, role playing, rehearsal, and verbal feedback. Such conditioning concepts as stimulus generalization, extinction, counterconditioning, and contingent reinforcement are commonly encountered in the behavior therapy literature. Stimuli may be presented in vivo (e.g., a real dog in the room, a stranger with whom the client tries to converse) or through imagery (e.g., imagine yourself handling a live snake; imagine yourself studying the night before an important exam).

Behavior therapy has been successfully employed at all age levels and with persons of diverse educational and cultural backgrounds. It has been used with schizophrenics, juvenile delinquents, and mental retardates, as well as with highly sophisticated adult clients. In its various forms, it has proved effective in the elimination of a wide variety of unwanted feelings and behaviors, such as phobias, anxiety in public speaking, enuresis, alcoholism, and overeating; and in the acquisition and improvement of desirable behaviors, such as self-assertion and interpersonal skills. The procedures followed in behavior therapy frequently combine different techniques and draw upon several learning principles. The available techniques, variants, and combinations are quite numerous. For surveys of these techniques and of the types of problems to which they have been applied, the reader is referred to such sources as Franks (1969), Mikulas (1972), Rimm and Masters (1974), and Suinn & Weigel (1975). As illustrations, four widely used procedures are described in the following sections.

Systematic Desensitization. A major application of the principles of classical, or respondent, conditioning is to be found in systematic desensitization (Rimm & Masters, 1974, Ch. 2; Wolpe, 1973). Although successfully employed in treating a variety of problems, this procedure is most commonly used in overcoming abnormal fears and anxiety. It involves essentially three processes. First, the client is taught *progressive muscle relaxation,* usually by a method based on the early work of Jacobson (1938). Second, an *anxiety hierarchy* is constructed jointly by client and therapist. In this process, representative stimulus situations are chosen and arranged in rank order from least to most anxiety-arousing. For example, in the case of a fear of dogs, the situations could range from looking through a closed window at a quiet dog being walked on a leash to being alone in a room with a lively, unrestrained dog. At this stage, the client may also be given practice in visualizing the relevant situations clearly and vividly, since imagined scenes are frequently employed in the actual desensitization. The third step is *countercondi-tioning,* whereby the relaxation response is associated with the feared or anxiety-arousing stimulus. In this process, it is important to begin with the mildest situation and proceed to the next item in the hierarchy only when the respondent reports little or no anxiety. The object, of course, is to replace the anxiety response with the incompatible relaxation response.

Systematic desensitization has been the subject of extensive research (Franks, 1969, Chs. 2–4). One question concerns the operation of counterconditioning and extinction in anxiety reduction. Controlled experiments have shown that the complete desensitization procedure, including the pairing of relaxation with the successive items in the anxiety hierarchy, is more effective than exposure to the anxiety hierarchy alone. Nor is relaxation training alone as effective as the complete procedure. It has been suggested, however, that relaxation may serve merely to facilitate the person's exposure to stimuli that would otherwise be found intolerable. The probable contribution of operant conditioning has also been noted, insofar as therapist attention and approval reinforce the reduction of reported anxiety. Moreover, anxiety reduction provides intrinsic reinforcement through self-observed improvement, and this self-reinforcement continues outside the clinic situation. It should also be noted that the effects of suggestion and nonspecific treatment expectancies have not been adequately ruled out in most studies of the outcome of desensitization therapy (Kazdin & Wilcoxon, 1976). This methodological point will be considered more fully in Chapter 14.

Whatever the underlying mechanisms, however, outcome studies of systematic desensitization have reported an impressive array of positive results. Both case studies and experimental investigations provide extensive evidence for the genera-lization of effects from imagined to real-life stimuli and from the clinic to extratherapeutic settings, as well as for the retention of effects after therapy is discontinued. There is also evidence that successful desensitization may be associated with a generalized reduction in anxiety and improvement in overall adjustment.

Contingency Management. Involving the carefully planned application of operant conditioning principles (Skinner, 1953), contingency management resembles most closely the behavior modification procedures employed in industrial settings (Chs. 4–6). It involves essentially the systematic provision of response-contingent reinforcement, thereby increasing the likelihood that the desired responses will be repeated (Franks, 1969, Ch. 5; Rimm & Masters, 1974, Ch. 5). For example, a solitary, lonely preschool child can be "rewarded" by friendly attention from the teacher whenever he approaches another child or makes any effort to join in social play. By making such reinforcement contingent upon the desired responses— however minimal and rudimentary—the child's behavior is gradually shaped in the direction of the target behavior.

It should be noted that giving the child special attention when he remains alone and avoids contact with others (as is often done) serves only to reinforce the unwanted isolate behavior. The crux of contingency management is that reinforcement is employed systematically, with full awareness of its effects, rather than haphazardly. The withholding or reduction of reinforcement can likewise be utilized in the elimination of undesirable behavior, such as temper tantrums. Contingency management is often implemented by training parents, teachers, institutional personnel, or other persons in the client's naturalistic environment to act as adjunct therapists.

A form of contingency management that is being employed increasingly in many settings is the *token economy* (Ayllon & Azrin, 1968; Franks, 1969, Ch. 6; Kazdin, 1977; Rimm & Masters, 1974, Ch. 6). In this procedure, a system is set up whereby desired behaviors are rewarded with tokens (or points recorded on a card, or some other convenient symbol), which may be exchanged for goods or privileges. The tokens thus serve as "money" which the individual may spend to obtain desired rewards or reinforcers. Token economies have proved effective in the home, in school, in community centers, and in residential facilities for delinquents, mental retardates, and mentally disturbed persons. Encouraging results have been obtained, for example, with chronic schizophrenics in such areas as self-care, verbal communication, interpersonal behavior, and occupational training.

When employed in an institutional setting, token economies are often incorporated in a therapeutic community, as part of a coordinated *milieu therapy* (Fairweather, 1964; Freedman et al., 1975, pp. 1990–1995; Rapoport, 1961). In sharp contrast to the predominantly custodial atmosphere of earlier institutions, milieu therapy is an attempt to utilize all the individual's daily experiences for therapeutic purposes. Considerable emphasis is placed on the cooperation of all personnel who may come in contact with patients, from the director of the institution to ward attendants and janitors. The attitudes of staff members toward patients is a major aspect of milieu therapy.

Activity on the part of patients is likewise stressed in a therapeutic environment. Patients are encouraged to keep busy in self-care, occupational training, and a variety of recreational activities. The content and nature of the activity program should be adapted to the needs and characteristics of the individual. For some, a highly structured environment with rigid schedules may be desirable; for others, maximum freedom in the choice and scheduling of activities may be most effective. Treating each patient as an individual and boosting morale by improving the patient's own appearance and that of the surroundings are additional aspects of milieu therapy. Increasing emphasis is also being placed on patient government, through regular group discussions, committees, and other techniques for patient participation in planning and decision making. Another relevant feature is the establishment of small residential facilities in a community setting, in contrast to the large and relatively isolated state mental hospital (Fairweather, Sanders, Maynard, Cressler, & Black, 1969).

Modeling and Related Techniques. Derived largely from the research of Bandura (1969) and other social-learning theorists, modeling is a procedure for vicarious learning through observation and imitation of others (Rimm & Masters, 1974, Ch. 4). The model may be presented live, on film, or even as a cartoon character. The behavior observed includes overt motor responses and verbalizations in the relevant situation and is usually reinforced. The reinforcement, however, need not be external but may consist of a clear expression of pleasure and satisfaction on the part of the model following the performance of the desired behavior. In either case, the observer receives vicarious reinforcement by watching the model.

As a technique of behavior therapy, modeling is most effective when the required response is not in the client's repertoire or when it rarely occurs spontaneously. In general, modeling is more successful when model and observer are not too dissimilar in such characteristics as age, sex, and initial status with regard to the target behavior. In treating a child's dog phobia, for example, a film of a child approaching a dog slowly and then displaying obvious pleasure when petting the animal would be more appropriate than one of an adult engaging in vigorous play with an exuberantly active dog.

Modeling is often used in conjunction with other techniques, such as systematic desensitization, relaxation training, coaching by the therapist, role playing by client and therapist, and rehearsal of the desired behavior in real-life situations. The combination of modeling with some of these techniques is illustrated by training in self-assertiveness (McFall & Lillesand, 1971; McFall & Twentyman, 1973; Rich & Schroeder, 1976; Rimm & Masters, 1974, Ch. 3). The goal of assertiveness training is the appropriate expression of feeling in ways that protect the individual's rights without humiliating or demeaning other persons. Effective self-assertion avoids the extremes of timidity and submission, on the one hand, and aggression or devious means of control, on the other. It focuses on honest, forthright communication combined with sensitivity for the feelings of others. Apart from protecting the individual against exploitation, the cultivation of assertiveness helps to eliminate several forms of undesirable interpersonal behavior. Examples include accumulated resentment against a family member or other close associate, self-pity and the "martyr" role, and behavior designed to induce guilt feelings in others. Assertive training also tends to inhibit anxiety and promote a feeling of well-being.

Self-control. Little-known prior to the mid-1960s, self-control training as a form of behavior therapy has shown dramatic growth. The sharp upsurge of interest in this approach is illustrated by the appearance of texts and manuals on behavior change through self-control procedures (Glasgow & Rosen, 1978; Goldfried & Merbaum, 1973; Thoresen & Mahoney, 1974; Watson & Tharp, 1972) and by recent national and international conferences devoted to this topic (W. A. Hunt, 1973; Stuart, 1977). Among the problems to which such techniques have most frequently been applied are overeating and obesity, smoking, excessive drinking, inability to study, and difficulties in social contacts. Although several behavior therapy techniques are applicable to self-control, the most common approach is based on the principles of operant conditioning (Rimm & Masters, 1974, Ch. 7). Within this framework, self-control can be defined as the systematic management of environmental circumstances and response-contingent reinforcements by the clients themselves.

Self-control programs are especially useful when the individual's environment provides no immediate, potent reinforcers for the desired behavior change. This condition is likely to hold when the desired behavior yields long-term rewards, while the alternative behavior to be replaced offers some immediate gratifications. Self-control programs may be combined with other procedures, such as systematic desensitization, modeling, role playing, rehearsal, and direct instruction by therapist (e.g., diet planning, tips on efficient studying).

In a typical self-control training program, the therapist begins by giving the client a general orientation regarding the nature of the program and the relevant learning principles. It is important at this stage to explain that self-control is not a matter of "willpower" but is achieved through the effective management of stimulus situations and response contingencies in the everyday environment. The second step is the establishment of a baseline for the target behavior, covering a period of a week or two prior to any intervention. Systematic record keeping is begun during this period. The record should show frequency and duration of the behavior in question, circumstances under which it occurs, and other pertinent details. It is noteworthy that this self-monitoring itself is often accompanied by some improvement in target behavior.

The third step involves the preparation of the training program jointly by therapist and client. The program usually includes changes in the stimulus environment (e.g., studying alone rather than with friends), identifying alternative competing responses (e.g., taking a walk instead of having an afternoon snack), selecting effective immediate rewards for self-reinforcement, setting a realistic terminal goal, and specifying easily attainable small steps for reaching that goal. In the fourth step, the program is put into practice. Self-monitoring and record keeping continue, together with periodic meetings with the therapist to review progress and alter procedures when necessary.

Both case reports and experimental studies have yielded promising results regarding the efficacy of self-control procedures. The data with regard to obesity control are especially encouraging. In general, however, more research is needed for an adequate evaluation of this approach. A word of caution should also be added regarding the rapidly proliferating do-it-yourself behavior therapy programs, as well as other self-help techniques, administered without professional consultation (Goldiamond, 1976; Rosen, 1976). These programs, in the form of printed manuals, sound recordings, and other instructional materials, are often marketed prior to empirical validation. Consequently, their effectiveness cannot be assumed.

A significant trend in all behavior therapy, but more particularly in self-control therapy, is a broadening of both theoretical orientation and implementation, manifested in at least two ways. First, behavioral and cognitive approaches are gradually being merged, with the increasing introduction of verbal and ideational procedures for the self-control of behavior. Second, the target of behavior modification is shifting from the elimination or enhancement of narrowly defined behaviors to the development of broadly applicable coping skills and what has been termed "stress inoculation" training (Meichenbaum, 1976). It might also be noted that some research has been done on a behavioral analysis of Zen meditation practices, their relation to behavioral self-control procedures, and possible ways of combining the two approaches (Shapiro & Zifferblatt, 1976).

COMMUNITY PSYCHOLOGY

Nature and Origins. Contemporary community psychology is a broad and as yet loosely defined area of professional activity that cuts across clinical and social psychology. In its general orientation, it touches many other fields, including social work, economics, political science, public administration, and urban planning, among others. In dealing with human problems, it may utilize elements or adaptations of any of the intervention procedures described in this chapter, together with several newly developing approaches. Conversely, it has had an impact on the practice of clinical psychology as a whole and is thus reflected in various ways in the content of these three chapters.

Among the influences contributing to the emergence of community psychology was the mounting dissatisfaction with the large state mental hospitals, which traditionally had been so organized as to serve principally a custodial rather than a therapeutic function. With their overcrowding and understaffing, their emphasis upon security and restraint, and their deadening inactivity, such institutions often contributed to the deterioration of chronic cases in the back wards. Sitting idly on benches from morning till night is not therapeutic. The longer persons remain in such a psychological vacuum, the farther they retreat from reality. The widespread introduction of psychotherapeutic drugs in the 1950s helped pave the way for altering the nature of mental hospitals and for returning more patients to community living. Tranquilizing drugs undoubtedly contributed significantly to the ensuing improvement in both staff attitudes and administrative practices. It should be noted, however, that tranquilizers were introduced in American hospitals at a time when the mental health professions were ready for the many procedural innovations that were facilitated by these drugs.

Another significant event was the enactment of the Mental Health Study Act of 1955 by the Congress of the United States and its implementation by the Joint Commission on Mental Illness and Health (Ewalt, 1961). With the help of 36 participating organizations representing many disciplines, this commission conducted extensive investigations of the country's mental health problems and available resources for meeting them. On this basis, the commission submitted a set of recommendations for action. Although incorporating many features now identified with community psychology, the Joint Commission report still followed the disease model and focused on the treatment of major mental dysfunctions. Its chief practical consequence was the enactment of the Community Mental Health Centers Act of 1963, providing for the establishment of community mental health facilities (Smith & Hobbs, 1966).

While these various influences were contributing to the "mental health movement," a number of psychologists were evolving a much broader approach to the enhancement of human well-being. To identify this approach, the term "community psychology" was introduced in 1965 at the Boston Conference on the education of psychologists for community mental health (Bennett, 1965; Bennett et al., 1966). Spearheaded largely by the participants at this conference, the APA Division of Community Psychology was established in 1967, thus providing more visibility for this emerging professional specialty. Within the next decade, community psychology underwent vigorous growth and achieved a distinct identity, as exemplified by the 1975 National Conference on Training in Community Psychology (Iscoe, 1975; Iscoe, Bloom, & Spielberger, 1977).

Major Objectives. Community psychology shares many features with the community mental health movement, especially as these features were presented in the Joint Commission report (Ewalt, 1961). But community psychology is broader in scope, reorders its priorities and emphases, and tends to reject the medical model of mental dysfunction. Its operations are typically *community based.* Problems are handled at the local level, with minimal disruption of the individual's normal activities and interpersonal contacts.

A major goal of community psychology is *prevention* of psychological dysfunction. In this regard it endeavors to follow a public health model rather than the predominantly therapeutic, medical model (Cowen, 1973; Kelly, Snowden, & Muñoz, 1977; Kessler & Albee, 1975). In its broadest sense, the preventive model includes three levels, designated as primary, secondary, and tertiary prevention. The most direct attack is through primary prevention, that is, forestalling even minor dysfunctions and promoting psychological well-being. This objective requires that the experiences of persons in general—especially in childhood—be so structured as to strengthen their ability to withstand the strains and stresses of daily living. It has been repeatedly observed that mental health is a way of reacting to problems rather than an absence of problems (Ewalt, 1961). Happy, well-adjusted persons may have many worries, but they know how to cope with them. Secondary prevention can be illustrated by such procedures as identifying and handling incipient dysfunctions in young children, attending to minor disorders at any age, and treating acute conditions early in their onset. Tertiary prevention refers to efforts to minimize long-term, residual effects.

Community psychology is oriented toward the positive goal of enhancing *psychological well-being and competency*, as contrasted to the negative goals of preventing and treating dysfunctions. Both this objective and that of primary prevention call for a marked extension in the types of persons to be reached. Moreover, rather than waiting for the client to seek help, this approach requires the development of alternative mechanisms for identifying persons in need of services and for facilitating communitywide interventions.

Probably the most basic difference between the earlier, mental health movement and community psychology is the latter's *systems orientation.* In contrast to individual psychotherapy, with its one-to-one relation between therapist and client and its concern with the treatment of established dysfunction, community psychologists are interested in broad-based intervention programs directed toward improving the operation of social systems, such as family life, education, or employment. Training programs for marriage and parenthood provide an opportunity for ameliorating not only child-rearing practices but also all interpersonal relations within the family. The schools can contribute much to mental health through both curricular and extracurricular activities, through interpersonal relations of the children with their peers, and through teacher-pupil relations. Much of what was said in Chapters 5 and 6 regarding employee motivation, supervisory practices, and organizational structure is obviously relevant to the promotion of mental health.

Some community psychologists think in even broader terms, to include community development and the application of mental health principles to large-scale social planning. Crime, delinquency, and even war, they argue, are in part problems of mental health. We can certainly grant that such conditions represent malfunctions in interpersonal systems, to borrow a concept from engineering psychology. On the other hand, premature efforts to implement overambitious goals and the overselling of community psychology can only lead to disappointment and skepticism as its achievements are realistically assessed.

As a recognized professional specialty, community psychology is of very recent origin. It is not surprising that progress has been slowest in its most innovative features, namely, primary prevention and the systems approach. Another major limitation is a weak research base for its activities, many of which evolved in crash programs with little planning. On the positive side, community psychology has taken the most rapid strides with regard to diversification of services and target populations, environmental interventions, and increase in the number and variety of therapeutic agents utilized. Each of these developments will be briefly examined in the next sections.

Diversification of Services. While still operating largely within a person-oriented rather than a systems-oriented model, community psychology has substantially expanded its reach to include target populations that had been relatively untouched by traditional individual psychotherapy (Kelly et al., 1977). Among such populations are children, the aged, ethnic minorities, the poor, mental retardates, delinquents, and prisoners. Community psychology has also expanded its coverage over certain problem areas, notably alcoholism, drug addiction, and suicide.

Of particular interest are the various procedures for *crisis intervention* (Caplan, 1964; McGee, 1974). Crises are highly disruptive experiences that tax an individual's coping skills. They may be sudden and unanticipated, such as death of a loved one, serious accident or illness, loss of job; or they may be predictable transitional or developmental crises, such as starting school, birth of a sibling, marriage, a new job, retirement. Relatively brief interventions at the time of crisis may avert later disastrous consequences. A noteworthy example is provided by the growing suicide prevention movement, launched by the pioneer efforts of Farberow and Shneidman (1961) and by the establishment of their prototype crisis intervention center (Shneidman & Farberow, 1965).

Crisis intervention represents an application of secondary prevention. Timely availability may be ensured through such facilities as 24-hour telephone hot lines, storefront consultation centers, and other walk-in community agencies. Crisis intervention comprises a variety of functions, ranging from an empathic listener, through various forms of brief psychotherapy, to needed practical services (e.g., homemaker to care for family while mother is in the hospital, financial counseling for widows). The goal is to enable the individual to master the problem by facing it and concentrating on task-oriented activity.

Another approach is based on "anticipatory guidance," designed to train individuals in appropriate coping skills for handling predictable crises (Caplan, 1964). Other related procedures involve systematic learning experiences as general preparation for dealing with all crises and stressful events (Cumming & Cumming, 1966; Poser, 1970; W. G. Smith, 1971).

Environmental Interventions. Characteristically, community psychology gives considerable attention to the role of environmental variables in the individual's psychological development and functioning. Environmental interventions may take many forms. The Joint Commission report strongly recommended the conversion of state mental hospitals from custodial institutions to *therapeutic communities*, in which every facet of the individual's daily experiences and interpersonal contacts is designed to advance rehabilitation. Such milieu therapy was cited in an earlier section of this chapter. Both the use of tranquilizers and the establishment of token economies contributed to the implementation of therapeutic environments.

A more recent, related movement pertains to the legal rights of the mentally handicapped (Mental Health Law Project, 1973). Concerned with such questions as the right to treatment, right to education, compensation for institution-maintaining labor, right to refuse treatment, the provision of the least restrictive alternative care, and the protection of confidentiality and privacy, this movement is contributing further to the reexamination of institutional environments for the mentally disturbed and the mentally retarded. It should be noted that the issues are not simple. For example, some have argued for the abolition of all involuntary hospitalization for mental patients (Ennis, 1972; Szasz, 1963). Others have observed that such a generalization is too sweeping and may conflict with the right for adequate treatment in individual cases (Rachlin, Pam, & Milton, 1975).

A second aspect of the environmental approach is a systematic effort to *minimize institutionalization*, especially in large, remote state hospitals. Such institutionalization isolates the individual from family and community contacts and disrupts normal educational, domestic, and occupational activities. A related goal is to facilitate the individual's return to normal community living. The implementation of these objectives is indicated by the establishment of day hospitals, night hospitals, weekend hospitals, halfway houses, and other arrangements for partial institutional treatment (Freedman et al., 1975, pp. 1995–2003). In a day hospital, the patient reports for therapy from 9 to 5 on weekdays, while continuing to live at home. Still less disruption of normal living is involved in the night hospital, which enables patients to continue with their jobs or other regular daytime activities, while reporting to the hospital in the evenings for treatment. Depending upon their specific needs, the patients may remain overnight at the hospital or return home after the evening sessions. Halfway houses are designed to aid in the rehabilitation of former mental hospital patients and to facilitate their transition to community living. With developments such as these, the sharp distinction between inpatient and outpatient care is disappearing. Instead, there are now available a wide variety of therapeutic schedules, from a one-hour therapy session to complete hospitalization, which may be adapted to the needs of the individual patient.

Other facilities available for both mentally disturbed and mentally retarded persons include sheltered workshops, boarding homes, and home care of discharged patients. Continued counseling and follow-up services are essential components of all these arrangements. There is also evidence that a substantial proportion of severely disturbed schizophrenics may be successfully maintained entirely on a home-care program, with the aid of tranquilizing drugs, periodic visits by a public health nurse, and access to a community health center on an outpatient basis (Davis, Dinitz, & Pasamanick, 1974; Pasamanick, Scarpitti, & Dinitz, 1967). It should be emphasized, however, that no program for community care of seriously disturbed persons, whether in their own families or in community centers, can succeed in the absence of adequate community resources for continuing consultation, supervision, and service. Returning chronic mental patients to the community without such resources is likely to prove detrimental to the patient, the family, and the community (Rachlin, 1976).

A third type of environmental intervention consists of *changes introduced in the ordinary contexts of daily life*. To reduce stress and provide a more wholesome milieu, the therapist may recommend a change of jobs for an adult client. For a child, the therapist may arrange a transfer to a different school or to another class within the same school. When the child's home is highly unfavorable and resistant to improvement, foster home placement may be indicated as a last resort. In other cases, clients may be guided into recreational activities specially suited to their needs. Joining a club, going to camp, participating in sports, or cultivating a hobby might each have therapeutic value for a given individual. An important aspect of environmental therapy involves counseling with significant persons in the client's life, such as parents, spouse, teachers, and employers. Modifying the attitudes of these associates toward the client and giving them a better understanding of the client's problems may go a long way toward reducing stress and interpersonal conflicts. The previously discussed family therapy is an example of procedures for restructuring the interpersonal home environment in the effort to resolve individual problems of one or more family members.

At a more basic level, community psychology is typically concerned with *broad-based environmental interventions*, directed not to selected individuals but to an entire target population. This type of intervention may relate to almost any aspect of the physical and psychological environment throughout the life span (Carson & Driver, 1966; Cowen, 1973; Kessler & Albee, 1975). Relevant programs may range from the provision of prenatal care to the design of housing for the aged. Although community psychologists argue convincingly for the need to restructure social institutions, such as the schools and the correctional system, implementation thus far has been limited to more narrowly defined problem areas. Furthermore, most of this work is at the stage of pilot studies or demonstration projects. Outstanding examples include several projects on enriched early childhood education for culturally disadvantaged populations, some extending down to infancy (Cowen, 1973; J. McV. Hunt, 1969, 1975; Stanley, 1972, 1973). Promising results have also been reported for some well-designed programs for emotionally disturbed children and for inner-city multiproblem youth (Cowen, 1973; Fishman, Denham, Levine, & Shatz, 1969; Hobbs, 1969).

Therapeutic Agents. One of the strongest stimuli for the community mental health movement was provided by the data demonstrating the vast discrepancy between the need for mental health services and the trained personnel available to meet this need (Albee, 1959, 1968). The Joint Commission report (Ewalt, 1961) recommended the utilization of nonprofessional aides and mental health counselors for many mental health functions. The intervening years have witnessed an impressive expansion in the recruiting of therapeutic agents from many sources (Cowen, 1973; Guerney, 1969; Kelly et al, 1977; Suinn & Weigel, 1975). The groups explored for this purpose range widely in age, education, socioeconomic level, occupation, ethnic identity, and experiential backgrounds. Not only does the utilization of such diverse therapeutic agents greatly extend the service reach of the professionally trained specialist, but it also yields important fringe benefits for both the recipient and the provider of services. The latter effect has been called the "helper therapy principle" (Riessman, 1969).

College student volunteers have been among the first nonprofessional therapeutic workers. There are currently a large number of programs in which college students serve as companions for chronic patients in mental hospitals. In other projects, college students have worked as companions, counselors, play therapists, behavior therapists, and tutors with a wide variety of target populations including children, adolescents, and adults (Goodman, 1972; Gruver, 1971; Rappaport, Chinsky, & Cowen, 1971). Not only have these programs generally proved successful, but there is also evidence indicating beneficial psychological effects on the student therapists (Gruver, 1971).

Still younger change agents are represented by high school students and school-age children (Gartner, Kohler, & Riessman, 1971). These groups often serve as tutors either for younger children or for their own peers. The latter programs are reminiscent of the successful adult peer-instruction programs cited in Chapter 4. Studies have shown that children's own learning is strengthened and their motivation improved when they teach others. This finding is also supported by research on siblings, in which older siblings' tendency to excel in intellectual development has been attributed in part to their opportunities to transmit skills and knowledge to their younger siblings (Zajonc & Markus, 1975).

Other groups include homemakers trained to do psychotherapy under limited conditions (Rioch et al., 1963), retired persons used as child-aides for maladapting schoolchildren (Cowen, Leibowitz, & Leibowitz, 1968), and needy aged persons serving as "foster grandparents" for emotionally disturbed, dependent, or neglected children (Guerney, 1969, pp. 231–244). Another promising source is provided by persons who have themselves experienced the type of problems presented by the target population. These include such groups as former mental patients, prisoners, delinquents, drug addicts, and alcoholics. Increasing attention is also being given to the development and utilization of local support systems and mutual help groups for coping with normal life crises (Caplan & Killilea, 1976). Examples of such groups include Parents without Partners and the Widow-to-Widow Program, as well as religious denominations, family groups, and other natural societal support systems.

A rapidly growing type of help agent is the *indigenous nonprofessional*. This category comprises persons drawn from the local community and members of the same ethnic, cultural, or socioeconomic population as the clients to be served (Cowen, 1973; Fishman et al., 1969; Padilla et al., 1975; Pearl & Riessman, 1965). The utilization of such indigenous personnel has a dual advantage. First, because the help agent is part of the client's culture, such a person may have a better understanding of the problem from the client's viewpoint and is more likely to be accepted by the client and to elicit cooperation. Second, the program provides vocational training, immediate jobs, and—if properly designed—a career ladder for economically disadvantaged persons.

Still another context for the development of nonprofessional change agents is to be found in *filial therapy* (Guerney, 1969). This is a procedure whereby small groups of parents are trained to conduct a Rogerian type of play therapy with their own emotionally disturbed children. In a related approach, followed increasingly in recent years, parents are taught to carry out behavior modification programs with their children.

In addition to the training and supervision of nonprofessional change agents, an important role of the community psychologist is that of consultant for established community *caregiver groups* (Caplan, 1970; Cowen, 1973). This role opens up extensive opportunities for trained professionals to extend the reach of their services through persons frequently called upon to deal with mental health problems in the course of their normal duties. Chief among these are members of the clergy, family physicians, attorneys, nurses, and teachers. Any other communi- ty members whose work brings them into frequent contact with persons who may have problems could be added to the list (e.g., bartenders, taxi drivers). Surveys (e.g., Ewalt, 1961) have shown that persons with emotional problems are much more likely to seek advice and help from familiar figures (especially members of the clergy and physicians) than from professionals trained in mental health.

Another category of workers in key positions are *urban agents*, such as welfare and law-enforcement personnel. Such persons often have to deal with acute and sudden crisis situations. An outstanding example of the effective utilization of urban agents is provided by the work of Bard (1970, 1971a) in training police officers for family crisis intervention in deprived inner-city areas of New York City. Mention should also be made of the role of *consultant at the systems level*, whereby the community psychologist participates in planning and policy making. In this role, which is as yet relatively undeveloped, the psychologist could consult with representatives from an almost unlimited variety of fields, such as urban planning, architecture, education, industry, the military, and government.

SUMMARY

The many kinds of available intervention procedures for the prevention and remediation of psychological dysfunctions may be grouped under somatic thera- pies, individual psychotherapy, group therapy and other group-related procedures, behavior therapy, and community psychology. Somatic therapies, requiring the services of a licensed physician, are illustrated by psychosurgery, shock therapy, and psychotherapeutic drugs. The introduction of tranquilizers led to a spectacular rise in the recovery rate of American mental hospital patients. A major factor in these results appears to be the role of tranquilizers in making patients more amenable to psychotherapy and in facilitating improvements in institutional environments.

Psychotherapy is practiced in many forms, reflecting the varied theoretical orientation of the therapists. In the most general terms, it can be described as the use of verbal or other means of communication in a nonthreatening situation, which facilitates the alleviation of anxiety and the elimination of maladaptive behavior through a learning process. Two widely known types of psychotherapy are psychoanalysis and client-centered therapy. Play therapy is commonly utilized with children, in lieu of the predominantly verbal techniques employed with adults. Increasing use is being made of many forms of brief psychotherapy, which focuses on treating the client's immediate psychological problem.

Group therapy is widely employed either in place of individual therapy or in conjunction with it. Among its many variants are psychodrama and role playing, personal development groups, and self-help groups organized around special problems. Family therapy follows a systems approach to improving the operation of a family unit. Marital therapy and child therapy are among its chief applications.

Behavior therapy is essentially the direct application of learning principles to therapeutic intervention. Among its major procedures are systematic desensitiza- tion, contingency management (illustrated by token economies and often incorpo- rated in milieu therapy), modeling, and self-control programs.

Community psychology cuts across clinical and social psychology and has significant contacts with many other disciplines. Evolving from the mental health movement of the 1960s, it is characteristically community based and systems oriented. Its primary goals are prevention of dysfunction and advancement of psychological well-being. Among its chief accomplishments are the expansion of clinical services to cover a diversity of target populations and problem areas, the development of environmental interventions at various levels, and the utilization of a wide variety of nonprofessional therapeutic agents.

RESEARCH IN CLINICAL AND COMMUNITY PSYCHOLOGY

FOURTEEN

N THE PRECEDING CHAPTERS, attention was called to the pressing need for research in many areas of clinical and community psychology. This need stems partly from the fact that few techniques currently in use for assessment or intervention purposes have been adequately validated. In addition, it is hoped that basic research will open up new approaches to problems of mental health. The Joint Commission on Mental Illness and Health emphasized the importance of basic research in mental health programs (Ewalt, 1961). The continuing interest in clinical research is illustrated by a number of special conferences and surveys dealing with research is psychotherapy (Bergin & Strupp, 1972; Rubinstein & Parloff, 1959; Shlien, 1968; Strupp & Luborsky, 1962). A major contributor to the growth of research in clinical psychology has been the National Institute of Mental Health (NIMH) of the U. S. Department of Health, Education, and Welfare. NIMH had advanced research both through its own intramural projects and by its grants to universities and other institutions. A comprehensive overview of this dual program is provided by *Research in the Service of Mental Health* (Segal, 1975), an account of the first 25 years of operation of NIMH. This book is also useful as a broad survey of the current state of knowledge in clinical psychology.

It is in research that clinical psychologists, as contrasted to other mental health professionals, can make their most distinctive contribution. Even in their service functions, clinical psychologists with a research orientation can operate more effectively than those who are trained only as practitioners. With research training, they are better able to evaluate innovations and to incorporate new developments into their practices. In a field that is rapidly evolving, rigid commitment to existing techniques can only retard progress.

INTEGRATION OF CLINICAL AND EXPERIMENTAL APPROACHES

Before 1950, the gap between clinical and experimental psychology was very wide. The rapid growth of clinical psychology since that time has been accompanied by some rapprochement between the two fields. The gap is still evident, but it has narrowed. To be sure, psychologists differ in their reaction to this gap. Some deplore its existence and urge further narrowing. Others insist it is inevitable and argue for a realistic acceptance of two kinds of psychologists. Nevertheless there are promising signs that psychologists *can* function effectively in the dual role of scientist-practitioner. Clinicians, on the one hand, have become more critical about their techniques and more willing to test their hypotheses (Bergin & Strupp, 1972, p. 11). Experimentalists, on the other, have been doing more and more research on problems arising out of clinical contexts.

There are several indications that the roles of clinician and experimentalist are merging. Rogerian, client-centered therapists were among the first to introduce systematic recording and data-gathering procedures during therapeutic sessions and to investigate the relation between several therapist and client variables. Among behavior therapists, the fusion of therapeutic and research procedures is especially evident.

From another angle, the introduction of research procedures may itself function as a therapeutic intervention and thus alter the subsequent behavior of individuals. In industrial and organizational psychology, this effect was first observed in the Hawthorne studies (Ch. 5) and has subsequently been noted repeatedly by consultants in organizational development (Ch. 6). Merely providing feedback on survey results obtained within an organization often leads to perceptible improvements. Similar effects were observed in an investigation of 231 dating couples in a college population (Rubin & Mitchell, 1976). This study was designed as basic research on the establishment, maintenance, and dissolution of close interpersonal relationships. The procedures included the completion of questionnaires at several points over a two-year period. There was evidence suggesting that participation in this research had affected the relationships of the couples in at least two ways: (1) by inducing participants to examine their own feelings and define the relationship, and (2) by indirectly promoting communication between partners about the relationship. In several ways, this study illustrated a blurring of the distinction between couples research and premarital counseling.

A clear sign of the rapprochement between clinical and experimental orientations can be seen in the increasing attention to experimental designs and statistical techniques suitable for clinical data (Campbell & Stanley, 1966; Chassan, 1967; Kiesler, 1971; Shontz, 1965). Of particular interest are the techniques designed for the intensive study of single cases (Gottman, 1973; Hersen & Barlow, 1976; Leitenberg, 1973). An example is the interrupted time series, illustrated in Figure 14-1. At a minimum, this type of design includes a series of observations constituting the base period (Stage 1), an intervention, and another series of observations constituting the experimental period (Stage 2). The data in Figure 14-1 were obtained in the course of treating the hyperactivity of a 4-year-old

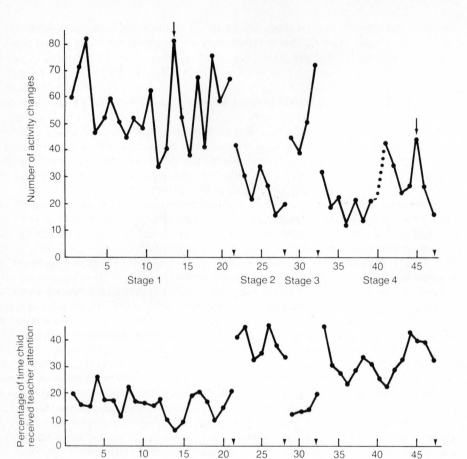

Figure 14-1. Interrupted time-series design in the treatment of a hyperactive child by social reinforcement of attending behavior. Upper graph shows number of activity changes during 50-minute periods; lower graph shows percentage of time child received teacher attention. Stage 1, baseline of activity changes under noncontingent attention. Stage 2, teacher attention contingent on child sustaining attention for one minute. Stage 3, return to baseline condition. Stage 4, contingent attention as in Stage 2; at dotted line, criterion for sustained attention raised to two minutes. Arrows indicate days child's mother visited. *(Adapted from Allen, Henke, Harris, Baer, & Reynolds, 1967, p. 234. Copyright © 1967 by American Psychological Association. Reproduced by permission.)*

preschool child (Allen, Henke, Harris, Baer, & Reynolds, 1967). In Stage 2, the child was given social reinforcement whenever he attended to a single activity for more than one minute. The complete design of this case included also a reversal, or return to baseline conditions, in Stage 3 and a reinstatement of contingent reinforcement in Stage 4; midway in Stage 4 (dotted line), the child's required period of sustained attention was increased to two minutes. Testing the statistical significance of the intervention effect in such a design requires a determination of the trend of results over time during baseline and intervention periods, as well as the deviations of individual observations from the expected trend values (Chassan, 1967, Ch. 7; Gottman, 1973).

A more fully controlled design involves two persons, each following the interrupted time series, but with the intervention introduced later in the series for the second person. This "*N*-of-two" design rules out the possible effects of other events that may have occurred at the time of the interventions. Even when data are gathered from many cases, it has been suggested that analyses of changes within each case ("*N*-of-one-at-a-time research") may substantially enhance the understanding of group results (Gottman, 1973). It should be added that the type of analysis illustrated by time series is applicable not only to the evaluation of intervention techniques but also to the monitoring of intervention effects for the guidance of the therapist in treating an individual case. In other words, these procedures can be incorporated in clinical practice as well as in research.

More and more, psychologists are coming to realize that no one type of investigation can provide definitive answers to the questions raised in clinical psychology. A whole spectrum of experimental designs is needed, ranging from naturalistic observations and the intensive case studies represented by *N*-of-one research to highly controlled, simplified, analogue studies. In fact, the combination of these two extreme research strategies in a cycle of hypothesis development and hypothesis testing provides one of the most promising approaches (Bergin & Strupp, 1972, pp. 432–434; Bordin, 1974, Ch. 4). Each strategy can serve a dual function: (1) to suggest new hypotheses and new intervention techniques, and (2) to test hypotheses and techniques arising out of the other strategy. The simplification strategy in clinical research is illustrated both by laboratory investigations with human participants and by animal experiments. It can also be applied in a clinic or other naturalistic setting by artificially controlling the conditions so as to focus on the operation of a single variable in any one study.

A pioneer research program to bridge the gap between clinical and experimental psychology by combining these two strategies was presented by Dollard and Miller (1950) in their book *Personality and Psychotherapy* and was more fully developed in later publications by Miller and others (Elder, Noblin, & Maher, 1961; N. E. Miller, 1958; Miller & Murray, 1952; Murray & Berkun, 1955; Murray & Miller, 1952). These investigators first reformulated common psychoanalytic concepts such as repression, displacement, and transference in terms of the conditioned-reaction learning theory developed by Hull (1943). Together with a group of their associates and students at Yale University, they then designed and conducted controlled animal experiments to test the various hypotheses generated by these theoretical formulations. Finally, they checked clinical observations of the behavior of patients in psychotherapy against their experimental findings. The recent, large-scale development of behavior therapy represents a more direct merging of laboratory research with clinical research and practice. Still another major example of the contribution of basic research to clinical psychology is provided by both human and animal studies on the causes of behavioral dysfunctions, to be discussed in a later section of this chapter.

VALIDATION OF ASSESSMENT TECHNIQUES

A major area of applied research in clinical psychology pertains to the validation of tests and other appraisal techniques. The basic validation procedures were described in Chapter 2. Criterion-related and construct validity are the types most generally applicable to clinical instruments. Because of the extensive use of projective techniques in clinical practice and the many unverified claims made about them, these techniques have presented a special challenge to validation research. Since the validation of these instruments is also beset with many methodological pitfalls, it provides good illustrative material for the purposes of this chapter (see Anastasi, 1976, Ch. 19).

Overestimating Validity. Inadequate experimental designs or inappropriate statistical analyses may have the effect of producing spurious evidence of validity where none exists. An example is the *contamination* of either criterion or test data. The criterion judges may have access to the client's test protocols. Conversely, the examiner may have obtained cues about the client's behavior from remarks made by the client while taking the test, or from case-history material or other nontest sources. The best control for the latter type of contamination in validation studies is provided by blind analysis in which the test record is interpreted by a scorer who had had no contact with the client and who has no information about the client other than that contained in the test protocol.

A more subtle source of error is illustrated by *stereotype accuracy*. Certain descriptive statements, such as might occur in a Rorschach protocol, may apply widely to persons in general, or to young men, or to hospitalized mental patients, or to whatever category of persons is sampled by the particular investigation. Agreement between criterion and test data with regard to such statements would therefore yield a spurious impression of validity. Some control for this error is needed, such as a measure of congruence between the test evaluation of one examinee and the criterion evaluation of another examinee in the same category (see, e.g., L. H. Silverman, 1959, p. 9). The spurious validity arising from stereotype accuracy will be recognized as somewhat similar to the "Barnum effect" described in Chapter 1.

Another common source of error, arising from reliance on clinical experience in the validation of diagnostic signs, is what Chapman (1967) labeled "*illusory validation.*" This type of error may account in part for the continued clinical use of techniques and systems of diagnostic signs for which empirical validity findings are predominantly negative. In a series of experiments to test this phenomenon, Chapman and Chapman (1967, 1969) presented college students with a set of human figure drawings, similar to those obtained in the Machover Draw-a-Person Test (D-A-P). Each drawing was accompanied by brief descriptions of two symptoms supposedly manifested by the person who made the drawing. For example, one pair included: (1) is suspicious of other people; (2) is worried about how manly he is. The students had no previous familiarity with the D-A-P test or its rationale. The symptoms chosen were those most frequently linked with certain drawing characteristics by a group of clinicians previously surveyed in a mail questionnaire. They were thus part of the clinical lore associated with the use of the D-A-P. In the experiment itself, however, the symptoms were randomly assigned to drawings, each subject receiving a different combination of drawings and symptoms. Thus the subject's learning experience did *not* support the traditional, stereotyped associations of symptoms and drawing signs.

Following the learning session, subjects were given a list of symptoms and asked to describe, under each symptom, the drawing characteristics they had found to be associated with it. The results showed that subjects responded in terms of preestablished popular stereotypes, even though these associations were not supported by the data presented during their learning experience. For example, they listed atypical eyes as being associated with suspiciousness, large head with worry about intelligence, and broad shoulders with concern about manliness. Not only were the interpretations unrelated to the empirical associations which the subjects had studied, but in other experiments these stereotyped cultural associations also proved to be resistant to change under intensive training conditions designed to establish counter associations. In other words, subjects retained their a priori expectations even when exposed to contradictory observations.

Illusory correlation is a special example of the mechanism that underlies the survival of superstitions. We tend to notice and recall whatever fits our expectations, and we tend to ignore and forget whatever is contrary to our expectations. This mechanism may actually interfere with the discovery and use of valid diagnostic signs in the course of clinical observation by clinicians who are strongly identified with a particular diagnostic system. The original research of Chapman and Chapman with the D-A-P has been corroborated by similar studies with the Rorschach (Chapman & Chapman, 1967, 1969; Golding & Rorer, 1972) and with the Incomplete Sentences Blank (Starr & Katkin, 1969).

From a different angle, an individual's responses may depend more upon the *specific testing technique* employed than upon his or her general behavioral characteristics. Insofar as behavioral descriptions based upon a single testing technique have validity, they should exhibit stability across techniques. To check on this aspect of validity, Campbell and Fiske (1959) proposed a multitrait-multimethod validation process whereby the correlations of the same traits measured by different methods are compared with the correlations of different traits measured by both the same and different methods. Common variance due to method might result from response sets and other test-taking attitudes that would increase the uniformity of the respondent's performance on a particular test or type of test. Unless the trait correlations are appreciably higher than the method correlations, there is obviously no point in describing an individual in terms of the given trait categories. For example, if aggressiveness and obsessiveness as measured by Test A correlate higher than do measures of aggressiveness derived from Test A and B, there is some question about the value of the construct "aggressiveness" as measured by these two tests.

Meehl (1960) described an adaptation of the Campbell-Fiske procedure involving essentially the correlation between Q sorts of two persons evaluated by a clinician on the same test (e.g., the Rorschach) and the correlation between Q sorts of that same person evaluated on two different tests (e.g., Rorschach and TAT). The first correlation would show the degree of similarity between the trait patterns of two different persons and would reflect stereotypes and sorting bias arising from the test and the scorers. The second correlation would show the degree of similarity between the trait patterns of the same person as measured by two different tests. The latter could be scored by the same or different scorers.

Still another source of spurious validity is failure to *cross-validate* (see Ch. 2). Because of the large number of possible diagnostic signs that can be derived from most projective techniques, it is likely that by chance alone some of them will discriminate significantly between criterion groups. It should be recalled that by chance approximately 5% of the diagnostic signs investigated ought to discriminate at the 5% level of significance, 1% at the 1% level, and so on. The validity of a scoring key based on such diagnostic signs, however, would collapse to zero when the test is cross-validated in a new sample.

The traditional interpretations of many projective test responses are expressed in the form of *dispositional constructs* (Sarbin et al., 1960, p. 229), such as "unconscious feelings of inferiority." Such interpretations cannot be fully validated unless reformulated in terms of observable behavior as, for example, "will buy a more expensive car than she can afford" or "will drop names of important persons" (Sarbin et al., 1960, p. 229). Without these behavioral predictions, we can determine only whether two independent observers or scorers arrive at the same dispositional construct by applying different diagnostic procedures to the same individual. Agreement under these conditions may be looked upon as a first step toward validation. But such validation must be regarded as tentative, because the agreement may simply reflect a common theoretical bias on the part of the two observers, a bias that is broad enough to encompass different diagnostic techniques.

Underestimating Validity. Inadequacies of experimental design may also have the effect of underestimating the validity of a diagnostic instrument. One example is provided by the use of an *inadequate criterion*. In Chapter 12 we noted various objections to the application of such traditional psychiatric categories as schizophrenia and anxiety hysteria. If this type of diagnostic category is used as the sole criterion for checking the validity of a personality test, negative results are inconclusive. A lack of correspondence in this case might indicate the weakness of the criterion rather than the invalidity of the predictor. Another important question pertains to the skill, training, and experience of the *clinician* who interprets the test protocol. Because of the active part played by the clinician in this interpretation, test validity cannot be evaluated independently of certain clinician variables.

Insignificant validity coefficients may also result from a failure to take *interaction effects* into account. For example, the hypothesized relation between aggression in fantasy (as revealed, for instance, in TAT stories) and aggression in overt behavior may be too complex to be tested by a single validity coefficient. Depending upon other concomitant personality characteristics, high aggression in fantasy may be associated with either high or low overt aggression. There is some evidence to suggest that, if strong aggressive tendencies are accompanied by high anxiety or fear of punishment, expressions of aggression will tend to be high in fantasy and low in overt behavior. When anxiety and fear of punishment are low, however, high fantasy aggression is associated with high overt aggression (Harrison, 1965; Mussen & Naylor, 1954; Pittluck, 1950). A lack of significant correlation between expressions of aggression in TAT stories and in overt behavior in a random sample of cases would thus be consistent with the stated hypothesis, since the relation is positive in some individuals and negative in others. Obviously, however, such a lack of correlation is also consistent with the hypothesis that the TAT has no validity in detecting aggressive tendencies. What these problems require, of course, is more complex experimental designs that permit the measurement of interaction effects through an analysis of results in previously identified subgroups.

Still another condition that may lower the validity indices obtained with projective techniques pertains to the *unevenness of coverage* of such procedures. Because of their unstructured nature, projective techniques may provide different kinds of information regarding different individuals—or even regarding the same individual when evaluated by different scorers (Meehl, 1960). One person's TAT responses, for example, may reveal a good deal about his aggression and little or nothing about his achievement drive; another person's TAT record may permit a thorough assessment of the strengh of her achievement drive, while indicating little about her aggression. This lack of uniformity in the kinds of information yielded in individual cases may help to explain the low validities found when projective test responses are analyzed for a single trait across a group of persons.

Much of the published literature on the evaluation of projective tests is inconclusive because of one or more of the methodological difficulties mentioned above or because of the use of inappropriate statistical techniques. A few studies reflect the increasing rapprochement of clinical and experimental psychology in the sophistication of their experimental designs (see, e.g., Golden, 1964; Henry & Farley, 1959; Little & Shneidman, 1959; L. H. Silverman, 1959). While differing in the type of persons tested and in the specific problems they set out to investigate, these studies point to a common conclusion: when experienced clinicians are given an opportunity to examine and interpret in their own way examinees' protocols from such projective tests as the Rorschach and TAT, their evaluations of the examinees' personalities tend to match independent case history evaluations significantly better than chance. Insofar as can be ascertained, however, the obtained relations are low. Moreover, the relationship appears to be a function of the particular clinician and client, a number of individual matches being no better than chance. There is also little agreement among evaluations based on different projective techniques or among different clinicians using the same technique.

More recently, it has been argued that *any* attempt to validate an instrument as a broad measure of the total personality is fundamentally unrealistic, however sophisticated the methodology. Attention has therefore concentrated on the validation of proposed indices of more specifically defined variables, such as hostility, anxiety, or organic brain damage (Goldfried, Stricker, & Weiner, 1971; Klopfer & Taulbee, 1976). At the same time, surveys of the ways in which clinicians actually use projective tests in their practice indicate that a sizable proportion do not score such tests at all; among those who do score them, the large majority rely on personally developed and rather subjective interpretations (Exner & Exner, 1972). When so employed, projective techniques serve, not as psychometric instruments, but as interviewing aids to the experienced clinician, as was noted in Chapter 12.

STUDIES OF THE PROCESS OF PSYCHOTHERAPY

Research on the process of psychotherapy has been concerned with such questions as the effect of therapist variables upon the psychotherapeutic process, the specific ways in which therapists function, and the changes in client behavior that occur in the course of psychotherapy. In contrast to studies of the outcome of psychotherapy, to be discussed in the next section, this research is limited to what goes on during the psychotherapeutic sessions themselves. Most of this process research was initiated by client-centered psychotherapists (Rogers & Dymond, 1954), although the same procedures have been applied to a more limited extent to psychoanalytic and other forms of psychotherapy. More recently, the behavior therapists have conducted extensive research in the course of therapy. In fact, the recording of data on stimulus situations and client responses throughout the threapeutic program is an integral part of behavior therapy. Much of the behavior therapy research, however, is concerned with the effectiveness of therapy in modifying target behavior, both within the therapy sessions and in extratherapeu-tic contexts; it includes the monitoring of the particular behavior of interest throughout the duration of therapy, as well as during follow-up periods after therapy is discontinued. When process research deals with therapeutic effective-ness, it actually represents only one stage or one phase of outcome research. As such, it can be more appropriately considered in the later section on outcome studies.

Observations in the Course of Therapy Sessions. Process research has been greatly advanced by the application of two techniques, namely the recording of psychotherapeutic sessions and content analysis. With the client's permission, therapeutic sessions are tape-recorded and then transcribed. When these records are employed for either research or teaching purposes, of course, all identifica-tions of individual clients are eliminated. Content analysis is a technique for classifying the meaningful content (as opposed to grammatical and other formal properties) of the verbal responses of client and therapist. Several schemas of classification have been worked out for this purpose, the specific categories varying with the objectives of the study and the theoretical framework of the investigator (G. Marsden, 1971).

An early study conducted with client-centered psychotherapy will serve to illustrate the procedure. Seeman (1949) analyzed over 6,500 client and therapist statements taken from 60 therapeutic sessions with 10 clients. Using a previously developed schema, he classified client responses into four categories: (1) expres-sions of problems or symptoms, (2) simple acceptances of therapist response, (3) indications of understanding or insight, and (4) discussions or explorations of plans for the future. The frequency of each of the four types of response was determined separately for successive fifths of the psychotherapeutic process in order to reveal any changes that occurred during therapy. The results can be seen in Figure 14-2. In the course of psychotherapy, the percentage of statements dealing with problems or symptoms declined sharply, while the percentage of those showing understanding or insight rose. Discussions of future plans also increased during the later sessions. Simple acceptance of therapist response rose in the early part of therapy and then declined slowly.

As a further index of the effectiveness of psychotherapy, Seeman computed the ratio between number of statements showing understanding or insight and the sum of these statements and those expressing problems or symptoms. When the data from all clients were combined, this ratio rose from the first to the last fifth of the psychotherapeutic process. Moreover, the rise tended to be greater for those clients whom the therapists rated as most improved than for those rated as least improved. The latter finding, however, may be a methodological artifact, since the therapist's rating of client improvement was probably influenced by client state-ments in the course of therapy. Another finding of the same study was that attitudes expressed by clients in the present tense tended to become more positive and less negative in the course of therapy, while attitudes expressed in the past tense showed the reverse change. Apparently the past was viewed with less favor and the present with increasing optimism following therapy.

Several other progressive changes have been identified in the course of psychotherapy. Defensiveness tends to decrease as therapy proceeds (Haigh, 1949; E. J. Murray, 1954). Similarly, expressions of hostility increase as the anxiety associated with such feelings is reduced through therapy (E. J. Murray, 1954). Such

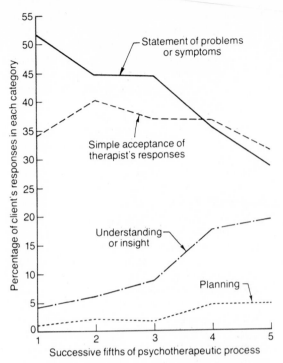

Figure 14-2. Changes in client responses during client-centered psychotherapy. *(Data from Seeman, 1949, p. 161.)*

findings suggest an increasing ability to recognize and express feelings freely in the course of therapy. It should be added, however, that neither the results nor the interpretations are consistent in all studies. Changes in such variables as anxiety, hostility, and defensiveness during therapy are related to type of therapy, as well as to client and therapist characteristics.

A number of studies by psychologists of the client-centered school were concerned with changes in the client's self-concept. With therapy, the self-concept tends to become more favorable and comes to resemble more closely the individual's self-ideal concept, or the way he would like to be. These changes have been investigated by having the client perform a Q sort with reference to his real self as he perceives it and his ideal self, at different stages of therapy. In one study of 25 cases (Butler & Haigh, 1954), the mean correlation between self-sorts and ideal sorts before therapy was −.01, as contrasted with a mean correlation of .58 found with normal control subjects. After therapy, the mean client correlation rose to .38. In a follow-up after an interval of six months to a year, this mean showed a negligible drop to .31. The mean control correlation remained virtually unchanged over the time intervals covered.

Although the observed changes in self-acceptance in the course of psychotherapy are consistent with the underlying rationale of client-centered therapy, their interpretation is not so simple as might seem at first sight (see Crowne & Stephens, 1961). One difficulty arises from the fact that different indices of self-acceptance do not correlate very highly with each other and hence may be measuring different constructs. Much more information is needed on the generality of self-acceptance with reference to measuring techniques, traits or items, situations, and time. Another difficulty is that the meaning of high self-acceptance scores is ambiguous. In such scores, self-acceptance may be confounded with defensiveness, lack of insight into one's emotional difficulties, or the tendency to choose socially desirable answers on personality inventories.

Therapist Variables. In the effort to learn more about the therapeutic relationship, some investigators have studied the effects of therapist characteristics and therapist responses upon client behavior and feelings during therapy (Meltzoff & Kornreich, 1970, Ch. 14; Orlinsky & Howard, 1975; Truax & Mitchell, 1971). For example, certain characteristics of the therapist's responses, such as the accuracy with which he reflects client feelings or the degree of his unconditional positive acceptance of the client, have proved to be significantly related to the extent of intrapersonal exploration that the client undertakes during group therapy (Truax, 1961). Some studies of individual psychotherapy have found that "insight" and "discussion of plans" by the client are more likely to follow nondirective than directive therapist responses and that resistance to the therapist and to the therapeutic process more often follow directive responses (Rubinstein & Parloff, 1959, pp. 247–259).

Of particular interest is the evidence of *interaction* among client, therapist, and process variables. These findings suggest that, because of their individual personality characteristics, some therapists may function more effectively with one type of therapy while others may function more effectively with a different type. Similarly, pretherapy personality characteristics of clients affect their responses to different therapists and to different therapeutic processes. The importance of compatibility between therapist and client is indicated by this research. There is also evidence of a close correspondence between client's feelings toward therapist and therapist's feelings toward client. In an intensive study of the psychotherapeutic relationship between one therapist and 20 clients (Snyder, 1961), both therapist and clients filled out specially constructed "affect scales" pertaining to their feelings toward each other, following each therapeutic session. For all sessions combined, the correlation between client and therapist affect for the 20 cases proved to be .70.

Still another approach is illustrated by an investigation of the effect of therapist response upon the frequency of client responses in different content categories (E. J. Murray, 1956). This study is of particular interest because it demonstrates that even in nondirective therapy the subtle approval or disapproval implicit in the therapist's remarks influences the subsequent frequency of various kinds of client responses. Among the response categories that were consistently approved by the therapist were expressions of client independence; among those that were disapproved were intellectual defenses and feelings of anxiety about independence. A comparison of the pooled categories of approved responses with the pooled categories of disapproved responses over eight hours of psychotherapy yielded the results shown in Figure 14-3. It can be seen that the proportion of approved responses rose sharply, while the proportion of disapproved responses dropped sharply, in the course of therapy. That subtle verbal reinforcement by the therapist will significantly affect the subsequent course of the client's responses has been repeatedly confirmed by other investigators. Also relevant is the research of Matarazzo and his associates (Matarazzo & Wiens, 1972), which was cited in Chapter 3. These studies, too, provided evidence of the effect of interviewer's (or

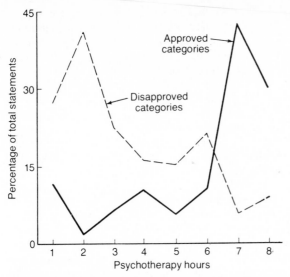

Figure 14-3. Effect of therapist approval or disapproval upon frequency of client statements in different categories. *(From Murray, 1956, p. 11. Copyright © 1956 by American Psychological Association. Reproduced by permission.)*

therapist's) behavior on client responses. Thus the speed and duration of client verbal responses were significantly related to length of interviewer utterances, nodding and other expressions of interviewer attention, and the neutral-versus-interpretive nature of interviewer comments.

Behavior therapy programs characteristically put considerable emphasis on situational or environmental variables encountered in the course of therapy. The investigation of therapist (or trainer) behavior, however, has only recently begun to receive attention (Loeber & Weisman, 1975). Although the reinforcement to be provided by the trainer and the reinforcement schedule are specified when a behavior modification program is set up, what the trainer actually does may deviate from the plan. This problem assumes special importance in view of the increasing use of a wide variety of therapeutic agents or trainers in contingency management programs, such as parents, teachers, or hospital attendants.

The questions raised in trainer research concern the trainee or client behavior to which the trainer actually responds with the designated reinforcement, the nature of the trainer's response, and the sort of reinforcement the trainer herself or himself receives from the trainee's behavior. For example, suppose the target behavior to be reinforced is social play in a shy, withdrawn preschool child. Does the teacher give the child attention when he responds to other children and ignore him when he engages in solitary play? Does the teacher show attention in ways that are perceived as rewarding by the child? Does the child's behavior after joining a group create new problems for the teacher, thereby decreasing the teacher's likelihood of reinforcing the child's subsequent social behavior? The trainer-therapist is more than a passive machine for administering reinforcement; and the trainee can—intentionally or unintentionally—influence the trainer's behavior. One is reminded in this connection of the old joke about the rat in the Skinner box confiding to a companion, "I really have this fellow trained—every time I press the bar, he drops me some food."

Physiological Measures. The research considered thus far has dealt predominantly with verbal responses. Considerable information is also available regarding changes in physiological indices of anxiety during psychotherapy. Both laboratory and clinical studies provide extensive evidence showing that such physiological measures as galvanic skin reaction, heart rate, blood pressure, muscle tension, and gastric motility can serve as indicators of emotional conflict areas during therapeutic sessions, can indicate quantitatively the extent of emotional involvement, and can reflect changes in client behavior as therapy progresses (Lang, 1971). Such physiological changes can be detected in moment-by-moment comparisons within a single therapy session, as well as in the comparison of different sessions. Behavior therapists sometimes include physiological indices of anxiety and other emotional states in the therapeutic program, particularly in monitoring the effects of systematic desensitization.

It would seem that physical indices of anxiety should provide a good measure of the effectiveness of therapy. Several difficulties arise, however, when the indices are employed for this purpose (Lang, 1971; Martin, 1961). First, the intercorrelations among different anxiety indicators are rather low. There is considerable specificity in the autonomic response pattern of different persons (Lacey & Lacey, 1958). Thus one individual might consistently show his maximal response to stress in blood pressure rise, another in heightened muscle tension, and a third in increased finger sweating. It would therefore be misleading to employ a single physiological variable for all cases.

A second difficulty stems from the fact that physiological indicators of anxiety cannot be taken directly as indices of therapeutic effectiveness but must be interpreted in the light of other behavioral data. For instance, physiological measures cannot differentiate between the reduction of stress resulting from neurotic defenses and that resulting from the resolution of conflicts. Some psychotherapists maintain that anxiety should rise and then decline in the course of therapy, as defensive symptom systems are broken down and new responses are developed. It is apparent that anxiety indicators need to be considered in combination with other information about the client and interpreted against previously formulated theoretical expectancies.

A final limitation is common to all measures taken during the therapeutic process, whether they be physiological or verbal. Any change observed in the course of psychotherapy may be restricted to the therapeutic situation. The therapist's nonthreatening and accepting attitude, for instance, may gradually lead to a reduction in the anxiety the client experiences *while talking to the therapist about emotional problems.* It is, of course, an underlying assumption of therapeutic practice that these response changes will generalize from talking to other behavior and from the therapeutic situation to other situations of daily living. On theoretical grounds, there is good reason to expect this generalization to occur. But it must be recognized that process studies as such can provide no evidence for such generalization.

EVALUATING THE OUTCOME OF THERAPY

A particularly difficult field of clinical research is that concerned with the evaluation of therapy. Although hundreds of studies have been published in this area, few have yielded conclusive results. Serious methodological problems make it difficult to determine the effectiveness of drug therapies as well as psychotherapy. Surveys of published research reveal conflicting results from different studies (Auerbach & Kilman, 1977; Bergin & Garfield, 1971; Bergin & Suinn, 1975; Franks, 1969). The overall picture provides only moderately positive evidence of the effectiveness of available forms of therapy. To be sure, that which is unproved is not thereby disproved. Inadequate experimental designs and procedural deficiencies may not only yield spurious positive results but may also fail to detect genuine effects of therapeutic interventions. It should also be noted that, since the mid-1960s, outcome studies have shown a marked increase in methodological sophistication.

Criteria of Outcome. One of the most persistent problems in outcome research centers around the criteria of outcome. How can we judge whether or not the individual has improved? One way is to ask the client about his or her own feelings. Such information could be obtained either through an informal report or through a standardized self-evaluation, as in a personality inventory or *Q* sort. A difficulty with this approach arises from defense mechanisms, which may make the client's self-report totally misleading. Another source of error has been described as the "hello-goodbye" effect (Hathaway, 1948). When clients are seeking therapy, they are likely to exaggerate their difficulties because of a subtle social obligation to justify their appeal for help; when about to terminate therapy, on the other hand, they are likely to overestimate their improvement and satisfaction out of courtesy and gratitude toward the therapist. For many persons, it may be difficult to say they feel no better after a professionally trained therapist has devoted many hours to helping them. Suggestion would also operate, insofar as the individual expects to benefit from therapy.

If we rely upon the therapist's evaluation of the patient's improvement, we encounter similar difficulties. Being ego-involved in the therapeutic process, the therapist cannot be considered an unbiased observer. Having diligently applied a form of therapy in whose efficacy she or he believes, the therapist certainly expects to find improvement. Although not subject to this bias, objective measures of verbal and physiological changes during therapy, such as those employed in process research, have the limitation that they may be specific to the therapeutic situation and unrelated to external indices of progress.

A fourth type of outcome criterion is based upon the ward behavior of institutionalized patients. Several objective rating scales have been developed to evaluate this behavior (Lyerly, 1973). Such scales generally list specific items to be marked by nurses or attendants in reporting on the patient's ward behavior during a specified period. In token-economy and other behavior therapy programs, records of specific target behaviors are regularly available throughout the program. To what extent improved adjustment to the sheltered institutional environment will generalize to behavior outside the institution must, of course, be checked for specific therapies and for different kinds of patients (Erickson, 1975).

A fifth and final type of outcome index utilizes follow-up data regarding the individual's behavior in real-life situations. Such data may range from length of time the individual remains outside the hospital to evidence of job and family adjustment and associates' evaluations of interpersonal behavior. Although theoretically this type of criterion would seem to be the most satisfactory, it is difficult to apply because of inequalities in the environments to which different persons must adjust. The experimenter has no control over the circumstances of the individual's life and little knowledge about them. A patient may return to the hospital within six months or may fail to adjust to a job, not because of the inadequacy of the therapy, but because of the unusually stressful nature of the patient's environment.

In view of the many special problems presented by each criterion of outcome, it is not surprising to find that the intercorrelations among different types of criteria are often low. A person may be greatly improved according to one criterion and unimproved according to another. In a well-controlled study of the relative effectiveness of three forms of psychotherapy with patients in a Veterans Administration hospital, there was little relation between outcome criteria based on ward behavior and those based on a six-month follow-up after discharge; and there was little relation between these criteria of outcome and those based on self-report inventories or Q sorts (Fairweather et al., 1960). Even among follow-up criteria, moreover, the relative effectiveness of different therapies differed depending upon whether a hospitalization or an employment criterion was chosen.

The time at which outcome data are obtained may also substantially affect the results (Erickson, 1975; Kiesler, 1971). Studies that focus on single points in time, yielding a pretherapy and a posttherapy measure, may present a misleading picture. For a proper assessment of the effect of a therapeutic program, data should be obtained regarding changes in feelings and behavior throughout the duration of therapy and at repeated follow-ups over several years. Different types of therapy may produce a different pattern of improvement and relapse at different stages in this period.

It should also be noted that the choice of a criterion of outcome involves some value judgment (Ehrlich & Wiener, 1961). The question of what constitutes mental health is relevant to the evaluation of therapy. Therapists differ, for example, in the relative value they place upon individual freedom and upon conformity and adjustment as goals of therapy. Clients also vary with regard to these values, partly as a function of socioeconomic background and other cultural factors. Such value differences represent one of the variables in the compatibility of client and therapist that may in turn affect the success of psychotherapy. All of the foregoing problems indicate the desirability of investigating the outcome of therapy in terms of multiple criteria and of specifying fully the criteria employed in each study.[1] This is especially important when evaluating different types of therapy, such as behavior modification, short-term supportive psychotherapy, and classical psychoanalysis. These therapies are likely to yield substantially different results if the criterion of outcome is based on overt behavior, client feelings, or therapist assessment of personality restructuring (Strupp & Hadley, 1977).

Selection of Cases. A second major methodological question pertains to the choice of both treated and control cases. Because of the likelihood of interaction between client variables and types of therapy, it is important to work with groups or subgroups that are homogeneous with regard to relevant variables. Which variables are relevant depends somewhat upon the type of therapy under investigation and the objectives of the study. Client characteristics that are likely to make a difference can be identified in part from earlier empirical findings and in part from the theoretical rationale underlying the therapy. Any study, however, should probably control, as a bare minimum, such variables as age, sex, socioeconomic

---

[1]A survey of different types of change measures for assessing the outcome of psychotherapy, together with a suggested core battery, can be found in Waskow and Parloff (1975).

level, duration of illness, type of onset (sudden or gradual), and diagnostic category. The expected improvement and recovery rates among untreated cases vary as a function of these patient characteristics. For instance, the base rate of improvement is considerably higher for manic-depressives than for schizophrenics (Staudt & Zubin, 1957). Similarly, an extensive survey of published data on neurotics led to the conclusion that recovery rates of untreated cases are likely to be symptom-specific and may vary from 0% to 90% (Lambert, 1976).

In any evaluation of therapy, it is particularly important to use a control group matched with the treated group in all of the previously mentioned variables. It is the function of the control group to indicate what improvement (or deterioration) would occur in the absence of the specific therapy under investigation. Changes occurring in the control group should reflect so-called spontaneous remission occurring as a result of nonspecific treatments (such as institutionalization) and of the many uncontrolled and unknown events in the individual's day-to-day experiences. Unless special care is exercised in matching treated and control groups, selective bias is likely to influence group assignments. In institutional samples, there is a strong tendency to place in the control groups cases with poorer prognosis. For example, an analysis of published research on schizophrenics revealed that the recovery rate of control groups used in studies of somatic therapies was significantly lower than that of the general untreated mental hospital population prior to the introduction of these specific therapies (Staudt & Zubin, 1957).

In research with outpatients, control cases are often drawn from waiting lists. This procedure presents several difficulties. It is likely that many such cases will obtain help elsewhere, especially if the waiting period is long. On the other hand, the fact that they have not been accepted for therapy may heighten the feeling of rejection that so often characterizes their interpersonal attitudes. In any event, a number may lose contact with the clinic and thus be unavailable for follow-ups. A somewhat more effective approach is to treat the waiting period as an own-control for cases later accepted for therapy. This procedure, which is being used increasingly, represents an application of the previously described N-of-one-at-a-time designs, calling for time-series analyses in the evaluation of outcome.

Experimental Design. There are many problems of experimental design that must be considered in planning or evaluating any study on the effects of therapy (Azrin, 1977; Bergin & Strupp, 1972, pp. 64–82; Bordin, 1974; Kiesler, 1971; Uhr & Miller, 1960, Chs. 5 & 6). Some of these problems are common to all outcome research in clinical psychology; others are specific to the evaluation of a particular form of treatment. As examples, we shall consider problems pertaining to needed control data in assessing the effects of drug therapy and of different psychological therapies.

In the evaluation of drug therapies, control procedures must be such as to rule out the *placebo effect* (Loranger, Prout, & White, 1961; Uhr & Miller, 1960, Ch. 6). The term "placebo," derived from a Latin verb meaning "to please" or "to placate," originally referred to a pharmaceutically inactive substance prescribed when no specific remedy was available for the patient's condition. Placebos are employed in drug experiments to control the effects of suggestion and expectation on both subjects and observers. The customary procedure is to administer a placebo to some subjects and the experimental drug to others in a form that makes the two indistinguishable. In the *double-blind technique*, the identity of drug and placebo (or control) cases is not revealed to either subjects or observers (e.g., therapists, nurses, attendants, examiners). Some drugs present a more difficult control problem because they produce recognizable side effects, such as dizziness or motor incoordination. It would thus be an easy matter for subjects and observers to determine who had received the placebo and who had received the drug. Under these circumstances, it is desirable to use an "active placebo," which simulates the side effects of the drug but does not contain the specific pharmaceutical agent under investigation.

With regard to psychotherapy, it is difficult to separate the influence of a specific therapy from the more general effect of any sort of therapeutic attention. For this reason, several special controls have been devised; these are variously described as attention placebo, minimal therapy, or pseudotherapy, as contrasted to a no-treatment control. In addition, behavior therapists have frequently designed investigations in which a composite therapeutic program has been dissected and separate elements have been presented to different experimental groups or introduced in stages to different groups in a time-series design (Bandura, Blanchard, & Ritter, 1969; Rachman, 1965). An increasing number of investigators, moreover, have argued that a more fruitful approach is the comparative investigation of alternative types of therapy.

A particularly well-designed study illustrating this comparative design was conducted by Paul (1966, 1968). The subjects were 96 college students who had requested treatment for anxiety in public speaking. All took an initial and final test battery assessing anxiety in a variety of interpersonal situations as well as other pertinent personality traits. For experimental purposes, these subjects were assigned to the following five treatment groups:

1. Systematic desensitization ($N = 15$).
2. Insight-oriented psychotherapy ($N = 15$)—traditional psychotherapy reflecting psychoanalytic and Rogerian influences.
3. Attention-placebo ($N = 15$). This psychotherapy was presented to the participants as "stress tolerance training." It included a placebo pill described as a fast-acting tranquilizer and an auditory signal detection task. Nonspecific aspects of therapy, such as rapport, explanation of rationale, and therapist attitude were closely similar for the first three groups.
4. No-treatment, waiting-list control ($N = 29$). This group received no treatment but, like the first three groups, underwent an individual stress assessment at the beginning and end of the experiment, which included a sample speech performance.
5. No-contact control ($N = 22$). Although selected so as to be equated with the other four groups, these subjects were unaware of their being included in the experiment, since they were administered the initial and final group battery with all other students registered in the speech classes.

The examiners who conducted the individual pretreatment and posttreatment stress assessments were unaware of the group assignment of individuals, thus preserving the double-blind control. Treatments were carried out by five therapists experienced in insight therapy, who were given intensive training in the systematic desensitization and attention-placebo procedures. Therapist variables were equated by assigning each of the therapists to three subjects in each of the three treatment groups. Analysis of results immediately after completion of the five-week program, as well as in a follow-up six weeks later, showed that all three treatment groups had improved significantly more than the controls, but the desensitization group improved significantly more than the other two. In a later, two-year follow-up, the treated groups showed continued improvement, and the relative position of the different groups was maintained.

A more recent study (Sloane, Staples, Cristol, Yorkston, & Whipple, 1975) followed a somewhat different and less fully controlled approach. The subjects were clients at a university outpatient clinic and had a variety of emotional problems. They were randomly assigned to brief psychoanalytic therapy, behavior therapy, or a waiting-list control group. In this investigation, each of the two types of therapy was conducted by clinicans highly experienced in that particular form of therapy. Although in certain respects behavior therapy proved more effective, the overall differences in outcome were minor. Of particular interest was the finding that what the two types of therapists did in the course of therapy, especially with regard to interpersonal relations with the client, revealed more similarities between them than are generally expected.

There is also some evidence that, when a sufficiently convincing and impressive pseudotherapy is used, it may be just as effective as systematic desensitization in overcoming a phobia (McReynolds, Barnes, Brooks, & Rehagen, 1973). A special feature of this study was the use of naive therapists who were themselves unable to differentiate between the pseudotherapy and the true therapy. Thus the double-blind technique was extended to include not only subjects and assessors but also therapists (triple-blind?). It might be added that a survey of published research on desensitization led to the conclusion that the majority of studies had failed to rule out differential expectation of improvement between the desensitization and control groups (Kazdin & Wilcoxon, 1976).

Interaction. In outcome research, we again encounter the interaction of variables and the desirability of a systems approach. In lieu of the general—and unanswerable—question, "Is psychotherapy effective?" Bergin and Strupp (1972, p. 8) propose the following reformulation: "What specific therapeutic interventions produce specific changes in specific patients under specific conditions?" In other words, outcome depends on interactions among variables of therapeutic techniques, of the client (specific complaints as well as relevant personality and background characteristics), and of the therapist (personality, training, experience, etc.). Moreover, outcome itself may vary depending upon the particular improvement criterion employed.

It is noteworthy that Bergin and Strupp had originally visualized a composite, collaborative research program in which a large number of such interacting variables and multiple assessment procedures could be investigated simultaneously. Following an extensive interview survey of leading clinical researchers, however, they abandoned that approach and instead recommended an essentially dual attack from two angles:

1. Highly controlled studies of the operation of individual variables, to provide theoretical guidelines for the development of various therapeutic programs.
2. Evaluation of intact therapeutic programs within particular contexts. These evaluations should in turn provide insights regarding higher order interactions, as data from many diverse studies accumulate.

It will be recognized that this dual attack on the problem of interactions coincides with the most feasible approach described in Chapter 4, regarding the investigation of interacting variables in training programs. Essentially the same conclusion was reached by Cronbach (1975) in a survey of learner, task, method, and instructor variables in education, as well as by the HumRRO investigators working with job training programs in military contexts (Bialek et al., 1973). A basic obstacle in the way of a comprehensive, broadly generalizable investigation is that lower order interactions (involving only two or three interacting variables) may be confounded by the unmeasured effects of higher order interactions, and the identification of statistically significant higher order interactions requires excessively large samples.

PROGRAM EVALUATION

Nature and Uses. Program evaluation is a rapidly growing professional specialty (Bernstein & Freeman, 1975; Mikawa, 1975; Perloff & Sussna, 1976; Roen, 1971). Its explosive development in the 1970s is reflected in the proliferation of books, journals, conferences, symposia, training institutes, and university programs devoted to procedures for conducting program evaluations and for evaluating the evaluations. A major stimulus for such evaluations is the pressure for accountability, especially in federally funded programs. The results of such evaluations are often used in reaching decisions about resource allocation. Two areas in which program evaluation has been especially prominent are education and community mental health. Although program evaluation is a multidisciplinary specialty, involving such fields as economics, accounting, education, industrial engineering, sociology, political science, and urban affairs, we shall focus on the contributions of psychologists.

Despite the recent emergence of program evaluation as a professional specialty, applied psychologists have for several decades been conducting empirical evaluations of their procedures as an integral part of their functions. Examples include the validation of personnel selection and classification instruments (Ch. 2), the evaluation of industrial training programs (Ch. 4), and the process and outcome studies of therapy, discussed earlier in this chapter. Much that was said about those topics is relevant to program evaluation.

In a survey of program evaluation in the *Annual Review of Psychology*, Perloff, Perloff, and Sussna (1976) describe its purpose as an investigation of the "extent to which a program achieved one or more of its objectives, the reasons it may not have achieved them, and the relationships among program effects and a variety of input variables and program characteristics" (p. 570). As in the assessment of training (Ch. 4), a distinction can be made between formative and summative program evaluations (Scriven, 1967). *Formative evaluation* is best adapted for program development. It is an ongoing evaluation, usually conducted from the outset by internal program staff. It provides continuing feedback for modifying and improving the program. An initial stage, especially in community mental health programs, may include an assessment of community needs, with special reference to nature of problems, client populations, and availability and current utilization of facilities.

Summative evaluation is most appropriate for the purposes of accountability. It usually involves an external, independent evaluation of overall program effectiveness. Certain major national projects have been subjected to secondary evaluations, performed by a second group of independent researchers. This is illustrated by the reevaluation of the children's television program, "Sesame Street," conducted by Cook and his staff (1975). The original evaluation had been done by Educational Testing Service (Bogatz & Ball, 1971).

Another familiar distinction that can be applied to program evaluation is that between process and outcome (or impact) research (Bernstein & Freeman, 1975). In this context, *process* research can be illustrated by an evaluation of how well the program was implemented. Examples of the questions that might be asked in process evaluation of a community mental health center include the extent to which the facility is actually used, the source of referrals, and the distribution of clients with regard to target populations. *Outcome* or *impact evaluation*, on the other hand, concerns the effects of the intervention in solving the problems for which the program was designed. It thus serves essentially the same purposes as the previously discussed outcome studies of psychotherapy.

Procedures. The specific procedures employed in program evaluation are extremely varied, ranging from superficial, subjective, anecdotal assessments to highly sophisticated and complex quantitative analyses. Interviews, questionnaires, and rating forms have been used with project staff, clients, and other community members. Clinical data, naturalistic observations, and field survey methods all have a place in such research. Evaluation of client progress utilizes all the sources of information available in clinical practice, including self-reports and reports by family members, teachers, social workers, and other observers.

Whatever the specific procedures or the purposes of the evaluation, one point deserves special emphasis: evaluation should be planned before the program is put into effect and should be an integral part of the program. All too often, no serious thought is given to evaluation procedures until the program is well under way or near completion. At that stage, it may be virtually impossible to gather meaningful evaluation data. For this reason, most fund-granting agencies now require that evaluation be built into the initial project proposal.

Without attempting to survey specific procedures that have been employed in program evaluation, we shall call attention to four common problems of particular importance, namely, objectives, experimental design, criteria of outcome, and cost-benefit analysis. To evaluate the effectiveness of any program requires the clear formulation of specific *program objectives*. Unless we can state in clear, readily observable or measurable terms what the program is trying to accomplish, it is obviously impossible to determine how well it has performed its function.

The concern for *experimental design* is based on the desire to make causal attributions. If certain changes (in clients, institutions, community, etc.) occur in the course of the program, can they be attributed to the program or could they have resulted from other conditions? Because it is difficult to follow ideal experimental designs in real-life community settings, researchers have proposed certain quasi-experimental designs (Campbell & Stanley, 1966; Cook & Campbell, 1976). Examples include the previously discussed time-series designs and the nonequivalent-control-group designs, in which both pretest and posttest data are obtained from available control and intervention groups, even though they cannot be matched on all relevant variables. Because any one method selected within the realistic constraints of evaluation studies is likely to have some limitations, the use of multiple methods representing different approaches is highly desirable. The same can be said about the choice of *criteria of outcome*. When single criteria are employed, different evaluators are likely to reach opposite conclusions about the effectiveness of the same program. It is important to apply multiple criteria which are tied to each of the specified program objectives. It is also advisable to look into possible adverse side effects of the program that may or may not have been anticipated.

Finally, some *cost-benefit analysis* of the program is needed, involving a comparative evaluation of this program with alternative ongoing or proposed programs. When questions of resource allocation are involved, such comparisons are obviously required. Considerations of cost-effectiveness are also relevant to formative evaluation and program development (see Ch. 4 for training program examples). Cost-benefit analysis may require a comprehensive decision-theory approach, in which subjective value judgments are expressed quantitatively and entered into the overall evaluation (see Ch. 2).

Potential Hazards. Although evaluation studies have been proliferating at an astounding rate, the large majority are poorly designed and inconclusive (Bernstein & Freeman, 1975). Yet their results are used in making important decisions regarding the initiation, continuation, or termination of major programs (Mushkin, 1973). An effective intervention program may be rejected because a poorly planned and weak evaluation failed to detect its impact, This would be an example of what is known as a Type II error in hypothesis testing.

A more far-reaching hazard is that the negative results may be attributed neither to the inadequate evaluation nor to the ineffectiveness of a particular intervention program but to the nature of the problem itself (Perloff et al., 1976). As an example, suppose that a poorly designed evaluation of a compensatory education program for culturally disadvantaged children failed to detect improvement in academic skills. The conclusion might be drawn not only that such compensatory education programs are futile but also that children from the population under investigation are genetically inferior and hence incapable of profiting from further help.

A different sort of hazard arises when the criteria of program effectiveness are chosen because of ready availability of data or ease of measurement, rather than for intrinsic importance. Thus some major program objectives may be overlooked and the evaluation may be unduly influenced by relatively minor outcomes. In this case, the mechanics of the evaluation process may not only lead to a distorted assessment of program effectiveness but may also adversely influence subsequent program operation and services. Under these circumstances, the attitudes and future behavior of the program staff may alter in the direction of whatever provides a more favorable evaluation result.

From another angle, a favorable outcome from a program about which the project personnel are enthusiastic and the clients hopeful must be viewed with caution. Both the Hawthorne effect (Ch. 5) and the many attention-placebo studies in clinical psychology warn against the premature acceptance of such positive results, unless adequate controls are employed. The danger in this situation is that, as the novelty and excitement of the program wear off, the decline in effectiveness may lead to disillusionment and to the abandonment of further intervention efforts. Still another type of participant attitude, which has been labeled the "John Henry effect," may influence results in the opposite direction (Saretsky, 1972). If the participating staff perceive the experimental innovation as a threat (to their job security, their traditional work patterns, etc.), they may expend extraordinary efforts to raise the performance level of the control group, thereby masking any potential advantage of the experimental program.

NATURE AND ETIOLOGY OF PSYCHOLOGICAL DYSFUNCTION

Investigations of the nature and causes of intellectual and emotional disorders constitute a large portion of the basic research underlying clinical psychology. The phenomenal growth of clinical psychology since midcentury has been accompanied by a vigorous and comprehensive attack on problems of etiology. This research has drawn upon a multitude of disciplines, from genetics and biochemistry to sociology and communication theory. Because the major emphasis in this book is on applied rather than on basic research, etiological studies will be sketched briefly, in order merely to suggest the varied approaches that are currently being explored and to illustrate methodological problems.

Epidemiology. Characterized by a preventive orientation, epidemiology is the study of the frequency and distribution of particular disorders with reference to various population characteristics (Dohrenwend & Dohrenwend, 1969, 1974a). The distribution of mental disorders has been investigated in both urban and rural communities by a variety of procedures.[2] Some researchers have surveyed institutionalized cases in both state mental hospitals and private clinics, as well as outpatients under treatment by individual therapists. Other studies have identified both treated and untreated cases through interviews of community samples to ascertain the presence of specific behavioral symptoms. This information is then used by clinicians to rate severity of disorder for each case. Such multiple approaches are designed to rule out selective biases which undoubtedly operate when only institutional samples are investigated.

Of particular interest is the greater prevalence of mental disorder among lower than among higher *socioeconomic levels.* This relation has been repeatedly demonstrated in a large number of studies conducted in several countries and following diverse procedures. Among the possible conditions contributing to these differences are child-rearing practices, educational level, amount of stress encountered in occupational and other adult activities, and class differences in attitudes toward mental health and therapy. A comparison of the socioeconomic level of the patients themselves with that of their parents sheds some light upon the probable influence of specific etiological factors. Surveys conducted in America reveal that the fathers of schizophrenics tend to be in the same occupational level as the patients (Hollingshead & Redlich, 1958). Hence the conditions associated with low socioeconomic level have been operative since the patient's childhood. In British surveys, on the other hand, the occupational distribution of the fathers is fairly typical of that found in the general population, while the schizophrenic sons tend to cluster in the unskilled labor level (Morrison, 1959). In both countries, however, the patients themselves tended to remain in the same occupational level throughout their own working life, rather than exhibiting a downward drift in their own job history. These analyses illustrate the complexity of conditions to be considered in interpreting epidemiological findings (see also Dohrenwend & Dohrenwend, 1974a).

Another noteworthy finding pertains to *cross-cultural differences* in the relative

---

[2]Some of the major projects are reported in: Hollingshead and Redlich, (1958); Langner and Michael (1963); Leighton, Harding, Macklin, Macmillan, and Leighton (1963); Pasamanick (1962); Srole and Fischer (1975); Srole, Langner, Michael, Opler, and Rennie (1962).

frequency of different syndromes, such as schizophrenia versus manic-depressive psychosis or anxiety hysteria versus conversion hysteria (Anastasi, 1958, Ch. 18; Dohrenwend & Dohrenwend, 1974a; Draguns & Phillips, 1972; Field, 1960; D. D. Jackson, 1960, Ch. 10; Ullman & Krasner, 1975, Ch. 10; Weinstein, 1962). Moreover, some syndromes appear to be specific to certain cultures and absent in others. The social history of our own culture shows temporal changes and "fashions in abnormality," as illustrated by the dancing manias of the Middle Ages and by the conspicuous decrease in the frequency of hysterical anesthesias and motor disorders between the two world wars. The whole problem is further complicated by the fact that behavior that is deviant or disabling in one culture may be accepted and even favored in another.

Even within the same diagnostic category, specific symptoms exhibit cultural differences. This finding is illustrated by comparative studies of American schizo-phrenics of Irish and Italian extractions (Fantl & Schiro, 1959; Singer & Opler, 1956; Zola, 1966). While closely equated in age, education, socioeconomic level, religion, and number of American generations, the two groups yielded significant differences in the nature of schizophrenic symptoms, as revealed in both personality test performance and ratings of ward behavior. The Irish-Americans showed a greater tendency toward imaginative and fantasy behavior and more inhibition of motor expression; the Italian-Americans were more overtly aggressive and impulsive. The investigators related these findings to subcultural differences in child-rearing practices and family constellation, as well as other cultural factors.

From a methodological viewpoint, it is important to examine the possible contribution of *diagnostic biases* to socioeconomic and cultural differences in the reported prevalence of mental disorders. In an investigation of the relative frequency of schizophrenia and manic-depressive psychosis in the United States and England, for example, part of the difference was found to result from the greater tendency of American psychiatrists to diagnose cases as schizophrenic, while British psychiatrists were more likely to use the manic-depressive diagnosis (Cooper et al., 1972). When this bias was eliminated through independent diagno-ses by a common project staff, however, substantial national differences in the prevalence of these syndromes remained.

With regard to socioeconomic classes, there is evidence that clinicians tend to attach less favorable diagnoses to the same behavior when manifested by a lower-class person than when manifested by a middle-class person (Haase, 1964). This tendency can be investigated by presenting the same test protocols, case histories, or interview recordings with the information that they were obtained from a lower-class or middle-class person. It should be noted, however, that this diagnostic bias was substantially controlled in those community surveys in which "blind" diagnoses were made from behavior records gathered by other project personnel. Moreover, there is evidence that this diagnostic bias is disappearing, especially among clinical psychologists (Koscherak & Masling, 1972; Smyth, 1973). As clinicians obtain more experience with lower-class clients and as they become sensitized to the possible operation of such a diagnostic bias, they learn to avoid it.

Heredity. The extent to which hereditary factors contribute to the etiology of mental disorders is still largely unknown. Since the experimentally controlled, selective-breeding procedures of animal genetics cannot be applied to human subjects, knowledge about human heredity must be derived from relatively indirect and uncontrolled sources. Thus human geneticists have investigated the extent of consanguinity (marriage of close relatives) in the families of persons with a given disorder, the incidence of a disorder in relatively isolated inbred communities, and the occurrence of a disorder in different members of the same family. Because of insufficient information about the operation of other factors, however, these approaches rarely provide conclusive evidence of hereditary influences.

Data on family resemblances in a given trait or condition are particularly difficult to interpret because families represent environmental as well as biological units. Even physical disorders may run in families without necessarily being hereditary. Beriberi shows high concentration in certain families, not because of a genetic basis, but because of a vitamin deficiency in the family diet. Members of the same family not only share many features of a common environment but also interact with each other. Hence there are many opportunities for mutual influence. Quite apart from heredity, an illiterate mother provides a less stimulating intellectual environment for her children than does a mother with a college degree. A more subtle but potentially effective factor is social expectancy. Since relatives are expected to resemble each other, any chance similarity between them is likely to be noticed and magnified. The expected similarities may in turn influence the individual's self-concept and subsequent psychological development.

It is only when a defect is transmitted according to a simple and easily identified hereditary mechanism that data on familial incidence can demonstrate its genetic origin. For example, if a characteristic depends upon a single recessive gene, its observed familial incidence can be checked against the expected distribution derived from Mendelian ratios. Such simple hereditary mechanisms have been identified for only a few human conditions. Among them are certain rare and extreme forms of mental retardation, such as phenylketonuria and Tay-Sachs disease. These types of mental retardation have also been traced to metabolic disorders, which in turn stem from biochemically defective genes. Knowledge about the many intervening physiological steps, from defective gene to behavior disorder, helps to clarify the hereditary basis of the disorder. For most psychological disorders, however, this type of information is unavailable.

In the effort to rule out some of the uncontrolled factors of familial studies, several investigators have worked with identical (monozygotic) and fraternal (dizygotic) twins. Since they develop from a single fertilized ovum, identical twins have identical sets of genes. Fraternal twins, on the other hand, are no more alike in heredity than ordinary siblings, although they are born at the same time. The usual procedure in twin studies is to locate individual cases of twins who manifest a particular disorder. The incidence of the disorder among the co-twins and other relatives of these "index cases" is then investigated. When both members of a pair of related persons (twins, siblings, parent-child, etc.) exhibit the same disorder, they are described as "concordant"; when only one member shows the disorder, the pair is described as "discordant."

The twin-study method has been employed in a number of major research projects on schizophrenia conducted in several countries (Rosenthal, 1971, Ch. 5). The earlier—and less adequately controlled—studies yielded very high estimates of monozygotic twin concordance (70%–80%), while the concordance rate for dizygotic twins was often no higher than that of siblings born singly. With increasing refinements in such research techniques as sampling procedures and definition of concordance, the monozygotic concordance rates dropped to the region of 25%–40%, although still exceeding the concordance rates for dizygotic twins (Rosenthal, 1971; Ullman & Krasner, 1975, Ch. 10). The interpretation of these results is still controversial. Most investigators agree that some hereditary factors are probably involved but that schizophrenia will not develop unless adverse environmental conditions are also present. Much remains to be learned about the nature and operation of specific hereditary and environmental mechanisms in the etiology of mental disorders.

A promising line of research is the systematic study of *discordant* monozygotic twin pairs (Wahl, 1976). There is some evidence suggesting that the twin who eventually developed schizophrenia weighed less at birth, had more often undergone birth complications, was perceived as more vulnerable, and was overprotected by parents. These early experiences in turn encouraged more dependency and a poorer self-concept on the child's part (Stabenau & Pollin, 1970). The investigation of such developmental influences is especially helpful in suggesting desirable intervention procedures in early childhood as a means of primary prevention of mental disorders.

Organic Factors. Any organic defects identified as causal factors in mental disorders may themselves have either a hereditary or an environmental origin. On the one hand, defective genes may produce metabolic disorders that ultimately lead to mental retardation or other behavioral dysfunctions. On the other hand, psychological disorders may result from a number of conditions in the prenatal environment, such as toxins, bacterial infections, nutritional inadequacies, and radiation. Brain injuries occurring during the birth process, as well as perinatal anoxia, may also cause intellectual defects and other psychological abnormalities. Severe diseases like meningitis or encephalitis in early childhood may have similar results.

The effects of many of these conditions have been investigated experimentally in animals as well as through follow-up studies of human infants. In a well-controlled animal experiment, for example, oxygen deprivation during gestation or immediately after birth significantly decreased the learning performance of rats and cats at maturity (Meier, Bunch, Nolan, & Scheidler, 1960). In another study (Graham, Ernhart, Thurston, & Craft, 1962), 355 newborn infants were classified into those who had had normal birth, those who had experienced anoxia, and those who had undergone other birth complications (prematurity, injuries, etc.). Three years later, the children were given neurological and psychological examinations. To control observer bias, the examiners had no knowledge of the subjects' original classification. The anoxia cases performed significantly more poorly on the Stanford-Binet and other psychological tests and showed signs of neurological impairment. Similar but more varied results were obtained with other birth complications. This study supported the view that "minimal brain damage," too slight to cause conspicuous disorders like cerebral palsy, may nevertheless produce behavioral deficiencies.

Following an extensive survey of many different complications of gestation and birth, Pasamanick and his associates (Knoblock & Pasamanick, 1959; Lilienfeld, Pasamanick, & Rogers, 1955) proposed a "continuum of reproductive casualty." By this they meant that varying degrees of prenatal or perinatal trauma will lead to a continuum of effects ranging from mild intellectual or emotional disorders to severe mental retardation, cerebral palsy, and death. The data for this survey were obtained retrospectively, by examining the birth certificates and obstetrical records of children whose subsequent condition was known. In the same survey (Pasamanick, Knoblock, & Lilienfeld, 1956), an analysis of results by socioeconomic level showed a marked excess of prenatal and perinatal abnormalities in lower socioeconomic levels, probably resulting from dietary deficiencies and inferior maternal care during pregnancy. These findings suggest a possible basis for some of the socioeconomic differences that are consistently found both in intelligence test performance and in the incidence of emotional disorders.

Organic factors have also been extensively investigated in connection with the etiology of schizophrenia (Groves & Rebec, 1976; D. D. Jackson, 1960; Kety, 1975; Reitan, 1976). Significant differences between schizophrenics and normals have been found in electroencephalograms, incidence of structural defects of cortical neurones, metabolic processes, blood chemistry, and endocrine functions. Several investigators have measured the toxicity of the serum of schizophrenics, using various animal forms as test objects. Research with psychotomimetic drugs, which simulate psychotic symptoms in normal persons, have suggested other biochemical hypotheses, which also help to explain the effect of certain antipsychotic drugs in terms of their specific biochemical action.

All this research activity is opening up promising new approaches to the etiology of schizophrenia and other psychological disorders. At this stage, however, conclusions would be premature. In interpreting the findings of any study in this area, we must bear in mind, first, that schizophrenia is a broad and loosely applied diagnostic category, which actually covers a variety of behavioral difficulties. Different forms of schizophrenia may have different etiologies. Even the same symptoms may result from different factors in different persons. It is generally recognized, too, that organic and experiential factors interact in the development of schizophrenic disorders. Thus either hereditary or environmentally produced organic dysfunctions may make the individual more vulnerable to psychological stress. In the absence of severely stressful experiences, however, behavioral disturbances may fail to develop even in one who is organically predisposed to them.

When organic differences are found between schizophrenics and normals, we must also consider the possibility that the differences may be a *result* of emotional stress, degree of activity, nutritional state, and other variables associated with either the psychotic condition itself or with institutionalization (Kety, 1975). Several alleged biochemical differences between schizophrenics and normals, for example, disappeared when rechecked in more adequately controlled studies. In some cases, the difference had resulted from deficiencies in the institutional diet. In order to minimize the influence of institutional conditions in comparative physiological studies of schizophrenics and normals, some large-scale projects have established special experimental wards (Kety, 1959, 1960). In such studies, schizophrenic patients remain for an extended period in the experimental ward, with controlled diet and uniform living conditions, while a group of normal control subjects live under approximately comparable conditions in a similar ward. With such an experimental design, however, it is still impossible to establish whether any observed organic difference represents a cause or a result of schizophrenia itself. Only longitudinal data can disentangle that relationship.

Experiential Factors. With the growing recognition of the important part that environment plays in the development and remediation of psychological dysfunctions, more and more research has been directed toward an analysis of experiential factors. What types of prior experiences differentiate mentally disturbed from effectively functioning persons and how do they operate in the etiology of dysfunction? The research on this question spans a wide variety of approaches, from clinical studies and questionnaire surveys to analogue experiments with human subjects and highly controlled investigations with animals. A few examples will be cited to illustrate the range of problems and methodology.

A large number of investigations have explored *child-rearing practices and early familial relations*. Data have been gathered from parents through interviews, questionnaires, and psychological tests, as well as through retrospective reports by adult patients (D. D. Jackson, 1960, Chs. 10–14). Some investigators have utilized a short situational test to observe interpersonal relations of parents and child (Garmezy, Farina, & Rodnick, 1960). Others have observed the family in the home or in a hospital setting for limited time periods. A more intensive and better controlled procedure is illustrated by the research of the Family Study Section of the National Institute of Mental Health (Bowen, 1960), in which schizophrenic patients and their parents lived together in a special ward for periods of six months to three years. Data were gathered through therapeutic family sessions as well as through daily observations by nurses and ward attendants.

Although these methods vary in dependability, each has certain shortcomings (Fontana, 1966; Frank, 1965). Procedures relying on reports by patients or other family members are subject to perceptual distortions and errors of recall, particularly for emotionally toned material. Direct observations of family interactions are preferable but subject to possible bias on the part of both observers and subjects: observers may be influenced by preconceptions, since the observing conditions are rarely "blind" with regard to subject identity, and the families may be influenced by awareness of being observed. A major difficulty is that of disentangling cause-and-effect relations. We do not know to what extent the abnormal behavior of the patient may have led to the disturbed family relations or to parental overprotectiveness, rejection, or other disruptive child-rearing practices.

In the light of such methodological problems, it is not surprising that nearly fifty years of research have failed to identify familial behavior patterns that consistently differentiated schizophrenics from other diagnostic categories or from normal controls (Frank, 1965). Some of the better controlled studies, however, provide guidelines for longitudinal studies, which can analyze causal relations more directly (Fontana, 1966). Another pertinent consideration is that of interaction of variables. It is reasonable to expect that any one child-rearing practice or any one pattern of familial relations may have a *different* effect when combined with different concomitant events or circumstances. Research on the families of psychologically disturbed children and adults may provide clues about such interactions which can be followed up in other types of studies.

In view of the recognized need for *longitudinal studies* to identify causal relations in the development of mental disorders, it is encouraging to find an upsurge of activity in this approach in the 1970s. Major longitudinal research projects are described in a series of volumes based on conferences of the Society for Life History Research (Roff & Ricks, 1970; Roff, Robins, & Pollack, 1972; Ricks, Thomas, & Roff, 1974; Wirt, Winokur, & Roff, 1976). Typically, these studies obtained follow-up adult data for individuals who had been examined many years earlier in child-guidance clinics and schools.

Those studies that began with schoolwide testing worked with an essentially unselected sample and were later able to identify the individuals with deviant outcomes. Most of the studies, however, employed largely case history material pertaining to children with problems of varying degrees of severity. An example is a study of 100 adult schizophrenics identified from a sample of about 15,000 cases who had been seen as children over a 50-year period in a single child-guidance clinic (Fleming & Ricks, 1970; Ricks & Berry, 1970). This group was compared with a normal control group of 100 cases selected on the basis of adequate work and social adjustment. The original childhood case records of both groups were examined for data on parental personalities, family relationships, and early childhood behavior patterns prior to the onset of schizophrenia.

An especially promising recent trend is the convergence of data from diverse types of basic research. An outstanding example is provided by major efforts to formulate a *comprehensive theory of depression* which integrates results from clinical observations with controlled analogue experiments on normal persons and on animals (e.g., Akiskal & McKinney, 1973; Hannum, Rosellini, & Seligman, 1976; Lewinsohn, 1975; Seligman, 1975). Applying the principles of reinforcement, this theory centers on the concept of learned helplessness as a basis for anxiety and depression. In essence the theory proposes that, if avoidance of an unpleasant situation and the attainment of positive reinforcement are no longer contingent on the individual's own responses, he learns to behave in a hopeless and helpless manner toward subsequent events. He feels incapable of influencing what happens to him and he stops trying.

Evidence from various sources suggests that, when the individual loses control over his sources of positive reinforcement, his behavior passes through three stages, described as protest, despair, and detachment or apathy. This behavior can be illustrated by the effects of separation from a significant object of attachment in early life. In experiments with infant monkeys, for example, behavior manifestations of severe depression have been observed following separation from the mother (Suomi & Harlow, 1977). Similar behavior occurs when the animal is separated from age peers or from a surrogate mother in the form of an inanimate object with which it was being reared. In species in which other adult females ("aunts") normally react to the infant as does its own mother, separation from all adult females has the same effect (Kaufman, 1973). Other experiments have shown that isolation, confinement, restraint, or other aversive stimulation that the animal is helpless to alter likewise lead to depression (Harlow & Harlow, 1971; Sidowski, 1971; Suomi & Harlow, 1977).

The extensive research program with monkeys conducted by Harlow and his associates at the University of Wisconsin included not only the experimental induction of behavior pathology but also the investigation of therapy and rehabilitation (Novak, 1978; Novak & Harlow, 1975; Suomi & Harlow, 1971, 1977). Both somatic and social-behavioral procedures have been explored. Examples of the latter include: gradual exposure to increased visual contact with another monkey through a wire mesh; the self-pacing of such visual stimulation, whereby the animal has limited control over the amount of visual contact it receives; and social experience with a monkey "therapist." The therapist monkeys were chosen on the basis of such characteristics as age (e.g., younger or the same age as the isolate) and their own rearing conditions so as to provide the behavioral stimulation most appropriate for the kind and severity of behavior pathology to be treated. Figure 14-4 shows a therapist monkey clinging to the back of an isolate during the early stages of rehabilitation. Active social play followed as therapy progressed, as illustrated in Figure 14-5. Repeated retests until the age of $3\frac{1}{2}$ years showed that recovery did not regress over time and normal behavior could be maintained if the monkeys were housed in groups. The monkey therapists in these experiments may

Figure 14-4. Therapist monkey clinging to back of isolate monkey with experimentally induced depression. *(From Suomi & Harlow, 1971, p. 524. Copyright © 1971 by Brunner/Mazel, Inc. Reproduced by permission. Photograph by courtesy of H. F. Harlow.)*

be regarded as one more example of the effective utilization of indigenous nonprofessional therapeutic agents!

An overview of research on the nature and causes of mental disorders points clearly to one conclusion: serious psychological pathology results from a *combination* of adverse conditions. No one factor, be it experiential, biochemical, or genetic, is sufficient to lead to severe mental dysfunction. Suppose that factor A occurs significantly more often in schizophrenics than in normals. Nevertheless, there will be some schizophrenics without this factor and some normals with it. This general finding offers a hopeful prospect for prevention and therapy. Although any one condition might be difficult or impossible to alter in a particular individual's life, other contributing factors are likely to be amenable to ameliorative manipulations.

SUMMARY

The gap between clinical practice and research has been narrowing since midcentury. Increasing use is being made of N-of-one and other quasi-

Figure 14-5. Isolate monkey (above) reciprocating play initiated by therapist monkey during later stages of therapy period. *(From Suomi & Harlow, 1971, p. 524. Copyright © 1971 by Brunner/Mazel, Inc. Reproduced by permission. Photograph by courtesy of H. F. Harlow.)*

experimental designs appropriate for clinical and community psychology. The integration of clinical investigations with highly controlled experiments with human and animal subjects is making significant progress.

A well-established type of clinical research is concerned with the validation of diagnostic procedures, particularly projective techniques and other special clinical instruments. In the validation of such instruments, special attention must be given to questions of blind analysis, stereotype accuracy, illusory correlation, multitrait-multimethod correlations, cross-validation, translation of test protocols into testable behavioral predictions, adequacy of criterion measures, interaction effects, and unevenness of coverage of the same test for different persons.

Investigations of the process of therapy deal with the way in which different therapists function, the effects of therapist characteristics and behavior upon client reactions, and progressive changes in client behavior within therapy sessions. Initiated largely by the client-centered school, process research is also an integral part of behavior therapy. Adequate assessment of the outcome of therapy requires repeated measurement at different stages before, during, and after therapy. Among the criteria of outcome employed for this purpose are client self-report, therapist's evaluation, objective records of behavior change during therapy sessions, ward behavior, and follow-up data in real-life situations. Representativeness and comparability of treated and control groups require special attention. There is also need for control procedures to identify placebo effects. In the design of outcome research and the interpretation of results, it is important to consider interactions among variables of client, therapist, and therapeutic technique and to recognize the specificity of outcome criteria.

Program evaluation, which is of special relevance to community psychology, has much in common with outcome research. It covers both formative and summative evaluations and both process and impact (or outcome) data. Utilizing a wide range of techniques, program evaluation needs to give special attention to the clear formulation of program objectives, the advance planning of suitable experimental designs, and comparative cost-benefit analyses.

Research on the causes of mental disorders is an interdisciplinary venture spanning many fields, from biochemistry to anthropology. The sources of behavioral pathology have been sought in heredity, organic conditions, and experiential factors. Epidemiology has identified socioeconomic and cross-cultural differences in the incidence of mental disorders and in the relative frequency of different syndromes and specific behavioral manifestations. Research on etiological factors is beset with methodological and interpretive problems. Although many biological and experiential variables have yielded significant differences between mentally disturbed persons and normal controls, it is evident that the development of serious psychological pathology requires a combination of adverse factors.

THE WORK OF THE
COUNSELING PSYCHOLOGIST

FIFTEEN

COUNSELING IS A BROAD TERM that covers many different functions. A professional counselor, moreover, may have been trained in psychology, social work, education, the ministry, or a number of other fields. It is only since the 1950s that the title of "counseling psychologist" was adopted to designate a fully trained psychologist, typically at the PhD level, who specializes in counseling functions. The term "counselor" is commonly employed more loosely to designate persons with varied backgrounds and relatively little specialized training in psychology.

Historically, counseling psychology originated in the vocational-guidance movement (Kitson, 1958). The early vocational counselors concentrated on the dissemination of information about jobs. Following the rapid growth of psychological testing after World War I, tests were widely employed to investigate the individual's qualifications for different kinds of work. Still later came the recognition that vocational choices and vocational adjustment are intimately related to personality development and to total life adjustment. As a result, the functions of the vocational counselor were broadened to include a study of the whole individual. Concurrently, the rise of the mental health movement, the introduction of employee counselors in industry, and other developments highlighted the need for counselors to deal with a number of personal problems other than those associated with vocational choice. At this stage, counseling merged with clinical psychology.

Some psychologists use the terms "clinical psychology" and "counseling psychology" interchangeably and recognize no essential difference between the two fields (see, e.g., F. McKinney, 1965; Patterson, 1973; Rogers, 1942, 1951). To be sure, there is much overlapping in the activities of most clinical and counseling psychologists. Among individual practitioners, moreover, some counseling psychologists can readily be found who in their functions resemble a particular clinical psychologist more closely than two clinical psychologists resemble each other. Nevertheless, the two fields as a whole *can* be differentiated in their relative emphases, as will be shown in a later section of this chapter. This differentiation has received formal recognition by the psychological profession. Thus the American Board of Professional Psychology issues separate diplomas in clinical and in counseling psychology. Similarly, the Education and Training Board of the American Psychological Association accredits university training programs independently in these two specialties, although there are many more programs in clinical than in counseling psychology. The American Psychological Association has also had separate divisions in the clinical and counseling fields since 1945, when a divisional structure was first introduced into the association, and it has published the *Journal of Counseling Psychology* since 1954. On the other hand, the overlap between clinical and counseling psychology is suggested by the similarity in actual course requirements in university training programs in these two fields (Paterson & Lofquist, 1960; Thompson & Super, 1964).

VARIETIES OF COUNSELING

Counseling psychologists work in many contexts. Schools and colleges represent one of the principal settings for their activities. An increasing number are being employed in industrial and business organizations, government agencies, and the armed services. Others work in hospitals, rehabilitation centers, correctional institutions, and a variety of community agencies. To a large extent, the setting in which counseling psychologists operate determines the type of problems with which they must deal.

Career counseling still represents a major part of the work of many counseling psychologists, particularly those employed in student counseling centers of high schools and colleges (Williamson, 1965). Because of its central position in the entire counseling field, career counseling will be discussed more fully in later sections of this chapter as well as in the next chapter.

A closely related area is that of *educational counseling.* Frequently the selection of a program of studies is implied in a vocational decision. In its own right, however, educational counseling is concerned with such decisions as whether or not to attend college, the choice of a particular college, what curriculum to pursue, or what specific courses to elect. Educational counselors may also deal with problems of study skills, learning disabilities, and other academic difficulties. Guidance functions are now regarded as an integral part of the daily classroom activity of elementary and high school teachers. Accordingly, guidance techniques are regularly included in teacher training programs, and several books on guidance have been directed specifically to the needs of teachers. Group counseling techniques suitable for use in a school situation have also been developed (Hoyt & Moore, 1960; M. R. Katz, 1959; Miller & Gelatt, 1971–1972). There is evidence that such group procedures may be as effective as individual counseling under certain circumstances. At the college level, counseling functions are generally integrated in the student personnel program, which covers also housing, student activities, student government, health services, and other extracurricular matters.

Employee counseling in industry was ushered in by the Hawthorne studies, discussed in Chapter 5. The growing recognition of the importance of employee morale led to the appointment of employee counselors in many industrial, business, and governmental organizations. The activities of such counselors are usually quite varied, ranging all the way from assistance in locating suitable housing to counseling on emotional problems. The problem need not be directly related to the job. For some maladjusted employees, the source of the difficulty may be at home or in some other problem arising off the job.

Depending upon the employee counselors' professional qualifications and the time available per client, they may handle problems themselves or make appropriate referrals. In any event, employee counselors would not themselves undertake long-term psychotherapy with seriously disturbed individuals. In order to establish an effective counseling relationship, employee counselors should have no administrative duties or authority. Only under these conditions would employees feel completely free to discuss their problems with the counselors. In some companies, employee counseling is carried on by independent consulting psychologists on a part-time basis. This practice is followed especially in the counseling of executive personnel.

Rehabilitation counseling is a rapidly expanding field of activity for the counseling psychologist (Lofquist, 1957, 1962; Neff, 1971; B. A. Wright, 1959). Its growth is reflected in the establishment and activities of the Division of Rehabilitation Psychology in the American Psychological Association. The rehabilitation counselor may work with the orthopedically handicapped, the blind, the deaf, the tubercular, the cardiac patient, the cancer patient, and the patient on hemodialysis for kidney failure, among others. There is also a growing body of psychological research dealing with the characteristics and problems of the physically handicapped (Bolton, 1976; Cruickshank, 1971; Cruickshank & Johnson, 1975; Telford & Sawrey, 1972; B. A. Wright, 1960).

Counseling of the physically handicapped must be closely coordinated with remedial and training programs. Such counseling may have several objectives. In the case of children, the physical disability is likely to have delayed psychological development through the curtailment of normal experiences. Such children may require not only special educational programs but also interpersonal experiences for normal personality growth. Handicapped persons of any age tend to have special emotional problems, such as feelings of insecurity or hostility and various types of defensive reactions. These reactions often stem from a feeling of being different from one's associates. An important goal of rehabilitation counseling is the development of a realistic and constructive attitude toward one's handicap. Emotional acceptance of prosthetic and other adaptive devices is a closely related problem.

The successful adjustment of the handicapped person often requires counseling with family, teachers, employers, and other associates who interact with the individual in significant ways. Vocational counseling is also an important aspect of the rehabilitation program. The physical disability limits the vocational opportunities available to a young person entering the world of work and often makes a return to the former job impossible for a previously employed worker. Satisfactory work adjustment can be achieved by a combination of intensive testing with realistic work samples, special training, experience in sheltered workshops, and eventual job placement. Such a program needs to be closely integrated with a medical evaluation of the limits set by the physical disability.

Patients who have been institutionalized for serious emotional disturbances may also require rehabilitation before resuming their normal activities. Today the scope of rehabilitation counseling has been broadened to cover mental as well as physical disabilities. A noteworthy development in this connection is the gradual inclusion of psychiatric patients in rehabilitation centers originally established to care for the physically disabled. The Institute for the Crippled and Disabled in New York City has successfully initiated such an extension of its services. Similar institutes throughout the country have begun to accept a few psychiatric patients, although no formal recognition of this function is included in their objectives. Since the physically disabled often have psychiatric problems, institutes designed to serve such patients may already have the facilities and experience for handling psychiatric disabilities.

Gerontological counseling is concerned with the occupational and personal guidance of elderly persons, with retirement problems, and with the special intellectual and emotional disorders associated with old age. Practical concern with the problems of advanced age has been stimulated by the relatively large number of older persons in our society. As medical progress and better living conditions lengthen the life span, the proportion of older persons in the population continues to increase. Gerontology, or the study of old age, and geriatrics, dealing with diseases of old age, are now thriving fields of research and professional specialization.

The active interest of psychologists in these fields is evidenced by the establishment of a Division of Adult Development and Aging in the American Psychological Association and by an increasing amount of research on the changes occurring beyond maturity in aptitudes, emotional reactions, interests, and attitudes (Eisdorfer & Lawton, 1973; Schaie & Gribbin, 1975). The use of longitudinal approaches, large representative samples, and improved experimental designs is beginning to clarify the nature and causes of these changes. Special attention has also been given to the industrial skills of older workers and to ways of maximizing their effective utilization. The adjustment problems of older persons provide a fertile field for the application of psychotherapy but one that has not yet been adequately explored. Counseling services for the aged, moreover, offer one more opportunity for the utilization of indigenous nonprofessional therapeutic agents, discussed in Chapter 13 (see, e.g., Pressey, 1973).

Another area in which psychologists can make a contribution is that of *marriage counseling*. Beginning with the pioneer work of Terman (1938), research has been conducted on psychological factors making for marital adjustment and compatibility (Jacobson & Martin, 1976; Tharp, 1963). Marital counseling itself spans many fields, including medicine, genetics, psychology, religion, social work, law, and home economics. The specific functions of marital counselors might range from planning a family budget to analyzing the hereditary transmission of a rare defect. Within this context, the psychologist is typically concerned with questions of compatibility in choice of marital partner and with the solution of interpersonal conflicts in family living. Problems of child rearing and parent-child relations are also of obvious relevance. The psychologist's approach to most of these familial problems utilizes the specialized techniques of family therapy described in Chapter 13.

Like clinical and community psychologists, counseling psychologists in the 1970s have made increasing efforts to reach diverse types of client populations. Several emerging varieties of counseling could be added to the examples already cited. Many publications have been appearing on the adaptation of counseling procedures to meet the special problems and needs of women, various cultural minorities, the urban and the rural poor, juvenile delinquents, alcoholics, drug abusers, and ex-offenders, among others.

Despite the many varieties of counseling, most clients need help in handling emotional difficulties, improving interpersonal relations, or developing problem-coping skills. Some may seek the services of a counselor explicitly because of an emotional problem. But even when the referral problem pertains to a career decision, an educational question, or some other specific and relatively "impersonal" matter, the root of the difficulty often lies in a personality problem. Moreover, personality difficulties frequently complicate and aggravate other problems. Counseling with regard to personality problems is usually designated as *personal counseling*, although it is also known as adjustment counseling or psychological counseling. It is in this area that psychologists can make their most distinctive contributions. Furthermore, counseling psychologists recognize the close interrelation of all adjustment problems and therefore function at a broad level regardless of the type of counseling involved. Their orientation tends always to be toward counseling the whole individual. It is in connection with personal counseling, too, that the work of the counseling psychologist comes closest to that of the clinical psychologist. Hence at this point it is appropriate to examine more fully the relation between these two fields.

RELATION BETWEEN CLINICAL AND COUNSELING PSYCHOLOGY

There are unquestionably many similarities between the functions of a clinical and a counseling psychologist. For both, the interpersonal relation between psychologist and client is of prime importance. As in clinical practice, the counseling relationship is nonthreatening, confidential, warm, and accepting (Bordin, 1968, Ch. 8; Tyler, 1969, Ch. 3). Similarly, counseling depends largely upon verbal communication. Most counseling psychologists employ some variant of the client-centered, or nondirective, approach discussed in Chapter 13, although many combine this approach with considerable information giving of a fairly directive type. Classical psychoanalysis is least likely to be used in a counseling situation. Some counseling psychologists, however, have adapted a psychoanalytic orientation to the counseling process (Bordin, 1968). The techniques of behavior modification are being employed increasingly in counseling situations, especially in the development of interpersonal and decision-making skills (Krumboltz, 1966a, 1966b).

What of the differences? Perhaps the primary difference is that the aim of clinical psychology is to *change* the individual's basic personality structure and personal constructs, while the aim of counseling psychology is to enable the individual to *utilize* his or her present resources most effectively in solving problems. Tyler (1960) introduced the concept of "minimum-change therapy" to characterize the counseling process. Its object is to bring about readjustment with a minimum of personality change rather than to delve into the sources of anxieties and conflicts. Because it does not undertake to restructure a client's personality or to provide insight into all the client's emotional conflicts, counseling characteristically requires less time than does traditional psychotherapy. In this regard, it resembles most closely the brief psychotherapies cited in Chapter 13.

While psychotherapy tries to alter a client's anxiety level, defensiveness, and other generalized response habits, counseling concentrates on the solution of specific current problems, such as poor study habits or lack of interpersonal skills, that may be interfering with effective functioning (Stefflre, 1972). It is also concerned with the making of decisions and plans regarding educational, vocational, and other courses of action. The counseling psychologist, however, does not as a rule give advice or tell the client what he should do. It is generally felt that to do so would reinforce habits of dependency rather than facilitate personal growth.

Another difference between clinical and counseling psychology is that the former focuses on weaknesses to be overcome, while the latter focuses on positive strengths to be developed (Stefflre, 1972). Typically, counselors are not concerned with ferreting out personality deficiencies that are adequately controlled. Rather they concentrate on the utilization of any available assets that they can identify in a particular client. Slight shifts in the direction in which an individual is moving may enable her or him to capitalize on these assets and to bypass obstacles. The counseling psychologist looks for the normalities found even in abnormal persons, whereas the clinical psychologist and, to a greater extent, the psychiatrist look for the abnormalities found even in normal persons. In its emphasis upon positive development and the prevention of dysfunction, counseling is consistent with the aims of community psychology (Ch. 13).

Unlike traditional psychotherapy, counseling frequently requires the giving of factual information. Thus, in educational and career counseling, individuals need information about job requirements and opportunities, suitable schools and courses of study, effective study skills, or test norms in terms of which they may evaluate their own performance. Such information should be provided when it will help the clients to think realistically and constructively about their problems. The counselors may impart the information themselves during an interview, or they may refer their client to appropriate persons or to readily available published sources. In any event, the information should be presented in such a way as to be understood and accepted. Effective communication, including sufficient feedback from the client, is essential to this aspect of counseling.

The counselors themselves also need to be familiar with up-to-date and dependable sources of information in their particular areas of operation. Since vocational counseling plays such an important part in the activities of most counselors, a knowledge of the world of work is a common requirement in the training of counseling psychologists. In fact, the inclusion or noninclusion of courses on occupational information often represents the principal difference between the basic training of counselors and clinical psychologists (Paterson & Lofquist, 1960; Thompson & Super, 1964).

The type of client with whom clinical and counseling psychologists work has often been cited as another difference between the two fields. It is certainly true that, in general, the counseling psychologist works with more nearly "normal" persons who may want help in making a specific decision or who may have minor emotional problems. Hahn (1955) summed it up by saying that the counseling psychologist is most often concerned with persons whose anxiety level is interfering and disruptive rather than disabling or disintegrative. To be sure, this distinction is only relative. On the one hand, some clinical psychologists will accept no severely disturbed cases for psychotherapy; they exclude all psychotics, as well as neurotics with symptoms of long standing. On the other hand, some counseling psychologists work with hospitalized psychotic patients. In the latter cases, however, the counseling psychologist is concerned with the patient's rehabilitation and career adjustment rather than with treatment of the psychotic condition. Frequently such counseling is introduced shortly before discharge, to enable the individual to make a more effective job and community adjustment. An example is the extensive program in counseling psychology conducted in Veterans Administration hospitals.

The difference between clinical and counseling psychology has also been described in terms of the characteristic orientations and attitudes of the psychologists who specialize in the two areas. It has been suggested, for example, that counseling psychologists resemble industrial psychologists more closely than they do clinical psychologists (Hahn, 1955). In contrast to the clinical psychologist, the counseling psychologist is more likely to rely upon objectively constructed tests and empirical norms than upon subjective qualitative approaches. She or he relies less on clinical judgment or projective tests and more on structured ability and interest tests. Counseling psychologists often have to work closely with members of other professions, as was apparent in the preceding section. They must therefore be able to function effectively in various settings and to cooperate with persons whose training and background are very unlike their own. In several of these contexts, counseling psychologists also tend to have administrative and managerial responsibilities.

Still another point of view about the relation of clinical and counseling psychology has been expressed by Vance and Volsky (1962). While maintaining that clinical and counseling *processes* can be differentiated, they argue that these two kinds of treatment are often required by the same client and hence should not be artificially separated in practice. On these grounds they advocate combined training in clinical and counseling processes for each practitioner. It should also be noted, as the reader has undoubtedly recognized by now, that most of the distinctive features of counseling psychology are also found in such recent developments as brief psychotherapy, behavior therapy, and—especially—community psychology. Counseling psychology differs most from classical psychoanalysis, which now represents a very small segment of clinical psychology.

USE OF TESTS IN COUNSELING

Types of Tests Used in Counseling. Tests may be helpful in any kind of counseling but are most often employed to facilitate educational and vocational decisions. All types of tests may be used in counseling and probably are, but certain types clearly predominate. For a more detailed treatment of these types of tests, the reader is referred to Anastasi (1976, Chs. 13–15, 18). The preliminary discussion of the use of tests in personnel selection and classification given in Chapter 3 is also relevant.

In counseling, certain general ability tests may be used to assess the individual's *level of intellectual development.* Designated by various names, this type of test is often loosely described as an "intelligence test." This term is avoided in the more recently developed instruments, however, because it has acquired excess meanings that may lead to misinterpretations of test scores. Most of these tests measure largely the individual's current level of development in verbal and numerical abilities. They are commonly designated as scholastic aptitude tests, since they correlate highly with educational level attained and in turn predict subsequent educational achievement.

Persons engaged in different occupations differ significantly in mean scores on such general ability tests. The clearest demonstration of these differences was provided by the analyses of test scores of large samples of men in the United States Army during both world wars (Fryer, 1922; N. Stewart, 1947). There are probably many reasons for these occupational differences, but a major factor is undoubtedly the educational level required for different types of work. The professions and other occupations calling for a high level of education typically show a higher average and a narrower range of scores on such tests than do routine clerical and manual occupations. For most educational or vocational counseling purposes, psychologists employ group tests of general intellectual development, which may, of course, be administered individually as well as in groups. These tests are available for different levels, from the primary grades to the graduate school. For more intensive analysis of individual cases, such clinical instruments as the Stanford-Binet or Wechsler scales may be administered (Ch. 12).

For educational counseling, scholastic aptitude tests are often supplemented with *achievement tests* in different areas. Of particular interest are tests of reading and arithmetic skills. Special disabilities in these skills—particularly in reading— may seriously interfere with over-all educational achievement. *Special aptitude tests* are frequently administered in individual cases as demanded by the particular circumstances. When considering a special educational program or making career plans, individuals may need information regarding their manual dexterity or other motor skills or about their mechanical, clerical, artistic, or musical aptitudes. Tests are available to aid evaluation in all these areas.

Multiple aptitude batteries are of particular relevance to counseling problems because they provide a profile of scores in relatively independent abilities. Combining the principal abilities covered by scholastic aptitude tests with other broad aptitude areas, they enable individuals to explore their major strengths and weaknesses. While a global score on a general ability test may indicate level of expected educational or vocational attainment, a profile of scores on a multiple aptitude battery is more helpful in the choice of a field of specialization.

A multiple aptitude battery that has been in use long enough to permit the accumulation of extensive validity data is the Differential Aptitude Tests (DAT). Sample items from each of the eight tests comprising this battery can be found in Figure 15-1 (A & B). Designed for Grades 8 through 12 and for unselected adults, this battery was prepared principally for use in educational and vocational counseling. Figure 15-2 shows a score profile on the DAT. The person's score on each of the tests is translated into a percentile and plotted as a percentile band (gray areas). The percentiles are spaced vertically on the graph so as to correspond to equal distances on a normal distribution curve. The percentile bands show the region within which the individual's score is likely to fluctuate on retesting, as predicted from the reliability coefficients of the tests. Users are cautioned not to attach undue significance to differences between abilities whose percentile bands overlap. The third column, based on the sum of the Verbal Reasoning and Numerical Ability scores, provides a single index of scholastic aptitude.

The General Aptitude Test Battery (GATB) developed by the United States Employment Service is used widely in State Employment Service offices for vocational counseling of adult workers.[1] By special arrangement, this battery can

---

[1] The GATB was described in Ch. 3 and its method of score interpretation illustrated in Ch. 2.

VERBAL REASONING

Choose the correct pair of words to fill the blanks. The first word of the pair goes in the blank space at the beginning of the sentence; the second word of the pair goes in the blank at the end of the sentence.

...... is to night as breakfast is to ......

    A. supper —— corner
    B. gentle —— morning
    C. door —— corner
    D. flow —— enjoy
    E. supper —— morning

The correct answer is E.

NUMERICAL ABILITY

Choose the correct answer for each problem.

Add	13	A	14	Subtract	30	A	15
	12	B	25		20	B	26
		C	16			C	16
		D	59			D	8
		N	none of these			N	none of these

The correct answer for the first problem is B; for the second, N.

ABSTRACT REASONING

The four "problem figures" in each row make a series. Find the one among the "answer figures" that would be next in the series.

PROBLEM FIGURES   ANSWER FIGURES

The correct answer is D

CLERICAL SPEED AND ACCURACY

In each test item, one of the five combinations is underlined. Find the same combination on the answer sheet and mark it.

TEST ITEMS   SAMPLE OF ANSWER SHEET

V.	AB	AC	AD	AE	AF
W.	aA	aB	BA	Ba	Bb
X.	A7	7A	B7	7B	AB
Y.	Aa	Ba	bA	BA	bB
Z.	3A	3B	33	B3	BB

	AC	AE	AF	AB	AD
V.				▌	
	BA	Ba	Bb	aA	aB
W.			▌		
	7B	B7	AB	7A	A7
X.	▌				
	Aa	bA	bB	Ba	BA
Y.		▌			
	BB	3B	B3	3A	33
Z.					▌

Figure 15-1A Sample items from the Differential Aptitude Tests. *(Reproduced by permission. Copyright © 1972 by The Psychological Corporation, New York, N.Y. All rights reserved.)*

MECHANICAL REASONING

Which man has the heavier load? (If equal, mark C.)

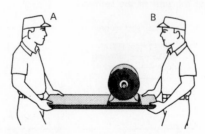

The correct answer is B.

SPACE RELATIONS

Which one of the following figures could be made by folding the pattern at the left? The pattern always shows the outside of the figure. Note the grey surfaces.

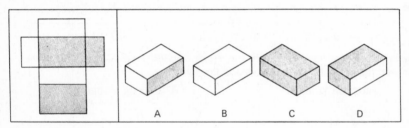

The correct answer is D.

SPELLING

Indicate whether each word is spelled right or wrong.

      W.   man

      X.   gurl

	R	W
W.	▌	
X.		▌

LANGUAGE USAGE

Decide which of the lettered parts of the sentence contains an error and mark the corresponding letter on the answer sheet. If there is no error, mark N.

  Y.   Ain't we / going to / the office / next week?
        A   B   C   D

	A	B	C	D	N
Y.	▌				

Figure 15-1B   Sample items from the Differential Aptitude Tests. *(Reproduced by permission. Copyright © 1972 by The Psychological Corporation, New York, N.Y. All rights reserved.)*

	Verbal Reasoning	Numerical Ability	VR+NA	Abstract Reasoning	Clerical Sp. & Acc.	Mechanical Reasoning	Space Relations	Spelling	Language Usage
Raw Score	21	30	51	43	38	44	39	96	40
Percentile	60	95	80	95	30	80	90	99	85

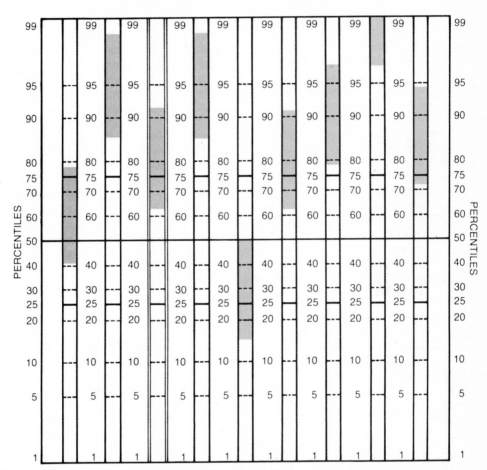

Figure 15-2 Score profile on the Differential Aptitude Tests. *(Fig. 2, Fifth Edition Manual, p. 73. Reproduced by permission. Copyright © 1973, 1974 by The Psychological Corporation, New York, N.Y. All rights reserved.)*

also be made available to such nonprofit organizations as high schools, community colleges, VA hospitals, and prisons. It consists of 12 tests which yield the following nine scores: General Learning Ability, Verbal Aptitude, Numerical Aptitude, Spatial Aptitude, Form Perception, Clerical Perception, Motor Coordination, Finger Dexterity, and Manual Dexterity.

Interest tests are undoubtedly one of the most popular counseling instruments. Essentially these tests are self-report inventories in which the respondents record their likes and dislikes or their relative preferences for many kinds of familiar activities, people, or objects. An outstanding example is the Strong-Campbell Interest Inventory (SCII) described in Chapter 3. This inventory yields scores for some 125 occupations. New occupational scoring keys are added as data on adequate samples become available. A high score on any given occupational key means that the individual's interests resemble those of persons engaged in that occupation. It suggests that he or she would find that occupation and his/her colleagues in it congenial and that he or she would fit in well with their way of life. For counseling purposes, the total pattern of occupational scores is customarily taken into account. It may be just as important to know which occupational groups the individual is most unlike as it is to know which groups he or she resembles most closely.

In addition to the occupational scores, the SCII yields scores on six general occupational themes, designated as Realistic, Investigative, Artistic, Social, Enterprising, and Conventional (Fig. 15-3). Each theme characterizes not only the person but also the type of working environment such a person would prefer. Still another set of scores, illustrated in Figure 15-4, is derived from 23 basic interest scales. These scales correspond to broad occupational categories, such as science, art, agriculture, and business management.

With regard to the use of the SCII in counseling, it should be noted that most of its keys pertain to occupations at the professional or higher business levels. Few are available for skilled trades, and none is available below that level. To fill this gap, the Minnesota Vocational Interest Inventory (MVII) was developed by a similar procedure but with tradesmen-in-general as a reference group. It provides scales for such occupations as baker, plumber, and radio-TV repairer, as well as area scales showing the examinee's liking for broader work activities, such as mechani-

General Occupational Themes				Administrative Indexes			
Theme	Std Score	Result		(for the use of the counselor)			
R-Theme	51	This is a MODERATELY HIGH	Score.	TOTAL RESPONSES		325	
				INFREQUENT RESPONSES		4	
I-Theme	63	This is a HIGH	Score.		Response %		
					LP	IP	DP
A-Theme	63	This is a HIGH	Score.	OCCUPATIONS	34	11	54
				SCHOOL SUBJECTS	42	11	47
S-Theme	26	This is a VERY LOW	Score.	ACTIVITIES	35	6	59
				AMUSEMENTS	67	10	23
E-Theme	35	This is a VERY LOW	Score.	TYPES OF PEOPLE	42	12	46
				PREFERENCES	40	47	13
C-Theme	41	This is a MODERATELY LOW	Score.	CHARACTERISTICS	86	7	7
				Special Scales: AOR: 60 IE: 53			

Figure 15-3 Portion of score profile on Strong-Campbell Interest Inventory, showing scores on six general occupational theme scales (Realistic, Investigative, Artistic, Social, Enterprising, Conventional), Administrative Indexes (used to detect carelessness and test-taking response sets), and Special Scales (Academic Orientation and Introversion-Extroversion). (Form reprinted from the Manual for the Strong-Campbell Interest Inventory, Form T325 of the STRONG VOCATIONAL INTEREST BLANK, SECOND EDITION, by David P. Campbell, with the permission of the publishers, Stanford University Press. Copyright © 1974, 1977 by the Board of Trustees of the Leland Stanford Junior University. Data by courtesy of Center for Interest Measurement and Research, University of Minnesota.)

Basic Interest Scales

	Scale	Std Score	Very Low	Low	Average	High	Very High
R-THEME	AGRICULTURE	39					
	NATURE	40	30	35	40 · 45 · 50 · 55	60 · 65	70
	ADVENTURE	67					
	MILITARY ACTIVITIES	55					
	MECHANICAL ACTIVITIES	55					
I-THEME	SCIENCE	59					
	MATHEMATICS	63					
	MEDICAL SCIENCE	68					
	MEDICAL SERVICE	38					
A-THEME	MUSIC/ DRAMATICS	61	30	35	40 · 45 · 50 · 55	60 · 65	70
	ART	53					
	WRITING	48					
S-THEME	TEACHING	43					
	SOCIAL SERVICE	26					
	ATHLETICS	45					
	DOMESTIC ARTS	41					
	RELIGIOUS ACTIVITIES	31					
E-THEME	PUBLIC SPEAKING	55					
	LAW/ POLITICS	51					
	MERCHAND'NG	44					
	SALES	42					
	BUSINESS MGMT.	40	30	35	40 · 45 · 50 · 55	60 · 65	70
C-TH	OFFICE PRACTICES	36					

Figure 15-4 Portion of score profile on Strong-Campbell Interest Inventory, showing scores on 23 basic interest scales, classified according to general occupational themes. Shaded bars refer to responses of 300 men, and open bars, to responses of 300 women in General Reference Group. Thick central portion covers range of middle 50%; thin portion, range of middle 80%. *(Form reprinted from the Manual for the Strong-Campbell Interest Inventory, Form T325 of the STRONG VOCATIONAL INTEREST BLANK, SECOND EDITION, by David P. Campbell, with the permission of the publishers, Stanford University Press. Copyright © 1974, 1977 by the Board of Trustees of the Leland Stanford Junior University. Data by courtesy of Center for Interest Measurement and Research, University of Minnesota.)*

cal tasks, food services, and electronics. Differentiation among occupations, however, is not so sharp with the MVII as with the SCII. This difference between the two instruments may reflect the nature of the occupations themselves. There is considerable evidence to suggest that, at higher job levels, job satisfaction is derived chiefly from intrinsic liking for the work, while at lower levels there is more reliance on factors extrinsic to the work itself (Darley & Hagenah, 1955).

The armamentarium of the educational and career counselor includes a large number of other measures of interests, motives, and personal values, Well-established examples include the Kuder Vocational Preference Record and the Allport-Vernon-Lindzey Study of Values, both described in Chapter 3. Although approaching the area from different theoretical orientations, these two instruments yield measures that have much in common with the SCII general occupational themes and basic Interest scales. Other versions of the Kuder scales include the Kuder General Interest Survey, a downward extension of the Kuder Vocational Preference Record designed for Grades 6 to 12; and the Kuder Occupational Interest Survey, which provides keys for specific occupations and college-major fields.

Because of their widespread use in career counseling, interest inventories have been the focus of considerable research on sex fairness in measurement (Diamond, 1975; Tittle & Zytowski, 1978). The studies cover a broad range of questions about the construction, scoring, interpretation, and use of interest inventories. A common goal of this research, however, was to facilitate career decisions that reflect the individual's qualifications and interests, rather than sex stereotypes and traditional roles.

Other types of *personality tests* are used to a more limited extent in counseling. The lack of adequate validity data about most of these instruments requires that they be interpreted with considerable caution and checked against other sources of information about the individual. Personality inventories may be employed as a preliminary screening device to identify persons who should be referred for psychotherapy. Or they may be used by counselors to focus discussion upon personal problems and to help the counselees to understand their own behavior.

Despite its original pathological orientation, the Minnesota Multiphasic Personality Inventory (MMPI), described in Chapter 12, has been used extensively in counseling normal persons and a considerable amount of relevant research has accumulated. On the basis of data obtained with this test from more than 4,000 students examined in a college counseling center, Drake and Oetting prepared a codebook for interpreting MMPI profiles in this context (1959). A few self-report inventories have been specially developed for normal persons, and their scores are expressed in terms of needs, motives, and interpersonal response modes rather than in terms of pathological deviations. Examples of such inventories include the California Psychological Inventory, the Comrey Personality Scales, the Edwards Personal Preference Schedule, and the Minnesota Counseling Inventory.

Integrating Tests into the Counseling Process. Counseling psychologists generally recognize the importance of the counseling process itself as a means of contributing to the client's development. In keeping with this viewpoint, several psychologists have given considerable attention to the way in which tests are introduced into the counseling process—how the tests are selected, when and how they are administered, and how the results are communicated to the counselees (Bordin, 1968; L. Goldman, 1971; Tyler, 1969). Some feel that what tests are chosen and how the individual scores on them are less important questions than how the tests are incorporated into the counseling process.

Taking tests is itself regarded as a significant experience for the counselee. It is envisaged, not as an independent activity, but as a part of the total counseling experience. As such, it is a kind of "reality testing," providing counselees with an opportunity to check their aspirations, plans, and self-concepts against objective standards. The individual's attitude toward taking tests may also be quite revealing and may in turn affect test performance. One student may feel threatened if she believes that the decision to enter the college of her choice hinges on her test score. Another may hope that a low test score will help to dissuade an overambitious father from pushing him into an occupation for which he has neither interest nor aptitude.

Unlike test scores obtained in other situations, the information obtained from counseling tests is primarily for the use of the clients themselves. In general, counseling tests should serve to stimulate client interest in areas or courses of action they have not previously considered and should provide them with the information they need to make decisions. Tests are not a substitute for decision making by the clients but should help to clarify the alternatives among which they must choose. Tests should therefore be introduced to answer specific questions or solve problems presented by the clients.

It should also be noted that test results are more helpful in making negative than in making positive decisions. It is easier to determine on the basis of test scores which occupations or courses of study to rule out than which to elect. This follows from the fact that a certain minimum aptitude, interest pattern, or whatever the test measures is a necessary but not a sufficient condition for success in a given area. Individuals lacking such a qualification are likely to fail. But those who meet the requirement are not assured of success, since the latter depends on many additional personal and situational factors.

In individual counseling, it is, of course, desirable to select tests to fit specific client needs. In most high school and college settings, batteries of tests are administered routinely to all students, and scores on these tests are already available to the counselor. Even in such cases, however, the counselor may wish to supplement these tests with other, specially chosen instruments. In any event, before tests are administered to an individual counselee—and certainly before the results of any tests are discussed with the counselee—the counselor should identify and clarify the kinds of questions for which the individual is seeking answers.

A possible difficulty may arise from misconceptions about the purpose of tests and incorrect notions about their nature, which many counselees have acquired from popular sources. The counselee may express a desire to take a test "to find out what kind of work I should do" or "to find out if I'm normal." Some may want to take tests as a means of evading a discussion of their real problems or for other defensive reasons. In all these cases, the counselor needs to pursue the matter sufficiently and possibly to provide appropriate information to cut through the superficial responses and enable the counselee to make a more intelligent decision about test taking.

On the positive side, client participation in the decision to take tests or to discuss available test results has important advantages. If the clients cannot see the relevance of tests to their immediate problems, they may simply drop out of counseling. The same result may follow if clients are not emotionally ready to submit to a reaslitic appraisal of themselves. When clients are convinced of the need for testing and understand its purpose, on the other hand, they will be better motivated to do their best on ability tests and to answer truthfully on self-report inventories. They will also be more likely to accept test findings, rather than reacting defensively toward them.

The way in which test findings are communicated to the client is another important consideration in the counseling process. Such communication must take into account what the test score will mean to the client in the light of the latter's individual attitudes, goals, anxieties, and conflicts. The counselor must be ready to detect expressions of rejection, hostility, and rationalization toward the test scores on the client's part. When such reactions occur, they must be accepted as one more fact regarding the client's behavior.

Test findings need not be reported in the form of scores, since these may be misunderstood by a psychometrically unsophisticated client. Rather they should be stated as expectancies or probabilities of concrete events, such as graduation from a given college, and should be directly related to the questions the client set out to answer. Test results should not be introduced until the client is ready to discuss them. Even then, the discussion should remain sufficiently flexible so that tangential topics brought up by the client may be followed up. The client should also be encouraged to integrate test findings with other self-knowledge, such as achievement in different academic courses, job experiences, interests in various activities, and the like. Such integration tends to dispel any "mystery" that attaches to psychological tests. When related to similar observations from everyday life, tests are more likely to be correctly perceived as behavior samples obtained under standardized conditions.

The counselor in a school or college has the opportunity to accumulate longitudinal data about each counselee over a period of several years. It is customary in such situations to keep a *cumulative record* for each individual, including test data, biographical information, and continuing observations of the student's reactions toward different teachers, courses, extracurricular activities, and other school experiences. Under these circumstances, moreover, the counselor has usually had repeated contacts with the individual over a long time span. When properly employed, the cumulative record should prove extremely helpful. It can provide a wealth of information and a picture of developmental trends that no cross-sectional counseling contacts could equal. In practice, however, there is danger that the keeping of cumulative records may become just one more mechanical chore in a busy schedule. The use of complicated and rigid forms may detract from the spontaneous recording of significant observations and the meaningful interpretation of developmental trends.

Another potential advantage available to counselors in school systems lies in their opportunity to do certain kinds of research. Because they have access to large numbers of students who go through similar criterion situations, such counselors are often in a better position than clinicians to conduct applied research with data already in their files. For example, entering students can be followed up through four years in the same college. The validity of tests and other predictors can thus be investigated, and empirical norms and cutoff scores can be established. Similar studies can be conducted with graduates of a single school who have entered a particular college in large numbers over a period of years—or possibly with groups that have been employed in a single community industry.

Finally, counselors should accumulate information regarding the criterion situations about which their clients must make predictions. In educational counseling, for example, they must keep up with current data regarding schools and colleges in which their clients may be interested. Routine information regarding admission requirements, curriculums, expenses, financial aid, student activities, and the like can be found in school and college catalogues and in a number of standard handbooks. A comprehensive source is *The College Handbook*, published by the College Entrance Examination Board (1977) and periodically updated.

There are many other characteristics of schools and colleges, however, that should be considered by a client. For example, it is well established that the average level and range of academic aptitude test scores vary widely among colleges. This type of data is available for a substantial number of colleges that submitted information for inclusion in the previously mentioned CEEB handbook. Colleges also differ in their psychological climate and in the kinds of environmental pressures they put upon the student. Research has revealed differences among colleges in such characteristics as relative strength of theoretical and practical values, emphasis placed upon social conformity and acceptance by others, extent of extracurricular participation, degree of student concern with social action and national problems, and pressure to achieve as contrasted to an easygoing atmosphere (Pace, 1960; Pace & Stern, 1958; G. C. Stern, 1970). Quite apart from intellectual qualifications, a student might be a misfit in one of these college environments and an outstanding leader in another.

In career counseling, knowledge about jobs is of such basic importance that it has received special attention from the earlierst beginnings of the vocational-guidance movement. This type of information will be considered in the next section.

OCCUPATIONAL INFORMATION

Because career decisions play a prominent part in the counseling process in schools, colleges, community agencies, Veterans Administration hospitals, and other contexts, the counseling psychologist must have ready access to dependable sources of occupational information. The scope and complexity of the modern world of work necessitate special efforts to organize and systematize such information.

Occupational information includes knowledge about available fields of work and types of jobs, nature of the work, worker qualifications, training requirements, pay rate, working schedules and hours, vacation provisions, retirement plans and other fringe benefits, characteristics of the working environment, and many other specific facts of interest to the potential worker. It involves knowledge about national trends as well as local conditions. Obviously, no one person could acquire all this information. Even if it could be done, moreover, such a store of knowledge would begin to go out of date at once. What the career counselor tries to do instead is to become familiar with *sources* of occupational information and with methods for evaluating it, keeping it up to date, and making it available to clients. Available sources of occupational information have been surveyed in a number of books (e.g., Hoppock, 1976). Such books are frequently used as texts in occupational information courses for counseling psychologists.

Counseling centers in schools, colleges, community agencies, and other settings generally maintain a library and file of occupational information materials for use by counselors and clients. Such collections include reference books and journals, as well as monographs, pamphlets, and leaflets dealing with specific fields, industries, or companies. Some texts on occupational information devote a whole chapter just to the question of how to classify and file these published materials so that they can be most readily located when needed. To keep their information up to date, counseling centers also subscribe to publication services which provide fresh material periodically.

Because of the tremendous quantity and uneven quality of occupational literature, the counselor needs to be selective. The principal requirements are recency, objectivity, and readability. Owing to the rapid obsolescence of occupational information, the date when information was obtained is a major consideration. Objectivity can often be evaluated by examining the source of the publication. Government agencies, such as the Department of Labor, as well as private publishing firms that prepare occupational materials, are usually motivated only to provide information. A specific industry or company, on the other hand, is likely to present a more biased picture because of its interest in recruitment. Popular sources are frequently concerned with the entertainment value of their material and may therefore give dramatized or glamorized versions. This does not imply, of course, that career material prepared by a popular magazine or by a company or industry is necessarily biased.

In publications to be used by clients, it is desirable that the information be interestingly presented and readily understood by the type of person for whom it is intended. By and large, occupational information materials tend to be too difficult for their readers. In one investigation, the Flesch formulas described in Chapter 11 were used to measure the reading ease and human interest of 78 occupational information booklets from a wide variety of government and private sources (Brayfield & Reed, 1950). Nearly two-thirds were rated as "very difficult," or at the level of a typical scientific magazine; another 32% were rated as "difficult." With regard to human interest, about two-thirds fell into the "dull" category and about a third into the "mildly interesting."

Among the general sources of occupational information available to the counselor, an outstanding publication is the *Occupational Outlook Handbook*, prepared by the United States Bureau of Labor Statistics (1976–1977). This book summarizes trends in the number of persons employed in different fields. For example, in recent decades the proportion of persons in the professions has been steadily increasing, as have the proportions of clerical and sales jobs. At the same time, the proportion of unskilled labor jobs has been decreasing, as machine production and automation have taken over more and more of their functions. The *Handbook* also contains detailed information regarding several hundred major occupations, chosen with special reference to the interests of students and other young people seeking guidance. The data given for each occupation include the nature of the work, number and nature of workers employed, where employed, training and qualifications, lines of advancement, employment trends and outlook, earnings and working conditions, and where to go for further information. To keep the material up to date, the *Handbook* is revised biennially. In addition, supplementary information is provided in a periodical, the *Occupational Outlook Quarterly*.

One of the major contributions to the organization and systematization of occupational information was the preparation of the *Dictionary of Occupational Titles* (DOT) by the United States Employment Service. Introduced in the 1930s, the DOT provided for the first time a comprehensive classification of jobs and a uniform numerical coding system. In the current edition (U.S. Department of Labor,

1977), the DOT describes many thousands of jobs and includes a large amount of additional information about job functions, worker qualifications, and working conditions. The development of the system of job classification used in the DOT represents the most ambitious occupational classification project yet undertaken. This system will be described more fully in Chapter 16.

As in the case of psychological tests, we may inquire into the ways in which occupational information can be incorporated into the counseling process (Hoppock, 1976; Tyler, 1969, Ch. 8). Like tests, occupational materials can be most effectively introduced when a specific need for them arises, to answer questions raised by the client. Generally, however, it is better to postpone the consideration of occupational data until after some preliminary interviewing and possibly testing. Otherwise, a detailed examination of a specific field may lead to a premature structuring of the client's problem around occupational questions or to a premature career choice.

Occupational information may serve several purposes in the process of career planning. One is the exploration of the world of work. The client may be looking for ideas about fields in which he or she would be interested and may want a general picture of the work performed in various jobs. It is in such cases that counselors often turn to comprehensive sources like the DOT and the *Occupational Outlook Handbook* to help clients investigate likely fields and identify jobs not previously familiar to them. A second use of such information is to aid the client in choosing among specific occupations. For this purpose, the client needs fuller information regarding the alternatives he or she is considering. Such information should not only cover obvious job characteristics but should also give some notion of the total way of life that a particular career choice implies. Finally, occupational information may be required to implement a career decision. For example, the client may need information about apprenticeships and union regulations in a skilled trade, about the educational requirements for law or medicine, about the offerings of different graduate schools in a particular field, or about the availability of scholarship aid in various colleges. A single client may require occupational information at any one or more of these stages in the process of choosing a career.

As for the method of presenting the information, the counselor may transmit the required data orally, refer the client to published sources, or combine the two procedures. Noting the client's reaction to the information and reflecting the client's feelings are important aspects of the counselor's contribution in this connection. Many supplementary methods can be employed to facilitate and augment the information-gathering process. Schools frequently conduct regular courses on occupations, which may utilize several techniques of group counseling. This approach is helpful in providing a preliminary overall view of the world of work and in encouraging the student to think about relevant questions. Other procedures include group conferences with representatives of different fields, plant tours, and part-time or summer jobs. Ideally, techniques such as these should supplement systematic counseling. If used alone, they may yield an inadequate or distorted picture of the occupations surveyed.

EVALUATING THE EFFECTIVENESS OF COUNSELING

Test Performance and Career Choice. Research on the effectiveness of counseling has been concerned with several aspects of the counseling process. Any data on the predictive validity of the tests employed in counseling are, of course, relevant. Several longitudinal investigations have analyzed the relation between test scores and later vocational choices or indices of vocational adjustment, when the tests were *not* administered in connection with counseling. An unusually extensive study of this type was conducted by Thorndike and Hagen (1959). In 1955 and 1956, these investigators sent a questionnaire to about 17,000 men who in 1943 had taken a comprehensive test battery when applying for cadet training in the United States Air Force. Approximately 10,000 responded. For purposes of analysis, the tests were grouped into five categories: general intellectual level or scholastic aptitude, numerical fluency, visual perception, mechanical ability, and psychomotor skills. Responses to a large number of items in a specially devised biographical inventory were also available. Initial test scores and biographical inventory responses were first analyzed in terms of the individual's present job. Within each job group, the predictors were then correlated with each of seven criteria of job adjustment, such as earned income and self-ratings for job success and for job satisfaction.

Among the 124 occupational categories analyzed, several could be clearly differentiated in terms of level and pattern of test scores, as well as in responses to biographical inventory items. For example, accountants and auditors averaged very high in numerical fluency and high in general intellectual level; they were about average in visual perception, below average in psychomotor skills, and very low in mechanical ability (Fig. 15-5). Architects were distinctly high in visual perception; carpenters scored higher in mechanical ability than in general intellectual tests. To be sure, individual differences in scores within each occupational group were large, and overlapping among groups was considerable. Moreover, there were a number of occupations that yielded flat profiles with no outstandingly high or low scores. Nevertheless, the results show considerable correspondence between the type of work in which these men were employed and their test performance some twelve years earlier.

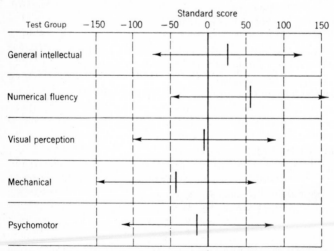

Figure 15-5 Means and standard deviations of 235 accountants and auditors on a multiple aptitude battery administered 12 years earlier. Vertical bar shows mean; distance between arrowheads corresponds to ±1 *SD*. *(From Thorndike & Hagen, 1959, p. 25. Copyright © 1959 by John Wiley & Sons, Inc. Reproduced by permission.)*

Neither test scores nor biographical inventory items, on the other hand, proved to have any validity in predicting degree of job success within any one occupation. The correlations with the various criteria of job adjustment were no different from what would be found by chance.

Despite its ambitious scope, this study had many limitations, which its authors described fully. As a result of self-selection as well as preliminary screening by the Air Force, the available sample was clearly unrepresentative of its age group. The proportion of nonrespondents leaves the way open for further bias in the final sample. The number of persons in single occupational groups was often quite small. Even when similar occupations were combined and the smallest groups eliminated, nearly half of the remaining categories contained fewer than 50 cases. At the same time, the men classified within each group were generally heterogeneous with regard to nature of work performed, even when their occupation was nominally the same. Finally, it is obvious that the criteria of job adjustment were crude. Most of these limitations are such as to reduce the likelihood of finding significant correlations between predictors and criterion measures. The differentiation of vocational groups in terms of initial aptitude patterns, on the other hand, was sufficiently pronounced to emerge despite these methodological handicaps.

It should be noted, furthermore, that other longitudinal studies of narrower scope have obtained similar results (Tyler, 1969, pp. 110–112). Both vocational and educational groups can be differentiated in terms of their initial score patterns on aptitude and interest tests. But, within such groups, the tests generally show little relation to degree of success.

A continuing longitudinal study of a national sample of high school students is yielding further data on the relation of test scores to subsequent career choices (Flanagan, Shaycoft, Richards, & Claudy, 1971). Known as Project TALENT, this research began in 1960 with the administration of a comprehensive battery of aptitude and achievement tests, as well as interest and personality inventories, to approximately 440,000 high school students. In comparison with earlier studies, this project provides a wider coverage of tests and a larger and more representative sampling of persons. The group was carefully chosen so as to yield a stratified sample of students enrolled in public, parochial, and private high schools throughout the country. In addition, in order to secure national norms for one complete age group, 15-year-olds not in high school were also tested. A 5-year follow-up analyzed the initial test scores of students who had either entered a chosen type of work or were seriously preparing to do so. The results showed a moderate differentiation of occupational fields in terms of aptitude and interest test profiles, with wide individual differences within occupations. The planned 11-year and 20-year follow-ups should provide additional relevant data.

On the basis of the 5-year follow-up and partial data from the 11-year follow-up, the Project TALENT investigators have developed a system of counseling aids, which will be refined as new data become available (Flanagan, 1973; Flanagan, Tiedeman, Willis, & McLaughlin, 1973; Rossi, Bartlett, Campbell, Wise, & McLaughlin, 1975). For this purpose, some 150 common occupations represented in the project sample were classified into 12 career-group clusters on the basis of similarities in training requirements and job functions. For each career group, a profile was prepared from the scores of the high school students who later entered that field. The profile covers values, interests, job information, and abilities. A battery of tests and questionnaires is also provided so that a student's own standing in these variables can be assessed on scales comparable to those employed in the TALENT profiles (American Institutes for Research, 1975, 1976). Computers can be utilized to score these instruments and to prepare interpretive forms for comparing the individual's profile with the profiles of the career-group clusters and of specific occupations within the clusters. The authors emphasize two important facts in their recommendations for the use of these occupational profiles (Rossi et al., 1975). First, individuals' profiles *can* change with further training and experience. Second, the profiles are *not* designed to match students to jobs but rather to facilitate the student's career exploration with a counselor. Perhaps the most distinctive feature of this approach to career counseling is that high school students compare their profiles with those of other high school students who later entered different vocations, rather than with those of employed adults.

The fact that tests can differentiate among occupational and educational groups probably reflects the selective processes that normally accompany admission and survival in these groups. Through self-sorting, screening, and subsequent dropping out, persons who are unsuited for a particular course of study or job are unlikely to remain in it long. It is the purpose of tests, of course, to reduce the waste in this natural selection by steering persons away from unsuitable choices in advance. Among those who meet the minimum prerequisites for survival in an educational or occupational category, however, the degree of success or satisfaction attained depends upon such a complex interplay of personal and situational variables that test scores alone are of little help in predicting it. This conclusion is supported by the common finding that negative prediction from test scores can be made with more accuracy than can positive prediction (Fisher, 1959).

Some investigations have been concerned more directly with the effect of using tests in the counseling process (Myers, 1971; Tyler, 1969, pp. 107–117). Although the results are often difficult to interpret because of methodological problems, there is suggestive evidence that the communication of test results by a counselor tends to make a counselee's career choices more realistic. Such findings probably reflect the influence of the counseling process itself. In the interaction between counselor and client, other relevant factors can be integrated with test scores in choosing a suitable course of action. Moreover, the individual's participation in the counseling process itself may have facilitated self-insight and personal development in ways that were beneficial to subsequent occupational adjustment. Tests provide opportunities for reality testing that may contribute to the effectiveness of this experience.

Global Studies of Counseling Effectiveness. Because many evaluations of counseling outcome are conducted in college counseling centers, a frequent criterion of counseling success is academic achievement and general adjustment to the college environment (Myers, 1971). An outstanding example of this type of research is provided by an investigation initially conducted at the University of Minnesota by Williamson and Bordin (1940) and followed up 25 years later by D. P. Campbell (1965). In the original study, the counseled group comprised 400 students who had come to the counseling center over a three-year period for assistance with educational, occupational, or other personal problems. These students were individually matched with control cases in college entrance scores on a scholastic aptitude test and an English proficiency test, high school rank, age, sex, size and type of high school, and college class. A year later, both groups were interviewed and evaluated. At this time, the counseled group had obtained significantly better grades and was better adjusted to college than the control group.

The later follow-up found that the counseled group retained its significant academic superiority, as indicated by subsequent grades, college graduation, academic honors, graduate school enrollment and performance, and similar indices. The counseled students also excelled in adjustment to college life, as illustrated by their more frequent election to student offices. Although the criteria of adult occupational and community achievements were admittedly crude, even in these regards the counseled group enjoyed slight advantages over the control group. It is interesting to note, however, that the members of the counseled group reported somewhat more anxiety and dissatisfaction with their adult life than did the control cases. This finding is consistent with the hypothesis that students who seek counseling tend to be more concerned about their achievement and adjustment than do students not voluntarily seeking such help. The same concern that made the counselees seek assistance while in college could make them more critical of their life as adults. Campbell found some support for this hypothesis in his analyses of available data.

Evaluation of Specific Counseling Procedures. Most of the traditional investigations designed to evaluate counseling effectiveness, like early studies on the outcome of psychotherapy, treated counseling as though it represented a uniform, global process. It is not surprising, therefore, that they often yielded conflicting results. Counseling covers a vast multiplicity of procedures, which undoubtedly vary in effectiveness. When Campbell (1965) approached his follow-up study from the methodologically more sophisticated vantage point of the 1960s, he was aware of this problem. Accordingly, he undertook to describe as fully as possible the procedures followed in the University of Minnesota counseling center at the time the initial data were gathered. In any investigation of counseling effectiveness, it is highly desirable to specify the *particular counseling procedures* that are being studied. Research initiated in the 1960s and 1970s has sometimes gone a step further by designing experiments to test the relative effectiveness of specific counseling procedures.

A related point is that the effectiveness of specific counseling procedures may vary as a function of the type of counseling problem, the characteristics of the counselees, and the criterion measure or index of outcome employed. Again we encounter the familiar concept of *interaction*, as we did in the comparable research on the evaluation of therapy. Modern research on counseling is showing a growing awareness of interaction effects (Myers, 1971).

Another major methodological problem in counseling research pertains to the choice of *control group*. Because of the setting in which most counseling research is conducted, this problem takes a somewhat different form than it does in psychotherapy research. The traditional study on counseling effectiveness drew its control cases from the population of students who did *not* seek help from a counseling center. As suggested in connection with the Campbell study, such control cases may differ in significant personality variables from the students who do seek counseling, even when the two groups are carefully matched in aptitude tests and other relevant variables. Apart from their stronger concern about personal problems, the volunteer counselees may manifest more "counseling readiness." They may be more open to counseling input, more willing to reexamine their self-concepts, and more amenable to altering their attitudes and behavior.

All of these initial motivational differences between those who do and those who do not voluntarily seek counseling could account for obtained group differences in outcome. In order to attribute outcome differences to the counseling itself, the investigator needs to rule out the effects of such motivational differences. There is evidence (Myers, 1971) that counseling outcomes are more favorable with volunteer help-seekers than with invited participants or with students who are assigned to counseling or required to participate (e.g., as a condition for a failing student to remain in college). The more carefully designed studies of counseling effectiveness select counseled and control cases from the same population with regard to counseling motivation. For example, both groups can be drawn from volunteer help-seekers, the controls being placed on a waiting list. This procedure is ethically justifiable if the treatment delay is short and if some delay is necessitated by the limitations of existing facilities. An alternative procedure is to employ only invited participants for research purposes and to assign to counseled and control groups random samples of those who accept the invitation.

A methodologically sound approach to counseling evaluation is illustrated in a series of studies by Krumboltz (1966b) and his associates. The participants were drawn from samples of college or high school students who were randomly assigned to treatment and control groups. In one of the studies on college students (Ryan & Krumboltz, 1964), the specific counseling outcome chosen for investigation was a widely recognized counseling goal, namely to promote behaviors that are instrumental in decision making. The specific counseling procedure employed was selected from the repertory of behavior modification. During a 20-minute interview, counselors used verbal approval to reinforce statements of deliberation in one group and statements of decision in another. The control group received no reinforcement during a similar interview. Despite the brevity of the treatement period, the two reinforced groups showed a significant increase in frequency of the reinforced verbal behavior during the interview. The group reinforced for decision statements also made more such statements in a subsequent story-completion task, although the effect of the reinforcement in the other group did not show such generalization of deliberation statements.

Other studies in the series employed a combination of verbal-reinforcement and modeling techniques to increase information-seeking behaviors of high school students relevant to their educational and career plans (Krumboltz & Schroeder, 1965; Krumboltz & Thoresen, 1964). The criterion of outcome was the frequency and amount of actual information-seeking behavior by the student during a three-week period following treatment. The results again demonstrated a significant effect of the procedures employed.

Another methodological innovation is illustrated by efforts to relate counseling processes to counseling outcomes in terms of specific quantifiable variables. For example, one study on college achievement compared not only the subsequent grades of counseled and control students randomly selected from the same population but also the degree of improvement among counseled students who had attended a varying number of counseling sessions, i.e., 8–11, 6–7, or 2–5 sessions (Spielberger, Weitz, & Denny, 1962). In another study of college underachievers, using similarly constituted counseled and control groups, counseling was provided in 24 small-group sessions extending over 12 weeks (Dickenson & Truax, 1966). All counseling sessions were recorded and rated on degree of "empathy," "unconditional positive regard," and "genuineness" manifested by the particular counselor. Again the counseled group improved more than the control group. In addition, those students who participated in sessions receiving high ratings in the counselor-behavior variables improved more than did those whose counseling sessions received moderate ratings.

Still other investigations have yielded suggestive results on the interaction of counseling procedures with student personality characteristics. For example, in one study on academic achievement, students with high autonomy needs improved more from group-structured, low-authority counseling, while those with high dependency needs improved more from leader-structured, high-authority counseling (Gilbreath, 1967).

The Role of Values in Counseling. At a different level of evaluation, psychologists, educators, and members of related disciplines have examined the goals, underlying assumptions, and philosophy of counseling. The rapid expansion of counseling activities and the increasing professionalization of counseling services since the mid-1950s led to some searching analyses of the responsibilities of the counselor. Typical of such examinations of the counselor's role is Wrenn's *The Counselor in a Changing World* (1962). Representing the report of a commission appointed to consider guidance in American schools, this book described needed developments in school counseling in the light of our pluralistic and changing culture. The author explored the implications of societal changes for the functions and training of counselors. Of particular interest is the analysis of the "culturally encapsulated counselor," who is unresponsive to both temporal changes and subcultural differences in the value systems he employs in his counseling practice. Furthermore, because counseling is typically concerned with the client's plans for the future, it is not enough for the counselor to evaluate his information in terms of its present accuracy; he must also check it against rate and direction of change.

Since discussions of the objectives of counseling reflect both the value systems and the theoretical orientations of the discussants, it is not surprising that the conclusions reached are quite divergent. This is one of the areas of current controversy and ferment alluded to in the opening of Chapter 12. The diversity of opinions held regarding the goals of counseling is richly illustrated in a series of articles published in a special issue of the *Harvard Educational Review* devoted to an examination of guidance (Carle, Kehas, & Mosher, 1962). Dealing principally with the functions of the counselor within a school setting, these articles cover such questions as: the role of counseling in shaping and modifying behavior, rather than merely predicting behavior; the influence of both the immediate school context and the broader societal setting upon counseling goals and practices; the unwitting "smuggling" into the counseling process of values that may not be explicitly recognized by the counselor; the impact of counseling upon education and its place in the total educational process; and the issue of social conformity versus spontaneity and individuality as counseling goals. With the rise of community psychology and the marked increase in diversity of client populations to be served by the counseling psychologist, these questions of values are even more cogent today than when they were first discussed (Pedersen, Lonner, & Draguns, 1976).

SUMMARY

Counseling psychologists work in many settings and perform a variety of functions. Although they may specialize in one type of counseling, such as career,

educational, employee, rehabilitation, gerontological, marriage, or personal counseling, fully trained counseling psychologists recognize the interrelation of all
adjustment problems and focus on the counseling of the whole person. While there
are many similarities between clinical and counseling psychology, the fields as a
whole can be differentiated in terms of objectives, type of client, duration of
professional relationship with client, extent of information giving, and orientation
of practitioners. In none of these variables, however, is the distinction so sharp as
to preclude overlapping of the two fields.

Among the types of tests most commonly used in counseling are tests of general
intellectual development, educational achievement tests, special aptitude tests,
multiple aptitude batteries, interest inventories, and personality inventories. Under
the influence of the client-centered approach, counseling psychologists have
placed increasing importance upon the ways in which tests are integrated into the
counseling process. In counseling, psychological tests are used chiefly for the
information of the clients themselves, to increase their self-knowledge and help
them in making decisions. Some counselors leave the choice of tests up to the
client. If applied within certain limits, this practice makes for a better counseling
relationship and a more effective utilization of test results by the client. Counselors
working in school systems generally have access to longitudinal data about their
counselees in the form of cumulative records.

Because of the importance of career decisions in most counseling activities,
counseling psychologists need to be familiar with sources of occupational information. An up-to-date and systematically organized library or file of occupational
materials should be available for the use of clients as well as counselors. The
Dictionary of Occupational Titles prepared by the United States Employment
Service provides a comprehensive, uniform classification and coding system for
occupations, with extensive information on job functions and worker qualifications. Like psychological tests, occupational information needs to be integrated
into the total counseling process.

Research on the effectiveness of counseling has been concerned with the
long-range predictive validity of counseling tests, the effect of using tests in the
counseling process, the overall success of counseling programs in terms of
follow-up criteria, and the evaluation of specific counseling procedures. Methodological problems in such research indicate the need to: recognize that counseling
covers a multiplicity of processes of varying effectiveness; consider the interaction
of counseling procedures with nature of counseling problem, counselee variables,
and criterion of outcome; and use control groups equated with counseled groups
in motivational variables. Thoughtful analyses of the underlying philosophy of
counseling point up the role of value systems and theoretical orientation of
counselors.

PSYCHOLOGY OF CAREER DEVELOPMENT

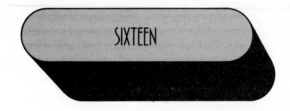

SIXTEEN

 HE MOST DISTINCTIVE area of research in counseling psychology is
that dealing with occupational choic-
es. What are the determinants of such choices? When and under what conditions
are career decisions made? What kinds of satisfactions do individuals seek in their
work? How do these satisfactions differ among persons who choose different
occupations? That counseling psychologists should focus upon occupations in
much of their research is understandable for a number of reasons. First, there is
the historical association of counseling with vocational problems. It will be recalled
that the vocational-guidance movement was the principal factor contributing to
the rise of counseling psychology. Even today, when the scope of counseling has
broadened considerably, many counseling psychologists still function predominantly in the occupational field.

To be sure, the counseling psychologist typically considers vocational problems
within the context of the client's overall psychological well-being. It is recognized
that the vocational problem presented by the client may itself arise from emotional
immaturity, insecurity, inability to face reality or make decisions, a difficult familial
situation, or other problems of personal adjustment. Conversely, there is increasing realization that occupation itself plays a central role in one's total life
adjustment. Emotional problems frequently stem from job tensions and frustrations, while absorbing and rewarding work can be highly therapeutic. Similarly,
maladjustments can often be prevented through satisfying work activities. Not only
the work itself, but also its many associated experiences, can contribute to the

individual's total adjustment. Of considerable importance to mental health, for instance, are acceptance by fellow workers and the feelings of security and belongingness that come from identification with an occupational group.

OCCUPATION AS A WAY OF LIFE

Rationale. Choosing an occupation is equivalent to choosing a way of life (Roe, 1956, Ch. 23; Super, 1957, Ch. 2). For one thing, a large proportion of one's waking time is spent on the job. But the influence of one's occupation extends well beyond working hours. For the vast majority of people in our culture, the nature of their work is the single most important determiner of social status. When trying to "place" a new acquaintance, people ask, "What *is* Wilson?" and are told that he or she is a lawyer, or a carpenter, or a hairdresser. The income derived from work helps to shape one's general style of living—the neighborhood in which one lives, the sort of house or apartment one occupies, the car one drives, the kind of vacation one can afford. One's job determines the distribution of work and leisure in both daily and seasonal schedules—as illustrated by the jobs of physician, long-distance truck driver, free-lance writer, schoolteacher, and bank clerk. Some jobs limit the places where one may live—as illustrated by the jobs of forest ranger, mining engineer, music critic, and investment broker. In many other kinds of work, some geographical mobility is required for maximal vocational advancement. A research chemist or a professor of history must be free to go where the best opportunities are available in his or her field of specialization. A person may be a native Californian with all family ties in the San Fernando valley, but the best job offer may come from Harvard.

Occupations differ in many other ways that may be significant to an individual worker. They may influence one's habitual dress, as witnessed by our stereotypes of white-collar and blue-collar jobs and by the many kinds of occupational uniforms with their widely recognized symbolic significance. They differ widely in the physical and psychological milieu in which the work is done. Contrast, for example, the neatness and order of the normal working environment of a surgeon with that of a construction supervisor, or the interpersonal contacts of a bill collector with those of a commercial artist. Friendships are often work-determined. People tend to spend their leisure hours with co-workers, business associates, or professional colleagues. Nor is it at all unusual for an individual to marry someone he or she has met through job contacts.

Many kinds of work are associated with characteristic sets of values that frequently extend into one's personal life. If some of these values are not consonant with the individual's own values, the resulting conflict may be quite disruptive. In view of the degree to which career decisions imply the choice of a whole way of life, it becomes easier to understand the success of interest tests such as the Strong-Campbell Interest Inventory. Persons in different occupations are in fact characterized by distinctive interest patterns and sets of values that reach beyond the work itself into nearly every aspect of daily living.

It might be added that it is not only the individual's own occupation but also that of his or her spouse that determines the familial way of life. Much has been written about the special problems and characteristic way of life of the wives of medical doctors, career officers in the military services, and high-level business executives. Although these examples have been widely publicized and dramatized, the same principle holds in all walks of life. The occupation of either or both spouses permeates and colors every facet of the family's world. With the increasing development of careers for married women, a fertile field of psychological research is the investigation of the summative and interaction effects of the occupations of the two spouses on the way of life of the entire family. Marriage counseling also needs to give increasing attention to possible conflicts between the value systems and way of life implicit in the career plans of the two partners.

From a different angle, the choice of an occupation can be seen as a way of establishing one's identity. Super (1953, 1957) has repeatedly pointed out that vocational choice is the implementation of a self-concept. He argues that "satisfaction in one's work and on one's job depends on the extent to which the work, the job, and the way of life that goes with them, enable one to play the kind of role that one wants to play" (1953, p. 189).

More specifically, occupations are chosen to meet needs. The economic need to earn one's livelihood is only one of many such needs. It can ordinarily be met by any one of many jobs, among which the individual chooses on the basis of other needs. For some persons, rate of pay may be so closely linked with one or more of their major goals that it will be the determining factor in a job decision. But, for most persons, other needs either determine or significantly affect career choices. Thus one person may put such a high value on personal freedom and independence that she can only be happy as a free-lance or self-employed worker. Another functions best when he is the center of attention—a need that could be satisfied by many occupations, ranging from actor to information clerk. Still others require the security that comes from working in a highly structured situation in which they are relieved of all responsibility for decision making.

These needs are not necessarily verbalized. The individual may simply feel that he or she *must* paint or that an office job would be intolerable, without being able to explain why. It is one of the objectives of counseling to make the individual aware of the motives underlying such convictions. When needs are recognized as such, they are more readily brought under rational control and less likely to lead to unrealistic decisions. Throughout such a process, however, the counselor must operate within the framework of the client's needs, which may differ from those of the counselor. This is one of the reasons why the counselor cannot choose a "suitable" occupation for the client without at least some interaction with the client. Parenthetically, the consideration of needs in career decisions highlights one difference between the characteristic approaches of clinical and counseling psychologists. If, for example, a client has a deep-rooted feeling of insecurity, the clinician typically attempts to change the client's personality in order to overcome the insecurity, whereas the counselor helps the client choose a vocation in which emotional insecurity is not a serious drawback.

Occupational Personality Patterns. There is a mounting accumulation of research literature dealing with personality differences among occupational groups. Summaries of portions of this literature prepared from different points of view can be found in several sources (Holland, 1973; Osipov, 1973, Ch. 6; Pietrofesa & Splete, 1975, Ch. 4; Super & Bohn, 1970, Ch. 5). Some of this research has been conducted by psychologists, although sociologists and members of other disciplines have contributed extensively to this topic. The methodology ranges from rather subjective biographical approaches to moderately well-controlled applications of questionnaires, interviewing techniques, personality inventories, and projective tests. A wide variety of occupations has been investigated, including those of scientists in a number of fields, mathematicians, engineers, medical students, psychiatric residents, schoolteachers, architects, nurses, office workers, and salespersons, among others. Some investigators have compared student groups specializing in different fields, such as accounting and creative writing. Others have worked with persons employed in the various occupations; a few have concentrated on scientists who have attained a high degree of eminence in their fields.

Data on developmental history and childhood experiences of persons in different occupations were generally obtained retrospectively during interviews with the adult subjects. A notable exception is the longitudinal study of a group of California children with initial Stanford-Binet IQs of 140 or higher, conducted by Terman and his associates. Among the many analyses of the voluminous follow-up data obtained in this project is a comparison of the men who eventually became physical scientists with those specializing in social science, law, or the humanities (Terman, 1954). Out of a total of about 500 items, including test scores, ratings, and biographical data, 108 differentiated between the two groups at the .05 level of significance or better. Most of these discriminating items dealt with interests, including evidence of early scientific interest in childhood and scores on the Strong Vocational Interest Blank (SVIB), precursor of the Strong-Campbell Interest Inventory (SCII).

The close association between vocational interests and other personality characteristics has been suggested by studies conducted over several decades with the SVIB (see Anastasi, 1976, pp. 541–543). An example is an investigation of 100 Air Force officers conducted at the University of California (see Darley & Hagenah, 1955, pp. 128–129). Each subject took a battery of tests, including the SVIB, and also underwent an intensive assessment program through interviews and other observational techniques. On the basis of all available information, subjects were described by eight clinical psychologists in terms of 76 given personality variables. Correlations of these trait ratings with each of the SVIB occupational keys revealed a number of statistically significant correlations. The personality descriptions associated with high scores on two of these keys are summarized below:

High scorers on Mathematician Key: Self-abasing, concerned with philosophical problems, introspective, lacking in social poise, lacking confidence in own ability, sympathetic, reacts poorly to stress, not persuasive in personal contacts, not an effective leader, not ostentatious, not aggressive or socially ascendant

High scorers on Real Estate Salesman Key; Self-indulgent, guileful, cynical, opportunistic, aggressive, persuasive, ostentatious, may arouse hostility in others, not sympathetic, not concerned with philosophical problems, not lacking confidence in own ability, not self-abasing

Available published research on occupational personality patterns provides a wealth of promising data. Interpretation of the results, however, requires a consideration of such procedural matters as the adequacy and comparability of control groups and the cross-validation of findings on new samples. Some personality patterns may be characteristic of occupational level and upward mobility in general rather than being associated with field of work. For instance, in Roe's (1951a, 1951b) studies of eminent scientists, the results pointed strongly to the importance of prestige motivation, strong inner drive, sustained effort, and absorption in work to the exclusion of other interests. There is no way of knowing to what extent these qualities are also typical of persons who have achieved distinction as artists, writers, business executives, statesmen, or workers in any other field. Even when significant personality differences are conclusively established between occupational groups, it is often difficult to analyze cause-effect relations. To what extent do salespersons become dominant and extroverted because of the demands of their jobs, and to what extent were they that way to begin with? Only longitudinal studies can adequately answer this kind of question.

At best, what occupational differences have been found in personality patterns represent only group trends. For many kinds of work, one could probably write personality sketches that would roughly fit a majority of persons in that occupation. This sort of information is useful in counseling insofar as it gives the counselees some idea of the kind of person with whom they are most likely to associate if they choose a given type of work. But, within any occupational group, the range of individual differences is fully as wide in personality variables as it is in aptitudes. Nor are these differences necessarily associated with different degrees of success. The breadth and flexibility of most occupations are such that different persons may succeed in them for different reasons. Individuals may choose specialties (as in law or medicine) that are consonant with their own needs, interests, and values. Even a single job can often be structured by the individual to fit his or her own aptitude and personality pattern. Moreover, the same job in different companies or under different supervisors may call for very different personality traits. Specific jobs as well as occupational fields undoubtedly vary in the degree of specialization and restructuring that they permit. This is one of the variables that should be considered in making career decisions.

Job Satisfaction and Worker Needs. Since mid-century, there have been increasing efforts to investigate the relation between a worker's reported job satisfaction and the degree to which the job fulfills those needs that are important to him or her. Scattered research on various occupational groups has provided suggestive evidence that job satisfaction is higher the closer the correspondence between what the job offers and what the individual seeks (e.g., Jacobson, Rettig, & Pasamanick, 1959; Rettig, 1960; Rettig, Jacobson, & Pasamanick, 1958; Schaffer, 1953). Among the personality variables studied are the needs for recognition, status and prestige, intellectual stimulation, self-expression, independence, pay, job security, and regular hours.

Although motivational factors undoubtedly play an important part in vocational adjustment, there is danger that they may be overemphasized at the expense of performance factors. As vocational counselors have moved in the direction of personal counseling, with its more nearly clinical orientation, they have tended to lose sight of the realistic goal of job performance. Brayfield (1961) cautioned against this de-emphasis of performance and advocated a closer integration of industrial and counseling psychology. He wrote, "We need the healthy antidote of a performance-oriented industrial psychology to balance the uncritical acceptance of the self-realization goal of vocational counseling" (p. 42).

A coordinated approach that covers both job performance and job satisfaction has been followed in the University of Minnesota Work Adjustment Project (Lofquist & Dawis, 1969). Spanning more than two decades of continuing research, this project is clearly outstanding in scope, comprehensiveness, and methodological sophistication. Although initially focused on the vocational rehabilitation of disabled workers, its contributions are equally applicable to career counseling in any context. A brief discussion of this project, with particular reference to the development of an instrument for measuring job satisfaction, was included in Chapter 5.

In their theory of work adjustment, the Minnesota investigators provide a conceptual framework and assessment procedures for conducting occupational counseling as well as for evaluating its outcome (Dawis et al., 1968; Lofquist & Dawis, 1969). Essentially, this theory defines work adjustment in terms of (1) job satisfaction and (2) worker satisfactoriness (i.e., satisfactory job performance). Worker satisfactoriness can be predicted from the correspondence between the individual's scores on appropriate aptitude tests and available information about job requirements. As major sources of both kinds of data, the investigators refer to the General Aptitude Test Battery (GATB) and the Occupational Ability Patterns (OAP), giving minimum scores in relevant aptitudes for each job. Both were developed by the USES and have been cited earlier (Chs. 2, 3, 15).

Within the Minnesota Work Adjustment Project, the following four instruments were developed for use in a coordinated approach to the problem:

1. Minnesota Satisfactoriness Scale (MSS) as a measure of worker *job performance;*
2. Minnesota Satisfaction Questionnaire (MSQ) as a measure of the individual's *job satisfaction*—how well the particular job fulfills the worker's needs (described in Ch. 5 and Table 5-3);
3. Minnesota Importance Questionnaire (MIQ) as a measure of the relative value of different *vocational needs* for the individual;
4. Minnesota Job Description Questionnaire (MJDQ) as a measure of the kinds and amounts of *reinforcers* provided by each job to meet the worker's needs.

The last three instruments contain parallel items relating to the same 20 needs (or reinforcers), such as advancement, creativity, variety of work, financial compensation, relations with co-workers and supervisors, and working conditions.

By having job supervisors (and in some jobs the workers themselves) apply the Minnesota Job Description Questionnaire to specific jobs in several hundred firms, the researchers of the Work Adjustment Project developed Occupational Reinforcer Patterns (ORPs) for 148 occupations (Borgen et al., 1968a, 1968b; Rosen, Weiss, Hendel, Dawis, & Lofquist, 1972). In effect, the ORPs provide the counselor with reinforcer patterns for each occupation, which can then be matched with individual worker needs. As the research continues, other occupations will be added to the ORP list. The available occupations have also been grouped into 12 occupational clusters having similar ORP profiles.

Still another element in the theory of work adjustment formulated by the Minnesota investigators pertains to the fact that the correspondence between worker needs and job environment is not static but subject to change over time. Thus insufficient correspondence may be improved by modifiability in either worker or job environment or both (Dawis & Lofquist, 1976).

THE CLASSIFICATION OF OCCUPATIONS

Dimensional Classifications. Psychological research on occupations has quite naturally led to attempts to classify occupations in terms of psychologically meaningful dimensions. This is admittedly a difficult task, not only because of the vast number and diversity of existing occupations, but also because occupations vary along several dimensions. The chief weakness of early classifications stemmed from their mixture of different dimensions or principles of classification. Beginning in the mid-1950s, counseling psychologists have tried to develop more refined systems of classification whereby each occupation could be classified in terms of two or more identifiable dimensions.

The most widely recognized occupational dimensions are level and field (Roe, 1956; Super, 1957). *Level* is identified with such occupational variables as income, social status and prestige, general educational requirements, degree of authority, freedom and independence of action, and amount of responsibility for decision making. Because these social and psychological variables are highly intercorrelated, it is feasible to classify occupations unidimensionally with regard to this composite definition of level. Although individual jobs might be differently ranked in terms of one or another of these variables, there is little difficulty in placing them in broad categories on this basis. It is noteworthy in this connection that prestige ratings of different occupations, obtained in surveys of large, representative samples of respondents, have revealed remarkable stability over periods of forty years or more (Hakel, Hollmann, & Dunnette, 1968). With regard to worker requirements, occupational levels are differentiated principally in terms of educational level and performance on tests of general intellectual development or scholastic aptitude.

Field of work refers to the type of activity performed. Although operating at the same level, for example, a bricklayer and an electrician are in different fields, as are a physiologist and a professor of English literature. Psychologically, field corresponds closest to differences in aptitude patterns and in interests, values, and related personality variables. Super (1957, Ch. 3) added a third dimension to this occupational classification, which he called *enterprise.* This dimension refers to the institutional or industrial setting in which the work is performed, such as agriculture, transportation, or government. Although not so basic psychologically as the classifications into level and field, choice of enterprise may be quite important in individual cases. A person who finds it oppressive to work indoors could profitably explore opportunities in agriculture and kindred occupations; one who has a deep-rooted aversion to bureaucratic procedures might be well advised to eschew employment in a government agency. Jobs in the same field and at the same level may appeal to quite different kinds of persons when performed in different settings. Compare, for example, the jobs of three chemists, one employed in a university, another in a government laboratory, and the third in a manufacturing plant.

Classification System of the Dictionary of Occupational Titles. In its later revisions, the *Dictionary of Occupational Titles* (DOT) incorporated the results of extensive research on the psychological requirements of different jobs (U.S. Department of Labor, 1977). The principal sources of data regarding individual jobs include ratings by job analysts derived from field observations, interviews, or job descriptions, as well as scores on the General Aptitude Test Battery (GATB). The job analysis summarized in Appendix C and briefly discussed in Chapter 2 illustrates the type of information recorded.

Each job title in the DOT is assigned a nine-digit code number which provides information useful in grouping and classifying jobs from several angles. The first three digits designate the *job content* or nature of work performed. In this set, the first digit corresponds to the broadest categories, as shown in Table 16-1. The next

TABLE 16-1
Broad Occupational Categories Corresponding to First Digit of
Numerical Code in Dictionary of Occupational Titles
(From U.S. Department of Labor, 1977, pp. xvi–xvii.)

First Digit of Code	Occupational Category
0⎱ 1⎰	Professional, technical, and managerial occupations
2	Clerical and sales occupations
3	Service occupations
4	Agricultural, fishery, forestry, and related occupations
5	Processing occupations
6	Machine trades occupations
7	Bench work occupations
8	Structural work occupations
9	Miscellaneous occupations

two digits reflect an increasing degree of detail with reference to such specifications as field, subject matter, material, product, service, or industry. For example, the three-digit code for the job of dough mixer for bakery products, described in Appendix C, is 520. The first digit, 5, represents processing occupations (Table 16-1); 52 designates occupations in the processing of food, tobacco, and related industries; and 520 adds to this designation the specific tasks of mixing, compounding, blending, kneading, shaping, and related activities.

The middle three digits of the DOT code indicate the *level* at which the worker functions in relation to data, people, and things, in that order. These digits provide information on the predominant subject-matter orientation characteristic of the job, as well as the level of complexity at which the worker operates. In the dough-mixer example, the entire nine-digit code is 520.562-010. The digits in the second set indicate that involvement with data is at the "copying" level (coded 5), with people at the level of "speaking-signaling" (coded 6), and with things at the level of "operating-controlling" (coded 2). The last three digits of the nine-digit code differentiate a particular occupation from all others.

As a further illustration, it may be of interest to note that the nine-digit codes for industrial, clinical, and counseling psychologists are 045.107-030, 045.107-022, and 045.107-026, respectively. The first digit (0) corresponds to professional occupations; 04 designates life sciences; and 045 specifies psychologists. The 107 code is shared by these types of applied psychologists with workers in other fields having the same profile of relationships with data, people, and things. Experimental psychologists, on the other hand, have an 061 code. The six-digit code (i.e., first six digits) makes it possible to group and regroup occupations in several significant ways in terms of common functions, technologies, and orientations across fields.

In addition to the basic nine-digit code for some 20,000 occupations, the DOT provides other information regarding groups of jobs classified according to worker interests, abilities, and other relevant characteristics (U.S. Department of Labor, 1978). In this classification, jobs are first grouped into 12 Occupational Interest

Areas of Work, as follows: Artistic, Scientific, Nature, Authority, Mechanical, Industrial, Business Detail, Persuasive, Accommodating, Humanitarian, Social-Business, and Physical Performing. These areas are further subdivided into groups of occupations with similar requirements in terms of general educational development, abilities, temperaments, and other appropriate characteristics. For each of the 65 job groups thus identified, the following worker requirements are reported:

General Educational Development—level of development in mathematics, reasoning, and language (reading, writing, and speaking);

Specific Vocational Preparation—extent of formal training, apprenticeship, or on-the-job demonstration or instruction;

Aptitudes—includes applicable coverage of GATB-based aptitude test batteries developed for specific occupation in the group;

Temperaments—typical job situations to which worker must adapt (e.g., performing a variety of duties and often changing tasks without loss of efficiency or composure);

Physical Demands—degree of strength and critical sensory or motor requirements.

The United States Employment Service (USES) has also developed an interest inventory that is geared for use in connection with the DOT (Droege & Hawk, 1977; U.S. Department of Labor, 1978). Its items are similar in nature to those of other widely used interest inventories, such as the Strong-Campbell and the Kuder described in Chapters 3 and 15. In the USES inventory, the counselee records "like," "dislike," or "?" in response to items listing: (1) job activities (e.g., serve meals in a restaurant), (2) occupational titles (e.g., typist), and (3) life experiences (e.g., repair a bicycle). In the construction of the inventory, a pool of 307 items was first prepared to sample a wide range of occupational activities. A factor analysis of the responses to these items by over 1,000 adult men and women led to the identification of 12 interest factors, such as mechanical, scientific, and artistic.[1] Revised forms of the inventory were then administered to representative national samples in order to develop final scales for measuring each of the 12 factors. These scales correspond to the 12 Occupational Interest Areas of Work now used to classify occupations in the *Guide to Occupational Exploration* which accompanies the fourth edition of the DOT (U.S. Department of Labor, 1978). Thus, in using the DOT, the counselee who has taken the USES Interest Inventory can begin by exploring those work areas that include occupations related to his or her measured interests.

Other Trait-Pattern Taxonomies. In connection with the discussion of the Strong-Campbell Interest Inventory (SCII) in Chapters 3 and 15, reference was made to Holland's classification of general occupational themes, which were incorporated in the SCII. This classification is the result of continuing research by Holland and others on the organization of interests and is represented by the hexagonal model reproduced in Figure 16-1. The model shows the empirically established degrees of relationship between the six types of interests. In general, the shorter the distance between any two interest types, the higher is the

[1]Only 11 factors were identified in the original analysis. A 12th scale, Physical Performing, was added later in order to cover a narrow category of jobs not elsewhere included, representing interest in physical activities performed before an audience.

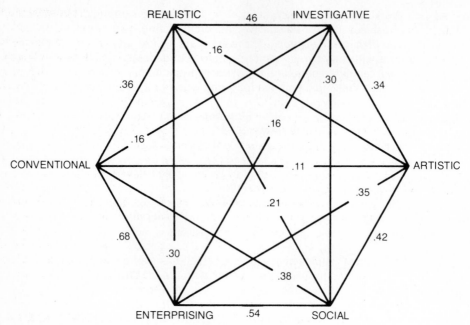

Figure 16-1. Holland's hexagonal model of general occupational themes, showing correlations between preference scores in the six areas in a sample of college students. *(From Holland, Whitney, Cole, & Richards, 1969, p. 4.)*

correlation between them. In following up this approach, Holland and his associates (Holland, 1973; Viernstein, 1972) developed a system for classifying all occupations in the DOT in terms of these six categories. For each occupation, Holland designates the. three predominant interests, in order of priority. For example, the job of electrical engineer (DOT code 003.061-010) is characterized by an IRE pattern, with high interests in the Investigative, Realistic, and Enterprising themes.

In the Self-Directed Search, designed by Holland (1971) as a preliminary counseling aid for high school, college, and adult populations, respondents record their interests and competencies in various activities on the basis of prior experience. They then score their own papers and find their three-letter interest codes, through which they can identify and explore suitable occupations. Under the appropriate three-letter codes, an accompanying booklet lists over 400 common occupations, which are said to account for about 95% of the labor force of the United States. It is characteristic of recent work on occupational classification that long-term, coordinated research programs are replacing the limited, piecemeal studies of an earlier period. In addition, there have been several systematic efforts to integrate the results of different investigations. Holland's application of his hexagonal model to the DOT jobs is one example. Conversely, the 12 Occupational Interest Areas of Work identified through the USES Interest Inventory have now been classified under the appropriate Holland occupational interest categories.

A more comprehensive approach is exemplified by the occupational taxonomy proposed by Dawis and Lofquist (1975) on the basis of their previously described theory of work adjustment. Essentially, this taxonomy represents an attempt to cross-classify occupations on the basis of the Occupational Aptitude Patterns (OAPs) of the DOT and the Occupational Reinforcer-pattern Clusters (ORCs) of the University of Minnesota Work Adjustment Project. The resulting clusters of occupations, each corresponding to a single OAP-ORC combination, have been labeled "Taxons." With the available data, only 77 Taxons could be identified by utilizing occupations for which both an OAP and an ORC were available; a total of 311 specific occupations are included in these 77 categories. Coverage will expand as additional occupations are described in terms of their aptitude and reinforcer patterns. The authors observe, however, that the occupations included in the joint taxonomy can best be regarded as "benchmark occupations" providing reference points for mapping the total occupational domain.

To facilitate further the utilization of available occupational data, the Minnesota Occupational Classification System (Dawis & Lofquist, 1974) not only gives the twofold Taxon for each job cluster but also summarizes additional data for each occupation within the cluster. This includes the six-digit DOT code, the interest, temperament, and physical demands of the job as reported in the DOT for the appropriate job group, the Holland interest pattern, and the interest inventories having an occupational key for that job (SCII and/or Kuder Occupational Interest Inventory).

CAREER DECISIONS

The Role of Decision Making in Counseling. One of the most important objectives of all counseling is to facilitate the making of effective decisions. In contrast to charlatans, who are likely to hand their clients ready-made solutions for their problems or to choose specific occupations for them, counseling psychologists concentrate on improving the individual's own decision making. Effective career decisions require accurate knowledge regarding both abilities and wants or needs. Tests help in this connection, as does much of the verbal interaction between counselor and counselee. In addition, effective decisions require knowledge about occupations, which counseling likewise tries to provide. Finally, they require the ability to think clearly—to combine available information in predicting outcomes, to weigh alternative courses of action, and to make choices that adequately reflect all relevant factors.

Career planning normally involves, not one decision, but a multitude of decisions, which typically extend over a period of several years. Many preliminary decisions may have to be made and implemented before the individual finally enters his or her chosen field of work. Moreover, people's wants and their suitability for different kinds of careers may change with time. Jobs also change. In our rapidly evolving society, new fields of work constantly emerge, and even familiar jobs may become drastically altered. All these circumstances call for flexibility in the occupational decisions made at any one stage. Also relevant is the multipotentiality of both persons and jobs, to which we have repeatedly alluded. Any one person is qualified for many different jobs, not just for a single job. Conversely, a given occupation may be successfully pursued in many different ways by different persons.

The goal of career counseling is *not* early commitment to an ultimate occupational choice. Rather, counseling contributes to career decisions in at least three ways. First, it helps individuals in making immediate decisions as demanded by their present environment. For instance, a junior high school student may have to choose among different types of schools, curricula, or courses; or the student may have to decide whether to continue in school or take a job. Such decisions require that the individual consider the general direction in which she or he wants to go and the major future implications of any decision. But there will be many opportunities for modifying the direction later and for making more specific choices in the light of subsequent experience.

In the second place, counseling may provide knowledge about oneself and about the world of work that will be used later—perhaps several years later—when the occasion demands it. At the time of counseling, one may have reached no decision at all. But as a result of the information acquired, one may accept or reject a specific job when it is offered. If it contributed to the wisdom of that decision, counseling was effective. Finally, the counseling process offers an opportunity to learn more effective procedures for decision making itself. This experience is designed to help the individual make wiser and more satisfying decisions in solving future problems of daily life.

Occupational choice represents a *synthesis* between wishes and reality, between what one wants and what one learns he or she can attain (Super, 1957, Ch. 21). Through continuing interaction with one's environment, the individual tests his or her personal needs, aptitudes, and other attributes against the demands and resources of society. In the process of growing up, the individual has an opportunity to explore different roles through fantasy, play activities, schoolwork, extracurricular functions, household tasks, and part-time or temporary jobs. Specific interests probably develop in much the same way. As Strong (1943, p. 682) put it, "An interest is an expression of one's reaction to his environment. The reaction of liking-disliking is a resultant of satisfactory or unsatisfactory dealing with an object." This resultant obviously depends upon the characteristics of the individual as well as upon the characteristics of the particular objects encountered and the circumstances under which he or she does so.

Tyler (1959; 1969, Chs. 2, 9; 1978) focused attention upon the important role of decisions in the individual's general development. Within any lifetime, only a small fraction of one's "potentialities" can be realized. A person may have the qualifications to become a distinguished surgeon, writer, *and* political leader, but there is not enough time to be all three. Choices must be made throughout life, and each in turn limits and determines the direction of subsequent development.

At the outset, these limits are set largely by external circumstances. For instance, newborn infants *could* learn any existing language—or even a nonexisting language that someone might devise. But what they actually learn to speak is quickly narrowed down to the language of their parents. As children become older, however, the limits of their development are established more and more by their own choices—whether they spend more time on schoolwork or play, whether they play baseball or collect stamps, the companions they choose, the books they read, and so forth. Although available opportunities, decisions by other persons, and their own physical and psychological attributes continue to set many limits upon their behavior, individuals themselves participate increasingly in the process. At every choice point they encounter, they help to set their own limits and to shape their future experiences.

In this concept of choice, Tyler sees a rationale for the successful predictions of occupational choice made with such instruments as the Strong Vocational Interest Blank. A high score on this inventory signifies that the individual's pattern of choices resembles that of persons in a given occupation. This in turn should help us to predict how this individual will choose in similar circumstances in the future.

The Application of Decision Theory. Career choice can be analyzed in the light of decision theory. There is a growing number of psychological experiments conducted within the framework of decision theory, which should provide some of the basic research for counseling. Decision theory began as an attempt to put the decision-making process into mathematical form so that available information may be used to arrive at the most effective decision under given circumstances. The mathematical procedures employed in decision theory are often quite complex, and few are in a form permitting their immediate application to psychological problems. Nevertheless, the basic concepts of decision theory help in formulating and clarifying the decision process. Surveys of the application of decision theory to psychological research on choice behavior can be found in Edwards (1961) and in Becker and McClintock (1967). The use of decision theory in personnel selection and classification was illustrated in Chapter 2.

Essentially, decisions are based upon: (1) predicted probability of different outcomes; (2) estimates of risks involved or seriousness of failure; and (3) consideration of the relative value or importance of different goals. In career decisions, information about the individual's capabilities, obtained from tests or other sources, together with job information, provides the data for predicting outcomes. Thus the individual, with the help of the counselor, might estimate his or her chances of completing an apprenticeship as machinist or of graduating from medical school. Expectancy tables (see Ch. 2) represent an effective way of presenting such probability data in counseling. In this context, they are often called experience tables, since they are based on prior experience with comparable samples of persons. The consequences of making a bad decision help to establish the certainty level we require to take action. If the consequences of failure are slight, we may be willing to try a course of action even though there is a high probability of failure.

Both decision theory and counseling psychology recognize the fundamental importance of values in the decision process. The fact that to be workable the individual's decisions must be consonant with his or her own value system provides one more reason why counselors cannot make decisions for clients. In decision theory, the mathematical expression of the relative values of different outcomes constitutes a particularly thorny problem. Values, however, inevitably enter into decision making; decision theory merely requires that they be made explicit.

Counseling psychologists have made increasing use of the concepts of decision theory as a framework for educational and occupational planning (Gelatt, 1962; M. R. Katz, 1966; Thoresen & Mehrens, 1967). Of special interest are the training programs designed to improve decision-making skills. An example is a workbook entitled *You: Today and Tomorrow* (M. R. Katz, 1959; Shimberg & Katz, 1962). Designed for a group guidance unit at the eighth- and ninth-grade level, this workbook introduces the student to career problems and provides exercises in self-appraisal, in the utilization of educational and occupational information, and in decision making. Data regarding abilities can be obtained from scholastic aptitude, multiple aptitude, or achievement tests administered in the regular school-testing program, as well as from the student's grade record. In addition, there is provision for students to consider their schoolwork, extracurricular activities, hobbies, and other experiences in the appraisal of their abilities, interests, and values. The workbook presents problems and information in an interesting and readable style. An excerpt is reproduced in Figure 16-2. With its accompanying teacher's guide, *You: Today and Tomorrow* is suitable for use by a classroom teacher in a program extending over about 30 class sessions. Its focus is

So we can see that the information we get from a forecast or prediction is only one fact that goes into making a wise decision. A lot does depend on the *chances* in our favor or against us. But a lot also depends on the *value* or importance of our goals; and a lot depends on the seriousness or danger of our *risks*.

A trackman who has jumped 21 feet in 8 out of 10 tries would be foolish to try to jump across a 20-foot chasm just to pick a few blueberries on the other side. But what if he were being chased by an angry grizzly bear?

So in deciding which high school course to take, or in setting goals for your future education and occupation, you will want to consider not only your chances of success or failure. You will want to consider also *how serious it would be to fail* and *how important it would be to succeed.*

Figure 16-2.   Excerpt from *You: Today and Tomorrow*—a group guidance program for junior high school students. *(From M. R. Katz, 1959, p. 34. Copyright © 1959 by Educational Testing Service. Reproduced by permission.)*

on the student's immediate task of choosing a high school curriculum, both for its direct effect on later career choices and for its value as a paradigm in decision making.

As part of a long-term plan for guidance services, the College Entrance Examination Board sponsored the development of a decision-making program for junior high school students (Gelatt, Varenhorst, & Carey, 1972; Miller & Gelatt, 1971–1972) and a more sophisticated program suitable for senior high school and college students and for out-of-school adults[2] (Gelatt, Varenhorst, Carey, & Miller, 1973). Both forms provide individual workbooks and a leader's guide. Major decision-making skills are taught through such techniques as written exercises, discussions, simulations, and role playing. The participants are helped to explore and clarify their personal values, gather and evaluate relevant information, and work out effective decision strategies for converting the information into action. The programs are concerned with educational, career, and personal decisions. They can serve as a basis for a semester course on decision-making skills, a unit in another course, or a major component of a group counseling program.

Another example is provided by the Life Career Game (Boocock, 1967), which can be used independently or incorporated into a more comprehensive program, such as the College Board program. This game can be played by any number of teams, each consisting of two to four players. The task is to plan the life of a fictitious student, with regard to education, occupation, family, and leisure. Each round of the game represents one year in the person's life. The object is to plan activities so as to maximize both present satisfaction and the chances of a satisfying life in the future. With the aid of tables incorporating census data and national surveys, "scores" representing the effect of decisions in each of the four areas are calculated at the end of each round. Realistically, chance elements are also incorporated in these scores. The team with the highest total score on all rounds wins. A minimum of 5 hours is required to complete the game, but a total of 10 hours is recommended. The rounds can be distributed over a period of days or weeks.

The development of training programs in decision-making skills was stimulated in part by the increasing number of options available to young people today, with the consequent need for more individual choices. Skillful decision making augments freedom of choice by enabling individuals to recognize available alternatives and to evaluate them in terms of their own needs and goals. It also gives them greater control over their lives by reducing the extent to which chance or external factors determine outcomes. It should thus help to reduce one's sense of helplessness about life events and foster what Rotter (1966) describes as a generalized expectancy for internal control of reinforcement.

Computer Utilization. Computers are being used increasingly both to assist in career counseling and—more broadly—to provide training in decision making (J. A. Harris, 1973; Hoppock, 1976; Pietrofesa & Splete, 1975; Super et al., 1970). Within the traditional career counseling process, computers can provide rapid and accurate information regarding educational and occupational opportunities and

---

[2]The latter program also formed the basis of a combined group and individual counseling project to aid low-income adults in continuing their education within a realistic career plan (Bromfield & Kilmurray, 1976).

requirements, as well as current job openings and predictions of future trends. With its enormous storage capacity and its procedures for almost instantaneous sorting and retrieval of relevant data, the computer can provide information tailored to the particular individual's needs. By assuming these mechanical but laborious tasks, it can free counselors for those functions they are best qualified to perform. For example, through verbal interchange with clients, counselors can help them to recognize and formulate their values, identify objectives, and assess the strength of personal commitment to particular goals. They can ensure that the clients choose with full cognizance of the probability of different outcomes and of the nature of the risks involved. Another important function of counselors is to detect when their clients have reached a genuine decision and when they are voicing a superficial, temporary decision to avoid facing up to their problems (Tyler, 1969, Ch. 9).

A more complex application of computers is provided by comprehensive, automated guidance systems. Several programs using sophisticated interactive computer systems are now in operation or in process of development. In effect, such programs permit the client to engage in a dialogue with the computer whereby information is provided in response to the client's questions. Besides general educational and occupational data, such computer programs can store and utilize data about the individual, such as test scores, grades, inventory responses, and the like. In addition, programmed learning techniques are employed to improve the client's decision-making skills.

As an example of available computerized guidance systems, we may consider

Figure 16-3. Keyboard and display panel of computer-based System of Interactive Guidance and Information (SIGI). *(Courtesy of Educational Testing Service.)*

the computer-based System for Interactive Guidance and Information (SIGI) developed at Educational Testing Service (ETS, 1974–1975; M. R. Katz, 1969, 1974). Originally designed to help community and junior college students to make career decisions and plans, this system has also been adapted for use with four-year college students. The student communicates by pressing appropriate keys on a keyboard and receives directions, questions, and information on a visual display panel, as illustrated in Figure 16-3. The student may also request a printout of any display by pressing a key marked PRINT.

SIGI allows considerable flexibility in the extent and manner in which each individual uses it. There are also several opportunities for the user to examine more information and to reconsider and alter his or her decisions at different stages. Table 16-2 summarizes the subsystems included in SIGI. Each subsystem raises a major question in the decision-making process and helps the student to answer it. Through this process, the student also receives training in essential decision-making skills.

TABLE 16-2
SIGI at a Glance: Subsystems of Computer-based System
of Interactive Guidance and Information
(Copyright © 1974, 1975 by Educational Testing Service,
Reproduced by permission)

Subsystem	What the Student Does	Questions Answered
Introduction	Learns concepts and uses of major sections listed below.	Where do you stand now in your career decision making? What help do you need?
I. Values	Examines 10 occupational values and weights importance of each one.	What satisfactions do you want in an occupation? What are you willing to give up?
II. Locate	Puts in specifications on 5 values at a time and gets lists of occupations that meet specifications.	Where can you find what you want? What occupations should you look into?
III. Compare	Asks pointed questions and gets specific information about occupations of interest.	What would you like to know about occupations that you are considering? Should you reduce your list?
IV. Prediction	Finds out probabilities of getting various marks in key courses of preparatory programs for occupations.	Can you make the grade? What are your chances of success in preparing for each occupation you are considering?
V. Planning	Gets displays of program for entering each occupation, licensing or certification requirements, and sources of financial aid.	How do you get from here to there? What steps do you take to enter an occupation you are considering?
VI. Strategy	Evaluates occupations in terms of the rewards they offer and the risks of trying to enter them.	Which occupations fit your values best? How do you decide between an occupation that is highly desirable but risky and one that is less desirable but easier to prepare for?

CAREER DEVELOPMENT

Rationale. The realization that career decisions are made over a period of many years has led to the concept of career development, which is now widely accepted by counseling psychologists (Bordin, Nachman, & Segal, 1963; Osipov, 1973; Super, Starishevsky, Matlin, & Jordaan, 1963; Tiedeman, O'Hara, & Baruch, 1963; Tyler, 1969). This developmental approach found its fullest expression in the work of Super (1957) and his associates. Drawing upon both developmental psychology and sociological analyses of occupational behavior, Super analyzed the process of occupational adjustment in terms of five stages. The first is the *growth* stage, extending from birth to the age of about 14 years. During this period, children begin to develop a self-concept. Through observation of parents and other adults in the family circle, they first become acquainted with different roles that a person may play in their culture. As they grow older, their available role models are augmented through contacts in school and in other situations outside the home. Still other roles may be encountered vicariously in books, movies, or television.

From an early age, children begin to "try on" different roles in play and fantasy. They may become in turn airplane pilots, police officers, teachers, auto racers, and fire fighters. At this level, needs are uppermost in the selection of roles. It is only later that one begins to consider interests, then abilities, and still later job requirements and opportunities. The apparently irrational occupational roles assumed in childhood make good sense when examined within their own context. Typically, young children are dominated by adults who restrict their freedom of action and protect them from danger. Against such a background, their needs for independence, for power over others, and for adventure find outlets in play. If asked what they want to be when they grow up, children are also likely to name an occupation from their limited repertory of knowledge that seems to fulfill these needs.

In recognizing that an occupational role *can* help to meet their needs, children have taken the first step in their career development. With time, they find increasing opportunities for realistic tryouts of occupational roles. As they carry out household chores, work in the neighbors' yard, baby-sit, tinker with mechanical gadgets, play baseball, take violin lessons, or study different subjects in school, the process of reality testing begins.

The second stage proposed by Super is that of *exploration,* spanning adolescence and early adulthood. This is a period of extensive reality testing, with consequent modification of the self-concept. It is at this stage that important educational decisions are first faced and career goals are first seriously examined. For these reasons, career counseling has traditionally focused on this period. At this stage the individual also undertakes more formal work-role tryouts through part-time, temporary, and trial jobs.

The third stage is that of *establishment.* After some preliminary trial-and-error and flouhdering, most persons show a tendency to settle down in a particular line of work. Stabilization and advancement are typical of this stage. Persons come to identify with their chosen fields of work; they accumulate experience that ties them more closely to that field; and they assimilate the general way of life associated with their jobs. The fourth stage is one of *maintenance.* Continuing in the same field of work, persons at middle age typically concentrate on retaining the positions they have attained on the job, at home, and in the community. They either enjoy the fruits of their labor or accept their frustrations. This stage leads finally to occupational *decline,* as indicated by reduction in job activity and eventual retirement.

Like any system of stages employed to describe human development, this schema is admittedly an oversimplification. While helping to focus attention on developmental sequences and on tendencies characterizing different life periods, it is limited in a number of ways. First, the developmental process is continuous, and any description of it in terms of discrete stages is at best an approximation. Second, there are wide individual differences in the time of onset and duration of each stage. In some persons, one or more stages may be skipped altogether. Individual career patterns, for example, vary in the number and nature of job shifts (Super, 1957, Ch. 5). These differences in mobility are also associated with the nature of the work. Thus for semiskilled or clerical work, changing jobs usually entails no loss and may represent a gain. For work requiring a long period of professional preparation or for jobs in which considerable premium is put on experience, on the other hand, earlier decisions are more nearly irrevocable, and the typical career pattern is very stable. Similar differences may be found at later stages. Some persons continue to advance in their work throughout life. For them, there never comes a time for mere maintenance of the *status quo* or for decline in productivity.

When these limitations are borne in mind, the above stages can provide a convenient framework for organizing a mass of discrete facts. They can serve to establish norms against which individual development can be evaluated. And they help to generate testable hypotheses for research.

A related concept is that of *developmental tasks* (Erikson, 1950; Havighurst, 1953; Super, Crites, Hummel, Moser, Overstreet, & Warnath, 1957). In career development as in other forms of human development, the individual encounters typical behavioral demands and problems at different life stages from the pre-school period to the age of retirement. Although both the problems and the appropriate reactions vary somewhat among cultures and subcultures, modal requirements can be specified within a given cultural setting. Each of the career life stages described above makes characteristic demands upon the individual. Mastery of the developmental tasks of earlier stages influences the individual's handling of the behavioral demands of the next.

Super and his associates (1957) have used this concept of developmental tasks in their treatment of *vocational maturity.* The individual's vocational maturity is measured in terms of his mastery of the vocational tasks of his age level or his effectiveness in coping with the characteristic problems of his life stage. For example, among the vocational developmental tasks of an elementary-school child are the choice of daily activities suited to one's capacities, the assumption of responsibility for one's acts, and the undertaking of cooperative enterprises. Vocational developmental tasks of a man in his sixties might include, among others, planning for any necessary curtailment of work load or change of functions, as well as realistic consideration of retirement prospects. In this context, *vocational adjustment* at any stage is the resultant of interaction between one's vocational maturity and the reality demands of the situations one encounters. Thus, while vocational maturity is defined in terms of the individual's behavior, vocational adjustment is defined in terms of the outcomes of that behavior (Super, 1957, p. 187). At any stage of development, moreover, vocational maturity implies sufficient flexibility to permit the individual to modify his or her occupational activities and life-style to meet the demands of changing personal and societal situations.

Career Development Studies. The concepts of developmental tasks and vocational maturity provided the theoretical framework for a 20-year longitudinal investigation of approximately 100 ninth-grade boys, initiated by Super and his associates (Super et al., 1957; Super & Overstreet, 1960). The students were all attending a public high school in an urban community in New York State, chosen as typical of American cities in many socioeconomic indices. A mass of data were gathered through tests, questionnaires, and a series of four semistructured interviews with each participant. Further data were obtained from records of school achievement, reports of extracurricular and community activities, peer ratings, interviews with parents, and other miscellaneous sources. Several indices of career development were formulated and applied to the group. The resulting measures were intercorrelated and factor analyzed. On the basis of these analyses, the following indices were identified as the best measures of the construct "vocational maturity" at this age level: concern with choice (awareness of need for choice and knowledge of factors affecting choice), acceptance of responsibility for choice and planning, specificity of planning for the preferred occupation, and use of resources in obtaining occupational information.

The findings suggested that the major career-development task at the junior high school level is that of preparing to make career choices. For the ninth-grade boy, vocational maturity is shown, not by the wisdom or consistency of the ultimate career goal he chooses, but rather by the way he handles the preliminary planning and exploration required at this stage. Correlations with many personal and background variables were also found in the effort to investigate factors associated with vocational maturity. As defined in this study, vocational maturity tended to be positively correlated with intellectual level, parental occupational level, extent of cultural stimulation provided in the home, level of boy's own occupational choice, and enrollment in a college-preparatory curriculum. It is thus possible that the indices chosen in this study may be more appropriate for assessing the vocational maturity of boys planning to enter higher level occupations than for those planning to enter lower level occupations. Other research on career development, by both cross-sectional and longitudinal approaches, has been contributing data that help to fill out the picture (Crites, 1965a, 1965b, 1969; Gribbons & Lohnes, 1968, 1969; Super, Kowalski, & Gotkin, 1967; Tiedeman et al., 1963).

A somewhat different orientation to career development is exemplified by a collaborative project of the College Board and five state education agencies (Kroll & Pfister, 1977). Based on the thesis that career development skills are learned and therefore teachable, this research led to the construction of the Career Skills Assessment Program designed to measure the skills individuals need to formulate and carry out career plans effectively. The six skill areas cover: self-evaluation and development, career awareness, career decision making, employment seeking, work effectiveness, and personal economics. In keeping with current, comprehensive approaches to career development, the program includes skills required not only for seeking and maintaining jobs but also for handling one's personal affairs—from paying bills to understanding insurance and investments. The Career Skills Assessment Program is designed for use in either individual or group counseling with secondary school, community college, and continuing adult education students. It can be used by both individuals and institutions to identify areas of strength and weakness and to plan learning programs.

Life-span Counseling. The increasing emphasis placed on career development, as contrasted to single occupational choices, is paralleled by a conception of career counseling as a continuing process. The value of life-span counseling is now widely recognized. Such counseling is needed to help children keep up with the developmental tasks of their age level in preparation for later occupational choices and to guide adolescents and young adults through their career explorations and successive approximations. Following entry into the world of work, other decisions must be made about specific jobs within one's chosen field and about job changes to improve job satisfaction, to facilitate career advancement, or for any number of individual reasons.

In special cases, a drastic reassessment of occupational choice may be required at any age. This is true of a person who discovers that he or she made an unsuitable choice at an earlier stage, or one whose needs and values have altered radically over time, or one who has suffered a physical disability through injury or disease. The tubercular, the heart patient, and the disabled war veteran are common examples of the need for career counseling during early or later maturity. Still other examples are provided by a married woman who is suddenly widowed or by an older woman whose children have grown up and who wants to enter or reenter the world of work.

Career counseling of older workers is now receiving more and more attention. The special problems encountered at this stage may revolve around changes in the nature or amount of work done on the present job, transfer to a more suitable type of job, or complete retirement from work. Research on problems of retirement has thus far concentrated on exploratory surveys of attitudes, problems, plans, and effects on both the individual and his or her family. The tools have been largely questionnaires or interviews (Streib & Thompson, 1958; Havighurst, 1973). A particularly well-designed instrument for assessing the satisfaction of retired men and women with important aspects of their lives is the Retirement Descriptive Index (P. C. Smith et al., 1969). Designed by the authors of the Job Descriptive Index discussed in Chapter 5, this instrument provides ratings of satisfaction in four areas: Activities and Work, Financial Situation, Health, and People.

Finally, it has been recommended that career counseling should not be limited to cross-sectional "crisis counseling," i.e., counseling given when the individual faces a serious problem. With its positive and preventive orientation, counseling should help to forestall crises. Moreover, counselors can function most effectively if they maintain continuing, long-term contact with the same client. Super (1957, Ch. 23) proposed that such a relationship might be comparable to the typical relationship one has with a family physician, dentist, minister, or lawyer. Individuals seek help when they feel the need for it and possibly for an occasional checkup. But on these occasions they continue to consult the same counselor, who thus accumulates enough background information to be of maximum service to the client. The continuing contacts that school counselors maintain with their counselees, as supplemented by cumulative records, approximate such a relationship. But in the counseling of adults, this pattern is thus far largely untried, except possibly in the case of employee counseling in certain industrial corporations.

The positive and preventive orientation of counseling is one of several ways in which it resembles the more recently evolving community psychology in its approach. Other examples of such similarities can be found throughout this and the preceding chapter. Like community psychology, counseling psychology is characterized by a focus on the constructive use of assets rather than extensive and drastic personality restructuring; the solution of immediate, specific problems; the imparting of relevant factual information; and the development of skills in such areas as interpersonal relations, effective study, and decision making. It requires less time than traditional psychotherapy, and it is adaptable to the needs of a wide diversity of client populations. It seems that, under the influence of community psychology, clinical psychologists may come to function more and more like counseling psychologists.

SUMMARY

A major area of research in counseling psychology concerns the process of occupational choice and the nature of career development. In selecting an occupation, the individual chooses a way of life. One's occupation is likely to affect not only income level and general social status but also many specific aspects of daily life. Job satisfaction and general emotional well-being are contingent upon the extent to which a person's work satisfies needs and values that are significant to her or him. There is a considerable accumulation of data on personality patterns characteristic of persons in different occupations, but the findings are often difficult to interpret because of procedural inadequacies. More promising is the investigation of job satisfaction in terms of the relation between the pattern of individual worker needs and the pattern of reinforcers provided by particular jobs.

Both occupational research and career counseling call for occupational classifications based upon psychologically meaningful categories. Dimensional classifications have utilized the concepts of level, field, and enterprise. Trait patterns have been employed in other classifications, such as those followed in the *Dictionary of Occupational Titles* and in the Minnesota Occupational Classification System.

Career choice involves, not one, but a series of decisions made over a period of years. It is one of the objectives of counseling to facilitate decision making by providing self-knowledge, occupational information, and training in the decision process. Occupational choice represents a synthesis between individual wants or needs and the demands and limitations of reality. An effective decision takes into account the probabilities of different outcomes, the risks involved, and the individual's value system. Throughout life, one's decisions set limits upon one's subsequent experiences and help to determine the direction of one's development. Programs designed to facilitate educational and career decisions and to enhance decision-making skills may utilize workbooks, simulation and gaming techniques, and interactive computer systems.

Counseling psychologists now emphasize the continuity of career development throughout life. In describing this developmental process, Super identifies five stages: growth, exploration, establishment, maintenance, and decline. Each stage presents its characteristic developmental tasks. An individual's vocational maturity is defined in terms of mastery of the vocational tasks appropriate to his or her age. There is increasing recognition of the need for life-span career counseling, since each life stage presents characteristic problems of its own. Vocational adjustment requires flexibility to reorient oneself to changing societal demands and individual capabilities throughout life.

PSYCHOLOGY AND OTHER PROFESSIONS

PART SIX

PSYCHOLOGY AND EDUCATION

SEVENTEEN

N THE NEXT THREE CHAPTERS we shall consider certain applications of psychology to other professional fields. In these roles, psychologists work predominantly (though not exclusively) through other professional personnel rather than directly with clients, applicants, employees, students, or other recipients of their services. They may function as consultants, making recommendations that are implemented by others. They may be engaged in the training of professional personnel in schools of education, medicine, business, home economics, social work, nursing, theology, and other specialties. Finally, they may conduct joint research with members of another profession, or they may serve on interdisciplinary teams in other capacities. The interprofessional contacts of any one psychologist may of course cover one or more of these types of relationships.

To be sure, some psychologists employed in schools, courts, hospitals, and other institutions do work directly with clients and may even devote most of their time to such immediate personal services. When they do so, however, their functions are so similar to those of clinical or counseling psychologists as to be virtually indistinguishable from them. In the present section, therefore, the focus will be on the interprofessional activities of psychologists working in these settings.

Mention should also be made of the extensive contributions of psychologists to testing programs for the selection of professional school students, the specialty certification of professional personnel, and the evaluation of applicants for professional posts. Examples of large-scale programs developed and administered by psychologically trained test specialists are provided by the Medical College Admission Test, the Law School Admission Test, and the National Teacher Examinations, among others (see, e.g., Anastasi, 1976, pp. 458–463). In these programs, psychologists function in the same way as they do in any personnel selection situation. Since the problems and techniques of personnel selection were discussed in Chapters 2 and 3, nothing further need be said about this role of psychologists in relation to other professions.

Although psychologists have established professional relationships with many fields and their contributions are being extended into ever-broadening areas (see, e.g., Woods, 1976), three fields have been singled out for special discussion. These are the fields of education, medicine, and law, each of which will be examined in a separate chapter. The potential contributions of psychology to each of these fields have been recognized for many decades. Except in limited areas, however, implementation proceeded haltingly and sporadically until the mid-sixties. Since then, the activities of psychologists in all three fields have undergone impressive development in nature, diversity, and scope.

ROLES OF PSYCHOLOGISTS IN THE SCHOOL SYSTEM

Psychologists who work in the field of education have been traditionally differentiated into school psychologists and educational psychologists. Although these two groups have much in common with regard to both training and functions, their distinctness is exemplified in the divisional structure of the American Psychological Association (Appendix A), which includes a Division of Educational Psychology (No. 15) and a Division of School Psychology (No. 16). Universities also offer separate training programs leading to graduate degrees in these two fields.

A third psychological specialty that is having an increasing impact on education is community psychology, described in Chapter 13. Also represented by their own APA division (No. 27), community psychologists are turning more and more to the schools as an appropriate context for the prevention of behavioral dysfunctions and the promotion of mental health in the general population.

The School Psychologist. The professional specialty of school psychology was originally modeled after clinical and counseling psychology, which it resembles in many ways. The central importance of the school context, however, is now generally recognized in the preparation for this specialty (Bardon, 1976; Bardon & Bennett, 1967, 1974; Gray, 1963). School psychologists are not merely clinical psychologists who work in a school building. They work not only *in* a school but *through* it. They serve as consultants to educational personnel; and they utilize the school environment as a therapeutic medium. For these reasons, they need an understanding of the educational process and some knowledge about the organization and administration of school systems, their available resources, and the roles of their specialized personnel.

The functions and responsibilities of school psychologists vary widely, depending in part upon the characteristics and resources of the school or school system that employs them. Nevertheless, certain common activities can be recognized (Holt & Kicklighter, 1971). A significant part of the school psychologist's time is occupied with diagnostic functions, broadly defined. These functions include the administration of psychological tests; fact-finding interviews with the student as well as with teachers, parents, and others who have significant contacts with the student; observation of the student in the classroom, on the playground, and in other school contexts; and study of the student's cumulative school record.

Although at one time school psychologists were principally mental testers or psychometrists, their area of operation has broadened considerably over the years. Today, consultation with teachers is probably their single most important function (Bardon & Bennett, 1974, Ch. 5). Such consultation may take several forms. Individual teacher consultations are the most common channel for implementing the interventions suggested by the diagnostic analysis of a particular child's problems. The kinds of problems for which children are referred to a school psychologist are quite varied. The most visible type is the behavior problem of an aggressive or disruptive nature that interferes with the normal operation of the school. Other kinds of emotional adjustment problems are also a common cause of referral. Learning difficulties of a general or specific nature, as in reading or arithmetic, are another frequent complaint. Some cases are referred because of physical handicaps that require special placement or adjustment in intructional techniques. The psychologist may be consulted, too, with regard to gifted children whose educational programs should be enriched or accelerated to suit their abilities.

Sometimes a teacher requests assistance in improving his or her classroom management or instructional effectiveness. In such cases, the resulting changes affect an entire class, rather than just individual children. Although directed specifically to the improvement of teaching performance, these recommended changes may have secondary therapeutic effects on the teacher, such as increased ability to cope with problems and enhanced self-confidence. In a broad sense, teacher consultation also occurs during in-service training programs conducted by school psychologists in a wide variety of areas, ranging from test administration and the interpretation of test scores, the use of behavior modification techniques in the classroom, and the handling of such controversial topics as sex education, to training in human relations skills and simple forms of group psychotherapy.

School psychologists may also engage in some individual or group psychotherapy with children. Except for crisis intervention, however, they usually have little time for these functions. Any individual requiring more than brief psychotherapy is likely to be referred to public or private community agencies. In such referrals, the psychologist's skill in communicating effectively with parents is especially important, since it is the parents who have to implement the recommended referral. In some instances, consultation with parents may be the principal intervention technique. This would be the case if the problem arises from some features of the child's home situation or parental relations. From time to time, the school psychologist may also consult with other professionals in the school system, such as school nurse or physician, social workers, guidance counselors, learning disabilities specialists, and teachers of special education.

The Community Psychologist. Like clinical psychologists, school psychologists are being influenced more and more by the orientation of community psychology (Bardon & Bennett, 1967; Traxler, 1967). This influence is reflected in the increasing efforts to deemphasize the one-to-one therapeutic model of operation in favor of comprehensive preventive programs. Nevertheless, school psychologists still devote most of their efforts to the individual pupils (or teachers) who come to their attention because they are having problems. The immediacy and urgency of such problems give them high priority, and there is often little time left to pursue the broader and more positive approach.

From the opposite angle, some community psychologists on university faculties are recognizing increasingly that schools are a particularly appropriate setting in which to implement the goals of community psychology (Kelly et al., 1977). Although not employed by school systems, such community psychologists may function as outside consultants to develop, install, and evaluate educational programs in close collaboration with school personnel. Some investigators have examined the organizational and interpersonal characteristics of the school context, together with their implications for effecting change (Sarason, 1971). Others have explored the utilization of a particular type of indigenous, nonprofessional change agent, namely, the children themselves, including both age peers and cross-age helpers (V. L. Allen, 1976; Lippitt, Lippitt, & Eiseman, 1972).

Of particular interest is a comprehensive, prototype project conducted by a group of community psychologists from the University of Connecticut (Allen, Chinsky, Larcen, Lochman, & Selinger, 1976). The project lasted 18 months and involved the joint participation of over 100 university and school personnel. While a small staff of university faculty and graduate students directed and coordinated the project, college student volunteers and teachers in the participating school were trained in the implementation of the programs. The active involvement of the teachers at every stage of the project helped to ensure that the general approach introduced by the investigators, as well as the specific procedures, would be continued.

The project was conducted in a public school located in a small New England town. A total of 483 third- and fourth-grade children in 19 home classrooms was employed. The experimental design involved the use of both control classes and control pupils within intervention classes. Combining the approach of community psychology with the techniques of behavior modification, the project was directed at three levels, representing primary, secondary, and tertiary prevention (see Ch. 13). Because the elementary school provides a particularly promising context for primary prevention and the promotion of mental health in the whole population, the investigators developed a problem-solving program to be conducted by the teachers in regular classes. A series of 24 problem-solving exercises dealing with social coping skills was worked out with the teachers, who also received training in such behavior modification techniques as role playing, modeling, and social reinforcement. Examples of the type of problem situations considered in these exercises include: wanting to join a game at recess to which the child has not been invited; and losing one's lunch money at school.

At the secondary prevention level, teachers nominated the three children in each of the 19 classes who were most withdrawn, socially isolated, and deficient in social skills. Each of these children was assigned a specially trained college student companion. The companion met informally with the target child twice weekly during lunch and recess periods. Effective interpersonal behavior was shaped through modeling and social reinforcement of the desired behavior.

Tertiary prevention, or therapeutic intervention, was represented by a systematic behavioral change program conducted by classroom teachers with children nominated as most disruptive, deficient in study skills, or both. Through a series of workshops, the teachers were trained in the use of several behavior modification techniques for altering these behaviors within the classroom context. Both concurrent and follow-up evaluations by a wide variety of procedures indicated a significant impact of the program at all three levels.

A later section of this chapter, dealing with behavior modification in the classroom, is especially germane to the activities of both school psychologists and community psychologists working in school systems. Further examples of the application of psychological methods and findings to school problems will be found in that section.

The Educational Psychologist. While school psychologists are professional psychologists practicing within a school system, educational psychologists are most likely to be found either on the faculty of a university department or school of education or in an educational research organization. Much of their work is in teacher training or research. Usually their principal content areas are either in the psychology of learning or in measurement and test development. To be sure, some psychologists who teach in schools of education may specialize in developmental, social, or other basic fields of psychology, but in such cases they are likely to identify with these specialties, rather than calling themselves educational psychologists. Textbooks of educational psychology reflect the same content emphases. The majority try to give the prospective teacher a comprehensive introduction to the most relevant areas of psychology (e.g., Cronbach, 1977). A few are deliberately more specialized in their orientation, focusing on learning (e.g., Ausubel, Novak, & Hanesian, 1978; Klausmeier & Goodwin, 1975).

Teacher training programs typically include several psychology courses. In addition to a general course often called "educational psychology" or "psychological foundations of education," the prospective teacher is usually introduced to more specialized areas. Courses in developmental, child, or adolescent psychology are designed to orient teachers toward developmental changes in behavior and to familiarize them with the particular age groups they expect to encounter. A closely related area is that of differential psychology. Knowledge regarding the nature, origin, and extent of individual differences helps in understanding the behavior of individual children in the classroom. Educators also need to consider the implications of physical and psychological sex differences and of the sex roles institutionalized by a particular culture. In a pluralistic society such as that of the United States, it is desirable for the teacher to have some familiarity with the diversity of ethnic and cultural backgrounds that may be represented in a classroom. In addition, the teacher needs special competencies in ways of educating all children for effective living in a multicultural environment (Epps, 1974; Grant, 1975; Ramirez & Castañeda, 1974; L. L. Schwartz, 1972). Teacher training programs may also include some social psychology, covering such topics as leadership, attitudes and prejudice, intergroup relations, competition and cooperation, interaction of individuals in face-to-face groups, conformity, and the internalization of social norms (see, e.g., Backman & Secord, 1968; Johnson & Johnson, 1975).

To function effectively in the modern school, the teacher must have considerable familiarity with psychological testing, with special reference to tests of scholastic aptitude and educational achievement. An elementary knowledge of the nature and interpretation of test scores and of simple statistical procedures for handling such scores is also helpful. Techniques for developing and evaluating classroom examinations are generally taught in this connection too.

The teacher also needs to be acquainted with the special problems and educational needs of several types of "exceptional children," including the intellectually gifted, the mentally retarded, the physically handicapped, and the emotionally disturbed. Many school systems have special classes for children in these various categories, taught by specially qualified teachers. Such teachers are usually required to have more training in psychology than are regular classroom teachers.

Modern education has for some time included among its major goals the promotion of mental health and the prevention of emotional disturbance. The development of community psychology stimulated interest in a reexamination of these goals. In its report, the Joint Commission on Mental Illness and Health (see Ch. 13) devoted a separate volume to the role of the schools in mental health (Allinsmith & Goethals, 1962). It is generally recognized that teachers need an elementary knowledge of common emotional problems. This background will help them in identifying children for referral to special services as well as in administering "psychological first aid" in the classroom. It should also help them in establishing effective teacher-pupil relations and in maintaining a classroom atmosphere conducive to mental health.

Many educational psychologists spend part or all of their time in *research and development.* Traditionally, educational psychologists have made their principal contributions in test construction and in the development of statistical methods for analyzing test results. In this area, educational psychologists have also attained a relatively high level of technical sophistication. The content of such publications as the *Journal of Educational Psychology, Educational and Psychological Measurement,* and the *Journal of Educational Measurement,* for instance, reveals both the predominant concern of educational psychologists with testing problems and the technical quality of their procedures in this area. Besides contributing to the development and validation of tests, psychologists have conducted considerable applied and basic research on a number of factors that affect test performance. For instance, several studies have been concerned with the influence of practice and coaching on test scores (see Anastasi, 1976, pp. 41–44). Another problem, with broad implications for educational practice, is that of "test anxiety." In studies of both schoolchildren and college students, extensive data were gathered on the origins of this anxiety, its effects on test performance and on school achievement, and its relation to anxiety in other situations (Gaudry & Spielberger, 1974).

A major area of educational research concerns the psychology of learning. After promising beginnings early in the century through the efforts of such pioneers as E. L. Thorndike and C. H. Judd, this type of research made slow progress for nearly half a century. It was not until the late 1950s that research in this area began to show new vigor. Melton (1959) pointed out that education bears the same relation to psychology that engineering bears to the physical sciences. Bridging the gap between education and psychology, the educational psychologist must design the curricula and teaching procedures that utilize the science of learning and must then carry out the necessary applied research to test the effectiveness of these procedures in school situations.

It was in the 1950s that psychologists trained in basic research on learning theory began to turn their attention to the applied psychology of school instruction. An important impetus for this movement came from the development of military training programs in which these psychologists had participated during World War II. Training research sponsored by the military services is continuing to make substantial contributions to the development of training procedures in both industry (Ch. 4) and education. By the 1970s, the growing activities of experimental psychologists in developing an applied instructional psychology began to bear fruit. Large-scale implementation of the research findings was launched in school settings. The nature of these applications will be examined in the sections on instructional psychology and educational technology.

MEASUREMENT AND EVALUATION

Not only do schools employ nearly every available kind of psychological test in their operational programs, but they are also the principal consumers of certain types of tests specially devised for educational purposes (Anastasi, 1976; Gronlund, 1976; Stanley & Hopkins, 1972). In the construction of these tests, psychologists and educators work in close collaboration. Tests developed to meet specific educational needs may be subsumed under two broad categories. The first covers a wide variety of predictive and diagnostic instruments designed for assessing educational readiness at different levels and in different areas. The second category includes instruments for assessing educational achievement, which may range from teacher-made classroom quizzes to standardized assessment techniques employed in national and even international surveys.

Assessing Educational Readiness. Essentially, educational readiness refers to the presence of prerequisite skills and knowledge that enable the learner to profit maximally from a certain kind of instruction. Individual differences in the *school readiness* of first-grade pupils provide a familiar example. At one time, readiness was considered largely in terms of maturation. To be sure, the attainment of certain minimum physical prerequisites facilitates some kinds of learning. Unless they can make the necessary auditory discriminations, children cannot learn to speak by the usual procedures; without the ability for fine motor coordination, they cannot manipulate a pencil in writing. Most school learning, however, is not so closely bound up with sensorimotor development. In the mastery of educational tasks, the importance of prior learning has come to be increasingly recognized. More and more emphasis is being placed upon the hierarchical development of knowledges and skills, whereby the acquisition of simpler concepts equips the individual for the learning of more complex concepts at any age.

Generally administered at the time of school entrance, school readiness tests cover what Hunt and Kirk (1974) have called the "entry skills" needed to cope with the learning situations encountered in the first grade. Although they have much in common with intelligence tests for the primary grade levels, readiness tests place more emphasis on the abilities found to be important in learning to read. Some attention is also given to the prerequisites of numerical thinking and to the sensorimotor control required in learning to write. Among the specific functions covered are visual and auditory discrimination, motor control, aural comprehension, vocabulary, quantitative concepts, and general information. A widely used example of this type of test is the Metropolitan Readiness Tests (1974).

Tests of general educational readiness beyond school entrance are usually designated as *academic or scholastic aptitude tests.* Designed for all educational levels—from elementary school to college and graduate school—such tests are used for the same purposes once served by group intelligence tests. In the newer tests, the term "intelligence" has been replaced by more specific designations, since "intelligence" has acquired too many excess meanings which may lead to misinterpretations of test scores. More recently developed tests also focus more directly on the prediction of academic performance, being based on detailed task analyses of actual school learning.

Specialized prognostic tests have also been developed to predict the individual's performance in specific areas of instruction, such as mathematics and foreign languages. An example of the latter is the *Modern Language Aptitude Test* (1967). A still more highly focused approach is represented by *diagnostic* and *criterion-*

referenced tests, which provide a precise description of what the individual has and has not mastered within a narrowly defined knowledge domain. Such tests are often used to prescribe subsequent instruction that is tailored to the individual's needs. Thus a child's performance on a diagnostic arithmetic test may indicate that he or she has mastered a particular unit of instruction and is ready to proceed to the next unit, or it may identify the specific concepts or skills in which the child needs further instruction before proceeding.

Finally, clinical and educational testing merge in the varied assessment instruments employed in *identifying specific learning disabilities* (Anastasi, 1976, pp. 478–482). The 1970s ushered in a wave of crash programs for the diagnosis and remediation of learning disabilities, as educators became increasingly aware of the high frequency of this type of handicap among schoolchildren. The term "learning disabilities" refers to pronounced difficulties in learning one or more basic educational skills (most often reading), together with various combinations of associated behavioral symptoms, such as perceptual disorders in one or more sense modalities, poor integration of input from different modalities, and disruption of sensorimotor coordination. Excluded from this category are children whose learning problems result primarily from sensory or motor handicaps, mental retardation, emotional disturbance, or environmental deprivation. The identification and treatment of learning disabilities generally require the collaborative efforts of a professional team, including classroom teacher, educational specialist on learning disabilities, and psychologist.

Assessing Educational Achievement. In contrast to the basically predictive or diagnostic use of tests discussed in the preceding section, the assessment of educational achievement is concerned with what has been learned in an educational program, course, or unit of study. Readiness or academic aptitude tests serve to forecast the quality of an individual's achievement in a new situation. Achievement tests, on the other hand, usually represent a terminal evaluation of the individual's status at the completion of training. The emphasis in such tests is on what one can do at the time.

It should be noted, however, that the distinction between aptitude and achievement tests is not as basic as was once assumed. Some aptitude tests closely resemble achievement tests, and some achievement tests may serve as effective predictors of future performance. For example, the progress a pupil has made in arithmetic, as shown by the pupil's present achievement test score, may be used to predict subsequent success in learning algebra. Similarly, achievement tests on premedical courses can serve as predictors of medical school performance. We should especially guard against the popular misconception that achievement tests measure the effects of learning, while aptitude tests measure "innate capacity" independent of learning.[1] All psychological tests measure current performance, which inevitably reflects the influence of prior learning. The fact that every test score has a "past," however, does not preclude its having a "future." While revealing the effects of past learning, test scores may also serve as predictors of future learning.

---

[1] For further discussion of the distinction between aptitude and achievement tests, see the conference report edited by D. R. Green (1974), especially the chapters by Humphreys (Ch. 8) and Ebel (Ch. 10), and the review of this report by Anastasi (1975).

Achievement tests, in the commonly accepted sense of terminal performance measures, serve several functions in the educational system. Their most familiar application is in *individual assessment*. This is the traditional, age-old function of school examinations, which is often fulfilled by teacher-made classroom tests. When used for this purpose, standardized achievement tests have the advantages of objectivity and uniformity. If properly constructed, they have other merits, such as adequacy of content coverage and reduction of the operation of irrelevant and chance factors in marking procedures. The periodic administration of well-constructed and properly chosen achievement tests serves to facilitate learning. Such tests reveal weaknesses in past learning, give direction to subsequent learning, and motivate the learner. The value of "knowledge of results," or feedback, has been repeatedly demonstrated by psychological experiments in many types of learning situations, with learners of widely varying age and education.

From another angle, achievement tests provide a means of adapting instruction to individual needs. Teaching can be most fruitful when it meets the learners at whatever stage they happen to be. Ascertaining what each individual is already able to do and what he or she already knows about a subject is thus a necessary first step for effective teaching. The growth of fall testing programs points up the increasing use of test results as a basis for planning what is to be taught to a class and what modifications or adjustments are needed in individual cases.

A second major use of achievement tests is in the *evaluation and improvement of instruction*. Achievement tests can provide information on the adequacy with which essential knowledge and skills are actually being taught. Such information can be used informally by individual teachers in increasing their teaching effectiveness. Achievement tests also constitute a major instrument in the formally organized, periodic self-studies conducted by entire schools or school systems.

Achievement tests play an important part in *program evaluation* and *educational accountability*. They provide one type of data needed to evaluate the effectiveness of innovative educational programs supported by government grants. Most grant applications now require that a clear statement of evaluation plans be included in the project proposal (Dyer & Rosenthal, 1974; Perloff et al., 1976). The increasing public demand for accountability requires the systematic collection of information on what schools as a whole are actually accomplishing. Although multiple sources of data are needed to answer these questions, well-designed achievement tests are an essential component of such assessments. The expertise of educational psychologists in experimental design and data analysis is likewise needed to cope with the multiplicity of interacting variables and methodological problems encountered in these studies (Anderson & Ball, 1978; Dyer, 1973; Gronlund, 1974, 1976; Lessinger & Tyler, 1971; Saretsky, 1972; Wrightstone, Hogan, & Abbott, 1972). It should be noted that a set of *Standards for Educational Evaluation*, comparable to the *Standards for Educational and Psychological Tests* (1974), is being prepared jointly by representatives from 12 national associations of educators and psychologists, including the American Psychological Association.

A related function of educational assessment instruments and procedures is represented by the growing interest in *educational indicators* (Gooler, 1976). Derived from the more global concept of social indicators, educational indicators are a means of reporting on the current educational state of the nation, as is done by the Gross National Product (GNP) and other familiar indicators with regard to its economic state. An important step toward the development of educational indicators is represented by the *National Assessment of Educational Progress* (NAEP), a national, longitudinal study of the attainment of educational objectives (Ahman et al., 1973; Tyler & Wolf, 1974, pp. 89–104; Womer, 1970). This survey involves the testing of representative samples of the American population in 10 subject-matter areas, such as reading, mathematics, science, and art. Testing is repeated at regular intervals in order to measure both current status and change in educational attainments over time. The ages sampled in any one time period include 9, 13, 17, and 26 to 35 years, chosen to correspond approximately to the end of primary, intermediate, secondary, and postsecondary education.

At a still broader level, the *International Study of Educational Achievement* has made a promising beginning in developing methods for uniform and comparable assessment of educational attainment across nations (Bloom, 1973; Thorndike, 1973). Such surveys have several important effects. They stimulate careful reexamination of educational goals and procedures in each country. And they may contribute toward an understanding of the influence of different variables on educational achievement, insofar as comparative achievement in different countries can be related to characteristics of their educational systems and other background data.

INSTRUCTIONAL PSYCHOLOGY

The effective management of learning is undoubtedly the central problem of education. To be sure, information from several other areas of psychology is relevant; but the value of such information to the educator stems chiefly from its application to the facilitation and guidance of learning. It should be noted, too, that learning covers much more than what is formally taught in school. The pupil, whether academically successful or unsuccessful, is constantly learning many things, such as attitudes toward peers and authority figures, habits of fair play and sportsmanship, neurotic symptoms, decision-making techniques, prejudices and superstitions, and a host of other reactions that may be desirable or undesirable. The teacher needs to be alerted to the vast multiplicity of learning that goes on in the school situation. An understanding of learning processes is thus relevant to every aspect of education, from the fostering of mental health to the choice of specific methods for teaching reading or arithmetic.

Yet for over half a century the gap between psychology and education was widest in the area of learning. It was not until the 1970s that this gap was truly bridged with the design of widely applicable instructional systems derived from applied learning research (Gagné, 1970; Glaser & Resnick, 1972; Travers, 1973). Much of the research conducted on military and industrial training yielded results that are also germane to school learning. The general guidelines summarized in Chapter 4 regarding motivation, stress and anxiety, active learner participation, feedback and immediacy of reinforcement, the distribution of learning, and the conditions affecting transfer of training are equally applicable to education. Of special relevance to academic instruction is the growing body of research on meaningful verbal learning, concept formation, and ideational problem solving (Cronbach, 1977, Chs. 11–13; Levin & Allen, 1976). In terms of a broadened, cognitive model, learning may occur not only through practice or reinforcement of overt behavior but also through such familiar procedures as observing a demonstration, listening to an explanation, or reading a book. These procedures, which are better adapted to the learning of complex meaningful materials, are receiving increasing attention in educational research (Wittrock & Lumsdaine, 1977).

Design of Instructional Programs. To bridge the gap between the experimental psychology of learning and the development of educational curricula requires specially designed applied research on the instructional process. There is need for studies that deal directly with educational subject matter, such as reading and mathematics. In one of the yearbooks of the National Society for the Study of Education, devoted entirely to this issue, Bruner (1964) called for a theory of instruction as distinguished from a theory of learning. The latter is essentially *descriptive,* focusing on how learning occurs. In contrast, a theory of instruction is chiefly *prescriptive,* insofar as it specifies procedures for optimizing the acquisition of skills and knowledge. Nevertheless, as Atkinson and Paulson (1972) point out, the investigator needs a reasonable model of the learning process to be optimized before instructional procedures can be designed. What is essential is that the research be done with educational subject matter, which is typically more complex than are the tasks employed in laboratory studies of learning.

As is true of the industrial training programs discussed in Chapter 4, *task analysis* is a major step in the design of instructional programs in education. Once the objectives, or desired outcomes, of a particular program or curriculum have been clearly formulated, the specific learning tasks required to achieve those objectives must be identified. These tasks obviously vary with the content of learning (e.g., reading, mathematics, art). However, some tasks are psychologically isomorphic, having similar characteristics with respect to optimal learning conditions although differing in subject matter. Taxonomies of learning tasks in terms of such common characteristics have played an important part in the design of instructional programs (Gagné, 1970; Melton, 1964).

Another major concept in instructional psychology is that of *learning hierarchies* (Gagné, 1970, 1973). Task analysis provides data on the demands each task makes on the learner, i.e., its prerequisite competencies. On the basis of such prerequisite relationships, the tasks can be arranged in an optimal sequence to form a learning hierarchy. The learner's entry point into the hierarchy is determined by his or her initial competencies—the prerequisite intellectual skills and cognitive strategies the learner brings to the learning situation.

The increasing rapprochement of psychological research and educational practice is evidenced by recent books which emphasize broad classroom applications of research findings (e.g., Bower, 1975, Chs. 1–3; Davis, Alexander, & Yelon, 1974; Levin & Allen, 1976), as well as by sophisticated psychological analyses of particular curricular areas, such as reading and writing (Gibson & Levin, 1975; Reber & Scarborough, 1977; D. E. P. Smith, 1976) and mathematics (Suppes, 1966; Suppes, Jerman, & Brian, 1968). Further examples are provided by current developments in educational technology, to be considered in a later section.

Within the field of education itself, the widespread emphasis on "performance-based education" (PBE) and "competency-based education" (CBE) likewise reflects the influence of task analysis, learning sequences, and other concepts of instructional psychology. Competency-based education is playing an important part not only in the design of elementary and high school curricula but also in teacher training and the evaluation of teaching performance (e.g., "Competency," 1974; Houston, 1974; Maucker, 1974; Schalock, 1975; Travers, 1973, Ch. 30). In research on competency-based teacher education, the effectiveness of teaching procedures is characteristically evaluated in terms of the resulting change in pupil performance (e.g., McDonald, 1976). Sophisticated experimental designs permit an analysis of the proportion of such change attributable to particular teacher behaviors, as well as the proportion attributable to other variables of the school, the home, and the community.

Interaction of Multiple Variables in Instructional Outcomes. In the design of instructional systems, there is no one best teaching method for all subject matter and all learners. In school learning, as in industrial training (Ch. 4), it is important to look for interactions among variables of the learner, the task, and the treatment or instructional procedure. For example, the optimal procedures for teaching reading and mathematics differ, as do the optimal procedures for teaching each of these subjects to second-grade and to fifth-grade schoolchildren.

There is an extensive body of educational research on Trait-Treatment Interactions (TTI) in learning (Berliner & Cahen, 1973; Bracht, 1970; Cronbach & Snow, 1977). Because of methodological difficulties, however, many studies have yielded negative or inconsistent results. One reason is to be found in the large number of interacting variables in most learning situations, a condition that requires the measurement of higher order interactions. For example, if the relative effectiveness of two teaching procedures depends both on subject matter and on some aptitude or personality trait of the learner, omitting any one of these three interacting variables may yield misleading results. The identification of statistically significant higher order interactions, however, requires unrealistically large samples (see Ch. 4).

Several procedures are being followed to resolve these difficulties. First, interactions can be investigated within narrowly defined contexts, such as a single grade level or a single type of learning task. The gradually accumulating findings from a number of such parallel studies can then be used to build up a more comprehensive picture. Second, the choice of variables to be investigated should not be haphazard but should be based on a sound theoretical rationale. This approach is illustrated in a well-designed study of the effect of reflective versus impulsive cognitive style on the learning performance of second-grade schoolchildren (Rhetts, 1974). The investigation began with a task analysis of two types of tasks that are basic to much of the school learning at this grade level, namely, visual discrimination, or matching, and paired associate learning. The learner variable, impulsivity-reflectivity, was chosen because it was plausibly related to the performance demands of these tasks. Finally, alternative instructional treatments were designed with the specific object of influencing the hypothesized performance differences among children.

The importance of choosing task-relevant learner variables was also demonstrated in a study of mathematics instruction with college students (Mayer, Stiehl, & Greeno, 1975). Significant interactions were found between treatment variables and learner status in specific knowledge and skills prerequisite to the task. But no interaction was found with learner scores on broad mathematical aptitude tests.

Another promising approach involves the use of clusters of variables for grouping learners into identifiable types, learning tasks into functional categories, and instructional procedures into coordinated programs. This method was illustrated in a comparison of fourth-grade pupils taught in "traditional," structured classrooms and in more informal, "open" classrooms (Solomon & Kendall, 1976). Several significant interactions were found between classroom type, representing different instructional treatments or teaching styles, and child type, as defined by the child's profile on measures of prior school achievement and personality variables. The effects also differed with outcome measures, such as academic achievement, creativity, and social attitudes.

In addition to aptitudes, many other learner traits have been investigated in TTI research, with populations ranging from first graders to college students. Among the traits included in these studies are anxiety level, achievement motivation, affiliation need, several cognitive styles, and internal-external locus of control, i.e., the extent to which individuals believe that what happens to them depends on their own behavior or on conditions beyond their control. The dependent variables include academic achievement in regular courses, performance on specially designed learning tasks, interpersonal behavior, attitudes, and student evaluations of college instructors using different teaching styles.[2]

EDUCATIONAL TECHNOLOGY

A major outcome of research in instructional psychology can be seen in the design of a number of instructional systems exhibiting varying degrees of individualization and automation. These systems illustrate the "development" phase of instructional "research and development" (R & D). Three principal features of current educational technology will be considered, namely, programmed learning, individualized instructional systems, and computer utilization. Although some instructional systems fall clearly into one or another of these categories, others incorporate two or all three features. Also cutting across specific instructional systems is the use of a variety of audiovisual media, such as films, tape recordings, and television. Some systems may rely predominantly on one of these media; others may use them as supplementary teaching aids. Regardless of how they are used, these media have been submitted to considerable psychological research and evaluation (Lumsdaine & May, 1965).

Programmed Learning. Like other developments in educational technology, programmed learning represents an application of learning principles to educational practice. It is essentially an instructional procedure that requires active learner participation, provides immediate feedback, and permits each individual to progress at his or her own pace. The technique stems largely from the work of Skinner (1968), being an outgrowth of his learning theory and his basic laboratory research with animals. In a typical Skinnerian learning program, the material to be learned is presented in small steps, or frames, so formulated as to reduce the probability of response errors to a minimum. Feedback follows immediately upon the completion of each response. The object of this technique is to elicit or "shape" the correct response by prompting or response cueing. The needed information is conveyed by the items themselves through a wide variety of ingenious prompts, a few of which are illustrated in Figure 17-1. By easy steps that

---

[2]Examples of such studies can be found in the previously cited surveys (Berliner & Cahen, 1973; Bracht, 1970; Cronbach & Snow, 1977) and in many subsequent publications (e.g., Dowaliby & Schumer, 1973; J. D. McKinney, 1975; Parent, Forward, Canter, & Mohling, 1975; P. L. Peterson, 1977; Sunshine & DiVesta, 1976).

---

1. **Manufacture** means to make or build. *Chair factories manufacture chairs.* Copy the word here:

    ☐ ☐ ☐ ☐ ☐ ☐ ☐ ☐ ☐ ☐

2. Part of the word is like part of the word **factory.** Both parts come from an old word meaning *make* or *build.*

    manu ☐ ☐ ☐ ☐ ure

3. Part of the word is like part of the word **manual.** Both parts come from an old word for *hand.* Many things used to be made by hand.

    ☐ ☐ ☐ ☐ facture

4. The same letter goes in both spaces:

    m ☐ nuf ☐ cture

5. The same letter goes in both spaces:

    man ☐ fact ☐ re

6. **Chair factories** ☐ ☐ ☐ ☐ ☐ ☐ ☐ ☐ ☐ ☐ ☐ chairs.

Figure 17-1. A set of frames used in programmed learning technique to teach spelling to a third- or fourth-grade schoolchild. *(From Skinner, 1958, p. 972.)*

virtually assure success and hence positive reinforcement of responses, the individual progresses from items providing maximal prompting to items providing minimal prompting. This process of progressive cue reduction is called "vanishing" and is basic to Skinner's method of shaping responses.

In the 1960s, programmed instruction was closely linked to so-called teaching machines, or mechanical contrivances for presenting the material and recording responses (Lumsdaine & Glaser, 1960). The initial reaction to such teaching machines was characterized by exaggerated expectations and overemphasis on gadgetry and hardware. More considered evaluations noted that it is not the machine or hardware that teaches but the software or instructional content of the program; and the latter needs to be evaluated from the standpoint of curriculum development and instructional psychology.[3] Programmed learning can be more simply—and just as effectively—presented in the form of programmed textbooks or printed booklets for small instructional units. Moreover, it is now most commonly used as an adjunct to other procedures, or to teach a particular unit within a course, or to provide remedial instruction to individual students. Modified versions have also been developed, which group the content into larger meaningful units than is done in the Skinnerian frames. For most educational purposes, the use of the typical program frame as a unit is too unwieldy and time-consuming.

Individualized Instructional Systems. A broader and more varied category of instructional systems can be characterized as individualized, personalized, or adaptive instruction (Klausmeier, Rossmiller, & Saily, 1977; Talmage, 1975). Some of these systems may include programmed learning as additional study aids or for special topics. The major teaching procedures, however, are typically less atomis-

---

[3]See, e.g., the joint statement issued by the American Psychological Association, the American Educational Research Association, and the Department of Audio-Visual Instruction of the National Educational Association ("Self-instructional Materials," 1961).

tic and more flexible than traditional programmed learning. Some systems leave a good deal of the detailed implementation to the individual teacher's discretion. Frequently, the content is acquired by the usual methods, such as reading text assignments, laboratory work, and individual study of specially prepared materials. Films, tapes, and other audiovisual aids may be included.

The essential distinguishing features of these systems are self-pacing and independent study, with short quizzes upon completion of each unit of study. If the student demonstrates mastery of the unit, he advances to the next unit; if he has failed to master it, he receives additional instruction on that unit. Thus the level of content mastery is approximately uniform for all learners, but the time required to complete a course may vary widely among individuals. The unit tests serve a dual function of routing the learner to appropriate material and providing a record of what he has mastered, with immediate feedback to the learner himself. Frequently, a composite examination is also administered at the end of the course as a summative evaluation of what has been learned and retained.

The design of these self-paced, individualized instructional systems stimulated the development of a type of assessment device commonly known as "criterion-referenced tests" (Anastasi, 1976, pp. 96–100; Cronbach, 1977, pp. 718–721; *Standards,* 1974, p. 19). Actually, "content-referenced" is a more accurate designation, since the chief feature of these tests is that they describe the individual's performance in terms of what he or she satisfactorily mastered, rather than in terms of what others can do, as in norm-referenced testing. For example, following mastery of a particular instructional unit, the child's performance would be described in terms of such specific instructional objectives as "multiplies three-digit by two-digit numbers" or "identifies the misspelled word in which the final *e* is retained when adding -*ing*."

Although individualized instructional systems have been widely adopted at the elementary school level, one system developed especially for college students has gained considerable popularity and has been applied in teaching a diversity of subjects, from mathematics, statistics, and engineering to psychology, biology, philosophy, and English. This is the Personalized System of Instruction (PSI), developed by Keller (1968, 1969). PSI is a set of basic procedures for planning and administering a course of study, which the individual instructor implements. The instructor's role includes selection, preparation, and organization of study materials (reading assignments, supplementary mimeographed materials, films, etc.), construction of unit tests and final examination, and supervision of instructional procedures. In planning the course content, the instructor follows specified procedures, including clear statement of course objectives, task analysis, and sequencing of learning units in terms of prerequisite demands. Students proceed at their own pace and receive immediate feedback after each unit. A special feature of PSI is the utilization of student assistants and student tutors, which permits one instructor to handle large classes while providing each student with considerable personal attention and tutoring. Although empirical studies have yielded favorable results in many contexts, the effectiveness of PSI varies for different kinds of subject matter and for different types of students and instructors (Johnson & Ruskin, 1977; McKeachie, 1974, pp. 171–172; Ryan, 1974; Sayre & Knightly, 1972). As with all other instructional procedures, these interactions must be taken into account in deciding when to use PSI. Moreover, the proper preparation of a PSI course requires considerable expenditure of time and effort and should not be undertaken lightly.

Computer Utilization. Both programmed learning and the broader types of individualized instructional systems described in the preceding section often utilize computers in various capacities. This is especially true of systems developed for large-scale applications at the elementary school level. While computers can be used to facilitate many administrative functions within school systems (Carter, 1961; Coulson, 1962), their principal contributions to instruction are of two types: computer-administered instruction (CAI) and computer-managed instruction (CMI).

In *computer-administered instruction,* the computer serves directly as the means of providing individually tailored instructional sequences to each learner (Holtzman, 1970; Hunter, Kastner, Rubin, & Seidel, 1975; Seidel & Rubin, 1977). The student works at a computer terminal, which may present material visually on a screen, or aurally through earphones, or both. Responses are usually given on a typewriter keyboard. A major advantage of computers is that each response can be scored immediately and stored. On the basis of the learner's stored response history, the computer chooses successive items and assembles exercises and instructional material appropriate to the learner's own past performance. Not only does each learner proceed at his or her own pace but also the instruction is completely adapted to the individual's own needs.

Several universities have CAI centers, which are used chiefly for remedial programs, as a supplementary learning aid, or for particular courses in which this approach has proved effective. Some progress is being made in the introduction of CAI at the high school level. Adoptions have been slow because of cost and because of problems involved in developing the required hardware and software and in training school personnel in the use of such instructional systems. A project conducted by the Human Resources Research Organization (Hargan, Hibbits, & Seidel, 1978) demonstrates some practical solutions to these difficulties. This project was conducted in a consortium of four District of Columbia secondary schools, which pooled their resources to install a CAI program.

An especially promising application at the elementary school level is illustrated by the Stanford University CAI reading program for children in the first three grades (Atkinson, 1974). The object of this program was "to develop low-cost . . . CAI that supplements classroom teaching and concentrates on those tasks in which individualization is critically important" (p. 169). The student terminal consists only of a teletypewriter with an audio headset. The central computer, housed at Stanford University, is connected by telephone lines to student terminals in several states as far away as Florida and Washington, D.C. The learner's response history is used by the computer to make trial-by-trial decisions regarding what instruction to present next.

A less costly and more widely applicable way of utilizing computers in teaching is through *computer-managed instruction* (Hambleton, 1974). In such systems, the learner does not interact directly with the computer. The role of the computer is to assist the teacher in carrying out a plan of individualized instruction, which may use self-instruction packages or more conventional types of instruction. A major contribution of the computer is to process the formidable mass of data accumulated daily regarding the performance of each student—in a classroom where each may be involved in a different activity—and to utilize these data in prescribing the next instructional step for each student.

A major example of CMI is provided by IPI (Individually Prescribed Instruction), developed at the University of Pittsburgh's Learning Research and Development

Center (Cooley & Glaser, 1969; Glaser, 1968; Glaser & Gow, 1964; Travers, 1973, Ch. 26). This center designs prototype models of instructional systems for elementary schools; prepares needed teaching materials; and provides assistance in installing the system, training school personnel, and evaluating results. The IPI approach was subsequently extended and broadened under the rubric of Adaptive Environments for Learning, or AEL (Glaser & Rosner, 1975).

CMI also underlies the PLAN system (Planning for Learning in Accordance with Needs), developed by the American Institutes for Research (Flanagan, 1971; Flanagan, Shanner, Brudner, & Marker, 1975). Adopted in several school districts throughout the country, the PLAN system covers instruction in elementary and high school subjects. It also provides a program of self-knowledge, individual development, and occupational planning. Still another widely implemented system is IGE (Individually Guided Education), developed at the University of Wisconsin Research and Development Center for Individualized Schooling (Klausmeier, Rossmiller, & Saily, 1977). This system combines individualized learning with cross-age tutoring and with small-group and large-group instruction. In all these instructional programs, teachers from participating schools assist in the initial formulation of course objectives, selection and preparation of teaching materials, development of unit tests, and other aspects of program development.

BEHAVIOR MODIFICATION IN THE CLASSROOM

Scope. Another example of the application of basic learning research to education is provided by behavior modification, also designated by such names as "behavior therapy," "learning therapy," and "applied behavior analysis." This application is the educational counterpart of the procedures by the same names employed in industrial training (Ch. 4) and in clinical interventions (Ch. 13). Since the mid-sixties, behavior modification has spread widely in the schools. The *Journal of Applied Behavior Analysis,* established in 1968, reports many studies conducted in educational settings. Portions of the extensive research literature have been summarized in repeated surveys (Hanley, 1970; Hayes, 1976; O'Leary & Drabman, 1971). The growing popularity of behavior modification in classroom management is evidenced by the plethora of guidebooks for teachers, ranging from simple, terse "how-to" manuals (e.g., Dollar, 1972; Sarason, Glaser, & Fargo, 1972) to more thorough presentations suitable as textbooks in teacher training courses (e.g., Ackerman, 1972; O'Leary & O'Leary, 1977; Walker & Shea, 1976). Illustrating a broader approach, Kazdin (1975) covers behavior modification in a variety of applied settings, including schools, and discusses procedures of applied research and program evaluation, as well as implementation.

Procedures. As in all its practical applications, behavior modification in the schools consists essentially in the use of operant conditioning principles to strengthen wanted behavior and to eliminate unwanted behavior. An important first step in such programs is to identify and clearly specify the target behavior to be altered. The major procedures for effecting the behavior changes are based on contingent reinforcement, i.e., providing rewards for the behavior to be strengthened and withholding rewards for the behavior to be weakened. The rewards or reinforcers may be social, such as attention from teacher or other children; they may be tangible objects, such as fruit, candy, trinkets, or games; or they may be intangibles, such as the privilege of reading a chosen magazine, watching a movie, or listening to one's favorite tape recordings. Both tangible and intangible reinforcers can be combined with a token economy, which is often incorporated in classroom programs of behavior modification. The tokens can be saved and exchanged at the appropriate time for the preestablished backup reinforcers. Tokens may be earned by individuals for their own use or for shared benefits in a team program. Team size may range from a pair of students to an entire class. In such group applications of token economy, there is opportunity for considerable peer influence through social pressure, cooperation, and peer tutoring (Hayes, 1976).

As in other contexts (Ch. 13), behavior modification in the classroom typically utilizes more than one of several available procedures, such as positive reinforcement, extinction, response cost (reward decrement or loss), time-out (removal of all positive reinforcement for a short period of time), modeling, verbal feedback, role playing, and rehearsal. Frequently, students participate in the formulation of behavior rules and contracts and in the selection of effective reinforcers. Although both rewards and punishments may be incorporated in behavior modification programs, available research shows the former to be more effective than the latter in most situations.

Of particular interest is the positive practice technique investigated by Azrin and Powers (1975). This technique was developed in an effort to reduce the classroom behaviors of speaking out and leaving one's seat, which often precede other disruptive actions. After each disruptive act, the child was required to engage in the positive action of asking for permission to speak out or to leave his seat. This procedure was tested in an intensive, six-week program with six boys, aged 7 to 11 years, who had been identified as extremely disruptive in their classrooms and severely deficient in academic skills. Disruptive actions in this group decreased by 98% when the positive practice was required immediately and by 95% when it was delayed. In contrast, disruptive actions remained at a high level during a verbal reminder and reprimand procedure; and they were reduced by only 60% through a loss-of-recess penalty procedure.

Applications. The types of behavioral objectives for which behavior modification procedures are commonly employed in schools include principally the elimination of disruptive classroom behavior and the improvement of academic performance. These two goals are closely intertwined. The reduction of disruptive behavior generally results in a rise in academic achievement as a by-product. Conversely, behavior modification programs designed to improve learning in such subjects as reading and arithmetic usually focus on relevant attitudes, motivation, attention control, and work habits (e.g., completing assignments, handing in homework regularly). Behavior modification techniques have been used with a wide diversity of child populations. In normal classroom groups, they can help in the primary prevention of emotional disturbance and in the development of coping skills and other positive behaviors. These applications were illustrated in the community psychology project described in the first section of this chapter. Behavior modification is also employed therapeutically with disruptive or academically deficient individuals within any classroom. It has likewise been successfully incorporated in the education of special populations, such as emotionally disturbed, autistic, hyperactive, delinquent, and mentally retarded children and those manifesting special learning disabilities.

Eclectic, Practical Orientation. Current educational applications emphasize a broad, eclectic approach and outcome-oriented strategies. It will be recalled that in the design of instructional systems, research on cognitive functions, information-processing strategies, and subject-matter structure was added to the basic principles of operant conditioning which underlay the initial efforts in programmed learning. In the same vein, the application of behavior modification to classroom management utilizes many procedures specially devised to fit the particular behavior and context involved. Contingent reinforcement is a major feature of most of these procedures. But it needs to be implemented in diverse ways in particular situations. The contrasting requirements of applied versus basic research in this area have been effectively presented by Azrin (1977), who is himself one of the most prolific contributors to the development of behavior modification procedures for a wide range of real-life problems and contexts.

An example of such a composite, outcome-oriented program is provided by a study of 10 matched pairs of fifth-grade public school children (Azrin, Azrin, & Armstrong, 1977). The class chosen for this project was one in which the teacher had requested assistance three months after the beginning of the school year because of uncooperative and fighting behavior. The experimental design included within-subject pretreatment and posttreatment comparisons, as well as a partial control for spontaneous behavior changes insofar as the new treatment was delayed one month for the 10 matched control cases.

The program was specifically directed toward maximizing the student's responsibility for his or her actions. It began with a set of rules for student actions and another set for teacher actions, both of which were jointly formulated and accepted by a consensus or near-consensus. A written behavioral contract was prepared for each child, which was reviewed and, if necessary, modified during teacher-student consultations. These consultations were regularly scheduled and frequent, and they provided specific feedback on the student's performance. The program utilized a token economy with a wide variety of self-selected reinforcers. Of particular interest was the inclusion of a makeup feature, providing for self-correction of mistakes in order to have one's rating raised. For repeated offenses, this was followed by the requirement of positive practice. Both makeup and positive practice procedures were tailored to the particular behavior. They might include apologizing to the person involved, appropriate actions to make restitution or otherwise correct the situation, stating what the child would do in similar future situations, and citing the appropriate action rule. Parental feedback on the child's progress was linked with further opportunities for positive reinforcement of desirable behavior. In comparison with both pretreatment and control group data, this composite behavior modification program resulted in significantly fewer problems, as reported by students, teachers, and project observers.

EARLY CHILDHOOD EDUCATION

The mid-sixties witnessed a sharp upsurge of interest in early childhood education. In large part, this interest was stimulated by the educational difficulties experienced by children from poverty and minority backgrounds. These children often entered school with serious deficiencies in prerequisite knowledge, cognitive skills, and motivation for school learning. Consequently, they were unable to profit fully from school instruction and fell farther behind in successive grades. In the meantime, suggestive research evidence of the modifiability of intelligence, especially in early childhood, had been gradually accumulating (J. McV. Hunt, 1975). Data were also available indicating marked group differences in child-rearing and parental behavior, which could account for the observed educational deficits.

Against this background, several developmental psychologists began to turn their attention to an instructional psychology of early childhood, designed to foster and enhance intellectual growth before school entrance. The rapid expansion of this area of educational psychology is evidenced by the number of scientific conferences devoted to the topic (e.g., Denenberg, 1970; Hess & Bear, 1968; Parker, 1972), the publication of books concerned specifically with the psychology of preschool education (e.g., Hom & Robinson, 1977), and the development of many new tests and other assessment techniques designed for use in early childhood education (see Anastasi, 1976, pp. 425–434).

Preschool Programs. A direct effect of the growing concern with early childhood education was the establishment of compensatory education programs for experientially disadvantaged children (Glaser & Resnick, 1972; J. McV. Hunt, 1975; Stanley, 1972, 1973). Many of these programs involve attendance at specially established preschools. Because the goal is to prepare children for school entrance, the activities center chiefly on cognitive development. Despite a diversity of specific content and teaching methods, the primary focus has shifted away from the free play and social adjustment of the traditional kindergarten and preschool, which were better adapted to the needs of middle-class children.

The most widely publicized and far-flung of these preschool projects was Head Start, supported by the federal government. Unfortunately, this program was initiated on a crash basis, with inadequate planning for either implementation or evaluation. Moreover, it actually comprised many local projects having little in common. Hence, any nationwide evaluation in terms of uniform criterion measures was necessarily ambiguous and inconclusive. Disappointment with the initial results of Head Start weakened popular confidence in the efficacy of early childhood education for culturally disadvantaged children (Payne, Mercer, Payne, & Davison, 1973).

A number of projects with more limited scope and more precisely defined goals, however, have been yielding more promising results (B. Brown, 1978; J. McV. Hunt, 1975; Palmer, 1978). A few of these were begun prior to Head Start (e.g., Deutsch, Taleporos, & Victor, 1974; Gray & Klaus, 1965). Some represent later follow-ups and better designed statistical analyses of particular Head Start projects. Others were initiated more recently and have benefited from the rapidly growing data base in the educational technology of early childhood. Some programs have concentrated on intensive training in the verbal and/or numerical skills required for school readiness (e.g., Bereiter & Engelmann, 1966; Wallach & Wallach, 1976). Others have been directed toward a broader based cognitive development, focusing on information-processing strategies, cognitive styles, or Piagetian stages of concept formation (e.g., Weikart, Rogers, Adcock, & McClelland, 1971). Still others have employed token economies to teach both academic skills and classroom behavior (e.g., Bushell, 1970). At least one program followed the procedures of task analysis, sequencing of skills in a learning hierarchy, and individualized, self-paced instruction (Resnick, Wang, & Rosner, 1977). The more successful programs include parental involvement as a means of supplementing the preschool experiences at home and ensuring their continuation after the program terminates (e.g., Gray

& Klaus, 1965). As a by-product, these programs also report beneficial effects on younger siblings, as well as on the parents themselves in the form of upgraded skills, enhanced self-confidence, and increased participation in community affairs.

In the effort to correct some of the chief deficiencies of the original Head Start project, several innovations were introduced with federal support (J. McV. Hunt, 1975). First, the approaches that had yielded the most promising results were followed in newly established preschool programs, with plans to evaluate each program in terms of its specific objectives. Second, in a new Project Follow-through, the educational techniques introduced by each of these projects were continued on a supplementary basis after school entrance, from kindergarten through the third grade. Third, parental training and lasting involvement were encouraged through the establishment of Parent and Child Centers. Thus, despite many administrative frustrations and missteps, a limited number of reasonably well-designed projects were launched in the hope that they would yield some objective data on what each type of program can accomplish.

Day-Care and Home Tutoring Programs. A focus on primary prevention is reflected in instructional programs designed for the infant level. These programs may be implemented through day-care centers, tutorial home visitors, or parental instruction. Two or all three of these approaches may be combined in a single program. Indigenous nonprofessionals have been successfully trained to instruct mothers in both home visits and day-care centers. In the home programs, instructional toys and books have been provided as gifts to the participating families. Home programs may begin shortly after birth. Age of admission to day-care centers varies from 1 to 6 months in different programs. Encouraging results have been reported from several programs utilizing day-care centers, home tutoring, or both (J. McV. Hunt, 1975, pp. 292–303). Essentially, the more successful programs provide the infant with the opportunity to observe and manipulate a variety of toy objects while the objects and their properties (colors, shape, size) are named and the manipulations are verbally described.

Among the various home tutoring programs launched in the 1960s and 1970s, one of the most fully developed and tested is the Mother-Child Home Program initiated by Levenstein (1977). Beginning with the premise that the acquisition of language is fundamental for the intellectual development of children from educationally disadvantaged homes, Levenstein chose the age of 2 years as the optimal time to introduce the program. The materials consist of a series of toys and books selected for their perceptual, motor, verbal, and conceptual properties. Home visitors, called Toy Demonstrators, work jointly with mother and child in the use of materials and in the accompanying verbal interactions. Levenstein has developed materials, instructional program, and demonstrator's handbook, and she has successfully trained paraprofessional aides as Toy Demonstrators.

Follow-up studies of children in the Mother-Child Home Program have shown substantial gains in IQ on several standard intelligence tests, while control children have shown no gain or slight losses. The IQ gains persisted at least until school entrance. The program children also excelled the control children in classroom behavior and peer relations. This program has proved to be transferable insofar as it has already been successfully introduced in several areas by different agencies. Beginning with a modest pilot study in 1965, the program has been growing stepwise in several dimensions. More research is planned, including later follow-ups, at least through the third grade.

SUMMARY

Chief among the fields in which psychologists work in a consulting or collaborative relation with other professional personnel are education, medicine, and law. Within the field of education, the roles of psychologists have been traditionally differentiated into those of school psychologist and educational psychologist. Although the functions of school psychologists vary widely from school to school, they consist largely in the diagnostic testing, interviewing, and observation of individual pupils, followed by recommendations for remedial action. Working through teachers and other educational personnel, the school psychologist utilizes the school environment as a therapeutic medium. The influence of community psychology is reflected in a shifting orientation of school psychologists away from individual remediation and toward broad-based preventive programs. In addition, community psychologists themselves are turning increasingly to the schools as an effective context for implementing the goals of positive mental health.

Educational psychologists are concerned principally with teacher training and educational research. Texts and courses on educational psychology focus upon the learning process, although attention is also given to tests and measurement, common emotional problems, and some aspects of developmental, differential, and social psychology. Educational psychologists have made major contributions to test construction and to the development of statistical methods for analyzing test results. In the area of learning, the necessary linkages between basic psychological research and the instructional process were long delayed; but by the 1970s, the gap was rapidly being closed.

While nearly every available kind of psychological test is used in the schools, two types specially designed for educational purposes are tests of educational readiness and tests of educational achievement. The first category includes school readiness tests, scholastic aptitude tests, prognostic tests in special subjects, diagnostic and criterion-referenced tests, and tests for identifying specific learning disabilities. Tests of educational achievement, measuring terminal performance after instruction, are used widely for individual assessment, for evaluation and improvement of instruction, for program evaluation, in meeting the demands for educational accountability, and in providing educational indicators in national and international surveys.

Instructional psychology is concerned with a prescriptive theory of instruction as contrasted with a descriptive theory of learning. There is an increasing amount of research on meaningful verbal learning and complex cognitive processes, as well as on learning in such academic areas as reading, writing, and mathematics. In the design of instructional systems, two major procedures are task analysis and sequencing of tasks into learning hierarchies. Learning outcomes depend upon interactions of instructional methods with variables of task, learner, and instructor. Relative effectiveness of instructional treatments also varies with the type of outcome assessed.

Developments in educational technology include programmed learning and a wide variety of individualized, self-paced instructional systems, ranging from the preschool to the college level. With the aid of computers, it is possible to provide individualized learning sequences, adapted to each person's own response history. In computer-assisted instruction (CAI), the learner works directly at a computer terminal. In computer-managed instruction (CMI), the computer processes the daily data on learner performance and utilizes these data in prescribing the next instructional step.

The use of behavior modification in the classroom has grown rapidly since 1970, chiefly for the elimination of disruptive behavior and the improvement of study habits. Token economies are commonly used to provide contingent reinforcement. Other procedures may include extinction, response cost, time-out, verbal feedback, role playing, and positive practice.

The upsurge in programs of early childhood education was largely stimulated by concern for the educational handicaps of children from poverty and minority families. A wide diversity of preschool programs has contributed to a greatly expanded knowledge base and instructional technology for early childhood education; several approaches have yielded promising results. In the interests of primary prevention, some programs have been directed to the infant level through the use of day-care centers and home tutoring. At both preschool and infant levels, the more successful programs have included parental instruction and involvement.

PSYCHOLOGY AND MEDICINE

EIGHTEEN

THE ROLE OF EMOTIONAL, motivational, and attitudinal factors in medical practice has long been recognized.
In fact, such recognition antedates modern scientific medicine, being of primary
significance in the ministrations of the medicine men of early preliterate
cultures. In more recent times, physicians have generally been aware of the
importance of many psychological factors in the daily practice of medicine.
Examples include the contribution of doctor-patient relations and of the placebo
effect[1] to the patient's recovery; the need for considering personality, familial, and
cultural factors in diagnosing a patient's condition; and the dependence of
physical improvement upon the individual patient's cooperation and motivation to
recover.

Despite the many potential applications of psychological knowledge to medicine, however, contacts between the two fields were negligible until quite recently.
Even books on the psychology of medical practice or the psychology of physical
illness were often written, not by psychologists, but by psychiatrists (e.g., Bellak,
1952; Hollender, 1958). This was also true of courses or units on psychology taught
in medical schools. With their strongly pathological orientation, psychiatrists are
likely to provide a distorted picture of the psychologically normal patients encountered in other branches of medicine. Moreover, the training and experience of
psychiatrists emphasize clinical practice rather than basic behavioral science.
Consequently, their notions of human behavior tend to derive from uncontrolled
personal observation and selected cases rather than from systematic and controlled experimentation.

---

[1]For a discussion of the placebo effect in the history of medicine, see Shapiro (1960).

It was not until the 1950s that professional contacts between psychology and medicine began to attain significant proportions, and even now the potential contributions of psychology in this field are largely undeveloped. Originally, the contacts occurred almost entirely between clinical psychologists and psychiatrists and were limited to psychodiagnostic functions. Later, an increasing number of referrals for psychodiagnosis started to come from other medical specialists, such as pediatricians, internists, neurosurgeons, plastic surgeons, obstetricians, and endocrinologists (Matarazzo, 1955). This trend reflected a growing realization among medical practitioners that a standardized assessment of the patient's emotional responses, intellectual functioning, and other psychological characteristics would in many cases facilitate the diagnosis of physical difficulties.

After midcentury, the role of psychologists in medical practice expanded to include consulting relations in other than diagnostic functions. The growth of collaborative psychological research in medical settings and of medical school teaching by psychologists was also characteristic of this period. And psychologists appeared increasingly as authors or editors of texts on psychological aspects of medical practice, often designed for use by medical students and other health professionals (e.g., Bowden & Burstein, 1974; Katz & Zlutnick, 1975; A. L. Knutson, 1965; Millon, 1975; Shontz, 1975). Furthermore, contacts with medicine were no longer limited to clinical psychologists but came to include counseling, social, developmental, physiological, experimental, and practically all other kinds of psychologists. A conspicuous development of the 1970s was the emergence of an independent psychological specialty on health-related behaviors (APA Task Force on Health Research, 1976). Although the number of psychologists identified with this specialty is still relatively small, there is a promising accumulation of behavioral research on health maintenance, disease prevention, pain control, and facilitation of treatment.

PSYCHOLOGY IN MEDICAL PRACTICE

In every major phase of medical practice, psychology can contribute in two principal ways: (1) by providing knowledge and orientations that improve the physician's performance of his or her own functions; (2) by providing the services of psychologists as consultants or as participating members of interprofessional teams. These two avenues of contact between psychology and medicine are not entirely distinct. Psychological orientations, for example, may be acquired by the physician, not only during medical school training, but also in the course of consulting and collaborative relationships with psychologists. In the present section, we shall illustrate the types of contributions psychology can make to diagnosis, treatment, rehabilitation, and preventive medicine.

Diagnosis. Mention has already been made of the increasing use of psychodiagnostic referrals in nearly every branch of medicine. In such cases, the physician integrates the psychodiagnostic data with medical data in arriving at a diagnosis. In their own diagnostic functions, moreover, all physicians rely at least in part upon information elicited from the patient through interviewing techniques. Training in effective interviewing procedures is thus as relevant to this field as it is to personnel selection (Ch. 3) or to the practice of clinical psychology (Ch. 12). Much can be accomplished by simply recording and playing back typical diagnostic interviews, thereby alerting the physician to common errors (see Kahn & Cannell, 1957, Chs. 1 & 10). Some familiarity with the findings of psychological research on interviewing procedures is also helpful.

For a variety of reasons, the medical interview presents special difficulties for effective communication and hence requires a particularly skillful interviewer (Bowden & Burstein, 1974, Ch. 2; Leventhal, 1975, pp. 138–145). For the patient, the situation is emotionally loaded and is likely to arouse ambivalent attitudes. On the one hand, the patient wants to communicate fully in order to obtain maximum help from the physician. On the other hand, he is reluctant to face the possibility that he may require long or unpleasant therapy or that he may be suffering from a serious disease. The combination of these conflicting tendencies may distort the patient's report in a number of ways. The patient's emotional involvement also heightens his suggestibility. He will thus be quick to respond to slight cues in the physician's queries that may suggest symptoms he had not really observed. He is also likely to read unintended meanings into the physician's remarks, tone of voice, and other expressive reactions. Communication is further obscured by differences in language between physician and patient (Shuy, 1976). Such differences may arise, not only from medical terminology and from the different connotations of common words to layman and physician, but also from possible differences in socioeconomic level, general education, and cultural background.

Mention should also be made of the extent to which medical diagnosis utilizes introspective report regarding the intensity, qualitative characteristics, and localization of pain, as well as other bodily sensations. The extensive psychological research on sensory and perceptual responses and on the factors influencing their accuracy is pertinent to an evaluation of such reports. A more specific example is provided by the detailed visual examinations conducted in ophthalmology. The standard psychophysical procedures of the psychological laboratory have much to contribute to these examinations.

From a different angle, computers are being used increasingly to facilitate and refine medical diagnosis (Glueck & Stroebel, 1975; Johnson & Williams, 1975; Kleinmuntz, 1975). Several of these applications parallel the utilization of computers in clinical psychology, discussed in Chapter 12. Computers permit the simultaneous processing of a multiplicity of data as they are being gathered in intake interviews and medical histories, as well as the rapid handling of longitudinal data about patient change over time. They can provide immediate analyses of instrumental records, such as electroencephalograms (EEG) and electrocardiograms (EKG). Another application is found in the development of problem-oriented patient records and classification systems. Computers are also being used to explore diagnostic problem solving in such fields as neurology. This procedure involves a sequential decision tree, consisting of a series of questions and answers about a patient's condition which elicit relevant diagnostic data and progressively narrow down the diagnosis.

Treatment. There has been a growing interest in the nature of the interpersonal relation between physician and patient and in the part which this relation plays in the recovery process (Kutner, 1960; Leventhal, 1975; Szasz & Hollender, 1975). Theoretical analyses of this relation have been proposed in terms of the attitudes of both patient and physician toward each other. The patient's attitudes, for example, may vary from passive dependence or awed admiration to skepticism or active resistance. The physician, on his part, may exhibit varying degrees of empathy and warmth or impersonal objectivity and aloofness. The physician-patient relationship may also be characterized in terms of a continuum ranging from authoritarian control, through guidance, to mutual participation. In all its aspects, the relationship varies as a function of the nature and severity of the patient's illness, the personality and intellectual characteristics of both patient and physician, the physician's reputation, the patient's earlier contacts with physicians, and other circumstances.

Although empirical data on the effects of the physician-patient relationship are meager, it seems evident that the nature of this relationship will be reflected in the patient's cooperation in carrying out medical orders. That the relationship itself may have therapeutic value is also widely recognized. Contact with a physician in whom the patient has confidence frequently provides an emotional "lift" accompanied by a noticeable amelioration of symptoms. In many cases, this effect may contribute to the patient's ultimate recovery.

From another angle, familiarity with a patient's cultural background may prove helpful to the physician. Behavior that might appear bizarre and irrational becomes intelligible when viewed against the frame of reference of the patient's own culture. Deep-rooted cultural beliefs and traditions may profoundly affect attitudes toward illness, doctors, hospitals, and other medical matters. A doctor who understands the patient's culture enjoys an advantage, not only in arriving at a correct diagnosis, but also in presenting required therapeutic procedures in ways that are acceptable to the patient.

The application of psychology to medical practice has been advanced by the movement to humanize and personalize health care (Hammond et al., 1959; Howard & Strauss, 1975; Matarazzo, 1955; Wexler, 1976). Medical schools have been introducing patient-centered curricula, training programs in comprehensive medical care, and a specialty in family medicine. Arising as a reaction against the increasing specialization of medical practice during the first half of the twentieth century, this approach focuses on the treatment of the total person. With the gradual disappearance of the family doctor, medicine was losing sight of the patient. Efforts are now being made to reverse this trend. Illness is viewed, not as a specific disorder of an isolated organ, but as a complex relation between the organism and its environment. The environmental stresses to which the organism is subjected may range from bacterial infection to interpersonal relations and cultural pressures. The resulting physiological and behavioral changes depend partly upon the nature of these environmental stresses and partly upon the state of the individual at the time. This state in turn reflects the individual's heredity and the residual effects of his or her previous life experiences.

A major problem in the medical treatment of chronic conditions is that of patient compliance and continuation in treatment. Surveys of both hospitalized and outpatient clinic cases of turberculosis and hypertension (high blood pressure) show that substantial proportions drop out of treatment (Baekeland & Lundwall, 1975). Although many variables were found to be associated with failure to persevere in treatment, a major factor was the patients' inadequate information about the consequences of discontinuing treatment and his or her failure to recognize that absence of symptoms does not signify cure. Among the therapist variables contributing to patient dropout were lack of interest in the patient as a person and inadequate communication.

Doctor-patient relations also affect compliance with prescribed medical regimens, including diet, medicines, and other preventive and therapeutic measures

(Leventhal, 1973, 1975). The likelihood that a patient will follow the appropriate procedures can be substantially increased by providing simple and clear explanations of why they are necessary, answering patient questions fully, and—most importantly—giving explicit action instructions to facilitate fitting the treatment into the patient's normal routine.

The alleviation of anxiety associated with a number of medical situations is another area to which psychologists have been contributing. For example, films employing familiarization and peer modeling can be effective in allaying children's fears about going to the dentist, entering a hospital, or undergoing surgery (e.g., Melamed, Howes, Heiby, & Glick, 1975; Melamed & Siegel, 1975). Some specific forms of treatment, as well as a few diagnostic procedures, entail a certain amount of physical discomfort and possibly pain. The extensive ongoing research on pain control, to be discussed in a later section, has much to contribute to this facet of medical practice.

As an illustration, we may consider an exploratory study of patients undergoing gastrointestinal endoscopic examination, a diagnostic test involving visual examination and photography of the upper gastrointestinal tract (Johnson & Leventhal, 1974). In this examination, the throat is swabbed with a local anesthetic and then the patient, who is sedated but not anesthetized, swallows a flexible fiber optic tube. On the basis of hypotheses formulated in prior research, the investigators constructed two types of preparatory messages: one provided accurate information about the sensations to be expected; the other provided detailed behavioral instructions and rehearsal of specific actions that facilitate the examination (mouth breathing, swallowing motions). Four groups of patients were studied, one of which was given the sensory information message; a second, the behavioral instructions; a third, a combination of the two; and a fourth, no preparatory information other than the standard explanation of procedure given to all patients by their physician prior to this type of examination. The results showed the combined message to be most effective both in minimizing aversive emotion and in enhancing coping responses. As hypothesized, accurate sensory information significantly reduced emotional reaction. The behavioral instruction message alone also lowered emotional responses, but its effect was weaker. For a significant improvement in coping responses, both messages were required.

The participation of psychologists themselves in medical treatment is exemplified by the appointment of psychologists in hospitals for orthopedic disabilities, tuberculosis, and other chronic disorders, as well as on obstetrical services and in renal dialysis units. There is a growing realization that in these settings the psychologist can function most effectively as a consultant to hospital physicians, nurses, and other staff members. Rather than spending a few hours a week with a handful of patients, the psychologist can thus help the hospital staff to deal more effectively with the daily problems arising in patient care. This staff-oriented approach is in line with the milieu therapy of psychiatric patients described in Chapter 13. It is also similar to the role of the school psychologist insofar as the latter works through teachers and other school personnel who are in daily contact with the child (Ch. 17).

Rehabilitation. In Chapter 15, rehabilitation counseling was described as one of the specialties in counseling psychology. The rehabilitation movement originated after World War I in an effort to facilitate the vocational readjustment of disabled war veterans. Following World War II, the movement underwent a significant expansion in scope and functions (Garrett & Levine, 1962; B. A. Wright, 1959). Its objectives were broadened to include not only vocational training and placement but also personal, familial, and community adjustment. The target populations were extended to include all persons of any age with sensory or motor handicaps, disabling physical injuries, and chronic diseases. Also included were patients convalescing from severe illness or surgery (e.g., mastectomy patients, burn victims) and discharged psychiatric patients. For such cases, it was recognized that the convalescent or transitional period should serve to prepare the individual for a return to community living. Depending upon the nature of the disorder, the duration of the illness, and the severity of residual handicap, the rehabilitation program could vary from a brief counseling session to a long period of intensive retraining.

Rehabilitation is typically carried on by teams of professional workers drawn from many fields, including physicians, nurses, physical therapists, occupational therapists, speech therapists, psychologists, social workers, vocational counselors, prosthetic specialists, and others. The focus is on the total adjustment of the individual to his or her environment, rather than on the disability as such. Moreover, it is generally recognized that the individual's reaction to the disability is often more important than the disability itself in determining work capacity and general adjustment. The attitudes of family, employers, teachers, and other significant associates are also major factors in the patient's progress. Research on attitudes toward disability, on the part of both disabled and nondisabled persons, has been gradually building a data base for use in rehabilitation programs (Kutner, 1971).

The psychologist's role on the rehabilitation team includes not only assessment and counseling of the patient but also consultation with other team members. Accurate assessment of motor and intellectual skills, emotional traits, motivation, and attitudes is of fundamental importance in planning the rehabilitation program, in determining the effectiveness of remedial procedures, and in detecting progressive changes in the patient. In severely disabled persons, even slight increments or decrements in function may drastically alter capacity for self-care, for job performance, and for other practical activities. Consequently, precise and repeated assessments of abilities are needed. On the basis of continuing evaluation of the patient through testing and interviewing, the psychologist can help in the planning and revision of the rehabilitation program at all stages. In consultative functions, he or she can also enhance the psychological orientation of the other team members, alerting them to the psychological aspects of the patient's adjustment to disability.

Rehabilitation counseling is now being absorbed into a more inclusive field of rehabilitation psychology, which covers basic and applied research, as well as the development and evaluation of procedures and equipment (Ince, 1976; Lofquist, 1962; Neff, 1971; Stubbins, 1977). Several psychological specialties contribute to this emerging area, including not only counseling and psychometrics but also physiological, experimental, social, educational, clinical, and engineering psychology. For example, a promising approach is the introduction of such behavior modification techniques as desensitization, modeling, operant conditioning, and token economies in therapeutic milieus and sheltered workshops. The management of depression and grieving associated with the onset of disability may also utilize learning therapy. The use of sensory feedback in retraining muscle control has met with some success with patients who did not respond to other forms of treatment.

In another area, engineering psychologists have contributed to the design and evaluation of prosthetic devices and environments for the severely disabled. Examples of devices for persons with extreme sensory and motor handicaps were described in Chapter 8. In the design of living environments for the handicapped, a major feature is the elimination of barriers to the motility of persons in wheelchairs. It is noteworthy that the American Association for the Advancement of Science and the American Psychological Association were among the professional societies that pioneered in adapting their annual convention environments to the needs of their handicapped members. One or more of the principal convention hotels provided such facilities as ramps, elevators, widened doorways, specially altered and equipped bedrooms and bathrooms, and elevator numbers in braille. Many public buildings and monuments in the nation's capital have been similarly adapted ("Freedom in a Wheelchair," 1976). Transportation facilities in several large cities and a number of hotel chains are likewise introducing provisions for the orthopedically handicapped. All these developments will undoubtedly be accelerated by the recently enacted legislation requiring such adaptations in public buildings.

Preventive Medicine. Like community psychology, preventive medicine focuses on primary prevention and the enhancement of health in the general public. In both individual medical practice and public health programs, preventive medicine needs the cooperation of the lay public. The availability of preventive medical techniques such as vaccination can be of no help if the public does not take advantage of them. Early detection and treatment of such conditions as cancer and tuberculosis likewise depend upon the knowledge and attitudes of the individual patients. To be effective, preventive medicine requires a well-informed public with appropriate attitudes toward disease prevention.

Several applications of psychological procedures to public health problems were cited in Chapter 11 as one facet of contemporary consumer psychology. The types of health-related behaviors investigated include seeking or avoiding early diagnosis and treatment of such conditions as cancer and tuberculosis; taking preventive measures such as inoculations; following positive health practices such as proper diet and dental hygiene; and avoidance or cessation of deleterious practices such as heavy smoking, alcoholism, or drug abuse.

Much research has been concerned with the characteristics of persons who engage in particular health-related behaviors and the situational variables that tend to reinforce or weaken such behaviors. It has been found, for example, that the eating behavior of many obese persons is controlled more by external cues, such as the sight and taste of food or the time of day, than by internal sensations of hunger (Shachter, 1971). Other studies on a variety of personality variables suggest a multiple etiology for obesity, with the pattern of contributing factors varying for different cases (Leon & Roth, 1977). A good deal of research has focused on the development and evaluation of behavior modification programs for the control of obesity (Stuart & Davis, 1971; Stunkard, 1972).

Several investigators have studied the reasons why people delay in seeking medical care for cancer and other serious illnesses. Among the most common reasons, they found inadequate information about symptoms, lack of confidence in physician or in medical practice generally, fear of diagnosis and/or treatment, and wishful thinking that the condition will simply go away (Gold, 1964; Kutner & Gordan, 1961; Leventhal, 1975; Shontz, 1972; 1975, Ch. 6). Essentially, whether or not a person seeks help for physical illness depends on how he or she perceives the situation; and this perception in turn depends on a myriad of personal and environmental variables.

In the development and evaluation of public health programs, psychologists have been contributing in a variety of ways. For example, in national tests of the prevention of coronary heart disease in high-risk persons, psychologists have collaborated in the recruitment of participants and in the design and evaluation of medication compliance procedures (Zifferblatt, 1976). In planning any public health campaign, data are needed about existing population attitudes or misinformation that may interfere with the adoption of any given preventive measure. Superstitions, cultural traditions, and deep-rooted emotional reactions that would cause resistance must be identified. For example, efforts have been made to investigate why people oppose community water fluoridation (Kegeles, 1960; Paul, Gawson, & Kegeles, 1961).

Public information campaigns in preventive medicine utilize the methodology and research findings of consumer psychology (Ch. 11). Psychologists have for some time been exploring the use of mass media to advance public health objectives (e.g., Evans, 1976). Among the types of media utilized are documentary films, public television programs, comedy sketches, animated cartoons, spot "commercials," booklets, and comic strips. Psychologists have been active in both the development of such programs and the evaluation of their effectiveness under experimentally controlled conditions. More broadly applicable, basic research has also been conducted on the relation between variables of health-related communications and public changes in attitudes and overt behavior. Such behavior modification techniques as modeling and the presentation of explicit action plans have proved promising. Repeated personal contacts and social support networks have been found to be especially effective in modifying health behavior (Kelly et al., 1977, p. 332).

The role of personal contacts was illustrated in a study of several types of communication about dental hygiene, conducted in six classes of junior high school girls (Evans, Rozelle, Noblitt, & Williams, 1975). All groups improved significantly over a 10-week observation period. But the most provocative result was that the control group improved as much as the other groups. The essential element, common to all groups, was the periodic reexamination by a member of the project staff. On these occasions, each participant completed a questionnaire about her current dental hygiene practices. In addition, a photographic record of tooth cleanliness was obtained with the aid of a tablet that dyes bacterial plaque red. The personal follow-up and periodic assessment of target behaviors were thus the key factors that accounted for improvement. In this connection, it may be recalled that, in self-control programs of behavior modification (Ch. 13), self-monitoring during the baseline periods is often accompanied by improvement in target behavior. Simply focusing the person's attention on the target behavior through systematic assessment and record keeping is itself a noteworthy technique of behavior change.

PSYCHOLOGY IN MEDICAL EDUCATION

Psychology in the Medical School Curriculum. Prior to midcentury, psychologists were rarely found on medical school faculties. What little psychology was included in medical school curricula was taught by psychiatrists. With the growth of clinical psychology during and following World War II, clinical psychologists began to teach in medical schools, usually on a part-time basis and within very limited areas. The 1950s and 1960s witnessed a mounting interest in the roles of psychologists in medical education, as evidenced by a plenitude of conferences, symposia, professional committees, and articles. Gradually, psychology came to be accepted as part of the basic science training for all medical students, rather than being limited as heretofore to those specializing in psychiatry. Its appropriateness in premedical education was also increasingly recognized.

Concurrently, the kinds of psychologists involved in medical education were increased to include not only clinical psychologists but also those in other specialties, such as experimental, physiological, social, and developmental psychology. On their part, psychologists began to build bridges between basic behavioral research and the realistic demands of medical practice. The gap remains, as in all applied fields, but substantial progress is being made in closing it (Wexler, 1976). The 1960s and 1970s saw an upsurge of psychological research on distinctly medical problems, such as patient care, medical diagnosis, the control of pain, and the contributions of psychological factors to both onset of disease and recovery. These developments were paralleled by a sharply rising trend in the number of psychologists employed on medical school faculties, as revealed by periodic surveys since the 1950s (Lubin, Nathan, & Matarazzo, 1978; Matarazzo & Daniel, 1957; Mensh, 1953; Wagner & Stegeman, 1964). By the 1970s, practically every American medical school had psychologists on its staff, and several had established well-rounded departments of behavioral science (Wexler, 1976). Psychologists are also participating more and more in the training of students in allied health professions and technical specialties, such as dentistry, nursing, and physical therapy.

Besides their direct involvement in medical school programs through formal course teaching, instruction of interns and residents, participation in case conferences, and individual counseling with students and staff, psychologists are contributing to medical education through research and development in areas that significantly affect medical students. Two examples of such activities have been selected because of their scope, diversity, and relevance to the process of medical education. They pertain to (1) evaluation and measurement in medical education and (2) the development and testing of patient-management skills.

Evaluation and Measurement. One of the earliest ways in which psychologists became involved in medical education was in the development and evaluation of tests and other assessment procedures for the selection of medical school applicants. The Medical College Admission Test (MCAT) is the product of continuing research and development by psychologists working with the Association of American Medical Colleges. In its current version, this test covers science knowledge in biology, chemistry, and physics acquired in premedical education; science problems requiring the application of such knowledge to problem solving; and two subtests tapping broader verbal and quantitative skills, respectively. The MCAT is typically employed together with college grade records, biographical information, and other data sources in assessing the student's qualifications for admission. In the development and evaluation of all these predictors, the same psychometric procedures are followed as in similar personnel selection and classification problems in other contexts (see Ch. 2).

At later stages of the training process, psychologists have been playing major roles in the construction of tests for use in the state licensing of medical practitioners and in the specialty certification administered by the various medical specialty boards. They are also actively contributing to the movement toward periodic relicensure and recertification of practitioners, necessitated by the rapid growth in medical knowledge (Shimberg, 1977). A noteworthy feature of this burgeoning movement is the development of self-assessment programs for use by the individual practitioner.[2] Such programs provide self-administered tests and detailed computer-generated feedback on the individual's performance. Also included are study guides and bibliographic references for updating information and closing gaps in one's knowledge.

A still different application of psychometric research is illustrated by studies of medical student characteristics (Gough, 1975a, 1975b; Gough & Ducker, 1977; Gough & Hall, 1973; Millon, 1975, pp. 29–68). Such research covers motivational and attitudinal traits of medical students as a group, changes in personality variables occurring in the course of medical training, differences among students electing different medical specialties, the distribution of reported specialty preferences, and the relation of socioeconomic level to several aspects of medical education. Other studies have concentrated on the variables associated with performance in the academic and in the clinical aspects of medical training and on the factors leading to dropout from medical school (Gough & Hall, 1975a, 1975b; Millon, 1975, pp. 29–68).

Patient-Management Skills. Even a cursory job analysis of medical practice reveals that a major—if not *the* major—activity of the physician consists of a chain of interrelated diagnostic and therapeutic decisions about the individual patient. Commonly designated by the term "patient management," this process includes questioning patients about their present complaint and relevant features of their medical history, performing or requesting medical tests (e.g., urine analysis, EKG), applying or prescribing specific treatment (e.g., antibiotics, surgery), observing the effects of the treatment, and (if necessary) modifying diagnosis and/or treatment on the basis of observed results.

Research on the nature of the patient-management process, reminiscent of the research on the nature of clinical judgment reported in Chapter 12, yields data that are germane to both medical training and performance evaluation. Wide individual differences have been found in the decision-making skills manifested in solving patient-management problems. Some research has focused on analyzing the decision process and identifying the decision rules followed by skilled practitioners. At the applied level, considerable effort has been devoted to designing both training programs for developing these clinical skills and tests for assessing them.

In a pioneer investigation of the patient-management problem, Rimaldi (1961) developed a prototype of the testing procedures now widely used for this purpose. Essentially, such a test begins with the examinee receiving preliminary information about a case, including admission data and chief complaints. The examinee then proceeds to request additional information as needed. The answer received to each question helps to narrow down the diagnosis of the case and in turn determines subsequent questions. In Rimaldi's original study, the examinee obtained the information by choosing appropriate cards. Test performance was

---

[2] E.g., American College of Physicians, Medical Knowledge Self-Assessment Program IV, 4200 Pine Street, Philadelphia, Pa. 19104.

evaluated on the basis of number and sequence of questions asked and the utility of the questions in reaching the final diagnosis. Unskilled diagnosticians generally ask more questions before reaching a diagnosis than do skilled diagnosticians. This results from the fact that the unskilled ask more irrelevant or redundant questions and tend more often to follow wrong clues. Such differences were demonstrated in exploratory research with junior and senior medical students and practicing physicians from five medical schools.

Subsequent research by other investigators led to considerable expansion and refinement of the patient-management problem (Berner, Hamilton, & Best, 1974; R. B. Friedman, 1973; Hubbard, 1964). With regard to the mechanics of testing, an important innovation consists of the use of printed test forms on which the answer to each question selected by the examinee is printed in invisible ink and is revealed by going over it with a special marker; or the process may involve erasing an inked overlay to uncover the answer. Figure 18-1 illustrates six items from different portions of a sample patient-management problem. The first three items deal with requested diagnostic procedures; the other three, with prescribed treatment steps.

The use of computer simulations of patient management permits much greater flexibility and realism both in presenting data and in processing responses than can be achieved with paper-and-pencil materials (e.g., R. B. Friedman, 1973). With such facilities, it is possible to have the examinees generate their own questions (or procedural steps) rather than selecting them from a given list. The examinees can also be given the results of prescribed treatments over time, as well as periodic data on changes in patient condition as shown on nurses' notes. Information on the availability, length, and cost of requested tests or procedures can likewise be

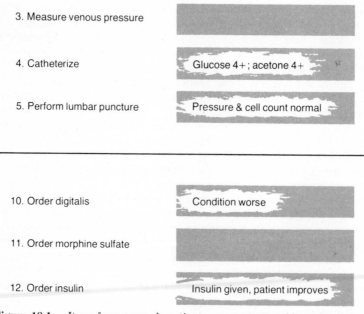

Figure 18-1. Items from a sample patient-management problem, showing spaces uncovered by a hypothetical examinee who chose diagnostic Steps 4 and 5 and treatment Steps 10 and 12. *(From Hubbard, 1964, p. 59. Copyright © 1964 by Educational Testing Service. Reproduced by permission.)*

provided. Still another variant employs a different kind of feedback to examinees: whenever they make an incorrect decision, they are told what information they should have requested and are given the correct data. Each decision point is thus unaffected by prior errors.

Besides the potential utilization of the patient-management problem in teaching clinical problem-solving skills, various forms of this problem have been incorporated in tests developed for licensure and certification. This type of problem is also included in some of the previously cited self-assessment tests for use in continuing education.

PSYCHOLOGY IN HEALTH RESEARCH

One of the chief contributions that psychologists can make to medicine is in the area of research. Both in medical schools and in other medical settings, the number of psychologists engaged in interdisciplinary research projects is growing rapidly. In this research, psychologists collaborate not only with medical practitioners but also with specialists in other basic sciences, such as physiology, neurology, biochemistry, and pharmacology. The effective collaboration of psychologists with medical personnel and other biological scientists is illustrated by the extensive research program on environmental stresses of space travel conducted for the National Aeronautic and Space Administration (Ch. 9). It is also noteworthy that one of the events leading to research on sensory deprivation was the observation that polio patients confined in respirators for long periods of time experienced feelings of strangeness, hallucinations, and other cognitive disturbances (Solomon, Leiderman, Mendelson, & Wexler, 1957).

Several examples of psychological research on health-related problems were cited in the first two sections of this chapter. Others will be given in the last two sections, dealing with psychosomatics and somatopsychology. The focus in the present section is on methodological contributions and on research areas that cut across several facets of medicine.

Psychopharmacology. A steadily expanding area of collaboration between psychology and medicine is to be found in psychopharmacology, or behavioral pharmacology (Claridge, 1970; Iverson & Iverson, 1975; Iverson, Iverson, & Snyder, 1978; Warburton, 1976). Much of the psychological research on drugs pertains to their use in the understanding and treatment of psychiatric disorders (Ch. 13). The total contribution of psychology to pharmacology, however, covers other medical uses of drugs, including relief of pain and specific therapies for physical disorders. It is being increasingly recognized, for example, that any drug designed for medical use should be tested for "behavioral toxicity," that is, for any adverse side effects it may have upon psychological functioning (Uhr & Miller, 1960, Ch. 7). For this purpose, almost every available kind of psychological test has been used, from measures of simple sensory and motor functions to tests of complex intellectual and personality traits.

In the testing of drugs prior to their release for medical use, psychological research techniques are being employed at every stage, from preliminary animal research, through experimental studies with human subjects, to clinical tests. In animal research, behavioral measures are proving more sensitive than physiological measures in detecting drug effects and are commonly employed for preliminary testing of new drugs. Skinner boxes and other sophisticated instruments for measuring animal behavior can now be found in the pharmacology departments of medical schools. Pharmaceutical companies also employ psychologists to conduct drug research with animals.

In both experimental studies on normal human volunteers and clinical field tests on patients, psychology has much to offer to methodology. Several relevant methodological points were discussed in Chapter 13, in connection with drug therapies for behavioral disorders, and in Chapter 14, in connection with procedures for evaluating the outcomes of therapy. Among psychology's contributions to drug research in general may be mentioned the use of psychological tests and rating scales for quantitative assessment of behavioral effects; the identification of relevant variables for selecting cases and assigning them to different treatment groups; and the use of the doube-blind technique to control for the influence of suggestion, or the placebo effect, on both subjects and observers (see Ch. 14). A particularly striking example of the placebo effect is illustrated in Figure 18-2. A group of student volunteers were given two differently colored placebos, a week apart. One was described as a sleep-producing or depressant drug, the other as a stimulant. The results showed significant differences from the baseline in the expected directions, the effects increasing consistently during the 50-minute observation period. As will be noted, the differences occurred not only in rated feelings but also in reaction time and physiological measures.

Another type of contribution pertains to the various experimental and quasi-

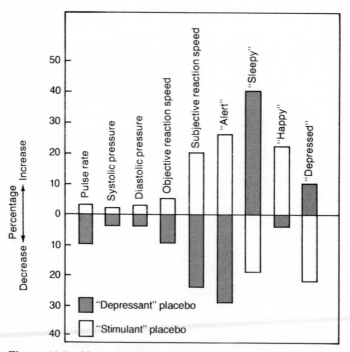

Figure 18-2. Mean percentage change from baseline level following administration of a "depressant" and a "stimulant" placebo. *(From Frankenhaeuser, Järpe, Svan, & Wrangsjö, 1963. Copyright © 1963 by Scandinavian Journal of Psychology. Reproduced by permission.)*

experimental designs, including own-control procedures and designs appropriate for analyzing data on single cases. Insofar as there are wide individual differences in both physiological and behavioral responses to drugs, psychological procedures for the measurement and analysis of individual differences are likewise relevant, as are techniques for investigating the personal variables associated with such response differences. There is also considerable evidence of interaction of drug effects with other independent variables acting upon the individual at the time, such as incentives, situational and context factors, and the behavior of associates (Claridge, 1970, Ch. 6).

Current societal and governmental developments are creating new opportunities for the participation of psychologists in programs on drug abuse and alcoholism (Goldberg, 1976; Wolfe, 1976). Increasingly, psychologists are coming to assume functions in these programs traditionally performed by either physicians or self-help lay groups. Potential contributions range from basic and applied research to treatment, rehabilitation, and preventive public health measures. Behavior modification programs, crisis intervention, group therapies, and family therapy are gradually being introduced into this area. Community psychologists include addicts among their target populations. Psychologists have also been active in the development and evaluation of public information programs regarding substance abuse.

At this stage, however, psychology's contributions to drug and alcohol research are more highly developed than are the emerging practice-oriented functions. For example, in a recent survey of assessment methods for the diagnosis of alcoholism, W. R. Miller (1976) concludes that the bulk of available research casts doubt on the unitary disease concept of alcoholism. He recommends multimodal, differential assessment to identify types and degrees of alcoholism as an alternative to the traditional binary classification of alcoholic versus nonalcoholic. Among the instruments available for such assessments are a variety of self-report scales covering either direct questions on drinking and alcohol-related behavior or more general, indirect personality items empirically shown to be correlated with alcoholism. Additional recommended assessment techniques include physiological measures (e.g., withdrawal symptoms, tolerance) and direct observation of consumption behaviors. The latter is especially germane to programs of behavior modification utilizing operant conditioning techniques. The need for longitudinal studies to determine the predictive validity of indices obtained prior to the development of alcoholism is also emphasized. Such information would permit the use of preventive measures with persons at high risk.

It is apparent that the same concepts and methodologies are pertinent to research on drug abuse. A sophisticated psychological approach to this problem is illustrated by a long-term project designed by Dunnette and his associates to test directional hypotheses about the causes and consequences of adolescent drug experiences (Dunnette & Peterson, 1977). There is considerable prior research evidence regarding personal correlates of adolescent drug use, such as low achievement orientation, high autonomy needs, and stronger orientation toward peer than toward parental norms (Gorsuch & Butler, 1976; Lettieri, 1975). But most studies followed a cross-sectional, correlational approach that does not permit an analysis of cause-and-effect relations. For example, is parental-adolescent alienation a cause or a consequence of adolescent drug use? Dunnette and his co-workers are investigating the directionality of such relations longitudinally, through repeated annual surveys of large groups of adolescents in several cities.

In the study of drug abuse, as in alcoholism research, investigators have repeatedly noted the lack of adequate measures for assessing drug-related behavior (Gorsuch & Butler, 1976; Walizer, 1975). As a step toward the needed quantification in this area, Dunnette and his associates devoted a major part of their project to the development and evaluation of suitable measuring instruments. Through a series of empirical steps, they constructed a set of scaled behavioral vignettes in order to provide a single index of extent and seriousness of drug involvement. Two questionnaires were also prepared. One concerns the respondent's drug experiences, including type of drugs used, frequency of use, age of first use, and immediate and long-term effects of use. The other samples a wide assortment of individual variables from the personality, social, behavioral, and biographical domains.

Research on psychopharmacology, as well as in other areas of medical and psychological collaboration, is also contributing to basic knowledge about behavioral science. From the standpoint of the research psychologist, collaboration with medicine opens up new research settings in hospitals, clinics, and other agencies and provides access to many types of subjects not heretofore available. It also permits the use of techniques such as drug administration that require medical collaboration. Apart from their therapeutic values, drugs are being used experimentally to produce temporary and limited "biochemical lesions" in the nervous system. By interfering with selected biochemical events these techniques can shed light on the operation of different parts of the nervous system in normal behavior. For this purpose, drugs have several advantages over earlier methods of extirpation and other types of surgical intervention. Not only is drug administration a simpler and better controlled procedure than surgical techniques, but the effects of drugs are also reversible. Because of this reversibility and the reduction of risk, some drug research can be safely conducted with human subjects. The precision with which drug administration can be controlled and manipulated, moreover, makes possible a clearer delineation of the physiological mechanisms underlying behavioral changes. The 1970s were characterized by impressive advances in the use of drug research to elucidate the functioning of the brain and other parts of the nervous system (Iverson, Iverson, & Snyder, 1978). Psychopharmacology thus illustrates the reciprocal contribution of collaborative research to both medical practice and psychological science.

Nature and Alleviation of Pain. The subject of pain is obviously of concern to medical practitioners, while falling clearly in the domain of psychological research. Pain and its relief have been investigated by psychologists, neurologists, anesthesiologists, and pharmacologists, among others (Liebeskind & Paul, 1977; Melzack, 1973; Weisenberg, 1977). Collaborative projects cutting across these fields, however, are of relatively recent origin. Specific studies have ranged from introspective analyses to the identification of sensory receptors and neurological correlates of pain. Their objectives have also varied widely, extending from the formulation of a basic theory of pain to the evaluation of individual techniques for its elimination or diminution.

There is a vast array of qualitatively different pain experiences. The pain of a burned hand is clearly different from that of a broken leg, a headache, or a toothache. Pain is a label that covers an endless diversity of experiences that vary along several dimensions. There are also wide individual and cultural differences in the response to pain. And the same person will respond differently at different times and in different situations. The meaning that the pain stimulus has for the individual affects the quality and intensity of pain felt. It is now generally recognized that any one pain experience is complex, including sensory, cognitive, and emotional components.

A noteworthy finding of much of the psychological research on pain is that pain-relieving agents may eliminate the discomfort and anxiety associated with pain without raising the pain threshold or altering pain sensations themselves (Barber, 1959; Beecher, 1959; Melzack, 1973). Thus the individual can still identify the pain, localize it, and discriminate it from other sensations such as touch or temperature, but he or she no longer finds it intolerable or distressing. Physiological reactions, such as blood pressure changes, ordinarily associated with the discomfort of pain may also disappear under these conditions.

The wide diversity of pain experiences—with regard to their causes, qualitative characteristics, duration, and intensity—points to the need for a multiplicity of therapeutic approaches. No one procedure will work for all kinds of pain or for all persons. Moreover, a combination of techniques will often yield the best results. This multidimensional approach is exemplified by the pain clinics which began to appear in the 1960s and are gradually being established throughout the country. Dealing largely with incapacitating chronic pains of long standing, these clinics utilize the joint services of many specialists, such as anesthesiologists, neurologists, psychologists, orthopedists, internists, pharmacologists, physical therapists, and nurses (Fordyce, 1976; Sternbach, 1974).

The principal somatic approaches to pain control comprise pharmacological and neurological procedures. Drugs employed for pain control include anesthetics, analgesics, sedatives, and tranquilizers. Anesthetics serve to eliminate all sensation temporarily, either locally or in the organism as a whole. The role of other types of drugs in pain relief is not completely understood; but controlled experiments strongly suggest that the placebo effect may account for much of the result (Claridge, 1970, Ch. 2).

The 1960s and 1970s have been a period of substantial progress in elucidating neurological mechanisms of pain reactions (Liebeskind & Paul, 1977; Melzack, 1973). Several treatment techniques have been developed as a result of this basic research, including limited neurosurgical procedures and electrical stimulation of specific nerves or central nervous system sites. Especially noteworthy is recent research identifying mechanisms of pain control in the medial brain stem (Liebeskind & Paul, 1977). In experiments with a wide assortment of pain tests and with species ranging from rat to human, stimulation within this region has produced analgesia closely equivalent to that obtained with large doses of morphine. It has been hypothesized that activation of such a central pain-inhibitory mechanism may underlie the analgesic effects of many psychological techniques that utilize suggestion and attention control.

Among psychological methods for pain control, there has been a vigorous resurgence of interest in hypnosis (Barber, Spanos, & Chaves, 1974; Hilgard, 1975; Hilgard & Hilgard, 1975). Although theories about its essential nature are still controversial, hypnosis is generally characterized by restriction of attention, relaxation, and suggestion. The extent to which each of these conditions is involved may vary with the operator, the subject, and the induction procedures. There are also wide individual differences in susceptibility to hypnosis, as illustrated in Figure 18-3. It is estimated that mild pain can be relieved by hypnotic techniques for the large majority of persons. In a few cases, sufficient depth of

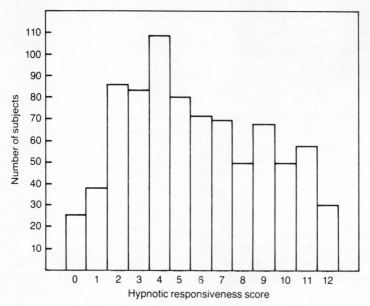

Figure 18-3. Distribution of 806 college students on the Stanford Hypnotic Susceptibility Scale, Form A. Scores are based on a combination of behavioral indices and range from least responsive (0) to most responsive (12). *(From Hilgard & Hilgard, 1975, p. 8. Copyright © 1975 by William Kaufmann, Inc. Reproduced by permission.)*

hypnosis can be achieved to perform major surgery without drugs. There is still disagreement about the extent to which hypnotic susceptibility can be modified by training. Hilgard and Hilgard (1975) describe successful uses of hypnosis for the relief of pain in terminal cancer patients, for facilitating childbirth, and as an adjunct to chemical anesthesia or (less often) as the sole anesthetic in surgery and dentistry.

Related techniques that probably depend on attention control to relieve pain include yoga exercises and various forms of transcendental meditation. Still other procedures rely chiefly on distraction, as in the use of intense auditory stimulation (white noise) and electrical stimulation of the skin. Again, such methods have been found to work only for some persons. Recent research on the ancient Chinese technique of acupuncture suggests that its pain-inhibitory effects, when present, may likewise result from distraction, suggestion, or both; some attention, however, is also being given to possible neurological mechanisms. Intense concentration of attention on competing activities may also account for the cases of football players, boxers, and soldiers in battle who experienced no pain while sustaining serious injuries (Beecher, 1959; Melzack, 1973).

Another approach, based on a different manipulation of attention, is described by Leventhal (1976). This approach begins with the premise that the individual's response to a pain-arousing stimulus may be characterized by two information-processing styles: (1) an objective style, directed to veridical observation of external events; and (2) a subjective or affective style which generates an emotional reaction to external events. This conception of the pain experience is consistent with the prevalent view of pain as a combination of a sensory or information component and an emotional or reactive component (Beecher, 1959; Melzack & Wall, 1965).

In the light of this theoretical model, Leventhal hypothesized that focusing a person's attention on the objective information-processing style should reduce the distress associated with the experience of pain. The hypothesis was tested in a series of studies that included both experimentally produced pain with laboratory subjects and work with hospitalized patients during childbirth. In some laboratory studies, the objective information-processing set was evoked by giving the subjects detailed prior information on the sensations they would experience. In other laboratory studies, as well as in the hospital study, subjects were instructed to observe their sensations carefully so that they could describe them later. In all these studies, the hypothesis was confirmed: the groups whose attention was concentrated on an objective observation of the sensory input reported significantly less distress than did the various control groups.

Operant conditioning techniques have also been successfully employed in the relief of pain, especially with the chronic pain patients treated in pain clinics. Fordyce (1976) describes a typical program based on the systematic use of contingent reinforcement. In such a program, each patient follows a schedule of individually designed exercises, such as walking; this schedule is adjusted to the patient's own empirically established "quota," so that he or she stops to rest before the pain becomes severe. Rest, which serves as the reinforcer in this situation, is thus made contingent upon achieving the exercise quota, rather than being contingent upon the pain as heretofore. Social attention from staff and family is likewise made contingent upon target behaviors and not upon such pain behaviors as moaning, complaining, and inactivity. Pain medication, which is a powerful reinforcer, is administered on a fixed schedule, rather than on a pain-contingent basis. At the outset, the patient is given sufficient amounts of all the needed analgesics to provide the desired pain relief. These medications are combined in a pleasantly flavored fruit drink, or "pain cocktail," which masks the taste. Drug content of this drink is gradually reduced—a procedure that was explained to the patient in advance, along with other features of the program. Some cases remain free from pain even when all medication has been withdrawn from the beverage.

This application of behavior modification to pain control has shown considerable promise in the treatment of certain types of chronic pain. Its underlying rationale is simple: since much of the sick behavior of chronic pain patients has probably been learned over the years, it can be unlearned by suitable rearrangement of contingencies. From a somewhat different angle, the contribution of operant conditioning to general nursing practice is being increasingly recognized (Berni & Fordyce, 1977).

Biofeedback. A significant breakthrough in learning research occurred in the 1960s with the successful operant conditioning of autonomic processes, i.e., visceral and glandular processes under the direct control of the autonomic nervous system. It had long been known that such processes were subject to classical or respondent conditioning. A familiar example is the Pavlovian experiment whereby dogs salivated to the sound of a bell that had been repeatedly accompanied by food. A similar conditioned salivary response can be evoked in any of us by the sight or smell of appetizing food or by a picture or verbal description of a delectable dish. Until recently, however, it was generally believed that operant conditioning was effective only for "voluntary" skeletal responses mediated by the central nervous system. The demonstration that autonomic responses were also modifiable by contingent reinforcement meant that persons might eventually be taught to control their own heart rate, blood pressure, digestive processes, and other physiological responses.

The pioneer animal research in operant conditioning of autonomic responses was conducted by Neal E. Miller and his associates (see N. E. Miller, 1969, 1975). By systematically reinforcing the target behavior whenever it occurred spontaneously in the animal, the experimenters were able to increase or decrease such processes as salivation, heart rate, intestinal contractions, blood pressure, and rate of urine formation. These findings stimulated a flood of research, including laboratory experiments with several species of animals and normal human volunteers, and clinical studies of patients with various physiological disorders.[3]

The encouraging results of much of this research, together with the development of sophisticated instruments that provide continuous visual and/or auditory records of various physiological processes (Paskewitz, 1975), led to the design of self-regulatory techniques known as "biofeedback." For example, a patient who is motivated to lower his blood pressure for health reasons observes a continuous record of his blood pressure in the form of a changing visual signal or a tone of varying loudness. He is instructed to try to bring the record down to a specified level and keep it there. The results suggest that it *can* be done, although the individual does not know how he does it. Moreover, there is evidence that the procedure may succeed equally well if the individual does not even know which particular physiological process is being modified, as long as he is rewarded whenever he emits changes in the target direction (Scott et al., 1973; G. E. Schwartz, 1973). This finding is not surprising, in view of the fact that the original animal experiments on operant conditioning of autonomic responses obviously did not involve such knowledge on the animal's part.

The term "biofeedback" is now used loosely to refer either to the monitoring of one's own body processes, or to the contingent reinforcement of such processes, or both. It should also be noted that, for a normally motivated human subject, performance feedback itself provides contingent reinforcement. Biofeedback techniques have been applied therapeutically to the control of cardiovascular conditions such as high blood pressure, chronic tachycardia (rapid heart rate), and irregularities in heart rhythm. Figure 18-4 illustrates the results obtained with a tachycardia patient, for whom a monetary reward was used to shape the target response. Besides the significant and substantial decrease in heart rate, which continued through the second baseline period when reinforcement was discontinued, the patient also reported that "he felt less anxious and stronger and that he was able to perform more household chores without tiring rapidly (Scott et al., 1973, p. 336).

Promising results have been obtained with biofeedback in the treatment of migraine, or vascular, headaches (Sargent, Walters, & Green, 1975). The strategy in such cases is to train the patient to decrease pressure in the enlarged blood

---

[3]The massive accumulation of research literature on this topic is reflected in the establishment of an interdisciplinary journal, *Biofeedback and Self-regulation,* the publication since 1971 of an annual, *Biofeedback and Self-control,* and the appearance of several edited books (e.g., Schwartz & Beatty, 1977).

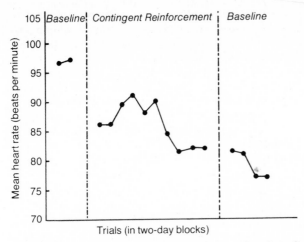

Figure 18-4. Deceleration of heart rate in a chronic tachycardia patient through operant conditioning. Each point represents the mean of two 20-minute trials on successive training days. *(From Scott, Blanchard, Edmunson, & Young, 1973, p. 337. Copyright © 1973 by Perceptual and Motor Skills, Reproduced by permission.)*

vessels of the scalp by increasing peripheral blood flow in the hand; feedback is provided by changes in fingertip temperature. Some patients become strikingly adept at thus warming the hands at will. For tension headaches, usually caused by sustained contraction of forehead and neck muscles, patients have been taught to relax specific muscles through feedback of the appropriate electromyography (EMG) recordings (Budzynski, Stoyva, Adler, & Mullaney, 1973). A particularly successful application of EMG biofeedback is found in the muscle reeducation of patients with disturbed or diminished neuromuscular control, especially cases of torticollis (wry neck) and stroke. This procedure is being used extensively at the Sensory Feedback Therapy Unit of the ICD Rehabilitation and Research Center in New York City (Brudny et al., 1974, 1976; Korein & Brudny, 1976).

Mention should also be made of the widely publicized alpha biofeedback training, which involves the use of electroencephalography (EEG) recordings. The object is to increase the occurrence of the alpha rhythm (8–13 Hz) in the EEG, a condition that in some persons is reportedly associated with relaxed, pleasant feelings (Kamiya, 1969; Nowlis & Kamiya, 1970). Results of this application of biofeedback have been inconsistent and inconclusive. Inadequate controls make it especially difficult to isolate specific treatment effects from general effects of distraction, suggestion, and relaxation, which could be achieved in other ways. Moreover, research to date has failed to demonstrate a genuine learning effect, since the positive results reported may have arisen from methodological artifacts (Leib, Tryon, & Stroebel, 1976).

The therapeutic uses of biofeedback are still at an exploratory stage (Blanchard & Young, 1974; Katz & Zlutnick, 1975; McCanne & Sandeman, 1976; N. E. Miller, 1975). To be sure, some applications are better developed and more promising than others; but there are still several unanswered questions and controversial interpretations, especially with regard to the particular mechanisms that mediate the obtained response changes. Methodological weaknesses and inadequate controls for placebo effects make for ambiguity in the results of a number of studies. Premature popularization, exaggerated claims, and commercial exploitation of hardware for do-it-yourself biofeedback (Schwitzgebel & Rugh, 1975) are likely to usher in a cycle of disillusionment and skepticism. Nevertheless, the basic research on operant conditioning of bodily processes has opened a promising route to understanding and unifying the vast area of behavioral self-regulation, including the results of such long-familiar processes as yoga, meditation, and hypnosis. Much research and development are still needed to bridge the gap between theory and practice. An excellent list of next steps for the researcher in this area is given by Neal Miller (1975), who concludes that at this stage "investigators should be bold in what they try but cautious in what they claim" (p. 363).

PSYCHOSOMATIC MEDICINE

Concept. The term "psychosomatic" has become familiar not only in medical and psychological literature but also in popular speech. Much publicity has been given to such "psychosomatic illnesses" as peptic ulcer, high blood pressure (essential hypertension), coronary heart disease, rheumatoid arthritis, and bronchial asthma.[4] The term was originally applied to those physical disorders in which emotional stresses have led to identifiable organic pathology. Such conditions were thus differentiated from those for which no organic basis could be found, as illustrated by "functional" or "hysterical" paralyses, "psychogenic" pain, and some cases of asthma. For several reasons, modern treatment approaches have tended to deemphasize this distinction. It is now recognized that patients suffering from a so-called functional disorder experience as much distress as do those for whom organic pathology is identifiable; and they are generally just as powerless to overcome their symptoms.

From another viewpoint, psychological therapies derived from learning principles, such as behavior modification and biofeedback, are equally applicable to both types of cases. To be sure, whenever organic pathology is found it should be treated by the appropriate medical means. Often, however, this is not sufficient to restore the patient to a normal condition; some psychological procedures may also be needed. A multidisciplinary approach to therapy, similar to that followed in the pain clinics, would seem to be optimal for such cases.

Historical Development. The concept of psychosomatic illness is an old one, dating from some of the earliest recorded writings (see H. I. Kaplan, 1975; Wittkower & Cleghorn, 1954, Ch. 3). Even the term psychosomatic is not very new, having been proposed at least as early as 1818 (Wittkower & Cleghorn, 1954, p. 41). Nevertheless, the psychosomatic movement in medicine and the widespread recognition of psychogenic factors in physical disorders are of relatively recent origin. The publication in 1935 of Dunbar's book on *Emotions and Bodily Changes,* which surveyed relevant world literature of both experimental and clinical nature,

---

[4]Current surveys of traditional psychosomatic disorders, with regard to both etiology and therapy, can be found in Freedman, Kaplan, and Sadock (1975, vol. 2, Ch. 6) and Katz and Zlutnick (1975).

did much to launch the movement. The first journal and the first association devoted to the study of psychosomatic problems were established within the next few years. The high incidence of psychosomatic disorders among military personnel and among civilians exposed to wartime stresses during World War II also contributed to the growing concern with these problems.

Several antecedent developments in psychology, physiology, and psychiatry contributed to the rise of the modern psychosomatic movement. A major contribution stems from research on the *effects of psychological factors on physiological functions,* as studied in both humans and animals. The pioneer animal experiments of Pavlov (1928) on the conditioned salivary reflex and of Cannon (1932) on physiological effects of intense emotional stimuli are outstanding examples of this research. The investigations of Selye (1946, 1973) on the "general adaptation syndrome" following prolonged exposure to any kind of stress shed further light on the role of certain hormones in mediating physiological responses to stress. More limited experimental studies on human subjects, as well as clinical observations on patients, provided additional data on changes in blood pressure, respiration, gastric motility, glandular secretions, and other physiological reactions resulting from emotional stress. Such research established that temporary and reversible physiological changes accompany anxiety and other emotional states. In addition, there was increasing evidence that excessive and continued emotional stress may lead to chronic disturbances of physiological functions and to permanent tissue damage. More recently, the case of psychosomatic etiology received strong theoretical support from the research of N. E. Miller (1969, 1975) and others on visceral learning through both respondent and operant conditioning of bodily processes.

Among the other developments that contributed to the emergence of psychosomatic medicine may be mentioned *constitutional type theories* (see Anastasi, 1958, Ch. 6). These typologies have a long history but are best known to psychologists through the work of Kretschmer (1925) and Sheldon (Sheldon & Stevens, 1942). The earliest expositions of constitutional type theories were concerned with the relation between body build and susceptibility to different diseases. In later formulations, body build came to be associated with characteristic personality patterns as well as with proneness to specific diseases. Such theories thus helped to stimulate investigations into the personality characteristics of persons suffering from given diseases.

Still another early influence, especially evident in psychiatric writings on psychosomatic medicine, was *psychoanalysis.* Beginning with Freud, many psychoanalysts proposed theories regarding the role of conflicts, repressions, and other psychoanalytic mechanisms in the development of physical diseases. These theoretical speculations, bolstered by selected examples from clinical practice, often led to descriptions of the typical personality of patients suffering from different psychosomatic disorders. Some psychoanalysts approached the problem through the symbolic psychoanalytic significance of different organ systems, which allegedly determined the specific psychosomatic disorders each person was likely to develop. Most of these symbolic interpretations, though ingenious, were more fanciful than empirical. Today this approach to psychosomatic illness has been largely abandoned in the light of subsequent research findings.

Research Methodology. Current research on psychosomatic problems reflects the influence of its diverse origins. Following the earlier exploratory work, *animal* *experiments* have been more directly concerned with the production and alleviation of specific psychosomatic symptoms (e.g., Ader, Tatum, & Beels, 1960; Beach, 1952; Brady, 1958; Lown, Verrier, & Corbalan, 1973; Sawrey, 1961; Weiss, 1972). By exposing rats, dogs, cats, monkeys, and other animals to conflictual and stressful situations, experimenters have been able to induce peptic ulcers, asthmalike symptoms, and other familiar psychosomatic disorders.

Short-term experiments of a milder nature have been performed with *human volunteers*. The subject is exposed to a stressful stimulus while various physiological measures are recorded and compared with those obtained under emotionally neutral circumstances. In clinical situations, the discussion of an emotionally charged topic may serve as the stressful situation. In such experiments, it is essential that the situation be one that has genuine emotional significance for the particular subject. This requires considerable knowledge about the individual's attitudes, values, and prior experiences. With suitable emotional stimuli, physiological changes have been demonstrated in a variety of bodily functions, including respiration, blood pressure, heart rate, sweat secretion, muscle potentials in different parts of the body, and acid secretion in the stomach.

Of particular interest are the studies of a few patients who as a result of injury or for therapeutic reasons have a gastric fistula that permits direct observation of the gastric mucosa, or inner lining of the stomach (Coddington, 1968; Engel & Reichsman, 1956; Stein, Kaufman, Janowitz, Levy, Hollander, & Winkelstein, 1962; Wolff & Wolff, 1953). Figure 18-5 illustrates results obtained with one of these patients during a conversation that aroused anger and hostility. It can be seen that stomach contractions were intensified, hydrochloric acid production was more then doubled, and the gastric mucosa reddened as it became engorged with blood.

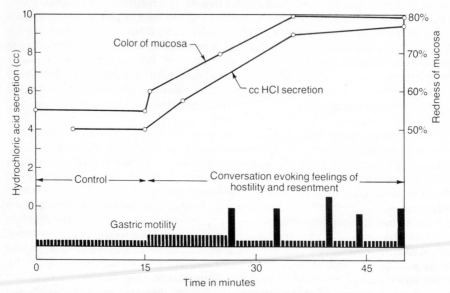

Figure 18-5. Changes in gastric mucosa observed in a patient with a gastric fistula during an emotionally stressful situation. *(Wolff & Wolff, 1953, p. 298. From* Contributions toward Medical Psychology, *edited by Arthur Weider. Copyright © 1953 by The Ronald Press Company. Reproduced by permission.)*

A third and related approach consists in the *longitudinal observation* of patients with psychosomatic disorders. Through such continuing observations, periods of remission or exacerbation of the physical symptoms can be correlated with life experiences. Published reports of such studies indicate a tendency for the patient's physical condition to worsen during periods of emotional stress. Because of the difficulty of maintaining contact with patients for long periods, an adaptation of this method utilizes case-history data (S. Cobb, 1953). Some investigators employed a "life chart" in which each row corresponds to a year in the patient's life. In appropriate columns on this chart, they recorded the patient's medical condition and any significant life events occurring during the year. Again published records indicate fairly close correspondence between experiential factors and the course of such disorders as peptic ulcer and rheumatoid arthritis (S. Cobb, 1953).

The analysis of life charts is less satisfactory than direct longitudinal observation, since it must rely upon the patient's report, and it leaves room for selective bias on the part of both patient and investigator. Both methods, moreover, are limited in that contact with the subject occurs after he or she is in an advanced stage of some somatic disorder. Physiological studies of individuals in the process of responding to life stresses, prior to the onset of pathology or during an early stage in the development of the disorder, are more illuminating, though more difficult to conduct. One such longitudinal study of Army inductees during World War II demonstrated that both physiological and personality variables contribute to the development of ulcers under stressful conditions (Weiner, Thaler, Reiser, & Mirsky, 1957).

A fourth approach analyzes the relation between *onset of illness and stressful life events* in large samples of persons (Gunderson & Rahe, 1974; Holmes & Rahe, 1967). A major stimulus for this research was the development of a quantitative scale for assessing the degree of change and readjustment associated with each of some 40 common life events. Rated on a proportionate scale of Life Change Units (LCU), these events range from death of a spouse (100), marriage (50), being fired from work (47), and pregnancy (40), to change of residence (20), going on a vacation (13), and minor violations of the law (11). The assumption is that life changes, whether favorable or unfavorable, demand adaptation and may therefore elicit varying degrees of stress. Using the Schedule of Recent Experience, the respondent indicates which events he or she has experienced within the last six months, one year, or some other specified period; the total LCU score is the sum of the weights of the reported events. This procedure has been followed with large normal samples of naval personnel in the United States and Norway. It has also been used with several patient samples and their matched normal controls. In all these studies, suggestive relations have been found between LCU score level in any given time period and the number and severity of illnesses occurring during the following period (Gunderson & Rahe, 1974).

Other research on stressful life events has explored the relation between death of the elderly and such occurrences as death of a significant other, relocation, and retirement (Rowland, 1977). The effect of these events on any one individual is a function of the type and amount of required readjustment in life pattern, as well as the individual's resources for coping with the crisis. Moreover, the results obtained with regard to retirement and relocation are often confounded by the person's health. For example, deteriorating health may account for one's early retirement or for a move to a relative's home or to a nursing home. From another angle, the effects of bereavement at any age have been receiving increasing attention (Glick, Weiss, & Parkes, 1974; Parkes, 1972). While there is abundant evidence that bereavement increases vulnerability to illness, much more research is needed to elucidate the specific ways in which the causal relationship may operate.

An excellent discussion of the conceptual and methodological problems involved in stressful life events is given by Dohrenwend and Dohrenwend (1974b, Chs. 1, 17, & 18). The area has attracted investigators from a number of medical and psychological specialties. A major problem pertains to the selection and classification of stressful life events. For instance, are the events differentiated with regard to such categories as favorable or unfavorable, within or outside the individual's control, and anticipated or unanticipated? Some of the reported events may be symptoms or consequences of a developing illness; others may themselves represent the individual's reaction to a stressful event (e.g., changes in eating or sleeping habits). Obviously the inclusion of such events will confound causal analyses, but it would facilitate prediction of illness in individual cases. Investigators also differ with regard to the evaluation of stressfulness of life events. All agree that the degree of stressfulness depends on how the event is perceived, but there is disagreement about *whose* perception should be considered. Should stressfulness be assessed in term's of each individual's perception or in terms of broader cultural or even universal standards? The answers to such questions may vary with the objectives of the particular study and the type of problem under investigation. There is encouraging evidence that research in this area is moving to a higher level of methodological and theoretical sophistication.

Still another type of research on the effect of life events focuses on a single major event that affects many persons. An example is a comprehensive study of the closing of a factory (Kasl & Cobb, 1970; Slote, 1977). Although workers differed widely in the way they coped with the resulting job terminations, approximately half developed such psychosomatic illnesses as ulcers, arthritis, and hypertension. At a more extreme level, studies of prisoners of war and survivors of concentration camps report a high frequency of persisting psychosomatic disorders, as well as cognitive and emotional disturbances (R. J. Arthur, 1974).

A fifth approach is that of *epidemiology.* By comparing the relative frequency of a disorder in different segments of the population, the epidemiologist can test hypotheses about causal influences. Analyses of the prevalence of certain diseases in different occupational groups provide one example of such an approach. It is noteworthy in this connection that surveys conducted in several countries have found peptic ulcer to be significantly more common among foremen than among craftsmen or higher level executives (Dunn & Cobb, 1962). Contrary to popular belief, it is not the top-level executive who is most likely to develop ulcers. Although much more information is needed to arrive at a causal interpretation of such findings, one of the proposed explanations is that role conflicts may increase the emotional stress of the foreman's job.

Along the same lines, a large-scale epidemiological study of Bell Telephone employees found that top executives who had been promoted rapidly had fewer and less serious heart attacks than did employees in lower level business jobs (Hinkle, Whitney, & Lehman, 1968). The same study revealed that persons who had college degrees at the time of employment had a lower incidence of heart attacks than did those without college degrees. Moreover, at the time of the study the college graduates were slimmer and were smoking less than their noncollege counterparts. It is evident that occupational differences in the incidence of psychosomatic illness can be understood only in the light of the many socioeconomic, educational, cultural, and other experiental variables associated with occupational level.

Epidemiological studies have generally found an association between poverty and high risk of psychosomatic disorders (Knapp, 1975). Also relevant are the stress and readjustments demanded by a shift from a rural to an urban environment. Of particular interest in this connection is a series of studies of the industrialization of a farming area in North Carolina (Cassel, Patrick, & Jenkins, 1960; Cassel & Tyroler, 1961; Tyroler & Cassel, 1964). As hypothesized, the "second-generation" factory workers, whose fathers were also employed in industry, had fewer health problems than did the "first-generation" employees, whose fathers were farmers. The emotional stresses accompanying the readjustments and culture conflicts of these first-generation factory workers were thus reflected in poorer health conditions.

From a different angle, psychiatrists and psychologists have investigated the *personality profile* of patients suffering from specific physical disorders. Whereas epidemiological and life-change studies focus on precipitating factors, personality profile studies concentrate on relatively durable predisposing conditions. Much of the early literature on psychosomatic medicine was concerned with the results of this type of study (Dunbar, 1954; S. Marshall, 1960; Watson & Schuld, 1977). Many of the published personality descriptions were derived from selected cases observed under uncontrolled clinical conditions. Data were usually gathered by interviewing. When tests were employed, they were often of questionable validity. More objective studies with random samples and moderately well-matched control groups have usually failed to confirm the hypothesized relations between personality variables and type of disorder.

A further difficulty in the application of this method is the impossibility of inferring causal relations. If, for example, coronary patients manifest excessive anxiety, we do not know whether this condition existed prior to the onset of the physical disability or whether it is the patient's reaction to the physical handicap and to the frustrations it imposes. Only a longitudinal study begun prior to the onset of the physical disorder can answer this question. A further complication arises from the possible behavioral effects of reduced blood supply to the brain, changes in blood content, and other physiological aspects of the disease itself. Drugs administered to treat the physical disorder may also influence emotional and intellectual responses.

Most of these methodological difficulties can be avoided by studying large normal samples, such as the employees of a department store or the members of a city fire department, and subsequently identifying those persons who develop a particular disease. This prospective, or predictive, approach was followed in some of the research on proneness to coronary heart disease in relation to so-called Type A and Type B personality patterns (Friedman & Rosenman, 1974; Jenkins, Rosenman, & Zyzansky, 1974). Type A, characterized by high coronary risk, is described as competitive, achievement oriented, highly involved in work and other activities subject to deadlines, and tending to react rapidly in speech and movements. Persons lacking these characteristics, designated as Type B, were found to be less prone to coronary disease. It might be noted that the description of Type A closely resembles the popular stereotype of upwardly mobile executives who, according to the previously cited Bell Telephone study, had relatively low coronary risk. Perhaps the psychosomatic stress results not so much from the striving itself as from the frustrations of motivated strivers whose achievements lag behind their ambition.

Current Trends. It is now widely recognized that the relation between emotional stress and somatic disorders is more complex than that implied in the personality-type theories. Because of methodological difficulties, studies purporting to show the association of characteristic personality profiles with specific psychosomatic syndromes are of questionable value. An examination of the proposed personality descriptions, moreover, reveals considerable similarity among the traits attributed to persons with different diseases, such as peptic ulcer, hypertension, and rheumatoid arthritis. Which specific syndrome develops is a resultant of (1) the suceptibility of different organ systems of the individual to pathology, (2) the individual's characteristic behavioral style for coping with psychological stress, and (3) the nature of environmental events—both physical and psychological—that precipitate the pathology.

A parallel trend in psychosomatic medicine is to regard *all* diseases as having both psychogenic and somatogenic components, rather than labeling a few as psychosomatic. As early as the 1950s, psychosomatic medicine began to include more and more specialties, such as surgery, gynecology, and ophthalmology (Dunbar, 1954, Chs. 1 & 17; Grinker, 1951). More recently, there has been considerable interest in the role of psychological factors in the etiology of cancer (Bahnson, 1969; Bahnson & Kissen, 1966; Cullen, Fox, & Isom, 1976). Another example is provided by bruxism, a nonfunctional gnashing and grinding of the teeth, which may lead to serious dental pathology (Glaros & Rao, 1977). Long neglected by psychologists, this condition is coming to be recognized as one that calls for a combined dental and behavioral approach.

Today, the concept of psychosomatic medicine has broadened to mean a consideration of the total reacting organism in its environment. Psychosomatic medicine thus stands for a point of view applicable to the practice of all medicine, rather than representing a branch of medicine. In recognition of the pronounced shift in orientation since the early phases of the psychosomatic movement, some medical writers now prefer the term "psychophysiological medicine" (e.g., H. I. Kaplan, 1975; Knapp, 1975). Moreover, the field is very broadly conceived as "a complex interface between the expanding bodies of behavioral and medical sciences" (Knapp, 1975, p. 1632). An equally broad conceptualization has been proposed by some psychologists (Lachman, 1972; L. Wright, 1977).

SOMATOPSYCHOLOGY

General Nature. Psychosomatic medicine began with investigations of the somatic effects of such psychological factors as emotional stress. Beginning at the opposite angle, some psychologists had been studying the individual's psychological reactions to physical illness or disability. Barker and his associates (Barker & Wright, 1954; Barker, Wright, Meyerson, & Gonick, 1953; B. A. Wright, 1960), coined the term "somatopsychology" for this field. More recently Lachman (1972) has discussed a similar relationship under the rubric of somatopsychic problems. Although this is a relatively unexplored research area, it has attracted increasing interest through its practical implications for rehabilitation programs.

In somatopsychology, the individual's body is regarded "as a tool for behavior, and as an object with social significance to himself and others" (Barker & Wright, 1954, p. 419). For example, an orthopedic disability that seriously affects locomotion and other motor responses will interfere with social interaction, with schooling, and with other normal childhood activities. Such experiential limitations, unless remedied by other means, will retard intellectual growth and influence personality development in various ways. Conspicuous physical anomalies may also affect psychological development through the reactions of associates. Pity, avoidance, oversolicitousness, rejection, repulsion, and many other emotionally charged attitudes tend to make the disabled individual's social environment different from that of physically normal persons. The individual's self-concept and his or her own attitude toward the disability are likely to be profoundly affected by such atypical experiences.

Long-term Psychological Effects. Exploratory studies have been conducted on the psychological effects of many types of physical disability, including deafness, blindness, amputation, facial disfigurement, tuberculosis, poliomyelitis, cerebral palsy, multiple sclerosis, and paraplegia, among others (Barker et al., 1953; Garrett & Levine, 1962; Kutner, 1971; Shontz, 1971; Siller & Silverman, 1958; B. A. Wright, 1960). Patients in these various categories have been investigated through intensive case studies, interviews, questionnaires, and projective tests. The results of such studies show that there is no consistent association between specific forms of disability and particular personality characteristics. There are no psychological traits that uniformly differentiate, let us say, the blind, the deaf, or the orthopedically handicapped from persons with other disabilities or from physically normal persons. As a group, the severely disabled tend to show some maladjustment, in the form of anxiety, depression, and social isolation. Even these group differences, however, are slight, and the overlapping with physically normal persons is extensive.

Studies of physically disabled *individuals,* on the other hand, reveal that the physical disability often has a profound effect upon behavior. The discrepancy between individual and group results arises from the fact that the psychological effect of disability takes many different forms in different persons. The end result in the individual's behavior depends upon a three-way interaction among: (1) nature and severity of handicap; (2) individual personality and ability variables; and (3) situational variables in home, school, job, and social contexts. Heterogeneity in the effects of specific physical disabilities upon individual behavior is one of the best-established findings of somatopsychology. The individual's attitude toward his or her disability is an important link in the chain of circumstances leading to particular behavioral effects.

Immediate Reactions to Illness. While the above research pertains to long-range and relatively permanent effects of physical disability upon intellectual and personality development, several investigators have been concerned with the individual's immediate response to illness, hospitalization, and treatment. Patient reactions to such conditions as tuberculosis, cancer, and heart disease have been investigated. Several studies have dealt with responses to surgery. Others have focused on specific types of treatment most likely to be psychologically disruptive, such as mastectomy, amputations, and hemodialysis.

Research on reactions to illness and hospitalization is illustrated by a series of studies undertaken cooperatively by psychologists in a number of Veterans Administration hospitals. In the first of these studies, data were obtained from nearly 800 male patients hospitalized for pulmonary tuberculosis (Vernier, Barrell, Cummings, Dickerson, & Hooper, 1961). This disease was chosen because it presents a particularly difficult adjustment problem during treatment. Inasmuch as the disease is contagious, the patient must be isolated. Treatment is slow and frustrating, the patients being hospitalized for long periods during which they may feel perfectly fit. In addition, the threats of possible lung surgery and permanent disability evoke anxiety and depression.

In the study, rating scales, interviews, and questionnaires were used to arrive at criterion indices of hospital adjustment and of subsequent community adjustment. These indices were correlated with biographical data and with scores on a battery of psychological tests. One of the suggestive findings of the study was that the type of person who adjusts well to the hospital tends to make a poorer community adjustment after discharge. Conversely, those making a good community adjustment tended to be more resistant to the regimentation and inactivity typical of the tuberculosis ward. The passivity, acquiescence, and dependence conducive to good hospital adjustment contrast sharply with the personal qualities demanded by the posthospital environment. Only one psychological variable, anxiety, was found to be detrimental to both hospital and community adjustment.

Patients' reactions to a diagnosis of cancer and to their subsequent hospitalization and treatment also provide a fruitful field for psychological research (B. Cobb, 1962). Because of the high mortality from some forms of this disease, insufficient knowledge about its nature, the possibility of disfiguring surgery, and the many superstitious beliefs associated with it, cancer engenders unusually high anxiety in most patients. Attitudes of relatives also play an important part in the patient's reaction to this disease. The psychologist in a cancer hospital can do much to reduce misunderstandings and allay anxieties.

Even with terminal cancer patients, psychological counseling for the acceptance of death has much to contribute to the patient's emotional well-being (B. Cobb, 1962; Feifel, Freilich, & Hermann, 1973). To perform effectively in this role, the psychologist needs considerable information about individuals' attitudes toward their own death. Largely neglected prior to the 1960s, psychological research on death and dying has been undergoing conspicuous expansion, as evidenced by the rapid accumulation of publications on the subject (Feifel, 1977; Kastenbaum & Aisenberg, 1976; Kastenbaum & Costa, 1977; Shneidman, 1976; Weisman, 1974). A substantial beginning has been made in exploring attitudes toward death held by individuals at different age levels, from early childhood to old age. Surveys of terminally ill patients suggest, among other findings, that feelings of being abandoned and rejected often augment the patient's dread. As might be anticipated, a given patient's reaction to imminent death depends upon many individual and situational variables. But most patients want to discuss their impending death and resent evasiveness and withdrawal by their associates. This finding was highlighted in the pioneer research of Feifel (1959) and has been repeatedly corroborated by subsequent investigators.

Relation between Patient Attitudes and Recovery. Still another type of investigation is concerned with the effect of patient attitudes upon recovery from illness. In the previously mentioned study of patients with pulmonary tuberculosis in Veterans Administration hospitals, biographical and test data were also correlated with indices of recovery as determined from x-ray films and bacteriological tests (Vernier et al., 1961). Favorable response to treatment was found to be significantly correlated with freedom from anxiety and with personal confidence. Rapid recovery also tended to be associated with an "experimenting," intellectual orientation as contrasted with a cautious and conservative attitude. Although these specific findings should be regarded as tentative and preliminary, the fact that patients in identical physical condition may respond very differently to treatment has long been recognized in clinical practice.

Similar observations have been reported by physicians treating cancer patients, and some exploratory research has been undertaken to identify psychological characteristics associated with differential recovery rate. Independent research projects conducted at different hospitals have provided suggestive evidence that patients' attitudes toward their illness and other personality characteristics are related to the likelihood of recovery from certain forms of cancer (B. Cobb, 1962; Gengerelli & Levine, 1962). Findings from joint psychological and biochemical research suggest the role of hormones as a possible mediating factor in this relationship.

Further data can be found in a well-designed study of the role of various psychological factors in recovery from acute myocardial infarction (Cromwell, Butterfield, Brayfield, & Curry, 1977). Length of hospital stay and susceptibility to further infarctions were found to be related to such variables as patient information about cardiac problems, the presence of diversion (e.g., television, reading matter), and participation in one's own treatment. There is also considerable clinical evidence that (1) recovery from surgery and other stressful forms of treatment is influenced by the patient's attitudes and expectations; and (2) depression, "giving up," and loss of the "will to live" may lead to death in a patient who is not critically ill (Kastenbaum & Costa, 1977, pp. 237–238; Secunda, 1973, p. 7; Weisman & Kastenbaum, 1968). This attitude of hopelessness has been linked to the "learned helplessness" syndrome identified by Seligman (1975) in his animal and human research (see Ch. 14).

With these studies on the effect of attitudes upon recovery from physical illness we have come full circle and are back to a psychosomatic relationship. By now it should be apparent that the separation of different types of relation between psychological factors and physical illness, while desirable for purposes of analysis, cannot be sharply maintained in practice. The way in which individuals adjust to the complex changes in their life patterns brought about by illness or physical disability depends to a large extent upon their pre-disability personality. The individual who has difficulty in coping with life stresses and as a result develops a physical illness may also have difficulty in coping with the discomforts and frustrations engendered by that illness, which further retards or prevents recovery in a continuing vicious circle. Both psychosomatic medicine and somatopsychology can thus be recognized as two aspects of a comprehensive psychophysiological approach to illness. This emerging field is coming to be identified by the term "behavioral medicine," as illustrated by the establishment in 1978 of the Academy of Behavioral Medicine Research and the publication of the *Journal of Behavioral Medicine*.

SUMMARY

Although the role of psychological factors in medical practice has been recognized for centuries, it was not until after World War II that contacts between psychology and medicine attained significant proportions. Even now, the potential contributions of psychology to medicine are largely undeveloped. In medical practice, psychology can aid in diagnosis, treatment, rehabilitation, and prevention. Apart from their utilization of psychodiagnostic data, physicians can profit from psychological knowledge in conducting medical interviews and in evaluating introspective reports by patients. Computers are being used increasingly to improve and facilitate several phases of the diagnostic process. In treatment, the role of interpersonal relations between physician and patient is widely recognized. The movement to humanize and personalize health care, with its emphasis on the whole patient in his or her environment, has advanced the application of psychology to medicine. Among the problems under investigation are compliance with prescribed regimens, continuation in treatment, and the alleviation of patient anxiety. In rehabilitation, the psychologist typically functions as a member of a team composed of health professionals from various fields. Rehabilitation psychology has broadened to cover not only counseling but also training and the design of prosthetic equipment and environments. Preventive medicine requires effective two-way communication between lay public and public health personnel. In this respect, its problems have much in common with those of consumer psychology. Other psychological contributions to preventive medicine range from basic research on health-related behaviors to the development of behavior modification programs.

Since midcentury, the participation of psychologists in medical school teaching has grown rapidly in terms of both the number of psychologists so employed and the scope of their functions. Psychologists have long been involved in the development and evaluation of tests and other assessment procedures for medical school admission, licensing, and certification. The patient-management problem provides a promising technique for both training and assessment. A major contribution that psychology can make to medicine is in research. Among the most active areas of collaborative research are psychopharmacology, the nature and relief of pain, and biofeedback.

Modern psychosomatic medicine dates from the mid-thirties. Its antecedents stem from such varied sources as physiological psychology, constitutional type theories, and psychoanalysis. Current research techniques include the artificial production of psychosomatic disorders in animals, experimental investigation of the effects of stress upon human physiological functions, longitudinal observations and case studies of patients with psychosomatic disorders, analysis of the relation between onset of illness and stressful life events, epidemiological surveys, and personality studies of patients with different physical syndromes.

Somatopsychology begins from the opposite angle, focusing upon the psychological effects of physical illness and disability. It is concerned with both long-range effects upon intellectual and personality development and immediate responses to illness, hospitalization, treatment, and impending death. Some suggestive data have been reported on the effect of patients' attitudes and other personality characteristics upon recovery from such illnesses as tuberculosis and cancer. Both somatopsychology and psychosomatic medicine may be regarded as two aspects of a comprehensive psychophysiological approach to illness.

PSYCHOLOGY AND LAW

ITH ITS HEAVY RELIANCE upon precedent, the practice of law is characteristically resistant to change. Current laws as well as judicial procedures are often based upon outdated theories of human behavior and are at variance with experimentally established facts. This cultural inertia is generally defended on the grounds that law, dealing as it does with matters that may have serious consequences for the persons involved, must move cautiously. Thus it is argued that "new" findings, concepts, and techniques provided by a rapidly developing science such as psychology cannot be accepted as guides in legal practice until they have become so firmly established as to meet with virtual unanimity among psychologists themselves.

The effect of this policy, however, is that the psychological principles actually followed in legal practice are sometimes so manifestly obsolete as to be almost unanimously rejected by psychologists. [1] In all practical action, decisions must be made in the absence of complete certainty. Under such circumstances, wisdom requires that all the information available at the time be utilized in choosing the best course of action. Modern medicine provides a good example of this approach. For most diseases, there is no therapy that guarantees 100% success. Nor would there be complete agreement about the best therapy to follow in any particular case. Yet this state of affairs is not used to justify a continuation of the medical practices of the Middle Ages.

Today there are several indications within the field of law that efforts are being made to bring legal practice into closer touch with developments in both natural and social sciences. Among law professors, jurists, and law enforcement officers, a few outstanding individuals have encouraged research into social problems and have introduced techniques and findings of modern science into their own work.

[1] This dilemma is reminiscent of what in statistics are known as Type I and Type II errors.

RESURGENCE OF A MULTIFACETED FIELD

Within psychology, there was an early period of vigorous research and publication on certain aspects of legal psychology, followed by a steady decline from the 1930s to the 1970s. Oddly enough, the psychology of testimony represents one of the earliest areas of applied psychology. Among the pioneers in this research was William Stern, who not only conducted studies of his own but also edited a journal on this topic, *Beiträge zur Psychologie der Aussage,* published at Leipzig during the first decade of this century.[2] During the same period, Alfred Binet, of intelligence test fame, was also conducting research and publishing on the psychology of testimony (Binet, 1905). In America, Harvard professor Hugo Münsterberg (1908) wrote *On the Witness Stand,* a book summarizing relevant psychological studies. Between 1909 and 1917, the *Psychological Bulletin* published annual reviews on the psychology of testimony, prepared by G. M. Whipple. Research on problems of testimony continued until the early 1930s, after which activity lapsed for some 30 years.

From another angle, as early as 1909, Healy established the first psychological clinic attached to a juvenile court and soon initiated continuing research on juvenile delinquency (Healy & Bronner, 1936). Such early books as Burtt's *Legal Psychology* (1931) and E. S. Robinson's *Law and the Lawyers* (1935) illustrated a variety of ways in which psychologists could contribute to law. Still other facets of this diversified field were sketched in later books such as *Psychology for Law Enforcement Officers* (Dudycha, 1955) and *Legal and Criminal Psychology* (Toch, 1961). The intervening decades since 1930, however, produced only sporadic and meager research. Interest in the interface of psychology and law declined, as evidenced by the drop in the proportion of psychological publications dealing with this field (Brodsky, 1976; Tapp, 1976). It was not until the 1970s that Gormally and Brodsky (1973) were able to write, "The 40-year downward trend toward diminished involvement of psychologists in justice work seems to have stopped and been reversed" (p. 928).

Like most fields of applied psychology, that of psychology and law took a quantum leap in the late 1960s and early 1970s (Tapp, 1976). This growth spurt extends from basic research to program development and a wide spectrum of service functions. It is evidenced by conspicuous development in publications, conferences, societies, and academic programs. The participants are drawn from such specialties as clinical, counseling, community, social, experimental, and child psychology. A substantial number of psychologists are now members of such burgeoning organizations as the American Psychology-Law Society, the International Academy of Forensic Psychology, and the American Association of Correctional Psychologists. Among its other functions, the American Psychology-Law Society has sponsored and cosponsored an increasing number of programs at the annual convention of the American Psychological Association. These conventions have shown a marked upswing in the number of symposia, workshops, paper sessions, and invited addresses by both psychologists and lawyers on a wide array of topics of common interest. Within the APA there has also been a proliferation of

[2]This journal was superseded in 1908 by the much broader *Zeitschrift für angewande Psychologie,* also edited by Stern. It is interesting to note that the first journal of applied psychology evolved from a publication initially devoted to the psychology of testimony.

task forces and committees on specialized psycholegal areas; and psychologists have been appointed on committees in various legal associations.

Among the new journals established in the 1970s are *Criminal Justice and Behavior* and *Law and Human Behavior,* the latter launched in 1977 with the collaboration of the American Psychology-Law Society. There is also evidence of a growing rapprochement of the two fields in academic institutions, with the establishment of several joint programs at both graduate and undergraduate levels (Brodsky, 1976; Tapp, 1976). And there is increasing involvement of psychologists as principal investigators in federally funded research projects on law-related problems.

In the present chapter, the diversified contributions of psychologists will be illustrated within four broad areas concerned with (1) the judicial process, as represented by court procedures; (2) the nature, sources, and development of antisocial behavior; (3) the professional roles of psychologists in the criminal justice system; and (4) applications of psychology in the development of laws and policy at the national and international levels.

PSYCHOLOGY AND THE JUDICIAL PROCESS

From its earliest beginnings at the turn of the century to its resurgence in the 1970s, psycholegal research has been concerned with several aspects of court procedures. The problems investigated have been as specific as the effect of the grammatical form of the question upon the accuracy of testimony (Loftus & Zanni, 1975) and as broad as the relative strengths and weaknesses of the adversary and inquisitorial systems of judicial procedures (Thibaut & Walker, 1975). In this section we shall consider: research on eyewitness testimony, which has had a long history but minimal impact on legal practice; the overpopularized techniques of so-called lie detection; and the recent flurry of interest in jury research. Finally, we shall take a look at the utilization of psychologists as expert witnesses, which represents still another way of applying the research data-base of psychology in court proceedings.

Eyewitness Testimony. Much of what psychology can contribute to the evaluation of courtroom testimony is derived from established facts of sensation, perception, memory, and other familiar areas of experimental psychology (Burtt, 1931, Chs. 2–4; J. Marshall, 1966). Among the most relevant findings are those pertaining to: localization of sounds; visual illusions, such as the overestimation of vertical as contrasted to horizontal distances, the overestimation of filled as contrasted to unfilled spaces, and the influence of contextual factors upon length estimation as illustrated by the Müller-Lyer illusion; estimation of short time intervals and of the speed of moving vehicles; and adaptation phenomena, such as shifts between light-adapted and dark-adapted vision and adaptation effects in the perception of odors, temperature, and other continuing stimuli. In another area, studies of incidental memory suggest that more reliance can be placed upon the testimony of a witness who realized she or he might later have to report on the events observed than on one who observed them casually and with no effort to memorize facts. Of particular relevance to legal testimony is the finding that strong emotion at the time of observation or subsequent report tends to increase the probability of error.

A specific example of the bearing that psychological research on perception may have upon the evaluation of legal testimony is provided by the case of a Canadian hunter who, mistaken for a deer, was shot and killed by his companions (Sommer, 1959). The victim was wearing faded red coveralls and was seen just before sunset on a very overcast day. The first pertinent psychological observation derives from the Purkinje phenomenon. As illumination diminishes, colors at the red end of the spectrum decrease in brightness faster than do those at the blue end. Consequently, red objects are among the first to lose their color as light fades. A second relevant psychological fact concerns the effect of set, or expectation, upon the perception of an ambiguous stimulus. The hunters, who were eagerly scanning the landscape for deer, perceived the moving object as a deer. When a policeman later observed a man under the same conditions, knowing it was a man, he perceived the object as a man.

Experiments designed specifically with reference to legal testimony typically employ a simulation procedure introduced by William Stern (1939). In such experiments, the subjects may be shown a short film depicting a robbery, a traffic accident, or an attempted kidnapping. Or a brief and exciting episode may be unexpectedly enacted before them. For example, during a class period, a stranger may rush into the classroom and engage in an angry altercation with the instructor. In every case, the subjects are subsequently asked to report on what they witnessed.

By these procedures, accuracy of report has been investigated in relation to a number of variables, such as length of delay, prior instructions, suggestion, degree of emotional involvement, and observer characteristics (Lipton, 1977; J. Marshall, 1966, Ch. 2). One of the principal findings of this research is that errorless reports are rare. The usual reaction is to fill in the gaps in one's observation or recall of the scene with plausible details that are consistent with the individual's general perception of the event. The subject is often certain that he or she actually observed such a detail, although it was only suggested by the context. Under these conditions, moreover, agreement among several witnesses is no guarantee of factual correctness, nor is it evidence of collusion. Such spurious consistency may result simply from constant errors that affect the responses of different persons. Thus another deep-rooted legal tradition regarding the validity of testimony is called into question.

For the usual reason of accessibility, most of these studies have been conducted with college students. Some efforts have been made, however, to work with other, more representative or appropriate populations, such as law students, police academy trainees, and groups sampling different educational and socioeconomic levels (J. Marshall, 1966). The increasing collaboration of psychologists and lawyers in such research has also encouraged the design of more realistically oriented procedures. It is interesting to note that William Stern (1939) recommended the use of such testimony tests in the training of law students. By observing their own performance in the role of witness, prospective lawyers could thus gain a realistic understanding of the limitations of courtroom testimony.

Among the conditions commonly investigated in eyewitness research is the method of eliciting information from the witness (Bingham et al., 1959, Ch. 10; Burtt, 1931, Chs. 5 & 6; Lipton, 1977; Loftus, 1975; Loftus & Zanni, 1975). Several experiments have demonstrated that with free narration, in which witnesses report the incident in their own words, accuracy is higher than with direct questioning. When asked specific questions, most persons give more details than in a free recital, but a larger percentage of their report is wrong. Under the more hostile or confusing type of questioning involved in cross-examination, accuracy tends to drop still further.

Some data are also available regarding the form of the question. Leading questions that suggest a particular answer obviously tend to encourage false recall. Questions containing a hidden assumption likewise have a strong suggestive effect. If asked whether the defendant held the gun in his right or left hand, witnesses may honestly come to believe they saw a gun that was not actually there. Even the grammatical form of a question may exert an influence upon the response "Wasn't there a car parked in front of the bank?" is a more suggestive question than "Was there a car parked in front of the bank?" Directing attention to the witnesses themselves as observers tends to increase response accuracy and caution. "Did you see a car?" is more likely to elicit a correct response than "Was there a car?" Even such an apparently minor difference as the use of definite or indefinite articles affects the accuracy of testimony. In an experiment in which students viewed a short film depicting a multicar accident, half were asked questions of the form, "Did you see *a* broken headlight?" For the other half, the corresponding questions were of the form, "Did you see *the* broken headlight?" The results showed that subjects who were asked "the" questions were more likely to report having seen an item— whether or not it had really appeared in the film—than were those who were asked "a" questions (Loftus & Zanni, 1975).

A problem that has received considerable attention in current psycholegal research is that of eyewitness identification (Brown, Deffenbacher, & Sturgill, 1977; Buckhout, 1974; Leippe, Wells, & Ostrom, 1978; Levine & Tapp, 1973). The problem concerns the identification of suspects by crime victims or witnesses from mugshots and/or police lineups. Studies in both laboratory and field settings have highlighted many common sources of inaccuracy in such identifications. For example, a carefully designed series of laboratory experiments demonstrated that observers are much better able to recognize a face than to recall where they saw it (E. Brown et al., 1977). In one of these experiments, live models were employed both in the initial ("criminal") observation period and in the later lineup; in addition, mugshot photos of the same persons were presented along with those of persons not previously seen. Of particular interest was the finding that suspects who had been seen only in the mugshots were often identified as the "criminal" in the subsequent lineup. The same investigation found a lack of correlation between the accuracy of eyewitness identification and reported confidence. On the basis of experiments such as these, some psychologists have recommended the type of cautions that should be observed in obtaining eyewitness identification in order to guard against common sources of suggestion and confusion.[3]

Lie Detection. The preceding section was concerned with testimony given by a witness who is motivated to be accurate and truthful. In many types of interrogation, however, the respondent tries to conceal or disguise facts or to mislead the investigator in other ways. The procedures discussed in this section share the common objective of obtaining correct information under the latter conditions. So-called lie detectors are now employed for this purpose in many countries

[3]*E.g., How fair is your lineup? A reliability checkup for lineups.* Center for Responsive Psychology, Brooklyn College of the City University of New York, Brooklyn, N. Y. 11210.

throughout the world (Barland & Raskin, 1973). They are being used not only in police departments but also in military services, government agencies, and many types of commercial enterprises. In all these contexts, a lie detector should be used only on a voluntary basis and with the examinee's full knowledge of what the procedure is designed to accomplish. The ethical questions of invasion of privacy and informed consent are clearly relevant to this situation.

As ordinarily employed in criminal investigation, the lie detector serves to narrow down the field of suspects and to channel further investigation in the most promising directions. Its greatest potential benefit is to protect the innocent from prolonged harassment and possibly false imprisonment (Lykken, 1974). It offers a safeguard against the hazards of false eyewitness identification discussed in the preceding section. In occupational settings, lie detectors have been used not only in internal investigations of employee thefts but also in screening applicants for certain types of jobs, such as those involving access to money, drugs, or classified information. For these purposes, their application is more questionable, for at least two reasons. First, as will be seen shortly, employment screening precludes the utilization of the more effective methodological designs. Second, in these contexts, *final* decisions about hiring and firing have often been made on the basis of lie detector results. This is not a defensible practice, especially in the light of the less valid procedures used with job applicants, and it has in fact been outlawed in several states (Coghill, 1968; Lykken, 1974).

Scientific efforts to differentiate between truthful and deceptive statements through concurrent bodily changes date back nearly a century (Barland & Raskin, 1973; Burtt, 1931, Chs.9-11; Orne, Thackray, & Paskewitz, 1972; Podlesny & Raskin, 1977). From the vast array of physiological processes thus investigated, those most commonly included in current lie detectors are respiration, blood pressure, and galvanic skin response (GSR). It has long been known that changes in respiration and blood pressure occur during emotional arousal. The use of the GSR is based on the fact that even slight increases in secretion of the sweat glands can be detected by a rise in the electrical conductivity of the skin. The typical commercial polygraphs used in lie detection provide simultaneous, continuous monitoring of all three processes.

Basically, the lie detector paradigm involves a comparison of the individual's responses to critical and neutral stimuli. The critical stimuli or questions refer specifically to the crime or incident under investigation. They will presumably arouse more emotional excitement than will the innocuous neutral stimuli. Of course, innocent subjects are also likely to respond more emotionally when asked whether they stole the money from the cash box than when asked the date of their birth. For this reason, most polygraph techniques also include "control" questions, designed to be intrinsically emotion-arousing but unrelated to the present crime. The assumption is that the responses of the guilty person to critical and control items will differ, while those of the innocent will not. Much depends on the feasibility of devising control and critical items that are truly comparable in their emotional impact on the innocent suspects.[4]

It should be noted that, while some psychologists are engaged in lie detection research and consultation, the large majority of polygraph practitioners are

---

[4]For detailed descriptions of standard procedures and their many variants, see Barland and Raskin (1973).

nonpsychologists. The polygraph schools recognized by the American Polygraph Association, including commercial and military centers, rarely have psychologists on their regular staff. Insofar as polygraph techniques represent an application of physiological psychology and psychometrics, however, there is an obvious need for the closer involvement of psychologists in consultation, research, and training in this area.

Field studies of the effectiveness of polygraphic techniques generally report extremely high rates of correct identification. Some highly experienced practitioners claim close to 100% accuracy for the records that they can interpret with confidence, after excluding doubtful or ambiguous cases. The high optimism engendered by these surveys must be tempered by a consideration of the unsystematic and uncontrolled nature of the data on which they are based (Barland & Raskin, 1973; Lykken, 1974). A common limitation of field studies is that for many of the cases there is no independent, objective criterion of guilt against which the polygraph findings can be properly validated. An even more serious difficulty—shared by field studies and laboratory studies of simulated "crimes" that use the standard lie detection procedure—is that the examiner who interprets the polygraph records also has access to additional sources of information about the subject. These include case records, extensive pretest and posttest interviewing, and continuous observation of the subject's behavior during the polygraph test.

One of the rare studies that analyzed the conclusions reached by experienced polygraph practitioners on the basis of polygraph records alone failed to support the usual optimistic claims (Horvath, 1977). Blind judgments of the polygraph records of 112 criminal suspects by 10 field-trained practitioners agreed with the original examiner's judgments, on the average, in only 63% of the records (against a chance expectancy of 50%). Agreement of the "blind" evaluators with each other was substantially higher. The findings strongly suggest that field examiners are normally influenced by cues extraneous to the polygraph records.

In a searching critique of the typical lie detection technique, Lykken (1974) concluded that (1) empirical reports of high success rates are open to serious question; and (2) a theoretical analysis of the customary procedures indicates that the expected probability of valid judgments is very low. As a viable alternative, he recommends a variant of the *guilty knowledge technique*. Essentially, this general approach utilizes a set of stimuli which would all be neutral for the innocent, but some of which would be critical for the guilty person. For example, suppose the crime under investigation is the theft of a green purse containing, among other things, $34 in cash, a card with the name Henry Donohue, and a book of matches from the Morningside Coffee Shop. In this case, the terms "green," "34," "Henry Donohue," and "Morningside" represent critical stimuli, whose association with the crime is known only to the culprit. To be sure, this implies that such details have not been publicized by the media or otherwise communicated to innocent suspects. But, as Lykken observes, if details that are intrinsically trivial are selected for this purpose, it should be feasible to find a sufficient number that have not been publicized. The technique, however, is not applicable to the screening of job applicants, in which no particular "crime" is being investigated.

The specific procedure designed by Lykken consists of a set of multiple-choice questions, one for each critical item. An example could be, "Was the color of the purse: black, brown, blue, green, red?" The subject could be instructed to give some predetermined verbal response to each alternative; or he could be required simply to listen while his polygraph responses are recorded. The expectation is that, for each item, the guilty suspect is likely to show the largest polygraph response to the critical alternative (i.e., green). As Lykken (1974) points out, the probability of this occurring by chance for an innocent suspect is $\frac{1}{5}$ or .2 for each item. The probability that it would occur on three items is $(\frac{1}{5})^3$ or .008; and on six items, the chances are less than 1 in 1,000. Experimental studies of this technique with both college student and prisoner samples have thus far yielded highly promising evidence of its validity (Ben Shakhar, Lieblich, & Kugelmass, 1970; Davidson, 1968; Lieblich, Ben Shakhar, & Kugelmass, 1976; Lykken, 1959, 1960). The technique offers a fruitful avenue for further exploration and merits trial in real-life criminal investigations.

Jury Research. Studies of the variables that influence the jury's *decision process* were conducted since the early decades of the century and continued as a trickle of scattered research through the 1950s and early 1960s (Burtt, 1931, Ch. 7; Toch, 1961, Ch. 5). Like other aspects of psycholegal research, such studies exhibited renewed vitality in the late 1960s, spearheaded by the publication of *The American Jury* (Kalven & Zeisel, 1966), a major report from the University of Chicago Jury Project. This type of research utilizes two principal procedures: (1) interviewing or mailing questionnaires to jurors or judges after trial, and (2) presenting simulated trials (or selected aspects of court procedure) to mock juries of college or law students or more representative samples drawn from actual jury pools (Bermant, Nemeth, & Vidmar, 1976, Chs. 1 & 7–12; Davis, Bray, & Holt, 1977; Gerbasi, Zuckerman, & Reis, 1977; Saks, 1977; Tapp, 1976).

Among the variables investigated are demographic characteristics of jurors, such as education, occupation, and sex, in relation both to jury behavior (e.g., amount of participation in discussion, influence on other jurors) and to type of verdict. Attitudinal variables, such as authoritarianism and internal-external locus of control, have been similarly studied. The effect of victim and defendant characteristics on jury decisions and their interaction with juror variables have also been investigated.

Considerable research has been concerned with the influence of various court procedures on jurors' decisions. For example, judges' instructions to ignore inadmissible evidence presented during the trial were found to have no significant effect on jury verdict. On the other hand, the number and severity of decision alternatives given to the jury does affect the proportion of guilty versus nonguilty verdicts. For instance, if the only options are first-degree murder and not guilty, a much larger percentage of jurors will choose "not guilty" than when the options are manslaughter and not guilty or when more options are available.

Also relevant are jurors' conceptions of what constitutes "reasonable doubt," as a basis for a not-guilty verdict in a criminal trial. In a questionnaire study, respondents were asked to state what would have to be the probability that the defendant had actually committed the crime to justify a guilty verdict. The reported probabilities were higher for judges and students than for real jurors. They also varied with the nature of the crime: for jurors, the mean required probability ranged from .95 for murder to .75 for petty larceny (Simon & Mahan, 1971). Among the other variables investigated are size of jury (12, 9, or 6), decision rule (unanimous or two-thirds majority), and videotaped versus live presentation of evidence.

Several studies, usually conducted with student groups, have dealt with more specialized questions, such as the effect of order of presentation upon persuasiveness of evidence (Hovland, 1957; Lawson, 1969; W. J. McGuire, 1964; Miller & Campbell, 1959; V. Stone, 1969; Walker, Thibaut, & Andreoli, 1972; Weld & Roff, 1938). In a typical experiment (Weld & Roff, 1938), a detailed report of a criminal case was divided into sections and read to groups of prelaw students acting as jurors. At the end of each section, the subjects rated their belief in the defendant's innocence or guilt on a 9-point scale. Figure 19-I shows the median rating assigned by the group after each installment of evidence was heard. It can be seen that the judgment of guilt rose with successive presentation of prosecution evidence and dropped with successive presentation of defense evidence. To test the effect of order of presentation, the same evidence was presented in a different order to each of two groups, A and B. When all the prosecution evidence was given first and the defense second, the final median guilt rating was 2.3. When the series began and ended with prosecution items, with the defense items sandwiched in between, the final median guilt rating was 5.4. In the latter arrangement, the prosecution evidence had more influence because of a recency effect. This is the practice currently followed in most states (Lana, 1972).

In general, all this research suggests that a variety of extraneous variables—both individual and procedural—may significantly affect jury verdicts. Conclusions must still be regarded as tentative, however, because of methodological limitations. When student groups are used, the obvious population differences are likely to limit generalizability of findings. Another limitation arises from the fact that several studies report individual verdicts rather than a group consensus as reached by the typical jury deliberation. To be sure, a number of studies *have* used representative samples from jury pools and group consensus; but even in such cases, the conditions are certainly not identical to those encountered in a real trial. Posttrial interviews of real juries, based on recall and verbal reporting, also have obvious limitations.

A more specialized involvement of psychologists in the judicial process, which

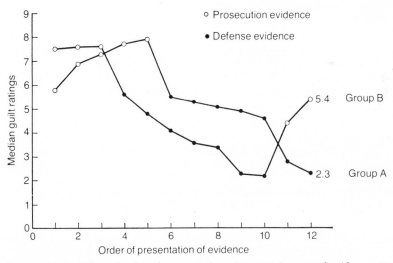

Figure 19-1. Effect of order of presentation on persuasiveness of evidence. *(Data from Weld & Roff, 1938, pp. 619, 622.)*

attracted considerable attention in the 1970s, is the use of psychological techniques as an aid in *jury selection* (Bermant et al., 1976, Chs. 1, 13, & 14; Tapp, 1976).
Essentially, this involves the participation of social psychologists as consultants to
attorneys in the exercise of peremptory challenges during the *voir dire* process of
jury selection.

As described by one of its chief exponents (Christie, 1976), the process utilizes
three major procedures in the effort to predict juror behavior. First, surveys are
conducted in the community in which the trial is scheduled. The object is to
investigate the relation between various demographic variables (e.g., age, occupation) within that community and the attitudes judged to be most relevant to the
ongoing trial (e.g., authoritarianism, civil-libertarian beliefs). Second, through a
network of local community contacts, information is gathered about the known
orientation of individual jurors with reference to general issues pertinent to the
trial. Third, the responses and general behavior of the jurors in the courtroom
during the *voir dire* process are observed. Finally, with the help of both regression
equations and global qualitative judgments, the psychologist tries to predict not
only the reactions of individual jurors but also their interpersonal relations with
other jurors, the extent of each juror's susceptibility to influence and likelihood of
influencing others, clique formation within the jury, and other aspects of small
group operation.

Some efforts to validate such selection procedures have been made by conducting intensive posttrial interviews with jurors, alternates, and potential jurors
eliminated during *voir dire.* The findings appear to show good predictive value of
the selection indices when evaluated in terms of subsequent behavior. However,
the available data are meager. Furthermore, it is impossible to rule out the
influence of the normal jury selection procedures and thus assess the incremental
validity attributable to the contributions of the social psychologist. The whole
question of social scientist participation in jury selection is still controversial with
regard to both its effectiveness and its broad societal and ethical implications.

Expert Witness. As long ago as 1911, Judge Learned Hand wrote in one of his
decisions:

> How long we shall continue to blunder along without the aid of unpartisan and
> authoritative scientific assistance in the administration of justice, no one knows; but all
> fair persons not conventionalized by provincial legal habits of mind ought, I should think,
> unite to effect some such advance (cited in Geiser & Newman, 1961, p. 685).

One of the means whereby scientific assistance may be made available to judges
and juries is through the testimony of expert witnesses. In law, an expert in a given
field is one who by virtue of training and experience has "the power to draw
inferences from the facts which a jury would not be competent to draw" (Louisell,
1955, part I, p. 244).

Psychology is one of the most recent sciences to be recognized by the courts as
providing such special training and experience. To be sure, individual psychologists have testified as experts since early in this century. This was particularly true
in Germany, where such eminent psychologists as Karl Marbe, William Stern, and
Kurt Bondy were called upon to testify on a variety of questions for which their
training in experimental psychology qualified them (see McCary, 1956; W. Stern,
1939). Nevertheless, it is only since midcentury that psychologists began to make

an appreciable contribution in this role. In the decades of 1950 and 1960, American courts broadened and clarified their practices regarding the admissibility of expert testimony by psychologists. In a number of cases in which psychological testimony was rejected by the trial judge, moreover, the decision was reversed by appelate courts (Hoch & Darley, 1962; McCary, 1956; Rodnick & Hoch, 1961). These developments were facilitated by certain advances within the profession of psychology itself, such as state certification and licensing of psychologists, specialty certification by the American Board of Professional Psychology, standardization and evaluation of training programs, and formulation of a code of professional ethics (see Ch. I).

In an increasing number of cases, psychologists have been appointed as expert witnesses in both federal and state courts, either by the court itself or by the parties to the suit. Psychologists have testified, in both civil and criminal cases, regarding many aspects of human behavior. Clinical psychologists have been called upon to assess intellectual and emotional conditions of children and adults in connection with commitment for mental retardation or insanity, contested wills, adoption into foster homes, and determination of legal responsibility for criminal acts. They have made similar contributions in accident cases where the extent of behavioral damage resulting from brain injury was to be ascertained.

Although clinical psychologists are the most likely to be called upon to testify, psychologists in other areas of specialization are also being utilized increasingly for such purposes. Consumer psychologists, for example, can be of service in cases involving brand-name and trademark infringement (Ch. 11), misleading advertising, and other questions that pertain basically to consumer reactions or to public opinion (Geiser & Newman, 1961, Louisell, 1955). For these purposes, relevant data can be gathered from a representative sample of the appropriate population and presented to the court with interpretations by the psychologist.

Experimental psychologists also have much to contribute, especially in the area of perception and memory. It was with perceptual and memory problems that some of the earliest court testimony by psychologists was concerned. A more recent illustration is provided by the case cited earlier in this chapter, in which a hunter was inadvertently shot by his companions (Sommer, 1959). So far, however, the utilization of experimental psychologists as expert witnesses has been minimal. Mention should also be made of the testimony of social psychologists in connection with such matters as school desegregation and other civil rights issues (K. B. Clark, 1953, 1955). In the 1960s and 1970s, specialists in differential psychology, test construction and validation, and selection procedures have been in increasing demand, particularly in cases dealing with the civil rights of women and ethnic minorities.

Testifying as expert witnesses is an activity in which most psychologists are still quite inexperienced. For this reason, a number of publications have set forth the pitfalls that may be encountered, as well as providing guidelines for effective testimony (Langhorne & Hoch, 1960; Liebenson & Wepman, 1964; McCary, 1956; Olinger, 1961; G. P. Rice, 1961; Ziskin, 1970). Several symposia, workshops, and mock trials have also been held at annual APA conventions to sensitize the potential expert witness to the demands of the role. When psychologists testify for one side in a court trial, they must submit to cross-examination, in which they are called upon to defend not only the validity of their evidence but also their qualifications as experts. This is true of any expert who testifies within the adversary system of court procedure, whatever the field of specialization. The psychologist, however, may encounter additional difficultues, arising from the lack of clarity that still characterizes the position of psychology among the learned professions and its relation to medicine. Moreover, the psychologist should always bear in mind that interpretations of research findings are often controversial and that several testing instruments, especially among those used by clinical psychologists, cannot be adequately defended on the basis of objective validation.[5]

Besides testifying in court, psychologists may also participate in pretrial hearings and serve as expert consultants to assist lawyers in their preparation of a case. Still another way in which they may contribute their specialized knowledge is to testify as *amicus curiae* (friend of the court), a procedure that removes them from the adversary role. This procedure has been employed especially by associations, such as the APA, which are in a position to provide professional or scientific information for the guidance of the court. The relevant facts and interpretations may be presented either through oral testimony of by filing a written *amicus curiae* brief. Since this practice has been followed particularly in test cases with relatively broad social implications, it will be illustrated more fully in a later section of the chapter in connection with psychology's contributions to the development of laws.

PSYCHOLOGICAL FACTORS IN ANTISOCIAL BEHAVIOR

Studies of Offenders. For at least a century, anthropologists, sociologists, psychiatrists, psychologists, and other specialists have been studying the characteristics of delinquents and criminals in the effort to identify the causes of antisocial behavior (Burtt, 1931; Toch, 1961). Among the first to pursue such investigations was Lombroso (1911a, 1876/1911b), a nineteenth-century Italian anthropologist who proposed that the criminal was a throwback to an earlier, more primitive stage of human evolution. In support of this doctrine, he gathered extensive data on physical anomalies, or "stigmata of degeneracy," that he observed in prison populations. Examples include prognathous jaw, receding chin, low forehead, flattened nose, facial asymmetry, deformities of teeth and palate, and malformations of the ears. This theory of a hereditary "criminal type" enjoyed considerable popularity until control observations revealed equal incidence of these physical defects among comparable noncriminal populations.

After the turn of the century, the emphasis shifted to mental retardation as the major cause of crime (Goddard, 1910; Goring, 1913; J. O. Smith, 1962). This hypothesis was bolstered by investigations of such families as the Jukes[6] and Kallikaks,[6] which showed a high concentration of mental retardation along with crime, delinquency, alcoholism, psychosis, pauperism, and other social and behavioral problems over many generations. Early interpretations of these familial studies stressed poor heredity, failing to take into account the extremely unfavorable home and community environments in which each successive generation of children had been reared.

That intellectual defect cannot account for a substantial proportion of crimes was demonstrated by two extensive surveys of the intelligence test performance of men in state penitentiaries (Murchison, 1926; Tulchin, 1939). Both studies found

[5]Jeffery (1964) gives a sobering report of actual cross-examinations of psychologists who were overconfident and inadequately prepared to discuss the tests they had used.

[6]These are pseudonyms by which these families have become well-known in the psychological literature.

the distribution of Army Alpha scores of the penitentiary samples to be virtually identical with that of the total World War I army draft from the same states. As might be anticipated, there was a significant relation between intelligence and type of crime. Individuals committed for fraud obtained the highest mean scores, while those committed for sex crimes obtained the lowest. The proportion of all crimes that could be attributed to mental retardation, however, was quite small.

Surveys of juvenile delinquents have yielded a somewhat greater incidence of low intelligence test performance (Caplan & Siebert, 1964). The deficiency is particularly apparent on verbal tests, which are highly correlated with school achievement (Prentice & Kelly, 1963). The juvenile delinquent's typical hostility toward school is noteworthy in this connection. The intellectually handicapped child naturally experiences more failure and frustration in school. Such frustration tends to engender aggressive behavior. At the same time, the antagonism of juvenile delinquents toward authority and restrictions makes them poor school learners and may in turn account for their retarded intellectual development. This is an example of the difficulty of unraveling cause-effect relations in delinquent careers. From a practical standpoint, however, the important implication is that mental retardation is not a major factor in juvenile delinquency. The mean difference between delinquent and nondelinquent groups, though statistically significant, is small, and the overlap is extensive.

Beginning in the 1930s, the focus of research again shifted, in at least two ways: from intellectual to personality variables and from predominantly hereditary to predominantly environmental etiological factors. Concurrently, there was a steady rise in the number of studies concerned with juvenile delinquents as contrasted with adult offenders.

All these trends are illustrated in the series of studies conducted by the Gluecks over nearly four decades (E. T. Glueck, 1966; S. Glueck & E. T. Glueck, 1930, 1934, 1943, 1950, 1959, 1962). A major finding of the Glueck research pertains to the early home and community backgrounds of the offenders, which were characterized by many adverse social and psychological conditions. Parental education and socioeconomic level were typically low; economic dependency, overcrowding, and insanitary living conditions were common; and broken homes, parental neglect, and criminal influences were prevalent. These results are typical of those obtained in other studies of the early environments of delinquents. While recognizing the influence of such broad environmental factors, the Gluecks in their later work tended to emphasize the individual's own personality traits as a major determinant of his or her behavior both before and after correctional treatment. An important influence contributing to the development of these traits is the nature of parent-child relations during early childhood. The role of these interpersonal factors was brought out in a study in which 500 delinquent boys were compared with a nondelinquent group matched with them in age, general intelligence, national and ethnic origin, and residence in underprivileged neighborhoods (S. Glueck & E. T. Glueck, 1950). The investigators hoped thereby to help explain why some children turn to delinquency while others remain law-abiding even when reared in the same neighborhoods.

An even more direct methodological approach to this question is provided by the earlier study of Healy and Bronner (1936), in which extensive case-history data were gathered on 105 juvenile delinquents and on their nondelinquent siblings. The gross environmental variables characterizing the socioeconomic, cultural, and educational level of the family were thus automatically held constant. In comparison with their nondelinquent siblings, many more delinquent children showed strong dislike for school and for individual teachers. The delinquents manifested more discontent and emotional disturbance and more often reported feelings of rejection, insecurity, and inferiority. When nondelinquents experienced comparable emotional difficulties, there were usually counterbalancing satisfactions that made their situations more tolerable.

A limitation of most delinquency studies is that observations begin after the subjects are identified as delinquents. Retrospective studies of childhood experiences are always subject to error, even when skilled interviewers and caseworkers gather the data. Moreover, it is difficult to disentangle causal relations under these circumstances. If delinquents are backward in school, hostile toward authority, emotionally insecure, and so on, we cannot determine to what extent these reactions may result from the delinquent behavior itself, as well as from the experience of arrest and institutional commitment.

One way to avoid this difficulty is to begin a longitudinal study *before* delinquent behavior occurs. This requires the gathering of data on a large sample of children, who are then followed up to see who becomes delinquent and who does not. A few psychologists have followed this approach by surveying large samples of elementary and high school pupils by means of personality tests and rating scales, such as the Minnesota Multiphasic Personality Inventory (Hathaway & Monachesi, 1953, 1957; Wirt & Briggs, 1959), Haggerty-Olson-Wickman Behavior Rating Schedules (Olson, 1959), and other self-report inventories and rating scales (J. E. Anderson et al., 1961). Despite the initial examination of large groups, however, the number of delinquents studied in these samples is too small to permit conclusive generalizations. A somewhat different approach is illustrated by an intensive six-year longitudinal study of 400 eighth-grade boys from an inner-city school, all of whom were socially and educationally maladjusted when chosen for the project (Ahlstrom & Havighurst, 1971).

Several procedures were combined in a well-designed investigation conducted with 10th-grade boys in the Denver, Colorado, public schools (Conger & Miller, 1966; Conger, Miller, & Walsmith, 1975). Within the total available sample of some 2,400 cases, the investigators identified those individuals who, prior to age 18, had committed one or more offenses that brought them to juvenile court. These cases were individually matched with nondelinquents from the same sample on the basis of age, socioeconomic status, residential neighborhood characteristics, school attended, and ethnic group membership. The two groups were then compared on measures that had been gathered on the entire school sample from kindergarten through the 10th grade. The data available for both groups included teacher ratings on a set of personal-social behaviors, supplemented by a systematic content analysis of recorded teacher comments. Statistical analyses were conducted on these data for Grades 3, 6, and 9. In addition, the ninth-grade data included scores on self-report inventories covering a sizable array of emotional, social, and attitudinal variables. The final matched groups for which all necessary data were available included 86 delinquents and 86 nondelinquents.

Although the specific findings of the study by Conger and his associates are too numerous to summarize, a few major trends may be cited. Significant differences in behavior ratings between the subsequent delinquents and the controls emerged in the earliest school grades and increased in number and magnitude in the later grades. The behavior ratings, teacher comments, and self-report inventory scores converged to highlight certain distinctive personality differences between the two groups. Thus, from the outset, the future delinquents had manifested significant deficiencies in their sense of responsibility and their regard for the rights and feelings of their peers. They showed poorer attitudes toward authority and less understanding or acceptance of the need for rules and regulations in a social group. They had more emotional problems, poorer work habits, and more difficulty in maintaining attention on the task at hand and in persisting until its completion. Some suggestive results were also obtained on *interactions* between certain personality-social variables and both intelligence and socioeconomic status. Thus some personality characteristics were differently related to delinquency at different intellectual or socioeconomic levels, and the largest differences between delinquents and nondelinquents were found in the socioeconomically deprived groups.

The search for test scores or other indicators that significantly differentiate delinquent from nondelinquent groups goes on (see, e.g., Riddle & Roberts, 1977). All such research adds to our understanding of the nature and sources of delinquency and crime. At the same time, most investigators now emphasize the multiple etiology of antisocial behavior. Moreover—and more importantly—the causes of any one individual's antisocial behavior reflect complex interactions of many personal, experiential, and situational variables. At this stage in the development of the research data base, the most fruitful approach to identifying young persons "at risk" of potential criminal behavior seems to be a clinical procedure whereby the individual's assets and liabilities, his or her coping mechanisms, adverse situational variables, special sources of stress, and available positive environmental resources can be evaluated in terms of their total impact on probable behavioral outcome.

Research on Aggression. The years since the mid-sixties yielded an avalanche of reports by committees, task forces, and commissions, as well as multiauthored books, dealing with the problem of aggression and violence. Concurrently, there was a sharp rise in both basic and applied research in this area. Among the signs of the times was the establishment in 1974 of a new multidisciplinary journal, *Aggressive Behavior,* as the official organ of the International Society for Research on Aggression. Undoubtedly this upsurge of activity was stimulated by the widespread increase in both individual and group violence that characterized the decades of the 1960s and the 1970s.

The terms "aggression" and "violence" are sometimes used interchangeably and sometimes with different emphases. For example, some writers include verbally expressed hostility under aggression, while limiting violence to physical forms of aggression. In relation to crime and delinquency, both aggression and violence are generally defined so as to be in some ways less and in other ways more inclusive in their coverage. Thus the term "aggression," as well as "violence," generally excludes several types of criminal acts, such as theft or fraud; at the same time, it is often defined so as to include legalized and institutionalized violence, as in wars and law enforcement. The sources of violence are being explored in many fields, ranging from genetics, neurophysiology, and endocrinology to the psychology of learning, cognitive psychology, and social psychology.[7]

[7]For an overview of the diversity of approaches, the reader is referred to such sources as Bandura (1973), Berkowitz (1969), Geen and O'Neal (1976), Johnson, (1972), J. F. Knutson (1973), Mark and Ervin (1970), Moyer (1976), Ribes-Inesta and Bandura (1976), J. P. Scott, (1975), Singer (1971), and Toch (1969).

The methods used by psychologists to investigate aggressive behavior are extremely varied. There is a mass of data obtained through both laboratory experiments and naturalistic observations of animals from such varied species as mice, rats, chickens, fish, dogs, wolves, monkeys, and baboons. A common finding in a number of animal behavior studies was that an increase in violence and destructive fighting followed "social disaggregation," or disruption of the normal social organization of the species by any of a variety of conditions (J. P. Scott, 1975). It is noteworthy that naturalistic observations of human groups provide many examples of a parallel phenomenon. Human research extends from nursery school children to adults in various educational, occupational, and sociocultural categories. Specific procedures include the arousal of mild degrees of aggression in laboratory situations, observations of real-life events, and personality studies of participants in violent acts. Both structured personality inventories and projective techniques have been employed in the search for predictors of violent behavior or "dangerousness," with generally disappointing results (Megargee, 1970; Monahan, 1976). As in the prediction of criminal behavior in general, no single measure could be identified as a dependable indicator or predictor of violent behavior. However, the accumulated data base on variables associated with violence offers general guidelines for a more sophisticated approach to prediction, involving a pattern of several test variables together with life-history data and situational factors. Shah (1978) gives an incisive analysis of the concept of dangerousness and the methodological problems involved in its application to legal policies and practices.

Several investigators have called attention to the varieties of aggressive behavior that need to be differentiated in the further study of etiology and prediction. For example, one distinction is that between instrumental aggression, which is a means to an end, and expressive or angry aggression, which may occur in direct response to frustration, perceived inequity, or some other interpersonal instigation. Some research has focused on special contributory factors. Among them are environmental conditions, such as heat, noise, and crowding (Geen & O'Neal, 1976, pp.169–192); the portrayal of violence on television, in its effect on both children and adults (Bandura, 1973; Liebert & Schwartzberg, 1977, pp. 156–160; *"Television,"* 1972; Turner, 1977); and the use of marijuana (Abel, 1977). Special forms of aggression have been investigated, such as child abuse and other intrafamilial violence (Bard, 1971b). Studies have also been conducted on crime victims and on bystanders (Heinzelmann, 1976; Hindelang, 1976; Walker & Brodsky, 1976). Still other investigators have surveyed attitudes toward various forms of violence in representative samples of American men, as well as in special groups, such as Quakers, parents of battered children, and rioters (Blumenthal, Kahn, Andrews, & Head, 1972; Blumenthal, Chadiha, Cole, & Jayaratne, 1976).

With regard to psychological techniques for the control of aggression, some efforts have been made at both the individual level and the community or broader societal level. The former can be illustrated by a promising behavior modification program for the control of anger, which utilizes a combination of desensitization/relaxation and cognitive self-instructional techniques (Novaco, 1975). Small group programs using token economies, modeling, and other behavior modification techniques report significant reduction in aggression and disruptive behavior in several settings, including schools, community recreational facilities, rehabilitative residential centers, and the child's own family home (Pierce & Risley, 1974; Ribes-Inesta & Bandura, 1976, Chs. 5–9). Another approach, combining the orientations of community and educational psychology, was based on the premise that the peer group is a natural setting for teenagers (Berkovitz, 1975). Accordingly, groups were formed in secondary schools under the leadership of specially trained counselors who could help adolescents to work through their common problems. The proponents of this program report considerable success in actual practice with both majority and minority students.

For the alleviation of group aggression, ranging from wars and labor disputes to racial conflicts, student protests, and other types of group confrontations that peaked in the 1960s, considerable attention has been given to the development of nonviolent procedures for conflict resolution (McNeil, 1965; Osgood, 1962; Rubin & Brown, 1975; C. G. Smith, 1971). By focusing on the conflict process, the problem situation can be identified and resolved before it deteriorates into violence. It has been repeatedly observed that conflict as such need not be destructive but can form the basis for constructive social change that enhances human well-being.

The problem of conflict resolution was encountered in Chapter 6, in connection with union-management relations and other sources of industrial strife. The same basic strategies for effective bargaining and negotiation developed in that context are applicable to the nonviolent resolution of other group conflicts. Among the procedures employed in research on intergroup hostility and conflict resolution are longitudinal field studies of genuine but limited conflict situations, including direct observation of events and interviews with representative samples of participants (D. Katz, 1961; Rinde & Rokkan, 1959; Rubin & Brown, 1975). In the effort to test hypotheses under more nearly controlled conditions, some investigators have utilized contrived but realistic simulations (Sherif, 1961). Others have made extensive and systematic use of bargaining games (Morton Deutsch, 1973; Guetzkow, 1962; Guetzkow, Kotler, & Schultz, 1972, Ch. 7; Rubin & Brown, 1975).

Several major suggestions for constructive strategies emerge from these various investigations. An example is the identification of a "superordinate" or common goal that is in the interests of both sides and thus serves to unify their efforts. Other strategies involve the use of intergroup communication to modify each party's perceptions, interpretations, and causal attributions regarding the actions and demands of the opposing party. Mediation by a third party who represents the public interest and is acceptable to both sides is a particularly effective technique. That this strategy is widely recognized as a promising approach to conflict resolution is evidenced by the establishment of several organizations that provide mediation services as well as training and consultation in settling disputes (see Spiegel & Levin, 1975). Although some of these organizations operate at a national or international level, most of them function at the community level, where many conflicts originate. The development of negotiating skills is also receiving increasing attention in the training of lawyers and police (Bard, 1971b; Bard & Shellow, 1976, Ch. 3; Bermant et al., 1976, Ch. 6).

Legal Socialization. Approaching the problem of antisocial behavior from the opposite angle, several psychologists have been studying the process of legal socialization. This refers to the development of the child's attitudes and behaviors toward the law. An unusually extensive investigation of legal socialization was conducted by Tapp and her associates in collaboration with interdisciplinary local teams in each of six countries, namely Denmark, Greece, Italy, India, Japan, and the United States (Hess & Tapp, 1969; Minturn & Tapp, 1970; Tapp & Levine, 1974).

By means of group-administered instruments and open-ended interviews, data were gathered from some 5,000 preadolescents in Grades 4, 6, and 8. The inquiry focused on the child's "legal reasoning" about norms of conduct and compliance in a multiplicity of legal or "rule" systems, including family, school, church, and peer groups, as well as local and national government. A second part of the project dealt with children's judgments of aggressive confrontation. In subsequent studies, similar procedures were followed with younger and older children, groups differing in socioeconomic level, and a variety of adult samples, such as law students, teachers, prisoners, and jurors.

Tapp and Levine (1974) organize their developmental data on legal socialization into three levels. Reflecting the influence of both Piaget (1932) and Kohlberg (1969), these levels are characterized essentially as: (1) preconventional, "law-obeying" level, at which compliance to laws is based on fear of authority and deference to power; (2) conventional, "law-maintenance" level, at which laws are justified in terms of the need to regulate society; and (3) postconventional, "lawmaking" level, at which laws are justified through abstract and personally defined conceptions of justice. The modal orientation of most adult groups was found to be at the second level. There was also some evidence that the socializing setting influences the rate and ultimate level of the individual's development.

Hogan (1975, 1976) has criticized Tapp's approach as being unduly rationalistic and giving inadequate consideration to emotional and motivating factors. He observes that the model concerns how people think they should or would behave rather than how they actually behave. He also takes issue with the extremely individualistic orientation underlying level 3, arguing that "man's well-being depends on social interaction, a predictable environment, and competition" (Hogan, 1975, p. 537). In place of this model, Hogan proposes an alternative legal socialization model that also recognizes three developmental stages or levels. In the first stage, the infant and young child *becomes attuned to the existence of rules* and learns compliance through benevolent and supportive parental guidance. Moreover, the attitudes the child develops toward his or her parents at this stage tend to generalize to other authority figures encountered later. In a deliberately simplified but admirably pithy statement, Hogan (1976, p. 70) observes:

> Generally speaking, a child will be most attuned to rules if it is treated in a warm but restrictive fashion—that is, if it receives love and nurturance combined with prompt and consistent disapproval for disobedience. Warm but permissive parents, on the other hand, produce self-confident children who are not attuned to rules. Parents who are cold and restrictive tend to have children who are hostile toward authority, but who publicly conform to rules. Parents who are cold and permissive tend to produce delinquent children.

The second stage is that of *sensitivity to social expectation* and concern for the well-being of others. As the child's contacts with parents gradually give way to contacts with age peers, he or she learns to accommodate to the norms of the peer group. If the children are properly supervised, these norms will approximate those of adult society. Concepts of reciprocity and fairness are acquired at this stage through games and other group activities.

The third stage, *ideational maturity,* provides for social change and progress through constructive nonconformity. At this stage, the individual is able to evaluate the norms currently popular within a particular group and to integrate the possibly conflicting norms of different groups (e.g., home, school, peers). The individual achieves autonomy, not with regard to basic social rules and principles, but with regard to particular reference groups. As a means of facilitating the attainment of this level of legal socialization, Hogan cites the "authoritative" as contrasted with "authoritarian" child-rearing practices investigated by Baumrind (1971). In addition, if the parents have reached this level in their own legal socialization, they can provide an important developmental influence through modeling.

Psychological research on legal socialization is in a state of ferment, in which different routes are being explored. An extensive data base is accumulating, and much productive effort is being directed to the formulation and evaluation of diverse hypotheses, interpretations, and theories. All this activity is slowly contributing to our understanding of the processes and circumstances that lead to the development of a socially effective human being—one who will follow constructive and creative strategies in meeting problems, frustrations, and conflicts.

ROLES OF PSYCHOLOGISTS IN THE CRIMINAL JUSTICE SYSTEM

Besides the broad range of research and consultation on psycholegal problems provided by psychologists from predominantly academic settings, more and more psychologists are being employed full time in different branches of the criminal justice system. These include three major categories, namely police-department, court, and correctional psychologists. As in educational and medical contexts, the psychologists working in the criminal justice system perform a dual role. They carry out their specialized functions as effectively as possible within the existing system while trying to improve the system itself through consultation, staff training, and participation in administrative and policy-making conferences.

Police-Department Psychologists. The participation of psychologists in police-department activities, both as external consultants and as internal staff, represents a recent but expanding professional role (Bard & Shellow, 1976; Mann, 1973; Reiser, 1972; Schlossberg, 1974; Woods, 1976, Chs. 13 & 14). A few large metropolitan centers, such as New York City, have fully organized psychology units in their police departments. One of the first areas in which psychologists were utilized, generally as consultants on a project basis, was in the development and evaluation of *selection procedures.* Programs for assessing applicant and officer qualifications for different levels and types of police work have been established in several state and local police agencies throughout the country (Dunnette & Motowidlo, 1975; Eisenberg & Murray, 1974; Gorham, 1977; Landy, Farr, Saal, & Freytag, 1976; Landy & Goodin, 1974; Rosenfeld & Thornton, 1976; Tordy, Eyde, Primoff, & Hardt, 1976). The development of these programs utilized many of the techniques discussed in Chapters 2 and 3, such as systematic and detailed job analyses, the collection of critical incidents, behaviorally anchored rating scales, the identification of differentiable job elements or components, content validation, and criterion-related validation. The selection instruments include specially developed tests in the cognitive, psychomotor, and affective domains; biographical inventories and other procedures for gathering background information; and simulation exercises for use in assessment centers. All these procedures not only serve in the selection process but can also provide information useful in recruiting, training, placement, transfers, promotions, and other phases of the total personnel system.

Other ways in which psychologists are functioning in police departments include counseling with individual officers, training, and participation in the design of operational programs (Woods, 1976, Chs. 13 & 14). Because of the special physical and emotional stresses that characterize police work, there is particular need for *counseling and clinical services* including diagnostic testing and interviewing, recommendations regarding job modifications and reassignments, individual psychotherapy, and group therapy.

Psychologists have been playing an active part in *training,* both in the design of curricula and in conducting special training programs at preservice and in-service levels. Several books have been written for this purpose by psychologists familiar with police work (Bard & Shellow, 1976; E. J. Green, 1976; Wicks, 1974). Bard and Shellow (1976) point out that a major but often unrecognized part of the police officer's role stems from his or her being the first to arrive at the scene of a crisis or disaster. Police are thus in a position to diagnose and treat a social or behavioral disruption. Yet this aspect of police work, actually occupying about 80% of the officer's time, has been largely neglected in the traditional training programs, which focus on law enforcement and the apprehension of criminals. In much of their day-by-day activities, what police officers need is skill in first aid, counseling, mediation, and crisis intervention.

Closely related to training is the application of psychological knowledge and methods to improvement of *operational procedures.* For example, psychologists can contribute to the solution of crimes by developing more effective techniques for interviewing crime victims, witnesses, and suspects. In some cases, psychologists have employed available clues in an effort to formulate a personality profile of the suspect. An important way in which psychologists have collaborated with experienced police officers is in designing procedures for crowd control, suicide prevention, managing hostage situations, family crisis intervention, and psychological first aid for the victims of crimes and disasters. Psychologists have also been giving some attention to the public image of the police and to the improvement of public cooperation in law enforcement, not through special "public relations" units or activities, but through altering the day-by-day contacts of police officers with members of their public.

Court Psychologists. Most court systems today have access to consultants in psychology and other relevant specialties, such as psychiatry, social work, and education (Toch, 1961, Ch. 11; Woods, 1976, Ch. 13). The principal function of such specialists is to help in the *understanding of the offender,* so that the disposition of the case can be adapted to the characteristics of the individual as well as to the nature of the crime. Referrals for psychological evaluations of children and adults may be made prior to trial or prior to sentencing. Juvenile courts in large cities usually have their own psychology unit, whose staff carries on these functions. Such units are also attached to some domestic relations courts and to a few criminal courts.

Like most clinical psychologists, court psychologists began as mental testers. Early court psychologists did little more than administer the Stanford-Binet or other intelligence tests to find the individual's "IQ." Slowly their functions have been broadening to cover a comprehensive diagnostic evaluation of the individual through a variety of testing and interviewing techniques. By these procedures, court psychologists try to identify the mentally retarded, psychotic, brain-damaged, or other pathological offender. They provide information regarding personal characteristics and background that helps to clarify the individual offender's motivations and attitudes and facilitates the prediction of subsequent behavior. They also evaluate the individual's potential for education, vocational training, and job placement.

On the basis of their findings, court psychologists may also make recommendations regarding disposition and treatment. In some court clinics, the psychologist does a limited amount of counseling and short-term psychotherapy. With children, the court clinic can serve a preventive function by prescribing remedial and therapeutic programs. Thus the youthful offender may be salvaged at an early stage without formal adjudication as a delinquent or institutional commitment. As in all clinical work with children, interviewing and counseling of parents and other significant adult associates are an integral part of the process. Remedial instruction, readjustments in school placement, recreational programs, foster home placement, and other types of environmental therapy may be arranged upon the psychologist's recommendation.

Through consultation, training, and the reporting of research findings, court psychologists can serve a broader function in the *communication of psychological knowledge* to both law enforcement professionals and community groups. They are often called upon to address meetings of parents, teachers, religious workers, and community mental health organizations. In this broader role, they are actively contributing to the reevaluation of legal procedures for handling various special groups, such as alcoholics, drug abusers, sex offenders, and juvenile delinquents. Existing procedures for the disposition of juvenile cases, for example, have been widely criticized on at least two counts. On the one hand, the rights of juveniles are not protected by due process as fully as are the rights of adult offenders. On the other hand, juvenile perpetrators of serious crimes are often returned to the community because of their age. This is obviously a situation calling for objective knowledge about human behavior, both in the disposition of individual cases and in the reformulation of general policy.

Correctional Psychologists. The psychologist working in a correctional setting is typically a clinical or counseling psychologist with special experience in dealing with problems of delinquency and crime (Brodsky, 1972; Woods, 1976, Ch. 13). Often he or she functions as a member of a team, which includes a psychiatrist and a social worker. In order to make effective recommendations, the psychologist needs to be familiar with penal institutions, social agencies, and other community facilities. It should also be noted that a community-psychology orientation is especially applicable to the work of the correctional psychologist.

Although the first organized psychological service in an American prison was established as early as 1919 (J. D. Jackson, 1950), the number of adequately qualified psychologists so employed remained extremely low for some 50 years. Currently, most correctional facilities have at least one psychologist on their staff and many have more than one. Institutions for juveniles usually have a larger psychologically trained staff than do those for adult offenders. Although until recently correctional psychologists were performing very limited functions, they are now better integrated into the correctional system and are serving in a broader capacity. Despite these general signs of progress, however, most correctional institutions are still noticeably understaffed in this area. In a survey conducted by Gormally and Brodsky (1973), the ratio of psychologists (and other mental health personnel) to inmates fell short of the minimum recommended by the American Correctional Association.

Several conditions make the task of the correctional psychologist difficult and have tended to discourage well-qualified psychologists from working in correctional settings. A major obstacle stems from a fundamental ambiguity of objectives. In the effort to reconcile the goal of deterrence and social control of crime, on the one hand, with rehabilitation and therapeutic objectives, on the other, correctional institutions are pulled in opposite directions. In part, this conflict reflects a theoretical controversy regarding the nature of antisocial behavior. In an analysis of this conflict, Shah (1972, p. 97) observed, "It is not very clear how one set of societal processes for defining and dealing with deviant behavior (the concept of mental disease and mental health handling) are to be related to another set of societal processes for dealing with social deviance (the concept of crime and the criminal justice system)."

Although confusion and controversy are certainly rampant in discussions about crime, it should be noted that rehabilitation as such need not imply a "mental disease" etiology or a medical model of criminal behavior. For example, training in occupational and interpersonal skills could increase the probability of normal community functioning on the part of at least some offenders, regardless of the ultimate source of their present predicament. But the many-sided theoretical controversy about both causes and treatment of antisocial behavior continues. Nor can available empirical data on the effects of alternative treatments help to resolve the argument. Because of conditions that hamper and limit their implementation, neither rehabilitation nor deterrence has been adequately tested in practice (Gibbs, 1975; Tapp, 1976).

Against this background of uncertain and conflicting goals, correctional psychologists are nevertheless performing a variety of functions that contribute to a better utilization of available facilities (Silber, 1974; Woods, 1976). One of the traditional functions of the correctional psychologist is the diagnostic testing and interviewing of new admissions. This assessment is often conducted at a central diagnostic and reception center, so that the results can be considered in assigning individuals to particular institutions. The results are likewise used in the assignment of persons to appropriate work functions, educational programs, or vocational training within the institution. For this reason, the testing of adult prisoners puts considerable emphasis on the measurement of vocational aptitudes, skills, and interests. In connection with the evaluation of parole candidates, the psychologist again conducts a comprehensive assessment, with special reference to the individual's readiness for community living and the prediction of his or her subsequent behavior.

In institutions for juvenile offenders, more emphasis is placed on the assessment and treatment of interpersonal and emotional problems. Educational programs are also of particular importance because of the juvenile delinquent's frequent educational retardation and poor school adjustment. In one attempt to overcome negative attitudes toward teachers and academic contexts, some promising results were obtained from the use of programmed learning and teaching machines (McKee & Watkins, 1962).

Increasingly, correctional psychologists are also providing several kinds of therapeutic interventions, which are usually available on a voluntary basis. Among them are short-term psychotherapy, crisis intervention, and walk-in clinics. Group techniques are especially useful for a variety of purposes, ranging from the control of disruptive behavior and the resolution of emotional problems to the acquisition of social skills and information needed for reentry into community living. Behavior modification programs and the organization of therapeutic environments are receiving increasing attention for use in correctional settings (Kohlberg, Scharf, & Hickey, 1971; Ribes-Inesta & Bandura, 1976; Tapp, 1976). While presenting a realistic picture of the practical problems to be faced in carrying out such programs, Repucci and Saunders (1974) describe a successful behavior modification program established in a correctional facility for delinquent boys. The program involved an institutionwide, round-the-clock token economy, in which points were used as tender for the purchase of all goods and privileges. Local staff was trained to implement the program, and certain organizational changes were introduced to ensure that all levels of staff and residents participated in decision making.

Mention should also be made of the role of psychologists in partial-release and postrelease settings, such as work-release programs and halfway houses. Although available facilities for psychological services in these settings are meager, there is special need for counseling, group therapy, social support, and crisis intervention during these difficult transitional periods. A noteworthy development in this connection is the establishment of self-help peer organizations for mutual aid and support. Such groups were mentioned in Chapter 13 to illustrate the utilization of nonprofessional change agents in community psychology. Of particular interest in the present connection is the Delancey Street Foundation, a self-help residential and therapeutic community in San Francisco, organized and operated by ex-convicts and ex-addicts (Hampden-Turner, 1976). This organization provides a residential facility for several hundred men and women and includes among its services intensive group therapy sessions; opportunities for high school, college, and vocational education; and participation in several business enterprises which it operates.

✓ CONTRIBUTIONS OF PSYCHOLOGISTS TO POLICY FORMATION AND THE DEVELOPMENT OF LAWS

Psychologists and the Legislative Process. Although social psychologists have been traditionally identified with efforts to apply psychological knowledge to the solution of broad societal problems, psychologists in other specialties have been contributing more and more to such applications. Since by its very nature the law deals with human behavior, psychology obviously should have much to contribute to the formulation, revision, and interpretation of laws. Yet psychology has, until recently, had little impact in this area.

The specific channels whereby psychological facts and methods bearing on a particular issue can be transmitted to lawmakers are gradually coming to be identified and utilized by psychologists (Brayfield, 1976; D. M. Fraser, 1970). Some psychologists serve as legislative aides on the personal staffs of congressmen or state legislators. Others are employed by such organizations as the American Bar Foundation and by a large variety of government agencies and public-interest groups that influence the development or implementation of laws. Another effective means of communicating information relevant to a specific issue is through the preparation of position papers by groups of experts. A number of such papers have been prepared under the auspices of the American Psychological Association. Psychologists may also assist the courts in their testing and interpretation of laws by testifying either as *amicus curiae* or as expert witnesses for one of the parties to the suit.

Functioning in these various capacities, psychologists have been involved in the development of laws pertaining to a wide spectrum of subjects, as illustrated by education (from preschool to professional level), health, delinquency, drug abuse, vocational rehabilitation, problems of the elderly, aviation, cultural minorities, traffic safety, protection of privacy, and foreign aid. One area of extensive and continuing activity pertains to civil rights, particularly in relation to women and cultural minorities. For several decades and in several roles, psychologists have contributed to the development and implementation of legislation in this area. An early example is provided by the participation of psychologists as expert witnesses in cases dealing with educational segregation. These cases culminated in the momentous decision of May 17, 1954, when the Supreme Court of the United States ruled that state laws requiring or permitting racial segregation in public education are unconstitutional. In support of its conclusion that "segregated educational facilities are inherently unequal," the Court cited materials that had been submitted by psychologists in an Appendix to the Appellants' Briefs (K. B. Clark, 1955, pp. 227–235). More recently, experts on psychological testing have participated in several capacities in the effort to ensure that various official guidelines for the fair use of tests for educational and vocational purposes reflect current psychological knowledge and methodological developments (e.g., Diamond, 1975; Tittle & Zytowski, 1978; see also Appendix D).

Psychologists have also been particularly concerned with a set of interrelated questions pertaining to (1) the judicial definition of "insanity" and its relation to the establishment of legal responsibility for crime; (2) the implications of involuntary hospitalization and treatment of mentally disturbed persons (whether criminal or noncriminal); and (3) the right to treatment of persons institutionalized for mental illness or mental retardation. Although some progress has been made, confusion, inconsistency, and controversy are still rampant in the handling of these problems.[8]

Political Psychology. By the 1970s, there were several signs that the emerging area of political psychology had begun to achieve recognition as a distinct subdiscipline by both political scientists and psychologists. This was evidenced by research, publications, university training programs, and association activities (Abeles, 1976). In contrast to the early, scattered writings on political psychology, which focused on psychopathology and psychoanalytic interpretations of political behavior, the political psychology of the seventies drew largely from social, developmental, and normal personality psychology (Elms, 1976; J. N. Knutson, 1973; W. F. Stone, 1974).

The books written by psychologists on this topic have generally had a dual purpose: (1) to familiarize the political scientist with relevant psychological material, and (2) to summarize the available psychological research on political behavior as such. The latter is illustrated by studies of voting behavior and other types of political participation by the general public, including the motivations for such participation; political attitudes and attitude change; the psychological dimension of liberalism-conservatism; and the psychological construct of the authoritarian personality. Other research has been concerned with the process of political socialization and with the phenomena of political alienation and social unrest. A number of studies have delved into the problem of political leadership

[8]See, e.g., Rachlin (1974), Rachlin, Pam, and Milton (1975), D. N. Robinson (1974), Silber (1974), H. Silverman (1969), Szasz (1963, 1970), Watson (1975).

and the personality of political leaders, with reference to strengths and weaknesses, coping mechanisms, and personality styles. Increasing attention is also being given to the interaction between personality and sociocultural variables in shaping leadership style.

A related development is the establishment of graduate training programs for the preparation of "public affairs psychologists" who can function effectively in legislative or other governmental settings (e.g., Brayfield, 1976). Similarly, some consideration has been given to what psychologists should know about political science and the practical arts of government if they are to have a significant impact on the formation of public policy (e.g., Bauer, 1966; D. M. Fraser, 1970).

International Relations. The decade of the 1960s was characterized by an upsurge of activity on problems of international relations and "peace research" by social psychologists. Stimulated by the general fear of a nuclear war, the efforts of these psychologists were reflected in a sharp rise in committees, conferences, symposia, and publications which tried to identify and communicate what psychology could offer toward the reduction of international tension (Kelman, 1965; Klineberg, 1964; Osgood, 1962, 1964; Solomon, 1964; Stagner, 1967). Among the topics covered in these surveys are: the images that persons have of their own nation and of other nations; the factors that affect national stereotypes and the conditions under which intergroup attitudes change; the effects of exchange programs (in education, performing arts, sports, etc.) and other intercultural contacts; techniques of communication and persuasion; bargaining, negotiation, and other methods of conflict resolution; and conditions that increase or decrease intergroup hostility.

The Psychologist Role. While many promising beginnings have been made in psychological research on matters pertaining to public policy, it is apparent that there is still a wide gap between such research and the solution of practical problems. Nevertheless, some psychologists, as well as other behavioral scientists, have proposed action programs in the effort to apply what knowledge is available. Although such recommendations are not based wholly upon experimentally verified facts, it is felt that psychologists, as experts on human behavior, have an obligation to contribute what they can to problems of such immediate urgency. Even in the absence of directly relevant data, it is argued, the informed opinion of technically trained specialists on matters falling within their area of competence are bound to be more nearly correct than the opinions of laypersons on the same matters.

When functioning in this gray area, psychologists must exercise special caution to avoid possible pitfalls (D. M. Fraser, 1970; Russell, 1962). First, they must bear in mind that the solution of complex societal problems requires the collaboration of specialists in many fields. Within psychology itself, they must recognize the limits of their own competence. They must also carefully differentiate between opinions (however well informed) and facts, and they must make this distinction clear in communicating with others. Above all, it is important to separate personal beliefs and preferences from one's contribution as a scientist. To promote personal ideas under the guise of science would be both unethical and self-defeating. It is by retaining their scientific objectivity, their awareness of factors that may distort perceptions, and their research orientation toward human problems that psychologists can make their most distinctive contribution as psychologists. This is true in the field of public affairs, as it is in every other field of applied psychology.

SUMMARY

Although the origins of psycholegal research and services date back to the turn of the century, a lull of several decades' duration preceded the renewed activity of the late 1960s and 1970s. Psychological research can contribute to several aspects of the judicial process. A considerable body of data is available regarding the accuracy of courtroom testimony and of eyewitness identification of suspects. Lie detection relies principally on continuous physiological records of emotion, especially changes in blood pressure, respiration, and galvanic skin response. Jury research comprises studies of the jury's decision process as well as the use of psychological data as an aid in jury selection. The participation of psychologists as expert witnesses provides still another channel for utilizing psychological facts and methods in judicial proceedings.

The search for psychological factors leading to antisocial behavior has produced a mass of research representing diverse approaches and theoretical orientations. The early studies of delinquents and criminals focused on hereditary etiology and intellectual deficits. Later research placed increasing emphasis on environmental factors and on emotional, motivational, and attitudinal variables. Most importantly, however, research findings point to the multiple causation of antisocial behavior and the complex interactions of personal, experiential, and situational variables in each individual case.

A large body of research has been concerned with the broader problem of aggression and violence, as it occurs in animals as well as humans, and in organized and/or legitimized group activities as well as in individual behavior. The sources of aggression are being actively explored by many methods and through diverse fields, including genetics, neurophysiology, endocrinology, and the psychology of learning, cognition, personality, and social processes. Among the procedures for aggression control, psychologists have investigated various behavior modification techniques with individuals and groups, the formation and utilization of adolescent peer groups, and several techniques for nonviolent conflict resolution. Some investigators have approached the problem from another direction by studying the process and stages of legal socialization, i.e., the development of the individual's attitudes, concepts, and behaviors pertaining to rules, regulations, and laws.

The expanding roles of psychologists in the criminal justice system are exemplified by the work of the police-department, court, and correctional psychologists. In police departments, psychologists are engaged in the development and evaluation of personnel programs, in counseling and clinical services, in training, and in the development of special operational procedures. Court psychologists conduct clinical assessments of offenders and make recommendations regarding disposition and treatment. Increasingly, they are also serving a broader function in communicating psychological knowledge to law enforcement professionals and community groups. Psychologists in correctional settings perform diagnostic testing and interviewing of new admissions and provide several kinds of therapeutic interventions, ranging from individual and group therapies to behavior modification and the organization of therapeutic environments.

Psychologists are beginning to apply their expertise to the solution of broad societal problems through several channels, such as service on legislative staffs and committees and testimony on many specific issues before congressional committees. The emerging area of political psychology is concerned both with research at the interface of psychology and political science and with the effective participation of psychologists in public affairs. The peaceful resolution of international conflicts has been the focus of concentrated research and publication by a group of social psychologists, particularly in the decade of the sixties. In public affairs roles, as in other fields of applied psychology, psychologists can function most effectively if they define for themselves and clearly communicate to others the limits of their own area of expertise wherein they can make a distinctive contribution.

THE AMERICAN PSYCHOLOGICAL ASSOCIATION

APPENDIX A

Founded in 1892, the APA is the major psychological organization in the United States. With some 50,000 members, it includes most of the qualified psychologists in the country. The APA Central Office, to which inquiries may be addressed, is located at:

1200 Seventeenth Street, N.W.
Washington, D.C. 20036

The APA publishes a biographical directory of its members, giving such member data as address, present position, highest academic degree, licensure or certification, and areas of specialization, as well as information about the Association itself.

The APA is currently organized into the following 36 divisions:[1]

1. Division of General Psychology
2. Division on the Teaching of Psychology
3. Division of Experimental Psychology
5. Division of Evaluation and Measurement
6. Division of Physiological and Comparative Psychology
7. Division on Developmental Psychology
8. Division of Personality and Social Psychology
9. The Society for the Psychological Study of Social Issues—A Division of the APA (SPSSI)
10. Division of Psychology and the Arts
12. Division of Clinical Psychology
13. Division of Consulting Psychology
14. Division of Industrial and Organizational Psychology
15. Division of Educational Psychology

[1]There are no divisions numbered 4 or 11.

16. Division of School Psychology
17. Division of Counseling Psychology
18. Division of Psychologists in Public Service
19. Division of Military Psychology
20. Division of Adult Development and Aging
21. The Society of Engineering Psychologists—A Division of the APA
22. Division of Rehabilitation Psychology
23. Division of Consumer Psychology
24. Division of Philosophical Psychology
25. Division for the Experimental Analysis of Behavior
26. Division of the History of Psychology
27. Division of Community Psychology
28. Division of Psychopharmacology
29. Division of Psychotherapy
30. Division of Psychological Hypnosis
31. Division of State Psychological Association Affairs
32. Division of Humanistic Psychology
33. Division of Mental Retardation
34. Division of Population and Environmental Psychology
35. Division of the Psychology of Women
36. Psychologists Interested in Religious Issues—A Division of the APA (PIRI)
37. Division on Child and Youth Services
38. Division of Health Psychology

ETHICAL STANDARDS OF PSYCHOLOGISTS[1]

APPENDIX B

PREAMBLE

Psychologists[2] respect the dignity and worth of the individual and honor the preservation and protection of fundamental human rights. They are committed to increasing knowledge of human behavior and of people's understanding of themselves and others and to the utilization of such knowledge for the promotion of human welfare. While pursuing these endeavors, they make every effort to protect the welfare of those who seek their services or of any human being or animal that may be the object of study. They use their skills only for purposes consistent with these values and do not knowingly permit their misuse by others. While demanding for themselves freedom of inquiry and communications, psychologists accept the responsibility this freedom requires: competence, objectivity in the application of skills, and concern for the best interests of clients, colleagues, and society in general. In the pursuit of these ideals, psychologists subscribe to principles in the following areas: 1. Responsibility, 2. Competence, 3. Moral and Legal Standards, 4. Public Statements, 5. Confidentiality, 6. Welfare of the Consumer, 7. Professional Relationships, 8. Utilization of Assessment Techniques, and 9. Pursuit of Research Activities.

[2]A student of psychology who assumes the role of a psychologist shall be considered a psychologist for the purpose of this code of ethics.

PRINCIPLE 1. RESPONSIBILITY

In their commitment to the understanding of human behavior, psychologists value objectivity and integrity, and in providing services they maintain the highest standards of their profession. They accept responsibility for the consequences of their work and make every effort to insure that their services are used appropriately.

a. As scientists, psychologists accept the ultimate responsibility for selecting appropriate areas and methods most relevant to these areas. They plan their research in ways to minimize the possibility that their findings will be misleading. They provide thorough discussion of the limitations of their data and alternative hypotheses, especially where their work touches on social policy or might be construed to the detriment of persons in specific age, sex, ethnic, socioeconomic, or other social groups. In publishing reports of their work, they never suppress disconfirming data. Psychologists take credit only for the work they have actually done.

Psychologists clarify in advance with all appropriate persons or agencies the expectations for sharing and utilizing research data. They avoid dual relationships which may limit objectivity, whether political or monetary, so that interference with data, human participants, and milieu is kept to a minimum.

b. As employees of an institution or agency, psychologists have the responsibility of remaining alert to and attempting to moderate institutional pressures that may distort reports of psychological findings or impede their proper use.

c. As members of governmental or other organizational bodies, psychologists remain accountable as individuals to the highest standards of their profession.

d. As teachers, psychologists recognize their primary obligation to help others acquire knowledge and skill. They maintain high standards of scholarship and objectivity by presenting psychological information fully and accurately.

e. As practitioners, psychologists know that they bear a heavy social responsibility because their recommendations and professional actions may alter the lives of others. They are alert to personal, social, organizational, financial, or political situations or pressures that might lead to misuse of their influence.

f. Psychologists provide adequate and timely evaluations to employees, trainees, students, and others whose work they supervise.

PRINCIPLE 2. COMPETENCE

The maintenance of high standards of professional competence is a responsibility shared by all psychologists in the interest of the public and the profession as a whole. Psychologists recognize the boundaries of their competence and the limitations of their techniques and only provide services, use techniques, or offer opinions as professionals that meet recognized standards. Psychologists maintain knowledge of current scientific and professional information related to the services they render.

a. Psychologists accurately represent their competence, education, training, and experience. Psychologists claim as evidence of professional qualifications only those degrees obtained from institutions acceptable under the Bylaws and Rules of Council of the American Psychological Association.

b. As teachers, psychologists perform their duties on the basis of careful preparation so that their instruction is accurate, current, and scholarly.

c. Psychologists recognize the need for continuing education and are open to new procedures and changes in expectations and values over time. They recognize differences among people, such as those that may be associated with age, sex, socioeconomic, and ethnic backgrounds. Where relevant, they obtain training, experience, or counsel to assure competent service or research relating to such persons.

d. Psychologists with the responsibility for decisions involving individuals or policies based on test results have an understanding of psychological or educational measurement, validation problems, and other test research.

e. Psychologists recognize that their effectiveness depends in part upon their ability to maintain effective interpersonal relations, and that aberrations on their part may interfere with their abilities. They refrain from undertaking any activity in which their personal problems are likely to lead to inadequate professional services or harm to a client; or, if engaged in such activity when they become aware of their personal problems, they seek competent professional assistance to determine whether they should suspend, terminate, or limit the scope of their professional and/or scientific activities.

PRINCIPLE 3. MORAL AND LEGAL STANDARDS

Psychologists' and moral, ethical, and legal standards of behavior are a personal matter to the same degree as they are for any other citizen, except as these may compromise the fulfillment of their professional responsibilities, or reduce the trust in psychology or psychologists held by the general public. Regarding their own behavior, psychologists should be aware of the prevailing community standards and of the possible impact upon the quality of professional services provided by their conformity to or deviation from these standards. Psychologists are also aware of the possible impact of their public behavior upon the ability of colleagues to perform their professional duties.

a. Psychologists as teachers are aware of the diverse backgrounds of students and, when dealing with topics that may give offense, treat the material objectively and present it in a manner for which the student is prepared.

b. As employees, psychologists refuse to participate in practices inconsistent with legal, moral, and ethical standards regarding the treatment of employees or of the public. For example, psychologists will not condone practices that are inhumane or that result in illegal or otherwise unjustifiable discrimination on the basis of race, age, sex, religion, or national origin in hiring, promotion, or training.

c. In providing psychological services, psychologists avoid any action that will violate or diminish the legal and civil rights of clients or of others who may be affected by their actions.

As practitioners, psychologists remain abreast of relevant federal, state, local, and agency regulations and Association standards of practice concerning the conduct of their practice. They are concerned with developing such legal and quasi-legal regulations as best serve the public interest and in changing such existing regulations as are not beneficial to the interests of the public and the profession.

d. As researchers, psychologists remain abreast of relevant federal and state regulations concerning the conduct of research with human participants or animals.

PRINCIPLE 4. PUBLIC STATEMENTS

Public statements, announcements of services, and promotional activities of psychologists serve the purpose of providing sufficient information to aid the consumer public in making informed judgments and choices. Psychologists represent accurately and objectively their professional qualifications, affiliations, and functions, as well as those of the institutions or organizations with which they or the statements may be associated. In public statements providing psychological information or professional opinions or providing information about the availability of psychological products and services, psychologists take full account of the limits and uncertainties of present psychological knowledge and techniques.

a. When announcing professional services, psychologists limit the information to: name, highest academic degree conferred, date and type of certification or licensure, diplomate status, address, telephone number, office hours, and, at the individual practitioner's discretion, an appropriate brief listing of the types of psychological services offered and fee information. Such statements are descriptive of services provided but not evaluative as to their quality or uniqueness. They do not contain testimonials by quotation or by implication. They do not claim uniqueness of skills or methods unless determined by acceptable and public scientific evidence.

b. In announcing the availability of psychological services or products, psychologists do not display any affilitations with an organization in a manner that falsely implies the sponsorship or certification of that organization. In particular and for example, psychologists do not offer APA membership or fellowship as evidence of qualification. They do not name their employer or professional associations unless the services are in fact to be provided by or under the responsible, direct supervision and continuing control of such organizations or agencies.

c. Announcements of "personal growth groups" give a clear statement of purpose and the nature of the experiences to be provided. The education, training, and experience of the psychologists are appropriately specified.

d. Psychologists associated with the development or promotion of psychological devices, books, or other products offered for commercial sale make every effort to insure that announcements and advertisements are presented in a professional, scientifically acceptable, and factually informative manner.

e. Psychologists do not participate for personal gain in commercial announcements recommending to the general public the purchase or use or any proprietary or single-source product or service.

f. Psychologists who interpret the science of psychology or the services of psychologists to the general public accept the obligation to present the material fairly and accurately, avoiding misrepresentation through sensationalism, exaggeration, or superficiality. Psychologists are guided by the primary obligation to aid the public in forming their own informed judgments, opinions, and choices.

g. As teachers, psychologists insure that statements in catalogs and course outlines are accurate and sufficient, particularly in terms of subject matter to be covered, bases for evaluating progress, and nature of course experiences. Announcements or brochures describing workshops, seminars, or other educational programs accurately represent intended audience and eligibility requirements, educational objectives, and nature of the material to be covered, as well as the education, training, and experience of the psychologists presenting the programs, and any fees involved. Public announcements soliciting subjects for research, and in which clinical services or other professional services are offered as an inducement, make clear the nature of the services as well as the costs and other obligations to be accepted by the human participants of the research.

h. Psychologists accept the obligation to correct others who may represent the psychologist's professional qualifications or associations with products or services in a manner incompatible with these guidelines.

i. Psychological services for the purpose of diagnosis, treatment, or personal advice are provided only in the context of a professional relationship, and are not given by means of public lectures or demonstrations, newspaper or magazine articles, radio or television programs, mail, or similar media.

PRINCIPLE 5. CONFIDENTIALITY

Safeguarding information about an individual that has been obtained by the psychologist in the course of his teaching, practice, or investigation is a primary obligation of the psychologist. Such information is not communicated to others unless certain important conditions are not met.

a. Information received in confidence is revealed only after most careful deliberation and when there is clear and imminent danger to an individual or to society, and then only to appropriate professional workers or public authorities.

b. Information obtained in clinical or consulting relationships, or evaluative data concerning children, students, employees, and others are discussed only for professional purposes and only with persons clearly concerned with the case. Written and oral reports should present only data germane to the purposes of the evaluation and every effort should be made to avoid undue invasion of privacy.

c. Clinical and other materials are used in classroom teaching and writing only when the identity of the persons involved is adequately disguised.

d. The confidentiality of professional communications about individuals is maintained. Only when the originator and other persons involved give their express permission is a confidential professional communication shown to the individual concerned. The psychologist is responsible for informing the client of the limits of the confidentiality.

e. Only after explicit permission has been granted is the identity of research subjects published. When data have been published without permission for identification, the psychologist assumes responsibility for adequately disguising their sources.

f. The psychologist makes provisions for the maintenance of confidentiality in the prevention and ultimate disposition of confidential records.

PRINCIPLE 6. WELFARE OF THE CONSUMER

Psychologists respect the integrity and protect the welfare of the people and groups with whom they work. When there is a conflict of interest between the client and the psychologist's employing institution, psychologists clarify the nature and direction of their loyalties and responsibilities and keep all parties informed of their commitments. Psychologists fully inform consumers as to the purpose and nature of an evaluative, treatment, educational, or training procedure, and they freely acknowledge that clients, students, or participants in research have freedom of choice with regard to participation.

a. Psychologists are continually cognizant of their own needs and of their inherently powerful position *vis a vis* clients, in order to avoid exploiting their trust and dependency. Psychologists make every effort to avoid dual relationships with clients and/or relationships which might impair their professional judgment or increase the risk of client exploitation. Examples of such dual relationships include treating employees, supervisees, close friends, or relatives. Sexual intimacies with clients are unethical.

b. Where demands of an organization on psychologists go beyond reasonable conditions of employment, psychologists recognize possible conflicts of interest that may arise. When such conflicts occur, psychologists clarify the nature of the conflict and inform all parties of the nature and direction of the loyalties and responsibilities involved.

c. When acting as a supervisor, trainer, researcher, or employer, psychologists accord informed choice, confidentiality, due process, and protection from physical and mental harm to their subordinates in such relationships.

d. Financial arrangements in professional practice are in accord with professional standards that safeguard the best interests of the client and that are clearly understood by the client in advance of billing. Psychologists are responsible for assisting clients in finding needed services in those instances where payment of the usual fee would be a hardship. No commission, rebate, or other form of remuneration may be given or received for referral of clients for professional services, whether by an individual or by an agency. Psychologists willingly contribute a portion of their services to work for which they receive little or no financial return.

e. The psychologist attempts to terminate a clinical or consulting relationship when it is reasonably clear that the consumer is not benefiting from it. Psychologists who find that their services are being used by employers in a way that is not beneficial to the participants or to employees who may be affected, or to significant others, have the responsibility to make their observations known to the responsible persons and to propose modification or termination of the engagement.

PRINCIPLE 7. PROFESSIONAL RELATIONSHIPS

Psychologists act with due regard for the needs, special competencies, and obligations of their colleagues in psychology and other professions. Psychologists respect the prerogatives and obligations of the institutions or organizations with which they are associated.

a. Psychologists understand the areas of competence of related professions, and make full use of all the professional, technical, and administrative resources that best serve the interests of consumers. The absence of formal relationships with other professional workers does not relieve psychologists from the responsibility of securing for their clients the best possible professional service nor does it relieve them from the exercise of foresight, diligence, and tact in obtaining the complementary or alternative assistance needed by clients.

b. Psychologists know and take into account the traditions and practices of other professional groups with which they work and cooperate fully with members of such groups. If a consumer is receiving services from another professional, psychologists do not offer their services directly to the consumer without first informing the professional person already involved so that the risk of confusion and conflict for the consumer can be avoided.

c. Psychologists who employ or supervise other professionals or professionals in training accept the obligation to facilitate their further professional development by providing suitable working conditions, consultation, and experience opportunities.

d. As employees of organizations providing psychological services, or as independent psychologists serving clients in an organizational context, psychologists seek to support the integrity, reputation, and proprietary rights of the host organization. When it is judged necessary in a client's interest to question the organization's programs or policies, psychologists attempt to effect change by constructive action within the organization before disclosing confidential information acquired in their professional roles.

e. In the pursuit of research, psychologists give sponsoring agencies, host institutions, and publication channels the same respect and opportunity for giving informed consent that they accord to individual research participants. They are aware of their obligation to future research workers and insure that host institutions are given adequate information about the research and proper acknowledgement of their contributions.

f. Publication credit is assigned to all those who have contributed to a publication in proportion to their contribution. Major contributions of a professional character made by several persons to a common project are recognized by joint authorship, with the experimenter or author who made the principal contribution identified and listed first. Minor contributions of a professional character, extensive clerical or similar nonprofessional assistance, and other minor contributions are acknowledged in footnotes or in an introductory statement. Acknowledgement through specific citations is made for unpublished as well as published material that has directly influenced the research or writing. A psychologist who compiles and edits material of others for publication publishes the material in the name of the originating group, if any, and with his/her own name appearing as chairperson or editor. All contributors are to be acknowledged and named.

g. When a psychologist violates ethical standards, psychologists who know first-hand of such activities should, if possible, attempt to rectify the situation. Failing an informal solution, psychologists bring such unethical activities to the attention of the appropriate local, state, and/or national committee on professional ethics, standards, and practices.

h. Members of the Association cooperate with duly constituted committees of the Association, in particular and for example, the Committee on Scientific and Professional Ethics and Conduct, and the Committee on Professional Standards Review, by responding to inquiries promptly and completely. Members taking longer than 30 days to respond to such inquiries shall have the burden of demonstrating that they acted with "reasonable promptness." Members also have a similar responsibility to respond with reasonable promptness to inquiries from duly constituted state association ethics committees and professional standards review committees.

PRINCIPLE 8. UTILIZATION OF ASSESSMENT TECHNIQUES

In the development, publication, and utilization of psychological assessment techniques, psychologists observe relevant APA standards. Persons examined have the right to know the results, the interpretations made, and, where appropriate, the original data on which final judgments were based. Test users avoid imparting unnecessary information which would compromise test security, but they provide requested information that explains the basis for decisions that may adversely affect that person or that person's dependents.

a. The client has the right to have and the psychologist has the responsibility to provide explanations of the nature and the purposes of the test and the test results in language that the client can understand, unless, as in some employment or school settings, there is an explicit exception to this right agreed upon in advance. When the explanations are to be provided by others, the psychologist establishes procedures for providing adequate explanations.

b. When a test is published or otherwise made available for operational use, it is accompanied by a manual (or other published or readily available information) that fully describes the development of the test, the rationale, and evidence of validity and reliability. The test manual explicitly states the purposes and applications for which the test is recommended and identifies special qualifications required to administer the test and to interpret it properly. Test manuals provide complete information regarding the characteristics of the normative population.

c. In reporting test results, psychologists indicate any reservations regarding validity or reliability resulting from testing circumstances or inappropriateness of the test norms for the person tested. Psychologists strive to insure that the test results and their interpretations are not misused by others.

d. Psychologists accept responsibility for removing from clients' files test score information that has become obsolete, lest such information be misused or misconstrued to the disadvantage of the person tested.

e. Psychologists offering test scoring and interpretation services are able to demonstrate that the validity of the programs and procedures used in arriving at interpretations are based on appropriate evidence. The public offering of an automated test interpretation service is considered as a professional-to-professional consultation. The psychologist makes every effort to avoid misuse of test reports.

PRINCIPLE 9. PURSUIT OF RESEARCH ACTIVITIES

The decision to undertake research should rest upon a considered judgment by the individual psychologist about how best to contribute to psychological science and to human welfare. Psychologists carry out their investigations with respect for the people who participate and with concern for their dignity and welfare.

a. In planning a study the investigator has the responsibility to make a careful evaluation of its ethical acceptability, taking into account the following additional principles for research with human beings. To the extent that this appraisal, weighing scientific and humane values, suggests a compromise of any principle, the investigator incurs an increasingly serious obligation to seek ethical advice and to observe stringent safeguards to protect the rights of the human research participants.

b. Responsibility for the establishment and maintenance of acceptable ethical practice in research always remains with the individual investigator. The investigator is also responsible for the ethical treatment of research participants by collaborators, assistants, students, and employees, all of whom, however, incur parallel obligations.

c. Ethical practice requires the investigator to inform the participant of all features of the research that might reasonably be expected to influence willingness to participate, and to explain all other aspects of the research about which the participant inquires. Failure to make full disclosure imposes additional force to the investigator's abiding responsibility to protect the welfare and dignity of the research participant.

d. Openness and honesty are essential characteristics of the relationship between investigator and research participant. When the methodological requirements of a study necessitate concealment or deception, the investigator is required to insure as soon as possible the participant's understanding of the reasons for this action and of a sufficient justification for the procedures employed.

e. Ethical practice requires the investigator to respect the individual's freedom to decline to participate in or withdraw from research. The obligation to protect this freedom requires special vigilance when the investigator is in a position of power over the participant, as, for example, when the participant is a student, client, employee, or otherwise is in a dual relationship with the investigator.

f. Ethically acceptable research begins with the establishment of a clear and fair agreement between the investigator and the research participant that clarifies the responsibilities of each. The investigator has the obligation to honor all promises and commitments included in that agreement.

g. The ethical investigator protects participants from physical and mental discomfort, harm, and danger. If a risk of such consequences exists, the investigator is required to inform the participant of that fact, secure consent before proceeding, and take all possible measures to minimize distress. A research procedure must not be used if it is likely to cause serious or lasting harm to a participant.

h. After the data are collected, the investigator provides the participant with information about the nature of the study and removes any misconceptions that may have arisen. Where scientific or humane values justify delaying or withholding information, the investigator acquires a special responsibility to assure that there are no damaging consequences for the participant.

i. When research procedures may result in undesirable consequences for the individual participant, the investigator has the responsibility to detect and remove or correct these consequences, including, where relevant, long-term after effects.

j. Information obtained about the individual research participants during the course of an investigation is confidential unless otherwise agreed in advance. When the possibility exists that others may obtain access to such information, this possibility, together with the plans for protecting confidentiality, is explained to the participants as part of the procedure for obtaining informed consent.

k. A psychologist using animals in research adheres to the provisions of the Rules Regarding Animals, drawn up by the Committee on Precautions and Standards in Animal Experimentation and adopted by the American Psychological Association.

l. Investigations of human participants using drugs should be conducted only in such settings as clinics, hospitals, or research facilities maintaining appropriate safeguards for the participants.

REFERENCES

Psychologists are responsible for knowing about and acting in accord with the standards and positions of the APA, as represented in such official documents as the following:

American Association of University Professors. Statement of Principles on Academic Freedom and Tenure. *Policy Documents & Report,* 1977, 1–4.

American Psychological Association. *Guidelines for Psychologists for the Use of Drugs in Research.* Washington, D.C.: Author, 1971.

American Psychological Association. *Principles for the Care and Use of Animals.* Washington, D.C.: Author, 1971.

American Psychological Association. Guidelines for conditions of employment of psychologists. *American Psychologist,* 1972, *27,* 331–334.

American Psychological Association. Guidelines for psychologists conducting growth groups. *American Psychologist,* 1973, *28,* 933.

American Psychological Association. *Ethical Principles in the Conduct of Research with Human Participants.* Washington, D.C.: Author, 1973.

American Psychological Association. *Standards for Educational and Psychological Tests.* Washington, D.C.: Author, 1974.

American Psychological Association. *Standards for Providers of Psychological Services.* Washington, D.C.: Author, 1977.

Committee on Scientific and Professional Ethics and Conduct. Guidelines for telephone directory listings. *American Psychologist,* 1969, *24,* 70–71.

AN EXAMPLE OF A JOB ANALYSIS

APPENDIX C

DOUGH MIXER (BAKERY PRODUCTS)[1]

Description of Tasks (with estimated % of time required for each major task)

1. Dumps ingredients into mixing machine: Examines production schedule to determine type of bread to be produced, such as rye, whole wheat, or white. Refers to formula card for quantities and types of ingredients required, such as flour, water, milk, vitamin solutions, and shortening. Weighs out, measures, and dumps ingredients into mixing machine. (20%)

2. Operates mixing machine: Turns valves and other hand controls to set mixing time according to type of dough being mixed. Presses button to start agitator blades in machine. Observes gages and dials on equipment continuously to verify temperature of dough and mixing time. Feels dough for desired consistency. Adds water or flour to mix measuring vessels and adjusts mixing time and controls to obtain desired elasticity in mix. (55%)

3. Directs other workers in fermentation of dough: Prepares fermentation schedule according to type of dough being raised. Sprays portable dough *Trough* with lubricant to prevent adherence of mixed dough to trough. Directs DOUGH-MIXER HELPER in positioning trough beneath door of mixer to catch dough when mixing cycle is complete. Pushes or directs other workers to push troughs of dough into fermentation room. (10%)

4. Cuts dough: Dumps fermented dough onto work table. Manually kneads dough to eliminate gases formed by yeast. Cuts dough into pieces with hand cutter. Places cut dough on proofing rack and covers with cloth. (10%)

5. Performs miscellaneous duties: Records on work sheet number of batches mixed during work shift. Informs BAKERY SUPERVISOR when repairs or major adjustments are required for machines and equipment. (5%)

---

[1]Adapted from U. S. Department of Labor, 1972, pp. 42–45. The particular Dough Mixer job described in this job analysis requires a higher functional level with respect to people, involving directing activities not included in the more general DOT-defined job. Hence its code is 520.562-010 rather than 520.582-010 as given in the 4th edition of the *Dictionary of Occupational Titles* (US Dept. of Labor, 1977, p. 316).

WORKER FUNCTION RATINGS (lower numbers correspond to more complex functions)

D. Data—5 (Copying)
P. People—6 (Speaking—Signaling)
T. Things—2 (Operating—Controlling)

WORKER REQUIREMENTS

General Educational Development (Levels are precisely defined in terms of reading, writing, speaking, mathematical, and reasoning requirements)
(low) 1   (2)   3   4   5   6 (high)
Level marked corresponds to six years of elementary school or equivalent

Specific Vocational Preparation
(low) 1   2   3   (4)   5   6   7   8   9 (high)
Requires six months on-the-job training or one year as a dough-mixer helper

Temperaments (Worker must adapt to one or more of 10 described work situations)
(M)—Adaptability to making generalizations, evaluations, or decisions based on sensory or judgmental criteria
(T)—Adaptability to situations requiring the precise attainment of set limits, tolerances, or standards

Physical Demands
Strength: Sedentary   Light   Medium   (Heavy)   Very Heavy
(3)—Stooping, kneeling, crouching, and/or crawling
(4)—Reaching, handling, fingering, and/or feeling
(6)—Seeing

Environmental Conditions
(1)—Inside
(5)—Noise and/or vibration

UNIFORM GUIDELINES ON EMPLOYEE SELECTION PROCEDURES (1978)[1]

APPENDIX D

GENERAL PRINCIPLES

SECTION 1. *Statement of purpose.*—A. *Need for uniformity—Issuing agencies.* The Federal government's need for a uniform set of principles on the question of the use of tests and other selection procedures has long been recognized. The Equal Employment Opportunity Commission, the Civil Service Commission, the Department of Labor, and the Department of Justice jointly have adopted these uniform guidelines to meet that need, and to apply the same principles to the Federal government as are applied to other employers.

B. *Purpose of guidelines.* These guidelines incorporate a single set of principles which are designed to assist employers, labor organizations, employment agencies, and licensing and certification boards to comply with requirements of Federal law prohibiting employment practices which discriminate on grounds of race, color, religion, sex, and national origin. They are designed to provide a framework for determining the proper use of tests and other selection procedures. These guidelines do not require a user to conduct validity studies of selection procedures where no adverse impact results. However, all users are encouraged to use selection procedures which are valid, especially users operating under merit principles.

C. *Relation to prior guidelines.* These guidelines are based upon and supersede previously issued guidelines on employee selection procedures. These guidelines have been built upon court decisions, the previously issued guidelines of the agencies, and the practical experience of the agencies, as well as the standards of the psychological profession. These guidelines are intended to be consistent with existing law.

[1]From *Federal Register*, Vol. 43, No. 166—Friday, August 25, 1978, pp. 38296–38309.

SEC. 2. *Scope.*—A. *Application of guidelines.* These guidelines will be applied by the Equal Employment Opportunity Commission in the enforcement of title VII of the Civil Rights Act of 1964, as amended by the Equal Employment Opportunity Act of 1972 (hereinafter "Title VII"); by the Department of Labor, and the contract compliance agencies until the transfer of authority contemplated by the President's Reorganization Plan No. 1 of 1978, in the administration and enforcement of Executive Order 11246, as amended by Executive Order 11375 (hereinafter "Executive Order 11246"); by the Civil Service Commission and other Federal agencies subject to section 717 of Title VII; by the Civil Service Commission in exercising its responsibilities toward State and local governments under section 208(b)(1) of the Intergovernmental-Personnel Act; by the Department of Justice in exercising its responsibilities under Federal law; by the Office of Revenue Sharing of the Department of the Treasury under the State and Local Fiscal Assistance Act of 1972, as amended; and by any other Federal agency which adopts them.

B. *Employment decisions.* These guidelines apply to tests and other selection procedures which are used as a basis for any employment decision. Employment decisions include but are not limited to hiring, promotion, demotion, membership (for example, in a labor organization), referral, retention, and licensing and certification, to the extent that licensing and certification may be covered by Federal equal employment opportunity law. Other selection decisions, such as selection for training or transfer, may also be considered employment decisions if they lead to any of the decisions listed above.

C. *Selection procedures.* These guidelines apply only to selection procedures which are used as a basis for making employment decisions. For example, the use of recruiting procedures designed to attract members of a particular race, sex, or ethnic group, which were previously denied employment opportunities or which are currently underutilized, may be necessary to bring an employer into compliance with Federal law, and is frequently an essential element of any effective affirmative action program; but recruitment practices are not considered by these guidelines to be selection procedures. Similarly, these guidelines do not pertain to the question of the lawfulness of a seniority system within the meaning of section 703(h), Executive Order 11246 or other provisions of Federal law or regulation, except to the extent that such systems utilize selection procedures to determine qualifications or abilities to perform the job. Nothing in these guidelines is intended or should be interpreted as discouraging the use of a selection procedure for the purpose of determining qualifications or for the purpose of selection on the basis of relative qualifications, if the selection procedure had been validated in accord with these guidelines for each such purpose for which it is to be used.

D. *Limitations.* These guidelines apply only to persons subject to Title VII, Executive Order 11246, or other equal employment opportunity requirements of Federal law. These guidelines do not apply to responsibilities under the Age Discrimination in Employment Act of 1967, as amended, not to discriminate on the basis of age, or under sections 501, 503, and 504 of the Rehabilitation Act of 1973, not tc discriminate on the basis of handicap.

E. *Indian preference not affected.* These guidelines do not restrict any obligation imposed or right granted by Federal law to users to extend a preference in employment to Indians living on or near an Indian reservation in connection with employment opportunities on or near an Indian reservation.

SEC. 3. *Discrimination defined: Relationship between use of selection procedures and discrimination*—A. *Procedure having adverse impact constitutes dis-*

crimination unless justified. The use of any selection procedure which has an adverse impact on the hiring, promotion, or other employment or membership opportunities of members of any race, sex, or ethnic group will be considered to be discriminatory and inconsistent with these guidelines, unless the procedure has been validated in accordance with these guidelines, or the provisions of section 6 below are satisfied.

B. *Consideration of suitable alternative selection procedures.* Where two or more selection procedures are available which serve the user's legitimate interest in efficient and trustworthy workmanship, and which are substantially equally valid for a given purpose, the user should use the procedure which has been demonstrated to have the lesser adverse impact. Accordingly, whenever a validity study is called for by these guidelines, the user should include, as a part of the validity study, an investigation of suitable alternative selection procedures and suitable alternative methods of using the selection procedure which have as little adverse impact as possible, to determine the appropriateness of using or validating them in accord with these guidelines. If a user has made a reasonable effort to become aware of such alternative procedures and validity has been demonstrated in accord with these guidelines, the use of the test or other selection procedure may continue until such time as it should reasonably be reviewed for currency. Whenever the user is shown an alternative selection procedure with evidence of less adverse impact and substantial evidence of validity for the same job in similar circumstances, the user should investigate it to determine the appropriateness of using or validating it in accord with these guidelines. This subsection is not intended to preclude the combination of procedures into a significantly more valid procedure, if the use of such a combination has been shown to be in compliance with the guidelines.

SEC. 4. *Information on impact.*—A. *Records concerning impact.* Each user should maintain and have available for inspection records or other information which will disclose the impact which its tests and other selection procedures have upon employment opportunities of persons by identifiable race, sex, or ethnic group as set forth in subparagraph B below in order to determine compliance with these guidelines. Where there are large numbers of applicants and procedures are administered frequently, such information may be retained on a sample basis, provided that the sample is appropriate in terms of the applicant population and adequate in size.

B. *Applicable race, sex, and ethnic groups for recordkeeping.* The records called for by this section are to be maintained by sex, and the following races and ethnic groups: Blacks (Negroes), American Indians (including Alaskan Natives), Asians (including Pacific Islanders), Hispanic (including persons of Mexican, Puerto Rican, Cuban, Central or South American, or other Spanish origin or culture regardless of race), whites (Caucasians) other than Hispanic, and totals. The race, sex, and ethnic classifications called for by this section are consistent with the Equal Employment Opportunity Standard Form 100, Employer Information Report EEO–1 series of reports. The user should adopt safeguards to insure that the records required by this paragraph are used for appropriate purposes such as determining adverse impact, or (where required) for developing and monitoring affirmative action programs, and that such records are not used improperly. See sections 4E and 17(4), below.

C. *Evaluation of selection rates. The "bottom line."* If the information called for by sections 4A and B above shows that the total selection process for a job has an adverse impact, the individual components of the selection process should be evaluated for adverse impact. If this information shows that the total selection process does not have an adverse impact, the Federal enforcement agencies, in the exercise of their administrative and prosecutorial discretion, in usual circumstances, will not expect a user to evaluate the individual components for adverse impact, or to validate such individual components, and will not take enforcement action based upon adverse impact of any component of that process, including the separate parts of a multipart selection procedure or any separate procedure that is used as an alternative method of selection. However, in the following circumstances the Federal enforcement agencies will expect a user to evaluate the individual components for adverse impact and may, where appropriate, take enforcement action with respect to the individual components: (1) where the selection procedure is a significant factor in the continuation of patterns of assignments of incumbent employees caused by prior discriminatory employment practices, (2) where the weight of court decisions or administrative interpretations hold that a specific procedure (such as height or weight requirements or no-arrest records) is not job related in the same or similar circumstances. In unusual circumstances, other than those listed in (1) and (2) above, the Federal enforcement agencies may request a user to evaluate the individual components for adverse impact and may, where appropriate, take enforcement action with respect to the individual component.

   D. *Adverse impact and the "four-fifths rule."* A selection rate for any race, sex, or ethnic group which is less than four-fifths ($^4/_5$) (or eighty percent) of the rate for the group with the highest rate will generally be regarded by the Federal enforcement agencies as evidence of adverse impact, while a greater than four-fifths rate will generally not be regarded by Federal enforcement agencies as evidence of adverse impact. Smaller differences in selection rate may nevertheless constitute adverse impact, where they are significant in both statistical and practical terms or where a user's actions have discouraged applicants disproportionately on grounds of race, sex, or ethnic group. Greater differences in selection rate may not constitute adverse impact where the differences are based on small numbers and are not statistically significant, or where special recruiting or other programs cause the pool of minority or female candidates to be atypical of the normal pool of applicants from that group. Where the user's evidence concerning the impact of a selection procedure indicates adverse impact but is based upon numbers which are too small to be reliable, evidence concerning the impact of the procedure over a longer period of time and/or evidence concerning the impact which the selection procedure had when used in the same manner in similar circumstances elsewhere may be considered in determining adverse impact. Where the user has not maintained data on adverse impact as required by the documentation section of applicable guidelines, the Federal enforcement agencies may draw an inference of adverse impact of the selection process from the failure of the user to maintain such data, if the user has an underutilization of a group in the job category, as compared to the group's representation in the relevant labor market or, in the case of jobs filled from within, the applicable work force.

   E. *Consideration of user's equal employment opportunity posture.* In carrying out their obligations, the Federal enforcement agencies will consider the general posture of the user with respect to equal employment opportunity for the job or group of jobs in question. Where a user has adopted an affirmative action program, the Federal enforcement agencies will consider the provisions of that program, including the goals and timetables which the user has adopted and the progress which the user has made in carrying out that program and in meeting the goals and timetables. While such affirmative action programs may in design and execution be race, color, sex, or ethnic conscious, selection procedures under such programs should be based upon the ability or relative ability to do the work.

Sec. 5. *General standards for validity studies.*—A. *Acceptable types of validity studies.* For the purposes of satisfying these guidelines, users may rely upon criterion-related validity studies, content validity studies, or construct validity studies, in accordance with the standards set forth in the technical standards of these guidelines, section 14 below. New strategies for showing the validity of selection procedures will be evaluated as they become accepted by the psychological profession.

B. *Criterion-related, content, and construct validity.* Evidence of the validity of a test or other selection procedure by a criterion-related validity study should consist of empirical data demonstrating that the selection procedure is predictive of or significantly correlated with important elements of job performance. See section 14B below. Evidence of the validity of a test or other selection procedure by a content validity study should consist of data showing that the content of the selection procedure is representative of important aspects of performance on the job for which the candidates are to be evaluated. See section 14C below. Evidence of the validity of a test or other selection procedure through a contruct validity study should consist of data showing that the procedure measures the degree to which candidates have identifiable characteristics which have been determined to be important in successful performance in the job for which the candidates are to be evaluated. See section 14D below.

C. *Guidelines are consistent with professional standards.* The provisions of these guidelines relating to validation of selection procedures are intended to be consistent with generally accepted professional standards for evaluating standardized tests and other selection procedures, such as those described in the Standards for Educational and Psychological Tests prepared by a joint committee of the American Psychological Association, the American Educational Research Association, and the National Council on Measurement in Education (American Psychological Association, Washington, D.C., 1974) (hereinafter "A.P.A. Standards") and standard textbooks and journals in the field of personnel selection.

D. *Need for documentation of validity.* For any selection procedure which is part of a selection process which has an adverse impact and which selection procedure has an adverse impact, each user should maintain and have available such documentation as is described in section 15 below.

E. *Accuracy and standardization.* Validity studies should be carried out under conditions which assure insofar as possible the adequacy and accuracy of the research and the report. Selection procedures should be administered and scored under standardized conditions.

F. *Caution against selection on basis of knowledges, skills, or ability learned in brief orientation period.* In general, users should avoid making employment decisions on the basis of measures of knowledges, skills, or abilities which are normally learned in a brief orientation period, and which have an adverse impact.

G. *Method of use of selection procedures.* The evidence of both the validity and utility of a selection procedure should support the method the user chooses for operational use of the procedure, if that method of use has a greater adverse impact than another method of use. Evidence which may be sufficient to support the use of a selection procedure on a pass/fail (screening) basis may be insufficient to support the use of the same procedure on a ranking basis under these guidelines. Thus, if a user decides to use a selection procedure on a ranking basis, and that method of use has a greater adverse impact than use on an appropriate pass/fail basis (see section 5H below), the user should have sufficient evidence of validity and utility to support the use on a ranking basis. See sections 3B, 14B (5) and (6), and 14C (8) and (9).

H. *Cutoff scores*. Where cutoff scores are used, they should normally be set so as to be reasonable and consistent with normal expectations of acceptable proficiency within the work force. Where applicants are ranked on the basis of properly validated selection procedures and those applicants scoring below a higher cutoff score than appropriate in light of such expectations have little or no chance of being selected for employment, the higher cutoff score may be appropriate, but the degree of adverse impact should be considered.

I. *Use of selection procedures for higher level jobs*. If job progression structures are so established that employees will probably, within a reasonable period of time and in a majority of cases, progress to a higher level, it may be considered that the applicants are being evaluated for a job or jobs at the higher level. However, where job progression is not so nearly automatic, or the time span is such that higher level jobs or employees' potential may be expected to change in significant ways, it should be considered that applicants are being evaluated for a job at or near the entry level. A "reasonable period of time" will vary for different jobs and employment situations but will seldom be more than 5 years. Use of selection procedures to evaluate applicants for a higher level job would not be appropriate:

(1) If the majority of those remaining employed do not progress to the higher level job;

(2) If there is a reason to doubt that the higher level job will continue to require essentially similar skills during the progression period; or

(3) If the selection procedures measure knowledges, skills, or abilities required for advancement which would be expected to develop principally from the training or experience on the job.

J. *Interim use of selection procedures*. Users may continue the use of a selection procedure which is not at the moment fully supported by the required evidence of validity, provided; (1) The user has available substantial evidence of validity, and (2) the user has in progress, when technically feasible, a study which is designed to produce the additional evidence required by these guidelines within a reasonable time. If such a study is not technically feasible, see section 6B. If the study does not demonstrate validity, this provision of these guidelines for interim use shall not constitute a defense in any action, nor shall it relieve the user of any obligations arising under Federal law.

K. *Review of validity studies for currency*. Whenever validity has been shown in accord with these guidelines for the use of a particular selection procedure for a job or group of jobs, additional studies need not be performed until such time as the validity study is subject to review as provided in section 3B above. There are no absolutes in the area of determining the currency of a validity study. All circumstances concerning the study, including the validation strategy used, and changes in the relevant labor market and the job should be considered in the determination of when a validity study is outdated.

Sec. 6. *Use of selection procedures which have not been validated.*—A. *Use of alternate selection procedures to eliminate adverse impact.* A user may choose to utilize alternative selection procedures in order to eliminate adverse impact or as part of an affirmative action program. See section 13 below. Such alternative procedures should eliminate the adverse impact in the total selection process, should be lawful, and should be as job related as possible.

B. *Where validity studies cannot or need not be performed.* There are circumstances in which a user cannot or need not utilize the validation techniques contemplated by these guidelines. In such circumstances, the user should utilize selection procedures which are as job related as possible and which will minimize or eliminate adverse impact, as set forth below.

(1) *Where informal or unscored procedures are used.* When an informal or unscored selection procedure which has an adverse impact is utilized, the user should eliminate the adverse impact, or modify the procedure to one which is a formal, scored, or quantified measure or combination of measures and then validate the procedure in accord with these guidelines, or otherwise justify continued use of the procedure in accord with Federal law.

(2) *Where formal and scored procedures are used.* When a formal and scored selection procedure is used which has an adverse impact, the validation techniques contemplated by these guidelines usually should be followed if technically feasible. Where the user cannot or need not follow the validation techniques anticipated by these guidelines, the user should either modify the procedure to eliminate adverse impact or otherwise justify continued use of the procedure in accord with Federal law.

SEC. 7. *Use of other validity studies.*—A. *Validity studies not conducted by the user.* Users may, under certain circumstances, support the use of selection procedures by validity studies conducted by other users or conducted by test publishers or distributors and described in test manuals. While publishers of selection procedures have a professional obligation to provide evidence of validity which meets generally accepted professional standards (see section 5C above), users are cautioned that they are responsible for compliance with these guidelines. Accordingly, users seeking to obtain selection procedures from publishers and distributors should be careful to determine that, in the event the user becomes subject to the validity requirements of these guidelines, the necessary information to support validity has been determined and will be made available to the user.

B. *Use of criterion-related validity evidence from other sources.* Criterion-related validity studies conducted by one test user, or described in test manuals and the professional literature, will be considered acceptable for use by another user when the following requirements are met:

(1) *Validity evidence.* Evidence from the available studies meeting the standards of section 14B below clearly demonstrates that the selection procedure is valid;

(2) *Job similarity.* The incumbents in the user's job and the incumbents in the job or group of jobs on which the validity study was conducted perform substantially the same major work behaviors, as shown by appropriate job analyses both on the job or group of jobs on which the validity study was performed and on the job for which the selection procedure is to be used; and

(3) *Fairness evidence.* The studies include a study of test fairness for each race, sex, and ethnic group which constitutes a significant factor in the borrowing user's relevant labor market for the job or jobs in question. If the studies under consideration satisfy (1) and (2) above but do not contain an investigation of test fairness, and it is not technically feasible for the borrowing user to conduct an

internal study of test fairness, the borrowing user may utilize the study until studies conducted elsewhere meeting the requirements of these guidelines show test unfairness, or until such time as it becomes technically feasible to conduct an internal study of test fairness and the results of that study can be acted upon. Users obtaining selection procedures from publishers should consider, as one factor in the decision to purchase a particular selection procedure, the availability of evidence concerning test fairness.

C. *Validity evidence from multiunit study.* If validity evidence from a study covering more than one unit within an organization satisfies the requirements of section 14B below, evidence of validity specific to each unit will not be required unless there are variables which are likely to affect validity significantly.

D. *Other significant variables.* If there are variables in the other studies which are likely to affect validity significantly, the user may not rely upon such studies, but will be expected either to conduct an internal validity study or to comply with section 6 above.

Sec. 8. *Cooperative studies.*—A. *Encouragement of cooperative studies.* The agencies issuing these guidelines encourage employers, labor organizations, and employment agencies to cooperate in research development, search for lawful alternatives, and validity studies in order to achieve procedures which are consistent with these guidelines.

B. *Standards for use of cooperative studies.* If validity evidence from a cooperative study satisfies the requirements of section 14 below, evidence of validity specific to each user will not be required unless there are variables in the user's situation which are likely to affect validity significantly.

SEC. 9. *No assumption of validity.*—A.. *Unacceptable substitutes for evidence of validity.* Under no circumstances will the general reputation of a test or other selection procedures, its author or its publisher, or casual reports of its validity be accepted in lieu of evidence of validity. Specifically ruled out are: assumptions of validity based on a procedure's name or descriptive labels; all forms of promotional literature; data bearing on the frequency of a procedure's usage; testimonial statements and credentials of sellers, users, or consultants; and other nonempirical or anecdotal accounts of selection practices or selection outcomes.

B. *Encouragement of professional supervision.* Professional supervision of selection activities is encouraged but is not a substitute for documented evidence of validity. The enforcement agencies will take into account the fact that a thorough job analysis was conducted and that careful development and use of a selection procedure in accordance with professional standards enhance the probability that the selection procedure is valid for the job.

SEC. 10. *Employment agencies and employment services.*—A. *Where selection procedures are devised by agency.* An employment agency, including private employment agencies and State employment agencies, which agrees to a request by an employer or labor organization to devise and utilize a selection procedure, should follow the standards in these guidelines for determining adverse impact. If adverse impact exists the agency should comply with these guidelines. An employment agency is not relieved of its obligation herein because the user did not request such validation or has requested the use of some lesser standard of validation than is provided in these guidelines. The use of an employment agency does not relieve an employer or labor organization or other user of its responsibilities under Federal law to provide equal employment opportunity or its obligations as a user under these guidelines.

B. *Where selection procedures are devised elsewhere.* Where an employment agency or service is requested to administer a selection procedure which has been devised elsewhere and to make referrals pursuant to the results, the employment agency or service should maintain and have available evidence of the impact of the selection and referral procedures which it administers. If adverse impact results, the agency or service should comply with these guidelines. If the agency or service seeks to comply with these guidelines by reliance upon validity studies or other data in the possession of the employer, it should obtain and have available such information.

SEC. 11. *Disparate treatment.* The principles of disparate or unequal treatment must be distinguished from the concepts of validation. A selection procedure–even though validated against job performance in accordance with these guidelines– cannot be imposed upon members of a race, sex, or ethnic group where other employees, applicants, or members have not been subjected to that standard. Disparate treatment occurs where members of a race, sex, or ethnic group have been denied the same employment, promotion, membership, or other employment opportunities as have been available to other employees or applicants. Those employees or applicants who have been denied equal treatment, because of prior discriminatory practices or policies, must at least be afforded the same opportunities as had existed for other employees or applicants during the period of discrimination. Thus, the persons who were in the class of persons discriminated against during the period the user followed the discriminatory practices should be allowed the opportunity to qualify under less stringent selection procedures previously followed, unless the user demonstrates that the increased standards are required by business necessity. This section does not prohibit a user who has not previously followed merit standards from adopting merit standards which are in compliance with these guidelines; nor does it preclude a user who has previously used invalid or unvalidated selection procedures from developing and using procedures which are in accord with these guidelines.

SEC.12. *Retesting of applicants.* Users should provide a reasonable opportunity for retesting and reconsideration. Where examinations are administered periodically with public notice, such reasonable opportunity exists, unless persons who have previously been tested are precluded from retesting. The user may however take reasonable steps to preserve the security of its procedures.

SEC. 13. *Affirmative action.*—A. *Affirmative action obligations.* The use of selection procedures which have been validated pursuant to these guidelines does not relieve users of any obligations they may have to undertake affirmative action to assure equal employment opportunity. Nothing in these guidelines is intended to preclude the use of lawful selection procedures which assist in remedying the effects of prior discriminatory practices, or the achievement of affirmative action objectives.

B. *Encouragement of voluntary affirmative action programs.* These guidelines are also intended to encourage the adoption and implementation of voluntary affirmative action programs by users who have no obligation under Federal law to adopt them; but are not intended to impose any new obligations in that regard. The agencies issuing and endorsing these guidelines endorse for all private employers and reaffirm for all governmental employers the Equal Employment Opportunity Coordinating Council's "Policy Statement on Affirmative Action Programs for State and Local Government Agencies" (41 FR 38814, September 13, 1976). That policy statement is attached hereto as appendix, section 17.

TECHNICAL STANDARDS

SEC. 14. *Technical standards for validity studies.* The following minimum standards, as applicable, should be met in conducting a validity study. Nothing in these guidelines is intended to preclude the development and use of other professionally acceptable techniques with respect to validation of selection procedures. Where it is not technically feasible for a user to conduct a validity study, the user has the obligation otherwise to comply with these guidelines. See sections 6 and 7 above.

A. *Validity studies should be based on review of information about the job.* Any validity study should be based upon a review of information about the job for which the selection procedure is to be used. The review should include a job analysis except as provided in section 14B(3) below with respect to criterion-related validity. Any method of job analysis may be used if it provides the information required for the specific validation strategy used.

B. *Technical standards for criterion-related validity studies.*—(1) *Technical feasibility.* Users choosing to validate a selection procedure by a criterion-related validity strategy should determine whether it is technically feasible (as defined in section 16) to conduct such a study in the particular employment context. The determination of the number of persons necessary to permit the conduct of a meaningful criterion-related study should be made by the user on the basis of all relevant information concerning the selection procedure, the potential sample, and the employment situation. Where appropriate, jobs with substantially the same major work behaviors may be grouped together for validity studies, in order to obtain an adequate sample. These guidelines do not require a user to hire or promote persons for the purpose of making it possible to conduct a criterion-related study.

(2) *Analysis of the job.* There should be a review of job information to determine measures of work behavior(s) or performance that are relevant to the job or group of jobs in question. These measures or criteria are relevant to the extent that they represent critical or important job duties, work behaviors, or work outcomes as developed from the review of job information. The possibility of bias should be considered both in selection of the criterion measures and their application. In view of the possibility of bias in subjective evaluations, supervisory rating techniques and instructions to raters should be carefully developed. All criterion measures and the methods for gathering data need to be examined for freedom from factors which would unfairly alter scores of members of any group. The relevance of criteria and their freedom from bias are of particular concern when there are significant differences in measures of job performance for different groups.

(3) *Criterion measures.* Proper safeguards should be taken to insure that scores on selection procedures do not enter into any judgments of employee adequacy that are to be used as criterion measures. Whatever criteria are used should represent important or critical work behavior(s) or work outcomes. Certain criteria may be used without a full job analysis if the user can show the importance of the criteria to the particular employment context. These criteria include but are not limited to production rate, error rate, tardiness, absenteeism, and length of service. A standardized rating of overall work performance may be used where a study of the job shows that it is an appropriate criterion. Where performance in training is used as a criterion, success in training should be properly measured and the

relevance of the training should be shown either through a comparsion of the content of the training program with the critical or important work behavior(s) of the job(s), or through a demonstration of the relationship between measures of performance in training and measures of job performance. Measures of relative success in training include but are not limited to instructor evaluations, performance samples, or tests. Criterion measures consisting of paper and pencil tests will be closely reviewed for job relevance.

(4) *Representativeness of the sample.* Whether the study is predictive or concurrent, the sample subjects should insofar as feasible be representative of the candidates normally available in the relevant labor market for the job or group of jobs in question, and should insofar as feasible include the races, sexes, and ethnic groups normally available in the relevant job market. In determining the representativeness of the sample in a concurrent validity study, the user should take into account the extent to which the specific knowledges or skills which are the primary focus of the test are those which employees learn on the job.

Where samples are combined or compared, attention should be given to see that such samples are comparable in terms of the actual job they perform, the length of time on the job where time on the job is likely to affect performance, and other relevant factors likely to affect validity differences; or that these factors are included in the design of the study and their effects identified.

(5) *Statistical relationships.* The degree of relationship between selection procedure scores and criterion measures should be examined and computed, using professionally acceptable statistical procedures. Generally, a selection procedure is considered related to the criterion, for the purposes of these guidelines, when the relationship between performance on the procedure and performance on the criterion measure is statistically significant at the .05 level of significance, which means that it is sufficiently high as to have a probability of no more than one (1) in twenty (20) to have occurred by chance. Absence of a statistically significant relationship between a selection procedure and job performance should not necessarily discourage other investigations of the validity of that selection procedure.

(6) *Operational use of selection procedures.* Users should evaluate each selection procedure to assure that it is appropriate for operational use, including establishment of cutoff scores or rank ordering. Generally, if other factors remain the same, the greater the magnitude of the relationship (e.g., correlation coefficent) between performance on a selection procedure and one or more criteria of performance on the job, and the greater the importance and number of aspects of job performance covered by the criteria, the more likely it is that the procedure will be appropriate for use. Reliance upon a selection procedure which is significantly related to a criterion measure, but which is based upon a study involving a large number of subjects and has a low correlation coefficient will be subject to close review if it has a large adverse impact. Sole reliance upon a single selection instrument which is related to only one of many job duties or aspects of job performance will also be subject to close review. The appropriateness of a selection procedure is best evaluated in each particular situation and there are no minimum correlation coefficients applicable to all employment situations. In determining whether a selection procedure is appropriate for operational use the following considerations should also be taken into account: the degree of adverse impact of the procedure, the availability of other selection procedures of greater or substantially equal validity.

(7) *Overstatement of validity findings.* Users should avoid reliance upon

techniques which tend to overestimate validity findings as a result of capitalization on chance unless an appropriate safeguard is taken. Reliance upon a few selection procedures or criteria of successful job performance when many selection procedures or criteria of performance have been studied, or the use of optimal statistical weights for selection procedures computed in one sample, are techniques which tend to inflate validity estimates as a result of chance. Use of a large sample is one safeguard; cross-validation is another.

(8) *Fairness*. This section generally calls for studies of unfairness where technically feasible. The concept of fairness or unfairness of selection procedures is a developing concept. In addition, fairness studies generally require substantial numbers of employees in the job or group of jobs being studied. For these reasons, the Federal enforcement agencies recognize that the obligation to conduct studies of fairness imposed by the guidelines generally will be upon users or groups of users with a large number of persons in a job class, or test developers; and that small users utilizing their own selection procedures will generally not be obligated to conduct such studies because it will be technically infeasible for them to do so.

(a) *Unfairness defined*. When members of one race, sex, or ethnic group characteristically obtain lower scores on a selection procedure than members of another group, and the differences in scores are not reflected in differences in a measure of job performance, use of the selection procedure may unfairly deny opportunities to members of the group that obtains the lower scores.

(b) *Investigation of fairness*. Where a selection procedure results in an adverse impact on a race, sex, or ethnic group identified in accordance with the classifications set forth in section 4 above and that group is a significant factor in the relevant labor market, the user generally should investigate the possible existence of unfairness for that group if it is technically feasible to do so. The greater the severity of the adverse impact on a group, the greater the need to investigate the possible existence of unfairness. Where the weight of evidence from other studies shows that the selection procedure predicts fairly for the group in question and for the same or similar jobs, such evidence may be relied on in connection with the selection procedure at issue.

(c) *General considerations in fairness investigations*. Users conducting a study of fairness should review the A.P.A. Standards regarding investigation of possible bias in testing. An investigation of fairness of a selection procedure depends on both evidence of validity and the manner in which the selection procedure is to be used in a particular employment context. Fairness of a selection procedure cannot necessarily be specified in advance without investigating these factors. Investigation of fairness of a selection procedure in samples where the range of scores on selection procedures or criterion measures is severely restricted for any subgroup sample (as compared to other subgroup samples) may produce misleading evidence of unfairness. That factor should accordingly be taken into account in conducting such studies and before reliance is placed on the results.

(d) *When unfairness is shown*. If unfairness is demonstrated through a showing that members of a particular group perform better or poorer on the job than their scores on the selection procedure would indicate through comparison with how members of other groups perform, the user may either revise or replace the selection instrument in accordance with these guidelines, or may continue to use the selection instrument operationally with appropriate revisions in its use to assure compatibility between the probability of successful job performance and the probability of being selected.

(e) *Technical feasibility of fairness studies*. In addition to the general conditions needed for technical feasibility for the conduct of a criterion-related study (see section 16, below) an investigation of fairness requires the following:

(i) An adequate sample of persons in each group available for the study to achieve findings of statistical significance. Guidelines do not require a user to hire or promote persons on the basis of group classifications for the purpose of making it possible to conduct a study of fairness; but the user has the obligation otherwise to comply with these guidelines.

(ii) The samples for each group should be comparable in terms of the actual job they perform, length of time on the job where time on the job is likely to affect performance, and other relevant factors likely to affect validity differences; or such factors should be included in the design of the study and their effects identified.

(f) *Continued use of selection procedures when fairness studies not feasible.* If a study of fairness should otherwise be performed, but is not technically feasible, a selection procedure may be used which has otherwise met the validity standards of these guidelines, unless the technical infeasibility resulted from discriminatory employment practices which are demonstrated by facts other than past failure to conform with requirements for validation of selection procedures. However, when it becomes technically feasible for the user to perform a study of fairness and such a study is otherwise called for, the user should conduct the study of fairness.

C. *Technical standards for content validity studies.*—(1) *Appropriateness of content validity studies.* Users choosing to validate a selection procedure by a content validity strategy should determine whether it is appropriate to conduct such a study in the particular employment context. A selection procedure can be supported by a content validity strategy to the extent that it is a representative sample of the content of the job. Selection procedures which purport to measure knowledges, skills, or abilities may in certain circumstances be justified by content validity, although they may not be representative samples, if the knowledge, skill, or ability measured by the selection procedure can be operationally defined as provided in section 14C(4) below, and if that knowledge, skill, or ability is a necessary prerequisite to successful job performance.

A selection procedure based upon inferences about mental processes cannot be supported solely or primarily on the basis of content validity. Thus, a content strategy is not appropriate for demonstrating the validity of selection procedures which purport to measure traits or constructs, such as intelligence. aptitude, personality, common sense, judgment, leadership, and spatial ability. Content validity is also not an appropriate strategy when the selection procedure involves knowledges, skills, or abilities which an employee will be expected to learn on the job.

(2) *Job analysis for content validity.* There should be a job analysis which includes an analysis of the important work behavior(s) required for successful performance and their relative importance and, if the behavior results in work product(s), an analysis of the work product(s). Any job analysis should focus on the work behavior(s) and the tasks associated with them. If work behavior(s) are not observable, the job analysis should identify and analyze those aspects of the behavior(s) that can be observed and the observed work products. The work behavior(s) selected for measurement should be critical work behavior(s) and/or important work behavior(s) constituting most of the job.

(3) *Development of selection procedures.* A selection procedure designed to measure the work behavior may be developed specifically from the job and job analysis in question, or may have been previously developed by the user, or by other users or by a test publisher.

(4) *Standards for demonstrating content validity.* To demonstrate the content validity of a selection procedure, a user should show that the behavior(s) demonstrated in the selection procedure are a representative sample of the behavior(s) of the job in question or that the selection procedure provides a representative sample of the work product of the job. In the case of a selection procedure measuring a knowledge, skill, or ability, the knowledge, skill, or ability being measured should be operationally defined. In the case of a selection procedure measuring a knowledge, the knowledge being measured should be operationally defined as that body of learned information which is used in and is a necessary prerequisite for observable aspects of work behavior of the job. In the case of skills or abilities, the skill or ability being measured should be operationally defined in terms of observable aspects of work behavior of the job. For any selection procedure measuring knowledge, skill, or ability the user should show that (a) the selection procedure measures and is a representative sample of that knowledge, skill, or ability; and (b) that knowledge, skill, or ability is used in and is a necessary prerequisite to performance of critical or important work behavior(s). In addition, to be content valid, a selection procedure measuring a skill or ability should either closely approximate an observable work behavior, or its product should closely approximate an observable work product. If a test purports to sample a work behavior or to provide a sample of a work product, the manner and setting of the selection procedure and its level and complexity should closely approximate the work situation. The closer the content and the context of the selection procedure are to work samples or work behaviors, the stronger is the basis for showing content validity. As the content of the selection procedure less resembles a work behavior, or the setting and manner of the administration of the selection procedure less resemble the work situation, or the result less resembles a work product, the less likely the selection procedure is to be content valid, and the greater the need for other evidence of validity.

(5) *Reliability.* The reliability of selection procedures justified on the basis of content validity should be a matter of concern to the user. Whenever it is feasible, appropriate statistical estimates should be made of the reliability of the selection procedure.

(6) *Prior training or experience.* A requirement for or evaluation of specific prior training or experience based on content validity, including a specification of level or amount of training or experience, should be justified on the basis of the relationship between the content of the training or experience and the content of the job for which the training or experience is to be required or evaluated. The critical consideration is the resemblance between the specific behaviors, products, knowledges, skills, or abilities in the experience or training and the specific behaviors, products, knowledges, skills, or abilities required on the job, whether or not there is close resemblance between the experience or training as a whole and the job as a whole.

(7) *Content validity of training success.* Where a measure of success in a training program is used as a selection procedure and the content of a training program is justified on the basis of content validity, the use should be justified on the relationship between the content of the training program and the content of the job.

(8) *Operational use.* A selection procedure which is supported on the basis of content validity may be used for a job if it represents a critical work behavior (i.e., a behavior which is necessary for performance of the job) or work behaviors which constitute most of the important parts of the job.

(9) *Ranking based on content validity studies.* If a user can show, by a job analysis or otherwise, that a higher score on a content valid selection procedure is likely to result in better job performance, the results may be used to rank persons who score above minimum levels. Where a selection procedure supported solely or primarily by content validity is used to rank job candidates, the selection procedure should measure those aspects of performance which differentiate among levels of job performance.

D. *Technical standards for construct validity studies.—* (1) *Appropriateness of construct validity studies.* Construct validity is a more complex strategy than either criterion-related or content validity. Construct validation is a relatively new and developing procedure in the employment field, and there is at present a lack of substantial literature extending the concept to employment practices. The user should be aware that the effort to obtain sufficient empirical support for construct validity is both an extensive and arduous effort involving a series of research studies, which include criterion-related validity studies and which may include content validity studies. Users choosing to justify use of a selection procedure by this strategy should therefore take particular care to assure that the validity study meets the standards set forth below.

(2) *Job analysis for construct validity studies.* There should be a job analysis. This job analysis should show the work behavior(s) required for successful performance of the job, or the group of jobs being studied, the critical or important work behavior(s) in the job or group of jobs being studied, and an identification of the construct(s) believed to underlie successful performance of these critical or important work behaviors in the job or jobs in question. Each construct should be named and defined, so as to distinguish it from other constructs. If a group of jobs is being studied the jobs should have in common one or more critical or important work behaviors at a comparable level of complexity.

(3) *Relationship to the job.* A selection procedure should then be identified or developed which measures the construct identified in accord with subparagraph (2) above. The user should show by empirical evidence that the selection proce-dure is validly related to the construct and that the construct is validly related to the performance of critical or important work behavior(s). The relationship between the construct as measured by the selection procedure and the related work behavior(s) should be supported by empirical evidence from one or more criterion-related studies involving the job or jobs in question which satisfy the provisions of section 14B above.

(4) *Use of construct validity study without new criterion-related evidence.—*(a) *Standards for use.* Until such time as professional literature provides more guidance on the use of construct validity in employment situations, the Federal agencies will accept a claim of construct validity without a criterion-related study which satisfies section 14B above only when the selection procedure has been used elsewhere in a situation in which a criterion-related study has been con-ducted and the use of a criterion-related validity study in this context meets the standards for transportability of criterion-related validity studies as set forth above in section 7. However, if a study pertains to a number of jobs having common critical or important work behaviors at a comparable level of complexity, and the evidence satisfies subparagraphs 14B (2) and (3) above for those jobs with criterion-related validity evidence for those jobs, the selection procedure may be used for all the jobs to which the study pertains. If construct validity is to be generalized to other jobs or groups of jobs not in the group studied, the Federal

enforcement agencies will expect at a minimum additional empirical research evidence meeting the standards of subparagraphs section 14B (2) and (3) above for the additional jobs or groups of jobs.

(b) *Determination of common work behaviors.* In determining whether two or more jobs have one or more work behavior(s) in common, the user should compare the observed work behavior(s) in each of the jobs and should compare the observed work product(s) in each of the jobs. If neither the observed work behavior(s) in each of the jobs nor the observed work product(s) in each of the jobs are the same, the Federal enforcement agencies will presume that the work behavior(s) in each job are different. If the work behaviors are not observable, then evidence of similarity of work products and any other relevant research evidence will be considered in determining whether the work behavior(s) in the two jobs are the same.

DOCUMENTATION OF IMPACT AND VALIDITY EVIDENCE

SEC. 15. *Documentation of impact and validity evidence.*—A. *Required information.* Users of selection procedures other than those users complying with section 15A(1) below should maintain and have available for each job information on adverse impact of the selection process for that job and, where it is determined a selection process has an adverse impact, evidence of validity as set forth below.

(1) *Simplified recordkeeping for users with less than 100 employees.* In order to minimize recordkeeping burdens on employers who employ one hundred (100) or fewer employees, and other users not required to file EEO-1, et seq., reports, such users may satisfy the requirements of this section 15 if they maintain and have available records showing, for each year:

(a) The number of persons hired, promoted, and terminated for each job, by sex, and where appropriate by race and national origin;

(b) The number of applicants for hire and promotion by sex and where appropriate by race and national orgin; and

(c) The selection procedures utilized (either standardized or not standardized).

These records should be maintained for each race or national origin group (see section 4 above) constituting more than two percent (2%) of the labor force in the relevant labor area. However, it is not necessary to maintain records by race and/or national origin (see section 4 above) if one race or national origin group in the relevant labor area constitutes more than ninety-eight percent (98%) of the labor force in the area. If the user has reason to believe that a selection procedure has an adverse impact, the user should maintain any available evidence of validity for that procedure (see sections 7A and 8).

(2) *Information on impact.*—(a) *Collection of information on impact.* Users of selection procedures other than those complying with section 15A(1) above should maintain and have available for each job records or other information showing whether the total selection process for that job has an adverse impact on any of the groups for which records are called for by section 4B above. Adverse impact determinations should be made at least annually for each such group which constitutes at least 2 percent of the labor force in the relevant labor area or 2 percent of the applicable workforce. Where a total selection process for a job has an adverse impact, the user should maintain and have available records or other information showing which components have an adverse impact. Where the total selection process for a job does not have an adverse impact, information need not

be maintained for individual components except in circumstances set forth in subsection 15A(2)(b) below. If the determination of adverse impact is made using a procedure other than the "four-fifths rule," as defined in the first sentence of section 4D above, a justification consistent with section 4D above, for the procedure used to determine adverse impact should be available.

(b) *When adverse impact has been eliminated in the total selection process.* Whenever the total selection process for a particular job has had an adverse impact, as defined in section 4 above, in any year, but no longer has an adverse impact, the user should maintain and have available the information on individual components of the selection process required in the preceding paragraph for the period in which there was adverse impact. In addition, the user should continue to collect such information for at least two (2) years after the adverse impact has been eliminated.

(c) *When data insufficient to determine impact.* Where there has been an insufficient number of selections to determine whether there is an adverse impact of the total selection process for a particular job, the user should continue to collect, maintain, and have available the information on individual components of the selection process required in section 15A(2)(a) above until the information is sufficient to determine that the overall selection process does not have an adverse impact as defined in section 4 above, or until the job has changed substantially.

(3) *Documentation of validity evidence.*—(a) *Types of evidence.* Where a total selection process has an adverse impact (see section 4 above) the user should maintain and have available for each component of that process which has an adverse impact, one or more of the following types of documentation evidence:

(i) Documentation evidence showing criterion-related validity of the selection procedure (see section 15B, below).

(ii) Documentation evidence showing content validity of the selection procedure (see section 15C, below).

(iii) Documentation evidence showing construct validity of the selection procedure (see section 15D, below).

(iv) Documentation evidence from other studies showing validity of the selection procedure in the user's facility (see section 15E, below).

(v) Documentation evidence showing why a validity study cannot or need not be performed and why continued use of the procedure is consistent with Federal law.

(b) *Form of report.* This evidence should be compiled in a reasonably complete and organized manner to permit direct evaluation of the validity of the selection procedure. Previously written employer or consultant reports of validity, or reports describing validity studies completed before the issuance of these guidelines are acceptable if they are complete in regard to the documentation requirements contained in this section, or if they satisfied requirements of guidelines which were in effect when the validity study was completed. If they are not complete, the required additional documentation should be appended. If necessary information is not available the report of the validity study may still be used as documentation, but its adequacy will be evaluated in terms of compliance with the requirements of these guidelines.

(c) *Completeness.* In the event that evidence of validity is reviewed by an enforcement agency, the validation reports completed after the effective date of these guidelines are expected to contain the information set forth below. Evidence denoted by use of the word "(Essential)" is considered critical. If information denoted essential is not included, the report will be considered incomplete unless the user affirmatively demonstrates either its unavailability due to circumstances beyond the user's control or special circumstances of the user's study which make the information irrelevant. Evidence not so denoted is desirable but its absence will not be a basis for considering a report incomplete. The user should maintain and have available the information called for under the heading "Source Data" in sections 15B(11) and 15D(11). While it is a necessary part of the study, it need not be submitted with the report. All statistical results should be organized and presented in tabular or graphic form to the extent feasible.

B. *Criterion–related validity studies.* Reports of criterion–related validity for a selection procedure should include the following information:

(1) *User(s), location(s), and date(s) of study.* Dates and location(s) of the job analysis or review of job information, the date(s) and location(s) of the administration of the selection procedures and collection of criterion data, and the time between collection of data on selection procedures and criterion measures should be provided (Essential). If the study was conducted at several locations, the address of each location, including city and State, should be shown.

(2) *Problem and setting.* An explicit definition of the purpose(s) of the study and the circumstances in which the study was conducted should be provided. A description of existing selection procedures and cutoff scores, if any, should be provided.

(3) *Job analysis or review of job information.* A description of the procedure used to analyze the job or group of jobs, or to review the job information should be provided (Essential). Where a review of job information results in criteria which may be used without a full job analysis (see section 14B3), the basis for the selection of these criteria should be reported (Essential). Where a job analysis is required a complete description of the work behavior(s) or work outcome(s), and measures of their criticality or importance should be provided (Essential). The report should describe the basis on which the behavior(s) or outcome(s) were determined to be critical or important, such as the proportion of time spent on the respective behaviors, their level of difficulty, their frequency of performance, the consequences of error, or other appropriate factors (Essential). Where two or more jobs are grouped for a validity study, the information called for in this subsection should be provided for each of the jobs, and the justification for the grouping (see section 14B(1) should be provided (Essential).

(4) *Job titles and codes.* It is desirable to provide the user's job title(s) for the job(s) in question and the corresponding job title(s) and code(s) from U.S. Employment Service's Dictionary of Occupational Titles.

(5) *Criterion measures.* The bases for the selection of the criterion measures should be provided, together with references to the evidence considered in making the selection of criterion measures (Essential). A full description of all criteria on which data were collected and means by which they were observed, recorded, evaluated, and quantified, should be provided (Essential). If rating techniques are used as criterion measures, the appraisal form(s) and instructions to the rater(s) should be included as part of the validation evidence, or should be explicitly described and available (Essential). All steps taken to insure that criterion measures are free from factors which would unfairly alter the scores of members of any group should be described (Essential).

(6) *Sample description.* A description of how the research sample was identified and selected should be included (Essential). The race, sex, and ethnic composition of the sample, including those groups set forth in section 4A above, should be

described (Essential). This description should include the size of each subgroup (Essential). A description of how the research sample compares with the relevant labor market or work force, the method by which the relevant labor market or work force was defined, and a discussion of the likely effects on validity of differences between the sample and the relevant labor market or work force, are also desirable. Descriptions of educational levels, length of service, and age are also desirable.

(7) *Description of selection procedures.* Any measure, combination of measures, or procedure studied should be completely and explicitly described or attached (Essential). If commercially available selection procedures are studied, they should be described by title, form, and publisher (Essential). Reports of reliability estimates and how they were established are desirable.

(8) *Techniques and results.* Methods used in analyzing data should be described (Essential). Measures of central tendency (e.g., means) and measures of dispersion (e.g., standard deviations and ranges) for all selection procedures and all criteria should be reported for each race, sex, and ethnic group which constitutes a significant factor in the relevant labor market (Essential). The magnitude and direction of all relationships between selection procedures and criterion measures investigated should be reported for each relevant race, sex, and ethnic group and for the total group (Essential). Where groups are too small to obtain reliable evidence of the magnitude of the relationship, results need not be reported separately. Statements regarding the statistical significance of results should be made (Essential). Any statistical adjustments, such as for less than perfect reliability or for restriction of score range in the selection procedure or criterion, should be described and explained; and uncorrected correlation coefficients should also be shown (Essential). Where the statistical technique categorizes continuous data, such as biserial correlation and the phi coefficient, the categories and the bases on which they were determined should be described and explained (Essential). Studies of test fairness should be included where called for by the requirements of section 14B(8) (Essential). These studies should include the rationale by which a selection procedure was determined to be fair to the group(s) in question. Where test fairness or unfairness has been demonstrated on the basis of other studies, a bibliography of the relevant studies should be included (Essential). If the bibliography includes unpublished studies, copies of these studies, or adequate abstracts or summaries, should be attached (Essential). Where revisions have been made in a selection procedure to assure compatibility between successful job performance and the probability of being selected, the studies underlying such revisions should be included (Essential). All statistical results should be organized and presented by relevant race, sex, and ethnic group (Essential).

(9) *Alternative procedures investigated.* The selection procedures investigated and available evidence of their impact should be identified (Essential). The scope, method, and findings of the investigation, and the conclusions reached in light of the findings, should be fully described (Essential).

(10) *Uses and applications.* The methods considered for use of the selection procedure (e.g., as a screening device with a cutoff score, for grouping or ranking, or combined with other procedures in a battery) and available evidence of their impact should be described (Essential). This description should include the rationale for choosing the method for operational use, and the evidence of the validity and utility of the procedure as it is to be used (Essential). The purpose for which the procedure is to be used (e.g., hiring, transfer, promotion) should be

described (Essential). If weights are assigned to different parts of the selection procedure, these weights and the validity of the weighted composite should be reported (Essential). If the selection procedure is used with a cutoff score, the user should describe the way in which normal expectations of proficiency within the work force were determined and the way in which the cutoff score was determined (Essential).

(11) *Source data.* Each user should maintain records showing all pertinent information about individual sample members and raters, where they are used, in studies involving the validation of selection procedures. These records should be made available upon request of a compliance agency. In the case of individual sample members these data should include scores on the selection procedure(s), scores on criterion measures, age, sex, race, or ethnic group status, and experience on the specific job on which the validation study was conducted, and may also include such things as education, training, and prior job experience, but should not include names and social security numbers. Records should be maintained which show the ratings given to each sample member by each rater.

(12) *Contact person.* The name, mailing address, and telephone number of the person who may be contacted for further information about the validity study should be provided (Essential).

(13) *Accuracy and completeness.* The report should describe the steps taken to assure the accuracy and completeness of the collection, analysis, and report of data and results.

C. *Content validity studies.* Reports of content validity for a selection procedure should include the following information:

(1) *User(s), location(s), and date(s) of study.* Dates and location(s) of the job analysis should be shown (Essential).

(2) *Problem and setting.* An explicit definition of the purpose(s) of the study and the circumstances in which the study was conducted should be provided. A description of existing selection procedures and cutoff scores, if any, should be provided.

(3) *Job analysis.—Content of the job.* A description of the method used to analyze the job should be provided (Essential). The work behavior(s), the associated tasks, and if the behavior results in a work product, the work products should be completely described (Essential). Measures of criticality and/or importance of the work behavior(s) and the method of determining these measures should be provided (Essential). Where the job analysis also identified the knowledges, skills, and abilities used in work behavior(s), an operational definition for each knowledge in terms of a body of learned information and for each skill and ability in terms of observable behaviors and outcomes, and the relationship between each knowledge, skill, or ability and each work behavior, as well as the method used to determine this relationship, should be provided (Essential). The work situation should be described, including the setting in which work behavior(s) are performed, and where appropriate, the manner in which knowledges, skills, or abilities are used, and the complexity and difficulty of the knowledge, skill, or ability as used in the work behavior(s).

(4) *Selection procedure and its content.* Selection procedures, including those constructed by or for the user, specific training requirements, composites of selection procedures, and any other procedure supported by content validity, should be completely and explicitly described or attached (Essential). If commercially available selection procedures are used, they should be described by title,

form, and publisher (Essential). The behaviors measured or sampled by the selection procedure should be explicitly described (Essential). Where the selection procedure purports to measure a knowledge, skill, or ability, evidence that the selection procedure measures and is a representative sample of the knowledge, skill, or ability should be provided (Essential).

(5) *Relationship between the selection procedure and the job.* The evidence demonstrating that the selection procedure is a representative work sample, a representative sample of the work behavior(s), or a representative sample of a knowledge, skill, or ability as used as a part of a work behavior and necessary for that behavior should be provided (Essential). The user should identify the work behavior(s) which each item or part of the selection procedure is intended to sample or measure (Essential). Where the selection procedure purports to sample a work behavior or to provide a sample of a work product, a comparison should be provided of the manner, setting, and the level of complexity of the selection procedure with those of the work situation (Essential). If any steps were taken to reduce adverse impact on a race, sex, or ethnic group in the content of the procedure or in its administration, these steps should be described. Establishment of time limits, if any, and how these limits are related to the speed with which duties must be performed on the job, should be explained. Measures of central tendency (e.g., means) and measures of dispersion (e.g., standard deviations) and estimates of reliability should be reported for all selection procedures if available. Such reports should be made for relevant race, sex, and ethnic subgroups, at least on a statistically reliable sample basis.

(6) *Alternative procedures investigated.* The alternative selection procedures investigated and available evidence of their impact should be identified (Essential). The scope, method, and findings of the investigation, and the conclusions reached in light of the findings, should be fully described (Essential).

(7) *Uses and applications.* The methods considered for use of the selection procedure (e.g., as a screening device with a cutoff score, for grouping or ranking, or combined with other procedures in a battery) and available evidence of their impact should be described (Essential). This description should include the rationale for choosing the method for operational use, and the evidence of the validity and utility of the procedure as it is to be used (Essential). The purpose for which the procedure is to used (e.g., hiring, transfer, promotion) should be described (Essential). If the selection procedure is used with a cutoff score, the user should describe the way in which normal expectations of proficiency within the work force were determined and the way in which the cutoff score was determined (Essential). In addition, if the selection procedure is to be used for ranking, the user should specify the evidence showing that a higher score on the selection procedure is likely to result in better job performance.

(8) *Contact person.* The name, mailing address, and telephone number of the person who may be contacted for further information about the validity study should be provided (Essential).

(9) *Accuracy and completeness.* The report should describe the steps taken to assure the accuracy and completeness of the collection, analysis, and report of data and results.

D. *Construct validity studies.* Reports of construct validity for a selection procedure should include the following information:

(1) *User(s), location(s), and date(s) of study.* Date(s) and location(s) of the job analysis and the gathering of other evidence called for by these guidelines should

be provided (Essential).

(2) *Problem and setting.* An explicit definition of the purpose(s) of the study and the circumstances in which the study was conducted should be provided. A description of existing selection procedures and cutoff scores, if any, should be provided.

(3) *Construct definition.* A clear definition of the construct(s) which are believed to underlie successful performance of the critical or important work behavior(s) should be provided (Essential). This definition should include the levels of construct performance relevant to the job(s) for which the selection procedure is to be used (Essential). There should be a summary of the position of the construct in the psychological literature, or in the absence of such a position, a description of the way in which the definition and measurement of the construct was developed and the psychological theory underlying it (Essential). Any quantitative data which identify or define the job constructs, such as factor analyses, should be provided (Essential).

(4) *Job analysis.* A description of the method used to analyze the job should be provided (Essential). A complete description of the work behavior(s) and, to the extent appropriate, work outcomes and measures of their criticality and/or importance should be provided (Essential). The report should also describe the basis on which the behavior(s) or outcomes were determined to be important, such as their level of difficulty, their frequency of performance, the consequences of error, or other appropriate factors (Essential). Where jobs are grouped or compared for the purposes of generalizing validity evidence, the work behavior(s) and work product(s) for each of the jobs should be described, and conclusions concerning the similarity of the jobs in terms of observable work behaviors or work products should be made (Essential).

(5) *Job titles and codes.* It is desirable to provide the selection-procedure user's job title(s) for the job(s) in question and the corresponding job title(s) and code(s) from the United States Employment Service's Dictionary of Occupational Titles.

(6) *Selection procedure.* The selection procedure used as a measure of the construct should be completely and explicitly described or attached (Essential). If commercially available selection procedures are used, they should be identified by title, form, and publisher (Essential). The research evidence of the relationship between the selection procedure and the construct, such as factor structure, should be included (Essential). Measures of central tendency, variability, and reliability of the selection procedure should be provided (Essential). Whenever feasible, these measures should be provided separately for each relevant race, sex, and ethnic group.

(7) *Relationship to job performance.* The criterion-related study(ies) and other empirical evidence of the relationship between the construct measured by the selection procedure and the related work behavior(s) for the job or jobs in question should be provided (Essential). Documentation of the criterion-related study(ies) should satisfy the provision of section 15B above or section 15E(1) below, except for studies conducted prior to the effective date of these guidelines (Essential). Where a study pertains to a group of jobs, and on the basis of the study, validity is asserted for a job in the group, the observed work behaviors and the observed work products for each of the jobs should be described (Essential). Any other evidence used in determining whether the work behavior(s) in each of the jobs is the same should be fully described (Essential).

(8) *Alternative procedures investigated.* The alternative selection procedures

investigated and available evidence of their impact should be identified (Essential). The scope, method, and findings of the investigation and the conclusions reached in light of the findings should be fully described (Essential).

(9) *Uses and applications.* The methods considered for use of the selection procedure (e.g., as a screening device with a cutoff score, for grouping or ranking, or combined with other procedures in a battery) and available evidence of their impact should be described (Essential). This description should include the rationale for choosing the method for operational use and the evidence of the validity and utility of the procedure as it is to be used (Essential). The purpose for which the procedure is to be used (e.g., hiring, transfer, promotion) should be described (Essential). If weights are assigned to different parts of the selection procedure, these weights and the validity of the weighted composite should be reported (Essential). If the selection procedure is used with a cutoff score, the user should describe the way in which normal expectations of proficiency within the work force were determined and the way in which the cutoff score was determined (Essential).

(10) *Accuracy and completeness.* The report should describe the steps taken to assure the accuracy and completeness of the collection, analysis, and report of data and results.

(11) *Source data.* Each user should maintain records showing all pertinent information relating to its study of construct validity.

(12) *Contact person.* The name, mailing address, and telephone number of the individual who may be contacted for further information about the validity study should be provided (Essential).

E. *Evidence of validity from other studies.* When validity of a selection procedure is supported by studies not done by the user, the evidence from the original study or studies should be compiled in a manner similar to that required in the appropriate section of this section 15 above. In addition, the following evidence should be supplied:

(1) *Evidence from criterion-related validity studies.*—a. *Job information.* A description of the important job behavior(s) of the user's job and the basis on which the behaviors were determined to be important should be provided (Essential). A full description of the basis for determining that these important work behaviors are the same as those of the job in the original study (or studies) should be provided (Essential).

b. *Relevance of criteria.* A full description of the basis on which the criteria used in the original studies are determined to be relevant for the user should be provided (Essential).

c. *Other variables.* The similarity of important applicant pool or sample characteristics reported in the original studies to those of the user should be described (Essential). A description of the comparison between the race, sex, and ethnic composition of the user's relevant labor market and the sample in the original validity studies should be provided (Essential).

d. *Use of the selection procedure.* A full description should be provided showing that the use to be made of the selection procedure is consistent with the findings of the original validity studies (Essential).

e. *Bibliography.* A bibliography of reports of validity of the selection procedure for the job or jobs in question should be provided (Essential). Where any of the studies included an investigation of test fairness, the results of this investigation should be provided (Essential). Copies of reports published in journals that are not commonly available should be described in detail or attached (Essential). Where a user is relying upon unpublished studies, a reasonable effort should be made to obtain these studies. If these unpublished studies are the sole source of validity evidence they should be described in detail or attached (Essential). If these studies are not available, the name and address of the source, an adequate abstract or summary of the validity study and data, and a contact person in the source organization should be provided (Essential).

(2) *Evidence from content validity studies*. See section 14C(3) and section 15C above.

(3) *Evidence from construct validity studies*. See sections 14D(2) and 15D above.

F. *Evidence of validity from cooperative studies*. Where a selection procedure has been validated through a cooperative study, evidence that the study satisfies the requirements of sections 7, 8, and 15E should be provided (Essential).

G. *Selection for higher level job*. If a selection procedure is used to evaluate candidates for jobs at a higher level than those for which they will initially be employed, the validity evidence should satisfy the documentation provisions of this section 15 for the higher level job or jobs, and in addition, the user should provide: (1) a description of the job progression structure, formal or informal; (2) the data showing how many employees progress to the higher level job and the length of time needed to make this progression; and (3) an identification of any anticipated changes in the higher level job. In addition, if the test measures a knowledge, skill, or ability, the user should provide evidence that the knowledge, skill, or ability is required for the higher level job and the basis for the conclusion that the knowledge, skill, or ability is not expected to develop from the training or experience on the job.

H. *Interim use of selection procedures*. If a selection procedure is being used on an interim basis because the procedure is not fully supported by the required evidence of validity, the user should maintain and have available (1) substantial evidence of validity for the procedure, and (2) a report showing the date on which the study to gather the additional evidence commenced, the estimated completion date of the study, and a description of the data to be collected (Essential).

DEFINITIONS

SEC. 16. *Definitions*. The following definitions shall apply throughout these guidelines:

A. *Ability*. A present competence to perform an observable behavior or a behavior which results in an observable product.

B. *Adverse impact*. A substantially different rate of selection in hiring, promotion, or other employment decision which works to the disadvantage of members of a race, sex, or ethnic group. See section 4 of these guidelines.

C. *Compliance with these guidelines*. Use of a selection procedure is in compliance with these guidelines if such use has been validated in accord with these guidelines (as defined below), or if such use does not result in adverse impact on any race, sex, or ethnic group (see section 4, above), or in unusual circumstances, if use of the procedure is otherwise justified in accord with Federal law. See section 6B, above.

D. *Content validity*. Demonstrated by data showing that the content of a selection procedure is representative of important aspects of performance on the job. See section 5B and section 14C.

E. *Construct validity*. Demonstrated by data showing that the selection procedure measures the degree to which candidates have identifiable characteristics which have been determined to be important for successful job performance. See section 5B and section 14D.

F. *Criterion-related validity*. Demonstrated by empirical data showing that the selection procedure is predictive of or significantly correlated with important elements of work behavior. See sections 5B and 14B.

G. *Employer*. Any employer subject to the provisions of the Civil Rights Act of 1964, as amended, including State or local governments and any Federal agency subject to the provisions of section 717 of the Civil Rights Act of 1964, as amended, and any Federal contractor or subcontractor or federally assisted construction contractor or subcontractor covered by Executive Order 11246, as amended.

H. *Employment agency*. Any employment agency subject to the provisions of the Civil Rights Act of 1964, as amended.

I. *Enforcement action*. For the purposes of section 4 a proceeding by a Federal enforcement agency such as a lawsuit or an administrative proceeding leading to debarment from or withholding, suspension, or termination of Federal Government contracts or the suspension or withholding of Federal Government funds; but not a finding of reasonable cause or a conciliation process or the issuance of right to sue letters under title VII or under Executive Order 11246 where such finding, conciliation, or issuance of notice of right to sue is based upon an individual complaint.

J. *Enforcement agency*. Any agency of the executive branch of the Federal Government which adopts these guidelines for purposes of the enforcement of the equal employment opportunity laws or which has responsibility for securing compliance with them.

K. *Job analysis*. A detailed statement of work behaviors and other information relevant to the job.

L. *Job description*. A general statement of job duties and responsibilities.

M. *Knowledge*. A body of information applied directly to the performance of a function.

N. *Labor organization*. Any labor organization subject to the provisions of the Civil Rights Act of 1964, as amended, and any committee subject thereto controlling apprenticeship or other training.

O. *Observable*. Able to be seen, heard, or otherwise perceived by a person other than the person performing the action.

P. *Race, sex, or ethnic group*. Any group of persons identifiable on the grounds of race, color, religion, sex, or national origin.

Q. *Selection procedure*. Any measure, combination of measures, or procedure used as a basis for any employment decision. Selection procedures include the full range of assessment techniques from traditional paper and pencil tests, performance tests, training programs, or probationary periods and physical, educational, and work experience requirements through informal or casual interviews and unscored application forms.

R. *Selection rate*. The proportion of applicants or candidates who are hired, promoted, or otherwise selected.

S. *Should*. The term "should" as used in these guidelines is intended to connote action which is necessary to achieve compliance with the guidelines, while recognizing that there are circumstances where alternative courses of action are open to users.

T. *Skill*. A present, observable competence to perform a learned psychomotor act.

U. *Technical feasibility*. The existence of conditions permitting the conduct of meaningful criterion-related validity studies. These conditions include: (1) An adequate sample of persons available for the study to achieve findings of statistical significance; (2) having or being able to obtain a sufficient range of scores on the selection procedure and job performance measures to produce validity results which can be expected to be representative of the results if the ranges normally expected were utilized; and (3) having or being able to devise unbiased, reliable and relevant measures of job performance or other criteria of employee adequacy. See section 14B(2). With respect to investigation of possible unfairness, the same considerations are applicable to each group for which the study is made. See section 14B(8).

V. *Unfairness of selection procedure*. A condition in which members of one race, sex, or ethnic group characteristically obtain lower scores on a selection procedure than members of another group, and the differences are not reflected in differences in measures of job performance. See section 14B(7).

W. *User*. Any employer, labor organization, employment agency, or licensing or certification board, to the extent it may be covered by Federal equal employment opportunity law, which uses a selection procedure as a basis for any employment decision. Whenever an employer, labor organization, or employment agency is required by law to restrict recruitment for any occupation to those applicants who have met licensing or certification requirements, the licensing or certifying authority to the extent it may be covered by Federal equal employment opportunity law will be considered the user with respect to those licensing or certification requirements. Whenever a State employment agency or service does no more than administer or monitor a procedure as permitted by Department of Labor regulations, and does so without making referrals or taking any other action on the basis of the results, the State employment agency will not be deemed to be a user.

X. *Validated in accord with these guidelines or properly validated*. A demonstration that one or more validity study or studies meeting the standards of these guidelines has been conducted, including investigation and, where appropriate, use of suitable alternative selection procedures as contemplated by section 3B, and has produced evidence of validity sufficient to warrant use of the procedure for the intended purpose under the standards of these guidelines.

Y. *Work behavior*. An activity performed to achieve the objectives of the job. Work behaviors involve observable (physical) components and unobservable (mental) components. A work behavior consists of the performance of one or more tasks. Knowledges, skills, and abilities are not behaviors, although they may be applied in work behaviors.

Appendix

SEC. 17. *Policy statement on affirmative action* (see section 13B). The Equal Employment Opportunity Coordinating Council was established by act of Congress in 1972, and charged with responsibility for developing and implementing agreements and policies designed, among other things, to eliminate conflict and inconsistency among the agencies of the Federal Government responsible for administering Federal law prohibiting discrimination on grounds of race, color, sex, religion, and national origin. This statement is issued as an initial response to the requests of a number of State and local officials for clarification of the Government's policies concerning the role of affirmative action in the overall equal employment opportunity program. While the Coordinating Council's adoption of this statement expresses only the views of the signatory agencies concerning this important subject, the principles set forth below should serve as policy guidance for other Federal agencies as well.

(1) Equal employment opportunity is the law of the land. In the public sector of our society this means that all persons, regardless of race, color, religion, sex, or national origin shall have equal access to positions in the public service limited only by their ability to do the job. There is ample evidence in all sectors of our society that such equal access frequently has been denied to members of certain groups because of their sex, racial, or ethnic characteristics. The remedy for such past and present discrimination is twofold.

On the one hand, vigorous enforcement of the laws against discrimination is essential. But equally, and perhaps even more important are affirmative, voluntary efforts on the part of public employers to assure that positions in the public service are genuinely and equally accessible to qualified persons, without regard to their sex, racial, or ethnic characteristics. Without such efforts equal employment opportunity is no more than a wish. The importance of voluntary affirmative action on the part of employers is underscored by title VII of the Civil Rights Act of 1964, Executive Order 11246, and related laws and regulations—all of which emphasize voluntary action to achieve equal employment opportunity.

As with most management objectives, a systematic plan based on sound organizational analysis and problem identification is crucial to the accomplishment of affirmative action objectives. For this reason, the Council urges all State and local governments to develop and implement results-oriented affirmative action plans which deal with the problems so identified.

The following paragraphs are intended to assist State and local governments by illustrating the kinds of analyses and activities which may be appropriate for a public employer's voluntary affirmative action plan. This statement does not address remedies imposed after a finding of unlawful discrimination.

(2) Voluntary affirmative action to assure equal employment opportunity is appropriate at any stage of the employment process. The first step in the construction of any affirmative action plan should be an analysis of the employer's work force to determine whether percentages of sex, race, or ethnic groups in individual job classifications are substantially similar to the percentages of those groups available in the relevant job market who possess the basic job-related qualifications.

When substantial disparities are found through such analyses, each element of the overall selection process should be examined to determine which elements operate to exclude persons on the basis of sex, race, or ethnic group. Such elements include, but are not limited to, recruitment, testing, ranking certification, interview, recommendations for selection, hiring, promotion, etc. The examination of each element of the selection process should at a minimum include a determination of its validity in predicting job performance.

(3) When an employer has reason to believe that its selection procedures have the exclusionary effect described in paragraph 2 above, it should initiate affirmative steps to remedy the situation. Such steps, which in design and execution may be race, color, sex, or ethnic "conscious," include, but are not limited to, the following:

(a) The establishment of a long-term goal, and short-range, interim goals and timetables for the specific job classifications, all of which should take into account the availability of basically qualified persons in the relevant job market;

(b) A recruitment program designed to attract qualified members of the group in question;

(c) A systematic effort to organize work and redesign jobs in ways that provide opportunities for persons lacking "journeyman" level knowledge or skills to enter and, with appropriate training, to progress in a career field;

(d) Revamping selection instruments or procedures which have not yet been validated in order to reduce or eliminate exclusionary effects on particular groups in particular job classifications;

(e) The initiation of measures designed to assure that members of the affected group who are qualified to perform the job are included within the pool of persons from which the selecting official makes the selection;

(f) A systematic effort to provide career advancement training, both classroom and on-the-job, to employees locked into dead end jobs; and

(g) The establishment of a system for regularly monitoring the effectiveness of the particular affirmative action program, and procedures for making timely adjustments in this program where effectiveness is not demonstrated.

(4) The goal of any affirmative action plan should be achievement of genuine equal employment opportunity for all qualified persons. Selection under such plans should be based upon the ability of the applicant(s) to do the work. Such plans should not require the selection of the unqualified, or the unneeded, nor should they require the selection of persons on the basis of race, color, sex, religion, or national origin. Moreover, while the Council believes that this statement should serve to assist State and local employers, as well as Federal agencies, it recognizes that affirmative action cannot be viewed as a standardized program which must be accomplished in the same way at all times in all places.

Accordingly, the Council has not attempted to set forth here either the minimum or maximum voluntary steps that employers may take to deal with their respective situations. Rather, the Council recognizes that under applicable authorities, State and local employers have flexibility to formulate affirmative action plans that are best suited to their particular situations. In this manner, the Council believes that affirmative action programs will best serve the goal of equal employment opportunity.

TEST PUBLISHERS

APPENDIX E

Below are the names and addresses of some of the larger American publishers and distributors of psychological tests. Catalogues of current tests can be obtained from these publishers on request. Manuals and specimen sets of tests can be purchased by qualified users. For names and addresses of other test publishers, see the Publishers Directory in the latest *Mental Measurements Yearbook.*

Addison-Wesley Testing Service, 2725 Sand Hill Road, Menlo Park, Calif. 94025.

American Guidance Service, Inc., Publishers' Building, Circle Pines, Minn. 55014

Bobbs-Merrill Company, Inc., 4300 West 62nd Street, Indianapolis, Ind. 46268

Bureau of Educational Research and Service, University of Iowa, Iowa City, Iowa 52240

CTB/McGraw-Hill, Del Monte Research Park, Monterey, Calif. 93940

Consulting Psychologists Press, Inc., 577 College Avenue, Palo Alto, Calif. 94306

Educational and Industrial Testing Service, P. O. Box 7234, San Diego, Calif. 92107

Ginn and Company, 191 Spring Street, Lexington, Mass. 02173

Houghton Mifflin Company, 110 Tremont Street, Boston, Mass. 02107

Industrial Relations Center, University of Chicago, 1225 East 60th Street, Chicago, Ill. 60637

Institute for Personality and Ability Testing, 1602 Coronado Drive, Champaign, Ill. 61820

Psychological Corporation—A subsidiary of Harcourt Brace Jovanovich, Inc., 757 Third Avenue, New York, N. Y. 10017

Psychological Test Specialists, Box 1441, Missoula, Mont. 59801

Psychometric Affiliates, Box 3167, Munster, Ind. 46321

Scholastic Testing Service, Inc., 480 Meyer Road, Bensenville, Ill. 60106

Science Research Associates, Inc., 259 East Erie Street, Chicago, Ill. 60611

Sheridan Psychological Services, P. O. Box 6101, Orange, Calif. 92667

C. H. Stoelting Company, 1350 South Kostner Avenue, Chicago, Ill. 60623

Western Psychological Services, 12031 Wilshire Boulevard, Los Angeles, Calif. 90025

REFERENCES

AAKER, D. A., & DAY, G. S. A dynamic model of relationships among advertising, consumer awareness, and behavior. *Journal of Applied Psychology,* 1974, *59,* 281–286.

ABEL, E. L. The relationship between cannabis and violence: A review. *Psychological Bulletin,* 1977, *84,* 193–211.

ABELES, R. P. An old, yet young interdisciplinary marriage. *Contemporary Psychology,* 1976, *21,* 1–3.

ACKERMAN, J. M. *Operant conditioning techniques for the classroom teacher.* Glenview, Ill.: Scott, Foresman, 1972.

ADAMS, J. A. Human tracking behavior. *Psychological Bulletin,* 1961, *58,* 55–79.

ADAMS, J. A. Preface to special issue of *Human Factors* on flight simulators. *Human Factors,* 1973, *15,* 501.

ADAMS, J. S. Inequity in social exchange. In L. Berkowitz (Ed.), *Advances in experimental social psychology* (Vol.2). New York: Academic Press, 1965. Pp. 267–299.

ADCOCK, C. J. *Factorial analysis for non-mathematicians.* New York: Cambridge University Press, 1954.

ADER, R., TATUM, R., & BEELS, C. C. Social factors affecting emotionality and resistance to disease in animals. *Journal of Comparative and Physiological Psychology,* 1960, *53,* 446–458.

ADVERTISING RESEARCH FOUNDATION. *The measurement and control of the visual efficiency of advertisements.* New York: Author, 1962.

AHLSTROM W. M., & HAVIGHURST, R. J. *400 losers.* San Francisco: Jossey-Bass, 1971.

AHMAN, J. S., et al. A look at the analysis of National Assessment data. In W. E. Coffman (Ed.), *Frontiers of educational measurement and information systems, 1973.* Boston: Houghton Mifflin, 1973. Pp. 89–111.

AKISKAL, H. S., & McKINNEY, W. T., JR. Depressive disorders: Toward a unified hypothesis. *Science,* 1973, *182,* 20–29.

ALBEE, G. W. *Mental health manpower trends.* New York: Basic Books, 1959.

ALBEE, G. W. Conceptual models and manpower models in psychology. *American Psychologist,* 1968, *23,* 317–320.

ALBEE, G. W. Emerging concepts of mental illness and models of treatment: The psychological point of view. *American Journal of Psychiatry,* 1969, *125,* 870–876.

ALBIG, W. *Modern public opinion.* New York: McGraw-Hill, 1956.

ALBRIGHT, L. E., et al. Federal government in psychological testing: Is it here? A symposium. *Personnel Psychology,* 1976, *29.* 519–557.

ALBRIGHT, L. E., SMITH, W. J., & GLENNON, J. R. A follow-up on some "invalid" tests for selecting salesmen, *Personnel Psychology,* 1959, *12,* 105–112.

ALDERFER, C. P. Organization development. *Annual Review of Psychology,* 1977, *28,* 197–223.

ALLEN, C. L. Photographing the TV audience. *Journal of Advertising Research,* 1965, *5*(1), 2–8.

ALLEN, G. J., CHINSKY, J. M., LARCEN, S. W., LOCHMAN, J. E., & SELINGER, H. E. *Community psychology and the schools: A behaviorally oriented multilevel preventive approach.* New York: Erlbaum, 1976.

ALLEN, K. E., HENKE, L. B., HARRIS, F. R., BAER, D. M., & REYNOLDS, N. J. Control of hyperactivity by social reinforcement of attending behavior. *Journal of Educational Psychology,* 1967, *58,* 231–237.

ALLEN, V. L. (ED.). *Children as teachers: Theory and research on tutoring.* New York: Academic Press, 1976.

ALLINSMITH, W., & GOETHALS, G. W. *The role of schools in mental health.* New York: Basic Books, 1962.

ALLISON, R. I., & UHL, K. P. Influence of beer brand identification on taste perception. *Journal of Marketing Research,* 1964, *1*(3), 36–39.

ALLPORT, G. W., VERNON, P. E., & LINDZEY, G. *A Study of Values (3rd ed.): Manual.* Boston: Houghton Mifflin, 1970.

ALLUISI, E. A., & MORGAN, B. B., JR. Engineering psychology and human performance. *Annual Review of Psychology,* 1976, *27,* 305–330.

ALTMAN, I. *The environment and social behavior: Privacy, personal space, territory, and crowding.* Monterey, Calif.: Brooks/Cole, 1975.

AMERICAN INSTITUTES FOR RESEARCH. *Planning Career Goals.* Monterey, Calif.: CTB/McGraw-Hill, 1975, 1976.

AMERICAN PSYCHIATRIC ASSOCIATION. *Diagnostic and statistical manual of mental disorders, second edition* (DSM-II). Washington, D. C.: Author, 1968. (DSM-III in preparation, 1978)

AMERICAN PSYCHOLOGICAL ASSOCIATION (TASK FORCE ON EMPLOYMENT TESTING OF MINORITY GROUPS). Job testing and the disadvantaged. *American Psychologist,* 1969, *24,* 637–650.

AMERICAN PSYCHOLOGICAL ASSOCIATION. Guidelines for psychologists conducting growth groups. *American Psychologist,* 1973, *28,* 933.

AMERICAN PSYCHOLOGICAL ASSOCIATION (DIVISION OF INDUSTRIAL-ORGANIZATIONAL PSYCHOLO-GY). *Principles for the validation and use of personnel selection procedures.* Dayton, Ohio: The Industrial-Organizational Psychologist, 1975. (a)

AMERICAN PSYCHOLOGICAL ASSOCIATION (TASK FORCE ON STANDARDS FOR SERVICE FACILITIES). Standards for providers of psychological services. *American Psychologist,* 1975, *30,* 685–694. (b)

AMERICAN PSYCHOLOGICAL ASSOCIATION (TASK FORCE ON HEALTH RESEARCH). Contributions of psychology to health research: Patterns, problems, and potentials. *American Psychologist,* 1976, *31,* 263–274.

ANASTASI, A. *Differential psychology* (3rd ed.). New York: Macmillan, 1958.

ANASTASI, A. On the formation of psychological traits. *American Psychologist,* 1970, *25,* 899–910.

ANASTASI A. Harassing a dead horse: Review of D. R. Green (Ed.), *The aptitude-achievement distinction. Review of Education,* 1975, *1,* 356–362.

ANASTASI, A. *Psychological testing* (4th ed.). New York: Macmillan, 1976.

ANASTASI, A., & SCHAEFER, C. E. Biographical correlates of artistic and literary creativity in adolescent girls. *Journal of Applied Psychology,* 1969, *33,* 267–273.

ANDERSON, C. W. The relation between speaking times and decision in the employment interview. *Journal of Applied Psychology,* 1960, *44,* 267–268.

ANDERSON, J. E., et al. *The prediction of adjustment over time.* Minneapolis: University of Minnesota Press, 1961.

ANDERSON, J. F., & BERDIE, D. R. Effects on response rates of formal and informal questionnaire follow-up techniques. *Journal of Applied Psychology,* 1975, *60,* 255–257.

ANDERSON, S. B., & BALL, S. A. *The profession and practice of program evaluation.* San Francisco: Jossey-Bass, 1978.

ANDREWS, F. M., & WITHEY, S. B. *Social indicators of well-being: Americans' perceptions of life quality.* New York: Plenum, 1976.

APPLEY, L. A. Executive decision making: A new strategy. *Think,* 1957, *23*(10), 2–6.

ARGYRIS, C. *Behind the front page.* San Francisco: Jossey-Bass, 1974.

ARNDT, J. *Word of mouth advertising.* New York: Advertising Research Foundation, 1967.

ARONOW, E., & REZNIKOFF, M. *Rorschach content interpretation.* New York: Grune & Stratton, 1976.

ARTHUR, A. Z. Diagnostic testing and the new alternatives. *Psychological Bulletin,* 1969, *72,* 183–192.

ARTHUR, R. J. Extreme stress in adult life and its psychic and psychophysiological consequences. In E. K. E. Gunderson & R. H. Rahe (Eds.), *Life stress and illness.* Springfield, Ill.: Charles C Thomas, 1974. Ch. 12.

ASHFORD, N. A. *Crisis in the workplace: Occupational disease and injury.* Cambridge, Mass.: Massachusetts Institute of Technology Press, 1976.

ASHRAE handbook of fundamentals. New York: American Society of Heating, Refrigerating, and Air-Conditioning Engineers, 1972.

ASKER, D. A., & DAY, G. S. (Eds.). *Consumerism: Search for the consumer interest* (2nd ed.). New York: Free Press, 1974.

ASSAEL, H. Constructive role of interorganizational conflict. In H. J. Leavitt & L. R. Pondy (Eds.), *Readings in managerial psychology* (2nd ed.). Chicago: University of Chicago Press, 1973. Pp. 542–556.

ASSAEL, H., KOFRON, J. H., & BURGI, W. Advertising performance as a function of print ad characteristics. *Journal of Advertising Research,* 1967, *7*(2), 20–26.

ATHEY, K. R., COLEMAN, J. E., REITMAN, A. P., & TANG, J. Two experiments showing the effect of interviewer's racial background on responses to questionnaires concerning racial issues. *Journal of Applied Psychology,* 1960, *44,* 244–246.

ATKINSON, J. W., RAYNOR, J. O. et al. *Motivation and achievement.* Washington, D. C.: Winston, 1974.

ATKINSON, R. C. Teaching children to read using a computer. *American Psychologist,* 1974, *29,* 169–178.

ATKINSON, R. C., & PAULSON, J. A. An approach to the psychology of instruction. *Psychological Bulletin,* 1972, *78,* 49–61.

AUERBACH, S. M., & KILMANN, P. R. Crisis intervention: A review of outcome research. *Psychological Bulletin,* 1977, *84,* 1189–1217.

AULCIEMS, A. Some observed relationships between the atmospheric environment and mental work. *Environmental Research,* 1972, *5,* 217–240.

AUSUBEL, D. P., NOVAK, J. D., & HANESIAN, H. *Educational psychology: A cognitive view* (2nd ed.). New York: Holt, Rinehart & Winston, 1978.

AYLLON, T., & AZRIN, N. H. *The token economy: A motivational system for therapy and rehabilitation.* New York: Appleton-Century-Crofts, 1968.

AZRIN, N. H. A strategy for applied research: Learning based but outcome oriented. *American Psychologist,* 1977, *32,* 140–149.

AZRIN N. H., FLORES, T., & KAPLAN, S. J. Job-finding club: A group-assisted program for obtaining employment. *Behaviour Research and Therapy,* 1975, *13,* 17–22.

AZRIN, N. H., & POWERS, M. A. Eliminating classroom disturbances of emotionally disturbed children by positive practice procedures. *Behavior Therapy,* 1975, *6,* 525–534.

AZRIN, V. B., AZRIN, N. H., & ARMSTRONG, P. M. The student-ortiented classroom: A method of improving student conduct and satisfaction. *Behavior Therapy,* 1977, *8,* 193–204.

BABARIK, P. Automobile accidents and driver reaction patterns. *Journal of Applied Psychology,* 1968, *52,* 49–54.

BACK, K. W. *Beyond words: The story of sensitivity training and the encounter movement.* New York: Russell Sage Foundation, 1972.

BACK, K. W. Intervention techniques: Small groups. *Annual Review of Psychology*, 1974, *25*, 367–387.

BACKMAN, C. W., & SECORD, P. F. *A social psychological view of education.* New York: Harcourt Brace Jovanovich, 1968.

BAEHR, M. E., & WILLIAMS, G. B., Underlying dimensions of personal background data and their relationship to occupational classification. *Journal of Applied Psychology*, 1967, *51*, 481–490.

BAEKELAND, F., & LUNDWALL, L. Dropping out of treatment: A critical review. *Psychological Bulletin*, 1975, *82*, 738–783.

BAHNSON, C. B. (Ed.). Second conference on psychophysiological aspects of cancer. *Annals of the New York Academy of Sciences*, 1969, *164*, 307–364.

BAHNSON, C. B., & KISSEN, D. M. (Eds.). Psychophysiological aspects of cancer. *Annals of the New York Academy of Sciences*, 1966, *125*, 773–1055.

BAKAN, D. Clinical psychology and logic. *American Psychologist*, 1956, *11*, 655–662.

BALMA, M. J. The concept of synthetic validity. *Personnel Psychology*, 1959, *12*, 395–396.

BALTES, M. M., & HAYWARD, S. C. Application and evaluation of strategies to reduce pollution: Behavioral control of littering in a football stadium. *Journal of Applied Psychology*, 1976, *61*, 501–506.

BANDURA, A. Psychotherapy as a learning process. *Psychological Bulletin*, 1961, *58*, 143–159.

BANDURA, A. *Principles of behavior modification.* New York: Holt, Rinehart & Winston, 1969.

BANDURA, A. *Aggression: A social learning analysis.* Englewood Cliffs, N. J.: Prentice-Hall, 1973.

BANDURA, A., BLANCHARD, E. B., & RITTER, B. The relative efficacy of desensitization and modeling approaches for inducing behavioral, affective, and attitudinal changes. *Journal of Personality and Social Psychology*, 1969, *13*, 173–199.

BARBER, T. X. Toward a theory of pain: Relief of chronic pain by prefrontal leucotomy, opiates, placebos, and hypnosis. *Psychological Bulletin*, 1959, *56*, 430–460.

BARBER, T. X., SPANOS, N. P., & CHAVES, J. F. *Hypnosis, imagination, and human potentialities.* Elmsford, N. Y.: Pergamon, 1974.

BARCLAY, W. D. The Semantic Differential as an index of brand attitude. *Journal of Advertising Research*, 1964, *4*(1), 30–33.

BARD, M. *Training police as specialists in family crisis intervention.* Washington, D. C.: U. S. Government Printing Office, 1970.

BARD, M. The role of law enforcement in the helping system. *Community Mental Health Journal*, 1971, *7*, 151–160. (a)

BARD, M. The study and modification of intrafamilial violence. In J. L. Singer (Ed.), *The control of aggression and violence: Cognitive and physiological factors.* New York: Academic Press, 1971. Pp. 149–164. (b)

BARD, M., & SHELLOW, R. *Issues in law enforcement: Essays and case studies.* Reston, Va.: Reston, 1976.

BARDON, J. I. The state of the art (and science) of school psychology. *American Psychologist*, 1976, *31*, 785–791.

BARDON, J. I., & BENNETT, V. C. Preparation for professional psychology: An example from a school psychology training program. *American Psychologist*, 1967, *22*, 652–656.

BARDON, J. I., & BENNETT, V. C. *School psychology.* Englewood Cliffs, N. J.: Prentice-Hall, 1974.

BARKER, R. G. *Ecological psychology: Concepts and methods for studying the environment of human behavior.* Stanford, Calif.: Stanford University Press, 1968.

BARKER, R. G., & WRIGHT, B. A. Disablement: The somatopsychological problem. In E. Wittkower & R. Cleghorn (Eds.), *Recent developments in psychosomatic medicine.* Philadelphia: Lippincott, 1954. Pp. 419–435.

BARKER, R. G., WRIGHT, B. A., MEYERSON, L., & GONICK, M. R. *Adjustment to physical handicap and illness: A survey of the social psychology of physique and disability* (Rev. ed.). New York: Social Science Research Council, 1953.

BARLAND, G. H., & RASKIN, D. C. Detection of deception. In W. F. Prokasy & D. C. Raskin (Eds.),

Electrodermal activity in psychological research. New York: Academic Press, 1973. Ch. 9.

BARNES, R. M. *Motion and time study: Design and measurement of work* (6th ed.). New York: Wiley, 1968.

BARNES, R. M., MUNDEL, M. E., & MACKENZIE, J. M. Studies of one- and two-handed work. *University of Iowa Studies in Engineering*, No. 21, 1940.

BAROFF, G. S. *Mental retardation: Nature, causes, and management.* New York: Wiley, 1974.

BARON, R., & LAWTON, S. Environmental influence on aggression: The facilitation of modeling effects by high ambient temperatures. *Psychonomic Science*, 1972, *26*, 80–82.

BARRETT, G. V., & BASS, B. M. Cross-cultural issues in industrial and organizational psychology. In M. D. Dunnette (Ed.), *Handbook of industrial and organizational psychology.* Chicago: Rand McNally, 1976. Ch. 37.

BARRETT, G. V., & THORNTON, C. L. Relationship between perceptual style and driver reaction to an emergency situation. *Journal of Applied Psychology*, 1968, *52*, 169–176.

BARRETT, G. V., THORNTON, C. L., & CABE, P. A. Relation between embedded figures test performance and simulator behavior. *Journal of Applied Psychology*, 1969, *53*, 253–254.

BARROW, J. C. Worker performance and task complexity as causal determinants of leader behavior style and flexibility. *Journal of Applied Psychology*, 1976, *61*, 433–440.

BARTEN, H. H. *Brief therapies.* New York: Behavior Publications, 1971.

BASS, B. M. The leaderless group discussion. *Psychological Bulletin*, 1954, *51*, 465–492.

BASS, B. M. Interface between personnel and organizational psychology. *Journal of Applied Psychology*, 1968, *52*, 81–88.

BASS, B. M., & BASS, R. Concern for the environment: Implications for industrial and organizational psychology. *American Psychologist*, 1976, *31*, 158–166.

BASS, B. M., & VAUGHAN, J. A. *Training in industry: Management of learning.* Belmont, Calif.: Wadsworth, 1966.

BASSIN, A. Red, white, and blue poker chips: An AA behavior modification technique. *American Psychologist*, 1975, *30*, 695–696.

BATTEN, BARTON, DURSTINE, & OSBORN ADVERTISING AGENCY. *The repetition of advertising: A survey of eighty years of research on repetition and its effect on the consumer.* New York: Author, 1967.

BAUER, R. A. Social psychology and the study of policy formation. *American Psychologist*, 1966, *21*, 933–942.

BAUER, R. A., & FENN, D. H., JR. *The corporate social audit.* New York: Russell Sage Foundation, 1972.

BAUMRIND, D. Current patterns of parental authority. *Developmental Psychology Monographs*, 1971, *4*(1, Pt. 2).

BAVELAS, A., & BARRETT, D. An experimental approach to organizational communication. *Personnel*, 1951, *27*, 367–371.

BEACH, F. A. "Psychosomatic" phenomena in animals. *Psychosomatic Medicine*, 1952, *14*, 261–276.

BEARDEN, W. O., & WOODSIDE, A. G. Interaction of consumption situations and brand attitudes. *Journal of Applied Psychology*, 1976, *61*, 764–769.

BECHTEL, R. B. Human movement and architecture. In H. M. Proshansky, W. H. Ittelson, & L. G. Rivlin (Eds.), *Environmental psychology: Man and his physical setting.* New York: Holt, Rinehart & Winston, 1970. Pp. 642–645.

BECKER, B. W., & MYERS, J. G. Yeasaying response style. *Journal of Advertising Research*, 1970, *10*(6), 31–37.

BECKER, G. M., & MCCLINTOCK, C. G. Value: Behavioral decision theory. *Annual Review of Psychology*, 1967, *18*, 239–286.

BEDFORD, T. Thermal factors in the environment which influence fatigue. In W. F. Floyd & A. T. Welford (Eds.), *Symposium on fatigue.* London: Lewis, 1953. Pp. 7–17.

BEECHER, H. K. *Measurement of subjective responses.* New York: Oxford University Press, 1959.

BELL, C. R. Psychological versus sociological variables in studies of volunteer bias in surveys. *Journal of Applied Psychology,* 1961, *39,* 375–381.

BELLAK, L (ED.). *Psychology of physical illness; psychiatry applied to medicine, surgery, and the specialties.* New York: Grune & Stratton, 1952.

BELLAK, L. *The TAT, the CAT, and the SAT in clinical use* (3rd ed.). New York: Grune & Stratton, 1975.

BELLAK, L., & SMALL, L. *Emergency psychotherapy and brief psychotherapy.* New York: Grune & Stratton, 1965.

BELLOWS, R. M., & ESTEP, M. F. *Employment psychology: The interview.* New York: Holt, Rinehart & Winston, 1954.

BENNETT, C. C. Community psychology: Impressions of the Boston conference on the education of psychologists for community mental health. *American Psychologist,* 1965, *20,* 832–835.

BENNETT, C. C., et al. *Community psychology: A report of the Boston conference on the education of psychologists for community mental health.* Boston: Boston University, 1966.

BENNETT, G. K., & DOPPELT, J. E. *Test Orientation Procedure.* New York: Psychological Corporation, 1967.

BEN SHAKHAR, G., LIEBLICH, I., & KUGELMASS, S. Guilty knowledge technique: Application of signal detection measures. *Journal of Applied Psychology,* 1970, *54,* 409–418.

BEREITER, C., & ENGELMANN, S. *Teaching disadvantaged children in the preschool.* Englewood Cliffs, N. J.: Prentice-Hall, 1966.

BERG, D. H. An enquiry into the effect of exposure to advertisements on subsequent perception of similar advertisements. *Journal of Applied Psychology,* 1967, *51,* 503–508.

BERGIN, A. E., & GARFIELD, S. L. (Eds.). *Handbook of psychotherapy and behavior change: An empirical analysis.* New York: Wiley, 1971.

BERGIN, A. E., & STRUPP, H. H. *Changing frontiers in the science of psychotherapy.* Chicago: Aldine, 1972.

BERGIN, A. E., & SUINN, R. M. Individual psychotherapy and behavior therapy. *Annual Review of Psychology,* 1975, *26,* 509–556.

BERGUM, B. O., & LEHR, D. J. Vigilance performance as a function of interpolated rest. *Journal of Applied Psychology,* 1962, *46,* 425–427.

BERKOVITZ, I. H. (Ed.). *When schools care: Creative use of groups in secondary schools.* New York: Brunner/Mazel, 1975.

BERKOWITZ, L. (Ed.). *Roots of aggression: A re-examination of the frustration-aggression hypothesis.* New York: Atherton, 1969.

BERKSHIRE, J. R., & HIGHLAND, R. W. Forced-choice performance rating: A methodological study. *Personnel Psychology,* 1953, *6,* 355–378.

BERLINER, D. C., & CAHEN, L. S. Trait-treatment interactions and learning. In F. N. Kerlinger (Ed.), *Review of research in education.* Itasca, Ill.: Peacock, 1973.

BERMANT, G., NEMETH, C., & VIDMAR, N. (Eds.). *Psychology and the law: Research frontiers.* Lexington, Mass.: Lexington Books, 1976.

BERNARDIN, H. J., & WALTER, C. S. Effects of rater training and diary-keeping on psychometric error in ratings. *Journal of Applied Psychology,* 1977, *62,* 64–69.

BERNER, E. S., HAMILTON, L. A., & BEST, W. R. A new approach to evaluating problem-solving in medical students. *Journal of Medical Education,* 1974, *49,* 666–671.

BERNI, R., & FORDYCE, W. E. *Behavior modification and the nursing process* (2nd ed.). St. Louis, Mo.: Mosby, 1977.

BERNSTEIN, I. N., & FREEMAN, H. E. *Academic and entrepreneurial research: The consequences of diversity in federal evaluation studies.* New York: Russell Sage Foundation, 1975.

BERRY, C. A. Weightlessness. In *Bioastronautics data book* (2nd ed.) (National Aeronautics and Space Administration, NASA SP-3006). Washington, D. C.: U. S. Government Printing Office, 1973. Ch. 8.

BETTMAN, J. R. Relation of information-processing attitude structures to private brand purchasing behavior. *Journal of Applied Psychology,* 1974, *59,* 79–83.

BETTMAN, J. R. Information integration in consumer risk perception: A comparison of two models of component conceptualization. *Journal of Applied Psychology*, 1975, *60*, 381–385.

BHATIA, N., & MURRELL, K. F. H. An industrial experiment in organized rest pauses. *Human Factors*, 1969, *11*, 167–174.

BIALEK, H. M., TAYLOR, J. E., & HAUKE, R. N. *Instructional strategies for training men of high and low aptitude.* (HumRRO Tech. Rep. 73-10). Alexandria, Va.: Human Resources Research Organization, April 1973.

BJERI, J., et al. *Clinical and social judgment: The discrimination of behavioral information.* New York: Wiley, 1966.

BIJOU, S. W., & PETERSON, R. F. Functional analysis in the assessment of children. In P. McReynolds (Ed.), *Advances in psychological assessment* (Vol. 2). Palo Alto, Calif.: Science and Behavior Books, 1971. Pp. 63–78.

BILODEAU, E. A. (Ed.). *Principles of skill acquisition.* New York: Academic Press, 1969.

BINET, A. La science du témoignage. *Année psychologique*, 1905, *11*, 128–137.

BINGHAM, W. V., MOORE, B. V., & GUSTAD, J. *How to interview* (4th ed.). New York: Harper, 1959.

BLACKFORD, K. M. H., & NEWCOMB, A. *The job, the man, the boss.* Garden City, N. Y.: Doubleday, 1919.

BLACKWELL, H. R. Development and use of a quantitative method for specification of interior illumination levels on the basis of performance data. *Illuminating Engineering*, 1959, *54*, 317–353.

BLACKWELL, H. R. Development of visual task evaluators for use in specifying recommended illumination levels. *Illuminating Engineering*, 1961, *56*, 543–544.

BLACKWELL, O. M., & BLACKWELL, H. R. Visual performance data for 156 normal observers of various ages. *Journal of Illuminating Engineering Society*, 1971, *1*, 3–13.

BLACKWELL, R. D., ENGEL, J. F., & KOLLAT, D. T. *Cases in consumer behavior.* New York: Holt, Rinehart & Winston, 1969.

BLACKWELL, R. D., HENSEL, J. S., PHILLIPS, M. B., & STERNTHAL, B. *Laboratory equipment for marketing research.* Dubuque, Iowa: Kendall Hunt, 1970.

BLACKWELL, R. D., HENSEL, J. S., & STERNTHAL, B. Pupil dilation: What does it measure? *Journal of Advertising Research*, 1970, *10*(4), 15–18.

BLAIWES, A. S., PUIG, J. A., & REGAN, J. J. Transfer of training and the measurement of training effectiveness. *Human Factors*, 1973, *15*, 523–533.

BLAKE, B. F., ZENHAUSERN, R., PERLOFF, R., & HESLIN, R. The effect of intolerance of ambiguity upon product perceptions. *Journal of Applied Psychology*, 1973, *58*, 239–243.

BLAKE, R. R., MOUTON, J. S., & SLOMA, R. L. The union-management intergroup laboratory: Strategy for resolving intergroup conflict. *Journal of Applied Behavioral Science*, 1965, *1*, 25–57.

BLAKE, R. R., SHEPARD, H. H., & MOUTON, J. S. *Managing intergroup conflict in industry.* Ann Arbor, Mich.: Foundation for Research in Human Behavior, 1964.

BLANCHARD, E. B., & YOUNG, L. D. Clinical applications of biofeedback training: A review of evidence. *Archives of General Psychiatry*, 1974, *30*, 573–589.

BLISS, J. C., KATCHER, M. H., ROGERS, C. H., & SHEPARD, R. P. Optical-to-tactile image conversion for the blind. *IEEE Transactions on Man-Machine Systems*, 1970, MMS-*11*(1), 58–65.

BLISS, J. C., & MOORE, M. W. The Optacon reading system: Parts 1–3. *Education of the Visually Handicapped*, 1974, *6*(4), 98–102; 1975, *7*(1), 15–21; 1975, *7*(2), 33–39.

BLOCK, J. *The Q sort method in personality assessment and psychiatric research.* Springfield, Ill.: Charles C Thomas, 1961.

BLOOM, B. S. The International Study of Educational Achievement (IEA): Comments following the paper by Dr. Thorndike. In W. E. Coffman (Ed.), *Frontiers of educational measurement and information systems, 1973.* Boston: Houghton Mifflin, 1973. Pp. 83–87.

BLUMENTHAL, M. D., CHADIHA, L. B., COLE, G. A., & JAYARATNE, T. E. *More about justifying violence: Methodological studies of attitudes and behavior.* Ann Arbor, Mich.: Institute for Social Research, 1976.

BLUMENTHAL, M. D., KAHN, R. L., ANDREWS, F. M., & HEAD, K. B. *Justifying violence: Attitudes of American men.* Ann Arbor, Mich.: Institute for Social Research, 1972.

BOEHM, V. R. Differential prediction: A methodological artifact? *Journal of Applied Psychology,* 1977, *62,* 146–154.

BOGATZ, G. A., & BALL, S. A. *A summary of the major findings in the second-year assessment of Sesame Street: A continuing evaluation.* Princeton, N. J.: Educational Testing Service, 1971.

BOGDEN, R., & TAYLOR, S. The judged, not the judges: An insider's view of mental retardation. *American Psychologist,* 1976, *31,* 47–52.

BOGGS, D. H., & SIMON, J. R. Differential effect of noise on tasks of varying complexity. *Journal of Applied Psychology,* 1968, *52,* 148–153.

BOLSTER, B. I., & SPRINGBETT, B. M. The reaction of interviewers to favorable and unfavorable information. *Journal of Applied Psychology,* 1961, *45,* 97–103.

BOLTON, B. *Psychology of deafness for rehabilitation counselors.* Baltimore: University Park Press, 1976.

BOOCOCK, S. S. The Life Career Game. *Personnel and Guidance Journal,* 1967, *46,* 328–334.

BORDIN, E. S. *Psychological counseling* (2nd ed.). New York: Appleton-Century-Crofts, 1968.

BORDIN, E. S. *Research strategies in psychotherapy.* New York: Wiley-Interscience, 1974.

BORDIN, E. S., NACHMAN, B., & SEGAL, S. J. An articulated framework for vocational development. *Journal of Counseling Psychology,* 1963, *10,* 107–117.

BORGEN, F. H., WEISS, D. J., TINSLEY, H. E. A., DAWIS, R. V., & LOFQUIST, L. H. *Occupational reinforcer patterns:* I. (Minnesota Studies in Vocational Rehabilitation: XXIV). Minneapolis: University of Minnesota, Work Adjustment Project, 1968. (a)

BORGEN, F. H., WEISS, D. J., TINSLEY, H. E. A., DAWIS, R. V., & LOFQUIST, L. H. *The measurement of occupational reinforcer patterns.* (Minnesota Studies in Vocational Rehabilitation: XXV). Minneapolis: University of Minnesota, Work Adjustment Project, 1968. (b)

BORMAN, W. C. Effects of instructions to avoid halo error on reliability and validity of performance evaluation ratings. *Journal of Applied Psychology,* 1975, *60,* 556–560.

BORMAN, W. C., & DUNNETTE, M. D. Behavior-based versus trait-oriented performance ratings: An empirical study. *Journal of Applied Psychology,* 1975, *60,* 561–565.

BOUCHARD, T. J., BARSALOUX, J., & DRAUDEN, G. Brainstorming procedure, group size, and sex as determinants of the problem-solving effectiveness of groups and individuals. *Journal of Applied Psychology,* 1974, *59,* 135–138.

BOWDEN, C. L., & BURSTEIN, A. G. *Psychosocial basis of medical practice: An introduction to human behavior.* Baltimore: Williams & Wilkins, 1974.

BOWEN, M. A family concept of schizophrenia. In D. D. Jackson (Ed.), *The etiology of schizophrenia.* New York: Basic Books, 1960. Ch. 12.

BOWEN, M. Family therapy and family group therapy. In H. I. Kaplan & B. J. Sadock (Eds.), *Comprehensive group psychotherapy.* Baltimore: Williams & Wilkins, 1971. Pp. 384–421.

BOWER, G. H. (Ed.). *The psychology of learning and motivation: Advances in research and theory* (Vol. 9). New York: Academic Press, 1975.

BRACHT, G. A. Experimental factors related to aptitude-treatment interactions. *Review of Educational Research,* 1970, *40,* 627–645.

BRADFORD, L. P., GIBB, J. R., & BENNE, K. D. (Eds.). *T-group theory and laboratory method: Innovation in re-education.* New York: Wiley, 1964.

BRADY, J. V. Ulcers in "executive" monkeys. *Scientific American,* 1958, *199*(4), 95–104.

BRAY, D. W., CAMPBELL, R. J., & GRANT, D. L. *Formative years in business: A long-term AT&T study of managerial lives.* New York: Wiley, 1974.

BRAY, D. W., & GRANT, D. L. The assessment centers in the measurement of potential for business management. *Psychological Monographs,* 1966, *80*(17, Whole No. 625).

BRAYFIELD, A. H. Vocational counseling today. In M. S. Viteles, A. H. Brayfield, & L. E. Tyler, *Vocational counseling: A reappraisal in honor of Donald G. Paterson.* Minneapolis: University of Minnesota Press, 1961. Pp. 22–58.

BRAYFIELD, A. H. How to create a new profession: Issues and answers. *American Psychologist,* 1976, *31,* 200–205.

BRAYFIELD, A. H., & CROCKETT, W. H. Employee attitudes and employee performance. *Psychological Bulletin,* 1955, *52,* 396–424.

BRAYFIELD, A. H., & REED, P. A. How readable are occupational information booklets? *Journal of Applied Psychology,* 1950, *34,* 325–328.

BREWER, J. M., et al. *History of vocational guidance: Origins and early development.* New York: Harper, 1942.

BRIGGS, G. E., & NAYLOR, J. C. The relative efficiency of several training methods as a function of transfer task complexity. *Journal of Experimental Psychology,* 1962, *64,* 505–512.

BRILL, H., & PATTON, R. E. Analysis of population reduction in New York State mental hospitals during the first four years of large-scale therapy with psychotropic drugs. *American Journal of Psychiatry,* 1959, *116,* 495–509.

BRODSKY, S. L. (Ed.). *Psychologists in the criminal justice system.* Marysville, Ohio: American Association of Correctional Psychologists, 1972.

BRODSKY, S. L. Psychology and criminal justice. In P. J. Woods (Ed.), *Career opportunities for psychologists: Expanding and emerging areas.* Washington, D. C.: American Psychological Association, 1976. Pp. 152–156.

BROMFIELD, S., & KILMURRAY, J. A. Learning to decide: New way to counsel nontraditional students. *College Board Review,* 1976, No. 100, 26–28.

BROPHY, A. L., & DURFEE, R. A. Mail-order training in psychotherapy. *American Psychologist,* 1960, *15,* 356–360.

BROWN, B. Long-term gains from early intervention: An overview of current research. In B. Brown (Ed.), *Found: Long-term gains from early intervention.* Boulder, Col.: Westview Press, 1978. Pp. 169–185.

BROWN, B. S., WIENCKOWSKI, L. A., & BIVENS, L. W. *Psychosurgery: Perspectives on a current issue* (DHEW Publication No. (HSM) 73-9119). Rockville, Md.: National Institute of Mental Health, 1973.

BROWN, E., DEFFENBACHER, K., & STURGILL, W. Memory for faces and the circumstances of encounter. *Journal of Applied Psychology,* 1977, *62,* 311–318.

BROWN, P. L., & BERDIE, R. F. Driver behavior and scores on the MMPI. *Journal of Applied Psychology,* 1960, *44,* 18–21.

BROWN, P. L., & PRESBIE, R. J. *Behavior modification in business, industry, and government.* New Paltz, N. Y.: Behavior Improvement Associates, 1976.

BROWN, S. R. Bibliography on Q technique and its methodology. *Perceptual and Motor Skills,* 1968, *26,* 587–613.

BRUDNY, J., et al. Sensory feedback therapy as a modality of treatment in central nervous system disorders of voluntary movement. *Neurology,* 1974, *24,* 925–932.

BRUDNY, J., et al. EMG feedback therapy: Review of treatment of 114 patients. *Archives of Physical Medicine and Rehabilitation,* 1976, *57,* 55–61.

BRUNER, J. S. Some theorems on instruction illustrated with reference to mathematics. In E. R. Hilgard (Ed.), *Theories of learning and instruction: The Sixty-Third Yearbook of the National Society for the Study of Education.* Chicago: University of Chicago Press, 1964. Pp. 306–335.

BRUVOLD, W. H. Scales for rating the taste of water. *Journal of Applied Psychology,* 1968, *52,* 245–253.

BRUVOLD, W. H. Laboratory panel estimation of consumer assessments of taste and flavor. *Journal of Applied Psychology,* 1970, *54,* 326–330.

BRUVOLD, W. H. Affective response toward uses of reclaimed water. *Journal of Applied Psychology,* 1971, *55,* 28–33.

BRUVOLD, W. H., & GAFFEY, W. R. Rated acceptability of mineral taste in water: II. Combinatorial effects of ions on quality and action tendency ratings. *Journal of Applied Psychology,* 1969, *53,* 317–321.

BRYAN, G. L., & NAGAY, J. A. Use in the military and government agencies. In R. Glaser (Ed.), *Teaching machines and programmed learning: II. Data and directions.* Washington, D. C.: National Education Association, 1965.

BUCKHOUT, R. Pollution and the psychologist: A call to action. In J. F. Wohlwill & D. H. Carson (Eds.), *Environment and the social sciences: Perspectives and applications.* Washington, D.C.: American Psychological Association, 1972, Pp. 75–81.

BUCKHOUT, R. Eyewitness testimony. *Scientific American,* 1974, *231*(6), 23–31.

BUCKNER, D. N., & McGRATH, J. J. (Eds.). *Vigilance: A symposium.* New York: McGraw-Hill, 1963.

BUDZYNSKI, T. H., STOYVA, J. M., ADLER, C. S., & MULLANEY, D. J. EMG biofeedback and tension headache: A controlled outcome study. *Psychosomatic Medicine,* 1973, *35,* 484–496.

Building a better mousetrap. *Time,* May 2, 1969, pp. 46, 51.

BURCHINAL, L. G. Personality characteristics and sample bias. *Journal of Applied Psychology,* 1960, *44,* 172–174.

BURDICK, H. A., GREEN, E. J., & LOVELACE, J. W. Predicting trademark effectiveness. *Journal of Applied Psychology,* 1959, *43,* 285–286.

BURDOCK, E. I., & HARDESTY, A. S. *Structured clinical interview.* New York: Springer, 1969.

BURGESS, R. L. Communication networks: An experimental reevaluation. *Journal of Experimental Social Psychology,* 1968, *44,* 324–337.

BURKE, J. B., HANSEN, J. H., HOUSTON, W. R., & JOHNSON, C. *Criteria for describing and assessing competency based programs.* Syracuse, N. Y.: National Dissemination Center for Performance-Based Education, Syracuse University, 1975.

BURKE, R. J., & WILCOX, D. S. Effects of different patterns and degrees of openness in superior-subordinate communication on subordinate job satisfaction. In B. M. Bass & S. D. Deep (Eds.), *Studies in organizational psychology.* Boston: Allyn & Bacon, 1972. Pp. 180–189.

BUROS, O. K. (Ed.). *Eighth Mental Measurements Yearbook.* Highland Park, N. J.: Gryphon Press, 1978.

BUROS, O. K. (Ed.). *Tests in print II.* Highland Park, N. J.: Gryphon Press, 1974.

BUROS, O. K. *Vocational tests and reviews.* Highland Park, N. J.: Gryphon Press, 1975.

BURROWS, A. A. Acoustic noise, an informational definition. *Human Factors,* 1960, *2*(3), 163–168.

BURT, C., COOPER, W. F., & MARTIN, J. L. A psychological study of typography. *British Journal of Statistical Psychology,* 1955, *8*(pt. 1), 29–58.

BURTON, A. *Modern humanistic psychotherapy.* San Francisco: Jossey-Bass, 1967.

BURTON, A. (Ed.). *Encounter: Theory and practice of encounter groups.* San Francisco: Jossey-Bass, 1970.

BURTT, H. E. *Legal psychology.* Englewood Cliffs, N. J.: Prentice-Hall, 1931.

BUSHELL, D., JR. *The behavior analysis classroom.* Lawrence, Kansas: University of Kansas, Department of Human Development, 1970.

BUTLER, J. M., & HAIGH, G. V. Changes in the relation between self-concepts and ideal concepts consequent upon client-centered counseling. In C. R. Rogers & R. F. Dymond (Eds.), *Psychotherapy and personality change: Coordinated research studies in the client-centered approach.* Chicago: University of Chicago Press, 1954. Ch. 4.

CAFFYN, J. M. Psychological laboratory techniques in copy research. *Journal of Advertising Research,* 1964, *4*(4), 45–50.

CAHILL, M.-C. Interpretability of graphic symbols as a function of context and experience factors. *Journal of Applied Psychology,* 1975, *60,* 376–380.

CAHILL, M.-C. Design features of graphic symbols varying in interpretability. *Perceptual and Motor Skills,* 1976, *42,* 647–653.

CAHOON, R. L. Auditory vigilance under hypoxia. *Journal of Applied Psychology,* 1973, *57,* 350–352.

CAMPBELL, A., CONVERSE, P. E., & RODGERS, W. L. *The quality of American life: Perceptions, evaluations, and satisfactions.* New York: Russell Sage Foundation, 1976.

CAMPBELL, D.P. *The results of counseling: Twenty-five years later.* Philadelphia: Saunders, 1965.

CAMPBELL, D. P. *Handbook for the Strong Vocational Interest Blank.* Stanford, Calif.: Stanford University Press, 1971.

CAMPBELL, D. P. *Manual for the Strong-Campbell Interest Inventory.* Stanford, Calif.: Stanford University Press, 1974.

CAMPBELL, D. T. The indirect assessment of social attitudes. *Psychological Bulletin,* 1950, *47,* 15–38.

CAMPBELL, D. T., & FISKE, D. W. Convergent and discriminant validation by the multitrait-multimethod matrix. *Psychological Bulletin,* 1959, *56,* 81–105.

CAMPBELL, D. T., & STANLEY, J. C. *Experimental and quasi-experimental designs for research.* Chicago: Rand McNally, 1966.

CAMPBELL, J. P., & DUNNETTE, M. D. Effectiveness of T-group experiences in managerial training and development. *Psychological Bulletin,* 1968, *70,* 73–104.

CAMPBELL, J. P., DUNNETTE, M. D., ARVEY, R. D., & HELLERVIK, L. V. The development and evaluation of behaviorally based rating scales. *Journal of Applied Psychology,* 1973, *57,* 15–22.

CAMPBELL, J. P., DUNNETTE, M. D., LAWLER, E. E., III, & WEICK, K. E., JR. *Managerial behavior, performance, and effectiveness.* New York: McGraw-Hill, 1970.

CAMPBELL, J. T., CROOKS, L. A., MAHONEY, M. H., & ROCK, D. A. *An investigation of sources of bias in the prediction of job performance: A six-year study.* Princeton, N. J.: Educational Testing Service, 1973.

CANNON, W. B. *The wisdom of the body.* New York: Norton, 1932.

CANTRIL, H. *Gauging public opinion.* Princeton, N. J.: Princeton University Press, 1944.

CAPLAN, G. *Principles of preventive psychiatry.* New York: Basic Books, 1964.

CAPLAN, G. *Theories of mental health consultation.* New York: Basic Books, 1970.

CAPLAN, G., & KILLILEA, M. (Eds.). *Support systems and mutual help: Multidisciplinary explorations.* New York: Grune & Stratton, 1976.

CAPLAN, N. S., & SIEBERT, L. A. Distribution of juvenile delinquent intelligence test scores over a thirty-four-year period. *Journal of Clinical Psychology,* 1964, *20,* 242–247.

CAPLAN, R. D., COBB, S., & FRENCH, J. R. P., JR. Relationships of cessation of smoking with job stress, personality, and social support. *Journal of Applied Psychology,* 1975, *60,* 211–219.

CAPLAN, R. D., ROBINSON, E. A. R., FRENCH, J. R. P., JR., CALDWELL, J. R., & SHINN, M. *Adhering to medical regimens: Pilot experiments in patient education and social support.* Ann Arbor, Mich.: Institute for Social Research, 1976.

Careers in psychology. Washington, D. C.: American Psychological Association, 1975.

CAREY, A. The Hawthorne studies: A radical criticism. *American Sociological Review,* 1967, *32,* 403–416.

CARLE, R. F., KEHAS, C. D., & MOSHER, R. L. (Eds.). Guidance—An examination. *Harvard Educational Review,* 1962, *32*(4).

CARLSON, R. E. Degree of job fit as a moderator of the relationship between job performance and job satisfaction. *Personnel Psychology,* 1969, *22,* 159–170.

CARLSON, R. E. Effect of interview information in altering valid impressions. *Journal of Applied Psychology,* 1971, *55,* 66–72.

CARLSON, R. E., THAYER, P. W., MAYFIELD, E. C., & PETERSON, D. A. Improvements in the selection interview. *Personnel Journal,* 1971, *50,* 268–275.

CARLUCCI, C., & CRISSY, W. J. E. How readable are employee handbooks? *Personnel Psychology,* 1951, *4,* 383–395.

CARO, P. W. Aircraft simulators and pilot training. *Human Factors,* 1973, *15,* 502–509.

CARO, P. W., ISLEY, R. N., & JOLLEY, O. B. *Research on synthetic training: Device evaluation and training program development* (HumRRO Tech. Rep. 73-20). Alexandria, Va.: Human Resources Research Organization, September 1973.

CARROLL, J. B., DAVIES, P., & RICHMAN, B. *Word frequency book.* Boston: Houghton Mifflin, 1971.

CARROLL, S. J., JR., & TOSI, H. L., JR. *Management by objectives.* New York: Macmillan, 1973.

CARSON, D. H., & DRIVER, B. L. A summary of an ecological approach to environmental stress. *American Behavioral Science,* 1966, *10,* 8–11.

CARTER, L. F. Automated instruction. *American Psychologist,* 1961, *16,* 705–710.

CASSEL, J., PATRICK, R., & JENKINS, D. Epidemiological analysis of the health implications of culture change: A conceptual model. *Annals of the New York Academy of Sciences,* 1960, *84,* 938–949.

CASSEL, J., & TYROLER, H. A. Epidemiological studies of culture change. *Archives of Environmental Health,* 1961, *3,* 25–33.

CASSENS, F. P. *Cross cultural dimensions of executive life history antecedents.* Greensboro, N. C.: Center for Creative Leadership, 1966.

CATALANELLO, R. E., & KIRKPATRICK, D. L. Evaluating training programs—The state of the art. *Training and Development Journal,* 1968, *22*(5), 2–9.

CATT, V., & BENSON, P. L. Effect of verbal modeling on contributions to charity. *Journal of Applied Psychology,* 1977, *62,* 81–85.

CAUTELA, J. R., & KASTENBAUM, R. A reinforcement survey schedule for use in therapy, training, and research. *Psychological Reports,* 1967, *20,* 1115–1130.

CHALL, J. S. *Readability: An appraisal of research and applications.* Columbus, Ohio: Ohio State University Press, 1958.

CHAPANIS, A. *Man-machine engineering.* Belmont, Calif.: Wadsworth, 1965.

CHAPANIS, A. (Ed.). *Ethnic variables in human factors engineering.* Baltimore: John Hopkins University Press, 1975.

CHAPANIS, A. Engineering psychology. In M. D. Dunnette (Ed.), *Handbook of industrial and organizational psychology.* Chicago: Rand McNally, 1976. Ch. 16.

CHAPANIS, A., GARNER, W. R., & MORGAN, C. T. *Applied experimental psychology.* New York: Wiley, 1949.

CHAPANIS, A., & LINDENBAUM, L. A reaction time study of four control-display linkages. *Human Factors,* 1959, *1*(4), 1–7.

CHAPANIS, A., & MANKIN, D. A. Test of ten control-display linkages. *Human Factors,* 1967, *9,* 119–126.

CHAPMAN, C., & RISLEY, T. R. Anti-litter procedures in an urban high-density area. *Journal of Applied Behavior Analysis,* 1974, *7,* 377–383.

CHAPMAN, L. J. Illusory correlation in observational report. *Journal of Verbal Learning and Verbal Behavior,* 1967, *6,* 151–155.

CHAPMAN, L. J., & CHAPMAN, J. P. Genesis of popular but erroneous psychodiagnostic observations. *Journal of Abnormal Psychology,* 1967, *72,* 193–204.

CHAPMAN, L. J., & CHAPMAN, J. P. Illusory correlation as an obstacle to the use of valid psychodiagnostic signs. *Journal of Abnormal Psychology,* 1969, *74,* 271–280.

CHASSAN, J. B. *Research design in clinical psychology and psychiatry.* New York: Appleton-Century-Crofts, 1967.

CHRISTIANSEN, D. Hawthorne revisited. *IEEE Spectrum,* 1975, *12*(1), 35.

CHRISTIE, R. Probability v. precedence: The social psychology of jury selection. In G. Bermant, C. Nemeth, & N. Vidmar (Eds.), *Psychology and the law: Research frontiers.* Lexington, Mass.: Lexington Books, 1976. Ch. 13.

CIALDINI, R. B., & ASCANI, K. Test of a concession procedure for inducing verbal, behavioral, and further compliance with a request to give blood. *Journal of Applied Psychology,* 1976, *61,* 295–300.

CLARIDGE, G. *Drugs and human behavior.* Baltimore: Penguin, 1970.

CLARK, B., & GRAYBIEL, A. *Disorientation: A cause of pilot error.* USN School of Aviation Medicine, Research Report No. NM 001 110 100.39, 1955.

CLARK, B., & GRAYBIEL, A. Vertigo as a cause of pilot error in jet aircraft. *Journal of Aviation Medicine,* 1957, *28,* 469–478.

CLARK, K. B. The social scientist as an expert witness in civil rights litigation. *Social Problems,* 1953, *1,* 5–10.

CLARK, K. B. (Ed.). A symposium on desegregation in the public schools. *Social Problems,* 1955, *2*(4).

CLARK, R. D., III. Group-induced shift toward risk: A critical appraisal. *Psychological Bulletin,* 1971, *76,* 251–270.

CLARK, R. N., BURGESS, R. L., & HENDEE, J. C. The development of anti-litter behavior in a forest campground. *Journal of Applied Behavior Analysis,* 1972, *5,* 1–5.

CLUM, G. A. Intrapsychic variables and the patient's environment as factors in prognosis. *Psychological Bulletin,* 1975, *82,* 413–431.

COBB, B. Cancer. In J. F. Garrett & E. S. Levine (Eds.), *Psychological practices with the physically disabled.* New York: Columbia University Press, 1962. Pp. 231–260.

COBB, S. Technique of interviewing a patient with psychosomatic disorder. In A. Weider (Ed.), *Contributions toward medical psychology.* New York: Ronald, 1953. Ch. 10.

COCH, L., & FRENCH, J. R. P., JR. Overcoming resistance to change. *Human Relations,* 1948, *1,* 512–532.

CODDINGTON, R. D. Study of an infant with a gastric fistula and her normal twin. *Psychosomatic Medicine,* 1968, *30,* 172–192.

COGHILL, M. A. *The lie detector in employment.* Ithaca, N.Y.: Cornell University, School of Industrial and Labor Relations, 1968.

COHEN, K. J., DILL, W. R., KUEHN, A. A., & WINTERS, P. R. *The Carnegie Tech Management Game: An experiment in business education.* Homewood, Ill.: Irwin, 1964.

COLEMAN, E. B., & KIM, I. Comparison of several styles of typography in English. *Journal of Applied Psychology,* 1961, *45,* 262–267.

COLEMAN, M., & LIAU, T. L. A computer readability formula designed for machine scoring. *Journal of Applied Psychology,* 1975, *60,* 283–284.

COLEMAN, P., RUFF, C., & SMITH, K. U. Effects of feedback delay on eye-hand synchronism in steering behavior. *Journal of Applied Psychology,* 1970, *54,* 271–277.

COLLEGE ENTRANCE EXAMINATION BOARD. *The college handbook.* New York: Author, 1977.

COLQUHOUN, W. P. (Ed.). *Biological rhythms and human performance.* New York: Academic Press, 1971.

COLQUHOUN, W. P. (Ed.). *Aspects of human efficiency: Diurnal rhythm and loss of sleep.* London: English University Press, 1972.

Competency/performance based teacher education. *Phi Delta Kappan,* 1974, *55*(1). (Special issue)

COMREY, A. L. A factor analysis of variables related to driver training. *Journal of Applied Psychology,* 1958, *42,* 218–221.

CONDIE, S. J., WARNER, W. K., & GILLMAN, D. C. Getting blood from collective turnips: Volunteer donations in mass blood drives. *Journal of Applied Psychology,* 1976, *61,* 290–294.

CONGER, J. J., & MILLER, W. C. *Personality, social class, and delinquency.* New York: Wiley, 1966.

CONGER, J. J., MILLER, W. C., & WALSMITH, C. R. Antecedents of delinquency: Personality, social class, and intelligence. In P. H. Mussen, J. J. Conger, & J. Kagan (Eds.), *Basic and contemporary issues in developmental psychology.* New York: Harper & Row, 1975. Pp. 433–450.

CONNER, R. F. Toward a consumer evaluation of government services. *Contemporary Psychology,* 1976, *21,* 179–180.

COOK, T. D., et al. *"Sesame Street" revisited.* New York: Russell Sage Foundation, 1975.

COOK, T. D., & CAMPBELL, D. T. The design and conduct of quasi-experiments in field settings. In M. D. Dunnette (Ed.), *Handbook of industrial and organizational psychology.* Chicago: Rand McNally, 1976. Ch. 7.

COOLEY, W. W., & GLASER, R. The computer and individualized instruction. *Science,* 1969, *166,* 574–582.

COOPER, J. E., et al. *Psychiatric diagnosis in New York and London: A comparative study of mental hospital admissions.* New York: Oxford University Press, 1972.

COOPER, R. High aptitude, low aptitude—training must fit the man. *Training,* 1974, *11*(11), 42–43; 58–60.

COPLEY, F. B. *Frederick W. Taylor, father of scientific management* (2 vols.). New York: Harper, 1923.

CORSINI, R. J. (Ed.). *Current psychotherapies.* Itasca, Ill.: Peacock, 1973.

COUCH, A., & KENISTON, K. Yeasayers and naysayers: Agreeing response sets as a personality variable. *Journal of Abnormal and Social Psychology,* 1960, *60,* 151–174.

COULSON, J. E. (Ed.). *Programmed learning and computer-based instruction.* New York: Wiley, 1962.

COWEN, E. L. Social and community interventions. *Annual Review of Psychology,* 1973, *24,* 423–472.

COWEN, E. L., LEIBOWITZ, E., & LEIBOWITZ, G. The utilization of retired people as mental health aides in the schools. *American Journal of Orthopsychiatry,* 1968, *38,* 900–909.

COX, D. F. (Ed.). *Risk taking and information handling in consumer behavior.* Cambridge, Mass.: Harvard University Press, 1967.

CRAIK, K. H. The assessment of places. In P. McReynolds (Ed.), *Advances in psychological assessment* (Vol. 2). Palo Alto, Calif.: Science and Behavior Books, 1971. Ch. 3.

CRAIK, K. H. Environmental psychology. *Annual Review of Psychology,* 1973, *24,* 403–422.

CRAIK, K. H., & ZUBE, E. H. (Eds.). *Perceiving environmental quality: Research and applications.* New York: Plenum, 1976.

CRAWFORD, J. W. *Advertising: Communications from management.* Boston: Allyn & Bacon, 1960.

CRAWFORD, M. P. Military psychology and general psychology. *American Psychologist,* 1970, *25,* 328–336.

CRITES, J. O. Measurement of vocational maturity at adolescence: 1. Attitude test of the vocational development inventory. *Psychological Monographs,* 1965, *79*(2, Whole No. 595). (a)

CRITES, J. O. Research frontier: The vocational development project at the University of Iowa. *Journal of Counseling Psychology,* 1965, *12,* 81–86. (b)

CRITES, J. O. *The maturity of vocational attitudes in adolescence.* Iowa City: University of Iowa, 1969.

CROMWELL, R. L., BUTTERFIELD, E. C., BRAYFIELD, F. M., & CURRY, J. J. *Acute myocardial infarction: Reaction and recovery.* St. Louis: Mosby, 1977.

CRONBACH, L. J. Proposals leading to analytic treatment of social perception scores. In R. Tagiuri & L. Petrullo (Eds.), *Person perception and interpersonal behavior.* Stanford, Calif.: Stanford University Press, 1958. Pp. 353–379.

CRONBACH, L. J. *Essentials of psychological testing* (3rd ed.). New York: Harper & Row, 1970.

CRONBACH, L. J. Beyond the two disciplines of scientific psychology. *American Psychologist,* 1975, *30,* 116–127.

CRONBACH, L. J. *Educational psychology* (3rd ed.). New York: Harcourt Brace Jovanovich, 1977.

CRONBACH, L. J., & GLESER, G. C. *Psychological tests and personnel decisions* (2nd ed.). Urbana: University of Illinois Press, 1965.

CRONBACH, L. J., & SNOW, R. E. *Aptitudes and instructional methods: A handbook for research on interactions.* New York: Irvington, 1977.

CROWNE, D. P., & STEPHENS, M. W. Self-acceptance and self-evaluative methodology. *Psychological Bulletin,* 1961, *58,* 104–121.

CRUICKSHANK, W. M. (Ed.). *Psychology of exceptional children and youth* (3rd ed.). Englewood Cliffs, N. J.: Prentice-Hall, 1971.

CRUICKSHANK, W. M., & JOHNSON, G. O. (Eds.). *Education of exceptional children and youth* (3rd ed.). Englewood Cliffs, N. J.: Prentice-Hall, 1975.

CULLEN, J. W., FOX, B. H., & ISOM, R. N. (Eds.). *Cancer: The behavioral dimensions* (DHEW

Publication No. (NIH) 76-1074). Washington, D. C.: U. S. Department of Health, Education, and Welfare, 1976.

CUMMING, J., & CUMMING, E. *Ego and milieu: Theory and practice of environmental therapy.* New York: Atherton, 1966.

CUMMINS, R. C. Relationship of initiating structure and job performance as moderated by consideration. *Journal of Applied Psychology,* 1971, *55,* 489–490.

CURETON, E. E. Validity, reliability, and baloney. *Educational and Psychological Measurement,* 1950, *10,* 94–96.

DAFTUAR, C. N. The role of human factors engineering in underdeveloped countries, with special reference to India. In A. Chapanis (Ed.), *Ethnic variables in human factors engineering.* Baltimore: Johns Hopkins University Press, 1975. Ch. 6.

DAHLE, T. L. Transmitting information to employees: A study of five methods. *Personnel,* 1954, *31,* 243–246.

DAHLSTROM, W. G., WELSH, G. S., & DAHLSTROM, L. E. *An MMPI handbook.* Vol. I, *Clinical interpretation.* Minneapolis: University of Minnesota Press, 1972.

DAHLSTROM, W. G:, WELSH, G. S., & DAHLSTROM, L. E. *An MMPI handbook.* Vol. II, *Research developments and applications.* Minneapolis: University of Minnesota Press, 1975.

DAILEY, C. A. The life history as a criterion of assessment. *Journal of Counseling Psychology,* 1960, *7,* 20–23.

DARLEY, J. G., & HAGENAH, T. *Vocational interest measurement: Theory and practice.* Minneapolis: University of Minnesota Press, 1955.

DATTA, S. R., & RAMANATHAN, N. L. Ergonomic comparison of seven modes of carrying loads on the horizontal plane. *Ergonomics,* 1971, *14,* 269–278.

DAVIDS, A. Therapeutic approaches to children in residential treatments: Changes from the mid-1950s to the mid-1970s. *American Psychologist,* 1975, *30,* 809–814.

DAVIDSON, P. O. Validity of the guilty-knowledge technique: The effects of motivation. *Journal of Applied Psychology,* 1968, *52,* 62–65.

DAVIES, D. R., & TUNE, G. S. *Human vigilance performance.* New York: Elsevier, 1969.

DAVIS, A. E., DINITZ, S., & PASAMANICK, B. *Schizophrenics in the new custodial community: Five years after the experiment.* Columbus: Ohio State University Press, 1974.

DAVIS, H. L. Dimensions of marital roles in consumer decision making. *Journal of Marketing Research,* 1970, *7*(2), 168–177.

DAVIS, H. L. (Ed.). Human factors in industry. *Human Factors,* 1973, *15,* 103–177; 195–268.

DAVIS, H. L., FAULKNER, T. W., & MILLER, C. I. Work physiology. *Human Factors,* 1969, *11,* 157–166.

DAVIS, J. H., BRAY, R. M., & HOLT, R. W. The empirical study of decision processes in juries: A critical review. In J. L. Tapp & F. J. Levine (Eds.), *Law, justice, and the individual in society: Psychological and legal issues.* New York: Holt, Rinehart & Winston, 1977. Pp. 326–361.

DAVIS, K. A method of studying communication patterns in organizations. *Personnel Psychology,* 1953, *6,* 301–312.

DAVIS, K. Success of chain-of-command oral communication in a manufacturing management group. In B. M. Bass & S. D. Deep (Eds.), *Studies in organizational psychology.* Boston: Allyn & Bacon, 1972. Pp. 190–199.

DAVIS, R. H., ALEXANDER, L. T., & YELON, S. L. *Learning system design: An approach to the improvement of instruction.* New York: McGraw-Hill, 1974.

DAWES, R. M., & CORRIGAN, B. Linear models in decision making. *Psychological Bulletin,* 1974, *81,* 95–106.

DAWIS, R. V., & LOFQUIST, L. H. *Minnesota occupational classification system.* Minneapolis: University of Minnesota, Department of Psychology, 1974.

DAWIS, R. V., & LOFQUIST, L. H. Toward a psychological taxonomy of work. *Journal of Vocational Behavior,* 1975, *7,* 165–171.

DAWIS, R. V., & LOFQUIST, L. H. Personality style and the process of work adjustment. *Journal of Counseling Psychology,* 1976, *23,* 55–59.

DAWIS, R. V., LOFQUIST, L. H., & WEISS, D. J., *A theory of work adjustment (A revision).* (Minnesota Studies in Vocational Rehabilitation: XXIII). Minneapolis: University of Minnesota, Work Adjustment Project, 1968.

DEARBORN, D. C., & SIMON, H. A. Selective perception: A note on the departmental identifications of executives. *Sociometry,* 1958, *21,* 140–144.

DE LA MARE, G., & WALKER, J. Factors influencing the choice of shift rotation. *Occupational Psychology,* 1968, *42,* 1–21.

DENENBERG, V. H. (Ed.). *Education of the infant and young child.* New York: Academic Press, 1970.

DE SILVA, H. R. *Why we have automobile accidents.* New York: Wiley, 1942.

DEUTSCH, M(ARTIN), TALEPOROS, E., & VICTOR, J. A brief synopsis of an initial enrichment program in early childhood. In S. Ryan (Ed.). *A report on longitudinal evaluations of preschool programs* (Vol. 1) (DHEW Publication No. (OHD) 74–24). Washington, D. C.: U. S. Department of Health, Education, and Welfare, 1974. Ch. 3.

DEUTSCH, M(ORTON). *The resolution of conflict: Constructive and destructive processes.* New Haven, Conn.: Yale University Press, 1973.

DIAMOND, E. E. (Ed.). *Issues of sex bias and sex fairness in career interest measurement.* Washington, D. C.: National Institute of Education, 1975.

DIAMOND, M. J., & BOND, M. H. The acceptance of "Barnum" personality interpretation by Japanese, Japanese-American, and Caucasian-American college students. *Journal of Cross-Cultural Psychology,* 1974, *5,* 228–235.

DICHTER, E. *Handbook of consumer motivations.* New York: McGraw-Hill, 1964.

DICKENSON, W. A., & TRUAX, C. B. Group counseling with college underachievers. *Personnel and Guidance Journal,* 1966, *45,* 243–247.

DICKSON, C. R. Role of assessment in behavior therapy. In P. McReynolds (Ed.). *Advances in psychological assessment* (Vol. 3). San Francisco: Jossey-Bass, 1975. Ch. 9.

DILL, W. R. Management games for training decision makers. In E. A. Fleishman & A. R. Bass (Eds.), *Studies in personnel and industrial psychology* (3rd ed.). Homewood, Ill.: Dorsey, 1974. Pp. 157–168.

DILLEHAY, R. C., BRUVOLD, W. H., & SIEGEL, J. P. On the assessment of potability. *Journal of Applied Psychology,* 1967, *51,* 89–95.

DILLMAN, D. A., & FREY, J. H. Contribution of personalization to mail questionnaire response as an element of a previously tested method. *Journal of Applied Psychology,* 1974, *59,* 297–301.

DIMOND, R. E., HAVENS, R. A., & JONES, A. C. A conceptual framework for the practice of prescriptive eclecticism in psychotherapy. *American Psychologist,* 1978, *33,* 239–248.

DINITZ, S., LEFTON, M., ANGRIST, S., & PASAMANICK, B. The post-hospital functioning of female mental patients: An exploration in prognosis. *Psychiatric Research Reports,* 1962, *15,* 154–163.

DOERINGER, P. B. (Ed.). *Programs to employ the disadvantaged.* Englewood Cliffs, N. J.: Prentice-Hall, 1969.

DOHRENWEND, B. P., & DOHRENWEND, B. S. *Social status and psychological disorder: A causal inquiry.* New York: Wiley, 1969.

DOHRENWEND, B. P., & DOHRENWEND, B. S. Social and cultural influences in psychopathology. *Annual Review of Psychology,* 1974, *25,* 417–452. (a)

DOHRENWEND, B. S., & DOHRENWEND, B. P. (Eds.). *Stressful life events: Their nature and effects.* New York: Wiley, 1974. (b)

DOLLAR, B. *Humanizing classroom discipline: A behavioral approach.* New York: Harper & Row, 1972.

DOLLARD, J., & MILLER, N. E. *Personality and psychotherapy: An analysis in terms of learning, thinking, and culture.* New York: McGraw-Hill, 1950.

DOOB, A. N., FREEDMAN, J. L., & CARLSMITH, J. M. Effects of sponsor and prepayment on compliance with a mailed request. *Journal of Applied Psychology,* 1973, *57,* 346–347.

DOWALIBY, F. J., & SCHUMER, H. Teacher-centered versus student-centered mode of college classroom instruction as related to manifest anxiety. *Journal of Educational Psychology,* 1973, *64,* 125–132.

DOWNEY, R. G. *Associate evaluations: Nominations vs. ratings.* U. S. Army Research Institute for the Behavioral and Social Sciences, Technical Report 253, September 1974.

DOWNEY, R. G., MEDLAND, F. F., & YATES, L. G. Evaluation of a peer rating system for predicting subsequent promotion of senior military officers. *Journal of Applied Psychology,* 1976, *61,* 206–209.

DRAGUNS, J. G., & PHILLIPS, L. *Culture and psychopathology: The quest for a relationship.* Morristown, N. J.: General Learning Press, 1972.

DRAKE, C. A. Accident proneness: A hypothesis. *Character and Personality,* 1940, *8,* 335–341.

DRAKE, L. E., & OETTING, E. R. *An MMPI codebook for counselors.* Minneapolis: University of Minnesota Press, 1959.

DREYFUS, H. *Symbol sourcebook.* New York: McGraw-Hill, 1972.

DROEGE, R. C., & HAWK, J. Development of a U. S. Employment Service interest inventory. *Journal of Employment Counseling, 1977, 14*(2), 65–71.

DRUCKER, P. *The practice of management.* New York: Harper, 1954.

DUBIN, R. Assaulting the tower of Babel (Review of *Behind the front page* by C. Argyris). *Contemporary Psychology,* 1975, *20,* 881–882.

DUDYCHA, G. J. (Ed.). *Psychology for law enforcement officers.* Springfield, Ill.: Charles C Thomas, 1955.

DUNBAR, F. *Emotions and bodily changes.* New York: Columbia University Press, 1954. (1st ed., 1935.)

DUNCAN, G. J., & MORGAN, J. N. (Eds.). *Five thousand American families—patterns of economic progress* (Vol. 5). Ann Arbor, Mich.: Institute for Social Research, 1977.

DUNHAM, R. B. The measurement and dimensionality of job characteristics. *Journal of Applied Psychology,* 1976, *61,* 404–409.

DUNN, J. P., & COBB, S. Frequency of peptic ulcer among executives, craftsmen, and foremen. *Journal of Occupational Medicine,* 1962, *4,* 343–348.

DUNNETTE, M. D. Use of the sugar pill by industrial psychologists. *American Psychologist,* 1957, *12,* 223–225.

DUNNETTE, M. D. A modified model for test validation and selection research. *Journal of Applied Psychology,* 1963, *47,* 317–323. (a)

DUNNETTE, M. D. A note on the criterion. *Journal of Applied Psychology,* 1963, *47,* 251– 254. (b)

DUNNETTE, M. D. Multiple assessment procedures in identifying and developing managerial talent. In P. McReynolds (Ed.), *Advances in psychological assessment* (Vol. 2). Palo Alto, Calif.: Science and Behavior Books, 1971.

DUNNETTE, M. D. (Ed.). *Handbook of industrial and organizational psychology.* Chicago: Rand McNally, 1976.

DUNNETTE, M. D., ARVEY, R. D., & BANAS, P. A. Why do they leave? *Personnel,* 1973, *50,* 25–39.

DUNNETTE, M. D., & BORMAN, W. C. Personnel selection and classification systems. *Annual Review of Psychology,* 1979, *30* (in press).

DUNNETTE, M. D., CAMPBELL, J. P., & HAKEL, M. D. Factors contributing to job satisfaction and job dissatisfaction in six occupational groups. *Organizational Behavior and Human Performance,* 1967, *2,* 143–174.

DUNNETTE, M. D., CAMPBELL, J. P., & JAASTAD, K. The effect of group participation on brainstorming effectiveness for two industrial samples. *Journal of Applied Psychology,* 1963, *47,* 30–37.

DUNNETTE, M. D., & KIRCHNER, W. K. *Psychology applied to industry.* New York: Appleton-Century-Crofts, 1965.

DUNNETTE, M. D., McCARTNEY, J., CARLSON, H. C., & KIRCHNER, W. K. A study of faking behavior on a forced-choice self-description checklist. *Personnel Psychology,* 1962, *15,* 13–24.

DUNNETTE, M. D., & MOTOWIDLO, S. J. *Development of a personnel assessment and career assessment system for police officers in patrol, investigative, supervisory, and command positions: Final report.* Minneapolis: Personnel Decisions, Inc., June 1975.

DUNNETTE, M. D., & PETERSON, N. G. *Causes and consequences of adolescent drug experiences: A progress report and research perspective.* (Institute Report 14). Minneapolis: Personnel Decisions Research Institute, March 1977.

DYER, H. S., *How to achieve accountability in the public schools.* Bloomington, Ind.: Phi Delta Kappa Educational Foundation, 1973.

DYER, H. S., & ROSENTHAL, E. Assessing education at the state level: Overview of the survey findings. In R. W. Tyler & R. M. Wolf (Eds.), *Crucial issues in testing.* Berkeley, Calif.: McCutchan, 1974. Pp. 105–127.

EBEL, R. L. Must all tests be valid? *American Psychologist,* 1961, *16,* 640–647.

EBEL, R. L. *Essentials of educational measurement.* Englewood Cliffs, N. J.: Prentice-Hall, 1972.

EDUCATIONAL TESTING SERVICE. *SIGI: A computer-based System of Interactive Guidance and Information.* Princeton, N. J.: Author, 1974, 1975.

EDWARDS, W. Behavioral decision theory. *Annual Review of Psychology,* 1961, 12, 473–498.

EFRON, D. H. (Ed.). *Psychopharmacology: A review of progress 1957–1967* (PHS Publication No. 1836). Washington, D. C.: Public Health Service, 1968.

EHRLICH, R., & WIENER, D. N. The measurement of values in psychotherapeutic settings. *Journal of General Psychology,* 1961, *64,* 359–372.

EISDORFER, C., & LAWTON, M. P. (Eds.). *The psychology of adult development and aging.* Washington, D. C.: American Psychological Association, 1973.

EISENBERG, T., & MURRAY, J. M. Selection. In O. G. Stahl & R. A. Staufenberger (Eds.), *Police personnel administration.* Washington, D. C.: Police Foundation, 1974. Pp. 69–100.

ELDER, T., NOBLIN, C. D., & MAHER, B. The extinction of fear as a function of distance versus dissimilarity from the original conflict situation. *Journal of Abnormal and Social Psychology,* 1961, *63,* 530–533.

ELMS, A. C. *Personality in politics.* New York: Harcourt Brace Jovanovich, 1976.

EMERY, F. E., & THORSRUD, E. *Form and content in industrial democracy.* London: Tavistock, 1969.

EMERY, F. E., & TRIST, E. L. The causal texture of organizational environments. *Human Relations,* 1965, *18,* 21–32.

Encyclopedia of occupational health and safety (2 vols.). Geneva, Switz.: International Labor Office, 1971.

ENGEL, G. L., & REICHSMAN, F. A study of an infant with a gastric fistula: I. Behavior and the rate of total hydrochloric acid secretion. *Psychosomatic Medicine,* 1956, *18,* 374–398.

ENGEL, J. F., KOLLAT, D. T., & BLACKWELL, R. D. *Consumer behavior* (2nd ed.). New York: Holt, Rinehart & Winston, 1973.

ENGEL, J. F., & WALES, H. G. Spoken *versus* pictured questions to taboo topics. *Journal of Advertising Research,* 1962, *2*(3), 11–17.

ENGLAND, G. W. *Development and use of weighted application blanks.* Minneapolis: University of Minnesota, Industrial Relations Center, 1971.

ENNIS, B. *Prisoners of psychiatry.* New York: Harcourt Brace Jovanovich, 1972.

EPPS, E. G. (Ed.). *Cultural pluralism.* Berkeley, Calif.: McCutchan, 1974.

EQUAL EMPLOYMENT OPPORTUNITY COMMISSION (EEOC). Guidelines on employee selection procedures. *Federal Register,* 1970, *35*(149), 12333–12336.

ERICKSON, G. D., & HOGAN, T. P. (Eds.). *Family therapy: An introduction to theory and technique.* Monterey, Calif.: Brooks/Cole, 1972.

ERICKSON, R. C. Outcome studies in mental hospitals. *Psychological Bulletin,* 1975, *82,* 519–540.

ERIKSON, E. H. *Childhood and society.* New York: Norton, 1950.

ETZEL, M. J., & WALKER, B. J. Effects of alternative follow-up procedures on mail survey response rates. *Journal of Applied Psychology,* 1974, *59,* 219–221.

EVANS, C. E., & LASEAU, L. N. My Job Contest—an experiment in new employee relations methods. Parts I-IV. *Personnel Psychology,* 1949, *2,* 1–16; 185–227; 311–367; 461–474.

EVANS, R. I. (Chair). *Mass media in effecting public health: What are psychologists contributing?* Discussion and film program presented at the meeting of the American Psychological Association, Washington, D. C., September 1976.

EVANS, R. I., ROZELLE, R. M., LASATER, T. M., DEMBROSKI, T. M., & ALLEN, B. M. Fear arousal, persuasion, and actual versus implied behavioral change: New perspective utilizing a real-life dental hygiene program. *Journal of Personality and Social Psychology,* 1970, *16,* 220–227.

EVANS, R. I., ROZELLE, R. M., NOBLITT, R., & WILLIAMS, D. L. Explicit and implicit persuasive communications over time to initiate and maintain behavior change: New perspective utilizing a real-life dental hygiene situation. *Journal of Applied Social Psychology,* 1975, *5,* 150–156.

EWALT, J. *Action for mental health: Final report of the Joint Commission on Mental Illness and Health.* New York: Basic Books, 1961.

EXNER, J. E., JR., & EXNER, D. E. How clinicians use the Rorschach. *Journal of Personality Assessment,* 1972, *36,* 403–408.

FAIRWEATHER, G. W. *Social psychology in treating mental illness: An experimental approach.* New York: Wiley, 1964.

FAIRWEATHER, G. W., et al. Relative effectiveness of psychotherapeutic programs: A multicriteria comparison of four programs for different patient groups. *Psychological Monographs,* 1960, *74*(5, Whole No. 492).

FAIRWEATHER, G. W., SANDERS, D. H., MAYNARD, H., CRESSLER, D. L., & BLACK, D. J. *Community life for the mentally ill: An alternative to institutional care.* Chicago: Aldine, 1969.

FANTL, B., & SCHIRO, J. Cultural variables in the behavior patterns and symptom formation of 15 Irish and 15 Italian female schizophrenics. *International Journal of Social Psychiatry,* 1959, *4,* 245–253.

FARBEROW, N. L., & SHNEIDMAN, E. S. (Eds.). *The cry for help.* New York: McGraw-Hill, 1961.

FARRIS, G. F., & LIM, F. G., JR. Effects of performance on leadership, cohesiveness, influence, satisfaction, and subsequent performance. *Journal of Applied Psychology,* 1969, *53,* 490–497.

FAULKNER, T. W., & MURPHY, T. J. Lighting for difficult visual tasks. *Human Factors,* 1973, *15,* 149–162.

FEAR, R. A. *The evaluation interview* (2nd ed.). New York: McGraw-Hill, 1973.

FEIFEL, H. (Ed.). *The meaning of death.* New York: McGraw-Hill, 1959.

FEIFEL, H. (Ed.). *New meanings of death.* New York: McGraw-Hill, 1977.

FEIFEL, H., FREILICH, J., & HERMANN, J. Death fear in dying heart and cancer patients. *Journal of Psychosomatic Research,* 1973, *17,* 161–166.

FESTINGER, L. *A theory of cognitive dissonance.* Evanston, Ill.: Row, Peterson, 1957.

FHANÉR, G., & HANE, M. Seat belts: Changing usage by changing beliefs. *Journal of Applied Psychology,* 1975, *60,* 589–598.

FIEDLER, F. E. *A theory of leadership effectiveness.* New York: McGraw-Hill, 1967.

FIEDLER, F. E., & CHEMERS, M. M. *Leadership and effective management.* Glenview, Ill.: Scott, Foresman, 1974.

FIEDLER, F. E., & FIEDLER, J. Port noise complaints: Verbal and behavioral reactions to airport-related noise. *Journal of Applied Psychology,* 1975, *60,* 498–506.

FIEDLER, F. E., MITCHELL, T., & TRIANDIS, H. C. The culture assimilator: An approach to cross-cultural training. *Journal of Applied Psychology,* 1971, *55,* 95–102.

FIELD, M. J. *Search for security: An ethno-psychiatric study of rural Ghana.* Evanston, Ill.: Northwestern University Press, 1960.

FINCHER, C. Personnel testing and public policy. *American Psychologist,* 1973, *28,* 489–497.

FINKELMAN, J. M., & GLASS, D. C. Reappraisal of the relationship between noise and human performance by means of a subsidiary task measure. *Journal of Applied Psychology*, 1970, *54*, 211–213.

FINKLE, R. B. Managerial assessment centers. In M. D. Dunnette (Ed.). *Handbook of industrial and organizational psychology*. Chicago: Rand McNally, 1976. Ch. 20.

FINKLE, R. B., & JONES, W. S. *Assessing corporate talent: A key to managerial manpower planning*. New York: Wiley-Interscience, 1970.

FINN, R. H., & LEE, S. M. Salary equity: Its determination, analysis, and correlates. *Journal of Applied Psychology*, 1972, *56*, 283–292.

FISHER, J. The twisted pear and prediction of behavior. *Journal of Consulting Psychology*, 1959, *23*, 400–405.

FISHMAN, J. R., DENHAM, W. H., LEVINE, M., & SHATZ, E. O. *New careers for the disadvantaged in human service: Report of a social experiment*. Washington, D. C.: Howard University, Institute for Youth Studies, 1969.

FISKE, D. W. The subject reacts to tests. *American Psychologist*, 1967, *22*, 287–296.

FISKE, D. W., & COX, J. A., Jr. The consistency of ratings by peers. *Journal of Applied Psychology*, 1960, *44*, 11–17.

FITTS, P. M. A study of location discrimination ability. In P. M. Fitts (Ed.), *Psychological research on equipment* (AAF Aviation Psychology Program, Research Reports, No. 19.). Washington, D. C.: U. S. Government Printing Office, 1947, Pp. 207–217.

FITTS, P. M., & DEININGER, R. L. S-R compatibility; Correspondence among paired elements within stimulus and response codes. *Journal of Experimental Psychology*, 1954, *48*, 483–492.

FITTS, P. M., & SEEGER, C. M. S-R compatibility: Spatial characteristics of stimulus and response codes. *Journal of Experimental Psychology*, 1953, *46*, 199–210.

FLANAGAN, J. C. Scientific development of the use of human resources: Progress in the Army Air Forces. *Science*, 1947, *105*, 57–60.

FLANAGAN, J. C. Critical requirements: A new approach to employee evaluation. *Personnel Psychology*, 1949, *2*, 419–425.

FLANAGAN, J. C. The critical incident technique. *Psychological Bulletin*, 1954, *51*, 327–358.

FLANAGAN, J. C. The PLAN system for individualizing education. *NCME Measurement in Education*, 1971, *2*(2), 1–8.

FLANAGAN, J. C. The first 15 years of project TALENT: Implications for career guidance. *Vocational Guidance Quarterly*, 1973, *22*, 8–14.

FLANAGAN, J. C., SHANNER, W. M., BRUDNER, H. J., & MARKER, R. W. An individualized instructional system: PLAN*. In H. Talmage (Ed.), *Systems of individualized education*. Berkeley, Calif.: McCutchan, 1975. Ch. 5.

FLANAGAN, J. C., SHAYCOFT, M. F., RICHARDS, J. M., JR., & CLAUDY, J. G. *Five years after high school*. Palo Alto, Calif.: American Institutes for Research, 1971.

FLANAGAN, J. C., TIEDEMAN, D. V., WILLIS, M. B., & MCLAUGHLIN, D. H. *The career data book*. Palo Alto, Calif.: American Institutes for Research, 1973.

FLEISHMAN, E. A. An experimental consumer panel technique. *Journal of Applied Psychology*, 1951, *35*, 133–135.

FLEISHMAN, E. A. The description of supervisory behavior. *Journal of Applied Psychology*, 1953, *37*, 1–6. (a)

FLEISHMAN, E. A. Leadership climate, human relations training, and supervisory behavior. *Personnel Psychology*, 1953, *6*, 205–222. (b)

FLEISHMAN, E. A. Factor structure in relation to task difficulty in psychomotor performance. *Educational and Psychological Measurement*, 1957, *17*, 522–533.

FLEISHMAN, E. A. Attitude versus skill factors in work group productivity. *Personnel Psychology*, 1965, *18*, 253–266.

FLEISHMAN, E. A. On the relation between abilities, learning, and human performance. *American Psychologist*, 1972, *27*, 1017–1032.

FLEISHMAN, E. A. Toward a taxonomy of human performance. *American Psychologist*, 1975, *30*, 1127–1149.

FLEISHMAN, E. A., & BASS, A. R. (Eds.). *Studies in personnel and industrial psychology* (3rd ed.). Homewood, Ill.: Dorsey, 1974.

FLEISHMAN, E. A., & HARRIS, E. F. Patterns of leadership behavior related to employee grievances and turnover. *Personnel Psychology, 1962, 15,* 43–56.

FLEISHMAN, E. A., HARRIS, E. F., & BURTT, H. E. *Leadership and supervision in industry.* Columbus, Ohio: Ohio State University, 1955.

FLEMING, P., & RICKS, D. F. Emotions of children before schizophrenia and before character disorder. In M. Roff & D. F. Ricks (Eds.), *Life history research in psychopathology* (Vol. 1). Minneapolis: University of Minnesota Press, 1970. Pp. 240–264.

FLESCH, R. *The art of plain talk.* New York: Harper, 1946.

FLESCH, R. *The art of readable writing.* New York: Harper, 1949.

FLESCH, R. *A new way to better English.* New York: Harper, 1958.

FOLLEY, J. D., JR. Determining training needs of department store sales personnel. *Training Development Journal, 1969, 23*(7), 24–27.

FONTANA, A. F. Familial etiology of schizophrenia: Is a scientific methodology possible? *Psychological Bulletin, 1966, 66,* 214–227.

FORBES, T. W. The normal automobile driver as a traffic problem. *Journal of General Psychology, 1939, 20,* 471–474.

FORBES, T. W. (Ed.). *Human factors in highway traffic safety research.* New York: Wiley, 1972.

FORD, R. N. *Motivation through the work itself.* New York: American Management Association, 1969.

FORDYCE, W. E. *Behavioral methods for chronic pain and illness.* St. Louis: Mosby, 1976.

FOREHAND, G. A., & GILMER, B. von H. Environmental variation in studies of organizational behavior. *Psychological Bulletin, 1964, 62,* 361–382.

FORER, B. The fallacy of personal validation: A classroom demonstration of gullibility. *Journal of Abnormal and Social Psychology, 1949, 44,* 118–123.

FORTUIN, G. J. Age and lighting needs. *Ergonomics.* 1963, *6,* 239–245.

FOWLER, O. S. *Human science or phrenology.* Philadelphia: National, 1873.

FOX, W. F. Human performance in the cold. *Human Factors, 1967, 9,* 203–220.

FRANK, G. H. The role of the family in the development of psychopathology. *Psychological Bulletin, 1965, 64,* 191–205.

FRANKENHAEUSER, M., JÄRPE, G., SVAN, H., & WRANGSJÖ, B. Psychophysiological reactions to two different placebo treatments. *Scandinavian Journal of Psychology, 1963, 4,* 245–250.

FRANKS, C. M. (Ed.). *Behavior therapy: Appraisal and status.* New York: McGraw-Hill, 1969.

FRASER, D. M. Congress and the psychologist. *American Psychologist, 1970, 25,* 323–327.

FRASER, T. M. Sustained linear acceleration. In *Bioastronautics data book* (2nd ed.) (National Aeronautics and Space Administration, NASA SP-3006). Washington, D. C.: U. S. Government Printing Office, 1973. Ch. 4.

FREDERIKSEN, N. Factors in in-basket performance. *Psychological Monographs, 1962, 76*(22, Whole No. 541).

FREDERIKSEN, N. Validation of a simulation technique. *Organizational Behavior & Human Performance, 1966, 1,* 87–109.

FREDERIKSEN, N. & EVANS, F. R. Effects of models of creative performance on ability to formulate hypotheses. *Journal of Educational Psychology, 1974, 66,* 67–82.

FREDERIKSEN, N., SAUNDERS, D. R., & WAND, B. The in-basket test. *Psychological Monographs, 1957, 71,*(9, Whole No. 438).

FREEBERG, N. E. Relevance of rater-ratee acquaintance in the validity and reliability of ratings. *Journal of Applied Psychology, 1969, 53,* 518–524.

FREEDMAN, A. M., KAPLAN, H. I., & SADOCK, B. J. (Eds.). *Comprehensive textbook of psychiatry*-II (2 vols.). Baltimore: Williams & Wilkins, 1975.

FREEDMAN, J. L. *Crowding and behavior.* New York: Viking Press, 1975.

Freedom in a wheelchair. *Time,* June 21, 1976, p. 44.

FREEMAN, G. L. Changes in tension-pattern and total energy expenditure during adaptation to "distracting" stimuli. *American Journal of Psychology,* 1939, *52,* 354–360.

FREEMAN, W., & WATTS, J. *Psychosurgery in the treatment of mental disorders and intractable pain* (2nd ed.). Springfield, Ill.: Charles C Thomas, 1950.

FRENCH, J. R. P., JR., ROSS, I. C., KIRBY, S., NELSON, J. R., & SMYTH, P. Employee participation in a program of industrial change. *Personnel,* 1958, *35,* 16–29.

FRENCH, W. L., & BELL, C. H. *Organization development.* Englewood Cliffs, N. J.: Prentice-Hall, 1973.

FRIEDLANDER, F. Comparative work value systems. *Personnel Psychology,* 1965, *18,* 1–20.

FRIEDLANDER, F., & BROWN, L. D. Organization development. *Annual Review of Psychology,* 1974, *25,* 313–341.

FRIEDMAN, M., & ROSENMAN, R. H. *Type 'A' behavior and your heart.* New York: Knopf, 1974.

FRIEDMAN, M. P. Consumer confusion in the selection of supermarket products. *Journal of Applied Psychology,* 1966, *50,* 529–534.

FRIEDMAN, M. P. Consumer price comparisons of retail products: The role of packaging and pricing practices and the implications for consumer legislation. *Journal of Applied Psychology,* 1972, *56,* 439–446.

FRIEDMAN, R. B. A computer program for simulating the patient-physician encounter. *Journal of Medical Education,* 1973, *48,* 92–97.

FROST, C. F., WAKELEY, J. H., & RUH, R. A. *The Scanlon Plan for organization development: Identity, participation, and equity.* East Lansing: Michigan State University Press, 1974.

FRYER, D. H. Occupational intelligence standards. *School and Society,* 1922, *16,* 273–277.

FRYER, D. H., & HENRY, E. R. (Eds.). *Handbook of applied psychology* (2 vols.). New York: Rinehart, 1950.

GAEL, S., GRANT, D. L., & RITCHIE, R. J. Employment test validation for minority and nonminority clerks with work sample criteria. *Journal of Applied Psychology,* 1975, *60,* 420–426. (a)

GAEL, S., GRANT, D. L., & RITCHIE, R. J. Employment test validation for minority and nonminority telephone operators. *Journal of Applied Psychology,* 1975, *60,* 411–419. (b)

GAGNÉ, R. M. *The conditions of learning* (2nd ed.). New York: Holt, Rinehart & Winston, 1970.

GAGNÉ, R. M. Learning and instructional sequence. *Review of Research in Education,* 1973, *1,* 3–33.

GANGULI, S., BOSE, K. S., DATTA, S. R., CHATTERJEE, B. B., & ROY, B. N. Biomechanical approach to the functional assessment of the use of crutches for ambulation. *Ergonomics,* 1974, *17,* 365–374.

GANS, H. *The urban villagers.* New York: Free Press, 1962.

GARFIELD, S. L. *Clinical psychology: The study of personality and behavior.* Chicago: Aldine, 1974.

GARFIELD, S. L., & KURTZ, R. Clinical psychologists in the 1970's. *American Psychologist,* 1976, *31,* 1–9.

GARMEZY, N., FARINA, A., & RODNICK, E. H. Direct study of child-parent interactions: I. The structured situational test. A method for studying family interaction in schizophrenia. *American Journal of Orthopsychiatry,* 1960, *30,* 445–452.

GARRETT, J. F., & LEVINE, E. S. (Eds.). *Psychological practices with the physically disabled.* New York: Columbia University Press, 1962.

GARTNER, A., KOHLER, M. C., & RIESSMAN, F. *Children teach children.* New York: Harper & Row, 1971.

GATEWOOD, R. D., & PERLOFF, R. An experimental investigation of three methods of providing weight and price information to consumers. *Journal of Applied Psychology,* 1973, *57,* 81–85.

GAUDRY, E., & SPIELBERGER, C. D. *Anxiety and educational achievement.* New York: Wiley, 1974.

GAY, E. G., WEISS, D. J., HENDEL, D. D., DAWIS, R. V., & LOFQUIST, L. H. *Manual for the*

Minnesota Importance Questionnaire (Minnesota Studies in Vocational Rehabilitation: XXVIII). Minneapolis: University of Minnesota, Work Adjustment Project, 1971.

GEACINTOV, T., & PEAVLER, W. S. Pupillography in industrial fatigue assessment. *Journal of Applied Psychology,* 1974, *59,* 213–216.

GEEN, R. G., & O'NEAL, E. C. (Eds.). *Perspectives on aggression.* New York: Academic Press, 1976.

GEISER, R. L., & NEWMAN, R. W. Psychology and the legal process: Opinion polls as evidence. *American Psychologist,* 1961, *16,* 685–690.

GELATT, H. B. Decision-making: A conceptual frame of reference for counseling. *Journal of Counseling Psychology,* 1962, *9,* 240–245.

GELATT, H. B., VARENHORST, B., & CAREY, R. *Deciding: A leader's guide.* New York: College Entrance Examination Board, 1972.

GELATT, H. B., VARENHORST, B., CAREY, R., & MILLER, G. P. *Decisions and Outcomes: A leader's guide.* New York: College Entrance Examination Board, 1973.

GELLER, E. S., CHAFFEE, J. L., & INGRAM R. E. Promoting paper recycling on a university campus. *Journal of Environmental Systems,* 1975, *5,* 39–57.

GELLER, E. S., WITMER, J. F., & TUSO, M. A. Environmental intervention for litter control. *Journal of Applied Psychology,* 1977, *62,* 344–351.

GENGERELLI, J. A., & LEVINE, E. S. (Eds.). *Psychological practices with the physically disabled.* New York: Columbia University Press, 1962.

GERBASI, K. C., ZUCKERMAN, M., & REIS, H. T. Justice needs a new blindfold: A review of mock jury research. *Psychological Bulletin,* 1977, *84,* 323–345.

GHISELLI, E. E. Differentiation of individuals in terms of their predictability. *Journal of Applied Psychology,* 1956, *40,* 374–377.

GHISELLI, E. E. The generalization of validity. *Personnel Psychology,* 1959, *12,* 397–402.

GHISELLI, E. E. Differentiation of tests in terms of the accuracy with which they predict for a given individual. *Educational and Psychological Measurement,* 1960, *20,* 675–684.

GHISELLI, E. E. Moderating effects and differential reliability and validity. *Journal of Applied Psychology,* 1963, *47,* 81–86.

GHISELLI, E. E. *The validity of occupational aptitude tests.* New York: Wiley, 1966.

GHISELLI, E. E. Interaction of traits and motivational factors in the determination of the success of managers. *Journal of Applied Psychology,* 1968, *52,* 480–483.

GHISELLI, E. E., & BROWN, C. W. *Personnel and industrial psychology* (2nd ed.). New York: McGraw-Hill, 1955.

GHISELLI, E. E., & HAIRE, M. The validation of selection tests in the light of the dynamic character of criteria. *Personnel Psychology,* 1960, *13,* 225–231.

GIBB, J. R. Communication and productivity. *Personnel Administration,* 1964, *27,* 8–13; 45.

GIBBS, J. P. *Crime, punishment, and deterrence.* New York: Elsevier, 1975.

GIBSON, D. L., WEISS, D. J., DAWIS, R. V., & LOFQUIST, L. H. *Manual for the Minnesota Satisfactoriness Scales* (Minnesota Studies in Vocational Rehabilitation: XXVII). Minneapolis: University of Minnesota, Work Adjustment Project, 1970.

GIBSON, E. J., & LEVIN, H. *The psychology of reading.* Cambridge, Mass.: Massachusetts Institute of Technology Press, 1975.

GILBREATH, S. H. Group counseling, dependence, and college male underachievement. *Journal of Counseling Psychology,* 1967, *14,* 449–453.

GILBRETH, F. B. *Bricklaying system.* New York: Clark, 1909.

GILBRETH, F. B. *Motion study.* New York: Van Nostrand, 1911.

GILBRETH, F. B., & GILBRETH, L. M. *Fatigue study.* New York: Sturgis & Walton, 1916.

GILBRETH, F. B., & GILBRETH, L. M. *Applied motion study.* New York: Sturgis & Walton, 1917.

GILLET, B., & SCHWAB, D. P. Convergent and discriminant validities of corresponding Job Description Index and Minnesota Satisfaction Questionnaire scales. *Journal of Applied Psychology,* 1975, *60,* 313–318.

GINNOTT, H. G. *Group psychotherapy with children: The theory and practice of play therapy.* New York: McGraw-Hill, 1961.

GLAROS, A. G., & RAO, S. M. Bruxism: A critical review. *Psychological Bulletin,* 1977, *84,* 767–781.

GLASER, R. Adapting the elementary school curriculum to individual performance. *Proceedings of the 1967 Invitational Conference on Testing Problems, Educational Testing Service,* 1968, 3–36.

GLASER, R., & GOW, J. S., JR. The learning research and development center at the University of Pittsburgh. *American Psychologist,* 1964, *19,* 854–858.

GLASER, R., & RESNICK, L. B. Instructional psychology. *Annual Review of Psychology,* 1972, *23,* 207–276.

GLASER, R., & ROSNER, J. Adaptive environments for learning: Curriculum aspects. In H. Talmage (Ed.), *Systems of individualized education.* Berkeley, Calif.: McCutchan, 1975. Ch. 4.

GLASGOW, R. E., & ROSEN, G. M. Behavioral bibliotherapy: A review of self-help behavioral therapy manuals. *Psychological Bulletin,* 1978, *85,* 1–23.

GLASS, D. C., & SINGER, J. E. *Urban stress: Experiments on noise and social stressors.* New York: Academic Press, 1972.

GLENNON, J. R., ALBRIGHT, L. E., & OWENS, W. A. *A catalog of life history items.* Greensboro, N. C.: Center for Creative Leadership, 1966.

GLICK, I., WEISS, R. S., & PARKES, C. M. *The first year of bereavement.* New York: Wiley-Interscience, 1974.

GLICKMAN, A. S., & BROWN, Z. B. *Changing schedules of work: Patterns and implications.* Washington, D. C.: American Institutes for Research, 1973.

GLICKMAN, A. S., HAHN, C. P., FLEISHMAN, E. A., & BAXTER, B. *Top management development and succession.* New York: Macmillan, 1968.

GLICKMAN, A. S., & VALLANCE, T. R. Curriculum assessment with critical incidents. *Journal of Applied Psychology,* 1958, *42,* 329–335.

GLOVER, J. D., HOWER, R. M., & TAGIURI, A. *The administrator: Cases on human aspects of management* (5th ed.). Homewood, Ill.: Irwin, 1973.

GLUECK, B. C., & STROEBEL, C. F. Computers and clinical psychiatry. In A. M. Freedman, H. I. Kaplan, & B. J. Sadock (Eds.), *Comprehensive textbook of psychiatry-II* (Vol. 1). Baltimore: Williams & Wilkins, 1975. Pp. 413–428.

GLUECK, E. T. A more discriminative instrument for the identification of potential delinquents at school entrance. *Journal of Criminal Law, Criminology, and Police Science,* 1966, *57*(1), 27–30.

GLUECK, S., & GLUECK, E. T. *500 criminal careers.* New York: Knopf, 1930.

GLUECK, S., & GLUECK, E. T. *One thousand juvenile delinquents.* Cambridge, Mass.: Harvard University Press, 1934.

GLUECK, S., & GLUECK, E. T. *Criminal careers in retrospect.* New York: Commonwealth Fund, 1943.

GLUECK, S., & GLUECK, E. T. *Unraveling juvenile delinquency.* New York: Commonwealth Fund, 1950.

GLUECK, S., & GLUECK, E. T. *Predicting delinquency and crime.* Cambridge, Mass.: Harvard University Press, 1959.

GLUECK, S., & GLUECK, E. T. *Family environment and delinquency.* Boston: Houghton Mifflin, 1962.

GODDARD, H. H. *The criminal imbecile.* New York: Macmillan, 1910.

GOHEEN, H. W., & MOSEL, J. N. Validity of the employment recommendation questionnaire: II. Comparison with field investigations. *Personnel Psychology,* 1959, *12,* 297–301.

GOLD, M. A. Causes in patients' delay in diseases of the breast. *Cancer,* 1964, *17*(5), 564–577.

GOLDBERG, F. J. Opportunities for psychologists in drug and alcohol programs. In P. J. Woods (Ed.), *Career opportunities for psychologists: Expanding and emerging areas.* Washington, D. C.: American Psychological Association, 1976. Ch. 11.

GOLDEN, M. Some effects of combining psychological tests on clinical inferences. *Journal of Consulting Psychology,* 1964, *28,* 440–446.

GOLDFRIED, M. R., & DAVISON, G. C. *Clinical behavior therapy.* New York: Holt, Rinehart & Winston, 1976.

GOLDFRIED, M. R., & MERBAUM, M. (Eds.). *Behavior change through self-control.* New York: Holt, Rinehart & Winston, 1973.

GOLDFRIED, M. R., STRICKER, G., & WEINER, I. B. *Rorschach handbook of clinical and research applications.* Englewood Cliffs, N. J.: Prentice-Hall, 1971.

GOLDIAMOND, I. Singling out self-administered behavior therapies for professional overview: A comment on Rosen. *American Psychologist,* 1976, *31,* 142–147.

GOLDING, S. L., & RORER, L. G. Illusory correlation and subjective judgment. *Journal of Abnormal Psychology,* 1972, *80,* 249–260.

GOLDMAN, L. *Using tests in counseling* (2nd ed.). New York: Appleton-Century-Crofts, 1971.

GOLDMAN, R. B. *A work experiment: Six Americans in a Swedish plant.* New York: Ford Foundation, 1976.

GOLDSMITH, D. B. The use of the personal history blank as a salesmanship test. *Journal of Applied Psychology,* 1922, *6,* 149–155.

GOLDSTEIN, I. L. *Training: Program development and evaluation.* Monterey, Calif.: Brooks/ Cole, 1974.

GOLDSTEIN, M. Brain research and violent behavior. *Archives of Neurology,* 1974, *30,* 1–35.

GOODALE, J. G., & AAGAARD, A. K. Factors relating to varying reactions to the 4-day workweek. *Journal of Applied Psychology,* 1975, *60,* 33–38.

GOODALE, J. G., & BURKE, R. J. Behaviorally based rating scales need not be job specific. *Journal of Applied Psychology,* 1975, *60,* 389–391.

GOODENOUGH, D. R. A review of individual differences in field dependence as a factor in auto safety. *Human Factors,* 1976, *18,* 53–62.

GOODMAN, G. *Companionship therapy: Studies of structured intimacy.* San Francisco: Jossey-Bass, 1972.

GOODMAN, P. S., & FRIEDMAN, A. An examination of Adams' theory of inequity. *Administrative Science Quarterly,* 1971, *16,* 271–288.

GOOLER, D. D. The development and use of educational indicators. *Proceedings of the 1975 ETS Invitational Conference,* 1976, 11–27.

GORDON, M. A. *A study of the applicability of the same minimum qualifying scores for technical schools to white males, WAF, and Negro males* (Tech. Rep. 53–54). Lackland Air Force Base, Texas: Air Force Human Resources Research Center, 1953.

GORHAM, W. A. (Chair). *Alternative choices in job-related police examining: What is correct?* Symposium presented at the meeting of the American Psychological Association, San Francisco, August 1977.

GORING, C. *The English convict: A statistical study.* London: H. M. Stationery Office, 1913.

GORMALLY, J., & BRODSKY, S. L. Utilization and training of psychologists in the criminal system. *American Psychologist,* 1973, *28,* 926–928.

GORSUCH, R. L., & BUTLER, M. C. Initial drug abuse: A review of predisposing social psychological factors. *Psychological Bulletin,* 1976, *83,* 120–137.

GOTTMAN, J. M. N-of-one and N-of-two research in psychotherapy. *Psychological Bulletin,* 1973, *80,* 93–105.

GOTTSCHALK, L. A., & DAVIDSON, R. S. Sensitivity groups, encounter groups, training groups, marathon groups, and the laboratory movement. In H. I. Kaplan & B. J. Sadock (Eds.), *Comprehensive group psychotherapy.* Baltimore: Williams & Wilkins, 1971. Pp. 422–459.

GOUGH, H. G. Factorial study of medical specialty preferences. *British Journal of Medical Education.* 1975, *9*(2), 78–85. (a)

GOUGH, H. G. Specialty preferences of physicians and medical students. *Journal of Medical Education,* 1975, *50,* 581–588. (b)

GOUGH, H. G., & DUCKER, D. G. Social class in relation to medical student performance and choice of specialty. *Journal of Psychology,* 1977, *96,* 31–43.

GOUGH, H. G., & HALL, W. B. A prospective study of personality changes in students in medicine, dentistry, and nursing. *Research in Higher Education,* 1973, *1,* 127–140.

GOUGH, H. G., & HALL, W. B. An attempt to predict graduation from medical school. *Journal of Medical Education,* 1975, *50,* 940–950. (a)

GOUGH, H. G., & HALL, W. B. The prediction of academic and clinical performance in medical school. *Research in Higher Education,* 1975, *3,* 301–314. (b)

GOUGH, H. G., MISITI, R., & PARISI, D. Contrasting managerial perspectives of American and Italian public administrators. *Journal of Vocational Behavior,* 1971, *1,* 255–262.

GRAHAM, F. K., ERNHART, C. B., THURSTON, D., & CRAFT, M. Development three years after perinatal anoxia and other potentially damaging newborn experiences. *Psychological Monographs,* 1962, *76*(3, Whole No. 522).

GRAHAM, N. E. The speed and accuracy of reading horizontal, vertical, and circular scales. *Journal of Applied Psychology,* 1956, *40,* 228–232.

GRANDJEAN, E. Fatigue: Its physiological and psychological significance. *Ergonomics,* 1968, *11,* 427–436.

GRANDJEAN, E., et al. Papers presented at International Symposium on Sitting Posture. *Ergonomics,* 1969, *12,* 113–367.

GRANDJEAN, E. W., HUNTING, W., WOTZKA, G., & SHÄRER, R. An ergonomic investigation of multipurpose chairs. *Human Factors,* 1973, *15,* 247–255.

GRANT, C. A. (Ed.). *Sifting and winnowing: An exploration of the relationship between multi-cultural education and CBTE.* Madison, Wis.: Teacher Corps Associates, 1975.

GRANT, D. L., & BRAY, D. W. Validation of employment tests for telephone company installation and repair occupations. *Journal of Applied Psychology,* 1970, *54,* 7–14.

GRANT, D. L., KATKOVSKY, W., & BRAY, D. W. Contributions of projective techniques to assessment of management potential. *Journal of Applied Psychology,* 1967, *51,* 226–232.

GRAY, S. W. *The psychologist in the schools.* New York: Holt, Rinehart & Winston, 1963.

GRAY, S. W., & KLAUS, R. A. An experimental preschool program for culturally deprived children. *Child Development,* 1965, *36,* 887–898.

GREEN, D. R. (Ed.). *The aptitude-achievement distinction: Proceedings of the Second CTB/McGraw-Hill Conference on Issues in Educational Measurement.* New York: McGraw-Hill, 1974.

GREEN, E. J. *Psychology for law enforcement.* New York: Wiley, 1976.

GREENBLATT, M. (Ed.). *Drugs in combination with other therapies.* New York: Grune & Stratton, 1975.

GREENE, C. N. Causal connections among managers' merit pay, job satisfaction, and performance. *Journal of Applied Psychology,* 1973, *58,* 95–100.

GREENE, C. N. The satisfaction-performance controversy. In R. M. Steers & L. W. Porter (Eds.), *Motivation and work behavior.* New York: McGraw-Hill, 1975, Pp. 242–253.

GRIBBONS, W. D., & LOHNES, P. R. *Emerging careers.* New York: Teachers College Press, 1968.

GRIBBONS, W. D., & LOHNES, P. R. *Career development from age 13 to age 25* (Final Report, Project No. 6-2151). Washington, D. C.: U. S. Office of Education, 1969.

GRIFFITT, W. Environmental effects on interpersonal affective behavior: Ambient effective temperature and attraction. *Journal of Personality and Social Psychology,* 1970, *15,* 240–244.

GRINKER, R. R. *Psychosomatic research* (Rev. ed.). New York: Grove Press, 1951.

GRONLUND, N. E. *Determining accountability for classroom instruction.* New York: Macmillan, 1974.

GRONLUND, N. E. *Measurement and evaluation in teaching* (3rd ed.). New York: Macmillan, 1976.

GROSS, A. L., & SU, W. H. Defining a "fair" or "unbiased" selection model: A question of utilities. *Journal of Applied Psychology*, 1975, *60*, 345–351.

GROSS, B. M. What are your organization's objectives? A general-systems approach to planning. *Human Relations*, 1965, *18*, 195–215.

GROSSMAN, H. (Ed.). *Manual on terminology and classification in mental retardation* (1973 revision). Washington, D. C.: American Association on Mental Deficiency, 1973.

GROVES, P. M., & REBEC, G. V. Biochemistry and behavior: Some central actions of amphetamine and antipsychotic drugs. *Annual Review of Psychology*, 1976, *27*, 91–128.

GRUBE, C. S. How the public learned to pronounce "Suchard." *Advertising and Selling*, October 1947, p. 68.

GRUVER, G. G. College students as therapeutic agents. *Psychological Bulletin*, 1971, *76*, 111–127.

GUERIN, P. J., JR. (Ed.). *Family therapy: Theory and practice.* New York: Gardner Press, 1976.

GUERNEY, B. G., JR. (Ed.). *Psychotherapeutic agents: New roles for nonprofessionals, parents, and teachers.* Holt, Rinehart & Winston, 1969.

GUETZKOW, H. Inter-nation simulation: An example of a self-organizing system. In M. C. Yovits, G. T. Jacobi, & G. D. Goldstein (Eds.), *Self-organizing systems.* Washington, D. C.: Spartan Books, 1962. Pp. 79–92.

GUETZKOW, H., KOTLER, P., & SCHULTZ, R. L. (Eds.). *Simulation in social and administrative science: Overviews and case examples.* Englewood Cliffs, N. J.: Prentice-Hall, 1972.

GUILFORD, J. P. *Personality.* New York: McGraw-Hill, 1959.

GUILFORD, J. P., & FRUCHTER, B. *Fundamental statistics in psychology and education* (6th ed.). New York: McGraw-Hill, 1978.

GUION, R. M. *Personnel testing.* New York: McGraw-Hill, 1965. (a)

GUION, R. M. Synthetic validity in a small company: A demonstration. *Personnel Psychology*, 1965, *18*, 49–63. (b)

GUION, R. M., & GOTTIER, R. F. Validity of personality measures in personnel selection. *Personnel Psychology*, 1965, *18*, 135–164.

GUNDERSON, E. K. E., & RAHE, R. H. (Eds.). *Life stress and illness.* Springfield, Ill.: Charles C Thomas, 1974.

HAASE, W. The role of socioeconomic class in examiner bias. In F. Riessman, J. Cohen, & A. Pearl (Eds.), *Mental health of the poor.* New York: Free Press, 1964. Pp. 241–247.

HACKMAN, J. R., LAWLER, E. E., III, & PORTER, L. W. (Eds.). *Perspectives on behavior in organizations.* New York: McGraw-Hill, 1977.

HACKMAN, J. R., & OLDHAM, G. R. Development of the Job Diagnostic Survey. *Journal of Applied Psychology*, 1975, *60*, 159–170.

HAHN, M. E. Counseling psychology, *American Psychologist*, 1955, *10*, 279–282.

HAIGH, G. Defensive behavior in client-centered therapy. *Journal of Consulting Psychology*, 1949, *13*, 181–189.

HAIRE, M. Projective techniques in market research. *Journal of Marketing*, 1950, *14*, 649–656.

HAIRE, M., GHISELLI, E. E., & PORTER, L. W. *Managerial thinking: An international study.* New York: Wiley, 1966.

HAKEL, M. D., DOBMEYER, T. W., & DUNNETTE, M. D. Relative importance of three content dimensions in overall suitability ratings of job applicants' resumés. *Journal of Applied Psychology*, 1970, *54*, 65–71.

HAKEL, M. D., HOLLMANN, T., & DUNNETTE, M. D. Stability and change in the social status of occupations over 21 and 42 year periods. *Personnel and Guidance Journal*, 1968, *46*, 762–764.

HALPERIN, K., SNYDER, C. R., SHENKEL, R. J., & HOUSTON, B. K. Effects of source status and message favorability on acceptance of personality feedback. *Journal of Applied Psychology*, 1976, *61*, 85–88.

HAMBLETON, R. K. Testing and decision-making procedures for selected individualized instructional programs. *Review of Educational Research*, 1974, *44*, 371–400.

HAMMOND, K. R., et al. *Teaching comprehensive medical care: A psychological study of a change in medical education.* Cambridge, Mass.: Harvard University Press, 1959.

HAMMOND, K. R., & ALLEN, J. M. *Writing clinical reports.* Englewood Cliffs, N. J.: Prentice-Hall, 1953.

HAMNER, W. C. Reinforcement theory and contingency management in organizational settings. In H. L. Tosi & W. C. Hamner (Eds.), *Organizational behavior and management: A contingency approach.* Chicago: St. Clair Press, 1974. Pp. 86–112.

HAMPDEN-TURNER, C. *Sane asylum: Inside the Delancey Street Foundation.* San Francisco: San Francisco Book Co., 1976.

HANEY, W. V. *Communication patterns and incidents.* Homewood, Ill.: Irwin, 1960.

HANLEY, E. M. Review of the research involving applied behavior in the classroom. *Review of Educational Research,* 1970, *40,* 597–625.

HANNUM, R. D., ROSELLINI, R. A., & SELIGMAN, M. E. P. Learned helplessness in the rat: Retention and immunization. *Developmental Psychology,* 1976, *12,* 449–454.

HARARI, O., & ZEDECK, S. Development of behaviorally anchored scales for the evaluation of faculty teaching. *Journal of Applied Psychology,* 1973, *58,* 261–265.

HARGAN, C., HIBBITS, N., & SEIDEL, R. J. *D. C. secondary schools project for adopting computer-aided education.* (HumRRO FR-ED 78–11). Alexandria, Va.: Human Resources Research Organization, August 1978.

HARLOW, H. F., & HARLOW, M. K. Psychopathology in monkeys. In H. D. Kimmel (Ed.), *Experimental psychopathology: Recent research and theory.* New York: Academic Press, 1971. Pp. 203–229.

HARMAN, H. H. *Modern factor analysis* (3rd ed.). Chicago: University of Chicago Press, 1976.

HARRIS, D. H. Predicting consumer reaction to product designs. *Journal of Advertising Research,* 1964, *4*(2), 34–37.

HARRIS, D. H., & CHANEY, F. B. *Human factors in quality assurance.* New York: Wiley, 1969.

HARRIS, E. F., & FLEISHMAN, E. A. Human relations training and the stability of leadership patterns. *Journal of Applied Psychology,* 1955, *39,* 20–25.

HARRIS, J. A. The computer: Guidance tool of the future. In W. E. Coffman (Ed.), *Frontiers of educational measurement and information systems—1973.* Boston: Houghton Mifflin, 1973. Ch. 7.

HARRIS, R. J. *A primer of multivariate statistics.* New York: Academic Press, 1975.

HARRISON, R. Thematic apperception methods. In B. B. Wolman (Ed.), *Handbook of clinical psychology.* New York: McGraw-Hill, 1965. Pp. 562–620.

HARTLEY, D., ROBACK, H. B., & ABRAMOWITZ, S. I. Deterioration effects in encounter groups. *American Psychologist,* 1976, *31,* 247–255.

HASHIMOTO, K., KOGI, K., & GRANDJEAN, E. (Eds.). *Methodology in human fatigue assessment.* London: Taylor & Francis, 1971. (Also in *Ergonomics,* 1971, *14*(1), 1–186.)

HASKINS, J. B. Validation of the abstraction index as a tool for content-effects analysis and content analysis. *Journal of Applied Psychology,* 1960, *44,* 102–106.

HASS, J. W., BAGLEY, G. S., & ROGERS, R. W. Coping with the energy crisis: Effects of fear appeals upon attitudes toward energy consumption. *Journal of Applied Psychology,* 1975, *60,* 754–756.

HATHAWAY, S. R. Some considerations relative to nondirective counseling as therapy. *Journal of Clinical Psychology,* 1948, *4,* 226–231.

HATHAWAY, S. R., & MONACHESI, E. D. (Eds.). *Analyzing and predicting juvenile delinquency with the MMPI.* Minneapolis: University of Minnesota Press, 1953.

HATHAWAY, S. R., & MONACHESI, E. D. The personality of predelinquent boys. *Journal of Criminal Law and Criminology,* 1957, *48,* 149–163.

HAUCK, M., & STEINKAMP, S. *Survey reliability and interviewer competence.* Urbana: University of Illinois Press, 1964.

HAVIGHURST, R. J. *Human development and education.* New York: Longmans, Green, 1953.

HAVIGHURST, R. J. Social roles, work, leisure, and education. In C. Eisdorfer & M. P. Lawton (Eds.), *The psychology of adult development and aging.* Washington, D. C.: American Psychological Association, 1973, Pp. 598–618.

HAYDUK, L. A. Personal space: An evaluative review. *Psychological Bulletin,* 1978, *85,* 117–134.

HAYES, L. A. The use of group contingencies for behavioral control: A review. *Psychological Bulletin*, 1976, *83*, 628–648.

HAYES, S. C., & CONE, J. D. Reducing residential electrical energy use: Payments, information, and feedback. *Journal of Applied Behavior Analysis*, 1977, *10*, 425–435.

HEALY, W., & BRONNER, A. F. *New light on delinquency and its treatment*. New Haven, Conn.: Yale University Press, 1936.

HECKER, D., GREEN, D., & SMITH, K. U. Dimensional analysis of motion: X. Experimental evaluation of a time-study problem. *Journal of Applied Psychology*, 1956, *40*, 220–227.

HEIMSTRA, N. W., & McFARLING, L. H. *Environmental psychology*, Monterey, Calif.: Brooks/Cole, 1974.

HEINZELMANN, F. (Chair). *Citizen response to a crime: Behavior of victims and witnesses.* Symposium presented at the meeting of the American Psychological Association, Washington, D. C., September 1976.

HEITLER, J. B. Preparatory techniques in initiating psychotherapy with lower-class, unsophisticated patients. *Psychological Bulletin*, 1976, *83*, 339–352.

HELLER, F. A., & CLARK, A. W. Personnel and human resources development. *Annual Review of Psychology*, 1976, *27*, 405–435.

HELMREICH, R., BAKEMAN, R., & RADLOFF, R. The LIfe History Questionnaire as a predictor of performance in Navy divers training. *Journal of Applied Psychology*, 1973, *57*, 148–153.

HEMPHILL, J. K. Job descriptions for executives. *Harvard Business Review*, 1959, *37*, 55–67.

HEMPHILL, J. K., GRIFFITHS, D., & FREDERIKSEN, N. *Administrative performance and personality.* New York: Teachers College Press, 1962.

HENRY, H. *Motivation research.* New York: Ungar, 1958.

HENRY, W. E., & FARLEY, J. The validity of the Thematic Apperception Test in the study of adolescent personality. *Psychological Monographs*, 1959, *73*(17, Whole No. 487).

HEROLD, D. M. Interaction of subordinate and leader characteristics in moderating the consideration-satisfaction relationship. *Journal of Applied Psychology*, 1974, *59*, 649–651.

HERSEN, M., & BARLOW, D. H. *Single case experimental designs: Strategies for studying behavior change.* Elmsford, N. Y.: Pergamon, 1976.

HERTZBERG, H. T. E. Engineering anthropology. In H. P. Van Cott & R. G. Kinkade (Eds.), *Human engineering guide to equipment design* (Rev. ed.). Washington, D. C.: U. S. Government Printing Office, 1972. Ch. 11.

HERZBERG, F. *Work and the nature of man.* Cleveland: World, 1966.

HERZBERG, F. One more time: How do you motivate employees? *Harvard Business Review*, 1968, *46*(1), 53–62.

HERZBERG, F., MAUSNER, B., & SNYDERMAN, B. B. *The motivation to work* (2nd ed.). New York: Wiley, 1959.

HESS, R. D., & BEAR, R. M. (Eds.). *Early education: Current theory, research, and action.* Chicago: Aldine, 1968.

HESS, R. D., & TAPP, J. L. *Authority, rules, and aggression: A cross-national study of the socialization of children into compliance systems—Part I.* Washington, D. C.: U. S. Department of Health, Education, and Welfare, 1969.

HIGBEE, K. L. Fifteen years of fear arousal: Research on threat appeals, 1953–1968. *Psychological Bulletin*, 1969, *72*, 426–444.

HIGGINS, J., & PETERSON, J. C. Concept of process-reactive schizophrenia: A critique. *Psychological Bulletin*, 1966, *66*, 201–206.

HILDUM, D. C., & BROWN, R. W. Verbal reinforcement and interviewer bias. *Journal of Abnormal and Social Psychology*, 1956, *53*, 108–111.

HILGARD, E. R. Hypnosis. *Annual Review of Psychology*, 1975, *26*, 19–44.

HILGARD, E. R., & HILGARD, J. R. *Hypnosis in the relief of pain.* Los Altos, Calif.: Kaufmann, 1975.

HILL, C. R. Haire's classic instant coffee study—18 years later. *Journalism Quarterly*, 1968, *45*(8), 466–472.

HILL, P. *Towards a new philosophy of management.* New York: Barnes and Noble, 1971.

HINDELANG, M. J. *Criminal victimization in eight American cities: A descriptive analysis of common theft and assault.* Cambridge, Mass.: Ballinger, 1976.

HINKLE, L. E., JR., WHITNEY, L. H., & LEHMAN, E. W. Occupation, education, and coronary heart disease. *Science,* 1968, *161,* 238–246.

HINRICHS, J. R. Comparison of "real life" assessments of management potential with situational exercises, paper-and-pencil ability tests, and personality inventories. *Journal of Applied Psychology,* 1969, *53,* 425–432.

HINRICHS, J. R. Measurement of reasons for resignation of professionals: Questionnaire versus company and consultant exit interviews. *Journal of Applied Psychology,* 1975, *60,* 530–532.

HIRSH, I. J. *The measurement of hearing.* New York: McGraw-Hill, 1961.

HITCHCOCK, E., LAITINEN, L., & VAERNET, K. (Eds.). *Psychosurgery.* Springfield, Ill.: Charles C Thomas, 1972.

HOBBS, N. Reeducation, reality, and community responsibility. In J. W. Carter (Ed.), *Research contributions from psychology to community mental health.* New York: Behavioral Publications, 1969. Pp. 7–18.

HOBBS, N. (Ed.). *Issues in the classification of children* (2 vols.). San Francisco: Jossey-Bass, 1975.

HOCH, E. L., & DARLEY, J. G. A case at law. *American Psychologist,* 1962, *17,* 623–654.

HOCH, E. L., ROSS, A. O., & WINDER, C. L. *Professional preparation of clinical psychologists* (Chicago Conference). Washington, D. C.: American Psychological Association, 1966.

HOGAN, R. Theoretical egocentrism and the problem of compliance. *American Psychologist,* 1975, *30,* 533–540.

HOGAN, R. Legal socialization. In G. Bermant, C. Nemeth, & N. Vidmar (Eds.), *Psychology and the law: Research frontiers.* Lexington, Mass.: Lexington Books, 1976. Ch. 3.

HOLLAND, J. L. *The Self-Directed Search: A counselor's guide.* Palo Alto, Calif.: Consulting Psychologists Press, 1971.

HOLLAND, J. L. *Making vocational choices: A theory of careers.* Englewood Cliffs, N. J.: Prentice-Hall, 1973.

HOLLAND, J. L., WHITNEY, D. R., COLE, N. S., & RICHARDS, J. M., JR. An empirical occupational classification derived from a theory of personality and intended for practice and research. *American College Testing Program, Research Report* No. 29, 1969.

HOLLANDER, J., & ERDMAN, W. The controlled-climate chamber. In S. Licht (Ed.), *Medical climatology.* Baltimore: Waverly Press, 1964.

HOLLANDER, J., & YEOSTROS, S. The effect of simultaneous variations of humidity and barometric pressure on arthritis. *Bulletin of the American Meteorological Society,* 1963, *44,* 489–494.

HOLLENDER, M. H. *The psychology of medical practice.* Philadelphia: Saunders, 1958.

HOLLINGSHEAD, A. B., & REDLICH, F. C. *Social class and mental illness: A community study.* New York: Wiley, 1958.

HOLLINGWORTH, H. L. *Advertising and selling.* New York: Appleton, 1913.

HOLMES, T. H., & RAHE, R. H. The social readjustment rating scale. *Journal of Psychosomatic Research,* 1967, *11,* 213–218.

HOLT, F. D., & KICKLIGHTER, R. H. (Eds.). *Psychological services in the schools: Readings in preparation, organization, and practice.* Dubuque, Iowa: Brown, 1971.

HOLTZMAN, W. H. Holtzman Inkblot Technique. In A. I. Rabin (Ed.), *Projective techniques in personality assessment.* New York: Springer, 1968. Pp. 136–170.

HOLTZMAN, W. H. (Ed.). *Computer-assisted instruction, testing, and guidance.* New York: Harper & Row, 1970.

HOLTZMAN, W. H. New developments in Holtzman Inkblot Technique. In P. McReynolds (Ed.), *Advances in psychological assessment* (Vol. 3). San Francisco: Jossey-Bass, 1975. Ch. 6.

HOM, H. L., JR., & ROBINSON, P. A. (Eds.). *Psychological processes in early education.* New York: Academic Press, 1977.

HOPKINSON, R., & COLLINS, J. *The ergonomics of lighting.* London: McDonald, 1970.

HOPPOCK, R. *Occupational information: Where to get it and how to use it in career education, career counseling, and career development* (4th ed.). New York: McGraw-Hill, 1976.

HORVATH, F. The effect of selected variables on interpretation of polygraph records. *Journal of Applied Psychology,* 1977, *62,* 127–136.

HOUSE, R. J., & WIGDOR, L. A. Herzberg's dual-factor theory of job satisfaction and motivation: A review of the evidence and a criticism. *Personnel Psychology,* 1967, *20,* 369–389.

HOUSTON, W. R. (Ed.). *Competency assessment, research, and evaluation.* Syracuse, N. Y.: National Dissemination Center for Performance Based Education, Syracuse University, 1974.

HOVLAND, C. I. (Ed.). *The order of presentation in persuasion.* New Haven, Conn.: Yale University Press, 1957.

HOWARD, J., & STRAUSS, A. (Eds.). *Humanizing health care.* New York: Wiley, 1975.

HOWE, E. S. Quantitative motivational differences between volunteers and nonvolunteers for a psychological experiment. *Journal of Applied Psychology,* 1960, *44,* 115–120.

HOYT, K. B., & MOORE, G. D. Group procedures in guidance and personnel work. *Review of Educational Research,* 1960, *30,* 158–167.

HUBBARD, J. P. Programmed testing in medicine. *Proceedings of the 1963 Invitational Conference on Testing Problems, Educational Testing Service,* 1964, 49–63.

HUBER, J. T. *Report writing in psychology and psychiatry.* New York: Harper, 1961.

HUCK, S. W., & GLEASON, E. M. Using monetary inducements to increase response rates from mailed surveys: A replication and extension of previous research. *Journal of Applied Psychology,* 1974, *59,* 222–225.

HUFF, E. M., & NAGEL, D. C. Psychological aspects of aeronautical flight simulation. *American Psychologist,* 1975, *30,* 426–439.

HULIN, C. L., & BLOOD, M. R. Job enlargement, individual differences, and worker responses. *Psychological Bulletin,* 1968, *69,* 41–55.

HULL, C. L. *Aptitude testing.* Yonkers, N. Y.: World Book Co., 1928.

HULL, C. L. *Principles of behavior.* New York: Appleton-Century-Crofts, 1943.

Human factors engineering, USAF, AFSC Design Handbook, Series 1-0, General, AFSC DH 1-3 (3rd ed.), January 1, 1977.

HUMAN RESOURCES RESEARCH ORGANIZATION. *Functional literacy.* Alexandria, Va.: Author, 1978.

HUNT, J. McV. *The challenge of incompetence and poverty.* Champaign: University of Illinois Press, 1969.

HUNT, J. McV. Reflections on a decade of early education. *Journal of Abnormal Child Psychology,* 1975, *3,* 275–330.

HUNT, J. McV., & KIRK, G. E. Criterion-referenced tests of school readiness: A paradigm with illustrations. *Genetic Psychology Monographs,* 1974, *90,* 143–182.

HUNT, W. A. (Ed.). New approaches to behavioral research on smoking. *Journal of Abnormal Psychology,* 1973, *81*(2), 107–198. (Special issue)

HUNTER, B., KASTNER, C. S., RUBIN, M. J., & SEIDEL, R. J. *Learning alternatives in U. S. education: Where student and computer meet.* Englewood Cliffs, N. J.: Educational Technology Publications, 1975.

HUNTER, J. E., & SCHMIDT, F. L. Critical analysis of the statistical and ethical implications of various definitions of *test bias. Psychological Bulletin,* 1976, *83,* 1053–1071.

HUNTER, J. E., & SCHMIDT, F. L. Differential and single-group validity of employment tests by race: A critical analysis of three recent studies. *Journal of Applied Psychology,* 1978, *63,* 1–11. (See also replies on pp. 12–21.)

HUNTER, J. E., SCHMIDT, F. L., & RAUSCHENBERGER, J. M. Fairness of psychological tests: Implications of four definitions for selection utility and minority hiring. *Journal of Applied Psychology,* 1977, *62,* 245–260.

HUNTINGTON, E. *Civilization and climate* (3rd ed.). New Haven, Conn.: Yale University Press, 1924.

IES lighting handbook (5th ed.). New York: Illuminating Engineering Society, 1972.

INCE, L. P. *Behavior modification in rehabilitation medicine.* Springfield, Ill.: Charles C Thomas, 1976.

ISCOE, I. National Training Conference in Community Psychology. *American Psychologist,* 1975, *30,* 1193–1194.

ISCOE, I., BLOOM, B. L., & SPIELBERGER, C. D. (Eds.). *Community psychology in transition.* Washington, D. C.: Hemisphere, 1977.

ITTELSON, W. H., PROSHANSKY, H. M., RIVLIN, L. G., & WINKEL, G. H. *An introduction to environmental psychology.* New York: Holt, Rinehart & Winston, 1974.

IVANCEVICH, J. M. Effects of the shorter workweek on selected satisfaction and performance measures. *Journal of Applied Psychology,* 1974, *59,* 717–721.

IVANCEVICH, J. M., & LYON, H. L. The shortened workweek: A field experiment. *Journal of Applied Psychology,* 1977, *62,* 34–37.

IVERSON, L. L., IVERSON, S. D., & SNYDER, S. H. (Eds.). *Handbook of psychopharmacology: Human psychopharmacology* (Vols. 10–14). New York: Plenum, 1978.

IVERSON, S. D., & IVERSON, L. L. *Behavioral pharmacology.* New York: Oxford University Press, 1975.

JABLONSKY, S. F., & DEVRIES, D. L. Operant conditioning principles extrapolated to the theory of management. *Organizational Behavior and Human Performance,* 1972, *7,* 340–358.

JACKSON, D. D. (Ed.). *The etiology of schizophrenia.* New York: Basic Books, 1960.

JACKSON, J. D. Prisons and penitentiaries. In D. H. Fryer & E. R. Henry (Eds.), *Handbook of applied psychology.* New York: Rinehart, 1950.

JACOBS, R., & SOLOMON, T. Strategies for enhancing the prediction of job performance from job satisfaction. *Journal of Applied Psychology,* 1977, *62,* 417–421.

JACOBSON, E. *Progressive relaxation.* Chicago: University of Chicago Press, 1938.

JACOBSON, F. N., RETTIG, S., & PASAMANICK, B. Status, job satisfaction, and factors of job satisfaction of state institution and clinic psychologists. *American Psychologist,* 1959, *14,* 144–150.

JACOBSON, N. S., & MARTIN, B. Behavioral marriage therapy: Current status. *Psychological Bulletin,* 1976, *83,* 540–556.

JACOBY, J. Personality and innovation proneness. *Journal of Marketing Research,* 1971, *8,* 244–247.

JACOBY, J. Consumer psychology as a social psychological sphere of action. *American Psychologist,* 1975, *30,* 977–987.

JACOBY, J. Consumer and industrial psychology: Prospects for theory corroboration and mutual contribution. In M. D. Dunnette (Ed.), *Handbook of industrial and organizational psychology.* Chicago: Rand McNally, 1976. Ch. 24. (a)

JACOBY, J. Consumer psychology: An octennium. *Annual Review of Psychology,* 1976, *27,* 331–358. (b)

JACOBY, J. *The handbook of questionnaire construction.* Boston: Lippincott, 1978.

JACOBY, J., OLSON, J. C., & HADDOCK, F. A. Price, brand name, and product composition characteristics of perceived quality. *Journal of Applied Psychology,* 1971, *55,* 570–579.

JAMES, L. R., ELLISON, R. L., FOX, D. G., & TAYLOR, C. W. Prediction of artistic performance from biographical data. *Journal of Applied Psychology,* 1974, *59,* 84–86.

JAMES, L. R., & JONES, A. P. Organizational climate: A review of theory and research. *Psychological Bulletin,* 1974, *81,* 1096–1112.

JEALOUS, F. S., BIALEK, H. M., PITPIT, F., & GORDON, P. *Developing the potential of low ability personnel.* (HumRRO Rep. FR-WD-Calif-75-6). Alexandria, Va.: Human Resources Research Organization, June 1975.

JEFFERY, R. The psychologist as expert witness on the issue of insanity. *American Psychologist,* 1964, *19,* 838–843.

JENKINS, C. D., ROSENMAN, R. H., & ZYZANSKY, S. J. Prediction of clinical coronary heart disease by a test for the coronary-prone behavior pattern. *New England Journal of Medicine,* 1974, *290,* 1271–1275.

JENKINS, G. D., JR., NADLER, D. A., LAWLER, E. E., III, & CAMMAN, C. Standardized observations: An approach to measuring the nature of jobs. *Journal of Applied Psychology,* 1975, *60,* 171–181.

JENKINS, W. O. The tactual discrimination of shapes for coding aircraft-type controls. In P. M. Fitts (Ed.), *Psychological research in equipment design* (AAF Aviation Psychology Program, Research Reports, No. 19). Washington, D. C.: U. S. Government Printing Office, 1947. Pp. 199–205.

JOHNSON, D. J., & MYKLEBUST, H. R. *Learning disabilities: Educational principles and practices.* New York: Grune & Stratton, 1967.

JOHNSON, D. W., & JOHNSON, R. T. *Learning together and alone: Cooperation, competition, and individualization.* Englewood Cliffs, N. J.: Prentice-Hall, 1975.

JOHNSON, J. E., & LEVENTHAL, H. Effects of accurate expectations and behavioral instructions on reactions during a noxious medical examination. *Journal of Personality and Social Psychology,* 1974, *29,* 710–718.

JOHNSON, J. H., & WILLIAMS, T. A. The use of on-line computer technology in a mental health admitting system. *American Psychologist,* 1975, *30,* 388–390.

JOHNSON, K. R., & RUSKIN, R. S. *Behavioral instruction: An evaluative review.* Washington, D. C.: American Psychological Association, 1977.

JOHNSON, R. D., & WALLIN, J. A. *Employee attendance: An operant conditioning intervention in a field setting.* Paper presented at the meeting of the American Psychological Association, Washington, D. C., September 1976.

JOHNSON, R. N. *Aggression in man and animals.* Philadelphia: Saunders, 1972.

JOHNSON, T. W., & STINSON, J. E. Role ambiguity, role conflict, and satisfaction: Moderating effects of individual differences. *Journal of Applied Psychology,* 1975, *60,* 329–333.

JONES, H. H., & COHEN, A. Noise as a health hazard at work, in the community, and in the home. *USPHS, Public Health Reports,* 1968, *83*(7), 533–536.

JONES, M. C. Albert, Peter, and John B. Watson. *American Psychologist,* 1974, *29,* 581–583.

JONES, M. H. Pain thresholds for smog components. In J. H. Wohlwill & D. H. Carson (Eds.), *Environment and the social sciences: Perspectives and applications.* Washington, D. C.: American Psychological Association, 1972. Pp. 61–65.

JONES, R. E., MILTON, J. L., & FITTS, P. M. *Eye fixations of aircraft pilots: IV. Frequency, duration, and sequence of fixations during routine instrument flight.* USAF AF TR 5975, 1949.

KAFAFIAN, H. *Study of man-machine communication systems* (Vol. III, Final Report). Washington, D. C.: Cybernetics Research Institute, 1973.

KAHN, R. L., & CANNELL, C. F. *The dynamics of interviewing: Theory, technique, and cases.* New York: Wiley, 1957.

KAHNEMAN, D., BEN-ISHAI, R., & LOTAN, M. Relation of a test of attention to road accidents. *Journal of Applied Psychology,* 1973, *58,* 113–115.

KALVEN, H., & ZEISEL, H. *The American jury.* Chicago: University of Chicago Press, 1966.

KAMIYA, J. Operant control of the EEG alpha rhythm and some of its reported effects on consciousness. In C. Tart (Ed.), *Altered states of consciousness.* New York: Wiley, 1969. Pp. 519–529.

KANFER, F. H. Assessment for behavior modification. *Journal of Personality Assessment,* 1972, *36,* 418–423.

KANFER, F. H., & SASLOW, G. Behavioral diagnosis. In C. M. Franks (Ed.), *Behavior therapy: Appraisal and status.* New York: McGraw-Hill, 1969. Ch. 12.

KANTOR, R. E., & HERRON, W. G. *Reactive and process schizophrenia.* Palo Alto, Calif.: Science & Behavior Books, 1966.

KANUNGO, R. N. Brand awareness: Effects of fittingness, meaningfulness, and product utility. *Journal of Applied Psychology,* 1968, *52,* 290–295.

KANUNGO, R. N. Brand awareness: Differential roles of fittingness and meaningfulness of brand names. *Journal of Applied Psychology,* 1969, *53,* 140–147.

KANUNGO, R. N., & PANG, S. Effects of human models on perceived product quality. *Journal of Applied Psychology,* 1973, *57,* 172–178.

KAPLAN, H. I. History of psychophysiological medicine. In A. M. Freedman, H. I. Kaplan, & B. J.

Sadock (Eds.), *Comprehensive textbook of psychiatry—II* (Vol. 2). Baltimore: Williams & Wilkins, 1975. Pp. 1624–1631.

KAPLAN, H. I., & SADOCK, B. J. (Eds.). *Comprehensive group psychotherapy.* Baltimore: Williams & Wilkins, 1971.

KAPLAN, L. B., SZYBILLO, G. J., & JACOBY, J. Components of perceived risk in product purchase: A cross-validation. *Journal of Applied Psychology,* 1974, *59,* 287–291.

KAPLAN, R. J. (Ed.). Human factors in highway transportation: Parts I-IV. *Human Factors,* 1976, *18,* 209–272; 313–407; 417–515; 521–600.

KARGER, D. W., & BAYHA, F. H. *Engineered work measurement* (2nd ed.). New York: Industrial Press, 1965.

KASL, S. V., & COBB, S. Blood pressure changes in men undergoing job loss: A preliminary report. *Psychosomatic Medicine,* 1970, *32,* 19–38.

KASSARJIAN, H. H. Personality and consumer behavior: A review. *Journal of Marketing Research,* 1971, *8,* 409–418.

KASTENBAUM, R., & AISENBERG, R. *The psychology of death (Concise ed.).* New York: Springer, 1976.

KASTENBAUM, R., & COSTA, P. T., JR. Psychological perspectives on death. *Annual Review of Psychology,* 1977, *28,* 225–249.

KASTL, A. J., & CHILD, I. L. Emotional meaning of four typographical variables. *Journal of Applied Psychology,* 1968, *52,* 440–446.

KATONA, G. What is consumer psychology? *American Psychologist,* 1967, *22,* 219–226.

KATONA, G. *Psychological economics.* New York: Elsevier, 1975.

KATZ, D. Current and needed psychological research in international relations. *Journal of Social Issues,* 1961, *17*(3), 69–78.

KATZ, D., GUTEK, B. A., KAHN, R. L., & BARTON, E. *Bureaucratic encounters: A pilot study in the evaluation of government services.* Ann Arbor, Mich.: Institute for Social Research, 1975.

KATZ, M. R. *You: Today and tomorrow* (3rd ed.). Menlo Park, Calif.: Addison-Wesley Testing Service, 1959.

KATZ, M. R. A model of guidance for career decision-making. *Vocational Guidance Quarterly,* 1966, *15,* 2–10.

KATZ, M. R. Can computers make guidance decisions for students? *College Board Review,* 1969, No. 72, 13–17.

KATZ, M. R. Career decision-making: A computer-based System of Interactive Guidance and Information (SIGI). *Proceedings of the 1973 Invitational Conference on Testing Problems, Educational Testing Service,* 1974, 43–69.

KATZ, R. C., & ZLUTNICK, S. (Eds.). *Behavior therapy and health care: Principles and applications.* New York: Pergamon, 1975.

KATZELL, R. A. Contrasting systems of work organization. *American Psychologist,* 1962, *17,* 102–108.

KATZELL, R. A., & DYER, F. J. Differential validity revived. *Journal of Applied Psychology,* 1977, *62,* 137–145.

KAUFMAN, I. C. Mother-infant separation in monkeys. In J. P. Scott & E. C. Senay (Eds.), *Separation and depression: Clinical and research aspects.* Washington, D. C.: American Association for the Advancement of Science, 1973. Pp. 33–52.

KAVRUCK, S. Thirty-three years of test research: A short history of test development in the U. S. Civil Service Commission. *American Psychologist,* 1956, *11,* 329–333.

KAZDIN, A. E. *Behavior modification in applied settings.* Homewood, Ill.: Dorsey, 1975.

KAZDIN, A. E. *The token economy: A review and evaluation.* New York: Plenum, 1977.

KAZDIN, A. E., & WILCOXON, L. A. Systematic desensitization and nonspecific treatment effects. A methodological evaluation. *Psychological Bulletin,* 1976, *83,* 729–758.

KEENAN, V., KERR, W., & SHERMAN, W. Psychological climate and accidents. *Journal of Applied Psychology,* 1951, *35,* 108–111.

KEGELES, S. S. (Chair). *Social and psychological phenomena related to the acceptance of community fluoridation.* Symposium presented at the meeting of the American Psychological Association, Chicago, September 1960. (See also *American Psychologist,* 1960, *15,* 439–440.)

KELLER, F. S. "Goodbye teacher . . ." *Journal of Applied Behavior Analysis,* 1968, *1,* 79–89.

KELLER, F. S. *Learning: Reinforcement theory* (2nd ed.). New York: Random House, 1969.

KELLY, J. G., SNOWDEN, L. R., & MUÑOZ, R. F. Social and community interventions. *Annual Review of Psychology,* 1977, *28,* 323–361.

KELMAN, H. C. (Ed.). *International behavior: A social-psychological analysis.* New York: Holt, Rinehart & Winston, 1965.

KENDELL, R. E. *The role of diagnosis in psychiatry.* Oxford, England: Blackwell Scientific, 1975.

KENKEL, W. F. Decision making and the life cycle: Husband-wife interaction in decision making and decision choices. *Journal of Social Psychology,* 1961, *54,* 255–262.

KERR, W. A. Experiments on the effects of music on factory production. *Applied Psychology Monographs,* 1945, No. 5.

KERR, W. A. Complementary theories of safety psychology. *Journal of Social Psychology,* 1957, *45,* 3–9.

KESSLER, M., & ALBEE, G. W. Primary prevention. *Annual Review of Psychology,* 1975, *26,* 557–591.

KETY, S. S. Biochemical theories of schizophrenia. Parts I and II. *Science,* 1959, *129,* 1528–1532; 1590–1596.

KETY, S. S. Recent biochemical theories of schizophrenia. In D. D. Jackson (Ed.), *The etiology of schizophrenia.* New York: Basic Books, 1960. Ch. 4.

KETY, S. S. Biochemistry of the major psychoses. In A. M. Freedman, H. I. Kaplan, & B. J. Sadock (Eds.), *Comprehensive textbook of psychiatry-II* (Vol. 1). Baltimore: Williams & Wilkins, 1975. Pp. 178–187.

KHALIL, T. M. An electromyographic methodology for the evaluation of industrial design. *Human Factors,* 1973, *15,* 257–264.

KIBBEE, J. M., CRAFT, C. J., & NANUS, B. (Eds.). *Management games: A new technique for executive development.* New York: Reinhold, 1961.

KIESLER, D. J. Experimental designs in psychotherapy research. In A. E. Bergin & S. L. Garfield (Eds.), *Handbook of psychotherapy and behavior change: An empirical analysis.* New York: Wiley, 1971. Pp. 36–74.

KILMANN, P. R., & SOTILE, W. M. The marathon encounter group: A review of the outcome literature. *Psychological Bulletin,* 1976, *83,* 827–850.

KIM, J. S., & HAMNER, W. C. Effect of performance feedback and goal setting on productivity and satisfaction in an organizational setting. *Journal of Applied Psychology,* 1976, *61,* 48–57.

KINDALL, A. F. *Personnel administration: Principles and cases* (3rd ed.). Homewood, Ill.: Irwin, 1969.

KINSLINGER, H. J. Application of projective techniques in personnel psychology since 1940. *Psychological Bulletin,* 1966, *66,* 134–149.

KIRCHNER, W. K., & REISBERG, D. J. Differences between better and less effective supervisors in appraisal of subordinates. *Personnel Psychology,* 1962, *15,* 295–302.

KIRMAN, J. H. Tactile communication of speech: A review and an analysis. *Psychological Bulletin,* 1973, *80,* 54–74.

KITSON, H. D. Psychology in vocational adjustment. *Personnel and Guidance Journal,* 1958, *36,* 314–319.

KLARE, G. *The measurement of readability.* Ames, Iowa: Iowa State Press, 1963.

KLAUSMEIER, H. J., & GOODWIN, W. *Learning and human abilities: Educational psychology* (4th ed.). New York: Harper & Row, 1975.

KLAUSMEIER, H. J., ROSSMILLER, R. A., & SAILY, M. (Eds.). *Individually guided elementary education: Concepts and practices.* New York: Academic Press, 1977.

KLEINMUNTZ, B. The computer as clinician. *American Psychologist,* 1975, *30,* 379–387.

KLEITMAN, N. *Sleep and wakefulness.* Chicago: University of Chicago Press, 1963.

KLIER, S., & LINSKEY, J. W. *Selected abstracts from the literature on stress.* U. S. Naval Training Devices Center, Technical Report No. 565-1, 1960.

KLINEBERG, O. *The human dimension in international relations.* New York: Holt, Rinehart & Winston, 1964.

KLOPFER, W. G. *The psychological report: Use and communication of psychological findings.* New York: Grune & Stratton, 1960.

KLOPFER, W. G., & TAULBEE, E. S. Projective tests. *Annual Review of Psychology,* 1976, *27,* 543–567.

KNAPP, P. H. Current theoretical concepts in psychophysiological medicine. In A. M. Freedman, H. I. Kaplan, & B. J. Sadock (Eds.), *Comprehensive textbook of psychiatry*-II (Vol. 2). Baltimore: Williams & Wilkins, 1975. Pp. 1631–1637.

KNOBLOCH, H., & PASAMANICK, B. Syndrome of minimal cerebral damage in infancy. *Journal of the American Medical Association,* 1959, *170,* 1384–1387.

KNOOP, P. A. Advanced instructional provisions and automated performance measurement. *Human Factors,* 1973, *15,* 583–597.

KNUTSON, A. L. *The individual, society, and health behavior.* New York: Russell Sage Foundation, 1965.

KNUTSON, J. F. (Ed.). *The control of aggression: Implications from basic research.* Chicago: Aldine, 1973.

KNUTSON, J. N. (Ed.). *Handbook of political psychology.* San Francisco: Jossey-Bass, 1973.

KOHLBERG, L. Stage and sequence: The cognitive-developmental approach to socialization. In D. Goslin (Ed.), *Handbook of socialization: Theory and research.* Chicago: Rand McNally, 1969. Pp. 347–480.

KOHLBERG, L., SCHARF, P., & HICKEY, J. Justice structure of the prison. *Prison Journal,* 1971, *51,* 3–14.

KOHLENBERG, R., PHILLIPS, T., & PROCTOR, W. A behavioral analysis of peaking in residential electrical-energy consumers. *Journal of Applied Behavior Analysis,* 1976, *9,* 13–18.

KONEČNI, V. J., EBBESEN, E. B., & KONEČNI, D. K. Decision processes and risk taking in traffic: Driver response to the onset of yellow light. *Journal of Applied Psychology,* 1976, *61,* 359–367.

KOPONEN, A. *Mock readership survey.* New York: J. Walter Thompson, 1956.

KOPONEN, A. *Personality profile projects.* New York: J. Walter Thompson, 1958.

KOPONEN, A. Personality characteristics of purchasers. *Journal of Advertising Research,* 1960, *1*(1), 6–11.

KOREIN, J., & BRUDNY, J. Integrated EMG feedback in the management of spasmodic torticollis and focal dystonia: A prospective study of 80 patients. In M. D. Yahr (Ed.), *The basal ganglia.* New York: Raven, 1976. Pp. 385–424.

KORMAN, A. K. Consideration, initiating structure, and organizational criteria: A review. *Personnel Psychology,* 1966, *19,* 349–363.

KORMAN, A. K. Task success, task popularity, and self-esteem as influences on task liking. *Journal of Applied Psychology,* 1968, *52,* 484–490.

KORNHAUSER, A. W. *Mental health of the industrial worker.* New York: Wiley, 1965.

KOSCHERAK, S., & MASLING, J. Noblesse oblige effect: The interpretation of Rorschach responses as a function of ascribed social class. *Journal of Consulting and Clinical Psychology,* 1972, *39,* 415–419.

KOSSORIS, M. D., & KOHLER, R. F. Hours of work and output. *U. S. Department of Labor, Bureau of Labor Statistics, Bulletin No. 917,* 1947.

KRAEMER, A. J. *Development of a cultural self-awareness approach to instruction in intercultural communication* (HumRRO Tech. Rep. 73-17). Alexandria, Va.: Human Resources Research Organization, July 1973.

KRAEMER, A. J. *Workshop in intercultural communication: Handbook for instructors* (HumRRO Tech. Rep. 74-13). Alexandria, Va.: Human Resources Research Organization, June 1974.

KRAEMER, A. J. Cultural self-awareness and communication. *International Educational and Cultural Exchange,* 1975, *10*(3), 13–16.

KRETSCHMER, E. *Physique and character* (Trans. from 2nd ed. by W. J. H. Sprott). New York: Harcourt, Brace, 1925.

KROLL, A. M., & PFISTER, L. A. Assessing career skills: A new approach. *College Board Review,* 1977, No. 105, 18–24.

KRUGMAN, H. E. Some applications of pupil measurement. *Journal of Marketing Research,* 1964, *1*(4), 15–19.

KRUGMAN, H. E. A comparison of physical and verbal responses to television commercials. *Public Opinion Quarterly,* 1965, *29,* 323–325.

KRUGMAN, H. E. Processes underlying exposure to advertising. *American Psychologist,* 1968, *23,* 245–253.

KRUMBOLTZ, J. D. Behavioral goals for counseling. *Journal of Counseling Psychology,* 1966, *13,* 153–159. (a)

KRUMBOLTZ, J. D. Promoting adaptive behavior: New answers to familiar questions. In J. D. Krumboltz (Ed.), *Revolution in counseling.* New York: Houghton Mifflin, 1966. (b)

KRUMBOLTZ, J. D., & SCHROEDER, W. W. Promoting career planning through reinforcement. *Personnel and Guidance Journal,* 1965, *44,* 19–25.

KRUMBOLTZ, J. D., & THORESEN, C. E. The effect of behavioral counseling in group and individual settings on information-seeking behavior. *Journal of Counseling Psychology,* 1964, *11,* 324–333.

KRYTER, K. D. An example of "engineering psychology": The aircraft noise problem. *American Psychologist,* 1968, *23,* 240–244.

KRYTER, K. D. *The effects of noise on man.* New York: Academic Press, 1970.

KUBIS, J. F., & MCLAUGHLIN, E. J. Skylab task and work performance (experiment M-151—time and motion study). *Acta Astronautica,* 1975, *2,* 337–349.

KUDER, G. F. A rationale for evaluating interests. *Educational and Psychological Measurement,* 1963, *23,* 3–10.

KUDER, G. F. The occupational interest survey. *Personnel and Guidance Journal,* 1966, *45,* 72–77.

KUDER, G. F. Some principles of interest measurement. *Educational and Psychological Measurement,* 1970, *30,* 205–226.

KURTH, R. Testing the significance of consumer complaints. *Journal of Marketing Research,* 1965, *2,* 283–284.

KURTZ, A. K. A research test of the Rorschach test. *Personnel Psychology,* 1948, *1,* 41–51.

KUTNER, B. Physician-patient relationships: A theoretical framework. In J. G. Peatman & E. L. Hartley (Eds.), *Festschrift for Gardner Murphy.* New York, Harper, 1960. Pp. 258–273.

KUTNER, B. The social psychology of disability. In W. S. Neff (Ed.), *Rehabilitation psychology.* Washington, D. C.: American Psychological Association, 1971. Pp. 143–167.

KUTNER, B., & GORDAN, G. Seeking care for cancer. *Journal of Health and Human Behavior,* 1961, *2,* 171–178.

LACEY, J. I., & LACEY, B. C. Verification and extension of the principle of autonomic response stereotype. *American Journal of Psychology,* 1958, *71,* 50–73.

LACHMAN, S. J. *Psychosomatic disorders: A behavioristic interpretation.* New York: Wiley, 1972.

LAMBERT, M. J. Spontaneous remission in adult neurotic disorders: A revision and summary. *Psychological Bulletin,* 1976, *83,* 107–119.

LANA, R. E. Persuasion and the law: A constitutional issue. *American Psychologist,* 1972, *27,* 901–902.

LANDY, F. J., FARR, J. L., SAAL, F. E., & FREYTAG, W. R. Behaviorally anchored scales for rating the performance of police officers. *Journal of Applied Psychology,* 1976, *61,* 750–758.

LANDY, F. J., & GOODIN, C. V. Performance appraisal. In O. G. Stahl & R. A. Staufenberger (Eds.), *Police personnel administration.* Washington, D. C.: Police Foundation, 1974. Pp. 165–184.

LANG, P. J. The application of psychophysiological methods to the study of psychotherapy and behavior modification. In A. E. Bergin & S. L. Garfield (Eds.), *Handbook of psychotherapy and behavior change: An empirical analysis.* New York: Wiley, 1971. Ch. 3.

LANGHORNE, M. C., & HOCH, E. L. Psychology in the states. *American Psychologist,* 1960, *15,* 632–634.

LANGNER, T. S., & MICHAEL, S. T. *Life stress and mental health.* New York: Glencoe Free Press, 1963.

LATHAM, G. P., & KINNE, S. B., III. Improving job performance through training in goal setting. *Journal of Applied Psychology,* 1974, *59,* 187–191.

LATHAM, G. P., WEXLEY, K. N., & PURSELL, E. D. Training managers to minimize rating errors in the observation of behavior. *Journal of Applied Psychology,* 1975, *60,* 550–555.

LAUER, A. R. *The psychology of driving: Factors of traffic enforcement.* Springfield, Ill.: Charles C Thomas, 1960.

LAUER, J., & PATERSON, D. G. Readability of union contracts. *Personnel,* 1951, *28,* 36–40.

LAURU, L. The measurement of fatigue. *Manager,* 1954, *22,* 299–304; 369–375.

LAWLER, E. E., III. Equity theory as a predictor of productivity and work quality. *Psychological Bulletin,* 1968, *70,* 596–610.

LAWLER, E. E., III. Job design and employee motivation. *Personnel Psychology,* 1969, *22,* 426–435.

LAWLER, E. E., III. *Motivation in work organizations.* Monterey, Calif.: Brooks/Cole, 1973.

LAWLER, E. E., III., & SUTTLE, J. L. A causal correlational test of the need hierarchy concept. *Organizational Behavior and Human Performance,* 1972, *7,* 265–287.

LAWSHE, C. H. Employee selection. *Personnel Psychology,* 1952, *5,* 31–34.

LAWSHE, C. H., & BALMA, M. J. *Principles of personnel testing* (2nd ed.). New York: McGraw-Hill, 1966.

LAWSON, R. G. The law of primacy in the criminal courtroom. *Journal of Social Psychology,* 1969, *77,* 121–131.

LAZARUS, A. A. *Behavior therapy and beyond.* New York: McGraw-Hill, 1971.

LAZARUS, A. A. *Multimodal behavior therapy.* New York: Springer, 1976.

LAZARUS, A. A. Has behavior therapy outlived its usefulness? *American Psychologist,* 1977, *32,* 550–554.

Learning to fly—with advanced audiovisuals and simulators. *Training,* 1977, *14*(11), 59–61.

LEAVITT, H. J. Some effects of certain communication patterns on group performance. *Journal of Abnormal and Social Psychology,* 1951, *46,* 38–50.

LEAVITT, H. J. *Managerial pscyhology: An introduction to individuals, pairs, and groups in organizations* (3rd ed.). Chicago: University of Chicago Press, 1972.

LEAVITT, H. J., & MUELLER, R. A. H. Some effects of feedback on communication. *Human Relations,* 1951, *4,* 401–410.

LEBO, D. Degrees for charlatans. *American Psychologist,* 1953, *8,* 231–234.

LEE, G. C., & PARKER, G. Y. *Ending the draft: The theory of the all-volunteer force* (HumRRO FR-PO-77-1). Alexandria, Va.: Human Resources Research Organization, April 1977.

LEE, R., & BOOTH, J. M. A utility analysis of a weighted application blank designed to predict turnover for clerical employees. *Journal of Applied Psychology,* 1974, *59,* 516–518.

LEGROS, L. A., & WESTON, H. C. On the design of machinery in relation to the operator. *Industrial Fatigue Research Board Report No. 36,* 1926.

LEIB, W., TRYON, W. W., & STROEBEL, C. S. Alpha biofeedback: Fact or artifact? *Psychobiology,* 1976, *13,* 541–545.

LEIGHTON, D. C., HARDING, J. S., MACKLIN, D., MACMILLAN, A. M., & LEIGHTON, A. H. *The character of danger.* Vol. III, *The Sterling County study of psychiatric disorder and socio-cultural environment.* New York: Basic Books, 1963.

LEIPPE, M. R., WELLS, G. L., & OSTROM, T. M. Crime seriousness as a determinant of accuracy in eyewitness identification. *Journal of Applied Psychology,* 1978, *63,* 345–351.

Leitenberg, H. The use of single-case methodology in psychotherapy research. *Journal of Abnormal Psychology,* 1973, *82,* 87–101.

Leon, G. R., & Roth, L. Obesity: Psychological causes, correlations, and speculations. *Psychological Bulletin,* 1977, *84,* 117–139.

Lerner, J. W. *Children with learning disabilities: Theories, diagnosis, and teaching strategies.* Boston: Houghton Mifflin, 1971.

Lessinger, L. M., & Tyler, R. W. (Eds.). *Accountability in education.* Worthington, Ohio: Charles A. Jones, 1971.

Le Sueur advertisement. *The New Yorker,* February 10, 1962, p. 88.

Lettieri, D. J. (Ed.). *Predicting adolescent drug abuse: A review of issues, methods, and correlates,* (DHEW Publication No. (ADM) 76-299). Rockville, Md.: National Institute on Drug Abuse, 1975.

Levenstein, P. The mother-child home program. In M. C. Day & R. K. Parker (Eds.), *The preschool in action: Exploring early childhood programs* (2nd ed.). Boston: Allyn & Bacon, 1977. Pp. 28–49.

Leventhal, H. Fear appeals and persuasion: The differentiation of a motivational construct. *American Journal of Public Health,* 1971, *61,* 1208–1224.

Leventhal, H. Changing attitudes and habits to reduce risk factors in chronic disease. *American Journal of Cardiology,* 1973, *31,* 571–580.

Leventhal, H. The consequences of depersonalization during illness and treatment: An information-processing model. In J. Howard & A. Strauss (Eds.), *Humanizing health care.* New York: Wiley, 1975. Ch. 7.

Leventhal, H. *Sensory information and attention in the control of pain.* Paper presented at the meeting of the American Psychological Association, Washington, D. C., September 1976.

Leventhal, H., Jones, S., & Trembly, G. Sex differences in attitude and behavior change under conditions of fear and specific instruction. *Journal of Experimental Social Psychology,* 1966, *2,* 387–399.

Leventhal, H., Watts, J. C., & Pagano, F. Effects of fear and instructions on how to cope with danger. *Journal of Personality and Social Psychology,* 1967, *6,* 313–321.

Levin, J. R., & Allen, V. L. (Eds.), *Cognitive learning in children: Theories and strategies.* New York: Academic Press, 1976.

Levine, F. J., & Tapp, J. L. The psychology of criminal identification: The gap from Wade to Kirby. *University of Pennsylvania Law Review,* 1973, *121,* 1079–1131.

Levine, S. L., & Silvern, L. C. The evolution and revolution of the teaching machine, Parts 1 and 2. *Journal of the American Society of Training Directors,* 1960, *14*(12), 4–16; 1961, *15*(1), 14–26.

Lewin, K. *Field theory in social science.* New York: Harper, 1951.

Lewinsohn, P. M. The behavioral study and treatment of depression. In M. Hersen, R. M. Eisler, & P. M. Miller (Eds.), *Progress in behavior modification.* New York: Academic Press, 1975. Pp. 19–64.

Lichtman, C. M., & Hunt, R. G. Personality and organization theory: A review of some conceptual literature. *Psychological Bulletin,* 1971, *76,* 271–294.

Liebenson, H. A., & Wepman, J. M. *The psychologist as a witness.* Chicago: Callaghan, 1964.

Lieberman, M. A., Yalono, I. D., & Miles, M. *Encounter groups: First facts.* New York: Basic Books, 1973.

Liebert, R. M., & Schwartzberg, N. S. Effects of mass media. *Annual Review of Psychology,* 1977, *28,* 141–173.

Liebeskind, J. C., & Paul, L. A. Psychological and physiological mechanisms of pain. *Annual Review of Psychology,* 1977, *28,* 41–60.

Lieblich, I., Ben Shakhar, G., & Kugelmass, S. Validity of the guilty knowledge technique in a prisoners' sample. *Journal of Applied Psychology,* 1976, *61,* 89–93.

Life Insurance Marketing and Research Association. *Improved validity for the Aptitude Index Battery.* (Research Rep. 1973-3). Hartford, Conn.: Author, 1973.

LIFE INSURANCE MARKETING AND RESEARCH ASSOCIATION. *Aptitude Index Battery, Form 2: Manual; Questionnaire.* Hartford, Conn.: Author, 1975.

LIKERT, R. *New patterns of management.* New York: McGraw-Hill, 1961.

LIKERT, R. *The human organization: Its management and value.* New York: McGraw-Hill, 1967.

LIKERT, R., & BOWERS, D. G. Organizational theory and human resource accounting. *American Psychologist,* 1969, *24,* 585–592.

LILIENFELD, A. M., PASAMANICK, B., & ROGERS, M. Relationship between pregnancy experience and the development of certain neuropsychiatric disorders in childhood. *American Journal of Public Health,* 1955, *45,* 637–643.

LINDER, R. Diagnosis: Description or prescription? A case study in the psychology of diagnosis. *Perceptual and Motor Skills,* 1965, *20,* 1081–1092.

LINDHEIM, R. Factors which determine hospital design. *American Journal of Public Health,* 1966, *56,* 1668–1675.

LIN-FU, J. S. *Lead poisoning in children* (DHEW, Children's Bureau Publication No. 452). Washington, D. C.: U. S. Government Printing Office, 1967.

LINK, H. C. *The new psychology of selling and advertising.* New York: Macmillan, 1932.

LINN, R. L. Single-group validity, differential validity, and differential prediction. *Journal of Applied Psychology,* 1978, *63,* 507–512.

LIPPITT, P., LIPPITT, R., & EISEMAN, J. *Cross-age helping package.* Ann Arbor, Mich.: Institute for Social Research, 1972.

LIPTON, J. P. On the psychology of eyewitness testimony. *Journal of Applied Psychology,* 1977, *62,* 90–95.

LISSITZ, R. W., & GREEN, S. B. Effect of the number of scale points on reliability: A Monte Carlo approach. *Journal of Applied Psychology,* 1975, *60,* 10–13.

LITTLE, K. B., & SHNEIDMAN, E. S. Congruencies among interpretations of psychological test and anamnestic data. *Psychological Monographs,* 1959, *73*(6, Whole No. 476).

LITTMAN, R. A., & MANNING, H. M. A methodological study of cigarette brand discrimination, *Journal of Applied Psychology,* 1954, *38,* 185–190.

LOCKE, E. A. Motivational effects of knowledge of results: Knowledge or goal setting? *Journal of Applied Psychology,* 1967, *51,* 324–329.

LOCKE, E. A. Toward a theory of task performance and incentives. *Organizational Behavior and Human Performance,* 1968, *3,* 157–189.

LOCKE, E. A. Personnel attitudes and motivation. *Annual Review of Psychology,* 1975, *26,* 457–480.

LOCKE, E. A. The nature and consequences of job satisfaction. In M. D. Dunnette (Ed.), *Handbook of industrial and organizational psychology.* Chicago: Rand McNally, 1976. Pp. 1297–1349.

LOCKE, E. A., & BRYAN, J. F. Performance goals as determinants of level of performance and boredom. *Journal of Applied Psychology,* 1967, *51,* 120–130.

LOCKE, E. A., BRYAN, J. F., & KENDALL, L. M. Goals and intentions as mediators of the effects of monetary incentives on behavior. *Journal of Applied Psychology,* 1968, *52,* 104–121.

LOCKE, E. A., SIROTA, D. E., & WOLFSON, A. D. An experimental case study of the successes and failures of job enrichment in a government agency. *Journal of Applied Psychology,* 1976, *61,* 701–711.

LOCKHART, J. M. Extreme body cooling and psychomotor performance. *Ergonomics,* 1968, *11,* 249–260.

LOCKHART, J. M., & KEISS, H. O. Auxiliary heating of the hands during cold exposure and manual performance. *Human Factors,* 1971, *13,* 457–465.

LOEBER, R., & WEISMAN, R. G. Contingencies of therapist and trainer performance: A review. *Psychological Bulletin,* 1975, *82,* 660–688.

LOFQUIST, L. H. *Vocational counseling with the physically handicapped.* New York: Appleton-Century-Crofts, 1957.

LOFQUIST, L. H. (Ed.). *Psychological research and rehabilitation.* Washington, D. C.: American Psychological Association, 1962.

LOFQUIST, L. H., & DAWIS, R. V. *Adjustment to work: A psychological view of man's problems in a work-oriented society.* New York: Appleton-Century-Crofts, 1969.

LOFTUS, E. F. Leading questions and the eyewitness report. *Cognitive Psychology,* 1975, *7,* 560–572.

LOFTUS, E. F., & ZANNI, G. Eyewitness testimony: The influence of the wording of a question. *Bulletin of the Psychonomic Society,* 1975, *5,* 86–88.

LOMBROSO, C. *Crime: Its causes and remedies.* Boston: Little, Brown, 1911. (a)

LOMBROSO, C. *Criminal man.* New York: Putnam, 1911. (b) (1st Italian ed., 1876.)

LOMRANZ, J. Cultural variations in personal space. *Journal of Social Psychology,* 1976, *99,* 21–27.

LOPEZ, F. M., JR. Evaluating executive decision making: The in-basket technique. *American Management Association Research Study No. 75,* 1966.

LORANGER, A. W., PROUT, C. T. & WHITE, M. A. The placebo effect in psychiatric drug research. *Journal of the American Medical Association,* 1961, *176,* 920–925.

LORION, R. P. Socioeconomic status and traditional treatment approaches reconsidered. *Psychological Bulletin,* 1973, *79,* 263–270.

LORION, R. P. Patient and therapist variables in the treatment of low-income patients. *Psychological Bulletin,* 1974, *81,* 344–354.

LORR, M. (Ed.). *Explorations in typing psychotics.* Elmsford, N. Y.: Pergamon, 1966.

LORR, M., KLETT, C. J., & MCNAIR, D. M. *Syndromes of psychosis.* Elmsford, N. Y.: Pergamon, 1963.

LORSCH, J. W., & MORSE, J. J. *Organizations and their members: A contingency approach.* New York: Harper & Row, 1974.

LOUISELL, D. W. The psychologist in today's legal world. Parts I & II. *Minnesota Law Review,* 1955, *39,* 235–272: 1957, *41,* 731–750.

LOVELESS, N. E. Direction-of-motion stereotypes: A review. *Ergonomics,* 1962, *5,* 357–383.

LOWIN, A. Participative decision making: A model, literature, and prescriptions for research. *Organizational Behavior and Human Performance,* 1968, *3,* 68–106.

LOWIN, A., & CRAIG, J. R. The influence of level of performance on managerial style: An experimental object lesson on the ambiguity of correlational data. *Organizational Behavior and Human Performance,* 1968, *3,* 440–458.

LOWN, B., VERRIER, R., & CORBALAN, R. Psychologic stress and threshold for repetitive ventricular response. *Science,* 1973, *182,* 834–836.

LUBIN, B., NATHAN, R. G., & MATARAZZO, J. D. Psychologists in medical education: 1976. *American Psychologist,* 1978, *33,* 339–343.

LUCAS, D. B. A rigid technique for measuring the impression value of specific magazine advertisements. *Journal of Applied Psychology,* 1940, *24,* 778–790.

LUCAS, D. B. The ABC's of ARF's PARM. *Journal of Marketing,* 1960, *25*(1), 9–20.

LUCAS, D. B., & BRITT, S. H. *Measuring advertising effectiveness.* New York: McGraw-Hill, 1963.

LUMSDAINE, A. A., & GLASER, R. (Eds.). *Teaching machines and programmed learning.* Washington, D. C.: National Education Association, 1960.

LUMSDAINE, A. A., & MAY, M. A. Mass communication and educational media. *Annual Review of Psychology,* 1965, *16,* 475–534.

LUTHANS, F., & KREITNER, R. *Organizational behavior modification.* Glenview, Ill.: Scott, Foresman, 1975.

LUTZ, K. A., & LUTZ, R. J. Effects of interactive imagery on learning: Application to advertising. *Journal of Applied Psychology,* 1977, *62,* 493–498.

LYERLY, S. B. *Handbook of psychiatric rating scales* (2nd ed.) (DHEW Publ. No. HSM 73-9061). Rockville, Md.: National Institute of Mental Health, 1973.

LYKKEN, D. T. The GSR in the detection of guilt. *Journal of Applied Psychology,* 1959, *43,* 385–388.

LYKKEN, D. T. The validity of the guilty knowledge technique: The effects of faking. *Journal of Applied Psychology,* 1960, *44,* 258–262.

Lykken, D. T. Psychology and the lie detection industry. *American Psychologist,* 1974, *29,* 725–739.

Lyman, H. B. Flesch count and readership in a midwestern farm paper. *Journal of Applied Psychology,* 1949, *33,* 78–80.

Maas, J. B. Patterned scaled expectation interview: Reliability studies on a new technique. *Journal of Applied Psychology,* 1965, *49,* 431–433.

Macek, A. J., & Miles, G. H. IQ score and mailed questionnaire response. *Journal of Applied Psychology,* 1975, *60,* 258–259.

MacKinney, A. C. The assessment of performance change: An inductive example. *Organizational Behavior and Human Performance,* 1967, *2,* 56–72.

Mackworth, N. H. Effects of heat on wireless operators hearing and recording Morse messages. *British Journal of Industrial Medicine,* 1946, *3,* 143–158.

Mackworth, N. H. Researches on the measurement of human performance. In H. W. Sinaiko (Ed.), *Selected papers on human factors in the design and use of control systems.* New York: Dover, 1961. Ch. 7.

MacPhillamy, D. J., & Lewinsohn, P. M. Depression as a function of levels of desired and obtained pleasure. *Journal of Abnormal Psychology,* 1974, *83,* 651–657.

MacPhillamy, D. J., & Lewinsohn, P. M. *Manual for the Pleasant Events Schedule.* Unpublished manuscript, 1976. (Available from P. M. Lewinsohn, Human Neuropsychology Laboratory, University of Oregon, Eugene, Oregon, 97403.)

Madsen, D. B., & Finger, J. R., Jr. Comparison of a written feedback procedure, group brainstorming, and individual brainstorming. *Journal of Applied Psychology,* 1978, *63,* 120–123.

Maher, J. R. (Ed.). *New perspectives in job enrichment.* New York: Van Nostrand Reinhold, 1971.

Mahoney, M. J. *Cognition and behavior modification.* Cambridge, Mass.: Ballinger, 1974.

Mahoney, M. J. Reflections on the cognitive-learning trend in psychotherapy. *American Psychologist,* 1977, *32,* 5–12.

Maier, M. H. *Effects of educational level on prediction of training success with the ACB.* U.S. Army Research Institute for the Behavioral and Social Sciences, Technical Research Note 225, June 1972.

Maier, M. H., & Fuchs, E. F. *Development and evaluation of a new ACB and aptitude area system.* U.S. Army Research Institute for the Behavioral and Social Sciences, Technical Research Note 239, September 1972.

Maier, M. H., & Fuchs, E. F. *Effectiveness of selection and classification testing.* U.S. Army Research Institute for the Behavioral and Social Sciences, Research Report 1179, September 1973.

Maier, N. R. F. *The appraisal interview: Objectives, methods, and skills.* New York: Wiley, 1958.

Maier, N. R. F. *Psychology in industrial organizations* (4th ed.). Boston: Houghton Mifflin, 1973.

Maier, N. R. F., Solem, A. R., & Maier, A. A. *Supervisory and executive development: A manual for role playing.* New York: Wiley, 1957.

Makens, J. C. Effect of brand preference upon consumers' perceived taste of turkey meat. *Journal of Applied Psychology,* 1965, *49,* 261–263.

Malaviya, Pratibha, & Ganesh K. Individual differences in productivity across type of work shift. *Journal of Applied Psychology,* 1977, *62,* 527–528.

Maloney, M. P., & Ward, M. P. Ecology: Let's hear from the people: An objective scale for the measurement of ecological attitudes and knowledge. *American Psychologist,* 1973, *28,* 583–586.

Maloney, M. P., Ward, M. P., & Braucht, G. N. A revised scale for the measurement of ecological attitudes and knowledge. *American Psychologist,* 1975, *30,* 787–790.

Mancuso, J. R. Why not create opinion leaders for new product introductions? *Journal of Marketing,* 1969, *33*(3), 20–25.

MANDEL, D. R., & BARON, R. M. *Environmental determinants of student study habits.* Paper presented at the meeting of the American Psychological Association, Washington, D. C., September 1976.

MANN, P. A. *Psychological consultation with a police department: A demonstration of cooperative training in mental health.* Springfield, Ill.: Charles C Thomas, 1973.

MARGULIES, S., & EIGEN, L. D. (Eds.). *Programed instruction: Uses in industry and the armed services.* New York: Wiley, 1962.

MARITZ, J. S. On the validity of inference drawn from the fitting of Poisson and negative binomial distributions to observed accident data. *Psychological Bulletin,* 1950, *47,* 434–443.

MARK, V. H., & ERVIN, F. R. *Violence and the brain.* New York: Harper & Row, 1970.

MARROW, A. J., BOWERS, D. G., & SEASHORE, S. E. *Management by participation: Creating a climate for personal and organizational development.* New York: Harper & Row, 1967.

MARSDEN, A. M. Visual performance—CIE style. *Light and Lighting,* April 1972, 132–135.

MARSDEN, G. Content-analysis studies of psychotherapy: 1954 through 1968. In A. E. Bergin & S. L. Garfield (Eds.), *Handbook of psychotherapy and behavior change: An empirical analysis.* New York: Wiley, 1971. Ch. 10.

MARSHALL, J. *Law and psychology in conflict.* New York: Bobbs-Merrill, 1966.

MARSHALL, S. Personality correlates of peptic ulcer patients. *Journal of Consulting Psychology,* 1960, *24,* 218–223.

MARTIN, B. The assessment of anxiety by physiological behavioral measures. *Psychological Bulletin,* 1961, *58,* 234–255.

MASLOW, A. H. A theory of motivation. *Psychological Review,* 1943, *50,* 370–396.

MASLOW, A. H. *Eupsychian management.* Homewood, Ill.: Irwin, 1965.

MASLOW, A. H. *Motivation and personality* (2nd ed.). New York: Harper & Row, 1970.

MATARAZZO, J. D. The role of the psychologist in medical education and practice: A challenge posed by comprehensive medicine. *Human Organization,* 1955, *14*(2), 9–14.

MATARAZZO, J. D. The interview. In B. B. Wolman (Ed.), *Handbook of clinical psychology.* New York: McGraw-Hill, 1965.

MATARAZZO, J. D. *Wechsler's measurement and appraisal of adult intelligence.* Baltimore: Williams & Wilkins, 1972.

MATARAZZO, J. D., & DANIEL, R. S. The teaching of psychology by psychologists in medical schools. *Journal of Medical Education,* 1957, *32,* 410–415.

MATARAZZO, J. D., & WIENS, A. N. *The interview: Research on its anatomy and structure.* Chicago: Aldine, 1972.

MATTESON, M. T. Type of transmittal letter and questionnaire color as two variables influencing response rates in a mail survey. *Journal of Applied Psychology,* 1974, *59,* 535–536.

MAUCKER, J. W. (Ed.). *Achieving the potential of performance-based teacher education.* Washington, D. C.: American Association of Colleges for Teacher Education, 1974.

MAYER, R. E., STIEHL, C. C., & GREENO, J. G. Acquisition of understanding and skill in relation to subjects' preparation and meaningfulness of instruction. *Journal of Educational Psychology,* 1975, *67,* 331–350.

MAYO, E. *The human problems of an industrial civilization.* New York: Macmillan, 1933.

MCBAIN, W. N. Noise, the "arousal hypothesis," and monotonous work. *Journal of Applied Psychology,* 1961, *45,* 309–317.

MCCANNE, T. R., & SANDEMAN, C. A. Human operant heart rate conditioning: The importance of individual differences. *Psychological Bulletin,* 1976, *83,* 587–601.

MCCARTHY, J. J., & MCCARTHY, J. F. *Learning disabilities.* Boston: Allyn & Bacon, 1969.

MCCARY, J. L. The psychologist as an expert witness in court. *American Psychologist,* 1956, *11,* 8–13.

MCCLELLAND, D. C. *Assessing human motivation.* New York: General Learning Press, 1971.

MCCORMICK, E. J. Application of job analysis to indirect validity. *Personnel Psychology,* 1959, *12,* 395–420.

McCORMICK, E. J. *Human factors engineering* (3rd ed.). New York: McGraw-Hill, 1970.

McCORMICK, E. J. *Human factors in engineering and design* (4th ed.). New York: McGraw-Hill, 1976. (a)

McCORMICK, E. J. Job and task analysis. In M. D. Dunnette (Ed.), *Handbook of industrial and organizational psychology.* Chicago: Rand McNally, 1976, Ch. 15. (b)

McCORMICK, E. J., JEANNERET, P. R., & MECHAM, R. C. A study of job characteristics and job dimensions as based on the Position Analysis Questionnaire (PAQ). *Journal of Applied Psychology,* 1972, *56,* 347–368.

McCORMICK, E. J., & TIFFIN, J. *Industrial psychology* (6th ed.). Englewood Cliffs, N. J.: Prentice-Hall, 1974.

McDONALD, F. J. Report on Phase II of the beginning teacher evaluation study. *Journal of Teacher Education,* 1976, *27*(1), 39–42.

McFALL, R. M., & LILLESAND, D. B. Behavior rehearsal with modeling and coaching in assertion training. *Journal of Abnormal Psychology,* 1971, *77,* 313–323.

McFALL, R. M., & TWENTYMAN, C. T. Four experiments on the relative contributions of rehearsal, modeling, and coaching to assertion training. *Journal of Abnormal Psychology,* 1973, *81,* 199–218.

McFARLAND, R. A. Psychophysiological studies at high altitudes in the Andes. Parts I to IV. *Journal of Comparative Psychology,* 1937, *23,* 191–225, 227–258; *24,* 147–188, 189–220.

McFARLAND, R. A. *Human factors in air transport design.* New York: McGraw-Hill, 1946.

McFARLAND, R. A. Fatigue in industry: Understanding fatigue in modern life. *Ergonomics,* 1971, *14,* 1–10.

McFARLAND, R. A., & MOSELEY, A. L. *Human factors in highway transport safety.* Boston: Harvard School of Public Health, 1954.

McGEE, R. K. *Crisis intervention in the community.* Baltimore: University Park Press, 1974.

McGEHEE, W., & GARDNER, J. E. Music in a complex industrial job. *Personnel Psychology,* 1949, *2,* 405–417.

McGEHEE, W., & OWEN, E. B. Authorized and unauthorized rest pauses in clerical work. *Journal of Applied Psychology,* 1940, *24,* 605–614.

McGEHEE, W., & THAYER, P. W. *Training in business and industry.* New York: Wiley, 1961.

McGRAW-HILL RESEARCH, LABORATORY OF ADVERTISING PERFORMANCE. *How repeat advertisements affect readership.* Data Sheet 3040, 1962.

McGREGOR, D. An uneasy look at performance appraisal. *Harvard Business Review,* 1957, *35*(3), 89–94.

McGREGOR, D. *The human side of enterprise.* New York: McGraw-Hill, 1960.

McGUIRE, F. L. The nature of bias in official accident and violation records. *Journal of Applied Psychology,* 1973, *57,* 300–305.

McGUIRE, W. J. Inducing resistance to persuasion. In L. Berkowitz (Ed.), *Advances in experimental social psychology* (Vol. 1.). New York: Academic Press, 1964. Pp. 191–229.

McKEACHIE, W. J. Instructional psychology. *Annual Review of Psychology,* 1974, *25,* 161–193.

McKECHNIE, G. E. *ERI manual: Environmental Response Inventory.* Palo Alto, Calif.: Consulting Psychologists Press, 1974.

McKEE, J. M., & WATKINS, J. C. *A self-instructional program for youthful offenders.* Unpublished report, Draper Correctional Center, Elmore, Alabama, May 1962.

McKINNEY, F. *Psychology of personal adjustment* (3rd ed.). New York: Wiley, 1960.

McKINNEY, F. *Understanding personality: Cases in counseling.* Boston: Houghton Mifflin, 1965.

McKINNEY, F., LORION, R. P., & ZAX, M. *Effective behavior and human development.* New York: Macmillan, 1976.

McKINNEY, J. D. Problem-solving strategies in reflective and impulsive children. *Journal of Educational Psychology,* 1975, *67,* 807–820.

McLARNEY, W. F., & BERLINER, W. M. *Management training: Cases and principles* (5th ed.). Homewood, Ill.: Irwin, 1970.

McMURRY, R. N. Validating the patterned interview. *Personnel,* 1947, *23,* 263–272.

McNeil, E. B. (Ed.). *The nature of human conflict.* Englewood Cliffs, N. J.: Prentice-Hall, 1965.

McNemar, Q. On so-called test bias. *American Psychologist,* 1975, *30,* 848–851.

McReynolds, W. T., Barnes, A. R., Brooks, S., & Rehagen, N. J. The role of attention-placebo influences in the efficacy of systematic desensitization. *Journal of Consulting and Clinical Psychology,* 1973, *41,* 86–92.

Meehl, P. E. *Clinical vs. statistical prediction: A theoretical analysis and a review of the evidence.* Minneapolis: University of Minnesota Press, 1954.

Meehl, P. E. Wanted—a good cookbook. *American Psychologist,* 1956, *11,* 263–272.

Meehl, P. E. The cognitive activity of the clinician. *American Psychologist,* 1960, *15,* 19–27.

Megargee, E. I. The prediction of violence with psychological tests. In C. D. Spielberger (Ed.), *Current topics in clinical and community psychology* (Vol. 2). New York: Academic Press, 1970. Pp. 97–156.

Meichenbaum, D. Toward a cognitive theory of self-control. In G. E. Schwartz & D. Shapiro (Eds.), *Consciousness and self-regulation: Advances in research* (Vol. 1). New York: Plenum, 1976. Ch. 6.

Meier, G. W., Bunch, M. E., Nolan, C. Y., & Scheidler, C. H. Anoxia, behavioral development, and learning ability: A comparative-experimental approach. *Psychological Monographs,* 1960, *74*(1, Whole No. 488).

Melamed, B. G., Howes, R. R., Heiby, E., & Glick, J. Use of filmed modeling to reduce uncooperative behavior during dental treatment. *Journal of Dental Research,* 1975, *54,* 797–801.

Melamed, B. G., & Siegel, L. J. Reduction of anxiety in children facing hospitalization and surgery by use of film modeling. *Journal of Consulting and Clinical Psychology,* 1975, *43,* 511–521.

Melton, A. W. The science of learning and the technology of educational methods. *Harvard Educational Review,* 1959, *29,* 96–106.

Melton, A. W. *Categories of human learning.* New York: Academic Press, 1964.

Melton, A. W. Visitor behavior in museums: Some early research in environmental design. *Human Factors,* 1972, *14,* 393–403.

Meltzoff, J., & Kornreich, M. *Research in psychotherapy.* New York: Atherton, 1970.

Melzack, R. *The puzzle of pain.* New York: Basic Books, 1973.

Melzack, R., & Wall, P. D. Pain mechanisms: A new theory. *Science,* 1965, *150,* 971–979.

Menne, J. W., McCarthy, W., & Menne, J. A systems approach to the content validation of employee selection procedures. *Public Personnel Management,* 1976, *5,* 387–396.

Mensh, I. N. Psychology in medical education. *American Psychologist,* 1953, *8,* 83–85.

Mental Health Law Project. *Basic rights of the mentally handicapped.* Washington, D. C.: Author, 1973.

Merrens, M. R., & Richards, W. S. Acceptance of generalized versus "bona fide" personality interpretations. *Psychological Reports,* 1970, *27,* 691–694.

Merrill, H. F. (Ed.). *Classics in management.* New York: American Management Association, 1960.

Metropolitan Readiness Tests. New York: Psychological Corporation, 1976.

Meyer, H. H. The validity of the in-basket test as a measure of managerial performance. *Personnel Psychology,* 1970, *23,* 297–307.

Michelson, W. (Ed.). *Behavioral research methods in environmental design.* Stroudsberg, Pa.: Dowden, Hutchinson, & Ross, 1975.

Mihal, W. L., & Barrett, G. V. Individual differences in perceptual information processing and their relation to automobile accident involvement. *Journal of Applied Psychology,* 1976, *61,* 229–233.

Mikawa, J. K. Evaluation in community mental health. In P. McReynolds (Ed.), *Advances in psychological assessment* (Vol. 3). San Francisco: Jossey-Bass, 1975. Pp. 389–432.

Mikulas, W. L. *Behavior modification: An overview.* New York: Harper & Row, 1972.

Miller, G. A. The magical number seven, plus or minus two: Some limits on our capacity for processing information. *Psychological Review,* 1956, *63,* 81–97.

MILLER, G. P., & GELATT, H. B. Deciding: The decision-making program. *College Board Review*, 1971–1972, No. 82, D1–D16.

MILLER, J. W., & ROWE, P. M. Influence of favorable and unfavorable information upon assessment decisions. *Journal of Applied Psychology*, 1967, *51*, 432–435.

MILLER, M., RANSOHOFF, J., & TICHAUER, E. R. Ergonomic evaluation of a redesigned surgical instrument. *Applied Ergonomics*, 1971, *2*(4), 194–197.

MILLER, N., & CAMPBELL, D. T. Recency and primacy in persuasion as a function of the timing of speeches and measurements. *Journal of Abnormal and Social Psychology*, 1959, *59*, 1–9.

MILLER, N. E. Liberalization of basic S-R concepts; Extensions to conflict behavior, motivation, and social learning. In S. Koch (Ed.), *Psychology: A study of a science* (Vol. 2). New York: McGraw-Hill, 1958. Pp. 198–292.

MILLER, N. E. Learning of visceral and glandular responses. *Science*, 1969, *163*, 434–445.

MILLER, N. E. Applications of learning and biofeedback to psychiatry and medicine. In A. M. Freedman, H. I. Kaplan, & B. J. Sadock (Eds.), *Comprehensive textbook of psychiatry—II* (Vol. 1). Baltimore: Williams & Wilkins, 1975. Pp. 349–365.

MILLER, N. E., & MURRAY, E. J. Displacement and conflict: Learnable drive as a basis for the steeper gradient of avoidance than of approach. *Journal of Experimental Psychology*, 1952, *43*, 227–231.

MILLER, W. R. Alcoholism scales and objective assessment methods: A review. *Psychological Bulletin*, 1976, *83*, 649–674.

MILLON, T. (Ed.). *Medical behavioral science*. Philadelphia: Saunders, 1975.

MILTON, J. L., JONES, R. E., & FITTS, P. M. *Eye fixations of aircraft pilots: V. Frequency, duration, and sequence of fixations when flying selected maneuvers during instrument and visual flight conditions. USAF AF TR* 6018, 1950.

MINDAK, W. A. Fitting the Semantic Differential to the marketing problem. *Journal of Marketing*, 1961, *25*(4), 28–33.

MINER, J. B. The concurrent validity of the PAT in the selection of tabulating machine operators. *Journal of Projective Techniques*, 1960, *24*, 409–418.

MINER, J. B. The validity of the PAT in the selection of tabulating machine operators: An analysis of predictive power. *Journal of Projective Techniques*, 1961, *25*, 330–333.

MINER, J. B. Personality and ability factors in sales performance. *Journal of Applied Psychology*, 1962, *46*, 6–13.

MINER, J. B., & CULVER, J. Some aspects of the executive personality. *Journal of Applied Psychology*, 1955, *39*, 348–353.

MINER, J. B., & DACHLER, H. P. Personnel attitudes and motivation. *Annual Review of Psychology*, 1973, *24*, 379–402.

MINTURN, L., & TAPP, J. L. *Authority, rules, and aggression: A cross-national study of children's judgments of the justice of aggressive confrontations—Part II.* Washington, D. C.: U. S. Department of Health, Education, and Welfare, 1970.

MINTZ, A., & BLUM, M. L. A re-examination of the accident proneness concept. *Journal of Applied Psychology*, 1949, *33*, 195–211.

MINUCHIN, S. *Families and family therapy*. Cambridge, Mass.: Harvard University Press, 1974.

MIRVIS, P. H., & LAWLER, E. E., III. Measuring financial impact of employee attitudes. *Journal of Applied Psychology*, 1977, *62*, 1–8.

MISCHEL, W. *Personality and assessment*. New York: Wiley, 1968.

MITCHEL, J. O. Assessment center validity: A longitudinal study. *Journal of Applied Psychology*, 1975, *60*, 573–579.

MITCHELL, M. B. *Time disorientation and estimation in isolation*. USAF ASD-TDR 60-277, 1962.

MITCHELL, T. R. Expectancy models of job satisfaction, occupational preference, and effort: A theoretical, methodological, and empirical appraisal. *Psychological Bulletin*, 1974, *81*, 1053–1077.

Moderator variables (Feature section). *Journal of Applied Psychology*, 1972, *56*, 245–270.

Modern Language Aptitude Test. New York: Psychological Corporation, 1967.

MONAHAN, J. The prevention of violence. In J. Monahan (Ed.), *Community mental health and the criminal justice system.* New York: Pergamon, 1976. Pp. 13–34.

MOOS, R. H. *The Social Climate Scales: An overview.* Palo Alto, Calif.: Consulting Psychologists Press, 1974.

MOOS, R. H. Assessment and impact of social climate. In P. McReynolds (Ed.), *Advances in psychological assessment* (Vol. 3). San Francisco: Jossey-Bass, 1975. Ch. 1. (a)

MOOS, R. H. *Evaluating correctional environments: With implications for community settings.* New York: Wiley, 1975. (b)

MOOS, R. H. *The human context: Environmental determinants of behavior.* New York: Wiley, 1976.

MOOS, R. H., & GERST, M. S. *University Residence Environment Scales.* Palo Alto, Calif.: Consulting Psychologists Press, 1974.

MORAN, M. J. Reduced-gravity human factors research with aircraft. *Human Factors,* 1969, *11,* 463–472.

MORENO, J. L. Psychodrama. In H. I. Kaplan & B. J. Sadock (Eds.), *Comprehensive group psychotherapies.* Baltimore: Williams & Wilkins, 1971. Pp. 460–500.

MORENO, J. L. Psychodrama. In A. M. Freedman, H. I. Kaplan, & B. J. Sadock (Eds.), *Comprehensive textbook of psychiatry—II* (Vol.2). Baltimore: Williams & Wilkins, 1975. Pp. 1891–1909.

MORGAN, C. T., & KING, R. A. *Introduction to psychology* (5th ed.). New York: McGraw-Hill, 1975.

MORRISON, R. F., OWENS, W. A., GLENNON, J. R., & ALBRIGHT, L. E. Factored life history antecedents of industrial research performance. *Journal of Applied Psychology,* 1962, *46,* 281–284.

MORRISON, S. L. Principles and methods of epidemiological research and their application to psychiatric illness. *Journal of Mental Science,* 1959, *105,* 999–1011.

MORSE, J. J., & LORSCH, J. W. Beyond Theory Y. *Harvard Business Review,* 1970, *48*(3), 61–68.

MORSH, J. E. Job analysis in the United States Air Force. *Personnel Psychology,* 1962, *37,* 7–17.

MOSCOWITZ, H. R. Subjective ideals and sensory optimization in evaluating perceptual dimension in food. *Journal of Applied Psychology,* 1972, *56,* 60–66.

MOSEL, J. N., & GOHEEN, H. W. Use of the "ERQ" in hiring. *Personnel Journal,* 1958, *36,* 338–340. (a)

MOSEL, J. N., & GOHEEN, H. W. The validity of the employment recommendation questionnaire in personnel selection. I. Skilled traders. *Personnel Psychology,* 1958, *11,* 481–490. (b)

MOSEL, J. N., & GOHEEN, H. W. The employment recommendation questionnaire: III. Validity of different types of references. *Personnel Psychology,* 1959, *12,* 469–477.

MOSES, J. L. The development of an assessment center for the early identification of supervisory potential. *Personnel Psychology,* 1973, *26,* 569–580.

MOSES, J. L., & BOEHM, V. R. Relationship of assessment center performance to management progress of women. *Journal of Applied Psychology,* 1975, *60,* 527–529.

MOTT, P. E., MANN, F. C., McLAUGHLIN, Q., & WARWICK, D. P. *Shift work: The social, psychological, and physical consequences.* Ann Arbor, Mich.: University of Michigan Press, 1965.

MOWRER, O. H. *Learning theory and personality dynamics.* New York: Ronald, 1950.

MOYER, K. E. *The psychobiology of aggression.* New York: Harper & Row, 1976.

MUECHER, H., & UNGEHEUER, H. Meteorological influence on reaction time, flicker fusion frequency, job accidents, and use of medical treatments. *Perceptual and Motor Skills,* 1961, *12,* 163–168.

MÜNSTERBERG, H. *On the witness stand.* New York: McClure, 1908.

MÜNSTERBERG, H. *Psychology and industrial efficiency.* Boston: Houghton Mifflin, 1913.

MURCHISON, C. *Criminal intelligence.* Worcester, Mass.: Clark University Press, 1926.

MURRAY, D. C., & DEABLER, H. L. Colors and mood-tones. *Journal of Applied Psychology,* 1957, *41,* 279–283.

MURRAY, E. J. A case study in a behavioral analysis of psychotherapy. *Journal of Abnormal and Social Psychology,* 1954, *49,* 305–310.

MURRAY, E. J. A content-analysis method for studying psychotherapy. *Psychological Monographs,* 1956, *70*(13, Whole No. 420).

MURRAY, E. J., & BERKUN, M. M. Displacement as a function of conflict. *Journal of Abnormal and Social Psychology,* 1955, *51,* 47–56.

MURRAY, E. J., & MILLER, N. E. Displacement: Steeper gradient of generalization of avoidance than of approach with age of habit controlled. *Journal of Experimental Psychology,* 1952, *43,* 222–226.

MURRAY, H. A. *Thematic Apperception Test.* Cambridge, Mass.: Harvard University Press, 1943.

MURRAY, H. A., et al. *Explorations in personality.* New York: Oxford University Press, 1938.

MURRELL, K. F. H. *Human performance in industry.* New York: Reinhold, 1965.

MUSHKIN, S. Evaluations: Use with caution. *Evaluation,* 1973, *1,* 30–35.

MUSSEN, P. H., & NAYLOR, H. K. The relationships between overt and fantasy aggression. *Journal of Abnormal and Social Psychology,* 1954, *49,* 235–240.

MYERS, R. A. Research on educational and vocational counseling. In A. E. Bergin & S. L. Garfield (Eds.), *Handbook of psychotherapy and behavior change: An empirical analysis.* New York: Wiley, 1971. Pp. 863–891.

NAMIAS, J. A. A method to detect specific causes of consumer complaints. *Journal of Marketing Research,* 1964, *1*(3), 63–68.

National register of health service providers in psychology. Washington, D. C.: Council for the National Register of Health Service Providers in Psychology, 1975.

NAYLOR, J. C. *Parameters affecting the relative efficiency of part and whole practice methods: A review of the literature.* U. S. Naval Training Devices Center, Technical Report No. 950-1, 1962.

NAYLOR, J. C., & BRIGGS, G. E. Effects of task complexity and task organization on the relative efficiency of part and whole training methods. *Journal of Experimental Psychology,* 1963, *65,* 217–224.

NEFF, W. S. (Ed.). *Rehabilitation psychology.* Washington, D. C.: American Psychological Association, 1971.

NEU, D. M. Measuring advertising recognition. *Journal of Advertising Research,* 1961, *1*(6), 17–22.

NEWMAN, R. I., HUNT, D. L., & RHODES, F. Effects of music on employee attitude and productivity in a skateboard factory. *Journal of Applied Psychology,* 1966, *50,* 493–496.

NORD, W. R. Beyond the teaching machine: The neglected area of operant conditioning in the theory and practice of management. *Organizational Behavior and Human Performance,* 1969, *4,* 375–401.

NORD, W. R. Improving attendance through rewards. *Personnel Administration,* 1970, *33*(6), 37–41.

NORD, W. R. Job satisfaction reconsidered. *American Psychologist,* 1977, *32,* 1026–1035.

NORD, W. R., & COSTIGAN, R. Worker adjustment to the four-day week: A longitudinal study. *Journal of Applied Psychology,* 1973, *58,* 60–66.

NOVACO, R. W. *Anger control: The development and evaluation of an experimental treatment.* Lexington, Mass.: Lexington Books, 1975.

NOVAK, M. A. Social recovery of monkeys isolated for the first year of life. II. Long-term assessment. *Developmental Psychology,* 1979, *15,* 50–61.

NOVAK, M. A., & HARLOW, H. F. Social recovery of monkeys isolated for the first year of life: I. Rehabilitation and therapy. *Developmental Psychology,* 1975, *11,* 453–465.

NOVICK, M. R., & ELLIS, D. D., JR. Equal opportunity in educational and employment selection. *American Psychologist,* 1977, *32,* 306–320.

NOVICK, M. R., & JACKSON, P. H. *Statistical methods for educational and psychological research.* New York: McGraw-Hill, 1974.

NOWLIS, D. P., & KAMIYA, J. The control of electroencephalographic alpha rhythms through auditory feedback and the associated mental activity. *Psychophysiology,* 1970, *6,* 476–485.

NUNNALLY, J. C. *Psychometric theory.* New York: McGraw-Hill, 1968.

O'BRIEN, G. E., & PLOOIJ, D. Comparison of programmed and prose culture training upon attitudes and knowledge. *Journal of Applied Psychology,* 1977, *62,* 499–505.

OCCUPATIONAL SAFETY AND HEALTH ADMINISTRATION (OSHA). Occupational safety and health standards. *Federal Register,* 1971, *36*(105), Part II.

O'CONNOR, E. J., WEXLEY, K. N., & ALEXANDER, R. A. Single-group validity: Fact or fallacy? *Journal of Applied Psychology,* 1975, *60,* 352–355.

OLDHAM, G. R., HACKMAN, J. R., & PEARCE, J. L. Conditions under which employees respond positively to enriched work. *Journal of Applied Psychology,* 1976, *61,* 395–403.

O'LEARY, K. D., & DRABMAN, R. Token reinforcement programs in the classroom. *Psychological Bulletin,* 1971, *75,* 379–398.

O'LEARY, K. D., & O'LEARY, S. G. (Eds.). *Classroom management: The successful use of behavior modification* (2nd ed.). Elmsford, N. Y.: Pergamon, 1977.

OLINGER, L. B. The psychodiagnostician as expert witness. *Journal of Projective Techniques,* 1961, *25,* 81–86.

OLMSTEAD, J. A. *Small-group instruction: Theory and practice.* Alexandria, Va.: Human Resources Research Organization, 1974.

OLMSTEAD, J. A., CLEARY, F. K., LACKEY, L. L., & SALTER, J. A. *Development of leadership assessment simulations.* U. S. Army Research Institute for the Behavioral and Social Sciences, Technical Paper 257, October 1974.

OLSON, P. L., WACHSLER, R. A., & BAUER, H. J. Driver judgments of relative car velocities. *Journal of Applied Psychology.* 1961, *45,* 161–164.

OLSON, W. C. *Child development* (2nd ed.). Boston: Heath, 1959.

On bias in selection. *Journal of Educational Measurement,* 1976, *13*(1). (Special issue)

On-the-spot size-up of package design. *Modern Packaging,* 1973, *46*(9), 24.

OPSAHL, R. L., & DUNNETTE, M. D. The role of financial compensation in industrial motivation. *Psychological Bulletin,* 1966, *66,* 94–118.

ORLINSKY, D. E., & HOWARD, K. I. *Varieties of psychotherapeutic experiences: Multivariate analyses of patients' and therapists' reports.* New York: Teachers College Press, 1975.

ORNE, M. T., THACKRAY, R. I., & PASKEWITZ, D. A. On the detection of deception: A model for the study of physiological effects of psychological stimuli. In N. Greenfield & R. Sternbach (Eds.), *Handbook of psychophysiology.* New York: Holt, Rinehart & Winston, 1972. Pp. 743–785.

OSBORN, A. F. *Applied imagination* (3rd ed.). New York: Scribner, 1963.

OSGOOD, C. E. *An alternative to war or surrender.* Urbana: University of Illinois Press, 1962.

OSGOOD, C. E. The psychologist in international affairs. *American Psychologist,* 1964, *19,* 111–118.

OSGOOD, C. E., SUCI, G. J., & TANNENBAUM, P. H. *The measurement of meaning.* Urbana: University of Illinois Press, 1957.

OSIPOV, S. H. *Theories of career development* (2nd ed.). New York: Appleton-Century-Crofts, 1973.

OWENS, W. A. Background data. In M. D. Dunnette (Ed.), *Handbook of industrial and organizational psychology.* Chicago: Rand McNally, 1976. Ch. 14.

OWENS, W. A., & HENRY, E. R. *Biographical data in industrial psychology: A review and evaluation.* Greensboro, N. C.: Center for Creative Leadership, 1966.

PACE, C. R. Five college environments. *College Board Review,* 1960, *41,* 24–28.

PACE, C. R., & STERN, G. G. An approach to the measurement of psychological characteristics of college environments. *Journal of Educational Psychology,* 1958, *49,* 269–277.

PADILLA, A. M., RUIZ, R. A., & ALVAREZ, R. Community mental health services for the Spanish-speaking/surnamed population. *American Psychologist,* 1975, *30,* 892–905.

PAGE, J. D. *Psychopathology: The science of understanding deviance* (2nd ed.). Chicago: Aldine, 1975.

PAINE, F. T., NASH, A. N., HILLE, S. J., & BRUNNER, G. A. Consumer attitudes toward auto versus public transport alternatives. *Journal of Applied Psychology,* 1969, *53,* 472–480.

PALMER, F. H. The effects of early childhood intervention. In B. Brown (Ed.), *Found: Long-term gains from early intervention.* Boulder, Col.: Westview Press, 1978. Pp. 11–35.

PALMER, M. H., LLOYD, M. E., & LLOYD, K. E. An experimental analysis of electricity conservation procedures. *Journal of Applied Behavior Analysis,* 1977, *10,* 665–671.

PARENT, J., FORWARD, J., CANTER, R., & MOHLING, J. Interactive effects of teaching strategy and personal locus of control on student performance and satisfaction. *Journal of Educational Psychology,* 1975, *67,* 764–769.

PARKER, J. F., JR., & FLEISHMAN, E. A. Use of analytical information concerning task requirements to increase the effectiveness of skill training. *Journal of Applied Psychology,* 1961, *45,* 295–302.

PARKER, R. K. (Ed.). *Conceptualizations of preschool curricula.* Boston: Allyn & Bacon, 1972.

PARKES, C. M. *Bereavement.* New York: International Universities Press, 1972.

PARSONS, F. A. *Choosing a vocation.* Boston: Houghton Mifflin, 1909.

PARSONS, H. M. (Ed.). Environmental design. *Human Factors,* 1972, *14*(5), 369–482. (Special issue) (a)

PARSONS, H. M. *Man-machine system experiments.* Baltimore: Johns Hopkins University Press, 1972. (b)

PARSONS, H. M. What happened at Hawthorne? *Science,* 1974, *183,* 922–932.

PASAMANICK, B. A survey of mental disease in an urban population. VII. An approach to total prevalence by race. *American Journal of Psychiatry,* 1962, *119,* 299–305.

PASAMANICK, B., KNOBLOCH, H., & LILIENFELD, A. M. Socioeconomic status and some precursors of neuropsychiatric disorders. *American Journal of Orthopsychiatry,* 1956, *26,* 594–601.

PASAMANICK, B., SCARPITTI, F. R., & DINITZ, S. *Schizophrenics in the community: An experimental study in the prevention of hospitalization.* New York: Appleton-Century-Crofts, 1967.

PASKEWITZ, D. A. Biofeedback instrumentation: Soldering closed the loop. *American Psychologist,* 1975, *30,* 371–378.

PATERSON, D. G. *Physique and intellect.* New York: Century, 1930.

PATERSON, D. G., & LOFQUIST, L. H. A note on the training of clinical and counseling psychologists. *American Psychologist,* 1960, *15,* 365–366.

PATTERSON, C. H. Predicting success in trade and vocational courses: Review of the literature. *Educational and Psychological Measurement,* 1956, *16,* 352–400.

PATTERSON, C. H. *Theories of counseling and psychotherapy* (2nd ed.). New York: Harper & Row, 1973.

PAUL, B. D., GAWSON, W. A., & KEGELES, S. S. (Eds.). Trigger for community conflict: The case of fluoridation. *Journal of Social Issues,* 1961, *17*(4). (Special issue)

PAUL, G. L. *Insight vs. desensitization in psychotherapy: An experiment in anxiety reduction.* Stanford, Calif.: Stanford University Press, 1966.

PAUL, G. L. A two-year follow-up of systematic desensitization in therapy groups. *Journal of Abnormal Psychology,* 1968, *73,* 119–130.

PAVLOV, I. P. *Lectures on conditioned reflexes* (W. H. Gantt, trans.). New York: International Publishing Company, 1928.

PAYNE, J. E., MERCER, C. D., PAYNE, A., & DAVISON, R. G. *Head Start: A tragicomedy with epilogue.* New York: Behavioral Publications, 1973.

PAYNE, R., & PUGH, D. S. Organizational structure and climate. In M. D. Dunnette (Ed.), *Handbook of industrial and organizational psychology.* Chicago: Rand McNally, 1976. Ch. 26.

PEARL, A., & RIESSMAN, F. *New careers for the poor.* New York: Free Press, 1965.

PEDALINO, E., & GAMBOA, V. U. Behavior modification and absenteeism: Intervention in one industrial setting. *Journal of Applied Psychology*, 1974, *59*, 694–698.

PEDERSEN, P., LONNER, W. J., & DRAGUNS, J. G. (Eds.). *Counseling across cultures*. Honolulu: University Press of Hawaii, 1976.

PERLOFF, R. Consumer analysis. *Annual Review of Psychology*, 1968, *19*, 437–466.

PERLOFF, R., PERLOFF, E., & SUSSNA, E. Program evaluation. *Annual Review of Psychology*, 1976, *27*, 569–594.

PERYAM, D., POLEMIS, B., KAMEN, J., EINDHOVEN, J., & PILGRIM, F. *Food preferences of men in the U. S. armed forces*. Chicago: Armed Forces Food and Container Institute, 1960.

PETERSEN, N. S. *An expected utility model for "optimal" selection*. American College Testing Program, Technical Bulletin No. 24, 1974.

PETERSEN, N. S., & NOVICK, M. R. An evaluation of some models for culture-fair selection. *Journal of Educational Measurement*, 1976, *13*, 3–29.

PETERSON, D. R. *The clinical study of social behavior*. New York: Appleton-Century-Crofts, 1968.

PETERSON, P. L. Interactive effects of student anxiety, achievement orientation, and teacher behavior on student achievement and attitude. *Journal of Educational Psychology*, 1977, *69*, 779–792.

PETERSON, R. A., & JOLIBERT, A. J. P. A cross-national investigation of price and brand as determinants of perceived product quality. *Journal of Applied Psychology*, 1976, *61*, 533–536.

PHILLIPS, L., & DRAGUNS, J. G. Classification of the behavior disorders. *Annual Review of Psychology*, 1971, *22*, 447–482.

PIAGET, J. *The moral development of the child*. Glencoe, Ill.: Free Press, 1932.

PIERCE, C. H., & RISLEY, T. R. Recreation as a reinforcer: Increasing membership and decreasing disruptions in an urban recreation center. *Journal of Applied Behavior Analysis*, 1974, *7*, 403–411.

PIETROFESA, J. J., & SPLETE, H. *Career development: Theory and research*. New York: Grune & Stratton, 1975.

PIGORS, P., & PIGORS, F. *Case method in human relations: The incident process*. New York: McGraw-Hill, 1961.

PINDER, C. C. Statistical accuracy and practical utility in the use of moderator variables. *Journal of Applied Psychology*, 1973, *57*, 214–221.

PITTLUCK, P. *The relation between aggressive fantasy and overt behavior*. Unpublished doctoral dissertation, Yale University, 1950.

PODLESNY, J. A., & RASKIN, D. C. Physiological measures and the detection of deception. *Psychological Bulletin*, 1977, *84*, 782–799.

POFFENBERGER, A. T. *Principles of applied psychology* (2nd ed.). New York: Appleton-Century, 1942.

POLITZ, ALFRED, MEDIA STUDIES. *The Rochester study*. Philadelphia: Curtis, 1960.

PORTER, L. W. Turning work into nonwork: The rewarding environment. In M. D. Dunnette (Ed.), *Work and nonwork in the year 2001*. Monterey, Calif.: Brooks/Cole, 1973. Ch. 7.

PORTER, L. W., & LAWLER, E. E., III. Properties of organization structure in relation to job attitudes and behavior. *Psychological Bulletin*, 1965, *64*, 23–51.

PORTER, L. W., & LAWLER, E. E., III. *Managerial attitudes and performance*. Homewood, Ill.: Irwin, 1968.

PORTER, L. W., LAWLER, E. E., III., & HACKMAN, J. R. *Behavior in organizations*. New York: McGraw-Hill, 1975.

PORTER, L. W., & ROBERTS, K. H. Communication in organizations. In M. D. Dunnette (Ed.), *Handbook of industrial and organizational psychology*. Chicago: Rand McNally, 1976. Ch. 35.

PORTER, L. W., & STEERS, R. M. Organizational, work, and personal factors in employee turnover and absenteeism. *Psychological Bulletin*, 1973, *80*, 151–176.

POSER, E. G. Toward a theory of behavioral prophylaxis. *Journal of Behavior Therapy and Experimental Psychiatry.* 1970, *1*, 39–45.

POULTON, E. C. Searching for newspaper headlines printed in capitals or lower-case letters. *Journal of Applied Psychology,* 1967, *51*, 417–425.

POULTON, E. C. Skimming lists of food ingredients printed in different sizes. *Journal of Applied Psychology,* 1969, *53*, 55–58. (a)

POULTON, E. C. Skimming lists of food ingredients printed in different brightness contrasts. *Journal of Applied Psychology,* 1969, *53*, 498–500. (b)

POULTON, E. C. *Environment and human efficiency.* Springfield, Ill.: Charles C Thomas, 1970.

POULTON, E. C. *Tracking skill and manual control.* New York: Academic Press, 1974.

PRENTICE, N. M., & KELLY, F. J. Intelligence and delinquency: A reconsideration. *Journal of Social Psychology,* 1963, *60*, 327–337.

PRESBREY, F. S. *The history and development of advertising.* Garden City, N. Y.: Doubleday Doran, 1929.

PRESSEY, S. L. Age counseling: Crises, services, potentials. *Journal of Counseling Psychology,* 1973, *20*, 356–360.

PRIEN, E. P. Development of a clerical position description questionnaire. *Personnel Psychology,* 1965, *18*, 91–98.

PRIEN, E. P. Dynamic character of criteria: Organization change. *Journal of Applied Psychology,* 1966, *50*, 501–504.

PRIEN, E. P., & RONAN, W. W. Job analysis: A review of research findings. *Personnel Psychology,* 1971, *24*, 371–396.

PRIEN, R. F., CAFFEY, E. M., & KLETT, C. J. Prophylactic efficacy of lithium carbonate in manic-depressive illness. *Archives of General Psychiatry,* 1973, *28*, 337–341.

PRIMOFF, E. S. Empirical validations of the *J*-coefficient. *Personnel Psychology,* 1959, *12*, 413–418.

PRIMOFF, E. S. *Job element methods. Volume 3: The J-coefficient.* Washington, D. C.: Personnel Research and Development Center, U. S. Civil Service Commission, 1975.

PRITCHARD, R. D. Equity theory: A review and critique. *Organizational Behavior and Human Performance,* 1969, *4*, 176–211.

PRITCHARD, R. D., DUNNETTE, M. D., & JORGENSON, D. O. Effects of perceptions of equity and inequity on worker performance and satisfaction. *Journal of Applied Psychology Monograph,* 1972, *56*, 75–94.

PROSHANSKY, H. M. Environmental psychology and the real world. *American Psychologist,* 1976, *31*, 303–310.

PROSHANSKY, H. M., ITTELSON, W. H., & RIVLIN, L. G. (Eds.). *Environmental psychology: People and their physical settings* (2nd ed.). New York: Holt, Rinehart & Winston, 1976.

Psychology—law, rules, and information. (Handbook 51, Professional Education, University of the State of New York.) Albany, N. Y.: State Education Department, 1967.

PUGH, D. S. Modern organization theory: A psychological and sociological study. *Psychological Bulletin,* 1966, *66*, 235–251.

RACHLIN, S. With liberty and psychosis for all. *Psychiatric Quarterly,* 1974, *48*, 410–420.

RACHLIN, S. The case against closing of state hospitals. In P. I. Ahmed & S. C. Plog (Eds.), *State mental hospitals.* New York: Plenum, 1976. Pp. 31–44.

RACHLIN, S., PAM, A., & MILTON, J. Civil liberties versus involuntary hospitalization. *American Journal of Psychiatry,* 1975, *132*, 189–192.

RACHMAN, S. Studies in desensitization. I. Separate effects of relaxation and desensitization. *Behaviour Research and Therapy,* 1965, *3*, 245–252.

RADLOFF, R., & HELMREICH, R. *Groups under stress: Psychological research in Sealab II.* New York: Appleton-Century-Crofts, 1968.

RAIMY, V. C. (Ed.). *Training in clinical psychology* (Boulder Conference). New York: Prentice-Hall, 1950.

RAMIREZ, M., & CASTAÑEDA, A. *Cultural democracy, biocognitive development, and education.* New York: Academic Press, 1974.

RAPOPORT, R. N. *Community as doctor: New perspectives on a therapeutic community.* Springfield, Ill.: Charles C Thomas, 1961.

RAPPAPORT, J., CHINSKY, J. M., & COWEN, E. L. *Innovations in helping chronic patients: College students in a mental hospital.* New York: Academic Press, 1971.

RASMUSSEN, J. E. (Ed.). *Man in isolation and confinement.* Chicago: Aldine, 1973.

RAVEN, J. C. *Guide to using Progressive Matrices.* London: Lewis, 1956. (U. S. distributor, Psychological Corporation.)

RAY, M. L., & WILKIE, W. L. Fear: The potential of an appeal neglected by marketing. *Journal of Marketing,* 1970, *34*(1), 54–62.

REBER, A. S., & SCARBOROUGH, D. L. (Eds.). *Toward a psychology of reading: The proceedings of the CUNY conference.* Hillsdale, N.J.: Erlbaum, 1977.

REID, D. H., LUYBEN, P. L., RAWERS, R. J., & BAILY, J. S. Newspaper recycling behavior: The effects of prompting and proximity of containers. *Environment and Behavior,* 1976, *8,* 471–482.

REILLY, R. R. A note on minority group test bias studies. *Psychological Bulletin,* 1973, *80,* 130–132.

REISER, M. *The police department psychologist.* Springfield, Ill.: Charles C Thomas, 1972.

REITAN, R. M. Neurological and physiological bases of psychopathology. *Annual Review of Psychology,* 1976, *27,* 189–216.

Report of the National Advisory Commission on Civil Disorders. New York: Bantam Books, 1968.

REPUCCI, N. D., & SAUNDERS, J. T. Social psychology of behavior modification: Problems of implementation in natural settings. *American Psychologist,* 1974, *29,* 649–660.

RESNICK, L. B., WANG, M. C., & ROSNER, J. Adaptive education for young children: The primary education project. In M. C. Day & R. K. Parker (Eds.), *The preschool in action: Exploring early childhood programs.* Boston: Allyn & Bacon, 1977. Pp. 220–251.

RETTIG, S. Status and job satisfaction of the professional: A factor analysis. *Psychological Reports,* 1960, *6,* 411–413.

RETTIG, S., JACOBSON, F. N., & PASAMANICK, B. *The motivational pattern of the mental health professional.* Washington, D. C.: American Psychiatric Association, 1958.

RHETTS, J. E. Task, learner, and treatment variables in instructional design. *Journal of Educational Psychology,* 1974, *66,* 339–347.

RIBES-INESTA, E., & BANDURA, A. (Eds.). *Analysis of delinquency and aggression.* Hillsdale, N.J.: Erlbaum, 1976.

RICE, G. P. The psychologist as expert witness. *American Psychologist,* 1961, *16,* 691–692.

RICE, S. A. Contagious bias in the interview. *American Journal of Sociology,* 1929, *35,* 420–423.

RICH, A. R., & SCHROEDER, H. E. Research issues in assertiveness training. *Psychological Bulletin,* 1976, *83,* 1081–1096.

RICKS, D. F., & BERRY, J. C. Family and symptom patterns that precede schizophrenia. In M. Roff & D. F. Ricks (Eds.), *Life history research in psychopathology* (Vol. 1). Minneapolis: University of Minnesota Press, 1970. Pp. 31–50.

RICKS, D. F., THOMAS, A., & ROFF, M. (Eds.). *Life history research in psychopathology* (Vol. 3). Minneapolis: University of Minnesota Press, 1974.

RIDDLE, M., & ROBERTS, A. H. Delinquency, delay of gratification, recidivism, and the Porteus Maze Tests. *Psychological Bulletin,* 1977, *84,* 417–425.

RIESSMAN, F. The "helper" therapy principle. In B. G. Guerney, Jr. (Ed.), *Psychotherapeutic agents: New roles for nonprofessionals, parents, and teachers.* New York: Holt, Rinehart & Winston, 1969. Pp. 87–95.

RIMALDI, H. J. A. The test of diagnostic skills, *Journal of Medical Education,* 1961, *36,* 73–79.

RIMM, D. C., & MASTERS, J. C. *Behavior therapy: Techniques and empirical findings.* New York: Academic Press, 1974.

RINDE, E., & ROKKAN, S. Toward an international program of research on handling of conflicts: Introduction. *Journal of Conflict Resolution,* 1959, *3,* 1–5.

RIOCH, M. J. et al. National Institute of Mental Health pilot study in training mental health counselors. *American Journal of Orthopsychiatry,* 1963, *33,* 678–689.

ROBINSON, D. D. Prediction of clerical turnover in banks by means of a weighted application blank. *Journal of Applied Psychology,* 1972, *56,* 282.

ROBINSON, D. N. Harm, offense, and nuisance. Some first steps in the establishment of an ethics of treatment. *American Psychologist,* 1974, *29,* 233–238.

ROBINSON, E. S. *Law and the lawyers.* New York: Macmillan, 1935.

ROBINSON, I. M., BAER, W. C., BANERJEE, T. K., & FLASCHBART, P. G. Trade-off games. In W. Michelson (Ed.), *Behavioral research methods in environmental design.* Stroudsburg, Pa.: Dowden, Hutchinson, & Ross, 1975. Pp. 79–118.

ROBINSON, J. P., ATHANASIOU, R., & HEAD, K. B. *Measures of occupational attitudes and occupational characteristics.* Ann Arbor, Mich.: Institute for Social Research, 1969.

ROBINSON, N. M., & ROBINSON, H. B. *The mentally retarded child* (2nd ed.). New York: McGraw-Hill, 1976.

A robot redesigns Vicks. *Modern Packaging,* March 1961, *34*(7), 90–91.

RODNICK, E. H., & HOCH, E. L. . . . and justice for all. *American Psychologist,* 1961, *16,* 718–719.

ROE, A. A psychological study of eminent biologists. *Psychological Monographs,* 1951, *65*(14, Whole No. 331). (a)

ROE, A. A psychological study of physical scientists. *Genetic Psychology Monographs,* 1951, *43,* 121–135. (b)

ROE, A. *The psychology of occupations.* New York: Wiley, 1956.

ROE, A., GUSTAD, J. W., MOORE, B. V., ROSS, S., & SKODAK, M. (Eds.). *Graduate education in psychology* (Miami Conference). Washington, D. C.: American Psychological Association, 1959.

ROEBUCK, J. A., JR., KROEMER, K. H. E., & THOMSON, W. G. *Engineering anthropometry methods.* New York: Wiley, 1975.

ROEN, S. R. Evaluative research and community mental health. In A. E. Bergin & S. L. Garfield (Eds.), *Handbook of psychotherapy and behavior change: An empirical analysis.* New York: Wiley, 1971, Ch. 20.

ROETHLISBERGER, F. J., & DICKSON, W. J. *Management and the worker.* Cambridge, Mass.: Harvard University Press, 1939.

ROFF, M., & RICKS, D. F. (Eds.). *Life history research in psychopathology* (Vol. 1). Minneapolis: University of Minnesota Press, 1970.

ROFF, M., ROBINS, L. N., & POLLACK, M. (Eds.). *Life history research in psychopathology* (Vol. 2). Minneapolis: University of Minnesota Press, 1972.

ROGERS, C. R. *Counseling and psychotherapy: Newer concepts in practice.* Boston: Houghton Mifflin, 1942.

ROGERS, C. R. *Client-centered therapy: Its current practice, implications, and theory.* Boston: Houghton Mifflin, 1951.

ROGERS, C. R. *On becoming a person: A therapist's view of psychotherapy.* Boston: Houghton Mifflin, 1961.

ROGERS, C. R., & DYMOND, R. F. (Eds.). *Psychotherapy and personality change.* Chicago: University of Chicago Press, 1954.

ROGERS, C. R., & ROETHLISBERGER, F. J. Barriers and gateways to communication. *Harvard Business Review,* 1952, *30*(4), 46–52.

ROHMERT, W. (Ed.). An international symposium on objective assessment of work load in air traffic control tasks. *Ergonomics,* 1971, *14*(5), 545–672. (Special issue)

RONAN, W. W., LATHAM, G. P., & KINNE, S. B., III. Effects of goal setting and supervision on worker behavior in an industrial situation. *Journal of Applied Psychology,* 1973, *58,* 302–307.

RONAN, W. W., & PRIEN, E. P. *Toward a criterion theory: A review and analysis of research and opinion.* Greensboro, N. C.: Center for Creative Leadership, 1966.

ROSCOE, S. N. Airborne displays for flight and navigation. *Human Factors,* 1968, *10,* 321–332.

ROSEN, G. M. The development of nonprescription behavior therapies. *American Psychologist,* 1976, *31,* 139–141.

ROSEN, S. D., WEISS, D. J., HENDEL, D. D., DAWIS, R. V., & LOFQUIST, L. H. *Occupational reinforcer patterns* (Vol. 2) (Minnesota Studies in Vocational Rehabilitation: XXIX). Minneapolis: University of Minnesota, Work Adjustment Project, 1972.

ROSENFELD, M., & THORNTON, R. F. *The development and validation of a multijurisdictional police examination.* Gaithersburg, Md., & Chicago: International Association of Chiefs of Police and International Personnel Management Association, 1976.

ROSENTHAL, D. *Genetics of psychopathology.* New York: McGraw-Hill, 1971.

ROSSI, R. J., BARTLETT, W. B., CAMPBELL, E. A., WISE, L. L., & MCLAUGHLIN, D. H. *Using the TALENT profiles in counseling: A supplement to the career data book.* Palo Alto, Calif.: American Institutes for Research, 1975.

ROTTER, J. B. Generalized expectancy for internal versus external control of reinforcement. *Psychological Monographs,* 1966, *80*(1, Whole No. 609).

ROURKE, B. P. Brain-behavior relationships in children with learning disabilities: A research program. *American Psychologist,* 1975, *30,* 911–920.

ROWLAND, K. F. Environmental events predicting death for the elderly. *Psychological Bulletin,* 1977, *84,* 349–372.

ROZELLE, R. M., & CAMPBELL, D. T. More plausible rival hypotheses in the cross-lagged panel correlation technique. *Psychological Bulletin,* 1969, *71,* 74–80.

RUBIN, J. Z., & BROWN, B. R. *The social psychology of bargaining and negotiation.* New York: Academic Press, 1975.

RUBIN, Z., & MITCHELL, C. Couples research as couples counseling: Some unintended effects of studying close relationships. *American Psychologist,* 1976, *31,* 17–25.

RUBINSTEIN, E. A., & PARLOFF, M. B. (Eds.). *Research in psychotherapy.* Washington, D. C.: American Psychological Association, 1959.

RUCH, W. W. *A re-analysis of published differential validity studies.* Paper presented at the meeting of the American Psychological Association, Honolulu, September 1972.

RUDOLPH, H. J. *Attention and interest factors in advertising.* New York: Funk & Wagnalls (in assoc. with Printers' Ink Publ. Co.), 1947.

RUNYON, K. E. Some interactions between personality variables and management styles. *Journal of Applied Psychology,* 1973, *57,* 288–294.

RUSSELL, R. W. Can psychologists contribute? In G. S. Nielsen (Ed.), *Psychology and international affairs: Can we contribute?* Copenhagen: Munksgaard, 1962. Pp. 48–58.

RYAN, B. A. *PSI—Keller's Personalized System of Instruction: An appraisal.* Washington, D. C.: American Psychological Association, 1974.

RYAN, T. A., & KRUMBOLTZ, J. D. Effect of planned reinforcement counseling on client decision-making behavior. *Journal of Counseling Psychology,* 1964, *11,* 315–323.

RYTERBRAND, E. C., & BARRETT, G. V. Managers' values and their relationship to the management of tasks: A cross-cultural comparison. In B. M. Bass, R. C. Cooper, & J. A. Haas (Eds.), *Managing for accomplishment.* Lexington, Mass.: Heath, 1970. Pp. 226–260.

SAKS, M. J. *Jury verdicts: The role of group size and social decision rule.* Lexington, Mass.: Lexington Books, 1977.

SALIPANTE, P., JR., & GOODMAN, P. Training, counseling, and retention of the hard-core unemployed. *Journal of Applied Psychology,* 1976, *61,* 1–11.

SAMPSON, H. *A history of advertising from the earliest times.* London: Chatto & Windus, 1875.

SANDS, W. A. A method for evaluating alternative recruiting-selection strategies: The CAPER model. *Journal of Applied Psychology,* 1973, *57,* 222–227.

SARASON, I. G., GLASER, E. M., & FARGO, G. A. *Reinforcing productive classroom behavior: A teacher's guide to behavior modification.* New York: Behavioral Publications, 1972.

SARASON, S. B. *The culture of the school and the problem of change.* Boston: Allyn & Bacon, 1971.

SARBIN, T. R., TAFT, R., & BAILEY, D. E. *Clinical inference and cognitive theory.* New York: Holt, Rinehart & Winston, 1960.

SARETSKY, G. The OEO P.C. experiment and the John Henry Effect. *Phi Delta Kappan,* 1972, *53,* 579–581.

SARGENT, J. D., WALTERS, E. D., & GREEN, E. E. Psychosomatic self-regulation of migraine headache. In R. C. Katz & S. Zlutnick (Eds.), *Behavior therapy and health care: Principles and applications.* New York: Pergamon, 1975. Pp. 385–402.

SAUNDERS, D. R. Moderator variables in prediction. *Educational and Psychological Measurement,* 1956, *16,* 209–222.

SAWREY, W. L. Conditioned responses of fear in relation to ulceration. *Journal of Comparative and Physiological Psychology,* 1961, *54,* 347–348.

SAWYER, J. Measurement *and* prediction, clinical *and* statistical. *Psychological Bulletin,* 1966, *66,* 178–200.

SAYRE, J. L., & KNIGHTLY, J. J. (Eds.). *The personalized system of instruction in higher education: Readings on PSI—the Keller plan.* Enid, Okla.: Seminary Press, 1972.

SCHACHT, T., & NATHAN, P. E. But is it good for the psychologists? Appraisal and status of DSM-III. *American Psychologist,* 1977, *32,* 1017–1025.

SCHACHTER, S., WILLERMAN, B., FESTINGER, L., & HYMAN, R. Emotional disruption and industrial productivity. *Journal of Applied Psychology,* 1961, *45,* 201–213.

SCHAFFER, R. H. Job satisfaction as related to need satisfaction in work. *Psychological Monographs,* 1953, *67*(14, Whole No. 364).

SCHAIE, K. W., & GRIBBIN, K. Adult development and aging. *Annual Review of Psychology,* 1975, *26,* 65–96.

SCHALOCK, H. D. (Ed.). *Closing the knowledge gap: CBTE programs as a focus and context for research in education.* Syracuse, N. Y.: National Dissemination Center for Performance-Based Education, Syracuse University, 1975.

SCHAPPE, R. H. Motion element synthesis: An assessment. *Perceptual and Motor Skills,* 1965, *20,* 103–106.

SCHEIN, V. E., MAURER, E. H., & NOVAK, J. F. Impact of flexible working hours on productivity. *Journal of Applied Psychology,* 1977, *62,* 463–465.

SCHLOSSBERG, H. *Psychologist with a gun.* New York: Coward, McCann, & Geoghegan, 1974.

SCHMIDT, D. E., GOLDMAN, R. D., & FEIMER, N. R. Physical and psychological factors associated with perceptions of crowding: An analysis of subcultural differences. *Journal of Applied Psychology,* 1976, *61,* 279–289.

SCHMIDT, F. L., BERNER, J. G., & HUNTER, J. E. Racial differences in validity of employment tests: Reality or illusion? *Journal of Applied Psychology,* 1973, *58,* 5–9.

SCHMIDT, F. L., & HUNTER, J. E. Racial and ethnic bias in psychological tests: Divergent implications of two definitions of test bias. *American Psychologist,* 1974, *29,* 1–8.

SCHMIDT, F. L., & HUNTER, J. E. Development of a general solution to the problem of validity generalization. *Journal of Applied Psychology,* 1977, *62,* 529–540. (a)

SCHMIDT, F. L., & HUNTER, J. E. *Development and test of a general solution to the problem of validity generalization.* Paper presented at the meeting of the American Psychological Association, San Francisco, August, 1977. (b)

SCHMIDT, F. L., HUNTER, J. E., & URRY, V. W. Statistical power in criterion-related validation studies. *Journal of Applied Psychology,* 1976, *61,* 473–485.

SCHMIDT, F. L., & TIFFIN, J. Distortion of drivers' estimates of automobile speed as a function of speed adaptation. *Journal of Applied Psychology,* 1969, *53,* 536–539.

SCHMUCKLER, E. *Age differences in biographical inventories: A factor analytic study.* Greensboro, N. C.: Center for Creative Leadership, 1966.

SCHNEIDER, D. E., & BAYROFF, A. G. The relationship between rater characteristics and validity of ratings. *Journal of Applied Psychology,* 1953, *37,* 278–280.

SCHOENFELDT, L. F. Utilization of manpower: Development and evaluation of an assessment-classification model for matching individuals with jobs. *Journal of Applied Psychology,* 1974, *59,* 583–595.

SCHREIBER, F. R. *Sybil.* Chicago: Regnery, 1973.

SCHULTZ, D. P. *Sensory restriction: Effects on behavior.* New York: Academic Press, 1965.

SCHUTZ, H. G. A food action rating scale for measuring food acceptance. *Journal of Food Science,* 1965, *30,* 365–374.

SCHUTZ, H. G., & KAMENETSKY, J. Response set in measurement of food preference. *Journal of Applied Psychology,* 1958, *42,* 175–177.

SCHWAB, D. P., & CUMMINGS, L. L. Theories of performance and satisfaction: A review. In R. M. Steers & L. W. Porter (Eds.), *Motivation and work behavior.* New York: McGraw-Hill, 1975. Pp. 223–241.

SCHWARTZ, G. E. Biofeedback as therapy: Some theoretical and practical issues. *American Psychologist,* 1973, *28,* 666–673.

SCHWARTZ, G. E., & BEATTY, J. (Eds.). *Biofeedback: Theory and research.* New York: Academic Press, 1977.

SCHWARTZ, L. L. *Educational psychology: Focus on the learner.* Boston: Holbrook, 1972.

SCHWITZGEBEL, R. L., & RUGH, J. D. Of bread, circuses, and alpha machines. *American Psychologist,* 1975, *30,* 362–370.

SCOTT, J. P. *Aggression* (2nd ed.). Chicago: University of Chicago Press, 1975.

SCOTT, R. W., BLANCHARD, E. B., EDMUNSON, E. D., & YOUNG, L. D. A shaping procedure for heart-rate control in chronic tachycardia. *Perceptual and Motor Skills,* 1973, *37,* 327–338.

SCOTT, W. D. *Psychology of advertising.* Boston: Small, Maynard, 1908.

SCRIVEN, M. The methodology of evaluation. In R. W. Tyler, R. M. Gagné, & M. Scriven (Eds.), *Perspectives of curriculum evaluation.* Chicago: Rand McNally, 1967.

SEASHORE, S. E., & BOWERS, D. G. Durability of organizational change. *American Psychologist,* 1970, *25,* 227–233.

SEASHORE, S. E., INDIK, B. P., & GEORGOPOULOS, B. S. Relationships among criteria of job performance. *Journal of Applied Psychology,* 1960, *44,* 195–202.

SEAVER, W. B., & PATTERSON, A. H. Decreasing fuel oil consumption through feedback and social commendation. *Journal of Applied Behavior Analysis,* 1976, *9,* 147–152.

SECORD, P. F., & MUTHARD, J. E. Personality in faces. IV. A descriptive analysis of the perception of women's faces and the identification of some physiognomic determinants. *Journal of Psychology,* 1955, *39,* 269–278.

SECUNDA, S. K. et al. *The depressive disorders: Special report,* 1973 (DHEW Publication No. HSM 73-9157). Washington, D. C.: U. S. Government Printing Office, 1973.

SEEMAN, J. A study of the process of non-directive therapy. *Journal of Consulting Psychology,* 1949, *13,* 157–168.

SEGAL, J. (Ed.). *Research in the service of mental health: Report of the task force of the National Institute of Mental Health.* Rockville, Md.: National Institute of Mental Health, 1975.

SEIDEL, R. J., & RUBIN, M. (Eds.). *Computers and communication: Implications for education.* New York: Academic Press, 1977.

Self-instructional materials and devices. *American Psychologist,* 1961, *16,* 512.

SELIGMAN, C., & DARLEY, J. M. Feedback as a means of decreasing residential energy consumption. *Journal of Applied Psychology,* 1977, *62,* 363–368.

SELIGMAN, M. E. P. *Helplessness: On depression, development, and death.* San Francisco: Freeman, 1975.

SELLS, S. B., & BERRY, C. A. (Eds.). *Human factors in jet and space travel: A medical psychological analysis.* New York: Ronald, 1961.

SELYE, H. The general adaptation syndrome and the diseases of adaptation. *Journal of Clinical Endocrinology,* 1946, *6,* 117–230.

SELYE, H. The evolution of the stress concept. *American Scientist,* 1973, *61,* 692–699.

SEXTON, R., & STAUDT, V. Business communication: A survey of the literature. *Journal of Social Psychology,* 1959, *50,* 101–118. (a)

SEXTON, R., & STAUDT, V. The communication clinic: A proposed solution to the business communication problem. *Journal of General Psychology,* 1959, *60,* 57–62. (b)

SHACHTER, S. Some extraordinary facts about obese humans and rats. *American Psychologist,* 1971, *26,* 129–144.

SHAFFER, L. F., & SHOBEN, E. J., JR. *The psychology of adjustment: A dynamic and experimental approach to personality and mental hygiene* (2nd ed.). Boston: Houghton Mifflin, 1956.

SHAH, S. A. The criminal justice system. In S. E. Golann & C. Eisdorfer (Eds.), *Handbook of community mental health.* New York: Appleton-Century-Crofts, 1972. Pp. 73–105.

SHAH, S. A. Dangerousness: A paradigm for exploring some issues in law and psychology. *American Psychologist,* 1978, *33,* 224–238.

SHAPIRA, Z., & BASS, B. M. Settling strikes in real life and simulations in North America and different regions of Europe. *Journal of Applied Psychology,* 1975, *60,* 466–471.

SHAPIRO, A. K. A contribution to a history of the placebo effect. *Behavioral Science,* 1960, *5,* 109–135.

SHAPIRO, D. H., JR., & ZIFFERBLATT, S. M. Zen meditation and behavioral self-control: Similarities, differences, and clinical applications. *American Psychologist,* 1976, *31,* 519–532.

SHAW, M. E., & WRIGHT, J. M. *Scales for the measurement of attitudes.* New York: McGraw-Hill, 1967.

SHAW, W. A., & KLINE, L. H. A study of muscle action potentials during the attempted solution by children of problems of increasing difficulty. *Journal of Experimental Psychology,* 1947, *37,* 146–158.

SHELDON, W. H., & STEVENS, S. S. *The varieties of temperament.* New York: Harper, 1942.

SHEPARD, H. A. The psychologist's role in union-management relations. *Personnel Psychology,* 1961, *14,* 270–279.

SHERIF, M. *Intergroup conflict and cooperation: The Robbers Cave Experiment.* Norman, Okla.: University Book Exchange, 1961.

SHERMAN, A. W., JR. The image of psychology: Some implications for teaching. *American Psychologist,* 1960, *15,* 465.

SHERRICK, C. E. The art of tactile communication. *American Psychologist,* 1975, *30,* 353–360.

SHETH, J. N., & ROSCOE, A. M., JR. Impact of questionnaire length, follow-up methods, and geographical location on response rate to a mail survey. *Journal of Applied Psychology,* 1975, *60,* 252–254.

SHETH, J. N., & WRIGHT, P. L. (Eds.). *Marketing analysis for societal problems.* Urbana-Champaign: University of Illinois Press, 1974.

SHIMBERG, B. Continuing education and licensing. In D. W. Vermilye (Ed.), *Relating work and education: Current issues in higher education.* San Francisco: Jossey-Bass, 1977. Pp. 154–166.

SHIMBERG, B., & KATZ, M. R. Evaluation of a guidance text. *Personnel and Guidance Journal,* 1962, *41,* 126–132.

SHLIEN, J. M. (Ed.). *Research in psychotherapy* (Vol. 3). Washington, D. C.: American Psychological Association, 1968.

SHNEIDMAN, E. S. (Ed.). *Death: Current perspectives.* Palo Alto, Calif.: Mayfield, 1976.

SHNEIDMAN, E. S., & FARBEROW, N. L. The Los Angeles Suicide Prevention Center: A demonstration of public health feasibilities. *American Journal of Public Health,* 1965, *55,* 21–26.

SHOBEN, E. J., JR. Psychotherapy as a problem in learning theory. *Psychological Bulletin,* 1949, *46,* 366–393.

SHOEMAKER, H. A., & HOLT, O. H. Use in industry. In R. Glaser (Ed.), *Teaching machines and programmed learning: II. Data and directions.* Washington, D. C.: National Education Association, 1965.

SHONTZ, F. C. *Research methods in personality.* New York: Appleton-Century-Crofts, 1965.

SHONTZ, F. C. Physical disability and personality. In W. S. Neff (Ed.), *Rehabilitation psychology.* Washington, D. C.: American Psychological Association, 1971. Pp. 33–73.

SHONTZ, F. C. The personal meanings of illness. *Advances in Psychosomatic Medicine,* 1972, *8,* 63–85.

SHONTZ, F. C. *The psychological aspects of physical illness and disability.* New York: Macmillan, 1975.

SHORE, C. W., & MARION, R. *Suitability of using common selection test standards for Negro and white airmen* (AFHRL-TR-72-53). Lackland Air Force Base, Tex.: Personnel Research Division, Air Force Human Resources Laboratory, May 1972.

SHUY, R. W. The medical interview: Problems in communication. *Primary Care,* 1976, *3,* 365–386.

SIDOWSKI, J. B. Psychopathological consequences of induced social helplessness during infancy. In H. D. Kimmel (Ed.), *Experimental psychopathology: Recent research and theory.* New York: Academic Press, 1971. Pp. 231–248.

SILBER, D. E. Controversy concerning the criminal justice system and its implications for the role of mental health workers. *American Psychologist,* 1974, *29,* 239–244.

SILLER, J., & SILVERMAN, S. Studies of the upper-extremity amputee: VII. Psychological factors. *Artificial Limbs,* 1958, *5*(2), 88–116.

SILVERMAN, H. Determinism, choice, responsibility, and the psychologist's role as an expert witness. *American Psychologist,* 1969, *24,* 5–9.

SILVERMAN, L. H. A Q-sort study of the validity of evaluations made from projective techniques. *Psychological Monographs,* 1959, *73*(7, Whole No. 477).

SILVERMAN, R. E. Learning theory applied to training. In C. P. Otto & O. Glaser (Eds.), *The management of training.* Reading, Mass.: Addison-Wesley, 1970, Ch. 8.

SIMKIN, W. E. Positive approaches to labor peace. *Industrial Relations,* 1964, *4,* 37–44.

SIMON, J. R., MEWALDT, S. P., ACOSTA, E., JR., & HU, JING-MEI. Processing auditory information: Interaction of two population stereotypes. *Journal of Applied Psychology,* 1976, *61,* 354–358.

SIMON, R., & MAHAN, L. Quantifying burdens of proof. *Law and Society Review,* 1971, *5,* 319–330.

SIMPSON, C. J., ROSENTHAL, T. L., DANIEL, T. C., & WHITE, G. M. Social-influence variations in evaluating managed and unmanaged forest areas. *Journal of Applied Psychology,* 1976, *61,* 759–763.

SINGER, J. L. (Ed.). *The control of aggression and violence: Cognitive and physiological factors.* New York: Academic Press, 1971.

SINGER, J. L., & OPLER, M. K. Contrasting patterns of fantasy and motility in Irish and Italian schizophrenics. *Journal of Abnormal and Social Psychology,* 1956, *53,* 42–47.

SKELLY, F. R. Interviewer-appearance stereotypes as a possible source of bias. *Journal of Marketing,* 1954, *19,* 74–75.

SKINNER, B. F. *Science and human behavior.* New York: Macmillan, 1953.

SKINNER, B. F. Teaching machines. *Science,* 1958, *128,* 969–977.

SKINNER, B. F. *The technology of teaching.* Englewood Cliffs, N. J.: Prentice-Hall, 1968.

SLEIGHT, R. B. The effect of instrument dial shape on legibility. *Journal of Applied Psychology,* 1948, *32,* 170–188.

SLIVNICK, P., KERR, W., & KOSINAR, W. A study of accidents in 147 factories. *Personnel Psychology,* 1957, *10,* 43–51.

SLOANE, R. B., STAPLES, F. R., CRISTOL, A. H., YORKSTON, N. J., & WHIPPLE, K. *Psychotherapy versus behavior therapy.* Cambridge, Mass.: Harvard University Press, 1975.

SLOTE, A. *Termination: The closing at Baker plant.* Ann Arbor, Mich.: Institute for Social Research, 1977. (1st published, 1969).

SMALL, L. *The briefer psychotherapies.* New York: Brunner/Mazel, 1971.

SMITH, C. G. (Ed.). *Conflict resolution: Contributions of the behavioral sciences.* Notre Dame, Ind.: University of Notre Dame Press, 1971.

SMITH, D. E. P. *A technology of reading and writing. Vol. 1: Learning to read and write: A task analysis.* New York: Academic Press, 1976.

SMITH, G. H. *Motivation research in advertising and marketing.* New York: McGraw-Hill, 1954.

SMITH, H. C. Music in relation to employee attitudes, piece-work production, and industrial accidents. *Applied Psychology Monographs,* 1947, No. 14.

SMITH, J. O. Criminality and mental retardation. *Training School Bulletin,* 1962, *59,* 74–80.

SMITH, K. U. *Delayed sensory feedback.* Philadelphia: Saunders, 1962.

SMITH, M. B., & HOBBS, N. The community and the community mental health center. *American Psychologist,* 1966, *21,* 499–509.

SMITH, P. B. Controlled studies of the outcome of sensitivity training. *Psychological Bulletin,* 1975, *82,* 597–622.

SMITH, P. C. The prediction of individual differences in susceptibility to industrial monotony. *Journal of Applied Psychology,* 1955, *39,* 322–329.

SMITH, P. C. The development of a method of measuring job satisfaction: The Cornell studies. In E. A. Fleishman & A. R. Bass (Eds.), *Studies in personnel and industrial psychology* (3rd ed.). Homewood, Ill.: Dorsey, 1974. Pp. 272–279.

SMITH, P. C., & KENDALL, L. M. Retranslation of expectations: An approach to the construction of unambiguous anchors for rating scales. *Journal of Applied Psychology,* 1963, *47,* 149–155.

SMITH, P. C., KENDALL, L. M., & HULIN, C. L. *The measurement of satisfaction in work and retirement: A strategy for the study of attitudes.* Chicago: Rand McNally, 1969.

SMITH, W. G. Critical life-events and prevention strategies in mental health. *Archives of General Psychiatry,* 1971, *25,* 103–109.

SMYTH, R. L. *The role of internal diagnostic bias, experience level, socioeconomic class, and antecedent diagnosis in clinical judgment, specifically current diagnosis and the perception of pathology.* Unpublished doctoral dissertation, Fordham University, 1973.

SNIDER, J. G., & OSGOOD, C. E. (Eds.). *Semantic Differential technique: A sourcebook.* Chicago: Aldine, 1969.

SNYDER, C. R., & LARSON, G. R. A further look at student acceptance of general personality interpretations. *Journal of Consulting and Clinical Psychology,* 1972, *38,* 384–388.

SNYDER, W. U. *Casebook of non-directive counseling.* Boston: Houghton Mifflin, 1947.

SNYDER, W. U. *The psychotherapy relationship.* New York: Macmillan, 1961.

SOLOMON, D., & KENDALL, A. J. Individual characteristics and children's performance in "open" and "traditional" classroom settings. *Journal of Educational Psychology,* 1976, *68,* 613–625.

SOLOMON, L. N. The Committee on Psychology in National and International Affairs. *American Psychologist,* 1964, *19,* 105–110.

SOLOMON, P., LEIDERMAN, P. H., MENDELSON, J., & WEXLER, D. *Sensory deprivation: A review.* *American Journal of Psychiatry,* 1957, *114,* 357–363.

SOMMER, R. The new look on the witness stand. *Canadian Psychologist,* 1959, *8*(4), 94–100.

SOMMER, R. Hawthorne dogma. *Psychological Bulletin,* 1968, *70,* 592–595.

SOUDER, J. J., CLARK, W. E., ELKIND, J. I., & BROWN, M. B. *Planning for hospitals: A systems approach using computer-aided techniques.* Chicago: American Hospital Association, 1964.

SPARKS, D. L., & TUCKER, W. T. A multivariate analysis of personality and product use. *Journal of Marketing Research,* 1971, *8,* 67–70.

SPENCE, H. E., & MOINPOUR, R. Fear appeals in marketing—a social perspective. *Journal of Marketing,* 1972, *36*(3), 39–43.

SPIEGEL, J. P., & LEVIN, M. A. Social violence and aggression. In A. M. Freedman, H. I. Kaplan, & B. J. Sadock (Eds.), *Comprehensive textbook of psychiatry—II* (Vol. 2). Baltimore: Williams & Wilkins, 1975. Pp. 2479–2484.

SPIELBERGER, C. D., WEITZ, H., & DENNY, J. P. Group counseling and the academic performance of anxious college freshmen. *Journal of Counseling Psychology,* 1962, *9,* 195–204.

SPITZER, R. L., & ENDICOTT, J. An integrated group of forms for automated psychiatric case records. *Archives of General Psychiatry,* 1971, *24,* 540–547.

SQUIRES, P. C. *The shape of the normal work area.* USN Bureau of Medicine and Surgery, Medical Research Laboratory, Report No. 275, 1956.

SROLE, L., & FISCHER, A. K. (Eds.). *Mental health in the metropolis: The Midtown Manhattan study* (Rev. ed.). New York: Harper & Row, 1975.

SROLE, L., LANGNER, T. S., MICHAEL, S. T., OPLER, M. K., & RENNIE, T. A. C. *Mental health in the metropolis: The Midtown Manhattan study.* New York: McGraw-Hill, 1962.

STABENAU, J. R., & POLLIN, W. Experiential differences for schizophrenics as compared with their nonschizophrenic siblings: Twin and family studies. In M. Roff & D. F. Ricks (Eds.), *Life history research in psychopathology,* Minneapolis: University of Minnesota Press, 1970. Pp. 94–126.

STAGNER, R. The gullibility of personnel managers. *Personnel Psychology,* 1958, *11,* 347–352.

STAGNER, R. *Psychological aspects of international conflict.* Belmont, Calif.: Wadsworth, 1967.

STAGNER, R., & ROSEN, H. *Psychology of union-management relations.* Belmont, Calif.: Wadsworth, 1965.

Standards for educational and psychological tests. Washington, D. C.: American Psychological Association, 1974.

STANLEY, J. C. (Ed.). *Preschool programs for the disadvantaged: Five experimental approaches to early education.* Baltimore: Johns Hopkins University Press, 1972.

STANLEY, J. C. (Ed.). *Compensatory education for children, ages two to eight.* Baltimore: Johns Hopkins University Press, 1973.

STANLEY, J. C., & HOPKINS, K. D. *Educational and psychological measurement and evaluation.* Englewood Cliffs, N. J.: Prentice-Hall, 1972.

STANLEY, T. J., & SEWALL, M. A. Image inputs to a probabilistic model: Predicting retail potential. *Journal of Marketing,* 1976, *40*(3), 44–83.

STARCH, D. *An analysis of 5,000,000 inquiries.* New York: Daniel Starch and Staff, 1930.

STARCH, D. Why readership of ads has increased 24%. *Advertising and Selling,* 1946, *39*(8), pp. 47; 154.

STARCH, D. How do size and color of advertisements affect readership? *Starch Tested Copy,* 1956, No. 74.

STARCH, D. Readership and size of advertisement. *Starch Tested Copy,* 1957, No. 82.

STARCH, D. *An analysis of 12 million inquiries.* Evanston, Ill.: Media/Scope, 1959.

STARCH, D. How does repetition of advertisements affect readership? *Starch Tested Copy,* 1960, No. 89, Pt. 1. (a)

STARCH, D. Should outdoor posters be repeated? *Starch Tested Copy,* 1960, No. 89, Pt. 2 (b)

STARCH, D. Do inside positions differ in readership? *Starch Tested Copy,* 1961, No. 94. (a)

STARCH, D. *Measuring product sales made by advertising.* Mamaroneck, N. Y.: Daniel Starch and Staff, 1961. (b)

STARCH, D. *Measuring advertising readership and results.* New York: McGraw-Hill, 1966.

STARCH, D., & STAFF. Is preferred position worth it? *Starch Tested Copy,* 1961, No. 94.

STARK, E. *Of acceptable risk: Science and the determination of safety.* Los Altos, Calif.: Kaufmann, 1976.

STARR, B. J., & KATKIN, E. S. The clinician as aberrant actuary: Illusory correlation and the Incomplete Sentences Blank. *Journal of Abnormal Psychology,* 1969, *74,* 670–675.

STAUDT, V. M., & ZUBIN, J. A biometric evaluation of the somatotherapies in schizophrenia. *Psychological Bulletin,* 1957, *54,* 171–196.

STEERS, R. M., & PORTER, L. W. The role of task-goal attributes in employee performance. *Psychological Bulletin,* 1974, *81,* 434–452.

STEERS, R. M., & PORTER, L. W. *Motivation and work behavior.* New York: McGraw-Hill, 1975.

STEFFLRE, B. Function of theory in counseling. In B. Stefflre & W. H. Grant (Eds.), *Theories of counseling* (2nd ed.). New York: McGraw-Hill, 1972.

STEIDL, R. E. Difficulty factors in homemaking tasks: Implications for environmental design. *Human Factors,* 1972, *14,* 471–482.

STEIN, A., KAUFMAN, M. R., JANOWITZ, H. D., LEVY, M. H., HOLLANDER, F., & WINKELSTEIN, A. Changes in hydrochloric acid secretion in a patient with a gastric fistula during intensive psychotherapy. *Psychosomatic Medicine,* 1962, *24,* 427–458.

STEIN, M. I. *Stimulating creativity.* Vol. 1, *Individual procedures.* Vol. 2, *Group procedures.* New York: Academic Press, 1974, 1975.

STEINKAMP, S. W. Some characteristics of effective interviewers. *Journal of Applied Psychology*, 1966, *50*, 487–492.

STEPHENSON, W. *The study of behavior: Q-technique and its methodology.* Chicago: University of Chicago Press, 1953.

STERN, G. C. *People in context: Measuring person-environment congruence in education and industry.* New York: Wiley, 1970.

STERN, W. The psychology of testimony. *Journal of Abnormal and Social Psychology,* 1939, *34*, 3–20.

STERNBACH, R. A. *Pain patients: Traits and treatment.* New York: Academic Press, 1974.

STEWART, N. AGCT scores of army personnel grouped by occupation. *Occupations,* 1947, *26*, 5–41.

STEWART, R. *Managers and their jobs: A study of the similarities and differences in the ways managers spend their time.* London, Macmillan, 1967.

STEWART, R. G. Reported driving speeds and previous accidents. *Journal of Applied Psychology,* 1957, *41*, 293–296.

STICHT, T. G. (Ed.). *Reading for working: A functional literacy anthology.* Alexandria, Va.: Human Resources Research Organization, 1975.

STODGILL, R. M., & COONS, A. E. *Leader behavior: Its description and measurement.* Columbus: Ohio State University, 1957.

STONE, V. A primacy effect in decision-making by jurors. *The Journal of Communication,* 1969, *19*, 239–247.

STONE, W. F. *The psychology of politics.* New York: Free Press, 1974.

STREIB, G. F., & THOMPSON, W. E. (Eds.). Adjustment in retirement. *Journal of Social Issues,* 1958, *14*(2). (Special issue)

STRONG, E. K., JR. *Vocational interests of men and women.* Stanford, Calif.: Stanford University Press, 1943.

STRONG, E. K., JR. *Vocational interests 18 years after college.* Minneapolis: University of Minnesota Press, 1955.

STRUMPEL, B. (Ed.). *Economic means for human needs: Social indicators of well-being and discontent.* Ann Arbor, Mich.: Institute for Social Research, 1976.

STRUPP, H. H., & HADLEY, S. W. A tripartite model of mental health and therapeutic outcomes, with special reference to negative effects of psychotherapy. *American Psychologist,* 1977, *32*, 187–196.

STRUPP, H. H., & LUBORSKY, L. (Eds.). *Research in psychotherapy* (Vol. 2). Washington, D. C.: American Psychological Association, 1962.

STRYKER, P. Is there an executive face? *Fortune,* 1953, *48*, 145–147; 162–168.

STUART, R. B. (Ed.). *Behavioral self-management: Strategies, techniques, and outcomes.* New York: Brunner/Mazel, 1977.

STUART, R. B., & DAVIS, B. *Slim chance in a fat world: Behavioral control of obesity.* Champaign, Ill.: Research Press, 1971.

STUBBINS, J. (Ed.). *Social and psychological aspects of disability: A handbook for practitioners.* Baltimore: University Park Press, 1977.

STUNKARD, A. J. New therapies for the eating disorders: Behavior modification of obesity and anorexia nervosa. *Archives of General Psychiatry,* 1972, *26*, 391–398.

SUDMAN, S. On the accuracy of recording of consumer panels. *Journal of Marketing Research,* 1964, *1*(2), 14–20; (3), 69–83.

SUDMAN, S., & BRADBURN, N. M. *Response effects in surveys: A review and synthesis.* Chicago: Aldine, 1974.

SUINN, R. M., & WEIGEL, R. G. (Eds.). *The innovative psychological therapies: Critical and creative contributions.* New York: Harper & Row, 1975.

SUINN, R. M., & WEIGEL, R. G. (Eds.). *Innovative medical-psychiatric therapies.* Baltimore: University Park Press, 1976.

SUMMERS, G. F. (Ed.). *Attitude measurement.* Chicago: Rand McNally, 1970.

SUNDBERG, C. W., & FERAR, M. Design of rapid transit equipment for the San Francisco Bay Area Rapid Transit System. *Human Factors,* 1966, *8*, 339–346.

SUNDBERG, N. D. The acceptability of "fake" versus "bona fide" personality test interpretations. *Journal of Abnormal and Social Psychology,* 1955, *50,* 145–147.

SUNDBERG, N. D., TYLER, L. E., & TAPLIN, J. R. *Clinical psychology: Expanding horizons* (2nd ed.). Englewood Cliffs, N. J.: Prentice-Hall, 1973.

SUNSHINE, P. M., & DIVESTA, F. J. Effects of density and format on letter discrimination by beginning readers with different learning styles. *Journal of Educational Psychology,* 1976, *68,*.15–19.

SUOMI, S. J., & HARLOW, H. F. Abnormal social behavior in young monkeys. In J. Hellmuth (Ed.), *Exceptional infant: Studies in abnormalities* (Vol. 2). New York: Brunner/Mazel, 1971. Pp. 483–529.

SUOMI, S. J., & HARLOW, H. F. Production and alleviation of depressive behaviors in monkeys. In J. Maser & M. E. P. Seligman (Eds.), *Psychopathology: Experimental models.* San Francisco: Freeman, 1977. Pp. 131–173.

SUPER, D. E. A theory of vocational development. *American Psychologist,* 1953, *8,* 185–190.

SUPER, D. E. *The psychology of careers: An introduction to vocational development.* New York: Harper, 1957.

SUPER, D. E., et al. *Computer-assisted counseling.* New York: Teachers College Press, 1970.

SUPER, D. E., & BOHN, M. J., JR. *Occupational psychology.* Belmont, Calif.: Wadsworth, 1970.

SUPER, D. E., CRITES, J. O., HUMMEL, R. C., MOSER, H. P., OVERSTREET, P. L., & WARNATH, C. *Vocational development: A framework for research.* New York: Teachers College Press, 1957.

SUPER, D. E., KOWALSKI, R. S., & GOTKIN, E. H. *Floundering and trial after high school* (Career Pattern Study, Monograph IV). New York: Teachers College Press, 1967.

SUPER, D. E., & OVERSTREET, P. L. *The vocational maturity of ninth grade boys.* New York: Teachers College Press, 1960.

SUPER, D. E., STARISHEVSKY, R., MATLIN, N., & JORDAAN, J. P. *Career development: Self-concept theory.* New York: College Entrance Examination Board, 1963.

SUPPES, P. Mathematical concept formation in children. *American Psychologist,* 1966, *21,* 139–150.

SUPPES, P., JERMAN, M., & BRIAN, D. *Computer-assisted instruction: Stanford 1965-66 Arithmetic Program.* New York: Academic Press, 1968.

SURVEY RESEARCH CENTER STAFF. *Interviewer's manual, revised edition.* Ann Arbor, Mich.: Institute for Social Research, 1976.

SWAN, J. A. Public response to air pollution. In J. F. Wohlwill & D. H. Carson (Eds.), *Environment and the social sciences: Perspectives and applications.* Washington, D. C.: American Psychological Association, 1972. Pp. 66–74.

SWANSON, C. E. Readability and readership. *Journalism Quarterly,* 1948, *25,* 339–343.

SWANSON, C. E., & FOX, H. G. Validity of readability formulas. *Journal of Applied Psychology,* 1953, *37,* 114–118.

SZASZ, T. S. *The myth of mental illness.* New York: Hoeber-Harper, 1961.

SZASZ, T. S. *Law, liberty, and psychiatry.* New York: Macmillan, 1963.

SZASZ, T. S. *The manufacture of madness: A comparative study of the Inquisition and the mental health movement.* New York: Harper & Row, 1970.

SZASZ, T. S., & HOLLENDER, M. C. A contribution to the philosophy of medicine: The basic models of the doctor-patient relationship. In T. Millon (Ed.), *Medical behavioral science.* Philadelphia: Saunders, 1975. Pp. 432–440.

SZYBILLO, G. J., & JACOBY, J. Intrinsic versus extrinsic cues as determinants of perceived product quality. *Journal of Applied Psychology,* 1974, *59,* 74–78. (a)

SZYBILLO, G. J., & JACOBY, J. Effects of different levels of integration on advertising preference and intention to purchase. *Journal of Applied Psychology,* 1974, *59,* 274–280. (b)

TAFT, R. Multiple methods of personality assessment. *Psychological Bulletin,* 1959, *56,* 333–352.

TALMAGE, H. (Ed.). *Systems of individualized education.* Berkeley, Calif.: McCutchan, 1975.

TANNENBAUM, P. H., JACOBSON, H. K., & NORRIS, E. L. An experimental investigation of typeface connotations. *Journalism Quarterly,* 1964, *41*(1), 65–73.

TAPP, J. L. Psychology and the law: An overture. *Annual Review of Psychology,* 1976, *27,* 359–404.

TAPP, J. L., & LEVINE, F. J. Legal socialization: Strategies for an ethical legality. *Stanford Law Review,* 1974, *27,* 1–72.

TAYLOR, C. L. *Human tolerance for short exposures to heat and humidity.* USAF, Aero Medical Laboratory, Engineering Division, T SEAA-695-56B, Memorandum Report 12, February 1946.

TAYLOR, C. W. (Ed.). *Climate for creativity; Report of the Seventh National Research Conference on Creativity.* New York: Pergamon, 1972.

TAYLOR, C. W., & ELLISON, R. L. Predictors of scientific performance. *Science,* 1967, *155,* 1075–1079.

TAYLOR, D. W., BERRY, P. C., & BLOCK, C. H. Does group participation when using brainstorming facilitate or inhibit creative thinking? *Administrative Science Quarterly,* 1958, *3,* 23–47.

TAYLOR, E. K., & WHERRY, R. J. A study of leniency in two rating systems. *Personnel Psychology,* 1951, *4,* 39–47.

TAYLOR, F. V. Psychology and the design of machines. *American Psychologist,* 1957, *12,* 249–258.

TAYLOR, F. W. *The principles of scientific management.* New York: Harper, 1911.

TAYLOR, H. C., & RUSSELL, J. T. The relationship of validity coefficients to the practical effectiveness of tests in selection: Discussion and tables. *Journal of Applied Psychology,* 1939, *23,* 565–578.

TAYLOR, J. E., MICHAELS, E. R., & BRENNAN, M. F. *The concepts of performance-oriented instruction used in developing the Experimental Volunteer Army Training Program* (HumRRO Tech. Rep. 72-7). Alexandria, Va.: Human Resources Research Organization, March 1972.

TAYLOR, J. E., & STAFF. *Establishing the concepts and techniques of performance-oriented training in army training centers: A summary report.* (HumRRO Tech. Rep. 75–21). Alexandria, Va.: Human Resources Research Organization, June 1975.

Television and growing up: The impact of televised violence. (Report to the Surgeon General, United States Public Health Service.) Washington, D. C.: U. S. Government Printing Office, 1972.

TELFORD, C. W., & SAWREY, J. M. *The exceptional individual: Psychological and educational aspects* (2nd ed.). Englewood Cliffs, N. J.: Prentice-Hall, 1972.

TERMAN, L. M. *Psychological factors in marital happiness.* New York: McGraw-Hill, 1938.

TERMAN, L. M. Scientists and nonscientists in a group of 800 gifted men. *Psychological Monographs,* 1954, *68*(7, Whole No. 378).

TERMAN, L. M., & MERRILL, M. A. *Stanford-Binet Intelligence Scale: 1972 norms edition.* Boston: Houghton Mifflin, 1973.

THARP, R. G. Psychological patterning in marriage. *Psychological Bulletin,* 1963, *60,* 97–117.

THARP, R. G., & WETZEL, R. J. *Behavior modification in the natural environment.* New York: Academic Press, 1969.

THELEN, M. H., VARBLE, D. L., & JOHNSON, J. Attitudes of academic clinical psychologists toward projective techniques. *American Psychologist,* 1968, *23,* 517–521.

THEOLOGUS, G. C., & FLEISHMAN, E. A. *Development of a taxonomy of human performance: Validation study of ability scales for classifying human tasks.* Washington, D. C.: American Institutes for Research, 1971.

THEOLOGUS, G. C., WHEATON, G. R., & FLEISHMAN, E. A. Effects of intermittent, moderate intensity noise stress on human performance. *Journal of Applied Psychology,* 1974, *59,* 539–547.

THIBAUT, J., & WALKER, L. *Procedural justice: A psychological analysis.* Hillsdale, N. J.: Erlbaum, 1975.

THIGPEN, C. H., & CLECKLEY, H. M. *The three faces of Eve.* New York: McGraw-Hill, 1957.

THOMAS, K. Conflict and conflict management. In M. D. Dunnette (Ed.), *Handbook of industrial and organizational psychology.* Chicago: Rand McNally, 1976. Ch. 21.

THOMPSON, A. S., & SUPER, D. E. (Eds.). *The professional preparation of counseling psychologists.* New York: Teachers College Press, 1964.

THORESEN, C. E., & MAHONEY, M. J. *Behavioral self-control.* New York: Holt, Rinehart & Winston, 1974.

THORESEN, C. E., & MEHRENS, W. A. Decision theory and vocational counseling: Important concepts and questions. *Personnel and Guidance Journal,* 1967, *46,* 165–172.

THORNDIKE, E. L., & LORGE, I. *The teacher's word book of 30,000 words.* New York: Columbia University, Teachers College, Bureau of Publications, 1944.

THORNDIKE, R. L. The problems and profits of empirical comparative education. In W. E. Coffman (Ed.), *Frontiers of educational measurement and information systems, 1973.* Boston: Houghton Mifflin, 1973. Pp. 67–81.

THORNDIKE, R. L., & HAGEN, E. *Ten thousand careers.* New York: Wiley, 1959.

THORNTON, G. R. The effect of wearing glasses upon judgments of personality traits of persons seen briefly. *Journal of Applied Psychology,* 1944, *28,* 203–207.

THUMIN, F. J. Identification of cola beverages. *Journal of Applied Psychology,* 1962, *46,* 358–360.

THURSTONE, L. L., & CHAVE, E. J. *The measurement of attitude.* Chicago: University of Chicago Press, 1929.

TICHAUER, E. R. Some aspects of stress on forearm and hand in industry. *Journal of Occupational Medicine,* 1966, *8*(2), 63–71.

TIEDEMAN, D. V., O'HARA, R. P., & BARUCH, R. W. *Career development: Choice and adjustment.* New York: College Entrance Examination Board, 1963.

TIFFIN, J., & WALSH, F. X. Readability of union-management agreements. *Personnel Psychology,* 1951, *4,* 327–337.

TINKER, M. A. Trends in illumination standards. *Illuminating Engineering,* 1948, *43,* 866–881.

TINKER, M. A. Light intensities preferred for reading. *American Journal of Optometry,* 1954, *31,* 55–66.

TINKER, M. A. Brightness contrast, illumination intensity, and visual efficiency. *American Journal and Archives of the Optometric Academy,* 1959, *36,* 221–236.

TINKER, M. A. *Legibility of print.* Ames, Iowa: Iowa State University Press, 1963.

TITTLE, C. K., & ZYTOWSKI, D. G. (Eds.). *Sex-fair interest measurement: Research and implications.* Washington, D. C.: National Institute of Education, 1978.

TOCH, H. (Ed.). *Legal and criminal psychology.* New York: Holt, Rinehart & Winston, 1961.

TOCH, H. *Violent men: An inquiry into the psychology of violence.* Chicago: Aldine, 1969.

TORDY, G. R., EYDE, L. D., PRIMOFF, E. S., & HARDT, R. H. *Job analysis of the position of New York State Trooper: An application of the job element method.* Albany, N. Y.: New York State Police, 1976.

TOSI, H. L., & HAMNER, W. C. (Eds.). *Organizational behavior and management: A contingency approach.* Chicago: St. Clair Press, 1974.

TRAVERS, R. M. W. (Ed.). *Second handbook of research on teaching.* Chicago: Rand McNally, 1973.

TRAXLER, A. J. State certification of school psychologists. *American Psychologist,* 1967, *22,* 660–666.

TRIANDIS, H. C., FELDMAN, J. M., WELDON, D. E., & HARVEY, W. M. Designing preemployment training for the hard to employ: A cross-cultural psychological approach. *Journal of Applied Psychology,* 1974, *59,* 687–693.

TRIST, E. L., & BAMFORTH, V. Some social and psychological consequences of the longwall method of coal-getting. *Human Relations,* 1951, *4,* 3–38.

TROLDAHL, V., & JONES, R. Predictors of newspaper advertising readership. *Journal of Advertising Research,* 1965, *5*(1), 23–27.

TROUTON, D., & EYSENCK, H. J. The effects of drugs on behavior. In H. J. Eysenck (Ed.), *Handbook of abnormal psychology.* New York: Basic Books, 1961. Ch. 17.

TRUAX, C. B. The process of group psychotherapy: Relationships between therapeutic conditions and intrapersonal exploration. *Psychological Monographs,* 1961, *75*(No. 7, Whole No. 511).

TRUAX, C. B., & MITCHELL, K. M. Research on certain therapist interpersonal skills in relation to process and outcome. In A. E. Bergin & S. L. Garfield (Eds.), *Handbook of psychotherapy and behavior change: An empirical analysis.* New York: Wiley, 1971. Ch. 9.

TRYON, W. W. A system of behavioral diagnosis. *Professional Psychology,* 1976, *7,* 495–506.

TULCHIN, S. H. *Intelligence and crime.* Chicago: University of Chicago Press, 1939.

TURNER, C. W. Television and social behavior: Three contrasting perspectives. *Contemporary Psychology,* 1977, *22,* 290–292.

TYLER, L. E. Toward a workable psychology of individuality. *American Psychologist,* 1959, *14,* 75–81.

TYLER, L. E. Minimum change therapy. *Personnel and Guidance Journal,* 1960, *38,* 475–479.

TYLER, L. E. *The work of the counselor* (3rd ed.). New York: Appleton-Century-Crofts, 1969.

TYLER, L. E. *Individuality: Human possibilities and personal choice in the psychological development of men and women.* San Francisco: Jossey-Bass, 1978.

TYLER, R. W., & WOLF, R. M. (Eds.). *Crucial issues in testing.* Berkeley, Calif.: McCutchan, 1974.

TYROLER, H. A., & CASSEL, J. Health consequences of culture change: II. The effect of urbanization on coronary heart mortality in rural residents. *Journal of Chronic Diseases,* 1964, *17*(2), 167–177.

UHLANER, J. E. *Human performance, jobs, and systems psychology—the systems measurement bed.* U. S. Army Behavior and Systems Research Laboratory, Technical Report S-2, October 1970.

UHLANER, J. E. Human performance effectiveness and the systems measurement bed. *Journal of Applied Psychology,* 1972, *56,* 202–210.

UHR, L., & MILLER, J. G. (Eds.). *Drugs and behavior.* New York: Wiley, 1960.

UHRBROCK, R. S. Attitudes of 4430 employees. *Journal of Social Psychology,* 1934, *5,* 365–377.

UHRBROCK, R. S. Music on the job: Its influence on worker morale and productivity. *Personnel Psychology,* 1961, *14,* 9–38. (a)

UHRBROCK, R. S. 2000 scaled items. *Personnel Psychology,* 1961, *14,* 375–420. (b)

ULLMANN, L. P., & KRASNER, L. *A psychological approach to abnormal behavior* (2nd ed.). Englewood Cliffs, N. J.: Prentice-Hall, 1975.

ULRICH, L., & TRUMBO, D. The selection interview since 1949. *Psychological Bulletin,* 1965, *63,* 100–116.

ULRICH, R., STACHNIK, T., & STAINTON, R. Student acceptance of generalized personality interpretations. *Psychological Reports,* 1963, *13,* 831–834.

U. S. BUREAU OF LABOR STATISTICS. *Occupational outlook handbook.* Washington, D. C.: U. S. Government Printing Office, 1976–1977.

U. S. DEPARTMENT OF LABOR, EMPLOYMENT AND TRAINING ADMINISTRATION. *Dictionary of occupational titles* (4th ed.). Washington, D. C.: U. S. Government Printing Office, 1977.

U. S. DEPARTMENT OF LABOR, EMPLOYMENT AND TRAINING ADMINISTRATION. *Guide to occupational exploration.* Washington, D. C.: U. S. Government Printing Office, 1978.

U. S. DEPARTMENT OF LABOR, MANPOWER ADMINISTRATION. *Pretesting orientation exercises (Manual; Test booklet).* Washington, D. C.: U. S. Government Printing Office, 1968.

U. S. DEPARTMENT OF LABOR, MANPOWER ADMINISTRATION. *Manual for the USES General Aptitude Test Battery.* Washington, D. C.: U. S. Government Printing Office, 1970. (a)

U. S. DEPARTMENT OF LABOR, MANPOWER ADMINISTRATION. *Pretesting orientation on the purpose of testing. (Manual; Illustrations).* Washington, D. C.: U.S. Government Printing Office, 1970. (b)

U. S. DEPARTMENT OF LABOR, MANPOWER ADMINISTRATION. *Doing your best on aptitude tests.* Washington, D. C.: U. S. Government Printing Office, 1971. (a)

U. S. DEPARTMENT OF LABOR, MANPOWER ADMINISTRATION. *Doing your best on reading and arithmetic tests.* Washington, D. C.: U. S. Government Printing Office, 1971. (b)

U. S. DEPARTMENT OF LABOR, MANPOWER ADMINISTRATION. *Handbook for analyzing jobs.* Washington, D. C.: U. S. Government Printing Office, 1972.

VALVERDE, H. H. A review of flight simulator transfer of training studies. *Human Factors,* 1973, *15,* 510–523.

VANCE, F. L., & VOLSKY, T. C., JR. Counseling and psychotherapy: Split personality or siamese twins? *American Psychologist,* 1962, *17,* 565–570.

VAN COTT, H. P., & KINKADE, R. G. *Human engineering guide to equipment design* (Rev. ed.). Washington, D. C.: U. S. Government Printing Office, 1972.

VAN ZELST, R. H. The effect of age and experience upon accident rate. *Journal of Applied Psychology,* 1954, *38,* 313–317.

VELASQUEZ, T. *Correlation between altitude and consciousness time in high-altitude natives.* USAF School of Aviation Medicine, Report No. 60-8, 1959.

VERNIER, C. M., BARRELL, R. B., CUMMINGS, J. W., DICKERSON, J. H., & HOOPER, H. E. Psychosocial study of the patient with pulmonary tuberculosis: A cooperative research approach. *Psychological Monographs,* 1961, *75*(6, Whole No. 609).

VERNON, H. M. The speed of adaptation of output to altered hours of work. *Industrial Fatigue Research Board (Great Britain), Report No. 6,* 1920.

VERNON, H. M., & BEDFORD, T. The influence of rest pauses on light industrial work. *Industrial Fatigue Research Board (Great Britain), Report No. 25,* 1924.

VIERNSTEIN, M. C. The extension of Holland's occupational classification to all occupations in the Dictionary of Occupational Titles. *Journal of Vocational Behavior,* 1972, *2,* 107–121.

VROOM, V. H. Some personality determinants of the effects of participation. *Journal of Abnormal and Social Psychology,* 1959, *59,* 322–327.

VROOM, V. H. *Work and motivation.* New York: Wiley, 1964.

WAGNER, N. N., & STEGEMAN, K. L. Psychologists in medical education: 1964. *American Psychologist,* 1964, *19,* 689–690.

WAHL, O. F. Monozygotic twins discordant for schizophrenia: A review. *Psychological Bulletin,* 1976, *83,* 91–106.

WAINWRIGHT, W. H. Cultural attitudes and clinical judgment. *International Journal of Social Psychiatry,* 1958, *4,* 105–107.

WALD, A. *Statistical decision function.* New York: Wiley, 1950.

WALIZER, D. G. The need for standardized scientific criteria for describing drug-using behavior. *International Journal of the Addictions,* 1975, *10,* 927–936.

WALKER, J. E., & SHEA, T. M. *Behavior modification: A practical approach for educators.* St. Louis: Mosby, 1976.

WALKER, L., THIBAUT, J., & ANDREOLI, V. Order of presentation at trial. *Yale Law Journal,* 1972, *82,* 216–226.

WALKER, M. J., & BRODSKY, S. L. (Eds.). *Sexual assault: The victim and the rapist.* Lexington, Mass.: Lexington Books, 1976.

WALLACE, S. R. Criteria for what? *American Psychologist,* 1965, *20,* 411–417.

WALLACH, M. A., KOGAN, N., & BEM, D. J. Diffusion of responsibility and level of risk taking in groups. *Journal of Abnormal and Social Psychology,* 1964, *68,* 263–274.

WALLACH, M. A., & WALLACH, L. *Teaching all children to read.* Chicago: University of Chicago Press, 1976.

WALLIN, J. A., & JOHNSON, R. D. The positive reinforcement approach to controlling employee absenteeism. *Personnel Journal,* 1976, *55,* 390–392.

WANAUS, J. P. Effects of a realistic job preview on job acceptance, job attitudes, and job survival. *Journal of Applied Psychology,* 1973, *58,* 327–332.

WANAUS, J. P. A causal-correlational analysis of the job satisfaction and performance relationship. *Journal of Applied Psychology,* 1974, *59,* 139–144.

WARBURTON, D. M. *Brain, behaviour, and drugs: Introduction to the neurochemistry of behavior.* New York: Wiley, 1976.

WARD, L. M., & SUEDFELD, P. Human responses to highway noise. *Environmental Research,* 1973, *6,* 306–326.

WARD, S., & WACKMAN, D. Children's purchase influence attempts and parental yielding. *Journal of Marketing Research,* 1972, *9,* 316–319.

WARRICK, M. J. Direction of movement in the use of control knobs to position visual indicators. In P. M. Fitts (Ed.), *Psychological research in equipment design* (AAF Aviation Psychology Program, Research Reports, Rep. No. 19). Washington, D. C.: U. S. Government Printing Office, 1947. Pp. 137–146.

WARWICK, D. P., & LININGER, C. A. *The sample survey: Theory and practice.* New York: McGraw-Hill, 1975.

WASKOW, I. E., & PARLOFF, M. B. (Eds.). *Psychotherapy change measures* (DHEW Publ. No. ADM 74-120). Rockville, Md.: National Institute of Mental Health, 1975.

WATSON, A. S. Forensic psychiatry. In A. M. Freedman, H. I. Kaplan, & B. J. Sadock (Eds.), *Comprehensive textbook of psychiatry—II* (Vol. 2). Baltimore: Williams & Wilkins, 1975. Pp. 2421–2436.

WATSON, C. G., & SCHULD, D. Psychosomatic factors in the etiology of neoplasms. *Journal of Consulting and Clinical Psychology,* 1977, *45,* 455–461.

WATSON, D. L., & THARP, R. G. *Self-directed behavior: Self-modification for personal adjustment* (2nd ed.). Monterey, Calif.: Brooks/Cole, 1977.

WATSON, J. B., & WATSON, R. R. Studies in infant psychology. *Scientific Monthly,* 1921, *13,* 493–515.

WEAVER, C. N., HOLMES, S. L., & GLENN, N. D. Some characteristics of inaccessible respondents in a telephone survey. *Journal of Applied Psychology,* 1975, *60,* 260–262.

WEBB, E. J., CAMPBELL, D. T., SCHWARTZ, R. D., & SECHREST, L. *Unobtrusive measures: Nonreactive research in the social sciences.* Chicago: Rand McNally, 1966.

WEBSTER, E. C. *Decision making in the employment interview.* Montreal: McGill University Industrial Relations Centre, 1964.

WECHSLER, D. *Wechsler Preschool and Primary Scale of Intelligence.* New York: Psychological Corporation, 1967.

WECHSLER, D. *Wechsler Intelligence Scale for Children—Revised.* New York: Psychological Corporation, 1974.

WECHSLER, D. *Wechsler Adult Intelligence Scale—Revised.* New York: Psychological Corporation, 1978.

WEED, S. E., MITCHELL, T. R., & MOFFITT, W. Leadership style, subordinate personality, and task type as predictors of performance and satisfaction with supervision. *Journal of Applied Psychology,* 1976, *61,* 58–66.

WEHRKAMP, R., & SMITH, K. U. Dimensional analysis of motion: II. Travel-distance effects. *Journal of Applied Psychology,* 1952, *36,* 201–206.

WEIKART, D. P., ROGERS, L., ADCOCK, C., & McCLELLAND, D. *The cognitively oriented curriculum.* Urbana: University of Illinois Press, 1971.

WEINER, H., THALER, M., REISER, M. F., & MIRSKY, I. A. Etiology of duodenal ulcer. I. Relation of specific psychological characteristics to rate of gastric secretion (serum pepsinogen). *Psychosomatic Medicine,* 1957, *19,* 1–10.

WEINGARTEN, K., HUNGERLAND, J. E., & BRENNAN, M. F. *Development and implementation of a quality-assured, peer-instructional model* (HumRRO Tech. Rep. 72-35). Alexandria, Va.: Human Resources Research Organization, November 1972.

WEINSTEIN, E. A. *Cultural aspects of delusions: A psychiatric study of the Virgin Islands.* New York: Free Press, 1962.

WEINSTEIN, S., FISHER, L., RICHLIN, M., & WEISINGER, M. Bibliography of sensory and perceptual deprivation, isolation, and related areas. *Perceptual and Motor Skills,* 1968, *26,* 1119–1163.

WEISENBERG, M. Pain and pain control. *Psychological Bulletin,* 1977, *84,* 1008–1044.

WEISMAN, A. D. *The realization of death.* New York: Aronson, 1974.

WEISMAN, A. D., & KASTENBAUM, R. *The psychological autopsy: A study of the terminal phase of life.* New York: Behavioral Publications, 1968.

WEISS, D. J., DAWIS, R. V., ENGLAND, G. W., & LOFQUIST, L. H. *Manual for the Minnesota Satisfaction Questionnaire* (Minnesota Studies in Vocational Rehabilitation: XXII). Minneapolis: University of Minnesota, Work Adjustment Project, 1967.

WEISS, J. M. Psychological factors in stress and disease. *Scientific American,* 1972, *226,* 104–113.

WEISSKOPF-JOELSON, E., & ELISEO, T. S. An experimental study of the effectiveness of brainstorming. *Journal of Applied Psychology,* 1961, *45,* 45–49.

WEITZ, J. Verbal and pictorial questionnaires in market research. *Journal of Applied Psychology,* 1950, *34,* 363–366.

WEITZ, J. Selecting supervisors with peer ratings. *Personnel Psychology,* 1958, *11,* 25–35.

WEITZ, J. A study of trade name confusion. *Journal of Marketing,* 1960, *25*(2), 54–56.

WELD, H. P., & ROFF, M. A study of the formation of opinion based upon legal evidence. *American Journal of Psychology,* 1938, *51,* 609–628.

WELDON, R. J., & PETERSON, G. M. Effect of design on accuracy and speed of operating dials. *Journal of Applied Psychology,* 1957, *41,* 153–157.

WELFORD, A. T., et al. *Skill and age: an experimental approach.* London: Oxford University Press, 1951.

WELLS, W. D. The influence of yeasaying response style. *Journal of Advertising Research,* 1961, *1*(4), 1–12.

WELLS, W. D., & LOSCIUTO, L. A. Direct observation of purchasing behavior. *Journal of Marketing Research,* 1966, *3,* 227–233.

WELLS, W. D., & TIGERT, D. J. Activities, interests, and opinions. *Journal of Advertising Research,* 1971, *11*(4), 27–35.

WEST, A., RAMAGGE, F., WEST, J., & JONES, H. The quality of railway carriage environments. *Applied Ergonomics,* 1973, *4,* 194–198.

WEXLER, M. The behavioral sciences in medical education: A view from psychology. *American Psychologist,* 1976, *31,* 275–283.

WEXNER, L. B. The degree to which colors (hues) are associated with mood-tones. *Journal of Applied Psychology,* 1954, *38,* 432–435.

WHITEHEAD, B., & ELDARS, M. Z. An approach to the optimum layout of single-storey buildings. *The Architects' Journal,* June 17, 1964, *139,* 1373–1380. (SfB Ba4: UDC 721.011.)

WICKS, R. J. *Applied psychology for law enforcement and correction officers.* New York: McGraw-Hill, 1974.

WIGGINS, J. S. *Personality and prediction: Principles of personality assessment.* Reading, Mass.: Addison-Wesley, 1973.

WILCOX, B. L., & HOLAHAN, C. J. Social ecology of the megadorm in university student housing. *Journal of Educational Psychology,* 1976, *68,* 453–458.

WILLIAMS, J. S., JR., KARP, S. A., & WILSON, P. T. *Pollution: Its impact on mental health—a literature survey and review of research* (DHEW Publication No. HSM 72-9135). Rockville, Md.: National Institute of Mental Health, 1972.

WILLIAMSON, E. G. *Vocational counseling.* New York: McGraw-Hill, 1965.

WILLIAMSON, E. G., & BORDIN, E. S. Evaluating counseling by means of a control group experiment. *School and Society,* 1940, *52,* 434–440.

WINETT, R. A., KAGEL, J. H., BATTALIO, R. C., & WINKLER, R. C. Effects of monetary rebates, feedback, and information on residential electricity conservation. *Journal of Applied Psychology,* 1978, *63,* 73–80.

WING, J. F. *A review of the effects of high ambient temperature on mental performance.* USAF, AMRL, TR 65-102, September 1965.

WINKEL, G. H., & SASANOFF, R. An approach to an objective analysis of behavior in architectural space. In H. M. Proshansky, W. H. Ittelson, & L. G. Rivlin (Eds.), *Environmental psychology: People and their physical settings* (2nd ed.). New York: Holt, Rinehart & Winston, 1976. Pp. 351–363.

WIRT, R. D., & BRIGGS, P. F. Personality and environmental factors in the development of delinquency. *Psychological Monographs,* 1959, *73*(15, Whole No. 485).

WIRT, R. D., WINOKUR, G., & ROFF, M. (Eds.). *Life history research in psychopathology* (Vol, 4). Minneapolis: University of Minnesota Press, 1976.

WITKIN, H. A., DYK, R. D., FATERSON, H. F., GOODENOUGH, D. R., & KARP, S. A. *Psychological differentiation: Studies of development.* New York: Wiley, 1962.

WITMER, J. F., & GELLER, E. S. Facilitating paper recycling: Effects of prompts, raffles, and contests. *Journal of Applied Behavior Analysis,* 1976, *9,* 315–322.

WITTKOWER, E., & CLEGHORN, R. (Eds.). *Recent developments in psychosomatic medicine.* Philadelphia: Lippincott, 1954.

WITTROCK, M. C., & LUMSDAINE, A. A. Instructional psychology. *Annual Review of Psychology,* 1977, *28,* 417–459.

WOHLWILL, J. F. The emerging discipline of environmental psychology. *American Psychologist,* 1970, *25,* 303–312.

WOHLWILL, J. F. Adapting to a noisy world. (Review of *Urban stress: Experiments on noise and social stressors* by D. C. Glass & J. E. Singer). *Contemporary Psychology,* 1975, *20,* 385–387.

WOHLWILL, J. F., & CARSON, D. H. (Eds.). *Environment and the social sciences: Perspectives and applications.* Washington, D. C.: American Psychological Association, 1972.

WOLFE, J. C. Psychologists in and out of the alcoholism field. In P. J. Woods (Ed.), *Career opportunities for psychologists: Expanding and emerging areas.* Washington, D. C.: American Psychological Association, 1976. Ch. 12.

WOLFF, S., & WOLFF, H. G. Life situations, emotions, and gastric function: A summary. In A. Weider (Ed.), *Contributions toward medical psychology.* New York: Ronald, 1953. Ch. 13.

WOLK, R. L., & WOLK, R. B. *Manual: Gerontological Apperception Test.* New York: Behavioral Publications, 1971.

WOLPE, J. *The practice of behavior therapy* (2nd ed.). New York: Pergamon, 1973.

WOLPE, J., & LANG, P. J. A fear survey schedule for use in behavior therapy. *Behaviour Research and Therapy,* 1964, *2,* 27–30.

WOMER, F. B. *What is National Assessment?* Ann Arbor, Mich.: National Assessment of Educational Progress, 1970.

WOODS, P. J. (Ed.). *Career opportunities for psychologists: Expanding and emerging areas.* Washington, D. C.: American Psychological Association, 1976.

WOODSIDE, A. G. A shopping list experiment of beer brand images. *Journal of Applied Psychology,* 1972, *56,* 512–513.

WOODSIDE, A. G. Relation of price to perception of quality of new products. *Journal of Applied Psychology,* 1974, *59,* 116–118.

WOOL, H., & FLYER, E. S. Project 100,000. In P. B. Doeringer (Ed.), *Programs to employ the disadvantaged.* Englewood Cliffs, N.J.: Prentice-Hall, 1969. Ch. 8.

WRENN, C. G. *The counselor in a changing world.* Washington, D. C.: American Personnel and Guidance Association, 1962.

WRIGHT, B. A. *Psychology and rehabilitation.* Washington, D. C.: American Psychological Association, 1959.

WRIGHT, B. A. *Physical disability: A psychological approach.* New York: Harper, 1960.

WRIGHT, L. Conceptualizing and defining psychosomatic disorders. *American Psychologist,* 1977, *32,* 625–628.

WRIGHT, O. R., JR. Summary of research on the selection interview since 1964. *Personnel Psychology,* 1969, *22,* 391–413.

WRIGHTSTONE, J. W., HOGAN, T. P., & ABBOTT, M. M. *Accountability in education and associated measurement problems* (Test Service Notebook 33). New York: Harcourt Brace Jovanovich, 1972.

WYATT, S., FROST, L., & STOCK, F. G. L. Incentives in repetitive work. *Industrial Health Research Board (Great Britain), Report No. 69,* 1934.

XINTORAS, C., JOHNSON, B. L., & DE GROOT, I. (Eds.). *Behavioral toxicology: Early detection of occupational hazards* (DHEW NIOSH Report No. 74-126). Washington, D. C.: U. S. Department of Health, Education, and Welfare, 1974.

YOELL, W. A. Make your advertising themes match consumer behavior. *Printers' Ink,* 1952, *238*(12), 82–87.

YUKL, G., WEXLEY, K. N., & SEYMORE, J. D. Effectiveness of pay incentives under variable ratio and continuous reinforcement schedules. *Journal of Applied Psychology,* 1972, *56,* 19–23.

ZAJONC, R. B., & MARKUS, G. B. Birth order and intellectual development. *Psychological Review,* 1975, *82,* 74–88.

ZEDECK, S. Problems with the use of "moderator" variables. *Psychological Bulletin,* 1971, *76,* 295–310.

ZEDECK, S., IMPARATO, N., KRAUSZ, M., & OLENO, T. Development of behaviorally anchored rating scales as a function of organizational level. *Journal of Applied Psychology,* 1974, *59,* 249–252.

ZEISEL, J. *Sociology and architectural design.* New York: Russell Sage Foundation, 1975.

ZIFFERBLATT, S. M. (Chair). *Assisting national coronary heart disease trials through behavioral research.* Symposium presented at the meeting of the American Psychological Association, Washington, D. C., September 1976.

ZILLER, R. C. Individuation and socialization: A theory of assimilation in large organizations. *Human Relations,* 1964, *17,* 341–360.

ZIMET, C. N., & WELLNER, A. M. Health service providers in psychology: The National Register. In B. B. Wolman (Ed.), *International encyclopedia of psychiatry, psychology, psychoanalysis, and neurology* (Vol. 5). New York: Van Nostrand Reinhold, 1977. Pp. 329–332.

ZISKIN, J. *Coping with psychiatric and psychological testimony.* Beverly Hills, Calif.: Law and Psychology Press, 1970.

ZOLA, I. K. Culture and symptoms: An analysis of patients' presenting complaints. *American Sociological Review,* 1966, *31,* 615–630.

ZUBEK, J. P. *Sensory deprivation: Fifteen years of research.* New York: Appleton-Century-Crofts, 1968.

INDEXES

AUTHOR INDEX

Saal, F. E., 521, **610**
Sadock, B. J., 316, 352, 492*n*, **581, 594, 597, 598, 607, 608, 609, 619, 620, 633, 641**
Saily, M., 462, 465, **608**
Saks, M. J., 510, **628**
Salipante, P., Jr., 114, **628**
Salter, J. A., 88, **622**
Sampson, H., 251, **628**
Sandeman, C. A., 491, **616**
Sanders, D. H., 358, **592**
Sands, W. A., 47, **628**
Sarason, I. G., 465, **628**
Sarason, S. B., 452, **628**
Sarbin, T. R., 323, 324, 350, 374, **629**
Saretsky, G., 388, 457, **629**
Sargent, J. D., 490, **629**
Sasanoff, R., 246, 247, **642**
Saslow, G., 338, **606**
Saunders, D. R., 48, 62, **594, 629**
Saunders, J. T., 525, **626**
Sawrey, J. M., 401, **637**
Sawrey, W. L., 494, **629**
Sawyer, J., 324, **629**
Sayre, J. L., 463, **629**
Scarborough, D. L., 459, **626**
Scarpitti, F. R., 363, **623**
Schacht, T., 316, **629**
Schachter, S., 174, **629**
Schaefer, C. E., 79, **575**
Schaffer, R. H., 429, **629**
Schaie, K. W., 402, **629**
Schalock, H. D., 459, **629**
Schappe, R. H., 183, **629**
Scharf, P., 525, **609**
Scheidler, C. H., 392, **618**
Schein, V. E., 181, **629**
Schiro, J., 390, **592**
Schlossberg, H., 521, **629**
Schmidt, D. E., 243, **629**
Schmidt, F. L., 35, 38, 53, 193, **604, 629**
Schmuckler, E., 80, **629**
Schneider, D. E., 77, **629**
Schoenfeldt, L. F., 48, **629**
Schreiber, F. R., 316, **629**
Schroeder, H. E., 358, **626**
Schroeder, W. W., 422, **610**
Schuld, D., 497, **641**
Schultz, D. P., 240, **630**
Schultz, R. L., 519, **600**
Schumer, H., 461*n*, **590**
Schutz, H. G., 276, 277, **630**
Schwab, D. P., 128, 130, **596, 630**
Schwartz, G. E., 490, **618, 630**
Schwartz, L. L., 453, **630**
Schwartz, R. D., 279, **641**
Schwartzberg, N. S., 518, **612**
Schwitzgebel, R. L., 492, **630**
Scott, J. P., 517*n*, 518, **607, 630**

Scott, R. W., 490, 491, **630**
Scott, W. D., 4, 251, **630**
Scriven, M., 386, **630**
Seashore, S. E., 36, 146, 147, **616, 630**
Seaver, W. B., 308, **630**
Sechrest, L., 279, **641**
Secord, P. F., 76, 453, **577, 630**
Secunda, S. K., 315, 317, 343, 345, 501, **630**
Seeger, C. M., 207, **593**
Seeman, J., 376, 377, **630**
Segal, J., 368, **630**
Segal, S. J., 442, **581**
Seidel, R. J., 464, **601, 604, 630**
Seligman, C., 308, **630**
Seligman, M. E. P., 395, 501, **601, 630**
Selinger, H. E., 452, **575**
Sells, S. B., 232, **630**
Selye, H., 493, **630**
Senay, E. C., **607**
Sewall, M. A., 297, **634**
Sexton, R., 157, **630, 631**
Seymore, J. D., 137, **644**
Shachter, S., 478, **631**
Shaffer, L. F., 346, **631**
Shah, S. A., 518, 524, **631**
Shanner, W. M., 465, **593**
Shapira, Z., 161, **631**
Shapiro, A. K., 472*n*, **631**
Shapiro, D., **618**
Shapiro, H., Jr., 360, **631**
Sharer, R., 215, **599**
Shatz, E. O., 364, **593**
Shaw, M. E., 124, 125, **631**
Shaw, W. A., 173, **631**
Shaycoft, M. F., 419, **593**
Shea, T. M., 465, **640**
Sheldon, W. H., 493, **631**
Shellow, R., 519, 521, 522, **577**
Shenkel, R. J., 14*n*, **600**
Shepard, H. A., 161, 162, **631**
Shepard, H. H., 161, **580**
Shepard, R. P., 205, **580**
Sherif, M., 519, **631**
Sherman, A. W., Jr., 11, **631**
Sherman, W., 193, **607**
Sherrick, C. E., 205, **631**
Sheth, J. N., 253, 266, **631**
Shimberg, B., 437, 481, **631**
Shinn, M., 305, **584**
Shlien, J. M., 368, **631**
Shneidman, E. S., 362, 375, 500, **592, 613, 631**
Shoben, E. J., Jr., 346, 347, **631**
Shoemaker, H. A., 98, **631**
Shontz, F. C., 369, 473, 478, 499, **631, 632**
Shore, C. W., 53, **632**
Shuy, R. W., 474, **632**

Sidowski, J. B., 395, **632**
Siebert, L. A., 515, **584**
Siegel, J. P., 277, **589**
Siegel, L. J., 476, **618**
Silber, D. E., 524, 526*n*, **632**
Siller, J., 499, **632**
Silverman, H., 526*n*, **632**
Silverman, L. H., 372, 375, **632**
Silverman, R. E., 100, **632**
Silverman, S., 499, **632**
Silvern, L. C., 98, **612**
Simkin, W. E., 162, **632**
Simon, H. A., 159, **589**
Simon, J. R., 211, 237, **581, 632**
Simon, R., 510, **632**
Simpson, C. J., 307, **632**
Sinaiko, H. W., **615**
Singer, J. E., 237, 239, **597, 643**
Singer, J. L., 390, 517*n*, **577, 632**
Sirota, D. E., 152, **613**
Skelly, F. R., 268, **632**
Skinner, B. F., 357, 461, 462, **632**
Skodak, M., 6, **627**
Sleight, R. B., 202, **632**
Slivnick, P., 193, **632**
Sloane, R. B., 385, **632**
Sloma, R. L., 161, **580**
Slote, A., 496, **632**
Small, L., 349, **579, 632**
Smith, C. G., 519, **632**
Smith, D. E. P., 459, **632**
Smith, G. H., 269, 270, **632**
Smith, H. C., 239, **633**
Smith, J. O., 514, **633**
Smith, K. U., 183, 200, **586, 602, 633, 641**
Smith, M. B., 360, **633**
Smith, P. B., 111, **633**
Smith, P. C., 70, 71, 126, 175, 445, **633**
Smith, W. G., 362, **633**
Smith, W. J., 36, **575**
Smyth, P., 146, **595**
Smyth, R. L., 390, **633**
Snider, J. G., 338, **633**
Snow, R. E., 103, 460, 461*n*, **587**
Snowden, L. R., 361, **608**
Snyder, C. R., 14*n*, **600, 633**
Snyder, S. H., 344, 483, 486, **605**
Snyder, W. U., 351, 378, **633**
Snyderman, B. B., 132, **602**
Solem, A. R., 109, **615**
Solomon, D., 460, **633**
Solomon, L. N., 527, **633**
Solomon, P., 483, **633**
Solomon, T., 131, **605**
Sommer, R., 123, 506, 513, **633**
Sotile, W. M., 353, **608**
Souder, J. J., 217, **633**
Spanos, N. P., 487, **577**
Sparks, D. L., 273, **633**

SUBJECT INDEX